THEOLOGICAL DICTIONARY
OF THE
OLD TESTAMENT

THEOLOGICAL DICTIONARY

OF THE

OLD TESTAMENT

EDITED BY

G. JOHANNES BOTTERWECK,

HELMER RINGGREN,

AND

HEINZ-JOSEF FABRY

Translated by

DOUGLAS W. STOTT

Volume VIII

לָכַד - מֹר

lāḵaḏ – mōr

WILLIAM B. EERDMANS PUBLISHING COMPANY

GRAND RAPIDS, MICHIGAN / CAMBRIDGE, U.K.

THEOLOGICAL DICTIONARY OF THE OLD TESTAMENT
Volume 8
Translated from
THEOLOGISCHES WÖRTERBUCH ZUM ALTEN TESTAMENT
Band IV, Lieferungen 5-9
Published 1983-1984 by
Verlag W. Kohlhammer GmbH, Stuttgart, Germany

255 Jefferson Ave. S.E., Grand Rapids, Michigan 49503 /
P.O. Box 163, Cambridge CB3 9PU U.K.

Printed in the United States of America

05 04 03 02 01 00 99 98 97   7 6 5 4 3 2 1

Library of Congress Cataloging-in-Publication Data

Botterweck, G. Johannes
Theological dictionary of the Old Testament
Translation of Theologisches Wörterbuch zum Alten Testament.
Translated by Douglas W. Stott
Includes rev. ed. of v. 1-2.
Includes bibliographical references.
1. Bible. O.T. — Dictionaries — Hebrew. 2. Hebrew language — Dictionaries — English.
I. Ringgren, Helmer, 1917 — joint author. II. Title.
BS440.B5713   221.4'4   73-76170
ISBN 0-8028-2338-6 (set)

Volume VIII ISBN 0-8028-2332-7

CONSULTING EDITORS

George W. Anderson
Henri Cazelles
David Noel Freedman
Shemaryahu Talmon
Gerhard Wallis

CONTRIBUTORS

L. Alonso-Schökel, Rome
G. André, Uppsala
†C. Barth, Basel
A. Baumann, Wolfsburg
P. Beauchamp, Paris
R. E. Clements, Cambridge
J. Conrad, Leipzig
C. Dohmen, Bonn
†H. Eising, Münster
H.-J. Fabry, Bonn (Editor)
D. N. Freedman, Ann Arbor / San Diego
J. Gamberoni, Paderborn
H. Gross, Regensburg
H. Haag, Lucerne
J. Hausmann, Neuendettelsau
K.-J. Illman, Turku
A. S. Kapelrud, Oslo
B. Kedar-Kopfstein, Haifa
D. Kellermann, Tübingen
K. Koch, Hamburg
B. Levine, New York
E. Lipiński, Louvain
P. Maiberger, Mainz
G. Mayer, Zornheim
C. L. Meyers, Durham, NC
J. Milgrom, Berkeley
H.-P. Müller, Halstenbek
R. North, Rome
M. P. O'Connor, Ann Arbor
H. D. Preuss, Neuendettelsau
H. Ringgren, Uppsala (Editor)
R. Schmid, Lucerne
K.-D. Schunck, Rostock
H. Seebass, Ladbergen
K. Seybold, Basel
H. Simian-Yofre, Rome
L. A. Snijders, Huizen
P. Stenmans, Würzburg
S. Talmon, Jerusalem
S. Wagner, Leipzig
M. Weinfeld, Jerusalem
B. E. Willoughby, Ann Arbor
D. P. Wright, Waltham
H.-J. Zobel, Greifswald

CONTENTS

EDITORS' PREFACE TO VOLUME VIII

The original plan for the *Theological Dictionary of the Old Testament* provided for the completion of this multivolume work over the span of approximately a decade. Almost immediately such a swift realization proved to be utopian. The abundant influx of new insights in exegesis (e.g., pressing discussions concerning the Pentateuch, the Deuteronomistic history, the prophetic books, etc.), lexicography and semantics, comparative linguistics, ancient Near Eastern studies, and certainly not least archaeology with the discovery of new cultures (e.g., Tell Mardikh-Ebla) again and again forced to a standstill the otherwise unimpeded flow of work on the Dictionary. Many entries that had already been completed had to be reedited. Rightly so, several contributors and subscribers expressed their displeasure.

In the midst of this persistent grappling our venture encountered a serious blow. On April 15, 1981, Professor Gerhard Johannes Botterweck died. His profound knowledge of the Old Testament and its milieu, his vast experience in all practical matters associated with book production, his organizational skills, and above all his theological foresightedness had come to be of inestimable value to our undertaking. All this will be missing in the future. All colleagues acknowledge with gratitude the value of his accomplishments. R.I.P.

Dr. Heinz-Josef Fabry, a student of Professor Botterweck and an editorial colleague since 1971, has become the new co-editor. This should guarantee a continuity in the editorial work in keeping with the established principles.

Deliberation over fundamental matters is therefore unnecessary. The principal goal of the project remains the same (see the Preface to Volume I), to analyze the Hebrew words semantically. The presentation of the fundamental concepts intended by the respective words and terms, the traditions in which they occur, and the different nuances of meaning they have in each tradition stand at the focus of this analytical work, so that in the end one might ultimately bring together the individual building blocks of an Old Testament theology.

Helmer Ringgren/Heinz-Josef Fabry

ABBREVIATIONS

AANLR	*Atti dell' Academia Nazionale dei Lincei, Rendiconti,* Rome
AASOR	*Annual of the American Schools of Oriental Research,* New Haven, Ann Arbor, Philadelphia
AB	*The Anchor Bible,* ed. W. F. Albright-D. N. Freedman, Garden City
ABAW	*Abhandlungen der bayerischen Akademie der Wissenschaften,* Munich
ABD	*Anchor Bible Dictionary,* ed. D. N. Freedman, 6 vols. (New York, 1992)
ABL	R. F. Harper, *Assyrian and Babylonian Letters,* 14 vols. (Chicago, 1892-1914)
abr.	abridged
ABR	*Australian Biblical Review,* Melbourne
abs.	absolute
AC	*L'Antiquité classique,* Brussels
AcThD	*Acta theologica danica,* Århus, Copenhagen
adj.	adjective
adv.	adverb
AFNW	*Arbeitsgemeinschaft für Forschung des Landes Nordrhein-Westfalen,* Cologne
AfO	*Archiv für Orientforschung,* Graz
ÄgAbh	*Ägyptologische Abhandlungen,* Wiesbaden
AGSU	*Arbeiten zur Geschichte des Spätjudentums und Urchristentums,* Leiden
AGWG	*Abhandlungen der Gesellschaft der Wissenschaften zu Göttingen,* Berlin
AHDO-RIDA	*Archives d'histoire du droit oriental — Revue internationale des droits de l'antiquité,* Brussels
AHw	W. von Soden, *Akkadisches Handwörterbuch,* 3 vols. (Wiesbaden, 1965-1981)
AION	*Annali dell'Istituto Universitario Orientali di Napoli*
AJBA	*Australian Journal of Biblical Archaeology,* Sydney
AJBI	*Annual of the Japanese Biblical Institute* (*Seísho-gaku ronshī*), Tokyo
AJP	*American Journal of Philology,* Baltimore
AJSL	*The American Journal of Semitic Languages and Literatures,* Chicago
AJT	*American Journal of Theology,* Chicago
Akk.	Akkadian
AKM	*Abhandlungen für die Kunde des Morgenlandes,* Leipzig, Wiesbaden, Hildesheim
Amor.	Amorite
AnAcScFen	*Annales Academiae Scientarum Fennicae,* ser. B, Helsinki
AnAcScFen, DHL	———. *Dissertationes humanarum litterarum,* Helsinki
AnBibl	*Analecta biblica,* Rome
AncIsr	R. de Vaux, *Ancient Israel: Its Life and Institutions* (Eng. trans., New York, 1961, [2]1965)
ANEP	*The Ancient Near East in Pictures,* ed. J. B. Pritchard (Princeton, 1954, [2]1969)
ANET	*Ancient Near Eastern Texts Relating to the OT,* ed. J. B. Pritchard (Princeton, [2]1955, [3]1969)
AnOr	*Analecta orientalia,* Rome
AnSt	*Anatolian Studies,* Leiden
AO	*Der Alte Orient,* Leipzig

AOAT	*Alter Orient und AT,* Kevelaer, Neukirchen-Vluyn
AOB	*Altorientalische Bilder zum AT,* ed. H. Gressmann (Berlin, ^{2}1927)
AOS	*American Oriental Series,* New Haven
AP	A. E. Cowley, *Aramaic Papyri of the Fifth Century B.C.* (1923, repr. Osnabruck, 1976)
APNM	H. B. Huffmon, *Amorite Personal Names in the Mari Texts* (Baltimore, 1965)
Arab.	Arabic
Aram.	Aramaic
ArbT	*Arbeiten zur Theologie,* Stuttgart
ARM	*Archives royales de Mari. Textes cunéiformes,* Paris
ARM.T	———. *Transcriptions et traductions,* Paris
ArOr	*Archiv orientální,* Prague
ARW	*Archiv für Religionswissenschaft,* Freiburg, Leipzig, Berlin
AS	*Assyriological Studies,* Chicago
ASAE	*Annales du Service des Antiquités de l'Égypte,* Cairo
ASOR	American Schools of Oriental Research
ASTI	*Annual of the Swedish Theological Institute in Jerusalem,* Leiden
AT	Altes Testament, Ancien Testament, etc.
ATA	*Alttestamentliche Abhandlungen,* Münster
ATD	*Das AT Deutsch,* ed. V. Herntrich-A. Weiser, Göttingen
AThANT	*Abhandlungen zur Theologie des Alten und Neuen Testaments,* Zurich
ATR	*Anglican Theological Review,* Evanston
ATS	*Arbeiten zu Text und Sprache im AT,* St. Ottilien, Munich
AuS	G. Dalman, *Arbeit und Sitte in Palästina,* 7 vols. (1928-1942, repr. Hildesheim, 1964)
AUU	*Acta universitatis upsaliensis,* Uppsala
BA	*The Biblical Archaeologist,* New Haven, Ann Arbor, Philadelphia, Atlanta, Durham
Bab.	Babylonian, Babylonian Talmud
BAfO	*Beiheft zur AfO*
BAr	*Bulletin archéologique du comité des travaux historiques et scientifiques,* Paris
BAR	*Biblical Archaeology Review,* Washington
BA Reader	*Biblical Archaeologist Reader,* ed. D. N. Freedman, *et al.,* 3 vols. (1961-1970, repr. Winona Lake, 1975)
BASOR	*Bulletin of the American Schools of Oriental Research,* New Haven, Ann Arbor, Philadelphia, Baltimore
BBB	*Bonner biblische Beiträge*
BBET	*Beiträge zur biblischen Exegese und Theologie,* Frankfurt, Las Vegas
BCPE	*Bulletin du Centre Protestant d'Études,* Geneva
BDB	F. Brown-S. R. Driver-C. A. Briggs, *A Hebrew and English Lexicon of the OT* (Oxford, 1907; Peabody, Mass., ^{2}1979)
BDBAT	*Beiheft zur Dielheimer Blätter zum AT*
BdÉ	*Bibliothèque d'études,* Paris
Benz	F. L. Benz, *Personal Names in the Phoenician and Punic Inscriptions. StPohl,* 8 (1972)
BeO	*Bibbia e oriente,* Milan
BethM	*Beth mikra,* Jerusalem
BETL	*Bibliotheca ephemeridum theologicarum Lovaniensium,* Paris, Gembloux
BEvTh	*Beiträge zur evangelische Theologie,* Munich
BHHW	*Biblisch-historisches Handwörterbuch,* ed. L. Rost-B. Reicke, 4 vols. (Göttingen, 1962-1966; index and maps, 1979)
BHK	*Biblia hebraica,* ed. R. Kittel (Stuttgart, ^{3}1929)

BHS	*Biblia hebraica stuttgartensia,* ed. K. Elliger-W. Rudolph (Stuttgart, 1966-1977)
BHTh	*Beiträge zur historischen Theologie,* Tübingen
Bibl	*Biblica,* Rome
bibliog.	bibliography
BIES	*Bulletin of the Israel Exploration Society,* Jerusalem (= *Yediot*)
BietOr	*Biblica et orientalia,* Rome
BiLe	*Bibel und Leben,* Düsseldorf
BiLi	*Bibel und Liturgie,* Klosterneuberg
BiOr	*Bibliotheca orientalia,* Leiden
BJRL	*Bulletin of the John Rylands Library,* Manchester
BK	*Biblischer Kommentar AT,* ed. M. Noth-H. W. Wolff, Neukirchen-Vluyn
BL	*Bibel-Lexikon,* ed. H. Haag (Einsiedeln, 1951, ^{2}1968)
BLe	H. Bauer-P. Leander, *Historische Grammatik der hebräischen Sprache des ATs* (1918-1922, repr. Hildesheim, 1991)
BM	Tablet in the collections of the British Museum
BMAP	E. G. Kraeling, *The Brooklyn Museum Aramaic Papyri* (New Haven, 1953)
BN	*Biblische Notizien,* Bamberg
BOLZ	*Beigabe zur OLZ, Berlin*
BOT	*De Boeken van het OT,* Roermond en Maaseik
BRA	*Beiträge zur Religionsgeschichte des Altertums,* Halle
BRL	K. Galling, *Biblisches Reallexikon. HAT* (1937, ^{2}1977)
BSAW	*Berichte über die Verhandlungen der Sächsischen Akademie der Wissenschaften zu Leipzig*
BSt	*Biblische Studien,* Neukirchen-Vluyn
BT	*The Bible Translator,* London
BTB	*Biblical Theology Bulletin,* Rome
BThH	*Biblisch-Theologisches Handwörterbuch zur Lutherbibel und zu neueren Übersetzungen,* ed. E. Osterloh-H. Engelaed (Göttingen, 1954, ^{2}1959, ^{3}1964)
BuA	B. Meissner, *Babylonien und Assyrien,* 2 vols. (Heidelberg, 1920-25)
BWA(N)T	*Beiträge zur Wissenschaft vom Alten (und Neuen) Testament,* Leipzig, Stuttgart
BWL	W. G. Lambert, *Babylonian Wisdom Literature* (Oxford, 1960)
BZ	*Biblische Zeitschrift,* Paderborn
BZAW	*Beihefte zur ZAW,* Berlin
BZfr	*Biblische Zeitfragen,* Münster
ca.	*circa,* about
CAD	*The Assyrian Dictionary of the Oriental Institute of the University of Chicago* (1956–)
CahB	*Cahiers de Byrsa,* Paris
CahRB	*Cahiers de la RB,* Paris
CahTh	*Cahiers théologiques,* Neuchâtel
Can.	Canaanite
CAT	*Commentaire de l'AT,* Neuchâtel
CB	*Coniectanea biblica,* OT Series, Lund
CBC	*Cambridge Bible Commentary on the New English Bible,* Cambridge
CBQ	*Catholic Biblical Quarterly,* Washington
CD A,B	Damascus document, manuscript A, B
cf.	compare, see
ch(s).	chapter(s)
CH	Code of Hammurabi
CIH	*Corpus inscriptionum himyariticarum* (= *CIS,* IV)
CIJ	*Corpus inscriptionum judaicarum* (Vatican, 1936–)
CIL	*Corpus inscriptionum latinarum* (Berlin, 1862–)

CIS	*Corpus inscriptionum semiticarum* (Paris, 1881–)
CML	G. R. Driver, *Canaanite Myths and Legends* (Edinburgh, 1956; ^{2}1977, ed. J. C. L. Gibson)
coll.	collective
comm(s).	commentary(ies)
conj.	conjecture
const.	construct
ContiRossini	K. Conti Rossini, *Chrestomathia arabica meridionalis ephigraphica* (Rome, 1931)
Copt.	Coptic
CRAI	*Comptes rendus des séances de l'Academie des Inscriptions et Belles Lettres,* Paris
CT	*Cuneiform Texts from Babylonian Tablets in the British Museum* (London, 1896–)
CTA	A. Herdner, *Corpus des tablettes en cunéiformes alphabétiques découvertes à Ras Shamra-Ugarit,* 2 vols. (Paris, 1963)
CThM	*Calwer theologische Monographien,* Stuttgart
cyl.	cylinder
D	D (doubling) stem
DACL	*Dictionnaire d'archéologie chrétienne,* ed. F. Cabrol-H. Leclerq, 15 vols. (Paris, 1924-1953)
DAWB	*Deutsch Akademie der Wissenschaft zu Berlin, Schriften der Sektion für Altertumswissenschaft*
DAWW	Denschriften der (kaiserlichen) Akademie der Wissenschaften in Wien, Vienna
DB	*Dictionnaire de la Bible,* ed. F. Vigouroux, 5 vols. (Paris, 1895-1912)
DBS	*Dictionnaire de la Bible, Supplement,* ed. L. Pirot, *et al.* (Paris, 1926–)
DISO	J. F. Jean-J. Hoftijzer, *Dictionnaire des inscriptions sémitiques de l'ouest* (Leiden, 1965)
diss.	dissertation
DissAbs	Dissertation Abstracts International, Ann Arbor
DJD	*Discoveries in the Judean Desert* (Oxford, 1955–)
DMOA	*Documenta et monumenta orientis antiqui,* Leiden
DN	Deity name
DtrN	nomistic Deuteronomistic source
DTT	*Dansk teologisk Tidsskrift,* Copenhagen
E	Elohistic source
EA	Tell el-Amarna tablets
EAEHL	*Encyclopedia of Archaeological Excavations in the Holy Land,* ed. M. Avi-Yonah-E. Stern, 4 vols. (Englewood Cliffs, N.J., 1975-78)
Eb.	Eblaic
EB	*Die Heilige Schrift in deutscher Übersetzung.* Echter-Bibel, Würzburg
ed.	edition
EdF	*Erträge der Forschung,* Darmstadt
EDNT	*Exegetical Dictionary of the NT,* ed. H. Balz-G. Schneider, 3 vols. (Eng. trans., Grand Rapids, 1990-93)
Egyp.	Egyptian
EH	*Europäische Hochschulschriften,* Frankfurt, Bern
EHAT	*Exegetisches Handbuch zum AT,* Münster
EMiqr	*Enṣiqlōpedyā miqrā'it* (*Encyclopedia Biblica*) (Jerusalem, 1950–)
emph.	emphatic
EncJud	*Encyclopaedia judaica,* 16 vols. (Jerusalem, New York, 1971-72)
EnEl	Enuma Elish
Eng.	English
ERE	*Encyclopedia of Religion and Ethics,* ed. J. Hastings, 13 vols. (New York, 1913-1927)

ErIsr	*Eretz-Israel,* Jerusalem
esp.	especially
EstBíb	*Estudios bíblicos,* Madrid
EstEcl	*Estudios ecclesiásticos,* Madrid
ÉtB	*Études bibliques,* Paris
Eth.	Ethiopic
ETL	*Ephemerides theologicae Lovanienses,* Louvain
ETR	*Études théologiques et religieuses,* Montpellier
EvTh	*Evangelische Theologie,* Munich
ExpT	*Expository Times,* Edinburgh
fem.	feminine
fig.	figure
Fr.	French
fr.	fragment
FRLANT	*Forschungen zur Religion und Literatur des Alten und Neuen Testaments,* Göttingen
FThS	*Frankfurter theologische Studien,* Frankfurt am Main
FuF	*Forschungen und Fortschritte,* Berlin
FzB	*Forschung zur Bibel,* Würzburg
GaG	W. von Soden, *Grundriss der akkadischen Grammatik. AnOr,* 33 (1952, ^{2}1969 [with *Ergänzungsheft. AnOr,* 47])
Ger.	German
GesB	W. Gesenius-F. Buhl, *Hebräisches und aramäisches Handwörterbuch über das AT* (Berlin, ^{17}1921, ^{18}1987–)
GesTh	W. Gesenius, *Thesaurus philologicus criticus linguae hebraecae et chaldaeae Veteris Testamenti,* 3 vols. (Leipzig, 1829-1858)
Gilg.	Gilgamesh epic
Gk.	Greek
GK	W. Gesenius-E. Kautsch, *Hebräische Grammatik* (Halle, ^{28}1909) (= Kautsch-A. E. Cowley, *Gesenius' Hebrew Grammar* [Oxford, ^{2}1910])
GSAT	*Gesammelte Studien zum AT,* Munich
GThT	*Gereformeerd theologisch Tijdschrift,* Aalten, Kampen
GTTOT	J. J. Simons, *The Geographical and Topographical Texts of the OT. StFS,* 2 (1959)
Guillaume	A. Guillaume, *Hebrew and Aramaic Lexicography* (repr. Leiden, 1965)
H	Holiness Code
HAL	L. Koehler-W. Baumgartner, *The Hebrew and Aramaic Lexicon of the OT* (Eng. trans., Leiden, 1994–)
HAT	*Handbuch zum AT,* ser. 1, ed. O. Eissfeldt, Tübingen
Heb.	Hebrew
Herm	*Hermeneia,* Philadelphia, Minneapolis
HKAT	*Handkommentar zum AT,* ed. W. Nowack, Göttingen
HO	*Handbuch der Orientalistik,* Leiden
HS	*Die Heilige Schrift des AT,* ed. F. Feldmann-H. Herkenne, Bonn
HSM	*Harvard Semitic Monographs,* Cambridge, Mass.
HThR	*Harvard Theological Review,* Cambridge, Mass.
HThS	*Harvard Theological Studies,* Cambridge, Mass.
HUCA	*Hebrew Union College Annual,* Cincinnati
IB	*The Interpreter's Bible,* ed. G. A. Buttrick, 12 vols. (Nashville, 1952-57)
ICC	*The International Critical Commentary,* Edinburgh
IDB	*The Interpreter's Dictionary of the Bible,* ed. G. A. Buttrick, 4 vols. (Nashville, 1962); *Sup,* ed. K. Crim (Nashville, 1976)
IEJ	*Israel Exploration Journal,* Jerusalem

IKZ	*Internationale kirchliche Zeitschrift,* Bern
ILC	J. Pedersen, *Israel: Its Life and Culture,* 4 vols. in 2 (Eng. trans., Oxford, 1926-1940, ^{5}1963)
ILR	*Israel Law Review,* Jerusalem
impf.	imperfect
impv.	imperative
inf.	infinitive
in loc.	on this passage
Int	*Interpretation,* Richmond
Intro(s).	Introduction(s) (to the)
IPN	M. Noth, *Die israelitischen Personennamen im Rahmen der gemeinsemitischen Namengebung. BWANT,* 46[3/10] (1928, repr. 1980)
J	Yahwist source (J^1, earliest Yahwist source)
Ja.	Enumeration according to A. Jamme (OSA)
JA	*Journal asiatique,* Paris
JANES	*Journal of the Ancient Near Eastern Society of Columbia University,* New York
JAOS	*Journal of the American Oriental Society,* Baltimore, Boston, New Haven
JARG	*Jahrbuch für Anthropologie und Religionsgeschichte,* Saarbrücken
Jastrow	M. Jastrow, *A Dictionary of the Targumim, the Talmud Babli and Yerushalmi, and the Midrashic Literature* (1903; repr. 2 vols. in 1, Brooklyn, 1975)
JB	Jerusalem Bible (Garden City, 1966)
JBL	*Journal of Biblical Literature,* Philadelphia, Missoula, Chico, Atlanta
JBR	*Journal of Bible and Religion,* Boston
JCS	*Journal of Cuneiform Studies,* New Haven, Cambridge, Mass., Philadelphia, Baltimore
JDAI	*Jahrbuch des Deutschen Archäologischen Instituts,* Berlin
JE	Yahwist-Elohist source
JE	*The Jewish Encyclopedia,* ed. I. Singer, 12 vols. (New York, 1916)
JEA	*Journal of Egyptian Archaeology,* London
JEOL	*Jaarbericht van het Vooraziatisch-Egyptisch Genootschap 'Ex Oriente Lux,'* Leiden
Jer.	Jerusalem (Palestinian) Talmud
JES	*Journal of Ecumenical Studies,* Pittsburgh, Philadelphia
JJP	*Journal of Juristic Papyrology,* New York
JJS	*Journal of Jewish Studies,* London
JNES	*Journal of Near Eastern Studies,* Chicago
JNSL	*Journal of Northwest Semitic Languages,* Stellenbosch
JOS	*Journal of Oriental Studies*
Joüon	P. Joüon, *A Grammar of Biblical Hebrew,* 2 vols. *SPIB.B, biblica,* 14/1 (Eng. trans., Rome, 1991)
JP	*Journal of Philology,* London
JPES	Jewish Palestine Exploration Society, Jerusalem
JPOS	*Journal of the Palestine Oriental Society,* Jerusalem
JQR	*Jewish Quarterly Review,* Philadelphia
JRAS	*Journal of the Royal Asiatic Society,* London
JSOT	*Journal for the Study of the OT,* Sheffield
JSS	*Journal of Semitic Studies,* Manchester
JTS	*Journal of Theological Studies,* Oxford
Jud	*Judaica,* Zurich
K	*Kethibh*
KAI	H. Donner-W. Röllig, *Kanaanäische und aramäische Inschriften,* 3 vols. (Wiesbaden, ^{2}1966-69, ^{3}1971-76)

KAT	*Kommentar zum AT,* ed. E. Sellin-J. Herrmann, Leipzig, Gütersloh
KBANT	*Kommentare und Beiträge zum Alten und Neuen Testament,* Düsseldorf
KBL	L. Koehler-W. Baumgartner, *Lexicon in Veteris Testamenti Libros* (Leiden, ^{1}1953, ^{2}1958, ^{3}1967–)
KD	C. F. Keil and F. J. Delitzsch, *Comm. on the OT,* 10 vols. (Eng. trans., repr. Grand Rapids, 1954)
KEHAT	*Kurzgefasstes exegetisches Handbuch zum AT,* ed. O. F. Fridelin (Leipzig, 1812-1896)
KHC	*Kurzer Hand-Commentar zum AT,* ed. K. Marti, Tübingen, Leipzig
KlSchr	*Kleine Schriften* (A. Alt [Munich, 1953-59, ^{3}1964]; O. Eissfeldt [Tübingen, 1962-1979])
KTU	*Die keilalphabetischen Texte aus Ugarit,* I, ed. M. Dietrich-O. Loretz-J. Sanmartín. *AOAT,* 24 (1976)
KUB	*Keilschrifturkunde aus Boghazköi,* Berlin
KuD	*Kerygma und Dogma,* Göttingen
Kuhn	K. G. Kuhn, *Konkordanz zu den Qumrantexten* (Göttingen, 1960); Nachträge, *RevQ,* 4 (1963-64), 163-234
l(l).	line(s)
Lane	E. W. Lane, *An Arabic-English Lexicon,* 8 vols. (London, 1863-1893, repr. 1968)
LAPO	*Littératures anciennes du Proche-Orient,* Paris
LÄS	*Leipziger ägyptische Studien,* Glückstadt
Lat.	Latin
LD	*Lectio divina,* Paris
Leslau, *Contributions*	W. Leslau, *Ethiopic and South Arabic Contributions to the Hebrew Lexicon* (Los Angeles, 1958)
LexÄg	W. Helck-E. Otto, *Lexikon der Ägyptologie* (Wiesbaden, 1975–)
LexHebAram	F. Zorrell, *Lexicon hebraicum et aramaicum Veteris Testamenti* (Rome, 1958, repr. 1968)
LexLingAeth	A. Dillmann, *Lexicon linguae aethiopicae* (Leipzig, 1865)
LexSyr	C. Brockelmann, *Lexicon syriacum* (Halle, 1928, ^{2}1968)
LidzEph	M. Lidzbarski, *Ephemeris für semitische Epigraphik* (Giessen, 1900-1915)
Lisowsky	G. Lisowsky, *Konkordanz zum hebräischen AT* (Stuttgart, 1958, ^{2}1966)
lit.	literally
LThK	*Lexikon für Theologie und Kirche,* ed. M. Buchberger, 10 vols. (Freiburg, 1930-38); ed. J. Höfer-K. Rahner, 10 vols. with index, 3 sups. (^{2}1957-1968, ^{3}1966-68)
LXX	Septuagint (LXX^{A}, Codex Alexandrinus; LXX^{B}, Codex Vaticanus; LXX^{R}, Lucianic recension; LXX$^{S[1,2]}$, Codex Sinaiticus, correctors 1, 2, etc.)
MAH	*Mélanges d'archéologie et d'histoire de l'école française de Rome,* Paris
Mand.	Mandaic
MarThSt	*Marburger theologische Studien,* Marburg
MÄSt	*Münchener Ägyptologische Studien,* Berlin
masc.	masculine
MdD	E. S. Drower-R. Macuch, *Mandaic Dictionary* (Oxford, 1963)
MEE	*Materiali Epigrafica di Ebla,* ser. maior, Naples
mg.	margin
Midr.	Midrash
MKAW	*Mededelingen der Koninklijke Nederlandse Akademie van Wetenschapen,* Amsterdam
Moab.	Moabite
Mon.	Monograph

MPG	J. P. Migne, *Patrologia graeca,* 167 vols. (Paris, 1857-1866); index, 2 vols. (1928-1936)
MPL	J. P. Migne, *Patrologia latina,* 221 vols. (Paris, 1841-1864); sup., 5 vols. (1958-1970)
MRS	*Mission de Ras Shamra,* Paris
MS(S).	manuscript(s)
MT	Masoretic Text
MThS	*Münchener theologische Studien,* Munich
Mur	Wadi Murabbaʿat text(s)
Mus	*Muséon,* Louvain
MVÄG	*Mitteilungen der Vorderasiatisch-Ägyptischen Gesellschaft* (Berlin), Leipzig
n(n).	note(s)
N	name
Nab.	Nabatean
NEB	*Die Neue Echter-Bibel,* Würzburg
NedGTT	*Nederduitse gereformeerde teologiese Tydskrif,* Kaapstad
NedThT	*Nederlands theologisch Tijdschrift,* Wageningen
NGWG	*Nachrichten von der Gesellschaft der Wissenschaften zu Göttingen,* Berlin
NJB	The New Jerusalem Bible (New York, 1985)
no(s).	number(s)
NRSV	New Revised Standard Version (New York, 1989)
NRTh	*Nouvelle Revue Théologique,* Louvain, Paris
N.S.	New Series
NT	New Testament, Neues Testament, etc.
NTS	*New Testament Studies,* Cambridge
NTT	Norsk teologisk Tidsskrift, Oslo
OBO	*Orbis biblicus et orientalis,* Fribourg, Göttingen
OBT	*Overtures to Biblical Theology,* Philadelphia, Minneapolis
obv.	obverse of a papyrus or tablet
OIP	*Oriental Institute Publications,* Chicago
OLZ	*Orientalistische Literaturzeitung,* Leipzig, Berlin
Or	*Orientalia,* Rome
OrAnt	*Oriens antiquus,* Rome
OrBibLov	*Orientalia et biblica Lovaniensia,* Louvain
OrSuec	*Orientalia Suecana,* Uppsala
OSA	Old South Arabic
OT	Old Testament, Oude Testament, etc.
OTL	*The Old Testament Library,* Philadelphia, Louisville
OTS	*Oudtestamentische Studiën,* Leiden
OuTWP	*Ou testamentiese werkgemeenskap in Suid-Afrika,* Pretoria
p(p).	page(s)
P	Priestly source (P^G, Priestly *Grundschrift* ["basic material"; P^S, secondary Priestly source])
Palmyr.	Palmyrene
PAPS	*Proceedings of the American Philosophical Society,* Philadelphia
par.	parallel/and parallel passages
pass.	passive
PCRHP	*Publications du Centre de Recherches d'histoire et de philologie. Hautes études orientales,* Geneva
PEQ	*Palestine Exploration Quarterly,* London
perf.	perfect
Phil.-hist. Kl.	Philosophische-historische Klasse

Phoen.	Phoenician
PJ	*Palästinajahrbuch,* Berlin
pl(s).	plate(s)
pl.	plural
PLO	*Porta linguarum orientalium,* Wiesbaden
PN	Personal name
PNU	F. Grondähl, *Die Personennamen der Texte aus Ugarit. StPohl,* 1 (1967)
prep.	preposition
PRU	*Le Palais royal d'Ugarit,* ed. C. F.-A. Schaeffer-J. Nougayrol. *MRS*
ptcp.	participle
Pun.	Punic
PW	A. Pauly-G. Wissowa, *Real-Encyclopädie der classischen Altertumswissenschaft,* 6 vols. (Stuttgart, 1839-1852); sup., 11 vols. (1903-1956); ser. 2, 10 vols. (1914-1948)
Q	Qere
Q	Qumran scroll (preceded by arabic numeral designating cave)
QuaestDisp	*Quaestiones disputatae,* ed. K. Rahner-H. Schlier (Eng. ed., New York, 1961–)
R (preceded by roman numeral)	text in H. C. Rawlinson, *The Cuneiform Inscriptions of Western Asia,* 5 vols. (London, 1861-1884)
R	Redactor (R^D, Deuteronomistic; R^P, Priestly)
R.	Rabbi
RA	*Revue d'assyriologie et d'archéologie orientale,* Paris
RAC	*Reallexikon für Antike und Christentum,* ed. T. Klauser (Stuttgart, 1950–)
RAcc	F. Thureau-Dangin, *Rituels accadiens* (Paris, 1921)
RÄR	H. Bonnet, *Reallexikon der ägyptischen Religionsgeschichte* (Berlin, 1952, ^{2}1971)
RB	*Revue biblique,* Paris
RdM	*Die Religionen der Menschheit,* ed. C. M. Schröder, Stuttgart
REJ	*Revue des études juives,* Paris
repr.	reprint, reprinted
RÉS (with number of text)	*Répertoire d'épigraphie sémitique* (Paris, 1900–)
RevBíbl	*Revista bíblica,* Buenos Aires
RevExp	*Review and Expositor,* Louisville
RevQ	*Revue de Qumrân,* Paris
RGG	*Die Religion in Geschichte und Gegenwart* (Tübingen, ^{2}1927-1931, ed. H. Gunkel-L. Zscharnack, 5 vols.; ^{3}1957-1965, ed. K.Galling, 6 vols.)
RHPR	*Revue d'histoire et de philosophie religieuses,* Strasbourg, Paris
RHR	*Revue de l'histoire des religions,* Paris
RivBiblCalz	*Rivista biblica, Rafael Calzada,* Argentina
RLA	*Reallexikon der Assyriologie,* ed. E. Ebeling-B. Meissner (Berlin, 1932–)
RLV	*Reallexikon der Vorgeschichte,* ed. M. Ebert, 15 vols. (Berlin, 1924-1932)
RoB	*Religion och Bibel,* Stockholm
RS	Ras Shamra text
RSO	*Rivista degli studi orientali,* Rome
RSP	*Ras Shamra Parallels: The Texts from Ugarit and the Hebrew Bible,* ed. L. R. Fisher, *et al.,* I, *AnOr,* 49 (1972); II, *AnOr,* 50 (1975); III, *AnOr,* 51 (1981)
RSV	Revised Standard Version (New York, 1946, 1952)
RT	*Receuil de travaux relatifs à la philologie et à l'archeologie égyptiennes et assyriennes,* Paris
rto.	recto, on the obverse of a papyrus or tablet

RyNP	G. Ryckmans, *Les noms propres sud-sémitiques,* 3 vols. *Bibliothèque de muséon,* 2 (Louvain, 1934-35)
SAHG	A. Falkenstein and W. von Soden, *Sumerische und akkadische Hymnen und Gebeten* (Zurich, 1953)
Sam.	Samaritan
SAT	*Die Schriften des ATs im Auswald,* ed. H. Gunkel–H. Gressmann (Göttingen)
SAW	*Sitzungsberichte der Österreichischen Akademie der Wissenschaften in Wien,* Vienna
SBFLA	*Studii biblici franciscani liber annus,* Jerusalem
SBL	Society of Biblical Literature
SBLSBS	*SBL Sources for Biblical Study,* Chico, Atlanta
SBM	*Stuttgarter biblische Monographien*
SBOT	*Sacred Books of the OT,* ed. P. Haupt (London, 1893)
SBS	*Stuttgarter Bibel-Studien*
SBT	*Studies in Biblical Theology,* London, Naperville
ScrHier	*Scripta hierosolymitana,* Jerusalem
SDAW	*Sitzungsberichte der Deutschen Akademie der Wissenschaften zu Berlin*
SEÅ	*Svensk exegetisk Åarsbok,* Lund
Sem	*Semitica,* Paris
ser.	series
Seux	J. M. Seux, *Epithètes royales akkadiens et sumériennes* (Paris, 1967)
sg.	singular
SHAW	*Sitzungsberichte der Heidelberger Akademie der Wissenschaften*
SIDA	*Scripta Instituti Donneriani Aboensis,* Stockholm
SJ	*Studia Judaica,* Berlin
SJT	*Scottish Journal of Theology,* Edinburgh
SKG.G	*Schriften der Königsberger Gelehrten Gesellschaft, Geisteswissenschaftliche Klasse,* Halle
SNumen	*Sup to Numen,* Leiden
SNVAO	*Skrifter utgitt av det Norske Videnskaps-Akademi i Oslo*
Sond	Sonderband, Sonderheft
SOTS	Society for Old Testament Studies, Cambridge
SPAW	*Sitzungsberichte der Preussischen Akademie der Wissenschaften,* Berlin
SSN	*Studia semitica neerlandica,* Assen
st.	status
StAns	*Studia Anselmiana,* Rome
StANT	*Studien zum Alten und Neuen Testament,* Munich
St.-B.	H. L. Strack-P. Billerbeck, *Kommentar zum NT aus Talmud und Midrasch,* 6 vols. (Munich, 1922-1961, ^{5}1969)
StDI	*Studia et documenta ad iura orientis antiqui pertinentia,* Leiden
STDJ	*Studies on the Texts of the Desert of Judah,* Leiden, Grand Rapids
StFS	*Studia Francisci Scholten memoriae dicata,* Leiden
StJLA	*Studies in Judaism in Late Antiquity,* Leiden
STLI	*Studies and Texts.* Philip W. Lown Institute of Advanced Judaic Studies, Brandeis University, Cambridge, Mass.
StOr	*Studia orientalia,* Helsinki
StPb	*Studia Postbiblica,* Leiden
StPohl	*Studia Pohl,* Rome
StSem	*Studi semitici,* Rome
StT	*Studi e testi,* Rome
StTh	*Studia theologica,* Lund, Århus
StudGen	*Studium generale,* Berlin

StUNT	*Studien zur Umwelt des NTs,* Göttingen
subst.	substantive
suf.	suffix
Sum.	Sumerian
Sup	Supplement(s) (to)
s.v.	*sub voce* (*vocibus*), under the word(s)
SVT	*Supplements to VT,* Leiden
Synt	C. Brockelmann, *Hebräische Syntax* (Neukirchen-Vluyn, 1956)
Syr.	Syriac
Syr	*Syria: Revue d'art oriental et d'archéologie,* Paris
SZ	*Kurzgefasster Kommentar zu den heiligen Schriften Alten und Neuen Testamentes,* ed. H. L. Strack-O. Zöckler (Nordlingen, 1886-1898)
TAD	*Textbook of Aramaic Documents from Ancient Egypt,* ed. B. Porten-A. Yardin, 4 vols. (Jerusalem, 1986).
TAik	*Teologinen aikakauskirja,* Helsinki
Targ.	Targum
TCL	*Textes cunéiformes du Musée du Louvre,* 31 vols. (Paris, 1910-1967)
TDNT	*Theological Dictionary of the NT,* ed. G. Kittel-G. Friedrich, 10 vols. plus index (Eng. trans., Grand Rapids, 1964-1976)
ThArb	*Theologische Arbeiten,* Berlin
THAT	*Theologisches Handwörterbuch zum AT,* ed. E. Jenni-C. Westermann, 2 vols. (Munich, 1971-79)
ThB	*Theologische Bücherei,* Munich
ThLZ	*Theologische Literaturzeitung,* Leipzig, Berlin
ThQ	*Theologische Quartalschrift,* Tübingen, Stuttgart
ThSt	*Theologische Studien,* Zurich
ThStKr	*Theologische Studien und Kritiken,* Hamburg, Gotha, Leipzig
ThViat	*Theologia viatorum,* Berlin
ThZ	*Theologische Zeitschrift,* Basel
Tigr.	Tigriña
TigrWb	E. Littmann-M. Höfner, *Wörterbuch der Tigre-Sprache* (Wiesbaden, 1962)
trans.	translation, translated by
TRE	*Theologische Realenzyklopädie,* ed. G. Krause-G. Müller-H. R. Balz, 22 vols. (Berlin, 1977-1992)
TrThZ	*Trierer theologische Zeitschrift*
TU	*Texte und Untersuchungen der altchristlichen Literatur,* Leipzig, Berlin
TWNT	*Theologisches Wörterbuch zum NT,* ed. G. Kittel–G. Friedrich, 10 vols. plus index (Stuttgart, 1933-1979)
UCPNES	University of California Publications in Near Eastern Studies, Berkeley
UF	*Ugarit-Forschungen,* Neukirchen-Vluyn
Ugar.	Ugaritic
UM	C. H. Gordon, *Ugaritic Manual. AnOr,* 35 (1955)
UT	C. H. Gordon, *Ugaritic Textbook. AnOr,* 38 (1965, ^{2}1967)
UUÅ	*Uppsala Universitets årsskrift*
v(v).	verse(s)
VAB	*Vorderasiatische Bibliothek,* 7 vols. (Leipzig, 1907-1916)
VAS	*Vorderasiatische Schriftdenkmäler der königlichen Museen,* Berlin
VAWA	*Verhandelingen der Koninklijke Akademie van Wetenschappen,* Amsterdam
VG	C. Brockelmann, *Grundriss der vergleichenden Grammatik der semitischen Sprachen,* 2 vols. (1908-1913, repr. Hildesheim, 1961)
VIOF	*Veroffentlich. Institut für Orientforschung,* Berlin
vo.	verso, on the reverse of a papyrus or tablet

VT — *Vetus Testamentum,* Leiden
Vulg. — Vulgate
VVAW.L — *Verhandelingen van de Koninklijke Vlaamse Academie voor Wetenschappen, Letteren en Schone Kunsten van België,* Klasse der letteren, Brussels
WbÄS — A. Erman-H. Grapow, *Wörterbuch der ägyptischen Sprache,* 6 vols. (Leipzig, 1926-1931, repr. 1963)
WbMyth — *Wörterbuch der Mythologie,* ed. H. W. Haussig (Stuttgart, 1965–)
WBTh — *Wiener Beiträge zur Theologie,* Vienna
Wehr — H. Wehr, *A Dictionary of Modern Written Arabic,* ed. J. M. Cowan (Ithaca, 1961, ^{3}1971, ^{4}1979)
Whitaker — R. E. Whitaker, *A Concordance of the Ugaritic Language* (Cambridge, Mass., 1972)
WMANT — *Wissenschaftliche Monographien zum Alten und Neuen Testament,* Neukirchen-Vluyn
WO — *Die Welt des Orients,* Göttingen
WTM — J. Levy, *Wörterbuch über die Talmudim und Midraschim,* 4 vols. (Leipzig, ^{2}1924, repr. 1963)
WUS — J. Aistleitner, *Wörterbuch der ugaritischen Sprache. BSAW,* Phil.-hist. Kl., 106/3 (1963, ^{4}1974)
WZ Halle — *Wissenschaftliche Zeitschrift der Martin-Luther-Universität Halle-Wittenberg,* Halle
WZ Leipzig — *Wissenschaftliche Zeitschrift der Karl-Marx-Universität Leipzig*
WZKM — *Wiener Zeitschrift für die Kunde des Morgenlandes,* Vienna
ZA — *Zeitschrift für Assyriologie,* Leipzig, Berlin
ZÄS — *Zeitschrift für ägyptische Sprache und Altertumskunde,* Leipzig, Berlin
ZAW — *Zeitschrift für die alttestamentliche Wissenschaft,* Giessen, Berlin
ZBK — *Zürcher Bibelkommentare,* Zurich, Stuttgart
ZDMG — *Zeitschrift der Deutschen Morgenländischen Gesellschaft,* Leipzig, Wiesbaden
ZDPV — *Zeitschrift des Deutschen Palästina-Vereins,* Leipzig, Stuttgart, Wiesbaden
ZKTh — *Zeitschrift für katholische Theologie,* Innsbruck
ZNW — *Zeitschrift für die neutestamentliche Wissenschaft,* Giessen, Berlin
ZRFOP — *Zion Research Foundation, Occasional Publications*
ZRGG — *Zeitschrift für Religions- und Geistesgeschichte,* Cologne
ZS — *Zeitschrift für Semitistik und verwandte Gebiete,* Leipzig
ZThK — *Zeitschrift für Theologie und Kirche,* Tübingen
ZWTh — *Zeitschrift für wissenschaftliche Theologie,* Jena
→ — cross-reference within this Dictionary
< — derived from
> — whence derived, to
* — theoretical form

TRANSLITERATION

VOWELS

◌ַ	a
◌ֲ	ᵃ
◌ָ	ā
◌ָה	â
◌ָיו	āw
◌ַי	ay
◌ָי	āy
◌ֶ	e
◌ֱ	ᵉ
◌ֶי	ey
◌ֵ	ē
◌ֵי	ê
◌ְ	ᵉ
◌ִ	i
◌ִי	î
◌ִיּ	iyy
◌ָ	o
◌ֳ	ᵒ
◌ֹ	ō
◌וֹ	ô
◌ֻ	u, ū
◌וּ	û

CONSONANTS

א	ʾ
בּ	b
ב	ḇ
גּ	g
ג	ḡ
דּ	d
ד	ḏ
ה, הּ	h
ו	w
ז	z
ח	ḥ
ט	ṭ
י	y
כּ, ךּ	k
כ, ך	ḵ
ל	l
מ, ם	m
נ, ן	n
ס	s
ע	ʿ
פּ	p
פ, ף	p̄
צ, ץ	ṣ
ק	q
ר	r
שׂ	ś
שׁ	š
תּ	t
ת	ṯ

לָכַד *lāḵaḏ;* לֶכֶד *leḵeḏ;* מַלְכֹּדֶת *malkōḏeṯ*

Contents: I. The Root *lkd*: 1. Statistics; 2. LXX; 3. Qumran. II. OT Usage: 1. Original Usage; 2. Metaphorical Application; 3. "Capture, Seize"; 4. Cast Lots; 5. Occurrences in Job.

I. The Root lkd. The verb *lkd* exhibits the basic meaning "capture, catch" and is used in the OT with reference to both animals and human beings. In Akkadian the same root *lakādu(m)* means to "run," while Akk. *kašādu(m)* corresponds to Heb. *lkd.*[1] The Aramaic term *l^eḵaḏ* in the Targumim (Est. 1:8; Eccl. 7:27) shifts the original meaning to "seize, take hold of." The stem has a similar meaning in Phoenician,[2] while Arab. *lakida* means "stick, cleave to."

1. *Statistics.* The root *lkd* occurs altogether 117 times in the OT: 83 times in the qal, 32 times in the niphal, and twice in the hithpael. By far the most numerous occurrences of *lkd* are in the historical writings, especially in the Deuteronomistic history and, probably influenced by these, in Jeremiah. The overall distribution of the verb breaks down as follows: 7 occurrences in the Pentateuch, 55 in the Deuteronomistic history, 10 in Chronicles, 1 in Nehemiah, 3 in the Psalms, 4 in Job, 5 in Proverbs, 1 each in Ecclesiastes and Lamentations, 4 in Isaiah, 21 in Jeremiah, 2 each in Daniel and Amos, 1 in Habbakuk. In addition, Prov. 3:26 attests the noun *leḵeḏ,* "snare," derived from the verb, and Job 18:10 the noun *malkoḏeṯ,* "trap." The verb *lkd* also occurs in the Hebrew text of Sir. 9:3d and in MS. D in 37:11b.

2. *LXX.* The LXX generally renders the root *lkd* with *lambánein* and its compounds *katalambánein, prokatalambánein,* and *syllambánein,* although there is no apparent reason for the differences prompting the choice of the simple or compound forms.

3. *Qumran.* The root *lkd* occurs 3 times in the Qumran texts: In 1QpHab 4:4, the term refers to the taking of fortifications, and in 1QH 2:29; 8:34, to a foot being caught in a snare (or net).

II. OT Usage.

1. *Original Usage.* The root *lkd* probably originally referred to the capturing of wild animals: according to Jgs. 15:4 Samson captured three hundred foxes. Besides human beings, predatory animals also occasionally occur as the subject of such capturing, e.g., a lion in Am. 3:4. According to Am. 3:5, birds are captured in a trap or snare. It is not surprising that at an early stage the original meaning of *lkd* was transferred to the capture of human beings in war, the common elements being the use of force and the

1. *AHw,* I (1965), 459b-461b, 529a.
2. *DISO,* 138.

deprivation of freedom; cf. Josh. 11:17; Jgs. 7:25; 8:12,14; 2 S. 8:4; 2 Ch. 22:9; 33:11; Job 36:8; Jer. 6:11; Lam. 4:20.

2. *Metaphorical Application.* The use of *lkd* is transposed into the religious and especially the ethical sphere above all in the prophetic writings and Wisdom Literature. Prov. 6:2 uses *lkd* metaphorically to refer to the obligation arising through promises and pledges.

Both God and sin in various guises appear as the subject of the verb, which is placed primarily in the service of divine judgment. According to Jer. 5:26, the sin of Jerusalem's inhabitants is that they seek to capture human beings, and according to Jer. 18:22 the prophet is threatened with capture. The inhabitants of Jerusalem (Jer. 6:11; 8:9), Moab (48:44), and Babylon (51:56) are threatened with capture as a part of divine judgment. According to Isa. 8:15, God himself will become a snare entrapping Jerusalem's inhabitants, and according to Job 5:13 God captures the wise in their own craftiness. With *lkd* he thus initiates the act-consequence relationship.[3] Thus it happens that at God's own initiative the wicked are caught in their own net (Ps. 9:16[Eng. v. 15]; 35:8). Prov. 5:22 means the same thing when the blasphemer is ensnared by his own iniquity (cf. Jer. 18:22). Thus the psalmist, too, can hope that his antagonists will be trapped in their own pride (Ps. 59:13[12]). Prov. 11:6 makes the same kind of statement in asserting that the treacherous are ensnared by their own lust. This idea also forms the background to the observation that a man taken in by feminine guile has gone astray from life (Eccl. 7:26); Sir. 9:3 similarly warns against the snares of a loose woman.

3. *"Capture, Seize."* In the majority of cases *lkd* refers to capturing and conquering cities and countries (altogether 71 times). We first encounter the verb in this meaning in the Pentateuch in Nu. 21:32; 32:39,41f.[4] In Nu. 32:39-42, *lkd* describes the conquest of the territory east of the Jordan, particularly Gilead. This pericope is probably one of the oldest Pentateuchal traditions.

The verb occurs 3 times in the recapitulation of the events starting with Israel's departure from Horeb and ending with their arrival in the territory east of the Jordan (Dt. 2:34f.; 3:4). In the first two instances it stands in context with → חרם *ḥāram* and serves as the prerequisite for the consecrated extermination of the entire male population. This explains why *lkd* (usually with *ḥrm* or *nkh*), judged against its frequency and meaning, becomes virtually a terminus technicus for the conquest of the land as portrayed in Joshua. This connection with *ḥrm* can already be discerned in its first occurrence in Josh. 6:20f., the conquest of Jericho. The taking of Ai (Josh. 8:19,21) also precedes its consecration to destruction (8:24). In 10:28,32,35, this zeugma becomes a standard expression. Josh. 10:37 reports that the same fate befell Hebron, and

---

3. Cf. G. von Rad, *OT Theology,* I (Eng. trans., New York, 1962), 264-66, 384-87, 411-13.
4. According to M. Noth, *Numbers.* OTL (Eng. trans. 1968), 165f., "Num. 21:32aβ, with an expression which is out of context and incomplete, must be an addition."

likewise v. 39 for Debir and all its towns. Finally, 10:42 uses *lkd* to summarize Joshua's subjugation of the entire southern region (= southern Palestine).

Josh. 11:10-12 reports further that Israel dealt similarly with Hazor and its royal cities in the north (= northern Palestine). In Josh. 15:16f. (cf. Jgs. 1:12f.), *lkd* refers to the taking of Kiriath-sepher. The conquest concludes with the taking of Leshem and the destruction of its inhabitants (Josh. 19:47). Jgs. 1:18 adds that Judah took three Philistine cities; according to 9:45 the usurper Abimelech took Shechem, although ultimately the siege and taking of Thebez was his undoing (vv. 50-57).

In 2 S. 5:7, *lkd* describes David's taking of the stronghold of Zion (cf. 1 Ch. 11:5), and in 2 S. 12:26-29 his siege and taking of Rabbah of the Ammonites. In addition to 1 K. 9:16; 16:18; and 2 K. 12:18(17), mention should be made especially of the conquest of Samaria in 2 K. 17:6 (cf. 18:10) and the fall of the northern kingdom. The verb *lkd* occurs with similar meaning in 2 Ch. 12:4; 13:19; 15:8; 17:2; 28:18; 32:18; Isa. 20:1. Influenced by the Deuteronomistic history and in retrospect of Samaria's fate, Jeremiah uses the same term to announce the threat of Jerusalem's own conquest by Nebuchadnezzar (Jer. 32:3,24,28; 34:22; 37:8; 38:3) as Yahweh's irreversible judgmental decree. The same fate then overtakes Babylon itself (Jer. 50:2,9,24; 51:31,41).

Preparatory measures for a successful siege include seizing vital water sources and cutting them off from the enemy; this action, too, is described by *lkd* in Jgs. 3:28; 7:24; 12:5.

4. *Casting Lots.* An additional, more narrow and specialized meaning for *lkd* is attested in Joshua and 1 Samuel: "to cast lots, to take by lots." In the pericope Josh. 7:14-18, *lkd* occurs 8 times with this specific meaning, 4 times each in the qal and niphal. The specialized use of *lkd* here suggests that the conquest of Ai depends on the complete consecration to destruction of all booty. Thus according to the laws of holy war a unique kind of "conquest" and "capture" must be applied to the guilty Achan; he along with his entire property is subjected to the most severe punishment: utter annihilation by fire. The text is reporting specifically a covenant transgression. The translation "cast lots, take by lots" is derived from the sense of the text. The Hebrew text itself does not attest the equivalent for "lots"; rather, the entire process is expressed by the single verb *lkd,* and thus the specifics of the inquiry and proceedings cannot be discerned.

In 1 S. 10:20f., *lkd* in the niphal is used 3 times to refer to Samuel's official appointment of Saul as the king of Israel. In a manner similar to Josh. 7:14-18, this determination by lots also proceeds from the larger unity of the entire people down to the actual chosen individual. Here too, however, there is no indication of the exact nature of this oracular determination by lots. The verb *lkd* suggests that the power of God stands behind Saul's appointment as king, a power deciding through almost physical intervention. 1 S. 14:47 uses the same root to describe Saul's assumption of kingship (cf. the same situation in Dnl. 6:1[5:31]; 7:18, where Aram. *qabbēl* is used). Finally, in 1 S. 14:41f. the casting of lots serves as a final means of determining who has transgressed against Saul's oath (v. 24) not to eat food until evening. After inquiries to God yield no answer (v. 37), the casting of lots decides as the ultimate authority; it falls on the royal house itself, whereas the people go free. Further casting of lots finally specifies Jonathan, who exhibits no hesitation about accepting death. Only the intervention of the people on his behalf spares his life.

5. *Occurrences in Job.* The 2 occurrences of *lkd* in the hithpael recall the general occurrences of *lkd* by expressing the same kind of tenacity or firmness otherwise resulting from an act of seizing or grasping. Thus Job 38:30 can say of the surface of water that frost causes it to become hard as a stone. Job 41:9(17) says that the impenetrable scales of the crocodile are firmly fastened and cannot be separated.

This confirms that the background of the broad and various uses of *lkd* is always the idea of the application of force and of the resulting firmness or stability.

Gross

לָמַד *lāmaḏ;* לִמּוּד limmûḏ; מַלְמָד malmāḏ; תַּלְמִיד talmîḏ

Contents: I. Ancient Near East. II. OT Usage and Qumran: 1. Qal; 2. Piel; 3. Late Occurrences; 4. Qumran; 5. Derivations. III. Summary. IV. LXX.

I. Ancient Near East. The verb *lmd* is used in Ugaritic texts to mean "learn, practice" or "instruct."[1] The corresponding pass. ptcp. *lmd,* "apprentice," occurs several times.[2] Apprentices clearly constituted a broad category in ancient Ugarit. In Akkadian the verb *lamādu* had approximately the same meaning as *yd'* in Hebrew: "experience, acquire, learn, understand, comprehend, know (a woman)," D "instruct, teach."[3] A *lāmid pirišti* was a "knower of mysteries," a soothsaying priest, possibly an ecstatic.[4] Peculiarly, *talmīdu* means not only "apprentice" but also "(broken-in) plow."[5]

---

lāmaḏ. W. Barclay, *Educational Ideals in the Ancient World* (1959, repr. Grand Rapids, 1974); H. Brunner, *Altägyptische Erziehung* (Wiesbaden, 1957); L. Dürr, *Das Erziehungswesen im AT und im antiken Orient. MVÄG,* 36/2 (1932); H.-J. Fabry, "Gott im Gespräch zwischen den Generationen," *Katechetische Blätter,* 107 (1982), 754-760; H. Gese, *Lehre und Wirklichkeit in der alten Weisheit* (Tübingen, 1958); J. C. Greenfield, "Ugaritic *mdl* and Its Cognates," *Bibl,* 45 (1964), 527-534; E. Jenni, "למד *lmd* lernen," *THAT,* I, 872-75; A. Klostermann, "Schulwesen im alten Israel," *Theologische Studien. Festschrift T. Zahn* (Leipzig, 1908), 193-232; A. Lemaire, *Les écoles et la formation de la Bible dans l'ancien Israël. OBO,* 39 (1981); E. Lohse, *Die Ordination im Spätjudentum und im NT* (Berlin, 1950/51); H. Torczyner (Tur Sinai), *Die Bundeslade und die Anfänge der Religion Israels* (Berlin, ²1930); Ḥ. Yalon, "The Meaning of ידע, למד," *Tarbiz,* 36/4 (1966-67), 396-400.

1. *KTU,* 1.6 VI, 55; 1.18 I, 29; 1.6 VI, 54; 1.18 VI, 29.
2. *WUS,* no. 1469.
3. *AHw,* I (1965), 531f.; *CAD,* IX (1973), 53ff.
4. *AHw,* I, 531b; *CAD,* IX, 55.
5. *AHw,* III (1981), 1311.

The term is used in Semitic languages with slight variations of meaning. The Arabic term *lamada* means "subject oneself,"[6] and Eth. *lamada* means "learn, accustom oneself." These meanings suggest that in the ancient Semitic world learning and teaching were not conducted totally without disciplinary measures.[7] Yet another semantic development occurs in Old South Arabic and Syriac. In Old South Arabic the word means "pull over, paste over,"[8] while in Syriac it means "cleave to."[9]

II. OT Usage and Qumran.

1. *Qal.* The Hebrew verb *lmd* means "learn" in the qal and "teach" in the piel. The underlying meaning appears to be "have experiences," perhaps also[10] "accustom oneself to something, become familiar with something." It is easy to see that this familiarization often took place with the aid of a whip (esp. in Proverbs).[11]

As might be expected, the verb occurs most frequently in the prophetic writings, the Psalms, and Deuteronomy. The relatively infrequent mention of learning in the historical writings is due to the fact that ancient Israel had no organized system of education of the kind familiar to us from ancient Sumer and Babylonia. Israel had nothing comparable to the "tablet house" of the Mesopotamian cultures. Instruction was usually provided by one's father (Dt. 6:20ff.).[12] In contrast, the frequent mention of learning in the poetic writings and Deuteronomy results from the fact that these writings understand it religiously. Here it usually does not refer to the appropriation of general knowledge or of knowledge applicable to daily life, but rather to the acquisition of specialized insights.

Whenever "disciples" are mentioned, the reference is not to pupils in a school, but rather usually to the followers of a prophet (2 K. 2:3ff.; Isa. 8:16; 50:4).

The semantic element "learn" manifests itself particularly in the qal. An old admonition in Isa. 1:17 exhorts the people to "learn to do good." Similar expressions also occur in later sections of the book. Through God's judgment the people will "learn righteousness," whereas the wicked do not learn righteousness (Isa. 26:9f.). Those who go astray will come to understanding, "learn (RSV 'accept') instruction (*leqaḥ*)," and fear Israel's God (Isa. 29:24). In God's future human beings will never again lift up swords or learn to wage war (Isa. 2:4 par. Mic. 4:3). The book of Jeremiah also conceives learning religiously: "Thus says Yahweh: 'Do not learn the way of the nations, or be dismayed at the signs of the heavens' " (Jer. 10:2).[13] Foreign nations are

---

6. Cf. Guillaume, 4.
7. Cf. the basic meaning proposed by *HAL,* "prick, spur on."
8. ContiRossini, 171.
9. *LexSyr,* 367.
10. So L. Koehler.
11. Cf. also M. H. Goshen-Gottstein, " 'Ephraim is a well-trained heifer' and Ugaritic *mdl,*" *Bibl,* 41 (1960), 64-66.
12. Cf. the discussion of Fabry.
13. Cf. M. Dahood, "Hebrew-Ugaritic Lexicography IV," *Bibl,* 47 (1966), 410.

given the opportunity to "diligently learn the ways of my people"; only then will they be incorporated into the holy people (Jer. 12:16). In the song of the lioness, Ezekiel speaks about the young lion who learned to catch prey (Ezk. 19:3,6), a metaphor for young Israel.

Deuteronomy emphasizes the importance of learning. Learning should especially be directed to God's law and regulations, whose significance is repeatedly underscored. "Hear, O Israel, the statutes and ordinances that I am addressing to you today; you shall learn them and observe them diligently" (Dt. 5:1). Deuteronomy views this kind of learning as essential for life: "Assemble the people for me, and I will let them hear my words, so that they may learn to fear me as long as they live on the earth, and may teach their children so" (Dt. 4:10). Similar statements occur in Dt. 14:23; 17:19; 31:13, whereas 18:9 shifts the emphasis of the admonition elsewhere: "When you come into the land that Yahweh your God is giving you, you must not learn to imitate the abhorrent practices of those nations."

In Wisdom Literature learning is directed primarily to the acquisition of proper insight: "I have not learned wisdom, nor have I knowledge of the holy ones" (Prov. 30:3). This is also clear in Ps. 119: "I will praise you with an upright heart, when I learn your righteous ordinances" (v. 7); "it is good for me that I was humbled, so that I might learn your statutes" (v. 71); and "your hands have made and fashioned me; give me understanding that I may learn your commandments" (v. 73).

2. *Piel.* The verb is often used in the piel with the meaning "teach someone something"; here, too, the religious understanding predominates. As with the qal, the Psalms and Deuteronomy attest the most occurrences. Among the prophets only Jeremiah uses the verb with any frequency; otherwise it hardly occurs in the prophetic writings, perhaps because they considered teaching useless and without significance.

The term is introduced in a thoroughly characteristic fashion in Dt. 4:1: "So now, O Israel, give heed to the statutes and ordinances that I am teaching you to observe, so that you may live to enter and occupy the land that Yahweh, the God of your ancestors, is giving you." Virtually the same words and sense recur in Dt. 4:5,10,14; 5:31; 6:1. The negative form of the admonition occurs in Dt. 20:17f.: "You shall annihilate them — the Hittites and the Amorites, the Canaanites and the Perizzites, the Hivites and the Jebusites — just as Yahweh your God has commanded, so that they may not teach you to do all the abhorrent things that they do for their gods, and you thus sin against Yahweh your God."

Dt. 11:19 is concerned with teaching children, and says of God's words: "Teach them to your children, talking about them when you are at home and when you are away, when you lie down and when you rise." Yahweh decrees that one should teach what is known as the Song of Moses to the Israelites: "Now therefore write this song, and teach it to the Israelites; put it in their mouths, in order that this song may be a witness for me against the Israelites" (Dt. 31:19). Shortly thereafter we read: "That very day Moses wrote this song and taught it to the Israelites" (v. 22). 2 S. 1:18 is also concerned with the teaching of a song, in this case a lament composed by David: "He ordered that it be taught to the people of Judah." Otto Eissfeldt,[14] however, thinks this refers to "training in the use of tools of war." In another Davidic song we read: "He trains my hands for war, so that my arms can bend a bow of bronze" (2 S. 22:35 par. Ps. 18:35[Eng. v. 34]). Jgs. 3:2 also states clearly that Yahweh taught the Israelites how to wage war.

Ps. 25 speaks of a different teaching activity: "Make me to know (*yd'* hiphil) your ways, O Yahweh; teach me (*lmd* piel) your paths. Lead me in your truth, and teach me, for you are the God of my salvation" (vv. 4,5). "Good and upright is Yahweh; therefore he instructs sinners in the way. He leads the humble in what is right, and teaches the humble his way" (vv. 8f.). Ps. 34:12(11) reflects this same wisdom tradition: "Come, O children, listen to me; I will teach you the fear of Yahweh." Ps. 51:15(13) mentions the instruction of sinners: "Then I will teach transgressors your ways, and sinners will return to you." The words "for instruction" in the superscription to Ps. 60, a lament and petition, are more puzzling. Perhaps this is referring to the kind of teaching of God's deeds and great works of which Ps. 71:17 speaks: "O God, from my youth you have taught me, and I still proclaim your wondrous deeds. So even to old age and gray hairs."

Ps. 94 also refers to being taught by God: "He who disciplines the nations, should he not chastise, he who teaches knowledge to humankind?" (v. 10); "happy are those whom you discipline, O Yahweh, and whom you teach out of your law (*tôrâ*)" (v. 12). In both cases *lmd* stands together with → יסר *yāsar;* in v. 12 one should note that Yahweh's → תורה *tôrâ* serves as the medium of instruction.

In the unique Ps. 132, a so-called "song of ascents" (*šîr hamma'^a lôṯ*) which functioned perhaps as a festival liturgy, one encounters the idea that the king and his sons were taught by Yahweh: "Yahweh swore to David a sure oath . . . : 'One of the sons of your body I will set on your throne. If your sons keep my covenant and my decrees that I shall teach them, their sons also, forevermore, shall sit on your throne' " (Ps. 132:11f.). In Ps. 144:1 as well, the teaching is directed to the king, and the teacher is God, who teaches the king how to wage war: "Blessed be Yahweh, my rock, who trains my hands for war, and my fingers for battle." This reflects older conceptions that — as we saw above — also appear in Ps. 18:35(34).

As expected, God's instruction in Psalm 119, a wisdom psalm, extends to the laws and statutes which among the wise were always the primary object of all teaching: "Blessed are you, O Yahweh; teach me your statutes!" (v. 12; cf. vv. 26,64,66, 108,124,135,171). A different idea occurs in v. 99: "I have more understanding than all my teachers, for your decrees are my meditation." Obviously God is not conceived as the teacher here, something unusual for this psalm.

Among the prophets the verb is used in Hos. 10:11 to characterize Ephraim: He was like a "trained [i.e., tamed] heifer." The same metaphor is used in Jer. 31:18, although

14. "Zwei verkannte militärtechnische Termini im AT," *VT,* 5 (1955), 235-38 = *KlSchr,* III (1966), 356-58.

Ephraim is there compared with an untamed calf. Human commandments learned by rote (*lmd* pual) are rejected in Isa. 29:13.

Although in the book of Jeremiah teaching is conceived in an extremely wide and varied sense, it is nonetheless almost always directed toward the religious dimension in life. The people had forgotten God and grown accustomed to transgression (*lmd* piel; Jer. 2:33). Their neighbors had taught the people to swear by Baʿal (12:16). Indeed, their ancestors had taught the chosen people to follow the baʿals (9:13[14]). They had taught their tongues to speak lies (9:4[5]). Thus did Yahweh's word come to the lamenting women: "Teach to your daughters a dirge, and each to her neighbor a lament" (9:19[20]). It had to end with disaster: "What will you say when they set as head over you those whom you have trained (*lmd* piel) to be your allies?" (13:21). Though the people were persistently taught, they did not listen (32:33). Though chastisement had to come, one day a new covenant would be made: "No longer shall they teach one another, or say to each other, 'Know Yahweh,' for they shall all know me" (31:34). External teaching (*lmd*) is replaced by inward knowledge (*ydʿ*).

3. *Late Occurrences.* In later poetic writings as well as in the late historical writings the idea of learning and teaching loses something of the special significance the verb exhibited in the qal and piel in the older literature. Although the word is used in a more general sense, the reference to teaching and learning of the law still often resonates. In Proverbs one is instructed to avoid strange women (Prov. 5:13). The instruction mentioned in Cant. 8:2 (MT contra LXX and Syr.): "I would lead you and bring you into the house of my mother, who instructed me" (*tᵉlammᵉḏēnî*), apparently refers only to the youth's daily life. Cant. 3:8 speaks of the swordbearers who were trained in war (*mᵉlummᵉḏê milḥāmâ*). Qoheleth is called a wise person who "taught the people knowledge" (Eccl. 12:9).

It is said that Ezra set his heart on teaching the people Yahweh's law and justice in Israel (Ezr. 7:10). King Jehoshaphat also sent people to the cities of Judah to teach the people the law (2 Ch. 17:7,9). In David's time, people — sons of Asaph, Jeduthun, and Heman — were trained in singing for Yahweh (1 Ch. 25:7). In Dnl. 1:4, the instruction of the young Israelites is intended to teach them the letters and language of the Chaldeans. In Job 21:22, Job asks who could claim to teach God, considering that God himself rules over all creation.

4. *Qumran.* The verb occurs several times in the Qumran writings. The War scroll emphasizes that God will drive out the enemies; he had, after all, from time immemorial taught the generations to wage war (1QM 10:2). He will also teach limp hands how to fight (14:6). Even the horses had to be prepared for war (6:12) and the riders well trained in riding (6:13). The people were a people of the saints of the covenant, instructed in the laws (10:10).

The Qumran psalms speak of learning wisdom; this is learning brought about by God, and wisdom placed into the heart (1QH 2:17). 1QS 3:13 emphasizes that the *maśkîl* should both instruct (*byn* hiphil) and teach (*lmd* piel) all the sons of light. All who entered into the covenant were to promise that they would teach their adversaries

(1QS 10:26–11:1). The Rule of the Congregation decrees that each person in Israel be instructed in the precepts of the covenant from youth onward in the book *hgw* (1QSa 1:6f.).

5. *Derivations.* The term *limmûḏ* refers to a pupil who receives instruction or is otherwise introduced to something. In Isa. 8:16, the reference is to the prophet's disciples among whom the prophet will seal the torah.[15] Deutero-Isaiah mentions someone who has been taught by God and can teach others himself (Isa. 50:4). This disciple is identified with Yahweh's servant. The same book, however, speaks of other disciples as well, *limmûḏê YHWH,* whose *šālôm* will be great (Isa. 54:13).

The ancient prophets knew, however, that a person could also be a "disciple of evil" (Jer. 13:23).[16]

The Qumran writings speak of "disciples of God" (1QH 2:39). Yet another psalm recalls Isa. 50:4. The psalmist compares his own tongue with the *limmûḏîm* of God who are to instruct the heart (1QH 7:10,13f.). The Damascus document mentions the *limmûḏê 'el,* "those taught by God" (CD 20:4), a self-characterization of the community itself.

The term *malmāḏ* is attested only in Jgs. 3:31. There it refers to the means whereby Ehud (MT 'Shamgar') slew six hundred Philistines: an oxgoad of the kind used by drovers, i.e., of the kind used to teach oxen to move on (cf. the basic meaning above!).

The term *talmîḏ* occurs only in 1 Ch. 25:8, which speaks of temple musicians who were taught to sing for Yahweh. A *talmîḏ* was a person trained in this manner.

III. Summary. The verb *lmd* refers to learning and instruction of all sorts, and appears to have been the customary word for such activity and experience from an extremely early period. From his father or mother a young man could learn either what was useful or necessary for life, or particular skills such as how to wage war. Animals were also capable of learning, e.g., a young lion from an older one, or a young heifer from a human being. This everyday usage of the word, however, did not determine its characteristic OT usage.

The predominating idea is that God is the ultimate teacher. In the earliest period he is viewed as the teacher of any special skill. In time, however, this view shifted to one of God as the teacher of the Torah and of all the regulations applying to ethical and cultic life. He was the source of all instruction concerning these vital questions. This also meant, however, that he was the teacher of all wisdom, and was the only one capable of mediating this insight into the heavenly mysteries. Whoever was a *limmûḏ YHWH* was instructed by the highest authority and was thus in a position to instruct others as well.

---

15. Cf. W. G. E. Watson, review of J. Jensen, *The Use of tôrâ by Isaiah. CBQ Mon.,* 3 (1973), *Bibl,* 56 (1975), 275.

16. According to *KBL*[1,3] the occurrence of the word in Jer. 2:24 is due to scribal error.

IV. LXX. The LXX is remarkably consistent in its rendering of *lāmaḏ* and its derivatives: *didáskein* and *manthánein* predominate, although *deiknýein* and *paideía* are used in a few instances. *Malmāḏ* is rendered by the technical terms *apotrópous* and *árotron.*

Kapelrud

לָעַג *lāʿag;* לַעַג *laʿag;* *לָעֵג *lāʿēg*

Contents: I. 1. Etymology; 2. Occurrences; 3. Semantic Field; 4. Versions. II. 1. Mockery from One's Enemies; 2. Yahweh as Subject; 3. Mockery from the Pious.

I. 1. *Etymology.* Apart from Biblical Hebrew, the root *lʿg* is attested with certainty only in Jewish Aramaic, Syriac, and Middle Hebrew. Perhaps the Arabic term *laʿağa,* "burn, be painful," also belongs to this group, and may even suggest the basic meaning. In late Biblical Hebrew *lʿg* appears to have been displaced by Aram. *lʿb,* "mock."[1] It is generally agreed that *lʿg* originally meant "stutter, stammer."[2] This meaning is attested in Isa. 28:11; 33:19 (probably also Hos. 7:16) and is suggested by Syr. *lʿg,* "stutter," Syr. and Middle Heb. *lagleg,* "stutter," Mand. *lʿg,* "barbarian," Arab. *lağlağ,* "stutter," Eth.-Tigr. *lāʿlaʿa,* "stutter, stammer"; this is also confirmed to a certain extent in secondary forms and modifications of the root (*lʿʿ* I, "speak confusedly, without thinking," *lʿz,* "speak incomprehensibly," *ʿlg,* "stammer").[3] The semasiological derivation "stutter" > "mock," however, is not convincing. The meaning "stutter" and similar variations belong to an independent root which in view of its numerous secondary forms in Northwest and Southern Semitic idioms one can characterize as onomatopoetic.

2. *Occurrences.* Among the 27 occurrences of the root, 18 attest the verbal form, 7 the noun *laʿag*. The uncertain term **lāʿēg* attests 2 further occurrences (Isa. 28:11; Ps. 35:16).[4]

The verb *lāʿag* occurs overwhelmingly (12 times) in the qal (2 K. 19:21; Isa. 37:22;

---

lāʿag. O. Michel, "Verspottung," *BHHW,* III (1966), 2098f.; H. D. Preuss, *Die Verspottung fremder Religionen im AT. BWANT,* 92[5/12] (1971) 141-153; L. Ruppert, *Der leidende Gerechte und seine Feinde* (Würzburg, 1973), 111-148; W. Vischer, "Der im Himmel Thronende lacht," *Freude am Evangelium. Festschrift A. de Quervain. BEvTh,* 44 (1966), 129-135.

1. *HAL,* II (1995), 532, on the basis of M. Wagner, *Die lexikalischen und grammatikalischen Aramaismen im alttestamentlichen Hebräisch. BZAW,* 96 (1966), no. 147; cf. W. Rudolph, *Chronikbücher. HAT,* XXI (1955), 336, on 2 Ch. 36:16.

2. Cf. *LexHebAram;* Guillaume, 27.

3. According to *KBL*[2] metathesis to *lʿg*.

4. But cf. *HAL.*

Jer. 20:7; Job 9:23; 11:3; 22:19; Ps. 2:4; 59:9[Eng. v. 8]; 80:7[6]; Prov. 1:26; 17:5; 30:17). Additional occurrences of the qal forms emerge if in Ps. 25:2 one reads LXX ילעגו instead of יעלצו, and in Ps. 35:16 LXX לעגו לעוג instead of לעגי מעוג. The hiphil occurs 5 times (Job 21:3; Ps. 22:8[7]; Neh. 2:19; 3:33[4:1]; 2 Ch. 30:10; cf. also 2 Ch. 36:16; on *lʿb* see above I.1). The niphal occurs only once (Isa. 33:19), and this is the only passage where the verb is attested with the meaning "stammer" or something similar. The noun *laʿag,* built on the form *qaṭl,* occurs almost always in the singular (Job 34:7; Ps. 44:14[13]; 79:4; 123:4; Ezk. 23:32; 36:4; with suf. Hos. 7:16). Only Isa. 28:11 (*laʿagê,* stative const., pl. of *laʿag,*[5]) and Hos. 7:16[6] attest the meaning "stammering."

By far, then, the root occurs most frequently in the poetic books or poetic genres of the OT. Wisdom and cultic poetry (8 times each) and, influenced by them, also various prophetic genres (5 times) are well represented. Only at a late period, and then noticeably infrequently (2 Ch. 30:10 with 36:16; Neh. 2:19; 3:33[4:1]; always hiphil), does *lʿg* also appear in narrative prose.

Later use (Sir. 4:1; 34:22; 1QpHab 4:2,6; 1QM 12:7; emended text 1QH 4:16) shows no change over against the OT.

3. *Semantic Field.* The meaning of *lʿg,* "mock," is illuminated by numerous synonyms and parallel terms in the various contexts. Verbs and nouns accompanying *lʿg* include those of → שחק *śāḥaq,* "laugh" (2 Ch. 30:10; Ps. 2:4; 59:9[8]; Prov. 1:26; Jer. 20:7; 1QpHab 4:1f.,6f.; *ṣāḥaq,* Ezk. 23:32), → שמח *śāmaḥ,* "rejoice" (Job 22:19; Ps. 35:19,24; Prov. 17:5; 1QpHab 4:1f.), → בזה *bāzâ,* "despise," בוז *bûz,* "contempt" (2 K. 19:21 par. Isa. 37:22; 2 Ch. 36:16; Neh. 2:19; Ps. 22:7[6]; 123:3; Prov. 30:17; Ezk. 36:4 [read *lāḇôz*]; 1QpHab 4:1f.; 1QM 12:7f.); → חרף *ḥārap̱,* "revile" (2 K. 19:21f. par. Isa. 37:22f.; Ps. 22:7f.[6f.]; 44:14,17[13,16]; 79:4; Prov. 17:5; Jer. 20:8), → קלס *qālas,* "scoff, mock" (Ps. 44:14[13]; 79:4; Jer. 20:8; 1QpHab 4:1f.; 1QM 12:7f.), → גדף *gādap̱,* "revile" (2 K. 19:21f. par. Isa. 37:22f.; Ps. 44:17[16] [with v. 14(13)]), and → כלם *kālam,* "rebuke, humiliate" (Ps. 44:16[15]; Ezk. 36:6 [with v. 4]); cf. further *tāʿaʿ,* "make fun of, mock" (2 Ch. 36:16; 1QpHab 4:2), and *hāṯal,* "scoff at" (1 K. 18:27; Job 17:2).

The semantic field also includes the typical gestures of mockery: *hēnîaʿ rōʾš,* "shake one's head" (2 K. 19:21 par. Isa. 37:22; Ps. 22:8[7]; cf. Ps. 44:15[14]; 80:7[6]; also Job 16:4; Ps. 109:25; Jer. 18:16; Lam. 2:15; Sir. 13:7; 12:18; Mk. 15:29), *ḥāraq šinnayim,* "gnash one's teeth" (Job 16:9; Ps. 35:16; cf. 37:12; 112:10; Lam. 2:16; 1QH 2:11), *qāraṣ ʿayin,* "wink with one's eyes" (Ps. 35:19; cf. Prov. 6:13; 10:10), and *hip̱ṭîr baśśāp̱â,* "make a wry mouth, pull a face" (Ps. 22:8[7]).

The noun *laʿag* is often accompanied by an expression indicating that an individual or collective "becomes" the object of mockery or is "made" into such an object. The expressions *hāyâ laʿag* (Ps. 79:4), *hāyâ lᵉlaʿag* (Ezk. 23:32; 36:4), and *śîm laʿag* (Ps.

5. Cf. B. Duhm, *Das Buch Jesaia. HKAT* (⁵1968), 173.
6. Cf. W. Rudolph, *Hosea. KAT,* XIII/1 (1966), 152.

44:14f.[13f.]) find parallels in combinations with *ḥerpâ, bûz, qeles, māšāl,* and others (esp. frequent in Jeremiah, Ezekiel, Lamentations, Nehemiah, and Psalms).

The subject and object of "mockery" characterized by *lʿg* vary according to context. As a rule it is human "enemies"[7] or hostile nations and neighbors who "mock" Israel/Judah/Jerusalem, a psalmist, or a prophet. Less frequently it is God or his representatives who mock the enemies.

4. *Versions.* The LXX renders the verb *lāʿag* 6 times with *myktērízein* and twice with *ekmyktērízein,* although without distinguishing between the qal and hiphil. The noun *laʿag* is rendered accordingly 3 times with *myktērismós.*[8] The verb is rendered 4 times with *katagelán,* "laugh at, deride," twice with *ekgelán,* "laugh out loud," and once each with *katachaírein,* "express malicious/excessive pleasure," *exouthenoún* and *katamōkásthai,* "mock." Although the Targumim use the same root for *lʿg,* it is rendered in the majority of instances by the synonymous *lʿb.* The renderings of the Vulg. and Jerome coincide almost exactly (19 times) with *subsannare/subsannatio* (from *sanna,* "mocking or mimicking grimace"); renderings deviating from this (*despicere, de-/in-ridere,* and others) usually correspond to *katagelán* in the LXX.

II. 1. *Mockery from One's Enemies.* In the great majority of instances human enemies are the subject of mockery: either enemies of an individual (psalmist or prophet) or of all Israel/Judah/Jerusalem. Ps. 22:8(7) ("all who see me mock at me; they make mouths at me, they shake their heads") and 35:16 ("like the godless[9] [NRSV 'impiously'] they mock and mock [so LXX], gnashing at me with their teeth") represent a well-known motif in the individual lament.[10] Jer. 20:7 ("I have become a laughingstock all day long; everyone mocks me") also belongs within the framework of this genre. Such talk of mockery from one's enemies occupies a firm position in the lament of the people as well.[11] Next to texts lamenting ongoing mockery ("our soul has had more than its fill of scorn" [Ps. 123:4]; "we have become a taunt to our neighbors, mocked and derided by those around us" [Ps. 79:4], incorporated into the prophetic oracle of salvation in Ezk. 36:4, and also as an addition to the oracle of wrath in Ezk. 23:32) we find others in which the scorn of one's enemies is lamented as a punishment imposed by God himself ("you have made us . . . the derision and scorn of those around us" [Ps. 44:14(13); 80:7(6)]). Despite any differences, the ideas of the "scorned righteous person" and "scorned Israel" are closely related.

The occurrences in Nehemiah's memoirs (Neh. 2:19; 3:33[4:1]) refer to the derision of hostile neighbors concerning the Jews' reconstruction plans.

---

7. → **איב** *'āyaḇ* (*'āyabh*) (I, 212-18).

8. On *myktērízein,* which actually means "turn up one's nose," cf. G. Bertram, "μυκτηρίζω," *TDNT,* IV, 796-99.

9. So H. Gunkel, *Die Psalmen. HKAT,* II/2 (^{5}1968), *in loc.*

10. Cf. H. Gunkel and J. Begrich, *Einleitung in die Psalmen. HAT,* II/2 (1933), §6, no. 8 (esp. 198-99).

11. *Ibid.,* §4, no. 7, esp. 126.

The notion of the suffering prophet is given its classic formulation in the Deuteronomistic history (cf. 2 K. 17:13-15), although it is also documented in 2 Ch. 30:10 (Hezekiah's couriers, who exhort all Israel to return to Yahweh, are scorned and mocked); 36:16 ("they kept mocking [*l'b*] the messengers of God, despising [*bzh*] his words, and scoffing [*t'*'] at his prophets").

The occurrences in Wisdom Literature constitute a group unto themselves. Drawing from the teachings of Amenemope,[12] Prov. 17:5 warns against mocking the poor (cf. also Sir. 4:1). The drastic warning against mocking one's aged parents in Prov. 30:17 is related to the commandment concerning parents in Ex. 20:12 par.[13]; cf. also the advice against mocking the wise in Sir. 31(34):22.

2. *Yahweh as Subject.* "Mockery" is attributed not only to human beings, but to God as well. The oldest example is Ps. 2:4: "He who sits in the heavens laughs; Yahweh has them in derision." Laughter and mockery are the expression of unquestionable superiority over against the activities of earthly kings.[14] In the lament of an individual oppressed by both the deeds and words of his enemies (Ps. 59:9[8]) we read: "But you laugh at them, O Yahweh; you hold all the nations in derision." This statement, which functions as a motif of trust, is so similar to Ps. 2 that one can probably assume it was borrowed from that psalm.[15] Ps. 37:13, a wisdom psalm, also expresses this notion that Yahweh "laughs" at the wicked; thus Yahweh's own "counter-mockery"[16] negates the mockery of the wicked (v. 12). Personified Wisdom threatens just as does God: "Because I have called and you refused [to listen] . . . I also will laugh at your calamity; I will mock when panic strikes you" (Prov. 1:24,26). The tyrannical mockery of which Job accuses his friends' God is quite different: "When disaster brings sudden death, he mocks at the despondency of the innocent" (Job 9:23).[17]

3. *Mockery from the Pious.* It is noteworthy that only rarely does *l'g* refer to mockery by the "pious" or "righteous." Although Job 22:19 speaks of the justified mockery of the righteous at the inevitable fate of the wicked, it is not without significance that Eliphaz is the one representing such wisdom. Textual corruption makes it unclear in just what sense Job is associated with "mocking" or "mockery" in the speeches of Zophar (Job 11:3) and Elihu (34:7); the same is true of one of Job's own speeches (21:3). In the individual laments the righteous person anticipates the time when he can mock the exposed impotence of his enemies (e.g., Ps. 35:26f.; 52:8[6]; 58:11[10]; 64:11[10]). There are, however, no corresponding utterances in the thanksgiving psalms. Only the oracle to Sennacherib (2 K. 19:21-28 par. Isa. 37:22-29), secondarily

---

12. *ANET*^{3}, 424.
13. → כבד *kāḇēḏ* (VII, 13-22).
14. Cf. the comms. and Vischer, who refers to the Ugaritic texts *KTU,* 1.6 III, 16; 1.4 IV, 27-30; V, 20-27; 1.12 I, 12f.; 1.17 VI, 41; 1.3 II, 24-27.
15. Cf. H.-J. Kraus, *Psalms 1-59* (Eng. trans., Minneapolis, 1988) *in loc.*
16. Preuss, 144.
17. Following F. Horst, *Hiob. BK,* XVI/1 (^{4}1983), *in loc.;* cf. Job 12:21.

incorporated into the two stories of Jerusalem's deliverance from the Assyrians (2 K. 18:13–19:37 par. Isa. 36f.), exhibits the wording of genuine mockery with Zion/Jerusalem as the subject: "She despises you, she scorns you — virgin daughter Zion; she tosses her head — behind your back, daughter Jerusalem" (2 K. 19:21 par. Isa. 37:22). Human mockery thrives on "seeing" the impotence of the person mocked (cf. *rā'â* in Ps. 22:8[7]; 31:12[11]; 35:21; 52:8[6]; 69:33[32]; Lam. 1:7f.). The daughter Zion can credibly mock even within her own impotence only because she trusts in the one whose own power gives him reason to mock the Assyrian. In the same spirit the community of Qumran engages in mockery (1QM 12:7f.).

Barth†

לַעֲנָה *la'ᵃnâ*

Contents: I. Etymology. II. Meaning. III. Usage.

I. Etymology. The etymology of *la'ᵃnâ,* a word occurring 8 times in the OT (additionally Lam. 3:5 conjectured, not Sir 31:29 emended), is unclear. Possibly it arose from the phoneme *l' (+ n),* which in initial position almost always gutturally expresses disinclination, aversion, and repulsive disgust; a negative element of repugnance or revulsion thus accompanies the word. This suggests a possible relationship with Nab. *l'n, l'nh* and Arab. *la'ana, la'n,* "to curse; imprecation."[1]

II. Meaning. The traditional meaning "wormwood" is quite uncertain. The LXX, unable to give a specific, concrete meaning, thus circumscribed the term according to the context 3 times with *pikría,* "bitterness"; twice with *cholḗ,* "gall"; and once each with *odýnē,* "sorrow, grief," and *anánkai,* "calamities" (Am. 5:7 is not translated). The Targum offers *gîḏ* (sometimes pl.; not Dt. 29:17[Eng. v. 18]; similarly also Syr. and the rabbinic writings), usually translated with "absinth." Aquila renders the word 3 times (Prov. 5:4; Jer. 9:14[15]; 23:15) with *tó apsínthion,* and the Vulg. accordingly with *absinthium* in all instances except Dt. 29:17(18) (cf. Targumim). It remains questionable whether this indeed refers to "wormwood," specifically the plant *ar-*

---

la'ᵃnâ. G. Dalman, *AuS,* II (1932), 318: H. Frehen, "Wermut," *BL* 44², 1887f.; R. K. Harrison, "Healing Herbs of the Bible," *Janus,* 50 (1961; repr., Leiden, 1966); I. Löw, *Die Flora der Juden,* I/1 (Vienna, 1926), 379-390; W. McKane, "Poison, Trial by Ordeal and the Cup of Wrath," *VT,* 30 (1980), 478-487; H. N. Moldenke and A. L. Moldenke, *Plants of the Bible. Chronica Botanica,* 28 (New York, 1952), 48-50; C. H. Peisker, "Wermut," *BHHW,* III (1967), 2167; G. E. Post and J. E. Dinsmore, *Flora of Syria, Palestine and Sinai* (Beirut, ²1932/33), 66, 534; M. Zohary, *Plant Life of Palestine: Israel and Jordan. Chronica Botanica,* 33 (New York, 1962) 134.

1. *DISO;* Wehr.

temisia absinthium* or, since this hardly occurs in Palestine, to *artemisia herba alba,* which for its own part has long been considered a medicinal herb; similarly, any identification of this with *laʿ^{a}nâ* is highly questionable. G. Piovano[2] suggests *artemisia judaica.* The OT occurrences of the word yield three qualifying features for *laʿ^{a}nâ:* 1. It designates (probably in the vernacular) a plant or herbal substance (Dt. 29:17[18] par. *rōʾš;* cf. Hos. 10:4). 2. The implication is that this substance is genuinely or (judged by its bitterness) presumably[3] poisonous or at least dangerous. In 6 or 7 instances (Lam. 3:5 conj.) *laʿ^{a}nâ* occurs together with *rōʾš,* "poison"; in some instances mortal (life-threatening) consequences are anticipated (Jer. 23:15; Prov. 5:4 par. "sword";[4] Lam. 3:5 with death motifs). Targ. Pseudo-Jonathan translates Dt. 29:17(18): "bitter as deadly absinth(?)" (*kʾgdnʾ dmwt*'; cf. also He. 12:15). 3. It is presupposed that *laʿ^{a}nâ* is eaten, perhaps taken (also) in liquid form (Prov. 5:4 par. flowing honey; cf. Jer. 23:15; 9:14[15] *ʾkl*; in contrast, *rōʾš* is drunk); considering its bitterness and accompanying danger, this seems to have occurred primarily by mistake or out of ignorance (cf. 2 K. 4:38-41). In light of this, these occurrences suggest some poisonous plant or substance rather than a kind of *artemisia* and "wormwood."[5] Just which plant or herbal poison is meant has not yet been determined.[6]

III. Usage. The parallel use of *laʿ^{a}nâ* with *rōʾš* in 6 of 8 occurrences suggests the two terms were proverbially associated with one another (cf. "poison and gall"). This is consistent with the wisdom milieu of several passages as well as with the use of the word itself as an image, metaphor, or symbol. The *tertium* in these cases is the hidden danger and deleterious effects inhering in seemingly quite harmless, beneficial things. The sweet words of the temptress are like virgin honey and seem smoother than oil, but in reality are as dangerous as *laʿ^{a}nâ* and a two-edged sword (Prov. 5:4). The concrete reference can still be discerned in Dt. 29:17(18). Those who have fallen away from the Yahwistic faith are characterized in a general fashion as roots that bring forth *(prh)* poison and *laʿ^{a}nâ.* Even in passages in which God initiates the eating and drinking of such poisonous substances, however, this concrete concept still resonates. Such is the case in Jeremiah's oracle of woe to the false prophets. They, the "prophets of Jerusalem," will have to consume "false" (in the sense of "poisoned") food as punishment, since — according to the lex talionis — "falseness"[7] has gone forth from them into all the land (Jer. 23:15 and, dependent on it, 9:14[15]; cf. also 8:14). Is this a reference to carrying out a death sentence by means of poison? Similar ideas occur in the laments of Lam. 3 (vv. 5,15,19). The two passages from Amos (cf. also Hos. 10:4) should probably be understood such that in the metaphorical form of his accusation (Am. 6:12)

---

2. "Contributo alla flora sinaitica," *Giornalle botanica italiana,* 69 (1962), 239-241.
3. "Noxium vulgo creditum est," *GesTh,* 758.
4. → חרב *ḥereḇ* (V, 155-165).
5. McKane, 483-85.
6. Cf. M. Zohary, *Geobotanical Foundations of the Middle East. Geobotanica Selecta,* 3 (Stuttgart, 1973), II, 391ff.
7. *ḥ^{a}nuppâ,* → חנף *ḥānēp* (V, 36-44).

and cry of woe (5:7) the prophet is expressing the general assertion that the inherent goodness and beneficence of the traditional system of justice *(mišpāṭ)* as well as the overall impact of the traditional social order *(ṣᵉḏāqâ)* have been perverted[8] into their opposites. This came about presumably because of their unnatural and irrational subjection to the strictures of a new social situation (Am. 6:12a). The judicial system itself thus becomes incapable of guaranteeing justice, and its essence is perverted. The social contract is ignored, and the good fruits it once brought forth for everyone are now as pernicious as poison.

Seybold

8. → הפך *hāpaḵ (hāphakh)* (III, 423-27).

לָקַח *lāqaḥ;* לֶקַח *leqaḥ*

Contents: I. 1. Root; 2. Meaning; 3. Occurrences in the OT. II. Usage in the OT: 1. Initiative for Subsequent Action; 2. Taking Things at One's Disposal; 3. Taking a Wife; 4. Taking Away, Carrying Off; 5. God's Taking; 6. Poetic and Special Usage. III. *leqaḥ*.

I. 1. *Root. lqḥ* is an especially popular root in OT Hebrew; although it is common to the Semitic languages (Ugar. *lqḥ,* Akk. *lēqû,*[1] Phoen., Moab. *lqḥ,*[2] Aram. *lᵉqaḥ,* OSA *lqḥ,*[3] Arab. *laqiḥa,* Eth. *laqḥa,* "lend, borrow"[4]), its understanding is not necessarily dependent on linguistic comparisons.[5] Herbert H. Schmid has provided the excellent lexical foundation[6] from which further discussion must proceed.

2. *Meaning.* The fundamental meaning "take" displays considerable flexibility. Compared to roots occasionally used synonymously, this basic meaning does not appear

lāqaḥ. A. Cody, "Exodus 18:12: Jethro Accepts a Covenant with the Israelites," *Bibl,* 49 (1968), 153-166, esp. II: "Jethro 'Accepts' the Sacrifice (and the Covenant)," 159-161; G. Delling, "λαμβάνω," *TDNT,* IV, 5-15; J. C. Greenfield, "*našû, nadānū* and Its Congeners," *Memoirs of the Connecticut Academy of Arts and Sciences,* 19 (1977), 87-91; S. Kogut, "Double Meaning of the Biblical Root לקח," *Lešonénu,* 34 (1969/1970), 320 [Heb.; Eng. summary]; L. Kopf, "Arabische Etymologien und Parallelen zum Bibelwörterbuch," *VT,* 8 (1958), 161-215, esp. 182 = *Studies in Arabic and Hebrew Lexicography* (Jerusalem, 1976); A. Kretzer, "λαμβάνω," *EDNT,* II, 336-38.

1. *AHw,* I (1965), 544.
2. *DISO,* 139.
3. ContiRossini, 173.
4. Leslau, *Contributions,* 29.
5. Cf. *HAL,* II (1995), 534.
6. "לקח *lqḥ* nehmen," *THAT,* I, 875-79.

to be characterized as much by the idea of expending energy as is, e.g., *ḥzq* hiphil, "seize" in the sense of "support, strengthen, grab hold of," or *nāśā'*, "lift up"; neither, however, despite the few, seemingly contradictory occurrences, does the idea of force or violence seem to apply as with → בזז *bzz,* or → לכד *lāḵaḏ*. Rather, the extremely frequent use of this verb to anticipate a subsequent verb that actually describes the intended act (almost as a *verbum relativum*) suggests that the primary emphasis is on the responsibility of the subject for that act. As will be seen, it frequently evokes the idea or aspect of initiative regarding a person's actions.

3. *Occurrences in the OT.* The verb occurs 939 times in the qal[7] and is especially frequent in narrative writings and regulations concerning offerings (together accounting for three fourths of all occurrences). Significantly, it occurs neither in Canticles (contextually inappropriate) nor in Ecclesiastes and Daniel (replaced, according to Schmid, by other roots in later languages). The niphal (10 times) and pual (as passive of qal, 15 times) have a clearly limited meaning: "be taken, fetched, or brought away."[8] The hithpael (twice) has the specialized meaning "flicker back and forth" (referring to flames). Other specialized meanings include *malqôḥayim,* "gums" (Ps. 22:16[Eng. v. 15]), *melqāḥayim,* "snuffers" (6 times), *miqqāḥ,* "taking [of a bribe]" (Aram. inf., only 2 Ch. 19:7), *maqqāḥôṯ,* "wares" (Neh. 10:32[31]; from **malqāḥôṯ*), and *malqôaḥ,* "booty belonging to the victor in war," distinguished from what has been stolen or plundered (Nu. 31:11f.,26f.,32; Isa. 49:24f.; *šālāl* probably refers to the actual booty, *baz* what has been plundered). The term *malqôaḥ* was incorporated into Egyptian as a terminus technicus *(mrqḥ.t)*.[9] The personal name *liqḥî,* although textually secure, is yet unclear in its specifics.[10] Only the noun *leqaḥ* requires further discussion.[11]

II. Usage in the OT. In the qal the meaning of *lāqaḥ* extends from "take, seize, grab," "take for oneself" with the result "take away," to a more militant sense of "appropriate for oneself," although also "accept, receive," and finally "get, fetch." Although the object of the verb can be either persons or things, documentation of this particular feature does not reveal anything essential concerning the meaning. Of more significance is an understanding of the peculiarities in the way the verb is actually employed.

1. *Initiative for Subsequent Action.* Often *lāqaḥ* designates the initiative for subsequent action. 2 K. 11:2 (par. 2 Ch. 22:11) praises the meritorious action of Jehosheba, who took Joash from among the king's sons and hid him. Similarly, in 2 K. 11:4,19 (par. 2 Ch. 23:1,20) Jehoiada took Judah's captains in preparation for the revolt against

---

7. Schmid.
8. *HAL.*
9. *HAL,* II, 594; *WbÄS,* II, 113.
10. Cf. *HAL.*
11. See III below.

Athaliah. According to Jgs. 6:27, Gideon took ten men in order to destroy an altar of Baʿal secretly. Laban took his brothers along in pursuit of Jacob (Gen. 31:23). Jacob took a stone to set up as a boundary marker, and Laban and his kinsmen took stones for a heap to serve as a marker (Gen. 31:45f.). Jacob took a stone to consecrate as a massebah (Gen. 28:18). Samuel took the young, previously unknown Saul before those invited for a feast (1 S. 9:22). Saul took a yoke of oxen and cut them into pieces to call the people together for holy war (1 S. 11:7). Gideon took the elders of Succoth in order to scourge them with thorns because of their lack of support (Jgs. 8:16). Joseph took five of his brothers to present to Pharaoh (Gen. 47:2). The brothers took Joseph and cast him into the empty cistern; they took his robe and dipped it in blood in order to deceive their father (Gen. 37:24,31). Boaz took ten men to the gate in order to conduct legal business (Ruth 4:2). All the people of Judah took Azariah and made him king (2 K. 14:21; Jehoahaz 23:30; cf. 2 Ch. 26:1; 36:1).

One can easily add to these examples. Although almost all regulations concerning offerings fall into this category, several of the more subtle expressions deserve special mention. Abraham took the wood appropriated for the burnt offering and laid it on Isaac — underscoring the assertion: "God himself will provide" (Gen. 22:6-8). Preparing to kill Isaac as directed, Abraham took a knife meant for eating rather than for sacrificial slaughter (*ma'ᵃḵeleṯ*; Gen. 22:10). After the flood Noah took of *every* clean animal and offered burnt offerings (Gen. 8:20). Before the miraculous deliverance at the Reed Sea, the people complain to Moses: "You have taken us away to die in the wilderness" (Ex. 14:11). The Moabite king Balak took Balaam to pronounce a curse on Israel; Balaam, however, took (from God?) the command to bless (Nu. 23:11,20). Gen. 15:9f. is particularly noteworthy. Although Yahweh orders Abraham to take for Yahweh a series of sacrificial animals, the directive says nothing about the required ritual itself, which Abraham apparently already knows. Do the words "take for me" together with the list of animals indicate that the reference is not to an offering at all, but rather to some special ritual?

2. *Taking Things at One's Disposal.* Only a short distance separates the usage just discussed from the act of taking things standing at one's disposal. Terah took Abraham and Nahor, Abraham took his wife and possessions, Lot his family, Esau his wives, and Joseph his sons (Gen. 11:31; 12:5; 19:15; 36:6; 48:1,13), either for a trip of some sort or to go to one's father. King Abimelech took herds and servants in order to appease Abraham for having taken Sarah (Gen. 20:2,14). Abraham took a skin of water and other provisions for the exiled Hagar to eat along the way (Gen. 21:14). Abraham took Ishmael to circumcise him (Gen. 17:23). Abraham and Saul took servants with them (Gen. 22:3; 1 S. 9:3). Saul took along three thousand men to pursue David (1 S. 24:3[2]). 1 S. 8:11-17 warns against the consequences of being at the disposal of a king. According to 2 S. 20:6, David assigns command over the elite royal troops to Joab's brother Abishai: "Take!" Potiphar took Joseph and placed him into the security of the royal prison (Gen. 39:20). As a condition of the preliminary allegation of espionage, Joseph took Simeon as a hostage (Gen. 42:24). Jethro took a burnt offering for Elohim (Ex. 18:12).

The meaning does not change when God is the subject of the action. According to Ps. 75:3(2), God prescribes the appointed time (*môʿēḏ*). He is opposed by prophets who take their tongues to utter pronouncements (Jer. 23:31). Yahweh Elohim takes Adam and places him in a garden, etc. (Gen. 2:15,21,22).

A few examples come from the legal tradition. The community is instructed to take from the altar any person guilty of (willful) murder even though normally the altar is a place of asylum (Ex. 21:14; Dt. 19:12: in the case of intentional capital crimes, the community elders under whose jurisdiction the perpetrator is found are to take him and hand him over to the avenger of blood). A man who spurns his wife and alleges that she is not a virgin shall be taken by the elders and whipped (Dt. 22:18).

3. *Taking a Wife.* This term apparently includes the terminus technicus for marriage: to take a wife/take as one's wife (e.g., Gen. 4:19; 11:29; 20:2f.; 24:3f.). The man must take the initiative, since legally the woman becomes a member of her husband's family through marriage. Gen. 16:3 describes a subcategory. If the primary wife brings maidservants into the marriage, she is empowered to give one of these maids to her husband as a wife (cf. also Gen. 30:9). Gen. 21:21 notes that the apparently impressive woman Hagar (cf. Gen. 16:7-14) took a wife for her son.

Merely taking a woman, however, is a base act (Gen. 34:2). Subsequent marriage can rectify the situation, but is not compulsory. David, too, took Bathsheba before he was able to marry her (2 S. 11:4). In neither instance is force mentioned (contra NRSV). The term occurs so frequently, however, that when the context is unequivocal it can be replaced by simple taking. The regulation pertaining to military service is noteworthy. If a man is betrothed to a woman but has not yet "taken" her, he is given leave from military service until he has insured the continuation of his name (Dt. 20:7). To "take a daughter," an expression reflecting Persian customs, is related (Est. 2:7,15; it is doubtful whether adoption was known in Israel itself).

4. *Taking Away, Carrying Off.* When the action results in taking away or carrying off something, neither the *modus* (e.g., force, illegality, etc.) nor the element of privation seems to be emphasized, but rather that of seizure or acquisition for oneself (although the verb does occur in Jer. 20:5 par. "plunder" and 1 S. 2:16 expressly adds "by force"). Gen. 31:34; 1 Ch. 7:21 probably refer to something like stealing, and Gen. 27:35,36 emphasize the illegality of the appropriation. In principle, however, one must deduce the mode from the context; thus precisely in Gen. 27 the illegality does not result in any disadvantage for Jacob, since the patriarchal blessing is at stake, a blessing that could only be bestowed once.

Gen. 31:1 is typical. Laban's sons believe that Jacob has acquired everything that belonged to Laban; only the simple fact is of significance here, and no illegality is alleged. Leah's words to Rachel (Gen. 30:15) are also interesting: "Is it a small matter that you have taken away my husband?" This is not a matter of taking away, but rather only of the fact that Rachel was more attractive to Jacob, and that Leah thus pointedly avoids treating her with a gift of mandrakes as well. Similarly, Gen. 31:34 asserts that

Rachel was threatened by mortal danger (v. 26) because she had taken — and thus possessed — the teraphim.

Taking in time of war should also be included here. The prerogative of the victor enables David to take the crown for himself after his victory over the Ammonites (2 S. 12:30). Similarly, 2 K. 15:29 lists the cities that Tiglath-pileser III took for himself after his victorious campaigns. According to Gen. 34:28, Jacob's victorious sons took the Shechemites' livestock from the fields, while according to v. 29 they also robbed them, namely, of human beings and all that was in their houses. 1 K. 20:34 reports that the king of Syria wanted to return the Israelite cities that his father had taken for himself (cf. also Jgs. 11:13,15; 1 Ch. 2:23).

Gen. 38:23 is also highly instructive. Judah tries through a friend to retrieve the valuable pledges he left to be redeemed after lying with a (presumed) cult prostitute (*q*ᵉ*ḏēšâ*); when the woman cannot be found, he says: "Let her take them, lest we be laughed at." Chasing after pledges given to a harlot only results in ridicule. This would also suggest that Gen. 48:22 is not intended violently. The father Israel took a "shoulder" (mountain slope near Shechem?) from the hand of the Amorites for sword and bow, and thus as security for the pass at Shechem.

In judgment it can be stated (2 S. 12:11) that it is Yahweh who takes David's wives and who gives them to a neighbor, because David had taken the wife of Uriah. Entirely characteristic is the word of Hosea (Hos. 13:11) that Yahweh gave and took Israel's kings in his anger!

5. *God's Taking.* The most frequent assertion made of Yahweh is that he will fetch or take his people back from the dispersion (Dt. 30:4; Jer. 3:14; Ezk. 36:24; 37:21). This is consistent with the fact that Yahweh had taken Israel as his people from Egypt (Ex. 6:7) or Sinai on. This doubtlessly expresses the kind of naive understanding of election occurring also in Gen. 24:7 (Abraham); Josh. 24:3 (your father); 1 K. 11:31 (Jeroboam I); Jer. 43:10 (Nebuchadnezzar is taken to smite Egypt); Hag. 2:23 (Zerubbabel); 2 S. 7:8; 1 Ch. 17:7; Ps. 78:70 (David); Nu. 3:12,41,45; 8:16,18 (Levites). The way the same expression is used in the calling of Amos (Am. 7:15), however, shows that the emphasis is always less on a particular concept of election than on that element of surprise associated with being taken by God out of completely different circumstances. In laments Yahweh is variously implored to take the petitioner's life or *nep̱eš,* since a person should not violate or profane life (e.g., 1 K. 19:4; Jon. 4:3). In judgment, on the other hand, Yahweh announces to Ezekiel the symbolic act of taking away Ezekiel's delight (i.e., his wife; Ezk. 24:16). In Ezk. 3:14; 8:3, God's taking refers to visionary translation to a different place, and Gen. 5:24; 2 K. 2:3 speak of Enoch and Elijah being transported directly to God. Is this also the reference in Ps. 49:16(15); 73:24?[12]

Relatively speaking, however, God only rarely appears as the subject of this verb (according to Schmid just over 50 times). Thus the verb is more likely to reveal

---

12. → כבוד *kāḇôḏ* (VII, 22-38).

something about the OT understanding of human beings than to constitute a theonomic expression.

6. *Poetic and Special Usage.* Several poetically striking examples should not go unmentioned. In a kind of self-imprecation Job remarks (Job 3:6): "That night [of one's birth] — let thick darkness seize it!" A similarly somber turn is taken by the wisdom assertion in Job 12:20. God takes away the power of discernment (*ṭaʿam*) even of the elders. Eliphaz rebukes the lamenting Job: "Why does your heart carry you away?" (Job 15:12). The expression "take revenge" occurs only poetically (Jer. 20:10; of God: Isa. 47:3). Concerning Jeremiah's own poesy: "Let your ears receive (*lqḥ*) the word of his [Yahweh's] mouth" (Jer. 9:19[20]). And finally, two striking images from wisdom: Anything acquired by violence takes away the *nep̱eš* of its possessor (Prov. 1:19; cf. 11:30; 22:25); evildoers are like thorns — they cannot be taken with the hand (2 S. 23:6).

The particular focus of the prohibition against taking interest (Lev. 25:36) or profit (Ezk. 18:8,13,17) prompt its mention here. In contrast, Samuel's assertion (1 S. 12:3f.) that while in office he took nothing from anyone is exemplary.

III. leqaḥ. The term *leqaḥ* probably does not mean "teaching" or "persuasiveness,"[13] but rather that which a person has been able to acquire in the way of wisdom or teaching and is thus in a position to pass on to others. This seems to be the case especially in Prov. 7:21 in its summarization of the seductive speech of the loose woman. Prov. 16:23 expresses this in the following words: "The mind of the wise makes their speech judicious,/and adds understanding (*leqaḥ*) to their lips." Is Prov. 16:21 then to be read chiastically? "The wise of heart is called [one who is] perceptive,/and such understanding (*leqaḥ*) constitutes pleasant speech [lips]." This sense emerges quite naturally for Dt. 32:2; Job 11:4; Prov. 4:2; the sense of one's own acquisition of learning is reflected in Prov. 1:5; 9:9; Sir. 8:8. That is to say, *leqaḥ* is *qabbālā'*, "what is received"[14] in the most literal sense.

Seebass

13. So *HAL*; Prov. 7:21.
14. Cf. *HAL*.

לָקַט *lāqaṭ*

Contents: I. Etymology; Occurrences. II. OT Usage.

I. Etymology; Occurrences. The root *lqṭ* occurs in most Semitic languages with the meaning "gather in, pick." The verb occurs 30 times in the OT, 13 times in the qal, 15 in the piel, and once each in the pual and hithpael. A clear distinction between the qal and piel is probably not possible; the book of Ruth uses both the qal (Ruth 2:8) and the piel (all other occurrences) to refer to picking (actually gleaning) grain. According to Ernst Jenni,[1] the qal refers to simple gathering, while the piel, as a resultative, includes the nuance of completed or total gathering.

II. OT Usage. In all cases the verb refers to gathering in the literal sense. Jacob's kinsmen gather stones for a stone heap at Galeed (Gen. 31:46); flowers are gathered (Cant. 6:2); the prophet's disciples gather herbs for soup (2 K. 4:39); children gather wood so that their parents can present a burnt offering to the queen of heaven (Jer. 7:18); Adoni-bezek, defeated by the Israelites, looks back at the time when seventy kings picked up the scraps under his table (Jgs. 1:7); Jonathan's lad fetches the arrow his master has just shot (1 S. 20:38); Joseph gathers all the money the Egyptians have given in payment for grain and gives it to Pharaoh (Gen. 47:14).

Two groups of examples deserve special attention. First, Lev. 19:9; 23:22[2] prescribe that at harvest one is not to glean subsequently (*lqṭ* piel with *leqeṭ*), i.e., gather up the grain that has fallen to the ground; rather, this should be given to the poor and the *gerîm*. According to Lev. 19:10, the same holds true for grapes that have fallen to the ground during harvesting. This probably reflects an originally cultic custom that subsequently became a commandment concerning welfare for the poor.[3]

Reflecting this practice, Ruth gleans the grain on Boaz' field (Ruth 2:2,3,7,8, 15,19,23); Boaz even grants her certain gleaning privileges (v. 16). It is uncertain whether Ruth directly presupposes Lev. 19:9, since according to Ruth 2:2 she intends to glean only if she can secure the permission of the owner. In any case, a simple daily task thus serves to reveal Boaz' benevolence and becomes a part of God's guidance.[4]

The image of the harvest recurs in Isa. 17:5f. The fate of the northern kingdom is compared to a harvest at which among other things the reaper gleans grain in the Valley of Rephaim and knocks olives from the trees so that only a pitiful amount remains to be gleaned.

Second, *lqṭ* is used in the context of gathering manna (Ex. 16:4,5,16,18,21f.,26f.; Nu. 11:8). One gathers in the manna, but is permitted to gather only as much as one needs; if one gathers more, it spoils and becomes useless. The people are directed to God's care and must depend on that care completely. The same idea resonates in Ps. 104:28: "When you give to them, they gather it up; when you open your hand, they are filled with good things." God provides adequately for human beings; they can depend on that.

The only occurrence of the pual, Isa. 27:12, again uses the image of harvest, although here in the positive sense. God will gather in the dispersed Israelites like grain and lead

---

1. *Das hebräische Piʿel* (Zurich, 1968), 188f.
2. According to K. Elliger, *Leviticus. HAT,* IV (1966), 247, citing Lev. 19:9.
3. *Ibid.,* 257.
4. G. Gerlemann, *Ruth. BK* XVIII (1965), 10, where v. 12 is cited.

them back to their land. Usually, the verb → קבץ *qāḇaṣ* piel is used in such contexts, though a few times also *'āsap*.

The hithpael occurs only in Jgs. 11:3. All sorts of "worthless fellows" gather around Jephthah and depart with him.

Ringgren

לָשׁוֹן *lāšôn*

Contents: I. Etymology, Linguistic Considerations. II. Ancient Near East. III. Physiology. IV. Figurative Usage: 1. Metaphors; 2. Metonymy. V. Semantic Field. VI. Religio-Ethical Considerations.

I. Etymology, Linguistic Considerations. Despite variations in the individual languages, the word meaning "tongue" is common to the Semitic languages and attested even beyond them: Ebla *li-sa-nu,* Akk. *lišānu,*[1] Ugar. *lšn,*[2] Phoen. (in Greek transliteration) λασουν,[3] Arab. *lisān,* Palaeo-Aram. *lšn,*[4] Biblical Aram. *liššān,* Jewish Aram. *lᵉšānā',* Syr. *leššānā',* etc.[5]

A consideration of Egyp. *nś,* Copt. *las,* and Berber (Hamitic) *ils*[6] strongly suggests

---

lāšôn. J. Behm, "γλῶσσα," *TDNT,* I, 719-727; W. Brueggemann, "Tongue," *IDB,* IV, 670; W. Bühlmann, *Vom rechten Reden und Schweigen. OBO,* 12 (1976); E. Dhorme, *L'emploi métaphorique des noms de parties du corps en hébreu et en akkadien* (Paris, 1923, repr. 1963), 83-89; A. Erman and H. Ranke, *Life in Ancient Egypt* (Eng. trans., New York, 1894; repr. 1969), 354f.; J. Fichtner, *Die altorientalische Weisheit in ihrer israelitisch-jüdischen Ausprägung. BZAW,* 62 (1933), 21; K. Goldammer, *Die Formenwelt des Religiösen* (Stuttgart, 1960), 230-37; H. Holma, *Die Namen der Körperteile im Assyrisch-Babylonischen. AnAcScFen,* 7/1 (1911), 25ff., 185; A. Jeremias, *Handbuch der altorientalischen Geisteskultur* (Leipzig, ²1929), 92-95; A. R. Johnson, *The Vitality of the Individual in the Thought of Ancient Israel* (Cardiff, ²1964), 45-47, 68, 104; H. Kees, "Herz und Zunge als Schöpferorgane in der ägyptischen Götterlehre," *StudGen,* 19 (1966), 124-26; M. A. Klopfenstein, *Die Lüge nach dem AT* (Zurich, 1964), 25, 164; H. Lesêtre, "Langue," *DB,* IV (1908), 72-74; M. Lurker, *Wörterbuch biblischer Bilder und Symbole* (Munich, ²1978), 374f.; S. Mowinckel, *The Psalms in Israel's Worship* (Eng. trans., repr. Nashville, 1967), I, 199f., 227-29; II, 3f.; J. L. Palache, *Sinai en Paran* (Leiden, 1979), 107; R. C. Thompson, *Semitic Magic* (1908, repr. New York, 1971), 172f.; P. Volz, *Hiob und Weisheit. SAT,* III/2 (1911), 175f., 181-84; H.-D. Wendland, "Zunge," *BThH* (²1959), 733f.; H. W. Wolff, *Anthropology of the OT* (Eng. trans., Philadelphia, 1974), 77-78.

1. *AHw,* I (1965), 556.
2. *WUS,* no. 1484.
3. *DISO,* 140.
4. *Idem.*
5. *HAL,* II (1995), 536; *LexSyr,* 371; P. Fronzaroli, "Studi sul lessico comune semitico. II: Anatomia e Fisiologia," *AANLR,* VIII/19 (1964), 252, 270.
6. Cf. J. H. Greenberg, *The Languages of Africa* (Bloomington, Ind., 1963), 63.

that Proto-Semitic attested an originally two-consonant word here which in Palaeo-Semitic was expanded by the suf. *-ān* (which in Hebrew became *-ôn*).[7] One cannot determine whether for the initial form **lš* one should postulate a verbal root *lš, lšš, lšh/y,* or *lwš* with the meaning "to lick";[8] in any case, the initial consonant *l,* which also occurs in verbs describing some activity of the tongue *(lqq, lḥk, lḥš, lʿz),* seems to have resulted from onomatopoeia, and has apparently entered into the combination with *š* for the same reason.[9] Not surprisingly, nothing further is gained for a closer understanding of the concepts associated with *lāšôn* by considering its nominal forms *qaṭāl* (> *qāṭôl*[10]) or *qiṭāl.*[11] In its own turn, the suf. *-ān/-ôn* added to **lš* is ambiguous.[12] In the present instance this might subsume the onomatopoetic designation for the organ itself under the *nomina instrumenti* (cf. *paʿ^a^môn, gillāyôn*), i.e., the tongue as the instrument of speech. (This might then also be the case with the term *gārôn,* "throat," whose expansion from the original **gr* by means of the reduplicated construction *gargeret̲,* "neck," has been demonstrated.) These considerations are of no significance if one views *lāšôn* as a primary noun derived from a verbal stem.

The word occurs 117 times in the OT, 5 of those in the plural form (always written defectively) *l^e^šōnôt̲.* Although it exhibits dual gender, no substantive difference between the masculine (Ps. 35:28; Lam. 4:4) and feminine construction (Job 27:4; Ps. 137:6) emerges. The feminine form, however, does predominate.

The figurative usage "tongue of the sea" (see below) is construed only as masculine.

The thesis that the original gender was masculine, while the feminine understanding arose only after the word came to refer to the instrument of speech,[13] is hardly tenable in view of linguistic comparisons, statistical findings, etc. The original gender was more likely feminine,[14] and the masculine usage then arose in individual instances (e.g., through contamination: from *l^e^šônî tehgeh* [Ps. 71:24] and *pî . . . yehgeh* [Ps. 37:30] there developed *l^e^šônî yehgeh* [Job 27:4]).

In construct combinations the attendant *nomen rectum* functions either as *genetivus subjectivus* designating the person possessing the *lāšôn* (*l^e^šôn kaśdîm,* "language of the Chaldeans"; *l^e^šôn ʾillēm,* "tongue of the mute"), or, much more frequently, as *genetivus qualitatis* designating the particular characteristic of the *lāšôn* (e.g., *l^e^šôn šeqer,* "deceitful speech [NRSV 'lying tongue']"). This distinction, however, cannot always be strictly maintained: *l^e^šôn limmûd̲îm* (Isa. 50:4), literally, "tongue of the [instructed] disciples," means "practiced tongue."

---

7. *BLe,* §469.

8. Gesenius, *Thesaurus,* II, 763: Arab. *lassa,* "to lick"; cf. also E. König, *Historisch-kritisches Lehrgebäude der hebräischen Sprache,* II/1 (Leipzig, 1895), 123.

9. Cf. W. Eilers, "Zur Funktion von Nominalformen," *WO,* 3 (1964), 81.

10. E.g., *BLe, loc. cit.*

11. *VG,* I, 350.

12. *BLe,* §§498-500.

13. K. Albrecht, "Das Geschlecht der hebräischen Hauptwörter," *ZAW,* 16 (1896), 78f.

14. Cf. König, II/2 (1897), 162ff., 175; D. Michel, *Grundlegung einer hebräischen Syntax,* I (Neukirchen-Vluyn, 1977), 71-81.

The vocalization is at times contestable. Considering parallelism and similar passages in Proverbs, *lāšôn nok̲riyyâ* (Prov. 6:24) might be emended to *l^ešôn nok̲riyyâ* (thus not "foreign speech," but rather "speech of a foreign woman").[15] Also *lāšôn r^emiyyâ* (Ps. 120:2) should be emended to *l^ešôn r^emiyyâ*, "tongue of deceit," on the basis of the par. *ś^epat̲ šeqer* and Job 27:4. Instead of the subst. *r^emiyyâ* (as *nomen rectum*), the punctuators thought the homonymous adjective was intended ("slack, loose," as in the expression *qešet̲ r^emiyyâ*, "the slack, loose bow").[16]

Two denominative verbal forms with the root *lšn* (Prov. 30:10 hiphil; Ps. 101:5 poel)[17] mean "use the tongue (maliciously)," i.e., accuse or slander someone.

For the most part, the LXX translates with *glōssa*, the Vulg. with *lingua*. The literal meaning of both words, "tongue," underwent metonymical expansion to include such meanings as "speech, speech idiom," and as such they were able to offer a fairly consistent rendering of the Hebrew term. Occasionally the LXX will use other equivalents for *lāšôn* in the sense of "language": *diálektos* (Dan. 1:4), *léxis* (Est. 1:22), *phōnḗ* (Isa. 54:17: "and every voice that rises against you in judgment" instead of the crass personification of the Hebrew: "and every tongue . . ."). For the metaphorical "tongue of fire" in Isa. 5:24, the LXX uses *ánthrakos*, "charcoal, burning embers," and for "tongue of land" (Josh. 15:2) *lophiá*, "mountain ridge." At Josh. 7:21, the Vulg. renders the "tongue [bar] of gold" with *regula aurea*, "bar/ingot of gold."[18]

II. Ancient Near East. In many cultures the tongue symbolizes the human capacity for speech, human language, and its power. Venerated and feared, it becomes the object of magic and its accompanying ritual.[19]

The Akkadian word *lišānu*[20] refers to the body part of both human beings and animals. The human tongue as the organ of eating and speaking is mentioned in medical texts, that of animals in sacrificial instructions. Great power is attributed to the tongue: the dragon has seven tongues, the snake a forked tongue.[21] A person's mouth and tongue speak for him in prayer; he petitions Ishtar for protection. The goddess's mouth and tongue are good and enjoy religious veneration.

As a designation for the important organ of speech, *lišānu* also acquires the meaning "speech, discourse." The gods had a *lišānu*, i.e., "held converse."[22] The king constructs a network of streets so that *lišānu*, communication and exchange, will be possible between peoples.[23] Akk. *lišānu* is also the concrete statement itself, then

---

15. Cf. Vulg. *lingua extraneae;* Syr. *dlšnh dnwkryt'*.
16. Cf. *KBL*², 894; *BDB*, 941.
17. *BLe*, §281.
18. For further variations, see below.
19. J. G. Frazer, *The Golden Bough* (New York, ³1935), index *s.v.* "tongue"; J. Campbell, *The Masks of God: Primitive Mythology* (New York, 1959, repr. 1968), 211.
20. *CAD*, IX (1973), 209-215.
21. Cf. the Ugaritic dual form *lšnm; WUS*, no. 1484.
22. EnEl, III, 133; *ANET*, 66.
23. R. Borger, *Die Inschriften Asarhaddons, Königs von Assyrien. BAfO*, 9 (²1967), 26, VII, 41.

further the written text. In a legal matter, whosever *lišānu* agrees with the facts is declared in the right; the *lišānu* of an inscription may not be altered.[24] An evil tongue wreaks havoc both in private and juridical life; the word thus also acquires the meaning of "malicious rumor, slander." The petitioner implores: "in spite of the evil mouth (and) the evil tongue of men, may I be in good standing before you [the deity]."[25]

Since the tongue is the instrument of such malice, punishment is carried out on it either concretely or through magical curse. The recalcitrant son, the person who defaults on a contract, and the rebel all are to have their tongues cut out. This gruesome practice is illustrated in pictorial representations in which Assyrians carry this out on prisoners of war.[26]

Whenever speech is incomprehensible, either because of its puzzling complexity or its provenance in a foreign language, attention is directed anew to the instruments of speech, and *lišānu* acquires the meaning "language," particularly "foreign language, special (or technical) language." The meaning of *lišānu* is then expanded to "language group, nationality, people." A *bēl lišāni,* "master of the tongue," is someone who understands a foreign language (or "the conjurer"[27]). Akk. *ša lišāni* is a person who knows of something held secret. Finally, *lišānu* can thus refer to the person himself from whom such information is expected.

Akkadian also attests metaphors referring to the tongue of a flame, of a weapon (a blade or sword), or of a ploughshare, and to a tongue (bar, ingot) of gold.

The Egyptian word *nś*[28] refers to the tongue of both human beings and animals. As the organ of speech it is frequently mentioned together with the heart, i.e., as the tandem of utterance and reflection. Extraordinary power is attributed to both organs. In Memphite theology Ptah is considered the head of the nine gods, since he functions as their heart and tongue, organs which control all the other members and serve as the organs of creation. The heart thinks and the tongue commands whatever they want. Thoth is viewed as the tongue of Re or Atum. Extraordinary debilitation results from having one's tongue cut out.[29]

The splendid, skilled tongue on the one hand, and the deceptive, slandering tongue on the other are used as epithets for various persons.[30] One god can be viewed as the tongue, i.e., the mouthpiece, of another god.[31]

Any tongue should be the tongue of truth. A person should proceed just as cautiously with the tongue as with the reflections of the heart. The wisdom teacher also recognizes:

---

24. *CAD,* IX, 212.
25. *Ibid.,* 211.
26. F. Vigouroux, "Armées Etrangères," *DB,* I (1895), 989f.
27. Cf. Holma.
28. *WbÄS,* II, 320.
29. G. Posener, *Festschrift S. Schott* (Wiesbaden, 1968), 110f.
30. *Book of the Dead,* 172, 178.
31. H. Grapow, *Vergleiche und andere bildliche Ausdrücke im Ägyptischen. AO,* 21/1f.(1920, repr. 1983), 119.

"If the tongue of a man (be) the rudder of a boat, the All-Lord is its pilot."[32] "The tongue is a sword to [a man] and speech is more valorous than any fighting."[33] "A man may fall to ruin because of his tongue."[34]

Several of the Ahikar-sayings speak metaphorically about the tongue: "God shall twist the twister's mouth and tear out [his] tongue"; "soft is the tongue of a king, but it breaks a dragon's ribs."[35] Aramaic inscriptions mention *ḥrb* and *lšn,* sword and tongue, together (directed against the royal house?),[36] and the admonition is issued not to send a *lšn* among people or into one's house, i.e., not to sow discord.[37]

III. Physiology. The literal meaning of the word *lāšôn,* namely, as the designation of the physical organ in human beings and animals, emerges clearly in several biblical passages, although these are comparatively few compared to instances in which the word is used metaphorically. The tongue is located behind the opening to the mouth *(peh)* in the mouth's cavity *(ḥēḵ)* (Job 33:2); it can be stuck out of an open mouth (Isa. 57:4). A person can hold something on or under it (Prov. 31:26; Cant. 4:11) and can lap water with it the way a dog laps (Jgs. 7:5). A great thirst causes the tongue to cleave to the roof of the mouth (Lam. 4:4); when water is scarce it becomes parched (Isa. 41:17) and rots in one's mouth the way one's eyes rot in their sockets (Zec. 14:12).

Animals also have a *lāšôn.* The viper kills with its tongue (Job 20:16), a person tries in vain to bind a cord on the tongue of the crocodile (Job 40:25[Eng. 41:1], and the dog sharpens his tongue menacingly (Ex. 11:7).[38]

With regard to human beings, however, the tongue is viewed primarily as the most important organ of speech. The *lāšôn* mutters (*hgh,* Isa. 59:3), speaks (*dbr,* Ps. 12:4[3]), and sings aloud (*rnn,* Ps. 51:16[14]; Isa. 35:6). Already in physiological descriptions we find that in the context of the organism as a whole the *lāšôn* is delineated more sharply than the other body parts and in particular more sharply than the other parts of the mouth and throat (e.g., *gārôn,* "throat" in Ps. 5:10[9] and "neck" in Isa. 3:16). The role of the *lāšôn* in speaking is viewed as being more active than that of the other organs: "See, I open my mouth; the tongue in my mouth speaks" (Job 33:2). The mouth is filled with laughter, the tongue with shouts of joy (Ps. 126:2). Thus when the tongue is motionless, a person falls silent (Ezk. 3:26); conversely, a person who falls silent out of reverence is holding his own tongue motionless (Job 29:10).

---

32. Instruction of Amenemope, XVIII, 5f.; *ANET,* 424.
33. Instruction for King Merikare, 33; *ANET,* 415.
34. Instruction of Ani, VII, 9; *ANET,* 420.
35. *ANET,* 429.
36. *KAI,* 214, 9.
37. *KAI,* 224, 17/18, 21; cf. also R. A. Brauner, *A Comparative Lexicon of Old Aramaic* (Philadelphia, 1974), 323ff.
38. Just what is meant by this expression is not really clear. Heb. *ḥāraṣ lᵉšônô,* lit., "sharpens [points] his tongue," could refer either to the tongue hanging out or to the dog's growling or barking. The Vulg. reads *muttire,* "utter a low sound, grumble." Cf. *HAL,* II, 356; *BDB,* 358. Josh. 10:21 offers no help, since its text is uncertain; see *BHS.*

The expression for this silence is *dāḇaq-lᵉšônô lᵉḥikkô,* "the tongue cleaves to the roof of the mouth," as was the case above during great thirst. These are the two main functions which the tongue now is no longer carrying out: the taking in of nourishment, and speaking. The self-imprecation in Ps. 137:6 more likely refers to the petitioner falling silent than to dying of thirst: "Let my tongue cleave to the roof of my mouth, if I do not remember you [Jerusalem]." That is, I would rather fall completely silent than to fail to speak of Jerusalem.

IV. Figurative Usage.

1. *Metaphors.* The striking physical form of the tongue itself prompts the metaphorical usage of *lāšôn* for things with a more or less similar structure. The spit of land extending into the Dead Sea and serving thus as a boundary marker is called *lāšōn* (Josh. 15:2, written defectively). It can also be called *lᵉšôn hayyām* (Josh. 15:5), since it is the "tongue" actually belonging to the Dead Sea: *lᵉšôn yām-hammelaḥ* (Josh. 18:19). The topographically opposite phenomenon is intended in Isa. 11:15, which speaks of Yahweh's threat to destroy (or dry up[39]) the *lᵉšôn yām-miṣrayim.* This refers to a water-filled bay in Egypt, namely, the Gulf of Suez.

The expression *lᵉšôn zāhāḇ* (Josh. 7:21) refers to the approximately tongue-shaped bar of gold.[40] The expression *lᵉšôn 'ēš* (Isa. 5:24) was probably originally prompted less by external similarity in form (e.g., the licking of the flame) than to the flame's devastating activity. Since this personified fire devours *('kl)* whatever it seizes, a consuming tongue is attributed to it.

2. *Metonymy.* The metonymical expansions of meaning which the word *lāšôn* underwent are of greater consequence. Since they are more deeply seated in the word's overall semantic fabric than are the metaphors, they obligate the interpreter to undertake the important and often difficult task of determining the exact nuance of meaning.

As the designation for the most important organ of speech, *lāšôn* can also refer to what is actually produced in speech *(producens pro producto),* i.e., the words uttered in a particular context. One should beware of the smooth tongue of the foreign woman (Prov. 6:24), i.e., of the flattering words of the temptress. A soft tongue (Prov. 25:15), i.e., gentle persuasion, can break down the most obdurate resistance. The expression *maʿᵃnēh lāšôn* (Prov. 16:1) refers to the formed utterance in contrast to what is conjured in reflection. The *maḥᵃlîq lāšôn* (Prov. 28:23) produces flattery, and *lᵉšôn ʿᵃrûmîm* (Job 15:5) describes Job's responses, which his friends dismiss as sophistical and wily.

A person's characteristic manner of speaking is an expression itself of that person's character and personality; indeed, in the view of antiquity it is virtually identical with the person's character. This is an example of "synthetic thinking,"[41] which "does not

---

39. See *BHK.*

40. H. Weippert, "Geld," *BRL*², 89; M. Weippert, "Metall und Metallbearbeitung," *BRL*², 221; *AOB,* 126.

41. *ILC,* I-II, 170-76.

distinguish sharply between an organ and its function on the one hand, . . . and a person's manner of being and deportment on the other."[42] Combined with various qualifications *lāšôn* can thus be used to refer to a given lifestyle identified by a certain manner of speech. The expression *lᵉšôn šeqer* (Prov. 21:6) stands for the falseness and deception with which wealth is acquired, *lᵉšôn mirmâ* (Ps. 52:6[4]) for the malicious slander propagated by the petitioner's powerful enemy, and *lāšôn mᵉḏabbereṯ gᵉḏōlôṯ* (Ps. 12:4[3]) for boastful arrogance. On the positive side, *lᵉšôn ṣaddîq* (Prov. 10:20) refers to the prudence of the pious person, and *lᵉšōnô tᵉḏabbēr mišpāṭ* (Ps. 37:30) to his support of justice. These and similar passages show from context that *lāšôn* does not represent a one-time utterance, but rather a manner of being, albeit one actualized in speech.

Thus one and the same expression may have various meanings depending on the context. "Speaking against me with lying *lāšôn*" (Ps. 109:2) means "lying to me and deceiving me." "Yahweh hates . . . haughty eyes [and] a lying *lāšôn*" (Prov. 6:16f.), however, means that "Yahweh hates arrogance and mendacity."

The Hebrew term can also refer in a general fashion to the specific function of the tongue, namely, the human capacity for speech as such, or to the specific capacity of those schooled in speech. The statement "to me every knee shall bow, every *lāšôn* shall swear" (Isa. 45:23) asserts that every cultic gesture will direct itself to Yahweh, and every person capable of speech (i.e., every person) will swear loyalty to him. The speech facility of a person who is slow of speech and of tongue (Ex. 4:10) or who has a stammering tongue (Isa. 32:4) is considered deficient. That person is not an *'îš dᵉḇārîm.* The expression "they use (*lqḥ*) their *lāšôn*" (Jer. 23:31) describes how the professional prophets employ their practiced facility of the tongue. Jeremiah's adversaries want to smite him with the *lāšôn* (Jer. 18:18[43]), i.e., finish him off with cleverly formulated accusations.

Finally, *lāšôn* can also refer to a dialect, i.e., any of the symbolic systems in which human speech is actualized. The nations separated themselves according to their *lᵉšōnōṯ* (Gen. 10:5,31), and each people has its own *lāšôn* (Neh. 13:24). Men will come from all *lᵉšōnôṯ haggôyim* (Zec. 8:23), i.e., from all the language groups of the nations. Here the term *lāšôn* becomes identical with that of nation: ". . . to gather all *gôyim* and *lᵉšōnôṯ*" (Isa. 66:18), i.e., all peoples and nations.

One's own *lāšôn* is familiar (Est. 1:22), while a foreign language is an "alien (lit., 'other') *lāšôn*" (Isa. 28:11). Foreigners seem to have an awkward tongue (Ezk. 3:6); the incomprehensibility of their language causes them to seem especially menacing (Dt. 28:49).

The foreign enemy is *nilʿag lāšôn* (Isa. 33:19) and comes with *laʿᵃgê śāpâ,* par. *lāšôn* (Isa. 28:11). Interpreters generally understand the meaning of *lʿg* here as "stammer," drawing support from Syriac and the *hapax legomenon ʿlg* (Isa. 32:4): To the native inhabitants the person speaking a foreign language will appear to be stammering.

42. W. H. Schmidt, "Anthropologische Begriffe im AT," *EvTh,* 24 (1964), 387.
43. The textual emendation suggested by BHS is unnecessary.

In these two passages, however, it is not really necessary to posit a divergent meaning for the otherwise richly attested term *lʿg,* "mock, deride." The incomprehensible sounds of a foreign language can elicit mockery from us, just as in their own turn they seem to scoff at us. Here we must also recall the close relationship between a song of mockery on the one hand and magic on the other, and between magic and a foreign language.[44] The enemy thus comes to us with barbarous speech that seems to mock one's own *lāšôn.*

A foreign language must be learned. Thus Daniel and his companions are instructed in the letters and language of the Chaldeans (Dan. 1:4). The noteworthy sequence *sēp̱er* and then *lāšôn* is hardly accidental. Est. 1:22 also mentions *keṯāḇ* first, then *lāšôn.* The acquisition of strange letters and writings (for Daniel those of Sumerian) precedes any actual mastery of the language.

A person who masters the specialized idiom of magical incantation is called a *baʿal hallāšôn* (Eccl. 10:11). He can charm snakes or explain the miracles they effect (LXX *tṓ epádonti,* "to the conjurer").[45] It is less likely that *lāšôn* here refers to the snake's tongue,[46] whereby the magician would be described as master of the snake's tongue. The Vulg. understands this as "secret slanderer."

V. Semantic Field. We must yet determine the position of the word *lāšôn* in relationship with the other words in its semantic field. In its metaphorical usage this word is partially synonymous with → פה *peh,* → שפה *śāp̱â,* and the less frequently used *ḥēḵ* and *gārôn.* When *lāšôn* appears in *parallelismus membrorum* with one of these synonyms, it usually appears in the second part of the verse, suggesting that it is less stereotypical and thus more expressive.[47]

The word *peh* often fades to an abstract concept (cf. expressions such as *ʿal pî*). It is significant that *pî YHWH* became a frequently used expression for divine instruction, whereas Yahweh's *lāšôn* is mentioned only once (Isa. 30:27), and there in a stark portrayal of a theophany (an analogous relationship obtains between Yahweh's *yāḏ,* i.e., "power," over against Yahweh's *raglayim* [Ps. 18:10(9)]). Moreover, *lāšôn* does not refer to the sense of taste (*peh, ḥēḵ*) nor to a loud outcry or the act of swallowing or devouring (*gārôn*). As the symbol of speech *lāšôn* is characterized more by movement and activity than are the synonyms. Speech issues from a person's mouth and lips (Dt. 23:24[23]; 8:3), and the tongue can rise up (Isa. 54:17). Whereas the mouth and lips testify unwillingly against the speaker, he himself chooses the tongue (Job 15:5f.). In the case of speech impediment a person's lips are veiled, and the tongue slow (Ex. 6:12; 4:10).[48] A man's lips are with him; he prevails with his tongue (Ps.

44. See Erman-Ranke.
45. Cf. Sir. 12:13 LXX; *ANET,* 326.
46. So H. W. Hertzberg, *Der Prediger. KAT,* XVII/4 (1963), 185.
47. On what have been called "parallel pairs," see M. Dahood and T. Penar, "Ugaritic-Hebrew Parallel Pairs," *RSP,* I, 73-78; *peh-lāšôn,* 309f., no. 455; *śāp̱â-lāšôn,* 368, no. 579.
48. → כבד *kāḇēḏ* (VII, 13-22).

12:5[4]). A babbler is a man of lips (Job 11:2); the malicious inciter is a man of the tongue (Ps. 140:12[11]).

A dialect as such can also be called *śāp̱â* where it is viewed as a unity (Gen. 11:1,6; Zeph. 3:9). For a plurality of languages, however, this word offers no plural form. A splintering into different languages is designated by *lāšôn* or *lᵉšōnôṯ* (Est. 3:12; Gen. 10:20). This is also the case in a Qumran text (1QM 10:14): *blt lšwn wmprd ʿmym,* "confusion of tongues and division of peoples."

VI. Religio-Ethical Considerations. The religio-ethical estimation of *lāšôn* addresses a person's linguistic behavior and agrees in substance with statements addressing that behavior under a different rubric.[49] In statements about *lāšôn,* however, a negative or positive estimation prompts stronger accentuation, resulting in assertions that can hardly be formulated more evocatively: "Death and life are in the power of the *lāšôn*" (Prov. 18:21; cf. Sir. 37:18).

The concept of the enormous power of the tongue unites dynamistic-magical beliefs[50] with empirical wisdom of the world. The proverb just cited evokes equally the curses and blessings conjured by the *lāšôn* on the one hand, or the disaster or deliverance brought about in a practical sphere of life on the other. In any case, OT understanding inseparably associates the *lāšôn* with thought (Ps. 52:4[2]) and action (Isa. 3:8). The tongue is as powerful as a weapon (Isa. 54:17 par. *kᵉlî,* "instruments of war") and can be used to smite a person (Jer. 18:18). It is like a sharpened knife (Ps. 52:4[2]), a scourge (Job 5:21; Sir. 28:17), and a sharp sword (Ps. 57:5[4]; Sir. 28:18). It can be bent like a bow and becomes a sharpened arrow (Jer. 9:2,7[3,8]). On the other hand, the tongue can heal like balsam and be a tree of life (Prov. 12:18; 15:4).

One should not overestimate the frequent linguistic occurrence of the tongue as the subject of a verbal clause. It plots the malicious deed (Ps. 52:4[2]), speaks wickedly (Isa. 59:3), rises in judgment (Isa. 54:17), and makes great boasts (Ps. 12:4[3]), although it also expresses praise (Pss. 35:28; 119:172). One cannot really speak of any quasi-independent activity on the part of the *lāšôn.*[51] "My *lāšôn* speaks" (Job 33:2) is a circumscription for "I speak with my *lāšôn*" (Ps. 39:4[3]).

The wisdom writings in particular warn against imprudent and false *lāšôn*; both the psalms and the prophets lament the malicious *lāšôn* of blasphemers. In isolated passages we find those significant statements about one's own sins of the tongue. Neither the smooth-tongued flatterer (Prov. 28:23) nor the tongue of the slanderer (25:23) finds favor. Whoever whispers to a master something ill about a servant (*lšn* hiphil) will bring down the servant's curse upon himself (Prov. 30:10). A lying tongue does not last long (Prov. 12:19), and a perverse tongue will come to an evil end (17:20; 10:31). Riches accumulated with a lying tongue prove to be a mere fleeting vapor, or even a snare of death (Prov. 21:6). Wickedness tastes good to the blasphemer. Though he wants

49. See V above.
50. Mowinckel.
51. Behm, Wendland.

to hide it under his tongue, it will be transformed into the bitter poison of asps, and he will be killed by the viper's tongue (Job 20:12-16).

The tongue of blasphemers is the expression of their vile nature and deeds. They feel almighty (*gbr*) with their *lāšôn:* "Who is our master?"; their *lāšôn* makes great boasts (Ps. 12:4f.[3f.]). They set their mouths against the heavens, and their *lāšôn* struts through the land (Ps. 73:9). The villains make their tongue smooth so that their throat becomes an open sepulchre (Ps. 5:10[9]). They conceal injustice and violence beneath their tongues, then deviously crush the poor and the innocent (Ps. 10:7-9). The inclination of the powerful blasphemer to employ a deceiving tongue results from his loving evil more than good (Ps. 52:4-6[2-4]). The stringent condemnation of this kind of *lāšôn* is illustrated by the fact that it is mentioned in the same breath with theft, adultery (Ps. 50:18f.), and murder (Prov. 6:17; Isa. 59:3). Thus the *'îš lāšôn* (Ps. 140:12[11] par. *'îš-ḥāmās* [*rā'*]) is to be understood as someone who incites criminal activity and violence.[52]

The prophets condemn their people for precisely this sin. Everyone's tongue became accustomed to lying (Jer. 9:4[5]); they direct their *lāšôn* against one another like a bow and arrow (vv. 2,7[3,8]). Their *lāšôn* is deceitful in their mouth (Mic. 6:12), and they thus direct their *lāšôn* and their deeds against Yahweh (Isa. 3:8). The historical psalm asserts the same thing. Past generations were not dedicated to God and his covenant, although they deceived him with their *lāšôn* (Ps. 78:36). They pretended not to understand the words of the prophet, as if they were a foreign people with slow, alien *lāšôn* (Isa. 28:11). In the face of this strife of tongues (*rîḇ lᵉšōnôṯ,* Ps. 31:21[20]), God is the only refuge. The righteous person entreats God to give him shelter and deliver him from the deceitful tongues (Ps. 120:2).[53] May God split those tongues (*plg,* as in Gen. 10:25, which refers to the [linguistic?] division of the nations) and bring the blasphemers to ruin because of their own tongues (Ps. 55:10[9]; 64:9[8][54]). According to a Qumran psalm (1QH 5:15), God will draw the adversaries' tongue back like a sword into its sheath before they can smite anyone. For a lying tongue is an abomination to Yahweh (Prov. 6:16f.).

Thus the virtuous person will examine his own *lāšôn* to determine whether it has been deceitful (Job 27:4). The righteous person knows that he must guard his tongue not only to keep himself out of trouble (Prov. 21:23), but also to keep evil away from it (Ps. 34:14[13]). Only a person who has never slandered another with his *lāšôn (rgl,* Ps. 15:3; cf. Sir. 5:14; *lšn,* Ps. 101:5) may dwell in God's tent.

In this way the *lāšôn* can become what it should be: the means of communication between human beings and between human beings and God. A wise tongue deepens a person's insight (Prov. 15:2), and a gentle tongue persuades (25:15). The *lāšôn* of the righteous is precious silver (Prov. 10:20), for it speaks justly (Ps. 37:30). In the hour

---

52. The translation "braggart" (H.-J. Kraus, *Psalms 60-150* [Eng. trans., Minneapolis, 1989], though a similar interpretation already arises in Sir. 9:18 LXX, Vulg.) enfeebles the function of *lāšôn.*

53. Thus our interpretation; cf. F. Delitzsch, *The Psalms. KD,* V, III, 268f.

54. Cf. *BHK.*

of miraculous deliverance the *lāšôn* of stammerers will speak clearly (Isa. 32:4), and that of the mute will sing for joy (35:6). In Thanksgiving Psalms the *lāšôn* proclaims Yahweh's steadfastness and righteousness (Ps. 35:28; 51:16[14]; 71:24; 126:2). Yahweh, who knows a person's every deed, also knows every word on his *lāšôn* (Ps. 139:4). Texts from Qumran portray this similarly: "The spirit that lies in man's speech you did create, you have known all the words of man's tongue" (1QH 1:28f.); "God made the *lāšôn* and knows its word" (4Q185). He gives the tongue to the prophet (Isa. 50:4; 1QH 7:10 interprets: "a tongue according to God's commandments"); the appropriate answer of the tongue comes from God (Prov. 16:1). Here no room is left for determinism. Although a person can willfully take his own *lāšôn* and proclaim what is false (Jer. 23:31), whoever is seized by Yahweh's spirit senses that Yahweh's word is upon his *lāšôn* (2 S. 23:2).

Kedar-Kopfstein

לִשְׁכָּה *liškâ*

Contents: I. 1. Etymology; 2. Occurrences in the OT. II. 1. Sacrificial Hall; 2. Jerusalem Temple (Preexilic); 3. Function and Use; 4. Differentiation by Personal Names; 5. Priests' Chambers. III. Qumran. IV. LXX.

I. 1. *Etymology.* The Ugaritic term *lṯk*[1] in the expression *blṯk bt* might be related to Heb. *liškâ,*[2] particularly since the remnants of the poorly preserved tablets also mention gates *(ptḥ),* windows *(ḥlnm),* and rooms *(ḥdr);* one would, however, anticipate a feminine form. Also, since only sparce evidence is attested for the letter *ṯ,* and since a noticeably large space occurs between *blṯk* and *bt,* the precise reference cannot be determined with any certainty.[3] A Punic attestation of *lyškt* in a fragmentary inscription from Maktar[4] is likewise uncertain.[5] The Middle Hebrew (mishnaic) and Jewish-

---

liškâ. T. A. Busink, *Der Tempel von Jerusalem von Salomo bis Herodes,* II: *Von Ezechiel bis Middot. StFS,* 3 (1980), esp. 721-26, 729f., 739-748; K. Elliger, "Die grossen Tempelsakristeien im Verfassungsentwurf des Ezechiel (42,1ff.)," *Geschichte und AT. Festschrift A. Alt. BHTh,* 16 (1953), 80-102; K. Galling, "Die Halle des Schreibers: Ein Beitrag zur Topographie der Akropolis von Jerusalem," *PJ,* 27 (1931), 51-57; J. Maier, "Die Hofanlagen im Tempel-Entwurf des Ezechiel im Licht der 'Tempelrolle' von Qumran," *Prophecy. Festschrift G. Fohrer. BZAW,* 150 (1980), 55-67.

1. *UT,* no. 1151, 8.
2. Cf. *PRU,* II, 182; M. Dahood, "Hebrew Lexicography: A Review of W. Baumgartner's *Lexikon,* Volume II," *Or,* 45 (1976), 345.
3. *KTU,* 4.195, 8 has not incorporated this reading.
4. J. G. Fevrier, "Communication," *Bulletin archéologique du comité des travaux historiques et scientifiques,* 1950, 111f.
5. Cf. *DISO,* 138.

Aramaic (e.g., targumic) evidence is dependent on the biblical occurrences of the word *liškâ*.

The question concerning the relationship between Heb. *liškâ* and Gk. *léschē* is also of interest. It is highly unlikely that *léschē* is a Semitic loanword in Greek;[6] since there is some etymological evidence within Greek itself,[7] the Hebrew and Greek forms probably do not share a common root from Asia Minor.[8] Thus it is possible that the word was imported from the Greek by foreign peoples.[9] The alteration $l \rightarrow n$ in the initial position of *liškâ/niškâ* (as in Neh. 3:30; 12:44; 13:7, and 11QT), however, should not be taken as an indication of uncertainty in the rendering of a foreign word; rather, it reflects the familiar East Aramaic (esp. in the Talmud) transition from *l* to *n* and *vice versa*.[10]

2. *Occurrences in the OT.* As the designation for part of a building in the sense of room, cell, chamber, hall, chapel, etc., *liškâ* occurs altogether 47 times in the OT: 8 times in Jeremiah (only in chs. 35 and 36), 23 times in Ezekiel (in the temple plans, chs. 40ff.), 14 times in the Chronicler's history (where the secondary form *niškâ* also occurs 3 times), and also in 2 K. 23:11; 1 S. 9:22. In Ezk. 45:5, the *ʿeśrîm lᵉšāḵōṯ*, despite attestation in Syriac, Targumim, and Vulg., should be emended according to the LXX to *ʿārîm lāšāḇeṯ*. Additionally, the LXX version of 1 S. 1:18 implies a fuller (though not necessarily better) text over against MT. After her prayer and conversation with Eli, Hannah returns to the "hall" *(eis tó katályma [autḗs] = halliškāṯâ)*. This Hebrew recension may also have spoken in 1 S. 1:9 of the *liškâ* (*blškh* instead of *bšlh*) in which the sacrificial meal was taken (analogous to 1 S. 9:22).[11]

It is not surprising that P does not mention the *lᵉšāḵôṯ*, since P maintains the fiction associated with the wilderness sanctuary, namely, that no ancillary buildings were necessary.[12]

---

6. Cf. H. Lewy, *Die semitischen Fremdwörter im Griechischen* (1895, repr. Hildesheim, 1970), 94f.

7. Cf. H. Frisk, *Griechisches Etymologisches Wörterbuch. Indogermanische Bibliothek,* ser. 2, II (Heidelberg, 1970), 107f.

8. Contra E. Meyer, *Geschichte des Altertums,* I/2 (1913, repr. Darmstadt, 1981), §476, p. 705 n.

9. Cf. C. H. Gordon, "Homer and Bible," *HUCA,* 26 (1955), 60f.; *idem,* "The Role of the Philistines," *Antiquity,* 30 (1956), 23f. Gordon suggests that *liškâ/léschē* evidences "Minoan heritage in architecture" mediated through the Philistines. On a possible semantic connection and an interpretation of *léschē* as a "drinking-hall," cf. J. P. Brown, "The Mediterranean Vocabulary of the Vine," *VT,* 19 (1969), 151ff.

10. Cf. R. Macuch, *Handbook of Classical and Modern Mandaic* (Berlin, 1965), 50f., §27.

11. Cf. following A. Klostermann, *Die Bücher Samuelis und der Könige. SZ,* III (1887), esp. K. Budde, *Die Bücher der Samuel. KHC,* VIII (1902); and more recently R. de Vaux, *Les Livres de Samuel* (Paris, ²1961), *in loc.*

12. For a different view, see M. Haran, *Temples and Temple-Service in Ancient Israel* (Oxford, 1978), 24, 193.

II. 1. *Sacrificial Hall.* A *liškâ* can refer to a room in a sanctuary in which sacrificial meals are celebrated (1 S. 1:9 LXX; 9:22; cf. also Jer. 35:2; Ezk. 42:13). 1 S. 9:22 implies that there was room for *ca.* thirty participants. Presumably the definition offered by KBL^2 and KBL^3 (with reference to Arab. *līwān*)[13] is applicable to such a room: seating benches for the celebrants were located along three walls, while the fourth side opened up toward a court (cf. Vulg. 1 S. 9:22: *triclinium,* and the translation of *liškâ* in LXX by *exédra* [18 times] and in Vulg. by *exedra* [6 times]). Archaeological evidence for such rooms used for sacrificial meals is attested for many temples in the ancient Near East.[14]

2. *Jerusalem Temple (Preexilic).*

a. Information from the preexilic period is sparse concerning ancillary rooms designated as *liškâ* connected with the Jerusalem temple. In the account of measures taken in connection with Josiah's cultic reform, 2 K. 23:11 reports that Josiah removed the horses for the chariot (LXX; MT 'chariots') of the sun, and that these horses were located in the *liškâ* of the *śārîs* Nathan-melech. If this refers to living horses and not to reproductions (made of metal?), then the *liškâ* of Nathan-melech, located next to the entrance to the temple (and thus at the eastern edge of the platform in the *parwārîm*), served as a horse stall.

b. Jer. 35:2,4 reports that Jeremiah brought the abstinent Rechabites into the *liškâ* of the "sons of Hanan" (so MT), the son of Igdaliah, the man of God, in order to offer them wine to drink. This *liškâ* seems to refer to a larger room serving as the meeting place for a prophetic school, the disciples of Hanan. Our understanding of its location is not really enhanced by the text's subsequent, more specific information, namely, that it was located near the *liškâ* of the *śārîm* (or does this [and Ezk. 40:44], following MT, refer rather to *šārîm,* i.e., singers' guilds, as in 1 Ch. 9:33?), above the *liškâ* of Maaseiah the son of Shallum, keeper of the threshold.

c. Jer. 36:10,12,20f. refer[15] to a single building, more specifically an official state building distinguished by its access both to the temple outer court and to the palace court. If one follows the MT, however, then the reference is on the one hand to a *liškâ* of Gemariah, the son of the scribe Shaphan (v. 10), in the upper court at the new temple gate, and on the other to the *liškâ* of the scribe (v. 12) Elishama (vv. 20f.) in the royal palace, which may have had some official status.

d. If as 1 Ch. 28:12 suggests the *l^ešāḵôṯ* surrounding the outer courts can be traced back to David's own directive, and if as 2 Ch. 31:11 suggests Hezekiah had such chambers prepared, then we can deduce at least that the preexilic temple had ancillary rooms that served in particular as treasury rooms and storage halls.

---

13. Cf. S. Renart, *Lexikon der arabischen Welt* (Zurich, 1972), 665.

14. Cf. J. Starcky, "Salles de banquets rituels dans les sanctuaires orientaux," *Syr,* 26 (1949), 62-67.

15. So Galling.

3. *Function and Use.* The creation of these chambers along the outer wall of the temple area might have been a result of Babylonian influence, although these chambers may have resulted simply from the construction technique of building casemates along the city wall.[16] On the other hand, the plural form in Neh. 13:9 may not be interpreted such that the priest Eliashib had apportioned to Tobiah, the Ammonite enemy of Nehemiah, a "suite" of smaller chambers, i.e., a *liškâ* partitioned into several rooms (cf. v. 5, *liškâ gᵉḏôlâ*); rather, "Tobiah's chamber had so tainted the adjoining rooms with its uncleanness that they, too, had to be cleansed."[17]

A portion of the *lᵉšāḵôṯ*[18] was used as treasury rooms (1 Ch. 28:12; Ezr. 8:29) or as storerooms for offerings (Ezk. 42:12), tithes of fruit, grain, wine, and oil (Neh. 10:39f.[Eng. vv. 38f.]; similarly 12:44; 13:9), taxes and tithes (2 Ch. 31:11f.) or frankincense (Neh. 13:9), and especially for storing the sacred cultic vessels (Neh. 13:9; according to the current text, also 1 Ch. 28:12, where an addendum [vv. 14-18] enumerates the individual pieces).[19] According to Ezk. 46:19f., one of the rooms among the holy chambers for the priests facing north served as an offering kitchen for cooking the guilt and sin offerings and for baking the cereal offering (cf. also 1 Ch. 28:12f., where *mᵉleʾḵeṯ ʿᵃḇôḏaṯ bêṯ-YHWH* also probably refers to the boiling and cooking of the offering, just as Mishnah *Mid.* i.4 speaks of a *liškâ* of the guild of "them that made the Baken Cakes" *[lškt byt ʿwśh ḥbtyn]*). According to Ezk. 40:38, there was a *liškâ* opening toward the front hall of the inner north gate reserved as a washing room for rinsing the entrails and lower legs of the burnt offering.[20] The Mishnah tractate *Middoth* contains additional, very precise instructions concerning the use of specific cells. For example, there was one chamber in which priests who were unfit for other service because of physical blemishes looked for worms in the wood used for the altar fire, since such worm-infested wood would have defiled the sacrifice (ii.5).

At very least, 1 Ch. 9:33 reveals that the *lᵉšāḵôṯ* served as places where temple personnel stayed. One can understand *ballᵉšāḵōṯ pᵉṭûrîm* such that when the singers were not actually in service, they could linger in these cells; or, since they were free from other service, they lived in these cells in order to be on call day and night.[21] Or one can insert *lôʾ*[22] and proceed on the assumption that the text is specially praising these singers by emphasizing that they enjoyed no respite even in the cells, in contrast to the other Levites, who were able to relax in the temple sacristies when not actually in service.

4. *Differentiation by Personal Names.* It is noteworthy that several of these rooms associated with the Jerusalem temple are identified more specifically by the personal

---

16. Cf. Busink, 725f.
17. W. Rudolph, *Esra und Nehemia. HAT,* XX (1949), 204.
18. Maier, 58f., calculates 210 individual rooms for the complex of the outer court, and as many as 856 according to the Temple Scroll.
19. Cf. Mishnah *Mid.* ii.6a, which mentions cells for storing musical instruments.
20. Cf. Mishnah *Mid.* v.3: *lškt hmdyḥyn.*
21. J. W. Rothstein and J. Hänel, *Das erste Buch der Chronik. KAT,* XVIII/2 (1927), 179.
22. So W. Rudolph, *Chronikbücher. HAT,* XXI (1955), 90f.

names of their builder and/or present owner (or tenant) (cf. 2 K. 23:11; Ezr. 10:6; Jer. 35:4; 36:10,20f.; differently in Neh. 3:30[23]).

The *liškâ* of Johanan the son of Eliashib mentioned in Ezr. 10:6 has acquired special renown in scholarship. In particular, Albin van Hoonacker[24] and scholars subscribing to his hypothesis[25] viewed it as an important argument for reversing the chronological sequence Ezra-Nehemiah into Nehemiah-Ezra. According to Ezr. 10:6, Ezra withdraws at the end of the day into the *liškâ* of Johanan the son of Eliashib to spend the night in mourning and fasting. Since according to Neh. 12:10f.,22 a grandson of the high priest Eliashib bears the name Johanan, and since in both Neh. 12:23; Ezr. 10:6 this Johanan is called "son of Eliashib," the suspicion cannot be so quickly dismissed that the two passages are speaking of the same man. If, however, Eliashib was the high priest not only at the beginning of Nehemiah's activity (Neh. 3:1), but also after Nehemiah's return from Babylon (Neh. 13:4), one may assume that the time in which his grandson occupied a *liškâ* at the temple is to be put after the twelfth year of Nehemiah, and that thus what is reported in Ezr. 10:6 cannot have preceded the construction of the wall.

Wilhelm Rudolph,[26] however, justifiably objects that it is by no means certain that the untitled Eliashib (Ezr. 10:6) really was the high priest, nor that the untitled (according to Neh. 12:23) Johanan was his grandson. The names Eliashib and Johanan occur frequently in the postexilic period and are attested for various persons; thus there is "not the slightest reason to assume a reference to the high-priestly family in Ezr. 10:6, particularly since at least in the preexilic temple private individuals also owned temple cells,"[27] as already evident from the notices in 2 K. 23:11; Jer. 35:4; 36:10 presented earlier.

If in Neh. 3:30 the *niškâ* of Meshullam the son of Berechiah is to be understood as a secular edifice, namely, the priests' dwelling outside the temple area, then it is not clear which particular architectural features prompted the designation of the building as *niškâ*. Although the description of the wall construction can indeed be followed from vv. 28-31 the length of the temple area, it is not likely that v. 30 is referring to a temple cell. Rather, as in vv. 20f. concerning the house of the high priest Eliashib, the reference is probably to a priest's dwelling which was not (cf. v. 28) located in the vicinity of the temple.

5. *Priests' Chambers.* The large complex of temple sacristies in Ezekiel's temple vision[28] stands completely under the sign of a more fully developed theology of

23. See below.

24. "Néhémie et Esdras: Une Nouvelle hypothèse sur la chronologie de l'époque de la restauration," *Mus,* 9 (1890), 151-184, 317-351, 389-401.

25. H. Cazelles, *Histoire politique d'Israël. Petite Bibliothéque des sciences bibliques,* AT 1 (Paris, 1982); *idem,* ed., *Introduction critique à l'AT* (Paris, 1973).

26. *HAT,* XX, 67f.

27. So Rudolph.

28. Our understanding presupposes the interpretation of Elliger.

holiness. The three-story building (Ezk. 42:5f.) provides not only for optimal utilization of space for the varied needs associated with a temple cult,[29] it also serves above all to segregate the sacred area. Already "the layout of the buildings which reveal their bridging function in their terrace-like ascent from the lay sphere to the priestly sphere"[30] shows the sharpened concept of holiness in the architectural plan, as illustrated particularly in the expanded layers within Ezk. 40ff. Here the priests must change garments before leaving the interior of the temple area and proceeding out to the lay people (42:13; 44:19); this also prompts the cultic designation of the buildings as *liškôṯ haqqōḏeš* (42:13; 44:19; 46:19). "From this qualification of the sacristies as a sacred place there arise the subsequent regulations about behavior in this area, which at the end of v. 13 is once again specifically described as מקום קדש [*māqôm qāḏōš*]."[31] "At the same time, however, the danger which threatens to arise in this intensified guarding and delimiting of the sacred is not overlooked."[32]

III. Qumran. This word occurs in the Qumran texts 12 times in the form *nškh* or *nškwt,* although only in the Temple scroll[33] in the section about the outer court (11QT 40:5–45:6).[34]

IV. LXX. The LXX rendering vacillates between *exédra* (18 times in Ezekiel), *gazophylákion* (11 times, esp. Ezra-Nehemiah), and *pastophórion* (8 times, esp. 1-2 Chronicles). In addition to these, *oíkos* also occurs 6 times as an equivalent. Isolated equivalents such as *katályma* (1 S. 9:22), *aulḗ* (Jer. 35:2[LXX 42:2]), or *skēnḗ* (Ezr. 8:29) only attest the uncertainty in the search for the exact meaning. Jerome prefers the loanword *gazofilacium* (altogether 37 times) to *exedra* (6 times). Translations occurring only once, such as *triclinium* (1 S. 9:22), *cubiculum* (Ezr. 10:6), or *horreum* (2 Ch. 31:11), interpret the word on the basis of context. In the NT, Jn. 8:20 uses *gazophylakeíon* to refer to a *liškâ* specially identified as a treasury room, while the same word in Mk. 12:41,43; Lk. 21:1 probably refers rather to an alms box.[35]

Kellermann

29. See II.2 above.
30. W. Zimmerli, *Ezekiel 2. Herm* (Eng. trans. 1983), 401.
31. *Ibid.,* 400.
32. *Ibid.,* 401.
33. Cf. Y. Yadin, *Megillat hammiqdaš,* I-IIIA (Jerusalem, 1977); J. Maier, *The Temple Scroll. JSOT Sup,* 34 (Eng. trans. 1985).
34. Cf. Maier, *Festschrift G. Fohrer,* 58.
35. Cf. St.-B., II (1924), 37-41.

מְאֹד mᵉʾōḏ

Contents: I. Etymology. II. Occurrences. III. 1. Relationship Between the Various Functions; 2. Adverbial Function. IV. Substantive: 1. Doubtful Cases; 2. bᵉḵol mᵉʾōḏeḵā.

I. Etymology. The root *mʾd* with word constructions comparable in meaning to that of Heb. *mᵉʾōḏ* occurs in several Semitic languages. These findings supersede attempts by earlier lexicographers to understand *mᵉʾōḏ* as a compound from the prefix *m* and the root *ʾûd* (after the Arabic, meaning approximately "weigh on, burden something; a burden").[1] Mitchell Dahood's suggestion[2] that *mʾd* represents a dialect variation of *mʾz,* "of old," is unacceptable.

Akkadian[3] attests a verb *mâdu (maʾādu),* "be or become much, numerous," an adj. *mādu (maʾdu),* "much, numerous," a subst. *ʾmaʾdû (mādû),* "large quantity, plenty," and an adv. *mādiš,* "very." Ugaritic[4] attests the form *mʾd,* which means "much" (*mʾd ksp,* "much silver") and "very" (*ʿz mʾd,* "very strong"), as well as the subst. *mʾd,* "large quantity." It is doubtful that the form *mʾdy* is actually a suffixed noun ("my fullness").

Dahood has suggested repointing on the basis of Ugar. *mʾd* into *māʾēd,* and to translate as "Grand One" or "God Almighty" (thus in Ps. 21:2[Eng. v. 1]; 46:2[1]; 92:6[5]; 96:4; 97:9; 105:24; 109:30; 119:8,96,138,140,167; 142:7[6]; 145:3).[5] This was picked up by David Noel Freedman (on Ps. 78:59)[6] and Lorenzo Viganò (on Gen. 13:13).[7] One can object with Oswald Loretz,[8] however, that in the passages under discussion stichometric considerations already make any repointing difficult. On the other hand, David Marcus[9] has pointed out that Ugar. *mʾd* means "many, much," but

---

mᵉʾōḏ. M. Lambert, *Traité de grammaire hébraïque* (Hildesheim, ²1972), 388-391; J. Pedersen, *ILC,* I-II, 146f.; G. von Rad, *OT Theology,* I (Eng. trans., New York, 1962), 206f., 225f.; E. Ben Yehuda, *Thesaurus totius Hebraitatis,* VI (1948, repr. New York, 1960), 2745-2750 [Heb.].

1. *GesThes,* 35-37; P. A. de Lagarde, *Übersicht über die im aramäischen, arabischen und hebräischen übliche Bildung der Nomina. AGWG,* 35 (1889, repr. Osnabrück, 1972), 128.
2. "Hebrew-Ugaritic Lexicography IV," *Bibl,* 47 (1966), 413.
3. *AHw,* II (1972), 573f.; *CAD,* X/1 (1977), 4f., 19-27; X/2 (1977), 163.
4. *WUS,* no. 1498; *UT,* no. 1406; M. Dahood, "Ugaritic-Hebrew Parallel Pairs," *RSP,* I, no. 342a, 415.
5. "Comparative Philology Yesterday and Today," *Bibl,* 50 (1969), 79; *Psalms III. AB,* XVIIA (1970), 473; more cautiously in "Hebrew Lexicography: A Review of W. Baumgartner's *Lexikon,* Volume II," *Or,* 45 (1976), 346.
6. "God Almighty in Psalm 78:59," *Bibl,* 54 (1973), 268 = *Pottery, Poetry, and Prophecy* (Winona Lake, 1980), 347.
7. *Nomi e titoli di YHWH alla luce del semitico del Nord-Ovest. BietOr,* 31 (1976); cf. M. Dahood, "Northwest Semitic Notes on Genesis," *Bibl,* 55 (1974), 77f.
8. "ʿd mʾd 'Everlasting Grand One' in den Psalmen," *BZ,* N.S. 16 (1972), 245-48; *idem,* "Die Umpunktierung von *mʾd* zu *māʾēd* in den Psalmen," *UF,* 6 (1975), 481-84.
9. "Ugaritic Evidence for 'The Almighty/The Grand One'?" *Bibl,* 55 (1974), 404-7.

never "great." Hence a divine epithet with the meaning suggested above cannot be derived from the Ugaritic evidence.

Arabic attests the verb *ma'ada,* "begin to grow."

II. Occurrences. The word *m^e'ōḏ* occurs 253 times in the OT in this particular form, 6 times in the superlative doubling *m^e'ōḏ m^e'ōḏ,* 24 times in the prepositional forms *bim^e'ōḏ m^e'ōḏ* (6 times), *'aḏ m^e'ōḏ* (17), *'aḏ lim^e'ōḏ* (once), and twice as a suffixed substantive.[10] The LXX usually translates with *sphódra,* "extremely, very (much)" (including an imitation of the doubling: *sphódra sphódra*), less often with *lían,* "very much indeed, too much." The Vulg. renders the word quite often with *valde,* "to a large extent, very (much)," although also with *nimis,* "beyond measure, much too much." In several instances we also encounter a semantically accurate translation: *vehemens* (Jgs. 12:2), *festinus* (1 S. 20:19), etc.

III. 1. *Relationship Between the Various Functions.* The lexica[11] assume an originally substantival meaning for the word *m^e'ōḏ* and derive from it the meaning of the adverbial function. This view is justified from a diachronic perspective, since the word was probably originally a noun (nominal construction *guṭl*[12]), as suggested by linguistic comparisons and the accompanying prepositions *(b^e, 'aḏ).* In the present context, however, *m^e'ōḏ* functions almost exclusively as an adverb; thus a synchronic description must take this function as its point of departure and only then attempt to determine its substantival meaning.

2. *Adverbial Function.* When used in the accusative as an adverb (in the Qumran texts often [even against MT] as *m^e'ôḏâ*[13]), the word serves to strengthen or amplify a statement. The work of a single day of creation is described as *ṭôḇ,* while the work as a whole is described as *ṭôḇ m^e'ōḏ* (Gen. 1:31). Since the content of the word itself is neutral, it can be employed equally for positive or negative emphasis (Jer. 24:2,3). The term *m^e'ōḏ* can strengthen or amplify adjectives (Jgs. 3:17), finite verb forms (Jgs. 6:6), imperatives (Jer. 2:10), infinitives (2 S. 14:25), adverbs (Zec. 14:14), and entire sentences (Jgs. 12:2; Jer. 18:13). It also occurs after verbs of movement (1 S. 20:19; Jer. 49:30), where it must be understood in the sense of "promptly, straightaway," and after negations (Isa. 64:8[9]; Dt. 17:17), where it means in effect "completely," "exceedingly."

This word is very flexible as regards its position within sentence structure (cf. the rather distant positioning in Josh. 9:13; Jgs. 12:2; 1 K. 11:19; etc.), although in general it stands after the word to be emphasized or after the essential part of the statement (e.g., after the verb and its subject) (cf. Ezk. 37:10; 1 K. 2:12; 1 Ch. 21:13). Accord-

---

10. See IV.2 below.

11. *BDB,* 547; *GesB,* 392; *HAL,* II (1995), 538; E. König, *Hebräisches und aramäisches Wörterbuch zum AT* (Leipzig, 1910), 203.

12. Cf. *BLe,* §460.

13. Cf. E. Y. Kutscher, *The Language and Linguistic Background of the Isaiah Scroll (1QIsa^a). STDJ,* 6 (1974), 413f., 498-500.

ingly, the extremely rare initial positioning of *mᵉʼōḏ* (Ps. 47:10[9]; 92:6[5]; 97:9) functions as an effective amplification of the emphasis itself within poetic style.

IV. Substantive.

1. *Doubtful Cases.* In some occurrences the word seems to exhibit nominal characteristics. Thus in Ps. 119:138 it might be taken as a virtual adjective to *ʼᵉmûnâ,* and in Ps. 31:12(11) as a parallel to *ḥerpâ* and *paḥaḏ* (cf. also Isa. 47:9; Ps. 46:2[1]). In all these verses, however, it is simpler not to undertake any textual emendation. Rather than assuming some extraordinary meaning that might have been familiar to the original audience, one should interpret this as distant positioning and refer *mᵉʼōḏ* to a preceding verb.

2. *bᵉḵol mᵉʼōḏeḵā.* The only (and significant) instance of a clearly substantival use occurs in Dt. 6:5 (and in the text dependent on it, 2 K. 23:25). Apparently, however, this does not represent a recovery of one of the word's original meanings which had dropped from current usage, but is rather a linguistically daring expansion of the use of the familiar emphatic particle. The addition of the personal suffix and the parallel positioning with *lēḇāḇ* and *nepeš* effectively substantivize the word. The translation tradition that interprets the word as "power, might" (LXX *dýnamis, ischýs;* Vulg. *fortitudo, virtus;* rabbinic writing, however, suggests *māmôn,* "wealth," a possibility that must likewise be considered[14]) is basically on target. In Deuteronomy, however, we must reckon with an "intensity of inwardness," although also with "a certain intellectualization."[15] The desire to describe the engagement of a person's whole personality, with all the positive features of which it is capable "in great measure," generated this neologism: "You shall love Yahweh your God with all your heart, and with all your soul, and *bᵉḵol mᵉʼōḏeḵā* (with your utmost efforts; NRSV 'with all your might']" (Dt. 6:5).

Kedar-Kopfstein

---

14. *Ber.* 61b.
15. Von Rad.

מֹאזְנַיִם *mōʼzᵉnayim*

Contents: I. Ancient Near East: 1. Egypt; 2. Mesopotamia; 3. West Semites. II. OT Usage: 1. Concrete Meaning in Symbolic Prophetic Acts; 2. Maxims About Honesty in Commerce; 3. *peles, qāneh, zygós;* 4. Symbol of God's Cosmic Rule; 5. Human Worth in Job.

---

mōʼzᵉnayim. G. Bertram, "ζυγός in the LXX," *TDNT,* II, 896-98; B. Kisch, *Scales and Weights: A Historical Outline* (New Haven, 1965), 26-78; C. Seeber, *Untersuchungen zur Darstellung des Totengerichts im Alten Ägypten. MÄSt,* 35 (1976), esp. 67-83; H. Weippert, "Waage," *BRL²*, 355.

I. Ancient Near East.

1. *Egypt.* The Egyptian term *wdn,* which is perhaps related to *wzn,* means "heavy";[1] a "balance, scale" is called *mḫȝ.t,* referring primarily to the "standing scale,"[2] or *ỉwśw,* probably the "hand[-held] scale."[3] The standing scale appearing at the judgment of the dead is especially well known. The heart of the deceased is weighed against the symbol of Maat before the throne of Osiris and the forty-two attendant judges. Here Thoth functions as scribe, and Anubis operates the scale.[4] The strict honesty of the scalemaster is emphasized. Thus we read in the Protests of the Eloquent Peasant: "Do the hand-scales *(ỉwśw)* err? Does the stand-balance *(mḫȝ.t)* incline to the side? Is even Thoth indulgent?"[5] At the judgment of the dead "Maat represents the universal ethical norm established by God against which the human being is measured with the testimony of his personal life."[6]

2. *Mesopotamia.* The Akkadian term *zibānītu,* "balance, scale" (Syr. *zᵉḇan,* "purchase"? *wzn*?), also refers to the constellation Libra;[7] another term is *gišrinnu* (Sum. *giš-erín*).[8] According to *CAD,*[9] these refer to two different kinds of scales, whereby *zibānītu* was equipped with a special component or mechanism **zibānu.*[10]

3. *West Semites.* The Ugaritic term *mznm* derives from *wzn* (cf. Arab. *wazana,* "weigh"); the Hebrew orthography with ' results from the combination with *'ōzen,* "ear,"[11] or with *'āzēn,* "implement, tool" (Dt. 23:14[Eng. v. 13][12]; RSV "weapons"). Although the dual form actually refers to the two balance pans together, it is used *pars pro toto* for "scales." The term *mznm* occurs in the Nikkal-Kotharot text[13] in a context concerned with determining the bridal price, i.e., in a domestic context as in Jer. 7:18. In Ugarit the scale *(mznm)* is mentioned among other household items.[14]

The meaning of the Punic term *m'zn*[15] is disputed: "implement, tool" or "scale,

---

1. *WbÄS,* I, 390.
2. *WbÄS,* II, 130.
3. *WbÄS,* I, 57. For illustrations of standing scales, cf., e.g., *ANEP,* 111, 122, 133 (for gold); for a hand-held scale, cf. E. Siphron, "מֹזְנַיִם," *EMiqr,* IV, 540.
4. *ANEP,* 639; on its operation see Seeber.
5. Ll. 148ff.; *ANET,* 409.
6. Seeber, 75.
7. *AHw,* III (1981), 1523.
8. *AHw,* I (1965), 293.
9. *CAD,* XXI (1961), 100.
10. For an illustration of a standing scale, cf. *ANEP,* 350. The hand scale reproduced there (no. 117) is actually Hittite; cf. M. Riemschneider, *Die Welt der Hethiter* (Stuttgart, 1954), 9, pl. 76.
11. So C. H. Gordon, *UT,* no. 801.
12. *HAL,* I (1994), 28.
13. *KTU,* 1.24, 34, 35, 37.
14. *KTU,* 4.385, 5; for a reproduction of a scale from Ras Shamra see O. R. Sellers, "Balances," *IDB,* I, 343.
15. *KAI,* 81.3.

balance''?[16] Egyptian Aramaic attests *mwzn,*[17] Biblical Aramaic *mōʼzᵉnayyāʼ,* and Jewish Aramaic *môḏᵉnāʼ* and *môzanyāʼ,* "scales, balance" (also Christian-Palestinian and Mandaic). According to E. Y. Kutscher,[18] the orthography *m(w)znym* in 1QIs[a] 40:12 is an aramaism. The piel form *ʼizzēn* (Eccl. 12:9) is denominative.

Archaeological finds include scales from Lachish[19] and Beth-zur.[20] Otherwise only balance pans[21] and weights (with a margin for error of up to 6%[22]) have been found.

II. OT Usage.

1. *Concrete Meaning in Symbolic Prophetic Acts.* The clearly concrete references to *mōʼzᵉnayim* also occur in theologically significant contexts. In Jer. 32:10, Jeremiah weighs the silver used in the purchase of a field, and in the course of symbolic gestures in Ezk. 5:1 the prophet parts his hair with balances into three parts as a symbol of the people's coming fate.

2. *Maxims About Honesty in Commerce.* The inculcation of the use of "honest balances" (*mōʼzᵉnê-ṣeḏeq*) and "honest weights" (*ʼaḇnê-ṣeḏeq*) (Lev. 19:36; Ezk. 45:10) actually also includes honesty toward one's fellow human beings in the larger sense. More frequently, however, we hear of false or deceptive balances (*mōʼzᵉnê mirmâ*: Hos. 12:8[7]; Am. 8:5; Prov. 11:1; 20:23). In Prov. 20:23, these parallel *ʼeḇen wāʼeḇen,* "false (NRSV 'differing') weights," and in 11:1 the false scale contrasts with *ʼeḇen šᵉlēmâ,* a "full (RSV 'just,' NRSV 'accurate') weight." Mic. 6:11 reproves the evil-doers for their dishonest business: false scales *(moʼzᵉnê rešaʽ)* and false weights *(ʼaḇnê mirmâ);* Yahweh cannot consider such a person pure or innocent.[23]

3. *peles, qāneh, zygós.* Prov. 16:11 asserts: "Yahweh has *peles* and *mōʼzᵉnê mišpāṭ*"; although *peles* probably refers to a specific component of the scale (arm? needle?), it functions here as a metonym for the entire scale (as also in Isa. 40:12).[24] The Hebrew text presents this insistence on correct scales as a divine command; since the verse stands in a series of royal sayings, however, the king may be intended as the person responsible before God for honest commerce. In Isa. 46:6, the term *qāneh,* "scale beam," similarly stands for the scale as a whole. Sir. 42:4 recommends honesty in *zygós* and *státhmia* (= *mōʼzᵉnayim* and *peles*[25]).

4. *Symbol of God's Cosmic Rule.* In Deutero-Isaiah the balance symbolizes God's cosmic rule. Who (if not God) has weighed the mountains in the *peles* and the hills in

16. *DISO,* 141.
17. *DISO,* 144.
18. *The Language and Linguistic Background of the Isaiah Scroll. STDJ,* 6 (1974), 187.
19. O. Tufnell, *Lachish,* III (London, 1953), pl. 62.
20. O. R. Sellers, *The Citadel of Beth Zur* (Philadelphia, 1933), II, pl. 44.
21. See Weippert, 355.
22. D. Diringer, "The Early Hebrew Weights Found at Lachish," *PEQ,* 74 (1942), 86.
23. Read piel → זכה *zāḵâ* (*zākhāh*), esp. II.2 (IV, 62-64).
24. According to Weippert, 355, *mōʼzᵉnayim* could be a hand balance and *peles* a standing balance.
25. Y. Yadin, *The Ben Sira Scroll from Masada* (Jerusalem, 1965), 22.

a *mō'zᵉnayim* (Isa. 40:12)? According to Isa. 40:15, the nations are no more than dust on the scales;[26] this verse is cited both in Wis. 11:22 and 2 Mc. 9:8. This is already an example of weighing human beings, although the concern is with their power, not their merits. The words in Dan. 5:27 are directed to Belshazzar, king of Babylon: "You have been weighed on the scales and found wanting."

5. *Human Worth in Job.* According to Job 6:2, a person's misfortunes are laid in the balances and weighed (*nāśā'*, "lift up onto the balance pan"[27]): It is heavier than the sand of the sea (v. 3). Job 31:6 is the only relatively unequivocal example of weighing a person's merits: If God weighs Job in a just balance, he will recognize Job's integrity (*tummâ*[28]). This is a matter of "the destiny and worth of man."[29] In contrast, according to Ps. 62:10(9) human beings are too light in the balances and cannot assert themselves. This particular usage develops the ideas of the Egyptian Book of the Dead further and leads naturally to Sir. 21:25; 28:25a, which speaks of words being weighed in the *zygós* and *státhmos.* Finally, the soul itself is laid upon the scales (1[Eth.]En. 41:1; 61:8; 2(Slav.)En. 49:2; 4 Esd. 4:36; Apoc. Elijah 13:4; and Jer. *Pe'ah* 1.16b; 37). The OT *mō'zᵉnayim* as a symbol of general human righteousness toward one's fellow human beings is thus further related both to the person himself and to God.

North

---

26. Thus D. W. Thomas, " 'A Drop of a Bucket'? Some Observations on the Hebrew Text of Isaiah 40 ₁₅," *In Memoriam Paul Kahle. BZAW,* 103 (1968), 217, not "clouds" as suggested by H. Torczyner, "The Firmament and the Clouds: Rāqîaᶜ and Sheḥāqîm," *StTh,* 1 (1948), 190.
27. Cf. F. Stolz, 'נשׂא *nś'* aufheben, tragen," *THAT,* II, 110.
28. → תמם *tāmam.*
29. Bertram, 896, with reference to Ps. Sol. 5:4.

מאן *m'n*

Contents: I. 1. Etymology; 2. Occurrences; 3. Meaning; 4. LXX. II. OT Usage: 1. Normal Usage; 2. Theological Usage.

I. 1. *Etymology.* Outside Hebrew, the root *m'n* is attested only in Syriac (*mē'n,* "disgust someone, spoil something for someone") and Old South Arabic (*m'n*[1]). Although Ethiop. and Tigré *manana,* "refuse," is semantically similar, its etymology is uncertain. Alfred Guillaume[2] assumes the presence of metathesis and refers to Arab. *manaᶜa,* "hold up, hinder."[3]

---

1. See W. W. Müller, "Altsüdarabische Beiträge zum hebräischen Lexicon," *ZAW,* 75 (1963), 311.
2. Guillaume, 10, 27.
3. Cf., however, → מנע *mānaᶜ* (VIII, 396-401).

2. *Occurrences.* Only the piel form occurs in the OT. Of 45 occurrences, 6 refer to Pharaoh's refusal to let the Israelites go, and 12 are found in the book of Jeremiah. Otherwise the distribution is of little interest.

3. *Meaning.* Isa. 1:19f. is especially useful for determining the meaning. There → אבה *'āḇâ ('ābhāh),* "be willing," and *mē'ēn* are antithetical, the latter being explicated further by → מרה *mārâ,* "be rebellious" (similarly also 4QpPs[a] 2:3). The verb is usually translated by "refuse" or "be unwilling," whereby it is not always clear whether the reference is to simple unwillingness or the actual act of refusing. In 6 instances the verb stands absolutely; otherwise it is complemented by an infinitive with or without *l*[e].

4. *LXX.* The LXX usually translates the term with negated forms of *(e)thélein* (18 times), *boúlesthai* (9), or *eisakoúein* (4), although other translations occur in isolated instances.

II. OT Usage.

1. *Normal Usage.* Most of the occurrences in the narrative writings are theologically neutral. Joseph refuses to accept the offer of Potiphar's wife (Gen. 39:8). Jacob does not want to bless Manasseh even though Manasseh is the first-born (Gen. 48:19). Edom refuses to grant the Israelites passage through his land (Num. 20:21). Yahweh does not want to allow Balaam to go to Balak (Num. 22:13), and Balaam refuses to go along (v. 14). The people refuse to listen to Samuel, and wish instead for a king (1 S. 8:19). Because Asahel pursues Abner and refuses to leave him alone, Abner kills him (2 S. 2:23). A disciple of the prophets refuses to strike his fellow (1 K. 20:35). Naboth refuses to give the king his vineyard (1 K. 21:15). Elisha refuses to accept the reward offered by Naaman (2 K. 5:16). Queen Vashti refuses to appear before the king's guests (Est. 1:12).

Three times it is asserted that someone refuses to eat: 1 S. 28:23 (Saul refuses to eat what the diviner of spirits offers him); 2 S. 13:9 (Amnon); and expressed more poetically in Job 6:7: "My *nep̱eš* does not want to touch the food." One wisdom proverb declares that the sluggard does not want to work (Prov. 21:25).

In several instances *m'n* is used with *nḥm* niphal. Jacob refuses to be comforted over Joseph's alleged death (Gen. 37:35). A lament proclaims: "My soul refuses to be comforted" (Ps. 77:3[Eng. v. 2]). Rachel, who laments her sons (i.e., the fallen northern kingdom), also refuses to be comforted (Jer. 31:15).

In a few instances the verb is used in the context of marital law. It refers to a father's refusal to give his daughter away as a wife (Ex. 22:16[17]) or to a man's refusal to consummate the levirate marriage (Dt. 25:7).

2. *Theological Usage.* Accounts of the exodus record several references to Pharaoh's refusal to let the Israelites go (Ex. 4:23; 7:14,27[8:2]; 9:2; 10:3,4). This is a matter of resistance to God's will which must remain futile and ultimately serve Yahweh's own glorification. A similar expression occurs in Jer. 50:33 in reference to the enemies who keep Israel in captivity.

The word acquires special theological resonance when it refers to unrepentance or the refusal to hear God's word. Such occurrences are especially numerous in Jeremiah. Lustful Israel refused to be ashamed; although God warned it with drought, it continued with its harlotry (Jer. 3:3). Although God smote the people, they still refused to accept correction (*mûsār*); they made their faces hard as stone and refused to repent or return (*šûḇ,* 5:3). The same term, *šûḇ,* is used with *m'n* in 8:5 as well; they turn away (*šûḇ* polel + *m*ᵉ*šuḇâ*), hold fast to their deceit (*tarmîṯ*), and refuse to repent. They abide in deceit and refuse to know God[4] (9:5[6]). With regard to obduracy and the worship of idols, the fathers or the people itself refuse to hear God's word (11:10; 13:10).

In the great vision of Yahweh's cup of wrath (Jer. 25[5]) we read that although the people do indeed refuse to accept the cup, they will be forced to drink it (v. 28). The human act of refusal is powerless against Yahweh's wrath. Jer. 15:18 has a slightly different angle of vision. There the prophet laments: "My wound refuses to be healed." Jer. 38:21 is different yet. If Zedekiah insists on refusing to surrender, he should well consider the consequences Jeremiah foretells.

This refusal to repent also appears in Hos. 11:5. Because the people refused to return or repent, they will be enslaved once again. The refusal to listen appears again in Zec. 7:11 in a litany of expressions for obstinacy. They refused to hearken (*qšb* hiphil), turned a stubborn shoulder,[6] and stopped their ears. Cf. also the confession of sin in Neh. 9:17. The fathers refused to listen, were not mindful (*zāḵar*) of God's wonders, and stiffened their necks. The historical reflections in Ps. 78 speak of obstinacy and disobedience, and offer the following summary: "They did not keep God's covenant, but refused to walk according to his law" (v. 10). Here law and covenant are virtually synonymous as expressions of religious obligation.

In Isa. 1:19f., the prophet presents the people with the choice between willingness and refusal, between heeding and recalcitrance. Ultimately this choice will determine the people's fate.

In the prophetically informed[7] wisdom discourse in Prov. 1:20-33, we read in vv. 24f.: "I have called and you refused, have stretched out my hand and no one heeded (*qšb* hiphil), . . . you have ignored all my counsel and would have (*'āḇâ*) none of my reproof." This accumulation of expressions for unwillingness corresponds to the prophetic texts cited above.

Finally, Prov. 21:7 declares that the wicked refuse to do *mišpāṭ*.

Ringgren

---

4. → ידע *yāḏa'* (V, 448-481).
5. → כוס *kôs* (VII, 101-4).
6. On this kind of stiff-necked obstinacy, cf. B. Couroyer, " 'Avoir la nuque raide': Ne pas incliner l'oreille," *RB,* 88 (1981), 216-225.
7. Cf. H. Ringgren, *Sprüche. ATD,* XVI/1 (^{3}1980), 17.

מָאַס *mā'as*

Contents: I. Root, Occurrences, Usage, and Meaning. II. Secular Usage. III. Theological Usage: 1. Human Beings as Subject; 2. God as Subject. IV. Uncertain Occurrences. V. Qumran. VI. LXX.

I. Root, Occurrences, Usage, and Meaning. The root *m's* does not appear to be indigenous to the older textual evidence of the Semitic languages. It occurs in Middle Hebrew and Jewish Aramaic, and there is some possibility that Arab. *ma'asa,* "reject," is related to Heb. *m's.* Attempts to derive it from Akk. *mašû,* "forget,"[1] or *mêšu,* "disregard, undervalue,"[2] are etymologically difficult, although from the perspective of semantics a relationship might be assumed. The biblical occurrences accord with these findings, since in the overwhelming majority of cases *m's* occurs in texts from the exilic and postexilic periods. Regarding the few earlier passages in which the root occurs, one must determine whether they genuinely come from the preexilic period or belong rather to the history of interpretation and adaptation of preexilic textual statements. It is noteworthy that *m's* does not occur in the older strata of the Pentateuch (3 times in Lev. 26 and twice in Numbers), not even in Deuteronomy, although it does occur in certain passages in the Deuteronomistic history (once in Judges; 9 times in 1 Samuel; 3 times in 2 Kings). A certain concentration of occurrences can be observed in material from the tradition of Jeremiah (11 times) and Ezekiel (6 times). Neither should we overlook the accumulation of occurrences in Wisdom Literature (11 times in Job, twice in Proverbs) in which the root is used in contexts exhorting the acceptance of one thing and the rejection of another. Testimonies of piety also presuppose situations involving decision. This is true both of the occurrences in the Psalms (7 times) and in the prophetic traditions (besides Jeremiah and Ezekiel [see above] also First Isaiah [8 times], Deutero-Isaiah [once], Hosea [3 times], Amos [twice]). The root *m's* also plays an important role in laments (3 times in Lamentations; cf. also the occurrences in the discourses in Job).

Determining the basic meaning of *m's* is not so easy, since the various contexts require choosing from a wide assortment of possible translations. The Greek translation (LXX) seems to have dealt with this problem by using a surprisingly large

---

mā'as. H. Gross, "Verwerfung," *BL*², 1845f.; J. J. Jensen, "The Age of Immanuel," *CBQ,* 41 (1979), 220-239; L. J. Kuyper, "The Repentance of Job," *VT,* 9 (1959), 91-94; N. Lohfink, "Zu Text und Form von Os 4,4-6," *Bibl,* 42 (1961), 303-332; J. Reich, *Studien zum theologischen Problem der Menschenverachtung im AT* (diss., Leipzig, 1968) (reviewed in *ThLZ,* 96 [1971], 234-36); H. Wildberger, "מאס *m's* verwerfen," *THAT,* I, 879-892; *idem,* "Die Neuinterpretation des Erwählungsglaubens Israels in der Krise der Exilszeit," *Wort–Gebot–Glaube. Festschrift W. Eichrodt. AThANT,* 59 (1970), 307-324.

1. *AHw,* II (1972), 631.
2. *Ibid.,* 649.

number of equivalents.[3] In addition, *m's* occurs in functional theological contexts in which it circumscribes activity either from the perspective of God toward human beings or from that of human beings toward God. Although in a few passages *m's* is also used to refer to events in daily life, one cannot show that this secular usage reflects its original meaning. If one evaluates the older occurrences and attempts to extrapolate a meaning encompassing all the nuances of understanding, one might arrive at the English equivalent "to esteem, regard lightly." From this "basic meaning" one can then easily derive all the other variations, such as "reject," "despise," "refuse," "abhor," and many others. Lester J. Kuyper[4] sees the entire semantic scope of *m's* exhibited in the passages from Job, from "reject" to "regard of little value" to "disregard, disrespect" and "despise, abhor." Accordingly, *m's* describes a subjective attitude toward a person or thing acquired on the basis of some decision. This decision is itself based on certain standards and criteria which in most cases are explicitly mentioned or are at least clearly and intelligibly presupposed. The subjective nature of the decision, however, is not suspended. The root *m's* functions in contexts addressing personal relationships.

In the OT this root occurs only in verbal forms; no nominal constructions are attested. Only the qal and niphal are attested (the latter only 3 times). Two OT passages use the niphal of a root *m's* possibly as a secondary form of *mss* with the meaning "pass away," "dissolve" (Ps. 58:8[Eng. v. 7]; Job 7:5).[5]

II. Secular Usage. A proverb employed theologically in Ps. 118:22 provides a point of departure for understanding the secular usage of *m's.* Construction workers select stones for their building, the determining factor doubtlessly being that of appropriateness, usefulness, etc. The process of "regarding of little value," "rejecting," and "throwing away" corresponds to that of selecting.[6] Inappropriate stones are rejected, cast aside, and left behind, while others are accepted. This process of alternatives is circumscribed by *bḥr* and *m's.* The proverb itself is effective because of the surprising and unexpected esteem now accorded to the discarded stone, both in the face of its rejection by the builders and despite the decision which has already been made to discard it (Ps. 118:23: "This is Yahweh's doing").

Initially, the notion of the "rejected silver" also lacks theological tenor, the reference being to silver that has not passed the test of purity after the refining process (Jer. 6:30). A decision concerning acceptance and rejection, however, can also be directed toward a human being. Deutero-Isaiah describes God's compassion toward his people with the evocative imagery of the (re-)acceptance of a wife who has been "cast off" (*m's* niphal) (Isa. 54:6; cf. v. 4). Admittedly, *m's* is not typical of the terminology of marriage or divorce law (cf. Dt. 24:1ff.), since it is characterized by

---

3. See Wildberger, *THAT,* I, 880f.
4. P. 94.
5. See IV below.
6. → בחר *bāḥar (bāchar),* "choose," "select" (II, 73-87).

a strong emotional element. In a late text in Isaiah (Isa. 33:8), *m's* is mentioned in the connection with a broken covenant (rejection of witnesses [*m's;* the incomprehensible *'ārîm* should presumably be read as *'ēḏîm* with LXX][7] in connection with the breaking of a covenant [*prr* hiphil with *b^erîṯ*] and the disregard of people by the *šôḏēḏ* and *bôgēḏ* mentioned already in v. 1), which according to the context characterizes the situation of distress from which Yahweh's might will bring deliverance (v. 10). Neither, however, does this one occurrence permit any characterization of *m's* as a typical legal term.

Finally, the object of this decision can also be abstractions such as good and evil. The Immanuel pericope asserts that God's predicted action will already have come to pass even before Immanuel, born of the young woman, knows how to make rational distinctions and then also how to decide *(l^eḏa'tô* or *yēḏa')* to choose the good and refuse the evil (Isa. 7:15,16; opposite *bḥr*). The figure of speech with → ידע *yāḏa'*, is important, governing as it does the noteworthy infinitive absolute construction with *m's and bḥr*.

This figure of speech effectively circumscribes the educational ideal of wisdom didactics.[8] Prov. 3:11; 15:32 as well as several passages from Job attest the use of *m's* in wisdom contexts. The practical wisdom described by Prov. 15:32 is abstract in a secular sense; it asserts that the acceptance of correction is good and even vital, while despising it results in self-injury *(mô'ēs napšô).* The parallel concept to *m's* is *pr'*, "disregard," which supports the suggestion that the "basic meaning" of *m's* is "to esteem, regard lightly." Although it is difficult to date the passage, it probably contains older material. Prov. 3:11 belongs to what is probably the latest part of the book of Proverbs (chs. 1–9). This passage adds a theological element to the same maxim. It is wise not to regard Yahweh's discipline lightly (*'al-tim'as,* "do not despise, do not reject," par. *qûṣ,* "experience loathing, disgust"). The principle involved is stated in Prov. 3:12: Yahweh "reproves" only the person he loves. In his own wisdom pronouncement, Eliphaz considers that person blessed *('ašrê)* who accepts God's correction. Like Prov. 3:11, he advises not to regard too lightly the *mûsār* of the Almighty (Job 5:17), and he knows that God preserves, blesses, and nurtures whoever accepts his "educational and beneficial punishment"[9] (vv. 18-27).

The contempt directed toward a person by others or by groups (the husband's contempt for his wife; cf. Isa. 54:6) is occasionally expressed by *m's.* Job's own misery and suffering include pronouncements of contempt addressed to him by socially unworthy people (Job 19:18; 30:1). Job 30:1-8 describes his detractors more closely. They deride *(śḥq 'al)* him, who has been tested by suffering, and make him the subject of their *n^egînâ,* their mocking song. Their social insignificance (Job 30:8) manifests itself in the fact that earlier Job would not have respected them (*mā'astî,* v. 1). They belonged to a class which general community perception considered socially unworthy. In con-

---

7. See *BHS*.
8. Cf. further Jensen.
9. → יסר *yāsar,* VI, 134.

trast, according to the statements of his purification oath, Job well observed the rights *(mišpāṭ)* of the menservants and maidservants socially dependent on him (*'im-'em'as,* a stylistic feature of the oath formula), even when it was to his own disadvantage (Job 31:13).

In a more general sense, low esteem can obtain between different groups among the inhabitants of a country. In Jgs. 9:38, the Canaanite group in and around Shechem represented by Gaal "despises" Abimelech and his "people" (or Abimelech and his men) (cf. vv. 22-29, esp. 27f.). Respect or disrespect manifests itself here in subjection or rebellion. In this context *m's* can acquire a strong political-historical content. This particular passage may possibly be one of the oldest attestations of the root in the OT.

The theological sphere of meaning for the root incorporates descriptions of activity from the secular sphere. In the story of David's anointing by Samuel (1 S. 16:7), David's brothers precede him in passing before Samuel, and Samuel realizes that Yahweh has not chosen them (*lô'-bāḥar,* vv. 8-10). In this context, the root *m's* occurs once in the assertion that Yahweh has "rejected" Eliab (*kî mᵉ'astîhû,* v. 7). This probably refers to a simple act of making a choice; the person choosing must make this choice, i.e., he chooses or rejects. Behind this narrative we see clearly that *bḥr* and *m's* can be used to convey highly significant theological content.

The disregard for one's own life is attested in Job's grand and moving laments (Job 7:16; 9:21). The context presumably reveals both aspects of the motivation for these laments: on the one hand, resignation, discouragement, and disappointment that the lament is futile and goes unanswered, and that suffering can be explained neither from its own context nor by any recourse to God; and on the other hand, the defiance that demands justice for itself in lament and accusation, regardless of any consequences for one's own life and existence. Since all this is viewed in connection with God, who ultimately is identified as the cause of this disappointment and as the addressee for the accusations, these passages actually attest the theological use of *m's.* Nonetheless, we encounter here the conscious disregard for one's own life (*m's* in combination with a form of *ḥyh*), though not in the sense of suicide, but rather in the sense of surrendering all security in life. Such disregard for life allows for a mode of behavior which with no further consideration keeps all options open for one's own life in the future, and does so equally both through resignation and through a defiant, virtually blasphemous attitude.

III. Theological Usage.

1. *Human Beings as Subject.* The theological use of *m's* predominates in the OT, and many passages reveal a close connection between disregard of human beings and rejection of God. The convergence of these two aspects is illustrated especially well by the historico-theological conclusions drawn by the Deuteronomistic history in its portrayal of Israel's fall in 2 K. 17. God's rejection of his people (v. 20; cf. already Hos. 4:6, further 1 S. 15:23,26; 16:1) is prompted by the Israelites' own contempt for and rejection of all of God's statutes and covenantal agreements (2 K. 17:15). The root *m's* thus belongs to the vocabulary of the covenant tradition[10] and is defined by

a large number of parallel terms taken from familiar Deuteronomistic nomenclature to refer to both aspects, the human and the divine. The reproach that the earlier people of God despised God's revealed will was presumably long a part of the message of judgment delivered by the prophets, who used it to justify the disaster they were foretelling.[11] In a summary fashion similar to the conclusions drawn by the Deuteronomistic history, the promises of blessing and warnings of curse concluding the Holiness Code also preserve this connection between human rejection (*m's* is accompanied by *gʿl, prr,* etc.) of the revelation of the divine will (*ḥoq, mišpāṭ, miṣwâ, bᵉrîṯ,* etc.) on the one hand, and the divine's own reactive rejection on the other (Lev. 26:15,43,44). A whole litany of misdeeds characterizes the substantive sphere applicable to *m's* (Lev. 26:14ff.). The only new element here addresses the theological sphere. The extraordinary assurance given here is that ultimately God will neither "spurn" *(m's)* nor "abhor" *(gʿl)* those who have been condemned and punished to the extent they accept and make amends for[12] their *ʿāwōn,* i.e., God's judgment will not give them over to destruction (v. 44). Unfortunately, it is not possible to date this passage; thus nothing can be said regarding the age of these theological declarations either.

In any case,[13] various prophetic passages attest that God's lament over Israel and Judah's contempt for God's will was doubtlessly already the legitimizing element in prophetic oracles of judgment and exhortation to repentance. Among Amos's oracles against the nations, the oracle against Judah is generally held to be a secondary addition (Am. 2:4); the suspicion has arisen, however, that an older nucleus of Deuteronomistic additions may be discernible.[14] Because Judah has rejected the *tôraṯ YHWH,* Amos foretells disaster for them. For Hosea, too, forgetting God's torah is cause for announcing judgment (Hos. 4:6). The parallel to this is the rejection of *daʿaṯ,* which in this context must be understood in the comprehensive and established sense of "knowledge of God." God's reaction to this deficient behavior is that he for his own part forgets and rejects. This low estimation of the *tôraṯ YHWH* by the people of God is also a theme in First Isaiah (par. *'imrâ* with the verb *ni'ēṣ* [Isa. 5:24, the integrity of which is disputed[15]]). Isa. 30:8-13 is not disputed. There the people's disobedience with regard to the *tôraṯ YHWH* is demonstrated anew, and v. 12 presents the proof of guilt once again with reference to the people's contempt for the word *(dāḇār).* This and other behavior is disqualified as *ʿāwōn* (Isa. 30:13), which brings about disaster.

The Jeremianic corpus of sayings speaks twice about human rejection of the divine

---

10. H. Wildberger, *Isaiah 1–12* (Eng. trans., Minneapolis, 1991), 212.
11. Cf. Lohfink, 323.
12. *rṣh* II according to *KBL*[3].
13. See previous discussion.
14. W. Rudolph, *Amos. KAT,* XIII/2 (1971), 120f.; S. Wagner, "Überlegungen zur Frage nach den Beziehungen des Propheten Amos zum Südreich," *ThLZ,* 96 (1971), 653-670, esp. 663-68; contra H. W. Wolff, *Joel and Amos. Herm* (Eng. trans. 1977), *in loc.*
15. Wildberger (*Isaiah 1–12,* 212), however, considers it genuine.

word. Of these, Jer. 6:19 gives the impression of being a later Deuteronomistic interpretation of the oracle of woe (which follows in v. 21) in the sense of providing a precise reason for the disaster: Yahweh's torah has been too lightly esteemed and God's *dāḇār* has not been heeded (v. 19). Although one can easily sense that Jer. 6:19 is an insertion, it is not certain that the figure of speech regarding the rejection of "my torah" or "my word" is necessarily of Deuteronomistic provenance.[16] The other occurrence is presumably more secure as genuinely Jeremianic material (Jer. 8:9). It threatens the *sopᵉrîm, ḥᵃḵāmîm, nāḇî',* and *kōhēn* (cf. the context). They despise the *dᵉḇar YHWH* by making it into *šeqer* (Jer. 8:8,10) while proclaiming *šālôm* where there is no *šālôm* (v. 11). Since the formulaic expressions recounting the *bᵉmišpāṭay mā'āsû* and the failure to walk according to God's statutes also appear in Ezekiel (Ezk. 5:6b), suggestions have been made that these are additions "in somewhat more precise language,"[17] whereas the continuation of the justification for coming judgment in v. 7 more strongly reflects traditional formulaic elements. Although one might well suspect Deuteronomistic redaction here as well, a consideration of Ezk. 20:13,16,24 gives reason for caution. Except for minor adjustments everything remains within the same semantic field of *m's* and *lô' hālaḵ bᵉ* . . . and *mišpāṭ* and *ḥōq,* with the addition of what for the priest Ezekiel are the important considerations involving either keeping or profaning the Sabbath (*ḥll* piel). Ezekiel's historical summary, which taken as a whole serves to demonstrate the guilt incurred by the chosen people and thus to reveal the cause of the present oppressed circumstances of the (first) Babylonian exile, exhibits its own style despite any formulaic expressions, a style heavily informed by priestly thinking. To that extent one might assume a connection with P rather than with the Deuteronomistic tradition.[18] According to Ezekiel, this rejection of God's *mišpāṭîm* extends back to the sojourn in the wilderness.

The rejected *dᵉḇar YHWH* is also the concern in the remarkable story of Saul's rejection (1 S. 15:23,26), a story whose position within tradition history is difficult to assess. Since its redactional function is to prepare the transition of kingship from Saul to David, caution is advised in drawing any conclusions regarding the provenance of individual passages and formulations. The fact that Saul's transgression is allegedly his incorrect observance of a cultic directive, and that this is identified as the cause of his rejection, seems rather to be the result of later (Deuteronomistic) interpretation of what were otherwise poorly understood tensions between Samuel and Saul (or between the tribes represented by them); this later interpretation has employed historical examples for the kerygmatic purpose of emphasizing the commandment to heed God's word.[19] Although *dāḇār,* "thing, matter, affair," can refer comprehensively to an entire complex of events, here the term acquires the sense of "commandment, law, instruction of God." Human disregard and rejection corresponds to divine rejection, as developed in both

16. Cf. also W. Thiel, *Die deuteronomistische Redaktion von Jeremia 1–25. WMANT,* 41 (1973), 97ff.

17. W. Zimmerli, *Ezekiel 1. Herm* (Eng. trans. 1979), 175.

18. *Ibid., in loc.;* differently G. Fohrer, *Ezechiel. HAT,* XIII (1955), *in loc.*

19. Differently H. J. Stoebe, *Das erste Buch Samuelis. KAT,* VIII/1 (1973), 294f.

passages (and in 1 S. 16:1 as well, in the same thematic context). Thus *m's* and its expressions belong next to other verbs in the prophetic proclamation of judgment and repentance in which demonstration of guilt justifies the announced calamity. Similarly, the term also belongs to Deuteronomistic proclamation, which draws a balance, admonishes, and issues a warning, and as a way out exhorts the people to reestablish their previously neglected loyalty to God and to the revelation of his will.

According to the OT, it is not only through rejection of God's word that God himself is rejected, but also through disregard for God's other gifts and benefactions. Presumably something similar is intended by the image of the "waters of Shiloah that flow gently" which the people regarded too lightly in the Syro-Ephraimitic War (Isa. 8:6-8), namely, the disdain accorded Yahweh's assurances given through Isaiah in the politically explosive situation, assurances which Ahaz, the inhabitants of Jerusalem, and the Judeans were unable to believe.[20] This pronouncement from Isaiah underscores yet again the use of *m's* already in early prophetic proclamation. Contempt for God further manifests itself in the rejection of his beneficial gifts, e.g., that of the land itself (Nu. 14:31 [P], in the murmurings of the wilderness generation prompted by unfavorable reconnaissance of the land[21]), or in the murmurings against God's guidance in the wilderness, where during that sojourn the experience of lack and deficiency elicited the fundamental question concerning the meaning of the exodus and the possibility of returning to Egypt (Nu. 11:20: *ya'an kî-m^{e}'astem 'eṯ-YHWH*[22]). A postexilic historical psalm (Ps. 106:24) picks up this reference to "contempt for the land" from Nu. 14:31 anew and parallels it with lack of faith in God's word *(m's* and *lō' he'^{e}mîn;* the object is *dāḇār).* According to Deuteronomistic estimation, the Israelites' wish for a king during the time of Samuel is subject to the same theological disqualification (1 S. 8:7; 10:19). This wish implies not only distrust toward Samuel, but even more a rejection of Yahweh (1 S. 8:7 expresses this in God's direct discourse to Samuel: "For they have not rejected you, but they have rejected me from being king over them"; 10:19 expresses this in Samuel's pronouncement to the Israelites at the occasion of Saul's selection as king by lot at Mizpah: "But today you have scorned [NRSV 'rejected'] your God").

The production and veneration of idols or statue(tte)s is condemned as a special form of rejecting God. This is most clearly the case in (Deutero-)Isa. 44:9ff. (cf. Ps. 115:4-8). The reestablishment of Yahweh's honor and dignity demands that such objects be cast away, either in the course of judgment (Isa. 2:20, *šlk* hiphil) or as an expression of penitence at the commencement of Zion's age of justice achieved through Yahweh's victory (over Assyria) (Isa. 31:7, *m's* taking the same objects as in 2:20). While the first-mentioned passage from Isaiah is genuine, the authenticity of 31:7 is justifiably disputed. Isa. 31:6-7 represent the kerygmatic advice of a later preacher or prophet

20. Cf. Wildberger, *Isaiah 1–12,* 342-45.

21. Cf. M. Noth, *Numbers. OTL* (Eng. trans. 1968), *in loc.*

22. Noth *(idem)* considers v. 20 to be part of the basic narrative picked up by J; v. 20b, however, gives the impression of being a late theological value judgment.

whom we can no longer identify more closely, and who either is incorporating this central theme of Deuteronomistic theology into Isaiah's message (actually this ideological complex is not completely alien to Deutero-Isaiah) or is trying to warn and admonish his own contemporary community by actualizing Isaiah's pronouncement. Of course, another possibility is the school of Isaiah itself, which wanted Isa. 2:20 to be incorporated here as well. The demand to turn and repent in Isa. 31:6 is occasionally altered into an announcement.[23]

We also encounter directives governing how a person may encounter God in his holy sphere or in the future community of his salvation. As is well known, Ps. 15 (cf. 24:3-6) reproduces an "entry torah" in which individual *tôrôṯ* concerning behavior are given, including the directive that the *niḇzeh* (person deserving contempt, godless person) must be despised in the eyes of the person seeking admission (Ps. 15:4, *m's* niphal), whereas the person who fears God is to be honored (*kbd* niphal). Isa. 33:14-16 borrows a *tôrâ* of this kind; in addition to more general expectations such as walking in righteousness and speaking uprightly, this passage also addresses the social dimension more concretely in its exhortation to despise gains made through extortion (v. 15: *mō'ēs b^eḇeṣa' ma'^ašaqqôṯ;* this is presumably a late text[24]). In the larger sense a person should reject evil, and the fact that the godless person does not do this testifies against him (Ps. 36:5[4]: *ra' lō' yim'as*). Ps. 36 is a postexilic individual lament in which the petitioner's lament over the blasphemer's malice is juxtaposed with God's benevolence, which benefits the righteous person.

The overwhelming majority of passages that speak of human activity involving *m's* present this as human rejection of God; this most often appears in the form of rejection of God's word, law, or commandments, and in the form of contempt for his guidance through life as well as for his beneficent gifts. Even if a large portion of the occurrences is late (exilic, Deuteronomistic, postexilic), one does encounter individual attestations from the preexilic period, specifically in the justification of announcements of doom to be uttered by prophets. At the same time, *m's* is used in the theological evaluation of historical circumstances; contempt for God by his own people is identified as the cause of the oppressive postexilic existence of the people of God in Palestine and the Diaspora. Human activity involving *m's* which can be evaluated positively in a theological sense occurs whenever a person scorns evil, rejects injustice, and bids farewell to man-made idols of gold and silver.

The final literary disposition of the book of Job presents the ideal of making the choice for God and against oneself (Job 42:6). Subdued by God, Job confesses guilt and repents in dust and ashes, renounces his previous rebellious, accusatory, and judgmental attitude toward God, and "despises himself" (*'al-kēn 'em'as).* Here (in a completely singular fashion) *m's* functions as a term for penitence and is given a positive estimation. One passage in the wisdom discussion concerning human righteousness and God's injustice (Job-theme) proposes the (actually absurd) solution of reversing

23. Cf. O. Kaiser, *Isaiah 13–39. OTL* (Eng. trans. 1974), *in loc.*
24. *Ibid., in loc.*

roles (see Job 40:6-14): if human beings can govern the world better than God, then even God is willing to accommodate himself to them. Elihu sharply rejects such thinking, although he does ascertain that Job's own words and behavior aspire to such absurdity, and that in so doing Job is necessarily testifying against himself (Job 34:31-37). In this context, the different kinds of behavior include a hypothetical act of rejection on Job's part to which God would then have to accommodate himself (34:33). Here *m's* is merely *one* means of expression among others for this hypothetical-absurd despotic activity to which God would have to subject himself. Only when Job declares God unjust and thus effects this proposed reversal in a practical sense does this action, too, involving *m's* acquire a negative quality in Elihu's judgment.

2. *God as Subject.* God as the subject of a verbal form of *m's* has already been mentioned in the context of God's own punitive reaction to human rejection *(m's)* of God.[25] This can be seen quite clearly in the Deuteronomistic theology of history. When according to 2 K. 17:15,20 the people of Israel rejected Yahweh's commandments, Yahweh rejected the people by oppressing them and giving them over to plunderers. According to 1 S. 15:23,26; 16:1, Saul rejected Yahweh's word through his "disobedience," and Yahweh then prevented *(m's)* Saul from continuing as king. 2 K. 23:27 (cf. v. 26) portrays the rejection of Jerusalem, which Yahweh had chosen, and of its temple as a (late) consequence of the wrath which Manasseh's reign had already provoked in Yahweh. This passage seems out of place because it has been inserted into the context of the otherwise positively evaluated reign of Josiah (2 K. 23:25; v. 26 continues with the significant adv. *'aḵ*). Presumably the passage functions redactionally to anticipate within the portrayal itself the unfortunate conclusion to the reign of Josiah and his successors by mentioning this original provocation. The pattern is the same: disobedience and apostasy lead to rejection by Yahweh and to coerced removal from God's countenance. Already in the prophetic message of Hosea (Hos. 4:6), however, God's contempt for and forgetfulness of human beings correspond to the people's own forgetfulness of God, represented by the unidentified priest (*m's* and *škḥ* are used both times). Thus *m's* describes God's reactive judgment, either anticipated in the prophetic oracle of judgment or justified in light of the actual historical catastrophe itself.

Early classical prophecy also attests the strong emotional components which can accompany *m's*. The most obvious example occurs in Am. 5:21. Prompted by the overall context (grand celebrations and worship services against the foil of continued violation of social justice), the passage speaks of Yahweh's strong emotions in order to bring to expression his rejection of such cultic activity (besides *m's,* the text also uses *śānē',* *lō' hērîaḥ, lō' šāma',* etc.). Yahweh expresses exasperation and revulsion, disgust and feelings of aggression. Hos. 9:17 is not quite so strong; admittedly, after the harsh announcements of disaster prompted by apostasy from God (cultic transgressions: Ba'al-peor and Gilgal [Saul's rejection], vv. 10-17), it summarizes the prophetic sub-

25. See III.1 above.

sumption of the entire message of judgment as a wish: "May my God cast them off [evocation of 1 S. 15:23], because they have not listened to him; let them become wanderers among the nations." Here, as it were for his own part and in agreement with his God, Hosea lends inexorable momentum to the oracle of woe.

After Hosea it is especially Jeremiah who in several passages uses *m's* in various forms. The most concrete and, as far as imagery is concerned, most vivid passage is Jer. 4:30. In a long pericope describing the enemy's inexorable march down from the north, a pericope difficult to subdivide (vv. 5-31), a particularly grotesque image is described: Jerusalem (and Judah? cf. v. 5 and *passim*) thinks it can win over the conqueror as a lover by adorning itself as a prostitute. This undertaking must fail, however, because the "lovers" will despise the harlot, and will seek rather to end her life. Although *m's* here is a predicate of those afflicting the "daughter Zion" (v. 31), they are merely the extended arm of Yahweh, the real subject bringing about this disaster.

Jer. 6:30 resides in a pericope (vv. 27-30) that might belong in the context of prophetic calling. Yahweh engages Jeremiah as an "assayer" (*bḥn*[26]) whose task is to separate the good metal from the slag during the refining process. Yahweh's judgment over his people has already been made. Since the refining process has not removed the impurities *(rā'îm),* the people must be described as "reject[ed] silver" *(kesep̱ nim'ās),* since Yahweh himself has rejected it. The judgment discourse delivered through the prophet is the *m's*-process directed by Yahweh. Finally, the collection of Jeremianic oracles of woe (chs. 2–6) includes a passage in which the prophet condemns the politics of alliance and coalition undertaken by the Judean kings at the conclusion of the period of kings. Yahweh has rejected the substantive objects of trust (*miḇṭāḥayiḵ,* 2:37). The establishment of political alliances and dependencies in this particular period constitutes *de facto* mistrust toward Yahweh.

Finally, Yahweh's judgment over his people, circumscribed by *m's,* is reflected once again in lamentation. Collective lament confronts the fact of fulfilled judgment in direct discourse with the words: "You have rejected us" (or similar expressions). This is illustrated most clearly in Lamentations. In Lam. 3:45, for example, those left behind after the catastrophe ascertain that Yahweh "has made us filth and rubbish among the peoples" *(s^eḥî ûmā'ôs).* Here *m's* stands within a litany of negative terms describing the destruction of the people. The lament contains supplications that the distress be alleviated, confessions of guilt, and elements of confidence that Yahweh's wrath will not continue indefinitely. Thus in Lam. 5:22, in an alternative rhetorical question appended to the actual petition itself (v. 21), the incredulous realization comes to expression that Yahweh really could have rejected his people: "Restore us to yourself, O Yahweh . . . (v. 21), unless you have utterly rejected us!" (*kî 'im-mā'ōs m^e'astānû*; par. *qṣp,* "be wrathful"). Even though an element of hope has indeed been woven into this peculiar turn of phrase, this alternative rhetorical question in the course of the lament does confirm *de facto* the

26. Cf. C. Baldauf, *Läutern und Prüfen im AT* (diss., Greifswald, 1970), 36ff., 130ff.

actual present situation, a situation comprehensible to the petitioner only as rejection by Yahweh. This catastrophe can also be evoked in its specifics, e.g., in the lament over the destruction of the Davidic kingship (Ps. 89:39[38]: *wᵉʾattâ zānaḥtā wattimʾas*).

Jeremiah also seems to have used *mʾs* in the lament (Jer. 7:29), even though the verse, as a fragment from an originally authentic Jeremianic saying, now stands in a Deuteronomistic denunciation of sacrifices (vv. 21-29).[27] The addressee is Jerusalem or Judah, who are called to a ritual of penitence and mourning because Yahweh has forsaken *(nṭš)* and rejected *(mʾs)* the generation of his wrath. In a homiletically extremely effective fashion the announcement of disaster has been cloaked in the directive to penitence and lament. The authenticity of Jer. 14:19, also taken from a (national) lament (vv. 19-22), is disputed. It stands in an extensive sequence of variously constituted discourses, all of which seem to revolve around Yahweh's judgmental activity in the form of a great drought (14:1–15:4).[28] Indeed, vv. 19-21 are rather general and lack concrete contours, and not until v. 22 does any reference to the drought appear. V. 19 poses again the question so unsettling within the lament, namely, whether Yahweh really has rejected Judah *(hᵃmāʾōs māʾastā)* and whether his soul has come to loathe Zion *(gāʿal)*. The national lament then also contains the two additional elements of confession of sin and a plea for deliverance (cf. Lam. 5:22). Both resonate within this formulation: on the one hand recognition of a present situation of distress that can only be described as rejection, and on the other confidence that this might not be intended as final, as a kind of silent appeal to Yahweh's covenantal loyalty to his people. If one takes this as a genuinely Jeremianic witness, one must assume that Jeremiah appropriated the passage from a national lament.

In the historical reflections of wisdom didactics *mʾs* also fulfills the specific function of describing, legitimizing, and interpreting the facts of history. The destruction of the temple at Shiloh (Ps. 78:60-62: *wayyiṭṭōš miškan šilô*) is proclaimed to be Yahweh's wrathful rejection of Israel (v. 59, *ʿbr* hithpael next to *mʾs*) and is justified in fine Deuteronomistic fashion by reference both to worship in high places and to the trafficking with graven images (v. 58). The confrontation between the selection of the tribe of Judah, Zion, and the Davidic house on the one hand, and the "rejection" of the house of Joseph and — specially named — the tribe of Ephraim (vv. 67-70) on the other, is described in fine Chronistic fashion. In the present context (vv. 65-72), no further motivation is given for these circumstances. Through the two antithetical concepts *mʾs* and *bḥr* historical events are subjected here to theological (Deuteronomistic or Chronistic) interpretation. Considering the

27. Cf. Thiel, 121ff.; with different delimitation W. Rudolph, *Jeremia. HAT,* XII ([3]1968), *in loc.*

28. S. Mowinckel, *Zur Komposition des Buches Jeremiah* (Oslo, 1914), 22-23, discusses the suggestion that it represents a prophetic liturgy; Rudolph, *HAT,* XII, 91, suggests that, except for smaller verses from the Deuteronomistic redaction, it comes from Jeremiah's early period (*Urrolle,* Baruch's original scroll); Thiel, 178ff., considers it to be a Deuteronomistic composition, though uncertainties remain; cf. 193f.

theological disposition of this extensive didactic piece about history, this psalm should probably be assigned to the postexilic period.[29] One might suspect that with its designation as *maśkîl* this psalm should be considered an example of theological-wisdom-didactic dealing with history.[30]

The portrayal of Yahweh as the subject of activity involving *m's* actually belongs to his *opera aliena*; his *opus proprium* consists in *lō' mā'as.* A fundamental conviction of theological-wisdom thinking is that God does not reject the righteous person *(tām),* but turns away from evildoers and puts a stop to their activity (Job 8:20). Bildad shares this dogmatic conviction with Elihu, whose pronouncement according to the MT can exhibit even more general character: "Surely God is mighty and does not despise any; he is mighty in strength of heart" (Job 36:5). As is customary, the context again does speak of God's devotion to the innocent and alienation from the wicked, e.g., Job 36:6, so that already the LXX undertook the appropriate alteration. Various commentaries also suggest reformulations in this direction, and occasionally postulate dittographical errors in transmission. The general sense remains clear, even if a universally persuasive reconstruction has not yet been undertaken.

This more general notion, namely, that God does not "reject" without provocation, is implied by the logic of the theology of creation. How could God find pleasure in rejecting precisely *that* which he himself has created? The solidarity of God the creator with the "work of his hands" is grounded in the theology of creation (Job 10:3), and this makes possible an element of trust in the lament of the individual that issues into the petition for alleviation of the distress. God's beneficial devotion reverses itself with regard to evildoers. He scorns them when they oppress the innocent. This positive partisanship for his chosen people is specially emphasized when they are threatened with "being eaten" by *pō'ᵃlê 'āwen* (Ps. 53:5[4]). In such cases the oppressors succumb to God's disdain and rejection (*m's* and *pzr* piel, Ps. 53:6[5]). In this fragmentary postexilic national lament (Ps. 53; cf. Ps. 14) it will be possible for the oppressed people to put those to shame who are oppressing them (actually "besieging," *ḥnh*), since God has "rejected" them. Thus God's *m's*-activity is defined both from divine and from human actions.

Deutero-Isaiah personalizes the fact of election in his unqualified announcement of good news by underscoring Yahweh's *opus proprium,* namely, that God has chosen *('aḇdî-'attâ bᵉḥartîḵā)* rather than rejected his people (*wᵉlō' mᵉ'astîḵā,* Isa. 41:9; cf. vv. 8 + 10ff.). Although the calamity intended for Israel's enemies is not circumscribed verbally with any reference to *YHWH mā'as* (or *yim'as*), it is implied by the context (and with other verbs, vv. 10-12). In contrast, Israel's own good news is contained in the statement *lō' mā'as YHWH.* One cannot persuasively show whether Yahweh's *lō' mā'as*-activity is already a part of the preexilic prophetic announcement of good tidings. In view of Jer. 31:37; 33:24,26, this might be assumed, although the authenticity of these passages is hotly disputed. Jer. 33:24,26 presupposes the

29. Contra G. Fohrer, *Intro. OT* (Eng. trans., Nashville, 1968), 289.
30. → שׂכל *śāḵal.*

catastrophe of 587 B.C.,[31] when it certainly seemed as if Yahweh had (once and for all) rejected the two "families" Israel and Judah (whereby the scorn experienced from outside [*n'ṣ*], namely, that they were no longer permitted to be a unified people, interprets *m's,* v. 24).

In contradistinction to this, an unknown voice proclaims the unqualified change of fate and Yahweh's compassion (Jer. 33:26b) by referring to the inviolability of redemption inherent in the inviolability of the creation order guaranteed by the same God. This formulation is deeply indebted to the kind of elliptical thinking most strongly articulated in the oath formula (vv. 25-26). The following expression is formulated as direct divine discourse: "If I have not established my covenant with day and night and the ordinances of heaven and earth, then I will reject the descendants of Jacob and of David my servant" (v. 26a). Since Jer. 31:37 subscribes to the same manner of thinking and formulation (the verse belongs to the smaller saying-unit vv. 35-37), this occurrence probably also belongs to the exilic or even postexilic prophetic announcement of salvation.[32] The irreal conditional *'em'as* in the divine direct discourse just cited, for which here, too, Yahweh's creative power is made the touchstone, is used to express the election of the "seed of Israel" that endures even through the catastrophe. If Yahweh has not rejected, then *de facto* he adheres to the election (cf. Jer. 33:24, where *bḥr* and *m's* are juxtaposed). Here as elsewhere we notice the use of the theology of creation in the deductive-argumentative sense. Yahweh's mightiness with regard to nature guarantees his mightiness with regard to salvation, and the *'em'as* does not occur.

IV. Uncertain Occurrences. In passing we should also mention the 2 extremely difficult occurrences of *m's (mō'eseṯ)* from Ezk. 21:15,18(10,13), occurrences which in spite of many attempts so far elude any satisfactory interpretation.[33]

Mention should be made of the 2 passages that use *m's* niphal in the sense of *mss* niphal. Both come from the postexilic period and must be translated following *mss* by "flow away," "melt, dissolve," "break up."[34] Ps. 58:8(7) probably belongs to a lament in which the righteous (vv. 11f.[10f.], *ṣaddîq*) seem to have felt threatened and oppressed by the wicked (v. 4[3], *rāšā'*). In the face of this threat they solicit God's active aid (v. 11[10], *nāqām,* 'vengeance'), so that the wicked must flow away like water (*yimmā'ᵃsû kᵉmô-mayim,* v. 8[7]). The other passage also comes from a lament (in this case the lament of an individual) in which Job bemoans his horrible illness (Job 7:5). In the course of this ailment his skin loosens itself (from his body; *m's* niphal next to *rg',* "become encrusted").[35]

Wagner

---

31. Cf. W. Thiel, *Die deuteronomistische Redaktion von Jeremia 26–45. WMANT,* 52 (1981), 37, identifies it as a post-Deuteronomistic addendum to ch. 32.

32. Thiel (*ibid.,* 28) suggests post-Deuteronomistic provenance.

33. Cf. Zimmerli, *Ezekiel 1,* 426f.

34. Cf. Guillaume, 21.

35. G. R. Driver, "Problems in the Hebrew Text of Job," *Wisdom in Israel and in the Ancient Near East. Festschrift H. H. Rowley. SVT,* 3 (1955), 76, refers to Arab. *ma'asa,* "gaping wound."

V. Qumran. The Qumran texts attest 22 occurrences of *m's* (8 in CD), although only twice with God as the subject. The outsider (1QpHab 1:11; 4Q162 7; 4Q163 14) or the apostate (1QpHab 5:11) "despises" the torah. He is then punished by excommunication (1QS 3:5; CD 3:17; 7:9; 8:19; 19:5f.,32; 20:8), since his contempt for the torah implies that he cuts himself off from instruction and rejects the *b*^{e}*rîṯ* (self-designation for the community! 1QS 2:25; 1QH 15:18; CD 20:11). The term *m's* also occurs as an expression for the appropriate detachment of the Qumran community and as a component of Qumran-Essene esotericism when the community members are directed to appropriate in love *('hb),* hate *(śn'),* and rejection *(m's)* both God's (1QH 17:24; CD 2:15) and Moses' (1QS 1:4) standard. Beyond torah and covenant, all "trials" *(nswyym)* and "blows" *(ngy'ym)* sent by God are perceived as God's instruction (4QDibHam 6:6; cf. Lev. 26:40-44). The fact that he has himself not "rejected" these trials gives the Qumran Essene the confidence that his petition will be answered.

God abhors apostasy, and thus rejects the apostate while choosing his covenantal people (1Q34 3:2,4; cf. Ps. 53:6[5]). It is unclear whether the assertion that God neither rejects the seed of Judah *(m's)* nor disowns Israel despite violation of the covenant and subsequent judgment (*g'l,* 4QDibHam 5:6) constitutes a reflection on salvation history or expresses a new salvation consciousness centered on Qumran.

Fabry

VI. LXX. The LXX renders *mā'as* with a wide variety of terms. The most common translations are *apodokimázein* (7 times) and *exouthenoún* (10 times).

Wagner

מַבּוּל *mabbûl*

Contents: I. 1. Etymology; 2. Occurrences. II. Religio-historical Considerations. III. 1. *mabbûl*: a. The Flood Narrative; b. Occurrences Outside the Flood Narrative; c. Ps. 29:10; d. Indication of Time; 2. Semantic Development.

---

mabbûl. J. Begrich, "Mabbūl: Eine exegetisch-lexikalische Studie," *ZS,* 6 (1928), 135-153 = *GSAT. ThB,* 21 (1964), 39-54; T. H. Gaster, *Myth, Legend, and Custom in the OT* (New York, 1969); C. Houtman, *De Hemel in het OT* (Franeker, 1974); A. Jeremias, *Handbuch der altorientalischen Geisteskultur* (Leipzig, [2]1929); O. Kaiser, *Die mythische Bedeutung des Meeres in Ägypten, Ugarit und Israel. BZAW,* 78 ([2]1962); O. Keel, *The Symbolism of the Biblical World* (Eng. trans., New York, 1978); M. Metzger, "Himmlische und irdische Wohnstatt Jahwes," *UF,* 2 (1970), 139-158; G. Pettinato, "Die Bestrafung des Menschengeschlechts durch die Sintflut," *Or,* 37 (1968), 165-200; P. Reymond, *L'eau, sa vie, et sa signification dans l'AT. SVT,* 6 (1958); L. I. J. Stadelmann, *The Hebrew Conception of the World. AnBibl,* 39 (1970); A. J. Wensink, *The Ocean in the Literature of the Western Semites.* VAWA, N.S. 19/2 (1918, repr. 1968); C. Westermann, *Genesis 1–11* (Eng. trans., Minneapolis, 1984) (with extended bibliog.); → יבל *ybl* (V, 364-67).

I. 1. *Etymology.* The etymology of *mabbûl* is uncertain, since neither East nor West Semitic equivalents are attested. Since Joachim Begrich, older attempts at derivation have been rejected on the basis of phonological, philological, or substantive considerations. Such attempts included derivations of Heb. *mabbûl* from Akk. *abūbu,* "deluge, flood,"[1] *bubbūlu, biblu, bibbulu,* "deluge,"[2] or *nabālu I,*[3] or from the common Semitic root *bll*[4] (cf. Akk. *balālu,* "sprinkle, mix, alloy"). *KBL*³ has rejected the possible derivation from Heb. *nēḇel,* "jar," or similar terms.[5] The most plausible solution[6] is to view *mabbûl* as a *maqṭûl* form[7] of *ybl II,* "to rain hard."[8] The West Semitic root *ybl* corresponds to *(w)bl* in the other Semitic languages[9] (cf. also Egyp. *wbn,* "spring, fountain; to overflow"[10]).

2. *Occurrences.* The word *mabbûl* occurs 13 times in the OT and once in Sir. 44:17. Except for Ps. 29:10, all occurrences are in Genesis, and are distributed approximately equally between the actual story of the Flood (Gen. 6:17; 7:6,7,10,17) and other passages (9:11[twice],15,28; 10:1,32; 11:10). The various expressions are judged against the background of source, place, and semantic development of *mabbûl.* J uses *mabbûl* twice, both times in the expression *mê hammabbûl* (7:7,10). P only uses *mabbûl* qualified by the article (6:17; 7:6,17). In addition, the fixed expression *'aḥar hammabbûl* is attested 4 times. The LXX translates all occurrences with *kataklysmós.*

II. Religio-historical Considerations. Various attempts have been made to demonstrate the historicity of the biblical Flood.[11] One theory holds, e.g., that an inundation was accompanied by devastation of such proportions that the event was picked up as a literary theme.[12] These flood narratives are attested in great numbers and are found

---

1. P. Haupt; H. Holzinger, *Genesis. KHC,* I (1898), 69; O. Procksch, *Genesis. KAT,* I (1913, ²⁻³1924); cf. *AHw,* I (1965), 8.

2. H. Zimmern, *Akkadische Fremdwörter als Beweis für babylonischen Kultureinfluss* (Leipzig, ²1917).

3. C. F. Keil, *Genesis. KD,* I (Eng. trans. 1888-89); F. Delitzsch, *Prolegomena eines neuen hebräisch-aramäischen Wörterbuchs zum AT* (Leipzig, 1886), 122ff; E. König, *Hebräisches und aramäisches Wörterbuch zum AT* (Leipzig, 1910), 204; see *napālu I* ("ruin, pull down, destroy"), *AHw,* II (1972), 733.

4. K. Vollers, "Zur Erklärung von יָדוֹן Gen 6,3," *ZA,* 14 (1899), 355.

5. *KBL*³, 514, *contra KBL*², 491; cf. Begrich, 53.

6. *HAL,* II (1995), 541; Begrich, 53f.

7. Cf. *VG,* I, §203; *GK,* §61gη.

8. Cf. Arab. *wābil,* "cloudburst, downpour" (cf. Lane, Sup, 3048; Wehr, 1046); cf. also U. Cassuto, *A Commentary of the Book of Genesis,* II (Jerusalem, 1964), 66f.

9. → יבל *ybl* (V, 364-67).

10. *WbÄS,* I, 294; cf. also O. Rössler, "Das Ägyptische als semitische Sprache," in F. Altheim and R. Stiehl, eds., *Christentum am Roten Meer,* I (Berlin, 1971), 263-326, §§2, 32, 34.

11. E.g., A. Parrot, *The Flood and Noah's Ark. Studies in Biblical Archaeology,* 1 (Eng. trans., New York, 1955); M. E. L. Mallowan, "Noah's Flood Reconsidered," *Iraq,* 26 (1964), 62-82; R. L. Raikes, "The Physical Evidence for Noah's Flood," *Iraq,* 28 (1966), 52-63.

12. Parrot, 41.

in all parts of the world.[13] Consideration of their religio-historical background, however, suggests that the Flood Narrative, independent of individual archaeological findings that might document various local inundations, is not the report of a single historical event involving a flood that inundated the entire world. The biblical Flood Narrative is the OT text with the largest number of extrabiblical parallels, and the difficulty in determining its origin and possible dependence on other stories results from the fact that all the extant flood stories exhibit enormous similarity in their basic conception and motifs, and basically agree in the essentials. They belong to the "common property of humanity,"[14] and, independent of provenance and cultural milieu, narrate that primal event.

Various levels of reflection manifest themselves within these flood narratives. Whereas in the primitive stories the center of gravity is found in the event itself, in the more advanced cultures it shifts to the relationship between God (gods) — viewed as the initiator of the catastrophe — and human beings, so that one can speak of a "theologizing of the flood narrative."[15] God's decree of annihilation appears as the fundamental motif, often explained in retrospect as having been provoked by human depravity.[16]

Earlier scholarship focused on the relationship between human ethical failings on the one hand and the Flood as punishment on the other, confirmed by comparisons with the Gilgamesh epic and the Atraḫasis epic. For more recent scholarship, however, the sense of the Flood Narrative is the notion that the Creator can annihilate the human beings he himself has created.

III. 1. *mabbûl.* a. *The Flood Narrative.* Both earlier and (despite numerous critical annotations) more recent commentaries and dictionaries translate *mabbûl* almost without exception as "deluge" or "flood," doubtlessly on the basis of the predominating use of the term in the Flood Narrative itself. Begrich, however, already ascertained that the term *mabbûl* experienced different levels of usage and underwent a shift in meaning; he showed that *mabbûl* was not originally a term for the inundation, but rather an old designation for the heavenly ocean. Within the actual Flood Narrative itself, references to the *mabbûl* that came upon the earth (in J and P) indicate that *mabbûl* does not refer here to the catastrophe itself. The initial occurrence (Gen. 6:17 [P]; 7:10 [J]) presupposes that *mabbûl* is already familiar, something difficult to imagine in the case of the "catastrophe," which in addition is regularly rendered by *mayim*: "the waters (*mayim*) became mighty and increased greatly on the earth" (7:18 [P]); "the waters (*mayim*) became more mighty upon the earth" (7:19 [P]; cf. vv. 20,24; 8:1,3b,5,13a [P]); "the waters (*mayim*) increased, and bore up the ark" (7:17 [J]); "and the waters (*mayim*) gradually receded from the earth" (8:3a J; cf. vv. 7,8,9,11 [J]).

---

13. For a listing, see Gaster, 82-128.
14. Westermann, 395.
15. Cf., e.g., *ibid.*, 402-6.
16. Cf. C. Westermann, *Genesis 1–11. Erträge der Forschung,* 7 (Darmstadt, 1972), 84.

In contrast to references outside the actual Flood Story, the term *mabbûl* is mentioned only when the commencement of the catastrophe itself is described, namely, the coming of the waters upon the earth: "For my part, I am going to bring the *mabbûl* (a flood of waters) on the earth, to destroy from under heaven all flesh in which is the breath of life" (6:17 [P]); "Noah was six hundred years old when the *mabbûl* (flood of waters) came on the earth" (7:6 [P]); "the *mabbûl* continued forty days on the earth" (7:17 [P]); "after seven days the waters of the *mabbûl* came on the earth" (7:10 J); "and Noah went before the waters of the *mabbûl* into the ark" (7:7 [J]).

Besides these common elements in J and P, one can also ascertain distinctions in terminology pointing to "varying degrees of intensity accompanying the commencement of the catastrophe."[17] In both occurrences in J *mabbûl* appears in the construct expression *mê hammabbûl.* Construct expressions occur elsewhere with *mayim* as well (e.g., *mê hannāhār,* "the waters of the River [Euphrates]," Isa. 8:7; *mê-bôrô,* "water from his own cistern," Isa. 36:16; *mê šiḥôr,* "the waters of the Nile," Jer. 2:18], etc.), and a comparison with these forms suggests that *mê hammabbûl* is to be understood as "the waters from the *mabbûl.*" In J, with its narrow geographical view of the world, the catastrophe only commences by means of an event: a rain *(gešem)* lasting forty days pours down upon the earth (Gen. 7:12). According to J, this rain is the water from the *mabbûl,* the heavenly ocean.

The additional elements of the worldview of P emerge in terminological distinction over against the J portrayal. The rain lasting forty days (*mê hammabbûl* [J]) corresponds in P to the entire *mabbûl* that comes upon the earth. This also explains the problems with Gen. 6:17, where Eduard Sievers[18] sees evidence of a gloss in *hammabbûl,* contra Umberto Cassuto, who emends to *mayim ʿal-hāʾāreṣ* on the basis on the narrative context,[19] and Hermann Gunkel,[20] who views *mayim ʿal-hāʾāreṣ* as an interpretation of the word *mabbûl,* which P understood to be a foreign word. The construction *hammabbûl ʿal-hāʾāreṣ* (7:10 [J]; 7:17 [P]) suggests that only *mayim* is a gloss to *hammabbûl,* while *ʿal-hāʾāreṣ* is to be taken with the verb. One explanation for this notion, which to be sure is rather difficult to conceive in the P text, may have been suggested by Begrich: not just the waters from the heavenly ocean precipitate the catastrophe, but also the waters of the *t^ehôm*;[21] the upper and lower waters thus flow together again (cf. the Creation Story).

The notion of the heavenly ocean is also found in extrabiblical sources.[22] Such notions probably resulted from the fact that heaven and water are the same color on the one hand, and that water falls from heaven on the other.[23] Although extrabiblical

17. Begrich, 50.
18. *Metrische Studien,* II (Leipzig, 1904-5), 252.
19. "Since the term . . . *mabbûl* described something that had not yet come into existence" (p. 67).
20. *Genesis. HKAT,* I/1 (^{9}1977), 142.
21. Cf. C. Westermann, "תְּהוֹם *t^ehōm* Flut," *THAT,* II, 1026.
22. Cf., e.g., Kaiser, 26, 117, and *passim.*
23. Cf. Keel, 36-39.

cosmogonies do differ somewhat in the nuances of their understanding of this heavenly ocean (e.g., its origin), its existence is undisputed, just as is recognition of the danger accompanying its waters, whose sudden outpouring would cause a flood.[24]

b. *Occurrences Outside the Flood Narrative.* Outside the actual Flood Narrative, the term *mabbûl* unequivocally carries the meaning usually associated with the term: deluge (as portrayed in Genesis). In this context *mabbûl* no longer has the meaning "heavenly ocean."[25] Here the term circumscribes this singular catastrophe itself (Gen. 9:11,15; cf. Sir. 44:17).

c. *Ps. 29:10.* Ps. 29, one of the oldest psalms,[26] contains various images and ideas from the ancient Near East. Except for Sirach, it is the only place where *mabbûl* (v. 10) occurs outside Genesis. The problems attending this verse, which has undergone the most diverse interpretations, stem from the fact that the term *mabbûl* is understood from the perspective of the Flood Narrative. Yahweh is enthroned over the flood *(YHWH lammabbûl yāšāḇ).* Irregularities involving language and content accompanying this notion, however, can be avoided if here, too, *mabbûl* is understood as the heavenly ocean (v. 3).[27] On the notion of Yahweh's enthronement in the heavenly sphere cf. Ps. 2:4; 104:2f.; 123:1.

Extrabiblical parallels support this notion of enthronement above the heavenly ocean, e.g., a clay relief from the Neo-Assyrian sphere, whose paradigm extends back into the second half of the eleventh century. This relief portrays the sun-god enthroned over the heavenly ocean in his heavenly sanctuary.[28]

d. *Indication of Time.* In 4 instances *mabbûl* is used in the OT to indicate a point in time. The fixed expression *'aḥar hammabbûl,* "after the flood" (Gen. 9:28; 10:1,32; 11:10), is reflected in Mesopotamian literature as well.[29] There the term *abūbu* also occurs in expressions such as *ša lam abūbi* or *ša arki abūbi* as a temporal indicator.[30] Both in Sumerian-Babylonian king lists and in the OT this "indication

---

24. Cf., e.g., Jeremias, 152.

25. See preceding discussion.

26. Cf. H.-J. Kraus, *Psalms 1–59* (Eng. trans., Minneapolis, 1988), 344-351.

27. R. Hillmann, *Wasser und Berg* (diss., Halle, 1965), 132f., understands *mabbûl* here as a storm flood upon which the weather-god rides. This interpretation, however, accords neither with the other occurrences nor with the OT conceptual world in the larger sense.

28. Cf. Metzger; cf. also Keel, 174. Similarly also M. K. Wakeman, *God's Battle with the Monster* (Leiden, 1973), 101, who compares Ps. 29:10 with *KTU,* 1.4 IV, 20-23: El is enthroned where he can control the waters; cf. also L. R. Fisher and F. B. Knutson, "An Enthronement Ritual at Ugarit," *JNES,* 28 (1969), 157-167. On Yahweh's enthronement, cf. also W. Schmidt, *Königtum Gottes in Ugarit und Israel. BZAW,* 80 (²1966), 48; E. Otto, " 'El und JHWH in Jerusalem': Historische und theologische Aspekte einer Religionsintegration," *VT,* 30 (1980), 316-329; → ישׁב *yāšaḇ* (VI, 420-438). Begrich's position has been contested recently by Houtman, 185, who understands *mabbûl* again as a general, mythical entity, namely, as a chaotic water power. For a dissenting view, cf. A. Lawhead, *A Study of the Theological Significance of* yāšab *in the Masoretic Text* (diss., Boston, 1975, repr. 1977), 201-4.

29. Cf. H. Schmökel, "Geschichte des alten Vorderasiens," *HO,* II/3 (1957), 4-9.

30. *CAD,* I/1 (1964), 78; *AHw,* I, 8.

of time" serves to link legendary primeval or prehistory with historically documented time.[31]

2. *Semantic Development.* These observations suggest that *mabbûl* is neither a term specifically associated with the Flood Story[32] nor a term originally associated with the idea of an inundation that covered the entire earth. Rather, a semantic shift probably took place in the course of tradition away from the original notion of *mabbûl* as the heavenly ocean to that of an inundation. In J, the Flood is brought about by the waters of the heavenly ocean (*mê hammabbûl*[33]). The portrayal of the Flood in P, where the heavenly ocean itself comes upon the earth, picks up on Gen. 1 and describes how the waters separated there flow together again with the waters of the *t^ehôm* to form the Flood. The loss of the original meaning of *mabbûl* manifests itself in the gloss *mayim* (6:17; 7:6). The context still preserved in J (in 7:4 Yahweh announces the rain, and in v. 10 the waters of the *mabbûl* come upon the earth) is no longer seen. The opening of the heavenly sluices (7:11b [P]) is no longer associated with *mabbûl* in the sense that the actual descent of the waters of the *mabbûl* is being described here. The detachment of the term from the actual context effected the semantic shift, and the term *mabbûl* lost its original sense. Once associated with the material relating to the Flood Story, however, it was then understood as a term for the inundation itself.[34] This new meaning then became the only one possible outside the actual Flood Narrative itself.

Stenmans

31. Cf. also D. O. Edzard, "Königslisten und Chroniken. Sumerisch," *RLA,* VI (1983), 77-86.
32. Contra Gunkel, 67.
33. See III.1.a above.
34. Begrich, 51f.

מִבְצָר *mibṣār*

Contents: I. Meaning, Occurrences in the OT and LXX. II. *ʿîr mibṣār:* 1. Secular Usage; 2. Theological Usage. III. *mibṣār:* 1. Secular Usage; 2. Theological Usage. IV. Qumran.

I. Meaning, Occurrences in the OT and LXX. As Ugar. *bṣr,* "soar, fly high, rise,"[1] confirms, the fundamental meaning of the root *bṣr* is apparently "to be high" and thus "inaccessible," and further "to be impossible" (Gen. 11:6; Job 42:2). The *ʿîr b^eṣûrâ* is a strongly fortified, impregnable city.[2] This accounts for the place names

1. *KTU,* 1.19 I, 33; 1.18 IV, 20, 31, par. *rḫp*.
2. See II below.

beṣer (Dt. 4:43; Josh. 20:8; 21:36; 1 Ch. 6:63[Eng. v. 78]) and *boṣrâ* (in Edom: Gen. 36:33; 1 Ch. 1:44; Isa. 34:6; Jer. 49:13,22; Am. 1:12; cf. in Gen. 36:42; 1 Ch. 1:53 the Edomite tribe Mibzar; in Moab: Jer. 48:24): a city rendered inaccessible by its elevated location and/or its fortifications. In Ps. 108:11(10), the expression *ʿîr mibṣār* refers to Bozrah in Edom.[3]

Apart from the questionable passage Jer. 6:27, the noun *mibṣār* occurs 36 times in the Hebrew Bible, with few exceptions in the Deuteronomistic history and in the prophetic writings; an additional occurrence is in Sir. 36:29 (Heb.). These occurrences are equally divided between the absolute form *mibṣār* and the full form *ʿîr mibṣār.* While *ʿîr mibṣār,* synonymous with *ʿîr beṣûrâ,*[4] always designates the fortified settlement in contrast to the exposed one, the simple form *mibṣār* often exhibits the more narrow sense of fortress, bastion, refuge.

The LXX renders *mibṣār* with *ochyrós* and *ochýrōma,* and in isolated instances also with *ischyrós* and *periochḗ*.

II. ʿîr mibṣār.

1. *Secular Usage.* The Israelites considered the city of Tyre to be the fortified city par excellence.[5] Josh. 19:29 mentions it as a city of the tribe of Asher, in obvious dependence on 2 S. 24:7 (*mibṣār* abs.). It is especially in Ezekiel (Ezk. 26:4-12), however, that Tyre serves as the paradigm of a fortified city, with walls *(ḥōmôṯ),* towers *(migdālîm),* gates *(šeʿārîm),* streets *(ḥûṣôṯ),* and mighty houses *(bātê ḥemdâ).* The fortified cities in Dt. 3:5 are similarly characterized by high walls, gates, and bars. In the battle of Gibeon, the secure cities offer refuge to the defeated Canaanites (Josh. 10:20), whereas the single mention of secure cities in the case of Naphtali seems out of place in the description of borders (Josh. 19:35).[6] Fortified cities are attested not only for the Canaanites, but also for the Philistines (1 S. 6:18; 2 K. 18:8) and the Moabites (2 K. 3:19). However, the Israelites also had their secure cities, first the tribes of Gad and Reuben in the territory east of the Jordan (Nu. 32:17,36), then Samaria (2 K. 10:2; cf. 17:9). Among the fortified cities of Judah (Jehoshaphat places military forces in them [2 Ch. 17:2,19]), Lachish and Azekah are mentioned by name (Jer. 34:7).[7]

Fortified cities are occasionally the same as cities in general (cf. Nu. 32:16f.; Jer. 34:7). In 2 K. 3:19, the expression *ʿîr mibṣār* parallels *ʿîr mibḥôr,* "choice city." The opposite of *ʿîr mibṣār* in Dt. 3:5; 1 S. 6:18 is *ʿîr happerāzî,* "the open (NRSV 'unwalled') city"; in Nu. 32:16f.,36 *giḏrōṯ ṣō'n,* "sheepfolds"; and in 2 K. 17:9; 18:8

---

3. For further discussion of etymology, see O. Loretz, "Ugaritische und Hebräische Lexikographie," *UF,* 12 (1980), 279-282; W. von Soden, "Zum hebräischen Wörterbuch," *UF,* 13 (1981), 157f.

4. See *HAL,* I (1994), *s.v. bāṣûr*.

5. On the layout of Tyre, see *BRL*², 349f.; A. van der Born, "Tyrus," *BL*², 1788-1790, with map.

6. Cf. M. Noth, *Das Buch Josua. HAT,* VII (³1971), *in loc.*

7. On Lachish, see *BRL*², 196-98.

the simple watchtower or citadel tower, which in more sparsely settled areas replaced the fortified city as a place of refuge.[8] Ps. 108:11(10) articulates the hope for a new future in the petition to be brought to the "fortified city" and to Edom (an allusion to Bozrah in Edom[9]; the parallel passage Ps. 60:11[9] reads *'îr māṣôr* with the same sense).

2. *Theological Usage.* This already provides the transition to the theological use of *'îr mibṣār.* In Jer. 1:18, Yahweh makes the prophet into a "fortified city" capable of rejecting all attacks (in addition to "iron pillar" and "bronze walls"). Jer. 4:5 warns the people of Judah to flee into the fortified cities before the approaching catastrophe. Ultimately, however, even trust in these cities (Jer. 5:17) no longer offers protection against unavoidable judgment (8:14).

III. mibṣār.

1. *Secular Usage.* Even without the qualification *'îr,* the term *mibṣār* can refer to a fortified city.[10] Thus 2 S. 24:7 refers to the city of Tyre as *mibṣār.* Hazael will certainly burn the "fortresses" in Israel (2 K. 8:12). And in Isa. 17:3 the fortress of Ephraim, to which Yahweh will put an end, is the city of Samaria. As a rule, however, *mibṣār* refers less to the fortified city than to the protective bulwark or refuge. Cf. in Mic. 5:10(11) the juxtaposition of *'ārîm* and *mibṣārîm,* and in Isa. 25:12 the combination *mibṣār* and *miśgāb,* "refuge." Contrasting terms to *mibṣār* include *maḥaneh,* "the open place [of the camp and tents]" (Nu. 13:19), and *nāweh,* "pasture" (Lam. 2:2). Its parallels include *g^edērâ,* "stone wall" (Ps. 89:41[40]), and *'arm^enôt,* "the comfortable houses" (Isa. 34:13; Lam. 2:5).[11]

The book of Daniel attests several unique constructions. In addition to the simple *mibṣārîm,* the (Egyptian) fortresses against which Antiochus IV devises plans (Dnl. 11:24), v. 15 mentions the "city of bulwarks" (*'îr mibṣārôt*), i.e., the strongly fortified city (Sidon? Gaza?), and v. 39 speaks of the *mibṣ^erê mā'uzzîm,* "strong fortresses."

2. *Theological Usage.* Prompted by the stronger emphasis on human strength and self-confidence inhering in the simple term *mibṣār,* the theological usage predominates in the occurrences of this term. The sense of the difficult passage Am. 5:9 seems in any case to be the praise of Yahweh's rule both over nature (v. 8) and history ("destruction upon the fortress").[12] Again and again the fortress appears as

---

8. *BRL*², 81.

9. See preceding discussion.

10. H. Wildberger, *Jesaja 13–27. BK,* X/2 (1978), 643.

11. Cf. H. Haag, "Jerusalemer Profanbauten in den Psalmen," *ZDPV,* 93 (1977), 91f. = *Das Buch des Bundes. KBANT,* 1980.

12. On the suggestion that one should read the piel ptcp. *m^ebaṣṣēr* here in the sense "vintager" or the constellation Arcturus (*"vindemiator"*), cf. W. Gundel, *Sterne und Sternbilder im Glauben des Altertums und der Neuzeit* (1922, repr. Hildesheim, 1981), 66; G. R. Driver, "Two Astronomical Passages in the OT," *JTS,* N.S. 4 (1953), 208-212.

the embodiment of human self-assurance and absurd self-confidence. The preeminent example of such arrogance is Tyre (Ezk. 26:2–28:19). Its ruler has allegedly called himself a god (Ezk. 28:2,9). Such hubris provokes Yahweh's sovereign rule in judgment and redemption, which tolerates no resistance. The same assertion occurs in several passages in which instead of *mibṣār* the expression *ʿārîm (hab)beṣurôṯ* is used, an expression especially characteristic of the Deuteronomistic history (Dt. 3:5; 9:1; 2 K. 18:13; 19:25 par.; Hos. 8:14; Zeph. 1:16). Yahweh summons the Assyrians against the fortresses of Samaria (Hos. 10:14; Isa. 17:3) and the Babylonians against the strongholds of Judah (Mic. 5:10[11]; Hab. 1:10; Lam. 2:2,5), and he has laid the bulwarks of Jerusalem in ruins (Ps. 89:41[40]). Even the destruction of the strongholds of Moab (Jer. 48:18; Isa. 25:12) and Edom (Isa. 34:13) is his work.

Yahweh's power, however, does not reveal itself only in the fact that he storms impenetrable fortresses. In a reverse fashion he is also able to make weak human beings into strongholds, above all the prophets (Jer. 1:18[13]), though also a woman, who is the man's helper *(ʿēzer),* pillar of support *(ʿammûḏ mišʿān),* and place of refuge *(mibṣār)* (Sir. 36:29 Heb.). The context shows that the reference is not only to the maintenance of possessions, but even more to the man's security.

IV. Qumran. Among the Qumran texts, 1QpHab 4:3-8 provides a commentary to Hab. 1:10. Compared to the MT, the pesher provides the (better) reading *whwʾ lkwl mbṣr yśḥq wyṣbwr ʿapr wylkdhw* and explains: "Interpreted, this concerns the commanders of the Kittim who despise the fortresses of the peoples and laugh at them in derision. To capture them, they encircle them with a mighty host, and out of fear and terror they deliver themselves into their hands."[14] According to Karl Elliger,[15] this is referring at least primarily if not exclusively to the siege and storming of Jerusalem by Pompey.

In 1QH 3:6f., the petitioner (the community?) compares his spiritual suffering to a ship in distress and to a besieged city *(kʿyr mbṣr).* 1QH 6:35 speaks of a person swinging a scourge *(mʿbyr šwṭ šwtp)* who will be unable to penetrate into the fortress, whereby *mibṣār* apparently serves as a self-designation for the community confident in the protection of its God.[16]

H. Haag

---

13. See II.2 above.

14. Translation according to G. Vermes, *The Dead Sea Scrolls in English* (Sheffield, ^{3}1987), 285.

15. *Studien zum Habakuk-Kommentar vom Toten Meer. BHTh,* 15 (1953), 272f.

16. Cf. M. Delcor, *Les hymnes de Qumran (Hodayot)* (Paris, 1962), *in loc.*

מִגְדָּל *migdāl*

Contents: I. 1. Etymology; 2. Occurrences. II. 1. Preexilic Texts; 2. Exilic and Postexilic Texts; 3. The Tower of Babel; 4. Component in Place Names; 5. Tower as Metaphor. III. LXX and Qumran.

I. 1. *Etymology.* The noun *migdāl,* attested in OT Hebrew, is also attested in Ugaritic[1] with the meaning "tower"[2] and as a place name,[3] as well as in Moabite,[4] but not in Phoenician.[5] Attestations in Aramaic include occurrences in Jewish Aramaic (Targum), Christian Palestinian, and Syriac.[6] The two singular attestations from al-ʿUla (in Minean[7] and Liḥyanite inscriptions[8]) are presumably foreign words or loanwords which in both cases refer to inhabited buildings. In Arabic the term *miǵdal* is a loanword from Aramaic,[9] and it is noteworthy that the Classical Arabic lexicographers interpreted it as "citadel, palace." Modern topographical onomastics attests *miǵdal* as a component in place names within a well-defined region in Palestine-Phoenicia with only sparse distribution outside this region.[10] It is still questionable whether the name of the Moroccan port city eṣ-Ṣawīr/Mogador[11] can be taken as a Berber attestation of the word *migdāl;*[12] the city Agadir, located not far from Mogador, suggests that both names derive from the same root *gdr.*

The term *mktr* occurs as a Semitic loanword in Egyptian in connection with place

---

migdāl. K. Galling, "Migdal," *BRL* (381f.); B. Mazar, "מִגְדָּל," *EMiqr,* IV (1962), 633-35; W. Michaelis, "πύργος," *TDNT,* VI, 953-56; G. Morawe, "Turm," *BHHW,* III (1962), 2032-4.

1. *WUS,* no. 632; *UT,* no. 562.
2. M. Dahood, "Ugaritic-Hebrew Parallel Pairs," *RSP,* I (1972), §II, 343.
3. Cf. M. C. Astour, "Place Names," *RSP,* II (1975), §VIII, 58, 162; M. Dietrich, O. Loretz, and J. Sanmartín, "Zur ugaritische Lexikographie (XI): Lexikographische Einzelbemerkungen," *UF,* 6 (1974), 31.
4. Mesha inscription, *KAI,* 181, 22.
5. As *HAL,* II (1995), 543, suggests.
6. *LexSyr,* 105a.
7. *RÉS,* 3340, 5 (*mgdlnhn* dual).
8. Cf. W. Caskel, *Lihyan und Lihyanisch.* AFNW Geisteswissenschaften, 4 (Cologne, 1954), no. 26, 1, 88f. (*mg'dl* pl.). D. H. Müller, *Epigraphische Denkmäler aus Arabien. DAWW,* Phil.-hist. Kl., 37/2 (1889), reads *mmdl*; the photo of the reproduction hardly suggests the presence of an *aleph* between the second and third letters.
9. Cf. S. I. Fraenkel, *Die aramäischen Fremdwörter im Arabischen* (1886, repr. Hildesheim, 1962), 236f.; certainly not borrowed from OSA, as suggested by *HAL,* II, 543.
10. Cf. B. S. J. Isserlin, "Place Name Provinces in the Semitic-speaking Ancient Near East," *Proceedings of the Leeds Philosophical Society,* 8 (1956), 83-85.
11. See H. Stumme, "Gedanken über libysch-phönizische Anklänge," *ZA,* 27 (1912), 123f.
12. This remains the case despite repetition of this thesis in E. Jenni, "גָּדוֹל *gādōl* gross," *THAT,* I, 402.

names since the time of the eighteenth dynasty.[13] As a place name in Egypt it can be traced back to the Greco-Roman period as *Mágdōlos,*[14] and in Coptic as *meǵtōl.*[15] Herodotus' reference[16] to Megiddo as *Mágdōlos* testifies to the relative frequency with which the word was used in place names. The natural identification of the word *migdāl* as a *miqṭāl* construction from a root *gdl*[17] is problematical because only Canaanite attests the root *gdl* in the meaning "be large, high" (cf. in contrast Arab. *ǵadala,* "twist or pull tightly, plait"), and because the context of several OT occurrences (e.g., Isa. 5:2[18]) does not suggest something large and high. Thus there is some reason to follow the suggestion first articulated by William F. Albright that the word *migdāl* arose through metathesis from *midgāl* (cf. Akk. *madgaltu,* "watchtower, border post").[19]

2. *Occurrences.* The term *migdāl* occurs altogether 49 times in the OT. The passages include: Gen. 11:4,5; Jgs. 8:9,17; 9:46,47,49,51(twice),52(twice); 2 K. 9:17; 17:9; 18:8; 1 Ch. 27:25; 2 Ch. 14:6[Eng. v. 7]; 26:9,10,15; 27:4; 32:5; Neh. 3:1(twice),11,25,26,27; 8:4; 12:38,39; Ps. 48:13[12]; 61:4[3]; Prov. 18:10; Cant. 4:4; 5:13; 7:5[4](twice); 8:10; Isa. 2:15; 5:2; 30:25; 33:18; Jer. 31:38; Ezk. 26:4,9; 27:11; Mic. 4:8; Zec. 14:10; cf. also the *qere* to 2 S. 22:51. Among these, only the Chronicler's history seems to exhibit a certain accumulation (16 occurrences). The masc. pl. *migdālîm* is attested 9 times (2 Ch. 14:6[7]; 26:9,10,15; 27:4; Ps. 48:13[12]; Isa. 30:25; 33:18; Ezk. 26:4), the fem. pl. *migdālôṯ* 5 times (1 Ch. 27:25; 2 Ch. 32:5; Cant. 8:10; Ezk. 26:9; 27:11). An evaluation of the use of the two plural forms confirms the thesis of Diethelm Michel,[20] namely, that the plural form in *-îm* is to be understood as a "collective or group plural," the form in *-ôṯ* in contrast as a "plural conceived as a combination of individuals." In preexilic texts *migdāl* as a rule refers to the citadel or fortress of a city, while in exilic and postexilic texts it refers to a tower standing in some relationship with a gate or with the city walls.

II. 1. *Preexilic Texts.* In older texts *migdāl* refers to a fortified citadel inside the city itself offering a final place of refuge. Thus in the portrayal of Abimelech's siege of Thebez (Jgs. 9:50-57), although the city proper has already been taken, the inhabitants are still able to flee into the *migdāl.* Just as Abimelech is about to set fire to the "citadel

---

13. Cf. A. H. Gardiner, "The Ancient Military Road Between Egypt and Palestine," *JEA,* 6 (1920), 107ff.

14. Cf. Kees, "Magdolon, Magdolos," *PW,* XIV/1 (1928), 299f.

15. Cf. W. E. Crum, *A Coptic Dictionary* (Oxford, 1939), 214f.; J. Černý, *Coptic Etymological Dictionary* (Cambridge, 1976), 102; W. Westendorf, *Koptisches Handwörterbuch* (Heidelberg, 1965-1977), 114, notes seven additional orthographic variations.

16. *Hist.* ii.159.

17. So, e.g., *HAL,* II, 543; Jenni, 402.

18. Cf. also the illustration in *AuS,* IV (1935), fig. 93, 94.

19. *AHw,* II (1972), 572b; *CAD,* X/1 (1977), 16. This is the position of L. A. Sinclair, *An Archaeological Study of Gibeah (Tell el-Ful). AASOR,* 34f. (1954-56[1960]), 7; A. F. Rainey, "The Toponymics of Eretz-Israel," *BASOR,* 231 (1978), 5.

20. *Grundlegung einer hebräischen Syntax,* I (Neukirchen-Vluyn, 1977), 53f.

door" *(peṯaḥ hammigdāl),* his final fate overtakes him. Similarly, the problematical account of the destruction of Shechem suggests that the *migdal-šᵉḵem* (Jgs. 9:46) does not refer to a locale different from Shechem itself,[21] but rather to the citadel of Shechem, which may have been further equipped with a tower. From there the inhabitants then fled into the crypt of the temple of Baʿal-berith, where they were burned to death. This kind of citadel, located inside a city, was presumably the rule. In any case, there is literary evidence for such a citadel at Penuel (Jgs. 8:9,17, in connection with Gideon's campaign in the territory east of the Jordan) and Jezreel (2 K. 9:17) and archaeological evidence for such, e.g., at Tell el-Fûl (Gibeah) and Khirbet eṭ-Ṭubeiqah (Beth-zur).

A certain kind of small, independent citadel is also called a *migdāl.* These *migdālîm,* which according to 2 Ch. 26:10 Uzziah and according to 2 Ch. 27:4 also Jotham erected in the Negeb or in the hill country of Judah, represent such archaeologically attested forts,[22] i.e., isolated watchtowers serving as vantage points from which to oversee border traffic and roads, as well as citadels of refuge for exposed settlements. 1 Ch. 27:25, to take one example, offers an insight into the geographical layout of such settlements in its enumeration of *ʿārîm, kᵉpārîm,* and *migdālôṯ,* similarly also 2 K. 17:9; 18:8 (from the watchtower to the fortified city: *mimmigdal nôṣᵉrîm ʿaḏ-ʿîr miḇṣār.*[23]

2. *Exilic and Postexilic Texts.* In later texts *migdāl* refers to a tower standing in some relationship with a gate or wall. The directive in Ps. 48:13[12] to count the towers of Zion[24] shows that there must have been a considerable number of such towers (this imagery [counting towers] also occurs in Isa. 33:18b in a gloss; in its own turn, this gloss is probably reflecting on Isa. 22:10, which speaks of counting Jerusalem's houses). This can also be seen from Neh. 3, which recounts the construction of the wall. Several towers in Jerusalem bear specific names, presumably because of their special size or function: *migdal ḥᵃnan'el* (Jer. 31:38; Zec. 14:10; Neh. 3:1; 12:39); *migdal hattannûrîm* (Neh. 3:11; 12:38); *migdal hammēʾâ* (Neh. 3:1; 12:39); *migdal-ʿēḏer* (Mic. 4:8); and *migdal dāwîḏ* (Cant. 4:4); the location of these towers, however, can probably no longer be determined archaeologically. Since the account of the construction of the wall differentiates clearly between gates and towers, these are probably not gate-towers, but rather towers which reinforced and secured the wall fortifications at strategically important points. It is unlikely that these refer to towers situated "on" the wall itself, as suggested by Targ. and Vulg. for 2 Ch. 32:5.[25] 1QSb 5:23 also mentions a strong tower situated against or in (not "on" or "upon," as is usually translated) the wall *(bḥwmh).*

---

21. Contra J. A. Soggin, "Bemerkungen zur alttestamentlichen Topographie Sichems mit besonderem Bezug auf Jdc. 9," *ZDPV,* 83 (1967), 195-97.

22. Cf. Y. Aharoni, "Forerunners of the Limes: Iron Age Fortresses in the Negev," *IEJ,* 17 (1967), 1-17.

23. P. Welten, *Geschichte und Geschichtsdarstellung in den Chronikbüchern. WMANT,* 42 (1973), 25f., 63f.

24. Cf. H. Haag, "Jerusalemer Profanbauten in den Psalmen," *ZDPV,* 93 (1977), 92f. = *Das Buch des Bundes. KBANT,* 1980, 255f.

25. On the MT, cf. Welten, 68ff.

In the promise of the return of the Davidic dynasty in Mic. 4:8,[26] the reference to the "tower of the flock" *(migdal-ʿēḏer)* probably refers, in the postexilic period, to a tower standing among the ruins of the palace and Ophel area which now served for protection and as a watchtower with regard to the flocks (cf. 2 Ch. 26:10.). Presumably this same tower or its remnants are mentioned in Neh. 3:27 as a large, projecting tower *(hammigdāl haggāḏôl hayyôṣēʾ)* at the wall of Ophel, and perhaps also in Isa. 32:14, which speaks of the Ophel and the watchtower (referred to as *baḥan* only here).

Small watchtowers were erected for protecting vineyards (Isa. 5:2; Mt. 21:33), although they apparently served as observation posts only during the day, whereas the guards were able to spend the night in the *sukkâ* (Isa. 1:8). Luke's assertion that eighteen people were killed when the tower in Siloam fell (Lk. 13:4) gives an indication of the size of the edifice.

3. *The Tower of Babel.* The account of the construction of the tower of Babel (Gen. 11:1-9)[27] twice mentions the city and the tower together (vv. 4, 5) and once the city alone (v. 8). Although both LXX and Sam. mention the tower in v. 8 as well, this probably reflects secondary harmonization. If with Hermann Gunkel[28] one assumes the presence of two originally independent narratives, one concerned with the city, the other with the tower,[29] then one can discount the various attempts to solve the problem philologically either by translating "the city and especially the tower" (reading a *waw*-augmentativum: "and specifically"),[30] or by taking the phrase as a hendiadys in the sense of "city crowned by a tower."[31] This is the temple-tower of the Sumerian-Babylonian urban culture, the ziggurat, an edifice that narrowed toward the top and appeared to rise without end, presumably even the ziggurat of Babylon itself, Etemenanki, by which Marduk descended to receive human veneration and offerings in his sanctuary Esagil. From his own vantage point, the narrator of the story was unable to sanction the pious intentions accompanying the construction of the tower. "For him this great edifice was merely the embodiment of arrogance and titanic pride."[32]

4. *Component in Place Names.* The term *migdāl* is also attested as a component in many place names, including in the OT *migdal-ʾēl* (Josh. 19:38, in Naphtali), *migdal-gāḏ* (Josh. 15:37, in Judah = Khirbet el-Mejdeleh), and *migdal-ʿēḏer* (Gen. 35:21, near

---

26. Cf. W. Rudolph, *Micha. KAT,* XIII/3 (1975), 84f.; H. W. Wolff, *Micah* (Eng. trans., Minneapolis, 1990), 125.

27. Cf. C. Westermann, *Genesis 1–11* (Eng. trans., Minneapolis, 1984), 531-557; and the status of scholarship report in *idem, Genesis 1–11. Erträge der Forschung,* 7 (Darmstadt, 1972), 95-104.

28. *Genesis. HKAT* (⁶1964), 92f.

29. Cf. also G. Wallis, "Die Stadt in den Überlieferungen der Genesis," *ZAW,* 78 (1966), 141f.

30. E. König, *Die Genesis eingeleitet, übersetzt, erklärt* (Gütersloh, ³1925), 435.

31. E. A. Speiser, "Word Plays on the Creation Epic's Version of the Founding of Babylon," *Or,* 25 (1956), 322, n. 26 = *Oriental and Biblical Studies* (Philadelphia, 1967), 59, n. 26.

32. Wallis, 142. Cf. also W. von Soden, "Etemenanki vor Asarhaddon nach der Erzählung vom Turnbau zu Babel und dem Erra-Mythos," *UF,* 3 (1971), 253-263.

Bethlehem; according to Targ. Ps.-J. the place from which the Messiah will reveal himself at the end of days).[33] Cf. *Magdalēnē* in the NT (Mt. 27:56; Mk. 15:40, etc.), "the one from Magdala." With different vocalization, *migdōl* refers to one or several places in Egypt (Ex. 14:2; Nu. 33:7, Israelites' encampment during the exodus = Tell el-Ḥeir; Jer. 44:1; 46:14, Jewish colony in Egypt; Ezk. 29:10; 30:6, point on the Egyptian border).

5. *Tower as Metaphor.* The assertion in Prov. 18:10, namely, that "the name of Yahweh is a strong tower; the righteous runs into it and is safe," employs the same metaphor as Ps. 61:4(3), where the petitioner confesses to God, "You are my refuge, a strong tower against the enemy." Both passages compare the security provided by the fortress tower with the refuge provided by God (cf. also 1QH 7:8; 1QSb 5:23). The *qere* to 2 S. 22:51 has the same image in mind when it suggests reading *magdôl* instead of *magdîl,* so that Yahweh is called the "tower of salvation of his king." On the other hand, injustice and godlessness protrude into the present like a great tower, virtually insuperable (cf. T.Lev. 2:3; 4QTestim 26). Only in the end time will Yahweh rise up against all that is proud and haughty, "against every high tower, and against every fortified wall" (Isa. 2:15), so that towers will fall (30:25b).

Comparison with a tower can serve as a symbol of beauty (Cant. 4:4; 8:10),[34] whereas according to Sir. 26:22 a married woman is a *pýrgos thanátou,* a "tower of death," for her paramour. Even if the lost Hebrew text spoke instead of a deadly net *(mᵉṣûḏaṯ māweṯ),*[35] the metaphor of the woman as a tower whose besieger pays with his own life, a metaphor presumed to be familiar to a Greek audience, is certainly intelligible[36] (cf. also 2 Mc. 13:5ff.).

III. LXX and Qumran. The LXX translates almost exclusively with *pýrgos.*[37] 1QM 9:10,11,12(twice),13(twice),14(twice) uses the term *migdāl* in a very specific sense in the portrayal of tactical military figures and movements. In this context, "tower" is certainly not referring to a siege tower (as attested also for Palestine since approximately the Hellenistic period; cf. 1 Mc. 13:43f.), but rather a troup tower full of armed soldiers (borne by elephants), which in the Roman army, too, could be called a *turris.* In 1QH 7:8, the petitioner describes the position God has assigned him for the present with the statement: "Thou hast made me like a strong tower, a high wall."[38] In the blessing for the Prince of the Congregation (1QSb 5:23), the same imagery (tower and wall) expresses the eschatological function of the Prince. He will be a "strong tower and a high wall" and will smite the peoples with the power of his mouth.[39]

Kellermann

33. For further (altogether 11) examples, see *PW,* XV/2 (1932), 1549f.
34. Cf. H. Ringgren, *Das Hohelied. ATD,* XVI/2 (^{3}1981), 271, 288f.
35. So P. W. Skehan, "Tower of Death or Deadly Snare? Sir 26,22," *CBQ,* 16 (1954), 154.
36. Cf. R. Smend, *Die Weisheit des Jesus Sirach* (Berlin, 1906), 239.
37. Cf. Michaelis.
38. Translation by G. Vermes, *The Dead Sea Scrolls in English* (Sheffield, ^{3}1987), 184.
39. Cf. O. Betz, "Felsenmann und Felsengemeinde," *ZNW,* 48 (1957), 52, 69.

מָגֵן māḡēn; גָּנַן gānan; צִנָּה ṣinnâ; שֶׁלֶט šeleṭ

Contents: I. General. II. 1. Etymology; 2. *gnn*; 3. Homographs. III. 1. Ancient Near Eastern Panoply; 2. Shield as Defensive Weaponry. IV. Uses: 1. Combat; 2. Component in the Panoply; 3. Decoration; 4. Testudo Fortifications; 5. "Shield Bearer"; 6. Metaphors of Human Opposition to God; 7. Metaphors of Divine Warfare; 8. Metaphors of Human Wickedness; 9. Testudo Metaphors. V. Qumran. VI. Synonyms and Related Terms: 1. *ṣinnâ*; 2. *šeleṭ*. VII. *māḡēn* or *mōḡēn*?: 1. Divine Epithet; 2. Descriptions of Persons. VIII. LXX.

I. General. The word *māḡēn*, "shield," occurs 58 times in the OT, used literally, metonymically, and metaphorically to describe a piece of personal defensive weaponry. In translations, the simple term "shield" predominates; in fact, the weapon so designated is more strictly a round shield or buckler, often with embossed sheathing. In Hebrew, the larger shield covering the body is called *ṣinnâ*.[1] This distinction is standard in the ancient languages of the Mediterranean basin: *māḡēn* = Greek *aspís* = Latin *clipeus; ṣinnâ* = *thyreós* = *scutum.* However, other distinctions were made based on function and weight.

Obscure developments in the language conspired so that several homographs of *mgn* may have fallen together etymologically and lexically.

II. 1. *Etymology.* The noun *māḡēn* is derived from the geminate root *gnn*, "to cover, surround, defend, protect," as shown by the evidence of the other Semitic languages.

2. *gnn.* The verbal forms of *gānan* occur only in the latter part of First Isaiah (some of the material is also given in 2 Kings) and in Deutero-Zechariah, which may be dependent upon Isaiah. In the Isaiah passages, Yahweh "protects" Jerusalem (with the prep. *ʿal*). In Isa. 31:5, he does so *k^eṣipp^orîm ʿāpôt*, "like flying (or perhaps better,

---

māḡēn. M. Dahood, "Hebrew-Ugaritic Lexicography IV," *Bibl*, 47 (1966), 403-419; *idem*, review of *Sem*, 12 (1962), *Bibl*, 45 (1964), 129f.; *idem*, "Ugaritic Lexicography," *Mélanges E. Tisserant*, I, *StT*, 231 (1964), 81-104, esp. 94; F. E. Deist, "Aantekeninge by Gen. 15:1,6," *NedGTT*, 12 (1971), 100-102; M. Dietrich, O. Loretz, and J. Sanmartín, "Zur ugaritischen Lexikographie (XI): Lexikographische Einzelbemerkungen," *UF*, 6 (1974), 19-38; M. Kessler, "The 'Shield' of Abraham?" *VT*, 14 (1964), 494-97; O. Loretz, "*ʾjš mgn* in Proverbia 6,11 und 23,34," *UF*, 6 (1974), 476-77; *idem*, "*mgn* — 'Geschenk' in Gen 15,1," *UF*, 6 (1974), 492; *idem*, "Psalmenstudien III," *UF*, 6 (1974), 175-210, esp. 177-183; *idem*, "Stichometrische und textologische Probleme in den Thronbesteigungs-Psalmen: Psalmenstudien (IV)," *UF*, 6 (1974), 211-240; A. R. Millard, "Saul's Shield Not Anointed with Oil," *BASOR*, 230 (1978), 70; A. M. Snodgrass, *Arms and Armour of the Greeks* (London, 1967); *idem*, *Early Greek Armour and Weapons, from the End of the Bronze Age to 600 B.C.* (Edinburgh, 1964); W. von Soden, "Vedisch *magham*, 'Geschenk' — Neuarabisch *maǧǧānīja* "Gebührenfreiheit": Der Weg einer Wortsippe," *JEOL*, 18 (1964), 339-344; Y. Yadin, *The Art of Warfare in Biblical Lands in the Light of Archaeological Discovery* (Eng. trans., New York, 1963).

1. See VI.1 below.

'hovering'; cf. Dt. 32:11) birds"; coordinate verbs are *nṣl* hiphil, "to rescue," *psḥ,* "to deliver,"[2] and *mlṭ* hiphil, "to liberate" (cf. 1QIs^{a}, *hplyṭ*; MT is superior). In Isa. 37:35, Yahweh defends Jerusalem *l^{e}hôšîʿāh,* "to save it," for his own sake and the sake of his servant David (cf. 2 K. 19:34). In Isa. 38:6 (par. 2 K. 20:6), Yahweh promises that he will rescue *(hiṣṣîl)* and defend the city. The sequence of actions in the last two passages is thus rescue *(hiṣṣîl),* defense *(gānan),* and salvation *(hôšîaʿ).* At the time of the messianic restoration, Deutero-Zechariah proclaims, Yahweh will defend the children of Zion (Zec. 9:15, with the prep. *ʿal*); only in this passage is *gānan* used in an explicitly martial context, which has references to slings and arrows. In a further prophecy of the restoration (Zec. 12:8), Deutero-Zechariah declares again that Yahweh will defend the inhabitants of Jerusalem (with the prep. *b^{e}ʿaḏ*).

The Masoretes have parsed 5 of the occurrences of the verb as qal, 3 as hiphil. It is possible, however, that all are qal. The term *gānan,* then, is apparently tied to a clearly discernible Jerusalemite tradition. An obscure further connection with Jerusalem may be lurking in the form *h^{a}ḡînâ* (Ezk. 42:12).

The root *gnn* is used in a bilingual Neo-Punic–Latin dedicatory text from Leptis Magna[3] which records that the erector *t ʿmdm wt hmʿq'm* (Heb. *hammaqôm) ygn,* "had enclosed the pillars and the sacred site." There is no equivalent in the Latin portion of the text. In the Marseille sacrificial tariff,[4] the *ṣpr 'gnn* is perhaps a "caged [enclosed], i.e., domesticated bird." Finally, the root is also attested in two Punic personal names: *'srgn,* "Osiris protects,"[5] and *gnn,* perhaps "protector."[6] The root is not attested in Ugaritic texts, but there is an abundance of evidence to suggest it existed in that language. Finally, it occurs with the meaning "to cover, defend" in the various Aramaic dialects, and in the causative stem in Phoenician, Old South Arabic, and Arabic. In Akkadian the root has been limited in reference to the "confinement" of persons.

3. *Homographs.* The Phoenician and Ugaritic cognates of *māḡēn* are attested only once each. Ugar. *mgn* occurs in the jejune context of a list of materiel.[7] On the Phoenician orthostat-inscription of Karatepe, Azitawadda boasts *wpʿl 'nk ss ʿl ss wmgn ʿl mgn,* "I have added horse to horse, shield to shield."[8] Cognates are also attested in both Western and Eastern Late Aramaic dialects, and in Arabic. If the comparable Akkadian form, Late Bab. **maginnu,*[9] is to be associated with *māḡēn,* it is as an Aramaic loanword. The word is used in Achaemenid inscriptions to

---

2. Cf. H. Wildberger, *Jesaja 28–39. BK* X/3 (1982), 1236f.
3. *KAI,* 124.
4. *Ibid.,* 69, 11.
5. *CIS,* I, 821, 4.
6. Benz, 297.
7. *KTU,* 4.127, 3.
8. *ANET*^{3}, 653; *KAI,* 26A I, 6f. Cf. Jer. 46:3f.; Y. Avishur, "Word Pairs Common to Phoenician and Biblical Hebrew," *UF,* 7 (1975), 23.
9. *AHw,* II (1972), 576.

describe the *petasos,* the broad-rimmed felt headgear worn by one class of Ionians in the Persepolis reliefs.[10]

III. 1. *Ancient Near Eastern Panoply.* The basic range of materiel in the ancient Near East was not remarkably different from the range elsewhere in the ancient world.[11] Setting aside operational materiel like chariots, horses, and battering rams, we can distinguish two classes of weapons: Offensive weapons include sword and dagger *(ḥereḇ);* spear *(ḥ^{a}nîṯ, rōmaḥ, kîḏôn);* bow, arrow, and quiver *(qešeṯ, ḥēṣ, 'ašpâ);* mace and battle-ax *(garzen);* and slingshot and stones *(qelaʿ, 'aḇnê qelaʿ).* The defensive weapons are largely fitted to the body: helmet *(k/qôḇaʿ),* mail *(s/širyôn),* greaves *(miṣḥâ),* and shoe *(s^e'ôn).* These are complemented by shields, sometimes large *(ṣinnâ)* and sometimes small *(māḡēn).* In panoply lists the shield tends to be included. For example, Goliath appears in helmet, mail, and greaves, bearing both a light spear *(kîḏôn)* and a heavy one *(ḥ^{a}nîṯ);* he is preceded by a man bearing a body shield (*ṣinnâ*, 1 S. 17:5ff.; cf. 17:38f.).[12]

2. *Shield as Defensive Weaponry.* Body shields were oblong and generally covered either the entire body[13] or only from the neck to the feet.[14] Anthony M. Snodgrass shows examples of the various types of Greek body shields: figure-eight, rectangular, etc.[15] Smaller Egyptian body shields from the early second millennium are attested.[16] Large shields sometimes had a curved top[17] or a peaked top[18] to allow the shield bearer visibility around the edges, and sometimes a flat bottom to permit firm anchoring on the earth.[19] In other cases, the bottom was pointed, allowing the shield to be planted. Some shields had a concavo-convex shape to enclose the wearer's body.

The material was generally wood with leather stretched over it and sometimes with metal attachments,[20] or reed or wickerwork with leather and metal.[21] The large shield was either carried on the left side[22] or worn on the back.[23]

Small shields were generally round wood or wicker frames covered with leather.[24]

---

10. Cf. the Nakš-i-Rustam reliefs (W. von Soden, "Aramäische Wörter in neuassyrischen und neu- und spätbabylonischen Texten," *Or* 35 [1966], 19, 16).

11. Cf. A. Oepke, "ὅπλον," *TDNT,* V, 292-98.

12. For further discussion of weaponry terminology → נשק *nešeq;* → מלחמה *milḥāmâ* (VIII, 334-345); → כלי *k^{e}lî* (VII, 169-175).

13. *ANEP,* 368, 373 (Neo-Assyrian).

14. *Ibid.,* 300 (3rd millennium).

15. A. Snodgrass, *Arms and Armour* (1967), plates 2, 5, 12; cf. 19.

16. *ANEP,* 180; for the Late Bronze Age, cf. *ANEP,* 344.

17. *Ibid.,* 344f. (Late Bronze Age Egyptian).

18. *Ibid.,* 180.

19. *Ibid.,* 300, 368, 373.

20. *Ibid.,* 180 (Middle Kingdom Egyptian).

21. *Ibid.,* 368, 373 (Neo-Assyrian).

22. *Ibid.,* 180, 300, 345, 368, 373.

23. *Ibid.,* 344.

24. *Ibid.,* 59, 332 (Late Bronze Age); 164, 184, 369, and *passim* (1st millennium); for further examples, see Snodgrass, *Early Greek Armour.*

Dumbbell shields[25] and squarish shields[26] are also attested. The Greek *péltē* was crescent-shaped. Small shields were either worn on the left hand[27] or slung around the back.[28] *ANEP,* 164, clearly shows the specially prepared boss and rim. Many small shields are flat, but some belly outward sharply.[29] The center of a buckler was often a boss of metal, sometimes an animal's head, sometimes spiked, and sometimes simple enough to look like a cymbal. Shields with metallic facings and all-metal shields follow from the boss design, but the latter were never dominant in the ancient world. Urartu and Crete form the conduit for leading Western Asiatic developments in military technology into Greece.

Both large and small shields were originally defensive weapons for lance and spear warriors, and only later were they used by archers and slingers. Whereas spear, lance, and javelin troops defended themselves directly, archers and slingers were defended by special shield bearers. In the Late Bronze age, with the increased use of the composite bow and the battle-ax, armor became more sophisticated, and consequently the small shield became more important than the large shield, which was eventually relegated to defensive line work. Half-body-size shields were worn by wielders of axes and sickle-swords.[30] Warriors with battle-axes and mace were equipped with small shields.[31]

Shields were used not only for personal defense, but also in ad hoc fortifications (Latin *testudo* "tortoise"). Battlements on Iron Age cities were supplemented by wooden frames in time of war. These held shields and protected the defenders of the city. Such a frame is shown in the Neo-Assyrian relief of the siege of Lachish.[32] Such screens were often also mobile, and were used when a moving formation needed to be screened from above and on all sides.

Nonmilitary uses of shields are not well attested. Some hunting attendants of a Neo-Assyrian monarch carry small shields and bows.[33] Ornate small shields, some with animal head bosses, constituted the chief treasure plundered from an Urartean temple at Muṣaṣir by the troops of Sargon II.[34]

IV. Uses.

1. *Combat.* Both texts in which *māḡēn* is used to designate weaponry being prepared for combat are drawn from the Chronicler's work. In 2 Ch. 23:9, the Levites of Jehoiada's army are equipped with spears, "small shields" *(hammāḡinnôṯ)* and *haššᵉlāṭîm,* which belonged to David and had been kept in the temple. Whether and to

---

25. *Ibid.,* 36.
26. *Ibid.,* 60, 496.
27. *Ibid.,* 36, 59, 164, and *passim.*
28. *Ibid.,* 37.
29. *Ibid.,* 370.
30. *Ibid.,* 344.
31. *Ibid.,* 60, 164.
32. *Ibid.,* 373.
33. *Ibid.,* 184.
34. *Ibid.,* 370; cf. IV.3 below.

what extent the Chronicler meant to distinguish the last two types of materiel is not clear.[35] In this case the shields were not used in any combat, since the restoration of Joash was largely bloodless.

The men who rebuilt the walls of Jerusalem under Nehemiah were divided into two groups. The load-bearers and builders were lightly armed (with *šelaḥ,* "missile" [?] and sword), while the guards had spears and bows, wore mail, and carried shields (Neh. 4:10f.[Eng. vv. 16f.]).

2. *Component in the Panoply.* In some passages which catalog a range of materiel, the buckler is among the items which make up the panoply or the metonym of it. Of sixteen such panoply lists, three approach an entire panoply: 2 Ch. 26:14; Jer. 46:3f., which have six terms each, and Ezk. 38:4, which has seven. The remaining passages include two or three terms and serve as short forms of the panoply catalog. These lists frequently also include *māgēn* and *ṣinnâ.* Two other defensive weapons are mentioned: *q/kôḇaʿ, s/širyôn;* eight offensive weapons are mentioned: *ḥēṣ, qešeṯ, ʾašpâ, ʾaḇnê qelaʿ, maqqēl yāḏ, ḥereḇ, rōmaḥ,* and perhaps *šelaḥ.* Two additional terms for general weaponry are used: *milḥāmâ* and *nēšeq,* along with two other terms for military equipment: *sōlᵉlâ,* "earthworks," and *merkāḇâ,* "chariotry."

Only one of the three large catalogs is balanced. The Chronicler's description of Uzziah's army's weaponry (2 Ch. 26:14) is noteworthy because the equipment was supplied by the king and not the soldiers. It consisted of three defensive weapons *(māgēn, kôḇaʿ, širyôn)* and three offensive weapons *(rōmaḥ, qešeṯ, ʾaḇnê qelaʿ).*

Six catalogs contain only two terms and should probably be taken as related metonyms of a whole panoply. In Jgs. 5:8, Israel's lack of weaponry at the battle of Taanach is cited as an absence of *māgēn* and *rōmaḥ.* Not only is this pair metonymic of the panoply; it is also coherent in that it describes the equipment of a major class of warriors. Even this most common equipment is missing on Israel's side because Israel had no professional soldiers. Furthermore, Israel knew itself to be allied with the greatest warrior, Yahweh, who enters the battle with his weapons, the heavenly hosts. These angelic warriors seen in visions over Jerusalem during Antiochus IV's second invasion of Egypt (*ca.* 170 B.C.) are equipped with lance and shield (*aspís*) (2 Mc. 5:3). According to 2 Mc. 15:11, this pair of weapons was not needed; the noble words of Judas Maccabeus sufficed. This pair of implements is also cited in Sir. 29:13, where the poet claims that *eleēmosýnē,* "public charity, almsgiving," is better at fending off an enemy "than a stout shield and a ductile (or 'weighty') spear" *(hypèr aspída krátous kaì hypèr dóry holkḗs).*

Hezekiah's weaponry in connection with his measures against Sennacherib includes the defensive *māgēn* and the offensive counterpart *šelaḥ* (2 Ch. 32:5); for a further balance, cf. also bow *(qešeṯ)* and *māgēn* (2 S. 22:35f. par. Ps. 18:35f.[34f.]), discussed further in the next paragraph. Dt. 33:29 reads: "Your blessings, O Israel! Who is like you, a people saved by Yahweh? — are your succoring shield and [delete *ʾᵃšer*] your

35. Cf. VI.2 below.

glorious sword." The sword and shield here seem to be attributes, associated with succor in battle and the resultant glory.[36]

The balanced panoply in prophetic thought is attributed only to the enemies of Israel, and thus Jeremiah issues mock orders to some of the participants at the battle of Carchemish: "Let the warriors go forth: Cush and Put, who carry the shield *(māg̱ēn),* the Ludim, who grasp, who draw the bow *(qešeṯ)*" (Jer. 46:9).

A panoply of three pieces is mentioned in connection with the army of Gog, a great horde bearing the *māg̱ēn* and *ṣinnâ* as well as the sword *(ḥereḇ)* (Ezk. 38:4). Here, too, the weapons are cited in the order defensive-offensive.

Such weaponry sequences often include other military devices. In 2 K. 19:32 (par. Isa. 37:33), Yahweh promises concerning the king of Assyria: "He shall not come into this city, shoot an arrow *(ḥēṣ)* there, come before it with a shield *(māg̱ēn),* or cast up a siege-ramp against it." This catalog moves from small arrows to larger shields and ends with great siege-works *(sōlᵉlâ).* The oracle in Isa. 22:6 similarly looks forward to failed battle against Jerusalem; the text is difficult, but reference to quivers *('ašpâ),* chariotry *(reḵeḇ),* and shields *(māg̱ēn)* is clear (cf. Ezk. 38:4).

Only one of the panoply catalogs with *māg̱ēn* cites more offensive than defensive weapons. Ezk. 39:9 lists the weaponry which the Israelites will destroy after God has vanquished Gog. The list opens with the general weaponry term *nēšeq* and then specifies *māg̱ēn* and *ṣinnâ;* the four offensive weapons end the list: *qešeṯ, ḥiṣṣîm, maqqēl yāḏ,* and *rōmaḥ.* The mode of destruction is burning, but it cannot be supposed that this means that all or any of the weapons was flammable. The Assyrian panoply listed in Jdt. 9:7 is largely offensive. The remaining panoply catalogs are largely defensive. Jer. 46:3f. includes two sets of three terms. The first triad opens with *māg̱ēn* and *ṣinnâ* and ends with the generic weaponry designation *milḥāmâ,* while the second begins and ends with defensive weapons, *kôḇaʿ* and *širyôn,* and includes *rōmaḥ* in the middle. Ezk. 23:24 also cites defensive weapons only: *māg̱ēn, ṣinnâ, qôḇaʿ* (cf. also Ezk. 38:5).

A number of these panoply catalogs occur in the same context, and the differences between them may offer information concerning the course of battle. In Jeremiah's description of the battle of Carchemish (Jer. 46), the Egyptian army is rendered first in full panoply and later, as defeat grows closer, only with light weaponry. The wars of Gog show the opposite arrangement (cf. Ezk. 38). Finally, an unusual panoply catalog is enumerated in Ezk. 23:24. Oholibah's lovers, whom she once paid for making love to her, now take up arms against her, yet the arms are exclusively defensive (*māg̱ēn* is included; cf. Jer. 46:3; Ezk. 38:4,5).

3. *Decoration.* The advantages of using precious metal to make decorations which serve at the same time to store the metal prompted Solomon to deck the House of the Forest of Lebanon with gold shields. The text mentions three hundred *māg̱innîm* of beaten gold, each with 3 minas of gold on it, according to 1 K. 10:17 (*ca.* 150 shekels, *ca.* 1.7 kg. [3.7 lb.]). The Chronicler in a burst of modest pious exaggeration gives the

---

36. Cf. IV.1.

amount of gold per small shield as 300 shekels (*ca.* 3.4 kg. [7.6 lb.]; 2 Ch. 9:16). Solomon complemented this treasure with two hundred large shields, each with 600 shekels of beaten gold (1 K. 10:16 MT; LXX has three hundred large shields of 300 shekels each; 2 Ch. 9:15 follows MT). This large shield *(ṣinnâ)* was probably four times as large as a *māgēn* and bore four times the gold. Solomon used gold in other decorations in his hall (1 K. 10:18-21)[37] to such an extent that the historian in 1 K. 10:21 dizzily reports that in Solomon's time silver was thought of as "any old thing" *(mᵉ'ûmmâ).* The shield collection, with 1860 kilograms (4180 lb.) of gold, clearly dominated the scene. The biblical text is not clear on the point, but it is likely the metal took the form of a facing that covered the area of the shield's frame or core, rather than constituting the shield as such.[38]

During the invasion of 918, Pharaoh Shishak (Sheshonq I) took amid his plunder these gold shields (1 K. 14:26 par. 2 Ch. 12:9); although only the *māginnîm* are mentioned, he probably took the large shields as well. Rehoboam then replaced this loss with *māginnê nᵉḥōšeṯ,* "bronze shields" (1 K. 14:27 par. 2 Ch. 12:10). These actually were intended for military use, since the palace runners, who kept guard at the palace gate, used them. In addition, whenever the king went to the temple, the runners would carry the shields; thereafter they would be returned to the runners' chamber (*tā',* the location of this room in the palace or the House of the Forest of Lebanon is obscure; 1 K. 14:28 par. 2 Ch. 12:11). This great weapon collection may have been what the Chronicler had in mind in his story of Athaliah's overthrow,[39] but the association with David is hardly precise; the odd report of 1 S. 17:54 may have been influential.

The tradition of shield decoration makes its first appearance in the Chronicler's story of the tenth century. It reappears a little over a hundred years later in a confused report of Joash's succession. A century later, the Chronicler alludes to another hoard of wealth, this one belonging to Hezekiah, who "made for himself treasuries for silver, for gold, for precious stones, for spices, for shields [MT contra BHS], and for all kinds of costly objects" (2 Ch. 32:27). The parallel passages in the Deuteronomistic history were not interested in these treasuries.

A related phenomenon is the payment of client-kingdom tribute in the form of a shield. A gold *aspís,* weighing 1000 minas (= 571 kg. [1260 lbs.]), sealed the alliance of Simon Maccabee with Rome (1 Mc. 14:24; 15:18,20).[40]

4. *Testudo Fortifications.* Shields were arrayed around the tops of city towers and battlements during sieges to provide a flexible screen for the city's defenders.[41] The Romans called such a screen a testudo. In his oracle on the great ship Tyre, Ezekiel likens the city to a testudo. After the initial ship metaphor has been sketched, the prophet

---

37. → כסא *kissē'* (VII, 232-259).
38. Cf. Snodgrass, *Early Greek Armor and Weapons,* 23-25.
39. Cf. IV.1.
40. Cf. J. A. Goldstein, *I Maccabees. AB,* XLI (1976), 496.
41. Cf. III.2.

expands on the decoration of the city, which is largely martial in nature. Foreign soldiers hung (*tillû*) their shield (*māgēn*) and helmet in the city (Ezk. 27:10). The Arvadites occupied the city walls, Gamadites the towers: "They hung their shields *(šeleṭ)* all around your walls; they made perfect your beauty" (Ezk. 27:11). The prophet goes on to describe Tyre's other wealth, but pride of place is given to the shields. Whereas in Solomon's palace shields were symbols and economic guarantees of national peace, in Tyre they are functional, hung on testudo screens, ready for war.

5. *"Shield Bearer."* Shields are associated with certain groups of warriors. Although the specific functions of the various troop divisions cannot always be determined exactly, occasionally the appellation already suggests a specific function. The eleventh-century army of Reubenites, Gadites, and transjordanian Manassites included (a) *bᵉnê-ḥayil,* "soldiers"; (b) *'ᵃnāšîm nōśᵉ'ê māḡēn wᵉḥereḇ,* "men who bore shield and sword"; (c) *dōrᵉḵê qešeṯ,* "archers"; and (d) *lᵉmûḏê milḥāmâ,* "students of weaponry" (or perhaps "of war") (1 Ch. 5:18). Group (c) was certainly a distinct class; group (b) seems mixed, since swordsmen did not usually bear shields. Group (a), considering the generic nature of the term, probably included all soldiers, while group (d) designates only those with special skills.

The late tenth-century army of King Asa included (a) a Judean force of *ḥayil nōśē' ṣinnâ wārōmaḥ,* "troops that bore the large shield and spear," (b) a Benjaminite force of *nōśᵉ'ê māḡēn,* "shield bearers," and (c) *dorᵉḵê qešeṯ,* "archers" (2 Ch. 14:7[8]). These three groups are described in consonance with archaeological data. Groups (b) and (c) were used together. The tribal specialization of the forces may reflect ancient tradition. Cf. in this context 2 Ch. 17:17f., according to which the army of Jehoshaphat included Benjaminite *nōšᵉqê-qešeṯ ûmāḡēn,* "bearers of bow and buckler," and *ḥᵃlûṣê ṣāḇā',* "those equipped for war." This second group is difficult to identify more precisely (cf. Jer. 46:9; Ezk. 38:4,5).

Metaphorical usage of such terms is alien to the OT, although Sir. 37:5 claims that a true friend is one who "bears the small shield *(aspída)* against the enemy" of the recipient of Ben Sira's wisdom.

6. *Metaphors of Human Opposition to God.* Human opposition to God is sometimes treated in the language of warfare. In Ps. 76, God, who dwells in Salem-Zion, shatters "bow, shield, sword, and other weapons of war *(milḥāmâ),*" all belonging to an unspecified invader of the holy mountain (v. 4[3]). In his second discourse (Job 15), Eliphaz offers a piece of wisdom for which he claims the seal of tradition. The wicked oppressor lives in torment because "he stretched out his hand against El, against Shaddai he tried his strength; he ran against him stubbornly *(bᵉṣawwā'r)* with his thick-bossed shield *(gabbê māḡinnāyw)*" (Job 15:25-26; the Hebrew is plural — perhaps of majesty). In this case, as in the first, opposition to God is unsuccessful.

7. *Metaphors of Divine Warfare.* People who oppose God with human weaponry fail, but God can take up such weapons with success. Ps. 35:1-3 reads: "Contend, Yahweh, with those who contend with me; fight against those who fight against me!

Take hold of buckler *(māḡēn)* and shield *(ṣinnâ),* and rise up to help me. Draw lance *(ḥ^{a}nîṯ)* and battle-ax *(s^{e}ḡōr;* cf. 1QM 5:7) against my pursuers." Yahweh is here described as a first-millennium lance warrior, holding in his left hand a shield and in his right, a pike. The joint use of two terms for each implement warns against excessive concretization. This portrayal of a weapon-laden Yahweh may also have seemed quite alien to the psalmist, for he shifts to the passive voice in Ps. 35:4 and finally even views Yahweh's messenger at work (vv. 5-6; cf. Dt. 33:29). The Wisdom of Solomon also speaks of Yahweh's weapons (Wis. 5:17-22; cf. Eph. 6:10-17). The deity grasps first his defensive weapons and thereafter his sword, bow, and sling. The last of the defensive weapons is the *aspís,* "small shield," which is described as "invincible" *(akatamáchēton),* since it is God's "holiness" *(hosiótēta)* (Wis. 5:19).

8. *Metaphors of Human Wickedness.* In the climactic lines of Hos. 4, the prophet denounces Ephraim as a *ḥ^{a}ḇûr '^{a}ṣabbîm,* "confederate of idols," who is consequently given to sexual promiscuity (vv. 17-19). The greatest objection to this pattern of idolatrous behavior is not its illicit effects, but the pointlessness of it. In the difficult concluding lines, the prophet shows that Yahweh is stronger than the idols Ephraim worships. "He [Yahweh] constrains the Iniquity with its shields, the Spirit of Desire [read *'iwwāṯâ*] with its wings (scil., skirts)."[42] The cult figure described here is called first a *qālôn,* "iniquity," and then specified as a "spirit of desire." Its most arresting feature is its vesture: shields and wings, perhaps a description of flowing robes.

9. *Testudo Metaphors.* The testudo is the source of two metaphors, one of great power, the other of great beauty. The description of Leviathan (Job 40:25–41:26[41:1-34])[43] includes a detailed evocation of the creature's body, with particular attention to its back. According to 41:7[15], its back (read *gē[']wô*[44]) is a row of shields *(māḡinnîm),* a formation closed with a signet's seal. No space comes between them (read *rewaḥ*), and they are so closely bound that they cannot be separated (v. 8[16]). The image here is clearly of a tightly joined testudo, either on a stationary screen or in mobile formation. The poet of Job has enhanced beyond comprehension the notion of invincible military might in order to describe adequately this creature's power.

The testudo in Canticles is a more astonishing image. Ch. 4 opens with a catalog of feminine charms, proceeding from eyes like doves to hair like mountain goats and teeth like pregnant ewes, to lips, mouth, and cheek. The description of the neck evokes a testudo: "Your neck is like the tower of David, built in courses; on it hang a thousand bucklers *(māḡēn),* all of them shields *(šilṭê)* of warriors." Marvin H. Pope has suggested that "the erect and bold carriage of the lady's bespangled neck is likened to a commanding tower adorned with trophies of war. . . . with multiple layers remarkably

---

42. Cf. F. I. Andersen and D. N. Freedman, *Hosea. AB,* XXIV (1980), *in loc.* A completely different interpretation is offered by H. W. Wolff, *Hosea. Herm* (Eng. trans. 1974); W. Rudolph, *Hosea. KAT,* XIII/1 (1966).

43. → לויתן *liwyāṯān* (504-9).

44. So M. H. Pope, *Job. AB,* XV (^{3}1979), 339.

resembling courses of masonry."[45] This is nearly but not quite accurate. Shields were not hung on the towers as trophies, but on temporary wooden frames above the towers as a testudo in preparation for warfare.

V. Qumran. The richest war literature in the ancient dialects of Hebrew is found in 1QM. This scroll refers often and in detail to the shields and their use in the eschatological battle. The first shield mentioned (5:1) is that of the leader *(nāśî')* of the community; it is inscribed with his name, together with the names of Israel, Levi, Aaron, and the twelve tribes. The text is corrupt at the decisive point, and the lacuna may have contained *'wt* instead of *mgn.* According to 1QM 5:4, the basic infantry soldiers are holding *mgny nḥwšt mrwqh km'šh mr't pnym,* "bronze shields, polished like mirrors" (cf. 1 Mc. 6:39) with borders of interlaced and inlaid ornamentation. The border was probably an artistic design wrought of gold, silver, and bronze, with precious stones. The shield is 2.5 cubits long and 1.5 cubits wide (i.e., about 1 m. by .75 m. [3.5 ft. by 2.5 ft.]).

In the narration of battle that follows, the infantry attacks from a fixed position, using darts *(šᵉlāṭîm),*[46] an attack thought to reduce the enemy force considerably. Two infantry divisions then move forward to finish off the enemy troops; one of these divisions is armed with *ḥᵃnîṯ ûmāḡēn,* "spear and shield," the other with *māḡēn wᵉḵîḏôn,* "shield and lance" (1QM 6:5). It is not clear from the text whether any distinction was made between *ḥᵃnîṯ* and *kîḏôn.* In contrast to the foot soldier's rectangular shield, the cavalry carried *māḡinnê 'eḡlâ,* "round shields" (1QM 6:15).

Judging from 1QM 9, the Qumranites were also familiar with the testudo. They called them "towers," and used them to secure the flanks of unprotected troops. These towers were formed of shields similar to those carried by the infantry. Each testudo included three hundred shields, one hundred on each side. The text describes a series of four such formations, i.e., twelve hundred shields moving together. Each shield in the first testudo (on the south) is labelled "Michael"; in the second (east), "Gabriel"; in the third (north), "Sariel"; and in the fourth (west), "Raphael" (1QM 9:12-14).

There is little doubt that Roman military tactics informed this portrayal. Whether the weaponry can be identified with Roman equivalents is less clear. Yigael Yadin has suggested identifying the infantry shield as the *scutum,*[47] whereas the cavalry carried the lighter *clipeus* or the *parma.*

A specialized use of *māḡēn* appears in the psalms of Qumran. The speaker at one point compares himself in his relationship with God to one who has entered a fortified city, which no stranger *(zār)* can invade. For the gates of the city are *dalṯê māḡēn,* "gates of strength" (lit., "of the shield"), "and there is no entering them; their bars are firm and cannot be broken" (1QH 6:27). The extension in meaning from the concrete to abstract is not an unusual phenomenon, but it is associated with *māḡēn* only here.

---

45. *Song of Songs. AB,* VII C (1977), 465, 468.
46. Cf. VI.2.
47. Cf. J. van der Ploeg, *Le Rouleau de la Guerre. STDJ,* 2 (1959), 90-94.

VI. Synonyms and Related Terms.

1. *ṣinnâ.* The etymology of the term *ṣinnâ* is obscure. This full-length shield is mentioned 20 times in the OT, 10 of these together with *māḡēn* (cf. 1 K. 10:16[twice]; 2 Ch. 9:15[twice];[48] 2 Ch. 14:7;[49] Ps. 35:2;[50] Jer. 46:3; Ezk. 23:24; 38:4; 39:9.[51] The remaining 10 occurrences by and large fit the categories outlined above: 2 Ch. 11:12; 25:5 can be added to IV.2. Ezk. 26:8 is a related text which mentions, along with one offensive *(ḥereḇ)* and one defensive weapon *(ṣinnâ),* other war materiel as well: *sōlᵉlâ; dāyēq,* "bulwark"; *mᵉḥî,* "battering ram" (v. 9); and *sûsîm,* "horses" (v. 10). 1 Ch. 12:9 can be added to IV.5.[52] 1 Ch. 12:35[34] mentions *ṣinnâ* and *ḥᵃnîṯ* together. 1 S. 17:7,41 mention a single *ṣinnâ*-bearer. Both Ps. 5:13[12] (Yahweh's *rāṣôn,* "good will," enwraps the righteous person like a shield) and 91:4 (Yahweh hides his faithful in his wings, and his fidelity is *ṣinnâ wᵉsōḥērâ;* the last word is a hapax legomenon, apparently another word for "body shield"[53]) can be added to IV.7. The large shield of faith is also mentioned in Eph. 6:16.

2. *šeleṭ.* The word *šeleṭ* is obscure; derivation from Akk. *šalāṭu* and Arab. *salaṭa,* "to be powerful," is highly unlikely. The word occurs 7 times in the OT, 3 times together with *māḡēn:* 2 Ch. 23:9;[54] Ezk. 27:11;[55] Cant. 4:4.[56]

The text of 2 Ch. 23:9 is a duplicate of 2 K. 11:10, except that the latter does not use *māḡēn.* The retention of *šeleṭ* in both texts suggests that it replaced *māḡēn* in the postexilic texts (cf., however, the evidence from Qumran). Jer. 51:11 belongs with the texts of IV.2 above: *šeleṭ* is accompanied by *ḥiṣṣîm,* "arrows," and by the verb *mālē',* "to fill," and this fact has suggested that here *šeleṭ* means "quiver."[57] The decorative treasures discussed in IV.3 should be joined by those in 2 S. 8:7 par. 1 Ch. 18:7, a scene in which David plunders *šilṭê hazzāhāḇ,* "shields [?] of gold," from Hadadezer's Aramean kingdom of Zobah. Two additional factors obscure the meaning of *šeleṭ.* The word has an entirely different sense in 1QM than in the OT.[58] Further, the LXX translators were at best confused about the word, since they rendered it five ways in seven texts.[59]

Freedman — O'Connor

---

48. Cf. IV.3.
49. Cf. IV.5.
50. Cf. IV.7.
51. Cf. IV.2.
52. *BHS/BHK* read *'rky ṣnh wrmḥ,* but many editions prefer *'ōrḵê ṣinnâ ûmāḡēn;* cf. also 1 Ch. 12:25.
53. Cf. A. A. Macintosh, "Psalm XCI 4 and the Root סחר," *VT,* 23 (1973), 56-62.
54. IV.1.
55. IV.4.
56. IV.9.
57. Cf. R. Borger, "Die Waffenträger des Königs Darius," *VT,* 22 (1972), 385-398: "bow-case."
58. Cf. V above.
59. Cf. *AB,* VII C, 469.

VII. māḡēn or *mōḡēn?*

1. *Divine Epithet.* God is described as *māḡēn* 15 times in the OT (Gen. 15:1; 12 times in the Psalms [1 additional occurrence, Ps. 84:10(9), is ambiguous]; and twice in Proverbs). The various contexts suggest how this usage was understood. In Ps. 3:4[3], the psalmist addresses Yahweh as his *māḡēn,* his glory *(kᵉḇôḏ),* and the lifter of his head. In Ps. 7:11[10], God is the highest,[60] the psalmist's *māḡēn* and savior *(môšîaʿ).* Yahweh as the psalmist's strength and *māḡēn* is the object of trust in Ps. 28:7. Ps. 18:3[2] enumerates a series of epithets: rock *(selaʿ),* fortress *(mᵉṣûḏâ),* deliverer *(mᵉpalleṭ),* rock *(ṣûr), māḡēn,* horn of salvation, refuge *(miśgāḇ);* 2 S. 22:3 adds refuge *(mānôs)* and savior *(môšîaʿ).* Ps. 144:1f. offers a similar series (*ṣûr, mᵉlammēḏ, ḥeseḏ, mᵉṣûḏâ, miśgāḇ, mᵉpallēṭ, māḡēn,* "in whom I take refuge"). In Ps. 18:31[30] par., Yahweh is a *māḡēn* for all those who take refuge in him (*ḥōsîm*; vv. 32-33[31-32]: rock and giver of strength). Ps. 119:114 mentions a hiding place (*sēṯer*) and *māḡēn.* Ps. 59:12[11] petitions "our *māḡēn*" for the destruction of enemies — whereby one should recall that the shield is not an offensive weapon. After emphasizing the insufficiency of human power and military strength, Ps. 33:20 asserts that Yahweh is both succor *(ʿēzer)* and *māḡēn;* similarly also in Ps. 115:9f.

The 2 occurrences in Proverbs state merely that Yahweh is a *māḡēn* for those who walk in integrity (Prov. 2:7) or take refuge in him (*ḥōsîm,* 30:5). In Gen. 15:1, Yahweh calls himself Abraham's *māḡēn* and promises him "great reward."

It is noteworthy that *māḡēn* is associated both with passive terms such as "protection" and "refuge" and with active terms such as "deliver" and "give." Furthermore, Ps. 84:12(11) designates Yahweh both as *māḡēn* and as sun,[61] recalling that both the Egyptian pharaoh and the Hittite monarch were referred to as the sun by their vassal princes. Claus Westermann and Otto Kaiser[62] correctly cite an oracle of Ishtar of Arbela to Esarhaddon: "Esarhaddon, in Arbela I am your gracious shield."

Ringgren

Several scholars, most recently M. Kessler and Mitchell Dahood, have considered a different interpretation of this divine epithet. The point of departure is recognition of a root *mgn,* "give, grant," common to several Semitic languages, e.g., Phoen. *mgn,* "grant,"[63] Palmyr. *mgn, "gratis,"*[64] Jewish-Aram. and Syr. *maggānāʾ, "gratis,* for nothing, in vain,"[65] Akk. *magannu,* "gift, present,"[66] Ugar. *mgn,* "confer, present

---

60. See *BHS;* L. Viganò, *Nomi e titoli di YHWH alla luce del semitico del Nord-Ovest. BietOr,* 31 (1976), 41.

61. Cf. M. Dahood, "Hebrew-Ugaritic Lexicography XI," *Bibl,* 54 (1973), 361.

62. C. Westermann, *Genesis 12–36* (Eng. trans., Minneapolis, 1985), 218; O. Kaiser, "Traditionsgeschichtliche Untersuchung von Genesis 15," *ZAW,* 70 (1958), 113; cf. also M. Rose, " 'Entmilitarisierung des Kriegs'? (Erwägungen zu den Patriarchen-Erzählungen der Genesis)," *BZ,* N.S. 20 (1976), 199.

63. *KAI,* 29, 1; *DISO,* 142; perhaps also Pun. *bʿl mgnm,* "lord of gifts," *KAI,* 178, 3.

64. *DISO,* 142.

65. Cf. F. Rundgren, "Aramaica I," *OrSuec,* 14f. (1965-66), 81-83.

66. According to *AHw,* II, 574f., this is a loanword; cf. *CAD,* X/1 (1977), 31f.

with,"[67] Heb. *miggēn,* "give, give up" (Gen. 14:20; Prov. 4:9; Hos. 11:8; cf. also 1QM 18:13).[68]

In Gen. 15:1, one could then read *'ānōḵî mōgēn lᵉḵā śᵉḵārᵉḵā harbēh mᵉ'ōḏ,* "I am about to give you your very great reward" (so Kessler), which fits well with Abraham's question in v. 2, "what will you give me?" Dahood[69] cites Pun. *magōn* as a general's title (Lat. *imperator, dux,* though the passages are questionable) and postulates a Heb. *māgān,* "suzerain," which, e.g., is combined in Ps. 84:10[9] with *māšîaḥ,* in 89:19[18] with *meleḵ,* and in 84:12[11] with *šemeš.* He cites Ps. 7:11[10]; 18:31[30]; 47:10[9]; 59:12[11]; Gen. 15:1; Prov. 2:7; 30:5 as additional witnesses to this meaning.[70]

It would be more commensurate with Hebrew usage to assume a divine epithet *mōgēn,* "he who gives or grants." Participles occur frequently as divine epithets, e.g., in the Song of Hannah in 1 S. 2: *mēmîṯ, mᵉḥayyeh, môrîḏ, môrîš, maʿᵃšîr, mašpîl, mᵉrômēm.* This meaning is certainly possible in the previously mentioned passages from the psalms, and would be particularly appropriate in those cases in which God appears as an active participant.

2. *Descriptions of Persons.* In some cases this title is also applied to persons. If one translates Ps. 84:10[9], "Behold our donor (*mōgēn,* MT *māgēn*), O God; look on the face of your anointed," then *mgn* would parallel *māšiaḥ* and refer to the king. Similarly Ps. 89:19[18]: "For our 'donor' belongs to Yahweh, our king to the Holy One of Israel." Ps. 47:10[9] speaks of the princes of the earth *(mgny-'ereṣ)* as belonging to God; its parallel is *nᵉḏîḇê ʿammîm.*

Three additional texts are uncertain. 2 S. 1:21b, "For there the *mgn* of the mighty was defiled, the *mgn* [of] Saul, anointed with oil no more" might be rendered "the donor of the mighty" or "the donor Saul."[71] Nowhere else is Saul's shield mentioned, and the notion of anointing shields is uncertain. The word *mgn* must refer to a person. A banquet scene in Isa. 21:5 issues a "call to weapons": "Rise up, O officers, oil a shield!" Since the oiling of shields is otherwise unattested (see preceding discussion), the reference may be to the consecration of a leader. The reference to the red coloring of the *mgn* of Nineveh's heroes or warriors in Nah. 2:4[3] is extremely obscure. Does this refer to red clothes[72] and red shields,[73] or to red skin coloring[74]?

When the assertion is made in Prov. 6:11; 24:34 that poverty will come upon the

---

67. *WUS,* no. 1513.

68. Cf. F. Asensio, "La bondad de Dios en su papel de escudo a través de las paginas del AT," *EstBíb,* 9 (1950), 441-460.

69. *Psalms 1–50. AB,* XVI (1965), 16f.; cf. also Deist, 100ff.

70. For further discussion, see M. O'Connor, "Yahweh the Donor," *Aula Orientalis,* 8 (1988), 46-70; *idem,* "Semitic *mgn and its Supposed Sanskrit Origin," *JAOS,* 109 (1989), 25-32.

71. The text is uncertain; see D. N. Freedman, "The Refrain in David's Lament over Saul and Jonathan," *Ex Orbe Religionum. Festschrift G. Widengren. SNumen,* 21 (1972), 122 = *Pottery, Poetry, and Prophecy* (Winona Lake, 1980), 122f..

72. M. Dahood, "Northwest Semitic Notes on Genesis," *Bibl,* 55 (1974), 78.

73. K. J. Cathcart, *Nahum in the Light of Northwest Semitic. BietOr,* 26 (1973), 86f.

74. *KTU,* 1.14 IV, 203-8.

sluggard like an *'îš māgēn,* it is noteworthy that a defensive weapon is used in connection with an attack. Older interpretation holds that the expression "one armed with a shield" characterizes the attacker as a "highway bandit who comes unexpectedly."[73] Recent interpretation often cites Ugar. *mōgēn* or *maggān* and reads "beggar."[74]

VIII. LXX. The translators of the LXX apparently had no concrete notion of these shields. Ten different words are used to render the 20 occurrences of *ṣinnâ,* e.g., *thyreós* (11 times), *dóry, kóntos* (both meaning "spear") (1 K. 10:16; Ezk. 39:9). The rendering of *mgn* is more consistent: *thyreós* (9 times), *aspís* and *péltē* (5 times each). In 3 instances an abstract translation is used: 2 S. 22:36 (par. Ps. 18:36[35]) *hyperaspismós*; Dt. 33:29 uses a form of *hyperaspízein.* The divine epithet *hyperaspistēs* is used in 2 S. 22:3,31 (par. Ps. 18:3,31[2,30]); Ps. 28:7; 33:20; 59:12[11]; 115:9-11; 144:2. Forms of *hyperaspízein* occur in Gen. 15:1; Prov. 2:7; 30:5; *antilḗmptōr* in Ps. 3:4[3]; 119:114; *boḗtheia* in Ps. 7:11[10]. 1 S. 1:21; Isa. 21:5 attest *thyreós;* Nah. 2:4[3] *hóplon.* In contrast, Ps. 84:10[9] attests *hyperaspístēs,* Ps. 89:19[18] *antílēpsis,* and Ps. 47:10[9] *krataiós.*

Freedman — O'Connor

75. G. Wildeboer, *Die Sprüche. KHC,* XV (1897), 18.

76. W. F. Albright, "Some Canaanite-Phoenician Sources of Hebrew Wisdom," *Wisdom in Israel and in the Ancient Near East. Festschrift H. H. Rowley. SVT,* 3 (1955), 9f.; so also *KBL*[3].

מִדְבָּר *miḏbār;* עֲרָבָה *ʿarāḇâ*

Contents: I. Etymology. II. Meaning. III. Occurrences: 1. *miḏbār;* 2. *ʿarāḇâ;* 3. Other Synonyms; 4. Antonyms; 5. Parts of the *miḏbār.* IV. Usage: 1. Spatial Dimension; 2. *miḏbār* as an Ecological Term; 3. Place of Refuge. V. Historico-spatial Dimension Between the Exodus and Conquest. VI. Theological Connotations: 1. General Considerations; 2. History of Scholarship. VII. OT Usage: 1. Time-Space Connotations; 2. Two Stages in the Wilderness Wanderings; 3. Motif Variations. VIII. Qumran.

miḏbār. S. Abramsky, "The House of Rechab," *Festschrift E. L. Sukenik. ErIsr,* 8 (1967), 255-264 [Heb.]; Y. Aharoni, "דרכי המדבר בתקופת המקרא," *Sefer Tur-Sinai* (Jerusalem, 1991), 43-46; *idem,* "Forerunners of the Limes: Iron Age Fortresses in the Negev," *IEJ,* 17 (1967), 1-17; *idem* and J. Naseh, *Arad Inscriptions* (Eng. trans., Jerusalem, 1981); W. F. Albright, "Primitivism in Ancient Western Asia," in A. O. Lovejoy, *et al.,* eds., *A Documentary History of Primitivism,* I (Baltimore, 1935), 421-432; J. M. Allegro, *Qumrân Cave 4. DJD,* V (1968), 42-49, 53-57; W. M. Alston, Jr., *The Concept of the Wilderness in the Intertestamental Period* (diss., Union Theological Seminary in Virginia, 1868); B. W. Anderson, "The Book of Hosea," *Int,* 8 (1954), 290-303; *idem,* "Exodus Typology in Second Isaiah," *Israel's Prophetic Heritage. Festschrift J. Muilenburg* (New York, 1962), 177-195; R. T. Anderson, "The Role of the Desert in Israelite Thought," *JBR,* 27 (1959), 41-44; R. Bach, *Die Erwählung Israels in der Wüste* (diss., Bonn, 1951); B. Baentsch, *Die Wüste, ihre Namen und ihre bildliche Anwendung in den alttesta-*

mentlichen Schriften (diss., Halle, 1883); D. Baly, The Geography of the Bible (New York, 21974); C. Barth, "Zur Bedeutung der Wüstentradition," Volume de Congrès, Genève 1965. SVT, 15 (1966), 14-23; M. Y. Ben-Gavriêl, "Das nomadische Ideal in der Bibel," Stimmen der Zeit, 88/171 (1962/63), 253-263; P. L. Berger, "The Sociological Study of Sectarianism," Social Research, 21 (1954), 467; K. H. Bernhardt, "Nomadentum und Ackerbaukultur in der frühstaatlichen Zeit Altisraels," VIOF, 69 (1969), 31-40; W. Beyerlin, Origins and History of the Oldest Sinaitic Traditions (Eng. trans., Oxford, 1966); A. Biram, Sefer Orbakh (Jerusalem, 1955), 116-139; P. Bonnard, "La significance du désert selon le NT," Natur und Geist. Festschrift K. Barth, Hors série 2 (Zurich, 1946), 9-18; W. H. Brownlee, "John the Baptist in the New Light of Ancient Scrolls," in K. Stendahl, ed., The Scrolls and the NT (New York, 1957), 33-53; H. Bückers, "Zur Verwertung der Sinaitraditionen in den Psalmen," Bibl, 32 (1951), 401-422; K. Budde, "The Nomadic Ideal in the OT," New World, 4 (1895), 726-745; idem, Religion of Israel to the Exile. American Lectures on the History of Religions, ser. 4 (New York, 1899), 17ff.; R. P. Carroll, "Rebellion and Dissent in Ancient Israelite Society, ZAW, 89 (1977), 176-204; U. Cassuto, "הנביא הושע וספרי התורה," Festschrift Chajes (Vienna, 1930), 202ff.; A. Causse, Du groupe ethnique à la communauté religieuse (Paris, 1937), 15-31; D. J. Chitty, The Desert a City: An Introduction to the Study of Egyptian and Palestinian Monasticism under the Christian Empire (Oxford, 1966); G. W. Coats, "Conquest Traditions in the Wilderness Theme," JBL, 95 (1976), 177-190; idem, "An Exposition for the Wilderness Traditions," VT, 22 (1972), 288-295; idem, Rebellion in the Wilderness (Nashville, 1968); idem, "The Wilderness Itinerary," CBQ, 34 (1972), 135-152; R. Cohen, "The Excavations at Kadesh-barnea 1976-1978," BA, 44 (1981), 93-107; idem and W. G. Dever, "Preliminary Report of the Pilot Season of the 'Central Negev Highlands Project,' " BASOR, 232 (1978), 29-45; idem, "Preliminary Report of the Second Season [etc.]," BASOR, 236 (1979), 41-60; idem, "Preliminary Report of the Third and Final Season [etc.]," BASOR, 243 (1981), 57-77; J. C. Craviotti, "El Sinai Biblico," RivBiblCalz, 30 (1968), 77-82, 135-142; 31 (1969), 1-9; F. M. Cross, Jr., The Ancient Library of Qumran and Modern Biblical Studies (1958, repr. Grand Rapids, 1980); M. Dahood, Psalms I–III. AB, XVI, XVII, XVII A (1966-1970); J. Daniélou, The Dead Sea Scrolls and Primitive Christianity (Eng. trans., New York, 1958, repr. 1979), 16ff.; M. Delcor, "Quelques cas de survivances du vocabulaire nomade en hébreu biblique," VT, 25 (1975), 307-322; F. Delitzsch, Die Lese- und Schreibfehler im AT (Berlin, 1920); S. J. de Vries, "The Origin of the Murmuring Tradition," JBL, 87 (1968), 51-58; M. Dothan, "The Fortress of Kadesh-Barnea," IEJ, 15 (1965), 134-151; G. R. Driver, CML; A. Dupont-Sommer, The Essene Writings from Qumran (Eng. trans. 1961, repr. Gloucester, Mass., 1973); D. O. Edzard, "Altbabylonisch nawûm," ZA, N.S. 19 (1959), 168-173; O. Eissfeldt, "Das Gesetz ist zwischeneingekommen: Ein Beitrag zur Analyse der Sinai-Erzählung Ex 19–34," ThLZ, 91 (1966), 1-6 = KlSchr, IV (1968), 209-214; idem, "Die Komposition der Sinai-Erzählung Ex. 19–34," FuF, 40 (1966), 213-15 = KLSchr, IV (1968), 231-37; M. Eliade, Birth and Rebirth (Eng. trans., New York, 1958); I. Eph'al, The Ancient Arabs: Nomads on the Borders of the Fertile Crescent, 9th-5th Centuries B.C. (Jerusalem, 1982); J. W. Flight, "The Nomadic Idea and Ideal in the OT," JBL, 42 (1923), 158-226; M. V. Fox, "Jeremiah 2:2 and the 'Desert Ideal,' " CBQ, 35 (1973), 441-450; F. S. Frick, The City in Ancient Israel. SBL DissSer, 36 (Missoula, 1977), 209ff.; idem, "The Rechabites Reconsidered," JBL, 90 (1971), 279-287; V. Fritz, Israel in der Wüste. MarThSt, 7 (1970); R. W. Funk, "The Wilderness," JBL, 78 (1959), 205-214; T. H. Gaster, Thespis (New York, 1950); L. Gautier, A propos des Récabites (Lausanne, 1927); H. Gese, "Bemerkungen zur Sinaitradition," ZAW, 79 (1967), 137-154; ThLZ, 92 (1967), 245f.; N. Glueck, Explorations in Eastern Palestine, IV. AASOR, 25-28 (1945-49 [1951]); N. K. Gottwald, "Domain Assumptions and Societal Models in the Study of Pre-Monarchic Israel," Congress Volume, Edinburgh 1974. SVT, 28 (1975), 89-100; idem, The Tribes of Yahweh (Maryknoll, N.Y., 1979); J. Gray, "The Desert God 'Aṯtar in the Literature and Religion of Canaan," JNES, 8 (1949), 72-83; idem, "The Desert Sojourn of the Hebrews and the Sinai-Horeb Tradition," VT, 4 (1954), 148-154; K. Gross, Die literarische Verwandtschaft Jeremias mit Hosea (diss., Berlin, 1930); A. Haldar, The Notion of the Desert in

Sumero-Accadian and West-Semitic Religions. UUÅ, 1950/3; N. Hareuveni, אור חדש על ספר ירמיהו (Jerusalem, 1953); P. Humbert, "La logique de la perspective nomade chez Osée et l'unité de Osée II,4-22," *Vom AT. Festschrift K. Marti. BZAW,* 41 (1925), 158-166; *idem,* "Osée, le prophète bédouin," *RHPR,* 1 (1921), 97-118; E. Jacob, "L'héritage cananéen dans le livre du prophète Osée," *RHPR,* 43 (1963), 250-59; Y. Kaufmann, תולדות האמונה הישראלית, I/2 (Tel Aviv, 1937) = *The Religion of Israel* (Eng. trans. [abridged], Chicago, 1960); G. Kittel, "ἔρημος," *TDNT,* II, 657-660; R. Kittel, *Great Men and Movements in Israel* (Eng. trans., London, 1925) [preface]; J.-R. Kupper, *Les nomades en Mésopotamie en temps des rois de Mari* (Paris, 1957); G. Lanczkowsky, *Altägyptischer Prophetismus. ÄgAbh,* 4 (1960); V. Maag, "Malkût JHWH," *Congress Volume, Oxford 1959. SVT,* 7 (1960), 129-153 = *Kultur, Kulturkontakt und Religion* (Göttingen, 1980), 145-169; C. C. McCown, "The Scene of John's Ministry and Its Relation to the Purpose and Outcome of His Mission," *JBL,* 59 (1940), 113-131; S. McKenzie, "Exodus Typology in Hosea," *Restoration Quarterly,* 22 (1979), 100-8; A. Malamat, "Aspects of Tribal Societies in Mari and Israel," *Rencontre Assyriologique Internationale* (Liège, 1966), 129-138; *idem,* "Mari and the Bible: Some Patterns of Tribal Organization and Institutions," *JAOS,* 82 (1962), 143-150; H. H. Mallau, *Die theologische Bedeutung der Wüste im AT* (diss., Kiel, 1963); U. W. Mauser, *Christ in the Wilderness. SBT,* 39 (1963), 15-52; B. Meissner, *Die babylonisch-assyrische Literatur* (Potsdam, 1927); G. E. Mendenhall, *The Tenth Generation* (Baltimore, 1973); Z. Meshel and C. Meyers, "The Name of God in the Wilderness of Zin," *BA,* 39 (1976), 6-10; E. Meyer, *Die Israeliten und ihre Nachbarstämme* (1906, repr. Darmstadt, 1967), 129-141; J. A. Montgomery, *Arabia and the Bible* (1934, repr. New York, 1969); S. Moscati, *Ancient Semitic Civilizations* (Eng. trans., New York, 1957); *idem, The Semites in Ancient History* (Cardiff, 1959), 91ff.; E. W. Nicholson, *Exodus and Sinai in History and Tradition* (Richmond, 1973); M. Noth, *Überlieferungsgeschichtliche Studien,* I (Tübingen, 1943), 91ff. = *The Deuteronomistic History. JSOTSup,* 15 (Eng. trans. 1981), 84ff.; *idem, Die Ursprünge des alten Israel im Lichte neuer Quellen. AFNW,* 94 (1961); S. Nyström, *Beduinentum und Jahwismus* (diss., Lund, 1946); E. O. Oren, "Ziklag — A Biblical City on the Edge of the Negev," *BA,* 45 (1982), 155-166; J. Pedersen, *ILC,* I-II, 454ff.; III-IV, 728ff.; J. N. Porter, "Genesis XIX:30-38 and the Ugaritic Text of ŠḤR and ŠLM," *Proceedings of the Seventh World Congress of Jewish Studies* (Jerusalem, 1981), 1-8; G. von Rad, "The Wandering in the Wilderness," *OT Theology,* I (Eng. trans., New York, 1962), 280-89; P. A. Riemann, *Desert and Return to Desert in the Pre-exilic Prophets* (diss., Harvard, 1964); B. Rothenberg, צפונות נגב (Ramat-Gan, 1967); M. Sæbo, "Grenzbeschreibung und Landideal im AT Mit besonderer Berücksichtigung der min-ʿad Formel," *ZDPV,* 90 (1974), 14-37; J. Schildenberger, "Psalm 78(77) und die Pentateuchquellen," *Lex tua veritas. Festschrift H. Junker* (Trier, 1961), 231-256; W. Schmauch, *Orte der Offenbarung und der Offenbarungsort im NT* (Göttingen, 1956), 27-47; J. M. Schmidt, "Erwägungen zum Verhältnis von Auszugs- und Sinaitradition," *ZAW,* 82 (1970), 1-31; A. Schwarzenbach, *Die geographische Terminologie im Hebräischen des ATs* (Leiden, 1954), 93-112; M. S. Seale, *The Desert Bible* (New York, 1974); P. Seidensticker, "Prophetensöhne — Rechabiter — Nasiräer," *SBFLA,* 10 (1959/1960), 65-119; E. Sellin, *Das Zwölfprophetenbuch. KAT,* XII/1 (1922); M. Smith, "On the Differences Between the Culture of Israel and the Major Cultures of the Ancient Near East," *Festschrift T. H. Gaster. JANES,* 5 (1973), 389-395; M. Soloveitchik, "'המדבר' בתולדותיו והשקפת עולמו של עם ישראל,'" דביר, II (1927), 16-45; A. P. Stanley, *Sinai and Palestine, in Connection with Their History* (London, [2]1862); A. Stock, *The Way in the Wilderness: Exodus, Wilderness and Moses Themes in the OT and New* (Collegeville, Minn., 1969); S. Talmon, "The Ancient Hebrew Alphabet and Biblical Text Criticism," *Mélanges D. Barthélemy. OBO,* 38 (1981), 497-530; *idem,* "The Biblical Concept of Jerusalem," *JES,* 8 (1971), 300-316; *idem,* "The 'Desert Motif' in the Bible and in Qumran Literature," in A. Altmann, ed., *Biblical Motifs* (Cambridge, Mass., 1966), 31-63; *idem,* "Did There Exist a Biblical National Epic?" *Proceedings of the Seventh World Congress of Jewish Studies: Studies in the Bible and the Ancient Near East* (Jerusalem, 1981), 41-61; *idem,* " 'Exil' und 'Rückkehr' in der Ideenwelt des ATs," in R. Mosis, ed., *Exil-Diaspora-Rückkehr* (Düsseldorf, 1978), 30-54; *idem,*

I. Etymology. The etymology of *midbār* is obscure. A connection with → דבר *dābār,* "word, thing, matter," is highly unlikely, and the derivation from the root *dbr,* "be behind," Arab. *dabara, dubr,* "back," Akk. *dab/pāru,* "go away, drive away"[1] is disputed. Rather, one should probably assume a connection with *dōber* (Isa. 5:17; Mic. 2:12), "drift," "pasture land," with *dibbēr* (2 Ch. 22:10) — *hidbîr* (Ps. 18:48[Eng. v. 47]; 47:4[3]), "subjugate," "subdue,"[2] and also with *rbd* (Prov. 7:16)/*rbṣ,* "lie," "crouch, cower," especially in reference to wild animals (Gen. 49:9; Isa. 11:6; 13:21; Ezk. 19:2) and grazing animals (Gen. 29:2; Isa. 13:20; 27:10; Jer. 33:12; Ezk. 34:14; Zeph. 2:14). The word is also attested in other Semitic languages: Ugar. *'rṣ dbr* with the meaning "grazing land"[3] (cf. Dt. 32:10; Prov. 21:19) or as the place name *mdbr qdš,*[4] *mlbr 'lš'y;*[5] *p't mdbr,* "wilderness"(?);[6] Official Aram. and Syr. *dabrā', mdbr';*[7] Mand. *dibra,* "field"; Safaitic *mdbr;* West Semitic loanword in Akkadian *madbaru, mud(a)baru*[8] in connection with desert tribes — *arbaya rūqūti āšibūt mad-ba-ri,* "the remote Arabs who dwell in the steppe"[9] as opposed to cultivated land;[10] as the place

"'המה הקינים הבאים מחמת אבי בית־רכב' I Chronicles II,55," *IEJ,* 10 (Eng. trans., 1960), 174-180; *idem,* "The New Covenanters of Qumran," *Scientific American,* 225/5 (1971), 72-81; *idem,* "Die Samaritaner in Vergangenheit und Gegenwert," *Frankfurter Universitätsreden,* 42 (1971), 71-83; *idem,* "The Town Lists of Simeon," *IEJ,* 15 (1965), 235-241; *idem,* "Typen der Messiaserwartung um die Zeitenwende," *Probleme biblischer Theologie. Festschrift G. von Rad* (Munich, 1971), 571-588; E. Testa, "Il deserto come ideale," *SBFLA,* 7 (1956/57), 5-52; A. C. Tunyogi, *The Rebellions of Israel* (Richmond, 1969); R. de Vaux, *AncIsr; idem, The Early History of Israel* (Eng. trans., Philadelphia, 1978); K. H. Walkenhorst, *Der Sinai im liturgischen Verständnis der deuteronomistischen und priesterlichen Tradition. BBB,* 33 (1969); W. G. E. Watson, "Fixed Pairs in Ugaritic and Isaiah," *VT,* 22 (1972), 460-68; M. Weber, *Ancient Judaism* (Eng. trans., New York, 1952); M. Weinfeld, "Jeremiah and the Spiritual Metamorphosis of Israel," *ZAW,* 88 (1976), 17-56; M. Weippert, *The Settlement of the Israelite Tribes in Palestine. SBT,* ser. 2, 21 (Eng. trans., 1971); J. Wellhausen, *Reste arabischen Heidentums* (Berlin, ²1897, repr. 1927); W. Wiebe, *Die Wüstenzeit als Typus der messianischen Heilszeit* (diss., Göttingen, 1939); G. H. Williams, *Wilderness and Paradise in Christian Thought* (New York, 1962); D. J. Wiseman, *Chronicles of the Chaldaean Kings (626-556 B.C.) in the British Museum* (London, 1956, 1961); *idem,* "They Lived in Tents," *Biblical and Near Eastern Studies. Festschrift W. S. La Sor* (Grand Rapids, 1978), 195-200; H. W. Wolff, "Das Thema 'Umkehr' in der alttestamentlichen Theologie," *ZThK,* 48 (1951), 129-148 = *GSAT. ThB,* 22 (1964), 130-150; A. S. van der Woude, *Die messianischen Vorstellungen der Gemeinde von Qumrân. SSN,* 3 (1957).

1. *AHw,* I (1965), 177; *HAL,* II (1995), 546.
2. *HAL,* I (1994), 210.
3. *KTU,* 1.6 II, 19f.; 1.5 V, 18, and elsewhere; possibly also *KTU,* 1.23, 4; 1.92, 3.
4. *KTU,* 1.23, 65.
5. *KTU,* 1.12 I, 21f.; read *mdbr* with *CTA.*
6. *KTU,* 1.23, 68; 1:14 III, 1.
7. *LexSyr,* 140.
8. *CAD,* X/I (1977), 11f.; *AHw,* II (1972), 572a.
9. A. G. Lie, *The Inscriptions of Sargon II* (Paris, 1929), 121, 124, 189; E. A. W. Budge and L. W. King, *The Annals of the Kings of Assyria* (London, 1902), 356, III, 37; Wiseman, *Chronicles of the Chaldaean Kings,* 70 rto. 10; *TCL,* 3, 193, and elsewhere.
10. H. W. F. Saggs, "The Nimrud Letters, 1952: Part II," *Iraq,* 17 (1955), 160, no. 23:12, 15; 13, 110; 436:5, 9.

name *madbar kalāma*,[11] *māt madbar* (?)[12] (cf. Ugar. *'rṣ dbr*). Akkadian usually renders "wilderness" as *ṣēru*.[13]

II. Meaning. In both Biblical and, to a certain extent, Postbiblical Hebrew and other Semitic languages the term *miḏbār* covers a wide and varied semantic field. Despite this variety, the diverse aspects of the word and its synonyms can be traced back to the following fundamental meanings. The term *miḏbār* refers to arid or semiarid regions whose scarcity of water makes them unsuitable for agriculture and farming settlements. This desolate area is yet in the primeval state of chaos (Dt. 32:10) or was reduced again to such chaos as divine punishment for human transgressions (Isa. 64:9[10]; Jer. 22:6; Hos. 2:5[3]; Zeph. 2:13; Mal. 1:3). It evokes fear and revulsion.

To a certain extent, *miḏbār* terrain is suitable as pasture land for livestock, e.g., goats and sheep. This explains the use of the word as a terminus technicus for "grazing land" surrounding a permanent or semipermanent pastoral settlement *nāweh* (= *nawûm* in the Mari texts) or adjacent to villages or towns. This aspect of *miḏbār* carries positive connotations. Pastoral romanticism and love (Cant. 3:6; 8:5) blossom in these remote pastoral settings (Jer. 9:1[2]; Ps. 55:8[7]).

The variety shown by this semantic field attests an intensive, existential-ecological, and historical *miḏbār* experience in biblical Israel which is also reflected in the Qumran documents, and in rabbinic and early Christian writings (NT and Church Fathers), where it is accompanied by modifications corresponding to the changed circumstances. At the same time, the rich use of *miḏbār* terminology on such diverse conceptual levels reveals something of the socio-historical and religious world of ideas of biblical Israel.

III. Occurrences. 1. *miḏbār.* The term *miḏbār* occurs 271 times in the OT (always in the sg.); as might be expected, it occurs almost twice as often in Numbers (48 times) as in other books: 26 times in Exodus; 24 in Samuel; 21 in Jeremiah; 20 in the Psalms; 19 in Isaiah. It is mentioned 10-20 times in Deuteronomy (19 times); Joshua (15); Ezekiel (14); Chronicles (11); less than 10 times in Judges (8); Genesis (7); Kings, Hosea, Joel (5 each); Leviticus (4); Job, Lamentations (3 each); Canticles, Nehemiah (twice each); Zephaniah, Malachi, Proverbs (once each); it does not occur in the other books. The term *miḏbār* is used 23 times absolutely (e.g., in Dt. 32:10; Job 38:26; Isa. 16:8; 32:15; 35:1; Jer. 22:6); 34 times with the definite article (Ex. 14:3; 16:10; Nu. 14:25; Dt. 1:19; 2:7; 11:24; Josh. 16:1; Jgs. 11:22); 7 times with a preposition: *lᵉmiḏbār* (Ps. 107:33), *mimmiḏbar* (*hārîm*, Ps. 75:7[6]?); 126 times with a preposition and definite article: *bammiḏbār* (Gen. 16:7; 21:20; Ex. 3:18; 5:3; Job 24:5; Isa. 40:3), *kammiḏbār* (Ps. 106:9; Hos. 2:5[3]), *lammiḏbār* (2 Ch. 20:24), *mimmiḏbār* (Ex. 23:31; Nu. 21:18; Isa. 21:1; Ezk. 23:42; Hos. 13:15), *mēhammiḏbār* (Josh. 1:4; 1 S. 25:14); with *hē*-locale *miḏbārâ:* (1 Ch. 5:9; 12:9[8]; Isa. 16:1), and definite article (11 times):

---

11. Sargon, II Cyl. 13.
12. C. J. Gadd, "Inscribed Prisms of Sargon II from Nimrud," *Iraq,* 16 (1954), 192, 48.
13. For Ethiop. *dabra,* "mountain," → הר *har,* III, 427-29.

hammiḏbārâ (Ex. 4:27; Lev. 16:21; Jgs. 20:45/47); 21 times in the construct state as the *nomen rectum: 'ereṣ miḏbār* (Dt. 32:10; Prov. 21:19), *qᵉṣēh hammiḏbār* (Ex. 13:20; Nu. 33:6), *'aḇrôṯ (Q 'arḇôṯ) hammiḏbār* (2 S. 15:28; 17:16), *nᵉ'ôṯ miḏbār* (Ps. 65:13[12]; Jer. 9:9[10]; 23:10; Joel 1:19/20; 2:22; presumably also Mal. 1:3: *lin'ôṯ* instead of MT *lᵉṯannôṯ miḏbār*[14]), *dereḵ hammiḏbār* (Ex. 13:18; Josh. 8:15; Jgs. 20:42), *qôṣê hammiḏbār* (Jgs. 8:7,16), *rûaḥ miḏbār* (Jer. 13:24), *ḥereḇ* (*ḥōreḇ*?) *hammiḏbār* (Lam. 5:9); 24 times as *nomen regens,* associated primarily with a geographical name: *miḏbar šûr* (Ex. 15:22), *sîn* (16:1), *sînāy* (19:1), or *ṣin* (Nu. 20:1), *pā'rān* (1 S. 25:1), *qāḏēš* (Ps. 29:8); with geopolitical implications: *miḏbar mô'āḇ* (Dt. 2:8), *'ᵉḏôm* (2 K. 3:8), *yᵉhûḏâ* (Jgs. 1:16); with a place name: *miḏbar zîp* (1 S. 26:2), *giḇᵉ'ôn* (2 S. 2:24); with a preposition: *bᵉmiḏbār* (25 times), *lᵉmiḏbār* (3 times), *mimmiḏbar* (10 times); with *hē*-locale: *miḏbarâ bêṯ 'āwen* (Josh. 18:12), *miḏbarâ dammāšeq* (1 K. 19:15);[15] the term occurs only once with a possessive suffix, *miḏbārāh* (Isa. 51:3). Textually uncertain occurrences include *mēhammiḏbār wᵉhallᵉḇānôn,* read *'aḏ hallᵉḇānôn* (Josh. 1:4; cf. Ex. 23:31); *baśśāḏeh bammiḏbār,* possibly *(û)ḇammôrāḏ* (Josh. 8:24);[16] *'al-pᵉnê-dereḵ 'eṯ-hammiḏbār* (2 S. 15:23); *miḏbar-yām* (the LXX omits *yām;* Isa. 21:1); *hakkarmel hammiḏbār,* read *kammiḏbār* (Jer. 4:26; compare Isa. 14:17; Hos. 2:5[3]; Zeph. 2:13 and Isa. 51:3; 32:15) or *miḏbār* (cf. Isa. 64:9[10]).

The LXX (as also the NT) renders *miḏbār* 244 times with *érēmos,* so that these two words can be considered strict equivalents. The Greek term also encompasses synonyms of *miḏbār: ḥārēḇ* (31 times), *šāmēm* (26 times), and several derivatives from these roots; these are more often represented in Greek by other terms.[17] Only in isolated, in part textually uncertain cases does the LXX render *miḏbār* with *erēmikós* (Ps. 102:7[LXX Ps. 101]), *erēmoún* (Jer. 2:6), *agrós* (Job 24:5), *ánydros* (Isa. 41:19), *auchmōdēs* (1 S. 23:14,15?), *pedíon* (Joel 2:3; 4:19), and other terms. Occasionally it will transcribe the term as *madbar(e)ítis* (Job 5:15; 18:12).[18] The Vulg. uses *desertum* (e.g., Ex. 13:18; 1 S. 25:4; Ps. 78:52[Vulg. Ps. 77]; Isa. 64:9[10]; Ezk. 34:25) or *solitudo* (e.g., Gen. 14:6).

2. *'ᵃrāḇâ.* The most frequently used synonym for *miḏbār* is *'ᵃrāḇâ,* occurring 59 times (or 60 times if *naḥal hā'ᵃrāḇîm* in Isa. 15:7 is equated with *naḥal hā'ᵃrāḇâ* in Am. 6:14). The etymological derivation is uncertain. *KBL*³[19] favors a connection with OSA *'rb,* "retire, withdraw (to a remote area)" over one with Ethiop. *'rb,* "dry out."[20] In general, *'ᵃrāḇâ* refers to an arid region with saline soil (*mᵉlēḥâ,* Job 39:6) and little vegetation (Isa. 33:9; 35:6; 41:19; Jer. 17:6) populated by dangerous wild animals (Jer. 5:6; cf. Hab. 1:8; Zeph. 3:3; Job 24:5 is textually uncertain).

---

14. Talmon, *Mélanges D. Barthélemy,* 517.
15. *GK,* §§26h, 67o, 85h, 90i.
16. Delitzsch, 150c.
17. Funk, 206ff.
18. *Ibid.*
19. P. 733.
20. The latter suggested by Baentsch, 17.

a. The term *ʿ^{a}rāḇâ* occurs 7 times in *parallelismus membrorum* with *midbār,* 6 of those as the second member, e.g., Isa. 41:19: *'ettēn bammidbār 'erez . . 'āśîm bāʿ^{a}rāḇâ b^{e}rôš* (cf. Job 24:5; Isa. 35:1,6; 40:3; 51:3; Jer. 2:6), but only once in the reverse order (Jer. 17:6): *w^{e}hāyâ k^{e}ʿarʿār bāʿ^{a}rāḇâ . . . w^{e}šāḵan ḥ^{a}rērîm bammidbār* (in the LXX also in Zec. 14:10 + *kaí tḗn érēmon*). It occurs in apposition to *midbār* (Dt. 1:1; 1 S. 23:24), in a trio with *ṣiyyâ* (Jer. 50:12; cf. Isa. 35:1, LXX + *tá érēma toú Iordánou*); in the construct state in 2 S. 17:16; 15:28 *(Q): b^{e}ʿarḇôṯ (K b^{e}ʿaḇrôṯ) hammidbār;* once in the construct state with *'ereṣ* (+ *w^{e}šûḥâ,* Jer. 2:6). Like *midbār, (hā)ʿ^{a}rāḇâ* refers for the most part to the arid tracts in the deep south of Palestine (Dt. 1:7; 4:49; Josh. 8:14f.; 18:18), from the Sea of Chinnereth (Josh. 11:2; 12:3) to the *yam hāʿ^{a}rāḇâ,* the "Dead [Salt] Sea" (Dt. 3:17 = Josh. 12:3; Dt. 4:49; Josh. 3:16; 2 K. 14:25; cf. Ezk. 47:8), and beyond that to Ezion-geber and Elath (Dt. 2:8) and portions of this region such as *ʿarḇôṯ mô'āḇ, midbar māʿôn baʿ^{a}rāḇâ 'el y^{e}mîn hayy^{e}šîmôn* (1 S. 23:24; cf. 2 S. 2:29; 4:7; 2 K. 25:4,5, etc.), *ʿarḇôṯ y^{e}rîḥô* (2 K. 25:4,5; Jer. 39:4,5; 52:7,8). The expression *naḥal hāʿ^{a}rāḇâ* (Am. 6:14) is presumably to be identified with the (lower course of the) Wadi Qelt.

b. The use of *ʿ^{a}rāḇâ* follows that of *midbār* only with reference to the (negative) wilderness dimension and as regards general geological-geographical aspects. The (positive) reference "grazing land/drift" is not attested for *ʿ^{a}rāḇâ.* The word occurs as a geographical term in Dt. 1:7: *bāʿ^{a}rāḇâ bāhār ûḇašš^{e}p̄ēlâ ûḇannegeḇ ûḇ^{e}ḥôp̄ hayyām* (cf. Dt. 11:30; Josh. 11:2,16; 12:8; 15:61-62; 2 Ch. 26:10; Isa. 33:9; Zec. 14:10), as a border reference (Dt. 3:17; 4:49; Josh. 12:1,3; 18:18; 2 K. 14:25; Am. 6:14), and as a place name *ʿarḇôṯ y^{e}rî/êḥô* (Josh. 4:13; 5:10; 2 K. 25:5; Jer. 39:5; 52:8); along with *ʿarḇôṯ mô'āḇ* (Nu. 22:1; 26:3,63; 31:12; 33:48,49,50; 35:1; 36:13; Dt. 34:1,8; Josh. 13:32), *midbār mô'āḇ* also occurs once (Dt. 2:8). Like *midbār, ʿ^{a}rāḇâ* can also refer to the historico-geographical experience of the wilderness wanderings (Numbers).

The LXX transcribes *Araba-Arabṓth* with the exception of Job 39:6; Isa. 35:1; 51:3; Jer. 17:6; 50:12 (LXX 27:12), where (next to *m^{e}lēḥâ*) it is translated by *érēmos.* Josh. 8:14 *(lammôʿēḏ lipnê hāʿ^{a}rāḇâ)* is textually uncertain and not attested in the main LXX traditions. The Vulg. uses *solitudo* (e.g., Josh. 12:1,8), *terra inhabitabilis* (e.g., Jer. 2:6); Targ. and Syr. use *mēšrā'.*

3. All the other synonyms used along with *midbār* refer almost exclusively only to the ecological and geographical semantic sphere "wilderness — desert."[21] Terminological accumulations show that the biblical authors wanted to depict for the reader as vividly as possible the connotation of *midbār* as an awe-inspiring, howling wilderness: *'ereṣ midbār — tōhû — y^{e}šîmôn* (Dt. 32:10); *midbār — ṣiyyâ — ʿ^{a}rāḇâ* (Isa. 35:1; 41:18f.); *midbār — ʿ^{a}rāḇâ — šûḥâ — ṣiyyâ — ṣalmāweṯ* (Jer. 2:6f.); *midbār — 'ereṣ ṣiyyâ — ṣāmā'* (Ezk. 19:13; cf. Hos. 2:5[3]); *midbār — š^{e}māmâ — ḥôrbâ* (Isa. 64:9f.[10f.]); *š^{e}māmâ — ṣiyyâ — midbār — šammâ* (Zeph. 2:13-15), and especially Ps. 107:33ff. In many cases these terms occur in portrayals of the wanderings through the

21. Schwarzenbach, 99-112.

great wilderness situated southeast of Palestine, after the exodus from Egypt (Dt. 32:10; Ps. 78:17-19,40; 106:14), or in visions focusing on the postexilic return from Babylon (Isa. 35:2; 41:18f.; 43:19f.).

a. The term *yᵉšîmôn* occurs altogether 13 times in connection with *miḏbār* (and *ᶜᵃrāḇâ*), primarily within the framework of the trek narratives: in reference to specific regions (Nu. 21:20; 23:28; cf. 1 S. 23:19,24; 26:1,3); in retrospectives of the wilderness tradition (Dt. 32:10; Ps. 68:8[7]; 78:40; 106:14; 107:4); and in anticipation of the future transformation of the desert into a land of rivers (Isa. 43:19f.). Both in *parallelismus membrorum* (Dt. 32:10; Ps. 78:40; 106:14; Isa. 43:19f.) and in apposition (Ps. 107:4), *miḏbār* always precedes *yᵉšîmôn*.

b. The term *ṣiyyâ* appears 15 times as a synonym of *miḏbār,* including once in the plural expression *baṣṣiyyôṯ* (Ps. 105:41) and twice in Isaiah in the form *ṣāyôn* (Isa. 25:5; 32:2). It is also used along with other wilderness terminology: *ᶜᵃrāḇâ* (Jer. 51:43); *šammâ* (Jer. 51:43; Joel 2:20); *ṣāmā'* (Ezk. 19:13; Hos. 2:5[3]); *ṣimmā'ôn* (Ps. 107:33); *ḥōm* (Job 24:19); *ᶜāyēp/ᶜᵃyēp̄â* (Isa. 32:2; Ps. 63:2[1]; 143:6). Like *miḏbār* and *ᶜᵃrāḇâ*, it is also used in the construct state with *'ereṣ* (Isa. 41:18; Jer. 2:6; Ezk. 19:13; Hos. 2:5[3]; Ps. 63:2[1]; 107:35). In *parallelismus membrorum* (Isa. 41:18; Jer. 2:6; Ezk. 19:13; Hos. 2:5[3]; Ps. 107:35) and appositionally (Isa. 35:1; Jer. 50:12), *miḏbār* precedes *ṣiyyâ* (as it does *ᶜᵃrāḇâ* and *yᵉšîmôn*). Only Ps. 78:17-19; Zeph. 2:13 attest the reversed order. This shows that *miḏbār* is the primary term used to designate "wilderness — desert" in the biblical vocabulary.

c. The term *šᵉmāmâ* (57 occurrences, of which 4 are in the pl., always in the construct state with *ᶜôlām*, Jer. 25:12; 51:26,62; Ezk. 35:9) circumscribes *miḏbār* in the adjectival construct state (Jer. 12:10; Joel 2:3; 4:19[3:19]). In *parallelismus membrorum, šᵉmāmâ* (and *ṣiyyâ,* Joel 2:20) functions next to *miḏbār* as the first (*šᵉmāmâ — miḏbār,* Mal. 1:3; Joel 4:18f.[3:18f.]; Zeph. 2:13-15; cf. Ezk. 6:14) and second member (*miḏbār — šᵉmāmâ,* Isa. 64:9[10]; Jer. 9:9-11[10-12]). One stylistic peculiarity of the book of Ezekiel is the pleonasm employing *šᵉmāmâ* with *šammâ* (Ezk. 23:33), *mᵉšammâ* (6:14; 23:33; 33:28,29; 35:3), *nᵉšammâ* (32:15), and *šimmᵉmâ* (35:7).

The term *šᵉmāmâ* evokes only the negative aspect of *miḏbār* in reference to the devastation, through divine punishment, of settlements (Josh. 8:28; Isa. 1:7; 64:9[10]; Jer. 6:8; 9:10[11]; 34:22; 49:2; 50:13; 51:26,62; Ezk. 29:12; Zeph. 2:4,9,13), lands or parts of lands (Ex. 23:29; Lev. 26:33; Isa. 1:7; 6:11; 17:9; 62:4; Jer. 4:27; 12:10f.; 32:43; 44:6; 49:33; Ezk. 6:14; 12:20; 14:15,16; 15:8; 29:9,10,12; 32:15; 23:28,29; 35:3,4,7,9,12?,14,15; 36:34; Joel 2:3,20; 4:19[3:19]; Mic. 7:3; Mal. 1:3). It is noteworthy that only in the book of Jeremiah is the term *šᵉmāmâ* used in *parallelismus membrorum* with *mᵉᶜôn tannîm,* "lair of jackals" (Jer. 9:10[11]; 10:22; 49:33; 51:37). With the exception of the allusions possibly inhering in *ᵃšimmēm* (Ezk. 20:26), the term *šᵉmāmâ* (and other derivatives from *šmm*) evokes neither the historico-spatial connotations of *miḏbār* nor the positive aspects of "grazing land," "place of refuge," locus of theophany and of the covenant with God.

d. Of the 42 total occurrences of *ḥōreḇ-ḥorbâ,* "ruins, rubble field," 3 are drawn into the semantic field "aridity — wilderness — desert" through stylistic connections with *miḏbār* or one of the previously mentioned synonyms: *miḏbār — šᵉmāmâ — ḥorbâ*

(Isa. 64:9f.[10f.]; Ps. 102:7[6]), *ḥorbâ — miḏbār* + *ʿᵃrāḇâ* (Isa. 51:3); with *ṣāyôn* (Isa. 25:5) and *šammâ* (Jer. 25:9; cf. also Ps. 106:9; Isa. 50:2).

e. Both the lack of water Israel suffered during the wilderness wanderings and the scarcity of water generally associated with *miḏbār* are emphasized by additional synonyms: the hapex legomenon *ḥᵃrērîm* (Jer. 17:6), *yabbāšâ* (Isa. 44:3), *negeḇ* (Isa. 21:1), *šārāḇ* (Isa. 35:7; 49:10), *ṣaḥ* (Isa. 13:5; Jer. 4:11) — *ṣᵉḥîḥâ* (Ps. 68:7[6]) — *ṣaḥṣāḥôṯ* (Isa. 58:11), *ṣāmā'* (Ezk. 19:12f.; cf. Isa. 5:13; 40:3) — *ṣimmā'ôn* (= Akk. *ṣumāmu*) *'ᵃšer 'ên-mayim* (Dt. 8:15; Ps. 107:33) and *'ereṣ mᵉlēḥâ*, "salt land" (Jer. 17:6; Ps. 107:34; Job 39:6). The same terms are used to describe the distant land Bāzu/Bazzu (*bāṣu/baṣṣu*, "sand"[22]) as an "arid land, saline ground, a waterless region."[23]

f. The elements of chaos associated with *miḏbār* are emphasized by parallelism with mythically charged terms such as *tōhû* (Dt. 32:10), *wāḇōhû* (Jer. 4:23-26), *šō'â ûmᵉšō'â* (Job 38:27; cf. Isa. 6:11), *šûḥâ* (Jer. 2:6), and the hapex legomena *'ereṣ tal'uḇôṯ* (Hos. 13:5), *'ereṣ ma'pēlyâ* (Jer. 2:31), and *'ereṣ gᵉzērâ* (Lev. 16:22).

g. In the expression *baśśāḏeh bammiḏbār* (Josh. 8:24), *śāḏeh* can be understood as a synonym for *miḏbār* if this is a conflation of text variants (cf. Jer. 12:9; Ezk. 29:5). This may also be the case with *ya'ar* in *bammiḏbār — bayyᵉ'ārîm* (Ezk. 34:25).[24]

4. *Antonyms*. Consistent with the multilayered semantic field of *miḏbār* itself and its synonyms, its antonyms also embrace several aspects within the geographical-spatial-ecological and religious-cultic spheres, as well as in relation to motifs and as literary imagery.

a. The negative characteristics of *miḏbār* — namely, aridity, barrenness, and scarcity of vegetation — are contrasted by springs of water and luxuriant vegetation. Depending on human behavior or Israel's own conduct, God turns fruitful land into a wasteland (Ps. 107:33f.; Isa. 50:2; cf. Ps. 106:9) or causes water to flow in the wilderness (Isa. 43:20 [cf. v. 19]; 41:18 [cf. Ps. 107:35]; Ps. 78:15; on the matrix *miḏbār — tᵉhôm* see Isa. 63:13[25] and the allusions in Ps. 77:17-21[16-20]; 78:13-16 and elsewhere).

b. In contrast to the wilderness characterizing the south of Palestine, the north is identified with "mountainous land, hill country" — *kî lō' mimmôṣā' ûmimma'ᵃrāḇ* (east and west) *wᵉlō' mimmiḏbār [ûmē]hārîm* (Ps. 75:7[6]); *rō'š hārîm* and *sela'* contrast with *miḏbār* (Isa. 42:11; cf. Isa. 16:1; Lam. 4:19) and are inhabited by various groups of people (Gen. 14:6).

c. One particularly vivid contrast is that between *har* and its synonyms[26] with *miḏbār* and related terms as spatial terms within the historico-geographical context of the conquest. The "great and terrible wilderness" (*hammiḏbār haggāḏôl wᵉhannôrā' hahû'*, Dt. 1:19) is diametrically juxtaposed with that "goodly hill country" (*hāhār haṭṭôḇ*

---

22. A. Heidel, "A New Hexagonal Prism of Esarhaddon (676 B.C.)," *Sumer,* 12 (1956), prism III, 11ff.

23. Eph'al, 132f.

24. This is the view of Baly, 106; but see III.4.d below.

25. Dahood, *AB,* XVII, 240; Watson, 466.

26. → הר *har* (III, 427-447).

hazzeh), which is identical with the "good land" (*hā'āreṣ haṭṭôḇâ,* Dt. 3:25). The "fruitful hill country (RSV 'plentiful land'; *'ereṣ hakkarmel*)" is the positive foil for *miḏbār, 'ereṣ ʿarāḇâ wᵉšûḥâ, 'ereṣ ṣiyyâ wᵉṣalmāweṯ* (Jer. 2:6f.). Divine punishment for human transgression consists in the reduction of the fruitful hill country to a desolate wilderness: *rā'îṯî wᵉhinnēh hakkarmel hammiḏbār* (read *kam-*) . . . *mippᵉnê ḥarôn 'appô* (Jer. 4:26); Gilead and Lebanon will become a *miḏbār* abandoned by human beings (Jer. 22:6). This so moves the prophet that he laments their desolation in a *qînâ* (Jer. 9:9-11[10-12]). In contrast, divine grace and beneficence find expression in the transformation of the desolate wilderness into fruitful hills (Isa. 41:18; 32:15,16; cf. Ezk. 20:35f.,40).

d. Ridges and other elevations, designated by *har* and its synonyms, offer a measure of security in the otherwise threatening and fearful wilderness (2 Ch. 20:24). If even these fall into the hands of enemies (1 S. 13:18: *gᵉḇûl* = "hill"[27]) or of freebooters (*ʿal-kol-šᵉpāyim*[28] *bammiḏbār bā'û šōḏᵉḏîm),* the land is then marked for desolation (Jer. 12:12; cf. 4:9ff.). In this sense the term *śāḏeh*[29] is used as an antithesis to *miḏbār* (Josh. 8:24?; Jer. 12:9; Ezk. 29:5), in some cases also *yaʿar,*[30] i.e., "forested heights" (Josh. 17:15,18; Isa. 37:24) bordering on the *miḏbār* plain (Ezk. 34:25) — *yaʿar haśśāḏeh negeḇ* (Ezk. 21:2,3[20:46,47]), *śᵉḏēh yaʿar* (Ps. 132:6; compare 1 S. 6:21; 7:1,2 and Josh. 15:9,60; 18:14,15).

e. This positive estimation of *har* as compared with *miḏbār* culminates in the identification of the promised land with *hārîm:* "I will bring forth descendants from Jacob, and from Judah inheritors of my mountains; my chosen shall inherit it, and my servants shall settle there" (Isa. 65:9; cf. Jer. 2:7). "The *hārîm* shall drip sweet wine, the *gᵉḇāʿôṯ* shall flow with milk," while Egypt will become *lišmāmâ* and Edom *lᵉmiḏbar šᵉmāmâ* (Joel 4:18f.[3:18f.]; cf. Am. 9:13; Ps. 65:13[12]). Unlike the perpetually endangered grazing lands in the *miḏbār,* the hills offer secure drift for sheep and livestock (Ezk. 38:12f.; Ps. 65:14[13]?) and in a metaphorical sense peace and well-being for Israel (Ezk. 34:6-15). The opposition *miḏbār* — *har* as places of misfortune on the one hand and good fortune on the other culminates in the notion of Mt. Zion (Ezk. 34:26; 20:40) as the polar opposite of the *miḏbar hāʿammîm,* the "wilderness of the peoples" (Ezk. 20:35f.; cf. 1QM 1:3; 4Q161 A 1 and VIII below), an image evoking the antithesis *miḏbar sînay* — *har sînay* of the wilderness trek period (Ex. 3–10).

5. *Parts of the miḏbār.* The term *miḏbār* and its synonyms are used exclusively as comprehensive terms circumscribing an entire landscape or inclusive area. In contradistinction with → הר *har,*[31] no mention is made of different parts of the "wilderness," "desert," or "steppe." The one exception is *qᵉṣēh hammiḏbār* (cf. Ugar. *p't mdbr;*[32]

27. → הר *har* I (III, 427-29); III.3 (III, 431f.).
28. → הר *har* III (III, 430-32).
29. → הר *har* III.3 (III, 431f.).
30. → הר *har* IV.4 (III, 432).
31. III.4.
32. *KTU,* 1.14 III, 1; IV, 30f.; 1.23, 68.

p't mlbr[33]), whose 2 occurrences are bound to the place name *'ēṯām* (Ex. 13:20; Nu. 33:6). It is still an open question whether *miḏbar 'ēṯām* is to be taken as the designation of a larger wilderness area or of the grazing land bordering the village or town *'ēṯām.*[34] Neither is it certain whether *'aḇrôṯ-'arḇôṯ hammiḏbār* (2 S. 15:28; 17:6; cf. *hā'aḇārim* in Nu. 21:11) refers to a peripheral *miḏbār* area or to areas bordering on the *miḏbār* itself (*'arāḇâ;* cf. *penê hammiḏbār,* 2 Ch. 20:16; *'al hammiḏbār,* Gen. 14:6). In addition to mountains or hills in the *miḏbār,* adjacent heights or other elevations are also mentioned which at least in part overlook the *miḏbār: maṣṣāḏ* (1 Ch. 12:9[8]), *miṣpeh* (2 Ch. 20:24), *geḇûl* (1 S. 13:18).[35]

IV. Usage. 1. *Spatial Dimension.*

a. *Geography of Palestine and the Near East.* The majority of occurrences of *miḏbār, 'arāḇâ,* and their synonyms, as well as the varied portrayals of *miḏbār* landscapes evoking the topographical-geological realities of the Arabian-Palestinian countryside,[36] refer primarily to the arid or even completely barren, low-lying, level areas between the great mountain ranges running through Palestine from the south to the north. This region extends from the Red Sea through the depression of the Jordan valley to Lebanon, abuts in the south on the Arabian desert and issues in the north into the Beqa'.

It encompasses four of the six regions into which OT geographical references divide the "land" (Josh. 12:8; cf. 10:40; 11:16; Dt. 1:7): *'ašēḏôṯ* — the steep slopes dropping off into the Jordan depression; *'arāḇâ* — the depression of the Jordan valley from the Sea of Chinnereth to Elath; *miḏbār* — primarily the Judean wilderness between the Judean mountains and the Dead Sea; *negeḇ* — south of Beer-sheba, up to the great complex of the Arabian desert, the true wasteland (Nu. 21:20; 23:28; Dt. 32:10; 1 S. 23:19,24; 26:1,3; Ps. 78:40; 106:14; 107:4). After the conquest, the extended, variously configured wilderness terrain was familiar to the Israelites only partially from their own experience. The "great and terrible [sand] wilderness," the Sahara, and the Arabian desert[37] are all reflected in traditions recounting the wilderness wanderings after the exodus from Egypt (Dt. 1:19; 2:7; 8:15f.) and in the accompanying literary reflections, particularly in the writings of the prophets and the psalms (Isa. 21:1,11-15; Pss. 78,105,106,107).

Neither the dimensions of the comprehensive geographical complex evoked by *miḏbār* and its synonyms nor those of the subregions can be specified precisely. Variations in annual rainfall, temporary expansion of agricultural activity into peripheral areas of the wilderness, or — vice versa — nomadic incursions into the periphery of agricultural land all bring about ecological fluctuation. This state of affairs finds expression in biblical imagery that frequently refers to the desolation of villages or towns and cultivated fields (Ps. 107:33; Isa. 27:10; 50:2; 64:9[10]; Jer. 4:26; 12:7ff.;

33. *KTU,* 1.12 I, 21f.
34. See IV.2.d below.
35. → הר *har* III.3 (III, 431f.).
36. Baly, 101-11.
37. *erg, ibid.,* 102.

22:6; Mal. 1:3) as a curse motif (Isa. 14:17; Jer. 22:6; Joel 2:3), or the reverse, especially in Deutero-Isaiah, namely, the transformation of *miḏbār* into luxuriant and fruitful land as a blessing motif (Ps. 107:35; Isa. 32:15; 35:1,6; 41:18,19; 43:20; 51:3).

b. *As a Boundary Designation.* Because of the aforementioned fluctuations, wilderness areas are less suited for demarcation of political boundaries than are seas, rivers, and mountain ranges.[38] Despite this, *miḏbār* (and also *ʿᵃrāḇâ*) serves in the OT to demarcate the southern boundary of the "promised land" — next to *nᵉhar/nahal/gᵉḇûl miṣrayim* (Gen. 15:18; Ex. 23:31; Nu. 13:21; 34:3; Josh. 15:1; 1 K. 5:1[4:21]; 2 K. 24:7; 2 Ch. 9:26); this occurs in territorial representations of its dimensions: *min-hammiḏbār* (= south) *wᵉ[ʿaḏ]hallᵉḇānôn* (= north) *min-hannāhār nᵉhar pᵉrāṯ* (= east) *wᵉʿaḏ hayyām hāʾaḥᵃrôn* (Dt. 11:24) or *hayyām haggāḏôl mᵉḇôʾ haššemeš* (Josh. 1:4), "Mediterranean" (= west),[39] and in literary metaphor (Ps. 75:7[6]): *kî lōʾ mimmôṣāʾ* (= east) *ûmimmaʿᵃrāḇ* (= west) *wᵉlōʾ (mim)miḏbār* (= south) *[ûmē]-hārîm* (= north; cf. Nu. 13:21,22; 34:3; Zec. 8:7). Instead of *har (hallᵉḇānôn), hannāhār,* "Euphrates," can as the northern boundary be contrasted with *miḏbār* as the southern boundary (Ex. 23:31; cf. 1 Ch. 5:8f.; 2 K. 14:25; Am. 6:14). The juxtaposition of *har* and *miḏbār* (cf. Gen. 14:6) also occurs in Akkadian, though without any direct territorial-political implications: *šadû u mad-ba-ru irrapudū,* "(the mighty Manda, who) roved the mountains and the open country[?]."[40]

c. *Topographical Circumscription.* Enumerations transmitted down through tradition, e.g., in the oracles against foreign nations, exhibit a general acquaintance with the division of the great wilderness area into regions associated with various ethnic and political groups: *dᵉḏān, têmāʾ, qēḏār, ʿᵃrāḇ* (Jer. 3:2; 25:23f.; 49:28-30 [cf. Isa. 42:11]; Ezk. 23:42 [cf. Job 1:15]).

Beginning in Egypt itself and following the trek accounts, the wilderness in the south is divided into the following main regions: *miḏbar-šûr* (Ex. 15:22; cf. Gen. 16:7; 20:1; 25:18; 1 S. 15:7; 27:8); *miḏbar-sîn* (Ex. 16:1; 17:1; Nu. 33:11f.; cf. Ezk. 30:15,16); *miḏbar-pāʾrān* (Nu. 12:16; 13:3,26; Dt. 1:1; cf. Gen. 14:6; 21:21; 1 S. 25:1; 1 K. 11:18; cf. also Hab. 3:3, *har-pāʾrān*); *miḏbar-ṣîn* (Nu. 13:21; 20:1; 27:14; 33:36; 34:3; Dt. 32:51; cf. Josh. 15:1), which is also known by the name of its most important oasis, *qāḏēš* (Nu. 33:36; Ps. 29:8; *mdbr qdš* also occurs as a geographical reference in Ugaritic[41]). In the Exodus accounts, all these subregions are summarized by the comprehensive term (with altogether 23 occurrences) *miḏbar sînay* (e.g., Ex. 19:1; Lev. 7:38; Nu. 1:1,19). In so doing, the tradition draws attention to the *har sînay* situated in this desert, i.e., the mountain associated with the theophany and the giving of the law.[42]

The OT traditions offer more precise information concerning the *miḏbār* regions in the Syrian-Palestinian area. In addition to the previously mentioned division of West Jordan

---

38. → הר *har* IV.3 (III, 432).
39. See Saebø.
40. Lie, 189; *CAD*, X/1, 11f.
41. See I above.
42. See VII.2.a below.

into six regions (Josh. 12:8; cf. 2 Ch. 26:10; Ps. 75:7[6]), one of which is called a *miḏbār* and two further ones *ʿªrāḇâ* and *neḡeḇ,* references to Transjordan include mention of the *miḏbār* associated with Edom (2 K. 3:8; Isa. 16:1), Moab, and Ammon (Nu. 21:11,13,23; Dt. 2:8; Jgs. 11:18; Isa. 16:8). This includes mention of certain geographical subdivisions (*miḏbar qªḏēmôt,* Dt. 2:26). Of particular note is the Judean wilderness (Jgs. 1:16; 1 S. 13:18; 1 K. 19:4; Ps. 63:1[superscription]; 2 Ch. 24:9), whose parts or adjacent areas are called *ʿªrāḇâ* (2 S. 2:29; 4:7; 2 K. 25:4,5 par. Jer. 39:4,5; 52:7,8) or *yªšîmôn* (1 S. 26:3; cf. 23:24,25). These terms refer to the area between Hebron-Bethlehem-Jerusalem and the Dead Sea (Josh. 16:1), which is of only limited agricultural use. The political significance of these cities and their association with David, whose early life to a large extent took place in this area and the adjacent Negeb, prompted the biblical sources to offer particularly detailed accounts of these areas, e.g., in the account of Abner's retreat, who had pushed forward from Mahanaim in Transjordan to Gibeon in West Jordan (2 S. 2:12). After losing the battle against Joab's troops (vv. 17-23), Abner fled with his men through the *miḏbar giḇʿôn* (v. 24) into the *ʿªrāḇâ* and crossed the Jordan to return to Mahanaim by way of the *biṭrôn* (the transjordanian steppe, v. 29). David's own flight before Absalom took a similar course. He fled Jerusalem through the Kidron Valley (2 S. 15:14-18) into the *miḏbār* (*yªrušālayim?* v. 23) and from there to the *ʿarḇôt hammiḏbār* (v. 28; cf. 17:16) — presumably the strip of land between the *miḏbār* and the *ʿªrāḇâ* — to escape across the Jordan to Mahanaim (2 S. 17:22-24).

Accounts divide the Negeb of Judah (1 S. 27:10) or Jerusalem (Zec. 14:10) into ethnically separate zones: *neḡeḇ hayyªraḥmªʾēlî, haqqênî* (1 S. 27:10), *hakkªrēṭî,* and *neḡeḇ kālēḇ* (1 S. 30:14). The inhabitants here were small livestock herders and a semisedentery population, which, like Israel, were periodically subject to attacks by the desert nomads: Amalekites (1 S. 30:1f.,14,16; cf. Nu. 13:29; 14:45; Jgs. 3:13; 10:12), Midianites (Gen. 36:35; Jgs. 6:1; 7:12), Ishmaelites and Hagrites (Ps. 83:7[6]). One crux interpretum is *neḡeḇ kinªrôt* (Josh. 11:2).

In one series of occurrences, *miḏbār* refers to thinly inhabited open spaces adjacent to permanent villages or towns (*ʿîr*) of differing sizes, as well as on the periphery of semipermanent pastoral settlements (*nāweh;* cf. Akk. *nawûm*) or of temporary, open (shepherd-)encampments (*maḥªneh,* Nu. 13:19; Ex. 16:10-13?). The *miḏbār* spaces are viewed as an extension of the encampment or the settlement, but are not an ecological or administrative part of it. The sociological distinction between those dwelling permanently in the *miḏbār* and those dwelling in the various types of settlements finds clear expression in the biblical traditions and vocabulary.

As in the previously mentioned case of *ʾēṭām* (Ex. 13:20; Nu. 33:6-8), a *miḏbār*-area can acquire its name from the encampment (or settlement) adjacent to it. Comparable cases include *māʿôn, zîp,* and *karmel,* which serve as place names (Josh. 15:55; 16:24; 1 S. 25:2,4,5,14,21,40; 2 Ch. 11:8; cf. 1 Ch. 2:42; 1 S. 15:12) and as names of the corresponding *miḏbār* (1 S. 23:24,25; 25:1; cf. LXX). Mention should also be made of *miḏbar ʿên geḏî* (1 S. 24:2[1]), *miḏbar tªqôaʿ* (2 Ch. 20:20), and *miḏbar yªrûʾēl* (2 Ch. 20:16; cf. Gen. 15:13,14; 25:11 with respect to 16:12; 21:20).

At the battle of Ai the attacking Israelites under Joshua made the pretense of retreat into the open spaces — *miḏbār, ʿªrāḇâ* (Josh. 8:15,20) — in order to entice the inhabitants out of the city, and then dealt them a decisive defeat *baśśāḏeh bammiḏbār* (v. 24). Although the expression *miḏbar hā'ay* is not explicitly attested, it may be presupposed as implicit. This is supported by the fact that an adjacent *miḏbar bêṯ 'āwen* (Josh. 7:2; cf. 1 S. 13:5; Hos. 4:15; 5:8; 10:5) is explicitly mentioned (Josh. 18:12) with regard to the city of Bethel (Josh. 8:12) not far from Ai. The designation of the open spaces on the outskirts of a city as *miḏbār* is also attested in the cases of Beer-sheba (Gen. 21:14), Gibeon (2 S. 2:24), and Damascus (1 K. 19:15). Jgs. 20:42,45,47 allude to a *miḏbar giḇeʿaṯ binyāmîn,* and 1 K. 2:34 (cf. 2 S. 15:23,28; 17:16; Isa. 32:14-18) alludes to a *miḏbar yerušālayim* (cf. Ezk. 34:23-25 with regard to 1 S. 17:28), which is then explicitly named in the Qumran literature (1QM 1:3). This particular connotation of *miḏbār* is also attested in rabbinic literature. *Midr. Qoh.*[43] recounts that R. Ḥiyyah ben Dossa once went out *lemiḏbārâ šel ʿîrô* and found a stone, which he ground and polished and then brought to Jerusalem as a (sacrificial) offering.

d. *For Designating Location.* In some parts of the great open spaces, spaces characterized by differing degrees of desolation, the Israelites had villages or towns which were largely taken over from the local inhabitants, although in some instances they were newly founded. With regard to the Jordan rift, mention is made of *bêṯ hāʿarāḇâ, middîn, sekāḵâ, hanniḇšān, ʿên geḏî,* and *ʿîr hammelaḥ* (Sodom? Josh. 15:61,62).[44] They were more numerous in the regions of the Negeb originally allotted to the tribe of Simeon and subsequently annexed by Judah (Josh. 19:1-9; 15:20-32; Neh. 11:25-30; 1 Ch. 4:28-33; 1 S. 26:5ff.).[45] Further *miḏbār*-settlements were found in the region of the transjordanian tribes (Josh. 13:15-32). For the most part these served as local centers and military bases like the cities which Solomon (re)built: *baʿalāṯ* (?) and *K tāmār/Q taḏmōr bammiḏbār* (1 K. 9:18; 2 Ch. 8:4). Located on the border of the agricultural land,[46] *beṣer bammiḏbār be'ereṣ hammîšōr* in the territory of the tribe of Reuben (Dt. 4:43; Josh. 13:15-23) was a city of refuge (Josh. 20:8; 1 Ch. 6:63[78]), and thus simultaneously fulfilled a religious-juridical function.

Archaeological research in the wilderness of Judah, the Negeb, and the Sinai peninsula has not substantively changed the picture offered by the biblical accounts. These areas witnessed the emergence of villages or towns of limited size, especially during periods in which a relatively stable regime in the cultivated areas offered support against incursions by nomads as well as for guarding the wilderness roads.[47] One typical example is Arad. Excavations reveal its development from a tiny desert settlement at the end of the 2nd millennium to a central military base in the kingdom of Judah from the 8th century into the Persian epoch. From this base military units patrolled the eastern branch of the road leading from Judah to Egypt.[48] In contrast with Arad, archaeological

43. Ed. Ketav, IVf., 64.
44. Cf. F. M. Cross and G. E. Wright, "The Boundary and Province Lists of the Kingdom of Judah," *JBL,* 75 (1956), 213.
45. Talmon, *IEJ,* 15 (1965), 235-241.
46. Baly, 103.
47. Glueck, 356.
48. Aharoni-Naseh.

evidence in Kuntillat ʿAjrud in the northern Sinai can be attested only for the second(?) half of the 9th century.[49] The history of this small settlement has not yet been clarified. The pronounced sacral character of the structural remains found there, including pottery and inscriptions, suggests that this was perhaps a station for pilgrims (on the way to Mt. Horeb?), which for unknown reasons was abandoned *ca.* 800. Assyrian sources also mention isolated settlements in the wilderness.[50]

2. *midbār as an Ecological Term.*

a. *Wilderness and Wasteland.* The ecological character of the *midbār*/"wasteland" terrain is determined by the scarcity of rainfall (averaging 20-40 mm.[.8-1.6 in.] annually[51]), rainfall which in some years may not occur at all. Furthermore, the searing east wind *(rûaḥ qāḏîm)* blowing across the desert dries up this meager moisture completely (Hos. 13:15; cf. 12:2[1]), so that any vegetation withers (Gen. 41:6,23,27; Ezk. 17:10; 19:12). This wind often rages with devastating force *keṣûpôṯ* ("as whirlwinds," Isa. 21:1; 27:8; differently in Jon. 4:8), driving plants, animals, and people before it like chaff (Jer. 13:24; 18:17; cf. Ex. 10:13; 14:21; 27:8; Job 1:19; 27:21; Ps. 48:8[7]; 78:26; Ezk. 27:26). Only pitiful, barren shrubs (*ʿarʿār,* Jer. 17:6; 48:6? cf. Ps. 102:18[17]), thorns, and briars (*qôṣîm, barqānîm,* Jgs. 8:7,16), i.e., useless plants, can take hold in this saline wasteland. Cultivated plants which, like people (Gen. 21:14), "stray" (*tāʿû,* Isa. 16:8) or are placed into this wasteland (Ezk. 19:10-13) no longer bear fruit (Ezk. 19:12; cf. 17:5-10).

The fauna, like the flora, is also pitiful. The only animals able to exist in this wilderness and find refuge there (*māʿôn,* Jer. 9:10[11]; 10:22; 49:33; 51:37; cf. *newēh gemallîm,* Ezk. 25:5) are vermin — serpents and scorpions (Nu. 21:6; Dt. 8:15) — and a few living things that are considered unclean (Lev. 11:15-18; Dt. 14:14-17), including birds: *qāʾāṯ, kôs,* (Ps. 102:7[6]), *qippōḏ* (Zeph. 2:14), *yanšûp̱, ʿōrēḇ* (Isa. 34:11; cf. 1 K. 17:4,6; Job 38:4; Ps. 147:9), *qōrēʾ* (Jer. 17:11; cf. 1 S. 26:20), *yāʿēn/(baṯ) yaʿanâ* (Job 30:29; Isa. 13:21; 34:13; 43:20; Jer. 50:39; Lam. 4:3), and animals: camels (Jgs. 6:5; 7:12; 8:21,26; 1 S. 30:17; 1 Ch. 5:21; 27:30 and elsewhere), wild asses (*pereʾ,* Job 24:5; 39:5; Jer. 2:24), and jackals (*tannîm,* Lam. 4:3).

Biblical human beings, accustomed to village and town life, view the wilderness as a gaping void. No civilized person dwells in it (*ʾereṣ lōʾ-ʾîš midbār lōʾ-ʾāḏām bô,* Job 38:26; cf. Isa. 6:11), nor even passes through it (Jer. 2:6; 9:9-11[10-12]; 17:6; 22:6; 50:40; 57:43). The "great and terrible wilderness" *(hammiḏbār haggāḏôl wehannôrāʾ)* inspires revulsion and debilitating fear (Dt. 1:19; 8:15; Isa. 21:1; Lam. 5:9 [read *ḥōrēḇ* instead of *ḥereḇ*?]; Ezk. 6:14). Hunger and thirst (Nu. 20:2-5; 21:5; 33:14; 2 S. 17:14,29; 16:2; Ps. 107:4-6) weaken (*ʿāyēp̱,* Gen. 25:29,30) the person (Ps. 107:5; cf. Jgs. 8:4,5; 1 S. 14:28,31; Prov. 25:25; Isa. 29:8; Jer. 31:25) who is cast (Ex. 14:3; 1 S. 30:11f.; 1 K. 19:3f.) into the wasteland (*ʾereṣ ʿayēp̱â,* Isa. 32:2; Ps. 143:6; cf. 63:2[1]).

---

49. See Meshel-Meyers.

50. H. W. F. Saggs, "The Nimrud Letters 1952: Part VI," *Iraq,* 25 (1963), 79f., letter 70, l. 13; cf. F. M. Fales, *Censimenti e Catasti di Epoca Neo-Assira* (Rome, 1973), no. 9.

51. Baly, 42f.

There he searches aimlessly for water (Gen. 21:14; Nu. 14:33 [MT *rō'îm;* read *tō'îm*]; cf. Nu. 21:5; 1 K. 3:8f.; Ps. 107:40; 119:176), suffering from heat and thirst (*hiṯ'aṭṭēp,* Ps. 107:5; cf. 142:4; Lam. 2:9,11,12; *hiṯ'allēp,* Isa. 51:20; Am. 8:13; Jon. 4:8), and finally expiring (Ex. 14:11,12; 16:3; Nu. 14 *passim;* 16:13; 20:4,5; 26:65; Dt. 9:28; Hos. 2:5[3]). Only divine intervention offers deliverance from death (Ex. 15:23-25; 16 *passim;* Nu. 20:7-11; 21:16-18; Dt. 32:10; 2 K. 3:15-20; Ps. 107:9). The "civilized" person will come to an inescapable and bitter end (Job 6:18; cf. 12:24; Ps. 107:40) unless God helps such a person who has strayed into the *midbār* to find the right path (Ex. 13:17f.; Dt. 1:31; 8:15; Neh. 9:19; Ps. 78:52; 136:16; Isa. 35:8; 43:19; Jer. 2:6; Am. 2:10), or unless a desert dweller familiar with the wilderness terrain leads him to food and water (Isa. 21:13-15) and serves as his guide within this labyrinth, as Jethro the Midianite once did for the Israelites (*wᵉhāyîṯā lānû lᵉ'ênayim,* Nu. 10:31). Similar views are found among the neighboring cultures.[52]

b. *Wilderness Inhabitants.* Only nomadic tribes rove the great *midbār* (Jer. 9:25[26]; 25:23-24), collectively called *bᵉnê-qeḏem* (Jgs. 6:3; 8:10f.; Job 1:3; Jer. 49:28; Ezk. 25:4f.) or *'ᵃrāḇîm* (2 Ch. 17:11; 26:7; 22:1 [?]; Jer. 3:2; 25:24). They live in the open (Jer. 3:2) or dwell in tents (Ps. 83:7[6]; 120:5; Cant. 1:5; Isa. 13:20; Hab. 3:7) in open settlements *(ḥāṣēr/ḥᵃṣērîm),* like the *(bᵉnê) qēḏār* (Isa. 42:11; Jer. 9:25[26]; 25:23; 49:28 [?]). Other inhabitants mentioned include *sāḇā'îm* (Ezk. 23:42[53]), Sabeans (Job 1:15; Ps. 72:10; Isa. 60:6), Edomites (Job 1:3; 42:12; cf. *bûz[î],* Job 32:2; Jer. 25:23), *hagrî'îm* (1 Ch. 5:10,19,20; 27:31[30c]; Ps. 83:7[6]), and *yišmᵉ'ēlîm,* the descendants of Hagar and her son Ishmael (Gen. 21:14; 25 *passim* par. 1 Ch. 1:29-31; Gen. 28:9; 36:3; 37:25,27; Jgs. 8:24). They resemble the Midianites (Jgs. 6–8 *passim;* cf. Ps. 83:10[9]; Isa. 9:3[4]; 10:26) and Amalekites (Ex. 17:8-16; 1 S. 15 *passim;* 26:3; 1 Ch. 4:42f.; cf. vv. 39f.) so closely that these various designations can be used synonymously (compare Gen. 37:25-27; 39:1 with 37:28,36; Jgs. 6:1-6; 8:10-12; Ps. 83:7f.[6f.]). Desert dwellers can be recognized by the shorn hair of their temples (*qᵉṣûṣê pē'â,* Jer. 9:25[26]; 25:23; 49:32; RSV 'the corners of their hair') and, as is still the case today, by the jewelry (Ezk. 23:42; cf. Gen. 24:22,30; Ex. 32:2f.; Job 42:11) with which they also adorn their camels (Jgs. 8:24-26).

The sedentary Israelites' fear of the wandering nomads manifests itself in their portrayal as brigands (Gen. 16:12; 21:20; cf. Isa. 21:13-17) and robbers (*šōḏᵉḏîm,* Isa. 21:2; Jer. 12:12; 48:32; cf. 4:20; 10:20; Job 12:6; Prov. 24:15; Zec. 11:2f.). Their attacks were a constant threat to farmers and herdsmen (Jgs. 6:2-6; 7:12; 1 S. 30 *passim;* Job 1:15; Isa. 16:4; Jer. 25:36; 48:15-20; Ob. 5), whose riding animals could not match the speed of the nomads' camels (1 S. 30:17). These camels enabled the desert tribes to establish a monopoly over caravan trade along the roads criss-crossing the great wilderness tracts, roads to which they alone had access (Gen. 37:25-28; 39:1; 1 K. 10:2; 2 Ch. 9:1; Isa. 21:13; 30:6; 60:6; Jer. 6:20; Ezk. 27:21-23; 38:13).

---

52. Haldar, 13.31ff., 68ff.; Funk, 205; Eph'al, 133.

53. On the reconstruction of this text, see W. Zimmerli, *Ezekiel 1. Herm* (Eng. trans. 1979), *in loc.*

Temporary settlements, especially of small livestock herdsmen, are able to establish themselves in such areas only in places in which during the rainy season water collects from the mountain runoff (Gen. 37:22-24). Permanent settlements come about in isolated oases whose water springs render possible a seminomadic living based on small livestock and limited, periodic cultivation of grain, vegetables, and date palms. Such was the case with *'êlîm,* where during their wanderings the Israelites came upon twelve springs of water and seventy palm trees (schematic numbers; Nu. 33:9).

c. *Grazing Land.* In contradistinction with *y^{e}šîmôn* and *m^{e}lēḥâ,* which are of no use at all, fallow *miḏbār* spaces adjacent to villages and towns, in the borderland between cultivated land and desert (metaphorically: Ps. 65:13[12]), can serve as the grazing land par excellence, above all for the sheep and goat flocks of seminomadic small livestock herdsmen, although also for the livestock[54] of sedentary farmers. This connotation of *miḏbār,* which is best rendered by "drift," is also attested in rabbinic literature. The Mishnah (*B.Qam.* vii.7) prohibits the rearing of sheep and goats *(b^{e}hēmâ daqqâ)* in the "land" because they endanger fruits and trees by their grazing. One exception is *miḏbāriyyôṯ šebb^{e}'ereṣ yiśrā'ēl,* in which one is permitted to keep small livestock (cf. also Bab. *Beṣa* 40a-b; Jer. *Beṣa* v.3 (63d); Tosefta *Beṣa Yom Ṭob* iv.11).

In this context the use of *nāweh* as a designation for pasturage settlements is richly attested, although only once in the immediate context with *miḏbār.* The author of Isa. 27:10f. compares the besieged (read *n^{e}ṣûrâ* instead of *b^{e}ṣûrâ*) city (Jerusalem) with a desolate and forsaken *nāweh* (cf. Isa. 34:13; 35:7; Jer. 49:20; 50:45; Ezk. 25:5) in whose *miḏbār* cattle graze (cf. Jer. 12:10,11) and goats strip the bare branches (cf. Isa. 17:1f.; 33:8; Zeph. 2:13-15). The positive foil to this negative imagery (cf. Job 18:14f.) is found in Isa. 33:20, where Jerusalem is portrayed as *nāweh ša'^{a}nān* (cf. Isa. 32:18; 49:19; 50:24; Hos. 9:13), an immovable tent no longer subject to a nomadic fate *(bal-yiṣʿān).* In this comparison of the city of Jerusalem with a stable and secure *nāweh* as the counterpart of the unstable *miḏbār* there resonates an evocation of the temple itself, which is repeatedly circumscribed by the epithet *nāweh* (2 S. 15:26; Jer. 10:25 par. Ps. 79:7; Jer. 25:30; 31:23), the secure resting place (in contrast to 2 S. 7:6) to which God leads his people (Ex. 15:13; Jer. 23:3; 33:12; 50:7,19; Ezk. 34:14). These images and motifs (cf. also Job 18:15; Prov. 3:33; 21:20; 24; Job 5:3 is textually uncertain) reflect a socio-economic reality with which Jeremiah, from Anatoth in the *miḏbār* region of Jerusalem, was especially well acquainted.[55]

In the *ʿ^{a}rāḇâ,* in the Negeb, and in the "great (Sinai) desert" grazing land was limited to those *miḏbār* spaces in which or in whose vicinity the herdsmen had access to wells or cisterns *(maʿ^{a}yānôṯ — b^{e}'ērōṯ — bōrôṯ).* In the patriarchal traditions, which are themselves of a largely pastoral nature, water springs play a central role (Gen. 14:10; 16:14; 21; 24; 26; 37 *passim,* and 36:24, where one should perhaps read *mayim* instead of MT *yēmim* [cf. Syr.]). The same is true of the David narratives localized in the Negeb. It is reported that the Judahite King Uzziah built watchtowers in the *miḏbār* and hewed out

54. → בקר *bāqār* (II, 209-16).
55. Hareuveni.

many *bōrôṯ* for his numerous herds (2 Ch. 26:10; cf. 1 S. 13:6). In the wilderness such grazing lands were located near oases, *n^{e}ʾôṯ miḏbār* (Jer. 9:9[10]), which for that reason are also called *n^{e}ʾôṯ deše'* (Ps. 23:1f.; cf. Joel 2:22) or *n^{e}ʾôṯ rōʿîm* (Am. 1:2; cf. Ps. 65:13f.[12f.]; also Jer. 25:37: *n^{e}ʾôṯ šālôm* in an obviously pastoral context). If they were taken by enemies (Lam. 2:2), usually nomads (Ps. 83:12f.[11f.]), this put an end to the peaceful life of herdsmen (Jer. 9:9-11[10-12]; 23:10; 25:34-38; Joel 1:19,20; Mal. 1:3 and Ps. 74:20 are textually uncertain). This *miḏbār* milieu is reflected in the Moses narratives localized in Midian (Ex. 2:15-22; 3:1ff.), which are very closely related to the Mt. Sinai traditions (e.g., Ex. 4:27; 10:9; 18:5; 19:2f.). These narratives resonate both in biblical (Ps. 77:16[15]; 78:51; cf. Isa. 49:10) and postbiblical imagery (1[Eth.]En. 89:28-40).

3. *Place of Refuge.* Due to this geographical remoteness, people living in the wilderness are only to a limited extent affected by the institutions of civilization or subject to its laws. As a result, the *miḏbār* becomes the refuge of rebels and outlaws, and the asylum of outcasts and fugitives, both literally and as a literary topos. The prototype of the wandering nomad is the fratricide Cain, whom God drives out from the (cultivated) ground *(mēʿal p^{e}nê hāʾ^{a}ḏāmâ)* as punishment (Gen. 4:11-14). Hagar fled with her infant into the wilderness, driven out by her rival Sarah (Gen. 16:6-14). Moses escaped into the wilderness of Midian from Pharaoh's men (Ex. 2:15ff.; 3:1). David took to the *miḏbar y^{e}hûḏâ* (Ps. 63:1[superscription]) in his flight before Saul and became the captain of four hundred men who were "in distress . . . and . . . in debt," 1 S. 22:1f.), *wayyēšeḇ . . . bammiḏbār bamm^{e}ṣāḏôṯ . . . bāhār b^{e}miḏbar-zîp . . . baḥōr^{e}šâ* (1 S. 23:14f.; cf. 1 Ch. 12:9[8]). From there he escaped into the *miḏbar māʿôn bāʿ^{a}rāḇâ* (1 S. 23:24,25; cf. 25:1: MT *pāʾrān,* LXX *Maan*). The regional meaning of *miḏbar māʿôn* is specified by the proper noun *māʿôn/m^{e}ʿûnîm* (1 Ch. 4:41; cf. 2 Ch. 20:1 MT: *mēhāʿammônîm,* LXX *Minaíōn*), a desert tribe mentioned along with the Amalekites (Jgs. 10:12) and the *ʿ^{a}rāḇîm* (2 Ch. 26:7). David sought refuge from Absalom in the wilderness (2 S. 15:23ff.). Elijah saved himself by fleeing into the *miḏbar b^{e}ʾēr šeḇaʿ* (1 K. 19:3f.) and finally found refuge at Horeb, the mount of God (vv. 8ff.) in the "great wilderness," as did Moses in his own time. After the unsuccessful battle against the other tribes, the Benjaminites fled into the *miḏbār* near their city (*giḇ^{e}ʿâ,* Jgs. 20:42) just as the Israelites once did after the battle at Ai (Josh. 8:15ff.), and then retreated even deeper into the Judean wilderness (Jgs. 20:45ff.). The prophet Jeremiah exhorts the Moabites to flee for their lives into the desert before their advancing enemies (Jer. 48:6). In the *miḏbār* the despairing prophet intends to seek lodging (Jer. 9:1[2]), a wish echoed in the words of the psalmist "truly, I would flee far away; I would lodge in the wilderness" (*ʾālîn bammiḏbār,* Ps. 55:7f.[6f.]). Not always, however, does the *miḏbār* offer protection, since there, too, one's pursuers lie in wait (Lam. 4:19).

V. Historico-spatial Dimension Between the Exodus and Conquest. In over half its occurrences in the OT the term *miḏbār* exhibits not only spatial but also temporal connotations. In all these instances the term refers to the "forty years" of the wilderness wanderings between the exodus from Egypt and the conquest of Canaan. The portrayal of the events associated with this period, and their evaluation in the historico-social experience of Israel and of biblical faith in the larger sense, are the primary concerns of the Pentateuch (with the exception of Genesis) from the beginning of the book of Exodus to the end of Deuteronomy. Compared with the other three books, Leviticus offers only sparse factual information about the course of those events. In this component of the Pentateuch, interest focuses exclusively on the giving of the law as it affected the cult, a complex which only through occasional references is "dated" to the years after the exodus itself (Lev. 18:3; 19:34,36; 23:43; 25:38) and before the conquest (e.g., Lev. 14:34; 18:3; 19:23,33; 20:22-24) and localized at the mountain of God in the wilderness of Sinai (Lev. 7:38; 26:46; 27:34).

Detailed descriptions of the Israelites' itinerary through the various regions of the "great wilderness" and exact information concerning rest stations are found particularly in the books of Numbers and Deuteronomy.[56] The accounts differ in many details regarding the exact route, the onomasticon, and also the description of "historical" events. OT scholarship traces these differences back to differing sources and/or to what were once independent strands of tradition ("Sinai tradition" and "conquest tradition") available to the compiler of the Pentateuch and actually used in composing the work.[57] Deuteronomy especially seems yet to contain traces of otherwise lost traditions.[58]

These multilayered sources for the wilderness accounts in the Pentateuch are also reflected in the OT writings generally. What is decisive for the biblical understanding is that it ascribes prototypical significance to the unique experience of a wilderness period in the history of Israel. That *miḏbār* period acquires the character of a fulcral symbol and motif, a development that affected the entire context of *miḏbār* in the extrapentateuchal biblical literature, and to a significant extent in postbiblical literature as well.

VI. Theological Connotations.

1. *General Considerations.* The use of the *miḏbār* vocabulary within the tradition of the wilderness wanderings essentially determines its theological dimension. That epoch in Israel's history is characterized by two seemingly opposite and yet complementary phenomena revealing its estimation in OT belief. One primary element is the forceful emphasis on the immeasurable beneficence (Dt. 2:7; 32; Pss. 78,105,106), the fatherly forbearance, and the love which God manifests toward his people in the awe-inspiring, howling wilderness. The framework of the period of wilderness wanderings includes the miracles God performed to and for Israel, the renewal of his covenant with the fathers as a covenant with the entire people, and the giving of the law at Mt. Sinai. Diametrically opposed to this is the second main element: Israel's doubt that God's power would indeed be able to actualize the promise of land. In a series of episodes, the people's apostasy and rebellious behavior runs like a leitmotif through the majority of accounts of the wilderness wanderings.[59]

---

56. De Vaux, *The Early History of Israel,* 376-388.

57. G. von Rad, "The Form-Critical Problem of the Hexateuch," *The Problem of the Hexateuch* (Eng. trans. 1966; repr. London, 1984), 1-78.

58. Noth, *The Deuteronomistic History,* 59ff.

59. Carroll, 197.

These contrasting elements generate the enormously varying estimations the OT attests concerning that period and its significance for the development of Israelite faith. In the overwhelming majority of reminiscences, allusions, and literary imagery, the period of wilderness wanderings serves as a topos for Israel's sinfulness. It was the era of "rebellion" par excellence (Ex. 16:2; Nu. 14 *passim;* 16 *passim;* 20:1-13; 21:4ff.; 27:14; Dt. 9:7; 32:51; Ezk. 20:13ff.; Ps. 78:17-19,40; 95:8; 106:14),[60] rebellion which cannot be portrayed as merely a secondary motif,[61] and the age of a wicked generation the likes of which cannot be found a second time in biblical historiography. In contrast, a minority of witnesses exhibit a seemingly affirmative estimation of the period of wilderness wanderings. In the *midbār* God made the people his own (e.g., Dt. 32:10; Jer. 31:12; Hos. 9:10), guided them reliably through the wilderness (Dt. 8:15; 29:4[5]; Neh. 9:19-21; Ps. 136:16; Am. 2:10), protected them as does an eagle its brood (Dt. 32:10f.), and carried them in his arms as a father carries his child (Dt. 1:31). It was Israel's "bridal period," in which the people entrusted itself to God and followed him "with youthful love" into the barren wasteland without hesitation (Jer. 2:2f.).

2. *History of Scholarship.* OT scholarship has proposed various theses to explain these antithetical traditions. One traces them back to older portrayals and strands of tradition which were simply incorporated parallel without being harmonized. Another views them as signs of a diachronic, inner-biblical development in the estimation of the wilderness wanderings. The originally positive estimation resulted from the fact that in the earlier period the interest of the biblical thinkers and authors focused exclusively on God's "salvific deeds," paying scant attention to Israel's own behavior.[62] This situation changed dramatically after the conquest. In the struggle against pagan cults and rituals which had crept into biblical monotheism from the very beginning of contact with the Canaanite population (Nu. 25), the postexodus experience was embellished in contrast to the Israelite-Canaanite syncretism predominating in the "land." This experience was recognized and idealized retrospectively as the locus of the ideal relationship between God and his people.[63]

This idealization of the wilderness period is attributed especially to the preexilic prophets, who according to Ernst Sellin[64] viewed the period of wilderness wanderings as the "normal period" in Israel's history.[65] In the development of this thesis a significant role was played by the — today largely outdated or at least decisively revised — assumption of prophetic opposition to ritual and sacrificial cult. The wilderness wanderings were presented as a time during which the relationship between Israel and its God was based on a "pure faith" unencumbered by cultic institutions. Amos was considered to be a typical representative of this view; as the oldest writing prophet he allegedly rejected all formalized institutions of sacrificial worship not practiced in the "ideal"

60. Coats; Tunyogi.
61. Coats, *Rebellion in the Wilderness,* 249f.; Carroll.
62. Von Rad; Bach, 15f.
63. Barth, 15.
64. *KAT,* XIII (^{3}1922), 236.
65. Moscati, *Ancient Semitic Civilizations,* 136f.

stage of the wilderness wanderings. This allegation presupposes the hardly defensible hypothesis that Amos (like Hosea and Jeremiah) either did not know or genuinely rejected the entire Pentateuch tradition that so often mentions "sacrificing" and "sacrifices." Furthermore, this view rests on the extremely slender evidence of Am. 5:21ff. Contextual interpretation of this passage suggests that this does not constitute a complete rejection of the "external sacrificial cult" (JB mg. "religion of mere form"), but rather the hybrid cult that proliferated in Israel after the conquest especially in the northern kingdom. The decisive verse Am. 5:25 should be translated in conjunction with v. 26 approximately as follows: "Did you bring to me sacrifices and meal-offerings for forty years in the wilderness [cf. Jer. 7:22 without mention of *miḏbār*[66]] and did you then [at the same time] carry [about in processions the statue of] Sakkuth your [idol] king and . . . idols [and] star [images] which you made for yourselves?" With these rhetorical questions the prophet does indeed condemn the Israelites' syncretism, syncretism permeated with Canaanite and Mesopotamian idolatry (cf. Hos. 2:4-9,19[2-7,17]); such worship during his own time stood in sharp contrast to the pure Yahweh worship of the (first) exodus-Mt. Sinai phase of the wilderness wanderings and ultimately would result in the punishment of exile (Am. 5:27).

It is further suggested that at the end of the first temple period a renewed pessimistic-negative attitude developed toward *miḏbār* and life in the wilderness, an attitude reflected in the Pentateuch accounts of the wilderness wanderings and also evident, e.g., in the book of Ezekiel (ch. 20) and in several historiographical psalms (78,105,106).

These schematic models are hardly tenable. Although a decisively deprecatory attitude toward the period of wilderness wanderings and the phenomenon "wilderness" is indeed adequately attested by biblical texts, the postulated affirmative attitude — whether conceived as running parallel to the negative or as belonging to a "middle period" in a diachronic developmental schema — is based on a precarious interpretation of isolated biblical statements[67] representing the "middle period."

a. *"Desert Ideal."* Although the purely statistical evidence[68] shows that the thesis of a clearly positive OT wilderness tradition is untenable,[69] there has been a tendency in OT scholarship since the end of the nineteenth century to present the notion of "wilderness" and "nomadic life" as eminent components in OT faith and Israelite civilization. It is asserted that a return to the religious and social conditions of the *miḏbār* period was the eschatological ideal above all of the prophets. The impetus for this development was Karl Budde's rather cautious and fairly balanced presentation of the "desert" as a formative factor in what he termed the "nomadic ideal in the OT." Budde had taken as his point of departure a presentation of the hypothesis that the *bᵉnê bêṯ rēḵāḇ* (Jer. 35) were the proponents of a religious belief which conceived of the God of Israel as a typical god of the desert. Budde interpreted the Rechabites' abstinence from sedentary life, agriculture, and

66. H. W. Wolff, *Joel and Amos. Herm* (Eng. trans., 1977), 264-66.
67. Barth, 19; Fox, 448.
68. See III above.
69. Bach, 20-23.

viticulture, and their insistence on living in tents rather than fixed houses (Jer. 35:6f.) as indications that they intended this mode of life to recreate the "original" Israelite experience of God in the desert. Drawing into the discussion the genealogical note in 1 Ch. 2:55, which connects the Rechabites with the Kenites,[70] and also the theory that the Israelite religion emanated from a Kenite (or Midianite) Yahwism, Budde concluded that even during Jeremiah's time the *b^e nê bêṯ rēḵāḇ* served as missionaries of that desert religion. Because of the association of the eponym of the Rechabites Jonadab ben Rechab with Jehu (2 K. 10:15), Jehu himself was dubbed the " 'wilderness' king," and Jeremiah was pronounced a "later sympathizer" of the Rechabites and their worldview.[71]

According to Budde, the prophets rejected this primitive concept of Yahweh as a desert god. But Budde nevertheless agrees that the notion of an original, ideal historical desert period left clear traces in Israel's thinking. Paul Humbert took Budde's thesis further and asserted that "the desert is the classic home of Yahwism,"[72] and that a "return to the life conditions of the Mosaic period constitutes Hosea's program for the future."[73] This theory reached its peak in an essay by J. W. Flight,[74] who elevated the postulated prophetic "desert idea" to a "nomadic ideal" which believing Christians even today should adopt as the goal of their religio-social efforts.

The discovery of the Qumran literature provided a new impetus for this hypothesis. It is suggested that the *yaḥaḏ* commune, from which this literature emerged in the last two pre-Christian centuries, provides proof that the "desert ideal" represents not only the anticipated ultimate goal of the prophetic hopes for the future, but also a concept capable of being actualized historically and in fact actualized at the end of the OT era itself.[75]

b. *Traces of Nomadic Culture.* This hypothesis of an OT desert ideology is based on dubious socio-historical assumptions. Interpreters postulate a developmental stage in which Israel was a true nomadic society, a situation now reflected in presumed traces of nomadic culture or vocabulary[76] in the OT writings and echoed in prophetic eschatology. These conjectures can hardly be maintained. Apart from splinter groups which attached themselves to Israel in the course of its early history and which require a separate treatment, the OT offers no indications that the Hebrews in the narrower sense of this term ever passed through a stage of true nomadism.[77] As early as patriarchal times the Israelite society bears the imprint of semisettled life in which only occasionally reflections of nomadic life can be discerned.[78] Tradition ascribes to them an "agricultural orientation" similar to that of the postexodus generations.[79]

---

70. Talmon, *IEJ,* 10 (1960), 174-180.
71. Williams, 17; cf. Meyer, 136.
72. *RHPR,* 1 (1921), 106.
73. *Festschrift K. Marti,* 162; cf. Meyer, 129-141; Soloweitschik; Mauser, 45ff.
74. *JBL,* 42 (1923), 158-226.
75. *AncIsr,* 14.
76. Delcor.
77. Mendenhall, 150; contra Moscati, *The Semites in Ancient History,* 91.
78. Moscati, *Ancient Semitic Civilizations,* 155f.
79. Gottwald, *The Tribes of Yahweh,* 435-473.

Even in the accounts of the wilderness wanderings, the tribes of Israel are not presented in the organizational pattern of a typical nomadic society. The main characteristics of nomadic culture, as they were abstracted from an analysis of the pre-Islamic Arab tribes, find little expression in the Pentateuchal books which recount the *midbār* period. "Tribal solidarity, (nomadic) hospitality, and blood vengeance,"[80] insofar as they are reflected in OT literature, more frequently appear in the accounts of Israel's sedentary history in Canaan (e.g., the institution of "cities of refuge," Nu. 35:9-19; Dt. 19:1-3; Josh. 20f.; 1 Ch. 6:42ff.[57ff.]) than in those concerning the patriarchal period or the wilderness. The OT sources record only one case of executed blood vengeance during the monarchy against a clearly political background — Abner's murder by Joab (2 S. 3:27). The sagas of Cain and Lamech (Gen. 4:13-16,23f.) are set in hoary antiquity and cannot be viewed as reflections of historical Israel. The rallying of the sons of Levi to the help of Moses in the Golden Calf episode (Ex. 32:26; cf. Dt. 33:8f.) and Korah's rebellion (Nu. 16:1-35) at best reflect guild rather than tribal solidarity.

Also, the Rechabites themselves cannot be adduced in evidence of the presupposed prophetic desert ideology. Their mode of life was prompted by an anti-urbanism[81] reflecting a socio-economic reality, not a religious idea,[82] an occupation, not a vocation. Nowhere are we told of any missionary activity on their part. Neither is Jehu a "desert king," nor Jeremiah a "desert prophet" who has joined with the Rechabites. By way of a simile the prophet sets up the Rechabites before the nation as an example of steadfastness. However, the *tertium comparationis* lies not in the ideas they represent, but rather in the tenacity with which they follow the guidance of their human forefathers, whereas Israel flagrantly transgresses against divinely appointed ordinances. Although Jeremiah has respect for this tenacity, he by no means identifies with the primitive forms of Rechabite life, nor does he conclude from their behavior any guidelines for his own understanding of faith.[83] The formulations of the desert-ideal hypothesis did not consider that the biblical texts themselves exhibit no enthusiasm whatever for nomadic life,[84] nor that — quite the contrary — "the ideal of the Hebrew writers for themselves was agricultural."[85] God's works and activity are parabolically equated with the work rhythms of a farmer (Isa. 28:23-29). As Frank S. Frick correctly emphasizes,[86] it is a mistake to interpret prophetic criticism of the luxurious, socially reprehensible urban life rampant during the monarchy as an entreaty for a return to the kind of nomadic desert life with which Israel presumably was acquainted from the "golden age" of its early history, and which it allegedly highly regarded.[87]

---

80. Causse; Nyström; Moscati, *The Semites in Ancient History,* 94.
81. Frick, *JBL,* 90 (1971), 279-287; *idem, The City in Ancient Israel,* 210ff.; Carroll, 179.
82. Seidensticker, 119.
83. W. Eichrodt, *Theology of the OT,* II. *OTL* (Eng. trans. 1967), 353f.; Talmon, *Biblical Motifs,* 37; Fox, 450.
84. Causse, 74.
85. H. P. Smith, *The Religion of Israel* (New York, 1914), 12.
86. *The City in Ancient Israel,* 209ff.
87. *AncIsr,* 14.

The representatives of true nomadic culture in OT literature are non-Israelites: Cain, Ishmael, Esau — certainly no ideal types, Hagrites (Ps. 83:7[6]; 1 Ch. 5:9f.), Meunim, Amalekites (1 Ch. 4:41-43), Midianites (Jgs. 6–8), and Kenites (Jgs. 4:17-21; 5:24).

We cannot treat here the fundamental question whether during the stage of the conquest in Canaan the Israelite tribes are to be understood as a social group in transition from nomadism to sedentary life, or whether this process resulted from a "peasants' revolt." Nor can we investigate the solutions which suggest a combination of itinerant herdsmen and rudimentary agriculture (transhumant pastoralism).[88]

VII. OT Usage. Any interpretation of the semantic context of *midbār* and its word field must consider several factors not usually given sufficient attention in OT scholarship.

1. *Time-Space Connotations.* The recollection of a period of wilderness wanderings lends to the spatial concept *midbār* also a temporal aspect. This fusion of spatial and temporal dimensions is not attested for the use of equivalent concepts. Neither in the Hebrew vocabulary nor in the biblical worldview do spatial terms such as, e.g., *har, mîšôr, ʿēmeq, nāhār, yām* also exhibit a temporal dimension. Only two other antithetical terms exhibit such a corresponding fusion of spatial and temporal dimensions: *ʾereṣ kᵉnaʿan/yiśrāʾēl* as a designation of (the period of) sedentary life in the land, and *gôlâ/gālûṯ* as a circumscription of a time of exile spent in a foreign land.[89] The linguistic-conceptual uniqueness of these three terms underscores the estimation of the original *midbār* experience as a situational transitory stage between bondage in Egypt — the prototypical exile — and independence in Israel's own land.

The uniqueness of the period of wilderness wanderings as a transitory stage finds literary expression in the ring composition into which it is embedded. It is situated between the Passover Festival symbolizing the exodus (Ex. 12) and the Passover celebration in Gilgal, which is intended as the first sign of sedentary life in the land (Josh. 5:10-12). Of comparable note is its bracketing between the circumcision of Moses (son?) as a prelude to the Exodus Narrative (Ex. 4:24-26) and the carrying out of the circumcision commandment "on the whole people" in Gilgal (Josh. 5:2-8), in both cases before the celebration of the Passover Festival. During the wilderness wanderings themselves — an historical hiatus — the Israelites kept the first of these regulations only once (Nu. 9:1-5), and the other never, something the author of Joshua specially emphasizes (Josh. 5:5-7).

a. *Subordinate Significance of the Period of Wilderness Wanderings.* The subordinate position assigned by biblical historical understanding to the period of wilderness wanderings manifests itself in the relatively brief span of time allotted to it: *only* "forty years" (e.g., Ex. 16:35; Nu. 14:33,34; 32:13; Dt. 1:3; 2:7; 8:2; Josh. 5:6; 14:10; Am. 2:10; 5:25), the (schematic) life expectancy of a single generation (e.g., Nu. 32:13; Dt. 2:14; cf. Dt. 1:35; Ps. 78:8; 95:10; cf. Jgs. 3:11; 5:31; 8:28; 13:1; 1 S. 4:18). The

88. On the status of scholarship, cf. Mendenhall, Weippert, Gottwald.
89. Talmon, *Exil-Diaspora-Rückkehr,* 32ff.

comparison with the "bondage in Egypt," to which (again, schematically) "four generations" were allegedly subjected (Gen.15:16) and which in one version lasted 400 (Gen. 15:13) and in another 430 years (Ex. 12:41), underscores the relatively minor significance accorded to the period of wilderness wanderings in OT historical thinking. Comparison with the Babylonian exile, predetermined to last seventy years (2 Ch. 36:21; Jer. 25:11,12; 29:10; Dnl. 9:2; Zec. 1:12; 7:5), yields similar results.

Juxtaposition with the epoch of actual sedentary life, however, is even more striking. Biblical tradition figures the period from the exodus from Egypt to the construction of Solomon's temple at 480 years (1 K. 6:1),[90] i.e., at twelve generations of forty years each, of which only one was involved in the wilderness period.

The extreme differences between these schematic quantities offer a concrete impression of the limited significance attributed to the wilderness epoch in the biblical historical model.

b. *Provisional Period.* These features characterize the early *miḏbār* experience as a provisional period, and precisely that characterization carries over as a motif to all comparable situations later. The "wilderness" symbolizes passage from a negative pole (bondage, exile) to a positive one (promised land). As a provisional period the wilderness does not possess any historical substance as such; as a transitory stage it exhibits only derivative intrinsic value. Against this background it is highly unlikely that within OT thinking a new desert stage could acquire the status of a future goal, and even less that it would be propagated as the eschatological end stage of Israel's history.

2. *Two Stages in the Wilderness Wanderings.* It is important to remember that a portion of the biblical wilderness tradition does indeed offer some support for the development of a positive estimation of that epoch. Any consideration of this material must be mindful that all the strata of the basic Pentateuchal tradition subdivide the forty-year period of the wilderness wanderings into two stages of quite unequal length and significance.

a. *The Positive Stage.* The first stage, which tradition figures at just over one year (Nu. 10:11f.), encompasses Israel's experiences from the crossing of the Red Sea to its arrival at the mount of God (Ex. 3:12; 4:27; 18:5; 19:2). The finale and high point of this period are God's covenant with Israel "on the third new moon [stereotypical time frame] after the Israelites had gone out of the land of Egypt" (Ex. 19:1ff.), the Sinai theophany, and the giving of the law (Ex. 20:1ff.; 34:27ff.; Dt. 5). For this initial stage of the trek — from the Red Sea to the mount of God — tradition records no impudence or rebelliousness on Israel's part. Hence this year can with some justification be called Israel's "bridal time," a time during which in faith and devotion it "followed God in the wilderness *(miḏbār),* in a land not sown" (Jer. 2:2).

b. *The "Mount of the Covenant."* It must be emphasized that the locus of the making of the covenant was not the desert, but rather the "mount of God," Sinai (Ex. 19:3ff.; 34:1ff.) or Horeb (Dt. 5:2ff.; 28:69[29:1]), which to be sure was located in the wilder-

90. Noth, *The Deuteronomistic History,* 58ff.

ness. All mention of the tables of the covenant (Dt. 9:9,11,15) and of the Decalog (Ex. 34:28; Dt. 4:13) and all allusions to them reflect the divine revelation "on the mountain," which is localized conceptually not far from the Egyptian border in the wilderness (e.g., Ex. 3:18; 5:3; 8:24[28]; Jer. 31:31ff.; Ps. 78:12f.). Thus it is a distortion of the witness of the OT writings to portray the wilderness as the "most appropriate place for the revelation of the true God,"[91] or to conceive "Bedouinism and Yahwism" as not only historically related, but as existentially consanguineous phenomena as well.[92] Similarly, the biblical evidence renders untenable Max Weber's conclusion, based on "empirical studies," that a provenance from the borderland between desert and cultivated land is characteristic of the biblical prophets.[93] If a geographical characterization of Israel's God is permissible at all, he would have to be understood as a mountain deity,[94] not as a desert deity. This concept lingers on into the period of the monarchy, at least among the surrounding nations. According to an unaffected and hence especially trustworthy account, the servants of the Aramean King Ben-hadad explain the loss in the battle for the city of Samaria by pointing out that Israel's God is an *ʾelōhê hārîm;* they advise fighting the Samaritans in the *mîšôr,* where they surely can be defeated (1 K. 20:23,25). In this context, *mîšôr* cannot refer to the Moabite plain in Transjordan (Dt. 3:10; Josh. 13:9,16,17,21; Jer. 48:8,21), but rather must — similar to *miḏbār* — be understood as "flat country." The occasional synonymous nature of these two terms is shown in the mention of *mîšôr* along with *šᵉpēlâ* and *miḏbār* as typical grazing land (2 Ch. 26:10), and especially in the localization of the city of refuge Bezer *bammiḏbār bᵉʾereṣ hammîšôr* (Dt. 4:43; Josh. 20:8).

c. *The Negative Stage.* The second stage, which lasted around thirty-eight years (Dt. 2:14), begins with the account of the transition from the *miḏbar sînay* into the *miḏbar pāʾrān,* in the second year, on the twentieth day of the second month (after the exodus from Egypt, Nu. 10:11), and ends with the war against the Midianites (Nu. 31). This final skirmish which Israel conducts against a desert people before the conquest of Canaan (cf. Jgs. 6–8 and elsewhere) signals the finale of the wilderness period. According to the biblical account, immediately after this episode Israel entered the territories of the transjordanian states in which the tribes of Reuben, Gad, and Manasseh gained a foothold (Nu. 32).

Consistent with a historiographical model appearing repeatedly in OT literature (cf. Josh. 23f.; 1 S. 12; Neh. 9:6ff., and elsewhere), the author of the book of Numbers offers at this "critical point" in Israel's history a retrospective summary of the last period, namely, the "routes (and stages) of the people of Israel *(masʿê bᵉnê-yiśrāʾēl)* since they went forth out of the land of Egypt," a summary whose authorship he attributes to Moses (Nu. 33:1ff.; Dt. 1:1ff.). That second stage of thirty-eight years was the period of actual wilderness wanderings, the many years *(yāmîm rabbîm,* Josh. 24:7)

---

91. R. Kittel, 38f.
92. Nyström.
93. Talmon, *Biblical Motifs,* 48f.; Weber.
94. → הר *har* VI (III, 442-47).

of "wandering about" in the wasteland. The original divine plan for an exodus from Egypt, to be followed without delay by the giving of the land as promised to the fathers (Ex. 6:2-9), did not anticipate a long sojourn in the wilderness. The trek into the desert had but one goal. The people were to proceed along the quickest route, after "three days" (Ex. 3:18), to the divine mountain in the wilderness to sacrifice to their God and to serve him (e.g., Ex. 5:1; 7:16,26[8:1]; 8:16,23,24[20,27,28]; 9:13; 10:3,9).

The delay in reaching the goal of the conquest resulted from Israel's own sinfulness. All the traditions and literary-historical strata of the Pentateuch and their reflection in the extrapentateuchal writings reveal an understanding of this stage of wilderness wanderings as a time of affliction and tribulation imposed upon Israel as divine punishment for its transgressions *l^ema'an 'annōt^ekā* (Dt. 8:2,16). This stage is precisely identified: "And the length of time we had traveled from Kadesh-barnea until we crossed the Wadi Zered [the natural boundary between Edom and Moab] was thirty-eight years, until the entire generation of warriors had perished," who because of their lack of faith were not to participate in the taking of the land (Dt. 2:14-16; Josh. 5:4-6; Ps. 106:26; Hos. 9:10). Ezekiel views this period as the prototype of divine judgment which must precede any future covenant with Israel: "And I will bring you into the wilderness of the peoples (*midbar hā'ammîm,* cf. 1QM 1:3), and there I will enter into judgment with you face to face. As I entered into judgment with your ancestors in the wilderness of the land of Egypt, so . . . I will purge out the rebels among you, and those who transgress against me; I will bring them out of the land where they reside as aliens [exile], but they shall not enter the land of Israel" (Ezk. 20:35-38; cf. 39ff.).

The episodes of this — hardly "ideal" — period are surveyed comprehensively in what may be called "the book of Israel's failings," which comprises Nu. 11:1–31:5. This literary complex — which does not constitute a self-contained unity (cf., e.g., 26:1–30:17[16]) — is compositionally clearly set apart from the surrounding text. The preceding part of Numbers ends with the "war song of the ark" (Nu. 10:35f.; cf. Ps. 68:2[1]), which already in rabbinic tradition is considered a separate book (Bab. *Šabb.* 115b-116a; *'Aboth R. Nat.* version A. c.30; *Sifre* 22a[95]; *Sop.* vi.1). This "book of iniquities" concludes with an epilogue (Nu. 33:1-49), and the following material (Nu. 33:50–36:13) exhibits no substantive relationship with it.

It is noteworthy that in the twelve chapters constituting the heart of this textual complex (Nu. 11–17,20,21,25,31,33) the term *midbār* is mentioned 24 times, and in the other chapters of Numbers only 19 times. Furthermore, several of these latter occurrences refer directly to episodes recounted in the "book of failings." It is thus no wonder that the atmosphere predominating in this complex decisively influenced the notion of the wilderness period in the extrapentateuchal biblical literature, thereby either directly or indirectly determining both the biblical conception of the "desert" and the biblical attitude toward it.

It is likely that this influence on the overall conception was precipitated not only by isolated literary citations and allusions, but also — and perhaps even more decisively

95. Ed. M. Friedmann (Vienna, 1864).

— by the recitation of historical traditions, primarily within a cultic framework. This was doubtlessly the case regarding the "historical" or, perhaps better, "historiographical" psalms (e.g., Pss. 78,105,106),[96] and can be postulated with high probability at least for Nu. 11–21,33.

Such secondary employment of the wilderness tradition presupposes that its life setting *(Sitz im Leben)* was the cult of a community which itself had a completely different socio-historical form than the "Israel in the wilderness." It was a sedentary, agricultural, and urban society which found in the wilderness reminiscences primarily negative "archetypes"[97] rather than a reflection of its own life in history. This explains why the descriptive historical passages of the Pentateuch never employed the wilderness vocabulary in any figurative-literary fashion (motifs, material, imagery), as is the case in the retrospective extrapentateuchal OT literature. In the Pentateuch, the semantic field "wilderness" always refers to the thing itself, to a "reality," not an image. A few examples of "actual" *miḏbār* features are attested in the book of Job (1:19; 24:5; 38:26), which itself reflects a society resembling Israel in its developmental phase before the conquest. In contrast, the term *miḏbār* is used in Prov. 21:19 as a purely literary figure.

3. *Motif Variations*. The contrasting estimations of the period of wilderness wanderings in the "historical accounts," though especially in the nonhistoriographical parts of the Pentateuch (Dt. 32) and in extrapentateuchal writings, result at least in part from the amplification of the *miḏbār* motif with traditions and material from other areas of experience. Of particular importance are conceptions rooted in the mythic-cultic sphere of the ancient Near East, and the connotations of *miḏbār* as "grazing land," "drift."

a. *The Netherworld*. The fundamentally negative estimation of *miḏbār* in its connotation as "wasteland, wilderness" reflects notions attested in other ancient Near Eastern literatures. In the Egyptian Book of the Dead (175:2), Osiris complains about the desert, in which there is neither water nor air, which is limitless and completely dark, and in which a person can find not a single of love's joys. Babylonian-Assyrian mythology associates the "mistress of the desert" (the sister of Tammuz) with the netherworld, "where she occupies the office of a 'table scribe of hell.'"[98] In Ugaritic myth, the desert or the netherworld is the natural habitation of Mot, the antagonist of the creator-god Baʿal.[99] This explains how *mdbr* and *thmt* can be used synonymously in *parallelismus membrorum*.[100] The same pairing is used in Isa. 63:13; Ps. 78:15.[101] One can compare here Ps. 77, which in addition to the explicit mention of $t^eh\bar{o}m\hat{o}t$ (v. 17[16]) also contains an unmistakable allusion to the desert wanderings: "You led your people like a flock by the hand of Moses and Aaron" (v. 21[20]); and Ps. 29, where the mention

96. See Talmon, *Proceedings*.

97. Coats, Tunyogi.

98. Meissner, 33.

99. *KTU*, 1.4 VII, 55-57.

100. *KTU*, 1.92, 3-5.

101. Dahood, *AB*, XVII, 240; *AB*, XVIIA, 452; *idem*, and T. Penar, "Ugaritic-Hebrew Parallel Pairs," *RSP*, I, 256; Watson, 466.

of *miḏbār* and *miḏbar qāḏēš* (v. 8) is preceded by that of *mayim rabbîm* (v. 3; reference to *tᵉhôm;* cf. also Hab. 3:3-10).

The desert is full of phantomlike creatures.[102] Such mythical beings also populate the *miḏbār* in the OT understanding: *yēmîm* (Gen. 36:24), whom the midrash identifies as demonic beings; *'iyyîm, ṣiyyîm* (Isa. 13:21,22; 34:14; Jer. 50:39); and *lîlît*, the "night hag" (Isa. 34:14). There "*śᵉ'îrîm* [satyrs] will dance" (Isa. 13:21). The presence of such monsters indicates that the wilderness yet persists in the primeval state of chaos, of *tōhû wāḇōhû* (Dt. 32:10; Job 6:18f.; Isa. 34:11; Jer. 4:23-26; cf. Ps. 107:10), similar to the salt wasteland to which God reduced the wicked cities Sodom and Gomorrah (Dt. 29:22[23]; Isa. 13:19-22; Jer. 49:17f.; 50:39f.; Zeph. 2:9; cf. Joel 2:3). Into this godforsaken land[103] (*'ereṣ gᵉzērâ,* Lev. 16:22; cf. 2 Ch. 26:21; Ps. 31:23[22]), the antithesis of the "land of the living" (Isa. 53:8; Ps. 7:6[5]; Lam. 3:53f.; Ezk. 37:11; cf. Joel 2:5; further Gen. 4:14; Isa. 57:20), God himself casts the king of Egypt (*ûnᵉṭaštîḵā hammiḏbārâ*) so that he may perish there (Ezk. 29:5). One reflection of this mythic aspect of the wilderness in OT thought is the annual atonement ritual carried out on the Day of Atonement, when a goat (*śā'îr*) carries the sins of the entire people into the *'ereṣ gᵉzērâ . . . laᵃzā'zēl hammiḏbārâ* (Lev. 16:10,21,22), thereby symbolically guaranteeing the community new life for the coming year.

b. *The "Drift"-Connotation.* Within the semantic field of *miḏbār* as "grazing land" two main themes apparently underlie the predominating motif variations.

(1) *God as the "Shepherd of Israel."* In late prophetic literature and in some psalms, the notion of God as father (Dt. 32:6,18,19), protector, and caretaker of his people (Ex. 19:4; Dt. 32:10f.; also vv. 4,15,18,30,31), which has its roots in the period of wilderness wanderings, is fused with the image of God as "Israel's shepherd," a notion drawn from the semantic field "drift" but not attested in the Pentateuchal wilderness accounts: "Then he led out his people [from Egypt] like sheep, and guided them in the wilderness like a flock" (Ps. 78:52; cf. 77:21[20]; Isa. 40:11; 63:11-14, etc.).

(2) *Love in the miḏbār.* In Canticles, which reflects a pastoral milieu, we encounter the motif "love in the *miḏbār.*" The beloved maiden "comes up from the drift *(miḏbār),* like a column of smoke, perfumed with myrrh and frankincense [an allusion to the pillar of smoke of the wilderness tradition?] . . . leaning upon her beloved [shepherd]" (Cant. 3:6; 8:5).

Another possible source is Ugaritic myth. The 'Anat cycle offers a rather crude description of Ba'al's "love in *dbr*" with a heifer.[104] Considering the circumstances, *dbr* in this context cannot have the otherwise attested connotation "netherworld."[105]

c. *Love in the Post-Exodus miḏbār in Preexilic Prophets.* The fusion of the motif "love in the *miḏbār*" with the wilderness sojourn tradition, a fusion found in the book of Hosea and — presumably dependent on Hosea — in Jeremiah, played a decisive role in the formulation of the hypothesis of an OT "desert ideal." In Hos. 1–3, and in

---

102. Gaster, 132 and n. 19; Porter, 3; Wellhausen, 198ff.
103. Mauser, 44.
104. *KTU,* 1.5 V, 18-22.
105. Contra Driver, 107.

this precise form only in these chapters,[106] the relationship between Israel and its God is conceived as that between husband and wife. The unfaithful people (the wife) must be subjected anew to the wilderness experience so that it may atone its sins there and return in faithfulness to God (the husband) (Hos. 2:16-21[14-19]). This (return) trek into the wilderness, however, is not set up as an aim per se,[107] but rather again as a necessary transitional stage to be followed by reestablishment in the land: "From there [the wilderness] I will give [back to] her her vineyards, and make the Valley of Achor [an allusion to the Achan episode in Josh. 7, esp. v. 25] a door of hope" (Hos. 2:17[15]). This employment of the motif combination love-*miḏbār* is a subsidiary theme in the book of Hosea and cannot be interpreted as the expression of a presumably prophetic "desert ideal." It testifies to a literary process, not a theological or existential idea.

The question must be raised, however, whether or not such a concept can be discerned in Jeremiah. This prophet apparently inserted the God-people-love motif into the tradition of the historical wilderness wanderings with an emphasis on the "wasteland" aspect of *miḏbār* rather than the "drift" aspect. Whereas Hosea focuses on the husband's (God's) steadfast love for his spouse (Israel) (Hos. 2:16[14]; 13:5; cf. 9:10; Dt. 32:10), Jeremiah emphasizes the devotion of the young people to their God. Translated somewhat freely, and without the *parallelismus membrorum*, the text reads as follows: "I remember . . the love of your bridal period (*ḥeseḏ, 'ahᵃḇâ*), how you followed me into the *'ereṣ miḏbār*, in a land that was not sown" (Jer. 2:2). Jeremiah is referring here presumably to the first (positive) stage of wilderness wanderings, the stage between the exodus and the Sinai theophany. For him, too, the wasteland is neither a goal nor an ideal, but rather the transition from bondage to freedom, a situation Israel will experience again in the future (Jer. 31:2-6): "Thus says Yahweh: The people who survived the sword [again] found grace in the *miḏbār*, when I [God] let the people Israel come to rest [in its land] . . . I loved you with an everlasting love (*'ahᵃḇat 'ôlām 'ᵃhaḇtîk); therefore with steadfast love (*ḥeseḏ*) I have drawn you to me [cf. 2:2] . . . for a [the] day will come when sentinels will call [out] in the hill country of Ephraim: 'Arise, let us go up to Zion, to Yahweh our God' " (cf. Isa. 2:5). From this we can conclude that the book of Jeremiah also attests the understanding predominating in the OT writings of a sojourn in the *miḏbār* as a transitory stage and prelude to the conquest, and that it by no means is propagating any "desert ideal."

d. *miḏbār in Postexilic Prophetic Writing.* This is precisely the role played by the word field *miḏbār* in the imagery of Deutero-Isaiah, who uses it extensively. The prophet conceives postexilic events as a reflection of Israel's fundamental historical experience: exodus, wilderness, conquest,[108] though with a shift of emphasis prompted by the changed circumstances. Since with the destruction of the temple and the Babylonian exile Israel had already passed through the stage of catharsis (e.g., Isa. 40:1f.; cf. 4Q176; Jer. 31:1ff.), the new (typological) trek through the desert could be freed

---

106. Kaufmann, 93-95 [Heb.].
107. Contra Mauser, 44ff.; Wolff, *ZThK,* 48 (1951), 129-148.
108. B. W. Anderson, *Festschrift J. Muilenburg,* 177-195.

from the negative aspect of "rebellion" and the concomitant necessity of purification, and invested instead with images of promise and hope. The blossoming, verdant wasteland of the Isaianic vision of restitution (Isa. 35:1f.,6-10; 41:18f.; 43:19f.; 48:21; 51:3; cf. Ps. 107:33-38) contrasts with the *'ereṣ (miḏbār) lō' z^erû'â* (Jer. 2:2) of the early period (e.g., Dt. 32:10). God's mercy manifests itself in the restructuring of chaotic nature and in the restitution of Israel to its land under a ruler from the house of David (Isa. 55:3; cf. ch. 32; Jer. 17:25; 22:4; 23:5; 33:14-17; Hos. 3:5; Am. 9:11).[109] Neither here nor in any other postexilic prophet (Ezekiel, Haggai, Zechariah, Malachi) do we find an idealization of the desert or of the period of wilderness wanderings.

VIII. Qumran. The inclusion of the literature and theology of Qumran in a discussion of the semantic field and fundamental meaning of *miḏbār* in the OT is justified by the following considerations: (a) The *yaḥaḏ* commune exhibited a pronounced OT orientation culminating in its self-understanding as the reestablished postexilic Israel.[110] (b) The retreat of the founders of this group into the Judean desert, where they established their community center, has resulted in their association (without convincing evidence) with the Rechabites. (c) The messianic-millennial character of the *yaḥaḏ* of Qumran encouraged the interpretation of this group's desert life as an historical realization of the presumably OT eschatological desert ideal.[111]

Against this background it is striking that the term *miḏbār* occurs only rarely in the specific Qumran literature. K. G. Kuhn[112] records 12 occurrences of the word, some of which are in tiny, unintelligible fragments. Only one mention of *miḏbār* is a direct reminiscence of Israel's desert trek, and it cites, most significantly, the extermination of the unbelieving desert generation with direct mention both of Dt. 9:23; Ps. 106:25: "They hearkened not to the voice of their Maker . . . and they murmured in their tents . . . and the anger of God was kindled against their congregation" (CD 3:5-9). The authoritative character of CD prompts the conclusion that this isolated citation documents in a concentrated fashion the Qumranites' agreement with the majority of OT writers in their depreciative attitude toward this period of wilderness wanderings. This agreement also manifests itself in their understanding of their own retreat into the desert as a transitory and preparatory stage in the reexperience of (self-imposed) exile and of a renewed future establishment in the land, founded on the "New Covenant" which God established with the "community of saints," *yaḥaḏ b^enê 'ēl* (CD 6:19; 8:21; 1QpHab 2:3). The reestablishment of the "new Jerusalem" (Temple scroll) will be preceded by a purificatory stage conceived on the model of the OT portrayal of the wilderness wanderings: "At the end [of this new interim period] of forty years they [the wicked] shall cease to exist [*hammamrîm yittammû*] and no wicked man shall be found on earth" (4QpPs^a). The identification of the adversaries of the *yaḥaḏ* with the

---

109. Talmon, *Exil-Diaspora-Rückkehr,* 31-56.
110. Talmon, *Frankfurter Universitätsreden,* 42 (1971), 71-83.
111. See VI.2.a above.
112. Kuhn, *Konkordanz zu den Qumrantexten.*

evil desert generation is made explicit by the reference to "forty years" (cf. CD 20:14ff.) and is further fortified by the employment of typical terminology borrowed from the Pentateuchal traditions: *mamrîm* (Nu. 20:10,24; 27:14; Dt. 1:26,43; 9:7,23,24; 31:27; cf. Ps. 78:17,56; 106:7,33,43; 107:11; etc.) and *yittammû* (Nu. 14:34-45; Dt. 2:14-16).

Evocations of the *miḏbār* motif from Deutero-Isaiah also play a role here. The Qumranites applied to themselves the prophet's call to prepare God's way in the wilderness (Isa. 40:3) and to live there as "penitents of the desert" (*šāḇê hammiḏbār,* 4QpPs^a 3:1)[113] according to the laws which had been revealed to them (1QS 9:19f.). As "returners to the Torah" (*šāḇîm lattôrâ,* 4QpPs^a 2:1f.)[114] they will prepare themselves for the coming time of salvation: "They go into the desert for a season, to be born again as the New Israel."[115] The Qumran community did not develop any nomadic way of life based exclusively on small livestock herds, although they may naturally have kept sheep and goats to a limited extent. Archaeological evidence (water reservoirs and irrigation works) testifies to an agricultural economy adapted to the ecological conditions of the Judean desert and accommodated in the Qumran statutes (CD 10f.).[116]

Summarizing we can say that in the Qumran literature, consistent with OT evidence, various aspects of *miḏbār* are fused. The desert was initially a place of refuge from persecution for the *yaḥaḏ* believers. It became the locale of purification and preparation for the new conquest of the land. The Qumranites, too, viewed the sojourn in the desert as a provisional period, not as a goal, as an unavoidable hiatus along the way to their goal, a rite of passage.[117] Although John the Baptist presumably propagated a similar agenda, one reflected in early Christian sources, it was only with the development of the hermit movements that a theological conception crystallized within Christianity which attributed intrinsic value to the desert.

Talmon

---

113. Cf. H. J. Fabry, *Die Wurzel ŠûB in der Qumran-Literatur. BBB,* 46 (1975), 64-68.
114. Cf. *ibid.,* 28-32.
115. Cross, *The Ancient Library of Qumran,* 56.
116. For further discussion cf. F. F. Bruce, "Preparation in the Wilderness: At Qumran and in the NT," *Int,* 16 (1962), 280-291.
117. Talmon, *Biblical Motifs,* 62f.

מָדַד *māḏaḏ;* מִדָּה *middâ;* מַד *maḏ;* מֵמַד *mēmaḏ*

Contents: I. Etymology and Distribution: 1. Akkadian; 2. Ugaritic; 3. Other Semitic Languages; 4. Distribution in the OT; 5. Structural Variations; 6. Synonyms; 7. LXX. II. 1. Secular Usage; 2. Cultic Building Plans; 3. Land Measurement; 4. Legal Contexts; 5. Anthropological Contexts; 6. Theological Usage: a. Creation; b. Increase; c. Land Measurement in Zec. 2:5f.; d. Reprisal; 7. *maḏ.* III. 1. Qumran; 2. Rabbinic Judaism.

I. Etymology and Distribution. The root *mdd,* which in Hebrew constitutes the basis of the forms *māḏaḏ, middâ, maḏ,* and *mēmaḏ,* is attested in almost all the Semitic languages, although in many cases the verification of homographs is difficult, especially in Akkadian (*madādu* II/III, *nadānu*[1]), Ugaritic *(mūdûm),* and Hebrew *(middâ).* At a later stage in the development of Hebrew, the secondary prefixing of *aleph*-prosthe-ticum to the root generated the verbal root *'md.*[2]

1. *Akkadian.* The root *mdd* already occurs in several different forms in Old Akkadian texts. The verb *madādu I* (with no relation to *madādu II,* "to love," or *madādu III,* "to escape") means "to measure" in the broadest sense of the term,[3] with most of its attestations occurring in agricultural-mercantile contexts: measuring out grain,[4] beer,[5] measuring off wood,[6] a field,[7] or a boundary.[8] It thus includes not only the comparison of objects with given standards (a measuring reed[9]) and weights, but also the measuring and meting out of portions partitively from given quantities. The term *madādu* apparently encompasses the entire process.[10]

Measuring is an important activity in house construction.[11] Later texts also speak of the magical measuring of a person.[12] Marduk is said to measure the waters of the sea.[13] Several equivocal attestations use the verb to mean "measure off," perhaps in the sense of "to terminate": Enki is to "measure off (= interrupt)" a canal with sludge.[14] This semantic valence also manifests itself in the "mene tekel" passage in Dnl. 5:25ff.

In addition to the verb, Akkadian also attests several nominal forms: already Old Bab. *middatum/mindatum,* "measure," both in the sense of a standard unit and instrument of measurement as well as an overall measurement (e.g., of heaven).[15] Early

---

māḏaḏ. J. Reider, "מָדַד in Job 7 4," *JBL,* 39 (1920), 60-65; W. Thiel, "Zur gesellschaftlichen Stellung des *mudu* in Ugarit," *UF,* 12 (1980), 349-356; J. Trinquet, "Métrologie Biblique," *DBS,* V (1957), 1212-1250; P. Vargyas, "Le *mudu* à Ugarit: Ami du roi?" *UF,* 13 (1981), 165-179; O. Wahl, "Göttliches und menschliches Messen: Zur Botschaft von Sacharja 2,5-9," *Künder des Wortes. Festschrift J. Schreiner* (Würzburg, 1982), 255-272.

1. Cf. M. Ellenbogen, *Foreign Words in the OT* (London, 1962), 98.
2. Cf. *WTM,* I, 94.
3. *AHw,* II (1972), 571; *CAD,* X/1 (1977), 5-9.
4. Cf. *VAB,* 5 (1913, repr. 1971), 535.
5. *VAS* (1983), 6, 104, 14.
6. Cf. H. Zimmern, "Assyrische chemisch-technische Rezepte," *ZA,* N.S. 3[36] (1924/25), 202, 50.
7. G. Dossin, *Correspondence de Šamši-Addu et de ses fils. ARM,* I (1949, repr. 1978), 7, 44.
8. R. F. Harper, *ABL,* 621, 10.
9. S. H. Langdon, *Die neubabylonischen Königsinschriften. VAB,* 4 (1912), 62, 27.
10. See the entries in *CAD.*
11. G. Dossin, "Tablette administrative," *Textes divers. Festschrift A. Parrot. ARM,* XIII (1964), 7, 15.
12. *CT,* 17, 15, 21.
13. *RAcc,* 134, 241; 138, 309; cf. Job 38:5; Isa. 40:12.
14. *CT,* 32.4 XII, 25; cf. *BWL,* 36, 100.
15. *AHw,* II, 650.

occurrences are also attested for *namaddum/namandum,* "measuring vessel,"[16] and *namdattum,* "something measured."[17] Not until Middle Babylonian is the term *mādidu/mandidu,* "measuring official (for grain, etc.)," attested,[18] an official engaged in the immediate vicinity of the temple. His office *māditūtu/mandidūtu* was bestowed as sinecure or compensation.[19]

Herbert Huffmon has noted that Amorite personal names constructed from this verbal root also suggest the meaning "to help."[20]

2. *Ugaritic.* The root *mdd* itself does not occur in Ugaritic, although it might have provided the basis for the plural form *mdm*[21] and the noun *md,* "cloak."[22]

The term *md/mudu* occurs frequently in administrative texts from Ugarit, especially in lists of royal servants, where it refers perhaps to a vocational group of "surveyors,"[23] "measurers" or cultic custodians of weights and measures (since these were protected by divine sanction),[24] or more generally "courtiers."[25] This designation, however, is also frequently derived from Akk. *ēdû,* "to know,"[26] or *ydd,* "to love."[27] That this is not the case, however, is suggested by the lists themselves,[28] in which these officials are classified with status equal to that of craftsmen, especially builders and lower military officials, but below that of priests and merchants; thus the term is apparently not referring to the highest "counselors" and closest "friends" ("privy councilor") of the king.[29]

The reading "refugee," from *madādu III,* "to escape,"[30] does not fit the context in most cases. Although they are classified above all other groups in some lists,[31] this may be a result of the peculiar nature of the lists themselves. Winfred Thiel[32] identifies *mdm* as a specific vocational group (?) that was elevated from its previous status to a privileged position. However, this cannot be supported by more specific evidence, nor

---

16. *AHw,* II, 725.
17. *AHw,* II, 727.
18. *AHw,* II, 572.
19. For documentation, see *AHw.*
20. For a listing, see *APNM,* 229.
21. *UT,* no. 1427.
22. *UT,* no. 1423; *WUS,* no. 1516.
23. *UT,* no. 1427.
24. J. Gray, "Feudalism in Ugarit and Early Israel," *ZAW,* 64 (1952), 50f.; cf. *idem, The Legacy of Canaan. SVT,* 5 (^{2}1965), 214.
25. P. Xella, "Lexicographische Randbemerkungen," *UF,* 12 (1980), 452.
26. P. Jensen, "Akkadisch *mudū,*" *ZA,* N.S. 1[35] (1924), 124-132; T. N. D. Mettinger, *Solomonic State Officials. CB,* 5 (1971), 63-69.
27. M. L. Heltzer, *Semitskie jazyki,* 2/1 (1965), 335-358; J. Nougayrol, *PRU,* VI, 151.
28. E.g., *KTU,* 4.38; 4.47; 4.99.
29. E. A. Speiser, "Akkadian Documents from Ras Shamra," *JAOS,* 75 (1955), 163; cf. Vargyas: "one guild among others."
30. Cf. A. Goetze, *The Laws of Eshnunna. AASOR,* 31 (1956), 111.
31. *KTU,* 4.69; 4.103.
32. *UF,* 12 (1980), 349-355.

does it seem particularly probable. P. Vargyas[33] identifies *mdm* as a frequently mentioned social group belonging to a class of attendants with medium social status,[34] obligated to pay tributes or fees on the basis of certain investitures. Vargyas makes the etymological connection with the Nuzi term *muddu,* "amount of tribute, payment quota,"[35] from the root *madādu,* "measure." The geminate form, however, makes a precipitous comparison with *mdm* difficult.

Ugaritic also attests personal names with *mdd,* "measure, measure out, help," e.g., *ymd* and *ỉlmd,* the latter of which perhaps also reflects Akk. *ili-ma-addu,* "my god, verily, is Addu."[36]

3. *Other Semitic Languages.* This root is widely distributed in the other Semitic languages. Although Syr. *md,* "follow after, flee from,"[37] likely does not derive from this root[38] (cf. *madādu* III), South Semitic has preserved some interesting semantic aspects: OSA *mdd,* "to measure," "standard, time period";[39] Arab. *madda,* "spread out, stretch out," IV "to help, grant a respite," VI + VIII, "stretch, extend"; *madd,* "extension"; *mudd,* "measure of quantity"; *mudda,* "period of time"; *madad,* "succor, aid"; *madīd,* "extended," etc.; and Tigré *mᵃdda,* "spread out, stretch out," to "attack, strike."[40]

Within this South Semitic linguistic sphere the meaning "extend, stretch, stretch out" has preserved a semantic specification that undeniably belongs in the immediate vicinity of the original meaning, even if in view of the East Semitic findings it cannot actually constitute that meaning itself[41] (cf. the hithpael in Hebrew). This semantic component also justifies the etymological association of *maḏ,* "cloak,"[42] with *mdd* (= *madādu I*).

4. *Distribution in the OT.* The verb *māḏaḏ* occurs 52 times in the Hebrew OT[43]: 43 times in the qal, 3 in the niphal, 4 in the piel, and once each in the hiphil and hithpael. Abraham Even-Shoshan counts 53 occurrences, since he also counts Hab. 3:6.[44] As its distribution clearly shows, the verb definitely belongs to late OT vocabulary: 36 occurrences in Ezekiel (primarily Ezk. 40–42); one each in Deutero-Isaiah, Trito-Isaiah, Zechariah, Ruth, and Job; the few occurrences in the Pentateuch can be attributed to

33. *UF,* 13 (1981), 165-179.
34. *Ibid.,* 169.
35. M. Müller, "Einige bemerkenswerte Urkunden aus Tell al-Faḫḫār zur altmesopotamischen Rechts-, Sozial-, und Wirtschaftsgeschichte," *WO,* 9 (1977), 30.
36. *PNU,* 40.156.
37. *LexSyr,* 374.
38. Contra *HAL,* II (1995), 547.
39. ContiRossini, 175.
40. *TigrWb,* 141; Leslau, *Contributions,* 30.
41. Contra J. L. Palache, *Semantic Notes on the Hebrew Lexicon* (Eng. trans., Leiden, 1959), 43.
42. *KBL*³, 518; *DISO,* 142.
43. Lisowsky, 752f.
44. *A New Concordance of the OT* (Jerusalem, ²1990), 622.

P. Later redactors are also responsible for the occurrences in Dt. 21:2; Jer. 31:37; 33:22, as well as those in the Deuteronomistic history: 2 S. 8:2 (twice); 1 K. 17:21. The remaining occurrences are Hos. 2:1(Eng. 1:10);[45] Ps. 60:8(6); 108:8(7).[46] Thus Hos. 2:1(1:10) likely constitutes the earliest and perhaps only preexilic occurrence.

The term *middâ* also occurs 53 times and is part of late OT vocabulary (25 times in Ezekiel; 6 in P; 5 in the Deuteronomistic history; 11 in the Chronicler's history); *maḏ* occurs 12 times (7 in the Deuteronomistic history, also in P and Job); Ps. 109:18; 133:2 attest perhaps the earliest occurrences. Jer. 13:25 exhibits textual difficulties. Considering the parallels in the Chronicler's work, 2 S. 21:20; 23:21 should probably also read *middâ.*[47] Finally, the term *mēmaḏ* (cf. Akk. *namaddu,* "measuring vessel"[48]) occurs only in Job 38:5, and is thus also postexilic.

5. *Structural Variations.* In more than two thirds of its occurrences, the verb *māḏaḏ* is used in factitive, largely consecutive forms, and thus within the framework of narrative texts and descriptions. In most instances human beings are the subject: the Israelites (e.g., Ex. 16:18; Nu. 35:5; Ezk. 43:10); Boaz (Ruth 3:15); David (2 S. 8:2); the judges and elders (Dt. 21:2). The verb *māḏaḏ* thus refers to an actual procedure from the daily life of human beings. This is reflected in the fact that God occurs only 3 times as its subject: Isa. 65:7 (Yahweh); Ps. 60:8(6); 108:8(7) *(*'*ᵉlōhîm).* The *'îš* in Ezekiel's temple vision and in Zechariah's third vision, with 30 + 1 occurrences, constitutes more than half of all occurrences by itself. Considering this latter usage, one might suspect that *māḏaḏ* is a legal term.[49] Direct objects are usually given without the particle, though occasionally with *'el* (Dt. 21:2) or *'eṯ* (Zec. 2:6[2]; Ezk. 40). The process of measuring off something is indicated by *min* (Ezk. 40:23), that of measuring by comparison with a given standard by the particle *bᵉ* (Ex. 16:18) or *kᵉ* (Ezk. 40:35), and that of measuring out something by *'al* (Isa. 65:7).

The noun *middâ* is combined with the cardinal number *'aḥaṯ,* "one measure" (= "an equal measure"; e.g., Ex. 26:2,8; 36:9) and with the ordinal number *šēnîṯ,* "the second measure" (Neh. 3). A corresponding *hammiddâ hāri'šōnâ,* "the first [= earlier] standard" (2 Ch. 3:3), implies a purely historical connotation. Other construct combinations

---

45. This occurrence is considered a product of the exilic period by O. Procksch, *Theologie des ATs* (Gütersloh, 1950), 160 (cf. also *idem, Die kleinen prophetischen Schriften vor dem Exil. Erläuterungen zum AT,* 6 [Calw, 1910, repr. 1929]); K. Budde, *Geschichte der althebräischen Literatur* (Leipzig, ²1909), 73f. (cf. *idem, Das prophetische Schrifttum* [Tübingen, ²1922]); T. H. Robinson, *Die zwölf kleinen Propheten: Hosea bis Micha. HAT,* XIV (²1954), *in loc.* Both H. W. Wolff, *Hosea. Herm* (Eng. trans. 1974), 25-27, and W. Rudolph, *Hosea. KAT,* XIII/1 (1966), *in loc.,* think Hos. 2:1f.(1:10f.) reflects genuine words of the prophet Hosea used by a later compiler.

46. H.-J. Kraus, *Psalms 60-150* (Eng. trans., Minneapolis, 1989), *in loc.,* ascribes a provenance after 587. J. Wellhausen, *The Book of Psalms* (Eng. trans., New York, 1898), and W. Staerk, *Lyrik (Psalmen, Hoheslied, und Verwandtes). SAT,* III/1 (²1920), consider it a product of the Maccabean period.

47. Cf. *KBL*³, 519.

48. *AHw,* II, 725.

49. Cf. discussion below.

are *'îš middâ,* "man of stature" (Isa. 45:14) and *'anšê middôṯ* (Nu. 13:32); cf. also *bêṯ middôṯ,* "spacious house" (Jer. 22:14). These last examples show that *middâ* can take on adjectival properties. Further construct combinations include the designations for the various measuring instruments: *ḥeḇel middâ* (Zec. 2:5[1]), *qaw hammiddâ,* "measuring line" (Jer. 31:39), and *qᵉnēh hammiddâ,* "measuring reed" (Ezk. 40,42). The term *middâ* is used as *nomen rectum* to *yāmîm,* "measure of days" (= "span of life") (Ps. 39:5[4]), and to various objects associated with buildings: *ša'ar,* "gate" (Ezk. 40:21f.); *bayiṯ,* "temple" (Ezk. 42:15); *mizbēaḥ,* "altar" (Ezk. 43:13); and *gāzîṯ,* "hewn stones" (1 K. 7:9,11). Finally, Neh. 5:4 mentions *middaṯ hammelek,* "king's standard" (= "tax"; cf. also *'eḇen hammeleḵ,* "royal standard weight," in 2 S. 14:26[50]). Considering the preceding discussion,[51] it does not seem advisable to conclude on the basis of this passage the presence of an etymologically independent term *middâ* II.[52]

Aram. *middâ* or *mindâ* (Ezr. 4:13,20; 6:8; 7:24) also occurs with this meaning.

6. *Synonyms.* Synonyms for the verb include *zrh* II, "to measure off" (= "examine"); *kûl* in connection with measure of quantity, "to measure" (= "contain, hold"); and *tikkēn,* "determine the measure of something," whereby the connotation "examine" also clearly resonates. Of a purely descriptive nature is the term *nāṭâ,* "stretch out," used with *qaw* (e.g., Job 38:5; Isa. 44:13): "stretch out a measuring line" (as a legal term esp. in Isa. 34:11).

The subst. *middâ* apparently has no real synonyms, since *qaw, qāneh, pāṯîl, ḥeḇel,* and *ḥûṭ* all refer to measuring instruments, the latter ("line") occurring in this sense only in connection with the temple pillars (1 K. 7:15; Jer. 52:21). The only possibility is perhaps *maṯkōneṯ,* "measurement, proportion," which does, however, refer clearly to measurements in a cultic context (Ex. 30: anointing oil; Ezk. 45:11: standard measures in connection with offerings).

Finally, *maḏ* is a general term for "clothing" and is similar to terms such as → בגד *beged (beghedh),* → לבש *lāḇēš,* and *kᵉsûṯ.*

7. *LXX.* The LXX renders *māḏaḏ* largely with *metreín* (4 times) and its compounds *diametreín* (36 times!) and *ekmetreín* (3 times). In contrast, *middâ* is rendered by *métron* (36 times) and *diamétrēsis* (4 times); isolated renderings occur with *árithmos, geōmetrikós, symmetrós,* and other terms; *maḏ,* understood as a piece of clothing, is nonetheless given various interpretations: *mandýas* (5 times), *himátion* (twice), *lampḗnē,* and *chítōn* (once each); *mēmaḏ* is rendered by *métron.*

II. 1. *Secular Usage.* As the previous discussion suggested, *māḏaḏ* and *middâ* for the most part occur with the completely concrete meanings of "to measure" and

50. → אבן *'eḇen ('ebhen),* I, 50.
51. See I.1 above.
52. Cf. *GesB,* 399; *HAL,* II, 548; F. Altheim and R. Stiehl, "Haushalt und Heerwesen im aksümitischen Reich," *Jahrbuch für Wirtschaftsgeschichte,* 1967/2, 311f.

"measure, standard," frequently specified more closely by familiar units of measurement: cubit, bath, kor.[53] A purely secular usage of these terms can no longer be clearly distinguished. The most likely candidates are those occurrences in which *middâ* is used with quasi-adjectival force in construct combinations with the meaning of a genitive of quality.[54] Within the framework of the Yahwistic reconnaissance report a Priestly redactor calls the original inhabitants of Canaan "people of great size" (Nu. 13:32). 1 Ch. 20:6 also alludes to the colossal size of these people; the par. *māḏôn,* "quarrelsome," in 2 S. 21:20 should be emended according to 1 Chronicles. Isa. 45:14 calls the Sabeans of South Arabia "tall of stature," and 1 Ch. 11:23 mentions a giant Egyptian whom Benaiah, one of David's mighty men, slew. Here, too, the par. *mar'eh,* "[pleasing] of appearance" (2 S. 23:21) should be emended accordingly. All these examples disclose the narrator's intention of portraying Yahweh's salvific actions as ever greater and mightier. Any person, however, who intends to undertake something great "beyond measure," such as Jehoiakim's plans to build a *bêṯ middôṯ,* must be mindful of the criticism of the prophet (Jer. 22:14).

2. *Cultic Building Plans.* These terms occur with particular frequency in connection with cultic building plans and descriptions.

a. *Tabernacle and Ark.* In the Priestly account of the making of the holy tabernacle,[55] the ark,[56] and the tabernacle equipment (Ex. 25:10-40), the terms *māḏaḏ* and *middâ* do not occur despite numerous detailed dimensions. In all these cases the dimensions themselves are indicated numerically. Only 4 passages speak of curtains and drapes, which are to be made according to the "same measure" (*middâ 'aḥaṯ,* Ex. 26:2,8; 36:9,15). These are to serve the complicated covering above the *miškān,* and thus come from the redaction of P^S, which amplified the Priestly description of the holy tabernacle on the basis of the postexilic Second Temple. "Contrary to the intentions of the Priestly design, these additions make the tent sanctuary conform to the accoutrements of the postexilic temple. . . . This adaptation of the Priestly design to the realities of the temple shows that in the postexilic period the tent sanctuary of Sinai was understood as the prototype and reflection of the Jerusalem temple."[57] The wooden *miškān,* however, is yet ambiguous from an architectural perspective *(ṣᵉlāʿôṯ?)* regarding its intended counterpart within the edifice of the postexilic temple.[58]

b. *Solomonic Temple.* The consistency regarding standard dimensions characteristic of the Priestly writing is also emphasized in connection with the Solomonic temple. Both cherubim in the *dᵉḇîr* had the "same measure" and the "same form" (*qeṣeḇ 'eḥāḏ,* 1 K. 6:25), as did the ten stands (*mᵉḵōnôṯ,* 7:37, uncertain text?). The stones for

53. Cf. *BRL*², 204ff.
54. Cf. *GK* §128s,t.
55. → אהל *'ōhel* (I, 118-130).
56. → ארון *'ᵃrôn* (I, 363-374).
57. Cf. V. Fritz, *Tempel und Zelt. WMANT,* 47 (1977), 122, 165f.
58. On the construction of this span of curtains, cf. B. Pelzl, "Das Zeltheiligtum von Ex 25ff.," *UF,* 7 (1975), 379-387.

Solomon's palace were also to be hewn "with quadrilateral evenness" (NRSV "according to measure"; 1 K 7:9,11; 6:36 and 7:12 speak only of *gāzîṯ* for the stones of the encompassing walls), probably also the stones for the temple, which according to the problematical and perhaps secondary verse 1 K. 6:7 were already prepared at the quarry. Perhaps, however, the expression *'eḇen-šᵉlēmâ massāʿ* is describing the stones as "unhewn"[59] as a characterization of their numinous integrity and the builders' artistic and technical skill. Solomonic wall construction has been preserved especially in Megiddo.[60] An archaic standard (*middâ hāri'šônâ,* 2 Ch. 3:3) was probably still used in connection with the Solomonic temple.

c. *Ezekiel's "Draft Constitution."* The largest and most concentrated accumulation of occurrences of *māḏaḏ* and *middâ* is found in Ezekiel's "draft constitution" (Ezk. 40–48). In Ezekiel's great vision of the new temple and the new land, an *'îš* leads the prophet through the temple area and presents to him the layout in a series of silently executed measurement procedures explicated only by brief remarks. The prophet is probably concerned primarily with contrasting this new cultic layout — as the ideal, pure, and cultically appropriate locus of the cult — with the preexilic temple environs.

Chs. 40–48 do not constitute a literary-critical unit. Hartmut Gese[61] and after him Walther Zimmerli[62] have illuminated the literary prehistory involved and shown that the numerous additions to the text corrected the first draft of the vision "consistently according to the historical structures of the Second Temple."[63]

(1) As far as specifics are concerned, the text's basic layer consists of a "guidance vision" (40:1-37,47-49; 41:1-4) (with 26 occurrences of our root) which has been reworked and expanded at least five times. In contrast, Ernst Vogt[64] postulates a smaller fundamental text (40:1-2; 43:4-7a; 47:1-12) that underwent three expansions: 40–42 (extensive temple description); 44–46 (extensive collection of laws); and 47–48 (addendum concerning the holy land and holy city). Vogt's point of departure, however, is problematical, since even the literary-critical break he postulates in 40:2,3 cannot be carried through. Ezk. 40:3 follows upon 40:1 seamlessly through the stylistic device of repetition.[65] Actually, 40:2 does seem (contra Gese, Zimmerli, and Vogt) to contain a later insertion.

(2) An initial amplification inserts a description into the guidance vision (41:5-15a; 42:15-20; 47:1-12) (with 13 occurrences of our root), which complements the basic

---

59. *HAL,* II, 548; M. Noth, *Könige 1–16. BK,* IX/1 (^{2}1983), 116.

60. Cf. Y. Yadin, "New Light on Solomon's Megiddo," *BA,* 23 (1960), 62-68; *idem,* "The Megiddo Stables," *Nelson Glueck Memorial Volume. ErIsr,* 12 (1975), 57-62 [Heb.]; D. Ussishkin, "King Solomon's Palace and Building 1723 in Megiddo," *IEJ,* 16 (1966), 174-186. → אבן *'eḇen ('ebhen)* (I, 48-51); → חומה *ḥômâ (chômāh)* (IV, 267-271); → חצב *ḥāṣaḇ,* V, 126, II.3 (*gāzîṯ*).

61. *Der Verfassungsentwurf des Ezechiel (Kap. 40–48) traditionsgeschichtlich untersucht. BHTh,* 25 (1957).

62. W. Zimmerli, *Ezekiel 2. Herm* (Eng. trans. 1983), 547-553.

63. Gese, 108.

64. *Untersuchungen zum Buch Ezechiel. AnBibl,* 95 (1981).

65. Cf. C. Kuhl, "Die 'Wiederaufnahme' — ein literarkritisches Prinzip?" *ZAW,* 64 (1952), 1-11.

outline presented in the vision itself. Neither account mentions any dimensions regarding height!

(3) Within the later expansions (according to Zimmerli) one can distinguish a *nāśî'* ("prince") stratum (44:1-3; 45:21-25; 46:1-12) and a "Zadokite" stratum (44:6-16,28-30a; 45:13-15) with additions (44:17-27,30b,31; 45:1-9), all of which probably originated completely outside the context of the present tradition. Neither stratum contains any occurrences of our root, and neither contains any reminiscence of the numerous measuring procedures. Additions inserted possibly at the same time (43:1-11; 48:1-29) attest 2 occurrences of the root.

(4) Further redactional activity toward the end of the exile worked in additional texts reflecting the growing disputes concerning priorities between Zadokites and Levites, especially texts more sharply delimiting sacred areas within the sanctuary itself (42:1-14; 43:12-17; 45:1-9; 46:16-24; 48:30-35) (with 6 occurrences of our root).

(5) A fourth redaction stresses the notion of atonement in the postexilic cult (no occurrences of our root).

(6) The section encompassing 41:15b-26 (with 1 occurrence) offers a description of the temple interior and constitutes an extraneous element in the course of the narrative. Despite indications of dimensions (v. 22), *māḏaḏ* and *middâ* do not occur at all (cf., however, v. 17[66]).

Gese[67] already noticed that the alternation between stative and factitive verbal forms seems to exhibit literary-critical significance. Actually, this is even more evident than Gese suspected. The basic stratum uses the narrative *wayyāmōḏ* so consistently that Zimmerli speaks in this context of a "measurement formula" (cf. 40:5,6,8,9,10,13). In most instances the object is indicated by the accusative particle *'eṯ,* although this can be omitted even when the object is definite (e.g., 40:20).[68] Only twice does the basic stratum use the stative with *waw* (40:24,35), where accordingly the accusative particle *'eṯ* does not appear. These exceptions are apparently not caused by the immediately preceding guidance formula (cf. also 40:28,32; 41:1), nor are they secondary. In contrast, the first reworking (2) uses *māḏaḏ* consistently in the stative (41:13,15; 42:16-20), although not in 41:5 nor in the section 47:1-12, where factitive consecutives appear (47:3-5). While the isolated stative exceptions can be attributed to the increasing linguistic malleability of later Hebrew, the findings in 47:1-12 suggest that this section either belongs yet to the basic stratum itself or — if it does indeed belong to the first stratum of reworking — it has come from a different redactor.[69] As a parallel example, cf. 2 K. 23:4-20. The 2 occurrences within the *nāśî'* stratum (3) (Ezk. 43:10; 48:16) and the 6 occurrences in stratum (4) are strikingly different from the previous findings.

66. See following discussion.
67. Pp. 29ff.
68. Cf. *ibid.,* 15.
69. Concerning the displacement of narrative verbal forms by statives + *waw,* cf. G. Beer–R. Meyer, *Hebräische Grammatik* III (Berlin, ³1972), 46f. On the literary-critical valence of these forms, cf. W. Gross, "Otto Rössler und die Diskussion um das althebräische Verbalsystem," *BN,* 18 (1982), 68f. and n. 167.

The verb is used only twice. In 43:10, Israel is to measure, and in 45:3 Ezekiel; all the other occurrences involve the substantive. There the section encompassing 48:30-35 (4) is even more of an anomaly in that it uses *middâ* absolutely as a standard indication of "measure."

Finally, the use of *middôṯ* in stratum (6) in 41:17 is also of literary-critical significance, since here, apart from text-critical difficulties, the term must have a different meaning. Standing isolated at the end of the verse the term *middôṯ* is probably a secondary textual insertion, since it is not yet attested by the LXX tradition. G. R. Driver[70] and Zimmerli[71] have suggested various solutions. Zimmerli suspects that *middôṯ* here means "measured off area, strip, field," a "geometrical division of the ornamented area into precise fields."[72] However, this semantic peculiarity of *middâ* as a "(flat) surface dimension" raises serious questions, since it is otherwise understood only in the sense of "linear measurement" (it first occurs as a "[flat] surface dimension" only during the rabbinic period[73]); furthermore, the "impossible" insertion into the present context begs the question of its elimination.[74] Finally, *middôṯ* cannot be taken as part of v. 18,[75] i.e., "gigantic figures," since that prompts further changes in MT.[76]

Although it seems highly likely that the differing formal usage within the individual strata also generates semantic shifts, this is difficult to demonstrate.

Within the guidance vision, *mādaḏ* apparently serves as a structural element for the vision account itself, consolidated into the "measurement formula" especially in the form *wayyāmôḏ* (alongside the "guidance formula" *wayᵉḇîʼēnî,* 40:17,28,32,35,48; less frequently as *wayyāḇēʼ,* 40:1,3; *wayyôliḵēnî,* 40:24). Vogt takes a different view: "This activity of guiding and measuring is simply a stylistic device designed to render a vivid visual account of the carefully conceived temple outline. The temple outline itself was not given in a vision, but is rather the result of considerable reflection and precise calculations."[77] The *ʼîš* incorporates the prophet, as a witness of this proclamatory testimony, into the series of measurements, whereby this "measuring" now becomes a common activity shared by the *ʼîš* and the prophet. The measurement procedures extend from the external gates to the interior ones, and thence to the outer courts, aiming all the time at an overall survey of the temple edifice.

In three measurement processes its vestibule (vv. 48f.), main hall (41:1f.) and inner sanctuary (41:3f.) are described. In the case of this last structure, for the first time on the whole progress through the temple a brief word of interpretation is heard from the man

---

70. "Linguistic and Textual Problems: Ezekiel," *Bibl,* 19 (1938), 184f.; "Ezekiel: Linguistic and Textual Problems," *Bibl,* 35 (1954), 306.

71. P. 384.

72. *Ibid.,* 387.

73. Cf. *WTM,* III, 25.

74. With J. Ziegler, *Ezechiel. Septuaginta: Vetus Testamentum Graecum,* 16/1 (Göttingen, ²1977); H. F. Fuhs, *Ezechiel 2. EB* (1988); Gese, 176. Contra Zimmerli. There is no need then to eliminate the entire verse. Cf. W. Eichrodt, *Ezekiel. OTL* (Eng. trans. 1970), 535 and n. 11.

75. G. A. Cooke, *Ezekiel. ICC* (1936, repr. 1951), 450.

76. *Ibid.,* 455.

77. P. 137.

> who . . . has hitherto completed the whole process of guidance and measurement in silence. From the point of view of form, too, this is a goal of the whole leading of the prophet from the periphery of the temple buildings to the threshold of the innermost, central part.[78]

The actual measurement is carried out by means of a *pāṯîl* and a *qᵉnēh hammiddâ* (40:3,5; stratum 2 speaks of a *qaw,* 47:3; Zec. 2:5[2:1] speaks of a *ḥeḇel middâ*), measuring instruments suitable for both longer and shorter distances.[79] In what follows the unit of measurement is first the "rod" (*qāneh,* Ezk. 40:4-8), then consistently the "cubit" (*'ammâ).*[80] For any attempt at determining the theological significance of these relatively vivid measurement processes (exception: Ezk. 40:5), both the point of departure and goal of the measurements as well as the accompanying interpretation given by the *'îš* (41:4: *zeh qōḏeš haqqᵒḏāšîm,* "This is the most holy place") are of particular importance. The measured dimensions are also of consequence, since in addition to the individual valences (the number twenty-five and multiples; rhythm of creation, etc.)[81] they seem to express the "mysterious symmetry and proportion" relating to the temple complex.[82] Finally, one must also consider that the outer court and the *lᵉšāḵôṯ* along the outer wall are merely described, but not "measured" (40:17f.). This yields the following conclusions for the interpretation of *māḏaḏ:*

(1) In both proximity to and distance from tradition, these measurement processes reveal new proportions and pure dimensions. The term *māḏaḏ* becomes an indirect term of *revelation.*

(2) Zimmerli correctly points out[83] that the *'îš* is involved in measuring a divine work, not a human work, and to that extent this activity takes on the character of a *promise.*

(3) Ps. 48:13-15(12-14) shows that the goal of any precise examination of the temple is to proclaim Yahweh's greatness. Thus here, too, the activity of measuring is ultimately directed toward *proclamation* (cf. Ezk. 40:4: *haggēḏ*).

(4) The measuring process subdivides the overriding process of guidance from the outer gate to the holy of holies. In measured stages the human being draws closer and closer to that goal, so as to "measure" its significance for himself. "The orientation towards the holy is unmistakably expressed as guidance for man."[84]

(5) The process of measuring implies the process by which Yahweh *takes possession* of the temple complex as he enters his sanctuary from the east. Since the secular areas are not counted as part of this separated area, neither are they measured.

(6) Finally, this "measuring" could also become a representation of the *rhythm of creation.*

---

78. Zimmerli, 343.

79. For extrabiblical examples of these instruments, cf. E. D. Van Buren, "The Rod and Ring," *ArOr,* 17 (1949), 434-450.

80. Cf. R. B. Y. Scott, "Weights and Measures of the Bible," *BA,* 22 (1959), 22-40; Zimmerli, 349.

81. Vogt takes a different view of this.

82. Zimmerli, 344.

83. *Ibid.,* 361.

84. *Idem.*

The first redactional stratum functions to supply previously missing dimensions (41:5,13,15 concerning the temple itself, and 42:16-20 concerning the temple complex). Here the term *māḏaḏ* exhibits the additional connotation of a separation of the holy from the secular. In 47:3-5, the same (?) redaction portrays by means of ever increasing dimensions the rapid enlargement of the temple spring from its modest beginnings, employing the term *māḏaḏ* in a clearly disparate fashion.

The additions made in connection with the *nāśî'* stratum in 43:1-11 look back at the concluded measurements, pick up on them, and now speak explicitly of the entry of Yahweh's *kāḇôḏ* as he moves to take possession of the temple. In view of this theophany the following conclusion is drawn from the original proclamatory commission (40:4) to the prophet. The "measurement" (= proclamation) of the sanctuary and of the accompanying commencement of Yahweh's salvific activity along with the people's own measuring on the same pattern is intended to effect "shame" (43:10f.),[85] a renewed reflection on the appropriate way to conduct oneself with regard to the holy. Finally, 48:16 — completely aside from the intention of the original guidance vision and its initial amplification — speaks of the dimensions *(middôṯ)* of the city. Within the framework of a land allocation list the system of spheres of graded sanctity is to be extended beyond the actual temple area. The fourth stratum of additions also tries to accommodate itself stylistically to the traditional material here: 43:13 speaks of the *middôṯ* of the altar; a pre-Priestly addendum to the land allocation list (45:3, standing at the wrong location) speaks of "measuring off" land for the sanctuary from that apportioned the priests. This qualifies the priests' land as a sacred sphere (cf. 48:12).[86]

d. *Nehemiah.* In the postexilic period the term *middâ* in connection with construction plans is attested in Neh. 3. Here the term apparently refers to "sections" of the city wall which are not identified more specifically but whose location was probably familiar, and which were assigned to various city families for repair. Work on the city wall was distributed across many groups whose appointed sections variously were situated "next to the other" *(ʿal-yāḏô/yāḏām,* vv. 2,4,5, and *passim*). The list of those who built the wall is amplified by the insertion of a second list of those who — in stereotypical formulation — repaired a *middâ šēnîṯ* (vv. 11,19,20,21,24,27,30). This refers apparently to the repair of a "second section" after the corresponding builder had already fulfilled his construction quota (compare v. 21 with v. 4; v. 24 with v. 18; v. 27 with v. 5; v. 30 with v. 8). This second list of those who were over-zealous probably comes from a second listing which was unsystematically inserted. For vv. 19,20 the preceding "first section" is not mentioned, and for v. 11 it is added subsequently in vv. 23 and 31. Finally, two repair sections are reported for Meshullam in vv. 3 and 30 without either being designated as *middâ šēnîṯ*. This makes an additional semantic connotation for *middâ šēnîṯ* unlikely.

---

85. → כלם *klm,* IV.2.b (VII, 191-94).

86. On the special meaning of *middôṯ* in the sixth stratum of additions, see the previous discussion on Ezk. 41:17.

3. *Land Measurement.* It is astonishing that the terms *māḏaḏ* and *middâ* do not appear at all in the boundary and land registers concerning the land Israel. This may be because these land-register lists were already set long before our root became fixed in Hebrew language usage, although perhaps also because *māḏaḏ* is apparently not suited for secular application. This is supported by the fact that *māḏaḏ* occurs only in connection with the measuring off of levitical cities,[87] and in that context more specifically concerning the measuring off of the surrounding area (*migrāš,* Nu. 35:5). The parallel lists of levitical cities and cities of refuge (Josh. 21 and 1 Chr. 6) speak in nonspecific fashion of "given" instead of "measured off" *(nāṯan min,* e.g., Josh. 21:3 par. Nu. 35:2 par. 1 Ch. 6:40[55]). It seems that this measuring off, in contrast to the more neutral "marking a boundary" (*t'h,* Nu. 34:7,8,10), is to emphasize the functionally intended separation of these cities.

Although *māḏaḏ* occurs in the land allocation list in Ezk. 47:13–48:29 (at 47:18), it is obviously the result of scribal error; although it could be understood as an allusion to the measuring of the temple complex, it stands quite out of context in the present text.[88]

4. *Legal Contexts.* The terms *māḏaḏ* and *middâ* occur in a few legal contexts in the OT. In the Holiness Code, *middâ* is used in a prohibition against doing wrong in judgment, in *middâ,* weights *(mišqāl),* and quantity (*m*ᵉ*śûrâ;* Lev. 19:35). Although in this context *middâ* is easily understood as "linear measure," its appearance in this legal sequence is somewhat surprising, since the following, explicative v. 36 as well as the parallel stipulations in Dt. 25:13ff. speaks only of weights and measures of quantity (cf. also Ezk. 45:10ff.; in contrast, the cultic sphere is treated differently: 1 Ch. 23:29).

Dt. 21:2 uses *māḏaḏ* in what is apparently a very old legal passage: "If, in the land that Yahweh your God is giving you to possess, a body is found lying in open country, and it is not known who struck the person down, then your elders and your judges shall come out to *measure* the distances to the towns that are near the body." In this way one should determine which community is obligated to atone the capital guilt. Yet even the process of measuring off shows that this "magical procedure"[89] comes from a very early period in which the field areas were not yet legally fixed in land registers.

The 2 occurrences in 2 S. 8:2 (Deuteronomistic history) allude to the context of martial law. In a punitive sanction against the Moabites, David "measures" the prisoners so as to have two thirds put to death and one third spared. To view as an act of "mercy" David's stipulation that a "full" *(m*ᵉ*lō')* third be spared borders on sarcasm.[90] The division of prisoners into thirds was probably based on a stipulation of martial law no longer known to us in its specifics. Actually, the fact that David carried out this stipulation by measuring as opposed to counting off leaves more room for humanitarian mitigation.

---

87. → לֵוִי *lēwî,* IV (VII, 494-96); A. G. Auld, "The 'Levitical Cities': Text and History," *ZAW,* 91 (1979), 194-206.

88. E.g., Zimmerli, 520f.; J. Ziegler, *Das Buch Ezechiel. EB* (²1958), 144; W. Eichrodt, *Der Prophet Hesekiel. Kap. 19–48. ATD,* 22/2 (²1969), 417.

89. G. von Rad, *Deuteronomy. OTL* (Eng. trans. 1966), 136.

90. H. W. Hertzberg, *I & II Samuel. OTL* (Eng. trans. 1964), 291.

Conviction concerning the sacredness of the ark of the covenant prompts Joshua's stipulation that no one be permitted to approach nearer than a "distance" *(middâ)* of two thousand cubits (distance of a Sabbath day's journey; Josh. 3:4). The consequences of transgression against this stipulation are shown in 2 S. 6:7.

Passages such as Ex. 16:18; Ruth 3:15, which speak of "measuring out" foodstuffs, allude to the social regulations of ancient Israel.

5. *Anthropological Contexts.* The term *māḏaḏ* is scarcely attested in anthropological contexts. Job 7:4 is text-critically extremely problematical, and most translations prefer the LXX reading: "When I lie down, I say, 'When will day come, that I arise?' and when I arise, 'when will night come?' "[91] The LXX, however, has distanced itself considerably from the MT, so that a different solution for the difficult expression *ûmiddaḏ-ʿāreḇ* must be found. Georg Fohrer[92] suggests replacing it with *ûmiddê,* "and as soon as it is evening, I am sated with restlessness."[93] I think, however, that Robert Gordis's suggestion[94] is still worthy of consideration, namely, that the MT be maintained. To be sure, one would have to point a qal instead of piel[95] or an otherwise unattested (?)[96] poel **ûmodaḏ* and translate reflexively: "When I lie down, then I say, 'when will I arise?' and when the evening 'stretches [extends] itself,' then I am sated with restlessness till dawn." In this sense *mdd* poel accentuates the dimension of limitless duration in Job's misery (cf. vv. 13ff.). (Joseph Reider[97] also maintains the MT, although he does interpret *middaḏ* as crasis of *min* + *dad,* Arab. "front" = "and from early eve. . . ." This attempt is suspect, however, since in Hebrew *daḏ* has clearly been attested with a different meaning.[98]) The poel would have approximately the same meaning as the hithpael (cf. 1 K. 17:21, though here it is said concretely that the prophet Elijah "stretches himself" upon the dead youth [perhaps an ancient sympathetic rite of energy transfer?]).

In Ps. 39:5(4), the petitioner implores Yahweh to let him know the "measure" of his days. Despite figurative usage here, the parallel use of *qēṣ,* "end," and *ḥāḏēl,* "transient," renders the meaning of *middâ* immediately clear.

6. *Theological Usage.* a. *Creation.* In connection with God's creative activity, several OT passages also speak of a "measuring" of the waters (Job 28:25, par. "weighing" of the winds), of the earth (Job 38:5, *mēmaḏ*), and of the heavens (Jer. 31:37). Otto Wahl[99]

---

91. Cf. A. Weiser, *Das Buch Hiob. ATD,* XIII (1951, [7]1980), *in loc.*
92. *Das Buch Hiob. KAT,* XVI (1963), 163.
93. Cf. *HAL,* I (1994), 219; II, 547.
94. "Quotations as a Literary Usage in Biblical, Oriental and Rabbinic Literature," *HUCA,* 22 (1949), 182.
95. Cf. F. Horst, *Hiob. BK,* XVI/1 ([4]1983), 97: "and the evening extends itself."
96. Cf. the crux Hab. 3:6; also G. R. Driver, "Hebrew Notes," *ZAW,* 52 (1934), 51-56, esp. 54f.; J. Barr, *Comparative Philology and the Text of the OT* (1968, repr. Winona Lake, 1987), 252.
97. Pp. 61, 64.
98. *HAL,* II, 214.
99. P. 262.

points out that this measuring is an activity intended to render things "comprehensible, so that one is clear just how things really are." The human being confesses that only God is capable of this. Here Job 38 and Deutero-Isaiah converge: "Who has measured the waters in the hollow of his hand and marked off the heavens with a span, enclosed the dust of the earth in a measure, and weighed the mountains in scales and the hills in a balance?" (Isa. 40:12; cf. 4Q511 30:4). Despite parallels from the ancient Near East (Marduk as *mâdidi mê tāmtim,* "measurer of the waters of the sea"), Karl Elliger has emphasized that this should be taken as a circumscription of the enormous difference between God and human beings rather than as a description of God's creative activity: "No human being can presume to measure the dimensions of creation" (cf. Sir. 1:1-3), i.e., comprehend it.[100] Human beings can but stand in astonishment and reverence. As little as the heavens can be measured and the foundations of the earth be explored, just as little can Israel be cast off anew over Yahweh's steadfast love (Jer. 31:37).

b. *Increase.* In a formulation differing from that found in the promises of increase given to the patriarchs (cf. Gen. 15:5; 22:17; 32:13[12]), Hosea refers to the "immeasurability" of the sand of the sea to proclaim the eschatological increase of the people after the suspension of judgment (2:1[1:10]). A "Jeremianic" commentary (Jer. 33:14-26), emphasizing Yahweh's steadfastness through a rich collection of motifs, similarly predicts that the descendants of David and (!) of the levitical priests will be "immeasurable" as the sands of the sea. "The hyperbole is unmistakable."[101]

c. *Land Measurement in Zec. 2:5f.(1f.).* Just as in Ezekiel's constitution draft, so also in Zec. 2:5f.(1f.) an *'îš* appears, although here he "measures" Jerusalem with a "measuring line."[102]

These verses present enormous difficulties for any interpretation. The identity of this *'îš* is disputed. If dependence on Ezk. 40ff. is assumed,[103] then one can take this as an angelic being.[104] But how is one then to understand the "correction" following in Zec. 2:8f.(4f.)? This is why other interpreters take the *'îš* to be a person carrying out measurements in preparation for construction.[105] The "correction" given in vv. 8f.(4f.) has an "overriding"[106] function intended to clarify the true relationship between human and divine measure.[107] An additional point of contention involves just what is being "measured." The text states: *'eṯ-yᵉrûšālayim* with the further specification *lir'ôṯ kammâ-roḥbāh wᵉḵammâ 'orkāh.* The measuring of Jerusalem is to yield information concerning *rōḥaḇ,* "width," perhaps specifically "breadth," and *'ōreḵ,* "length." "Length and

---

100. *Deuterojesaja. BK,* XI/1 (1970), 49f.

101. W. Rudolph, *Jeremiah. HAT,* XII (³1968), 200.

102. On the relationship with Ezk. 40, cf. C. Jeremias, *Die Nachtgesichte des Sacharja. FRLANT,* 117 (1977), 164.

103. This is the position of Jeremias.

104. F. Horst, *Die zwölf kleinen Propheten: Nahum bis Maleachi. HAT,* XIV (²1954), 223f.

105. M. Bič, *Die Nachtgesichte des Sacharja. BSt,* 42 (1964), 19-22; W. Rudolph, *Sacharja 1–8. KAT,* XIII/4 (1976), *in loc.*

106. So Jeremias.

107. Wahl.

breadth" sooner suggest surface measurements[108] than a measuring of the length of the city wall.[109]

These interpretive antitheses become irrelevant if one takes this third vision of the prophet as the portrayal of role-playing intended to elucidate the imminent commencement of the end time and Jerusalem's function in this new epoch. On the one hand, the "measuring" signals the beginning of construction, just as in the case of preparations for construction (cf. Zec. 1:16); on the other hand, in correspondence to the "overriding correction" (vv. 8f.[4f.]) this "measuring" of earthly dimensions proclaims the "immeasurable" dimension of the end time. In this case the vision is concerned neither with the construction of the wall nor with the rebuilding of Jerusalem (cf. in contrast Jer. 31:39, where "measuring line" and *bānâ* are parallel). As in Ezk. 40ff., one can observe that here, too, *māḏaḏ* has the connotation of "taking possession."

This is consistent with the use of *māḏaḏ* piel in the oracle of good news in Ps. 60:8(6) par. 108:8(7). Yahweh divides *(ḥālaq)* the city of Shechem as war spoils and "measures" the Vale of Succoth. Both the implication of taking possession (cf. 60:10[8] par. and the rite of "casting one's shoe") and — indicated by the par. *ḥālaq* — the assignment to Israel constitute the meaning of *māḏaḏ* here.

d. *Reprisal.* Only once does *māḏaḏ* occur in the context of reprisal, in connection with the oracle of judgment in Isa. 65:7.[110] Yahweh will repay the apostates and "measure" their deeds *(pᵉʿullōṯ).*[111] This recalls the *mᵉnēʾ* of the "mene tekel" passage in Daniel (Dnl. 5:25).

7. *maḏ.* The term *maḏ* is for the most part theologically irrelevant. It refers to "battle dress" (of David, 1 S. 17:38f.; Jonathan, 18:4; Joab, 2 S. 20:8), whose complement included the sword *(ḥereḇ),* helmet *(qôḇaʿ),* and coat of mail *(širyôn).* Without these military accessories, *maḏ* probably designated an unexceptional piece of clothing (Jgs. 3:16; 1 S. 4:12).[112] According to Lev. 6:3(10), the *maḏ* and *miḵnēs,* "breeches," constitute the garments (*bᵉgāḏîm,* v. 4[9]) of the priests who are to clear away the ashes of the burnt offering. Ps. 133:2 uses the *maḏ* in an even more general sense to refer to priests' clothing. Ps. 109:18 uses the term metaphorically. The psalmist cites[113] the curses his enemies have directed against him, which now surround him like a "coat" *(maḏ),* "garment" *(beḡeḏ),* and "belt" (*mēzaḥ,* v. 19). Perhaps this is also an allusion to a protective "sphere of the curse" effected through "self-malediction."[114]

III. 1. *Qumran.* The root *mdd* occurs only rarely in Qumran texts. The great scrolls do not attest the verb at all, and it occurs only 3 times in 4Q. 4Q185 1f.II.10 speaks

108. So Rudolph and Jeremias.

109. So J. Rothstein, *Die Nachtgesichte des Sacharja* (Leipzig, 1910), 79f.

110. → פקד *pāqaḏ;* → שלם *šlm;* → שוב *šûḇ* hiphil.

111. Cf. *BMAP,* 5, 7, and also the textually problematical Jer. 13:25.

112. On the textually problematical term *middîn* in Jgs. 5:10, referring to "garments" or "carpets on which one sits," cf. *HAL,* II, 546.

113. Kraus, 338.

114. *Ibid.,* 340f.

of the "measure of goodness" *(mddt ṭb)* used as a standard for measurement. 4Q511 30:4 contains a citation from Isa. 40:12 in a characteristic Qumran-Essene reformulation (instead of *mayim* we now read *mê rabbâ,* etc.). The nominal form *mdh* occurs in Qumran with the meaning "tribute" (1QapGen 21:26f.), "garment" (1QS 4:8, the splendid garment as reward for the faithful), and "measure, standard." According to 1QS 8:4, "walking according to the standard of truth" is already one of the basic requirements of the Qumran founders. God's creative power manifests itself in the fact that he establishes words with the measuring line *(qaw)* and according to measure (*middâ;* 1QH 1:29). His *kāḇôḏ* (1QH 5:21) and his wisdom (9:17) are without measure. Finally, *middâ* occurs as expected in the Temple scroll (13 times); the verb does not occur, since the character of Ezekiel's guidance vision in 11QT is no longer given.[115]

2. *Rabbinic Judaism.* In rabbinic Judaism it was above all the nominal form *middâ/middôṯ* that experienced rich semantic extension. In addition to its former meanings,[116] it now also refers to the rules of exegetical interpretation of scripture,[117] though also to the various modes of behavior and characteristics of God,[118] his "righteousness" *(dîn)* and "mercy" *(raḥ^a^mîm),* on which the world is grounded (*Gen. Rab.* xii.15). The Mishnah tractate *Middoth* deals with the measurements and accoutrements of the temple.

Fabry

115. On the similarities with Ezekiel's draft, cf. J. Maier, "Die Hofanlagen im Tempel-Entwurf des Ezechiel im Licht der 'Tempelrolle' von Qumran," *Prophecy. Festschrift G. Fohrer. BZAW,* 150 (1980), 55-67.

116. Cf. *WTM,* III, 24-28.

117. Cf. H. L. Strack, *Introduction to the Talmud and Midrash* (Eng. trans. 1931, repr. New York, 1978), 93-104.

118. Cf. J. Maier and P. Schäfer, *Kleines Lexikon des Judentums* (Stuttgart, 1981), 210.

מהה *mhh;* אחר *'ḥr*

Contents: I. Occurrences and Distribution. II. LXX. III. 1. Human Tarrying; 2. Divine Tarrying. IV. *'ḥr.*

I. Occurrences and Distribution. Outside Hebrew, the root *mhh* is attested only in Arabic, although Arab. *mahah,* variously rendered as "slow, ambling pace,"[1] sooner suggests the nuance of "gentle, delicate."[2] It occurs 8 times in the Hebrew OT, always in the hithpalpel.[3] Almost all occurrences are preexilic. Although in Isa. 29:9aα MT

1. *GesB,* 402; *HAL,* II (1995), 552.

2. See M. Ibn Mukkarram Ibn Manẓur, *Lisān al-ʿArab* (Beirut, 1979), *s.v.*

3. *BLe,* §283v.

hiṯmahmᵉhû can be derived from *mhh,* scribal error from *hittammᵉhû*[4] is generally assumed on the basis of LXX *eklýthēte* and Vulg. *obstupescite,* as well as the parallelism with v. aβ. Occurrences are also found in Sir. 12:16; 14:12; 32:22 (= 35:18) as well as 2 in Qumran; 1QM 11:18 and 11QPs[a] 19:6 (Plea for Deliverance) attest the formative מהמה, which Jean Carmignac[5] derives from *mhh,* while Yigael Yadin[6] refers to the as-yet-unexplained *mhmhm* in Ezk. 7:11. The first Qumran text becomes comprehensible if one assumes defective spelling of *mᵉhûmâ,* "confusion, panic," while the second occurrence might be interpreted as *mēhēmmâ,* "from inside."

II. LXX. The LXX was unable to offer a genuine Greek equivalent for this word. The terms *bradýnein, epiménein, hypoménein, hystereín,* and *chroníxein* all belong to the general semantic field "delay, hesitate, come late." Twice the LXX reads a form of *mḥh, strateúein,* and twice it derives the form from *hwm, tarássein.* Also at Sir. 12:16 a distinction is evident between the Hebrew text *bśptyw ytmhmh ṣr,* "the enemy hesitates with his lips," and the *glykaneí* of the LXX, "the enemy speaks sweetly with his lips," which might presuppose a form such as *yamtîq* or *yiśmaḥ.* The verse's parallelism, however, permits all three possibilities.

III. 1. *Human Tarrying.* With few exceptions, human beings are always the subject of the *hiṯmahmah.* In certain cases the context permits ambiguity; this delay might sometimes refer to neutral waiting, in other instances to actual hesitation seeking to prolong a period of decision for the sake of delaying an unpleasant decision.

a. On their flight from the Egyptians the Israelites could not wait for the leavening of the dough (Ex. 12:34,39 [J¹]), and had to nourish themselves with unleavened bread. The expression *lōʾ yāḵᵉlû lᵉhiṯmahmēah* effects a circumscription of the situation of hasty flight, and simultaneously provides the historicizing element for the Yahwistic redactor, who thus fixes the location of the historically unbound rite of the unleavened bread within Israel's history of salvation (cf. Ex. 12:15-20).[7]

The independent, pre-Deuteronomic Ehud tradition in Jgs. 3:15b-26 reports that the servants of the Moabite King Eglon "wait" in the vestibule (*yāḥîlû,* v. 25), although during "their delay" (*hiṯmahmᵉhām,* v. 26) Ehud has already made his escape. The Levite (Jgs. 19:8) also "lingers" at his father-in-law's, though it is not clear for what

4. → תמה *tāmâ,* "be shocked"; cf. B. Duhm, *Das Buch Jesaja. HKAT,* III/1 (²1902); F. Delitzsch, *KD,* VII; *BHK, BHS;* H. W. Hoffmann, *Die Intention der Verkündigung Jesajas. BZAW,* 136 (1974), 51f.; H. Wildberger, *Jesaja 28–39. BK,* X/3 (1982), *in loc.*

5. J. Carmignac, *La Règle de la Guerre des Fils de lumière contre les Fils de ténèbres* (Paris, 1958), 169.

6. Y. Yadin, *The Scroll of the War of the Sons of Light against the Sons of Darkness* (Eng. trans., Jerusalem, 1957), 314.

7. On the literary-critical and tradition-critical problems, cf. J. Schreiner, "Exodus 12,21-23 und das israelitische Pascha," *Studien zum Pentateuch. Festschrift W. Kornfeld* (Vienna, 1977), 69-90; B. N. Wambacq, "Les origines de la *Pesaḥ* israélite," *Bibl,* 57 (1976), 206-224; *idem,* "II: Suite et fin," 301-326; *idem,* "Les *Maṣṣôt,*" *Bibl,* 61 (1980), 31-54.

he is waiting. He delays his journey home for several days although he has already reached the goal of his journey.

However, the *hiṯmahmah* is also attested as goal-oriented "lingering, patient waiting." Joseph's brothers assert, "if we had not delayed, we would now have returned twice" (Gen. 43:10). Based on the course of the Joseph narrative, their hesitation is variously motivated: fear of arrest because of actual failure to make payment; pressure because of Joseph's command to bring Benjamin to Egypt; delay in relaying this command to Jacob. That this hesitation ultimately serves to facilitate a decision is shown by the fact that only Judah's willingness to take complete responsibility brings this phase to an end and sets in motion a second journey to Egypt.

b. According to the pre-Deuteronomic Succession Narrative of David, after his flight from Absalom David waited at the "fords of the wilderness" for word from the priests (2 S. 15:28). This is first of all doubtlessly a sophisticated chess move enabling him to gain information from a secure distance concerning the political events in Jerusalem. At the same time, however, *hiṯmahmah* acquires a religious component inasmuch as David intends to await divine initiative. The word moves into the proximity of verbs of waiting[8] and hoping;[9] "the king is quite serious in his belief."[10] A reciprocal relationship between "delaying" and "believing" manifests itself both in the older passage Gen. 19:16 (J) and in the later passage Ps. 119:60 (postexilic[11]). It is not just Lot's curiosity that makes him delay leaving the threatened city Sodom (cf. Gen. 19:16); his objections (vv. 18ff.) and those of his sons-in-law (v. 14) show that he needs further reasons for making the grave decision of leaving his possessions behind. Finally, his lingering is the direct result of lack of faith. Gen. 19 does not clearly show just whether or when Lot recognizes the two *mal'āḵîm* as such so as to accept and obey their demand as Yahweh's salvific will. Yahweh, however, does not in any case allow human hesitation to impede his saving work, as Gen. 19 clearly shows. According to Ps. 119:60, "not delaying" is synonymous with "hastening" *(ḥûš).* The postexilic psalmist emphasizes the spontaneity of his Torah observance, which in connection with his "reflective self-observation"[12] (Ps. 119:59) in the face of the intrigues of his adversaries is a visible criterion of the integrity of his faith.

2. *Divine Tarrying.* Only in Sir. 32:22 (= 35:18) is God the explicit subject of *hiṯmahmah,* "delay." The *terminus classicus* for "God's tarrying" is *'ḥr,* here especially in Ps. 40:18(17).[13] Sirach emphasizes that God will not delay in smiting the unmerciful. According to Sir. 14:12, death does not tarry, but rather comes inescapably to all human beings.

---

8. → יחל *yāḥal* (VI, 49-55).
9. → שׂבר *śibbēr.*
10. H. W. Hertzberg, *I & II Samuel. OTL* (Eng. trans. 1964), 343.
11. H.-J. Kraus, *Psalms 60–150* (Eng. trans., Minneapolis, 1989), *in loc.*
12. *Ibid.,* 417.
13. See IV below.

It is said metaphorically of the *ḥāzôn* of the prophet Habakkuk that it is determined only for a certain time (Hab. 2:3). Through synthetic parallelism of the verbs *pûaḥ,* "hasten" (uncertain), *lō' kāzaḇ,* "not disappoint [expectations]," *ḥāḵâ,* "wait, look forward to impatiently," and *'ḥr,* "fail to appear, be delayed," the verse as a whole encompasses precisely the semantic field covered by *mhh.* This semantic concentration goes together with the commission to the prophet to write down the following tablet text,[14] "Behold, he whose spirit is not upright in him shall perish, but the righteous shall live by his faithfulness."[15] "The command to write down the words guarantees that this revelation will actually come to pass."[16] The certainty of this promise is thus so secure that any delay can be recognized precisely as such, and should not be permitted to discourage one's faith in the ultimate fulfillment.

IV. 'ḥr. The verb *'ḥr,* well attested in Akkadian, Arabic, and in the immediate linguistic vicinity of Hebrew, should probably be understood as a denominative from *'aḥar,* meaning "linger" (qal), "delay, hesitate" (piel), "be delayed" (hiphil).[17] It occurs 16 times in the OT, but cannot be assigned to a specific time period. The term is also attested in Qumran. The verb refers first of all to a person's "tarrying" during a normal or set period of time (cf. Gen. 32:5[4], par. *gûr*), then to similar lingering beyond the normal period (2 S. 20:5; Isa. 5:11; Prov. 23:30). It can also refer to "hesitation" in connection with reaching a decision (Gen. 24:56; 34:19) or to hesitation in the sense of failing to appear, which can also coincide with the expectation of another person (Jgs. 5:28, par. *bwš* pilel).

In connection with the cult, the prohibitive *lō' tᵉ'aḥēr,* "you shall not delay," occurs several times in connection with fulfilling the obligation of offerings (Ex. 22:28[29]) and vows (Dt. 23:22[21]; Eccl. 5:3[4]).

God knows no delay, hence all occurrences are negated that insinuate either implicitly or explicitly that God is the subject. One can recognize Yahweh in that he destroys "without delay" those that hate him (Dt. 7:10).

The term *'ḥr* occurs in the language of prayer only in connection with the plea for deliverance from extreme distress. In these situations the oppressed turns to God and implores him to render aid without delay: "hasten to me!" (*ḥûšâ* [textual emendation], Ps. 40:18[17]; cf. Ps. 70:6[5]); "hearken!" *(šᵉmā'â);* "forgive!" *(sᵉlāḥâ);* "take notice!" *(haqᵃšîḇâ);* "act!" (*'ᵃśēh,* Dnl. 9:19). The extreme urgency of these pleas is then intensified by the addition of the concluding prohibitive *'al-tᵉ'aḥar,* "do not tarry!" In a reverse fashion, God's own salvific promise is spoken into his people's most extreme mortal distress: "I bring near my deliverance, it is not far off, and my salvation will not tarry" (Isa. 46:13).

Fabry

---

14. For a delimitation, cf. P. Jöcken, *Das Buch Habakwuk. BBB,* 48 (1977), 520.

15. Cf. A. S. van der Woude, "Der Gerechte wird durch seine Treue leben. Erwägungen zu Habakuk 2,4f.," *Studia Biblica et Semitica. Festschrift T. C. Vriezen* (Wageningen, 1966), 367-375; W. T. In der Smitten, "Habakuk 2,4 als prophetische Definition des Gerechten," *Bausteine biblischer Theologie. Festschrift G. J. Botterweck. BBB,* 50 (1977), 291-300.

16. W. Rudolph, *Habakuk. KAT,* XIII/3 (1975), 215f.

17. *HAL,* I (1994), 34f.

מהר mhr; מְהֵרָה m^e^hērâ; מָהִיר māhîr

Contents: I. Etymology, Occurrences. II. Use as an "Auxiliary Verb" and as an Independent Verb. III. Theologically Interesting Examples: 1. Quick Inclination to Evil; 2. Quick Downfall; 3. God's Imminent Action; 4. Other Aspects; 5. Isa. 8:1-3. IV. Niphal. V. *māhîr.* VI. LXX.

I. Etymology, Occurrences. Hebrew attests two roots *mhr.* One is found in → מהר *mōhar,* "bridal money" (perhaps also as a verb in Ps. 16:4), while the other means "to hasten," a meaning attested only in Hebrew. In other Semitic languages *mhr* means "be practiced, skilled": Syr. *m^e^hîr,* "skilled," verb pael, "teach"; Arab. *mahara,* "be practiced, skilled"; Eth. *mahara,* "teach."[1] The verb occurs 78 times in the OT in the piel, 4 times in the niphal. The noun *m^e^hērâ* occurs 20 times, *māhîr* 4 times.

II. Use as an "Auxiliary Verb" and as an Independent Verb. The root *mhr* in the piel is often used together with another finite verb and functions then as an auxiliary verb with the meaning "quickly," e.g., *watt^e^mahēr wattōreḏ kaddāh . . . wattašqēhû,* "she quickly let down her jar . . . and gave him a drink" (Gen. 24:18; cf. vv. 20,46; similarly also 44:11; 45:13; Ex. 34:8; Josh. 4:10; 8:14,19, etc.[2]). The situation is similar in the imperative, e.g., *mahēr himmālēṭ,* "save yourself quickly" (Gen. 19:22); *mah^a^rû wa^ca^lû 'el-'āḇî,* "go up quickly to my father" (45:9); *mah^a^rû ^ca^śû kāmônî,* "do quickly, as I have done" (Jgs. 9:48). The inf. *mahēr* is also often employed adverbially in the sense of "quickly," e.g., *sārû mahēr,* "they have turned aside quickly" (Ex. 32:8; cf. Dt. 9:12,16); *'āḇôḏ tō'ḇēḏûn mahēr,* "you will quickly perish" (Dt. 4:26; cf. Dt. 9:3; 28:20); *riḏpû mahēr 'aḥ^a^rêhem,* "pursue them quickly" (Josh. 2:5).

The term *mhr* can also be used with an infinitive with or without *l^e^,* e.g., *maddûa^c^ miharten bô',* "why do you come so quickly" (Ex. 2:18); *mah-zzeh mihartā limṣō',* "how is it that you have found it so quickly" (Gen. 27:20); *way^e^mahēr la^ca^śôṯ 'ōṯô,* "he quickly prepared it" or "he hastened to prepare it" (Gen. 18:7; cf. also 41:32; Ex. 10:16; Isa. 51:14; 59:7; etc.).

In other instances *mhr* is used independently with the meaning "hasten to some-

---

mhr. P. Humbert, "Mahēr Šalāl Ḥāš Baz," *ZAW,* 50 (1932), 90-92; A. Jirku, "Zu 'Eilebeute' in Jes 8,1.3," *ThLZ,* 75 (1950), 118; S. Morag, "On Some Semantic Relationships," *Festschrift H. L. Ginsberg. ErIsr,* 14 (1978), 137-147 [Heb.]; S. Morenz, "Zu 'Eilebeute,' " *ThLZ,* 74 (1949), 697-99; L. G. Rignell, "The Oracle 'Maher-šalal-ḥaš-bas,' Is 8," *StTh,* 10 (1957), 40-52; E. Vogt, "Einige hebräische Wortbedeutungen," *Bibl,* 48 (1967), 57-74, esp. 63-69: " 'Eilig tun' als adverbielles Verb und der Name des Sohnes Isaias in Is. 8,1."

1. Cf. Heb. *māhîr,* V below; E. Ullendorff, "The Contribution of South Semitics to Hebrew Lexicography," *VT,* 6 (1956), 195 = *Is Biblical Hebrew a Language?* (Wiesbaden, 1977), 194.

2. *HAL,* II (1995), 553, incorrectly adduces Gen. 45:9; Ps. 102:3, which in fact belong to the next group with the imperative.

where," "come hurriedly," "bring quickly," and so on. According to Ernst Vogt,[3] this is often a case of ellipsis, i.e., the main verb is omitted: e.g., *mahᵃrû [qirʾû] ʾeṯ-hāmān,* "call Haman quickly" (Est. 5:5); *rāʿāṯô mihᵃrâ mᵉʾōḏ [lāḇôʾ],* "his doom comes quickly" (Jer. 48:16); *yᵉmahᵃrû [yēlᵉḵû] ḥômāṯāh,* "they will quickly go to the wall" (Nah. 2:6[Eng. v. 5]; cf. also Gen. 18:6; 1 K. 22:9).

III. Theologically Interesting Examples.

1. *Quick Inclination to Evil.* Human beings are quick to do evil. In Dt. 9:12, Yahweh says to Moses at Sinai that the people "have acted corruptly. They have been quick to turn from the way that I commanded them" (cf. Ex. 32:8). When Moses descends from the mountain he finds the golden calf and says: "You had been quick to turn from the way that Yahweh had commanded you" (Dt. 9:16). The people had allowed itself to be seduced with remarkable ease into apostasy and idolatry. The same expression recurs in the thematic introduction to the book of Judges (Jgs. 2:17): the people "played the harlot after other gods and bowed down to them. They quickly turned aside from the way in which their ancestors had walked." The people's inclination to engage in idolatry is thus described as "precipitousness." A similar notion occurs in Ps. 106:13 (probably with some Deuteronomistic influence): "They quickly forgot his works; they did not wait for his counsel." Although the exodus (Ps. 106:9-11) awakened the people to faith in God, in the wilderness they quickly forgot everything he had done for them, and dedicated themselves to idolatry in the form of the golden calf. Such inclination to evil is also qualified by *mhr* elsewhere. In a context that speaks of the people's sins as the cause of their misfortune, Isa. 59:7 asserts: "Their feet run to evil, and they rush to shed innocent blood." Prov. 6:18 speaks of "feet that hurry to run to evil" (the same expression is developed somewhat more fully in 1:16).

2. *Quick Downfall.* The consequence of apostasy is a quick downfall. Just as Yahweh had once promised to cast down the people of the land before Israel so that Israel might quickly destroy them (*wᵉhaʾaḇaḏtem mahēr,* Dt. 9:3), so also will he destroy Israel if it serves other gods (*ʾāḇōḏ tōʾḇēḏûn mahēr,* 4:26). Israel will be driven from the land (cf. *waʾᵃḇaḏtem mᵉhērâ,* Dt. 11:17; *wᵉhišmîḏᵉḵā mahēr,* 7:4). The two verbs *ʾbd* and *šmd* are combined in the curses in Dt. 28: *ʿaḏ hiššāmedḵā wᵉʿaḏ-ʾᵃḇoḏḵā mahēr* (v. 20: "until you are quickly destroyed and perish"). God's wrath ignites against any idolatry, and his judgment cannot be delayed.

3. *God's Imminent Action.* God's action is imminent. The day of Yahweh "is near, near and hastening fast" (*qārôḇ ûmahēr mᵉʾōḏ,* Zeph. 1:14). Yahweh's wrath will not hesitate; he will soon intervene. Joel's assertion concerning world judgment (Tyre, Sidon, and the Philistines are being addressed) is similar: "I will turn your deed back upon your own head swiftly and speedily *(qal mᵉhērâ)*" (Joel 4:4[3:4]). Concerning Moab, Jer. 48:16 asserts: "The calamity of Moab is coming soon *(qārôḇ lāḇôʾ),* and

---

3. Pp. 65f.

his doom approaches swiftly *(mih^{a}râ m^{e}'ōḏ)*" (again the combination *qārôḇ — mahēr*). In contrast, Isa. 5:26, where Yahweh "entices" the nations of the world to advance against Israel, employs the juxtaposition *qal m^{e}hērâ.*

Quick intervention, however, can also bring about a positive turn of events. Although Jeremiah does indeed castigate the false prophets who proclaim quick deliverance from Babylon (Jer. 27:16), Deutero-Isaiah asserts: "The oppressed shall soon (speedily) be released" (Isa. 51:14). Fundamental motifs from the lament resonate here,[4] especially the plea for quick response.[5] The salvation oracle asserts that Yahweh, the creator who "stirred" the sea, is also able to subdue the oppressor. Cf. also Isa. 58:8: "Then your healing shall spring up quickly"; although these expressions suggest a gradual process,[6] the imminent commencement of the healing process is emphasized.

Ps. 147:15 says in a general fashion that Yahweh's word "runs swiftly" *('aḏ-m^{e}hērâ yārûṣ),* i.e., it is quickly actualized. The context speaks of God's effective power within nature. Thus when the unbelievers say mockingly, "Let him make haste, let him speed *(y^{e}mahēr yāḥîšâ)* his work that we may see it" (Isa. 5:19; the context also attests the verbs *qrb* and *bô'*), this is an enormous presumption.

When it is a question of God's quick intervention, the word *piṯ'ōm* is frequently used, e.g., "whose crash comes suddenly" (Isa. 30:13); "suddenly the destroyer will come upon us" (Jer. 6:26); "[the Lord] will suddenly come to his temple" (Mal. 3:1). This emphasizes the unexpected nature of the action.

Pleas for quick intervention occur in several psalms of lament, usually in the expression *mahēr '^{a}nēnî,* "answer me (respond to me) quickly" (Ps. 69:18[17]; 102:3[2]; 143:7). However, other expressions occur as well: "Let your compassion come speedily *(mahēr)* to meet us" (Ps. 79:8); "rescue me speedily" *(m^{e}hērâ haṣṣîlēnî,* Ps. 31:3[2]). It is noteworthy that the synonymous term → חוש *ḥûš,* which occurs several times in psalms of lament and elsewhere is used with *mhr* (Isa. 5:19; 8:1), is not used here.

4. *Other Aspects.* Other aspects of quickness or swiftness emerge from the following examples. The tongues of the stammerers hasten, i.e., speak normally (Isa. 32:4). Just as the bird hastens into a snare, so also does the fool rush to his own ruin (Prov. 7:23). The sinners fade as quickly as the grass withers (Ps. 37:2). God is a swift witness *('ēḏ m^{e}mahēr;* according to Vogt,[7] one should emend *la'^{a}nôṯ:* "who immediately testifies") against the sorcerers and adulterers (Mal. 3:5). He is simultaneously both witness and judge, and swiftly carries out the trial.[8] "What your eyes have seen do not hastily bring into court," i.e., one should maintain control and not act prematurely (Prov. 25:7f.). This illustrates the wisdom ideal of self-control, just as in Eccl. 5:1(2): "Never be rash with your mouth, nor let your heart be quick to utter a word before God"; impetuous words only cause trouble.

---

4. C. Westermann, *Isaiah 40–66. OTL* (Eng. trans. 1969), 243f.
5. See discussion below.
6. Westermann, 338.
7. P. 65.
8. K. Elliger, *Das Buch der zwölf kleinen Propheten, II: Maleachi. ATD,* XXV (^{8}1982), 196.

5. *Isa. 8:1-3.* The symbolic name of Isaiah's son *mahēr šālāl ḥāš baz* (Isa. 8:1,3) presents several problems. The terms *mhr* and *ḥwš* are more or less synonymous,[9] as are *šālāl* and *baz.* The term *ḥāš* seems to be a participle, *mahēr* an imperative. The two verbs are thus not equivalents unless one takes *mahēr* as an abbreviated participle = *m^e^mahēr.* The imperative is supported by an Egyptian parallel appearing in the documents of the eighteenth dynasty where the two imperatives *is ḥ'ḳ* ("hasten, plunder") can also be used as substantives to refer to light booty.[10] Anton Jirku,[11] on the other hand, refers to Ugar. *mhr,* "servant, soldier," which leads to the translation "warrior of spoils, hastening for plunder." Vogt[12] understands *mahēr* adverbially and translates, "soon one will carry off spoils, and shortly plunder." Reference has also been made to Akk. *ḫumuṭ-tabal,* "quickly, take away," the name of the ferryman of the underworld,[13] where the imperatives of *ḫamāṭu,* "to hasten," and *tabālu,* "to take away,"[14] function as a personal name.

In and of itself *mahēr šālāl ḥāš baz* could be an Isaianic ad hoc construction. As far as the *l^e^* preceding the name is concerned, it could either refer to the possessor (*l^e^ possessoris)* as in Ezk. 37:16,[15] or merely function as an introductory colon to the inscription.[16] In any case, the sense of the name is clear enough: Assyria will soon "carry away the wealth of Damascus and the spoil of Samaria" (Isa. 8:4).

IV. Niphal. The niphal occurs only 4 times, and the passages concerned are fairly diverse. In Job 5:13, Eliphaz says that God thwarts all human hubris and "takes the wise in their own craftiness, so that the schemes of the wily dash headlong," i.e., are quickly frustrated. Isa. 32:4 predicts a time when "those who once acted rashly, reached false conclusions and carried out false acts,"[17] finally gain insight. Hab. 1:6 refers to the Chaldeans as a *gôy mar w^e^nimhār,* approximately "fierce and impetuous." In contrast, in Isa. 35:4 the *nimh^a^rê-lēḇ* are those who are anxious and despondent.

V. māhîr. The term *māhîr* means "skilled, experienced," and as such is closely related to the meaning of this root in the other Semitic languages.[18] Prov. 22:29 speaks of persons skillful in their work,[19] Ps. 45:2(1) of a skillful scribe; cf. also Ezr. 7:6, according to which

9. See previous discussion.
10. See Morenz, 697.
11. P. 118.
12. Pp. 66f.
13. *HAL,* II, 554; E. Ebeling, "Dämonen," *RLA,* II (1932), 111.
14. *AHw,* I (1965), 316; III (1981), 1297.
15. O. Kaiser, *Das Buch des Propheten Jesaja, Kapitel 1–12. ATD,* XVII (1960), 80, refers to a deed of purchase such as that in Jer. 32:16, which does not, however, use *l^e^*. Cf. also *idem, Isaiah 1–12. OTL* (²1983), 178.
16. On the *l^e^ inscriptionis,* cf. S. Moscati, *L'epigrafia ebraica antica 1935-1950. BietOr,* 15 (1951), 85-89; H. Wildberger, *Isaiah 1–12* (Eng. trans., Minneapolis, 1991), 335.
17. O. Kaiser, *Isaiah 13–39. OTL* (Eng. trans. 1974), 323.
18. See I above.

Ezra is *māhîr* in the law of Moses. Isa. 16:5 uses the expression *m*ᵉ*hîr ṣeḏeq* to refer to a judge who "seeks justice *(dōrēš mišpāṭ)* and is swift to do what is right."

VI. LXX. The LXX usually uses words such as *speúdein, táchos, tachýs, tachéōs,* and for *māhîr* the words *oxýgraphos, oxýs, speúdein,* and *tachýs.*

Ringgren

19. → מלאכה *m*ᵉ*lā'ḵâ* (VIII, 325-331).

מֹהַר *mōhar*

Contents: I. 1. Meaning; 2. Usage; 3. Legal Questions. II. Ancient Near East: 1. Ugarit. 2. Alalakh; 3. Mari and Mesopotamia; 4. Elephantine; 5. Hittites.

mōhar. S. Bialoblocki, *Materialien zum islamischen und jüdischen Eherecht* (Giessen, 1928); M. Burrows, "The Complaint of Laban's Daughters," *JAOS,* 57 (1937), 259-276; *idem, The Basis of Israelite Marriage. AOS,* 15 (1938); G. Cardascia, *Les lois assyriennes* (Paris, 1969), esp. 69-71, 165-170, 192-96; P. Cruveilhier, "Le droit de la femme dans la Genèse et le recueil de lois assyriennes," *RB,* 36 (1927), 350-376; M. David, *Vorm en wezen van de huwelijkssluiting naar de oud-oostersche rechtsopvatting* (Leiden, 1934); G. R. Driver–J. C. Miles, *The Assyrian Laws* (Oxford, 1935), 126-271; *idem, The Babylonian Laws,* I (Oxford, ²1956), 245-324; R. Dussaud, "Le 'mohar' israélite," *CRAI,* 1935, 142-151; A. Eberharter, "Was bedeutet Mohar?" *ThQ,* 95 (1913), 492ff.; *idem, Das Ehe- und Familienrecht der Hebräer. ATA,* 5/1f. (1914); T. Engert, *Ehe- und Familienrecht der Hebräer* (Munich, 1905); L. M. Epstein, *Marriage Laws in the Bible and the Talmud* (Cambridge, Mass., 1942); A. Falkenstein, *Die neusumerischen Gerichtsurkunden,* I. *ABAW,* N.S. 39 (1956), 78-81; A. Goetze, *The Laws of Eshnunna. AASOR,* 31 (1956), 75-89; C. H. Gordon, "The Status of Women Reflected in the Nuzi Tablets," *ZA,* N.S. 9[43] (1936), 146-169, esp. 157f.; *idem,* "The Story of Jacob and Laban in the Light of the Nuzi Tablets," *BASOR,* 66 (1937), 25-27; H. Holzinger, "Ehe und Frau im vordeuteronomischen Israel," *Studien zur semitischen Philologie und Religionsgeschichte. Festschrift J. Wellhausen. BZAW,* 27 (1914), 229-241; K. Kahana, *The Theory of Marriage in Jewish Law* (Leiden, 1966); W. Kornfeld, "Mariage I: Dans l'AT," *DBS,* V (1957), 905-926; V. Korošec, "Ehe," *RLA,* II (1938), 281-299; P. Koschaker, "Eheschliessung und Kauf nach alten Rechten, mit besonderer Berücksichtigung der älteren Keilschriftrechte," *ArOr,* 18/2 (1950), 210-296; B. Landsberger, "Jungfräulichkeit: ein Beitrag zum Thema 'Beilager und Eheschliessung,'' *Symbolae Iuridicae et Historicae. Festschrift M. David,* II (Leiden, 1968), 41-105; E. Lüddeckens, *Ägyptische Eheverträge. ÄgAbh,* 1 (1960); D. R. Mace, *Hebrew Marriage* (London, 1953); P. E. van der Meer, "Tirḫātu," *RA,* 31 (1934), 121-23; I. Mendelsohn, "On Marriage in Alalakh," *Essays on Jewish Life and Thought. Festschrift S. W. Baron* (New York, 1959), 351-57; J. Morgenstern, *Rites of Birth, Marriage, Death and Kindred Occasions among the Semites* (Cincinnati, 1966); Y. Muffs, *Studies in the Aramaic Legal Papyri from Elephantine. StDI,* 8 (1969; repr. New York, 1973), 51-56, 84ff., 163f.; J. Neubauer, *Beiträge zur Geschichte des biblisch-talmudischen Eheschliessungsrechts. MVÄG,* 24f. (1920); E. Neufeld, *Ancient Hebrew Marriage Laws* (London, 1944), 94-110; P. W. Pestman, *Marriage and Matrimonial Property in Ancient Egypt*

I. 1. *Meaning.* The word *mōhar* occurs only 3 times in the OT, always in older texts (Gen. 34:12; Ex. 22:16[Eng. v. 17]; 1 S. 18:25; LXX *dóma* and *phernē*). It also occurs in the texts of Ugarit,[1] in the Egyptian-Aramaic contracts of the Jewish community at Elephantine,[2] in the Targumim, and in rabbinic writings. The *mōhar* is also well known among the Arabs in Syria, Palestine, and the Transjordan, who use the words *mahr* or *mahar.* The term always refers to gifts which the bridegroom or his father must give to the father or guardian of the girl before she is "given over"[3] to her "lord."[4] The *mōhar* never occurs in the sense of an actual purchase price. The amount of the *mōhar* was determined by the claims of the father (Gen. 34:12) and the social situation of the family (1 S. 18:25), and was paid in silver or in kind (Ex. 22:16[17]). It does not appear that the validity of the marriage depended on actual payment of the *mōhar,* as, e.g., the payment of a purchase price was the *conditio sine qua non* for establishing the validity of a purchase contract. In fact, payment of the *mōhar* could be replaced by services rendered, as in the case of David before his marriage to Saul's daughter (1 S. 18:17-27) or Othniel before his marriage to Caleb's daughter (Josh. 15:16f.; Jgs. 1:12f.). The girl was then given as a reward. The *mōhar* could also be replaced by a longer period of work, as was the case before Jacob's two marriages (Gen. 29:15-30). The *mōhar* could even be dispensed with entirely if the marriageable daughters were simply exchanged (cf. the suggestion Jacob's sons make to the Shechemites, Gen. 34:16). The Arabs call this *badal,* "substitute."[5]

These various agreements show that the *mōhar* was understood as compensation granted the family for the loss of the girl as an economic asset, as a worker, or as a means to advantageous connections. It should not be forgotten that the girl performed economically important functions in her father's house, e.g., she tended the flocks (Gen. 29:6,9), went to the well and drew water (Gen. 24:11-16; 1 S. 9:11), and worked to

---

(Leiden, 1961), 13-20, 52; W. Plautz, "Die Form der Eheschliessung im AT," *ZAW,* 76 (1964), 298-318; A. van Praag, *Droit matrimonial assyro-babylonien* (Amsterdam, 1945), 128-160, 202f.; J. J. Rabinowitz, "Marriage Contracts in Ancient Egypt in the Light of Jewish Sources," *HThR,* 46 (1953), 91-97; *idem,* "The Puzzle of the 'Tirḫâtum bound in the bride's girdle,' " *BiOr,* 16 (1959), 188-190; H. F. Richter, *Geschlechtlichkeit, Ehe und Familie im AT und seiner Umwelt. BBET,* 10 (1978); A. van Selms, *Marriage and Family Life in Ugaritic Literature* (London, 1954); E. A. Speiser, "New Kirkuk Documents Relating to Family Laws," *AASOR,* 10 (1928/29), 1-73, esp. 23f.; E. Szlechter, "L'affranchissement en droit suméro-akkadien," *AHDO-RIDA,* N.S. 1 (1952), 127-195, esp. 136-144; R. de Vaux, *AncIsr,* 32-36; J. Wellhausen, "Die Ehe bei den Arabern," *NGWG,* 1893, 431-480; E. A. Westermarck, *The History of Human Marriage,* II (London, [5]1922), ch. 23; B. Wilanowski, "Une nouvelle interprétation du §31 du Recueil de Lois assyriennes," *JJP,* 4 (1950), 267-273; R. Yaron, "Aramaic Marriage Contracts from Elephantine," *JSS,* 3 (1958), 1-39; *idem, Introduction to the Law of the Aramaic Papyri* (Oxford, 1961), 45-50; C. Zaccagnini, "Lo scambio dei doni nel Vicino Oriente durante i secoli XV-XIII," *OrAnt,* 11 (1973), 12-32.

1. *KTU,* 1.10 I, 11; 1.24, 19; 1.100, 74f.
2. *TAD* B2.6; B3.8.
3. → מכר *māḵar* (VIII, 291-96), Gen. 31:15.
4. → בעל *baʿal* (II, 181-200).
5. Wehr, 58.

gather scattered grain behind the harvest workers (Ruth 2:2). Furthermore, a good marriage might bring appropriate respect to the girl's family, as well as honor and material advantages. It is self-evident that the *mōhar,* understood in this way, only made sense in a patrilocal society in which a married couple lived in the husband's community, so that the young woman left her parents' house in order to live at that of her husband.

The notion of economic compensation also determines the etymology of the term *mōhar.* The suggestion made by Heinrich Zimmern,[6] namely, that *mōhar* derives from Akk. *maḫīru,* "equivalent, going price,"[7] certainly misses the mark. Although the root *mhr* I is probably a variant of *mwr*[8] *or myr,* which in Aramaic means "to procure food for oneself," the Hebrew hiphil exhibits the more general sense of "to give in exchange for" *(hēmîr b^e).* The sense of the qal of *mhr* I would thus have to be "to procure for oneself through compensation." Precisely this interpretation fits Ex. 22:15(16): *māhōr yimhārennâ llô l^e'iššâ,* "he shall procure her for himself as his wife." Here the verb *māhar* does indeed imply an expenditure. The term *māhar* exhibits the same meaning in Ps. 16:4 even without the context of marriage: *yirbû 'aṣṣ^{e}ḇôṯām 'aḥēr māhārû,* "although their idols multiply, they have procured another for themselves." This yields an acceptable meaning despite suspected corruption of the MT[9]: not satisfied with the spontaneous increase of gods as alleged by theogonic myths, the psalmist's contemporaries commission yet another idol to be produced at their own cost. Thus *māhar* implies procurement involving expenditure, although one cannot speak of "price" or "purchase" in the normal sense. Hence *mōhar* in the literal sense could also refer to the "compensation" one could exact when a girl left her parents' house for the purpose of marriage.

One might counter that the expression *mōhar habb^{e}ṯûlōṯ* (Ex. 22:16[17]) refers rather to the *pretium virginitatis.*[10] In this case, the *mōhar* would be compensation to the girl for the loss of her virginity. This explanation, however, is unacceptable, since it proceeds on the assumption that the term *b^{e}ṯûlâ* means "virgin." This may doubtlessly be the case in many passages, but in Joel 1:8, *b^{e}ṯûlâ* refers to a married woman who had been "possessed" by her husband *(ba'al); b^{e}ṯûlâ* thus refers to a marriageable girl who was physically able to cope with a man, "taking her into his possession." Here the term *b^{e}ṯûlâ* says nothing about her virginity.[11] Ex. 22:16(17) *(kesep̱ yišqōl k^{e}mōhar habb^{e}ṯûlōṯ)* can thus be translated "he shall weigh out as much silver as is required for marriageable girls."

In this context we should point out that ancient Hebrew custom did not associate marriageability with puberty. In contrast to the marriageable girl *(b^{e}ṯûlâ),* the → עלמה *'almâ* refers to a girl in puberty capable of conception. Girls could in fact already be

6. *Akkadische Fremdwörter als Beweis für babylonischen Kultureinfluss* (Leipzig, ^{2}1917), 18.
7. → מחיר *m^{e}ḥîr* (VIII, 231-34).
8. *GesB,* 171.
9. H.-J. Kraus, *Psalms 1-59* (Eng. trans., Minneapolis, 1987), 233f., 237.
10. Cf. Neubauer and Eberharter.
11. → בתולה *b^{e}ṯûlâ (b^{e}thûlāh),* II, 340-43.

given in marriage long before actual physical maturity, perhaps even as young as five years old (cf. Lev. 27:5), and it did happen that marriages were already consummated with prepubescent girls. Thus the paragraphs of old legal codices concerning infertile women can also refer precisely to such prepubescent girls who were coerced into consummating the marriage.[12]

2. *Usage*. The stipulation in Ex. 22:15f.(16f.) presupposes that there was a customary price which could vary from village to village and from clan to clan. In the case of a marriage compelled by the "rape of a marriageable girl who is not yet married," Dt. 22:29 directs that 50 shekels of silver be paid; this might correspond to the highest price of the *mōhar,* or in any case to a higher price than was customary (cf. Ex. 22:16[17]). This sum is also significantly higher than the purchase sum for a slave. The killing of a female slave was requited with 30 shekels (Ex. 21:32). According to Lev. 27:4, the valuation of a woman was also 30 shekels, and a girl between the ages of five and twenty was even valued at a mere 10 shekels (v. 5). These differing sums show that ultimately the *mōhar* was not intended as a purchase sum. This becomes all the more obvious if one compares it with genuine purchase contracts, e.g., Ex. 21:7-11: a girl could be "delivered"[13] by her father to another man who could designate her to be his own or his son's concubine. In this case she became an *'āmâ,* "maidservant"; *de facto,* however, she was — like the Assyrian *ēsērtu*[14] — a second-class wife.[15] This legal status of a girl purchased as a "maidservant" with the obligation of "marital" relations is well known in the rest of the ancient Near East as well.[16] This *'āmâ* could also be sold again to others, though not to a foreign people (Ex. 21:8). Hos. 3:2 might contain such a case: the prophet buys the woman for 15 shekels of silver and a homer and a lethech of barley, which also corresponds to approximately 15 shekels of silver. Hosea thus pays the customary price for a female slave (cf. Ex. 21:32).

The biblical evidence does not allow the conclusion that the father of the girl kept the *mōhar* for himself.[17] Quite the opposite seems to have been the case when Rachel and Leah turn against their own father, who has "delivered" them after he "has been using up their money" (Gen. 31:15). The *mōhar* thus actually seems to have become a financial gift to the woman to secure her in case she was cast out or lost her husband. This is also the interpretation that emerges from the fifth-century-B.C. documents from Elephantine,[18] in which the *mōhar* is part of the dowry even though it was handed over to the girl's father or guardian. In a reverse fashion, this *mōhar* was no less distinguished

12. Cf. CH §§147, 163.

13. → מכר *mākar* (VIII, 291-96).

14. Cf. Middle Assyrian laws, A, §41.

15. Cf. N. Avigad, *Bullae and Seals from a Post-Exilic Judaean Archive. Qedem,* 4 (1976), 11-13, 31f. [Eng. and Heb.].

16. Cf. A. Jaussen, *Coutumes des Arabes au pays de Moab* (Paris, 1908, repr. 1948), 60f.; *idem, Coutumes palestiniennes,* 1; *Naplouse et son district* (Paris, 1927), 129f.

17. See II below.

18. *AP,* 15; *BMAP,* 7.

from the gifts which the father or the bridegroom gave to the girl at the wedding. On this distinction, cf., e.g., Gen. 34:12: *mōhar* and *mattān,* "gift." These gifts to the girl or to her relatives provide compensation as it were for the acceptance of the marriage proposal. After Rebekah's marriage, Abraham's servants give costly gifts both to her and to her relatives (brother and mother; Gen. 24:53), another indication that *mōhar* by no means implied a purchase sum.

3. *Legal Questions.* Full payment of the *mōhar* sealed the marriage, which from that moment on was considered *matrimonium ratum.* This emerges from 2 S. 3:14, where David demands that his wife Michal be handed over to him, having acquired her as his wife *('ᵃšer 'ēraśtî lî bᵉ)* for a hundred foreskins of the Philistines. Here he is doubtlessly alluding to a *mōhar* demanded by Saul (1 S. 18:25ff.). The conclusion of the *matrimonium ratum* is being demanded by use of the piel *'ēraś,* which is usually incorrectly translated by "to betrothe." From the moment of marriage, the legally married woman — even if she has not yet been "taken into possession" by her husband — is called *mᵉ'ōrāśâ* (pual ptcp.). Her rape is punished as adultery (Dt. 22:23-27), and this shows that the lawgivers already equate her status with that of a wife (Dt. 22:24; cf. 2 S. 3:14). The transition from *matrimonium ratum* to *matrimonium consummatum* was introduced by the formal transfer of the wife into the house of her husband (*lāqaḥ,* Dt. 20:7; 24:1; cf. Gen. 20:3), an act comparable to that of the *traditio puellae.* The actual marital act is circumscribed by *bāʿal,* "possess" (Dt. 21:13; 24:1; Mal. 2:11).[19] Thenceforth the wife is called *bᵉʿulaṯ-baʿal* (Gen. 20:3; Dt. 22:22) or *bᵉʿûlâ* (Isa. 54:1; 62:4; Sir. 9:9). Payment of the *mōhar* thus actualizes the agreement of all parties involved and emerges as the constitutive element of the *matrimonium ratum.* This yields the legal situation designated by the various forms of *'rś.* The legal situation was quite clear when the requisite *mōhar* was delivered to the girl's father all at once; the marriage was then considered immediately in effect. It did happen, however, that the *mōhar* was paid in several installments. Extrabiblical evidence, nevertheless, shows that the bridal father, after having accepted a portion of the *mōhar* — in whatever form — could no longer withdraw from the transaction without payment of a penalty. If he did so, however, the contract apparently was considered terminated.

II. Ancient Near East.

1. *Ugarit.* Similar customs are attested in other parts of the ancient Near East, especially among the Western Semites. The oldest attestation of the term *mōhar* is found in the Ugaritic poem on the marriage of the moon-god.[20] Here the moon-god Yariḫ asks for the hand of the goddess Nikkal: "I shall give her father her *mhr:* 1,000 shekels of silver and 10,000 of gold."[21] In addition, he promises the bride profuse wedding gifts.[22] The mediator Ḫirḫib suggests other girls with whom he would like to

19. → ידע *yāḏaʿ* (V, 448-481).
20. *KTU,* 1.24.
21. *KTU,* 1.24, 19-21.
22. *KTU,* 1.24, 21-23; cf. *mattān,* Gen. 34:12.

"wed" him. The expression is *trḫ lk,*[23] which corresponds exactly to Heb. *'ēraśtî lî* (2 S. 3:14). The bridegroom is accordingly called *trḫ,*[24] and the wife *mtrḫt,*[25] which corresponds to Heb. *m*e*'ōrāśâ.* In the second scene the family enters to accept the *mōhar.* The description here doubtlessly reflects the reality of daily life.

The word *mhr* also occurs in *KTU,* 1.10 I, 11, but in a fragmentary context. In contrast, the mythical narrative of the charm against snake-bite[26] contains an interesting reference to *mhr.* The god Ḥoron has taken the daughter of the sun-goddess as his wife. The daughter demands snakes from him as *mōhar,* and Ḥoron agrees.[27] The girl selects the *mōhar,* which is then given to her. This mythical case, however, can be evaluated only with some reservation with regard to any light it might throw on the conditions obtaining in the Ugaritic aristocracy.

The Akkadian word corresponding to the *mhr* is *te/irḫatu,*[28] which derives from the same root as Ugar. *trḫ* and refers to the "wedding gift." The word occurs in three Akkadian legal texts from Ugarit (14th century). In the first,[29] a woman receives "as her *terḫatu*" the house of her father from the hand of an unidentified person. In another,[30] we read that a woman has brought along 80 shekels; furthermore, if after the death of her husband she takes this back, she is considered to have settled the account of the *terḫatu.* Finally,[31] if a woman has joined a family "as daughter-in-law" *(ana kallūti)* and is not treated properly, she can leave and take her *terḫatu* with her. The term *kallūtu* derives from *kallatu,* which corresponds to Ugar. *mtrḫt* and Heb. *m*e*'ōrāśâ.* Hence in legal documents the term *terḫatu* refers to goods which the woman brings into the marriage from among the possessions of her father, but which she takes back if the marriage is dissolved. The father of the bride thus does not keep the *terḫatu* himself, but rather passes them on to the daughter, who then consigns them to her husband. The wife maintains the right to take them back if the marriage is dissolved. The same situation is reflected in the Elephantine documents, and is echoed in Gen. 31:15.

2. *Alalakh.* The Alalakh documents (15th century) attest a similar custom. Two of the five marriage documents refer explicitly to the *terḫatu,*[32] and in two others[33] it is perhaps implied. It must be pointed out, however, that the Code of Hammurabi[34] recognized marriages without *terḫatu.* The first Alalakh text[35] suggests that the father

---

23. *KTU,* 1.24, 28f.; cf. 18, 26, 33; *KTU,* 1.14 I, 14; 1.23, 64.
24. *KTU,* 1.14 II, 47; IV, 26.
25. *KTU,* 1.14 I, 24; 1.24, 10.
26. *KTU,* 1.100.
27. *KTU,* 1.73-76.
28. *AHw,* III (1972), 1341.
29. RS 16.158; *PRU,* III, 62.
30. RS 15.92; *PRU,* III, 54-56.
31. RS 16.141; *PRU,* III, 60.
32. D. J. Wiseman, *The Alalakh Tablets* (London, 1953), nos. 92, 93.
33. *Ibid.,* nos. 17, 4-6; 91, 4.
34. CH §189.
35. Wiseman, no. 92.

passed on the *terḫatu* to the daughter; in the case of divorce, the *terḫatu* went either to the husband or to the wife, depending on who was at fault in the divorce. The second text[36] mentions the giving of the *terḫatu* after the *traditio puellae,* which means either that the *terḫatu* was paid directly to the woman or that it was paid to the father-in-law only after the *traditio.*

3. *Mari and Mesopotamia.* Documents from Mari seem to attest just such a case. One[37] mentions the *terḫatu* brought to Zimri-Lim when his daughter was already residing in the palace of her husband Ibal-Addu.[38] The same situation seems to apply to the marriage between the son of Šamši-Adad and the daughter of the king of Qatna;[39] here Šamši-Adad raises the amount of the requisite *terḫatu* because he considers it insufficient for a woman from the royal family. Another text[40] mentions the *terḫatu* in connection with the consolidation of a peace treaty through marriage.

The Amarna letters also mention the *terḫatu,* first in the letters from the Mitanni king Tušratta to Amenophis III and IV,[41] then also in a letter from Amenophis III to King Tarḫundaradu of Arzawa.[42] Here, however, the exchange of gifts also involves political considerations.

It should be noted that the Code of Hammurabi[43] confirms the practice of Alalakh and Ugarit[44]: the father of the woman passed the *terḫatu* on to his daughter. This custom is perhaps of Amorite provenance, although its additional attestation in a marriage contract from Nuzi (15th-14th centuries) suggests that the Hurrians may be its source. The Assyrian laws[45] also presuppose that the woman kept either all or part of the *terḫatu,* and prohibit the husband from making any claim to it. It seems, by the way, that in Assyria the *terḫatu* was not paid until the final stage of the marriage negotiations, after the other gifts had been given (cf. Gen. 24:53-58).[46]

4. *Elephantine.* It is noteworthy that the custom attested in Alalakh and Ugarit reappears nine hundred years later in the Elephantine documents. Although one might expect a certain amount of influence from Egyptian marriage contracts, where the woman receives a *šp-n-sḥm.t* ("gift for a woman") or *šp-rnwt-sḥm.t* ("gift for a young

36. *Ibid.,* no. 93.

37. G. Dossin, *Correspondance féminine. ARM,* X (1978), no. 75, 5.

38. *Ibid.,* no. 74.

39. G. Dossin, *Correspondance de Šamši-Addu et de ses fils. ARM,* I (1949, repr. 1978), nos. 24, 46, 77.

40. C.-F. Jean, *Lettres diverses. ARM,* II (1959, repr. 1978), no. 40.

41. EA, 19, 48, 58; 27, 14, 64; 29, 23f.

42. EA, 31, 22.

43. CH §§136, 163, 164.

44. Driver-Miles, 253.

45. Middle Assyrian laws, A, §38.

46. On the situation in Nuzi, cf. K. Grosz, "Dowry and Bride Price in Nuzi," *Studies on the Civilization and Culture of Nuzi and the Hurrians. Festschrift E. R. Lacheman* (Winona Lake, 1981), 161-182.

girl"), here the father or guardian of the young woman is the formal recipient of the *mōhar.* Although this involves a legal fiction, it nonetheless means that the Jewish colonists clung to the older West Semitic tradition. The small sum is also noteworthy: 5[47] or 10 shekels;[48] the latter sum corresponds to the stipulation in Lev. 27:5.

5. *Hittites.* The Hittite laws[49] mention the term *kušata-,* which corresponds to *mōhar* and *terḫatu.* It seems that payment of the *kušata-* was required for marrying a free woman, and that it constituted the *matrimonium ratum* whereby the woman was "bound" *(ḫamank-)* to her husband.[50] Similarly, the daughter of King Tarḫundarada of Arzawa could not be taken to Egypt *(traditio puellae)* before Amenophis III had paid the *kušata-*.[51]

Lipiński

47. *TAD* B2.6.
48. *TAD* B3.8.
49. I, §§29, 30, 34-36.
50. §29.
51. EA, 31, 22; cf. II.3 above.

מוג *mûg*

Contents: I. 1. Etymology, Ancient Near East; 2. Meaning, Occurrences. II. Concrete Usage: 1. Surge, Melt, Dissolve; 2. Waver, Reel, Be Shaken. III. Figurative Usage: Melt with Fear, Go into a Panic.

I. 1. *Etymology, Ancient Near East.* The root *mwg* is attested only in later West Semitic languages, especially Arab. *mwǵ,* "to surge," *mauǵ,* "wave," Jewish-Aram. *mwg,* "to melt." This evidence as well as the semantic development of the root in Middle and Modern Hebrew suggests a common background, namely, the notion of the rolling sea or of ground becoming soft because of moisture.

2. *Meaning, Occurrences.* This fundamental meaning is also clearly discernible in the OT. In addition, however, the idea of earthquakes also became associated with *mwg.* Here the influence of → מוט *mwṭ* may have played a role, which in Ps. 46:7(Eng. v. 6) (perhaps also Ps. 46:3[2]) parallels *mwg* and attracted other verbs from the conceptual field of earthquakes, such as *rāʿaš*[1] (Nah. 1:5; from the semantic range of *mwg,* cf. also Jer. 49:21; Ps. 46:4[3]; Isa. 14:16) and in an extended sense also *hāmâ*[2] (Ps. 46:7[6]; cf. 1 S. 14:16).

mûg. P. Joüon, "Notes de lexicographie hébraïque: Verbe מוג," *Bibl,* 7 (1926), 165-68.

1. → רעשׁ *(rāʿaš).*
2. → המה *hāmâ (hāmāh)* (III, 414-18).

The root *mwg* occurs 17 times in the Hebrew OT (of these, Isa. 64:6[7] should probably not be counted, whereas the root should presumably be conjectured in Ps. 46:3[2]; cf. the comms.), 4 times in the qal, 6 in the niphal, twice in the pilel, and 3 times in the hithpolel. Of the 4 occurrences in the Qumran texts, 2 are niphal (1QM 14:6; 4QM[a] 4) and 2 hithpolel (1QH 3:34, 35). The root occurs almost exclusively in poetic texts; thus except for Ex. 15:15; Josh. 2:9,24; 1 S. 14:16, it occurs only in prophetic books and in Psalms and Job; a similar situation obtains for the Qumran texts.

For the most part, the LXX apparently translates according to the context. Only *tḗkō* and *saleúō* occur 3 times each, *tarássō* twice.

II. Concrete Usage. 1. *Surge, Melt, Dissolve.* In one series of passages, the association of *mwg* with the notion of the rolling of the sea is only barely discernible. In Ex. 15:15 — though also in Josh. 2:9 (cf. v. 10!),24 — the miracle of the Reed Sea provides the background. 1 S. 14:16 describes the surging to and fro of a multitude of people. In Nah. 2:7(6), the location of the palace "on the river" suggests the surging of masses of water. And in Ps. 46:3(2) (conj.), the mountains threaten to sink into the sea (cf. v. 4[3]).

Ps. 107:26 (or vv. 23-32 taken together), however, unequivocally addresses the situation of seafarers on the high seas who come into distress during a storm. V. 26 offers a dramatically pointed description of the up-and-down motion of the surging sea: the seafarers are heaved up to heaven and then pulled back down into the abyss. (An echo of this notion can be found in the description of the earthquake in Am. 9:5, where the quaking is compared with the rising and sinking of the Nile.) Similarly, the situation of a person in maritime distress during a storm probably also provides the background to Job 30:22, which speaks of being lifted up and tossed about in the wind.

The term *mwg,* however, refers not only to the waves of the sea, but also to the gently falling rain (or even dew) that softens the ground and makes it dissolve. The term *mwg* is used in this sense in Am. 9:13 together with *nṭp,* where it expresses the overflowing fruitfulness characterizing the time of salvation. (The similarly formulated statement in Joel 4:18[3:18] does not use *mwg.*) Here the notion of a great influx of water into the ground immediately suggests its logical consequence, namely, the overflowing fullness of the harvest, without any clear distinction being made between the two. The "rolling" of the grain in the fields and of the vines in the vineyards may have contributed to this manner of expression.

Ps. 65:11(10) attests the same notion, extensively described in vv. 10-14(9-13) (together with *rʿp* and *rwh*): the abundance of water from the falling rain causes the fields to overflow with the luxuriant growth of vegetation, becoming thus a symbol of divine blessing.

2. *Waver, Reel, Be Shaken.* Ps. 46:3-7(2-6) shows that there is a fluid transition from the notion of the surging sea to that of an earthquake. When the convulsions assume cosmic proportions, then not only the masses of water surge, but also the seemingly immovable mountains threaten to sink into the sea, and that means: into chaos. 1 S.

14:15f. also reveals that from the biblical perspective earthquakes and surging seas are actually two sides of the same coin, namely, the convulsion and dissolution of the order obtaining since the beginning of the world.

This explains why in some passages *mwg* can refer directly to an earthquake, thus approaching the meaning of *mwṭ,* whereby the notion of the anchoring of the earth in the sea variously rounds out the context (Am. 9:5f.; Nah. 1:4f.); Ps. 75:4(3) explicitly mentions the pillars on which the earth rests in the middle of the sea (cf. 1QH 3:34f.). In this context we also learn what the antithesis of *mwg* is, namely, a steady foundation (cf. *tkn* in Ps. 75:4[3]; cf. 1QM 14:6).

II. Figurative Usage: Melt with Fear, Go into a Panic. Whereas the surging of the sea and earthquakes affect the entire earth, thus becoming cosmic convulsions, it is the "inhabitants of the land" themselves who are also often explicitly mentioned as victims (Josh. 2:9,24; Ps. 75:4[3]; Am. 9:5; 1QH 3:34), or else the inhabitants of a specific land (the land of the Philistines in Isa. 14:31; Canaan in Ex. 15:15), or of a specific building (a palace in Nah. 2:7[6]). This external threat to their stability inevitably also affects them internally; the external convulsion causes the same to occur internally, the result then manifesting itself in fear and panic. Thus *mwg* repeatedly serves to describe such situations of fear and panic, conditions usually brought about by God's own intervention.

In some passages it is no longer immediately clear whether the reference pertains more to the external or to the internal disruption of stability. Nah. 2:7(6) might just as easily refer to the chaos resulting from the opening of the gates as to the fear caused by that opening. It is likely, however, that no real alternative is intended here: *mwg* encompasses both aspects. Our word "panic" functions similarly. 1 S. 14:15f. also describes this amalgam of internal and external panic in quite graphic terms. The endangered seafarers also melt from fear in their ship, which has become a plaything for the surging waves (Ps. 107:26; cf. Job 30:22).

The term *mwg* is also used in portrayals of fear caused by Yahweh's mighty intervention, although without the details of the situation itself being made clear. Ex. 15:15 employs a plethora of words portraying the fear of the nations (cf. vv. 14-16), similar to 1 S. 14:15f. Josh. 2:9,24 is also a general portrayal of fear drawing on the formulation of Ex. 15:15.

Isa. 14:31; Jer. 49:23; Ezk. 21:20(15); 1QH 3:34f.; and perhaps also Isa. 64:6(7) also employ the term *mwg* in descriptions of the panic generated by Yahweh's mighty intervention in history. In these cases, however, the meaning has faded somewhat and lacks clear contours.

In contrast, several expressions occur describing the effect of fear on the individual. In Ps. 107:26, it is the *nep̱eš* of the seafarers that is seized by panic. Ezk. 21:20(15) as well as Jer. 49:23 (according to an almost universally accepted textual emendation) says the same thing about the *lēḇ* of the affected individuals. This refers not merely to part of the person, but emphasizes rather that the entire person is seized by fear and panic. In contrast, when 1QM 14:6; 4QM[a] 4 speak of those whose knees have become weak, they are clearly referring to a specific part of the body. Yet even here the intention may still be a reference to the entire person whose panic manifests itself in knees that are no longer steady, and which tremble.

In all these examples *mwg* shows itself to be a root that has forfeited much of its original identity by being drawn into the context of Yahweh's struggle with the nations and with chaos. Its later semantic development in Hebrew does, however, show that this contextual shift only partially affected its meaning at large, and did so only for a time; the vernacular preserved the older fundamental meaning "to surge, waver, become soft."

Baumann

מוט *mwṭ;* מוֹט *môṭ;* מוֹטָה *môṭâ*

Contents: I. 1. Etymology, Ancient Near East; 2. Meaning, Occurrences. II. Secular Usage: 1. Totter, Become Unsteady; 2. Be Unable to Maintain Oneself. III. Religious Usage: 1. Creation Theology; 2. Polemic against Idolatry; 3. Dispute between the Righteous and the Godless; 4. Declarations of Trust and Asseverations of Innocence.

I. 1. *Etymology, Ancient Near East.* The root *mwṭ* is attested only in the West Semitic languages: in Jewish-Aramaic, Syriac, Aramaic, and Palmyrene *mwṭ* means "to totter, waver," in part also "to ponder (in the sense of to weigh)," "to sink." Arab. *myṭ* means "to deviate, retire," Ethiop. *mēṭa* "to turn, bend." The common notion seems to be the deviation from an accustomed position, of the kind observed, e.g., in the beam of a scale or in the bending of a pole.

This basic meaning provided a conceptual transition to the nouns *môṭ* and *môṭâ,* which are generally considered derivations of *mwṭ* and which both mean "carrying pole, yoke." The notion of a carrying pole bending up and down might have suggested this derivation. It is striking, however, that *mwṭ* and *môṭ/môṭâ* nowhere occur in the same context, suggesting that the kinship was not conscious. It is far more likely that the speaker sensed a relationship with → מטה *maṭṭeh,* "staff," "branch," which derives from the root *nṭh* and whose semantic field ("spread out, stretch out, turn from the way, turn away, deviate") exhibits a certain proximity to that of *mwṭ*. Perhaps the semantic development of *môṭ/môṭâ* and of *maṭṭeh* can also be traced back to the influence of Egyp. *mdw,* "staff," and Ugar. *mṭ,* "staff."

2. *Meaning, Occurrences.* The basic meaning of *mwṭ* is probably "totter, waver," whereby the reference is always to something firm, such as the human body or bodily

---

mwṭ. G. Bertram, "σαλεύω, σάλος," *TDNT,* VII, 65-70; H. A. Brongers, "Darum, wer fest zu stehen meint, der sehe zu, dass er nicht falle: 1 Kor X 12," *Symbolae biblicae et mesopotamicae. Festschrift F. M. T. de Liagre Böhl. StFS,* 4 (1973), 56-70.

parts, or the earth or its foundations. Since the notion of the surging of the sea is quite alien here, and since that of slackening or becoming soft does not really fit into the semantic field, the root is not suited for descriptions of fear in its external and internal manifestations. Rather, the root *mwṭ* suggests primarily the stability or firmness — threatened or secure — of a solid mass.

The root *mwṭ* occurs 40 times in the Hebrew OT, 14 times in the qal, 22 in the niphal, twice in the hiphil, once in the hithpolel. An additional occurrence might be in Ps. 99:1, whereas the occurrences in Ps. 140:11(Eng. v. 10); 55:4(3); Prov. 24:11 (in the latter case in favor of *nāṭâ*!) should probably be eliminated. The Qumran texts attest 4 additional occurrences (3 in the niphal, 1 in the hithpolel). Of the OT occurrences, 26 are in the Psalter alone, and of the rest only Lev. 25:35 represents a genuine prose text, whereas a certain concentration can also be observed in Isaiah (6 occurrences, 4 of those in Deutero-Isaiah) and Proverbs (4 occurrences).

The distribution of *môṭ* and *môṭâ* exhibits completely different results. The word *môṭ* occurs altogether 4 times, 3 of those in Numbers (Nu. 4:10,12; 13:23) with the meaning "carrying pole," and once in Nah. 1:13 meaning "yoke" (unless this latter occurrence is to be read as a form of *môṭâ*). Although *môṭâ* can also mean "carrying pole" (1 Ch. 15:15), the meaning "yoke, yoke collar" predominates by far: of 12 occurrences in all, 11 exhibit this meaning, whereby the word can be either a concrete (Isa. 58:6a,6b,9; Jer. 27:2; 28:10,12,13a,13b) or a figurative reference (Lev. 26:13; Ezk. 34:27). In Ezk. 30:18 one should probably read *maṭṭeh* instead of *môṭâ;* similarly, *môṭâ* probably fits better in Isa. 9:3(4). One notices that *môṭ* and *môṭâ* do not occur at all in the psalms, and that the other occurrences are also found in biblical books or literary contexts that are quite different from those of *mwṭ*. This confirms the earlier observation that no real awareness of any kinship between the root and its presumed derivations can be ascertained.

The LXX variously translates *mwṭ* on the basis of context. Special preference, however, is given to *saleúō* or *sálos* (which together count for 23 occurrences); a third of the occurrences of *mwṭ* is covered by *saleúō,* which in Greek refers to natural movement, especially of the sea, and is used to render no less than 23 Hebrew roots; this usage, of course, was not without consequences for the meaning of *saleúō* in the LXX.

Aside from *nwṭ,* whose only occurrence (Ps. 99:1) should probably be emended to a form of *mwṭ,* synonyms include especially → מוג *mûg* (which was augmented, probably under the influence of *mwṭ,* to include the meaning "waver, heave during earthquakes"), *nûḏ,* and *nûaʿ*, though also *mwš/myš* (cf. Isa. 54:10) and *mʿd.* Antonyms are influenced by the context and are thus discussed separately.[1]

II. Secular Usage. 1. *Totter, Become Unsteady.* A person's steadiness is threatened especially when his feet slip or otherwise become unsteady. Thus it is not surprising that human feet[2] are often associated with *mwṭ* (Dt. 32:35; Ps. 38:17[16]; 66:9; 94:18;

1. See III below.
2. → רגל *reg̱el.*

121:3), or a person's "gait" or "steps" (Ps. 17:5). The enormous emphasis on steadfastness in connection with the polemic against idolatry (cf. Isa. 40:20; 41:7)[3] points in the same direction. When the assertion is made without further specification that a person — or idol — does not totter, as a rule this is probably also referring to the steadiness of feet and legs. Here the fundamental meaning of *mwṭ* comes to expression most clearly.

2. *Be Unable to Maintain Oneself.* Lev. 25:35 uses *mwṭ* in a metaphorical sense. It is probably no accident that here, too, the term is associated with a bodily part that can contribute to steadiness, namely, with → יד *yāḏ,* "hand," although even this word is intended here in a metaphorical sense. Instead of referring merely to the "slipping of one's hand," the assertion is that a person's "wealth" is unable to maintain itself, or "cannot endure." The concern is with maintaining a minimum of economic independence when someone within the covenant community slips into poverty.

III. Religious Usage. The majority of the occurrences of *mwṭ* are found in the context of religious statements. Several areas of usage stand out: the context of creation theology, especially the threat posed to creation by chaos and by the assault of the nations; the mockery of alien religions, especially the polemic against idolatry; disputes between the righteous and the godless; and finally, declarations of trust and asseverations of innocence. Although some thematic overlapping does occur between these areas, it seems best to discuss the material within this general outline and sequence.

1. *Creation Theology.* The fundamental convictions of OT creation theology include the assertion that Yahweh "established"[4] the circle of the earth[5]; Ps. 93:1; 96:10; 1 Ch. 16:30 all associate this statement with the assertion that the earth will "not totter" (NRSV "be moved"). This rejection of the possibility that the earth might lose its stability simultaneously functions to emphasize precisely that stability. (The formula *lō' yimmôṭ/bal-timmôṭ* radiates out into other contexts as well and becomes one of the most frequent designations for stability in general.[6]) The same can be said of *leʿôlām,* which also is frequently used to underscore the notion of stability.[7]

However, precisely such strong emphasis on the stability of the cosmos reveals that this stability was by no means self-evident. Rather, creation is continually in danger of sinking back into the primal chaos constantly lurking about creation itself. The cultic traditions of Jerusalem long had access to expressive possibilities for dealing with these notions, possibilities whose main themes — the "struggle with the gods of chaos" and the "struggle with foreign nations" — emanate from many OT passages.[8] This same

---

3. See III.2 below.
4. → כון *kûn* (VII, 89-101).
5. → תבל *tēḇēl.*
6. See III.4 below.
7. See below.
8. Cf., e.g., F. Stolz, *Strukturen und Figuren im Kult von Jerusalem. BZAW,* 118 (1970).

thing can be observed in the contexts associated with *mwṭ*. An important consideration was apparently that *mwṭ* could also refer to the threat to the earth's stability posed by earthquakes, such as those constantly occurring in the Syro-Palestinian region. Earthquakes were doubtlessly perceived as a primal menace underscoring the immediacy of the dissolution of all order into primordial chaos.

Earthquakes are explicitly mentioned in Isa. 24:19, which recounts the destructive power of the quaking in an accumulation of expressions and then elaborates on it further in vv. 18-20., where recollections of the Flood also resonate. Such recollections of the Flood also provide the background for Isa. 54:9f., which explicitly states that the waters of Noah should no longer inundate the earth; this provides the proper perspective on the earthquake mentioned in v. 10: although mountains and hills may totter and give way *(mwš),* there is no real danger of a complete reversion to primordial chaos, since Yahweh's *ḥesed̲* will not totter or withdraw *(mwš)* from his people, just as according to Isa. 24:18-20 the earthquake is caused by Yahweh and thus can also be stopped by him. Earthquakes are also mentioned in Ps. 60:4(2); 82:5; 46:3(2). Ps. 104:5 in particular emphasizes the stability of the earth in connection with a retrospect of the Flood and the subsequent limits placed on the powers of chaos, which here are especially identified with the sea.

Ps. 46 closely associates the motif of the struggle with chaos with that of the struggle with the nations, motifs even more succinctly paralleled in Ps. 99:1. Ps. 46:3f.(2f.) speaks of earthquakes and of the danger of the mountains sinking in the sea. In 46:7(6) (with *hāmâ* and *mwg* as synonyms) it is the assault of the nations against Mt. Zion; and v. 6(5) asserts that the city of God will remain firm. All three verses employ *mwṭ,* which together with *mwg* provides the leitmotif of the whole: although everything else may totter and stagger, God himself and his city do not!

This general framework of the struggle with chaos also includes Job 41:15(23), which says of the primordial sea monster Leviathan that the "folds of its flesh" cling to it as if poured on, and that it "does not move." Here the immovability and invincibility of this power of chaos are briefly characterized, just as they are then more broadly described in vv. 16ff.(24ff.). Here, too, however, it is made clear that this monster is powerless against God: it is, after all, God's creature (v. 25[33])!

Despite all the drama provided by these motifs of struggles with chaos and the gods, drama confirmed by the experiences of earthquakes and war, these statements nonetheless persevere in the conviction that Yahweh, who established the earth itself, will also safeguard it from sinking back into chaos. Here *mwṭ* provides a key word inasmuch as it delineates the contrast between the defective stability of the powers of chaos and even of the seemingly immovable mountains on the one hand, and Yahweh's genuinely imperturbable stability and steadfastness on the other.

2. *Polemic against Idolatry.* Job 41:15(23) already insinuates that Yahweh's adversaries are not so much the powers of nature or the nations and their leaders, as other powers which themselves claim divinity. Ps. 82 addresses this opposition between God and the gods more clearly by tracing the world's own disorder back to its lack of knowledge and understanding, which causes it to fumble around in the dark; as a result,

the foundations of the earth itself shake and totter (v. 5). Dt. 32:35 announces the danger of slipping in connection with the accusation of apostasy to other gods.

In these passages *mwṭ* is used in an extended sense in the context of polemic against other gods. In two passages with close literary connections, however, *mwṭ* acquires a special meaning (Isa. 40:20; 41:7). Here *mwṭ* occurs in the context of polemic against idols,[9] polemic which in a gleeful portrayal of the actual production of such idols demonstrates the impossibility of these other religions. Here *mwṭ* fulfills an important function by drawing attention to the decisive weakness of an idol, namely, that it cannot provide for its own stability. Rather, it needs the help of an experienced craftsman so that it does not "totter" (40:20); but even when several master craftsmen strive together to insure an especially good rendering of the image, nails must still be used as an aid in securing it so that — in human estimation — it does not "wobble." Twice the statement *lō' yimmôṭ* stands emphatically at the conclusion. The OT is well acquainted with the notion that an idol can tip over (cf. 1 S. 5:1ff.). Since idols are such a shaky thing, how can one expect them to exhibit stability *(kwn)* or strength *(ḥzq)* when they themselves need stabilizing? Yahweh, of course, needs no such aid; he sits above the circle of the earth (Isa. 40:22) and is thus able to lend stability to everything else.

3. *Dispute between the Righteous and the Godless.* Yet another sphere of usage is revealed by the numerous passages from the psalms which use the word *mwṭ* to address the antithesis between the righteous (the *ṣaddîq*) and the godless (the *rāšā'*). The polemic against idols resonates here inasmuch as the impious also believe that they will never be shaken, and will be spared any misfortune (Ps. 10:6), just as in a reverse fashion the righteous, when shaken, are fearful before the rejoicing of their adversaries (Ps. 13:5[4]; 38:17[16]). Prov. 25:26 also considers it a great misfortune when a *ṣaddîq* gives way before the wicked. The adversarial relationship between God and the gods is continued in that between the righteous and the godless.

The righteous person, however, also realizes that he indulged in a false sense of security when he earlier asserted that in all eternity he would never totter (Ps. 30:7[6]). Never can a person acquire stability from within himself, but rather only from Yahweh. Thus precisely when the righteous person thought his stability was lost and that he would totter, Yahweh's *ḥesed* supported him (Ps. 94:18). The righteous person can thus also confidently cast his burdens upon Yahweh, always certain that Yahweh will never allow the *ṣaddîq* to stagger (Ps. 55:23[22]). Or he can express the conviction that he will always be mindful, and will never totter (Ps. 112:6). Prov. 10:30; 12:3 treat the same idea in a similar fashion by juxtaposing the fate of the *ṣaddîq* with that of the *rāšā'*. The righteous person can be certain of never staggering, while the wicked will never endure *(kwn),* and will not dwell in the land.

The occurrences of *mwṭ* in the Qumran texts evoke the same conceptual background. 1QS 11:12 considers the possibility of slipping (with *kāšal* as a synonym), anticipating

---

9. Cf. H. D. Preuss, *Verspottung fremder Religionen im AT. BWANT,* 92[5/12] (1971), 193ff., 201ff.

as does Ps. 94:18 the succor of the *ḥasd̲ê* or the *ṣid̲qat̲ 'ēl.* 1QH 6:21,27; 7:7 also speak of the staggering of the godless and of the imperturbability of the righteous, extensively described using the metaphor of a well-structured wall built on a firm foundation.

This field of usage removes *mwṭ* from the broader sphere of convulsions of cosmic proportions as illustrated by the struggles with chaos and the nations, and by earthquakes and war. Here the focus is rather on the personal fate of the individual. Yet even when literal reference is made to the slipping of a person's foot, the imperturbability of the righteous person could likely not be expressed so powerfully by the root *mwṭ* if the mode of expression shaped by the theology of creation, with its high valuation of Yahweh's secure establishment of the world, did not provide its background. In all probability this constitutes a later individualization of statements which originally encompassed a much wider sphere. Thus every emphasis on the stability and imperturbability of the righteous person resonates with the stability and firmness which Yahweh once bestowed upon the earth itself and which again and again he maintains against the myriad destructive forces of chaos.

4. *Declarations of Trust and Asseverations of Innocence.* The way in which this individualization came about can probably be deduced from Ps. 21:8(7). Here the king expresses his trust[10] in Yahweh as well as the confidence that he will himself never stagger through the *ḥesed̲* of the Most High. All this is said against the background of the king's obligation to take up arms against his enemies, which in vv. 9ff.(8ff.) are clearly identified as Yahweh's own enemies. Nonetheless, the declaration of trust is the primary focus, and is not being made in any polemical confrontation as was the case in the examples discussed in the previous section. Above all, an individual is being addressed here, even if as the king he represents the entire people.

This royal declaration of trust leads to expressions of trust made by pious individuals from a later time. In Ps. 16:8f., the psalmist proclaims his conviction that he will not totter if Yahweh, of whom he is continually mindful, is by his side. In Ps. 62:3,7(2,6), this same confidence is repeated like a refrain and augmented by the assertion that Yahweh is his rock, salvation, and fortress (cf. Ps. 46:8,12(7,11). This reference to the rock evokes Mt. Zion, which Ps. 125:1 calls a place of trust which bestows eternal stability. Such expressions of trust can also recall experiences in which God has kept the petitioners from slipping (Ps. 66:9), whereby here as in other passages it is uncertain whether the petitioners are being addressed as individuals or as a collective.

Ps. 15:5 uses *mwṭ* at the conclusion of an entry liturgy which enumerates the conditions under which the petitioners may enter Mt. Zion. In Ps. 121:3, *mwṭ* occurs within the framework of a dismissal ceremony. This and the great frequency with which the statement *lō'* or *bal-yimmôṭ,* "he will not totter," occurs (1 Ch. 16:30; Job 41:15[23]; Ps. 10:6; 15:5; 16:8; 21:8[7]; 30:7[6]; 46:6[5]; 62:3,7[2,6]; 93:1; 96:10; 104:5; 112:6; 125:1; Prov. 10:30; 12:3; Isa. 40:20; 41:7 — formulated in part also in the 1st person) suggest that it was a fixed formula often associated with statements concerning eternal

10. → בטח *bāṭaḥ (bāṭach)* (II, 88-94).

permanence such as *l^e^dōr wādōr* (Ps. 10:6), *l^eʿôlām* (e.g., Ps. 15:5; 112:6; 125:1; Prov. 10:30), or *l^eʿôlām w^eʿād* (Ps. 104:5). As such, the formula was apparently part of the framework of worship (perhaps entry or dismissal ceremonies) functioning as the expression directly pledging the stability and imperturbability mediated by trust in Yahweh.

Baumann

מוּל *mûl*; מוּלָה *mûlâ*

Contents: I. Linguistic Considerations; LXX. II. Ancient Near East. III. Usage: 1. The Rite; 2. Interpretation. IV. Qumran.

---

mûl. A. Allwohn, "Die Interpretation der religiösen Symbole, erläutert an der Beschneidung," *ZRGG,* 8 (1956), 32-40; Y. Blau, "The *ḥatan damim* (Ex IV:24-26)," *Tarbiz,* 26 (1956/57), 1-3 [Heb.], I [Eng. summary]; W. Bunte, "Beschneidung," *BHHW,* I (1962), 223-25; A. Caquot, "Pour une étude de l'initiation de l'ancien Israël," *Initiation. SNumen,* 10 (1965), 131-33; R. B. Culbreth, *A Historical Study of Circumcision* (diss., Southern Baptist Theological Seminary, Louisville, 1952); W. Dumbrell, "Exodus 4:24-26: A Textual Re-Examination," *HThR,* 65 (1972), 285-290; D. Flusser and S. Safrai, " 'Who Sanctified the Well-Beloved in (lit. from) the Womb,' " *Studies in Bible and the Ancient Near East* (Jerusalem, 1978), I, 193f. [Eng. summary], II, 329-336 [Heb.]; G. Fohrer, *Überlieferung und Geschichte des Exodus. BZAW,* 91 (1964), 45-48; H. O. Forshey, "Circumcision: An Initiatory Rite in Ancient Israel?" *Restoration Quarterly,* 16 (1973), 150-58; W. H. Gispen, "De Besnijdenis," *GThT,* 54 (1954), 148-157; 55 (1955), 9-16; P. Gordon, *L'Initiation sexuelle et l'évolution religieuse* (Paris, 1946), 63-68; R. Gradwohl, "Der 'Hügel der Vorhäute' (Josua V 3)," *VT,* 26 (1976), 235-240; L. H. Gray, *et al.,* "Circumcision," *ERE,* 3 (1910), 659-680; J. de Groot, "The Story of the Bloody Husband (Exodus IV 24-26)," *OTS,* 2 (1943), 10-17; M. Haran, "The Religion of the Patriarchs: An Attempt at a Synthesis," *ASTI,* 4 (1965), 30-55; J. Hehn, "Der 'Blutsbräutigam' Ex 4 24-26," *ZAW,* 50 (1932), 1-8; H.-J. Hermisson, *Sprache und Ritus im altisraelitischen Kult. WMANT,* 19 (1965), 64-76; S. B. Hoenig, "Circumcision: The Covenant of Abraham," *JQR,* 53 (1962/63), 322-334; E. Isaac, "Circumcision as a Covenant Rite," *Anthropos,* 59 (1964), 444-456; E. Junes, "Etude sur la circoncision rituelle en Israël," *Rev. Hist. Méd. Isr.,* 16 (1953), 37-57; 17 (1954), 91-104; 18 (1955), 159-168; H. Junker, "Der Blutbräutigam: Eine textkritische und exegetische Studie zu Ex 4 24-26," *Alttestamentliche Studien. Festschrift F. Nötscher. BBB,* 1 (1950), 120-28; H. Kosmala, "The 'Bloody Husband,' " *VT,* 12 (1962), 14-28; E. Kutsch, "Der sogenannte 'Blutbräutigam,' " *ZDMGSup,* 4 (1980), 122f.; R. Le Déaut, "Le thème de la circoncision du coeur (Dt. xxx 6; Jér iv 4) dans les versions anciennes (LXX et Targum) et à Qumrân," *Congress Volume, Vienna 1980. SVT,* 32 (1981), 178-205; F. R. Lehmann, "Bemerkungen zu einer neuen Begründung der Beschneidung," *Sociologus,* N.S. 7 (1957), 57-74; J. S. Licht, "mîlāh," *EMiqr,* IV (1962), 894-901; A. Lods, " 'La mort des incirconcis,' " *CRAI* (1943), 271-283; E. Meyer, "Zur Beschneidung der Phöniker," *ZAW,* 29 (1909), 152; R. Meyer, "περιτέμνω," *TDNT,* VI, 72-84; P. Middlekoop, "The Significance of the Story of the 'Bloody Husband' (Ex 4:24-26)," *South East Asia Journal of Theology,* 8/4 (1966/67), 34-38; J. Morgenstern, "The 'Bloody Husband' (?) (Exod. 4:24-26) Once Again," *HUCA,* 34 (1963), 35-70; M. Ohana, "Agneau pascal et circoncision: Le problème de la halakha prémishnaïque dans le Targum palestinien," *VT,* 23 (1973), 385-399; J. Preuss, *Biblical and Talmudic Medicine* (Eng. trans., New York, 1978);

I. Linguistic Considerations; LXX. The verb *mûl,* "circumcise," attested only in Hebrew, occurs 32 times in the Bible (13 times in the qal, 19 in the niphal). The postulation of a secondary form *mll* as an explanation for *mōl* (Josh. 5:2) and *n*^e^*maltem* (Gen. 17:11) is unconvincing.[1] Either the person himself is circumcised (so Gen. 17:10,12,13,26,27; 21:4; 34:15,22,24; Ex. 12:44,48; Josh. 5:2,3,4,5,7), or his *b*^e^*śar ʿorlâ* (Gen. 17:11,14,23,24,25; Lev. 12:3) or *ʿorlâ* (Jer. 9:24[Eng. v. 25]), i.e., the foreskin. In metaphorical usage *mûl* is used with *ʿorlaṯ l*^e^*ḇaḇkem* (Dt. 10:16; Jer. 4:4) or *lēḇāḇ* (Dt. 30:6) as objects. The Qumran texts twice attest the qal (1QS 5:5; 1QpHab 11:13), once the niphal (CD 16:6). 1QS 5:5 attests the infinitive construct (which does not occur in the Bible itself). The noun *mûlâ* occurs only in Ex. 4:26.

Synonyms include *krt* (Ex. 4:25) and *sûr* hiphil (Jer. 4:4).

Except for Dt. 30:6 *(perikatharízō)* and Josh. 5:4 *(perikathaírō),* the equivalent used by the LXX is *peritémnō* (also Ex. 4:25; Jer. 4:4).

II. Ancient Near East. In addition to Judah itself, Jer. 9:25(26) also mentions the Egyptians, Edomites, Ammonites, Moabites, and Arabs as people who practice circumcision. While no witnesses to the custom of circumcision in Mesopotamia have yet come to light,[2] Egyptian circumcision is richly documented,[3] although it does not seem to have been the general custom during all periods. The Egyptian practice itself is attested by Jer. 9:25(26), supported by Ezk. 32:19,28,32, perhaps also Josh. 5:9, as well as Herodotus and Philo.[4] Greek documents dealing with circumcision from the second

---

G. Richter, "Zwei alttestamentliche Studien. I. Der Blutbräutigam," *ZAW,* 39 (1921), 123-28; L. F. Rivera, "El 'esposo sangriento' (Ex 4,24-26)," *RevBíbl,* 25 (1963), 129-136; J. M. Sasson, "Circumcision in the Ancient Near East," *JBL,* 85 (1966), 473-76; H. Schmid, "Mose, der Blutbräutigam: Erwägungen zu Ex 4,24-26," *Jud,* 22 (1966), 113-18; J. Schmid, "Beschneidung. I. Biblisch," *LThK,* II, 289-291; I. Schur, *Wesen und Motive der Beschneidung im Lichte der alttestamentlichen Quellen und der Völkerkunde* (Helsinki, 1937); M. H. Segal, "The Religion of Israel Before Sinai. IV. The Origin of Circumcision in Israel," *JQR,* N.S. 52 (1961), 53-56; F. Sierksma, "Quelques remarques sur la circoncision en Israel," *OTS,* 9 (1951), 136-169; E. M. Smallwood, "The Legislation of Hadrian and Antoninus Pius Against Circumcision," *Latomus,* 18 (1959), 334-347; L. V. Snowman, "Circumcision," *EncJud,* V (1971), 567-575; B. Stade, "Miszellen. 14. Der 'Hügel der Vorhäute' Jos 5," *ZAW,* 6 (1886), 132-143; St. B., IV ([5]1969), 23-40; F. Stummer, "Beschneidung," *RAC,* II (1954), 159-169; S. Talmon, "The Bloody Husband," *ErIsr,* 3 (1954), 93-96 [Heb.], IV [Eng. summary]; R. de Vaux, *AncIsr,* 46ff.; *idem, The Early History of Israel* (Eng. trans., Philadelphia, 1978); G. Vermés, *Scripture and Tradition in Judaism. StPB,* 4 (1961), 178-192 ("Circumcision and Exodus IV 24-26"); C. Weiss, "A Worldwide Survey of the Current Practice of Milah," *Jewish Social Studies,* 24 (1962), 30-48; H. Wissmann, O. Betz, and F. Dexinger, "Beschneidung I-III," *TRE,* V (1980), 714-724; C. Westermann, *Genesis 12–36* (Eng. trans., Minneapolis, 1985), 263-69; → חתן *ḥtn* (V, 270-77); → ערל *ʿrl;* → לב *lēḇ* (VII, 399-437).

1. Cf. *BLe,* §56u″; 58t; W. Gesenius–G. Bergsträsser, *Hebräische Grammatik,* II ([29]1926, repr. Hildesheim, 1962), §28i; *KBL*[3] adduces Gen. 17:11 under both מול and מלל.
2. Cf. E. Ebeling, "Beschneidung," *RLA,* II (1938), 18.
3. Cf. *RÄR,* 109-11.
4. Herodotus *Hist.* ii.36f.; Philo *De spec. leg.* i.2.5; *Quaest. in Gen.* iii.47.

half of the 2nd century, however, mention only the circumcision of priests,[5] which agrees with the indications given by the church fathers.[6] In this respect, the oldest witnesses cannot be interpreted unequivocally. On a stela from Naga ed-Der in Middle Egypt (23rd century B.C.) the donor proclaims that he owes his success to this ritualistic operation, which was performed on him together with 120 others.[7] A funerary relief from Saqqārah (sixth dynasty) portrays a priest performing the rite of circumcision on a youth with a flint knife.[8] It seems certain that the age at which circumcision was performed was somewhere around puberty (rite of entering manhood?),[9] or in exceptional instances earlier.[10] In the later period circumcision of priests was obligatory.[11] The fact that during the Hasmonean period the Ammonites and Edomites do not practice circumcision (Jth. 14:10; Josephus *Ant.* xiii.9.1; in contrast to Jer. 9:25[26], although Ezk. 32:29 also describes the Edomites as circumcised) does not constitute a contradiction; it might be rather that the inhabitants of the regions of Idumea and Ammon had in the intervening period given up circumcision. Whereas circumcision among the Moabites is not mentioned elsewhere, it is a well-attested tradition among the Arabs (Gen. 17:25f.; Josephus *Ant.* i.12.2).[12] The oldest witness is probably the pericope Ex. 4:24-26, which recent exegetes suggest derives from a Midianite background.[13] Rabbinic literature views Ex. 4:24ff. as the *locus classicus* for the assertion that God tolerates no delay regarding circumcision (Bab. *Ned.* 31b). Beyond this, the oracle of woe against the prince of Tyre in Ezk. 28 reveals that the Judeans were also aware of circumcision among the Phoenicians (v. 10), which is attested in Sanchuniathon,[14] Herodotus,[15] and Aristophanes.[16] The fact that the Phoenicians do not appear in Jeremiah's enumeration might suggest that his selections were political in nature. Wilhelm Rudolph suggests an anti-Babylonian coalition under Egyptian leadership whose propagandistic vaunting of shared circumcision the prophet here deflates.[17]

III. Usage. 1. *The Rite.* Circumcision did not become legally regulated until the exilic and postexilic periods. After that, every male was to be circumcised (Gen.

---

5. L. Mitteis and U. Wilcken, *Grundzüge und Chrestomathie der Papyruskunde* (Leipzig, 1912), I/2, nos. 74-77.
6. F. Zimmermann, *Die ägyptische Religion nach der Darstellung der Kirchenschriftsteller und die ägyptischen Denkmäler* (Paderborn, 1912), 158-162.
7. *ANET*³, 326.
8. *ANEP,* 206; cf. also *ANET*³, 673.
9. K. Sudhoff, *Ärztliches aus griechischen Papyrus-Urkunden. Studien zur Geschichte der Medizin,* 5f. (Leipzig, 1907), 179: twelve to fourteen years old; Philo *Quaest. in Gen.* iii.47: fourteen years old.
10. Mitteis-Wilcken, no. 74: seven and eleven years old.
11. Cf. W. Westendorf, "Beschneidung," *LexÄg,* I (1975), 727-730.
12. J. Wellhausen, *Reste arabischen Heidentums* (Berlin, ²1897, repr. 1961), 174f.
13. So Kosmala, H. Schmid, Kutsch, Forshey; → חתן *ḥtn,* V, 276f.
14. Cited in Eusebius *Praep. ev.* i.10.33.
15. *Hist.* ii.104.
16. *Birds* 504ff.
17. *Jeremia. HAT,* XII (³1968), 64f.

17:10b,11a), the time of circumcision was set at the eighth day after birth (v. 12a), and the circle of those affected was expanded to include slaves (vv. 12b,13a) in order to guarantee the cultic purity of the larger family to which they belonged. The ordinances conclude in Gen. 17:14a with a sanction.[18] Individual elements reappear in other contexts. Ex. 12:43-50 mentions (vv. 44,48) allowing slaves and foreigners dwelling in the land to partake of the Passover if they are circumcised. The stipulation of the eighth day as the time of circumcision was incorporated into Lev. 12:1-8, a compendium of ordinances to be followed at the birth of a child (v. 3).

Circumcision itself can be traced back to the time before the country was unified (Josh. 5:2-9), back to the period of the conquest, and probably even as far back as the end of the patriarchal period (Gen. 34).[19] The presentation of P in Gen. 17; 21:4, which traces circumcision back to Abraham, accommodates itself to the historical framework of the period portrayed.[20] The flint knives mentioned in Ex. 4:25; Josh. 5:3 also suggest a very early date. The designation of the eighth day rendered impossible the kind of collective circumcision apparently customary in an earlier period (Josh. 5:2-9).[21] Comparisons with later circumstances yield only approximate details with which to amplify this picture.

The fundamental elements of the modern practice of circumcision were already fixed at the time of the Mishnah. Three stages of the operation are differentiated: 1. removal *(mîlâ)* of the foreskin *(ḥittûḵ);* 2. exposing the *glans penis* as far as the corona *(pᵉrîʿâ);* 3. sucking off the bleeding vessels *(mᵉṣîṣâ).* The *pᵉrîʿâ* can hardly have been a part of circumcision during the biblical period, since it obstructs operations which reestablish the foreskin of the kind familiar from the Hellenistic-Roman period (1 Mc. 1:15; *As.Mos.* 8:3; Josephus *Ant.* xii.5.1; 1 Cor. 7:18; *ʾAboth* iii.11). A later introduction of this element is also suggested by the fact that tradition explicitly tries to attribute it to Abraham (Bab. *Yoma* 28b). In general, a father probably circumcised his son, although in emergency situations anyone could perform the rite as long as he or she was a Jew. The modern mohel can also be represented by any Jew.

2. *Interpretation.* Until the end of the monarchy circumcision was a self-evident sign of ethnic identity (Gen. 34).[22] The need for religious interpretation emerged at the same time legal regulation became necessary, since it became clear that circumcision on the one hand and personal behavior on the other could very easily diverge. Deuteronomy (10:16; 30:6), Jeremiah (4:4; 9:25[26]), and Ezekiel (44:7,9) all believe that this could be rectified by a "circumcision of the heart" which would fulfill that of the flesh. "Circumcision is circumcision of the heart."[23] P then interprets circumcision as a sign of the covenant (Gen. 17:11) which manifests on the one hand God's steadfastness, and on the other Israel's

---

18. Westermann, 263, 267.
19. *Ibid.,* 540f.
20. De Vaux, *The Early History of Israel,* 286f.
21. Cf. also *ANET*³, 326.
22. → ערל *ʿrl.*
23. Hermisson, 76.

commitment. The Talmud expresses this by asserting that circumcision overrides all 613 commandments and prohibitions (Bab. *Ned.* 32a). A third interpretation emerges from the LXX rendering of Dt. 30:6; Josh. 5:4.[24] Circumcision is a condition for cultic purity. This apparently reflects the Egyptian understanding.[25]

IV. Qumran. The Qumran texts follow the interpretations of Deuteronomy, Jeremiah, Ezekiel, and P. An autonomous person omits circumcising the foreskin of his heart (1QpHab 11:13) or the foreskin of his evil inclinations and stiffness of neck (1QS 5:5). CD 16:6 views the day of Abraham's circumcision as the day the covenant was made.[26]

G. Mayer

24. See I above.
25. Herodotus *Hist.* ii.37; Philo *De Spec. Leg.* i.5).
26. → לב *lēḇ* (VII, 399-437).

מוֹלֶדֶת *môleḏeṯ*

Contents: I. 1. Grammatical Form; 2. Occurrences; 3. Meaning. II. Context: 1. Place of Birth, Home, Fatherland: a. *'ereṣ môleḏeṯ;* b. *môleḏeṯ;* 2.a. Birth; b. Descent, Origin; 3.a. Race; b. Descendants; c. Relatives.

I. 1. *Grammatical Form.* Among the abstract nouns derived from the root → ילד *yld* which occasionally exhibit concrete meaning, *môleḏeṯ* is the most important after *tôlāḏâ,* with which it is closely associated.[1] The non-segolate form *môlāḏâ* occurs only as a place name (Josh. 15:26; 19:2; 1 Ch. 4:28; Neh. 11:26).

2. *Occurrences.* The term *môleḏeṯ* occurs 22 times in the Hebrew Bible, although with uneven distribution (in particular, it occurs nowhere in the Deuteronomistic history, nor in the greater Ketubim). It occurs 9 times in Genesis (8 of those among the older narrators), 4 times in the remaining Tetrateuch; the rest occur in Jeremiah (twice), Ezekiel (3 times), Ruth (once), and Esther (3 times). Temporal distribution thus extends from the Yahwist to the Hellenistic period.

3. *Meaning.* Of the three semantic categories which the grammars generally attribute to substantives constructed with *ma-,* namely, place, instrument, and verbal-abstract,[2] the

1. On the construction with the preformative *ma- (maqṭal-t),* see *GK,* §85e-g; Joüon, §88 1.e; on the segolate ending cf. *GK,* §94g; Joüon, §89g.
2. Cf. esp. H. S. Nyberg, *Hebreisk Grammatik* (Uppsala, 1952), 205-8.

instrumental does not apply to *môleḏeṯ*. Accordingly, two fundamental meanings emerge: 1. place of birth, home, fatherland; 2. birth, and thence descent, lineage; or as *concretum pro abstracto:* a) tribe; b) descendants; c) persons of the same descent = relations, family.

In all these variations, however, the fundamental meaning of *yld* is always present. In contrast to the nomadic tribal and clan structures, which are often supported by artificial genealogies, *môleḏeṯ* is that identification and connection based on consanguinity and birth which still obtains even if the tribal and clan structures themselves are dissolved.[3]

For a consideration of the LXX renderings of *môleḏeṯ,* see the individual sections below.

II. Context. 1. *Place of Birth, Home, Fatherland.* a. *'ereṣ môleḏeṯ.* The meaning "place of birth, home" is to be read in particular in those passages that speak of *'ereṣ môleḏeṯ,* "homeland." It is not really accurate to understand *môleḏeṯ* here in the derivative sense of "kindred," in which case *'ereṣ môleḏeṯ* would be the "land of one's kindred."[4] Rather, *'ereṣ môleḏeṯ* is the land in which a person has his physical, though also his spiritual roots. Of the 7 passages with *'ereṣ môleḏeṯ,* 2 belong to the Abraham cycle, and one to the Jacob cycle. One fixed biblical tradition places Abraham's home in Mesopotamia. This is his *('ereṣ) môleḏeṯ,* which he gives up under Yahweh's guiding hand. As is well known, P deviates from this by having Abraham's father Terah's wanderings begin in Ur of the Chaldeans (Gen. 11:31), though significantly without calling it his home (*'ereṣ môleḏeṯ* does not occur in the P source). It is rather the Yahwist who considers Aram Naharaim and more specifically Haran to be Abraham's *'ereṣ môleḏeṯ.* This is doubtlessly his reference in Gen. 11:28, where "Ur of the Chaldeans" functions "merely to harmonize."[5] And in Gen. 24:7 (cf. v. 10) he formally names Aram Naharaim and the city of Nahor as Abraham's *'ereṣ môleḏeṯ,* i.e. (according to 27:43; 28:10; 29:4) Haran itself. As tenacious as the older narrators are in their association of not only Isaac (Gen. 24) but also Jacob (Gen. 29–33) with Haran as Abraham's *'ereṣ môleḏeṯ,* Jacob's *'ereṣ môleḏeṯ* is actually Canaan.[6] When in Gen. 31:13 (E) the angel of Elohim instructs Jacob to return to the *'ereṣ* of his *môleḏeṯ,* the reference is to Canaan. The "sons of Jacob" come from middle Palestine,[7] and the Jacob traditions already enjoy a fixed focal point in the sanctuary at Bethel.[8] This change in direction over against the Abraham cycle, however, also reveals the change that has taken place in the combinations and systematization of the patriarchal traditions from Abraham to

3. See II.1.a below.

4. R. de Vaux, "Les patriarches hébreux et les découvertes modernes," *RB,* 55 (1948), 322: "place where one's kindred dwells"; C. Westermann, *Genesis 12–36* (Eng. trans., Minneapolis, 1985), 139: the land of his kith and kin, the land where his kinsmen lived.

5. Westermann, 135.

6. Cf. H. Seebass, *Der Erzvater Israel und die Einführung der Jahweverehrung in Kanaan. BZAW,* 98 (1966), 33.

7. Cf. A. Lemaire, "Les Benê Jacob," *RB,* 85 (1978), 321-337.

8. Cf. A. de Pury, *Promesse divine et légende cultuelle dans le cycle de Jacob,* II. *ÉtB* (1975), esp. 559-585; E. Otto, "Jakob in Bethel," *ZAW,* 88 (1976), 165-190.

Jacob by the Israelite narrators and theologians. Whereas Abraham's *'ereṣ môleḏeṯ* is in Aram Naharaim, and Isaac similarly sojourns in Canaan as a foreigner (Gen. 26:3: *gûr;* cf. in P the *'ereṣ m^{e}gurîm:* Gen. 17:8, etc.; Abraham is a *gēr* and *tôšāḇ* in the land: Gen. 23:4), Jacob's wives already feel like *noḵriyyôṯ* in Aram Naharaim (Gen. 31:15); his *'ereṣ môleḏeṯ* is Canaan: the promise is taking form.

Not only the stories surrounding the figure of Abraham, but also the Ruth narrative make it clear that the *'ereṣ môleḏeṯ* is not the highest good, and that Yahweh may well demand of his elect that they give it up. By leaving father and mother Ruth is also leaving her *'ereṣ môleḏeṯ* in order to join the people of Yahweh, whom she earlier did not know (although her husband was, after all, one of them!) and among whom she was considered a *noḵriyyâ,* and to seek refuge under the wings of the God of Israel (Ruth 2:11f.). Despite the parallels to the Abraham tradition generally acknowledged by the commentaries, the theological shift cannot be overlooked. Yahweh is no longer the God who wanders with the fathers, as was the case with the older Pentateuch narrators (cf. esp. Gen. 28:20f.), but is rather bound to a specific land and to a specific people, and the foreigner who would enjoy Yahweh's protection must first leave his own *'ereṣ môleḏeṯ*.

Jeremiah twice uses the expression *'ereṣ môleḏeṯ* in the sense of country of birth, home. The successor to King Josiah, who fell in battle against Pharaoh Neco, was Jehoahaz, whom Neco took captive to Riblah and from there deported to Egypt, and to whom the prophet must then announce that he will never see his homeland again (Jer. 22:10); rather — so goes the explication — "in the place where they have carried him captive he shall die, and he shall never see this land again" (v. 12). Even if this statement was made in 622, the Deuteronomistic commentary reflects the homelessness of the exile, of the "foreign land" (*'aḏmaṯ nēḵār,* Ps. 137:4).[9] After the invasion of Egypt by Nebuchadnezzar, the foreign mercenaries in the Egyptian army (or the foreign merchants?[10]) flee the sinking ship by calling to one other: "Come, let us go back to our own people and to the land of our birth" (Jer. 46:16). For the first time here, *('ereṣ) môleḏeṯ* — as later in Esther[11] — is not a parallel to clan and patriarchal house, but rather to *'am.* The clans have been subsumed under peoples, and these peoples are now associated with their own homelands. The same set of circumstances is found in Ezekiel. He accuses Judah of allowing itself to be fooled by mere pictures of officers who looked like Babylonians and whose homeland was Chaldea (Ezk. 23:15). Here also nation and land are viewed as one.

In all these passages the LXX understands *'ereṣ môleḏeṯ* as the land of one's birth or origin, or descent (not of kindred). It translates *en tḗ gḗ hē egennḗthē* (Gen. 11:28, analogously 24:7), *tḗn gḗn (tḗs) genéseōs sou* (Gen. 31:13; Ruth 2:11), *patrís* (Jer. 22:10; 46:16[LXX 26:16]; Ezk. 23:15).

---

9. Cf. H.-J. Hermisson, "Jeremias Wort über Jojachin," *Werden und Wirken des ATs. Festschrift C. Westermann* (Göttingen, 1980), 267-270.

10. W. Rudolph, *Jeremia. HAT,* XII (^{3}1968), 272.

11. See below.

b. *môleḏeṯ.* The word *môleḏeṯ* by itself probably also has the meaning "place of birth, home" in the 5 passages (all J or J-source) in which it is construed with the preps. *min, 'el,* and *l*[e], particularly since in every case it stands in obvious proximity to *'ereṣ.* Even though the lexica,[12] translations, and commentaries largely advocate the rendering "kindred," it is difficult to understand *'ereṣ* + *môleḏeṯ* other than as *'ereṣ môleḏeṯ.* The call with which Yahweh begins human history anew in Gen. 12:1 demands that Abraham leave his land *('ereṣ),* his *môleḏeṯ,* and his father's house *(bêṯ 'āḇ).* This does not really constitute a heightening of elements, as various commentaries suggest, such that Abraham is to leave not only his land, but also his kindred, indeed, even his most intimate family circle (of which, by the way, he takes along a sizeable portion!). "Your country and your *môleḏeṯ*" stands here for "your *'ereṣ môleḏeṯ,*"[13] and the *'ereṣ môleḏeṯ* itself is for nomads automatically identical with the land of one's *bêṯ 'āḇ* (cf. Gen. 24:7, where *bêṯ 'āḇî* and *'ereṣ môlaḏtî* are synonymous). The pleonasm simply serves to emphasize the radical break with the past on the one hand, and the absolute new beginning on the other.

The same is true of Gen. 24:4 (J), where Abraham orders his servant: "Go to my country and to my *môleḏeṯ.*" Here, too, "land" and *môleḏeṯ,* as v. 7 shows, can mean nothing other than *'ereṣ môleḏeṯ* (indeed, the entire section vv. 1-9 emphasizes only the "land"; only *after* the encounter with Laban's family are the *bêṯ 'āḇ* and *mišpāḥâ* mentioned!). Similarly, a comparison with 31:13 (E)[14] — despite the fact that the two passages draw from different sources — makes it clear that in Gen. 31:3 (J) "to the land of your ancestors and to your *môleḏeṯ*" means the same as "to the land of your *môleḏeṯ.*" To be sure, for Jacob the basis of confidence is less the privileges of one's home which he enjoys in Canaan than Yahweh's support: "I will be with you" — the Yahwist's warning against false trust in the Davidic-Solomonic claims to power.[15] In the prayer at Jabbok in Gen. 32:10(9) Jacob cites Yahweh's own instructions *šûḇ l*[e]*'arṣ*[e]*ḵā ûl*[e]*môlaḏt*[e]*ḵā,* which echoes both *lēḵ-l*[e]*ḵā mē'arṣ*[e]*ḵā ûmim-môlaḏt*[e]*ḵā* (Gen. 12:1) and *šûḇ 'el-'ereṣ môlaḏt*[e]*ḵā* (Gen. 31:13). The sense is the same as that in Gen. 12:1. Finally, to Moses' request to guide his people through the wilderness, Hobab responds: "I will not go, but I will go back to my own land and to my *môleḏeṯ*" (Nu. 10:30 [J]), in short: to the land of my origin, to my home.

The LXX is inconsistent in these passages. In the sense discussed above it translates Gen. 32:10(9) *eis tḗn gḗn tḗs genéseōs sou,* while in Gen. 31:3; Nu. 10:30 it uses the ambiguous *geneá;* the use of *syngéneia* in Gen. 12:1 and *phylḗ* in 24:4 presupposes the meaning "kindred" for *môleḏeṯ.*

2. a. *Birth.* The law concerning forbidden degrees of relations in Lev. 18:9(twice),11 uses *môleḏeṯ* first in the sense of "birth." V. 9 prohibits relations with one's half-sister on both the father's and mother's side, whether it concerns a "house birth" *(môleḏeṯ bayiṯ)*

---

12. *GesB, KBL*[2], *KBL*[3], *HAL.*

13. Cf. *GesB* and *KBL*[3] *s.v. w*[e] with the example from Gen. 3:16: "your pain and your childbearing" = "the pain of your childbearing."

14. See a. above.

15. Cf. W. H. Schmidt, "Ein Theologe in salomonischer Zeit? Plädoyer für den Jahwisten," *BZ,* N.S. 25 (1981), 101f.

or a "birth abroad" *(môleḏeṯ ḥûṣ),* i.e., one born either at home or elsewhere, legitimate or illegitimate (LXX *endogenoús ḗ gegennēménēs éxō*). V. 11 extends the prohibition to include the daughter of a wife of the father from a different relationship. Of her, too, it is said: "(she is) the birth of (NRSV 'begotten by') your father *(môleḏeṯ 'āḇîḵā),* . . . she is your sister [LXX *homopatría adelphē*]," i.e., she is "declared to be 'a sister,' in a peculiar phrase — perhaps a later addition — because 'begotten by your father.' "[16]

The great discourse against Jerusalem in Ezk. 16 also speaks of birth, though now in a metaphorical sense: "Your origin and your birth (*m^{e}ḵōrōṯayiḵ ûmōl^{e}ḏōṯayiḵ;* pl. employed in lawsuit[17]) are of the land of the Canaanites" (v. 3). The repetition in v. 4 of *ûmôl^{e}ḏôṯayiḵ* ("and as for your birth") should doubtlessly be considered a case of disruptive dittography.[18] With the words "on the day you were born" v. 4 provides a meaningful and seamless transition from v. 3 and simultaneously specifies the sense of *môleḏeṯ* as "birth" (LXX *génesis*). Against the background of its Amorite-Hittite "birth" and the — theologically — hopeless future of the city, Jerusalem's election and disloyalty emerge in all their incomprehensibility. "For a pagan city and a state founded on such a city can make none of the claims that might accompany physical descent from Abraham. In and of themselves, Jerusalem and Judah are nothing special and can make no claims to privilege. What they were and are is based solely on Yahweh's obliging love."[19]

b. *Descent, Origin.* In Est. 2:10,20, *môleḏeṯ* exhibits the extended sense of "descent, ethnic identity, race," as shown by the parallelism with *'am:* Mordecai has charged Esther not to make known "her people or kindred." This usage is an example of the transition from the abstract to the concrete.

3. a. *Race.* This transition is completed in Est. 8:6, where there is no discernible difference between *'am* and *môleḏeṯ*. Esther laments: "For how can I bear to see the calamity that is coming on my people . . . the destruction of my race?"[20] The quantity that emerges from common descent is ultimately the people itself. This is a time in which national pride emerges victorious and in which the preservation and purity of the race is worthy of the believers' best efforts.

The LXX renders *môleḏeṯ* inappropriately in all 3 instances with *patrís,* "fatherland, home town."

b. *Descendants.* In one passage, Gen. 48:5f. (P), *môleḏeṯ* has the meaning of "descendants, posterity." At Jacob's deathbed, it emerges that Jacob's adoption of the sons of Joseph will be limited to Ephraim and Manasseh, and will not extend to Joseph's other sons: "Ephraim and Mannaseh shall be mine, just as Reuben and Simeon are. As for the descendants (NRSV 'offspring'; LXX *ékgona*) born to you after them, they shall be yours." The adoption of both Ephraim and Manasseh, based on divine revela-

---

16. M. Noth, *Leviticus. OTL* (Eng. trans. 1965), 135.
17. E. König, *Hebräisches und aramäisches Wörterbuch zum AT* (Leipzig, 1910).
18. Thus G. Fohrer, *Ezechiel. HAT,* XIII (1955); W. Eichrodt, *Ezekiel. OTL* (Eng. trans. 1970); *LexHebAram;* contra W. Zimmerli, *Ezekiel 1. Herm* (Eng. trans. 1979), 322.
19. Fohrer, 86.
20. On the change in social structures reflected in the par. *'am/môleḏeṯ,* see II.1.a above.

tion, as well as their inclusion in the promise, is thus emphasized more strongly than among older narrators against the claims made on behalf of natural descent.

c. *Relatives.* The meaning "kindred" = "one's relatives," which lexicographers and commentators also suggest for the passages mentioned under II.1.b, seems actually to apply only to Gen. 43:7 (J). Jacob's sons assert before him that the Egyptian "questioned us carefully about ourselves and our *môleḏeṯ*." The kindred (LXX *geneá*) about which Joseph inquires is, to be sure, limited to the immediate family: "Is your father still alive? Have you another brother?" Hence one might better translate *môleḏeṯ* here as "family" than as "kindred."

We have found that the semantic spectrum of *môleḏeṯ* revolves around the fundamental notion of birth (root *yld*) and expresses several relationships created through birth: place of birth, home, fatherland — descent, origin — race, descendants, family.

H. Haag

מוֹעֵד *môʿēḏ*

Contents: I. Occurrences and Semantic Intricacies. II. Human Interaction. III. *môʿēḏ* in the Natural and Cultic Calendar. IV. Future (and) Eschatological Divine Action at the *môʿēḏ* Time. V. *ʾōhel môʿēḏ*.

I. Occurrences and Semantic Intricacies.

1. Although *môʿēḏ* is attested in various genres from the oldest historical texts (Gen. 18:14; 1 S. 9:24) to the most recent apocalyptic utterances (Dnl. 12:7), certain focal points do emerge regarding its use. Of the 223 occurrences in the OT, 149 are in the section from Ex. 25 to Nu. 31, i.e., in the Priestly writing, as well as Gen. 1:14; 17:21; 21:2 (cf. Josh. 18:1; 19:51). The expression also occurs frequently in Chronicles (12 times) and in Lamentations (6 times), and later particularly in the Qumran writings (in addition to the 61 occurrences according to Kuhn,[1] 57 others[2] are found in 4Q and 10

---

môʿēḏ. J. Dus, "Zur bewegten Geschichte der israelitischen Lade," *AION,* 41 (1981), 351-385; M. Görg, *Das Zelt der Begegnung. BBB,* 27 (1967), 168-170; J. Macdonald, "An Assembly at Ugarit?" *Festschrift C. F. A. Schaeffer. UF,* 11 (1979), 515-526; E. T. Mullen, *The Assembly of the Gods: The Divine Council in Canaanite and Hebrew Literature. HSM,* 24 (1980); L. Rost, *Die Vorstufen von Kirche und Synagoge im AT. BWANT,* 76[4/24] (1938; ²1967), 35-38, 129-152; G. Sauer, "יעד *jʿd* bestimmen," *THAT,* I, 742-46; J. A. Thompson, "Expansions of the יעד Root," *JSS,* 10 (1965), 222-240; J. A. Wilson, "The Assembly of a Phoenician City," *JNES,* 4 (1945), 245; N. Zelnik, "מקראי קדש," *Shanah be-Shanah,* 1972, 266-272; for further bibliog. → אהל *ʾōhel,* I, 118f.; יעד *yāʿaḏ,* VI, 135; cf. "Festivals," *EncJud,* VI, 1237-1246.

1. Kuhn.

2. Cf. J. Allegro, *Qumrân Cave 4. DJD,* V (1968); M. Baillet, *Qumrân Grotte 4,* III *(4Q482–4Q520). DJD,* VII (1982).

in the Temple scroll). The term *môʿēḏ* occurs 146 times in a construct relationship with *ʾōhel* in reference to the Israelite tent sanctuary during the wilderness period, the "tabernacle"; of these, 133 are found between Ex. 25 and Nu. 31, and this special usage requires a separate discussion.[3]

Several instances of linguistic overlapping and thus presumably of close semantic associations point to the notion of a fixed point in time. "Days" and "years" occur in parallel (e.g., Gen. 1:14; Lam. 2:22), as also "feasts" or "festivals" (Hos. 9:4f.; Ezk. 46:11), or "time" in general (Ps. 102:14[Eng. v. 13]). In cultic contexts the terms "Sabbath and new moon" are often used in connection with it.[4] Usage involving the notion of "time" often employs construct combinations with *yôm* (Lam. 2:22; Hos. 9:5; 12:10), *ḥōḏeš* (Ex. 23:15; 34:18), or *šānâ* (Dt. 31:10). The term *qrʾ* ("solemnly convene/call together") occurs most often as a verbal compliment; a *môʿēḏ* is summoned against someone (Lam. 1:15), though much more frequently one's cultic associates are summoned together for the *môʿēḏ,* which is therefore called *miqrāʾ qōḏeš* (e.g., Lev. 23:2ff.). Various divine designations used as *nomens regens* frequently refer to God as the determinative element (Lev. 23:2ff.; Ps. 74:8; 2 Ch. 2:3[4]), as do the corresponding suffixes (e.g., Lev. 23:2; Ps. 74:4; Lam. 2:6).

2. The noun is related to the verb → יעד *yʿd,* with which it is also explicitly associated in Ex. 30:36; 2 S. 20:5. The term *yʿd* refers either to the making of an appointment between two equal partners, or to such action taken by one person over against another of lower standing; as a rule, both cases refer to a meeting at a specified time, and occasionally also at a specified place.[5]

3. All the West Semitic languages attest a noun *mʿd.* Arab. *mawʿid* means "place/time of an appointment,"[6] Aram. *mōʿaḏāʾ* means "appointed time, festival."[7]

II. Human Interaction. *HAL* lists "place for meeting, assembly point" as the first meaning of the basic word, and "meeting, assembly" as the second.[8] The passages adduced for the first meaning (Josh. 8:14; Job 30:23; Lam. 2:6; Ps. 74:4), however, can also be interpreted differently,[9] or at least can be taken to emphasize the connotation "appointed time, date," which *KBL*[3] does not list until third.

This can be demonstrated by the relatively rare instances where *môʿēḏ* refers to nonreligious human interaction. In Josh. 8:14 the warriors of Ai presumably do not meet "at an appointed place" (Martin Luther) at the *ʿarāḇâ,* but rather meet there at a time favorable for the united assault. The Israelite warriors do not just set an

---

3. See V below.
4. See III.2 below.
5. → יעד *yāʿaḏ* (V, 393-426).
6. Wehr, 1081.
7. *DISO,* 145; Jastrow, II, 745. On Ugar. *mʿd* see III.3 below.
8. *HAL,* II (1995), 557f.
9. See following discussion.

"appointment" (NJB "agreed") with "those of the ambush" separated from them for strategic purposes, but rather determine the decisive point in time at which to undertake collective action (Jgs. 20:38). Jonathan goes out into the field "at the *môʿēḏ* of David," referring to the time of meeting specified by David (1 S. 20:35); although this includes the place necessary for the meeting, it by no means refers only to the place. David becomes restless when Amasa delays beyond the "set time of the meeting" (2 S. 20:5).

This virtually exhausts the instances which attest nonreligious use of the lexeme. It is thus limited to preexilic writings and refers here to a time set between two partners for a meeting for the purpose of undertaking collective action; under certain circumstances the appointed time can be augmented by a specification of the meeting place as well. As a rule, the *môʿēḏ* is fixed and made binding by the first partner for the weaker one. This hierarchy in the relationship between the two partners emerges even more clearly in the religiously oriented contexts to be discussed later.

As the only later witness, Job 30:23 is generally understood "spatially"; the *bêṯ môʿēḏ* to which the dead descend in the underworld is usually translated in the sense of "place of assembly." If one does not point the text as *mûʿāḏ* ("the house appointed [for all living]),"[10] it seems more advisable to assume some influence from the Babylonian mythology of the underworld. There the underworld is frequently viewed as a "gloomy, dusty etc. house"[11] to which human beings sojourn in the days of their appointed fate *(ûmē šîmti).*[12]

III. môʿēḏ in the Natural and Cultic Calendar.

1. What is perhaps the oldest witness (Gen. 18:14 [J]) already equates *môʿēḏ* with the time at which the year comes full circle *(kāʿēṯ hazzeh).* The P parallel (17:21) expresses this even more clearly: "at this time (NRSV 'season'; *lammôʿēḏ hazzeh)* in the next year" (similarly also in 2 K. 4:16f.). The return of certain animals in rhythm with the course of the year also occurs at the "set time" which, e.g., the stork knows instinctively (Jer. 8:7). Similarly, the ripening of the fruit of the field also follows with a corresponding, fixed regularity (Hos. 2:11,13[9,11]).

2. The term has also long been used to refer to the appointed time and place of the more important cultic celebrations, i.e., feasts of worship. This is probably the sense of the cook's words to the astonished Saul at the cultic meal when he serves Saul a portion of the sacrifice (1 S. 9:24): "Eat, for it was kept for you until the feast"[13] (so also 1 S. 13:8,11?). In the Pentateuch the Feast of Passover-Mazzoth clearly emerges as the decisive annual *môʿēḏ,* celebrating the day of deliverance from Egypt, while the other festival times are occasionally mentioned alongside it and do

---

10. Cf. G. Fohrer, *Das Buch Hiob. KAT,* XVI (1963), 414, n. 23, following J. Reider, "Contributions to the Scriptural Text," *HUCA,* 24 (1952/53), 102f.
11. *BuA,* II (1925), 144f.
12. *AHw,* III (1981), 1239.
13. Görg, 169.

not receive such designation: Ex. 13:10; 23:15 (E); 34:18 (J); Nu. 9:2f.,7,13; Dt. 16:6; cf. 2 Ch. 30:22; Hos. 12:10(9). Yet in the majority of OT passages (aside from the combination *'ōhel mô'ēḏ*) it refers to the time of the (three) great annual festivals (Lev. 23:2ff.; Nu. 10:10; 15:3; 28:2; 29:39; 2 Ch. 8:13; Ps. 75:3[2]; Isa. 1:14; Lam. 1:4; 2:7,22; Ezk. 36:38; 44:24; 45:17; 46:9,11; Hos. 9:5; Zeph. 3:18; Zech. 8:19; cf. Dt. 31:10). In this connection it can also refer to the festival locale, the holy place on Zion (2 Ch. 30:22; Ps. 74:4,8; Isa. 33:20; Lam. 2:6), though it remains unclear whether the temporal or spatial reference is being emphasized. In its statements about the cultic festivals as *mô'ᵃḏîm,* the lexeme occurs surprisingly often together with the terms "sabbath and new moon" (Lev. 23:2ff.; Nu. 10:10; 1 Ch. 23:31; 2 Ch. 2:3[4]; 31:3; Isa. 1:14; Lam. 2:6; Hos. 2:13[11]; cf. Ezk. 36:38; 46:9,11; Hos. 9:5), so that the Sabbath and new moon, while apparently not referring to a *mô'ēḏ,* do designate a closely related quantity.

This last combination suggests that an inner relationship obtains between the usage of *mô'ēḏ* in reference to the recurring, more important temporal divisions within the natural year on the one hand and its usage in reference to the greater annual festivals on the other. This orientation in relationship to Sabbath and new moon demonstrates how even in the preexilic period the Hebrews were quite conscious that the Passover-Mazzoth (Weeks) and autumnal festivals were to take place at a time set by Yahweh through the course of the stars. The fixed seasons in the course of the year are at the same time the fixed times of festivals.

Though the moon plays an especially decisive role, the sun is also of consequence: "He made the moon for the *mô'ᵃḏîm;* the sun knows its (time for) rising" (Ps. 104:19). A similar sense is expressed by the famous passage Gen. 1:14, according to which the celestial bodies were created to be "for signs and for (regular) times of festivals and for days and years" (cf. Sir. 43:7). 1QS 9:26–10:8 extensively discusses the relationship between the natural and cultic year from the perspective of *mô'ēḏ*.

Festival dates are thus inviolably fixed by the course of the stars as seasonally significant temporal divisions. Since in the earlier period this is emphasized especially regarding the Passover-Mazzoth festival, the festival itself must have been oriented since a very early period to the course of the celestial bodies, not only of the moon (full moon), but also of the sun according to the equinox. This probably refutes the thesis of a purely lunar calendar in ancient Israel, since at least the cult was given a lunar-solar orientation.

However, it is not only as regards the natural cycle that these *mô'ēḏ*-times are thrown into relief; at the same time, they represent those days when God approaches Israel as the Creator and meets with his cultic community. Such times are thus filled with holiness (*qdš,* Ps. 74:3f.; Lev. 23:2ff. and *passim*), and such occasions are marked by solemn convocations (*qr',* Lev. 23:2ff.; Nu. 16:2; Lam. 1:4,15; 2:22 and *passim*). The community is required to make offerings at such times, whereas on other days such offerings are voluntary and can take place as acts prompted by a special occasion (Nu. 10:10; 15:3; 28:2; 2 Ch. 2:3[4]; 8:13; 31:3; Ezk. 45:17 and *passim*). The 10 occurrences in the Temple scroll fall under this rubric; there *mô'ēḏ* always means "festival date" and is explicitly distinguished from the "work day" as "day of weariness" (11QT 43:15).[14]

3. According to Isa. 14:13, the gods come together on a *har-mô'ēḏ,* where at one time the Babylonian king sojourned. This passage became the mythical prototype for the eschatological Har Magedon (Armageddon) of Rev. 16:16.[15] Exegetes unanimously take the sense of this expression to be "mount of assembly (of the gods)" and adduce the Ugaritic parallels in the Ba'al-Yamm myth, according to which the sea-god once sent his messengers "to the *pḫr m'd* in the midst of the Mount of Lala,"[16] where *pḫr* refers to the closed alliance of the gods and *m'd* here, too, is taken as "assembly."[17] However, both the Ugaritic and the OT contexts suggest rather a "fixed time for the assembly (of the gods)"; in neither instance is the reference to ad hoc meetings, but rather to regularly recurring occasions which presumably are to be celebrated concurrently as festivals on earth as well. This remains the case even if John Macdonald is correct in suggesting that one point as the passive participle "appointed."[18]

The account of the journey of the Egyptian Wen-amon mentions an extraordinary, brief meeting among human beings; Wen-amon reports that one day a prince of Byblos convened his *mw'd(wt)* (a Syrian word foreign to Egyptian) in order to stand in their midst and make certain decisions[19]. Reference is apparently being made to a kind of ministerial council or circle of representatives of the people, whose suggestion, however, is then rejected by the ruler. Does this passage allow us to conclude the existence of a people's assembly as a regular institution under the name of *mô'ēḏ* in Syria-Phoenicia?[20]

An element of ambiguity remains regarding the Aramaic inscription of Tell Deir 'Allā,[21] where a seer by the name of Balaam seems to be reporting a vision and speaks of *šdyn,* Shaddai gods (or cult servants?): *wnṣbw . . . mw'd,* "they take their places (*yṣb* as in Ex. 33:8; Nu. 11:16; Dt. 31:14) at the appointed time of meeting."[22] This can refer both to a specially convened assembly of deities and to a regularly conducted assembly.[23]

---

14. J. Maier, *The Temple Scroll. JSOTSup,* 34 (Eng. trans. 1985), 113; also G. Vermes, *The Dead Sea Scrolls in English* (Sheffield, ^{3}1987), 142.
15. J. Jeremias, "Ἅρ Μαγεδών," *TDNT,* I, 468; J. Gray, *The Legacy of Canaan. SVT,* 5 (^{2}1965), 24, n.1.
16. *KTU,* 1.2 I, 14-18, 31; *ANET,* 130.
17. *WUS,* no. 1619; *UT,* no. 1512; *CML*^{2}, 151.
18. P. 524; similarly Mullen, 129.
19. *ANET,* 29a.
20. Wilson, Macdonald, contra Mullen, 282.
21. J. Hoftijzer and G. van der Kooij, *Aramaic Texts from Deir 'Alla. DMOA,* 19 (1976).
22. *Ibid.,* I, 6.
23. This passage has been discussed most recently by H. and M. Weippert, "Die 'Bileam'-Inschrift von *Tell Dēr 'Allā,*" *ZDPV,* 98 (1982), 88, 103; and H.-P. Müller, "Die aramäische Inschrift von Deir 'Allā und die älteren Bileamsprüche," *ZAW,* 94 (1982), 217f., 224.

IV. Future (and) Eschatological Divine Action at the mô'ēḏ Time. It is not only through his creation of time itself that God established fixed *mô'ᵃḏîm* which his people are to keep and which serve the purpose of an encounter with God. Rather, his efficacious word establishes ever anew a *mô'ēḏ* for good fortune or disaster for human beings in history. This includes the appointed end of the pestilence in Israel during the time of David (2 S. 24:15) as well as the commencement of the fifth Egyptian plague (Ex. 9:5). In particular, the small book of Lamentations understands Judah's fall in 587/586 as a *mô'ēḏ* called upon them by Yahweh, and equates the element of cultic holidays which terrifies the godless — holy days which according to the language of the psalms bring about ruin for the wicked just as they do blessing for the righteous — with the destruction of the people as an enemy of God; the development of eschatological notions from a cultic context can be discerned here in an exemplary fashion (Lam. 1:4,15; 2:6f.,22).

In contrast, Ps. 102:14(13) pleads for a *mô'ēḏ* as a time when Yahweh will again have pity on Zion. The transition to the use of *mô'ēḏ* as an eschatological term includes Hab. 2:3, where the order for the prophet to write down what he has seen is given the following justification: *kî 'ôḏ ḥāzôn lammô'ēḏ,* which probably means that the vision extends itself (delays) "to the appointed time"[24] set for the turn of fortune in Israel's history, i.e., it will not occur immediately.

Yahweh also appoints significant times in the history of other peoples. A time was allowed for the Egyptian pharaoh to rage, although he let it pass by unused (Jer. 46:17). The book of Daniel allots to each of the Hellenistic Diadochian kings a (divinely determined) *mô'ēḏ* for their military campaigns; after a certain time, the *mô'ēḏ* ends and the kings lose their power (Dnl. 11:27,29,35). In these passages *mô'ēḏ* is probably not intended to be understood in an eschatological sense.[25]

This is the case, however, for Dnl. 8:19, where the angel says to Daniel: "I will tell you what will take place later in the period of wrath, *kî lᵉmô'ēḏ qēṣ.*" Regardless of whether one takes the two final words as a construct combination, "at the time fixed for the end,"[26] or as a nominal clause, "(so that) there is an end to the appointed time,"[27] in any case the preceding parallel *'aḥᵃrîṯ hazza'am* evokes an eschatological term. Dnl. 12:7 represents perhaps a middle position, where at the anxious question "how long" an angel swears by the life of the *'ôlām: lᵉmô'ēḏ mô'ᵃḏîm wāḥēṣî,* which is usually translated "a time, (two) times, and half a time." This rendering does, however, remain questionable, since *mô'ēḏ* otherwise never refers to temporal duration, but rather to an emphasized phase within a temporal continuum.

The Qumran writings frequently refer to the mysterious eschatological concluding phase of history as the *mô'ēḏ* of affliction (1QS 1:18; 4:18) or of judgment (*mišpāṭ,*

---

24. W. Rudolph, *Habakuk. KAT,* XIII/3 (1975), *in loc.*

25. On this discussion see B. Hasselberger, *Hoffnung in der Bedrängnis. ATS,* 4 (1977), 259, 261, 272.

26. *HAL,* II, 558.

27. On this discussion, see Hasselberger, 61.

1QS 4:20), or simply as the *mô'ēḏ* of God (*'ēl,* 1QM 1:7), etc. Many of these passages reveal a similarly close relationship between cultic and eschatological motifs.[28]

V. 'ōhel mô'ēḏ. The "tent of the *mô'ēḏ*" in the Pentateuch in (E?[29] and) P is discussed in I, 123-130, where mention is made of J. A. Wilson's suggestion to translate "tent of assembly for a festival" instead of the usual "tent of meeting (between God and human beings)," a rendering supported by modern personalistic theology. To be sure, this designation does include the notion that at the *mô'ᵃḏîm* God is closer to his people than at the usual, "normal time," and only in this tent, nowhere else, is Moses able to "speak face to face" with his God (Ex. 33:11; cf. also the verb *y'd* used in Ex. 29:42-45 to refer to God's meeting with the people). In addition, Ex. 25ff. simultaneously refers to the tent as *miškān,* "dwelling place," namely, for God. From time to time his glory descends upon this sanctuary (Ex. 40:34f.; Nu. 14:10; 16:19; 17:7[16:42]; 20:6); indeed, to the extent that this glory appears on earth at all, according to P it always abides in a cloud above the *mô'ēḏ*-tent. Yet at least in the Priestly writing it is no doubt intentional that the establishment of the holy tent in Ex. 40 is followed by the extensive sacrificial regulations of Lev. 1–16, which refer in particular to the festival times.[30] Even if the Pentateuch narrators were understandably less interested in recurring festival times than in unique, significant historical points in time, this does not exclude the possibility that the term *mô'ēḏ* has the same sense in its combination with "tent" that it does elsewhere in P,[31] i.e., a gathering or assembly for a festival.

Koch

---

28. Cf. J. Carmignac, "Précisions apportées au vocabulaire de l'hébreu biblique par la Guerres des fils de lumière contre les fils de ténèbres," *VT,* 5 (1955), 354; F. Nötscher, *Zur theologischen Terminologie der Qumran-Texts. BBB,* 10 (1956), 167-69; on *mw'd ht'nyt* in 4QpPs[a], "time of affliction," cf. R. B. Coote, " 'MW'D HT'NYT' in 4Q 171 (pesher Psalm 37), fragments 1-2, col. II, line 9," *RevQ,* 8 (1972), 81-85.

29. M. Haran, *Temples and Temple-Service in Ancient Israel* (Oxford, 1978), ch. xiv: "The Non-Priestly Image of the Tent of *mô'ēḏ.*"

30. In contradistinction from the literary-critical elimination of Lev. 1ff. from the basic P material (customary since Wellhausen), see K. Koch, *Die Priesterschrift von Exodus 25 bis Leviticus 16. FRLANT,* N.S. 53[71] (1959).

31. See discussion above.

מוֹפֵת *môp̄ēṯ*

Contents: I. Derivation, Interpretation, Occurrences, and Usage. II. Theological Use in the OT: 1. The Exodus Traditions; 2. "Prophetic Literature"; 3. Variations in Context and Meaning. IV. Qumran.

I. Derivation, Interpretation, Occurrences, and Usage. The OT attests 36 occurrences of the word *môp̄ēṯ,* which occurs only in its nominal form and whose etymological derivation is still completely uncertain. Neither does its use in Middle Hebrew, Samaritan, Jewish-Aramaic, or Phoenician offer any clue regarding its derivation and original meaning. The only Phoenician witness to date is uncertain,[1] since this passage also allows for a completely different interpretation of the letters *mpt.* Thus the witnesses in the OT constitute the earliest occurrences of this word at the present. The basic meaning is best rendered by the English equivalent "sign,"[2] while the individual context suggests the more precise rendering ("miracle," "sign of remembrance," "warning sign," "omen," "testing sign"). The term *môp̄ēṯ* frequently parallels → אות *'ôṯ,* though also *massâ,*[3] and occasionally *niplā'â*[4] and *mišpāṭîm.* The LXX translates the word in the majority of cases with *téras,* and in some instances with *sēmeíon.*

Among the few occurrences in the OT, the concentration in Deuteronomy (9 times), Exodus (5 times), Ezekiel (4 times), and the Psalms (5 times) is noteworthy. From the perspective of content and thematic material, the traditions surrounding the miraculous exodus from Egypt seem to have prompted the use of *môp̄ēṯ.* The Deuteronomic-Deuteronomistic view of these events employs *môp̄ēṯ* along with other terms (e.g., the term *'ôṯ* mentioned above). Another sphere of usage is discernible in the prophetic literature, where *môp̄ēṯ* can function as an affirming sign of the prophetic message or even, as its *verbum visibile,* constitute the content itself of that message. Most of the passages come from the later OT period (Deuteronomic-Deuteronomistic-Chronistic), and the two witnesses in Proto-Isaiah may be the oldest of them all. No secular usage of *môp̄ēṯ* is attested; the Hebrew term functions exclusively in theological contexts.

môp̄ēṯ. B. S. Childs, "Deuteronomic Formulae of the Exodus Traditions," *Hebräische Wortforschung. Festschrift W. Baumgartner. SVT,* 16 (1967), 30-39; J. Haspecker, "Wunder im AT," *Theologische Akademie,* 2 (1965), 29-56; C. A. Keller, *Das Wort OTH als "Offenbarungszeichen Gottes"* (Basel, 1946); S. V. McCasland, "Signs and Wonders," *JBL,* 76 (1957), 149-152; G. Quell, "Das Phänomen des Wunders im AT," *Verbannung und Heimkehr. Festschrift W. Rudolph* (Tübingen, 1961), 253-300; K. H. Rengstorf, "σημεῖον," *TDNT,* VII, 200-269; *idem,* "τέρας," *TDNT,* VIII, 113-126; G. Rinaldi, "Môfet," *BeO,* 22 (1980), 159; L. Sabourin, "OT Miracles," *BTB,* 1 (1971), 227-261; F. Stolz, "אות *'ōt* Zeichen," *THAT,* I, 91-95; → אות *'ôṯ* (*'ôth*) (I, 167-188).

1. Cf. *DISO,* 164; *KAI,* 30.
2. *KBL*[3]: *Wahrzeichen.*
3. → נסה *nsh.*
4. → פלא *pl'.*

II. Theological Use in the OT.

1. *The Exodus Traditions.* At least half of the OT passages which use *môpēṯ* (19 of 36) occur in an immediate or, in a few instances, indirect connection with the exodus event. The extraordinary signs that Moses and Aaron (or one of them) are to perform before Pharaoh in order to underscore effectively the plea for release of their people are called *môpēṯ* (along with other terms in the more immediate or extended context). The occurrences in Exodus are essentially a product of P (Ex. 7:3,9; 11:9,10); only the provenance of 4:21 remains uncertain (J or E,[5] or additions by J[6] or from an even later period). The problem with 4:21 is the context (vv. 21-23). From the perspective of content, it actually already oversees and encompasses the entire ensemble of plagues, and identifies the (theologically conceived) ultimate consequence of that ensemble (the slaying of the Egyptian first-born) as the result of Pharaoh's refusal to release Yahweh's first-born son, namely, Israel. This kind of theological interpretation of the events, namely, one that views the plague-complex together with the Passover tradition, could arise presumably only at a later stage of reflection, and not already at the time of J or E. Furthermore, the theological topoi have already been brought together which conceive of *môp^{e}ṯîm* in the larger sense without any concrete manifestation as miraculous signs, and which employ the accompanying divine hardening of Pharaoh's heart to reveal and confirm Yahweh's ultimate goal beyond this series of plagues: the Israelites' miraculous departure and exodus from Egypt.

In the course of the call story of Moses as formulated by P, the purpose of Moses' going to Pharaoh is to demand the people's release (Ex. 6:11). In connection with the attendant difficulties, the text mentions the hardening of Pharaoh's heart (the acting subject is Yahweh, *'^{a}nî 'aqšeh*), such that Yahweh will multiply his signs and wonders (Ex. 7:3; *'eṯ-'ōṯōṯay w^e'eṯ-môp^{e}ṯay*). Neither do the following verses depart from such generalities by asserting that Yahweh will lay his hand upon Egypt (*nāṯan 'eṯ-yāḏ b^e . . . ; nāṭâ 'eṯ-yāḏ ʿal . . . ;* vv. 4f.). The leading out of the Israelites occurs *bišpāṭîm g^{e}ḏōlîm* ("by great acts of judgment"), which interpret *môpēṯ* and *'ôṯ* yet again (v. 4). All subjective activity is attributed to Yahweh, and aims at prompting the Egyptians to recognize that Yahweh himself is acting against the Egyptians on behalf of the Israelites (v. 5).

In the extensive account of the plagues (Ex. 7:8–10:29), an account with an extremely complex traditio-historical background, Moses and Aaron prove through a "miraculous sign" that they are the legitimate messengers of their God: A rod cast to the ground turns into a serpent (Ex. 7:9). Although *môpēṯ* is indeed a miracle, it actually functions as a kind of "attestation of credentials"; its failure to be accepted as such is already an expression of Pharaoh's self-hardening (v. 13, *ḥzq lēḇ*). The conclusion to the plague narrative again recalls the situation of the call and sending of Moses (and of Aaron, 7:1): Pharaoh will not listen to the two messengers of Yahweh, Yahweh's *môp^{e}ṯîm* will (thereupon) be multiplied in the land of Egypt (*l^{e}maʿan r^{e}ḇôṯ . . . ,* Ex. 11:9), and Yahweh hardens the heart of Pharaoh (*ḥzq* piel) so that the Israelites will

---

5. G. Fohrer, *Überlieferung und Geschichte des Exodus. BZAW,* 91 (1964), 38-43.
6. M. Noth, *Exodus. OTL* (Eng. trans. 1962), 47.

not be released (11:10). The *lemaʿan* clause in v. 9 is noteworthy; one must almost understand this figure of speech such that Pharaoh's refusal, his "hardening," is brought about solely so that the *môpeṯîm* may be multiplied! Ex. 11:10 recounts in retrospect how Moses and Aaron performed all the *môpeṯîm* assigned them, whereby the position and sense of this statement can only be referring to the plagues. Everything presses forward to the final act, to the Passover, departure, and exodus (Ex. 12:1ff.).[7]

Various strata of Deuteronomy recall the events of the exodus from Egypt; this is the case in the creedlike summaries, e.g., in what is known as the little historical Credo in Dt. 26 (v. 8), which reduces the entire exodus event to a brief formula mentioning the *mōpeṯîm* together with the *'ōṯôṯ*, the mighty hand and outstretched arm of Yahweh, and Yahweh's terrible deeds. Yahweh is the only subject of the salvific deed between the harsh repression of Israel by the Egyptians and Yahweh's ultimate bestowal of the land upon Israel (vv. 6f., 9): *wayyôṣî'ēnû YHWH mimmiṣrayim* (v. 8).

The context of Dt. 29:2(Eng. v. 3) also seems to presuppose a worship situation, namely, that noteworthy covenant in the land of Moab (Dt. 28:69[29:1]) which justifies its admonitions to keep the covenant terms (29:8[9]) by recalling Yahweh's mighty deeds in Egypt (29:1[2]). Here Egypt, the pharaoh, his servants, and his entire land are mentioned explicitly. Those entering into the covenant are reminded of their role as eyewitnesses of those mighty signs and miracles (Dt. 29:2[3]; *'ōṯōṯ* and *môpeṯîm*). It is worth noting that these signs are also called *hammassôṯ haggedōlōṯ*, although the remark does not make it quite clear whether these powerful events represented trials and temptations for the Israelites or whether the designation refers to the Egyptians. V. 2(3) suggests the latter, v. 3(4) the former, i.e., trials and temptations for the Israelites inasmuch as they now (at the occasion of the present covenant) acquire what they did not know during the events themselves, namely, the ultimate understanding of Yahweh's mighty deeds.

Such recollection of the events in Egypt also plays a role in underscoring exhortation and admonishment in sermons and instruction (Dt. 6:22; 7:19). The listener is encouraged not to fear, but rather to recall Yahweh's mighty demonstrations of power (7:18f., *zkr;* the wording of vv. 18, 19a strongly evokes 29:1,2[2,3]; even the *massôṯ* resurface). The anticipated question of the son (6:20) regarding Yahweh's statutes and ordinances prompts a (catechetical) response that is a kind of paraphrase of the Credo (6:22 describes the *môpeṯîm* not only as mighty, but also as grievous, *rāʿîm*). Both types — sermon and catechism — also exhibit ideas strongly influenced by Deuteronomistic thinking, so that their origin or at least their final literary shape must be dated fairly late. Dt. 4 includes such Deuteronomistic sermonizing in its subjection of the facts of salvation history to homiletic interpretation, including the events in Egypt (v. 34, with *môpēṯ* and all the familiar parallel terms). They are said to have been performed expressly for (*le*, "for the benefit of") Israel. One notices that fixed formulas are employed (e.g., *leʿêneyḵā,* although the change from the 2nd to the 1st person still

7. These passages in Exodus are discussed in Noth; Fohrer; F. Hesse, *Das Verstockungsproblem im AT. BZAW,* 74 (1955).

cannot quite be explained). The goal of Yahweh's actions — we now read — was that Israel might finally understand that he, Yahweh, alone and exclusively was God (Dt. 4:35: "You, yes you have been made to see [*r'h* hophal] so that you might know . . . [*lāḏaʿaṯ kî* . . .]"). This passage strongly evokes Deutero-Isaiah in its solicitation of trust in God, whose salvific acts in history speak for him even though he has struck in judgment. This passage in Deuteronomy, however, does not stop at Deutero-Isaiah's unqualified assurance of salvation, but issues the challenge to keep Yahweh's commandments precisely so that things may go well for Israel (vv. 39f.).

The conclusion of Deuteronomy (ch. 34) has undergone similar Deuteronomistic redaction. Moses is characterized as a unique prophet, attested not least by all the miraculous deeds and demonstrations of power in Egypt before Israel's eyes, deeds for which Yahweh empowered Moses alone (34:11; the usual terms recur, cf. v. 12).[8]

The Deuteronomic-Deuteronomistic view of the miraculous signs in Egypt has also been incorporated into Jer. 32:20f., Jeremiah's prayer after the purchase of the field at Anathoth (vv. 17-25). The formulations here clearly recall the little historical Credo (Dt. 26:8f.).[9] A similar situation obtains in the historical summaries found in the psalms, e.g., Ps. 78:43, which also mentions individual plagues from the Exodus traditions under the rubric of the *môpᵉṯîm* and *'ōṯôṯ* (vv. 44ff.), including the slaying of the first-born of the Egyptians and the miraculous deliverance of the Israelites at the Red Sea (vv. 51-53).[10] This passage can be compared directly with Ps. 105:27 (vv. 26-36); Neh. 9:10, where fixed formulas are used (particularly noticeable in Nehemiah). Neh. 9:10 speaks with clarity unequalled in such contexts of how Yahweh made a name for himself through these miraculous deeds, a name such as that still venerated at the time when this passage was composed. The motif of obduracy is explicated: Pharaoh is hardened (or hardens himself) so that Yahweh's name might be glorified. Historical summaries apparently play a role in worship or in (wisdom discussion and) instruction (Ps. 78:4),[11] and in praise of Yahweh (Ps. 135:9), where the fundamental call is made for the assembled congregation to be mindful of God's signs, wonders, and mighty deeds (Ps. 105:5: *zikrû niplᵉ'ôṯāw 'ᵃšer-ʿāśâ mōpᵉṯāw ûmišpᵉṭê-pîhû,* par. 1 Ch. 16:12).[12] The formative power of the Deuteronomistic theology is also unmistakably present in these latter passages. Such cultic procedures and wisdom reflections probably represent the self-expression of the postexilic community. All praise, confession, and trust are to be directed to this God, and manifest themselves in performing his will. This is the sense of the appended parenesis.

---

8. Concerning the various passages from Deuteronomy, see the pertinent works by G. von Rad, including *Studies in Deuteronomy. SBT,* 9 (Eng. trans. 1953); *Deuteronomy. OTL* (Eng. trans. 1966). Concerning the little historical Credo see also L. Rost, "Das kleine geschichtliche Credo," *Das kleine Credo und andere Studien zum AT* (Heidelberg, 1965), 11-25; G. Wallis, "Die geschichtliche Erfahrung und das Bekenntnis zu Jahwe im AT," *ThLZ,* 101 (1976), 801-816; G. Braulik, *Sage, was du glaubst: Das älteste Credo der Bibel* (Stuttgart, 1979).

9. Cf. W. Thiel, *Die deuteronomistische Redaktion von Jeremia 26–45. WMANT,* 52 (1981), 29ff.

10. Cf. J. Kühlewein, *Geschichte in den Psalmen. CThM,* A/2 (1973), 146-151.

11. Cf. *ibid.,* 85-92.

12. Cf. W. Schottroff, *"Gedenken" im alten Orient und im AT. WMANT,* 15 (1964), 127ff.

2. *"Prophetic Literature."* The oldest occurrences of *môpēṯ* are found in Proto-Isaiah (Isa. 8:18; 20:3). Isa. 8:18 is generally considered to be authentic and to be a product of a period of withdrawal the prophet entered after his message during the Syro-Ephraimite War was not officially accepted in Jerusalem and Judah. This message is now passed on and entrusted to his circle of disciples (8:16). For now, attention is directed to the signs and portents which Yahweh established in "Israel" and which are still visible, namely, the children (presumably the physical ones) as an "element of proclamation" whose symbolic names (*šᵉʾār yāšûḇ,* 7:3; *mahēr šālāl ḥāš baz,* 8:1-3; and perhaps *ʿimmānû ʾēl* [if the *ʿalmâ* can be identified as the prophet's wife, 7:14], who is explicitly designated as *ʾôṯ*) represent the substance of the proclamation. The notion that the prophet himself is also a *môpēṯ* or *ʾôṯ* is not so easy to comprehend; this can only refer to the very fact of his existence, albeit his existence as a prophet (8:18).

The extraneous account in Isa. 20:3 attests that symbolic prophetic acts can be called *ʾôṯ* and *môpēṯ;* the prophet allegedly walked "naked" and barefoot for three years as a sign of the impending disaster posed by the Assyrian deportation of entire peoples. Here the term *môpēṯ* acquires the meaning of "omen" or "warning sign." The symbolic act itself becomes the nonverbal *verbum visibile;* worse yet: it anticipates the disaster.[13] This passage is doubtlessly non-Isaianic.[14]

Ezekiel, too, is commanded to symbolize by appropriate actions Jerusalem's deportation by the Babylonians (Ezk. 12:6,11). Here the situation is prefigured with exaggerated clarity even as far as the details are concerned, i.e., precisely the way it will occur on the day of judgment: baggage upon the exiles' shoulders, nocturnal departure, the covering of their faces, etc. (12:1-6). The symbolic action itself is carried out publicly and in all openness, though initially without words. Yahweh offers up Ezekiel in his entire being and actions as a *môpēṯ* for the house of Israel (v. 6). The background is presumably the deceptive faith of the exiles of 597 B.C. in the continued existence of Jerusalem prior to 587 (for them, too, a favorable set of circumstances). In Yahweh's eyes, however, the first exiles are also a disobedient and recalcitrant generation, and not only the portion of the population dwelling in Palestine. When the people question him, Ezekiel is then to tell them verbally that he is a *môpēṯ* for them, and that *gôlâ* and *šᵉḇî* are unavoidable (v. 11; v. 10 mentions specifically that this also applies to Jerusalem and its inhabitants, although it must also apply to those before whom it is acted out and uttered[15]). The symbolic quality of prophetic life (cf. Isa. 8:18) in its service to God extends even into the private sphere. The death of Ezekiel's wife and the subsequent behavior commanded by Yahweh, namely, not to follow the usual custom of mourning, both prefigure Jerusalem's destruction. It is Ezekiel's fate to become a *môpēṯ* himself (*lāḵem,* "to you," Ezk. 24:24,27). The reality of Yahweh's

---

13. Cf. G. Fohrer, *Die symbolischen Handlungen der Propheten. AThANT,* 25 (1953); 54 (²1968).

14. Cf. H. Wildberger, *Jesaja 13–27. BK,* X/2 (1978) *in loc.*

15. W. Zimmerli, *Ezekiel 1. Herm* (Eng. trans. 1979) *in loc.*

existence discloses itself in prediction and fulfillment; here, too, *môp̄ēṯ* is (also) an "omen," "warning sign," "portent," or even more: a proleptic realization of portended events that then do indeed subsequently come to pass.[16]

In the prophetic legends of the OT prophets do perform miraculous signs commissioned by Yahweh, as portrayed, e.g., in 1 Kgs. 13 (a chapter with a complicated transmission history). In the first of the two prophetic legends, an unknown prophet from Judah comes to Bethel and originally probably threatens the king (who was just then engaged in cultic activity) with a message of disaster. In the present, later version of the story the disaster is directed against the altar, which — we now read — the later Davidic king Josiah would defile and thus destroy (cf. 2 K. 23:16f.). As corroboration, a *môp̄ēṯ* is given *(nāṯan),* a sign consisting in a special divine oracle *(zeh hammôp̄ēṯ ʾᵃšer dibber YHWH).* This oracle predicts that the altar will be torn down and the (fat-) ashes[17] poured out (1 K. 13:3). When the king attempts to defend himself against the prophet and reaches for him, his outstretched hand becomes lame (v. 4; the previously unnamed king is now Jeroboam, doubtlessly a secondary insertion[18]), while the altar itself bursts and the ashes really are poured out. It is now remarked *expressis verbis* that all this took place according to the sign *(môp̄ēṯ)* given by the man of God *biḏḇar YHWH* ("in the word of Yahweh, by/through the word of Yahweh"; v. 5). In a short space here *môp̄ēṯ* acquires two identities: first, as the divine oracle accompanying the threat it symbolically foretells the destruction of the altar differently than the announced action of Josiah conceives it; and second, as the actual fulfillment of that accompanying oracle, it constitutes the event itself of the *môp̄ēṯ* according to the substance of its content. Here *môp̄ēṯ* legitimizes, corroborates, and executes the divine oracle already given. The passages using *môp̄ēṯ* belong to a later Deuteronomistic redaction of the material.[19]

Dt. 13:1-6(12:32–13:5) considers the possibility that a prophet or dreamer might employ his ability to perform signs and wonders to lend striking support and credibility to his own demand that Israel serve other gods (v. 2[1]: *wᵉnāṯan ʾēleyḵā ʾôṯ ʾô mōp̄ēṯ;* cf. 11QT 54:9). According to the Deuteronomist, it can even happen that these signs and wonders actually come to pass (v. 3[2]: *ûḇāʾ hāʾôṯ wᵉhammôp̄ēṯ*). This leads to the grievous situation in which even a prophet or dreamer not sent by Yahweh is able to augment his own message with such displays of power. The strict interdiction directs Israel not only not to listen to such a "man of God" (v. 4[3]), but to put him to death and thus purge the evil from its midst (v. 6[5]). The occurrence of such a distressful situation is addressed by v. 4(3) with the surprising explanation that such a "false prophet" is testing Israel for God (*nsh* piel) to determine whether it loves Yahweh with an undivided heart. The meaning of even these *môpᵉṯîm* and *ʾōṯôṯ* is set by God ultimately for the benefit of his own people, and they are by no means autonomous or effectively inimical to God.

---

16. Cf. also Zimmerli, 156f.; 502ff.
17. E. Würthwein, *Das erste Buch der Könige. ATD,* XI/1 (1977), *in loc.*
18. See BHS.
19. Cf. Würthwein, *in loc.;* A. Jepsen, "Gottesmann und Prophet: Anmerkungen zum Kapitel 1. Könige 13," *Probleme biblischer Theologie. Festschrift G. von Rad* (Munich, 1971), 171-182.

In its final section, Deuteronomy contains aphorisms both of blessing and of curse,[20] the latter addressing a person who does not keep Yahweh's commandments and statutes and does not obey Yahweh's voice (Dt. 28:45ff.). These curses become actualized in a terrible historical catastrophe (vv. 47-57), becoming thereby *môp̱ēṯ* and *'ôṯ* both for the person cursed and for his descendants *(zera')* forever, i.e., signs for remembrance and warning, a visible reminder of the curse (v. 46).

3. *Variations in Context and Meaning.* In a postexilic individual lament the petitioner describes his own lamentable situation as a "dreadful sign" to many (Ps. 71:7),[21] a sign which his enemies have understood as a signal of abandonment by God and thus as justification for persecuting the petitioner (vv. 10f.). The petitioner, however, turns to God full of trust and confidence (v. 12 and *passim*). In this instance, *môp̱ēṯ* is taken as a symbol of distress which can indicate to outsiders that even God has abandoned the person.

The versions of the story of Hezekiah both by the Chronicler and by the Deuteronomist mention the king's prayer that his serious illness be healed. Although the response itself has not been preserved, Yahweh does grant him a miraculous sign (*nāṯan môp̱ēṯ,* 2 Ch. 32:24). Unfortunately, this *môp̱ēṯ* is not specified more closely, though one can doubtlessly assume that this "sign" is referring to Hezekiah's miraculous recovery. The parallel account in 2 K. 20:1-10; Isa. 38:1-8,21-22, however, does actually mention a sign of confirmation for the healing predicted by Isaiah, a sign which Hezekiah himself seeks and which is granted by Yahweh. To be sure, the term *'ôṯ* is used in this passage, and the parallel accounts are unfortunately not quite consistent. The story of Sennacherib's siege of Jerusalem converges with the story of the illness such that the sign could also refer to the impending deliverance of Jerusalem. Be that as it may, the *'ôṯ* itself refers to an extraordinary sign that controverts natural laws (the shadow that goes backward instead of forward) and confirms impending deliverance.

The sense of *môp̱ēṯ* in the Chronicler's conclusion to the story of Hezekiah is not quite clear (2 Ch. 32:31); mention is made again of a (or the?) Babylonian envoy to Jerusalem who had been sent to inquire about the "miraculous sign" that had been done in the land (*liḏrōš hammôp̱ēṯ;* the Deuteronomistic conclusion says nothing of this, 2 K. 20:20f.). Here *môp̱ēṯ* can refer back both to the miraculous recovery of Hezekiah and to the surprising deliverance of Jerusalem from Assyrian encirclement. The comms. give the passage differing interpretations.[22]

According to Joel 3:3(2:30) the general outpouring of God's spirit will be accompanied by special signs in the heavens and on earth: blood and fire and smoke, apocalyptic signs. However, this use of *môp̱ēṯ* is quite singular, not in the apocalyptic

20. Cf. von Rad, *Deuteronomy.*

21. Thus the translation of *môp̱ēṯ* by H.-J. Kraus, *Psalms 60–150* (Eng. trans., Minneapolis, 1989), 72.

22. Cf. W. Rudolph, *Chronikbücher. HAT,* XXI (1955), *in loc.;* K. Galling, *Die Bücher der Chronik, Esra, Nehemia. ATD,* XII (1954), *in loc.;* NJB suggests that 2 Ch. 32:31 represents a "new interpretation" of 2 K. 20:12-19.

literature as such (if one follows the suggestion that certain portions of Proto-Zechariah are a product of early apocalyptic writing [Zec. 3:8][23]), but rather in this particular meaning. Any understanding of Zec. 3:8 poses considerable problems to the exegete, especially concerning the question of just who is meant by the *'anšê môpēṯ*. The formulation strongly suggests that it be the *rē'eyḵā* who are "sitting before" the high priest Joshua, who is being addressed. However, the complexity of the following text (are vv. 8b, 10 secondary? what does v. 9 mean with the "stone"?) makes it quite unclear to whom the "men of the sign" actually refer. If the reference is to the colleagues of the high priest, then it is conceivable that the reestablishment of the organized temple cult and the reinstallation of legitimate and consecrated priests (515 B.C.) would involve a pledge for the impending time of good fortune; the *'anšê môpēṯ* would then constitute this pledge.[24]

IV. Qumran. A surprising parallel to Zec. 3:8 is found in 1QH 7:21. There the Teacher of Righteousness is apparently viewed as a "father to the sons of grace" (l. 20) and as a "foster-father to men of the marvelous sign." The "sons of grace" and the "men of the marvelous sign" are presumably designations for the Qumran community itself, or at least for the adherents of the Teacher of Righteousness.[25] 1QH attests two further occurrences (13:16; 15:20). In both instances the notion is advanced that the godless person will be struck by God's wrath, becoming thus a (warning) sign to subsequent generations and serving ultimately to reveal God's greatness and strength (15:20). The use of *môpēṯ* in 4Q511 26:4; 48-51 II 5 follows the OT usage.

Finally, Sir. 48:12 uses *môpēṯ* in its praise of the fathers, and does so in reference to the miracles performed by Elisha. In this context *môpēṯ* can only refer to the prophet's miraculous, mighty acts in the Elisha legends. Additionally, a collective prayer of petition implores God to renew the signs and wonders so that the nations see that he, the God of Israel, is alone God (Sir. 36:6). The parallel terms in v. 6 (a strong arm, powerful hand, right arm, glorification of God's powers) remind us that the allusion here is to the exemplary events in Egypt (*môpēṯ* in the sg.!). Sir. 36:1-4 was a paradigm for liturgical pieces, especially for the New Year Festival during a later period.[26]

Wagner

---

23. H. Gese, "Anfang und Ende der Apokalyptik, dargestellt am Sacharjabuch," *ZThK,* 70 (1073), 20-49.

24. Cf. W. Rudolph, *Sacharja 1–8. KAT,* XIII/4 (1976), *in loc.;* F. Horst, *Die zwölf kleinen Propheten: Nahum bis Maleachi. HAT,* XIV (^{2}1954), *in loc.;* K. Elliger, *Das Buch der zwölf kleinen Propheten II: Sacharia. ATD,* XXV (^{8}1982), *in loc.*

25. G. Vermes, *The Dead Sea Scrolls in English* (Sheffield, ^{3}1987).

26. According to G. Sauer, *Jüdische Schriften in jüdisch-hellenistischer Zeit,* III/5: *Jesus Sirach* (Gütersloh, 1981), 591f.; cf. 627.

מור *mwr*

Contents: I. Etymology. II. Occurrences. III. OT Usage. IV. *t^e^mûrâ.* V. LXX. VI. Qumran.

I. Etymology. The root *mwr* I is found in Jewish-Aram. *'aph* with the meaning "to exchange," perhaps borrowed from the Hebrew; in contrast, Sam. *mwr* means "to shatter," and Syr. *mwr* "to import grain." Akk. (Neo-Bab.) *māru,* "to purchase," probably belongs together with "(an) exchange" and might represent a West Semitic loanword;[1] Arab. *māra(i),* "to supply with provisions, provide for," is probably also related. Ugar. *mr* means "to retire, give way," and belongs better with Arab. *marra,* "depart."[2] Alfred Guillaume refers to Arab. *ma'ara,* "raged, was in commotion."[3]

II. Occurrences. The OT attests the niphal once, "be changed"; the hiphil, "to exchange, change" (12 times); and the noun *t^e^mûrâ,* "exchange."

III. OT Usage. The only occurrence of the niphal is Jer. 48:11, which asserts that Moab has long enjoyed an undisturbed peace and has thus remain unchanged. Employing imagery from wine cultivation, the prophet notes that it has kept its taste *('āmaḏ ṭa'mô bô),* and its fragrance has not changed *(rêḥô lō' nāmār).* Moab resembles "a well-aged wine that has not lost its taste and bouquet through agitation."[4] Now, however, that time has come to an end: Yahweh will pour out the fine wine and shatter the jars; Moab will be completely destroyed.

The hiphil form, "to exchange," occurs first in Lev. 27:10,33. The first passage issues a prohibition against exchanging an animal vowed as a sacrifice for another, since the vowed animal has become holy; if a person nonetheless does exchange it, the substitute animal also becomes holy and belongs to the sanctuary. It is difficult to determine whether any distinction obtains between the two verbs used here (hiphil: *ḥlp, mwr*). "Perhaps חלך refers to an exchange of equals, מור to an exchange of unequals";[5] the passages discussed below might support this conclusion. Lev. 27:33 prescribes something similar concerning tithes, and additionally prohibits any redemption *(g'l).* A similar notion can be found in Ezk. 48:14. The land of the *t^e^rûmâ* apportioned to the priests and Levites is holy to Yahweh and may not be sold *(mkr)* or exchanged; it is not to pass into other hands.

Three other passages address exchanging God for useless idols. Hos. 4:7 reproves the priests for having sinned by "exchanging their glory *(kāḇôḏ)* for shame" (MT "I will exchange" is a tiqqun sopherim). Their glory is either Yahweh himself (cf. Ps.

1. *AHw,* II (1972), 616.
2. According to J. Aistleitner, *WUS,* no. 1658.
3. Guillaume, 21; → מהר *mōhar* (VIII, 142-49).
4. W. Rudolph, *Jeremia. HAT,* XII (³1968), 258.
5. K. Elliger, *Leviticus. HAT,* IV (1966), 387.

3:4[Eng. v. 3]), whom they have exchanged for Baʿal and other idols, or cultivation of the *daʿaṯ ʾᵉlōhîm,* in which they should have lived;[6] instead, they live "on the sin of my people" (Hos. 4:8) and engage in fornication (with Baʿal, v. 10). The first interpretation is supported by Ps. 106:20, which alleges that in the wilderness Israel "exchanged their glory *(kāḇôḏ)* for the image of an ox." Here, as v. 19 shows, the reference is to the golden calf. The image of an ox "that eats grass" is a useless idol. It is thus possible that Hosea is thinking of the images of oxen in Bethel and Dan. The same notion is expressed most emphatically in Jer. 2:11: no pagan people has exchanged its gods even though these are no gods at all (*lōʾ ʾᵉlōhîm*[7]) — yet Israel has exchanged its glory *(kāḇôḏ)* for something that is good for nothing *(lōʾ yôʿîl).* Jer. 2:13 makes it quite clear what is being addressed: Israel has exchanged its God Yahweh for useless idols, which is as foolish as depending on broken cisterns instead of fountains with "living" waters. Israel has committed the ultimate folly.

Ps. 15:4 is textually problematical. It is clear, however, that the reference is to a "change" from what a person has guaranteed with an oath (see the comms.). The text of Mic. 2:4 is in obvious disarray. A lament characterized as a *māšāl* speaks of enemies "exchanging" the land portions and dividing *(ḥlq)* the fields. The LXX apparently reads *yimmaḏ,* "is measured," instead of *yāmîr,* which fits better as a parallel to "divide." The rampaging enemies offer no recompense.

The occurrence in Prov. 3:35 (where one should perhaps read the hiphil ptcp. *mᵉmîrîm* instead of *mērîm*) is textually uncertain.[8]

IV. tᵉmûrâ. Among the passages already discussed, the noun *tᵉmûrâ* occurs first in Lev. 27:10,33. In Job 15:31 it refers to what a person receives if he trusts in emptiness *(šāwʾ),* and in Job 20:18 to the deceptive benefit of wealth. Job 28:17 asserts that wisdom cannot be acquired in exchange for gold. Finally, Ruth 4:7 recalls the old custom of removing one's shoe to attest a transaction involving redeeming *(gᵉʾûllâ)* or exchanging *(tᵉmûrâ).*

V. LXX. The LXX usually renders the verb with *allássein,* although alternate translations include *atheteín, katametreín, tarássein,* and *tithénai.* The noun *tᵉmûrâ* is rendered 3 times with *állagma* and once with *antállagma* (Ruth 4:7). Job 15:31 uses a form of *apobaínein;* Job 20:18 has *amásētos,* "unchewed"(?).

VI. Qumran. The 4 occurrences from Qumran, all of which are found in the Hodayoth, seem to be more or less dependent on Jer. 2:11. The adversaries of the Teacher of Righteousness have exchanged his teaching for uncircumcised lips and a foreign tongue (1QH 2:18); in contrast, he has not let himself be deceived into exchanging steadfastness *(yēṣer sāmûḵ)* for folly (2:36). The false interpreters have

---

6. H. W. Wolff, *Hosea. Herm* (Eng. trans. 1974), 81.
7. → אלהים *ʾᵉlōhîm* (I, 267-284).
8. Cf. V. Reider, "Etymological Studies in Biblical Hebrew," *VT,* 2 (1952), 123f.

exchanged God's law for flattery (4:10). Finally, in 14:20 the poet asserts that he would not exchange God's truth for riches *(hôn)* nor his precepts for bribes.

Ringgren

מוּשׁ/מִישׁ *mûš/mîš*

Contents: I. Etymology, Occurrences. II. Obedience to the Law, New Covenant. III. Transitive and Hiphil. IV. LXX. V. Qumran.

I. Etymology, Occurrences. There are two different roots *mwš.* One is a secondary form of *mšš,* "to touch, feel"; the other, which attests the secondary form *myš,* means "to move or depart from a given position." The only related words are in Middle Hebrew (pilpel) and Jewish Aramaic (palpel) with the same meaning. The latter root is attested in the MT 18 times in the qal and twice in the hiphil.

II. Obedience to the Law, New Covenant. Most of the occurrences refer to purely objective circumstances and exhibit no particular theological significance. Joshua does not "depart" (from) the tent of meeting (Ex. 33:11). Neither the ark nor Moses "depart[s]" (out of) the camp (Nu. 14:44). The pillar of cloud and pillar of fire did not "depart" from their place before the people (Ex. 13:22). Gideon says to the angel of Yahweh: "Do not depart from here" (Jgs. 6:18). The tent peg "gives way" and falls down (Isa. 22:25, oracle against Shebna). The idol "does not move" from its place, but remains where it has been placed (Isa. 46:7, as proof of the powerlessness of the images). The plunder of the enemy "does not end" (Nah. 3:1). The Mount of Olives will be split in two, and the two halves will "withdraw" northward and southward (Zec. 14:4). The tree planted by water "does not cease" to bear fruit (Jer. 17:8). Evil "does not depart" from the house of the person who returns evil for good (Prov. 17:13). Oppression *(tōḵ)* and fraud *(mirmâ)* "do not depart" from the wicked city (Ps. 55:12[Eng. v. 11]).

In the introductory parenesis to Joshua, Joshua is admonished never to let the book of the law "depart" out of his mouth, but rather to meditate on it *(hāḡâ)* day and night (Josh. 1:8). The concern here is thus obedience to the law in the sense of Ps. 1. In the same sense Job avers that he has never "departed" from God's commandments, but has rather treasured *(ṣāp̱an)* these words in his own bosom (read: *ḥēq;* Job 23:12). If obedience is the question, then God has no occasion to punish him.

Isa. 59:21 is a promise: God makes an eternal covenant with his people; the spirit and the words of Yahweh will never "depart" from him and his descendants. This possession of the spirit recalls Isa. 42:1; the people itself will thus be the servant of Yahweh. The "words" are perhaps the words of the law, and this thus reflects the obligation to keep the law as already attested in the passages just discussed. This may also be an allusion to Isa. 54:10, which also speaks of an eternal covenant: even if mountains may "depart" from their places, Yahweh's *ḥesed* will not "depart" from his people, nor will his covenant of peace waver. Jer. 31:36 makes a similar reference in connection with the new covenant: only when the laws *(ḥuqqîm)* of nature "depart," i.e., are suspended, will Israel cease *(šāḇat)* being a people (i.e., a people of God).

III. Transitive and Hiphil. In Zec. 3:9 *mûš* is used transitively in reference to the removal of the land's guilt. This meaning is otherwise rendered by the hiphil: this family cannot "remove" their necks from the disaster (Mic. 2:3); it cannot be avoided. Mic. 2:4 is problematical; one might translate *'êḵ yāmîš lî* "O how he takes from me (the land)."[1]

IV. LXX. The LXX does not offer a consistent translation. For the qal it uses *aphistánai, ekleípein* (twice), *kineín* (5 times), *klínein, methistánai, paúein, chōrízein;* and for the hiphil *kōlýein* (?) and *poieín.*

V. Qumran. Of the Qumran occurrences, 3 refer to the absence or delay of a person. A priest may not be absent from the meals (1QS 6:3), and wherever ten members are together, a proclaimer of the law may not be absent (1QS 6:6; cf. CD 13:2, which asserts that he must be instructed in the book *hgw*). 1QH 8:17 says that the teaching is like water which does not recede or cease, but rather becomes a rushing stream. The small fragment 1Q55 seems to contain a quote from Nah. 3:1.

Ringgren

1. H. W. Wolff, *Micah* (Eng. trans., Minneapolis, 1990), 68.

מוּת *mûṯ;* מָוֶת *māweṯ;* תְמוּתָה *tᵉmûṯâ;* מְמוֹתִים *mᵉmôṯîm*

Contents: I. Ancient Near East: 1. Egypt; 2. Mesopotamia; 3. West Semites. II. 1. Etymology; 2. Occurrences. III. The Experience of Death: 1. General Notion; 2. Before Death; 3. Death Wish; 4. After Death. IV. Death and Burial: 1. The Death-Burial Schema; 2. Lament for the Dead; 3. Special Places of Death. V. Death as a Temporal Designation: 1. Before, at, and after Death; 2. Succession; 3. Genealogy and Age. VI. Reasons for Death: 1. Why Death? 2. Sin; 3. Manner of Death. VII. Death as Consequence: 1. Qal; 2. Hiphil; 3. Hophal; 4. Other Expressions. VIII. 1. The Dead; 2. The Netherworld. IX. Death and Life. X. Qumran.

mûṯ. B. Alfrink, "L'expression שָׁכַב עִם אֲבוֹתָיו," *OTS,* 2 (1943), 106-118; *idem, "L'expression* נֶאֱסַף אֶל־עַמָּיו*," OTS,* 5 (1948), 118-131; F. A. Ali, "Death and Underworld in Cuneiform and the OT," *Bayn al-Nahrayn,* 7/27 (1979), 231-245; P. W. Armes, *The Concept of Dying in the OT* (diss., Southwestern Baptist Theological Seminary, 1981); L. R. Bailey, *Biblical Perspectives on Death. OBT* (1979); C. F. Barth, *Die Errettung vom Tode in den individuellen Klage- und Dankliedern des ATs* (Zollikon, 1947); A. Bertholet, *Die israelitischen Vorstellungen vom*

Zustand nach dem Tode (Tübingen, [2]1914); L. Bronner, "From Death to Life in the Bible in the Light of the Ugaritic Texts," *BethM,* 25 (1980), 202-12 [Heb.]; J. B. Burns, "The Mythology of Death in the OT," *SJT,* 26 (1973), 327-340; H. Christ, *Blutvergiessen im AT. Theologische Dissertationen,* 12 (Basel, 1977); G. R. Driver, "Plurima Mortis Imago," *Studies and Essays in Honor of Abraham A. Neuman* (Philadelphia, 1962), 128-143; *idem,* "The Resurrection of Marine and Terrestrial Creatures," *JSS,* 7 (1962), 12-22; G. Fohrer, "Das Geschick des Menschen nach dem Tode im AT," *KuD,* 14 (1968), 249-262 = *Studien zu alttestamentlichen Texten und Themen (1966-1972). BZAW,* 155 (1981), 188-202; G. Gerlemann, "מות *mût* sterben," *THAT,* I, 893-97; G. F. Hasel, "Resurrection in the Theology of OT Apocalyptic," *ZAW,* 92 (1980), 267-284; K.-J. Illman, *OT Formulas About Death* (Åbo, 1979); K. Jaroš, "Die Vorstellung Altisraels über Tod und Fortleben nach dem Tod," *BiLi,* 51 (1978), 219-231; O. Kaiser and E. Lohse, *Death and Life* (Eng. trans., Nashville, 1981); U. Kellermann, *Auferstanden in den Himmel. SBS,* 95 (1979); *idem,* "Überwindung des Todesgeschicks in der alttestamentlichen Frömmigkeit vor und neben dem Auferstehungsglauben," *ZThK,* 73 (1976), 259-282; A. F. Key, "The Concept of Death in Early Israelite Religion," *JBR,* 32 (1964), 239-247; R. Knierim, *Die Hauptbegriffe für Sünde im AT* (Gütersloh, 1965); B. Lorenz, "Bemerkungen zum Todeskult im AT," *VT,* 32 (1982), 229-234; O. Loretz, "Vom kanaanäischen Totenkult zur jüdischen Patriarchen- und Elternverehrung," *JARG,* 3 (1978), 149-204; *idem,* "Tod und Leben nach altorientalischer und kanaanäisch-biblischer Anschauung in Hos 6,1-3," *BN,* 17 (1982), 37-42; V. Maag, "Tod und Jenseits nach dem AT," *Kultur, Kulturkontakt und Religion* (Göttingen, 1980), 181-202; R. Martin-Achard, *From Death to Life* (Eng. trans., Edinburgh, 1960); *idem,* "Trois remarques sur la résurrection des morts dans l'AT," *De la Tôrah au Messie. Festschrift H. Cazelles* (1981), 301-317; E. M. Meyers, "Secondary Burials in Palestine," *BA,* 33 (1970), 2-29; L. M. Muntingh, "Life, Death and Resurrection in the Book of Job," *OuTWP,* 17f. (1974f., ed. 1977), 32-44; G. E. W. Nickelsburg, Jr., *Resurrection, Immortality and Eternal Life in Intertestamental Judaism. HThS,* 26 (1972); O. Plöger, "Tod und Jenseits im AT," in H.-J. Klimkeit, ed., *Tod und Jenseits im Glauben der Völker* (Wiesbaden, 1978), 77-85; H. D. Preuss, "Psalm 88 als Beispiel alttestamentlichen Redens vom Tod," in A. Strobel, ed., *Der Tod — ungelöstes Rätsel oder überwundener Feind?* (Stuttgart, 1974), 63-79; G. Quell, *Die Auffassung des Todes in Israel* (1925, repr. Darmstadt, 1967); J. W. Ribar, *Death Cult Practices in Ancient Palestine* (diss., Michigan, 1973); J. F. A. Sawyer, "Hebrew Words for the Resurrection of the Dead," *VT,* 23 (1973), 218-234; H. Schulz, *Das Todesrecht im AT. BZAW,* 114 (1969); H. Schüngel-Straumann, *Tod und Leben in der Gesetzesliteratur des Pentateuch, unter besonderer Berücksichtigung der Terminologie von "töten"* (diss., Bonn, 1969); J. A. Soggin, "Tod und Auferstehung des leidenden Gottesknechtes Jesaja 53_{8-10}," *ZAW,* 87 (1975), 346-355; G. Steiner, "Das Bedeutungsfeld 'TOD' in den Sprachen des Alten Orients," *Or,* 51 (1982), 239-248; G. Stemberger, "Auferstehung der Toten II: Judentum," *TRE,* IV (1979), 443-450; *idem, Der Leib der Auferstehung. AnBibl,* 56 (1972); R. Stola, "Zu den Jenseitsvorstellungen im alten Mesopotamien," *Kairos,* 14 (1972), 258-272; N. J. Tromp, *Primitive Conceptions of Death and the Nether World in the OT. BietOr,* 21 (1969); L. Wächter, *Der Tod im AT. ArbT,* 2/8 (1967); H. Wahle, "Die Lehren des rabbinischen Judentums über das Leben nach dem Tod," *Kairos,* 14 (1972), 291-309; P. L. Watson, "The Death of 'Death' in the Ugaritic Texts," *JAOS,* 92 (1972), 60-64; P. Welten, "Die Vernichtung des Todes und die Königsherrschaft Gottes," *ThZ,* 38 (1982), 129-146; J. V. M. Wijngaards, "Death and Resurrection in Covenantal Context (Hos. VI 2)," *VT,* 17 (1967), 226-239; J. Zandee, *Death as an Enemy according to Ancient Egyptian Conceptions. SNumen,* 5 (1960); W. Zimmerli, " 'Leben' und 'Tod' im Buche des Propheten Ezechiel," *ThB,* 13 (1957), 494-508 = *Gottes Offenbarung. Gesammelte Aufsätze,* I. *ThZ,* 19 ([2]1969), 178-191; for further bibliog. see *TWNT,* X/2 (1979), 1100-1103; *EDNT,* II (1991), 129.

I: B. Alster, ed., *Death in Mesopotamia: Papers Read at the XXVIe Rencontre Assyriologique Internationale* (Copenhagen, 1980); H. Bonnet, "Jenseitsgericht," *RÄR,* 333-341; *idem,* "Jenseitsglaube," *RÄR,* 341-355; E. Ebeling, *Tod und Leben nach den Vorstellungen der Babylonier,* I: *Texte* (Berlin, 1931); A. Gardiner, *The Attitude of the Ancient Egyptians to Death and the Dead*

I. Ancient Near East.

1. *Egypt.* The root *mt (mwt)* manifests itself in three different forms in Egyptian: the verb *mt,* "be dead, die," the adj. *mt,* "dead," and the subst. *mt,* "death." The semantic field emerges quite naturally from circumstances. The antithesis to "to live" (*ʿnḫ*) occurs frequently, and combinations such as "as a dead person or as a living person" ("dead or alive"), "not to die, but rather to live," "to love life and to hate death" are all frequently attested.[1] The term can refer both to human beings and to animals, to a sinking ship,[2] a sick bodily part,[3] or to poison that has lost its efficacy;[4] a child wounded by a poisonous animal is told, "Live, child! Die, poison!"[5] Metaphorical statements include "the earth lies in darkness, as if it were dead,"[6] "they lie down after the manner of those who die."[7] Frequently the speaker avoids mentioning death: Osiris is "tired" (in the sense of dead), the dead themselves are "the weary ones," and are also called "those who sleep."[8] The realm of the dead is called the "land of life." The expression "he went to his peace" means "he died."[9] Another noteworthy expression is *mt m whm,* "to die a second time," i.e., to die yet again in the beyond.

Death is visualized as "part of [the] cosmic order,"[10] and is considered inescapable: "When death comes, he steals away . . . the infant which is on its mother's lap like him who has reached old age."[11] "There is no messenger of god [i.e., of death] who receives gifts in order to neglect [the cause why] he was dispatched."[12] The deity determines the time of death of the individual: "Amon makes a lifetime long or shortens it."[13]

The attitude toward death vacillates between pessimism and optimism. "Generations pass away. . . . They that build buildings, their places are no more. . . . No one returns

---

(Cambridge, 1935); H. Kees, *Totenglauben und Jenseitsvorstellungen der alten Ägypter* (Berlin, 1926, ²1956); C. E. Sander-Hansen, *Der Begriff des Todes bei den Ägyptern* (Copenhagen, 1942); J. Spiegel, *Die Idee vom Totengericht in der ägyptischen Religion. LÄS,* 2 (1935); J. A. Wilson, "Egypt," in H. Frankfort, *et al., The Intellectual Adventure of Ancient Man* (Chicago, 1946), 31-121.

1. *WbÄS,* II, 165ff., with citations.
2. *Story of the Shipwrecked Sailor,* 171 = A. Erman, *The Ancient Egyptians* (Eng. trans., New York, 1966), 31.
3. G. Ebers, *Papyros Ebers* (Leipzig, 1875), 103.18.
4. W. Golénischeff, *Die Metternichstele in der Originalgrösse* (Leipzig, 1877), 69.
5. H. Grapow, *Vergleiche und andere bildliche Ausdrücke im Ägyptischen. AO,* 21/1f.(1920, repr. 1983), 138.
6. Hymn to the Sun 15; cf. Erman, 289.
7. N. de G. Davies, *The Rock Tombs of El Amarna,* IV (London, 1906), 28; Grapow, 138.
8. Grapow, 139.
9. *Ibid.,* 19, 138.
10. S. Morenz, *Egyptian Religion* (Eng. trans., Ithaca, N.Y., 1973), 186.
11. Instruction of Ani, v.2-4, cited by Morenz, 192 = *ANET,* 420.
12. G. Lefebvre, *Le Tombeau de Petosiris* (Cairo, 1923-24), II, 90 (no. 127), cited by Morenz, 192.
13. A. H. Gardiner, *The Admonitions of an Egyptian Sage from a Papyrus in Leiden* (*Pap. Leiden,* 344, recto) (Leipzig, 1909), I, 350, III, 17, cited by Morenz, 71, 185 = *ANET,* 369.

from (over) there."[14] "Lowly . . . for us is death; life we hold in high esteem."[15] One formula, in common use since the Middle Kingdom, was used as an appeal to the living; it begins: "O ye who love to live and hate to die, speak [the prayer for the dead]."[16] Death seems to be the only escape for the person who is weary of life. It is a condition in which one does without everything: water, food, consciousness, human company.[17] "The West [i.e., the realm of the dead], that is the land of slumber, a heavy darkness, the dwelling-place of those who are there [euphemism for 'the dead']. Sleeping is their occupation. They do not awaken to see their brothers. . . ."[18]

On the other hand, Egyptian belief is continually concerned with the hope of life in the beyond. The *ba* ("soul"), which departs the body at the moment of death, tarries in the vicinity of the dead person in the grave and maintains contact with the living, mediates funerary sacrifices, etc. The *ka* (second self, *Doppelgänger,* vital force) lives on, is depicted in the tomb, and secures the continuance of life in the beyond. Through burial rites the deceased becomes an *akh* ("transfigured one") and lives on with the gods. Here notions of differing provenance overlap. In the Old Kingdom one thought that the king was united with his father Re and participated in his eternal cycle in heaven. Another early notion is that the deceased becomes an Osiris and, like him, lives forever. This might be the background to the idea of the continual renewal of nature (of grain, etc.).

The Egyptians also entertained the notion of judgment in the beyond: The deceased was to plead his innocence before the court of Osiris and be pronounced just. "Thus justice was given to him who does what is liked and injustice to him who does what is disliked. Thus life was given to him who has peace and death was given to him who has sin."[19] However, attempts were made to circumvent this idea of compensation through magic: if one only knew the correct formula, he might be pronounced innocent and escape the dangers of the netherworld.

2. *Mesopotamia.* The Akkadian verb *mātu* can refer both to human beings and to animals and plants,[20] though also to tablets whose contents have become invalid. The adj. *mîtu,*[21] "dead," which often appears as the antithesis together with *balṭu,* "living," is also used both of animals and plants; in addition, it can designate the spirit of the dead, approximately = *eṭemmu.*[22] The subst. *mûtu,* "death,"[23] is often contrasted with *napištu* or *balāṭu,* "life," and can even be personified: "Death, the ruler of men, has taken his son."[24]

The divine epithet *muballiṭ mîtē,* "he who makes the dead live," is also of signifi-

14. Papyrus Harris 500 (British Museum Papyrus No. 10060), VI, 2-9, cited by Wilson, 104.
15. Instruction of Hor-dedef, cited by Morenz, 187 = *ANET,* 419.
16. Morenz, 187.
17. *Ibid.,* 188.
18. Stele BM 157, cited in Morenz, 188.
19. Shabaka inscription 57, cited by Morenz, 116.
20. *AHw,* II (1972), 634f.; citations in *CAD,* X/1 (1977), 421ff.
21. *AHw,* II, 663.
22. See discussion below.
23. *AHw,* II, 691.
24. *CAD,* X/2 (1977), 317; cf. Steiner, 247.

cance; it appears in contexts apparently dealing with the healing of (mortally) ill persons.

The gods have imposed death upon human beings: "When the gods created mankind, death for mankind they set aside, life in their own hands retaining" (*Gilg.* X, III, 3-5).[25] Cf. also: "No one can see death. No one can see the face of death. No one can hear the voice of death. But savage death snaps off mankind" (*Gilg.* X, VI, 13-16).[26] The Atraḫasis epic suggests that the reason for the establishment of death was the gods' wish to limit the increase in human beings, since the Flood had not been effective.[27]

The hour of a person's death depends on fate *(šīmtu);* a premature death occurs on a day that is not this day of fate.[28]

Death can be described by verbs such as "fall asleep" *(ṣalālu)* and "rest" *(nâlu, pašāḫu).*[29] The body *(zumru, pagru)* becomes a cadaver *(šalamtu),* and one's flesh disappears.[30] What remains is a breath or spirit *(zaqīqu, šâru),* a shadow *(ṣillu),* or, the usual designation, an *eṭemmu,* which as an evil spirit can harm the living who are left behind.[31]

The dead exist in the realm of the dead, often called *ᵏⁱerṣetu,* "earth," KI.GAL, "the great netherworld," or by the personal name Arallu. It is KUR.NU.GI.A = *erṣet lā târi,* "the land without return."[32]

The gods of the netherworld are sometimes called "judges" *(dayyānu),* but in this case "to judge" effectively means "to decide": they determine that the deceased is to remain in the netherworld and be subject to its laws. Thus this does not really represent the notion of any ethically focused judgment.[33]

The dying gods present a special problem. On the one hand, a god is killed in order to secure the life of human beings, who are created from loam; on the other hand, old gods are killed so as to be replaced by younger successors.[34] Finally, DUMU.ZI/Tammuz, as the god of nascent life and of vegetation, is a dying god.[35]

3. *West Semites.* The Ugaritic texts contain a few references to human death in a general sense. One text states that "Aqhat the Youth is dead *(mt),*"[36] another relates that the children of Keret die.[37] The general attitude toward death emerges from several lines in the Aqhat epic. Although ʿAnat has offered Aqhat eternal life in exchange for

25. *ANET,* 90.
26. Cited by W. G. Lambert in Alster, 54f.
27. *Ibid.,* 57f.
28. Steiner, 243.
29. Cited by Bottéro in Alster, 28; Steiner, 242, lists additional synonyms and euphemisms.
30. Cited by Bottéro in Alster, 27.
31. *Ibid.,* 28f.; Steiner, 245.
32. Bottéro in Alster, 29f.; cf. Friedrich Delitzsch, *Das Land ohne Heimkehr* (Stuttgart, 1911).
33. Bottéro in Alster, 34.
34. *Ibid.,* 45, n. 17.
35. H. Ringgren, *Religions of the Ancient Near East* (Eng. trans., Philadelphia, 1973), 65f.
36. *KTU,* 1.19 II, 42; *ANET,* 154.
37. *KTU,* 1.14 I, 16; *ANET,* 143.

his bow, he refuses with the rejoinder: "Further life — how can the mortal attain it? How can the mortal attain life enduring? . . . And I'll die as everyone dies, I too shall assuredly die."[38] Death is the inescapable lot of human beings; only the gods enjoy immortality. This generates the problem in the epic of King Keret. Keret falls ill, and those around him believe him to be close to death; since as king he is of divine origin, the question arises: "Wilt thou die, then, father, like the (other) mortals?"[39] and "Shall, then, a god die, an offspring of the Kindly One not live?"[40] As is well known, Ugaritic mythology attests a dying (and revivified) god, namely, Aliyan Baʿal, whose death at the hands of the god Mot (whose name itself probably means "death" and who represents the dying off of vegetation during the dry season) is proclaimed as follows: "For dead is Aliyan Baʿal, perished *(ḫlq)* the Prince, Lord of Earth."[41] The contrasting pronouncement at his revivification reads as follows: "Behold, alive is Aliyan Baʿal! And behold, existent (again) the Prince, Lord of Earth!"[42]

After Baʿal's victory, the death of Yam is proclaimed: "Yam is dead; Baʿal will reign."[43]

Ringgren

II. 1. *Etymology.* The root *mwt* is common to the Semitic languages and also occurs in Egyptian: Ugar. *mt;*[44] Can.,[45] Pun., Old Aram., Ya'udic, Egyptian Aram., Nab., Palmyr.,[46] Biblical Aram., Jewish Aram., Sam.,[47] Syr., Mand.,[48] OSA,[49] Arab. *mwt;* Ethiop., Tigriña, Akk. *mē/īt;*[50] Egyp. *mt.*[51]

2. *Occurrences.* In Hebrew the verb is attested in the qal (630 times[52]) with the meaning "die," additionally also in the polel (9 times), "kill off, give the death-blow, slay," as the polal ptcp. *mᵉmôṯāṯîm,* "those who should be killed,"[53] in the hiphil (138 times), "kill, have (someone) executed," in the hophal (68 times), "be killed, suffer death." The subst. *māweṯ* (150 occurrences[54]) means "death, dying," although it might

---

38. *KTU,* 1.17 VI, 34-37; *ANET,* 151.
39. *KTU,* 1.16 I, 3f., 18; *ANET,* 147.
40. *KTU,* 1.16 I, 22; *ANET,* 147f.
41. *KTU,* 1.5 VI, 9; *ANET,* 140; cf. also 139.
42. *KTU,* 1.6 III, 2f.; *ANET,* 140.
43. *KTU,* 1.2 IV, 31-34; cf. also *ANET,* 131.
44. *UT,* no. 1443; *WUS,* no. 1703.
45. EA, 1468.
46. *DISO,* 145.
47. Z. Ben Hayyim, *The Literary and Oral Tradition of Hebrew and Aramaic amongst the Samaritans,* II (Jerusalem, 1957), 503b [Heb.].
48. *MdD,* 263b.
49. ContiRossini, 176a.
50. *AHw,* II, 634b.
51. *WbÄS,* II, 165ff.
52. According to *THAT.*
53. *HAL,* II (1995), 563.
54. According to *THAT.*

be translated as the personification "god of death, Death (?)" (Jer. 9:20[Eng. v. 21], Hos. 13:14; Hab. 2:5; Ps. 18:5[4]; 49:15[14]; 116:3; Prov. 13:14)[55] or "realm of the dead" as a parallel to → שׁאול *šᵉʼôl* (Cant. 8:6; Isa. 28:15) and → שׁחת *šaḥaṯ* (e.g., Isa. 38:17f.; cf. Job 38:17). Other derivatives from *mwt* include *tᵉmûṯâ,* "dying, death" (Ps. 79:11; 102:21[20]) and *mᵉmôṯîm,* "death, type of death" (Jer. 16:4; Ezk. 28:8). Altogether we would have 1,000 occurrences of this root.[56]

The overwhelming majority of occurrences refer to human beings, although animals (Gen. 33:13; Ex. 7:18,21; 8:9[13]; 9:6f.; Lev. 11:31f.,39; Isa. 66:24) and plants (Job 14:8) also appear as subjects.

The distribution of these occurrences is interesting. The overwhelming majority are found in the narrative writings and refer to the simple fact of dying or death. Only 4 occurrences of the verb are found in the Psalms (compared to 18 occurrences of *māweṯ*), a situation probably resulting from the circumscription of death by typified imagery. Job attests 13 occurrences of the verb in the qal, Isaiah 12 occurrences, Jeremiah 27, Ezekiel 37, the Minor Prophets 9, Proverbs 6, Ecclesiastes 7.

Synonyms include → גוע *gāwaʻ,* → הלך *hālaḵ,* "go forth," *yṣʼ* with *nepeš, neʼᵉsap ʼel ʻammāw* or *ʼᵃḇōṯāw,*[57] → שׁכב *šāḵaḇ;* antonyms include → חיה *ḥāyâ,* "live." The hiphil is also rendered by → הרג *hāraḡ* and → רצח *rāṣaḥ.* In isolated instances death is described as sleep (Job 3:13; 14:12; Ps. 13:4[3]; Jer. 51:39,57; cf. Isa. 26:19; Dnl. 12:2).[58]

III. The Experience of Death.

1. *General Notion.* The synonyms just enumerated characterize death as the "departure of the *nepeš,* i.e., of life"; a person lies down (to sleep, *šāḵaḇ*) or departs *(hlk).* Some passages indirectly suggest a definition, e.g., Job 14:10: "But man *(geḇer)* dies, and is laid low *(ḥlš),* man breathes his last *(gāwaʻ),* and where is he?" Ps. 39:14(13) is even more unequivocal: "I depart and am no more *(ʼênennî)*"; cf. Ps. 103:16: "they are no more, and their place knows them no more." Another passage emphasizes the fact that the deceased will not return to life: "before I go *(ʼēlēḵ)* whence I shall not return (*wᵉlōʼ ʼāšûḇ*)" (Job 10:21); cf. Akk. *erṣet lā tāri,* "the land without return"[59]).

2. *Before Death.* Actual impending death can be expressed by various formulas: *wᵉšāḵaḇtî ʻim-ʼᵃḇōṯay,* "when I lie down with my fathers," or *ʼᵃnî neʼᵉsap ʼel-ʻammî,* "when I am gathered to my people" (Gen. 47:30; 49:29).[60] These statements occur in connection with the patriarchs' preparation for death, especially in the context of testamentary provisions. In this connection, however, the root *mwt* is also directly employed, e.g., the qal participle: *hinnēh ʼānōḵî mēṯ,* "behold, I am about to die" (Gen.

55. Cf. *HAL,* II.
56. *THAT.*
57. → אב *ʼāḇ (ʼābh),* I, 10.
58. → ישׁן *yāšēn* (VI, 438-441).
59. See I.2 above.
60. See IV.1 below.

48:21; 50:5), *kî 'ānōḵî mēṯ,* "for I am to die" (Dt. 4:22), with qal imperfect: *beṭerem 'āmûṯ,* "before I die" (Gen. 27:4; 45:28; Prov. 30:7), with the subst. *māweṯ: lip̱nê môṯô/môṯî,* "before his/my death" (Gen. 27:7,10; 50:16; Dt. 33:1; 1 Ch. 22:5). Besides the testamentary provisions, the dying person's last wish or the final measures before death are also mentioned here.

This context includes several expressions focusing on the inf. *lāmûṯ*. These include *wayyiqreḇû yemê-yiśrā'ēl lāmûṯ,* "and when the days drew near that Israel must die" (Gen. 47:29; cf. 1 K. 2:1 concerning David and Dt. 31:14 as an address to Moses), and *'ānōḵî hôlēḵ lāmûṯ,* "I am about to die" (Gen. 25:32). Mention should also be made here of the blessing[61] characteristic of the patriarchal narratives.

2 K. 20:1 (par. Isa. 38:1); 2 Ch. 32:24 mention a sickness unto death (although the sick king, Hezekiah, does recover), as does 2 K. 13:14, where King Joash visits the deathbed of the prophet Elisha. Here the verb *ḥālâ* is used with *mûṯ*.

3. *Death Wish.* The death wish is relatively rare in the OT. Twice the expression *wayyiš'al 'eṯ-nap̱šô lāmûṯ* occurs, "he wanted to die (RSV 'he asked that he might die' " (1 K. 19:4 referring to Elijah; Jon. 4:8 regarding Jonah). The second passage is clearly dependent on the first, although the situations are quite dissimilar. Twice the wish is expressed by the irreal idiom *mî yittēn* with the suffixed inf. *mûṯēnû* (Ex. 16:3) or *mûṯî* (2 S. 19:1[18:33]). In the first instance Israel laments, "would that we had died by the hand of Yahweh in the land of Egypt," and in the second David, "would I had died instead of you [i.e., Absalom]." A third expression, *tāmōṯ nap̱šî,* "let me die," does not refer to a death wish as such, but rather to the wish for the proper kind of death: Balaam concludes his first oracle concerning Israel with the words, "let me die the death of the upright" (Nu. 23:10), and Samson hopes to take the Philistines with him to death (Jgs. 16:30).

4. *After Death.* Recognition that death has occurred is usually expressed by the perf. *mēṯ* or the ptcp. *mēṯ* in various phrases, the shortest of which is *wehinnēh mēṯ,* "and (behold), he is dead" (e.g., 2 S. 4:10; 1 K. 3:21; 2 K. 4:32), whereby the name of the dead person is mentioned or presumed already familiar. When a slain person is discovered, the expression is *wehinnēh nōp̱ēl mēṯ,* "and (behold) he lies dead" (Jgs. 3:25 referring to Ehud; 4:22 regarding Sisera). In place of the perfect, two participles express a narrative element of surprise here. Much more frequently, however, a cognitive verb is combined with *mûṯ,* both often in the perfect. Examples include especially *šāma'* . . . *kî mēṯ,* "he heard . . . that (he) had died" (1 S. 25:39; 2 S. 4:1; 11:26; 1 K. 11:21; 21:16), and *rā'â* . . . *kî mēṯ,* "he saw . . . that (he) had died" (e.g., Gen. 50:15; Jgs. 9:55; 1 S. 17:51; 31:5; 2 K. 11:1). The verbs *ngd* (hiphil), *bîn,* and *yāḏa'* are used only once each with *mûṯ* (2 S. 12:18,19; 1:5). These are idioms which speak in a simple, natural way of the experience of death. Such expressions often provide the direct transition to additional actions which then constitute the real focus of the narrative. In

61. → ברך *brk* (II, 279-308).

direct discourse, such information concerning the death of a person only serves to emphasize something else; e.g., Joseph's death provides the motif for safeguarding Benjamin's life (Gen. 42:38; 44:20).

IV. Death and Burial.

1. *The Death-Burial Schema.* Death and burial are often encompassed within a schema whose primary elements are the consecutive forms *wayyāmoṯ . . . wayyiqqāḇēr,* "he died . . . and was buried." Besides these elements, the schema usually includes the subject and information concerning the hometown or place of burial. Additional information is frequently given as well, especially if the deceased was a significant person. The most basic form of this death-burial schema is found in the lists of what are known as the minor judges (Jgs. 10:1-5; 12:7-15). Further occurrences include 2 S. 17:23 (Ahithophel); Jgs. 8:32 (Gideon); and, with a feminine subject, Gen. 35:8 (Deborah), 19 (Rachel); Nu. 20:1 (Miriam). The schema incorporates small variations involving the second element in Josh. 24:29f. (Joshua); 1 S. 25:1 (Samuel); 2 K. 13:20 (Elisha); and 2 Ch. 24:15f. (Jehoiada). Dt. 34:5f., where Yahweh buries his servant Moses, is unique. Finally, two more extensive expositions concerning Abraham (Gen. 25:8f.) and Isaac (35:28f.) as well as Eleazar (Josh. 24:33) and Samuel (1 Sam. 28:3) belong under the rubric of this schema, although here the perf. *mēṯ* is used instead of the consecutive form. A further variation of the schema occurs in Gen. 48:7, where Jacob makes reference to Rachel's death.[62]

Within this schema itself, or in isolated instances, yet other formulaic elements are used. In Gen. 25:8; 35:29, the expression *wayyāmoṯ* is preceded by *wayyigwaʿ,* "he passed away, breathed his last." This is also the case in Gen. 25:17, although there the burial motif is missing. The formula *wayyēʾāsep̱ ʾel-ʿammāw,* "and (he) was gathered to his people" (Gen. 25:8,17; 35:29), is unique to the P stratum and can even replace the phrase *wayyāmoṯ* (as in Gen. 49:33; Nu. 20:24; Dt. 32:50) and appear with varying subjects (Gen. 49:29; Nu. 27:13; 31:2). Similar to → גוע *gwʿ, neʾesap . . .* can mean simply "to die" (Ps. 26:9; Isa. 57:1). Scholars have suggested that the original meaning of the formula refers to a uniting of the deceased with his forefathers in Sheol,[63] although it is to be differentiated from another formula, namely, *šāḵaḇ ʿim-ʾaḇôṯāw,* "sleep with his fathers," which is used almost exclusively to refer to kings who die a normal death (e.g., 1 K. 1:21; 2:10; 11:21 [David]; 2 K. 8:24 [Joram]). Both formulas, however, are used in reference to Jacob's death (cf. Gen. 47:30; 49:29,33), which shows that both have the same meaning or have already become fixed idioms in the Pentateuch. Thus they can occasionally be mixed, *ʿammāw* being replaced by *ʾaḇôṯāw* (Jgs. 2:10; 2 K. 22:20). One widely held view suggests that the second formula means "to be interred in the family grave," and Ludwig Wächter[64] believes this was also the original

62. Cf. → קבר *qeḇer.*

63. This is the view of Alfrink, Driver, and Tromp; → שׁאול *šeʾôl.*

64. P. 71, following Quell and L. Dürr, *Die Wertung des Lebens im AT und im antiken Orient* (Münster, 1926).

meaning of *wayyēʾāsep̱ ʾel-ʿammāw.* Carol L. Meyers, however, suggests combining the two meanings: archaeological excavations attest the practice of multiple (secondary) burials, whereby remains were interred in a common ossuary.[65] The formulas might then mean "die and descend into Sheol, where all Israel is gathered," thereby expressing literally this practice of multiple burials. Claus Westermann holds a differing opinion: "There is no thought of a state in which the dead find themselves such as could be imagined or represented; the idea is rather what they now mean for the living: they belong to the ancestors who have gone before and whose memory is preserved."[66]

Two additional formulas involving *mûṯ* should also be mentioned: *zāqēn ûśᵉḇaʿ yāmîm,* "an old man and full of years," occurs in Gen. 25:8 (Abraham); 35:29 (Isaac); 1 Ch. 23:1 (David; cf. 29:28; 2 Ch. 24:15); Job 42:17 (Job). Parallels can be found in both Akkadian and Egyptian texts.[67] According to Wächter,[68] the reference is not merely to "advanced age"; rather, the formula also served as a demonstration of virtue emphasized by the reference to numerous descendants and interment in the family grave. The formula *bᵉśêḇâ ṭôḇâ,* "in a good old age," is used to refer to Abraham (Gen. 15:15; 25:8), Gideon (Jgs. 8:32), and David (1 Ch. 29:28). It, too, expresses advanced age and a condition of fulfillment.

Gerhard von Rad is probably correct in asserting that especially the first formula "shows that in ancient Israel one accepted life not with a defiant claim to endlessness but from the start in resignation, as something limited, something assigned to man, in which then the state of satiation was to be reached. . . ."[69] This does not, however, allow far-reaching conclusions concerning the estimation of life and attitude toward death in the larger sense. It is noteworthy that no statements occur concerning God's intervention or participation in these deaths. This should come as no surprise in the case of such formulaic expressions, however, for only in exceptional instances does the narrator depart significantly from the schema. This happens only if the manner of death or burial itself was unusual, as was the case with Moses and Aaron, or if the person was a significant figure, such as Abraham, Jacob, or David. In the first case Yahweh himself brings about both the death and burial, and in the second the death-burial schema is amplified, expanded, or replaced by the formulas mentioned.

2. *Lament for the Dead.* Statements about the rite of lament for the dead are found both in connection with the death-burial schema and independent of it. 1 S. 25:1 recounts that "all Israel assembled and mourned for him [i.e., Samuel]"; cf. the somewhat shorter version in 28:3. It is also asserted that "all Israel" mourned Jeroboam's son Abijah (1 K. 14:13,18). In both instances this remark is incorporated into the framework of the schema. The lament for the dead is also mentioned in

---

65. Cf. A. Kuschke, "Grab," *BRL*², 122-29; M. Weippert, "Sarkophag, Urne, Ossuar," *ibid.,* 269-276.

66. C. Westermann, *Genesis 12–36* (Eng. trans., Minneapolis, 1985), 397.

67. Dürr, 13.

68. Pp. 65f.

69. *Genesis. OTL* (Eng. trans. ²1972), 262.

connection with *mûṯ* in Gen. 23:2 (Abraham-Sarah); 2 S. 11:26 (Bathsheba-Uriah). The ritual of lament also includes the element of consolation, which is mentioned in the immediate context of the report of death in Gen. 38:12; 2 S. 13:39. The perfect of *nḥm* designates the conclusion of the period of mourning.[70]

An indirect indication of the significance of the rites of mourning can be derived from passages which proscribe them or foretell their absence. Dt. 14:1 commands: "You shall not cut yourselves or make any baldness on your foreheads for the dead," a practice apparently viewed as pagan. In Jer. 22:10, the prophet admonishes the people not to mourn the dead King Josiah, but rather his successor Jehoahaz, who was to go into exile. Jer. 16:4-7 gives an extensive description of the awful death that will befall the inhabitants of Jerusalem, punctuated especially by the absence of any burial or mourning. The prophet forbids the survivors from entering the houses of mourning, since Yahweh has withdrawn his peace from his people. Similarly, Ezekiel is instructed to underscore the enormity of the impending catastrophe by omitting the mourning ritual for his own wife (Ezk. 24:16).[71]

3. *Special Places of Death.* Within the death-burial schema, the place of death is as a rule one's home; exceptions include those instances when death occurs during a journey (Gen. 35:8,19; Nu. 20:1), or when the place of death is unusual for some other reason. In that case, an emphatic *šām,* "there," can refer to the previously mentioned locale: Kadesh (Nu. 20:1); Mt. Hor (Nu. 20:26,28; 33:38); Moserah (Dt. 10:6); Mt. Nebo (Dt. 34:5). The threat of death in exile can also be expressed with *šām* (Isa. 22:18; Jer. 20:6; 22:12; 42:16; Ezk. 12:13). This underscores that exile by no means offers protection; on the contrary, precisely "there" will the people encounter death.

In some passages death in the wilderness is mentioned as something that has already occurred (Nu. 3:4; 27:3; Josh. 5:4), though only in the latter instance does the antithesis wilderness–promised land play a role. Only in connection with the motif of "murmuring in the wilderness"[72] is "death in the wilderness" emphasized as a specific motif of lament. In Nu. 14:2, to be sure, death either in Egypt or in the wilderness is considered preferable to an encounter with the alleged giants in the promised land. The Israelites also accuse Moses and Aaron of having led them out of Egypt merely to let them die in the wilderness (Ex. 14:11,12; Nu. 16:13; 21:5; Dt. 9:28).

These findings prompt the conclusion that the ideal was a death at an advanced age, sated and fulfilled by progeny, with burial in the family grave in one's home. The antithesis was a death in exile, in the wilderness, or in war,[73] since in these cases the appropriate interment and mourning would not take place.

---

70. → בכה *bāḵâ (bākhāh)* (II, 116-120); → ספד *sāpaḏ;* → נחם *nḥm;* cf. also P. Heinisch, *Die Totenklage im AT. BZfr,* 13/9f. (1931).

71. On the rituals of mourning, cf. E. Kutsch, *"Trauerbräuche" und "Selbstminderungsriten" im AT. ThSt,* 78 (1965), 25-42; P. Welten, "Bestattung II: AT," *TRE,* V (1980), 734-38.

72. → לון *lûn* (VII, 509-12).

73. Cf. VI.3 below.

V. Death as a Temporal Designation. Mention of the death of a person can also function as a temporal designation. The context can be that of the succession of various events, though also of changes in the age, epochs, connected chronologies, etc.

1. *Before, at, and after Death.* The expression *ʿaḏ-môṯ hakkōhēn haggāḏôl,* "until the death of the high priest," specifies the duration of exile imposed for unintentional manslaughter (Nu. 35:25,28[cf. v. 32]; Josh. 20:6). A different sort of asylum situation is involved when Jeroboam flees to Egypt "until the death of Solomon" (1 K. 11:40). The formula *ʿaḏ-yôm môṯô,* "to the day of his death," refers to the time remaining in a person's life (Jgs. 13:7; 1 S. 15:35; 2 S. 6:23; 2 K. 15:5 par. 2 Ch. 26:21; Jer. 52:11,34). The expression *yôm hammāweṯ* (Eccl. 7:1; 8:8) refers to the end of life in general and has no chronological function.

The expression *b^emôṯ* . . . , "at the death (of) . . . ," expresses either simultaneity (Gen. 21:16; Nu. 26:10; Prov. 11:7) or immediate succession (Jgs. 2:19; Est. 2:7). The expression *b^emôṯô,* "at his death," is as a rule amplified by specific indications of the age of the deceased in the death-burial schema: Nu. 33:39 (Aaron); Dt. 34:7 (Moses); 2 Ch. 24:15 (Jehoiada). The same expression is used to recount that "all Judah and the inhabitants of Jerusalem honored [King Hezekiah] at his death" (2 Ch. 32:33), and that Samson slew more men "at his death" than during his life (Jgs. 16:30). The expression *b^emôṯô* is also used in a general fashion in wisdom assertions: a person will take along nothing of his wealth "at his death" (Ps. 49:18[17]).

A point in time "after the death . . ." is indicated either by *ʾaḥ^arê môṯ* . . . or *kaʾ^ašer mēṯ.* The first expression is used in schemata marking the transition from one epoch to another: Abraham-Isaac (Gen. 25:11), Moses-Joshua (Josh. 1:1), Joshua-Judges (Jgs. 1:1), and Saul-David (2 S. 1:1). Chronological information is also being given in Nu. 35:28; 1 Ch. 2:24; 2 Ch. 24:17, etc. In addition to its temporal valence (Jgs. 8:33; 2 S. 12:21), the expression *kaʾ^ašer mēṯ* can also express a comparison (e.g., Dt. 32:50: "as Aaron your brother died").

2. *Succession.* Monarchical succession is indicated by two different schemata, one for peaceful and one for violent succession to the throne:

(1) *wayyāmoṯ-* . . . *wayyimlōḵ taḥtāw,* "when he died, . . . became king in his stead" (Gen. 36:33-39 par. 1 Ch. 1:44-50; 2 K. 1:17; 8:15; 13:24; 2 S. 10:1 par. 1 Ch. 19:1; 1 Ch. 29:28).

(2) *way^emîṯēhû* . . . *wayyimlōḵ taḥtāw,* "he killed him . . . and became king in his stead." The conspiracy schema contains a series of fixed elements that lead up to the murder and usurpation of the throne (1 K. 15:27f.; 16:10; 2 K. 15:10,14, 25,30).

These two schemata apparently have a chronological function. The first is used in the case of Israelite and Judaic as well as foreign kings. A middle group is represented by cases in which the consecutive *wayyāmoṯ* is preceded by expressions for killing (2 K. 12:21f.[20f.] par. 2 Ch. 24:25,27; cf. also 1 K. 15:27). The second schema is used only in the Deuteronomistic history, where it occurs in connection with six northern Israelite conspiracies.

3. *Genealogy and Age.* The expression *wayyāmoṯ* is also a fixed component in genealogical schemata, which themselves are part of the chronological framework of P.[74] This schema occurs 7 times in Gen. 5: "When A had lived x years, he became the father of B. A lived after the birth of B y years, and became the father of other sons and daughters. Thus A lived z years, and then he died." The striking element here is the interest in tracing the genealogy back as far as possible.[75] The sometimes extremely high indications of age (in number of years) can amplify this information.[76] Yet another schema is generated when the previously discussed death-burial schema is augmented by information concerning a person's age: "This is the length of Abraham's life, a hundred and seventy-five years. Abraham breathed his last and died . . ." (Gen. 25:7f.). Further examples are Gen. 11:32 (Terah); 23:1f. (Sarah); 25:17 (Ishmael); 35:28f. (Isaac); 47:28f. (Jacob/Israel); 50:22,26 (Joseph); Job 42:16f. (Job).

It is also worth noting that in some cases *wayyāmoṯ* is amplified by the remark that the deceased passed away "without a son/sons" (2 K. 1:17; 1 Ch. 2:30,32,34; 23:22). When 1 Ch. 2:34; 23:22 remarks that a certain person "had no sons, only daughters," it is clear that the reference is to a genealogical break that can be remedied through daughters only as a last resort. The even greater misfortune was childlessness; it is explicitly stated that Michal "had no child to the day of her death" (2 S. 6:23); the narrator interprets this as her punishment for having criticized her spouse King David.

VI. Reasons for Death.

1. *Why Death?* The frequent question why a person must die is in most cases a rhetorical one. When Qoheleth inquires, "Why should you die before your time?" (Eccl. 7:17), he presupposes that wickedness and folly can cut life short, and that a specific time is set for each life (cf. Job 22:16). That a person is not permitted to kill without reason emerges from 1 S. 20:32, where Jonathan objects to Saul's intention to kill David: "Why should he be put to death? What has he done?"

The rhetorical nature of such questions emerges clearly from several passages. The Egyptians ask Joseph why they should die before his eyes, since he very well could provide them with bread (Gen. 47:15,19). The Israelites entreat Moses to intervene as a mediator for them at Horeb so they will not be consumed by the fire (Dt. 5:25). The prophet asks why the king and his people should die instead of giving up their resistance to the Babylonians (Jer. 27:12f.). Ezk. 18:31; 33:11 are concerned with either individual or — more likely — collective guilt that will result in death if not atoned. In all these instances, the question functions to emphasize the danger of impending death, prompting the correct conclusions to be drawn.

---

74. Cf. S. Tengström, *Die Toledotformel und die literarische Struktur der priesterlichen Erweiterungsschicht im Pentateuch. CB,* 17 (1982).

75. E. A. Speiser, *Genesis. AB,* I (1964), 41.

76. On the function of these high indications of age as a representation of temporal extension in the early period, cf. C. Westermann, *Genesis 1–11* (Eng. trans., Minneapolis, 1984), 353f.

2. *Sin.* Sin and the resulting guilt are sometimes given as the reason for death. Especially in the book of Ezekiel this is expressed in formulaic expressions which according to Rolf Knierim[77] reflect declaratory formulas from legal language (e.g., Dt. 24:16), although they have been reformulated by the prophet himself. Examples include *hû' rāšā' ba'ᵃwōnô yāmûṯ,* "that wicked man shall die because of his iniquity" (Ezk. 3:18; 33:8), and *wᵉ'āśâ 'āwel ûmēṯ 'ᵃlêhem bᵉ'awlô 'ᵃšer-'āśâ yāmûṯ,* "and commits iniquity and dies, then he dies for the iniquity which he has committed" (Ezk. 18:26; 33:18; cf. further Ezk. 3:19; 7:16; 18:17,18; 33:9,13; Jer. 31:30). Although the actual presence of guilt can be questioned, the fatal consequences cannot once such qualified guilt has been established (so, e.g., 1 S. 20:8; 2 S. 14:32).

While *'āwōn* and especially *'āwel* are used specifically by Ezekiel, *ḥēṭ'* and *ḥaṭṭā'ṯ* seem to be more commonly cited as reasons for death: Nu. 27:3; Dt. 24:16; 2 K. 14:6 par. 2 Ch. 25:4; Ezk. 3:20; 18:4,20; Am. 9:10. The principle that each person dies for his own sins is brought into focus in various ways. In the case of Ezekiel it should be noted that life and death are extremely vague concepts. "Life" shifts between "stay alive, survive," on the one hand, and "enjoy the fullness of life with God in a functioning covenantal relationship" on the other. The antithesis is "die" or "death," expressed by the formulas of the death sentence.[78]

Other causes of death include touching sacred objects (Ex. 19:12; Nu. 4:15,20; 2 S. 6:7; cf. 1 S. 6:19 *nkh* hiphil). Actually seeing God is considered even more life threatening. "No one can see God and live" (Ex. 33:20). Thus after Yahweh's angel has revealed itself, Manoah says: "We shall surely die, for we have seen God" (Jgs. 13:22).

Termini technici for capital guilt are *mišpaṭ-māweṯ* (Dt. 19:6; Jer. 26:11,16), *ḥēṭ' māweṯ* (Dt. 22:26), and *ḥēṭ' mišpaṭ-māweṯ* (Dt. 21:22). The corresponding transgressions are murder (Dt. 19), sexual trespass (Dt. 22), and false prophecy (Jer. 26); in all cases guilt is debated or even negated. Sacral transgressions "bring down capital guilt" upon the perpetrator (e.g., Ex. 28:43; Nu. 18:22). According to Knierim,[79] the original life setting *(Sitz im Leben)* of these expressions is to be found in the community legal assembly as such, something still discernible in Dt. 21:22; 24:16. In Nu. 18:22; 27:3, however, one can discern a transition to the sacral-legal sphere. Although some passages do indeed attest legal formulations, they "no longer belong to the sphere of actual execution of justice, but rather of proclamation" (Am. 9:10; Dt. 24:16, and passages dependent on them: 2 K. 14:6; 2 Ch. 25:4; cf. Ezk. 18:4,20; 3:20).[80]

3. *Manner of Death.* Death also comes upon a person in war, by the sword, through pestilence, and through hunger. Because a warrior is especially exposed to the threat of death, he can under certain circumstances be relieved of military obligation "lest he die in battle" (Dt. 20:5-7). In poetry such death in battle is described by several parallel expressions: *ḥālāl* par. *mēṯ, ḥereḇ* par. *milḥāmâ* (Isa. 22:2), *rā'āḇ* par. *milḥāmâ,*

---

77. P. 217.

78. W. Zimmerli, *Ezekiel 1. Herm* (Eng. trans. 1979), 383f.; → חיה *ḥāyâ (chāyāh),* IV, 336f.

79. P. 49.

80. This is the view represented by Knierim.

māweṯ par. *ḥereḇ* (Job 5:20), etc. The "dead" has been "pierced," the "sword" is the instrument of war, and pestilence and famine follow as consequences of war.[81]

Amos threatens both Jeroboam and "all the sinners of my people" with death by the sword (Am. 7:11; 9:10); in contrast, Jeremiah foretells not death by the sword for Zedekiah, but rather death "in peace" ((Jer. 34:4f.), assuming, of course, that he hears Yahweh's words. Like the qal forms, the hiphil and hophal forms of *mûṯ* also enter into fixed combinations with *ḥereḇ*. To slay by the sword means essentially "to execute" (2 K. 11:15,20 par. 2 Ch. 23:14,21; cf. 1 K. 1:51; 2:8). The sword is considered the instrument of killing (e.g., Jgs. 9:54; Jer. 41:2); in contrast, when David kills Goliath it is emphasized that he was not holding the sword in his hand (1 S. 17:50), but rather only drew it afterward (v. 51). 1 K. 19:17 emphasizes the inescapability of judgment; escaping "from the sword" of one enemy only leads to death at the hands of another.

Hunger, thirst, and pestilence can be listed either individually or together as the means of death. Moses allegedly planned to kill the people through hunger (Ex. 16:3); the Philistines are threatened with such death (Isa. 14:30), and it is a threat to Jeremiah as a result of his own imprisonment (Jer. 38:9). According to the people's own lament, they will be killed by thirst as a result of having been led into the wilderness (Ex. 17:3). Samson also fears death by thirst (Jgs. 15:18). Sennacherib wants to let the besieged inhabitants of Jerusalem die from both hunger *and* thirst (2 Ch. 32:11). Jeremiah threatens the inhabitants of Jerusalem with pestilence (Jer. 21:6), while Ps. 78:50 uses "death" and "pestilence" in parallel in its description of the Egyptian plagues.

Sequential enumeration of several different kinds of death is a favorite device in Jeremiah's and — less frequently — Ezekiel's threats. "Sword" and "pestilence" are syntactically combined with *mûṯ* in Jer. 11:22; 44:12; without *mûṯ* in Jer. 14:15,16,18; 16:4; 42:16; 44:27; Lam. 4:9. Although Ezk. 33:27 mentions "sword" and "pestilence," these terms are separated by the expression "food for the wild beasts," which could be viewed as an adaptation of the triple schema, with "hunger" as the middle member.[82] Cf. also 1 K. 14:11 (repeated in 16:4; 21:24), where the dead within the city walls are described as food for the dogs, those in the open country as food for the birds. Here, too, we have a kind of double schema for the kinds of death that accompany war.

The triple schema *baḥereḇ — bārāʿāḇ — baddeḇer,* "by sword — famine — pestilence," occurs no fewer than 15 times in Jeremiah, 5 of those together with *mûṯ* (Jer. 21:9; 27:13; 38:2; 42:17,22). This sequence usually remains constant, although Ezekiel varies and augments the schema more extensively. In Ezk. 5:12; 6:12; 7:15, we encounter the combination with *mûṯ,* to which 2 additional passages without the verb can be adduced. Perhaps Ezekiel acquired the schema from Jeremiah and modified it in the process.[83] In any case, it probably functions as an expression of complete annihilation: "sword" is emblematic of war itself; "famine" and "pestilence" then come in its wake to complete the harvest of death.

---

81. → דבר *deḇer (debher)* (III, 125-27).
82. See discussion below.
83. So Wächter, 138f.

VII. Death as Consequence.

1. *Qal.* The qal perfect consecutive serves to designate death as a consequence. The form *wāmēṯ* can indicate the consequence of the establishment of guilt (Gen. 44:9), of a wicked disposition (1 K. 1:52), or of murder (often in combination with *nkh* hiphil) (Ex. 21:12,20,28,35; 22:1[2]; Dt. 19:11f.; 2 S. 11:15). A conceivable but avoidable consequence can also be expressed by *wāmēṯ* (Gen. 19:19; 33:13; 44:22,31). In some cases the peril results from touching sacred objects (Nu. 4:15,20),[84] or through inappropriate clothing (Ex. 28:43). Finally, *wāmēṯ* refers to the consequence of the death penalty itself, either specified as stoning (Dt. 13:11[10]; 17:5; 21:21; 22:21,24) or left unspecified (Dt. 17:12; 18:20; 22:25; 24:7). The difference is that in the first case *wāmēṯ* concludes the judgment formula, whereas in the second the formula is introduced by *ûmēṯ*.

Qal imperfect forms can also refer to the consequences of capital crimes. In two cases the guilty party is "brought out" to die (*wᵉyāmōṯ,* Jgs. 6:30; 1 K. 21:10). The paronomastic expression *môṯ tāmûṯ* can be used to refer both to threats and to proclamations of a death sentence. If we view the giving of reasons as the criterion for judgments, then, e.g., 1 S. 14:44; 22:16; 2 K. 1:4,6,16; Jer. 26:8; Ezk. 3:18; 33:8,14 represent such judgments formulated in legal language; in contrast, e.g., Gen. 2:17;[85] 20:7; 1 K. 2:37,42 should be viewed as threats. The corresponding formulations in the 3rd person, *môṯ yāmûṯ(û),* usually occur outside the actual corpus of laws (Nu. 26:65; 1 S. 14:39; 2 S. 12:14; 2 K. 8:10) and, like *môṯ tāmûṯ,* can be understood as judgments or as threats. In a completely different fashion, *môṯ nāmûṯ* refers to the inescapability of death. In Jgs. 13:22, Manoah speaks to his wife about the deadly consequences of having seen God,[86] and in 2 S. 14:14 the common lot of all human beings is expressed this way.

Negated qal imperfect forms frequently refer to the avoidance of death. In this case, the negation *lō'* is used when death is indeed prevented (Jgs. 6:23; 1 S. 20:2; 2 S. 12:13; 19:24[23]), whereas *wᵉlō'* is usually used in statements in which such avoidance is dependent on certain conditions (e.g., Ex. 9:4; 21:18; 28:35; Lev. 16:2,13; Jer. 11:21; 38:24). The negation *pen* also follows conditions (Gen. 3:3; Lev. 10:6), while *wᵉ'al* occurs once with conditions (1 S. 12:19) and once without (Dt. 33:6). These rules do show exceptions: Ex. 9:4; 21:18; Isa. 51:14, and in the synthetic expressions used as pendent to *ḥyh.*[87]

2. *Hiphil.* Hiphil perfect consecutive forms occur partly in direct threats (Isa. 14:30; 65:15; Hos. 2:5[3]; 9:16), partly in conditional commands (Ex. 1:16; 2 S. 13:28), or in other consecutive clauses (Ex. 21:29; Nu. 14:15; 2 S. 14:32). The same is true of the hiphil imperfect forms: direct threats issued by prophets (1 K. 19:17; Isa. 11:4), death sentences stipulated in casuistic laws (Nu. 35:19,21), self-imposed threats (Gen. 42:37),

84. See VI.2 above.
85. See VI.2 above.
86. See VI.2 above.
87. See IX below.

extradition commands (Jgs. 20:13; 1 S. 11:12), etc. The guarantees of life (i.e., of safety) attested by oaths constitute an interesting group[88]: the oath partner is assured that he will not *('im)* be killed (e.g., 1 S. 30:15; 1 K. 1:51; 2:8; Jer. 38:16). Apart from the oath formula as such, pledges of safety also occur both with attendant conditions (1 S. 5:11; Jer. 38:25) and without (Jgs. 15:13; 1 K. 2:26).

3. *Hophal.* The hophal imperfect forms occur much more frequently both in threats and in legal stipulations concerning the death penalty (in contrast, the hophal perfect occurs only twice: Dt. 21:22; 2 S. 21:9). The imperfect forms appear in apodictic (?) and in casuistic laws as act-consequence prescriptions at the end of clauses (Ex. 21:29; 35:2; Lev. 24:16,21; Nu. 1:51; 3:10,38; 18:7). In Deuteronomy and narrative texts, on the other hand, the syntactical position of the act-consequence prescription *yûmaṯ* varies (Dt. 13:6[5]; 17:6; 24:16; Jgs. 6:31; 1 S. 20:32; 2 S. 19:23[22]; 1 K. 2:24; 2 Ch. 23:14; Jer. 38:4). Only 3 passages use the negated hophal imperfect (Lev. 19:20; Dt. 24:16; 2 K. 14:6).

The paronomastic act-consequence prescription *môṯ yûmāṯ/yûmᵉṯû* occurs primarily in three different contexts:

(1) In the participial laws in the Book of the Covenant, e.g., *makkēh 'îš wāmēṯ môṯ yûmāṯ,* "whoever strikes a man so that he dies shall be put to death unconditionally" (Ex. 21:12; cf. 21:15,16,17; 22:18[19]). Such legal statements have been described as apodictic;[89] although Ex. 22:18[19] is similarly constructed, it stands in a context with casuistic laws, and it may be that this law, too, originally stood in the other series and was later separated.[90]

Illman

Hans Jochen Boecker has brought to an appropriate end the discussion concerning the designation of the *môṯ yûmāṯ* legal statements as casuistic or apodictic. Their repeated assignment to casuistry,[91] which follows the lead of Albrecht Alt,[92] is controverted by the fact that here the complicated conditional formulation is replaced by a concentrated participial construction. Stereotypical formulations and series construction militate further against casuistic qualification. "All these points taken together can lead to only one conclusion: the understanding of law here is quite different from that expressed in casuistic principles. Whereas the latter originally referred to an actual legal case, classified it, and made a judgement on it, the principles of the series under

88. Cf. G. Giesen, *Die Wurzel* שבע *"schwören." BBB,* 56 (1981), 90-105.
89. H. J. Boecker, *Law and the Administration of Justice in the OT and Ancient East* (Eng. trans., Minneapolis, 1980), 191-207.
90. *Ibid.,* 196.
91. H. Gese, "Beobachtungen zum Stil alttestamentlicher Rechtssätze," *ThLZ,* 85 (1960), 147-150; R. Kilian, "Apodiktisches und kasuistisches Recht im Licht ägyptischer Analogien," *BZ,* N.S. 7 (1963), 185-202; E. Gerstenberger, *Wesen und Herkunft des "apodiktischen Rechts." WMANT,* 20 (1965).
92. "The Origins of Israelite Law," *Essays on OT History and Religion* (Eng. trans., Oxford, 1966), 79-132.

discussion are independent of any actual event. The case is described in quite general and abstract terms. . . . These principles mark out a frontier which none may overstep."[93]

Fabry

(2) Lev. 20 with a series of similarly formulated laws, e.g., *'îš 'îš 'ašer yeqallēl 'eṯ-'āḇîw we'eṯ-'immô môṯ yûmāṯ,* "every one who curses his father or his mother shall be put to death unconditionally" (Lev. 20:9; cf. vv. 2,10,11,12,13,15,16,27). As a rule, this schema concludes with the bloodguilt formula *dāmāw bô,* "his blood is upon him," or *demêhem bām,* "their blood is upon them." While Lev. 20:9, like Ex. 21:17, prohibits cursing one's parents, Lev. 20:2,27 directs itself against foreign cultic practices and vv. 10-16 against sexual trespasses of various sorts. These laws probably reflect a later stage of development than does Ex. 21.

(3) Nu. 35:16,17,18,21,31 contain a further series of similarly formulated laws, although without the tight structure of the previously mentioned formulations. They have been "casuistically relaxed," and the act-consequence prescription *môṯ yûmāṯ* no longer has the legal community itself as subject, but rather the blood avenger (cf. vv. 19,21). With the exception of v. 31, the crime is intentional murder. The variations concern weapons used in the murder.

The *môṯ yûmāṯ* formula is also found in a series of other laws (Ex. 31:14,15; Lev. 24:16,17; 27:29; Nu. 15:35) and threats (Gen. 26:11; Jgs. 21:5; Ezk. 18:13). One striking observation is the presence of the participial form at the beginning and the act-consequence prescription at the end even in a narrative text such as Gen. 26:11, which shows that legal formulations exerted an influence far beyond legal contexts in the narrower sense. Ex. 19:12 occupies a middle position: whoever touches the holy mountain shall be put to death.[94]

Illman

The question of the origin of these *môṯ yûmāṯ* series of legal principles has drawn the attention of various scholars;[95] the results clearly reveal the nomadic origin of this type of law.[96] Whether the *môṯ yûmāṯ* formula is by origin a formulation of the death penalty[97] or whether because of a lack of concrete indicators concerning this punishment it more likely served as a declaration that a person was worthy of death[98] will probably be decided in the latter sense. This would mean, however, that in Israel the

---

93. Boecker, 196.

94. Cf. VI.2 above.

95. V. Wagner, *Rechtssätze in gebundener Sprache und Rechtssatzreihen im israelitischen Recht. BZAW,* 127 (1972); G. Liedke, *Gestalt und Bezeichnung alttestamentlicher Rechtssätze. WMANT,* 39 (1971); Schulz; W. Schottroff, *Der altisraelitische Fluchspruch. WMANT,* 30 (1969).

96. Wagner, 29.

97. Boecker, 197.

98. So H. U. Cazelles, *Études sur le code de l'alliance* (Paris, 1946); Schulz; H. Graf Reventlow, "Kultisches Recht im AT," *ZThK,* 60 (1963), 267-304.

death penalty originally ended without *mûṯ,* something not without consequences for semantic considerations concerning this root.

Fabry

4. *Other Expressions.* The subst. *māweṯ* is used in two combinations as an expression of a threat. One oath formula, beginning with *ḥay-YHWH,* "as Yahweh lives," and the threat formula *ben/b^e^nê-māweṯ,* "doomed to death (RSV 'deserves to die')," with a subject occurs in 1 S. 26:16; 2 S. 12:5 (cf. also 1 S. 20:31). Yet another threat formula is *'îš/'anšê-māweṯ* with the same meaning (2 S. 19:29[28]; 1 K. 2:26).

Combinations of various sorts frequently occur with *mûṯ* and other verbs. The observation *w^e^hinnēh nōpēl mēṯ* has already been mentioned.[99] The terms *mûṯ* and *npl* are used as a parallel and semantically equivalent pair in Jer. 44:12; Ezk. 5:12; 6:12; 33:27 within the framework of the triplet schema about death in war. In the synthetic parallelism *nāpal/wayyippōl . . . wayyāmoṯ,* "he fell . . . and died" (2 S. 1:4; 2:23), the two verbs refer to the same event. In 1 S. 31:5, *npl* apparently refers to a preceding act: Saul plunges into his own sword, after which he dies.

The situation of "seeking to kill" someone is expressed by variations of *biqqēš l^e^hāmîṯ* (Ex. 4:24; 1 S. 19:2; 2 Sam. 20:19; 1 K. 11:40; Ps. 37:32; Jer. 26:21). This is an idiom (cf. also Gen. 37:18 with a different verb for the attempt, *nkl* hithpael, "behave cunningly, deceitfully") expressing wickedness. Another idiom consists of combinations of *ḥāpēṣ,* "wish, delight in, be inclined toward," and *mûṯ: ḥāpēṣ l^e^hāmîṯ* (Jgs. 13:23; 1 S. 2:25) and *ḥāpēṣ b^e^môṯ* (Ezk. 18:23,32; 33:11), both with Yahweh as subject. But while the first passage still countenances the fact that Yahweh means to kill someone, Ezekiel completely excludes this possibility: God does not want the death of the sinner, but rather for the sinner to repent and stay alive.

Although the combination of *nkh* in the hiphil and *mûṯ* in the hiphil or qal does occur in legal texts, the overwhelming majority of occurrences are in narrative texts. In the first case we have expressions for striking someone so that he dies, and the consequences of the act: *wāmēṯ(û)* (Ex. 21:12,20; 22:1[2]; Dt. 19:11) and the sequence *hikkāhû wayyāmoṯ,* ". . . he struck him down so that he died" (Nu. 35:16,17,18,21) with the casuistic indication of the instrument used in striking. In the second case we have on the one hand the qal form *wayyāmoṯ* as consequence or complement to *hikkâ* (2 S. 1:15; 10:18; 11:21; 20:10; 2 K. 12:21f.[20f.]; 25:25), and on the other hand the combination of two synonyms: *wayyaḵ . . . wayyāmeṯ* (Josh. 10:26; 11:17; 1 S. 17:35,50; 2 S. 4:7; 14:6; 18:15; 21:17; 1 K. 16:10; 2 K. 15:25; Jer. 41:2; 52:27). To these we can add the previously mentioned conspiracy schemata.[100] In contrast with those schemata, the combinations with *hikkâ* and *mûṯ/hēmîṯ* are not formulaic in and of themselves, but sooner constitute synthetic parallels for death by striking, an observation also supported by a consideration of their extremely varied use.[101]

---

99. See III.4 above.
100. V.2.
101. → נכה *nkh.*

Yet another combination of two synonyms is that with → הרג *hārag* and *mûṯ*. In 2 Ch. 24:25, *hrg* takes the place of *hikkâ* in the conspiracy schema. In Jer. 18:21, we have two parallel constructions: *h^a^rugê māweṯ,* "slaughtered to death," and *mukkê-ḥereḇ,* "slain by the sword." In Prov. 24:11, *māweṯ* and *hereg* stand parallel. In Lev. 20:16, *w^e^hāragtā,* "you shall kill," anticipates proleptically the act-consequence prescription *mûṯ yûmāṯû,* and in Dt. 13:10 the expression *hārōg tahargennû,* "you shall kill him," precedes the inf. *lah^a^mîṯô,* "to put him to death." This does show at least that *hrg,* like *hikkâ* albeit less frequently, is used either in synthetic or synonymous parallelism with *mûṯ/hēmîṯ* or parallel and synonymously with it.

The legal prescriptions concerning stoning as a death penalty[102] have apparently also influenced several narratives about the actual carrying out of this penalty. 1 K. 21 (the stoning of Naboth) restates several times the combination *sql bā'^a^ḇānîm,* "to stone," and *mûṯ* (vv. 10,13,14,15); and 1 K. 12:18 (par. 2 Ch. 10:18) uses *rgm 'eḇen* and *mûṯ*. It is quite clear here that the carrying out of the death penalty was described without *mûṯ* hiphil. Here the presence of *mûṯ* merely ascertains the actual event of death itself as a result of stoning. Helen Schüngel-Straumann[103] points out that stoning occurs in those cases in which blood revenge is excluded. In neither case does the act of killing cause bloodguilt, which is also why stoning was preferred to killing with a sword.

The law does not sanction the trodding *(rms)* of the royal official *(šālîš)* in the gate at Samaria, although the prophet Elisha did foretell his death (2 K. 7:17-20). Benaiah's attack on Solomon's enemies (1 K. 2:25,34,46) is expressed by *pg'-b^e^* plus *wayyāmoṯ,* whereby the first verb should apparently be translated "strike down" (cf. v. 29). In contrast, in Nu. 35:19, where the right of the blood avenger is established, the expression *b^e^pig'ô-ḇô* sooner means "where he meets him," "when he meets him."

In summary we can say that despite clear distinctions between the legal prescriptions on the one hand and actual threats on the other, one can indeed discern the influence of legal formulations on narrative texts. The pronouncement of punishment in the latter texts is primarily *môṯ tāmûṯ* or *môṯ yāmûṯ(û),* whereas the laws themselves usually have *môṯ yûmāṯ(û)* in that position. The simple expression *yûmaṯ/yum^e^ṯû* is used in both types of texts, which could attest just this sort of influence, especially when the pronouncement of punishment or the act-consequence prescription stands at the end of the judgment.

VIII. 1. *The Dead.* When the dead person (*mēṯ* ptcp.) refers to someone slain in battle (Nu. 19:16,18; Isa. 22:2; Ezk. 28:8; Ps. 88:6[5]), the parallel expression *ḥālāl,* "pierced (RSV 'slain')," or something similar occasionally also occurs. In the realm of the dead the *mēṯîm* are also called *r^e^pā'îm,* "spirits of the dead, shadows" (e.g., Isa. 26:14,19; Ps. 88:11[10]).[104] The expression *k^e^mēṯê 'ôlām,* "like those long dead" (Ps.

---

102. Cf. VII.1 above.

103. P. 140.

104. On the discussion of this term, cf. W. J. Horwitz, "The Significance of the Rephaim," *JNSL,* 7 (1979), 37-43; J. F. Healy, "*MLKM/RP'UM* and the *KISPUM,*" *UF,* 10 (1979), 89-91; C. E. L'Heureux, *Rank Among the Canaanite Gods: El, Ba'al, and the Repha'im. HSM,* 21 (1979).

143:3; Lam. 3:6), similarly refers to the shadowy existence characterizing the realm of the dead.

Contact with a dead body causes uncleanness, against which certain legal prescriptions were formulated. Again, two schemata recur: *ng'*, "to touch" — *mēṯ* — *ṭm'*, "be unclean" (e.g., Lev. 11:31; Nu. 19:11,13,16), and *lō' yāḇô'* ("not visit, go in") — *mēṯ* — *ṭm'* (e.g., Lev. 21:11; Nu. 6:6f.; Ezk. 44:25). Whereas the first schema establishes uncleanness as the result of touching, the second is directed to the high priest (Lev. 21:11), "the levitical priests" (Ezk. 44:25), and the Nazirites (Nu. 6:6ff.) as groups especially obligated to exercise caution in such matters.

The expression *keleḇ mēṯ*, "a dead dog" (1 S. 24:15[14]; 2 S. 9:8; 16:9), is used in a comparison between the king and his (supposed) enemy, and serves as an extremely pejorative expression for a person.[105]

2. *The Netherworld.* Death *(māweṯ)* is also used as a designation for the realm of the dead or the "sphere of death," functioning as an equivalent to *šᵉ'ôl.* In this sense references are made to *ša'ᵃrê māweṯ*, "gates of death" (Ps. 9:14[13]; 107:18; Job 38:17; cf. *ša'ᵃrê šᵉ'ôl*, Isa. 38:10), *mišbᵉrê-māweṯ*, "waves of death," *ḥeḇlê-māweṯ*, "cords of death," *môqᵉšê-māweṯ*, "snares of death" (2 S. 22:5f. par. Ps. 18:5f. [4f.]; Ps. 116:3; Prov. 13:14; 14:27). Variations include *naḥᵃlê bᵉliyya'al*, "torrents of Belial," and *ḥeḇlê šᵉ'ôl*, "cords of Sheol" (2 S. 22:5f.). Additional metaphors for the netherworld are *kᵉlê-māweṯ*, "weapons of death" (Ps. 7:14[13]), *ḥaḏrê-māweṯ*, "halls, chambers of death" (Prov. 7:27), etc. These show that the realm of the dead was conceived on the one hand spatially ("gates," "halls"), and on the other as a chaotic, terrifying condition ("waves," "torrents," "cords," "snares," "weapons"). This was probably part of the common mythology of the Mediterranean world.

The parallel nature of *māweṯ* and *šᵉ'ôl* emerges from several other passages as well. Isa. 28:15,18 speaks of a "covenant with death" *(bᵉrîṯ 'eṯ-māweṯ)* and, parallel with that, of a "pact with Sheol" *(ḥāzûṯ 'eṯ-šᵉ'ôl).* Rather than thinking here, e.g., of the god of death Osiris, we should probably assume with Hans Wildberger[106] that Isaiah was able to use these expressions metaphorically "because people in Jerusalem at that time were familiar with rituals through which they believed they could protect themselves against the powers of death." Further combinations of *māweṯ* and *šᵉ'ôl* illustrate "the descent into the netherworld" (Ps. 55:16[15]; Prov. 5:5; 7:27), "the fate of the rich" (Ps. 49:15[14]), "the transitoriness of life" (Ps. 89:49[48]), "that no one praises God in Sheol" (Isa. 38:18), and "the strength of love" (Cant. 8:6).

Other parallels with *māweṯ* occur less frequently: *qeḇer*, "the grave" (Isa. 53:9), *'ᵃḇaddôn*, "the (place of) destruction" (Job 28:22; cf. 26:6). These, too, are expressions referring to the sphere of death.

The transitoriness of life comes to expression in Ps. 89:48f.(47f.): "Remember, O Lord, what the measure of life is, for what vanity thou hast created all the sons of men!

---

105. → כלב *keleḇ* (VII, 146-157).
106. *Jesaja (28-39). BK,* X/3 (1982), 1073.

What man can live and never see death *(māweṯ)*? Who can deliver his soul from the power of Sheol *(miyyaḏ-š^e'ôl)*?" The word *mûṯ* itself is often absent from such pessimistic observations. According to Ps. 90:3ff., the transitoriness of human beings is God's work: "Thou turnest man back to the dust, and sayest, 'Turn back, O children of men' " (v. 3). "Thou sowest them . . . they are like grass; in the morning it flourishes and is renewed; in the evening it fades and withers" (vv. 5f.). God's own wrath is given as the reason (vv. 7,11). "Man cannot abide in his pomp, he is like the beasts that perish" (Ps. 49:13[12]; cf. v. 21[20]).

In this context, Eccl. 12:7 follows Gen. 3:19: "You are dust *('āp̄ār)*, and to dust you shall return [i.e., you shall become dust again]." This statement was apparently taken as a general decree concerning mortality, since Gen. 3:22 refuses humans access to the tree of life, which could bestow "eternal" life. Thus the formula *môṯ tāmûṯ*[107] could also become a general statement concerning human mortality, human disobedience being given as the reason for this mortality.

A person should be mindful of the transitoriness of life: "So teach us to count our days that we may get a wise heart" (Ps. 90:12). The statement cited by Isaiah, "Let us eat and drink, for tomorrow we die" (Isa. 22:13), is condemned as frivolous thinking. On the other hand, Deutero-Isaiah admonishes his listeners not to fear "men who die [i.e., who are mortal]" (Isa. 51:12); only Yahweh, the creator, is to be feared.

Occasionally the general mortality of all human beings is juxtaposed with the unusual death of certain persons. Thus Moses says of Korah, Dathan, and Abiram: "If these men die the common death of all men, or if they are visited by the fate of all men, then Yahweh has not sent me" (Nu. 16:29). Yahweh's response follows in v. 33: "So they with all that belonged to them went down alive into Sheol." This apparently refers to a sudden death. The petitioner in Ps. 55:16(15) wishes the same upon his enemies, i.e., divine judgment attesting their injustice. Although it is the common lot of human beings that a person's name perishes with him in death (Ps. 41:6[5]), Prov. 11:7f. seems to presuppose a distinction between the righteous and the wicked regarding their hope beyond death (?). Just what this implies, however, remains unclear. In contrast, Eccl. 3:19 even asserts that there is no difference between human beings and beasts: "as one dies, so dies the other" *(k^emôṯ zeh kēn môṯ zeh)*.

IX. Death and Life. Besides a series of various combinations of *mûṯ/māweṯ* and its opposite *ḥyh/ḥayyîm,*[108] combinations juxtaposing "death" and "birth" occur only rarely. The examples "a time to be born, and a time to die" (*'ēṯ lāleḏeṯ w^e'ēṯ lāmûṯ,* Eccl. 3:2), and "a good name is better than precious ointment, and the day of death, than the day of birth" (Eccl. 7:1), are well known. Mention should also be made of Hos. 9:16, where the prophet punctuates his threat of childlessness in the prediction that even if children were to be born, Yahweh would slay them.

---

107. See VII.3 above.

108. → חיה *ḥāyâ (chāyāh)* (IV, 324-344).

The terms *ḥyh* and *mûṯ* are combined in the inclusive phrases "live and not die." Such clauses serve to underscore what has been said, either as an assurance of life or as the desire to preserve it (e.g., Gen. 42:2; 43:8; 47:19; Nu. 4:19; Dt. 33:6; 2 K. 18:32; Ps. 118:17 [concerning this psalm cf. also the content of Ps. 116:8f.]; Ezk. 18:21,28; 33:15). The reverse combination "die and not live" occurs less frequently (2 K. 20:1 par. Isa. 38:1; Job 14:14; Ps. 89:49[48]).

Other combinations present death and life as alternatives resulting from correct decisions (e.g., Gen. 19:19f.; 20:7; 42:18,20; Dt. 5:24-26; Jer. 27:12f.; Ezk. 18:23,32; 33:11). According to Deuteronomistic theology, the God of the covenant has given human beings the choice between life and death *(ntn lipnê . . . ḥayyîm/māweṯ),* good and evil, blessing and curse (Dt. 30:15,19), in the hope that a person will choose life. This can also be expressed by saying that the concern is with the correct choice of paths in a concrete situation (Jer. 21:8) or in the reflections of wisdom (Prov. 5:5; 8:35f.; 11:19; 12:28; 13:14; 14:27; 16:14f.; 18:21). The difference is that Deuteronomistic theology is addressing the people or cultic community as a whole, while the two-path teaching from the wisdom tradition is addressing the individual.

One frequent juxtaposition is that of the "living" and the "dead," expressed by the ptcps. *ḥay* and *mēṯ*. The reference is usually to a concrete situation without abstract significance (e.g., Ex. 21:35; Nu. 17:13[16:48]; 2 S. 12:18,21; 19:7[6]; 1 K. 3:22,23). Isa. 8:19, however, refers to the interrogation of the dead (i.e., of the spirits of the dead — *'ōḇôṯ* or *yiddeʿōnîm*) by the living, a practice punishable by death (Lev. 19:31; 20:6,27; Dt. 18:10f.) but nonetheless employed in critical situations (e.g., 1 S. 28).

A contradiction arises between Eccl. 4:2 and 9:5. In the first instance Qoheleth pronounces the dead more fortunate than the living, and in the second he says that the living are more fortunate because they at least know they are to die, whereas the dead know nothing at all. This leads to the proverb "a living dog is better than a dead lion" (9:4), which, intended ironically, seeks to disclose the questionable character of life.[109]

Job 14:14 poses the rhetorical question: "If a man die, shall he live again?" The obviously negative answer is given, e.g., in Isa. 26:14. The universal law that the dead do not live again is, however, limited here to enemies, so that an option emerges for Israel. Thus in Isa. 26:19 God's pledge is given that Israel's dead (cf. vv. 7,19,20) will nonetheless live again *(yiḥyû mēṯeyḵā).*[110] As an oracle of salvation responding to the preceding lament of the people (vv. 7-18), this statement is referring not to the resurrection of individuals, but rather metaphorically to the reestablishment of Israel itself.[111] The assertion in Ezk. 37 concerning the dead skeletons that are to live again can be understood similarly, although here the term *yāḇēš,* "dry," is used instead of *mēṯ.*[112] Cf. also Hos. 6:2; Am. 5:2.[113]

---

109. A. Lauha, *Kohelet. BK,* XIX (1978), *in loc.*

110. Cf. F. J. Helfmeyer, " 'Deine Toten — meine Leichen': Heilszusage und Annahme in Jes 26,19," *Bausteine biblischer Theologie. Festschrift G. J. Botterweck. BBB,* 50 (1977), 245-258.

111. So Wildberger, *in loc.*

112. Cf. E. Haag, "Ez 37 und der Glaube an die Aufweckung der Toten," *TrThZ,* 82 (1973), 78-92.

113. → חיה *ḥāyâ (chāyāh)* (IV, 324-344).

Yahweh is a God who "kills and makes alive" (Dt. 32:39; 1 S. 2:6; cf. 2 K. 5:7). It is difficult to determine whether this is to be understood as a sign of a certain duplicity in Yahweh's being, or rather as a bipolar expression of the fact that Yahweh is the ultimate cause of everything (cf. Isa. 45:6f.). Like earthly kings as well (Ex. 1:16; 2 S. 8:2; Est. 4:11), he is certainly lord of life and death. This also manifests itself in the fact that he can deliver *(hiṣṣîl)* a person from death (Ps. 33:19; 56:14[13]; 86:13; 116:8,9). This is not a reference to the resurrection of the dead, but rather more likely to the healing of certain illnesses which in and of themselves are already viewed as belonging to the sphere of death (cf. Akk. *muballiṭ mîtē*).[114] However, he can also plunge a person into Sheol (Job 30:23). One petition motif, namely, that God might deliver a person from Sheol, is generated by the fact that no praise of God is possible in Sheol, i.e., that the relationship with God is broken off (cf. Isa. 38:18,19). Just what is meant here concretely by the assertion that God will not give his faithful over to death in any final sense (e.g., Ps. 49:16[15]; 73:23-26) is still somewhat puzzling. Although it is clear *that* he will deliver a person, we are not told *how* this will happen.

Only apocalyptic texts assert that God will destroy death once and for all (*bl'* piel, Isa. 25:8; considering the context, this might perhaps refer rather to the elimination of weeping and all mourning) and will awaken individuals for judgment and eternal life (Dnl. 12:2). The notion of the immortality of the soul then establishes its presence in the Wisdom Literature outside the protocanonical writings.[115]

Illman

X. Qumran. The root *mwt* is attested with extraordinary frequency in the writings of Qumran, and a particular concentration can be discerned in the Temple scroll. The verb occurs 56 times (34 in 11QT), the noun 14 times (twice in 11QT). What is surprising is that except for 1QH (anthropological contexts) and CD the fundamental texts of the Qumran community do not use this root.

Although belief in a beyond was self-evident in Qumran,[116] and although the resurrection hope which grew rampantly especially during the intertestamental period had also been taken up,[117] the total absence of any mention of death or of dying in the community's significant texts is striking.[118] The Essene petitioner describes himself as a "worm of the dead" (1QH 6:34; 11:12), oppressed by the "waves of death" (1QH 3:8,9; 9:4), and

---

114. See I.2 above.

115. Cf. the extensive literature on the problem of resurrection, and Kellermann, *ZThK*, 73 (1976), 259ff.

116. Cf. R. B. Laurin, "The Question of Immortality in the Qumran 'Hodayot,'" *JSS*, 3 (1958), 344-355; J. van der Ploeg, "The Belief in Immortality in the Writings of Qumrân," *BiOr*, 18 (1961), 118-124.

117. Cf. K. Schubert, "Das Problem der Auferstehungshoffnung in den Qumrantexten und in der frührabbinischen Literatur," *WZKM*, 56 (1960), 154-167.

118. Cf. H. Lichtenberger, *Studien zum Menschenbild in Texten der Qumrangemeinde. StUNT*, 15 (1980), 219ff.

surrounded by Belial and his "cords of death" (3:28),[119] standing before the "gates of death" (6:24). CD and the Temple scroll use *mwt* almost exclusively in legal contexts, where the following focal points emerge: the death penalty is imposed in the case of crimes worthy of death (*dᵉḇar māweṯ,* CD 9:6,17), a penalty which peculiarly is to be carried out by pagans (CD 9:1), or in the case of capital crimes (*ḥṭ['] mšpṭ mwt,* 11QT 64:9) by stoning (11QT 64:6; 66:2,5) or by "hanging on a tree" (*tlh ʿlʿṣ,* 11QT 64:8,9,11; it is doubtful that this refers to punishment by crucifixion[120]); prescriptions against defilement resulting from contact with the dead occupy a great deal of space (CD 12:18; 11QT 49; 50). Qumran had a special law governing the establishment of cemeteries (11QT 48).

The root *mwt* also appears in the context of the voluntary oath obligating a person to community membership. The sodalist is not to break this oath even at the "price of death" (*ʿaḏ mᵉḥîr māweṯ,* CD 16:8).

1QSb 5:25 applies the notion of the power of the word, a concept also familiar to the OT itself (cf. Jer. 23:29; 51:20), to the teacher *(maśkîl):* he will smite the peoples with the power of his mouth and bring death to the ungodly with the breath of his lips (cf. Isa. 11:4).

Fabry

---

119. → חבל *ḥbl* (IV, 172-79).

120. This is the conclusion of J. M. Baumgarten, "Does *TLH* in the Temple Scroll Refer to Crucifixion?" *JBL,* 91 (1972), 472-481; *idem, Studies in Qumran Law. StJLA,* 24 (1977), 172-182; cf. also J. M. Ford, " 'Crucify him, crucify him' and the Temple Scroll," *ExpT,* 87 (1976), 275-78; L. D. Merino, *Estudios Eclesiasticos,* 51 (1976), 5-27; *idem,* "El Suplico de la cruz en la literatura judia intertestamental," *SBFLA,* 26 (1976), 48-69; J. Finegan, "Crosses in the Dead Sea Scrolls," *BAR,* 5/6 (1979), 41-49.

מִזְבֵּחַ *mizbēaḥ*

Contents: I. 1. Etymology; 2. Occurrences and Distribution; 3. LXX; 4. Hypostatization. II. 1. Religio-historical Considerations; 2. Ancient Near East; a. Egypt; b. Mesopotamia; c. Asia Minor; d. Syria; e. Arabia. III. OT: 1. General Considerations; 2. The Altar; a. The Patriarchal Period; b. The Mosaic Period; c. Prior to Construction of the Temple; d. Solomon's Temple; e. Prior to the Exile; f. Ezekiel's Draft Constitution; 3.a. Blood Rite; b. Altar Horns; c. Asylum; d. Altar Service; e. Idol Worship. IV. Qumran.

---

mizbēaḥ. Y. Aharoni, "The Horned Altar of Beer-sheba," *BA,* 37 (1974), 2-6; W. F. Albright, "The Babylonian Temple-Tower and the Altar of Burnt-offering," *JBL,* 39 (1920), 137-142; A. Biran, "An Israelite Horned Altar at Dan," *BA,* 37 (1974), 106f.; *idem,* ed., *Temples and High Places in Biblical Times* (Jerusalem, 1981); J. P. Brown, "The Sacrificial Cult and its Critique in Greek and Hebrew. II. The Altar and 'High Place,' " *JSS,* 25 (1980), 1-21; T. A. Busink, *Der Tempel von Jerusalem. StFS,* 3, I (1970); II (1980); M. Cogan, "The Ahaz Altar: On the Problem

I. 1. Etymology. The substantive form *mizbēaḥ* (*mäzbēḥ* with Babylonian pointing[1]) derives from the common Semitic root *zbḥ*;[2] consistent with the distribution of this root,[3] equivalents of *mizbēaḥ* are also attested throughout the Semitic linguistic sphere.[4] Following the semantic scope of Heb. *zāḇaḥ,* "slaughter, perform a *zeḇaḥ* ritual, sacrifice,"[5] *mizbēaḥ* can refer to the slaughter site, to the place of *zeḇaḥ,* and to the sacrificial site in the general sense. No original meaning emerges from this usage; rather, the element common to all these meanings stands in the foreground, and the

---

of Assyrian Cults in Judah," *Proceedings of the Sixth World Congress of Jewish Studies,* I (Jerusalem, 1977), 119-124 [Heb.]; D. Conrad, *Studien zum Altargesetz: Ex 20:24-26* (diss., Marburg, 1968); *idem,* "Einige (archäologische) Miszellen zur Kultgeschichte Judas in der Königszeit," *Textgemäss. Festschrift E. Würthwein* (Göttingen, 1979), 28-32; *idem,* "Der neugefundene Altar von Beerscheba," *ZDMGSup,* 4 (1980), 116; L. F. De Vries, *Incense Altars from the Period of the Judges and Their Significance* (diss., Southern Baptist Theological Seminary, 1975); B. Diebner and H. Schult, "Die Stellung der Jerusalemer Orthodoxie zu den Yhwh-Altären der Diaspora," *Diehlheimer Blätter,* 7 (1974), 33-37; M. Forte, "Sull' origine di alcuni tipi di altarini sud-arabici," *AION,* N.S. 17 (1967), 97-120; V. Fritz, *Tempel und Zelt. WMANT,* 47 (1977); N. H. Gadegaard, "On the So-called Burnt Offering Altar in the OT," *PEQ,* 110 (1978), 35-45; K. Galling, *Der Altar in den Kulturen des Alten Orients* (Berlin, 1925); N. Glueck, "Incense Altars," *ErIsr,* 10 (1971), 120-25 [Heb.], XII [Eng. summary]; M. Görg, "Der Altar — Theologische Dimensionen im AT," *Freude am Gottesdienst. Festschrift J. G. Plöger* (Stuttgart, 1983), 291-306; J. de Groot, *Die Altäre des salomonischen Tempelhofes. BWAT,* N.S. 6 (1924); M. Haran, *Temples and Temple-Service in Ancient Israel* (Oxford, 1978); J. Henninger, *Das Opfer bei den Arabern* (diss., Fribourg, 1944), abr. *Arabica Sacra = Contributions à l'histoire religieuse de l'Arabie et de ses régions limitrophes. OBO,* 40 (1981), 189-203; H. W. Hertzberg, "Der heilige Fels und das AT," Beiträge zur Traditionsgeschichte und Theologie des AT (Göttingen, 1962), 45-53; P. Kübel, "Epiphanie und Altarbau," *ZAW,* 83 (1971), 225-231; E. Kutsch, "Gideons Berufung und Altarbau Jdc 6,11-24," *ThLZ,* 81 (1956), 75-84; R. de Langhe, "L'autel d'or du temple de Jérusalem," *Bibl,* 40 (1959), 476-494; J. Morgenstern, *The Fire upon the Altar* (Leiden, 1963); E. W. Nicholson, "Blood-spattered Altars?" *VT,* 27 (1977), 113-17; H. T. Obbink, "The Horns of the Altar in the Semitic World, Especially in Jahwism," *JBL,* 56 (1937), 43-49; A. Parrot, "Autels de terre à Mari," *Archäologie und AT. Festschrift K. Galling* (Tübingen, 1970), 219-224; M. Popko, *Kultobjekte in der Hethitischen Religion nach Keilschriftlichen Quellen* (Warsaw, 1978); G. Rinaldi, "Mizbaḥ 'ădāmâ," *BeO,* 16 (1974), 192; E. Robertson, "The Altar of Earth (Exodus XX, 24-26)," *JJS,* 1 (1948), 12-21; G. Ryckmans, "Sud-arabe mḏbḥt = hébreu mzbḥ et termes apparentés," *Festschrift W. Caskel* (Leiden, 1968), 253-260; N. H. Snaith, "The Altar at Gilgal: Joshua XXII 23-29," *VT,* 28 (1978), 330-35; J. J. Stamm, "Zum Altargesetz im Bundesbuch," *ThZ,* 1 (1945), 304-6; F. J. Stendebach, "Altarformen im kanaanäisch-israelitischen Raum," *BZ,* N.S. 20 (1976), 180-196; E. Stern, "Note on a Decorated Limestone Altar from Lachish," *'Atiqot* 11 (1976), 107-9; E. D. Van Buren, "Akkadian Stepped Altars," *Numen,* 1 (1954), 228-234; *idem,* "Places of Sacrifice ('Opferstätten')," *Iraq,* 14 (1952), 76-92; P. H. Vaughan, *The Meaning of bāmâ in the OT. SOTS Mon, 3* (1974); L. H. Vincent, "L'autel des holocaustes et le caractère du temple d'Ezéchiël," *Analecta Bollandiana,* 67 1949), 7-20; H. W. Wiener, "The Altars of the OT," *BOLZ,* 1927; → זבח *zāḇaḥ (zābhach)* (IV, 8-29); → במה *bāmâ (bāmāh)* (II, 139-145).

1. Thus P. Kahle.
2. *BLe,* §61rζ.
3. → זבח *zāḇaḥ (zābhach),* IV, 8-11.
4. *HAL,* II (1995), 564.
5. → זבח *zāḇaḥ (zābhach),* IV, 11.

general translation "altar" is thus justified, especially since as a result of semantic transformation the term *mizbēaḥ* can in Hebrew also refer to the incense altar and similar structures.

2. *Occurrences and Distribution.* The noun *mizbēaḥ* occurs 401 times in the OT;[6] in Gen. 33:20 one should read *maṣṣēḇâ* with *BHS* instead of *mizbēaḥ,*[7] and in 2 Ch. 28:2 *mizbēaḥ* instead of → מסכה *massēḵâ* (III.1); to these can be added 4 occurrences in Sirach (Sir. 47:9; 50:11,14,19) and the Aramaic form *maḏbaḥ* in Ezr. 7:17. The majority of occurrences are in the Priestly writings (59 in Exodus; 87 in Leviticus; 29 in Numbers) and in the historical writings (35 in 1 Kings; 28 in 2 Kings; 10 in 1 Chronicles; 39 in 2 Chronicles); other books attesting high frequency are Genesis (13 times), Deuteronomy (10), Joshua (15), Judges (12), and Ezekiel (18).

3. *LXX.* The LXX renders *mizbēaḥ* primarily with *thysiastērion;* 23 times it uses *bōmós,* though only in reference to illegitimate pagan altars.[8]

4. *Hypostatization.* Among the cultic hypostases attested especially in the first millennium in the pantheon of ancient Syria[9] one also finds a deity called *mdbḥ.* J. T. Milik[10] views the personal name *'šm-mdbḥ* as evidence for the cult of this deity "altar." Veneration of an altar as *Zeús Mádbachos (mdbḥ)* is attested in proximity of Aleppo. "This god is not some *Zeús Bōmios* or Beʿel Madbachâ, i.e., a numen dwelling within the stone; rather, the altar stone itself is for this community the tangible manifestation of the highest god."[11] Similar interpretations are found in the case of Baítylos/Baitýlion within the Phoenician-Punic sphere.[12]

II. 1. *Religio-historical Considerations.* Historically, altars came about when a specific place was set apart for the bringing of offerings; this already encompasses the two features characteristic of altars, namely, the special place on the one hand and the offering on the other.[13] The altar is thus to be distinguished on the one hand from the marker stone which designates a significant locale and on the other from the cultic pedestal which supported the symbols of deities and similar objects, even if both occasionally could function cultically when sacrifices or offerings were placed either in front of or upon them. The

---

6. A. Even-Shoshan, *A New Concordance of the Bible* (Jerusalem, 1983), lists 400 occurrences, though this includes several incorrect listings.

7. On the restructuring of an old itinerary notice concerning the setting up of a marker stone, cf. C. Westermann, *Genesis 12–36* (Eng. trans., Minneapolis, 1985), 529.

8. Cf. S. Daniel, *Recherches sur le vocabulaire du culte dans la 'Septante'* (Paris, 1966), 15-53.

9. H. Gese, *Die Religionen Altsyriens, Altarabiens und der Mandäer. RdM,* 10/2 (1970), 169f.

10. "Les papyrus araméens d'Hermoupolis et les cultes syro-phéniciens en Égypte perse," *Bibl,* 48 (1967), 577f.

11. E. Meyer, "Untersuchungen zur phönikischen Religion," *ZAW,* 49 (1931), 13.

12. Cf. O. Eissfeldt, "Der Gott Bethel," *KlSchr,* I (Tübingen, 1962), 206-233.

13. Cf. C. H. Ratschow, "Altar," *RGG*^{3}, I, 251ff.

altar functions as a place for sacrifices or offerings. The significant character of the locale in and of itself (e.g., sacred boulder, tomb, locus of theophany, temple) suggests that ultimately this does not completely exhaust the function of altars.[14] The determination of the specific nature and significance of any given altar requires careful consideration of the notion and practice of sacrifice and offering associated with it.

2. *Ancient Near East.* a. *Egypt.* Since sacrifice in Egypt exhibited primarily the character of a meal for the gods,[15] the altar itself can also be understood as having been modeled on secular eating utensils such as the dining mat, table, bowl, etc. The original form of the altar in Egypt is that of the food plate placed at the cultic location. An offering mat *ḥtp*[16] portrayed with a loaf of bread also serves as a hieroglyph for offering as such.[17] Further structural developments of altars[18] are prompted by the various kinds of offerings involved.

This is confirmed as well by the various designations for altars *(ȝw.t; ʿbȝ; rȝ-nṯrw; ḫȝy.t; hȝ(w).t; smȝ; śm; ḳdf).* Since in Egypt altars served exclusively as a prop supporting offerings,[19] the Egyptian temples also retained a number of transportable altars which could be set up at the place of sacrifice according to the size of the sacrifice to be made.

Consistent with the lesser significance of burnt offerings,[20] only rarely do we encounter fixed altars; in contrast, censing in the cult by means of the most varied incense vessels is of great significance in Egypt.[21]

b. *Mesopotamia.* Although a number of different kinds of sacrifice and cultic appurtenances are known from Mesopotamia, we still possess no information concerning the performance and understanding of specific sacrifices.[22] As in Egypt, the primary notion is that of provision of food for the gods; thus altars also were incorporated into the furniture of the divine dwelling with this function in mind, and to a large extent correspond to the secular eating table both in terminology (semantic development from vessel to table) and form (cf. Akk. *paššūru,* Sum. *banšur*[23]). Besides the offering table designation *paššūru,* other terms associated with altars include the Sumerian loanword *guduttû,*[24] *garakku,*[25] *guḫšû,*[26] *kapru* II,[27] and numerous cultic vessels which served

---

14. Cf. also the "four basic relational forms": table, hearth, grave, and throne (*ibid.,* 252f.).
15. Cf. *RÄR,* 547-550; → זבח *zāḇaḥ (zābhach),* IV, 13-16.
16. *WbÄS,* III, 183.
17. *RÄR,* 557ff.
18. Cf. Galling, 1-16.
19. Cf. R. Stadelmann, "Altar," *LexÄg,* I (1975), 145-49.
20. Cf. A. Eggebrecht, "Brandopfer," *LexÄg,* I, 848-850.
21. Cf. O. Keel, "Kanaanäische Sühneriten auf ägyptischen Tempelreliefs," *VT,* 25 (1975), 424-436.
22. → זבח *zāḇaḥ (zābhach),* IV, 16f.
23. *AHw,* I (1965), 845f.; A. Salonen, *Die Möbel des Alten Mesopotamien nach sumerisch-akkadischen Quellen. AnAcScFen,* B, 127 (1963), 174-203.
24. *CAD,* V (1956), 120.
25. *AHw,* I, 281f.
26. *Ibid.,* I, 296.
27. *CAD,* VIII (1971), 190f.

the presentation of various sacrifices as well as censing: *nig̲nakk/qqu,*[28] *maqtārum,*[29] *kinūnu,*[30] libations: *adagur(r)u,*[31] *maqqītu,*[32] and other functions. It is questionable whether the various cultic pedestals *kigallu, manzāza,* or *nēmedu* are to be identified as altars.[33] In addition to these numerous temple altars,[34] we also find so-called "places of sacrifice" outside the temple; Van Buren postulates that here the remains of sacrificial offerings were regularly burned in the same place.[35] There is as yet no direct evidence from Mesopotamia concerning the significance of burnt offerings.

c. *Asia Minor.* As in Egypt and Mesopotamia, the Hittite temple represents a divine dwelling equipped with an inventory consistent with that of the palace itself consisting of throne, hearth, table, etc. Within the cult, the hearth area *ḫašša-*[36] occupies a special position; this is shown not only by the offerings brought to it, but especially by its orthography with a divine determinative. The term *ištanana-*[37] probably refers to a cultic pedestal (not to be associated with Heb. *'ašērâ*[38]) for the representation of the god[39] rather than to an altar, even if offerings were occasionally laid down beside, in front of, or even on it.[40] In front of this *ištanana-* usually stood the real, wooden (always with the determinative *GIŠ*) offering table *papu-* upon which the sacrificial meal was placed; it is often called the "table of the deity" (*GIŠBANŠUR DINGIRLIM*).[41] In a manner comparable to that of the Egyptian offering table, it could also be set up at other cultic places for certain types of offerings.[42] The offering itself was primarily food for the gods, and the occasionally mentioned sacrificial blood had no real significance in the cult.[43]

d. *Syria.* Although the cultures of ancient Syria exhibit considerable agreement with the OT concerning sacrifice,[44] such widespread terminological agreement should not be permitted to obscure manifest differences.[45] While the cult in ancient Syria includes provision of food for the gods, sacral meals, as well as the use of incense

---

28. *AHw,* II (1972), 787.
29. *Ibid.,* II, 608.
30. *Ibid.,* I, 481f.
31. *Ibid.,* I, 9.
32. *Ibid.,* II, 607.
33. Cf. D. Opitz, "Ein Altar des Königs Tukulti-Ninurta 1. von Assyrien," *AfO,* 7 (1931), 83-90. See II.1 above.
34. On the various types and forms, cf. esp. P. Lohmann in Galling, 17-53; E. Unger, "Altar," *RLA,* I (1932), 73-75; E. D. Van Buren, *Numen,* 1 (1954), 228-234.
35. *Iraq,* 14 (1952), 76-92.
36. Cf. Popko, 48-59.
37. *Ibid.,* 66-71.
38. Cf. O. R. Gurney, *Some Aspects of Hittite Religion* (Oxford, 1977), 37.
39. *KUB,* XXV, 22, II, 9.
40. *KUB,* XX, III, 2ff.
41. Popko, 78.
42. Concerning the archaeological evidence and types of Hittite altars, cf. Galling, 90-101.
43. Cf. Gurney, 28f.
44. → זבח *zāḇaḥ (zābhach),* IV, 17f.; Gese, 173-181.
45. Cf. H. Ringgren, *Israelite Religion* (Eng. trans., Philadelphia, 1966), 176f.

and libation, blood does not play any discernible role in the sacrificial cult;[46] furthermore, the sacrificial animals themselves were either completely or partially burned. However, the origin and extent of these types of sacrifice are uncertain;[47] next to terms for the more familiar types of sacrifice[48] in the texts from Ebla, possible parallels to Heb. *ʿōlâ* might be attested in the sacrificial designations *é-lum*[49] and *sà-ra-pa-tum.*[50]

The relationships obtaining between these various sacrificial types and the ancient Syrian sacrificial sites,[51] altars,[52] and cultic equipment[53] remain uncertain.

e. *Arabia.* Next to the enormous differences between the sacrificial customs of the northern and southern Arabs in antiquity,[54] there is a certain continuity extending even into the present regarding sacrifice among the Arabian semi- and full Bedouins.

Compared to the full Bedouins, whose sanctuaries are necessarily movable, the semi-Bedouins do have preferred places of sacrifice[55] such as ancestral graves, sacred stones and trees, etc.

Since the essential part of their sacrifice is the pouring of blood, the slaughtering must also take place at the sacrificial site itself. A pit for the spilled sacrificial blood was located at the foot of the stone *(nuṣub, nuṣb)* before which the slaughter was performed, and votive gifts were occasionally also placed into it.[56] The blood was applied to the stone (*anṣāb,* "blood-smeared stones") and also sprinkled in the direction of the recipients and bringers of the sacrifice.[57] As far as the meaning of the sacrifice is concerned, the concluding meal was less significant than this blood ritual. Thus genuine altars are not found; in place of the stone blocks customary elsewhere, the Bedouins of the Sinai peninsula used rock heaps.[58]

The same sacrificial customs familiar from the OT are also found in the ancient Arabic cultures: animal sacrifice, sacrificial meal, libation, incense, and perhaps also burnt offering.[59] According to Gonzague Ryckmans,[60] altar terms such as *mḏbḥ(t), mqṭr, mṣrb,* and *mslm* are not limited to the type of sacrifice evoked by the various root

---

46. → דם *dām,* III, 238f.
47. → זבח *zāḇaḥ (zābhach),* IV, 17-19.
48. Cf. the sacrificial terminology in G. Pettinato, "Culto ufficiale ad Ebla durante il regno di Ibbi-Sipiš," *OrAnt,* 18 (1979), 120-27.
49. *Ibid.,* 125.
50. *Ibid.,* 126.
51. → במה *bāmâ (bāmāh),* II, 139-145.
52. Cf. Galling, 54-79; Stendebach.
53. Cf. H. G. May, *Material Remains of the Megiddo Cult. OIP,* 26 (1935), 12-26.
54. Cf. J. Henninger, "Das Opfer in den altsüdarabischen Hochkulturen," *Anthropos,* 37-40 (1942-45), 805-810 = *Arabica Sacra = Contributions à l'histoire religieuse de l'Arabie et de ses régions limitrophes. OBO,* 40 (1981), 204-253.
55. Cf. S. J. Curtiss, *Primitive Semitic Religion Today* (Chicago, 1902), 133-143, 229-237.
56. Cf. Henninger, *Das Opfer bei den Arabern,* 66.
57. *Ibid.,* 177-184.
58. *Ibid.,* 66.
59. Cf. Henninger, *OBO,* 40 (1981), 204-253.
60. P. 259.

meanings, but rather vary both according to the context of the inscriptions in which they appear and according to the characteristics of the monuments designated by these names. However, the stela *qyf,* which is also of cultic significance, should be distinguished from these altars.[61]

III. OT. 1. *General Considerations.* Since the enormous semantic scope of Heb. *mizbēaḥ* (place of slaughter, sacrificial site, altar of burnt offering, incense altar, temple table, etc.) is paralleled by the multiplicity of archaeologically attested types and forms of altars in Palestine,[62] any association of archaeological evidence with textual situations must be undertaken with caution. One thing becomes clear: there was no definitive altar type in ancient Israel; on the other hand, as the most salient point of connection with sacrifice itself, and thus with the cultic center, the altar can also refer to the cultic locale in general, especially since altars are indeed possible apart from temples, while temples without altars are not. The notions associated with altars should be viewed in connection with the Israelite sacrificial cult, which itself underwent continual development as a result of admixture and delimitation.

2. *The Altar.*

a. *The Patriarchal Period.* The nomadic religion of the patriarchs[63] exhibits numerous parallels to the cult of pre-Islamic Arabs,[64] the focus of which was sacred stones and trees instead of specially constructed sanctuaries. Nonetheless, Genesis contains numerous accounts of altar construction by the patriarchs, usually expressed by the stereotypical formula *wayyiḇen šām [PN] mizbēaḥ (lᵉ-YHWH),* "and [PN] built there an altar to Yahweh."[65] Since besides this formula further details are never mentioned, such as the fact that sacrifices were offered there, it is clear that these are not descriptions of cultic acts; rather, this information has meaning only for the later time in which it was composed. As far as content is concerned, two groups emerge. One represents altar etiologies; the other seeks to trace what were originally Canaanite sanctuaries back to one of the patriarchs by means of the formula just cited. The formula usually stands in itineraries or independent units (Gen. 12:7,8; 13:4,18) and is followed by *wayyiqrā' bᵉšēm YHWH,* "and he called on the name of Yahweh," as a sign of worship and of the inauguration of the cult at that place. Both groups can additionally contain elements of theophany and promise.[66] Hence all these accounts originated during the time of sedenterization and of appropriation of the sanctuaries already extant in the land; this is also consistent with the partially

61. Cf. M. Höfner, "Kultobjekte und Kulthandlungen," *Die Religionen Altsyriens, Altarabiens und der Mandäer. RdM,* 10/2 (1970), 328ff.; Ryckmans, 259.

62. Cf. A. Reichert, "Altar," *BRL*², 5-10; Stendebach.

63. Cf. C. Westermann, *Genesis 12–50. EdF,* 48 (³1992), esp. 111-14.

64. See II.2.e above.

65. → בנה *bānâ (bānāh),* II, 175-78.

66. W. Richter, *Traditionsgeschichtliche Untersuchungen zum Richterbuch. BBB,* 18 (²1966), 134-37.

reworked altar etiologies in Jgs. 6:11-24; 13;[67] 1 S. 7:17; 14:35; 2 S. 24:18-25; 1 Ch. 21:18-28.[68]

b. *The Mosaic Period.* The larger discussion concerning the interdependence of the traditions of the tent sanctuary and the temple[69] in P includes the accounts of the altar of burnt offering in Ex. 27:1-8, the table for the bread of the Presence in Ex. 25:23-30, and the incense altar in Ex. 30:1-10. Because the altar of burnt offering had to be transportable, it is described as a wooden horned altar with a metal firepan, carrying poles, and an obscure *nik̲bār.*[70] Its measurements of 5 by 5 by 3 cubits recur in 2 Ch. 6:13 in reference to the *kiyyôr.*[71] The description of the incense altar in the addendum Ex. 30:1-10 follows that of the altar of burnt offering, although the table mentioned in Ex. 25:23-30[72] might already imply the setting up of incense vessels.[73] Apart from the accounts surrounding the holy tent, twice mention is made of altars erected by Moses himself (Ex. 17:15; 24:4).

The name of the altar Moses erected in Rephidim after the victory over the Amalekites has occasioned numerous textual emendations,[74] since the name Yahweh *nissî* (Ex. 17:15) does not seem to fit the explanation in v. 16, *kî-yāḏ ʿal-kēs yāh* (MT).[75] The reference here is probably not to a throne for the warlord Yahweh[76] (the notion of throne altars is attested nowhere in the OT). Rather, this altar probably represents for Israel the cultically venerated battle standards common to the entire ancient Near East since the second millennium, having originated in Egypt.[77] One would then have to consider whether in the addendum explaining the name (v. 16) *yāḏ* is used absolutely to refer to Yahweh's might,[78] whose dominion over Israel is expressed in the phrase *ʿal kissēʾ* (with Sam., Syr.); this accords with v. 16b, since the war against the Amalekites is always a war for *(l^e)* Yahweh. B. Couroyer[79] attempts to fuse the two statements by deriving *nissî*[80] from Egyp. *nś.t,* "throne," and understanding this as a gesture associated with a vow.

The altar Moses erects in Ex. 24:4 together with twelve marker stones as a response to the theophany[81] does not merely represent the divine covenantal partner;[82] rather, it

---

67. Cf. Kübel.
68. Cf. Fritz, esp. 15-20.
69. → אהל *ʾōhel* (I, 118-130); Fritz, 112-166.
70. Cf. Fritz, 147.
71. *Ibid.,* 146.
72. *Ibid.,* 139-143.
73. See III.2.d below.
74. Cf. B. Couroyer, "Un Egyptianisme en Exode, XVII,15-16: *YHWH-nissi,*" *RB,* 88 (1981), 333-39; A. R. Müller, "Ex 17,15f in der Septuaginta," *BN,* 12 (1980), 20-23.
75. Cf. M. Noth, *Exodus. OTL* (Eng. trans. 1962), 143.
76. → כסא *kissēʾ,* IV.1 (VII, 253-55).
77. Cf. H. Schaefer, *Klio* (1906), 393ff.
78. → יד *yāḏ* (V, 393-426).
79. Pp. 333-39.
80. → נס *nēs.*
81. Cf. E. Zenger, *Israel am Sinai* (Altenberge, 1982), 161.
82. Noth, 198f.

serves the sacrificial acts mentioned in v. 5 so that the blood rite[83] performed at the altar in v. 6 does not represent anything out of the ordinary. The actual covenant itself, however, is not fully concluded until the blood of the covenant is sprinkled on the people (v. 8).[84]

c. *Prior to Construction of the Temple.* The transition from seminomadic to settled life (conquest) was accompanied by progressive acquaintance with new cultic institutions and practices. In this early period of the people Israel numerous cultic sites belonging to the land's inhabitants are used concurrently or even appropriated from them. This period of religious syncretism involving the numerous legitimate sanctuaries (Bethel, Mamre, Shechem, etc.) includes the accounts of altar construction and sacrificial rites performed by prominent personalities.[85] Since some of these narratives still preserve remnants of earlier cultic rites without altars, rites unique to the nomadic lifestyle, we can conclude that the process of religious integration proceeded only slowly. This is reflected in the account of the sacrifice offered by the inhabitants of Beth-shemesh at the arrival of the ark (1 S. 6:13-15); no altar is mentioned, but rather only a great stone *('eḇen gᵉḏōlâ)* upon which the ark is placed and the blood probably applied. It is similarly recounted that Saul, after hearing of the people's ritual transgression, has a great stone *('eḇen gᵉḏōlâ)* brought for the rite of slaughtering (1 S. 14:33-35); the focus here is not the sacrifice itself, but rather the blood rite performed on the stone. 1 S. 14:35 comes from a later hand and refers to the stone, which could still be seen long afterward (cf. 6:18), as Saul's altar. In neither report does the great stone function as an altar, but rather resembles more the massebah. In contrast, Jgs. 6:11-24 mentions a rock functioning as an altar; Gideon places his sacrifice — understood as divine food — on the rock (cf. 13:19f.), and this rock later seems to have been the basis for a constructed altar (6:24).[86] Such rock altars,[87] next to altars made of earth, represent the simplest kind of altar in the OT. The close relationship between rock and altar characterizes many altars even up to the period of the Jerusalem temple itself.[88]

The → במה *bāmâ (bāmāh)* can be understood as one of the cultic institutions appropriated from the settled peoples. J. M. Grintz[89] has demonstrated the probability of its Moabite provenience;[90] more recent studies[91] have disclosed the close relationship and even frequent identity between *bāmâ* and altar. Leonhard Rost has shown that neither Moabite nor Babylonian sacrificial rites provide the background of the Balaam

83. See III.3.a below.

84. → דם *dām,* IV.4 (III, 248f.); cf. E. W. Nicholson, "The Covenant Ritual in Exodus xxiv 3-8," *VT,* 32 (1982), 74-86.

85. See III.2.a above; cf. G. Fohrer, *History of Israelite Religion* (Eng. trans., Nashville, 1972), 62-65.

86. Cf. Kutsch, Kübel.

87. On the archaeological evidence, cf. Reichert, 6ff.; Stendebach; Galling, esp. 59-64.

88. Cf. Hertzberg; also G. Bruns, "Umbaute Götterfelsen als kultische Zentren in Kulträumen und Altären," *JDAI,* 75 (1960), 100-111.

89. "Some Observations on the 'High-Place' in the History of Israel," *VT,* 27 (1977), 111-13.

90. Cf. also Vaughan, 36.

91. Vaughan, Haran.

narrative (Nu. 23).[92] It is certain that Israel used *bāmôṯ* both in the sense of sanctuaries and as places of sacrifice (altar) (cf. 1 K. 3:2,4). It remains unclear, however, whether the origin of burnt offering *(ʿōlâ)* should be associated with the *bāmâ,* and just what cultic use was made of the threshing floor *(gōren)* in the Canaanite area as suggested by the *hierós lógos* ("holy oracle") regarding the location of the Jerusalem temple (2 S. 24).[93]

The coincidence of cultic forms of nomads and settled peoples emerges most clearly in the altar legislation of Ex. 20:24-26 (Dt. 27:4-7).[94] Diethelm Conrad[95] has examined and precisely determined the sense of the notions and cultic practices against which this altar legislation directs itself. However, his findings regarding the *mizbaḥ ʾ^a^ḏāmâ* seem questionable, since the comparative archaeological evidence he adduces is associated with brick or tile altars of a different kind (temple, house, and street altars) and with correspondingly different notions of sacrifice than are the OT examples. Since the significance of the sacrificial blood remained central to the Israelite cult, a significance deriving from nomadic sacrifice, the temporal context of the Book of the Covenant here suggests that *mizbaḥ ʾ^a^ḏāmâ* more likely refers to a simple earthen place of sacrifice (slaughter) capable of guaranteeing the cultically fulcral destruction of the sacrificial blood, removing it thus from possible false manipulation; it seems unlikely that such altar legislation would have left this completely unaddressed, especially considering the extreme importance attributed to the sacrificial blood within the cult and in that context particularly in connection with the altar (Lev. 17:11). Thus the first commandment contains an element constitutive for every Israelite cultic act over against the two following commandments, which seek to differentiate.

d. *Solomon's Temple.* Despite the central position of altars in any temple, the account of the temple construction in 1 K. 6[96] mentions only the incense altar (vv. 20f.) before (?) the *d^e^ḇîr,* but not the altar of burnt offering in the outer court. This does not allow the conclusion, however, that the overall layout of the Jerusalem temple was conceived more as Yahweh's dwelling place than as a place of sacrifice,[97] since the temple design exhibits too few parallels with the genuine dwelling temples of the ancient Near East. The possibility does exist, however, that an altar or place of sacrifice was already located at this place before the temple structure itself, so that the construction account itself justifiably says nothing about it. Numerous questions have been raised concerning

---

92. "Fragen um Bileam," *Beiträge zur alttestamentlichen Theologie. Festschrift W. Zimmerli* (Göttingen, 1977), 377-387.

93. → גרן *gōren,* III, 64f.

94. Cf. E. König, "Stimmen Ex 20,24 und Dtn 12,13 zusammen?" *ZAW,* 42 (1924), 337-346; K.-H. Walkenhorst, *Der Sinai im liturgischen Verständnis der deuteronomistischen und priesterlichen Tradition. BBB,* 33 (1969), 147-160.

95. *Studien zum Altargesetz, Ex 20:24-26.*

96. Cf. K. Rupprecht, "Nachrichten von Erweiterung und Renovierung des Tempels in 1 Könige 6," *ZDPV,* 88 (1972), 38-52.

97. Fritz, 23.

both the form and the location[98] of the altar of burnt offering.[99] Niels H. Gadegaard's investigation shows the improbability of burnt offerings on the altars described in the OT and on some of those discovered in Palestine. Furthermore, the scope and succession of sacrifices described in the sacrificial laws bear no relationship to the altar described, a difficulty not eliminated by Johannes de Groot's incorrect assumption of a second altar. Since *bāmâ* was partially synonymous with *mizbēaḥ,*[100] the reference to the *bāmâ* as an altar form[101] does not offer merely a philological solution to the question of the actual place where the offering was burned. A substantive solution is also opened up by what Patrick H. Vaughan has designated as the second type of *bāmâ.*[102] This type of *bāmâ* is always associated with a temple and serves both as an altar itself and as the base for a regular altar.

Perhaps there was a type I *bāmâ*[103] in Jerusalem prior to the construction of the temple, one which was expanded in the course of the temple construction and then equipped with a *mizbēaḥ nᵉḥōšeṯ*. It seems certain that no burnt offerings were possible on this *mizbēaḥ nᵉḥōšeṯ,*[104] so that this altar functioned cultically either in connection with the blood rite,[105] which accords well with the eminent significance of blood within the Israelite cult, or should be associated with cult objects of the sort found in Phoenician/Punic inscriptions using the same designation.[106] We can no longer determine whether these two, the *bāmâ* and the altar standing upon it, are referred without distinction in the OT as *mizbēaḥ,* something which is certainly linguistically possible; or whether the two taken together are so designated, something probably intended in the expression occurring only in late texts, *mizbaḥ hāʿōlâ* (Ex. 30:28; 31:9; 35:16; 38:1; 40:6,10,29; Lev. 4:10; 1 Ch. 6:34[Eng. v. 49]; 16:40; 21:26; 2 Ch. 29:18).[107]

It is striking, however, that a great many of the acts associated with the altar use the prep. *ʿal* (next to *ʾel* and *lip̱nê* in reference to approaching and bringing forth)[108] without it becoming clear whether this is a spatial reference in the sense of "upon, over," or whether in all these cases *ʿal* merely indicates the relationship to the altar.[109] To this we can add the references to burning the offering in the construction *qṭr*

98. Not least the history of development of the altar itself militates for a location above the holy rock (see III.2.c above); cf. also Hertzberg; H. Schmid, "Der Tempelbau Salomos in religionsgeschichtlicher Sicht," *Archäologie und AT. Festschrift K. Galling* (Tübingen, 1970), 241-250.

99. Cf. Busink, I, 321-26.

100. Cf. Vaughan, 33.

101. Cf. Haran, 23ff.

102. Vaughan, 46-51.

103. *Ibid.,* 40-45.

104. Cf. Gadegaard, 36ff.

105. See III.3.a below.

106. Cf. *mzbḥ nḥšt* in *KAI,* 10, 4; 66, 1; → נחשת *nᵉḥōšeṯ*.

107. See III.2.f below.

108. Cf. the ascent to the altar in 1 S. 2:28; 1 K. 12:32,33 (cf. also H. W. Wolff, *Joel and Amos. Herm* [Eng. trans. 1977], 339); concerning the sprinkling of blood, see III.3.a below.

109. Cf. C. Dohmen, "על־(ה)מזבח — Zur Bedeutung und Verwendung von hebräisch על," *BN,* 16 (1981), 7-10.

hammizbēḥâ, from which only 2 Ch. 29:22(3 times),24 deviate, where *hammizbēḥâ* is associated with the blood rite. Consistent with the original sense of the accusative ending *-â*[110] indicating direction toward,[111] this linguistic construction might be based on a substantive distinction between *mizbēaḥ (bāmâ)* for burning and *mizbēaḥ* for the blood rite, whereby the altar itself was always the focal point.

Although the obscure *kiyyôr* in 2 Ch. 6:13 might also refer to the base of an altar,[112] the information there concerning dimensions and material is dependent on other traditions,[113] rendering impossible any reconstruction of the original.

The north side of the altar is of particular significance in the temple.[114] According to Lev. 1:11, the sacrificial animal is to be slaughtered *ʿal yereḵ hammizbēaḥ ṣāp̄ōnâ,* "on the north side of the altar" (cf. Lev. 4:24,29,33 concerning sin and guilt offerings), and the same formulation is used in 2 K. 16:14 to indicate the place to which Ahaz removed the older bronze altar. Ezk. 40:38-43 then reports that the tables for slaughtering stood in the north gate of the temple,[115] suggesting that this north side of the altar is to be identified with the north gate where the slaughtering took place. Thus Ahaz had the bronze altar placed together with these slaughtering tables in the north gate. Although 2 K. 12:10(9) also mentions an altar in the north gate,[116] this does not justify the hypothesis of a second altar in the temple; consistent with the semantic field of *mizbēaḥ,* this can be a reference to the slaughtering tables in the north gate. This same semantic association might be behind the erroneous (?) designation in Ezk. 8:5 of a north gate as the "altar gate" *(šaʿar hammizbēaḥ),* eliminating the need for the numerous conjectural attempts this has prompted.[117]

The temple construction account in 1 K. 7:48 mentions the table for the bread of the Presence and a golden altar.[118] Not only the variously answered question concerning the origin, age, and type of the incense altar associated with the Israelite cult,[119] but also substantive considerations have prompted Martin Noth[120] to doubt the existence of a special incense altar *(mizbaḥ haqqᵉṭōreṯ,* Ex. 30:27; 31:8; 35:15; 1 Ch. 6:34[49], etc.). He suspects that the table for the bread of the Presence and the golden altar are identical,[121] and that possibly a censer stood on the table; this accords with Ezk. 41:22, where the "table that stands before Yahweh" is called *kᵉmarʾēh hammizbēaḥ.*[122] It

110. Cf. also E. A. Speiser, "The Terminative-Adverbial in Canaanite-Ugaritic and Akkadian," *IEJ,* 4 (1954), 108-115; J. Hoftijzer, *A Search for Method* (Leiden, 1981).

111. *GK,* §90.2(a).

112. Cf. *KBL*³, 450; cf. *HAL,* II, 472.

113. Cf. Fritz, 25.

114. Cf. K. Elliger, *Leviticus. HAT,* IV (1966), 37.

115. Cf. W. Zimmerli, *Ezekiel 2. Herm* (Eng. trans. 1983), *in loc.*

116. Cf. W. McKane, "A Note on 2 Kings 12_{10} (Evv 12_9)," *ZAW,* 71 (1959), 260-65.

117. W. Zimmerli, *Ezekiel 1. Herm* (Eng. trans. 1979), *in loc.*

118. Cf. Busink, I, 288-293.

119. → קטר *qṭr;* Haran, 230-245.

120. *Könige 1–16. BK,* IX/1 (²1983), 122, 166.

121. For a different interpretation, see Fritz, 24.

122. Cf. Zimmerli, *Ezekiel 2, in loc.*

seems certain that incense was burned in the interior of the temple (Isa. 6:6).[123] Although Robert de Langhe has attempted on the basis of OSA *d̲hb,* "spice, incense,"[124] to explain the *mizbaḥ zāhāḇ* as an incense altar, this is not likely considering the context in which the materials are indicated.[125]

e. *Prior to the Exile.* The period before the division of the kingdom up to the exile is characterized by religious syncretism. Numerous cultic places were located outside Jerusalem, not just in the Jerusalem temple itself. This is made clear by the story of the Ahaz-altar in 2 K. 16;[126] Mordecai Cogan has shown that it is not a specific altar model that is the focus here (be it Assyrian, Phoenician, or Aramaic), but rather the interest in foreign gods and cults characteristic of the times. Peter Welten[127] distinguishes four categories of sanctuaries applicable to this period: central sanctuary, national temple, temple high place, and high place. The frequent mention of altars in the Deuteronomistic and Chronicler's accounts reflects this situation.[128] The focus is not, however, on the nature or various types of altars; rather, as the center of any cult the altar itself represents *pars pro toto* the sanctuary and its cult. The dispute over these sanctuaries and cults[129] is also reflected in the story of the altar at Bethel in 1 K. 13.[130] Similarly, the story in Josh. 22 concerning the altar in Gilgal on the west bank of the Jordan,[131] a story projected back into the period of Joshua,[132] reflects the dispute over a sanctuary located there;[133] it does not represent a postexilic legitimization on the part of Jerusalem orthodoxy of diaspora sanctuaries without sacrificial cults.[134] The translators of the LXX recognized the underlying dispute and also commented on it by rendering *mizbēaḥ* with *bōmós,* a term normally reserved for pagan altars.

One should assume with T. A. Busink that no altar for the sacrificial cult was erected on the rubble soon after the destruction of the Jerusalem temple in 587 B.C.[135] Not until

---

123. Cf. H. Wildberger, *Isaiah 1–12* (Eng. trans., Minneapolis, 1991), 44, 269.

124. → זהב *zāhāḇ (zāhābh),* IV.1 (IV, 39).

125. On the various objects associated with censing, cf. Glueck; de Vries; → חמם *ḥmm,* III (IV, 475-77).

126. Cf. R. Rendtorff, *Studien zur Geschichte des Opfers im alten Israel. WMANT,* 24 (1967), 46-50.

127. "Kulthöhe und Jahwetempel," *ZDPV,* 88 (1972), 19-37.

128. See III.3.e below.

129. Cf. A. Jepsen, "Gottesmann und Prophet: Anmerkungen zum Kapitel 1. Könige 13," *Probleme biblischer Theologie. Festschrift G. von Rad* (Munich, 1971), 171-182.

130. On this text, cf. E. Würthwein, "Die Erzählung vom Gottesmann aus Juda in Bethel: Zur Komposition von 1 Kön13," *Wort und Geschichte. Festschrift K. Elliger. AOAT,* 18 (Kevelaer, 1973), 181-89; on the end of the Bethel sanctuary (2 K. 23), cf. H. W. Wolff, "Das Ende des Heiligtums in Bethel," *Archäologie und AT. Festschrift K. Galling* (Tübingen, 1970), 287-298.

131. → ירדן *yardēn,* II.3 (VI, 327f.).

132. Cf. H. J. Hermisson, *Sprache und Ritus im altisraelitischen Kult. WMANT,* 19 (1965), 99ff.

133. Cf. Snaith.

134. Diebner-Schult.

135. Cf. Kosters, Kittel, Noth; see Busink, II, 777f.

Ezr. 3:2f. (cf. Hag. 2:14) do we read that an altar was built after the exile. Insufficient source material prohibits more specific determination of details concerning the altars of the Second Temple.[136]

f. *Ezekiel's Draft Constitution.* Scholarship has quite frequently augmented the lack of information concerning the altar of burnt offering, regarding the Solomonic and the Second Temple as well as the altar Ahaz had built, by drawing on the precise description of the altar provided by Ezekiel's draft constitution (Ezk. 43:13-27). Apart from the *opinio communis* regarding the overall disposition and layout of the altar, numerous and varying attempts have been made to explain specific terms, the resulting notions and reconstructions, parallels to the altar, and its possible origin.[137] Vaughan's remarks[138] in this regard are worth mentioning; a consideration of the terms *ḥêq* and *gaḇ* leads him to the notion of an altar construction resting on a base platform. In this sense the altar described in Ezekiel represents a further development of the previously mentioned association of *bāmâ* and altar; i.e., their functions — burnt offering and blood rite — can now take place together on the altar, a situation perhaps having something to do with the new orientation of the altar.[139] It is conceivable that this sort of "unified model" is also the basis for the Priestly conception in the sacrificial texts.[140]

3. a. *Blood Rite.* The enormous significance which has always been attributed to blood in the Israelite cult can be traced back to the nomadic sacrificial cult.[141] The blood of every sacrifice had to be applied to the altar itself (Dt. 12:27); depending on the type of sacrifice involved it was either thrown round about onto the altar, or the horns of the altar were smeared and the rest poured out onto the foundation of the altar.[142] During the blood rite the blood itself stood in offering basins *(mizrāq)*[143] at or on the altar (Ex. 24:6-8; 29:21; Lev. 8:30; Zec. 9:15). The application of blood had an expiatory effect,[144] not only on the altar itself as the locus of atonement,[145] but also regarding human beings and objects. Together with oil, blood was also used in connection with the variously mentioned consecration of the altar *(ḥ^{a}nukkaṯ hammizbēaḥ).*[146]

In connection with the absolute limitation of blood to the altar (Lev. 17:11), the altar represents the center of the cult itself; the reference here is thus to the exclusively cultic

136. On further descriptions, esp. in Josephus and the Mishnah, see Busink, II.

137. Cf. the presentations and critical comments in Busink, II, 730-36; Zimmerli, *Ezekiel 2,* 423-28.

138. Pp. 51-54.

139. Zimmerli, *Ezekiel 2,* 428.

140. See III.2.d above. On the incense altar in Ezk. 41:22, see III.2.d above.

141. See II.2.e above.

142. → זרק *zāraq* (IV, 162-65); → יצק *yāṣaq* (VI, 254-57); → שפך *šāpaḵ.*

143. → זרק *zāraq,* IV, 164.

144. → כפר *kpr* (VII, 288-303).

145. Zimmerli, *Ezekiel 2,* 433.

146. → חנך *ḥānaḵ,* V, 20f.

use of blood.[147] Allusions to the significance of the y^esôḏ also in connection with ritual[148] (not limited just to the orderly removal of the blood of the sacrifice) reflects perhaps the origins of the altar, which was built on or over a sacred rock.[149]

E. W. Nicholson[150] has shown clearly that *ʿārîm,* "cities, towns," in Jer. 2:28; 11:13; 19:15; Ezk. 6:6; Hos. 11:6; Mic. 5:13[14] cannot on the basis of Ugaritic parallels be traced back to a root **ʿārēh,* "blood-spattered altar."

b. *Altar Horns.* The origin of altar horns (*q^erānôṯ,* e.g., Ex. 27:2; 29:12; 30:2,3,10; Lev. 4:7,18,25; 1 K. 1:50f.; Jer. 17:1; Ezk. 43:20; Am. 3:14) cannot be determined with any certitude.[151]

One suggestion is that a massebah was quasi-quartered for technical reasons associated with sacrifice,[152] another that it was a holder for censers.[153] De Groot[154] associates the altar horns with the horned crowns of both gods and kings and considers their original significance to be apotropaic. Walter Andrae[155] interprets the comparable horns of the Babylonian ziggurat as "successors of the 'spar-bundles' of the oldest huts of the gods on the hill."[156] With F. J. Stendebach,[157] however, one should probably associate the altar horns with the cult of the bull, which was known throughout the ancient Near East, especially since evidence of actual bull horns from neolithic Çatal Hüyük[158] confirm this interpretation, and since a connection to the horn-pair attested in the Aegean (the so-called "horns of consecration"[159]) can be established. The practices of blood rite and asylum indicate that the horns of the Israelite altar were considered especially holy. In Jer. 17:1, ineradicable guilt is also described as being engraved on the horns of the altar.[160]

c. *Asylum.* Like most peoples, the Israelites recognized the right of asylum in the sanctuary.[161] Through contact with holy objects the person seeking asylum participates in their holiness (Ex. 29:37).[162] The altar itself, or its horns as the center of the sanctuary,

---

147. Cf. N. Füglister, "Sühne durch Blut — Zur Bedeutung von Leviticus 17,11," *Studien zum Pentateuch. Festschrift W. Kornfeld* (Vienna, 1977), 143-164.
148. → יסד *yāsaḏ* (VI, 111-121).
149. See III.2.c above.
150. *VT,* 27 (1977), 113-17.
151. On the distribution of horned altars, cf. Reichert, *BRL*², 9; → קרן *qeren.*
152. Galling, 67.
153. *ANEP,* 319.
154. Pp. 76-88.
155. *Das Gotteshaus und die Urform des Bauens im alten Orient. Studien zur Bauforschung,* 2 (Berlin, 1930), 59.
156. Cf. also Obbink.
157. P. 190.
158. Cf. J. Mellaart, *Çatal Huyuk: A Neolithic Town in Anatolia* (New York, 1967), 77-130, esp. 106ff.
159. Cf. W. Burkert, *Greek Religion* (Eng. trans., Cambridge, Mass., 1985), 37-39.
160. → לב *lēḇ,* V.6.c (VII, 426-29).
161. For an overview, cf. L. Delekat, *Asylie und Schutzorakel am Zionheiligtum* (Leiden, 1967).
162. Cf. J. Milgrom, "Sancta contagion and altar/city asylum," *Congress Volume, Vienna 1980. SVT,* 32 (1981), 278-310.

represents this holy place in the OT; not only does it function as a place of asylum (1 K. 1:50,51,53; 2:28f.), but due to its holy nature it is also the place where a decision or sign is expected after the swearing of an oath in the case of unsubstantiated transgressions (1 K. 8:31 par. 2 Ch. 6:22). In an oracle of judgment, the prophet Amos (Am. 3:14) expands the exclusion of the murderer from the right of asylum (Ex. 21:14) by announcing the destruction of all places of asylum, thus cutting off possibility of deliverance.[163]

d. *Altar Service.* As the center of the cult, the altar has also influenced the designations for priests; their task is the *mišmereṯ hammizbēaḥ,* referring to the entire service of the cult (e.g., Nu. 18:5; 1 S. 2:28; Ezk. 40:46) for which the priests are responsible.[164] It was considered a grievous cultic transgression for the king to appropriate for himself priestly functions[165] (1 K. 12:32; 2 Ch. 26:16) which went beyond those assigned to him (cf. 1 K. 8:22 par. 2 Ch. 6:12; 1 K. 8:54; 9:25, etc.).[166]

e. *Idol Worship.* In later historical writing the period of sedenterization and especially that of the later monarchy are characterized by the danger of religious syncretism.[167] The neighboring peoples' sanctuaries to be destroyed (Ex. 34:13; Dt. 7:5; Jgs. 2:2) are often described more specifically by → במה *bāmâ (bāmāh),* → אשרה *'ᵃšērâ (ᵃshērāh),* → מצבה *maṣṣēḇâ,* and → חמם *ḥammānîm.*[168] These enumerations never fail to include references to the altars, whose idolatrous function Isa. 17:8 skillfully exposes when it refers to them as "work of the hands," a characterization borrowed from the polemic against idols.

The apocalyptist in Isa. 19:19 sees all of Egypt as a "cult place" (not merely individual places in Egypt of the kind familiar to his own period) with an altar in the midst of the land *(bᵉṯôḵ)* and a massebah at its border *('ēṣel-gᵉḇûlāh).* This notion is then further expanded in vv. 23-25.

The central focus especially of prophetic criticism is the senseless multiplication of sanctuaries for offering sacrifices (Jer. 2:28; 11:13; Hos. 8:11; 10:1).[169] Not surprisingly, the majority of occurrences of the plural forms of *mizbēaḥ* is found in these texts. Hezekiah's reduction of cultic places to a single altar in the Jerusalem temple must have seemed to the pagans like a diminution of worship (2 K. 18:22; Isa. 36:7).

The destruction of altars and defilement of the cultic places (2 K. 11:18; 23:20; Ezk. 6:4f.,13) signal the anticipated end of the worship of idols.

---

163. Wolff, *Joel and Amos,* 201.

164. *Ibid.,* 31.

165. → כהן *kōhēn* (VII, 60-75).

166. Cf. Noth, *BK,* IX/1 (²1983), 220.

167. For a systematic presentation of the history of the Israelite cult within the Deuteronomistic history, cf. H.-D. Hoffmann, *Reform und Reformen. AThANT,* 66 (1980), *passim.*

168. Cf. K. Galling, "Baʿal Ḥammon in Kition und die Ḥammanîm," *Wort und Geschichte. Festschrift K. Elliger. AOAT,* 18 (1973), 65-70; V. Fritz, "Die Bedeutung von *Ḥammān* im Hebräischen und von *ḥmn'* in den palmyrenischen Inschriften," *BN,* 15 (1981), 9-20.

169. Cf. H. W. Wolff, *Hosea. Herm* (Eng. trans. 1974), 81, 144, 173.

IV. Qumran. Apart from rather fragmentary altar descriptions in the Temple scroll,[170] the term *mizbēaḥ* occurs only 8 times in the manuscripts from Qumran (11QPs[a] 18:9; 27:5 [DavComp]; CD 6:12,13; 11:17,19,20; 16:13). Consistent with the absence of any bloody sacrificial cult in Qumran,[171] *mizbēaḥ* is used on the one hand in a figurative sense; on the other hand, CD 11:17,19,20 seems to envision limited participation in the temple cult. Over against this stands CD 6:12,13, where the demand of Mal. 1:10 to do away with the temple service altogether rather than continue it in its unclean state is presented to the community members as a justification for their own separation from the official temple cult. Indeed, they should themselves be the ones to end this temple service (compare Mal. 1:10 with CD 6:12).

Dohmen

170. Cf. Y. Yadin, *M^{e}gillat hammiqdaš* (Jerusalem, 1977), I, 186; II, 37 [Heb.]; also Busink II, 1420-26.

171. Cf. G. Klinzing, *Die Umdeutung des Kultes in der Qumrangemeinde und im NT. StUNT,* 7 (1971), esp. 22-41.

מְזוּזָה m^e*zûzâ*

Contents: I. Etymology, Meaning. II. Ancient Near East. III. OT. IV. LXX.

I. Etymology, Meaning. The etymology of this word is still unknown. The post-OT verb *zwz,* "move, push to the side" is hardly appropriate. Neither can Akk. *manzāzu/mazzaztu,* nominal forms of *izuzzu,* "to stand,"[1] be cognates, since they exhibit no semantic affinity whatsoever and since the doubling of the *z* has left no traces in Hebrew (e.g., **mazzûzah*). Maximilian Ellenbogen[2] refers to Akk. *muzzāzu* (N-stem ptcp. of *zāzu*) with the meaning "doorpost."[3]

The term m^e*zûzâ* signifies either the "doorpost" (Ex. 21:6; Prov. 8:34; Isa. 57:8; Ezk. 43:8), the "gatepost" (of stone, Jgs. 16:3; Ezk. 46:2), or possibly the "door frame" (1 K. 6:31,33; Ezk. 41:21).

m^e*zûzâ.* I. M. Casanowicz, "Mezuzah," *JE,* VIII (1904), 531f.; J. Milgrom, "Israel's Sanctuary: The Priestly 'Picture of Dorian Gray,' " *RB,* 83 (1976), 390-99; E. Reiner, "Plague Amulets and House Blessings," *JNES,* 19 (1960), 148ff.; E. A. Speiser, "*Pālil* and Congeners: A Sampling of Apotropaic Symbols," *Festschrift B. Landberger. AS,* 16 (1965), 389-393; J. Trachtenberg, *Jewish Magic and Superstition* (New York, 1939, repr. 1975), esp. 146ff.; S. Yeivin, *EMiqr,* IV (1962), 780-82.

1. *AHw,* I (1965), 408-411; II (1972), 638.
2. *Foreign Words in the OT* (London, 1962), 99.
3. Cf. *AHw,* II, 692?

II. Ancient Near East. The importance of the *mezûzâ* can be traced to earliest historical times when symbols of identification and ownership were placed at or over house entrances. Chalcolithic ossuaries in the shape of houses, for example, with models of tools suspended over the entrance, show the owner's trade (?); Mesopotamian seals similarly place symbols of the deity above the entrance to his temple. Indeed, the identification of the occupants of tombs in ancient Egypt was proclaimed in inscriptions written on lintels or posts at their entrance. Similarly, Phoenician inscriptions were installed at sepulchre entrances to identify the interred (e.g., Yeḥimilk and Šipiṭbaʿal of Byblos).

Although Shemuel Yeivin asserts that the magico-cultic function of these entrance inscriptions is a subsequent development, there is no reason to doubt that this exorcistic-function was present from the beginning. In the ancient Near East the door/gatepost figured prominently in ritual and magical purifications. The house was considered most vulnerable at its entrance, since it was there that demonic incursion was most likely to take place. "No door can shut them out/no bolt can turn them back/through the door like a snake they slide/through the hinge like a wind they blow" (*Utukki limnuti,* V, 25-35). Hence, images of protector gods (*šēdu* and *lamassu*) were erected at the entrances: "I have made you stand at the gate, at right and left, to dispel them [the demons] from the house of PN."

III. OT. Such is clearly the intent of Ezk. 45:19, which calls for the daubing of the blood of the *ḥaṭṭā'ṯ,* the purification offering, on the doorposts of the temple and on the gates of the inner court, in addition to the four corners of the altar ledge. This procedure is similar in purpose to the use of the *ḥaṭṭā'ṯ* blood on Yom Kippur, when it was aspersed within the adytum and shrine and daubed on the horns of the altar.[4] Thus was the sanctuary to be purged[5] of impurity, not primarily of demonic, but more likely of human origin.

Blood smeared on doorposts had an apotropaic function as well as a purgative one. In the Exodus account it serves to ward off the destroyer (*mašḥîṯ,* Ex. 12:23; cf. 7:22). A vestige of this apotropaic notion can be seen in the specific levitical office of the *šōʿarîm,* the temple ostiaries, which were concerned primarily with guarding the entrances of the sanctuary against unauthorized intruders (1 Ch. 9:18; 26:1,12; 2 Ch. 23:19). Young Samuel in the Shilonite sanctuary seems to have performed this function. The importance of this function is further underscored by the fact that the priests serving as sanctuary guards (*šōmerê hassap̱,* lit., "guardians of the threshold") stood immediately after the high priest and his assistant in rank, to judge by the list of officials deported by the Babylonians (2 K. 25:18).

The apotropaic function of doorposts is further attested by amulets.[6] This custom is clearly the backdrop for the Deuteronomistic prescription to write verses "on the

---

4. See Milgrom.
5. → כפר אמ *kipper* (VII, 288-303).
6. Cf. Reiner.

doorposts of your house and on your gates" (Dt. 6:9; 11:20). Although in biblical wisdom such writing (e.g., "on the tablet of your heart," Prov. 7:3) is probably metaphoric, there is no reason to doubt that the Deuteronomistic injunction is to be taken literally. Just as D prescribes the wearing of phylacteries on the forearm and forehead and tassels on the outer garment (Dt. 22:12), so it must be understood as enjoining the inscribing of key Torah verses on the doors and gateposts. Precisely what these verses are, however, is not clear from the text. The earliest such *mᵉzûzâ* inscription comes from Cave 8 in Qumran.[7] It is a parchment 6.5 × 16 cm. (2.6 in. × 6.3 in.). containing Dt. 10:12–11:21. The passage prescribed by the rabbis, however, is briefer and differs slightly (Dt. 6:4-9; 11:13-21).

Their widespread use during this period is verified by Flavius Josephus (*Ant.* viii.213). Accordingly, the term *mᵉzûzâ* comes to signify these doorpost inscriptions. It is crucial, however, to be mindful of the overall development. Beginning with Deuteronomy, biblical Israel transformed what was originally a doorpost amulet into a reminder to the occupants of the dwelling that they should order their lives according to the Torah. Yet the apotropaic powers of the *mᵉzûzâ* were not forgotten. Onqelos the proselyte explained it to the Roman soldiers who came to arrest him: "In the case of the Holy One, his servants dwell within, while he stands guard over them from without" (*ʿAbod. Zar.* 11a; cf. *Menaḥ.* 33b; Targ. Onqelos on Cant. 8:3). And on the talmudic remark that affixing a *mᵉzûzâ* improperly may be a source of harm, the medieval commentator Rashi explains that such a house will not be protected against demons (*Menaḥ.* 32b).[8]

IV. LXX. The LXX renders *mᵉzûzâ* as *stathmós* (7 times), *stoá,* or *próthyron* (once each). Although the rendering *anaptýssein* in Ezk. 41:16 is semantically accurate, it is precisely here that the LXX has inserted an additional explanatory circumscription.[9]

Milgrom

7. Cf. M. Baillet, J. T. Milik, and R. de Vaux, *Les 'petites grottes' de Qumrân. DJD* III (1962).
8. For further *mᵉzûzôṯ* from Qumran, cf. also R. de Vaux and J. T. Milik, *Qumrân Grotte 4,* II: *Tefillin, Mezuzot et Targums. DJD,* VI (1977), 80-85.
9. W. Zimmerli, *Ezekiel 2. Herm* (Eng. trans. 1983), 383.

מָחָה *māḥâ*

Contents: I. Etymology. II. OT Usage: 1. Literal Meaning; 2. Figurative-theological Meaning; 3. Overview; 4. Special Cases. III. LXX.

māḥâ. R. Oberforcher, *Die Flutprologe als Kompositionsschlüssel der biblischen Urgeschichte* (Innsbruck, 1981), 150-54.

I. Etymology. The Hebrew term *māḥâ* corresponds to Ugar. *mḥy,* "wipe away,"[1] Phoen. *mḥh,* "extinguish, wipe off,"[2] and perhaps Akk. *ma'û,* "throw down, destroy, exterminate,"[3] Arab. *maḥa* (III. *w*), "wipe away."[4]

II. OT Usage. 1. *Literal Meaning.* Since the theological use of *māḥâ* constitutes a figurative understanding of the word's literal sense, it is advisable to begin with those cases in which *māḥâ* exhibits its physical aspect of action or process. These include:

a. *2 K. 21:13.* A dish "is wiped" inside and out; i.e., with the help of water and perhaps something else (object or substance) a spot or impurity is removed from an article or utensil. The text mentions both object and verb (dish and "wipe off"); the other factors, namely, spot or stain and water, are implied. The parallel expression "stretch the measuring line" is not synonymous, but serves rather as another image for destruction. The stain appears in a general form in v. 13, while v. 16 speaks of spilled blood. This text can be compared with Isa. 4:4, probably a later text which speaks of unclean blood and "washing" *(rāḥaṣ).* One further significant parallel with related imagery is Ezk. 24:11, which speaks of "melting the filthiness and consuming the rust" on the kettle defiled by spilled blood.

b. Nu. 5:23 is part of the law concerning jealousy. After the priest has pronounced a curse, he writes it down, perhaps on parchment; he then washes the document off with the water *(māḥâ 'el-mê)* so that the water eradicates the words; the accused woman drinks the water, thus taking the curse into her own body. The text thus mentions the material on which something is written, what is actually written, and the water that washes that writing away. The transition from formless spot or stain to writing is significant. Although the meaning of the writing does not really influence the physical process itself, it radically influences the sense of the statement.[5] Menaḥem Haran[6] believes that the use of *māḥâ* here and in similar contexts suggests the use of papyrus; the eradication of writing from parchment is indicated by the verb *grd.*

c. *Prov. 30:20.* The adulteress "eats, and wipes *(māḥᵃṯâ)* her mouth." Here the verb is used in its literal meaning in a context which when taken as a whole exhibits metaphorical or figurative meaning.

d. *Isa. 25:8.* "God will wipe away the tears." Here the physical act underlies the symbolic meaning. Here and in the previous case we find a person, a body instead of an object, something that stains or disrupts, and the act of wiping away *(māḥâ).* These

1. *WUS,* no. 1540; C. J. Labuschagne, "The Root MḪH Attested in Ugaritic," *VT,* 5 (1955), 312f.

2. *KAI,* 26 A, III, 13, 18; C, IV, 15; 1, 2; *DISO,* 147.

3. *AHw,* II (1972), 637; *CAD,* X/2 (1977), 321. The semantic field is covered by other verbs as well: "wipe away" = *kapāru, mašāšu;* "extinguish, eradicate": something written = *pašāṭu,* sins = *pasāsu.*

4. On the Ethiopic, see Leslau, *Contributions,* 30.

5. For an overview, cf. G. Giesen, *Die Wurzel* שׁבע *"schwören." BBB,* 56 (1981), 124ff.

6. "Book-Scrolls in Israel in Pre-Exilic Times," *JJS,* 33 (1982), 169.

latter two constitute theological symbols: reproachable ethical behavior, and an ultimate salvific act.

2. *Figurative-theological Meaning.* The theological meaning of the verb *māḥâ* appears only in contexts containing various individual or compound features: the object or person which is soiled or described; the image of the stain itself or of the writing which is to be eradicated. The factor that actually wipes away is less influential. This analysis permits the following corresponding classification. What is actually eradicated includes:

a. a name from a register;
b. sin/guilt: such as a stain from the person or inscribed guilt; virtue/merit: such as catalogued credit;
c. living beings from the face of the earth, objects of idolatry from the land.

a. *Registers.* In these cases eradication occurs either explicitly or implicitly (the uttering of a name can be the same as something written): Ex. 17:14; 32:32f.; Dt. 9:14; 25:6,19; 29:19(Eng. v. 20); Jgs. 21:17; 2 K. 14:27; Ps. 9:6(5); 69:29(28); Sir. 44:13. There is no difference between the qal, niphal, and hiphil. Synonyms in the wider sense include: *hišmîḏ, šāḵaḥ, sālaḥ, ʾibbēḏ, hiḵrîṯ;* antonyms include: *kāṯaḇ, hôšîaʿ, zāḵar, pālaṭ, ʿāmaḏ, qûm ʿal šēm.*

b. *Guilt (Sin) or Merit.* Neh. 3:37(4:5); 13:14; Ps. 51:3,11(1,9); 109:14; Prov. 6:33; Isa. 43:25; 44:22; Jer. 18:23 (conj.); Zec. 3:9 (conj.); Sir. 3:14; 1QS 11:3. No difference is discernible between the qal, niphal, and hiphil. Synonyms include: *nāšâ, kibbes, ṭihar, kissâ, kipper;* antonyms include: *zāḵar, nimṣāʾ.*

c. *Living Beings or Cultic Objects.* Gen. 6:7;[7] 7:4,23; Jgs. 21:17; Prov. 31:3; Ezk. 6:6; Sir. 31:1. The same meaning is exhibited in the qal and niphal. Synonyms include: *himṭîr, ḥrb, šmm, šbr, hišbîṯ, hēsîr;* antonyms include: *nišʾar.*

3. *Overview.* This classification yields the following brief overview. We began with two examples without identifying them chronologically, namely, the spot or stain that is washed out or wiped away, and the writing that is eradicated. It is always something external cleaving to a body. The example of writing leads us into the world of the word that names, registers, effects. Although the verb *kāṯaḇ* and the noun *sēper* are not frequently mentioned in the same context, they are presupposed in many instances. There is then an easy transition from writing to its oral equivalent: from the written to the spoken name, from the document to the register of a person's memory. In both cases the word can function either as solicitation or as simple verification: eradicating a name or guilt can have juridical status; forgetting a transgression constitutes forgiveness. The consequences of the act can also have an enduring effect, e.g., the wiping out of a name, or of remembrance *(šēm, zēḵer):* Ex. 17:14; Dt. 9:14; 25:6,19; 29:19(20);

7. Cf. Oberforcher.

2 K. 14:27; Ps. 9:6(5); 109:13. In this sense a person implores that his merit not be eradicated, but that his guilt be wiped away.

The semantic scope of *māḥâ* is illuminated by those texts that speak of ineradicable writing, e.g., Jer. 17:1: "The sin of Judah is written with an iron pen; with a diamond point it is engraved on the tablet of their hearts" (cf. also Job 19:23f.). The conceptual range of the notion of eradicating spots or stains is considerable; the passages initially cited are unequivocal (2 K. 21:13; Prov. 30:20; Isa. 25:8). Perhaps this group also includes Isa. 44:22 (the clouds are like spots in the heavens; cf. *ṭāhôr* as an epithet for heaven[8]) and Ps. 51:3(1) with its parallels *kbs* and *ṭhr* (v. 4[2]); Prov. 6:33 is more dubious (ineradicable disgrace). To which category do the living beings and human structures belong? One might assume the first, which proceeds from the notion of eradicating writing or of destroying something actual. One might also understand the human beings or objects as spots or stains on the earth that are to be eradicated. It is best, however, to dispense with any classification. The flood and its waters remove all living things from the earth (Gen. 6:7; 7:4,23), and systematic destruction eradicates all structures belonging to the cults of idols (Ezk. 6:6).

Three texts reveal the vague semantic fixation of *māḥâ* in connection with transgressions and persons. Ex. 32:32: When in a given instance a sin is not forgiven *(nāśā')*, a person or name is blotted out of the register. Ps. 109:13: When guilt is not similarly eradicated, descendants are annihilated. Dt. 29:19(20): The curses written down will be visited upon the guilty party and will blot out his name.

The term *māḥâ* occurs in various combinations in the theological semantic sphere. They can be classified as follows:

eradicate	something	from something
	writing	from a document
	spot/stain	from a body
	living beings/objects	from their normal place

Several texts illustrate the validity of this schema:

Gen. 6–7	living beings	from the face of the earth
Ex. 17:14	names/remembrance	from under heaven
Ex. 32:32	person/name	from the register (book)
Jgs. 21:17	a tribe	out of Israel
Isa. 25:8	tears	from a person's face
Dt. 25:6	his name	out of Israel

This schema does not hold up when a member of the second column occupies the position of the direct object, which normally corresponds to the first column, e.g., eradicate/wash off Jerusalem (2 K. 21:13), wipe off one's mouth (Prov. 30:20).

---

8. → טהר *ṭāhar* (V, 287-296).

4. *Special Cases.* This illustrates the theological use of *māḥâ,* its basic schema, and its semantic variations. It can be useful, however, to examine individually several problematic or especially interesting cases.

a. *Ex. 32:32f.; Ps. 69:29(28).* The consequences of blotting out a name depend on the kind of book in which it is registered in the first place. Being entered in the book of the elect registers and guarantees membership in the community; being entered in the book of the living guarantees life.

b. *Dt. 25:6.* If a person dies without progeny, "his name is blotted out"; this eradication is avoided if a firstborn comes who carries his name on *(yāqûm ʿal-šēm).* Sir. 44:13 must be understood similarly, except that *kāḇôḏ* is used instead of *šēm.*

c. *Ezk. 6:6.* The accoutrements of the worship of idols, *bāmôṯ,* altars, idols, *ḥammānîm,* defile the land and must be violently destroyed so that such works (not "deeds"[9]) of those who serve idols are "wiped out."

d. *Jgs. 21:17.* Due to scarcity of wives the men have no inheritance *(y^{e}ruššâ),* and a tribe "is blotted out." This is a reflection of reality, not a literary notice in a register; this passage is related to Dt. 25:6.

e. *Sir. 31:1.* The expression *ymḥh š'rw,* literally, "wipe away his flesh," refers to dissipating or debilitating one's health, allowing one's body to waste away.

f. *Prov. 31:3.* The variant *lamḥôṯ* is dubious. Similar to Sir. 31:1, the reference is to women who destroy or debilitate the health of kings. Compared with Dt. 25:6; Jgs. 21:17, this would mean that sexual deviation can "eradicate" a dynasty and bring about its end; this would yield an insightful but uncertain contrast: a tribe is extinguished because of scarcity of women; a dynasty is blotted out because of a superfluity of women.

III. LXX. The LXX does not translate consistently; the most frequent renderings are *exaleíphein* and *apaleíphein,* though *aponíptein, aphaírein, ektēkein,* and *epilanthánein* also occur.

Alonso-Schökel

---

9. So *KBL*[3].

מְחִיר m^eḥîr

Contents: I. Etymology. II. Usage. III. LXX.

---

m^{e}ḥîr. B. Landsberger, "Akkadisch-Hebräische Wortgleichungen," *Hebräische Wortforschung. Festschrift W. Baumgartner. Congress Volume 1967. SVT,* 16 (1967), 176-204, esp. 184f., n. 2; J. J. Rabinowitz, "Neo-Babylonian Legal Documents and Jewish Law," *JJP,* 13 (1961), 131-175, esp. 140f.

I. Etymology. The word m^{e}*ḥîr* derives from the root *mḫr,* which is common to all the Semitic languages. In South Arabian *mḫr* means "face, run toward."[1] In Classical and Literary Arabic the meaning of the verb *maḫara* has shifted from "advance towards" or "come over" to "cleave, traverse, plow through."[2] The basic meaning of the Akkadian verb *maḫāru* is "approach toward someone." Various substantives were derived from this term, e.g., *maḫīru,* "equivalent value, going price, purchase price, commercial activity, market place."[3] The verb *mḫr* > *mḥr* itself is not actually attested in the Northwest Semitic languages, although one does find there the nominal derivatives *mḫr/mḥ(y)r,* "equivalent value, correspondence," *mḫr,* "front (side)," like Akk. *maḫru,*[4] → מחר *māḥār,* "tomorrow," and the PN m^{e}*ḥîr*/Μαχιρ *(Machir)* (1 Ch. 4:11), which is probably a substitute name meaning "correspondence, equivalent." Hence there is no reason to understand m^{e}*ḥîr* as having been borrowed from Akkadian, particularly since the semantic fields of the two terms do not coincide. In Hebrew the term m^{e}*ḥîr* is always used in the sense of "equivalent value," a notion originating in the activity of barter. The translation "price" seldom evokes the real sense of the texts, although the terms "reward" and "payment" occasionally do justice to the context.

II. Usage. The oldest West Semitic material comes from the royal archives at Ugarit. One business letter[5] mentions *kl mḫrk,* "your delivery's total value," in reference to the payment due for a delivery of copper. At the end of an accounting document one finds the expression *ksp mḫrhn,* "silver of their value,"[6] referring to the ships purchased by the Ugaritic king mentioned in the body of the text. The same expression, *kesep̱* m^{e}*ḥîr,* also occurs in 1 K. 21:2; Job 28:15. In these cases it is self-evident that the reference is to payment made with a specific amount of silver. The context suggests that 2 S. 24:24 is to be understood in precisely the same way. There the expression *qānâ bimḥîr* occurs, "acquire for the equivalent value" or "acquire through payment." In 1 K. 10:28 par. 2 Ch. 1:16, the expression *lāqaḥ bimḥîr,* "take for an equivalent" or "take through payment," occurs in a context showing clearly that the reference is not to a gift, but rather to a business transaction. The expressions *bimḥîr,* "for an equivalent value" (Lam. 5:4; Dnl. 11:39; Mic. 3:11; Sir. 31:5), or *lō' bimḥîr* (Isa. 45:13; Jer. 15:13; 1QS 5:17) and b^{e}*lô'* m^{e}*ḥîr* (Isa. 55:1; 1Q27 1, II 6) with the same meaning, "without equivalent value," occur without any dependable indication of just what type of payment the author had in mind. The expression b^{e}*lō'-kesep̱ ûb*^{e}*lō'* m^{e}*ḥîr* in Isa. 55:1 accordingly seems to indicate that at least in this context m^{e}*ḥîr* does not refer to silver. The parallelism *kesep̱* — m^{e}*ḥîr* in Lam. 5:4 might sooner be synthetic and complementary than synonymous. Other parallelisms such as m^{e}*ḥîr* — *šōḥaḏ,* "equivalent value

1. Cf. Leslau, *Contributions,* 30.
2. Cf. Wehr, 1051.
3. Cf. *CAD,* X/1 (1977), 92-99.
4. *KTU,* 4.625, 2.
5. *KTU,* 2.32, 9.
6. *KTU,* 4.338, 18.

— reward" (Isa. 45:13), *šōḥaḏ* — *m*^e^*ḥîr* — *kesep̱* (Mic. 3:11), and *hôn* — *m*^e^*ḥîr* (Ps. 44:13[12]; 4Q160 7:3) all suggest even less that our term refers to a given amount of silver.

According to Ps. 44:12f.(Eng. vv. 11f.), God sold his people and delivered them for slaughter like sheep without any gain for himself and without enriching himself through the appropriate equivalent value. It cannot be shown that the psalmist is referring here to the sale of small livestock for its silver value. Even the enumeration *rkwš whwn wmḥyr,* "possession, wealth, equal value" (4Q160 7:3), does not disclose the true nature of the *m*^e^*ḥîr.* The same is true of ostracon 2 from Arad (7th century B.C.), until now the only known piece of writing of Hebrew provenience spelling *mḥr* without the mater lectionis. The letter writer demands an appropriate equivalent value for the delivery of two baths of wine and three hundred loaves of bread to Greek merchants or mercenaries: *whsbt mḥr,* "and you are to bring an equivalent value" (ll. 5f.). In any case, in Prov. 27:26 the "equivalent value" for a field consists of goats. When the transaction involved silver, the terminology regularly includes the expression *b*^e^*ḵesep̱* (Dt. 2:6,28; 14:25; 21:14; 2 S. 24:24; 1 K. 10:29; 16:24; 21:6,15; 2 K. 6:25; 1 Ch. 21:22,24; 2 Ch. 1:17; 25:6; Isa. 7:23; 43:24; Jer. 32:25,44; Lam. 5:4; Ezk. 27:12; Hos. 3:2; Am. 2:6; 8:6; Mic. 3:11). Correspondingly, the expressions *lōʾ b*^e^*ḵesep̱* (Isa. 48:10; 52:3; 55:1) and *b*^e^*lî-ḵesep̱* (Job 31:39) signal a transaction not involving payment in silver. Such claims to "equivalent value," however, were not merely raised in exchanges for movable or immovable goods, but also for services rendered. Thus one can speak of a *m*^e^*ḥîr* for priests (Mic. 3:11), male cult prostitutes (*m*^e^*ḥîr keleḇ,* Dt. 23:19[18]; "dog's wages"[7]), and prostitutes (*m*^e^*ḥîr zônâ,* Bab. *Soṭah* 26b, etc.). In these three cases *m*^e^*ḥîr* evokes a clearly pejorative estimation. Although the content of the *m*^e^*ḥîr* is not specified here, other examples give us an idea of what is meant. According to Gen. 38:17,20,23, Judah offers the supposed prostitute or hierodule Tamar a kid[8] as payment. The compensation to priests consists in a legislated portion of the sacrifice (Lev. 2:3,10; 6:9f.,19,22[16f.,26,29]; 7:6,10,14f.; 10:12-15).

One cannot, of course, expect any precise indication of the *m*^e^*ḥîr* in those texts that speak of *m*^e^*ḥîr* in a metaphorical sense. In Prov. 17:16, the wise person asks what use the *m*^e^*ḥîr* could possibly have in the hand of a fool, since the fool cannot buy wisdom with it. A similar notion occurs in the Book of Mysteries of the Qumran Essenes (1Q27 1, II 8): *wk[wl mḥ]yr lwʾ yšwh b[. . .],* "and there is no equivalent value that corresponds to. . . ." In Sir. 6:15, the expression *ʾên m*^e^*ḥîr* is the pendent to *ʾên mišqāl,* which might evoke the weighed amount of silver. However, *ʾên m*^e^*ḥîr* here means that there is no equal to a loyal friend. CD 16:8f. admonishes the Qumran Essenes to keep their oath *ʿaḏ m*^e^*ḥîr māweṯ,* "even at the price of death." 1QH 10:10 is also important: *lgbwrtkh ʾyn mḥyr,* "nothing is comparable to your strength." Such expressions signal a comparison of values and show that *m*^e^*ḥîr* maintained this meaning even into the postbiblical period.

---

7. Cf. G. J. Botterweck, → כלב *keleḇ* (146-157).
8. → גדי *g*^e^*ḏî (g*^e^*dhî),* II.3 (II, 386).

The few concrete examples in which *m*e*ḥîr* definitely implies payment in silver refer to commercial transactions in which at least one partner is a reigning sovereign: the kings of Ugarit and Byblos,[9] David (2 S. 24:24), Solomon (1 K. 10:28f.; 2 Ch. 1:16f.), Ahab (1 K. 21:2). This is probably no accident. Proper commercial activity only became customary in Israel at a late period, and even then wholesale trade was primarily a royal undertaking, whereas private citizens in Israel and Judah made do mainly with local barter activity. It was at the village square or city gate, where the market was located, that artisans sold their works and farmers their agricultural produce (2 K. 7:1). This kind of retail trade took place directly between the producer and consumer, without any intermediary. Although weighed silver was doubtlessly being used as a kind of currency (e.g., Gen. 23:15f.; 2 K. 6:25; 7:1,16; Jer. 32:9), barter was still the more customary form of trade. Jacob purchased a parcel of land in exchange for 100 *q*e*śîṭôt* (Gen. 33:19; Josh. 24:32), the tenant pays his lease with goats (Prov. 27:26). Judah pays Tamar with a kid (Gen. 38:17), and each of Job's friends pays him with a *q*e*śîṭâ* and a ring of gold (Job 42:11). The meaning of *q*e*śîṭâ* is known from the older translation "lamb" (11QtgJob *'imm*e*râ;* Targ. Onqelos *ḥûrpā';* LXX *amnós, amnás*) and from the etymology **qśṭ,* "shear" (cf. Arab. *qašaṭa,* "scrape off," Akk. *kašāṭu,* "cut off"). Because of the confusion regarding the roots *qśṭ* and *qšṭ,* "be right, true" (> Arab. *qsṭ*), however, commentaries have tended to view this as a specific weight or quantity (cf. Arab. *qiṣt,* "a measure") of gold or silver.[10] The term *m*e*ḥîr* refers in any case to payment in silver or in kind, or even at a later period also in services rendered (Dnl. 11:39). The division of the lands by Antiochus Epiphanes *bimḥîr* obviously was not carried out in exchange for a payment in silver or in kind. The background here is military service to be rendered as compensation by those who profited from the divided land *(gḗ klērouchikē).* This system was widespread among the Seleucids and Ptolemies.

III. LXX. The translation of *m*e*ḥîr* clearly caused difficulties for the LXX. In addition to *állagma* (5 times) and *antállagma* (3 times), the LXX also uses *anállagma, dṓron, lýtron, misthós, timḗ,* and *chrḗma* once each. In 2 Ch. 1:16, it translates *lāqaḥ bimḥîr* by *agorázein.*

Lipiński

9. *KTU,* 4.338, 18.
10. Cf. A. de Wilde, *Das Buch Hiob. OTS,* 22 (1981), 406.

מָחַץ *māḥaṣ*

Contents: I. Etymology. II. OT Usage: 1. Occurrences, Literal Meaning; 2. Theological Usage; 3. Combinations. III. LXX.

I. Etymology. This root is attested in most Semitic languages: Ugar. *mḫṣ,* "smash, smite,"[1] Akk. *maḫāṣu,* "strike; weave,"[2] Ethiop., Tigre *maḫaṣa,* "strike," Arab. *maḫaḍa,* "shake," Aram. *meḥāʾ/meḥâ* (< *meḥaʿ*), "strike."[3]

II. OT Usage. 1. *Occurrences, Literal Meaning.* The verb *māḥaṣ* and the subst. *maḥaṣ* occur only in poetic texts (the verb occurs in Jgs. 5, though not in the par. Jgs. 4), especially in hymns and similar genres. Discounting Ps. 68:24(Eng. v. 23) (scribal error *timḥaṣ* for *tirḥaṣ?*) and the duplicate involving Ps. 18 and 2 S. 22, the verb occurs 12 times and the noun once; i.e., this verb is relatively rare.

Considering the scarcity of material, it is noteworthy how relatively often *roʾš* (4 times) and *pēʾâ* (once) occur as objects, either in the literal sense or figuratively as "roof," "superior." If one additionally considers the object *mo̱tnayim* (1 occurrence), the fundamental meaning "strike, smash" seems most probable, and thence "conquer."

The physical quality emerges perhaps best in Jgs. 5:26, in a descriptive series of verbs.[4] Although this might evoke a shattering blow, the mention of an arrow as the instrument in Nu. 24:8 militates for a less specific meaning.

The object is usually personal or personified, and if a collective, a people or an army; the verb means to "conquer, overcome." The predominating meanings are thus "strike, smash" and "conquer."

2. *Theological Usage.* The subject determines the theological use of the verb. It never occurs with a secular or theologically neutral meaning; the subject is always God or his people, a fact aiding in evaluating the sparse material.

a. With God as the subject, *māḥaṣ* occurs antithetically with *rāp̄āʾ* in Dt. 32:39; Job 5:18; Isa. 30:26 (subst.); this antithesis expresses God's unlimited sovereignty, and the three passages are intended as arguments supporting the notion of hope. In Dt. 32:39, the pair *māḥaṣ — rāp̄āʾ* parallel the verbs of killing *(mwt* hiphil) and making alive *(ḥyh* piel). These three texts are related to Isa. 19:22 *(ngp — rpʾ);* Jer. 30:17 *(nkh* hiphil *— rpʾ);* Hos. 6:1 *(ṭrp — rpʾ),* and are best evaluated in connection

---

māḥaṣ. H. Schäfer, "Das Niederschlagen der Feinde: Zum Geschick eines ägyptischen Sinnbildes," *WZKM,* 54 (1957), 168-176.

1. *WUS,* no. 1547; by-form *mḫš, WUS,* no. 1550.
2. *AHw,* II (1972), 580.
3. *DISO,* 147.
4. See below.

with the notion of the healing God.[5] Here they also serve to draw *mḥṣ* into the semantic range of *nkh* and *ngp*.

b. With God as the subject in warfare, God fights against his or his people's enemies (Dt. 33:11; Ps. 68:22[21]; 110:5f.; Hab. 3:13) or against a mythical adversary (Job 26:12).

Although in Hab. 3:13 one might take *rō'š mibbêṯ* to be the "head of the family," the parallel word *yᵉsôḏ* shows that the reference is to a house, with its roof and foundation. The second expression, *'ārôṯ yᵉsôḏ,* recalls Ps. 137:7 *('ārâ);* Ezk. 13:14; Mic. 1:6 *(gālâ).* This sparse evidence does not allow the conclusion that *māḥaṣ rō'š* represents a fixed formula. The term *yᵉsôḏ* might adroitly be alluding to *sôḏ* for the sake of creating a play on words: roof and foundation, leader and counselor.

Ps. 110:5f. contains a series of chiastic correspondences which must be considered in any explanation of the text. A schematic presentation reveals several relationships:

mḥṣ mᵉlāḵîm
yāḏîn baggôyim
mḥṣ rō'š 'al-'ereṣ rabbâ
yārîm rō'š minnaḥal badderek̲
mᵉlāḵîm/gôyim, mᵉlāḵîm/rō'š
māḥaṣ rō'š/yārîm rō'š, mḥṣ/dyn

If we consider the common elements for *mḥṣ* and *dyn,* the sense is that of a victory with the character of judgment confusing the kings and their peoples. If we direct attention to the objects of *mḥṣ,* the first *rō'š* could be a defeated leader on a broad plain; if in contrast we consider the two verbs in connection with *rō'š,* the physical aspects emerge: a shattered head (collective) and a head that raises itself in victory. The poet combines the two aspects to attain a pregnant ambiguity or ambivalence.

In Ps. 68:22(21), *rō'š* can also be alluding to the leader, although the par. *qoḏqōḏ* suggests a physical connotation with descriptive value.

The texts of this group all belong to the notion of God as warrior.

c. Israel or its king is the subject of *mḥṣ* in Nu. 24:8,17; Ps. 18:39[38] par. 2 S. 22:39. In these cases God's intervention and even his warrior role are unequivocal, something also discernible in Nu. 24:17 from the parallelism and preceding oracles (cf. 1QM 11:6; 12:11). Thus for all practical purposes these texts can be subsumed under the previous group.

3. *Combinations.* Outside the context of holy war several series or parallels can be discerned.

Nu. 24:8: *yō'ḵal ṣārāw — yᵉgārēm 'aṣmōṯêhem — ḥiṣṣāw yimḥaṣ.* Because of insufficient correspondence between *ḥēṣ* and *'eṣem,* some interpreters emend the text to achieve a parallel to *ṣar* and *'eṣem;* in the MT, however, the third expression introduces a change in function, underscoring it with the alliteration *mḥṣ/ḥṣ.*

---

5. → רפא *rāp̄ā'.*

Jgs. 5:26: *hālam — māḥaq rō'š — māḥaṣ — ḥālap raqqāṯô*. This combination of expressions brings *māḥaṣ* into a parallel position with *hālam,* and assonance connects *hālam* and *ḥālap, māḥaq* and *māḥaṣ*.

Ps. 18:38f.(37f.): *rdp, hišmîḏ* (so 2 S. 22 contra Ps. 18 *nśg* hiphil), *klh, mḥṣ; lō' qûm, npl* is a series sooner attesting pleonasm than genuine differentiation; it describes emphatically the finality of the victory.

III. LXX. The LXX does not render *māḥaṣ* consistently. The only renderings that recur are *patássein* (3 times) and *synthlán* (4 times); the other occurrences use *bállein, báptein, ekthlíbein, thlán, thraúein, katagnýnai, katatoxeúein, paíein, strōnnýein, syntríbein,* and *tríbein.*

Alonso-Schökel

מָחָר *māḥār;* מָחֳרָת *moḥ°rāṯ*

Contents: I. 1. Etymology; 2. Meaning, Related Words, Distribution. II. OT Usage: 1. Departure; 2. Meals and the Cult; 3. Good Fortune or Disaster; 4. Drinking Songs and Proverbs; 5. The Children's Question. III. LXX.

I. 1. *Etymology.* The etymology of *māḥār* is disputed. Although Carl Brockelmann[1] postulates an original form **ma'ḥar* (root *'ḥr*),[2] this etymology is unlikely, since there is no trace of the '. G. R. Driver's suggestion[3] that *māḥār* belongs with Akk. *maḫāru,* "confront" (cf. *ina maḫri,* "before"), is doubtlessly preferable. Other related words are attested in Canaanite (EA *ūmi ma-ḫa-ri*)[4] and in several Aramaic dialects (Egyp.-Aram.,[5] Targ. *mᵉḥar, maḥrā',* Syr. *mᵉḥār*). This militates for derivation from *mḫr*.

2. *Meaning, Related Words, Distribution.* The term *moḥ°rāṯ* unequivocally means

---

māḥār. J. Barr, *Biblical Words for Time. SBT,* 33 (²1969); S. J. DeVries, "Temporal Terms as Structural Elements in the Holy-War Tradition," *VT,* 25 (1975), 80-105; *idem,* "The Time Word *māḥār* as a Key to Tradition Development," *ZAW,* 87 (1975), 65-79; *idem, Yesterday, Today and Tomorrow: Time and History in the OT* (Grand Rapids, 1975); J. Finegan, *Handbook of Biblical Chronology* (Princeton, 1964); G. Gerleman, "'Heute', 'Gestern' und 'Morgen' im Hebräischen," *TAik,* 72 (1967), 84-89; B. Halpern, "The Ritual Background of Zechariah's Temple Song," *CBQ,* 40 (1978), 167-190.

1. *VG,* I, 241.
2. So also *GesB.*
3. Review of P. Leander, *Laut- und Formenlehre des Ägyptisch-Aramäischen. Göteborgs Högskolas Årsskrift,* 34 (1928), *JRAS,* 1932, 178f.
4. *AHw,* III (1972), 580a.
5. *DISO,* 148.

"the following day," and follows upon *bayyôm hahû'* just as *māḥār* follows upon *hayyôm* (2 S. 11:12); *kol yôm hammoḥᵒrāṯ* follows upon *kol-hayyôm hahû' wᵉkol-hal-laylâ* (Nu. 11:32). The day between a specific day *(yôm ziḇḥᵃḵem)* and *yôm haššᵉlîšî* is *moḥᵒrāṯ* (Lev. 19:6). The day which in a given context is designated as *māḥār* (Ex. 9:5f.; 32:5f.; 1 S. 11:9-11) and follows upon a night (Gen. 19:34; Jgs. 6:38; 1 S. 30:17; Jon. 4:7; cf. v. 10) is *moḥᵒrāṯ*. Combinations containing *moḥᵒrāṯ* include *lᵉmoḥᵒraṯ hayyôm hahû'* (1 Ch. 29:21), *mimmoḥᵒraṯ haḥōḏeš* (1 S. 20:27), *mimmoḥᵒraṯ happesaḥ* (Nu. 33:3; Josh. 5:11), *mimmoḥᵒraṯ haššabbāṯ* (Lev. 23:11,15f.).

The term *māḥār* means "tomorrow, the morrow," and usually has the sense "tomorrow" = "on the following day," although it can sometimes be translated with "in the future" (Gen. 30:33; Ex. 13:14; Dt. 6:20; Josh. 4:6,21; 22:24,27,28). The connection with *bōqer* and *škm* hiphil shows that *māḥār* often means "early tomorrow morning" (Ex. 9:13-18; cf. 8:16-19[Eng. vv. 20-23]; 10:4-13; 16:23; cf. v. 24; Nu. 14:25; cf. v. 40; 16:5-7; Josh. 7:13-16; Jgs. 19:9; 1 S. 9:16-19; 11:9-11; 19:11; 2 S. 11:12-14; 2 K. 10:6-9; 2 Ch. 20:16-20). Combinations with *māḥār* include *kā'ēṯ māḥār,* "tomorrow about this time" (1 S. 9:16; 1 K. 19:2; 20:6; 2 K. 7:1,18; 10:6), and *māḥār kā'ēṯ hazzō'ṯ* (Josh. 11:6).

The use of *māḥār* and *moḥᵒrāṯ* is unequally distributed among the biblical books: 31 occurrences in the Pentateuch, 11 in Joshua, 5 in Judges, 24 in Samuel-Kings, 4 in the prophets, twice in Proverbs, 3 in Esther, 4 in Chronicles.

II. OT Usage. 1. *Departure.* A person can request of another (e.g., a Levite, Jgs. 19:9; Uriah, 2 S. 11:12; cf. v. 14) to stay the night and postpone departure until "tomorrow morning." The Israelites set out from Rameses "on the day after" the passover (Nu. 33:3; cf. Josh. 5:11f.); later they are instructed to set out on a different route "tomorrow" (morning) (Nu. 14:25; cf. v. 40).

2. *Meals and the Cult.* Esther prepared a dinner for the king "today" and "tomorrow" (Est. 5:8,12; cf. v. 4). Saul's intentions toward David are to be disclosed by David's absence from the Feast of the New Moon "tomorrow and the day after tomorrow" (1 S. 20:5,12,18f.,27). A great famine prompts a woman to propose: "Give up your son; we will eat him today, and we will eat my son tomorrow" (2 K. 6:28).

A thanksgiving offering *(zeḇaḥ tôḏaṯ šᵉlāmîm)* must be eaten on the day of the offering, and may not be left till the morning *(bōqer,* Lev. 7:15); a votive offering or a freewill offering is to be eaten on the day of the sacrifice or on the next day (Lev. 7:16; 19:6). A portion of the food prepared on the sixth day from the manna and quail was put aside for the following sabbath (Ex. 16:23). The first sheaf of the harvest is to be sacrificed as a wave offering on the day after the sabbath (Lev. 23:11,15,16). After a lament before God in Bethel the people arose early the next morning, built an altar, and offered sacrifices (Jgs. 21:4). When Aaron had built an altar before the golden calf, he announced: "Tomorrow *(māḥār)* shall be a *ḥag* to Yahweh," and early in the morning of the next day *(škm* hiphil; *mimmoḥᵒrāṯ)* the celebration took place with offerings, eating, drinking, and play (Ex. 32:5f.). On the following day Moses entreated Yahweh to forgive the people (32:30; on celebrating *māḥār,* cf. Ex. 16:23; 32:5; 1 S.

20:5,18). On the day after Moses tells his father-in-law about being delivered by God he appointed judges (Ex. 18:13-26). At an offering feast Solomon becomes coregent on the day after David's thanksgiving prayer for the generous contributions to the temple construction (1 Ch. 29:21). God announces Saul's arrival to Samuel: "Tomorrow about this time I will send to you a man . . . and you shall anoint him to be ruler" (1 S. 9:16).

Several texts speak of preparations for a divine sign and/or theophany which is to take place *māḥār,* "tomorrow" (Nu. 16:7,16; 17:6,23[16:41; 17:8]).

Four passages speak of consecration on the day before a proclamation of God's deeds: before the making of the covenant (the act is postponed until the *yôm haššᵉlîšî,* Ex. 19:10f.), the quail miracle (Nu. 11:18), the halting of the waters of the Jordan (Josh. 3:5; cf. 4:6,21), and the casting of lots to determine guilt (Josh. 7:13).

"Tomorrow" is an important concept in the account of the plagues (Ex. 7:8–11:10), although it does fulfill different functions in the various accounts and does not occur in them all. Yahweh declares: "this sign [flies] shall occur *lᵉmāḥār*" (8:19[23]). Yahweh set a time and said: "*māḥār* Yahweh will do this thing [cattle plague] in the land" (9:5). The expression *mimmoḥᵒrāṯ* is used in the account of the actual carrying out of the plagues (9:6).[6] Yahweh twice speaks in conditional terms: "If you oppose/refuse . . . *māḥār* I will cause the heaviest hail to fall/bring locusts" (9:17f.; 10:4). Moses promises to ask God to take away the flies *māḥār* (8:25[29]), and Pharaoh himself is permitted to set the time for the departure of the frogs. He answers "*lᵉmāḥār*" (8:6[10]). This precise agreement on the time excludes any possibility of chance.

Other texts use *kāʿēṯ māḥār* in threats and promises (1 S. 9:16; 1 K. 19:2; 20:6; 2 K. 7:1,18; 10:6; *māḥār kāʿēṯ hazzōʾṯ,* Josh. 11:6). These occurrences of *māḥār* suggest that Yahweh's theophany, signs, or intervention was announced the preceding day.

3. *Good Fortune or Disaster.* It is often said that the defeat of Israel's enemies and, concomitantly, Israel's victory will occur "tomorrow," or occurred on the following day/morning. In warfare God is *māḥār* (Ex. 17:9; Josh. 11:6; Jgs. 20:28; 1 S. 11:9f.; 2 K. 7:1,18; Est. 9:13; 2 Ch. 20:16f.) or *moḥᵒrāṯ* (1 S. 5:3f.; 11:11; 30:16) present in the midst of his victorious people (Josh. 11:6; 1 S. 11:11; cf. vv. 6,13; 2 K. 7:1,18; cf. 6:33; 7:6) with his rod (Ex. 17:9), with the ark of the covenant (Jgs. 20:27f.; 1 S. 5:1-4), with the ephod (1 S. 30:17; cf. v. 7f.), through hymn singers before the warriors (2 Ch. 20:14-26). The sign of deliverance (dew on the fleece of wool) also occurred *moḥᵒrāṯ* (Jgs. 6:38).

It also happens that disaster or defeat is predicted for "the following day" (Josh. 22:18; 1 S. 28:19; 1 K. 20:6). Defeat is brought about by Yahweh himself because of sin (Josh. 22:18; 1 S. 28:19). The day after Saul's death the Philistines defile his corpse (1 S. 31:8; 1 Ch. 10:8; cf. 2 K. 10:6). Jezebel threatens to kill Elijah "tomorrow" (1 K. 19:2). Saul tries to kill David (1 S. 19:11). To become king, Hazael kills Ben-hadad

---

6. See S. Ö. Steingrimsson, *Vom Zeichen zur Geschichte. CB,* 14 (1979), 227f.

the day after telling him "you will certainly recover" (2 K. 8:15f.). The plant under which Jonah sat withered the day after it sprouted (Jon. 4:7).

4. *Drinking Songs and Proverbs.* Despite an apparently similar formal background, the hedonistic exhortations in Isa. 22:13; 56:12 evoke different perspectives on the future. "Let us eat and drink, for tomorrow we die" (Isa. 22:13; cf. 1 Cor. 15:32) is the people's resigned reaction to the disaster. Instead of holding a lament, they celebrate with an excess of wine and flesh. "Come, let me get wine; let us fill ourselves with strong drink. And tomorrow will be like today, great beyond measure" (Isa. 56:12; cf. Am. 4:1) is spoken by the selfish shepherds of the people who do not comprehend the imminent threat of disaster. The common formal background is that of a drinking song (cf. Isa. 28:7-10). Several so-called harpists' songs from Egyptians tombs contain similar statements, e.g., "Celebrate a cheerful day, you noble one! Forget all that is bad and think only of joy, till the day when you come into the land that cherishes silence."[7]

Prov. 3:28 admonishes a person to be quick to lend aid: "Do not say . . . tomorrow I will give it [to you]" (cf. Dt. 24:14f.), and Prov. 27:1 to be mindful of the uncertainty of the morrow (cf. Ps. 39:5f.[4f.]; Sir. 18:26; Jas. 4:13-16). A similar maxim can be found on a statue of the twenty-second dynasty: "Put tomorrow clearly before us! What is in it is not known";[8] compare also the story of the Eloquent Peasant: "Do not prepare for tomorrow before it is come. One knows not what evil may be in it."[9]

5. *The Children's Question.* This question occurs in three variations: *kî-yišʾālᵉḵā binḵā māḥār lēʾmōr mah-* (Ex. 13:14; Dt. 6:20, Passover celebration), *kî-yišʾālûn bᵉnêḵem māḥār lēʾmōr mah-* (Josh. 4:6,21, stones), *māḥār yōʾmᵉrû bᵉnêḵem lᵉḇānênû lēʾmōr mah-* (Josh. 22:24,27,28, altar at Gilead). In the first case the son will inquire at the sacrifice of the firstborn[10] about its significance. His father will then recall God's killing of the Egyptian firstborn. In Josh. 4 the question "What do these stones mean to you?" is associated with two versions of the crossing of the Jordan.[11] The answer to v. 6 explains the twelve stones in the middle of the Jordan, while that to v. 21 addresses the Gilgal sanctuary. Both explanations are to recall the miracle of the water (Josh. 3). The context in Josh. 22 is different. The question in 22:24, "What have you to do with Yahweh, the God of Israel?" is intended as an accusation made to the eastern tribes, as shown by vv. 27f.: "You have no portion in Yahweh." To counter this

7. Cf. S. Schott, *Altägyptische Liebeslieder* (Zurich, [2]1950), 134.

8. *Kairo WB,* no. 49(58) = *WbÄS,* Belegst. V, 423[1]; cited in J. G. Griffith, "Wisdom About Tomorrow," *HThR,* 53 (1960), 219-221.

9. B 1, 183, A. Erman, *The Literature of the Ancient Egyptians* (Eng. trans., New York, 1927, repr. 1971); cf. F. Vogelsang, *Die Klagen des Bauern* (Berlin, 1904), 146.

10. M. Noth, *Exodus. OTL* (Eng. trans. 1962), 101f.

11. J. A. Soggin, *Joshua. OTL* (Eng. trans. 1972), 43-67; cf. also E. Otto, *Das Mazzotfest in Gilgal. BWANT,* 107[6/7] (1975), esp. II.2.

accusation in the future, the altar (the real reason behind the accusation) is erected as a witness to the common faith in Yahweh.[12]

III. LXX. The LXX usually translates *māḥār* with *aúrion* and *moḥ^{o}rāṯ* with *epaúrion,* although *moḥ^{o}rāṯ* is also rendered with *aúrion* (Lev. 7:16; 19:6), *metá tḗn aúrion* (Ex. 32:30; 1 S. 11:11), *hḗ echoménē* (*sic,* 1 Ch. 10:8), and *tó prōí* (1 S. 5:4). In Ex. 13:14 *māḥār* in the sense of "in time to come" is translated by *metá taúta.* The parallel in Dt. 6:20 has *aúrion.* The LXX gives no equivalent for *māḥār* in Josh. 4:21; 1 S. 20:12 or for *moḥ^{o}rāṯ* in Josh. 5:11,12; Jer. 20:3.

André

---

12. On the "children's question," cf. recently H.-J. Fabry, "Gott im Gespräch zwischen den Generationen," *Katechetische Blätter,* 107 (1982), 754-760.

מַטֶּה *maṭṭeh*

Contents: I. 1. Occurrences; 2. Etymology; 3. LXX. II. 1. Literal Meaning; 2. Literal Meaning with Overtones: a. Branch, Stem; b. Rod, Staff. III. Figurative Meaning: 1. Tribe; 2. Instrument of Might (Isaiah); 3. Power (Ezekiel). IV. Problematic Passages. V. 1. Qumran; 2. Post-OT Period.

I. 1. *Occurrences.* The word *maṭṭeh* (pl. *maṭṭôṯ*) occurs 252 times in the OT,[1] in the majority of cases with the sociological meaning "tribe." Of these, 111 are in Numbers, 59 in Joshua, 27 in Exodus, and 23 in 1 Chronicles. To these passages one should add the 6 occurrences in Sirach and the conjectures in Ps. 89:45(Eng. v. 44); Ezr. 9:13.[2] The most frequent combinations with *maṭṭeh* are *maṭṭēh-leḥem, maṭṭēh ʿōz, maṭṭeh* in parallelism with *šēḇeṭ,* in connection with the names of the tribes of Israel, and in the expression *maṭṭēh b^{e}nê . . . ,* further the expression *rāʾšê hammaṭṭôṯ.* Besides *maṭṭeh* and *šēḇeṭ,* other OT words with the meaning "stick, staff" include *m^{e}ḥōqēq* (Nu. 21:18; Gen. 49:10), which acquires the connotation "the ruler, authority" (Jgs. 5:14; Dt. 33:21)

---

maṭṭeh. S. Cavalletti, "La terminologia ebraica per 'bastone,'" *Antonianum,* 28 (1953), 411-424; W. Dietrich, *Jesaja und die Politik. BEvTh,* 74 (1976), 115-122, 125-28; A. H. J. Gunneweg, *Leviten und Priester. FRLANT,* N.S. 71[89] (1965), 95-98, 171-188; P. Humbert, "Étendre la main," *VT,* 12 (1962), 383-395; G. Sauer, "Mandelzweig und Kessel in Jer $1_{11ff.}$," *ZAW,* 78 (1966), 56-61; H. Valentin, *Aaron: Eine Studie zur vor-priesterlichen Aaron-Überlieferung. OBO,* 18 (1978), 72-81, 158-182; R. de Vaux, *AncIsr,* 4-10; P. Weimar and E. Zenger, *Exodus: Geschichten und Geschichte der Befreiung Israels. SBS,* 75 (1975); G. J. Wenham, "Aaron's Rod (Numbers 17_{16-18})," *ZAW,* 93 (1981), 280f.

1. A. Even-Shoshan, *A New Concordance of the OT* (Jerusalem, 1983), lists 251 occurrences.
2. See IV below.

and, through its association with Yahweh (Ps. 60:9[7] par. 108:9[8]), becomes one of Yahweh's titles, and also exhibits the connotation "judge" or "king,"[3] and *maqqēl,* "rod, branch, staff."[4]

2. *Etymology.* The word *maṭṭeh* probably derives from *nṭy.*[5] J. M. A. Janssen[6] views it as a loanword from Egyp. *mdw.* Akkadian attests the root *naṭû,* "strike,"[7] although neither the meaning "stretch forth" nor any subst. **maṭṭû* is attested. Of the substantives referring to the staff or scepter, *ḫaṭṭu* occurs most frequently; *šabbiṭu* (Heb. *šēḇeṭ*) occurs only in three texts.[8] In contrast, *maṭṭeh* occurs in Ugaritic[9] and has now also been attested in the Ebla texts.[10] In *KTU,*[11] *mṭm* stands parallel with *qšth,* as in Hab. 3:9.[12]

3. *LXX.* The LXX uses *stḗrigma* for "staff of bread" (Ps. 105:16; Ezk. 4:16; 5:16; 7:11), *skḗptron* in Hab. 3:9; 1 S. 14:27,43, *zygós* in Isa. 14:5, *plēgḗ* in Isa. 10:24, and *thymós* in Isa. 10:26. Jer. 31:17 uses *baktḗria; rábdos* is used in Gen. 38:18,25 and in the narratives in which the staff exhibits quasi-magical power (Ex. 7–10; 14:16; 17:5,9) or functions as a sign of Yahweh's might (Ex. 4). In all texts where *maṭṭeh* means "tribe" it is translated by *phýlē,* including Mic. 6:9, where the meaning is difficult to determine.[13]

II. 1. *Literal Meaning.* The term *maṭṭeh* occurs in its literal meaning without additional connotations in Gen. 38:18,25 as one of the pledges Judah gives Tamar; Jonathan, who is unaware of Saul's oath, carries one (1 S. 14:27,43), as do the Levites who transport the ark (1 Ch. 15:15). This group also includes the expression *maṭṭēh-leḥem* (Lev. 26:26; Ps. 105:16; Ezk. 4:16; 5:16; 14:13; cf. Sir. 48:2), in reference to the stick or staff on which the ring-shaped *ḥallâ*-bread was stacked to keep it away from mice, etc.,[14] or to the stalk (*lḥm* is attested in the meaning "corn, grain"[15]). Since *maṭṭēh-leḥem* is everywhere associated with the verb *šbr* and with the explicit mention

---

3. "חקק *ḥqq* einritzen, festsetzen," *THAT,* I, 628, 630.

4. On the staff and scepter as symbols of authority, cf. G. Fohrer, "Stab," *BHHW,* III, 1845; L. E. Toombs, "Scepter," *IDB,* IV, 234f. (with bibliog.); → שֵׁבֶט *šēḇeṭ;* → מקל *maqqēl* (VIII, 548-551).

5. *BLe,* §491n; *KBL*[3], 542.

6. *L'AT et l'Orient* (Louvain, 1957), 40; cf. also W. B. Kristensen, *MKAW,* 16/14 (1954), 591-610.

7. *AHw,* II (1962), 768.

8. *AHw,* III (1981) 1119.

9. *WUS,* no. 1551; Whitaker, 417; cf. M. Held, "*mḫṣ/*mḫš* in Ugaritic and Other Semitic Languages," *JAOS,* 79 (1959), 169f.

10. TM.75 G.2005 obv. III, 13-17 ^{giš}*gu-RU*^{urudu} = *ma-ṭì-um;* TM.75 G.1426 obv. III, 8-13 ^{giš}*gu-RU-kak*^{urudu} = *ma-ṭì-um;* references by G. Pettinato.

11. 1.3 III, 15f.

12. Cf. M. Dahood and T. Penar, "Ugaritic-Hebrew Parallel Pairs," *RSP,* I, 349.

13. See IV below.

14. *HAL,* II (1995), 573.

15. *KTU,* 1.16 III, 14 and Ps. 104:15; see M. Dahood, *Psalms III. AB,* XVIIA (1970), 40.

of famine in a city, the expression probably refers to a city's food supplies. The expression is always collective, with the exception of Ps. 105:16, "every *maṭṭēh-leḥem.*"[16]

2. *Literal Meaning with Overtones.* a. *Branch, Stem.* The expression *maṭṭēh/maṭṭôṯ ʿōz/ʿuzzāh* (3 times) occurs in the allegorical lament Ezk. 19:10-14 (a product of the school of Ezekiel that rounds off and concludes Ezk. 19:1-9) with the literal meaning "branch, stem"; it fashions the allegory by referring simultaneously also to the scepter of power and to descendants. Israel's ultimate victory is evoked by the image of the vine. The *maṭṭôṯ ʿōz* could transform themselves into *šiḇṭê mōšᵉlîm* (v. 11), but after chastisement, expressed in a general sense by the images of the east wind and fire, there is no longer any strong stem (descendants, tribe) able to transform itself into the ruler's scepter (v. 14). It is possible that this image has been influenced by the old Royal Psalm Ps. 110, with the expression *maṭṭēh-ʿuzzᵉḵā* (Ps. 110:2), where *maṭṭeh* serves more clearly than in any other OT text as the symbol of the royal dynasty Yahweh has chosen and protects. In Ezk. 19:10-14, *maṭṭeh* is simultaneously the symbol of the descendants (pl. *maṭṭôṯ,* v. 11) of Israel in general and of the royal dynasty in particular. In Jer. 48:17, the elegiac exclamation "how the *maṭṭēh-ʿōz* (par. *maqqēl*) [of Moab] is broken!" most closely resembles Isa. 14:5b. This image is a completely fixed expression and does not refer to the branch or descendants, but rather only to the authority evoked by the figure "staff of power."

b. *Rod, Staff.* The "staff" as a concrete object which nonetheless connotes a special power attributed to Yahweh occurs especially in Exodus and Nu. 17:20[5]. Ex. 4:2f. (J) is the oldest passage attesting this notion; both Ex. 7:15 ("the staff that was turned into a snake") and Ex. 17:5 ("the staff with which you struck the Nile"; cf. 7:17) then allude to it. In Ex. 4:2f., the rod that turned into a serpent is a symbol of Yahweh's powerful help, while in Ex. 4:17 it is the instrument of the manifestation of such power before Pharaoh. The demonstrative expression "this staff" seems to introduce an unknown element into the narrative; possibly the intention is to distance the object from Moses' possession, since it has become the instrument of divine action. This is also the sense of the E conclusion to the narrative (Ex. 4:20).

In the plague stories, *maṭṭeh* is mentioned 14 times in reference to Moses' or Aaron's staff; all occurrences belong to P with the exception of Ex. 7:15,17. Martin Noth[17] views these two passages as J; apparently, however, the new introduction "thus says Yahweh" in v. 17 seems contrived after vv. 14,16, and it remains unclear just who is carrying out the action, Moses or Yahweh. Verse 17 thus might contain the pre-Yahwistic source of the plague story in which Yahweh himself smites Egypt and the first-born (7:17; 12:29). As soon as the action shifts into the hand of Moses (as

16. Cf. further H. Schult, "Marginale zum 'Stab des Brotes,'" *ZDPV,* 87 (1971), 206-8; J. Schoneveld, "Het breken van de staf des broods," *NedThT,* 27 (1973), 132-145; → לחם *leḥem* (VII, 521-29) and the postbiblical metaphorical parallel construction "staff of living water" among the Mandeans; cf. K. Rudolph, *Die Mandäer,* II. *FRLANT,* N.S. 75[93] (1961), 33-37.

17. *Exodus. OTL* (Eng. trans. 1962), 72f.

Yahweh's instrument?), the rod is introduced. In the other passages in the plague story the ambiguity is striking; the rod of Moses (Ex. 9:23) or of Aaron (7:9f.) is mentioned. The sequence of events is confused; there is no connection between command and execution as regards the expressions "take/stretch forth the rod," "stretch forth one's hand," and "strike with the rod." Compare Ex. 7:19 with v. 20; 8:1(5) with v. 2(6); 8:12[16] with v. 13[17] and 9:22; 10:12 with 9:23; 10:13. Although the mention of Aaron in the plague story is universally viewed as a later addition, probably by P, the lack of consistency in the use of the expression does not permit the attribution to P of all texts in the plague story which mention *maṭṭeh.*[18] One might sooner assume a redaction JE which has combined the expression preferred by E, "stretch forth one's hand," with the motif of the powerful rod found in J. In the story of the crossing of the sea, the command "stretch out your hand" is given twice (14:16,26), and its execution is narrated in 14:21,27. In this context the mention of the raising of the rod seems displaced and to be a redactional attempt (by P?) to associate the crossing of the sea with the E account of the plagues.

The "staff of God in my hand" in Ex. 17:9 introduces an element of tension into the narrative of the victory over the Amalekites, where in the final analysis the rod has no real function. Moses' action is centered in holding up both hands (arms), although he does need the physical help of both Aaron and Hur. The introduction of the rod into this story might be intended to justify theologically a given action (holding hands up) as having been commanded by Yahweh ("staff of God"), an action which in the original version of the story, i.e., without any explicit commission by Yahweh, might have appeared to be an act of magic. In Nu. 20:1-13 (P) (water from the rock in the wilderness of Zin), *maṭṭeh* is mentioned 3 times (vv. 8,9,11) in the middle of the narrative. In contrast to the clear and logical exposition in the other version of the event in Ex. 17:1-7, Nu. 20 is characterized by an element of tension between the action focusing on the use of the *maṭṭeh* on the one hand and the information in v. 8 on the other: it is through the power of Moses' and Aaron's word that the rock will yield water to the assembled people. Here, too, P has attempted to correct the elements of the narrative of Ex. 17 as he found them by means of a theological commentary: Moses' and Aaron's action receives its power not through magic, but rather through Yahweh's will.

The expression *millipnê YHWH* in Nu. 17:24(9) is alluding to Aaron's rod in v. 25(10). In Nu. 17:17-26(2-11) (P), *maṭṭeh* occurs 16 times. The unified account of Aaron's budding rod cannot have been incorporated into the context of Nu. 16–17 as a positive counterpart in order to show, e.g., that the Aaronites are the only legitimate priests,[19] nor to produce an advantage for the Levites over against the laity by mentioning Aaron as the "head" of the tribe of Levi. Rather, the intention is more likely to integrate Aaron into the tribe of Levi as the genealogies do, thus resolving the old theoretical and practical problems associated with the relationship between Levi and

18. *Ibid.,* 67-84.
19. M. Noth, *Numbers. OTL* (Eng. trans. 1968), 130f.

Aaron. It is hardly conceivable that a rod was kept in the temple as a relic, as A. H. J. Gunneweg suggests.[20]

III. Figurative Meaning.

1. *Tribe.* The transition from the literal meaning "branch, rod" to the sociological meaning "tribe" is reflected perhaps in Nu. 18:2. The translation of *maṭṭēh lēwî* par. *šēḇeṭ 'āḇîḵā* might be "tribe of Levi, branch of your father." There is no persuasive reason simply to repeat the term "tribe." The sense of *maṭṭeh* as "tribe" is preferred not only because of the notion of the "*maṭṭeh* of power" under which all the members of a group are subsumed, but also because of the image of the different branches which belong to the same tree trunk (i.e., stem/trunk [Ger. "Stamm"] > tribe). A third component would be the sexual connotation of *maṭṭeh,* which is probably attested in several Ugaritic texts[21] and perhaps implied in Ps. 89:45(44) if one reads *maṭṭēh hārô,* "branch of procreation"; this variant might be supported by parallelism with vv. 30,37(29,36).[22]

There does not seem to be any difference between *maṭṭeh* and *šēḇeṭ* in the meaning "tribe," although *maṭṭeh* occurs predominantly in reference to the names of the traditional tribes.

a. P uses *maṭṭeh* systematically in its lists, although this does not imply that such usage is exclusive to P nor that P initiated the use of *maṭṭeh* in the sense of "tribe." This more likely reflects common exilic and postexilic usage.[23]

P lists in which *maṭṭeh* is used in the sense of "tribe" include: Nu. 1:20-46 (the census of the tribes); 2:3-31 (the arrangement of the tribes while encamped); 10:14-27 (the order of march out of the Sinai desert); 13:4-15 (the list of spies as representatives of the tribes); 34:18-28 (the lists of those commissioned to divide the land among the nine and one half tribes).

Nu. 1:20-46 probably represents the older document which served as the reference for 2:3-31; 10:14-27.[24] The list of spies seems to be an *ad hoc* construction by P based on the model of 1:5-15, whose order of tribes it essentially duplicates. In its own turn, Nu. 34:18-28 takes the two preceding lists as its model. The appearance of old names both in Nu. 13 and in Nu. 34 shows merely that the author had access to such names; it says nothing about the age of these lists. Because of their structure and the high overall numbers, Nu. 1:5-15; 26:5-51 seem to be the oldest documents from the period of the organization of the tribes. These served as the model for the lists of P, the former for the lists of the *n^e^śî'îm,* the latter for the lists of tribes. Neither of the two lists uses *maṭṭeh,* prompting the question whether the genuinely older element in Nu. 1:20-46

---

20. P. 184.

21. Cf. *KTU,* 1.23, 27, 40, 44, 47; other possible occurrences are listed in Whitaker, 417.

22. H.-J. Kraus, *Psalms 60–150* (Eng. trans., Minneapolis, 1989), 199, 200 reads *maṭṭēh hôḏô,* "his powerful scepter."

23. M. Noth, *Überlieferungsgeschichtliche Studien* (Tübingen, 1943), 184.

24. On the high numbers, cf. G. E. Mendenhall, "The Census Lists of Numbers 1 and 26," *JBL,* 77 (1958), 52-66.

does not consist in the simple mention of the tribe, *liḇnê* + number. The two later lists, 10:14-27 and 34:18-28, use *maṭṭeh* + *bᵉnê* + the name of the tribe.

b. In Josh. 13:15,29; 15:1–19:48 (with the exception of 17:1), the pattern is *maṭṭeh* + *bᵉnê* + name of the tribe. The expression is used consistently in the story of the division of the land, both in Transjordan and in Canaan, in the oldest stratum of the book of Joshua. The most uniform text is preserved in Josh. 18:11–19:48, where the description of the possessions of each tribe commences with the formula "the lot of the tribe of NN came up . . . ." and concludes with the formula "this is the inheritance of the sons of . . . according to their families." Despite the regularity of the formulation, *maṭṭeh* does not occur in 19:10,16; 19:17 (Issachar — the sons of Issachar); or in 19:32, where the "sons of Naphtali" is repeated before and after "and the sixth lot came out." With the exception of 19:10,16, the absence of *maṭṭeh* in the beginning or concluding formula generates an element of uncertainty suggesting the presence of textual corruption. The formula "tribe of the sons of . . ." seems to have been the one usually appearing in the source before the redactor. This is confirmed by the usage in 13:15,29b (distribution by Moses in Transjordan) and 15:1,20 (beginning and concluding formula of the distribution of land to Judah), in negative fashion also by 13:24, where the absence of the customary formula led to the repetition "tribe of Gad — sons of Gad."

Josh. 17:1 constitutes the only exception in the use of "tribe" within the narrative of the division of the land, a fact that might be explained by the complex relationship between Joseph, Ephraim, and Manasseh. Joseph is never referred to as a "tribe," but rather as a "house" (17:17) or "sons of" (16:1; 17:14,16; but cf. Nu. 36:5). Similar references are made to the "sons of Ephraim" (16:5,9) and the "sons of Manasseh" (16:9), although both are also referred to as "tribes." Hence *maṭṭeh* is usually used when the context involves a tribe's possessions.

The combination *maṭṭeh* + tribal name is used in Josh. 7:1,18; 13:24; 17:1; 20:8 (3 times); and in 21:4–22:1 (25 times), with the exception of 21:9. The three occurrences in 20:8 are additions to the nucleus of the text about cities of refuge (Josh. 20:7-9abα); the lists of the levitical cities in Josh. 21 doubtlessly belong to the post-Deuteronomistic period when Samaria had so receded from Jerusalem's purview that not a single locale in Samaritan territory is mentioned. In contrast, Josh. 7:1,18 belongs to the older stratum of the etiological story of Achan from the tribe of Judah, and 13:24 resulted from a possible textual corruption after the elimination of the formula "tribe of the sons of. . . ."

A comparison between the use of *maṭṭeh* + name of the tribes in Numbers and in Joshua leads to the conclusion that the oldest stratum in the lists did not contain the word *maṭṭeh;* a later usage is *maṭṭeh* + tribal name as in Nu. 1:21-43, and a third stage used *maṭṭeh* + *bᵉnê* + tribal name, although the postexilic texts revert to *maṭṭeh* + name (Josh. 21:4-38; 1 Ch. 6:45-65[60-80]). In 1 Chronicles, the expression *maṭṭeh* + *bᵉnê* + tribal name (3 times) is limited to 1 Ch. 6:50[65]).

"The heads of the fathers' houses of the tribes of the people of Israel" (*rā'šê 'ᵃḇôṯ hammaṭṭôṯ liḇnê yiśrā'ēl,* Nu. 32:28; Josh. 14:1; 19:51; 21:1) is a fixed expression (P) with reference to Eleazar and Joshua, the son of Nun. The P-character of the expression is unequivocal since the introduction of Eleazar in Ex. 6:25. 1 K. 8:1 par. 2 Ch. 5:2

unite in an undifferentiated enumeration "the elders of Israel, all the heads of the tribes, and the leaders of the fathers' houses of the people of Israel." A similar enumeration appears in the later addition to P in Nu. 7:2, where the leaders of Israel, the heads of the fathers' houses, and the leaders of the tribes are all mentioned.

2. *Instrument of Might (Isaiah).* Isa. 10:5,15, the most important text for the understanding of *maṭṭeh* in Isaiah, is an oracle against Assyria generally held to be genuine. The tandem *šēḇeṭ/maṭṭeh* (as *inclusio*) implies that Assyria is the instrument for chastisement by Yahweh, although this chastisement will not be ultimate. That instrument, however, sought independence and overstepped the bounds Yahweh imposed on its commission. Through its own destruction Assyria is to realize that Yahweh is the only master of history, and that the nations play but a limited roll in this drama. The chastisement of Assyria in Isa. 10:24-27a, an oracle of promise to Israel, completes 10:5-15. The pair *šēḇeṭ/maṭṭeh* (v. 26, *maṭṭeh-šôṭ*) undergoes a shift in meaning. Assyria is no longer the instrument, but rather the enemy who must be annihilated. The terms *šēḇeṭ* and *maṭṭeh,* now without *za'mî* and *'appî* (as in 10:5), are symbols of Assyrian aggression (v. 24) and of Yahweh's punishment (v. 26). The motif of the *maṭṭeh* has evoked the allusion to Midian in Isa. 10:26 through the association Midianites-Amalekites (Jgs. 7:12) with the story of Moses and the Amalekites (Ex. 17:9, rod of God). The expression *bᵉḏereḵ miṣrayim* in Isa. 10:24,26 is dependent on Ex. 14:16, since here, too, the raising of the staff is a sign of deliverance for Israel. The pair *maṭṭeh/šēḇeṭ* also appears in Isa. 9:3[4], integrated into the image of the yoke (cf. Isa. 10:27) in three-part parallelism with reference to oppression. Here, too, the image of the *maṭṭeh* (through literary dependence on Isa. 10:24-27a?) is associated with the day of Midian.[25]

It does not seem justified to draw on Isa. 14:5, "Yahweh has broken the staff of the wicked, the scepter of rulers," in the explanation of the "broken reed" in Isa. 42:3 (broken staff or broken reed as a symbol of those condemned to death = *rᵉšā'îm*[26]). The parallelism with *šēḇeṭ mōšᵉlîm* on the one hand, and the incorporation of the image into a text directed against the king of Babylon on the other, show clearly that the image is referring to the ruler's power. Isa. 14:5,20b,21 refer to a single addressee in contrast to the plural in vv. 4b + 6-20. The composition of 14:4b-20(21), however, is a unity. The point of departure is a mythological motif (vv. 12-15) which with the aid of various ideas has been assimilated to the Jerusalem theology. The whole shows the influence of Isaiah's theology, something clearly manifested in the favored motif *maṭṭeh-šēḇeṭ,* which is strongly colored by anti-Assyrian polemic. This does not mean, however, that the text aims directly at Assyria. Isa. 14 is directed not so much against a specific person or power as against any person or power that would usurp Yahweh's power. Two paradigms are portrayed. Verse 5 alludes to the hybris of the old enemy

---

25. → יוֹם *yôm* (VI, 7-32).

26. Cf. J. Begrich, "Zur Interpretation von Kap. 42,1-4," *Studien zu Deuterojesaja. BWANT,* 77[4/25] (1938), 164; repr. *ThB,* 20 (1963).

Assyria, while v. 12 contains a mythical motif, Helal, the son of dawn. Setting up one's throne on the Zaphon means setting it up on Zion (cf. Ps. 48); whether Assyria or Helal is the power attempting to install itself in Jerusalem, it will be punished.

The motif *šēḇeṭ-maṭṭeh* recurs in Isa. 30:31f. (usually considered post-Isaianic), apparently in the context of anti-Assyrian polemic. Here, however, the expression has lost its theological meaning and portrays a violent image within an apocalyptic description of Yahweh's advent to punish the nations. In Isa. 28:27, *maṭṭeh-šēḇeṭ* might be intended in the purely literal sense as an instrument used for certain agricultural tasks. The unit 28:23-29, however, contains other expressions ("Yahweh of hosts," *ʿēṣâ*), which Isaiah uses in a technical sense to describe Yahweh's political decisions. Quite possibly — and this is why the piece was inserted into the book of Isaiah — the substance of this wisdom parable from agricultural life might be genuinely Isaianic. Assyria had a commission to be carried out with rod and staff, but executed it with the wheels of its chariots instead. The implicit conclusion is the same as in Isa. 10:5-15; 10:24-27a; 14:5: Yahweh again takes control of the situation and chastises the person who has not understood what it means to be Yahweh's instrument. Behind this parable we note the perplexity of the Jerusalemites, who see that from a certain moment on (713?) Isaiah is announcing a message of good news or at least the destruction of the enemy.

3. *Power (Ezekiel).* Ezk. 7:10 needs no modification, since *maṭṭeh* can be understood as power *(concretum pro abstracto)* in direct parallelism with *hazzāḏôn.* The connotation of "power" which *maṭṭeh* usually has shifts to "act of violence" when it involves the power of the unrighteous. Ezk. 7:11 also says this: power arises and becomes the scepter of wickedness. Cf. also Isa. 14:5.

IV. Problematic Passages. Hab. 3:9aα: MT *šᵉḇuʿôṯ maṭṭôṯ ʾōmer* is unintelligible. The term *maṭṭôṯ* should be translated in parallelism with v. 9a as "arrow,"[27] while *ʾmr* is a noun with prothetic *aleph* from *mrr:* "strength, might."[28] The term *šᵉḇuʿôṯ* conceals a form of *śbʿ* with accusative: that with which a person sates himself, intended figuratively. The entire verse might be translated: "Your bow is completely bare, your arrows sated with power." Yahweh is ready to begin his acts of war. The meaning "arrow" can also be assumed in Hab. 3:14a; the general sense is clear.

A grammatically adequate resolution emerges in Ezr. 9:13 even without altering the consonantal text if one reads *lᵉmaṭṭeh* instead of *lᵉmaṭṭâ:* "Thou hast spared some of our evil deeds from the rod," whereby *m* is partitive and *lᵉ* separative instead of *min,* which is normally used with *ḥśk.* The pair *ḥśk-maṭṭeh* also appears in Prov. 24:11b (cf. in Prov. 13:24 *ḥśk šēḇeṭ*): "that you might spare the rods of execution," whereby *ʾim* is precatory as in Ps. 95:7: "O that. . . ."

Various translations are given for *maṭṭeh* in Mic. 6:9: "tribe" (NRSV) or "rod of

---

27. Cf. I.2 above.
28. Dahood, *AB,* XVIIA, 21.

correction" (Ger. *Zuchtrute*).[29] If one divides and points the words differently than the MT, one might translate: "If they hear him who guides [bends] them, who could accuse him?" Then *mṭh* would be the hiphil participle of *nṭh,* "bend, guide," which is used figuratively, e.g., in reference to the hearts of adversaries (2 S. 19:15[14]). This translation fits the forensic context well.[30]

Simian-Yofre

V. 1. *Qumran.* In contrast to the Mandeans,[31] the Qumran Essenes had no special use for a staff or scepter. The term *maṭṭeh* occurs more than 15 times, always in the meaning "tribe," unless one follows Jean Carmignac's suggestion that 1QM 5:1 is speaking of the scepter of the prince of Israel.[32] Usually, however, one reads *mgn,* "shield," in the lacuna, which seems more evident, since only a shield would have the necessary surface area upon which to write the names of the twelve tribes *(šiḇṭê)* of Israel. The use of *šēḇeṭ* (14 more times in 1QM) clearly recedes in the Temple scroll (3 times) behind *maṭṭeh,* which appears here especially in the sacrificial regulations (11QT 18–24), in synonymous parallelism with *šēḇeṭ* (11QT 18:16[?]; 21:2), with the "clans of Israel" (19:14f.), the "children of Israel" (22:12), and the "children of Jacob" (23:7).

2. *Post OT-Period.* In the post-OT period a rich matrix of associations developed especially regarding the rod of Moses, prompted essentially by the miraculous powers of this rod (cf. Ex. 4; 7; Nu. 20:11f.; cf. also Gen. 30:37ff.; 2 K. 4:19; 6:6). The Apocrypha views the rod of Moses as a branch from the trees of paradise or from the tree of life.[33] In rabbinic messianic expectation the rod of Moses is identical with the rod of the redeemer,[34] and in Christianity ultimately with the cross of Christ.[35]

Fabry

---

29. W. Rudolph, *Micha. KAT,* XIII/3 (1975), 114.

30. Cf. F. Frezza, *Ascendenze filologico-letterarie semitico-nordoccidentali* (diss., Rome, 1977), 120-22.

31. Cf. K. Rudolph, 33ff.

32. J. Carmignac, *La Règle de la Guerre des Fils de lumière contre les Fils de ténèbres* (Paris, 1958), 75.

33. G. Widengren, *The King and the Tree of Life in Ancient Near Eastern Religion. UUÅ,* 1951/4, 38f.; 55f.

34. Cf. B. Murmelstein, "Adam, ein Beitrag zur Messiaslehre (Forsetzung und Schluss)," *WZKM,* 36 (1929), 55.

35. Cf. Tertullian *De bapt.* ix; R. Reitzenstein, *Die Vorgeschichte der christlichen Taufe* (Leipzig, 1929), 381; K. Rudolph, *Die Mandäer II,* 36; C. Schneider, "ῥάβδος," *TDNT,* VI, 966-971, esp. 969f.

מָטָר māṭār; גֶּשֶׁם gešem; זֶרֶם zerem

Contents: I. The Various Words for Rain: 1. Frequency; 2. Meaning. II. Rain as a Natural Phenomenon. III. Yahweh and the Rain. IV. Yahweh/Baʿal and the Rain. V. Rain in Metaphors and Comparisons: 1. Secular References; 2. Religious References to Salvation and Judgment; 3. Apocalyptic Usage.

I. The Various Words for Rain.

1. *Frequency.* Biblical Hebrew has access to a series of words that refer to rain or to certain aspects of rain. According to frequency, the following nouns and verbs occur: *māṭār* (38 times), *gešem* (35 times), *zerem* (9 times), *malqôš* (8 times), *šeṭep̄* (6 times), *rᵉḇîḇîm* (6 times), *ḥāzîz* (3 times), *môreh* (3 times), and *yôreh* (2 times), as well as single occurrences of *gōšem, ṣagrîr, zarzîp̄, sāp̄îaḥ, śᵉʿîrîm,* and *ʿᵃrîp̄îm.* Specific verbs include *šṭp* (31 times), *mṭr* (16 times), *yrh* (3 times), *zrm* (2 times), and *gšm* (once). To these one can also add → טל *ṭal,* "drizzle, dew," or → מים *mayim,* "water,"[1] as well as *šemen* as a metaphorical expression for rain.[2]

Most of these words are attested throughout the Semitic languages: *māṭār* occurs in Syriac, Arabic, Aramaic, and Ugaritic, where it is by far the most common noun and verb. Ugaritic occasionally also attests the noun *rbb,* "drizzle," and the noun *yr,* "raindrops, rain," and once each the noun *gšm,* "cloudburst," and the verb *zrm,* "rain." Furthermore, Syr. *šēgma'* and Arab. *ǵasama* are related to Heb. *gšm;* Akk. *zunnu* (the usual word for "rain"), Arab. *zarama* IV, "to thunder," and Ethiop. *zĕnām,* "rain," are compared with Heb. *zrm;* Heb. *šṭp* corresponds to Arab. *saṭafa,* Heb. *ḥzz* to Arabic nouns, Heb. *spḥ* to Arabic words, Heb. *zrp* to Syriac, Arabic, and Ethiopic words, and Heb. *yrh/mrh* can also be compared to certain Arabic words. For the most part each of these words is attested at least once in another Semitic language. Since Ugaritic attests at least five of the fifteen different designations, one can assume that these words are typically West Semitic constructions.

2. *Meaning.* As regards the semantic nuances of these words, the most frequently

---

māṭār. G. Dalman, *AuS,* I (1928), *s.v.;* H. W. Hertzberg, "Regen," *BHHW,* III, 1568-1571; R. Hillmann, *Wasser und Berg: Kosmische Verbindungslinien zwischen dem kanaanäischen Wettergott und Jahwe* (diss., Halle, 1965); L. Köhler, "Hebräische Vokabeln II," *ZAW,* 55 (1937), 161-174; M. Noth, *The OT World* (Eng. trans., Philadelphia, 1966); J. van der Ploeg, "Prov xxv 23," *VT,* 3 (1953), 189-192; P. Reymond, *L'eau, sa vie, et sa signification dans l'AT. SVT,* 6 (1958); R. B. Y. Scott, "Meteorological Phenomena and Terminology in the OT," *ZAW,* 64 (1952), 11-25; E. F. Sutcliffe, "The Clouds as Water-Carriers in Hebrew Thought," *VT,* 3 (1953), 99-103; H.-J. Zobel, "Der bildliche Gebrauch von *šmn* im Ugaritischen und Hebräischen," *ZAW,* 82 (1970), 209-216.

1. Reymond, 23.
2. Zobel.

occurring one, *māṭār* (rendered consistently in the LXX as *hyetós*), is also the most general term for rain.[3] According to Dt. 11:14, it can be further subdivided into *yôreh,* "early rain," and *malqôš,* "latter rain" (also Job 29:23). In Isa. 30:23, rain is necessary for the growth of the seed and refers to the winter rain. The combination *māṭār sōḥēp̄* (Prov. 28:3) refers to something like a devastating "downpour." Also, *māṭār* is used in connection with *mayim,* "water" (Job 5:10), *'eglê ṭal,* "dewdrops" (Job 38:28), or simple *ṭal,* "dew" (Dt. 32:2), to circumscribe all sorts of moisture that comes from the heavens (2 S. 1:21; 1 K. 17:1). "Thunder" (*qōlôṯ;* 1 S. 12:17f.) or "lightning and thunder" (*ḥᵃzîz qōlôṯ;* Job 28:26; 38:25) are used together with *māṭār.* In Jer. 10:13 par. 51:16; Ps. 135:7, rain is associated with lightning and in Isa. 4:6 with a "storm" *(zerem).* The combination of rain, hail, and thunder occurs in Ex. 9:33f., and of rain, rainshower *(rᵉḇîḇîm),* and penetrating rain *(zarzîp̄)* in Ps. 72:6.

The next most frequent noun, *gešem,* exhibits a slightly different meaning.[4] It, too, can encompass the "early" and "latter" rains (*yôreh* and *malqôš,* Joel 2:23 [*BHS*]; the same series in Jer. 5:24; both words constitute a "specifying appositive" to *gešem;*[5] cf. Dt. 11:14), can be used together with *malqôš* (Hos. 6:3) or, given the temporal indication "three months before the harvest," can refer thus to the "latter rain" (Am. 4:7); it can also, however, refer to the winter rains (Cant. 2:11; cf. Isa. 55:10: par. *šeleg,* "snow") or to rain in a very general sense (Isa. 44:14; Jer. 14:4; 1 K. 17:7,14). Thus the plural form in Lev. 26:4 likely refers to the various seasonal rains.[6] More striking associations are those of clouds *(nāśî'* or *'āḇ),* storm *(rûaḥ),* and rain (1 K. 18:45; Prov. 25:14), winds and rain (2 K. 3:17; cf. Ezk. 13:11,13), or clouds and rain (Eccl. 11:3), since these allude to the actual meaning of *gešem* as "downpour" (cf. also Ezk. 1:28: the rainbow on the day of rain). Thus the plural form (Ezk. 34:26; Ezr. 10:9,13, and elsewhere) implies "heavy showers," as do the genitive combinations *mᵉṭar-gešem* (Zec. 10:1), *gešem māṭār,* and *gešem miṭrôṯ* (Job 37:6).[7] Finally, the expression *gešem šôṭēp̄,* "deluge of rain" (Ezk. 13:11,13; 38:22), and the rain of the flood story (Gen. 7:12; 8:2) should be noted.

As far as *zerem* is concerned, we have already anticipated its meaning as "cloudburst," "stormy weather." The combination *zerem mayim* (Isa. 28:2; Hab. 3:10; cf. *BHS*) circumscribes the strong downpour of a sudden cloudburst, *zerem bārāḏ* a destructive "hailstorm" (Isa. 28:2), and *zerem qîr* the "storm that dashes against a wall," threatening its stability (Isa. 25:4); the verb is used accordingly to refer to the pouring out of water from the clouds (Hab. 3:10 conj.; Ps. 77:18[Eng. v. 17]) and to rinsing or washing away (Ps. 90:5). In Isa. 30:30, *zerem* is associated with a preceding *nepeṣ,* "bursting, shattering,"[8] and mentioned together with "hailstones." Finally, Job 24:8; Isa. 4:6; 25:4; 32:2 speak of shelter from such violent weather. This overview shows

---

3. Cf. Scott, 23; Reymond, 22.
4. Cf. Scott, 23; Reymond, 22.
5. H. W. Wolff, *Joel and Amos. Herm* (Eng. trans. 1977), 55.
6. Scott, 23.
7. *Idem,* "the falling of rain, but possibly with the sense of heavy rain, showers."
8. Reymond, 23: hendiadys.

at least that *zerem* consistently evokes the negative aspects of the ravaging, threatening, or destructive results of such weather.

The term *malqôš* always refers to the "latter rains" in the spring.[9] It stands after *māṭār* (Dt. 11:14; Job 29:23; Zec. 10:1), after *gešem* (Hos. 6:3; Joel 2:23; also Jer. 5:24), and after *r^e^bîbîm* (Jer. 3:3). The combination "early and latter rains" appears in Dt. 11:14; Jer. 5:24; Joel 2:23. The expression *ʿāb malqôš,* "clouds of the latter rains," occurs in Prov. 16:15.

The counterpart of the latter rain is the "early rain" anticipated in autumn. In Joel 2:23 (twice); Ps. 84:7[6], this is replaced by *môreh;* in Zec. 10:1, the LXX amplifies with "at the time of the early rain."[10] In contrast, the form *yôreh* appears in Dt. 11:14; Jer. 5:24. Both words derive from the same root → ירה *yrh,* which in Hos. 6:3; 10:12; Prov. 11:25 means to "rain, moisten, refresh," yet in other contexts to "throw" and to "teach."[11] Wilhelm Rudolph[12] associates the first-mentioned *yrh* semantically with *rwh,* "drink one's fill,"[13] from which then *yôreh* and *môreh* also derive. In Joel 2:23a, the Targ. and Vulg. (probably also Qumran: Teacher of Righteousness) interpret *môreh* as "teacher" and thus derive it from the other root *yrh.* Gustaf Dalman[14] refers to Jewish tradition which interprets the early rain among other things also as "teacher," "because it teaches *(mōrē)* people to bring in their fruits [into the house] and to seal their roofs [against inclement weather]." The merely folk character of this ingenious etymology emerges in the rest of the citation, which interprets the early rain also "as a satiater that sates the earth *(marwē),* soaking it to the depths, but which also as . . . an archer aims at the earth, though not shooting *(yōrē)* in anger." Dalman himself suggests that "this latter interpretation . . . is basically on target," since the early rain is the "rain of the archer," arriving at the time "when the course of the sun advances through the zodiac sign of the 'archer' [Sagittarius]." This reference to the zodiac, however, shows that the etymological explanation only came about retrospectively. Thus the most probable solution is to derive both words from *yrh* as a by-form of *rwh.*[15]

The noun *šeṭep* refers in Job 38:25 to "torrents of rain,"[16] since it stands parallel here to *ḥ^a^zîz qōlôṯ,* which is used in Job 28:26 in parallelism with *māṭār.* Ps. 32:6 speaks of the "rush of many waters" *(šēṭep mayim rabbîm),* and Nah. 1:8 of an "overflowing flood" *(šeṭep ʿōḇēr).* Prov. 27:4 associates this noun with "anger" *(ʾap).* Concerning Dan. 9:26, "and its end will come with a flood"; 11:22, "empires of the flood shall be inundated," see the comms.

The root *šṭp,* which occurs much more frequently than the noun, means to "overflow,

---

9. Scott, 23, with etymological information.
10. Cf. the comms.
11. *HAL,* II (1995), 436.
12. *Hosea. KAT,* XIII/1 (1966), 132.
13. So also *KBL*³.
14. *AuS,* I/1 (1928), 122.
15. Cf. Scott, 23.
16. G. Fohrer, *Das Buch Hiob. KAT,* XVI (1963), 488.

flood" (Isa. 8:8; 10:22; Jer. 47:2; Ps. 69:3,16[2,15]; 124:4; Cant. 8:7; Dnl. 11:10, 22,26,40), though also "wash away, wash off, cleanse" (Lev. 6:21[28]; 15:11,12; 1 K. 22:38; Job 14:19; Isa. 43:2; Ezk. 16:9), and is used in reference to the flowing of streams (2 Ch. 32:4; Ps. 78:20). Quite often the ptcp. *šôṭēp̱* is associated with a noun: *gešem šôṭēp̱,* "pouring rain" (Ezk. 13:11,13; 38:22), *naḥal šôṭēp̱,* "overflowing stream" (Isa. 30:28; 66:12; Jer. 47:2), *zerem mayim kabbîrîm šōṭᵉpîm,* "storm of mighty, overflowing waters" (Isa. 28:2), and figuratively *sûs šôṭēp̱,* "plunging horse" (Jer. 8:6), and *šôṭ šôṭēp̱,* "overwhelming scourge" (Isa. 28:15,18).

The Hebrew *pluralia tantum rᵉḇîḇîm* probably refers to "rainshowers," a "sudden shower."[17] In Ps. 65:11(10), such showers refer to the early rains, since they "soften" the dried earth (*mwg* polel). Jer. 3:3 might mean something similar if this term is interpreted not as synonymous with *malqôš,*[18] but rather as a substantive counterpart to the latter rains. Such rainshowers, however, also fall upon the "herbs" (*ʿēśeḇ;* Dt. 32:2; Mic. 5:6[7]), causing them to grow. It stands parallel to *māṭār* in Ps. 72:6, to the root *gšm* in Jer. 14:22, and in connection with *ṭal* in Mic. 5:6[7]). Since the hapax legomenon *śᵉʿîrim* functions as a synonym of this term in Dt. 32:2, it probably has the same meaning,[19] "rainshower for the new fresh grass" *(deše').*

Am. 7:4 should be read *lirḇiḇ 'ēš,* "rain of fire."[20]

Before briefly addressing the other words that occur only once, we must yet consider the term *ḥᵃzîz. KBL*³ renders the plural in Zec. 10:1 (Sir. 35[32]:26) as "strong (gust of) wind," and the expression *ḥᵃzîz qōlôṯ* (Job 28:26; 38:25; Sir. 40:13) as "thunderclap."[21] Dalman[22] early saw that "although one's inclination is to associate Heb. *ḥāzīz* with a thunderclap, it probably refers rather to a thunderhead." With this reference in mind, Georg Fohrer[23] suggests the meaning "storm cloud," which can also be accompanied by "thunder." That this word does indeed refer to such clouds bringing the anticipated latter rains emerges clearly from Zec. 10:1, though it is also suggested by the two passages from Job. Georg Sauer[24] aptly renders this term in Sir. 35(32):26 with "rain" and in Sir. 40:13 with "thunderstorm."

Finally, Prov. 27:15 speaks of a "continual dripping on a rainy day" *(yôm sagrîr).* The term *zarzîp̱,* occurring only in Ps. 72:6, is almost always interpreted not as a noun,[25] but rather as a verbal form *(zirzᵉpû* or *yarzîpû).*[26] The term *sāp̱îaḥ* is attested only in Job 14:19 (pl. with 3rd fem. sg. suf.), where *GesB* translates it as "pouring rain" and

---

17. Cf. Scott, 23, also concerning etymology; Reymond, 22: Fr. *bruine,* "small drizzling rain."

18. So Scott, 23.

19. Scott, 23, n. 1; Reymond, 22: Fr. *pluie douce,* "soft rain."

20. Correctly so interpreted most recently by Wolff, 292.

21. Already so interpreted by Köhler, 173.

22. P. 215.

23. P. 392.

24. *Jüdische Schriften aus hellenistisch-römischer Zeit,* III/5 (Gütersloh, 1981).

25. Thus interpreted only by *GesB:* "strong, penetrating rain."

26. H. Schmidt, *Die Psalmen. HAT,* XV (1934), 136; *BHK;* H.-J. Kraus, *Psalms 60-150* (Eng. trans., Minneapolis, 1989), 74: "like showers that water the land"; similarly *HAL; BHS.*

KBL[3] as "downpour." Gustav Hölscher,[27] *BHK,* and Fohrer[28] suggest reading *s*[e]*ḥîp̄â* instead, which *KBL*[3] translates as "downpour" (though cf. also *BHS*). Perhaps *ʿ*[a]*rîp̄îm* in Isa. 5:30 should also be mentioned, which *KBL*[3] translates as "trickle, drip."

II. Rain as a Natural Phenomenon. The discussion has already either mentioned or alluded to the various kinds of rain, their intensity and seasonal sequence, and their meaning. At this point the OT evidence itself can be evaluated.[29]

The enthusiastic portrayal of the land where Israel is to dwell (Dt. 11) emphasizes the characteristic differences in a comparison between the promised land with Egypt. Whereas in Egypt one must water the fields "by foot" after sowing seeds (v. 10), Palestine is "a land of hills and valleys, which drinks water by the rain from heaven" (v. 11). The decisive factor affecting the land's yield is not human effort, but rather the rain, which is inaccessible to human control.

This high estimation of rain is also expressed by the fact that a season is named after the rain, and that various designations are used to refer to the rain associated with specific months. The "time of heavy rain" (Ezr. 10:13) is winter;[30] "winter" and "rain" belong together (Cant. 2:11). It was at this time, which included such rain, that all the people shivered in the open square before the temple on the twentieth day of the ninth month, which corresponds to our month of December (Ezr. 10:9).[31] According to Dalman,[32] this period of winter rains lasts from December to March.

It is noteworthy, however, that the OT emphasizes both the early[33] and latter rains much more strongly than the winter rains. Dalman[34] considers this an attestation to their crucial economic significance, and to the fact that on the whole the winter rains do come every year.

The early rains "water" the earth (*rwh* hiphil: Isa. 55:10), "soften it" (Ps. 65:11[10]), and make it fruitful (Isa. 55:10). They fall from the middle of October to the middle of November,[35] just as according to Jewish reckoning (Gen. 7:11) the flood began on Nov. 17, i.e., during the time of the early rains.[36] Zec. 14:17 gives the impression that participation in the Feast of Tabernacles in October involves an assurance of rain that must be referring at least to the early rains,[37] Saturation of the earth (cf. Job 38:27)

---

27. *Das Buch Hiob. HAT,* XVII (^{2}1952), 37.
28. P. 239.
29. Cf. the meteorological data in Noth, 28-32, 35; Scott, 12-16, 19; Hertzberg, 1569f., as well as the bibliographical information there.
30. Cf. Scott, 16; Reymond, 19-24; Hertzberg, 1568, 1571.
31. Dalman, 190.
32. *Ibid.,* 172; information concerning amounts of rain is given on pp. 173-77.
33. Cf. Reymond, 18f.; Hertzberg, 1571.
34. P. 177.
35. Dalman, 119; statistical data given on pp. 128-130.
36. *Ibid.,* 123.
37. Cf. also Lev. 26:3-5; K. Elliger, *Leviticus. HAT,* IV (1966), 365: "in all probability . . . part of the agenda of the autumnal festival."

means soaking to a depth of 40 centimeters (16 in.).[38] The early rain is followed by a pause in the rains, the earth dries up somewhat, and the farmer can begin planting.[39]

The latter rain is even more important for the land's yield.[40] It is with this rain and this rain only that the plea in Zec. 10:1 is concerned. It "refreshes, revives the earth" (Hos. 6:3 conj.; cf. Isa. 55:10), and "moistens" it (Ps. 72:6). The latter rain is expected three months before the harvest (Am. 4:7), i.e., after March/April. Jewish reckoning also dates the end of the Flood (Gen. 8:4,14) to the end of the rains and the time of drying, i.e., to the beginning of summer.[41] Although the latter rain occurs primarily during April, it can also continue to fall in May. Dalman[42] supplies information concerning levels of rain and draws attention to the fact that this latter rain is absolutely necessary for a good yield of grain crops,[43] as expressed by the Arabic proverb: "It is the life of human beings."[44]

How the rain falls is also important, something revealed by the various nouns themselves. The term *māṭār* is largely associated with the notion of an intensive, penetrating rain such as that which falls in winter (cf. Isa. 30:23; Ps. 72:6), though this might be contradicted by the comparison in Dt. 32:2, where the verb *ʿrp* is used, which means to "drizzle, drip." If the point of comparison is the constant evenness with which such rain falls, then the verb *ʿrp* might express the most essential feature of the winter rain as a longer lasting, steady rain. This is also suggested by the plural form of *gešem* used to refer to the winter rain in Ezr. 10:9,13. Other terms and combinations suggest that especially the early and latter rain, though also the winter rain, fall as brief downpours or showers. Thus, e.g., Prov. 16:15 can employ the image of the "clouds of the latter rains," and Ezk. 1:28 that of the rainbow after the downpour.

Human beings owe virtually everything to rain in the larger sense. Spring causes the flowers to bloom again; it is the "time of singing" (Cant. 2:12). "All green things" grow (Gen. 2:5; Dt. 32:2; 2 S. 23:4 conj.), and "the land shall yield its produce" (Lev. 26:4); rain is for the "seed" (Isa. 30:23), the "land," the "earth," the "mown grass" (Dt. 11:14,17; 1 K. 18:1; Jer. 14:4; Ps. 72:6; 147:8), or for "your land" (Dt. 28:12,24; 1 K. 8:36). The bounty of fields made fertile by the rain includes "grain, wine, and oil" (Dt. 11:14; Joel 2:24; cf. Ezk. 34:27), as well as "grass for your livestock" (Dt. 11:15), the fruit from the trees of the field (Lev. 26:4; Ezk. 34:27), and the oak or cedar. The rain is responsible for people having bread enough to eat their fill (Lev. 26:5; Isa. 55:10), and for the sower having seed again for sowing (Isa. 55:10). Dalman[45] views all this as evidence that while the seed-corn needs soft rain, the trees and cisterns need

38. Dalman, 127.
39. *Ibid.,* 157-160.
40. Cf. Reymond, 24; Hertzberg, 1571.
41. Dalman, 295f.
42. *Ibid.,* 291-94.
43. *Ibid.,* 291.
44. *Ibid.,* 299.
45. *Ibid.,* 186-88.

heavy rain, and that every kind of rain can be beneficial both for human beings and for animals.

The substance of these findings concerning rain is also expressed by various expressions and formulas. References are made to "rain in abundance" (Ps. 68:10[9]) and repeatedly to rain "in its season" (Dt. 11:14; 28:12; Jer. 5:24; Ezk. 34:26; cf. Zec. 10:1) or to the different rains "in their season" (Lev. 26:4). The proper season and adequate amounts are the essential prerequisites for speaking about "showers of blessing" (Ezk. 34:26).[46] Ps. 84:7[6] similarly asserts that the early rain covers the valley of Baca with blessings.

If the rain comes at the wrong time, however, it can bring disaster on both fields and animals.[47] Rain "at the harvest" (1 S. 12:17,18; Prov. 26:1) is such a disaster, though an even greater disaster is late rain (Jer. 3:3; Am. 4:7), and especially a total absence of rain (Dt. 11:17; 1 K. 8:35; 17:7; 2 Ch. 6:26; 7:13; Jer. 14:4; Ezk. 22:24).[48] The result is aridity (1 K. 17:7; Jer. 14:4; Ezk. 22:24; cf. also, e.g., Gen. 12:10; 45:6) and infertile fields (Dt. 11:17; Am. 4:7f.) with all the ravaging consequences for life. The image of the "rain of powder and dust" refers to such a drought in which the wind becomes clouds of dust (Dt. 28:24).[49] Thus it is quite understandable that the Israelites yearn for the rains and open their mouths for the spring rain (Job 29:23).

Of course, the opposite can also occur; too much rain or too heavy a rain can fall, bringing disruption and destruction. The rain of the flood lasted forty days and nights (Gen. 7:12). "Torrential rain" or a "downpour" (Isa. 28:2; Nah. 1:8; Hab. 3:10; Ezk. 38:22) can cause a wall to collapse after laying bare its foundations (Ezk. 13:11,13). This is the rain that can also be called a "wall torrent," as it dashes against a wall (Isa. 25:4).[50] What is essential is that such rain "leaves no food" (Prov. 28:3) and that it sends everyone running for shelter (Isa. 4:6; 25:4; 32:2; cf. Job 24:8). Such violent, mighty storms cause streams to overflow suddenly far beyond their banks, becoming a threat both for human beings and for animals (Isa. 30:28; Jer. 47:2; Ps. 69:3,16[2,15]; 124:4f.; compare 2 K. 3:16-20 and Job 14:19).[51] Finally, it should also be mentioned that merely sporadic or local rain can also constitute considerable misfortune.[52] While one city and one field receive rain, another city and another field do not (Am. 4:7f.). In his elegy over Saul and Jonathan, David asks that there be neither dew nor rain upon the mountains of Gilboa (2 S. 1:21). Neither should the clouds rain upon the vineyard (Isa. 5:6).

The final question concerns what the OT says about the origin of rain.[53] A somewhat

---

46. W. Eichrodt, *Ezekiel. OTL* (Eng. trans. 1970), 474 (Ger. "segenspendende Regengüsse"); W. Zimmerli, *Ezekiel 2. Herm* (Eng. trans. 1983), 210 (Ger. "gesegnete Regen").
47. Cf. Dalman, 116-18.
48. Cf. *ibid.,* 195-97, 297: "winters of meager rain."
49. *Ibid.,* 133f.
50. *Ibid.,* 188, 208.
51. See also *ibid.,* 201f., 207.
52. *Ibid.,* 131f.
53. Cf. the thorough work of Sutcliffe.

infrequent expression proceeds from the notion that rain "comes down from heaven" (Dt. 28:24; Jer. 14:22), whereby the "heavens are opened" (Dt. 28:12). The view in Job 36:27f. is a bit more complex. The drops of water are taken from the celestial reservoirs, trickle through the firmament, and collect into clouds which then finally cause the rain to fall.[54] Rain is most frequently associated with clouds (Job 26:8; Ps. 77:18[17]; 147:8; Prov. 16:15; Eccl. 12:2; Isa. 5:6). Elijah sees a small cloud rising out of the sea and knows that rain is coming (1 K. 18:44), and Qoheleth knows: "When the clouds are full, they empty rain on the earth" (Eccl. 11:3). Wind and rain, however, are also closely associated. Although there is neither wind nor rain, the valley is full of water (2 K. 3:17). The miraculous nature of this event draws attention to the fact that the wind is the harbinger of rain.[55] However, the assertion that the north wind brings rain (Prov. 25:23) fits the conditions in Egypt more than those in Palestine.[56] The complete picture unites the elements of clouds and wind with the rain (1 K. 18:45; Prov. 25:14) and adds lightning as well (Jer. 10:13 par. 51:16; Ps. 135:7).[57]

This notion is not really contradicted by the assertion that rain comes from the upper celestial ocean (Gen. 1:6-8; Ps. 104:2f.; 148:4) and falls to earth through sluices (Gen. 7:11; 8:2; Isa. 24:18).

According to E. F. Sutcliffe,[58] however, two other conceptions are attested in Job 38:25 and in Jer. 10:13c par. 51:16c; Ps. 135:7b. Behind the first we allegedly find the notion that God has cleft a groove or channel for the rain, guiding it down to earth and each individual drop to its specified place; according to the other conception, both the clouds and the wind come from the celestial repositories at Yahweh's command. It is questionable, however, whether these really constitute different conceptions.

III. Yahweh and the Rain. Job 28:26 asserts that at its origin and in its various manifestations rain follows a prescribed law *(ḥōq)* and a predetermined path *(dereḵ)*. The author of this "law" and "path" is none other than Yahweh. A similar notion occurs in Job 38:25: Yahweh has "cut a channel for the torrents of rain." Yahweh is always the subject of rain events. He is the only "bringer of rain" (Jer. 14:22); heaven cannot give rain of its own accord. Rain has no father (Job 38:28). The order human beings discern is thus a divine order, "Yahweh's order" (Isa. 8:7). "The Yahweh faith knows of no natural laws."[59]

All these statements reveal that it is Yahweh who through his abundant rain during the proper seasons renders a good life possible for his chosen people in the promised land (cf. esp. Dt. 11). Ps. 68:10(9) emphasizes this in a unique fashion: God sheds rain

---

54. Fohrer, 481.
55. Dalman, 103f., 154.
56. B. Gemser, *Sprüche Salomos. HAT,* XVI (^{2}1963), 92; H. Ringgren, *Sprüche. ATD,* XVI/1 (^{3}1980), 101; a different view is taken by van der Ploeg, 189f., who interprets *ṣāpôn* as an "unknown place."
57. Dalman, 304f.
58. P. 103.
59. W. Rudolph, *Jeremia. HAT,* XII (^{3}1968), 102.

in abundance, thereby restoring the land of his heritage. Such rain is a "dispensation of divine generosity,"[60] since rain is "never directly related to 'compassion' or 'grace,' "[61] even when Yahweh causes the water for watering the fields to flow out of the "river of God" *(peleg ᵉʾlōhîm)* (Ps. 65:10f.[9f.]).

A different notion is expressed by assertions that Yahweh or his "glory" offers "shelter from the storm and rain" (Isa. 4:6; 25:4; cf. Isa. 32:2). Despite the directness of this statement, recalling the protective function of the Jerusalem sanctuary,[62] this seems to be metaphorical usage (cf. also Nah. 1:8; Ps. 32:6; 69:3,16[2,15]; 124:4, where Yahweh provides deliverance from a torrential flood).

The distinction between object and metaphor is also fluid in those passages that speak of rain and other meteorological phenomena as Yahweh's "strength" (Job 37:6), as his weapons against Israel's enemies, against the wicked in Israel, or against the disobedient people itself. As early a text as Ex. 9:18,23 (J) mentions as the seventh plague a "very heavy rain of hail" upon Egypt, to which Ps. 105:32 then alludes. Ps. 77:18[17] uses various images to describe Yahweh's miraculous deeds during the Exodus, including the observation that "the clouds poured out water." From this perspective it is understandable that Isa. 30:30 portrays Yahweh's anticipated help for Israel in the form of a "cloudburst and tempest and hailstones" upon its enemies. Yahweh causes "coals of fire and brimstone" to rain down upon the wicked (Ps. 11:6), recalling Gen. 19:24 (J) (cf. also Job 20:23). Similar threats are directed toward "those who smear whitewash" (Ezk. 13:11-13).

Walther Zimmerli[63] correctly sensed that older forms of speech belonging to the context of the wars of Yahweh resonate in these passages. At the battle of Gibeon Yahweh threw down "huge stones from heaven" (Josh. 10:11), and in the Song of Deborah the actual battle is described with reference to the warring of the stars from heaven[64] and to the overflowing Kishon (Jgs. 5:20f.).

These figures of speech are picked up again with references in Isa. 28:2,17; Ezk. 38:22 to the storm of mighty, torrential waters, in Isa. 29:6 to thunder, quaking, tremendous noise, tempests, whirlwinds, and flames of fire, and in Ezk. 13:11, 13 to a deluge of rain, storm wind, and hailstones (cf. Jer. 23:19), though now directed against Israel itself. Thus does "Yahweh destroy the work of his enemies."[65]

Yet another perspective involves the incorporation of rain phenomena into theophany portrayals.[66] The appearance of Yahweh in the Song of Deborah includes the dripping of water from the heavens and clouds (Jgs. 5:4). Ps. 68:9(8) contains a similar reference to the heavens pouring down rain, and Hab. 3:10 associates Yahweh's appearance with a cloudburst and the rumbling of the *tᵉhôm.* In a reverse fashion, Am. 1:2 mentions the

60. Dalman, *304.
61. *Idem.*
62. H. Wildberger, *Isaiah 1–12* (Eng. trans., Minneapolis, 1991), 171f.
63. *Ezekiel 1. Herm* (Eng. trans. 1979), 295f.
64. Cf. *KTU,* 1.3 II, 41, IV, 34.
65. Zimmerli, *Ezekiel 1,* 295.
66. Cf. Dalman, 216-18; Reymond, 20f.

withering of the top of Carmel as one of the phenomena accompanying Yahweh's theophany. This "tumult of nature"[67] manifests itself in downpours or rainlessness. As Jörg Jeremias has persuasively demonstrated with regard to Jgs. 5, such theophany portrayals originally belonged to the thematic material associated with the wars of Yahweh,[68] and were developed out of this material.[69] This suggests that we should not really draw any distinctions in principle between the rain motif in the context of the wars of Yahweh and that in theophany portrayals.

The entire people of Israel is affected when Yahweh withholds rain because of disobedience (Dt. 11:16f.; 1 K. 8:35; 2 Ch. 6:26; Jer. 3:3; 5:24; Ezk. 22:24), which means that such absence of rain can also become the occasion of repentance for Israel (Jer. 5:24; Am. 4:7), or that each time Israel confesses its guilt before Yahweh the rains return (1 K. 8:35f.; 2 Ch. 6:26; 7:13; similarly also Ex. 9:33f.). This includes the notion that one can and should entreat Yahweh for rain. Both Samuel (1 S. 12:17f.) and Elijah (1 K. 18:42) did this successfully, and Zec. 10:1 (cf. the counterpart Zec. 14:17) also issues this exhortation. Hosea shows, however, that this can result in a false sense of security for Israel; he polemicizes against what is apparently an older priestly penitential song (Hos. 6:1-3) which presupposes that Yahweh can be found as soon as one looks for him, and that he will come to Israel as surely as the rain comes. Our attention is drawn to the cultic provenance of this rain motif by the fact that Solomon's temple dedication prayer (1 K. 8; 2 Ch. 6), the text of Zec. 14, and that of Hos. 6 all belong to the temple cult, and that the prayers of Samuel and Elijah constitute cultic or at least cultic-like actions.

Gerhard von Rad correctly emphasizes[70] that "cultic curse formulas" resonate in Dt. 11, formulas "in which it is traditional for the withholding of rain to play a great part (Deut. 28:12,24; Lev. 26:4)." In this context it is appropriate to refer again to Ezk. 34:26; Ps. 84:7(6),[71] which explicitly associate the gift of rain with the catchword "blessing." This shows that rain also belongs to the context of blessing and curse. Finally, we note the several references to Yahweh's wrath or anger (Dt. 11:17; Job 20:23; Ezk. 13:13; 22:24). Just as the gift of rain reflects Yahweh's love, so also does the absence of rain reflect divine anger. Yahweh's love toward his people also colors those passages which speak of the rain of bread (Ex. 16:4), manna (Ps. 78:24), and flesh (Ps. 78:27) during the period of wilderness wanderings.

It is also of significance that a whole series of statements about Yahweh as the lord of rain is either hymnically formed or appears in hymns themselves. This hymnic style is characterized by participial constructions in the statements functioning as predicates to Yahweh: "who gives rain . . . and sends waters" (Job 5:10); "who gives the 'early rain' " (Jer. 5:24). Similar statements occurring in hymns from the psalter include: "rain in abundance thou didst shed abroad" (Ps. 68:10[9]); "the clouds poured out water"

---

67. J. Jeremias, *Theophanie. WMANT,* 10 (^{2}1977), 15 and *passim.*
68. *Ibid.,* 142, 144.
69. *Ibid.,* 145-150.
70. *Deuteronomy. OTL* (Eng. trans. 1966), 85.
71. See II above.

(Ps. 77:18[17]); "the early rain covers it with blessing" (Ps. 84:7[6]); "he who makes the clouds rise . . . who makes lightnings for the rain" (Ps. 135:7); "he covers the heavens with clouds, he prepares rain for the earth" (Ps. 147:8); "rejoice in Yahweh . . . for he has given the early rain . . . he has poured down for you abundant rain" (Joel 2:23). Similar statements are made in the Thanksgiving Psalm 65:11(10) and the Historical Psalm 105:32. All these hymnic statements might be summarized by Jer. 14:22: "For it is you who do all this." Such power over the rain is a sign of Yahweh's power as creator, and the gift of rain an expression of his glory as creator.

IV. Yahweh/Baʿal and the Rain. The observation that the thematic "Yahweh and the rain" occurs in various contexts — Yahweh-war/theophany, cult, praise of the creator — needs some illumination. The OT contains several indications that Israel did not always subscribe unequivocally to the assertion "Yahweh provides rain"; rather, other gods fulfilled this function. The fact that in retrospect of the exile Israel never associated rain and the fear of Yahweh (Jer. 5:24)[72] can be interpreted in two ways. Either it understood rain as a natural phenomenon — which, as we have seen, was not the case — or the rain was derived from the "false gods of the nations" (Jer. 14:22). The reference to "harlotry" in Jer. 3:3 suggests this latter possibility. The postexilic text Zec. 10:1f. also speaks of teraphim and diviners who impart lies and deception to Israel. The reality behind Hos. 6:1-3 is more clearly discernible. When v. 3 refers to seeking and finding Yahweh, which would mean both God's advent and rain for Israel, "mythical motifs" of "seeking the absent or sleeping God" resonate,[73] motifs obviously associated with rain. Such statements are made unequivocally in 1 K. 18:27, where Elijah says in a mocking tone that Baʿal is either "musing, or he has gone aside, or he is on a journey, or perhaps he is asleep and must be awakened." It should be noted that the context here involves the question of the absence or presence of rain, Yahweh or Baʿal.

Although this makes it likely that the alternative Yahweh or Baʿal also constitutes the background of the other passages, Hos. 2 confirms this. Israel is persuaded that it must "go after its lovers," who give it bread and water, wool and flax, oil and drink (v. 7[5]), for it has not realized that it is Yahweh who gives it grain, wine, and oil (v. 10[8]). That these "lovers" mentioned in v. 7(5) are none other than Baʿal emerges from v. 10(8), where we find that the silver and gold Yahweh lavished upon the people was used to make an image of Baʿal. And since these gifts enumerated here are typically those provided by the rain,[74] the question becomes: Who provides that rain, Yahweh or Baʿal?

This interpretation is entirely confirmed and amplified by the texts from Ugarit. Rain is unequivocally associated with Baʿal. "Baʿal's rain [is] for the earth, and the rain of the sublime for the field" *(l'rṣ mṭr bʿl wlšd mṭr ʿly),*[75] repeated in ll. 7f.: "Baʿal's

72. Rudolph, 41.
73. H. W. Wolff, *Hosea. Herm* (Eng. trans. 1974), 119.
74. See II above.
75. *KTU,* 1.16 III, 5f.

rain is bliss for the earth, and the rain of the sublime for the field." Rain is the most wonderful of Baʿal's gifts, for it provides human beings with bread, wine, and oil: "Those plowing lift their heads, the grain farmers their heads high: the bread is consumed . . . the wine . . . the oil."[76] Another text reveals that Baʿal is indeed the lord of the rain: El has become old; his spouse therefore decrees: "From now on let Baʿal set the time of his rain *(wn'p ʿdn mṭrh bʿl yʿdn),* the time of becoming rigid as ice [?], the resounding of his voice from the clouds, the hurling of lightning to the earth."[77] Baʿal determines the times of the rains, of winter, of thunder, and of thunderstorms. The fact that a rainless summer follows upon the winter rain is explained by the assertion that Baʿal has gone to the world of the dead and taken along his clouds, his winds, his team of horses, and his rain *(ʿrptk rḥk mdlk mṭrk).*[78] The cry of anguish at the beginning of the dry season refers to this occurrence: "Aliyan Baʿal is dead! The Prince, the Lord of the Earth is perished!"[79] El himself joins in the dirge: "Baʿal is dead! What becomes of the people? Dagon's Son! What of the masses! After Baʿal I'll descend into earth!"[80] "The primary cause of this anxiety is . . . the fear of famine."[81]

The counterpart to this scene is the one in which the joy prompted by the first autumnal rains finds eloquent expression. ʿAnat relates a dream to El in which she realizes: "Alive is Aliyan Baʿal! Existent the Prince, the Lord of the Earth!";[82] for "the heavens fat did rain *(šmm šmn tmṭrn),*[83] the wadis flow with honey!"[84] El himself picks up this good news and spreads it further: "the springs of the fields babble . . a god has made them flow: the lord of the springs of the land."[85]

However, just as the gift of rain comes from Baʿal, so also the absence of rain. Danel's lament relates that "seven years shall Baʿal fail, eight the Rider of the Clouds; no dew *(ṭl),* no rain *(rbb),* no welling-up of the deep, no sweetness of Baʿal's voice!"[86] That Danel is addressing the clouds apparently results from the close relationship between Baʿal and the clouds, which are his vehicle: "O clouds! Bring rain. . . ! O clouds! Cause . . . rain to fall!" *(yr ʿrpt tmṭr).*[87]

Yet another scene shows that rain is a gift from Baʿal. After the goddess ʿAnat has befouled herself in a bloodbath, she bathes in "sky-dew *(ṭl),* fatness of earth *(šmn 'rṣ),* spray *(rbb)* of the Rider of the Clouds; dew that the heavens do shed, spray *(rbb)* that is shed by the stars."[88] Everything the heavens yield in the way of moisture is Baʿal's

---

76. *KTU,* 1.16 III, 12-16.
77. *KTU,* 1.4 V, 6-9.
78. *KTU,* 1.5 V, 7f.; *ANET,* 139.
79. *KTU,* 1.5 VI, 9f.; *ANET,* 139.
80. *KTU,* 1.5 VI, 23-25; *ANET,* 139.
81. Hillmann, 3.
82. *KTU,* 1.6 III, 2f.; *ANET,* 140.
83. Cf. Zobel, 210-12.
84. *KTU,* 1.6 III, 6f., 12f.; *ANET,* 140.
85. *KTU,* 1.6 III, 25-27, 36-38.
86. *KTU,* 1.19 I, 42-46; *ANET,* 153.
87. *KTU,* 1.19, I, 39-41; cf. *ANET,* 153.
88. *KTU,* 1.3 II, 39-41; *ANET,* 136; similarly also *KTU,* 1.3 IV, 33f.; cf. here Jgs. 5:20.

benefaction: dew, rain, drizzle. All this makes the earth fruitful and causes the streams to bubble. When one hears the thunder, the rushing of rain, and the bubbling of springs, a great relief comes over both the gods and the human beings of Ugarit, since they can now face the immediate future with joy and confidence. Baʿal will again bequeath grain, wine, and oil. His aids include *Rb,* the "goddess of the drizzling rain," mother of *Ṭly,* the "dew goddess," who is one of Baʿal's daughters.[89]

As far as our original question is concerned, we can see unequivocally that Yahweh became associated with life-giving rain only after the fact. That is, Baʿal's sphere was gradually attributed to Yahweh, who took over his function and was thereafter the only "giver of rain" for Israel. However, since the notion of God as creator also only became known to Israel during the course of its history, and only then was actually attributed to Yahweh, there is nothing unique about the present case either. In the meantime, rain seems to have been a part of theophany and of Yahweh-war from the very beginning, where it expresses Yahweh's sovereign power and strength as experienced by his people from the beginning of its history. Precisely because during the course of the exodus events and in his salvific intervention for his people both during and after the land conquest Yahweh always emerged as the more powerful, stronger God, the one superior to all others, this derivation of life-giving rain from Yahweh, who was now also venerated as the creator God, was a natural, necessary consequence.

V. Rain in Metaphors and Comparisons. The comparisons and imagery drawn from the notion of rain are as varied as the statements about rain itself.

1. *Secular References.* Extensive comparisons constructed with *kᵉ* occur in reference to Job and to the figure of the king. Job draws on images of the expectant anticipation of rain to describe the respect he enjoyed among his contemporaries and the high expectations they had of him: "They waited for me as for the rain; they opened their mouths as for the spring rain" (Job 29:23). And David's last words (2 S. 23:4) describe the king as the one who shines "like the sun shining forth upon a cloudless morning, like rain that makes grass to sprout from the earth" (cf. *BHS*). The goodwill and favorable predisposition of the king mean life-giving benefaction. The comparison in Ps. 72:6 draws similar images: the king is "like rain that falls on the mown grass, like showers that water the earth" (cf. *BHS*). When the king advances the welfare of his kingdom, he is like rain that fructifies the earth (cf. Hos. 6:3, referring to Yahweh). The comparison in Isa. 32:2 describes the protection afforded subjects by a just association of king and prince as "refuge from storm and downpour."

Considering the extraordinary significance rain has for human life, it is not surprising that Wisdom Literature attests a large number of comparisons and metaphorical expressions referring to rain. First it should be briefly noted that Eccl. 11:3; Prov. 25:23 contain what amounts to popular weather rules based on a extensive experience. But now to the Wisdom material itself. The favor of the king is compared with "clouds

89. *KTU,* 1.4 I, 17; IV, 56 and *passim.*

that bring the spring rain" (Prov. 16:15). The "didactic opening summons" in the Song of Moses (Dt. 32:2)[90] employs the typical language of wisdom sayings to compare the activity and positive effects of "teaching" and "speech" with the falling rain, the dripping dew, and the freshening of the tender grass and herbs by gentle rainshowers. Steady, continuing, uninterrupted instruction has a beneficial effect on the life of the listener and pupil. The metaphorical use of *yrh* and *rwh* in Prov. 11:25 is the final positively intended formulation: the person who blesses, is blessed; the person who refreshes, is refreshed; goodness is requited.

Other passages use cause and effect as points of comparison. "The north wind produces rain; and a backbiting tongue, angry looks" (Prov. 25:23); "like clouds and wind without rain is one who boasts of a gift never given" (v. 14).

The other comparisons and metaphors refer to those aspects of rain that are less pleasant for human beings. Prov. 27:15 compares a contentious woman with a leaky roof that drips on a rainy day.[91] Prov. 28:3 compares a poor man who oppresses those of lesser station with a beating rain that leaves no food because its waters run off too quickly. The wild impetuosity of human passion is the point of comparison in Jer. 8:6. A fool and honor are as compatible as rain and harvest (Prov. 26:1). Cant. 8:7 finds that love is stronger than mighty waters and overflowing rivers. And the description of the miserable lot of the inhabitants of the steppe, who are wet with rain from the mountains because they have no shelter (Job 24:8), probably also derives from didactic wisdom.[92]

2. *Religious References to Salvation and Judgment.* This imagery occurs more frequently in theological contexts. The image of Yahweh or of his → כבוד *kāḇôḏ* as a refuge from downpours and a shelter from storms (Isa. 4:6; 25:4) is a reference to the protection which his oppressed postexilic community finds in God against dangerous, life-threatening powers.[93] The other image, one occurring several times both in the Psalter and in exilic-postexilic prophets, is that of the protection of the individual or community against the life-threatening danger of being washed away and dying in torrents of water. A plea to Yahweh for succor in such disaster appears in Ps. 32:6; 69:3,16(2,15), and thanksgiving for deliverance from such danger in Ps. 124:4f. (cf. Ps. 40:3[2]; 88:7f.[6f.]; Lam. 3:53; Jon. 2:6[5]). Nah. 1:8 is formulated as a confession: Yahweh provides deliverance from an overflowing flood; Isa. 43:2 seeks to console: "When you pass through the waters . . they shall not overwhelm you." The expressiveness of the imagery of torrential rain and flooding water is so strong,[94] and their symbolism so extensive, that every danger and threat to the community and to the individual can be rendered and expressed, be it external affliction or inner temptation.

Only a few passages use the positive aspect of rain, that aspect so decisively

90. Von Rad, 196.
91. Dalman, 189.
92. Cf. Fohrer, 370.
93. Wildberger, 172f.
94. Cf. Dalman, 210f.

determinative for growth, as a metaphor or comparison involving Yahweh's salvific acts or presence. Isa. 55:10f. compares the efficacy and power of Yahweh's word with the rain that waters the earth. Yahweh's salvific deeds in Israel's history are summarized in the image of the abundant rain Yahweh sheds (Ps. 68:10[9]). He extends prosperity to his community like a flowing river (Isa. 66:12), in overflowing abundance. Whereas in its own self-deception Israel believed that one need only come to Yahweh and he, too, would come like rain watering the earth (Hos. 6:3), Hos. 10:12 assures the Israelites that Yahweh will come and rain salvation upon them only when they themselves sow righteousness.

The imagery of rain and storm is most strongly associated with the theme of judgment. This may have resulted from the fact that the substance of this imagery was always quite naturally incorporated into the theophany portrayals and the motif of the wars of Yahweh, and that the life-giving effects of rain were originally associated with Baʿal. Various points of focus can be discerned. Yahweh caused fire and brimstone to rain down upon Sodom (and Gomorrah) (Gen. 19:24 J). The annihilation was total. The same imagery is reflected in the rain of fire in Am. 7:4[95] as well as in Job 20:23; Ps. 11:6, where the wicked are met by a ravaging rain.

Other imagery employs elements of an exaggerated portrayal of thunderstorms or other destructive weather to express the unlimited might and irresistible power of Yahweh or of his emissary and his judgment. The oracle of doom concerning Ephraim is introduced by the announcement that Yahweh will send "one who is mighty and strong," something then elaborated in two similes: "like a storm of hail, a destroying tempest, like a storm of mighty, overflowing waters." The result is: "He will hurl them down to the earth [with violence]" (Isa. 28:2). This tripartite imagery occurs again in the announcement of judgment against "those who smear whitewash," the false prophets: a "deluge of rain," "hailstones," and "a stormy wind" will come upon them (Ezk. 13:11,13).

A third metaphor, perhaps drawing on the flood imagery, renders independent the element "deluge of rain," recasting it as an "inundation" and "overflowing" of the entire land by the waters of the Euphrates (Isa. 8:8; cf. the inauthentic verse Isa. 10:22) or by waters from the north (Jer. 47:2). The Jerusalemites will be crushed by a "torrential scourge" (Isa. 28:15,17f.). Yahweh's breath, however, will reach up to the neck of Israel's enemies "like an overflowing stream" (Isa. 30:28). Finally, the theme of rainlessness also belongs to the language of judgment (cf. Isa. 5:6; Ezk. 22:24). "Rain is blessing . . . and not to be rained upon is not to be blessed."[96]

Thus the promise is made that postexilic Israel will be "surrounded by many peoples . . . like dew from Yahweh, like showers on the grass," a gift from Yahweh bringing blessings to the nations (Mic. 5:6[7]).

3. *Apocalyptic Usage.* Ps. 90:5 describes the end of human life with the image of being swept away, and Job 14:19 describes the way Yahweh destroys human hopes

---

95. Wolff, *Joel and Amos,* 298.
96. J. Herrmann, *Ezechiel. KAT,* XI, (1924), cited by Zimmerli, *Ezekiel 1,* 468.

with the image of the cloudburst that washes away the soil of the earth. This imagery of the torrential flood seems to have been especially favored in apocalyptic writing because it effectively expresses the sudden, absolute end of the oppressor (Dnl. 9:26; 11:10,22,26,40).

Two passages show how the various metaphorical elements can be combined together or even accumulated: Ps. 105:32 mentions both "rain of hail" and "flaming fire," and Ezk. 38:22, "pestilence and bloodshed," "torrential rains and hailstones," and "fire and brimstone." This, too, seems to be a style closely related to that of apocalyptic writing.[97]

Zobel

---

97. Zimmerli, *Ezekiel 2,* 313.

מַיִם *mayim*

Contents: I. 1. Meaning; 2. Etymology; 3. Word Field; 4. Place Names; 5. LXX; 6. Ancient Near East. II. Secular Usage: 1. Natural Element; 2. Natural Properties; 3. Israelite Cosmology; 4. Sustenance; 5. Cleansing; 6. Food Preparation; 7. Metaphorical Usage. III. Religious Usage: 1. The Mythological Power of Chaos; 2. The Sanctity of Water; 3. Ritual Usage; 4. Legal Usage; 5. Religious Symbolism. IV. 1. Qumran; 2. The Mandeans.

---

mayim. T. Canaan, "Haunted Springs and Water Demons in Palestine," *JPOS,* 1 (1920), 153-170; *idem,* "Water and 'the Water of Life' in Palestinian Superstition," *JPOS,* 9 (1929), 57-69; U. Cassuto, "Baal and Mot in the Ugaritic Texts," *IEJ,* 12 (1962), 77-86; A. Causse, "Le jardin d'Elohim et la source de vie," *RHR,* 81 (1920), 289-315; B. S. Childs, *Myth and Reality in the OT. SBT,* 27 (1960); F. M. Cross, Jr., *Canaanite Myth and Hebrew Epic* (Cambridge, Mass., 1973); *idem* and D. N. Freedman, "A Royal Song of Thanksgiving — II Samuel 22 = Psalm 18," *JBL,* 72 (1953), 15-34; N. A. Dahl, "The Origin of Baptism," *Interpretationes ad VT Pertinentes. Festschrift S. Mowinckel. NTT,* 56 (1955), 36-52; M. Douglas, *Purity and Danger* (New York, 1966); O. Eissfeldt, *Baal Zaphon, Zeus Kasios und der Durchzug der Israeliten durchs Meer. BRA,* 1 (1932); *idem,* "Gott und das Meer in der Bibel," *Studia orientalia Ioanni Pedersen septuagenario* (Copenhagen, 1953), 76-84 = *KlSchr,* III (1966), 256-264; I. Engnell, " 'Planted by the Streams of Water,' " *Studia orientalia Ioanni Pedersen septuagenario,* 85-96; L. R. Fisher, "Creation at Ugarit and in the OT," *VT,* 15 (1965), 313-324; H. Frankfort, *Kingship and the Gods* (Chicago, 1948); *idem, et al., Before Philosophy* (Harmondsworth, 1949); B. Gemser, "*Beʿēber hayyardēn:* In Jordan's Borderland," *VT,* 2 (1952), 348-355; J. C. L. Gibson, ed., *Canaanite Myths and Legends* (Edinburgh, 1978); N. Glueck, *The River Jordan* (Philadelphia, 1946); L. Goppelt, "ὕδωρ," *TDNT,* VIII, 314-333; C. H. Gordon, "Leviathan: Symbol of Evil," *STLI,* 3 (1966), 1-9 = in A. Altmann, ed., *Biblical Motifs* (Cambridge, Mass., 1966), 1-9; J. Gray, *The Legacy of Canaan. SVT,* 5 ([2]1965); H. Gunkel, *Schöpfung und Chaos in Urzeit und Endzeit* (Göttingen, 1895, [2]1921); R. Hillmann, *Wasser und Berg: Kosmische Verbindungslinien zwischen dem kanaanäischen Wettergott und Jahwe* (diss., Halle, 1965); J. J.

I. 1. *Meaning.* The Hebrew subst. *mayim* derives from a biliteral base ל״י[1] or ל״ו.[2] The word is widely attested in the Hamito-Semitic languages,[3] and its Hebrew form should be taken as a *pluralia tantum* instead of as (an apparent) dual.[4] It occurs more than 500 times in the OT to describe "water" in a wide range of cosmic, ritual, and secular contexts. The distribution of these occurrences is unremarkable, although it occurs most frequently in the Pentateuch (more than 200 occurrences), with particular concentration in Gen. 7–9 (the Flood Narrative); Ex. 14f. (deliverance at the Reed Sea); Lev. 11 (regulations concerning clean and unclean animals); Nu. 19 (rites for the water of purification); and Nu. 20f. (desert wanderings from Meribah to Transjordan). The Deuteronomistic history attests *ca.* 100 occurrences, with particular concentration in Jgs. 7 (Gideon's water test at *'ên ḥ^a^rōḏ*) and 1 K. 13, 18; next in frequency are the Psalms (53 occurrences), Ezekiel (46, with 13 of those in Ezk. 47 [the temple stream]), Proto-Isaiah (33; 18 times in Deutero-Isaiah, 5 in Trito-Isaiah), Jeremiah (29), and Job (25).

2. *Etymology.* The base occurs in Aramaic and Syriac as *mayyā'*, *mayyin*,[5] and in Ugaritic as *my*, pl. *mym*.[6] Akkadian attests *mû*,[7] as well as the poetical usage in

---

Jackson, "The Deep," *IDB*, I, 813f.; O. Kaiser, *Die mythische Bedeutung des Meeres in Ägypten, Ugarit, und Israel. BZAW*, 78 (^{2}1962); A. S. Kapelrud, "King and Fertility: A Discussion of 2 Sam. 21:1-14," *Festschrift S. Mowinckel*, 113-122; R. Kratz, *Rettungswunder. EH*, 23/123 (1979); W. G. Lambert, "A New Look at the Babylonian Background of Genesis," *JTS*, N.S. 16 (1965), 287-300; R. Luyster, "Wind and Water: Cosmogonic Symbolism in the OT," *ZAW*, 93 (1981), 1-10; H. G. May, "Some Cosmic Connotations of MAYIM RABBÎM, 'Many Waters,'" *JBL*, 74 (1955), 9-21; M. Ninck, *Die Bedeutung der Wasser in Kult und Leben der Alten* (1921, repr. Darmstadt, 1967); S. I. L. Norin, *Er spaltete das Meer. CB*, 9 (Ger. trans. 1977); M. H. Pope, *El in the Ugaritic Texts. SVT*, 2 (1955); R. Press, "Das Ordal im alten Israel," *ZAW*, 51 (1933), 121-140, 227-255; P. Reymond, *L'eau, sa vie, et sa signification dans l'AT. SVT*, 6 (1958); *idem*, "Un tesson par 'ramasser' de l'eau à la mare (Esaie xxx,14)," *VT*, 7 (1957), 203-7; J. M. Sasson, "Nu 5 and the 'Waters of Judgement,'" *BZ*, N.S. 16 (1972), 249-251; W. H. Schmidt, *Königtum Gottes in Ugarit und Israel. BZAW*, 80 (^{2}1966); R. B. Y. Scott, "Meteorological Phenomena and Terminology in the OT," *ZAW*, 64 (1952), 11-25; E. A. Speiser, "'Ed in the Story of Creation," *BASOR*, 140 (1955), 9-11; E. F. Sutcliffe, "The Clouds as Water-Carriers in Hebrew Thought," *VT*, 3 (1953), 99-103; H. Torczyner, "The Firmament and the Clouds: Rāqîa' and Sheḥāqîm," *StTh*, 1 (1948), 188-196; B. Vawter, "A Note on 'The Waters Beneath the Earth,'" *CBQ*, 22 (1960), 71-73; M. K. Wakeman, *God's Battle with the Monster* (Leiden, 1973); A. J. Wensinck, *The Ocean in the Literature of the Western Semites. VAWA*, N.S. 19/2 (1918; repr. 1968); R. A. Wild, *Water in the Cultic Worship of Isis and Sarapis* (Leiden, 1981); H. Zimmern, "Lebensbrot und Lebenswasser im Babylonischen und in der Bibel," *ARW*, 2 (1899), 165-177; E. Zolli, "*'Eyn 'adām* (Zach. ix 1)," *VT*, 5 (1955), 90-92; → מבול *mabbûl* (VIII, 60-65).

1. Joüon, §98e.
2. *VG*, I, §85.
3. Cf. P. Fronzaroli, "Studi sul lessico comune semitico," *AANLR*, N.S. 20 (1965), 140, 146, 150; G. Bergsträsser, *Introduction to the Semitic Languages* (Eng. trans., Winona Lake, 1983), 214f.; *KBL*^{2}, 546.
4. Following Joüon, §§90f., 91f.; contra *BLe*, §78q, and *GK*, §88d.
5. *LexSyr*, 383; *"aqua; semen virile."*
6. *WUS*, no. 1559; *UT*, no. 1469; 21 occurrences in Ugaritic according to Whitaker, 417.
7. *AHw*, II (1972), 664; *CAD*, X/2, 149-156; *GaG*, §61h.

Middle/Neo-Babylonian of *mām/wū.*[8] The word *mē/ima,* "water," occurs in the Canaanite glosses in the Amarna letters.[9] The Paleo-Aramaic pl. const. *my* occurs in Sefire[10] in connection with *bîr,* "well water." The Siloam inscription (*ca.* 700 B.C.) mentions the flow of water *(hmym)* evidencing the successful breakthrough in the tunnel construction.[11] Finally, the base also occurs in Official Aramaic, Egyptian Aramaic, Nabatean, and Palmyrene. The emphatic *my'* also occurs in the Gnostic Aramaic letter "WAW."[12] Mandaic reads *mai* and *mia.*[13] South Semitic also widely attests the base: OSA *mū* (Minean *mh*);[14] Arab. *mā',* "water; liquid, fluid; juice";[15] Ethiop., Tigr. *māy.*[16] Similarly, the base occurs in Egyptian only as *pluralia tantum mw (myw),* "water,"[17] *mwy,* "urine, semen," metaphorically for "son"; *mwy.t,* "moisture."[18]

Fabry

3. *Word Field.* The element water is found in a wide range of natural sources, comprising the sea,[19] rivers,[20] wadis or seasonal stream-beds,[21] springs,[22] and wells.[23] The source of all these types of water in a more cosmic setting is the primordial ocean.[24]

The primary reference of *mayim* is to the colorless, usually tasteless liquid which occurs as a natural substance in these varied sources. It means "liquid" in the broader sense, and can appear as a euphemism for "urine" (cf. Ezk. 7:17; 21:12[Eng. v. 7], and *mêmê r^e^gālîm* in 2 K. 18:27 par. Isa. 36:12 *Q*); in Isa. 48:1, it is used (as in Syriac and Egyptian) in reference to *semen virile,*[25] although the reading probably follows 1QIs^a^, namely, *ûmimm^e^'ê,* "loins," instead of *ûmimmê* (cf. *BHS*).

Water was considered basic to the sustenance of life in Israel, and as such it soon acquired a strong cosmic importance in Israelite cosmology. Its presence in the

8. *AHw,* II, 601a; *CAD,* X/1, 202b.
9. J. A. Knudtzon, *Die El-Amarna-Tafeln. VAB,* 2/2 (1915, ²1964), 1547, and EA 148, 12, 31; 155, 10.
10. *KAI,* 222B, 33, 34.
11. *Ibid.,* 189, 5.
12. Published by A. Dupont-Sommer; *DISO,* 149.
13. *MdD,* 242, 265.
14. ContiRossini, 175.
15. Wehr (⁴1979), 1094.
16. *TigrWb,* 138.
17. *WbÄS,* II, 50ff.
18. *Ibid.,* II, 53.
19. → יָם *yām* (VI, 87-98).
20. → נהר *nāhār.*
21. → נחל *naḥal.*
22. → עין *'ayin.*
23. → באר *b^e^'ēr* (I, 463-66).
24. → תהום *t^e^hôm;* Akk. *ti'āmtum (tāmtu);* Ugar. *thm.*
25. Cf. P. Wernberg-Møller, "Notes on the Manual of Discipline (DSD) I 18, II 9, III 1-4, 9, VII 10-12, and XI 21-22," *VT,* 3 (1953), 201, and the additional occurrences adduced there from rabbinic writings and the Koran.

primordial ocean *(tᵉhôm)* thence took on a mythological aspect, giving it the force of a primal power and investing it with the attributes of will and intelligence.[26]

4. *Place Names.* The presence of water near a locale led to the identification of such sites through their water supply: sites near a well, e.g., *bᵉʾēr šeḇaʿ;* sites at a river, e.g., *ʾᵃram nahᵃrayim;* sites near springs, e.g., *ʿên ḥᵃrōḏ, ʿên rōḡēl, ʿên dōʾr, ʿên šemeš;* sites generally near water, e.g., *mê dîmôn* (Isa. 15:9), *mê yᵉrîḥô* (Josh. 16:1), *mê mᵉgiddô* (Jgs. 5:19), *mê mᵉrîḇâ* (Nu. 20:13), *mê nimrîm* (Isa. 15:6), *mê neptôaḥ* (Josh. 15:9), *mê zāhāḇ,* (Gen. 36:39),[27] and *mê hayyarqôn* (Josh. 19:46). The "city of waters" (*ʿîr hammayim,* 2 S. 12:26f.) refers to the lower city of Rabbath-Ammon.

5. *LXX.* The LXX almost always translates *mayim* with *hýdōr;*[28] Hebrew word combinations are rendered by *hydrophóros, hydragōgós, hygrasía, hydropoteín,* and *ánydros.* Occasionally the LXX will respond to the context and translate *pótos,* "drink," *pēgḗ,* "spring," *hyetós,* "rain," and *oúron,* "urine." In Nu. 24:7, it reads *goyim (éthnos),* and in Ps. 73:10 *yôm (hēméra).*

Clements

6. *Ancient Near East.*

a. *Mesopotamia.* In Mesopotamia water acquires a significance that can hardly be surveyed; contexts include daily life in connection with cleansing and food preparation,[29] in divination and conjuring,[30] and in medicine.[31] Since water was long regarded as a power, deification came more easily. Enki is the god of the waters of the deep, which emerge in springs and fructify the earth. Water monsters[32] also play a part in the Mesopotamian worldview, and are associated particularly with the name Tiamat. Mesopotamian cosmogony also attributed enormous significance to water. The gods were thought to have arisen from a mixture of the primordial waters Apsû and Tiamat (sweet and salt water).[33] This notion of the bisexual primordial water probably has its origin in Eridu in the south with its acquaintance with the mixture of sweet and salt water in the Delta. The counterpart to this conception is that from Nippur, according to which there was only one primal goddess, Nammu, the mother of Enki and Engur (Apsû).[34]

b. *Egypt.* Washing with water and natron was given priority within the framework of purification rites in Egypt; sacrificial priests, vessels, and sacrifices were additionally

---

26. Cf. Gunkel, 103f.; Eissfeldt, *KlSchr,* III, 256ff.
27. *HAL,* II (1995), 577.
28. Cf. Goppelt, 314ff.
29. Cf. *BuA,* I, 412ff.
30. *Ibid.,* II, 207ff.
31. *Ibid.,* II, 309.
32. → לויתן *liwyāṯān* (VII, 504-9).
33. EnEl, I, 1-10; *ANET,* 60-61.
34. Cf. W. G. Lambert, "Kosmogonie," *RLA,* VI (1983), 220f.

washed by having water poured over them, water being understood as the bearer of divine power,[35] graphically represented by the juxtaposition into jets of water of the hieroglyphs *ʿanḫ,* "life," and *ḏd,* "permanence."[36] The royal bath has mythological significance and symbolizes the morning cleansing of the sun-god in the celestial ocean. Because water was identified with the life-sustaining bodily fluids, a vivifying power was attributed to it in connection with the washing of the dead and with libations.[37]

According to Egyptian cosmogony, the primordial water bore the name Nuu or Nun, and from this the creator-god came forth. In Hermopolitan cosmogony, Nun and Naunet (masc. and fem.) are two of the eight primordial gods who beget the sun. Thus here, too, water is conceived as the primal element which as the eternal primordial material precedes even the creation of the world,[38] although at the same time it is also the element into which at the end of the age the world will sink like an island of the Nile.

c. *Ugarit.* The term *my* occurs 21 times in the texts of Ugarit.[39] Cosmic and theomachist elements are treated in connection with the "sea."[40] Water is hardly mentioned as a secular element: women draw water from springs and wells;[41] Danel's daughter Paghat bears the epithet "who bears water on her shoulders."[42] A city's access to plentiful water could also become an epithet, cf. Qor-Mayim, "water spring."[43] Water is understood as closely associated with fertility;[44] cosmologically it constitutes the limits of the world.[45] By means of a suffix water is associated with the goddess ʿAnat.[46] Finally, there is some dispute concerning the interpretation of the expression "pouring out her waters" (tears?), which parallels the "running out of her *nepeš.*"[47] Cyrus Gordon suggests that "water," like blood, is understood here as a vital substance.

Fabry

II. Secular Usage.

1. *Natural Element.* In a wide variety of contexts the noun *mayim* occurs as a description of the natural element occurring in seas, rivers, springs, and wells. The OT does not evidence any sharp distinction between the salt waters of the sea and the sweet waters of inland water sources. This contrasts strikingly with the more prominent distinction made between the two in Mesopotamian mythology.[48] Precisely the sea with

---

35. *RÄR,* 634.
36. Cf. the cleansing of Amenophis III by Horus and Seth, *ibid.,* 397.
37. On the cleansing and vivifying effects of baptism in the Isis mysteries, cf. *ibid.,* 636.
38. Cf. P. Derchain, "Kosmogonie," *LexÄg,* III (1980), 747-756, esp. 749.
39. *UT,* no. 1469; *WUS,* no. 1559.
40. → יָם *yām,* VI, 90f.
41. *KTU,* 1.14 III, 9f.
42. *Ibid.,* 1.19 II, 1, 6; IV, 28, 37.
43. *Ibid.,* 1.19 IV, 45f.
44. *Ibid.,* 1.1 IV, 9; 1.19 II, 1, 6.
45. *Ibid.,* 1.5 VI, 24; 1.6 I, 6f. (text?).
46. *Ibid.,* 1.3 II, 38; IV, 42, 86.
47. *Ibid.,* 1.16 I, 34.
48. Cf. W. F. Albright, "The Mouth of the Rivers," *AJSL,* 35 (1918/19), 190ff.

its mighty masses of water was variously evaluated: the presence of the water in the seas represents a basic feature of the order of creation (Gen. 1:10; Hab. 3:15), indicating that water itself was looked upon as a supra-mundane aspect of reality. As *mayim rabbîm*[49] it possessed the power to confer life, yet it was also regarded as a threatening power of chaos which could bring death, and could even threaten to disrupt or even overthrow the order divinely determined for creation (cf. Ps. 104:5-9). The waters of the primordial ocean could thereby be regarded as possessing a voice and a will which could challenge the cosmic purpose and order ordained by God (cf. Ps. 93:3f.). From this perspective these fundamental elements of the natural order easily acquired mythological character as cosmic forces.

In the traditions of the origins of the nation of Israel a primary importance is accorded to the crossing of the Reed Sea.[50] The passage of the escaping Hebrews, under the leadership of Moses, through the waters of the sea is viewed as the most significant act of divine salvation. It demonstrated the power of Yahweh to control even the natural order to ensure that his people were protected from the threats of their Egyptian pursuers (Ex. 14:28; 15:1). It is precisely the mythological aspects of the primordial waters that come to the fore here. The waters could become a shield of protection to the Hebrews on the one hand, but a cause of death and destruction to the Egyptians on the other (cf. also Isa. 51:9f.). The location of the Israelite crossing of the *yam sûp̱* can no longer be certainly established, although a site close to the Mediterranean seaboard, east of Suez and especially in the marshlands in the vicinity of the Sirbonian lake, is highly probable.[51]

Later Israelite tradition came greatly to magnify the event as a demonstration of the unique power of Yahweh and of his special relationship to Israel (Ex. 15:10,19; Dt. 11:4; Josh. 2:10; Ps. 78:13; 106:11; Isa. 63:12). Of the remaining references to the waters of the sea, the majority occur in a more neutral theological context. In Am. 5:8; 9:6, the violence of the rainstorm is described as the pouring out of the waters of the sea upon the face of the earth.[52] Yet the waters of the sea can also be portrayed less emotionally. They constitute the element through which ships pass (Ps. 107:23; cf. Ezk. 27:26,34; Ps. 18:16[15]). Isa. 57:20 focuses on the ceaseless motion of the waters of the sea; at the same time, the motion of the waves throws up mire and dirt.

The waters of rivers are also mentioned. The citizens of Babylon dwell by "many waters" *(mayim rabbîm),* which means the same as *nāhār* (Jer. 51:13 *[Q]*). The valleys of the Euphrates, and of the many subsidiary watercourses which flowed through the low-lying, flat Mesopotamian countryside, were of enormous significance for Babylon, and represented a marked contrast to the narrower, steeper valleys of the sparse water-

---

49. Cf. II.3 and III.1 below.

50. → יָם *yām,* VI, 94f.; → סוּף *sûp̱.*

51. Cf. M. Noth, "Der Schauplatz des Meereswunders," *Vom Ugarit nach Qumran. Festschrift O. Eissfeldt. BZAW,* 77 (1947), 181-190 = *Aufsätze zur biblischen Landes- und Altertumskunde* (Neukirchen-Vluyn, 1971), I, 102-110; Eissfeldt, *Baal Zaphon, passim.*

52. Cf. also Isa. 28:2; H. Gese, "Die strömende Geissel des Hadad und Jesaja 28,15 und 18," *Archäologie und AT. Festschrift K. Galling* (Tübingen, 1970), 127-134.

courses of the land of Israel. Similarly for the inhabitants of Nineveh, the waters of the Tigris were vital, so much so that they became emblematic of Assyrian power (Isa. 8:7). For Israel the Jordan was the only river of significant size, and even it remained fordable at many points during the entire year.[53] An important crossing point was located at Gilgal (Josh. 3:1-4,24),[54] near Jericho (Khirbet el-Mefjer?).

Because of its location the river Jordan[55] formed a natural political boundary to the land of Israel for much of its history (Josh. 13). Its value as a natural barrier enabled Gideon to use it as a checkpoint in order to cut off the escape route of marauding Midianites (Jgs. 7:24). In Josh. 16:1, the Jordan is described as "the waters of Jericho," and the river is the scene of a special demonstration of divine power through Elijah in 2 K. 2:6ff. The prophet used his cloak to divide the waters so as to allow Elijah and Elisha to cross over on dry ground.

The most imposing of the rivers of the world known to the Israelites was the Nile,[56] and the OT reflects an awareness of the great importance which this river possessed for the life, culture, and economy of Egypt (cf. Nah. 3:8; Jer. 46:7f.). The fertility of the land was especially dependent on the annual inundation of the Nile valley; its absence meant famine, and could thus be interpreted by a Judean prophet as the effects of a dire curse upon the Egyptian people (cf. Isa. 19:5). Two very prominent sign-actions are ascribed by Israelite tradition to Moses among the "signs and wonders" which accompanied deliverance from Egypt. The first of these consisted of the pouring out of water from the Nile upon dry ground so that it became blood (Ex. 4:9). The second involved the turning of all the water of the Nile into blood (Ex. 7:14-24). In company with the complicated and complex plague narratives,[57] these accounts have been subjected to a long theological development.[58] Nevertheless, behind the story there must lie some awareness of the peculiar phenomenon whereby the waters of the Nile took on a reddish-brown color in the flood season when they drew down heavy soil deposits from the Upper Nile region.[59]

The Syrian rivers Abana and Pharpar are mentioned in 2 K. 5:12. In Moab the water supply was drawn from the waters of Nimrim (Isa. 15:6; Jer. 48:34) and the waters of Dibon (Isa. 15:9).

In Jerusalem mention is made of the small spring of Gihon (1 K. 1:38; 2 Ch. 32:30),[60] and the water supply of the city of Jerusalem was already of utmost importance to the city in antiquity. This was thrown into even greater relief by an awareness of the meager

---

53. Cf. Glueck.

54. Cf. J. Muilenburg, "The Site of Ancient Gilgal," *BASOR,* 140 (1955), 11-27; "Gilgal," *IDB,* II, 398f.

55. → ירדן *yardēn* (VI, 322-330).

56. → יאר *yᵉʾōr* (V, 359-363).

57. Cf. J. L. Ska, "Les plaies d'Égypte dans le récit sacerdotal (Pᵍ)," *Bibl,* 60 (1979), 23-35; *idem,* "La sortie d'Égypte (Ex 7–14) dans le récit sacerdotal (Pᵍ) et la tradition prophétique," *Bibl,* 60 (1979), 191-215.

58. Cf. S. Ö. Steingrimsson, *Vom Zeichen zur Geschichte. CB,* 14 (1979), 50ff.

59. Cf. G. Hort, "The Plagues of Egypt," *ZAW,* 69 (1957), 84-103; 70 (1958), 48-59.

60. → גִּיחוֹן *gîḥôn (gîchôn)* (II, 466-68).

flow of the stream of Shiloah, especially compared with the abundant waters of the Tigris (Isa. 8:6). 2 Ch. 32:3f. mentions that Hezekiah endeavored to block off the flow of water from springs outside Jerusalem in order to prevent their use by the Assyrians. Isa. 22:9 refers to the waters of the "lower pool" at the lower end of the Kidron valley. The "Water Gate" *(šaʿar hammayim)* is mentioned in Neh. 3:26; 8:1,3,16; 12:37.

There is a reference to waters in a visionary stream in Dnl. 12:6f., and unnamed streams are referred to in Job 12:15; Ps. 42:2(1). Jer. 18:14 contrasts the permanent flow of water in the mountain rivers with the more seasonal and limited supply in the wadis *(naḥal),* which flowed with water only in the rainy season. These water-filled gullies could also suddenly turn into rushing torrents during the rainy season (Jgs. 5:4; 2 S. 21:10; 2 K. 3:20; Joel 4:18[3:18]) and so acquired significance in military tactics (Jgs. 5:19; 2 S. 17:20) when they became difficult, or impossible, to ford. Water then appeared as a threatening element not only in the seas, where storms could make it dangerous, but even in much smaller lakes and streams (cf. Ps. 66:12; Isa. 43:2; Hab. 3:10).

The presence of springs[61] in arid regions (cf. Gen. 24:13; Isa. 49:10) contributed to the emergence of particular religious traditions associated with such springs (cf. the waters of Merom, Josh. 11:5,7; *ʿên šemeš,* 15:7; the waters of Nephtoah, 15:9; 18:15; and *mê hayyarqôn,* 19:46). According to Josh. 15:19, the daughter of Caleb asked for a portion of land with springs of water *(gullōṯ).* 2 S. 12:27 refers to the Ammonite city of Rabbah as the "City of Waters." Finally, springs of water served as geographical landmarks (Jgs. 1:15; 1 K. 18:5; 2 K. 3:19f.,22,25; Ps. 107:33,35).

Two oases in the desert region of Sinai played an especially prominent role in Israelite tradition: Meribah (= Meribath-kadesh, Ezk. 47:19) and Marah. The name of the first of these (*m^e^rîḇâ,* "lawsuit, strife") suggests that this oasis functioned as the site for the hearing of lawsuits. Israelite tradition has developed this nomenclature through various etiological elaborations into a series of traditions concerning Israel's rebellion against the leadership of Moses, and thus ultimately against the authority of Yahweh (cf. Nu. 20:8,10,13,24; 27:14; Dt. 32:51; 33:8; Ps. 81:8[7]; 106:32).[62] Ps. 106:32f. links the names of the two oases so that the name "Marah" now indicates the distinctive "bitter" taste of the water, which evidently resulted from its mineral content and led to certain fears concerning its safety for use as drinking water. The tradition that Moses cast a tree into the water to make it drinkable (Ex. 15:23ff. [J]) became linked with this fear. In turn this tradition was elaborated by a divine promise to deliver Israel from the "diseases" of Egypt (Ex. 15:26).[63] For the healing of the "poisoned" water of springs we may note also the tradition of 2 K. 2:19ff. In Jgs. 15:19, we have a tradition in which a popular folk-motif involving Samson has become linked with the spring of *ʿên haqqōrē'.*

---

61. → עין *ʿayin.*

62. Cf. C. Barth, "Zur Bedeutung der Wüstentradition," *Volume de Congrès, Genève 1965. SVT,* 15 (1966), 14-23; G. W. Coats, *Rebellion in the Wilderness* (Nashville, 1968), 47ff.

63. Cf. H. F. Fuhs, "Qādes — Materialien zu den Wüstentraditionen Israels," *BN,* 9 (1979), 54-70, esp. 60.

Next to spring water, water from wells[64] was also of great importance (cf. Gen. 21:19,25; 24:11,13; 1 S. 9:11). All these passages refer to the widespread custom of sending the younger women to draw water from a well. Wells in arid regions made them especially important to travelers, and made them into social and religious centers of habitation and meeting (cf. Gen. 26:18-22 and the naming of wells with *ʿēśeq,* "quarrel," *śiṭnâ,* "enmity," and *r^eḥōḇôṯ,* "wide space"; *b^eʾēr-šeḇaʿ,* Gen. 26:32, and the Song of the Well in Nu. 21:16f.). The presence of a well in Bethlehem is attested by 2 S. 23:15-17, when David's soldiers evaded the Philistine guards in order to draw water from it for David. The remarkable way in which springs of water could flow from apparently barren rock was taken as a sign of divine providence (cf. Neh. 9:15; Ps. 78:16; Isa. 48:21). Water from springs could often be kept in pools or cisterns. A large pool of water was to be found at Gibeon (Jer. 41:12), and other pools are mentioned in Isa. 14:23; Eccl. 2:6.

Water occurs naturally in the form of rain,[65] and this formed the basis for religio-mythological reflection. Ancient Near Eastern cosmology explained the sources of rain in terms of large storehouses of water above the earth.[66] The primordial and formless earth from which creation sprang was viewed as an order in which there was no rain (Gen. 2:5). Prov. 8:24 asserts that there were no springs of water before God created the earth. However, the wholly unmythical link between rain and the clouds which brought it was clearly known and recognized (Job 26:8; Ps. 77:18[17]). In Dt. 11:11, dependence of the land upon the rain of heaven is interpreted as a mark of the special divine providence pertaining to it. In Job 5:10, God causes the rains to fall, and this is interpreted as a sign of his power which human beings cannot emulate (cf. Job 38:34). In Israel most rainfall took place in heavy showers pouring out from powerful storm-clouds, "a gathering of water" (2 S. 22:12; cf. Isa. 28:2); since such rains were frequently accompanied by electrical storms, they became associated with the topology of divine theophany (cf. Ps. 18:10ff.[9ff.]; 29:3; 77:16-19[15-18] *[Q]*).

These heavy rainstorms made a dramatic physical change to the appearance of the countryside, especially when the hills appeared to melt and to run with water (cf. Ps. 104:13). The force of the rainstorm provides the basis for the prophet's imagery of an attack by hostile powers (Isa. 28:17). After the rain a fine mist rises (Job 36:27; cf. Gen. 2:6).[67]

Aside from rain and mist, water also occurs in the form of dew.[68] The tradition of Gideon's call to serve Israel as a deliverer from the Midianites involved effects of the dew as a sign of Yahweh's power and of the authenticity of Gideon's call (Jgs. 6:36-40).

Finally, water could also occur in the form of snow (Job 9:30 *[Q];* Ps. 147:16, and elsewhere).[69]

---

64. → באר *b^eʾēr* (I, 463-66).
65. → מטר *māṭār* (VIII, 250-265).
66. Cf. further under II.3.
67. For Heb. *ʾēḏ,* see C. Westermann, *Genesis 1–11* (Eng. trans., Minneapolis, 1984), 200-201; Speiser.
68. → טל *ṭal* (V, 323-330).
69. → שלג *šeleg.*

The scope of *mayim* in the OT is rounded off when one considers that human tears also consist of water, so that for the eyes to "run with water" serves as a visible expression of great grief (Lam. 1:16; cf. 3:48).

2. *Natural Properties.* The necessity of water for the maintenance of virtually all forms of life is fully and frankly recognized in the OT, and its enormous importance encouraged its employment in a wide range of cultic activities.[70] The fertility of trees and plant life in its entirety is directly linked with the presence of abundant waters (Ps. 1:3; Ezk. 17:5,8; 19:10 [twice]; 31:5,7,14,16). Where there is no water, reeds cannot flourish (Job 8:11), and the earth is ever thirsty for water (Prov. 30:16). At the mere scent of water a tree will bud, even after it has been cut down (Job 14:9).

That water could appear in the form of snow has already been noted above, yet since snow quickly melted and turned to water, which quickly evaporated in the heat of the sun, it could easily evoke the notion of the transience of life (Job 24:19). Yet water could also become frozen, becoming as hard as stone (Job 38:30). The freezing of water was also ascribed to God: Job 37:10 considers God's breath responsible.

Finally, water could also boil (Isa. 64:1[2]), which was of great importance to its use in cooking. Such cooking enhanced the taste of food and made it digestible, but it was felt also to effect a certain purifying function.[71]

A series of didactic sayings addresses the sailing of ships upon the waters of the seas, wondering how they chart the correct course (Prov. 30:19). Although human beings can learn to swim, if a person is not careful or if the current is too strong, the unwary will be carried away and drowned (Job 22:11; 24:18; Ps. 69:3[2]).

It is the natural condition of rivers and seas to be full of fish and all sorts of animals, which God created to flourish there (Gen. 1:20ff.; Lev. 11:9ff.; Dt. 4:18; 5:8; 14:9f.).

3. *Israelite Cosmology.* The importance of water to human life and to the life of the entire created order, combined with the remarkable phenomena which often accompanied thunderstorms, downpours, and the power of the waves of the sea, enhanced the notion of water with rich cosmic significance. Much of this significance appears reflected in a wide range of mythological themes, images, and titles.[72] Nevertheless, it is difficult to distinguish sharply between mythological and cosmological frames of reference regarding water. There are indications that some of the more overtly mythological aspects of water as a cosmic force, personified as a monster or dragon,[73] have been modified so as to minimize the element of mythological religious association (cf. Ps. 104:26).[74]

In the Yahwist Creation Narrative (Gen. 2:4b–3:24), the creation of water is not

70. See below under III.2, 3.
71. See below under II.5, 6.
72. See below under III.1.
73. → לויתן *liwyāṯān* (VII, 504-9).
74. Childs, 36ff.

made the subject of a special divine action. The author affirms that, in the original unformed world, the world was made fertile not by the giving of rain, but by a "cloud of mist" *('ēḏ)* (Gen. 2:6). In the Priestly Creation account, a more fundamental role is ascribed to water, which appears as a primordial substance. As a primeval ocean *(t^ehôm),* it appears not to have lost entirely all vestiges of its mythological character as a cosmic power, although it is no longer vested with the personal qualities of will and intelligence which appear in the Babylonian Tiamat.[75] The Hebrew *t^ehôm* displays features of power and cosmic range capable of disrupting the divinely given order of creation (cf. Ps. 104:7-9) without the waters themselves threatening to overwhelm God. God establishes his own power over the waters by separating the upper from the lower waters at creation (Gen. 1:6ff.). Similarly, the provision of fixed boundaries and channels for the waters to flow in continually robs them of their authority and power (cf. Ps. 104:9; Prov. 8:29). This division of the waters can even be viewed as a fundamental feature of Israelite cosmology (cf. Gen. 1:6; Ex. 20:4; Dt. 5:8; Ps. 104:3; 136:6; 148:4).[76] The cosmic aspect of the sea was clearly related at some stage in the growth of Israelite religio-mythological tradition with the figure of the primeval dragon monster Leviathan (cf. Ps. 104:26; Isa. 27:1). The subterranean waters were believed to extend to the very boundaries of Sheol (Ezk. 31:15; Jon. 2:6f.[5f.]), and these waters formed a part of the world-embracing oceans, the *mayim rabbîm* (Ezk. 26:19). In this sense death itself could be viewed as a journey through the *mayim rabbîm* to Sheol (Lam. 3:54). There thus developed a close association between the threatening power of water, especially in its cosmic manifestation as *mayim rabbîm,* and the physical fact of death (cf. Ps. 124:5; 144:7; also Ps. 18:17[16]; 69:3,15f.[2,14f.]; Isa. 43:2).

Yahweh's power in establishing boundaries for the waters, and in gathering the waters together "as in a bottle," is mentioned in Ps. 33:7. According to Job 28:25; Isa. 40:12, Yahweh is able to measure out the waters. The cosmic boundary of the primeval waters could also be said to mark the division between the realms of light and darkness (Job 26:10).

The most striking of the OT narratives which reflect the cosmic range and threatening power of water is that of the Flood (Gen. 6:5–8:22).[77] Here a number of individual features point to some connection in the history of the tradition with that of the flood episode recounted in the Babylonian epic of Gilgamesh[78] and the Babylonian Atraḫasis epic.[79] The onset of the Flood[80] is described in the Israelite tradition as the bursting

75. Cf. A. Heidel, *The Babylonian Genesis* (Chicago, 1951), 100ff.

76. Cf. Kaiser, 48ff.

77. *Ibid.,* 120ff.

78. Cf. A. Heidel, *The Gilgamesh Epic and OT Parallels* (Chicago, ²1963), 224ff.; E. Fisher, "*Gilgamesh* and Genesis: The Flood Story in Context," *CBQ,* 32 (1970), 392-403; on this whole complex see also R. Oberforcher, *Die Flutprologe als Kompositionsschlüssel der biblischen Urgeschichte* (Innsbruck, 1981).

79. Cf. W. G. Lambert and A. R. Millard, *Atra-ḫasis: The Babylonian Story of the Flood* (Oxford, 1969); L. Matouš, "Die Urgeschichte der Menschheit im Atraḫasīs-Epos und in der Genesis," *ArOr,* 37 (1969), 1-7; see also *ANET,* 512-14.

80. → מבול *mabbûl* (VIII, 60-65).

forth of the waters of the great deep (Gen. 7:11) and as a heavy downpour (*gešem,* v. 12). The strongly mythological features of the account are evident at a number of points even though the story has been adapted to a historical form and has acquired a certain number of cultural historical associations. The waters over the earth (Gen. 7:10,17ff.,24) destroy all living creatures (Gen. 7:18ff.), leaving only Noah and those with him in the ark. After the earth had become dried up through the action of the wind (Gen. 8:1), God affirmed by an oath that such a catastrophe would not be repeated upon the earth (Gen. 9:15). This left a distinctive tradition in Israel concerning the "waters of Noah" (Isa. 54:9).

4. *Sustenance.* The primary importance of water for human life was as life-sustaining drink. As a consequence, threats of drought, thirst, and weakness caused by lack of water are reflected at a number of points in the biblical tradition. This inevitably drew to itself a close association with the climatological and geographical features of the land of Israel, much of which is of a semi-desert character. There thus also developed an Israelite tradition of the Sinai oases Massah and Meribah, associated with the spring at Kadesh (cf. Neh. 9:15,20).[81] The presence of springs and underground wells especially in the most arid regions made such sites important for Bedouins, travelers, and traders. Many of the most distinctive features of life in such regions, with the strong demarcation between the seasons by the amount of rainfall, are to be linked with the necessity of water to sustain life. As Israel came to be increasingly characterized by an agrarian economy, so the water supply, and the storage and transportation of water, became decisive factors.

The OT contains a plethora of references to the central necessity of an adequate supply of water: cf. Jgs. 4:19; 5:25 (Sisera); 7:4f. (Gideon); 1 S. 30:11; 2 S. 23:16f. (David); 1 K. 17:10 (Elijah); 18:4 (Obadiah); 18:13; 1 Ch. 11:17; Neh. 13:2; Hos. 2:7[5]; Ezk. 12:18f.; Dnl. 1:12. This need for water to sustain life is reflected in the form of the divine promise which God affirms to his people: "I will bless your bread and your water" (Ex. 23:25). The very essence of worthy hospitality consisted in offering the guest water (2 K. 6:22; Ps. 23:5; Isa. 21:14). To "eat bread and drink water" in another person's house was recognized as an acceptance of that person's hospitality, and in consequence it carried with it the effect of being open to the blessing *(bᵉrāḵâ)* or curse *('ālâ, qᵉlālâ)* which rested upon that house (1 K. 13:8f.,16ff.,22). To refuse to give an exhausted person food and water was interpreted as a reprehensible act of deliberate rebuff (Nabal toward David, 1 S. 25:11). Similarly, the hostility of the Edomites toward Israel was recalled and exemplified in the tradition that they had refused Israel water even when the Israelites offered to pay (Nu. 20:17,19; Dt. 2:6,28). A similar request was put to Sihon, king of the Amorites; he, too, rebuffed them (Nu. 21:23; cf. Dt. 23:5[4]). The need to buy water for money was viewed as a situation of deepest distress (Lam. 5:4).

---

81. Cf. V. Fritz, "Kades Barnea — Topographie und Siedlungsgeschichte im Bereich der Quellen von Kadesch und die Kultstätten des Negeb während der Königszeit," *BN,* 9 (1979), 45-50.

The experience of physical weakness and faintness caused by dehydration and lack of water is reflected in a number of OT traditions (cf., e.g., 1 S. 30:12; Ps. 107:4f.). Even the smith, traditionally a figure of considerable strength, could be weakened by lack of water (Isa. 44:12).

Because of the seasonal nature of rainfall in Israel, half the year essentially constituted a dry season. If the winter rains failed, the situation became life-threatening for human beings, animals, and plants. As a result there occurred periodically years of drought in which areas which had been cultivable were dried up and regular sources of water became dangerously depleted. The OT reflects experiences of such seasons of exceptional drought (Am. 4:8; Jer. 14:1-6; 38:6). At such times the storage of water became necessary (cf. Jer. 14:3 *[Q];* 15:18). Scarcity of water could also result from military siege, which cut off access to wells and springs outside the city, although such lack could be bridged for a time by careful rationing of water (Ezk. 4:11-17). The "water of affliction" (*mayim ṣār* [text?]; Isa. 30:20) probably refers to such a situation. The provision of an adequate water supply for the special needs of such times of distress consequently became an important aspect of the defense of cities, e.g., of Jerusalem (2 Ch. 32:3f.; Isa. 22:11; cf. also 2 K. 20:20; Isa. 3:1). Similarly, part of the deprivation which imprisonment brought was a lack of normal quantities of water (1 K. 22:27 par. 2 Ch. 18:26). During a period of fasting a person might also do without water (Ex. 34:28; Dt. 9:9,18; Ezr. 10:6; Jon. 3:7), although this was understandably regarded as unusual.

It was a mark of well-being and security to be in possession of a continuing and reliable water supply (Nu. 24:6f.; Isa. 33:16). The stealing of water was proscribed, and only a foolish woman might extol the sweet taste of stolen water (Prov. 9:17).

This overriding need for a good water supply made it essential that it should be kept wholesome and uncontaminated. Hence to drink clean water, and then to proceed to foul the remainder, like an uncomprehending animal, was seen as a mark of inhuman folly (Ezk. 34:18; cf. 26:12). The action here refers to ravaging soldiers who contaminate the cisterns after capturing a city. Of course, water could also become contaminated or poisoned by natural causes, something taken as a sign of divine judgment (Jer. 8:14; 9:14[15]; 23:15). However, even contaminated water supplies could be rendered drinkable again through appropriate measures. According to 2 K. 2:19-22, Elisha "healed" (*rippē'*) a supply of water in Jericho. Such prophetic power over water was manifested in Moses, who changed the water of the Nile into blood, rendering it unfit for drinking purposes (Ex. 7:14-24).

Different types of containers were used to store water and to carry it: jars (*kaḏ,* Gen. 24:15,17,43; 1 S. 26:11f.,16; 1 K. 19:6), troughs for watering sheep (*šeqeṯ, rahaṭ,* Gen. 30:38), bottles made of animal skin for use on a journey (*ḥēmeṯ,* Gen. 21:14f.,19), and cups for drinking purposes (*kôs*). Without the help of such a container a person might use a shard of broken pottery (Isa. 30:14) or his own hands, or even lie down and lap like a dog (Jgs. 7:5ff.). In order to draw water up from a well one might use a bucket (*d^e^lî,* Nu. 24:7) or storage jars (Gen. 24:14-17). For the drawing of water, see also Dt. 29:10[11]; Josh. 9:21,23,27.

For reasons of hygiene it was obviously necessary to ensure that all containers and pits used to store drinking water were also clean (Lev. 11:34,36,38). If these basic rules of cleanliness were not observed, the water itself was classified as unclean (Lev. 11:38). Finally, water could be mixed with wine so as to improve its taste and palatability.[82]

2 K. 8:15 has documented how water can become the instrument of murder. According to this tradition, Hazael dips a bed coverlet in water and spreads it across the face of the sick king Ben-hadad to induce asphyxiation.

5. *Cleansing.* The secular and cultic customs involving water are closely intertwined in its use for washing, since the concepts of holiness and purity were very closely related to each other. As a consequence, it is frequently impossible to separate the ritual from the secular in connection with the cleansing efficacy of washing.[83] The washing of Aaron and his sons for their consecration to the service of the priesthood involved both aspects (Ex. 29:4; 30:20).[84] Hygiene and ritual cleansing were not distinguished in the case of involuntary sexual emissions, normal sexual activity, emissions of blood from women, and the appearance of skin infections, as well as contact with lepers and the dead. Besides the removal of dirt, the washing of a child also included such ritual removal of uncleanness. Yet there was an awareness of a more directly secular necessity for washing off dirt, as is to be seen in the washing of the feet after a journey (Gen. 18:4; 24:32; 43:24). The relationship of a servant to his master could even be described as that of "pouring water on the hands" (cf. the relationship between Elisha and Elijah, 2 K. 3:11). It was also evidently usual to wash new items of clothing before wearing them; this notion lies behind the sign-action involving a linen waistcloth (Jer. 13:1-11) and explains why Jeremiah was prohibited from washing the waistcloth before using it.

Utensils for cooking and eating were doubtlessly washed before the preparation and consumption of food. We can only assume that the normal daily acts of washing and bathing (e.g., 2 S. 11:2) were not accorded any specific ritual significance.

6. *Food Preparation.* Water was used in the kitchen for boiling the food, including in some circumstances the meat of sacrificial animals. Although those parts of a sacrificial animal which were to be eaten would normally have been roasted (*ṣālâ,* 1 S. 2:15; Isa. 44:16,19; *ḥāraḵ,* Prov. 12:27), the meat could also be boiled (*bāšal,* Lev. 8:31; 1 K. 19:21; 2 K. 6:29; Ezk. 46:20,24) to render it more suitable for eating, and also to reduce the risk of food poisoning through deterioration. Even the Passover sacrifice, which might more commonly have been roasted (Ex. 12:8f.), could be boiled (Dt. 16:7; cf. 2 Ch. 35:13). Through a period of "seething" (*rāṯaḥ,* Job 30:27; 41:23[31]; Ezk. 24:5) one could boil various vegetables and herbs together (cf. also Ezk. 24:5; Job 41:23[31]).

7. *Metaphorical Usage.* Heb. *mayim* is also extensively used in metaphors and as a component in symbolical gestures.

---

82. On the metaphorical interpretation, cf. Isa. 1:22 and II.7 below.
83. Cf. Douglas, 7ff.
84. See further below under III.3.

a. The physical property of water as a fluid has occasioned its use as an image of weakness. After their defeat and the loss of thirty-six men at Ai, the Israelites became disheartened, i.e., "the *lēḇ* of the people melted and turned to water" (Josh. 7:1-5). The *nep̱eš* can also be poured out like water, an image for weakness and illness leading to the pronounced fear of death (Ps. 22:15[14]). The expression "all knees turn to water" (Ezk. 7:17; 21:12[7]) probably attests a drastically realistic background: "Men are no longer able to preserve the elementary aspects of self-control, like the infant and the dying man who passes water."[85] The wise woman of Tekoa is alluding to the ultimate human weakness leading to death when she says to David: "We must all die; we are like water spilled on the ground" (2 S. 14:14).

b. The formlessness and evanescence of water also invite metaphorical usage. The psalmist implores that his enemies "vanish like water that runs away" (Ps. 58:8[7]). Job 14:11 compares human beings with the water of a lake that dries up and disappears. Zophar uses this image in Job 11:16 to conceive of the sins of the person reconciled to God as having disappeared "as waters that have passed away" *(k^emayim ʿāḇ^erû).* In Nah. 2:9(8), Nineveh in its destruction is likened to a pool "whose waters (read: *mêmeyhā* with *BHS* mg.) run away." The reverse image of constancy can be attained through negation: the righteous of Israel will become "like a watered garden, like a spring of water, whose waters never fail" (Isa. 58:11; cf. 1:30).

c. The idea of the constant movement of water is employed by the wisdom poet to describe God's power over the king: "The king's heart is a stream of water in the hand of Yahweh; he turns it wherever he will" (Prov. 21:1).

d. There was also an awareness of the power and irresistible force of water, and of the difficulty in controlling it or containing it in a fixed place. This is probably in Amos' mind when he demands that social justice be like a cascading stream (Am. 5:24). In Mic. 1:4, the coming of God to his people in judgment is described with the aid of the imagery of a storm theophany; his presence causes the mountains to melt, "like waters poured down a steep place." The image of the destructive torrent of water also stands behind Job 27:20 (fear and terror overtake the wicked like a flood); 1 Ch. 14:11 (Yahweh overcomes the enemies like a bursting flood); Isa. 8:7; 17:12f.; Jer. 47:2. And just as the persistent dripping of water wears away stones, so is God able gradually to destroy human hopes (Job 14:19).

e. A consciousness of the fluidity and formlessness of water when poured out has led to its being used to convey the notion of excess and unlimited freedom. So the enemies of Jerusalem are said to have poured out the blood of its citizens like water (Ps. 79:3; cf. also Dt. 12:24; 15:23); according to Hos. 5:10, Yahweh threatens to pour out his wrath like water upon the princes of Judah. In a similar fashion the afflicted Job can describe his cries and groanings as "poured out like water" (Job 3:24), the point of the metaphor being to convey the idea of suffering beyond all measure (cf. also Lam. 2:19).

---

85. W. Zimmerli, *Ezekiel 1. Herm* (Eng. trans. 1979), 208.

f. Descriptions of grief also employ the image of water, associating water with tears. The eyes of the person who fails to observe the torah gush with water (Ps. 119:136; cf. Jer. 8:23[9:1]; 9:17[18]).

g. The depth of cisterns and the fact that they were fed by subterranean springs occasioned metaphorical usage. The wisdom teacher asserts that the words of a person's mouth are like deep waters (Prov. 18:4), and the purpose of a person's mind is like deep water (Prov. 20:5). Deep water conceals things. Just as a person can sink stones into such water, so were the Egyptians sunk in the Sea of Reeds (Ex. 15:1,5; Neh. 9:11).

h. Ps. 109:18 contains a vivid image for the act-consequence relationship. Just as water is able to soak into other substances, so also the man who loves to curse is so pursued by the consequences of his own actions that the curse is said to soak into his body.

i. Water that surrounds a person is understood as a threat (Ps. 88:18[17]). God's wrath surrounds a person like water (Ps. 69:2[1]; cf. v. 3[2] with different terminology, *šibbōleṯ*), till it reaches up to his neck. We can easily detect remnants of mythological features in such descriptions as these that draw on the threatening force of water, i.e., water as a power of chaos threatening the realm of creation. Yahweh's power, however, overcomes this threat (cf. Isa. 43:2).

Clements

j. The reflective surface of water serves the aphorism in Prov. 27:19: "Just as water reflects a face, so does the heart of a man reflect him."

A more controversial metaphorical application is to be found in Eccl. 11:1: "Cast your bread upon the waters, for you will find it after many days." Interpreters long suspected the presence here of a sexual motif from the cult of Adonis.[86] Willy Staerk[87] early suggested that this constituted an injunction to unreflected generosity and goodness, which would be rewarded in due time. Yet the peculiar expression *šallaḥ laḥmᵉḵā* repeatedly evoked the idea of encouragement to undertake a sea journey,[88] and this — with somewhat inconsistent interpretation — in its own turn evoked the challenge to accept the risk of confronting the uncertain.[89] As Hans Wilhelm Hertzberg[90] and Oswald Loretz[91] suggest, the proverb thus probably refers to an act that contrary to all expectation comes to a beneficial end.[92]

Fabry

k. A range of metaphorical applications relating to water is drawn from its importance as a drink, and consequently as a basic element necessary for the sustenance of life and vigor. Thus the image of drinking water *(šāṯâ)* frequently represents the acquisition

86. Cf. O. S. Rankin, "Ecclesiastes: Introduction and Exegesis, *IB,* V (1956), 81.
87. "Zur Exegese von Koh 10_{20} und 11_1," *ZAW,* 59 (1942), 216f.
88. Cf. R. Gordis, *Koheleth — The Man and His World* (New York, ²1955), 320.
89. Cf. also W. Zimmerli, *Prediger. ATD,* XVI/1 (³1980), 240.
90. *Der Prediger. KAT,* XVII/4 (1963), 200-202.
91. *Qohelet und der Alte Orient* (Freiburg, 1964), 88.
92. Contra A. Lauha, *Kohelet. BK,* XIX (1978), *in loc.*

of certain behavioral characteristics. The wicked person "drinks iniquity like water" (Job 15:16). Job himself, when faced with the rebukes and admonitions of his friends, is characterized as a person "who drinks up scoffing like water" (Job 34:7). The experience of drinking water from a cistern provides the basis of the didactic metaphor, "Drink water from your own cistern" (Prov. 5:15), an unmistakable admonition to remain sexually loyal to one's own wife. With the same overtone Cant. 4:15 describes the beloved as a "well of living water" (= a garden spring) and as "flowing streams from Lebanon." And again with mythological resonance, Cant. 8:7 refers to the constancy of true love, which even "many waters (*mayim rabbîm,* an allusion to the waters of chaos?[93]) cannot quench." Prov. 25:21 alludes to concepts of hospitality with its custom of giving a guest water to drink, enjoining that an enemy also be given water to drink and food to eat that he may thereby be brought to feel the shame of his enmity. Finally, the reception of good news from a distant land is likened to the eagerness with which a thirsty man accepts a drink of cool water (Prov. 25:25).

l. Water is important for fertility and high crop yield. The well-being of a righteous person is compared to a tree planted by streams of water (cf. Job 29:19; Ps. 1:3); the Egyptian pharaoh is likened to a well-watered cedar (Ezk. 31:4), and according to Isa. 12:3 the future Israel, when it has been restored to its land, is assured that with joy it will "draw water from the wells of salvation." And finally, the outpouring of God's spirit[94] upon the descendants of Israel is compared to the pouring out of water upon parched ground (Isa. 44:3; cf. 32:2; 44:4; 55:1; 58:11; Jer. 17:8; Ezk. 17:5,8; 19:10; 31:5,7).

Ps. 73:10 is probably alluding to the water supply system when it refers to the actions of the wicked: "abundant waters are drained by them." Several commentators here have sought an emendation of the text so as to eliminate any reference to *mayim,*[95] even though the MT is certainly intelligible. If the text is allowed to stand, the harmful activities of the wicked are compared to the blameworthy waste of a plentiful water supply.[96]

That God is a "fountain of living waters" becomes a readily explicable metaphor of the life-giving power of Yahweh, in his role as giver of fertility and of salvation and righteousness (Jer. 17:13). Yahweh is the source of life and blessing for his people. Thus in Jer. 2:13 the turning of Israel to Baʿal is described as having "forsaken me, the fountain of living water, and dug out . . . cracked cisterns that can hold no water."

A much more complex development of the imagery of water is to be found in Ezekiel's vision of the restored temple and its stream (Ezk. 47:1ff.). Here mythological, metaphorical, and traditional ritual associations of water have been combined into an image of the blessing which will be given to Israel through its restored cult. Notions of fertility, salvation, prosperity, and cultic blessing have been brought together in

---

93. Cf. III.1 below and H. Ringgren, *Das Hohelied. ATD,* XVI/2 (^{3}1981), *in loc.*

94. → רוח *rûaḥ.*

95. *BHS;* cf. H.-J. Kraus, *Psalms 60-150* (Eng. trans., Minneapolis, 1989), 83f., 87f.

96. Cf., however, the similar assertion about the demonic "gods," *KTU,* 1.23, 62f.; see H. Ringgren, "Einige Bemerkungen zum LXXIII. Psalm," *VT,* 3 (1953), 269.

imagery evoking the realization of the unthinkable: the waters of the Dead Sea will become fresh (vv. 8f.). On this notion of the temple spring that issues forth blessings, cf. also Zec. 14:8.[97]

The development of apocalyptic imagery involving water is further to be found in Zec. 9:11, where the redeemed of Israel are assured of deliverance from the pit, which a scribal addition has elaborated as being without water.

m. The extent and vastness of the sea have encouraged its use in similes expressing grandeur and completeness. The future eschatological age is described as one in which the whole earth will become full of the knowledge of Yahweh "as the waters cover the sea" (Isa. 11:9 par. Hab. 2:14). The contrast between the vastness of the seas and the smallness of a small branch floating upon it is to be found in Hos. 10:7. The imagery here is employed to describe the divine judgment coming upon the king of Samaria, although the text is uncertain;[98] some commentators understand *qeṣep* as (divine) "wrath."[99]

n. Finally, *mayim* occurs in various similes. In Jer. 6:7, Jerusalem is accused of keeping her wickedness fresh "as a well keeps its water fresh." The imagery of drinking water is also used by Jeremiah to denounce publicly the seeking of military and political alliances with Egypt and Assyria (Jer. 2:18). In a strange metaphor of purification, Ezekiel describes the coming divine judgment of Egypt as a time when Yahweh will cause the waters of the Nile to become clear and its rivers to run like oil (Ezk. 32:14). The description of the tribe of Reuben as "unstable as water" (Gen. 49:4) characterizes the tribe's restlessness and instability (or presumption?).

III. Religious Usage.

1. *The Mythological Power of Chaos.* Throughout the ancient Near East water was recognized as a primal element of creation and as an indispensable part of the process by which life came into being. Lack of it brought death and desolation, whereas its presence brought life and fertility. Its association with storms and the concomitant electrical phenomena added to this a sense of divine mystery and power. Instead of merely being regarded as one element that existed within creation, it came to be regarded as itself constituting a cosmic power. Alongside its beneficent potentialities for life and fertility it could also appear as a negative force threatening to disrupt the very order of the world and challenging Yahweh's sovereignty, characteristics also shared by the Mesopotamian dragon Tiamat.[100] The presence of water in the seas, its fruitful drenching of the earth, and its powers to achieve cleansing and renewal of life all conferred upon it a unique role in ancient Israel as a cosmic force which could even be set alongside God himself.[101]

---

97. → גיחון *gîḥôn (gîchôn)* (II, 466-68).
98. Cf. H. W. Wolff, *Hosea. Herm* (Eng. trans. 1974), 176.
99. F. I. Anderson and D. N. Freedman, *Hosea. AB,* XXIV (1980), 548, 538.
100. Cf. Wakeman, 166ff.; Norin, 42ff.
101. Cf. Kaiser, 1ff.; W. H. Schmidt, *Alttestamentlicher Glaube und seine Umwelt* (Neukirchen, 1968), 152ff.

In the Syrian-Canaanite sphere a number of varied forms of this cosmic role of water are to be found.[102] Ugaritic mythology reflects the notion of a conflict between Baʿal and the power of the cosmic seas[103] in the person of the *tpṭ nhr zbl ym,* "Judge River, Lord Sea."[104] Familiarity with such a myth is shown by a number of references in the OT (cf. Ps. 74:13; Isa. 51:9f.; Ps. 89). The personification of the primeval force of water could take on various names: Rahab (Isa. 30:7) and Leviathan (Isa. 27:1), among others. Ps. 104:26 speaks of Leviathan with much reduced powers playing in the waters of the seas, unable to pose any threat. These remnants attest the enormous significance this myth had in ancient Israel, although they represent only fragments of various mythological motifs. The extensive similarity between these mythological traces and the myths of the Mesopotamian-Syrian sphere excludes the possibility that Israel ever had its own version of this myth. Rather, the various fragments suggest that the Israelites adapted and varied different elements of the more widely attested mythology.

Further echoes of the myth of the conflict between God and the sea (water) resonate in several places in Israel, e.g., in the extremely sharp rebuke of water during creation and the limitation of its sphere (cf. Ps. 104:5-9; cf. also Ps. 46:4[3]; 65:10[9], where the waters of chaos threaten the dominion of Yahweh). A late literary development of this mythology is also to be found in Ezk. 32:2.

The concept of the primeval ocean in the guise of "mighty waters" *(mayim rabbîm)* is widely attested in the OT. At several points it retains marked overtones of its significance as a destructive cosmic power (cf. Ps. 93:4).[105] In Ex. 15:10, the waters of the *yam sûp̱* into which the Egyptians sank are described as *mayim rabbîm,* linking the ancient creation mythology with the exodus tradition (cf. Isa. 43:16).[106] Less clearly defined are the references to the challenge which the *mayim rabbîm* pose to the rule of Yahweh's sovereignty (2 S. 22:17 par.; Isa. 17:12f.; Ps. 29:3; 32:6; Jer. 51:55). In the latter instance the political threat to Israel posed by Babylon is compared to that which the *mayim rabbîm* pose to Yahweh (cf. also Jer. 10:13; 51:16; Ezk. 1:24). In Isa. 17:12f.; Ezk. 43:2, the roaring of hostile nations is compared to that of the primeval waters. Otherwise *mayim rabbîm* occurs only in poetical descriptions of the sea (Isa. 23:3; Ps. 18:17[16] par.; even here the cosmic-mythological dimension has not entirely disappeared). With slight terminological variation Ps. 124:4 portrays undefined hostile powers as *hammayim* and *naḥlâ,* "torrent."

2. *The Sanctity of Water.* The sense of a divine power that was working through water to bring fertility and to preserve life resulted in such sources of water being venerated as sacred places. Thus not only were the locations of wells and springs

---

102. Cf. Kaiser, 40ff.; H. Gese, *Die Religionen Altsyriens, Altarabiens und der Mandäer. RdM,* 10/2 (1970), 59ff., 134ff.

103. → יָם *yām* (VI, 87-98).

104. *KTU,* 1.2, *passim;* cf. I.6.c above and Gray, 23ff.; Schmidt, *Königtum Gottes in Ugarit und Israel,* 10ff.; → יָם *yām,* VI, 90f.

105. May, 9-21.

106. See also Norin, 77f.

frequently associated with shrines and holy places, but the very springs and wells themselves came to be regarded as particularly holy. Thus the well at Beer-sheba was a site of special holiness, both as the place of covenant making and as a source of water (cf. Gen. 21:30f.; 26:32ff.). The sanctity of wells is the focus of the Song of the Well (Nu. 21:17f.). The narrative concerning the role of Elisha in bringing about the healing from leprosy of Naaman reflects a belief in the sanctity of the water of a river (2 K. 5:1-14); in this case it is the water of the Jordan[107] that brings about the cleansing from leprosy (2 K. 5:10,12,14). The action of immersing oneself seven times recalls the ritual cleansing in running water.[108] The water itself was not conceived to possess this cleansing and life-renewing power, but rather to be the medium of such divine efficacy.

3. *Ritual Usage.* In antiquity the notion of purity[109] was closely associated with those of holiness[110] and wholeness.[111] The individual semantic fields overlap and are accommodated to one another: "Our rituals create a lot of little sub-worlds, unrelated. Their rituals create one single, symbolically consistent universe."[112] It is impossible in consequence to understand adequately the use of water in rites of washing and purification without being aware of the imprecise separation between sacred and profane, ritual and ordinary washing. Actions designed to promote the removal of dirt, of harmful influences and diseases, and of ritual impurity were so closely interconnected that they cannot be understood in isolation from one another.

So far as the apparatus of the cult was concerned, the most striking of all the vessels intended for ritual washing appears to have been the "bronze sea" (*yam mûṣāq,* 1 K. 7:23ff.); this was certainly a very large water receptacle, although we cannot know for sure in which ritual, if any, it was used. The only clue is its association with the Jerusalem temple inventory. Its designation as "sea" suggests cosmic and mythological symbolism.[113] The Jerusalem temple also contained ten bowls, or lavers (*kiyyōrôṯ,* 1 K. 7:38f.,43), which perhaps also contained water (cf. Ex. 30:18; 40:7,30).

Running water was definitely preferred for use in cultic ceremonies (Lev. 14:5f., 50ff.; Nu. 19:17ff.). The distinctive ritual associated with the cleansing of a leper called for the slaughter of a bird over an earthen vessel with fresh water (Lev. 14:5f., 50ff.). In other types of sacrificial offering as well, certain parts of the sacrifice (legs and entrails) were to be washed with water (Lev. 1:9,13; 8:21). Even the cultic personnel had to subject themselves to washing before embarking on the performance of the ritual activities. Similarly, the Aaronid priests were to be washed before their consecration to office (Lev. 8:6). A slight variation of this is to be found in Nu. 8:7, which required cleansing of the Levites as a part of their consecration to office by an act of sprinkling

107. → ירדן *yardēn* (VI, 322-330).
108. See III.3 below.
109. → טהר *ṭāhar* (V, 287-296).
110. → קדשׁ *qdš.*
111. → תמם *tmm;* cf. Douglas, 73ff.
112. Douglas, 69.
113. Cf. W. F. Albright, *Archaeology and the Religion of Israel* (Baltimore, ²1946), 148-150.

"water of expiation *(mê ḥaṭṭā'ṯ)*" (cf. also Nu. 19:21; Ezk. 36:25). This allows the conclusion that such washings represented symbolical action and simultaneously a substitute for complete washing of all bodily parts. In contrast with this, Lev. 16:4,24 calls for the priest to bathe his body completely in water before entering the holy place for the performance of the rites of the Day of Atonement, to be repeated after his return from within the sanctuary. For washings after the ritual of the slaughter of the red heifer and after the distribution of booty from a battle, cf. Nu. 19:9; 31:24.

Regulations concerning the cleansing of lepers laid down stringent demands for washing. A person adjudged to be clear of such disease was required to wash his entire body, as well as to shave off his hair and to wash his clothing (Lev. 14:8ff.). Similar regulations concerned those suffering various kinds of bodily discharge (Lev. 15:5f.,8ff.,18,21f.,27). Here the requirements for washing were extended to cover even bedding. No doubt these levitical regulations were intended to promote hygiene and to inhibit further infection, but these aims cannot be fully divorced from the ideas of ritual uncleanness. Hence the washing itself possessed a semiritual character. After contact with the dead carcass of an unclean animal the contaminated person had to wash both himself and his personal objects (i.e., especially his clothing) with water (Lev. 11:32,36). Contact with the corpse of a dead person also called for careful washing with water and extended to the washing of clothes and especially of the tent in which the person had died (Nu. 19:13ff.). Spoil taken in battle which could not be purged by fire had to be washed with water because of its contact with the forbidden and alien sphere of other deities (Nu. 31:23).

In connection with the dispute between Elijah and the prophets of Baʿal at Carmel (1 K. 18:20ff.) Elijah pours four jars of water around the altar (vv. 33ff.,38). This action does not, however, indicate any ritual use of water; it serves rather to show that the fire which consumed the sacrifice came directly from Yahweh.

Clements

4. *Legal Usage.* Water occurs only once in a juridically relevant context (Nu. 5:11-31), namely, the trial by ordeal of a woman suspected of adultery by her husband. Although various forms of trial by ordeal are evidenced elsewhere in ancient Mesopotamia,[114] no exact parallel to the practice described in Nu. 5:11ff. has been found.[115] The primary characteristic of such a form of legal examination and testing is to secure a situation in which the final verdict could be interpreted as a judgment of God.[116] Nu. 5 presupposes that water is able to effect the securing of such a divine judgment in two ways, first by its character as "holy water" (*mayim qᵉḏōšîm,* v. 17), a phrase which occurs uniquely here, and secondly by its power to mediate a curse. The husband who suspects his spouse of marital infidelity is instructed to bring his

---

114. Cf. Press; P. J. Budd, "Priestly Instruction in Pre-exilic Israel," *VT,* 23 (1973), 1-14.

115. For a comparison of Nu. 5:11 with CH §§131f., cf. M. Fishbane, "Accusations of Adultery: A Study of Law and Scribal Practice in Numbers 5:11-31," *HUCA,* 45 (1975), 25-45, esp. 36-39; G. Giesen, *Die Wurzel* שבע "schwören." *BBB,* 56 (1981), 124ff.

116. Cf. E. Kutsch, "Gottesurteil. II," *RGG³,* II, 1808f.

wife to the temple, where the ordeal is then carried out. The husband is required to bring "a grain offering of jealousy" (v. 15). The woman is then subjected to a test by being compelled to drink "holy water" into which particles of dirt from the sanctuary floor have been mixed. The water then becomes the "water of bitterness that brings a curse" (*mê hammārîm ham*ᵉ*'ār*ᵃ*rîm,* v. 19).

Jack M. Sasson[117] associates *mārîm* with *mrr III,* "bless,"[118] and views this designation of the water as a merism "consisting of 'waters that bless' and 'waters that curse,' hence 'waters of judgement.' " The goal of the ordeal thus remains fundamentally open to proof of the woman's *innocence.* In contrast, Georg Giesen[119] refers to the synonymous character of *'rr* and *mr* (Nu. 5:22f.) and considers the goal of the ordeal (contra Sasson) to be proof of the woman's *guilt.* The decidedly negative emphasis on the curse within the procedure seems to militate for this view. G. R. Driver[120] associates *mārîm* with *mrh,* "to be contentious, rebellious," and interprets *mê hammārîm* as "waters of contention, dispute." Herbert C. Brichto[121] refers to *yrh III,* "teach," and interprets this as "oracle-water."

The mediation of the curse by the water is strengthened by a very solemn oath which the woman accepts as binding through the repeated "Amen, Amen" (Nu. 5:19-22). If the woman is guilty, the curse comes upon her with its entire force after she drinks, causing bodily disorders (vv. 21f.).[122] The efficacy of the water in mediating the effects of the curse is further strengthened by the priest's writing down the words of the curse upon a document and washing them off into the water. The complex magical background is further evidenced when the priest unbinds the woman's hair (vv. 17f.).[123]

Fabry

A further fragmentary echo of the use of water in forms of trial by ordeal is suggested by the narrative tradition of the golden calf (Ex. 32:20). However, no other occurrences can be adduced to suggest any widespread use of such practices in ancient Israel.

5. *Religious Symbolism.* The promise in Ezk. 36:25 in which Yahweh avers to the renewed Israel that he will "sprinkle clean water" upon them to remove all their uncleanness reflects a complex blending of cult-ritual, mythological, and even metaphorical elements. The range of ideas that later led to the rite of Christian baptism owes its development to such symbolic language and such rituals. An extensive religious

---

117. *BZ,* N.S. 16 (1972), 249-251.

118. Cf. later M. Dietrich, O. Loretz, and J. Sanmartín, "Die ugaritischen Verben *mrr* I, *mrr* II und *mrr* III (Zur ugaritischen Lexikographie VIII)," UF, 5 (1973), 119-122.

119. P. 127, n. 270.

120. "Two Problems in the OT Examined in the Light of Assyriology," *Syr,* 33 (1956), 73-77.

121. "The Case of the *ŚÔṬĀ* and a Reconsideration of Biblical 'Law,' " *HUCA,* 46 (1975), 61.

122. → בטן *beṭen,* II, 98: "damage to the female reproductive organs, or, if she has conceived in an extramarital affair, then it could refer to loss of the child."

123. Cf. *AncIsr,* 157f.

symbolism was concerned with water from the beginning of OT times, although especially the cosmic-mythological aspect gradually fell into disuse. Finally, an example of complex symbolism is also found in the imagery of the river which flowed out from the threshold of the temple (Ezk. 47:1ff.), a prophetic image symbolic of the blessing and prosperity of the renewed Israel.

So we find that various features of a mythological and ritual heritage have been blended together to establish a fundamentally new type of religious symbolism. Once established in the literature of the OT, such symbolism came to be more extensively developed in late Judaism (especially in Qumran)[124] and Christianity (cf. Jn. 7:37-39).

Clements

IV. 1. *Qumran.* Given the archaeological evidence, it comes as no surprise that the word *mayim* occurs quite frequently in the Qumran writings (more than 110 times, 27 of those in 1QH alone, 11 in CD, 7 in 1QS, and 13 in 11QT; it does not occur in 1QM). The use of water in connection with ritual washings clearly predominates, something attested by the occurrences in 1QS (in which every occurrence can be attributed to the latest redaction!): the water of purification (*niddâ;* 3:4,9; 4:21; compare CD 10:10-13; 11:4; Ezk. 36:25) is like the spirit of truth for the sectaries, while outsiders and those unwilling to repent are not permitted to enter it (*bô';* cf. 1QS 3:4,5; 5:13). This terminology indicates that the reference is to ritual bathing.[125] Purification by water alone, however, is not enough; it must be complemented by repentance;[126] the reverse is also true.[127] Both the water of purification and the well rich in water, the latter as a metaphor for the Torah (CD 3:16; 19:34), were early integrated into the esoteric mysticism of the Essenes (1QH 8:13-19). Whereas the Temple scroll speaks almost exclusively within the context of laws pertaining to cleanness (11QT 45:16; 49:12-18; 50:2,14; 51:3ff.) and sacrificial regulations (20:1; 32:14; 52:12; 53:5), 1QH applies *mayim* to anthropological contexts: human beings as constructions of loam and water (1:21; 3:24; 13:15); adversaries are compared to the roaring of *mayim rabbîm* (2:16,27); water is a metaphor for danger (3:13-16,26; 6:24; CD 19:16); the heart[128] of the righteous melts like water (1QH 2:28; 8:32). The image of the righteous person as a tree planted beside "streams of water" (Ps. 1:3) is echoed in 1QH 8:4-9; 10:25. Finally, the rigoristic interpretation of the Sabbath commandment is noteworthy: CD 11:16

---

124. See IV.1 below.

125. Cf. O. Betz, "Die Proselytentaufe der Qumransekte und die Taufe im NT," *RevQ,* 1 (1958/59), 216-220; J. Gnilka, "Die essenischen Tauchbäder und die Johannestaufe," *RevQ,* 3 (1961/62), 185-207; J. Pryke, "The Sacraments of Holy Baptism and Holy Communion in the Light of the Ritual Washings and Sacred Meals at Qumran," *RevQ,* 5 (1964-66), 543-552; H. Thyen, *Studien zur Sündenvergebung im NT und seinen alttestamentlichen und jüdischen Voraussetzungen. FRLANT,* N.S. 78[96] (1970); A. T. Abraham, *The Baptismal Initiation of the Qumran Community* (Princeton, 1973).

126. Cf. H. J. Fabry, *Die Wurzel Šûḇ in der Qumran-Literatur. BBB,* 46 (1975), 297ff.

127. Cf. H. Braun, *Spätjüdisch-häretischer und frühchristlicher Radikalismus. BHTh,* 24 (1957), 29.

128. → לב *lēḇ* (VII, 399-437).

stipulates that if a living person should fall into a "water pit" on the Sabbath he shall not be pulled out.[129]

2. *The Mandeans.* The Mandeans developed their own cultic activities involving water, the primary constituents of which were baptism and cleansings. A necessary component was "living water" (in contradistinction with "murky" or "dark" water), i.e., running water with a connection to the world of light. Such water could be personified, and as the "Jordan"[130] acquires a messianic function. Just as water itself as a cosmic force is associated with the world of light, so is earthly baptism a "reflection of the heavenly baptism and simultaneously a symbol of the soul's belonging to the world of light. Baptism guarantees and grants to the fallen divine soul a real connection with the water that in its own turn comes from the beyond."[131]

Fabry

---

129. Cf. further J. Neusner, *The Idea of Purity in Ancient Judaism. StJLA,* 1 (1973); and J. M. Baumgarten, *Studies in Qumran Law. StJLA,* 24 (1977), 46-51, 88-97.
130. → ירדן *yardēn* (VI, 322-330).
131. Cf. K. Rudolph, *Die Mandäer II. FRLANT,* N.S. 75[93] (1961), 61ff., 93.

מִין *mîn*

Contents: I. 1. Etymology; 2. Meaning; 3. LXX. II. The Creation Narrative. III. Sirach. IV. Qumran.

I. 1. *Etymology.* The etymology of *mîn* is yet unclear. Various attempts derive the root from an Arabic etymon *myn* in the sense of "create; fruitfulness, procreation of living beings of the same species."[1] (Otherwise Arab. *māna[i]* means to "lie, tell a falsehood," though also "split, divide, plow";[2] cf. Ethiop. *mēna,* "lie."[3]) References have also been made to Akk. *mīnu,* "portion, number," and *minûtu,* "numbering, figuring"[4] or "number,

---

mîn. J. Barr, *The Semantics of Biblical Language* (1961, repr. Philadelphia, 1991), 76, 104f.; P. Beauchamp, *Création et Separation* (Paris, 1969), 240-47; H. Cazelles, "*MYN* — espèce, race ou ressemblance," *Mémorial du Cinquantenaire (1914-1964), École des Langues Orientales Anciennes de l'Institut Catholique de Paris. Coll. Trav. de l'Inst. Cath. de Paris,* 10 (Paris, 1969), 105-8; W. H. Schmidt, *Die Schöpfungsgeschichte der Priesterschrift. WMANT,* 17 (^{2}1967); O. H. Steck, *Der Schöpfungsbericht der Priesterschrift. FRLANT,* 115 (^{2}1981); C. Westermann, *Genesis 1–11* (Eng. trans., Minneapolis, 1984), 126.

1. Cazelles, with additional references to Christian Palestinian.
2. See the lexica and cf. A. M. Honeyman's review of *KBL, VT,* 5 (1955), 220.
3. *LexLingAeth,* 213; cf. also Barr.
4. *AHw,* II (1972), 656f.

amount; accounting; shape, figure" (probably from *manû,* "count").[5] William F. Albright's citation in *KBL*[3] (547) is incorrect, and the meaning of Ugar. *mnm* is similarly uncertain.[6] The only undisputed point is its etymological connection with *t^{e}mûnâ.*[7]

2. *Meaning.* In its meaning as "kind" or "species," *mîn* functions as a classification term used generally with reference to plants or animals, including human beings (cf. Sir. 13:16b, though a different view is taken by 1QS 3:14: *lkl myny rwḥwtm* with *twldwt* in context). In CD 4:16, *mîn* acquires the abstract meaning "category." With *l^e* it is distributive, "each kind in turn" or "according to the distinctiveness of the species," or in the singular "after its kind" (Lev. 11:14,19;[8] cf. CD 12:14: *bmynyhm,* "no matter what kind they are"; Sir. 43:25b, Gk. *poikilía*).

3. *LXX.* The LXX renders *mîn* with *hómoios* (20 times), *génos* (11 times), *homoiótēs,* and *poikilía* (once each).

II. The Creation Narrative. The distinctions between the various species is grounded in the plan of creation. Just as the immutable works are subjected to the principle of separation *(hiḇdîl),* so also are the mutable ones subjected to the principle of differentiation (*mîn;* 10 occurrences in Gen. 1:11f.,21,24f.).

In their own turn, separation and differentiation are closely related to law: the divine law that puts an end to chaos, the Mosaic law that is to prevent any mixing of species *(kil'ayim)* (Lev. 19:19; Dt. 22:9-11). Nonetheless, *kil'ayim* does not encompass the term *mîn,* though a different situation obtains in the list of clean and unclean animals (Lev. 11:14-16,19,22,29; Dt. 14:13-15,18). Thus it cannot be determined with any certainty whether the occurrences of *mîn* in the Creation Narrative of P contain direct references to regulations of the Torah.[9]

The occurrence of *mîn* is more likely an indication of the wisdom presuppositions of Gen. 1:1–2:4a: "In the context of P's careful distinction of the species of plants and animals, one can speak of a scientific interest, provided one distinguishes it from our idea of 'science.' "[10] As the differentiation between plants and animals in the proverbs of Solomon shows (1 K. 5:13[Eng. 4:33]), wisdom had long been interested in classification or "taxonomy." As far as animals are concerned, important clues to interpretation can be gleaned from the presuppositions evident in the texts.

---

5. *CAD,* X/2 (1977), 96f.

6. *KTU,* 1.4 I, 39; cf. A. Caquot, M. Sznycer, and A. Herdner, *Textes Ougaritique I. LAPO,* 7 (1974), 196; cf. also the controversy involving M. Dahood, "The Linguistic Position of Ugaritic in the Light of Recent Discoveries," *Sacra Pagina,* I *BETL,* 12f. (1959), 270f., and C. Rabin, "Etymological Miscellanea," *Studies in the Bible. ScrHier,* 8 (1961), 392f.

7. Cf. M. Dietrich and O. Loretz, "Die sieben Kunstwerke des Schmiedegottes in KTU 1.4 I 23-43," *UF,* 10 (1978), 62: "form, kind."

8. K. Elliger, *Leviticus. HAT,* IV (1966), *in loc.*

9. A different view is taken by Schmidt.

10. Westermann, 126.

The multiplicity of species is a predominating feature of the animal kingdom. The system of the "seven-day schema" juxtaposes animals and human beings: the multiplicity of animals is contrasted with the "unity" of human beings, an opposition also indicated by the consistent absence of *mîn* whenever references are made to human beings. Hence if *mîn* had something to do with the capacity of a living being to reproduce itself in a continuing sequence of generations,[11] then the term would indeed be applicable to human beings. Since this is not the case, however, greater attention needs to be directed to the background of this text. There one finds the contrast between the world of humans and that of animals, and the concomitant moral and religious implications. However, the content of this distinction is also of significance: neither the human being in and of itself constitutes a species or kind, nor does the multiplicity of human beings, races, and nations constitute a multiplicity of species or kinds. Yet humans are exhorted to multiply in a place already occupied by the world of animals (Gen. 1:26-28). Thus human "unity" is to exercise dominance over the multiplicity of animals. Both the Flood tradition (7 occurrences of *mîn* in Gen. 6:20; 7:14) and several prophetic texts (Isa. 11:1-9) confirm that humans have what is basically a political mission as regards the world of animals. Because of the relationship *t^e^mûnâ/mîn*[12] one can specify more precisely that this human mission is based on the similarity between human and divine "unity," and correspondingly on the dissimilarity between human beings and animals.

The Flood tradition reflects a reversal of this relationship, for now human being devours human being, just as animal devours animal, the human being now consciously setting himself up against his original purpose (Gen. 1:29f.). This is presupposed in any case by the Noahic law (Gen. 9:1-7 [P^G]). This makes it possible to enhance previous insights as well, whereby the allusions to Gen. 1:1–2:4a are rendered comprehensible and are confirmed by the Flood tradition (as they are later by Sirach).

III. Sirach. Sir. 13:15f. (Heb.) offers a commentary to Gen. 1:1–2:4a, perhaps also to Lev. 19:19f. (cf. Sir. 25:8). As in the animal world, human beings are devouring one another, or they group themselves together according to their own *mîn* (Sirach applies this term here to human beings, alluding thereby to the human status *after* the Flood). The sequence of the two commandments in Lev. 19:18f. is perhaps reflected in Sir. 13:15f.: to love one's kind while not mixing with others. Thus Sirach accommodates the use of *mîn* in Gen. 1:1–2:4a more to that of *kil'ayim* in the law.

Beauchamp

IV. Qumran. In Qumran the term *mîn* occurs only 3 times, in texts from a relatively early stage of the sect. Whereas CD 12:14 clearly picks up the meaning of *mîn* in Gen. 1:1–2:4a in formulating its dietary laws (the *ḥ^a^gāḇîm b^e^mînêhem,* "locusts, according to their various kinds," are designated unfit to eat), CD 4:16 applies *mîn* to a legal

11. So Cazelles.
12. *Ibid.*

context in designating Belial's "three kinds of [false] righteousness" *(mînê haṣṣeḏeq)*: fornication, riches, and profanation of the sanctuary. This pesher to Isa. 24:17 makes it clear that ultimately one cannot escape this alleged "righteousness," and thus cannot avoid incurring guilt. In what is probably an old *maśkîl* law (1QS 3:13ff.),[13] the term *mîn* is applied to human beings in consonance with later OT development. It is the task of the *maśkîl*[14] to evaluate and instruct the individual members of the sect according to *mînê rûḥôṯām,* "the kind of spirit which they possess" (1QS 3:14). The oldest *maśkîl* assignments speak only of *kᵉrûḥô,* "according to his spirit" (1QS 9:14).

Fabry

13. Cf. J. L.-Duhaime, "L'instruction sur les deux esprits et les interpolations dualistes à Qumrân (1QS III,13–IV,26)," *RB,* 84 (1977), 566-594.

14. Cf. H.-J. Fabry, "Der altorientalische Hintergrund des urchristlichen Diakonats," *Der Diakon. Festschrift A. Frotz* (Freiburg, ²1981), 15-26, esp. 16f.

מכר *mkr*

Contents: I. The Verb *mkr.* II. The Nouns *môḵēr* and *makkār.* III. The Nouns *meḵer, mimkar, mimkereṯ.* IV. Conclusions. V. LXX.

I. The Verb mkr. The verb *mkr* occurs 56 times in the qal, with a clear concentration in the Pentateuch (7 times in the Joseph narrative [Gen. 37–50]; 5 times in the Covenant Code in laws regarding slaves [Ex. 21]; 7 times in the regulations concerning the Jubilee Year [Lev. 25]) and 5 occurrences in Joel 4; the distribution of the remaining occurrences is unremarkable. The hiphil occurs 19 times, with 7 occurrences in Lev. 25 alone; the hithpael occurs 4 times. The usual translation of the Hebrew verb *mkr* is "to sell." This meaning can be traced back to the fifth century B.C. (Neh. 10:32[Eng. v. 31]; 13:15f.,20; Prov. 31:24) and is attested later in contracts from Wadi Murabbaʿat which date from A.D. 134 and 135.[1] A scrutiny of the use of *mkr* in older texts shows, however, that this verb does not apply specifically to the semantic field "buy/sell," but designates

mkr. Z. W. Falk, "Hebrew Legal Terms: II," *JSS,* 12 (1967), 241-44; B. Landsberger, "Akkadisch-Hebräische Wortgleichungen," *Hebräische Wortforschung. Festschrift W. Baumgartner. Congress Volume 1967. SVT,* 16 (1967), 176-204, esp. 176ff., 187f., 204; E. Lipiński, "Le mariage de Ruth," *VT,* 26 (1976), 124-27; *idem,* "Sale, Transfer, and Delivery in Ancient Semitic Terminology," *Gesellschaft und Kultur im Alten Vorderasien = Schriften zur Geschichte und Kultur des Alten Orients,* 15 (1982), 173-185; A. L. Oppenheim, "Old Assyrian *magāru* or *makāru?*" *Festschrift H. G. Güterbock* (Istanbul, 1974), 229-237; W. Plautz, "Die Form der Eheschliessung im AT," *ZAW,* 76 (1964), 298-318, esp. 312ff.

1. Mur 29:1,10; 30:1,4,10,20.

a delivery of goods, generally in return for valuables, with or without the intention of passing ownership. As late as talmudic times the verb *mkr* is still used to denote transfer of rights and claims for a predetermined period without actually transferring ownership. For instance, Bab. *B. Meṣ.* 79a-b discusses the case of a man who "*mwkr* his field for sixty years," on the expiration of which the land returns to its owner. Hence this is not a sale, but only a transfer of the right of usufruct. In other words, *mkr* signifies a transfer of possession which can, but must not necessarily, amount to a sale.

This is made clear by the use of the verb in the first half of the first millennium B.C. Although we have no evidence of its exact meaning in some cases (e.g., Lev. 27:28; Dt. 14:21; 24:7; 32:30; Prov. 23:23), a number of characteristic examples are to be found in other biblical texts. A man in serious financial difficulties "hands himself over" or "is handed over" *(yimmāḵēr)* to his creditor for six years (Dt. 15:12; Jer. 34:14) or until the next Jubilee Year (Lev. 25:39-42,47-54). Although a land parcel belonging to the patrimony can "be made over" *(timmāḵēr)* to the mortgagee or to a usufructuary until the next Jubilee Year (Lev. 25:23-28; 27:20f.,24), this by no means constitutes a sale.

Yahweh "hands over" *(yimkᵉrēm)* the Israelites to their enemies for a period of eight (Jgs. 3:8), twenty (Jgs. 4:2f.), or eighteen years (Jgs. 10:7f.). The translation "to sell" suits none of these passages, for the notion of selling implies an absolute transfer of the property, and not merely a usufruct limited to a predetermined number of years.

This is explicitly stated in Lev. 25:13-16, which deals not with the sale and purchase of cultivable land, as would appear from the usual translations, but with the acquisition of the right of holding in usufruct someone else's property until the next Jubilee Year (cf. esp. v. 16). In vv. 14-15, where *mkr* is used twice, it can only refer to the usufruct that is transferred for a certain price and a predetermined number of years. The same applies in Lev. 25:29-31 to the usufruct of houses, with the exception of the ones within a walled town, the possession of which was transferred by usucaption to the user after one year (redemption period) and which did not have to be returned during the Jubilee Year. Even in a text like Ezk. 7:12f. the *môḵēr* cannot be a seller, for v. 13 states that the time of doom is forthcoming, and then he, the *môḵēr,* will be unable to go back to the property given away. This means that he would do so in normal times and that he did not "sell" his property, but gave it in usufruct or as mortgage. All this finds confirmation also in Ruth 4:3-5, according to which Naomi intended to "make over" the piece of land that belonged to Elimelech, her deceased husband. The use of *mkr* just denotes that she was contemplating a transfer of the usufruct of Elimelech's land, limited by law to the period of her widowhood. She could not sell that land, since it would transfer by law to the closest relative (cf. Nu. 27:8-11) or to Elimelech's posthumously born child, which Ruth should bear him according to the custom of levirate marriage (Ruth 4:5). And this is precisely the reason why the closest relative renounced his right of marrying her: were he to beget a male descendant for the deceased, he would deprive himself at the same time of Elimelech's heritage. In talmudic times, as a matter of fact, the performance of the levirate marriage carried with it the right of inheritance (Bab. *Yebam.* 40a; *Ketub.* 81b, 82a); but this was not the case in earlier times if the story of Ruth really reflects ancient legal customs. In any case, the translation of *mkr* in Ruth 4:3 cannot be "to sell."

Biblical texts referring to human pledges and to the enslavement of defaulting debtors[2] show as well that *mkr* means something like "to hand over," "to give away." Speaking of the thief who is to restore the stolen goods, Ex. 22:2b(1b) states according to the usual translation: "If he has nothing, then he shall be sold for his theft." But Flavius Josephus (*Ant.* iv.8.27 [272]) still attests a tradition stating that the thief should be "handed over" to the person to whom he was adjudged to pay if he was unable to compensate for the stolen animal. This is also reflected by the terminology: *g^e^nēḇâ,* "stolen goods" (rather than "theft"), and from the use of the verb *mkr b^e^*, "handed over in exchange for" (cf. also Gen. 37:28; Lev. 27:27; Dt. 21:14; Isa. 50:1; Joel 4:3[3:3]; Am. 2:6; Nah. 3:4; 1Q27 1, II 6; 11QT 43:14). Therefore the phrase in question is to be rendered: "If he has nothing, he shall be handed over in exchange for the stolen goods." A similar meaning should be given to Isa. 50:1a; 52:3-5, where one can hardly translate "You will be sold gratuitously" (cf. 1Q27 1, II 6). Reference to unjustifiable enslavement enforced in consequence of dishonest claims and bribery is found in Am. 2:6, where *mkr* clearly means "to hand over." This translation is confirmed by the expression *māḵar b^e^yaḏ* (Jgs. 2:14; 3:8; 4:2,9; 10:7; 1 S. 12:9; Ezk. 30:12; Joel 4:8[3:8]), which never appears in a context implying an agreement on a price. The current rendering as "to sell" is thus simply wrong. The use of *mkr* with an indication of the place to which a person is "given away" (Gen. 45:4f.; Joel 4:7[3:7]),[3] or with *'el* followed by a place name (Gen. 37:36), also indicates that this verb originally had nothing to do with sale and purchase, although the idea of selling is sometimes connoted.

The verb *mkr* also covers the giving away of a daughter as a bride (Gen. 31:15) or concubine (Ex. 21:7f.), or of a brother as a slave (Gen. 37:27f.; Dt. 28:68; Ps. 105:17). In the first case at least, *mkr* does not mean "to sell," since the so-called "purchase marriage" is not attested in the West Semitic world of the second and first millennia B.C.[4]

But not even the "giving away" in slavery always implies a "sale," for a debtor could surrender a member of his family to the creditor as a pledge, and one could pledge oneself (cf. Dt. 28:68). Only persons or goods given *b^e^ḵesep* (Gen. 37:28; Dt. 21:14; Am. 2:6; 11QT 43:14) or *b^e^ʿēreḵ* (Lev. 27:27) are obviously sold. Only in this context does the verb *mkr* connote the idea of selling, although the verb as such still means "to give away, to hand over." There are also texts (Joel 4:3[3:3]; Nah. 3:4) where *māḵar b^e^* refers to a kind of barter. This wide meaning of *māḵar* explains why the verb can be used in Est. 7:4 in the sense of "giving up" to destruction, slaying, and annihilation.

---

2. Cf. recently I. Cardellini, *Die biblischen "Sklaven" — Gesetze im Lichte des keilschriftlichen Sklavenrechts. BBB,* 55 (1981), esp. 339.
3. Cf. also in Ugaritic *KTU,* 3.8, 16; 2.48, 5.
4. → מהר *mōhar* (VIII, 142-49).

Even in texts like Ex. 21:37(22:1a), which refers to the theft of an ox or a sheep that the robber has slaughtered or otherwise delivered up, the translation of *māḵar* by "to sell" is contradicted by the very wide interpretation of *mkr* found in the Tosefta *B. Qam.* vii.14: "If he stole it and bartered it, if he stole it and sanctified it, if he stole it then gave it as a gift, if he stole it and paid a debt with it, if he stole it then sent it as a betrothal present to his father-in-law's house, he makes the fourfold or fivefold payment."

A complementary argument is further found in the idiomatic use of the reflexive hithpael of *māḵar* in 1 K. 21:20,25; 2 K. 17:17, where the expression *hiṯmakkerkā la'ᵃśôṯ hāra'* must be translated "you let yourself be 'induced' to do what is wrong" (cf. also Sir. 47:24); the connotation "to sell" is utterly misleading.[5]

In conclusion, one could also refer to the use of Akk. *makāru,* which occurs primarily in Old Assyrian texts. There it never means "to sell";[6] in most cases it clearly refers to the amount of silver or gold which has or has not to be "given away" in order to acquire goods, which have in their turn to be transported and sold with profit.

II. The Nouns môḵēr and makkār. The Heb. ptcp. *môḵēr* is used not only in a verbal sense (Lev. 25:16; Nah. 3:4; Neh. 13:16), but also as a noun (Neh. 13:20; Isa. 24:2; Ezk. 7:12,13; Zec. 11:5), the usual translation of which is "trader" or "seller." This substantival form occurs only in relatively recent texts, the oldest being Ezk. 7:12f. Here, too, the usual translation does not make sense, for the seller is not supposed to go back to the property sold. In this particular case, therefore, the *môḵēr* refers to a "releaser" who temporarily gives his property over. Thus the participle *môḵēr* used substantively had a wider semantic scope than "seller."

The noun *makkār* that appears in 2 K. 12:6,8(5,7) has largely been rendered in translations as "acquaintance, friend," which derive it from the root *nkr* despite the Greek equivalent *prásis,* "sale." The LXX is certainly correct in relating the term in question to the root *mkr.*[7] The particular form *makkār* (constructed after the *qaṭṭāl* pattern) is a vocational designation. From the context of 2 K. 12 the *makkārîm* appear to have been business assessors of the temple; they are mentioned in later talmudic texts in what seems to be the same meaning (Jer. *Giṭ.* iii.45a; Bab. *Giṭ.* 30a; Bab. *Ḥul.* 133a). Even though we cannot determine any more what precise function the *makkārîm* had, it seems clear enough that the function enters the semantic field of the root *mkr* rather than that of *nkr.*

The noun *makkîr* that appears in Mur 30:3,16 is the participle of *nkr,* a form which one finds also in talmudic and midrashic literature. Here it designates the alienee to whom transfer of property is made, and not the "vendor" *môḵēr,* as wrongly suggested by former translators of Mur 30. In contrast, the clan name *māḵîr* is likely to have

5. Cf. D. W. Thomas, "The Root מכר in Hebrew," *JTS,* 37 (1936), 388f.; *idem,* "A Further Note on the Root מכר in Hebrew," *JTS,* N.S. 3 (1952), 214.

6. Cf. *CAD,* X/1, 126ff.: "to do business, to use (silver etc.) in business transactions."

7. *HAL,* II (1995), 582.

referred initially to a specific region, being constructed from the *mem-locale* and the root *kyr/kwr,* meaning perhaps something like "district" (cf. Arab. *kūra*).[8]

We do not know as yet whether the frequent Ugaritic noun *mkr* and the Punic noun *mkr* have to be related to the ptcp. *mākiru* or to the professional name *makkāru,* for the vocalization is so far unknown.[9] The same is true for the Canaanite loanword *mkr* in Egyptian[10]: its spelling does not allow us to decide whether it was pronounced *mākiru* or *makkāru.* As for the name of *Mákēris* (cf. Pausanias *Description of Greece* x.17), which could be explained both ways, it is not a deformation of the name of the deity Melqart, as commentators generally believe because of his identification with Heracles, but a Libyco-Berber divine name, well known in North Africa. However, an epithet "merchant," somewhat similar to the appellation *Hercules ponderum,*[11] might apply to Melqart, whose cult had become very popular with merchants. This would be the case perhaps if Makar, the legendary first settler in Lesbos,[12] was a Phoenician "merchant" rather than a Greek *Mákar,* "blessed one."

In any case, the Ugaritic and Punic *mkrm* deal with trade, and *mkr* is undoubtedly a professional name. Some of Ugarit's *mkrm* were very influential people and enjoyed considerable independence in their business activities, while the official status of other *mkrm* is clearly indicated by the fact of their receiving rations and wages from the royal palace.[13] They were royal dependents in their quality as "deliverers" and could also serve as messengers or accompany ambassadors sent with gifts and presents to other courts.[14] In this function they were similar to the Mesopotamian *tamkāru,* who was also a mercantile agent.[15] Distinctions of time and place should, however, be kept in mind.

The noun *mkr* is attested also in South Arabian,[16] where it seems to designate a person involved in trade activities. Judging from the later Arabic root *mkr,* the general rule *caveat emptor* was particularly well suited in ancient Arabia. In fact, in Classical Arabic *makara* means "to cheat"; *makr,* which corresponds to Heb. *meḵer,* is used in the sense of "deception, trickery," and a *makkār* or *mākir* is a "swindler."[17] To designate a merchant, Arabic uses instead the loanword *tāğir* (< Aram. *taggārā'* < Akk. *tamkāru*).

---

8. On the PN *māḵîr,* "Machir," cf. the different explanation of E. Täubler, "Haus Joseph: Machir," *Biblische Studien: Die Epoche der Richter* (Tübingen, 1958), 190ff., and *HAL,* II, 579f., both of which derive it from *mkr.* Since the gemination of the *k* in Mur 30 is not certain, some connection might exist between the two formatives. [Fabry]

9. Cf. also L. de Meyer, "L'étymologie de *Macellum* 'Marché,' " *AC,* 31 (1962), 148-152.

10. Cf. W. Helck, *Die Beziehungen Ägyptens zu Vorderasien im 3. und 2. Jahrtausend v. Chr. ÄgAbh,* 5 (1962), 563, no. 128.

11. *CIL,* VI, 336.

12. *Etymologicum Magnum,* ed. T. Gaisford (Oxford, 1848), *s.v.* "βρισαῖος" *(brisaíos).*

13. *KTU,* 4.38, 3; 4.263, 1; *PRU,* III, 200, A II, 12-46.

14. Cf. A. F. Rainey, "Business Agents at Ugarit," *IEJ,* 13 (1963), 315.

15. Cf. *AHw,* III (1981), 1314f.: "merchant, trader, financier."

16. *RÉS,* 3951, 2.

17. Cf. Wehr (^{4}1979), 1076.

III. The Nouns meḵer, mimkar, mimkereṯ. The noun *meḵer* (Nu. 20:19; Prov. 31:10) means "value, price," yet also designates goods for sale or merchandise in Neh. 13:16, and signifies "mortgaged estate" or "land sold" in Mur 22:1-9,12; 30:4,7,16, 17,22,24,28, as it does in the Mishnah (*Ketub.* xi.4) and Talmud (Bab. *Qidd.* 6b; 47a), where the traditional translation "sale of land" ought to be corrected in consideration of the deeds from Wadi Murabbaʿat. These three meanings of *meḵer* can hardly derive one from the other; they must have originated independently in different times or places. In particular, the use of *meḵer* in the sense of "land sold" obviously replaced the older use of the noun *mimkār,* the meaning of which had changed in the course of time.

The term *mimkār* first signified "landed property given in usufruct" or "mortgaged" (Lev. 25:14,25,27,28,29,33,50; Dt. 18:8; Ezk. 7:13; 11QT 60:15) and, exceptionally, "sold" (Neh. 13:20; Sir. 37:11). In fact, the Hebrew nominal pattern *miqṭal/miqṭāl* designates things used in performing an action, here that of "handing over" and "giving away" *(mkr).* The noun *mimkār* used later in CD 13:15 and in talmudic literature with the meaning "sale" (Bab. *B. Meṣ.* 79b; *B. Bat.* 155b) is, instead, a verbal noun deriving from the aramaizing inf. *miqṭāl.* The same applies to the noun *mimkereṯ* in Lev. 25:42 and in 4Q159 2–4:3, the meaning of which is also "sale" or, more generally, "transfer of possession."

In talmudic literature one finds also the noun *m^eḵîrâ,* "sale," constructed after the frequent postbiblical Hebrew pattern *q^eṭîlâ.*

IV. Conclusions. The root *mkr,* which was most used in Hebrew besides *ntn* in relation to transactions involving transfer or sale of movable or immovable goods, means "to give away," "to hand over," "to transfer," or "to deliver." The consequence of this action was normally legal possession or ownership, according to the terms and the substance of the contract. In earlier Hebrew sources, however, *mkr* mostly refers to the simple transfer of possession, while *ntn* is used in clauses stressing that a transfer of land was to be effective forever (Gen. 13:15; 17:8; 48:4).[18] On the other hand, the parallel use of both verbs in some texts (e.g., Gen. 25:33f. [cf. v. 31]; Dt. 14:21; Jgs. 2:14; Ps. 44:12f.[11f.]; Prov. 31:24; Ezk. 30:12; Joel 4:3[3:3]) precludes any definite judgment on their distinctive meaning and use. The verb *mkr* thus refers to the transfer of possession and the transfer of property with a gradual shift in the direction of the latter. In other words, *mkr* characterizes the form of the transaction, but does not specify its substance.

V. LXX. The LXX prefers to render the verb in the qal as *apodidónai* (39 times) and *pōleín* (8 times), in the niphal and hithpael as *pipráskein* (together 19 times). The nouns are in most passages rendered by *prásis.*

Lipiński

---

18. Cf. S. E. Loewenstamm, "Notes on the Alalakh Tablets," *IEJ,* 6 (1956), 222; R. Yaron, *ILR,* 3 (1968), 481.

מָלֵא *mālē'*; מְלֹא *m^e lō'*; מִלֻּאָה *millu'â*; מִלֻּאִים *millu'îm*; מִלּוֹא *millô'*

Contents: I. Occurrences: 1. Ancient Near East; 2. OT. II. Meaning. III. Expressions: 1. *mālē' hayyāmîm;* 2. *mālē' k^e bôḏ YHWH;* 3. *millē' 'aḥ^a rê YHWH;* 4. *millē' 'eṯ-hadd^e ḇārîm;* 5. *millē' 'eṯ-yāḏ.* IV. Derivatives: 1. *m^e lō';* 2. *millu'îm;* 3. *millô'.* V. Qumran.

I. Occurrences. 1. *Ancient Near East.* The root *ml'* is common to the Semitic languages. Akkadian attests the verb *malû,* "to be or become full,"[1] the subst. *mīlu,* "flood high water,"[2] and *tamlû,* "heap, terrace."[3] North and South Arabic[4] as well as Ethiopic attest *ml',* "to be full" or "to fill."[5] Both Phoenician and Aramaic offer parallels,[6] and Biblical Aramaic attests a peal of *mālē'* (Dnl. 2:35) and a hithpael, "become filled" (Dnl. 3:19).

2. *OT.* The verb *ml'* occurs altogether 246 times in the OT, 100 of which are qal, 108 piel, 36 niphal, 1 pual (Cant. 5:14), and 1 hithpael (Job 16:10).

The subst. *m^e lō'* or *m^e lô'* is once written without *aleph* (Ezk. 41:8), the verb twice: *mālû* (Ezk. 28:16), *mālēṯî* (Job 32:18). Twice *he* is written instead of *aleph* (Job 8:21; Ezk. 16:30; cf. also 3Q15 2:1; 3:8, 11). The name *yimlâ* (1 K. 22:8), "he will fill or be full," is written *yimlā'* in 2 Ch. 18:7. Isa. 23:2 should be read with 1QIs^a *mal'āḵeykā,* "your messengers," instead of *mil'ûḵ,* "they filled you" (?).

The adj. *mālē'* appears twice in somewhat obscure contexts. It is unclear whether these are forms of the verb or the adj. *mālē'.* Foregoing textual emendation, this word is interpreted adverbially: a "loud" cry (i.e., a "full" cry, Jer. 12:6); they are "fully" consumed (Nah. 1:10). Lacking parallels, however, this is a questionable solution. Jer. 12:6 is often compared with Jer. 4:5, though this is hardly appropriate.[7] Perhaps the vocalization should be *m^e lō'* instead of *mālē':* "fullness, entirety, multitude" (Gen. 48:19; Isa. 31:4). The translation would then be: "They too call together a multitude

---

mālē'. R. Borger, "Die Waffenträger des Königs Darius," *VT,* 22 (1972), 385-398; M. Delcor, "מלא *ml'* voll sein, füllen," *THAT,* I, 897-900; C. F. D. Moule, "Fulfillment-Words in the NT: Use and Abuse," *NTS,* 14 (1967), 293-320; M. Noth, "Office and Vocation in the OT," *The Laws in the Pentateuch* (Eng. trans., Philadelphia, 1967), 229-249; K. Rupprecht, "Quisquilien zu der Wendung מלא (את) יד פלוני und zum Terminus מלאים," *Sefer Rendṭorff. Festschrift R. Rendtorff. BDBAT,* 1 (1975), 73-93; D. W. Thomas, "מלאו in Jeremiah IV.5: A Military Term," *JJSt,* 3 (1952), 47-52.

1. *AHw,* II (1972), 597ff.
2. *Ibid.,* 652f.
3. *Ibid.,* III (1981), 1316.
4. ContiRossini, 177.
5. *LexLingAeth,* 148f.; *TigrWB,* 108.
6. *DISO,* 151.
7. For Jer. 4:5, see below.

after you [to pursue you]"; cf. Isa. 31:4: "the whole band of shepherds is called forth against him."

II. Meaning. The qal of *mālē'* can be either transitive or intransitive, "to fill" or "to be full." Examples include "she filled her jar" (Gen. 24:16), and "the houses of the Egyptians shall be filled with swarms of flies" (Ex. 8:17[Eng. v. 21]). The text does not always indicate with what something is filled, though the context usually supplies such information: "the jar [with water]" (Gen. 24:16), or "fill the waters in the seas [sc. with yourselves, i.e., animals]" (Gen. 1:22), "his train filled the entire temple [with itself]" (Isa. 6:1); cf. also Isa. 2:6: "they are full [of people, things] from the east."

The substance with which an object is filled functions grammatically as a second accusative, as accusative of material, and is occasionally qualified by *'eṯ*[8]: *watt^{e}mallē' 'eṯ-haḥēmeṯ mayim,* "she filled the skin with water" (Gen. 21:19); and *ûl^{e}mal'ām 'eṯ-pigrê hā'āḏām,* "to fill them [the houses] with dead bodies" (Jer. 33:5).

Usually something empty is filled: a bag with grain (Gen. 42:25), a horn with oil (1 S. 16:1), a house with smoke (Isa. 6:4), the cistern or valley with the slain (Ps. 110:6? read *gē'āyôṯ;*[9] Jer. 41:9; Ezk. 32:5f.). The opposite of "being full" is the wasteland, the wilderness, the land with no human beings (Ezk. 26:2: "I shall become full, the wasteland"[10]); "so shall the ruined towns be filled with flocks of people" (Ezk. 36:38). Naomi laments: "I went away full [i.e., with my whole family], but Yahweh has brought me back empty *(rêqām)*" (Ruth 1:21).

The word is also used in the sense of "fill up, complete": "Complete the week of this one [bride]" (Gen. 29:27). In Babylon the hour draws near when Israel's time of service is fulfilled, i.e., when the measure of suffering is complete (Isa. 40:2). The Jordan was filled beyond its banks: "it was filled to the top" (Josh. 3:15; cf. 1 Ch. 12:16[15]). David delivered the required foreskins and "filled them up in addition": he made their number full (1 S. 18:27). According to 2 K. 9:24, "Jehu filled his hand [= his strength] through the bow."[11]

Not only concrete things are used to fill, but immaterial ones as well. In a figurative sense a person is filled with wisdom (Dt. 34:9; 1 K. 7:14),[12] praise (Hab. 3:3), or indignation (Jer. 15:17). Zion is filled with righteousness (Isa. 33:5), a mouth with laughter (Job 8:21; Ps. 126:2), and loins with anguish (Isa. 21:3).

Hunger is like a hole; satisfying it means to fill that hole (Job 38:39; Ps. 107:9). People can be filled with drunkenness *(šikkārôn)* like "jars" with wine (Jer. 13:12f.).

The sense of "becoming filled," "being full," is amplified in certain contexts by the synonymous verb *śāḇa'*, "satisfy, sate" (Dt. 33:23; Ps. 17:14; 107:9; Ezk. 7:19).

---

8. *GK,* §117z.

9. Cf. H.-J. Kraus, *Psalms 60-150* (Eng. trans., Minneapolis, 1989), 344f.

10. Even if W. Zimmerli, *Ezekiel 2. Herm* (Eng. trans. 1983), 27, translates "She who was (once) full is now laid waste," the contrast remains the same.

11. See discussion below.

12. See further V. Sasson, "An Unrecognized Juridical Term in the Yabneh-Yam Lawsuit and in an Unnoticed Biblical Parallel," *BASOR,* 232 (1978), 57-63.

The same notion appears in the expression *zāqēn ûmᵉlē' yāmîm* and *zāqēn uśᵉba' yāmîm,* "old and full of/sated with days" (Gen. 35:29; Jer. 6:11; cf. Gen. 25:8; Job 42:17). The fulfillment of a time or the conclusion of a specific period is expressed not only by *mālē',* but also by the verb *tāmam,* "be complete or full, be at an end" (Lev. 25:29f.). In the expression "the word was fulfilled" *mālē'* can be replaced by *kālâ* (2 Ch. 36:21f.) and *hēḵîn* (Jer. 33:2). Similarly, *kālâ* can also be used when a certain time has been fulfilled or has come to an end (Ezk. 4:8; 5:2). The same thing can be expressed by the verb *šālēm,* "be finished, complete" (Isa. 60:20). The adj. *mālē',* "full" (= the qal ptcp. fem. *mᵉlē'â*) occurs 60 times in the OT. Granaries are full (Ps. 144:13), as are plates and bowls (Nu. 7 *passim*), etc. That with which something is full usually follows after the subject involved, less frequently in the reverse order: *tᵉšu'ōṯ mᵉlē'â 'îr,* "with shoutings the city is full" (Isa. 22:2).[13]

III. Expressions. The verb *mālē'* (and its derivatives) is the fixed component in a number of theologically significant expressions.

1. *mālē' hayyāmîm.* The expression *mālē' hayyāmîm,* "to fulfill the days," refers to a specified period of time that is, as it were, empty. One counts the days until the period is filled, the days complete, e.g., of pregnancy (Gen. 25:24), a service relationship (Gen. 29:21,27,28), embalming (Gen. 50:3), the duration of a vow (Nu. 6:5), the period of consecration for a priest (Lev. 8:33), or the period required for beautification in a harem (Est. 2:12). One also speaks of the duration of bondage: Seventy years (Jer. 25:12; 2 Ch. 36:21) that become "full" (cf. Jer. 29:10; Dnl. 9:2). A person lives a certain period of time, and for each person there comes the time when his "days are full" (Ex. 23:26; 2 S. 7:12; 1 Ch. 17:11). When our days are "full" or "fulfilled," then the end draws "near" or "has come" (Lam. 4:18). To make one's days full means to die. In contrast, it is considered a curse for a person to die before "his day" *(bᵉlō'-yômô)* (Job 15:32), or if an old man does not fulfill his days (Isa. 65:20); cf. the expression "old and full of days" (Jer. 6:11), or, frequently, "sated with days" (Gen. 25:8; 35:29; Job 42:17).[14]

2. *mālē' kᵉḇôḏ YHWH.* We often read that the *kᵉḇôḏ YHWH* fills a house or the land.[15] At the consecration of the temple a cloud filled the sanctuary in Jerusalem (1 K. 8:11; 2 Ch. 7:1,2), indicating the presence of God. It covered the tent of meeting, and the *kᵉḇôḏ YHWH* filled the *miškān,* the tabernacle (namely, with itself, Ex. 40:34f.). 2 Ch. 5:13f. varies this slightly: the house is filled with a cloud and with the *kᵉḇôḏ YHWH.* Similar statements are made in Ezk. 43:5; 44:4; Hag. 2:7. Ezk. 10 relates how Yahweh leaves the temple. The cloud comes out from the interior of the sanctuary and "fills" the court, and the *kᵉḇôḏ YHWH* rises up. The temple was "filled" with the cloud (niphal), and the court "was full" (qal) of the brightness of Yahweh's glory (v. 4).

---

13. On the expression *bᵉḵesep mālē'* in the sense of "pay the full equivalent value" (Gen. 23:9), cf. G. M. Tucker, "The Legal Background of Genesis 23," *JBL,* 85 (1966), 77-84.

14. See preceding discussion.

15. → כבוד *kāḇôḏ* (VII, 22-38).

Although Isaiah's vision does not speak of temple consecration (or profanation), the prophet does experience God's presence in a manner similar to such an occasion: he "saw Yahweh sitting on a throne, high and lofty; and his train filled the temple" (Isa. 6:1). Ps. 104:2 suggests a theophany involving light: the Lord's garment is light. Is it perhaps the brilliance of gold and silver that evokes the gleaming presence of the Lord in the assertion that the treasures of the nations fill the sacred house with "splendor" (Hag. 2:7)?

Several texts allude to God's presence in the land, in the world, or outside the temple, though in these cases one speaks differently than in the case of God's presence in the sanctuary. Hab. 2:14 asserts that knowledge *(da'aṯ)* of the *kāḇôḏ* will fill the earth, and Hab. 3:3 says that praise *(t^ehillâ)* of the name of Yahweh will fill the earth, the advent of the Lord calling forth this worship. The earth can also "be full" of Yahweh's *ḥeseḏ* (Ps. 33:5; 119:64), or of the divine beneficence in Israel's history and in mighty natural phenomena (Ps. 136).[16] The only passage directly asserting that God himself is omnipresent in the world is Jer. 23:24: "Do I not fill heaven and earth?" No person can hide before God, for he is not only a God at hand, but also a God that is afar off. Isa. 6:3 takes a different view, where the MT should be maintained contra the old translations that presuppose the reading *māl^e'â:* "The fullness of the whole earth is his *kāḇôḏ.*" If *mēlō'* is the subject,[17] the assertion is that everything that fills the earth — human beings and other creatures — contributes to and proclaims God's honor (as in Ps. 19:2[1]).[18] Certainly it remains true, however, that the earth is full of violence (Gen. 6:11), idols (Isa. 2:8), and bloody crimes (Ezk. 7:23). Yet this does not cloud the vision of the righteous person to the fact that the world is full of "God's mighty deeds."

Doubtful passages include Ps. 72:19; Nu. 14:21, where the MT attests a niphal form which is usually altered into an active form. If the MT is maintained, the interpretation is as follows: the *kāḇôḏ* of God will be fulfilled (will be full, will become total) with the whole world. The essence of Yahweh's glory consists not only in his presence in the sanctuary, but also in his works in the entire world, works with which Yahweh "fills" his *kāḇôḏ.*

3. *millē' 'aḥ^arê YHWH.* The expression *millē' 'aḥ^arê YHWH* is usually translated "to render complete obedience, to follow with one's whole heart," or similarly. This interpretation agrees with the rendering of this expression in the LXX *(epakoloutheín)* and suits the context well. The question remains, however, just how one is to complete the abbreviated expression. The addition of *lāleḵeṯ,* "in order to go," or *lihyôṯ,* "to be," is not quite satisfactory. The reference to *lēḇ,* "heart, will," in various passages offers a third possibility. In Josh. 14, e.g., Caleb is praised for his faithfulness. Whereas his brothers made the people's heart (will) falter, Caleb "filled [its heart] behind the Lord" (v. 8). Reference can also be made to 1 K. 11:4,6 with its assertion that Solomon's heart was not *šālēm,* "whole," with Yahweh. He did what was evil in the sight of

16. → חֶסֶד *ḥeseḏ,* V, 55.
17. See discussion below.
18. Cf. H. Wildberger, *Isaiah 1–12* (Eng. trans., Minneapolis, 1991), *in loc.*

Yahweh, and "did not fill [his heart] behind Yahweh," since he also worshipped Ashtoreth and Milcom. A person's heart can also "be full" to do evil (Eccl. 8:11), can "be full of booty" (Ex. 15:9) or filled with the spirit of truth (Dt. 34:9). These examples make the concise expression "fill behind Yahweh" more comprehensible. The heart contains nothing against Yahweh; it is fully, completely for or behind the Lord. As already indicated, the expression is applied several times to Caleb (Nu. 14:24; 32:11f.; Dt. 1:36; Josh. 14:8,14).

4. *millē' 'eṯ-hadd*ᵉ*ḇārîm.* Special attention should also be given those texts that speak of "fulfilling the words" *(millē' 'eṯ-hadd*ᵉ*ḇārîm).* We often hear that one fulfills with one's hand what has been promised with one's mouth (1 K. 8:15,24; 2 Ch. 6:4,15; 36:21; Jer. 44:25). The word (prophecy, vow, witness) is strengthened and actualized by an event (which can also consist of words). The "hand"[19] represents might or power, and the words are thus filled with power. In this expression *mālē'* can be replaced by *hēqîm,* "establish," and *šlm,* "complete, finish": "Who establishes [actualizes] *(mēqîm)* the word of his servant and carries out *(yašlîm)* the counsel of his messengers" (Isa. 44:26; cf. Nu. 23:19; 1 S. 3:12).

Nothing new occurs in such fulfillment; rather, a word is made full, or is empowered. It then acquires unavoidable validity and will certainly come to pass. Thus Martin Noth does not understand the expression in the sense of "substantively amplify" or "complete," but rather as "implement fully."[20]

Dnl. 4:30(33) shows clearly how closely related are prediction and occurrence: "In the same moment [that the voice sounded from heaven] the word was fulfilled upon Nebuchadnezzar." The word was implemented. It is not "empty," but rather brings about that which Yahweh has willed, and effects that for which he sent it (Isa. 55:11). For the immediate relationship between statement and fulfillment, cf. also 1 K. 2:27.

Finally, in 1 K. 1:14 Nathan says that he will come in to the king after Bathsheba, and while she yet speaks with the king he (Nathan) "will fulfill your words." His message is the same as that of Bathsheba, his story the same. For just this reason he lends her words power and validity, since through two or three witnesses a word or matter is "sustained" (*yāqûm dāḇār,* Dt. 19:15). Thus it is hardly correct when C. F. D. Moule denies the meaning "confirmation" and translates "I will tell the whole story," as if that story contained gaps to be filled.[21]

The LXX usually translates this expression with *plēróō tón lógon,* and once with *synteleíō,* "complete," "finish" (Dnl. 4:30[33]).

5. *millē' 'eṯ-yāḏ.*

a. The expression *millē' yaḏ hakkōhēn,* "fill the hand of the priest,"[22] occurs 16

---

19. → יד *yāḏ* (V, 393-426).
20. *Könige 1–16, BK,* IX/1 (²1983), 20.
21. P. 308.
22. → יד *yāḏ,* V, 409f.; → כהן *kōhēn* IV (70f.).

times in reference to the consecration of priests: Ex. 28:41; 29:9,29,33,35; 32:29; Lev. 4:5 (LXX); 8:33(twice); 16:32; 21:10; Nu. 3:3; Jgs. 17:5,12; 1 K. 13:33; 2 Ch. 13:9; 29:31. The LXX directs our attention toward a certain interpretation by translating *millē'* here not with *pímplēmi* (76 times) or *plēróō* (71 times), but rather with *teleióō,* "to complete, bring to an end." The object is plural: *tás cheíras.* In one case the LXX abbreviates the expression by omitting reference to the hands (Lev. 21:10). This passage prompts us to think of a ritual whereby the priest is made suitable or qualified to exercise his office. Gerhard Delling[23] understands the term to mean "to make free from stain, unblemished."

From Lev. 21:10 it becomes clear that "hands" refer *pars pro toto* to the priest as such, and that the concern is with the cultic purity of the entire person. The Vulg. translates as *consecrare,* "consecrate." Commentators generally refer to the Akkadian expression *mullû qātā,* "to commission a person with something, to empower a person for the priesthood."[24] Both Roland de Vaux[25] and Noth[26] adduce a Mari text[27] which refers to the filling of officers' hands with a portion of the spoils of war. *Mutatis mutandi* one might thus take this to refer in the OT to the priests' income. The earliest passage in which the expression *millē' 'eṯ-yāḏô* occurs (Jgs. 17:5,12) speaks of the salary of the Levite who has become priest in the house of Micah: ten pieces of silver a year, a suit of apparel, and his living (v. 10). The later, comprehensive description of the installation of priests (Ex. 29; Lev. 8) draws attention to the priests' portion of the sacrificial offering (Ex. 29:28). Thus it may well be that the distribution of a portion of the offering provides the background to this expression. Noth relates this to the witness in the Mari texts and suggests that the filling of the hand refers to the apportionment of a part of the sacrifices offered in the sanctuary.[28]

Konrad Rupprecht has objected to this thesis with some success. Although the passages in question do speak of the portions of the sacrifice allotted to the priest, and although this was doubtlessly of considerable importance for the priest, there is nowhere any indication that the pledge of income or any symbolic handing over of flesh, etc. ever constituted an actual celebratory part of the consecration ritual. The term is usually a general designation of priestly consecration and, when the latter is described in some detail (Ex. 29; Lev. 8), is associated with other rites as well; one should not be tempted into understanding the "filling of the hand" as a literal "giving into someone's hand." Various exegetes seek the origin of the expression in this direction,[29] pointing out that

---

23. *TDNT,* VIII, 82f. and n. 20.

24. *AHw,* II (1972), 598, *ana qāt X mullû;* cf. A. Dillmann, *Die Bücher Exodus und Leviticus. KeHAT,* 12 (Leipzig, ²1880), on Lev. 7:37; A. Malamat, "The Ban in Mari and the Bible," *Biblical Essays 1966. OuTWP* (Stellenbosch, 1966), 48, who directs attention to *ana mil qātišunu* as "a certain ritual nuance, referring to the appropriation of such objects."

25. *AncIsr,* 346f.

26. *The Laws in the Pentateuch,* 231-33.

27. C.-F. Jean, *Lettres diverses. ARM,* II (1959, repr. 1978), 13.

28. So also F. Michaeli, *Le livre de l'Exode. CAT,* II (1974), 257.

29. So U. Cassuto, *A Commentary on the Book of Exodus* (Eng. trans., Jerusalem, 1967), 386; J. H. Hertz, *Leviticus* (Oxford, 1936) 66; *AncIsr,* 346f.; Dillmann, *in loc.*

the actual consecration occurred when the priest performed the altar service for the first time, receiving thereupon the allotted portion of the sacrifice. The fact that an explicit distinction is made between consecration (Lev. 8) and the actual taking of office (Lev. 9) militates against this thesis. Furthermore, the word *yāḏ* is used in the singular, whereas the Hebrew in the phrase "to lay into a person's hand" uses *kap* or *ḥōpen* rather than *yāḏ*. When the priest actually fills his hand in the literal sense upon taking office, the expression is *wayᵉmallē' kappô* (Lev. 9:17; cf. Ex. 29:24; Ps. 129:7; Ezk. 10:2; etc.). Delling[30] correctly points out the difference in the LXX between *pímplēmi tás cheíras* (Lev. 9:17; 16:12) and *teleióō tás cheíras* (Ex. 29:9,29,33,35; Lev. 8:33), the latter having absolutely nothing to do with the former. The translator consciously rendered the two expressions differently.

In the regulations for the consecration of priests in Ex. 29; Lev. 8 we notice that in the first part of Ex. 29 the "filling of the hand" summarizes several different acts: the washing with water, the putting on of the sacred garments, the placing of the holy diadem, and the anointing with oil (vv. 4,7,9). In v. 35, too, this expression designates the entire seven-day consecration procedure. The same summarizing reference also occurs in Ex. 32:29; Nu. 3:3; 1 K. 13:33; 2 Ch. 13:9; 29:31. In other passages, however, the anointing and filling of the hand occur as two separate designations for the consecration of priests; Ex. 29:29; 28:41; Lev. 16:32 all mention "the anointed and hand-filled priest" (compare Lev. 21:10 and 4:5 with the LXX). Sir. 45:15 uses the reverse order: hand-filled and anointed. This distinction between anointing and *millē' 'eṯ-yāḏô* leads to the conclusion that these were two important components of the consecration of priests, each of which alone could serve as a designation of the consecration as such, though they were distinguished in the ceremony itself (in contrast, Ex. 29:9b refers only to the "hand filling," this designation including the act of anointing).

For the interpretation of the notion of "hand filling" it is important to consider what is said about what is called the *millu'îm* ram (Ex. 29:19-35). The pl. *millu'îm,* "filling, ordination," summarizes various parts of the service.[31] The word seldom occurs alone, but rather usually in connection with *'ayil,* ram" (Ex. 29:22,26,27,31; Lev. 8:22,29), *bāśār,* "flesh" (Ex. 29:34), *'ôlâ,* "offering" (Lev. 8:28), *sal,* "basket" (Lev. 8:31), and *yāmîm,* "days of hand-filling" (Lev. 8:33). It occurs once independently in a series of offering types (Lev. 7:37). It is not immediately clear just which of the previously mentioned offerings is meant.[32] The most likely candidate is suggested by Lev. 6:12-23, which in connection with the cereal offering mentions one tenth of an ephah of fine flour as the priest's cereal offering "on the day when one of them is anointed." Now Ex. 29; Lev. 8, the chapters concerned with the ordination of priests, both mention fine flour used to make cakes (Ex. 29:2,23; Lev. 8:3,26). These cakes were burned with the second ram, the *millu'îm* ram, as a *millu'îm* offering (Lev. 8:28). The cakes were placed

30. Pp. 80f., 82f.
31. *GK,* §124f.
32. Cf. K. Elliger, *Leviticus. HAT,* IV (1966), 103, 119.

into a basket and brought to the altar. In one instance this basket is called the "basket of hand-filling (NRSV 'of ordination offerings')" (Lev. 8:31). Thus in the above-mentioned passages the expression *millu'îm* is always associated with the ordination ritual of the priests, and especially with the offering of the second ram.

The offering of the second ram is thus of special significance in connection with the hand-filling of the priest. A distinction is made between the anointing, the ceremony of the bull offering, and the ram of the burnt offering (Ex. 29:10-18). After Aaron and his sons have laid their hands upon the head of the second ram,[33] its blood is put on the candidates' ear, thumb, and great toe (v. 20). Blood, mixed with oil, is then sprinkled on the priests and their garments (v. 21). Parts of the sacrifice are placed with the bread into their hands, waved back and forth, and then burned on the altar (vv. 22-25). The breast and thigh are given to the priests, to be eaten as a peace offering (vv. 26-28). These specific parts of the sacrifice are to be a perpetual due to the priests from the people of Israel (Lev. 7:34). Ex. 29:33 offers the explanatory remark that this food "fills their hand"; in this respect they are clearly distinguished from other people, who are not permitted to eat of it (v. 33). At the conclusion we find that the ceremony of the hand-filling lasts seven days in this form (v. 35), though the final sentence does not clarify whether the entire ritual extends over one week or whether everything is performed seven times, each day anew. Lev. 8 describes the ordination of priests in the same way.

The conclusion must be that *millē' 'eṯ-yāḏ* is either a general designation for the ordination of priests or constitutes an integral part of such ordination, namely, the application of blood, the apportionment of sacrificial flesh, and the meal. The rite of hand-filling refers *pars pro toto* to the consecration of priests. Thus the anointing of the priest is also a part of the ceremony (e.g., distinguished from the hand-filling in Lev. 16:32; Nu. 3:3), and is often the designation for the consecration or the condition as such of having been consecrated (Ex. 40:15; Lev. 4:3; 6:15[22]; Nu. 35:25). The ritual of hand-filling is a ritual of strengthening one's efficacy as priest, of "full" empowerment, of "filling" the soul, rendering it capable of performing the service at the altar; the word *yāḏ* in this context is thus to be understood in the sense of "efficacy, power"[34] (e.g., Lev. 25:35; Dt. 32:27; Jgs. 7:11; 9:24; 1 Ch. 29:24). G. te Stroete[35] correctly translates Ex. 29:9 as "you shall anoint them" (i.e., equip them with the power necessary to carry out the office), "give them power and consecrate them." Dt. 33:11 speaks of the "strength, efficacy" *(ḥayil)* of the priest.

It comes as no surprise that reference is made to filling the "hand" of the altar (Ezk. 43:26). The sanctuary, too, and especially the altar, possesses a "soul" that can be extinguished and must thus be "charged" anew. It is fortified by the sprinkling of blood and other atonement rites. (The LXX has misunderstood the passage, having not the "hand of the altar," but rather the "hands of the priest" be completed or filled.)

---

33. → סמך *sāmaḵ*.
34. Cf. A. S. van der Woude, "יָד *jāḏ* Hand," *THAT,* I, 667ff., sub c.
35. *Exodus. BOT,* I/2, (1963), 207.

Thus, too, it is not surprising that Ex. 32:29 exhorts the Levites, who have become unclean through contact with the dead, to renew themselves with efficacy and power, i.e., to fill their hand so as to receive blessing and power for their office.

b. The expression *millē' 'eṯ-yāḏô* is used in yet another context. In 1 Ch. 29:5, David invites the people to bring gold and silver to build the house of God. He asks: "Who then is willing to fill his hand for Yahweh?" David himself has acted commensurate with his own ability (*kōaḥ,* v. 2) by donating numerous precious things and even a second offering: thousands of talents of gold and silver. Who now also wishes to increase his own "strength" so as to be capable for the service of Yahweh? Who now wishes to "make his heart whole" *(šālēm)* for God (v. 9)? Understood in this way, 1 Ch. 29:5 is also speaking of a kind of "consecration."

A similar train of thought can help us clarify the expression *millē' yāḏ* in reference to military service. Warriors are in a special way consecrated to the Lord and "sacred." 2 K. 9:24 does not relate that Jehu "took his bow into hand," but rather that he "filled" his hand "with the bow" and shot Joram. This is likely saying that Jehu filled up his *yāḏ,* i.e., his strength or might, complemented with a weapon. Now he is removed from normal life and "consecrated" to a superhuman commission (cf. 2 S. 23:7: the worthless are like thorns which one does not touch with one's hand; rather let one "fill" [add: *yāḏ,* his hand] with iron). The weapon gives him strength and ability; through it he is full of power. Jer. 4:5 can be understood similarly: *qir'û mal'û* means to "call together, fill yourselves (with strength)." The decision must be made. The people should leave behind land and house and gather into the fortified cities in order to resist the enemy. This decision demands strength. Although this interpretation is preferable, one might also complete the phrase with the subst. *qôl:* "voice, sound." Thus the usual translation is "call (together), fill (your voice)," i.e., call with a full voice, with full sound.

Jer. 12:6 is also usually understood in this way. Here, too, the combination "call" and "fill" occurs. This sentence, however, has a different structure, since the subject changes (plural and singular), and the expression *qārᵉ'û mālē'* is split by the prep. *'aḥᵃreyḵā.* Hence the translation "to call with a full voice" is unsatisfactory. I would like to read here as follows: "For even your brothers and the house of your father, even they have dealt treacherously with you, they cry after you 'fill yourself' [with strength, *mallē'* piel impv., i.e., 'be strong'], but trust them not, though they speak fair words to you." That is, the brothers behave like the prophet's comrades: they encourage him to continue the struggle. Their intention, however, is to bring him down. D. Winton Thomas[36] suggests a different meaning for *mālē',* namely, "to gather together, mobilize." He points Jer. 12:6 as *mᵉlō',* "mass, multitude" (cf. Gen. 48:19; Isa. 31:4) or *mallē'* (piel inf. abs.), "mass together, assemble," and translates: "They have raised a hue and cry after him, they have massed together to hunt him down." G. R. Driver[37] interprets "help, everyone!" similarly when he suggests that the element "All together" is actualized in the root *ml'.* Among other reasons, Winton Thomas cites the LXX

36. Pp. 47ff.
37. "Jeremiah, XII,6," *JJS,* 5 (1954), 178.

rendering *synéchthēsan* in supporting the interpretation of Jer. 4:5 as "assemble, mobilize": "The phrase *qir'ū mal'ū* means literally proclaim, assemble a *m^{e}lō',* i.e. assemble an assembly, a phrase which is equivalent to 'proclaim mobilisation.' "[38] It seems rather peculiar, however, that "assembling" should be mentioned twice in immediate succession (cf. *hē'ās^{e}p̱û*). Furthermore, Winton Thomas also adds *m^{e}lō'* to the text (as others add *qôl*). In Jer. 4:5, as well as in many other passages, one can make do equally well with the usual meaning of *mālē'* in the sense of "to fill, be full" and add a *yāḏ,* "strength" (compare the *millē' 'eṯ-yāḏ* texts and Ezk. 43:26; 1 Ch. 29:5; 2 S. 23:7; 2 K. 9:24).

Rykle Borger[39] has clarified the interpretation of the cry "fill the shields!" (Jer. 51:11). He points out that the word *š^{e}lāṭîm,* which is almost always translated as "shield," is correctly rendered by the LXX as *pharétra,* "quiver." In all the biblical passages *šeleṭ* means "quiver," the only question being whether this refers only to comprehensive quivers for arrows and bow or also simply to the quiver for arrows.[40] Thus *mil'û* here exhibits the normal, concrete meaning: something empty is filled. Arrows will thus fill a quiver.

IV. Derivatives.

1. *m^{e}lō'*. The subst. *m^{e}lō',* "fullness," refers to that which fills something or makes it full, e.g., *m^{e}lō' kap,* "a handful" (1 K. 17:12; Eccl. 4:6). One especially frequent expression is *hā'āreṣ ûm^{e}lō'â,* "the earth and what fills it" (Dt. 33:16; Ps. 24:1; 50:12; Isa. 34:1; Jer. 8:16; 47:2; Ezk. 19:7; 30:12; cf. Ps. 89:12[11]). It can also mean "the land and its fullness" (Jer. 8:16; Ezk. 12:19; 19:7). Dt. 33:16; Isa. 24:1; Mic. 1:2 suggest that the reference here is to that which grows and lives upon the earth,[41] especially human beings and the various peoples (cf. Jer. 8:16; 47:2). Am. 6:8 speaks of the city and its fullness, i.e., its inhabitants. The opposite of the land with its fullness is the wasteland, the devastated earth (Ezk. 12:19; 30:12; 32:15; 36:38). In the first verse of Ps. 24, we find a parallel between the fullness of the earth and the inhabitants of the world (cf. Ps. 50:12; 89:12[11]; 98:7). It is God's commission to human beings to multiply and fill the earth (Gen. 1:28; 9:7). God is praised because he filled the land with the vine, i.e., with the people of Israel (Ps. 80:10[9]). Ezk. 36:38 promises "so shall the ruined towns be filled with flocks of people" (*m^{e}lē'ôṯ ṣō'n 'āḏām;* cf. Isa. 26:15); the psalmist is referring not only to human beings, but to all living things: "In wisdom you have made them all; the earth is full of your creatures" (Ps. 104:24). The formula *hayyām ûm^{e}lō'ô* is similar; the sea shelters the fishes and teams with living creatures: "God made the sea and all that is in it" (Ex. 20:11; Ps. 96:11; Isa. 42:10). This interpretation also closely approximates Gen. 48:19 with its assurance that Ephraim will be a "fullness (NRSV 'multitude') of nations," i.e., a multiplicity of tribes inhabiting the land. (In Rom. 11:12, one should follow the LXX and read *plēthos* rather

---

38. *Ibid.,* 177.
39. *VT,* 22 (1972), 385-398.
40. *Ibid.,* 397f.
41. A. Dillmann, *Die Bücher Numeri, Deuteronomium und Josua. KEHAT* XIII (^{2}1886), 426.

than *plērōma.*) Isa. 31:4 is similar with its reference to the "fullness of shepherds," i.e., the whole band, the totality of shepherds. And whereas we say "its full length" or "its full breadth," Hebrew refers to the "fullness of its length" and the "fullness of its breadth" (e.g., of the land; 1 S. 28:20; Isa. 8:8).[42]

2. *millu'îm.*[43] The term *millu'îm* is also used, like *millu'â,* to refer to the filling (of precious stones) in the oracular breastpiece of the high priest (Ex. 25:7; 35:9,27; 1 Ch. 29:2; Ex. 28:17,20; 39:13). One might ask whether the "setting" of the breastpiece is referring only to a technical act or perhaps also to spiritual strengthening and "ordination," a kind of consecration.

3. *millô'.* The term *millô',* "filling, solid fill, terrace, rampart" (Akk. *tamlû*) is generally taken to refer in Jgs. 9:6,20; 2 S. 5:9; 1 K. 9:15,24; 11:27; 1 Ch. 11:8; 2 Ch. 32:5 to a building or area in Shechem or Jerusalem. It is best not to translate the word, but rather to render it simply as "Millo." It refers to the acropolis of the old city of David, and in Solomon's time to the temple and palace area.[44] It is advisable here to allow the word's fundamental meaning to resonate, which suggests an elevation or filling up of a piece of property. As a rule a natural elevation was preferred, though such property often had to be restructured through artificial solid fill to render it more serviceable.[45] Uncertainty still surrounds the exact location of the Millo in Jerusalem. Kathleen M. Kenyon is inclined to understand the Millo as a terracelike, solid-fill platform on the eastern slope of the Ophel.[46] Manfred Görg[47] suggests a "parklike layout . . . in the southern part of the Solomonic temple area," and refers to the establishment of the "gardens of Aton" in Amarna.

Snijders

V. Qumran. The term *ml'* occurs quite frequently in the writings of Qumran. The verb *malē'* occurs about 40 times, the adj. *mālē'* 6 times (almost always spelled with *h* in the Temple scroll), the subst. *m^elô'* 5 times (uncertain reading in 4Q493 1:5). The term *millû'îm* occurs only in 11QT 15 (4 times), where it is associated with a consecration festival only the rudiments of which are yet identifiable in rabbinic sources[48] and which is dependent ritually on Lev. 8:14ff.; Ex. 29:1ff. The "hand-filling" was also practiced in Qumran within the framework of the consecration of priests (1QSb 5:17) and was considered a necessary prerequisite for priestly service (11QT 35:6).

---

42. Cf. also L. Prijs, "Ergänzungen zum talmudisch-hebräischen Wörterbuch," *ZDMG,* 120 (1970), 19.

43. For *millu'îm,* see also III.5 above.

44. K. Galling, "Jerusalem 3.b," *BRL*², 160.

45. Cf. K. Galling, "Akropolis," *BRL*².

46. Cf. the overview of K. R. Veenhof in "De muren van Jeruzalem," *Phoenix,* 11 (1965), 214-221.

47. *"kp* und *kp n rdwj," Göttinger Miszellen,* 20 (1976), 29f.

48. Cf. Y. Yadin, ed., *M^egillat hammiqdaš [The Temple Scroll],* I (Jerusalem, 1977), 75ff., 110ff.

Otherwise the term *ml'* occurs with the simple concrete meanings "filled up" (cisterns, 3Q15 2:1; a pot, 3Q15 4:8), and "in full strength, full number" (the military host, 1QM 5:3), with the figurative meaning "pregnant" (cattle, 11QT 52:5), "full of wind" (horses, 1QM 6:12), in the semantic sphere "completion or fulfillment of a specific time period, age, etc." (1QS 7:20,22; 1QSa 1:10,12; 1QM 17:9; CD 10:1), and in connection with statements about the theology of creation (1QH 16:3; 1QS 3:16; 1QM 12:12; 19:4; CD 2:11; 4QEn[e] 5).

Fabry

מַלְאָךְ *mal'āḵ*

Contents: I. Distribution. II. Etymology. III. Ancient Near East: 1. Ugarit; 2. Aramaic Evidence; 3. Mesopotamia; 4. Phoenicia. IV. Human Envoys: 1. Personal Envoys; 2. Political Envoys; a. *ml'k* (singular); b. *ml'k* (plural). V. Divine Envoys: 1. General; 2. Prophets; 3. Priests; 4. *mal'aḵ YHWH / mal'aḵ 'ᵉlōhîm.* VI. Metaphorical Usage. VII. Qumran.

I. Distribution. The word *mal'āḵ* occurs 213 times in the OT and refers to both human and divine "messengers." The meaning "messenger" is confirmed by the verbs with which *mal'āḵ* appears: *šlḥ,* "to send" (56 times), *bw',* "to come" (16 times), *'mr,* "to say" (29 times), *dbr,* "to speak" (11 times), *hlk,* "to go" (9 times), *šwb,* "to return" (6 times), as well as *qr',* "to call," *yṣ',* "to go out," *yrd,* "to go down," and *ngd* hiphil,

---

mal'āḵ. W. Baumgartner, "Zum Problem des 'Jahwe-Engels,' " *Zum AT und seiner Umwelt* (Leiden, 1959), 240-46; V. Calvianu, "Sesul expresiei 'trimisul lui Dumnezeu' (Malak-Jahve) in VT," *Studi Teologice Bucureşti,* 27 (1975), 226-231; J. L. Cunchillos, *Cuando los angeles eran dioses. Bibliotheca Salmanticensis* 14/12 (1976); *idem, "Étude philologique de mal'āk,"* *Congress Volume, Vienna 1980. SVT,* 32 (1981), 30-51; R. Ficker, "מַלְאָךְ *mal'āk* Bote," *THAT,* I, 900-908; B. Graham, *Angels: God's Secret Agents* (New York, 1975); S. M. Grill, "Synonyme Engelnamen im AT," *ThZ,* 18 (1962), 241-46; H. Gross, "Der Engel im AT," *Archiv für Liturgiewissenschaft,* 6 (1959), 28-42; F. Guggisberg, *Die Gestalt des Mal'ak Jahwe im AT* (diss., Neuenburg, 1979); W. G. Heidt, *Angelology of the OT* (Washington, 1949); V. Hirt, *Gottes Boten im AT* (diss., Leipzig, 1971); D. M. Irwin, *The Comparison of Tales from the OT and the Ancient Near East* (diss., Tübingen, 1977); A. Kniazef and V. Moustakis, "Ἄγγελος," *Threskeutike kai ethike enkyklopaideia* I (Athens, 1962), 172-196; J. S. Licht, "מלאך," *EMiqr,* IV (1962), 975-990; J. Michl, "Engel II (jüdisch)," *RAC,* V (1962), 60-97; R. North, "Separated Spiritual Substances in the OT," *CBQ,* 29 (1967), 419-449; M. Paulas, *Ursprung und Geschichte der kirchlichen Engelverehrung* (diss., Vienna, 1971); H. Röttger, *Mal'ak Jahwe — Bote von Gott. Regensburger Studien zur Theologie,* 13 (1978); A. Rofé, *Israelite Belief in Angels in the Pre-Exilic Period as Evidenced by Biblical Traditions* (diss., Jerusalem, 1969); H. Seebass, "Engel II: AT," *TRE,* IX, 583-86; J. Urquiza, *Jahweh und sein Mal'akh* (diss., Vienna, 1972); M. Valloggia, *Recherche sur les "messagers"* (wpwtyw) *dans les sources égyptiennes profanes. PCRHP,*2/6 (1976); A. S. van der Woude, "De *Mal'ak Jahweh:* een Godsbode," *NedThT* 18 (Wageningen, 1963), 1-13.

"to bring news, recount." Here *mal'āḵ* refers to an individual who is sent to someone for the purpose of conveying a message or of carrying out an order. The *mal'āḵ* speaks, receives a response, and returns to the one who sent him.

These messengers appear in both the human and divine spheres, though the difference seems to be more spatial than metaphysical; i.e., divine messengers are those sent by God from his heavenly abode, while human messengers are sent by earthly chieftains. The *mal'āḵ* does not report his own message; his function and message are dependent upon the will of the person who sends him. His significance derives not from who he is, but from who his superior is. This territorial distinction is evidenced by the role of the prophet, a human being who is a divine messenger. The prophet is a witness to what goes on in the heavenly council;[1] although he is to deliver God's message, he generally remains on earth.

The LXX translates *mal'āḵ* without distinction as *ángelos* in agreement with Classical Greek usage, whereas the Vulg. distinguishes between *nuntius* (a messenger of human beings) and *angelus* (a messenger of God).

II. Etymology. The subst. *mal'āḵ* derives like the abstract noun *mal'āḵûṯ* (Hag. 1:13) and → מלאכה *m^elā'ḵâ* from the verbal stem *l'k,* "to depute, minister, send a messenger,"[2] which, while attested neither in Hebrew nor in Akkadian, is probably attested in Ugarit and in the South Semitic languages.[3] The root *hlk* is probably related etymologically.[4]

III. Ancient Near East.

1. *Ugarit.* The Ugaritic evidence[5] is important for three reasons: First, it contains the only attestations of the verb *l'k;* second, *ml'k* is used in the dual; thus two messengers are always being sent; and third, *ml'k* is used to refer to both political and divine messengers. The verb is used to refer to the sending of messengers[6] or to the bringing of a message (*spr d lảkt*[7]). Based on this evidence *l'k* would be comparable to Heb. *šālaḥ.*

The subst. *ml'k* occurs in the Keret epic, where the exchange between Keret and King Pabil of Udm always takes place through messengers.[8] The context shows that the ending *-m* is to be taken as a marker of the dual. These messengers are political

1. → סוד *sôḏ.*
2. *HAL,* II (1995), 585.
3. *Ibid.,* II, 513.
4. On the etymology, cf. further E. L. Greenstein, "Trans-Semitic Idiomatic Equivalency and the Derivation of Hebrew *ml'kh," UF,* 11 (1979), 329-336.
5. *WUS,* no. 1423; *UT,* no. 1344.
6. *KTU,* 1.14 III, 19f.; 1.4 V, 42; 1.2 I, 22; 1.24, 16; in letters, e.g., 2.10, 10; 2.30, 17; this probably also includes *KTU,* 1.4 VII, 45, where *dll* probably means "broker" or something similar rather than "tribute"; see J. Sanmartín, "Zu den *'ad(d)*-Denominierungen im Ugaritischen," *UF,* 12 (1980), 347.
7. *KTU,* 2.14, 7.
8. *Ibid.,* 1.14 III, 19f.; IV 32f.; VI 35; see also *ANET,* 142-49.

envoys delivering messages. In the Baʿal-ʿAnat cycle, the *ml'k* appears as the companion of a god, especially of Yamm.[9]

Freedman-Willoughby

J. L. Cunchillos has shown that *l'k* does not mean merely "to send," but rather "to send a messenger/message." The *ml'k* functions as a connecting link between two persons or groups, thus bringing the two separated parties together. His specific functions range from that of a simple messenger or envoy to those of a fully empowered ambassador. Otherwise he does not identify himself with the person who sends him except when he actually carries out his mission. In that situation he speaks "in the name of," though without in any metaphysical sense actually being the person who sent him. Any identification is merely functional, and only in this sense does the *ml'k* "represent" the person who has commissioned him.

It is interesting to note that Akk. *mār šipri* (lit., "son of the message," i.e., messenger) is related to *šipru* with its double meaning "message" and "work" in the same way that *mal'āḵ* is related to *mᵉlā'ḵâ,* "work," though occasionally also "commission, message."[10]

Ringgren

2. *Aramaic Evidence.* The term *ml'k* occurs 5 times in the extant Aramaic literature: twice in the eighth-century-B.C. Old Aramaic Sefire inscriptions,[11] twice in the Biblical Aramaic of Daniel, and once in a Judean Aramaic inscription.[12] Both occurrences of *ml'k* in the Sefire inscriptions (*ml'ky,* "my ambassador," and *ml'kh,* "his ambassador") are employed with the verb *šlḥ,* "to send," and refer to political emissaries sent from one king to another to negotiate peace or to report important governmental decisions. The term seems to refer to an officer of the royal court whose responsibility is to bring information from and back to the king.

Biblical Aramaic evidence of *mal'āḵ* is found in Dnl. 3:28; 6:23[Eng. v. 22]. In both instances the term refers to an angel who rescues the innocent from unjust punishment. Here, too, it is used with *šlḥ:* God sent his angel to deliver Shadrach, Meshach, and Abednego from the fire (3:28) and Daniel from a den of lions (6:23[22]). The pl. const. *ml'ky* appears in Judean Aramaic with the same meaning.[13]

3. *Mesopotamia.* Akkadian evidence for this root is extremely uncertain. A *mālaku* appears in one Old Babylonian text[14] which reads: *PN mālakī aṭṭardakku šipātim mala tīšû . . . ṭurdam,* with the possible translation, "I am sending you PN, my messenger; send me all the wool which you have." If *mālaku* does indeed refer here to a "messenger," then the reference is to a personal envoy.

---

9. *KTU,* 1.2 I, 22, 26, 28, 30, 44; see also *ANET,* 129-142.
10. → מלאכה *mᵉlā'ḵâ* (VIII, 325-331).
11. *KAI,* 224, 8.
12. *DISO,* 151.
13. *JKF,* I, 203, 4.
14. *CT,* 29, 21, 19.

4. *Phoenicia.* Finally, *ml'k* appears in a Phoenician inscription from Maʿṣūb (222 B.C.).[15] The text mentions (l. 2) the *ml'k mlkʿštrt,* "the messenger of Milk Astarte" (a deity of the Phoenician pantheon). From the context, *ml'k* refers to a priest or prominent citizen who represented the community's relationship with its deity.

IV. Human Envoys.

1. *Personal Envoys.* The OT contains only 4 references to a personal envoy (2 sg., 2 pl.), two of which occur in the Wisdom Literature. Prov. 13:17 reads: *mal'āḵ rāšāʿ yippōl b^e^rāʿ w^e^ṣîr 'ᵉmûnîm marpē'.* The reading *yappîl* is recommended on grounds of parallelism, with the translation: "A bad messenger brings trouble, but a faithful envoy [brings] healing." This passage does not seem to deal with the content of the message, only with the character of the messenger. The author presumably has in mind the disruptive consequences of false reporting or failure on the part of the messenger to carry out his assignment.

Since the authority of the sender is bound up in the legate, this passage leaves open the question of how an unfavorable report by a faithful messenger can produce healing. The terms *ṣîr* and *mal'āḵ* are in synonymous parallelism here (cf. Isa. 18:2 with its plural forms), though *ṣîr,* "messenger, envoy," is a far less frequently used term in this sense.

The occurrence in Job 1:14 portrays a messenger in a realistic scene and exemplifies the basic, standard role of the messenger in delivering a message from a sender to a receiver.

Personal envoys (pl.) appear in Gen. 32:4,7(3,6), where Jacob sends *mal'āḵîm* to Esau to announce his return home and to inform Esau that Jacob's intentions are peaceful and conciliatory. Such a gesture was in order after the stealing of the blessing of the first-born and the resulting tension between the two.[16]

The paucity of examples of personal messengers in the OT is the result of an overt attempt by its authors to write about Israel as a political and social unity from the time of the exodus onward in which the *mal'āḵ* refers to an envoy of the local or national government. Since the common, everyday occurrences of the average citizen are of little interest, personal envoys rarely appear.

2. *Political Envoys.* The term *mal'āḵ* is employed in the singular 16 times and in the plural 72 times to refer to a government agent whose basic function is to convey messages either within the land itself or between lands. The abundance of the plural forms attests the common political practice of sending more than one messenger for reasons of security (to increase the possibility that the message would be delivered should the contingent of emissaries come under attack), of accuracy in delivering the message, and to underscore one's own status.

---

15. *KAI,* 19.

16. Cf. D. Thompson, *The Genesis Messenger Stories and Their Theological Significance* (diss., Tübingen, 1972).

a. *ml'k (singular).* Although it was customary to send more than one messenger, possibly accompanied by an interpreter or an entire retinue, there were circumstances when it was advisable to send only one messenger. One messenger comes to Saul and reports that the Philistines have raided the land (1 S. 23:27). It may be that he was the only person to escape the initial attack of the Philistines, or he traveled alone so he would be less conspicuous.[17] In addition, speed was of the essence.[18]

Only one messenger might be sent if the sender wished to restrict knowledge of the matter. Thus Joab sent an oral message to David by a lone envoy (2 S. 11:19,22,23,25), since he could only entrust to a single individual this volatile news of Uriah's death. Thus royal messengers could have a high position in the government and be among the king's closest and most trusted friends.[19] In the same passage, David sent details of his plan to kill Uriah in a written message to Joab. Certainly, the drama of the passage is heightened by the irony of Uriah, returning to the front lines of the battle, carrying his own death sentence. But it was not unusual for irregular messengers to be sent on occasion.[20] Thus such a message might be either written (v. 14f.) or oral (v. 19; cf. Isa. 37:14 par. 2 K. 19:14; Jer. 27:3).[21]

After Jehu had been anointed king over Israel, while Jehoram was still on the throne, the latter sent a messenger to Jehu to determine his true intentions (2 K. 9:18). This passage shows that a messenger could be sent back and forth several times, since the sender was expecting confirmation of his message.[22] Jehu had Jehoram and all Ahab's descendants put to death, and their death was reported to Jehu by a messenger (2 K. 10:8).

In addition to relaying messages, the *mal'āḵ* might also have additional duties, e.g., the arrest and transport of prisoners. Prov. 17:11 depicts a messenger who is authorized to arrest and detain an outlaw or even to inflict the punishment he pronounces in the name of a higher authority. This verse is an apt commentary on 1 S. 19:14: Saul sent messengers to arrest the rebellious David (cf. 2 K. 6:32, where the *mal'āḵ* is authorized to seize an opponent and escort him to the king). The *mar šipri* had the same function in EA, 54; 162.

In other passages where only one messenger is sent, the relevant factor may be the status of the receiver. Ahab summoned Micaiah to prophesy concerning a proposed war with Syria (1 K. 22:13; 2 Ch. 18:12); Jehoram sent a messenger to the prophet Elisha (2 K. 6:32[twice],33); Jezebel dispatched a messenger to Elijah (1 K. 19:2); Elisha sent a messenger to Naaman (2 K. 5:10). Naaman is offended at first because Elisha did not deliver the message in person. He assumes that a man of his rank has a right to a direct audience with the prophet. This shows that one may dispatch a messenger to an inferior to request his presence or to demand action (in 2 K. 18, 19

17. Cf. EA, 112, 40-50.
18. Cf. EA, 7, 51-60; Job 1:14.
19. Cf. EA, 24.
20. Cf. EA, 112, 40-50.
21. Cf. EA, 26, 10-18; 32, 1-6, 10-15.
22. On the *mal'āḵ* on horseback, cf. also EA, 7, 51-60.

the king of Assyria sends the Rabshakeh to demand the surrender of Jerusalem), but in response a person of superior status or rank expects a personal appearance from his inferior rather than an envoy.

Finally, according to Ezk. 23:40 it was customary to dispatch envoys into other nations in order to invite dignitaries to visit and to form alliances (cf. Isa. 14:32; 18:2; 30:4; 33:7; Ezk. 17:15; 23:16).

b. *ml'k (plural).* The pl. *mal'āḵîm* occurs 89 times in the OT, 72 times in reference to political envoys. These missions were both intrastate (Josh. 7:22; 1 S. 6:21) and international (Jgs. 11:17; 2 S. 5:11; 1 K. 20:2; 2 K. 16:7; 17:4; 19:9). Envoys were employed for communication between citizens (1 S. 6:21), kings (2 S. 5:11), generals (2 S. 3:26), and other administrative and military personnel. Although in fact anyone who was dispatched with a message could be a *mal'āḵ,* the frequent use of the term in political contexts (from the time of the tribal league onward) points to a conclusion that the term *mal'āḵ* also designated a government official, a "legate."

Besides delivering messages, the *mal'āḵîm* also occasionally gathered intelligence and arrested criminals. The men who were sent to spy out the land of Jericho *('ᵃnāšîm hamᵉraggᵉlîm)* are also called *mal'āḵîm* (Josh. 6:17,25). Both terms reflect the functions these men were to perform: to "foot about" the land and then return with their report.[23] According to Josh. 7:22, Joshua sent *mal'āḵîm* to find goods plundered from Jericho and to locate the guilty parties (cf. above Prov. 17:11 and EA 54; 2 K. 6:32; 1 S. 19:14). Josh. 6,7 show that the number of *mal'āḵîm* sent depended on the task and the responsibilities involved.

There are only 5 references to political envoys in the Pentateuch (4 of those occur in Numbers). Moses sends *mal'āḵîm* to the king of Edom and to Sihon, the king of the Amorites, to obtain safe passage through their land (Nu. 20:14; 21:21; Dt. 2:26). Balak summons Balaam through messengers (Nu. 24:12) to curse Israel (22:5). All 5 occurrences show the *mal'āḵîm* to be typical political legates.

In prophetic literature, *mal'āḵîm* appear as government officials dispatched for the purpose of initiating political alliances. Isaiah (Isa. 14:28-32) gave an oracle in the year King Ahaz died (715 B.C.) concerning the premature celebration of the Philistines, who were encouraged to rebel against Assyria because of Egyptian resurgence under the Ethiopian King Piankhy (the revolt did indeed take place the next year, led by Ashdod, but was crushed by Sargon). Isaiah's message is clear: Assyria will put down the rebellion. Thus he concluded his oracle with the following statement: *ûmah-yyaʿᵃneh mal'ᵃḵê-gôy kî YHWH yissaḏ ṣiyyôn ûḇāh yeḥᵉsû ʿᵃniyyê ʿammô,* "What will one answer the messengers of the nation? Yahweh has founded Zion, and the needy among his people will find refuge in her," or "What can the messengers of the nation respond, for Yahweh has founded Zion, and the needy among his people will find refuge in her." With the former (traditional) translation, Isaiah's conclusion is that the Philistine envoys who urged Judah to join the rebellion against Assyria will receive the reply: Yahweh himself is the security for Jerusalem and its inhabitants. Verse 32b is the answer in the

23. Cf. EA, 162.

form of indirect discourse *(kî)* to the question posited in v. 32a, and the evidence for such a conclusion is presented in the oracle itself. This analysis takes *mal'ᵃk̲ê* as the direct object of *ya'ᵃneh,* which itself lacks a definite subject.[24] In the second translation, *mal'ᵃk̲ê-gôy* is taken as a collective for the Philistine ambassadors. The phrase serves as the subject of *ya'ᵃneh,* while *kî* introduces a causal dependent clause. The effect of this analysis is that there is no reply that the ambassadors of Philistia can produce to counteract the evidence presented in the oracle.

The same historical context is the setting for Isa. 18:1-7, where Cushite envoys *(ṣîrîm)* have come to enlist Judah in the revolt. Isaiah admonishes these "swift messengers" *(mal'āk̲îm qallîm)* to depart for Egypt and declare to the Egyptians that Israel is prepared to wait for Yahweh. The function of the *ṣîrîm* and *mal'āk̲îm* is the same (cf. Prov. 13:17). Jer. 27:3; Ezk. 17:15; 23:16 also attest such internationally active political *mal'āk̲îm.*

A difficult passage occurs in Nah. 2:11-14(10-13), where the prophet describes the crimes of Nineveh which brought about its destruction. He speaks metaphorically, referring to Nineveh as a "cave" (*mᵉ'ārâ;* MT *mir'eh,* "pasture") from which the lion (the Assyrian army) kills its prey for its lioness and cubs. Although it is not uncommon for a predatory ruler or an aggressive nation to be compared with a lion (cf. Prov. 28:15; Jer. 50:17), Nah. 2:14(13) nonetheless seems out of place. It reads as follows:

hinᵉnî 'ēlayik̲ nᵉ'um YHWH ṣᵉb̲ā'ôt̲
wᵉhib̲'artî be'āšān rik̲bāh ûk̲ᵉpîrayik̲ tō'k̲al ḥāreb̲
wᵉhik̲rattî mē'ereṣ ṭarpēk̲ wᵉlō'-yiššāma' 'ôd̲ qôl mal'āk̲ēk̲ēh

"See, I am against you, says Yahweh of hosts, and I will burn your (MT 'her') chariots in smoke, and the sword shall devour your young lions; I will cut them off from the land of your prey; and the voice of your messengers shall be heard no more."

Three points of analysis can clarify the passage and the interpretation of *qôl mal'āk̲ēk̲ēh.* The peculiar suffix is the result[25] of scribal error from *mal'āk̲ayik̲* with dittography of the following *h* (Nah. 3:1). Textual emendation according to the LXX[26] is now no longer advisable considering the evidence of 4QpNah 2:1. First, the traditional translation of *hik̲rattî . . . ,* "I will cut off your prey from the earth," is in error. The phrase is parallel to *ûk̲ᵉpîrayik̲ tō'k̲al ḥāreb̲.* Just as the young lions devour their prey, so the tables will be turned, and the sword of Yahweh will devour the lions and cut them off from their prey. Yahweh will not destroy the prey, but the lions (i.e., the Assyrian army). The sword of Yahweh both devours and cuts, and the object of these actions is the same in both phrases: the young lions. Thus the object of both *tō'k̲al* and *wᵉhik̲rattî* is *kᵉpîrayik̲.* Yahweh "cuts off" with his sword which "devours." The phrase *mē'ereṣ ṭarpēk̲* is a construct chain.

Second, Nah. 2:14(13) is thematically related to 3:15, which reads: *šām tō'k̲ᵉlēk̲ 'ēš*

---

24. Cf. H. Wildberger, *Jesaja 13–27. BK,* X/2 (1978), 573ff.
25. So *GK,* §91l.
26. So *KBL*³; K. Elliger, *Das Buch der zwölf Kleinen Propheten, II: Nahum. ATD,* XXV (⁸1982).

takrîtēk ḥereb tō'kelēk kayyāleq, "There fire will devour you, sword will cut you off. It will devour you like a locust." Here, too, the object of the verbs is "you," i.e., not the prey, but the Assyrian army.

Third, there is a thematic chiasm in the verse. The metaphor with which Nahum begins the oracle reappears in the phrases *ûkepîrayik . . . ḥāreb* and *wehikrattî . . . ṭarpēk.* This chiastic pair is surrounded by *wehib'artî . . . rikbāh* and *welō' . . . mal'ākēkēh.* The expressions *rikbāh,* "chariots," and *mal'ākēkēh,* "messengers," link the metaphor with practical reality. The metaphor is thus concerned not with the destruction of Assyria in general, but of its military units. Hence *mal'ākēkēh* represent military heralds who blow their trumpets at the beginning of the battle, thereby initiating various tactical maneuvers.

The use of political envoys continues into the Persian period, and their basic function does not change. Neh. 6:3-9 records the interchange of messengers between Nehemiah and Sanballat. Among Sanballat's messages, the last was an "open letter" (*'iggeret petûḥâ,* v. 5) delivered by his "servant" *(na'ar).* While *na'ar* apparently refers to the status of this person, *mal'āk* refers to his function.

Of the 48 occurrences of the plural indefinite, 46 refer to political envoys, to "legates." Since the verb *šlḥ* appears 45 times, the standard idiom would seem to be *šlḥ mal'āk.* The *mal'ākîm* thus are officers of the government who are specifically trained to communicate between heads of state concerning war, political alliances, and other matters important to the administration of the state.

V. Divine Envoys.

1. *General.* A messenger of God is one whose message originates from and who is sent by God; this category includes both prophets and priests. Of the 120 occurrences of *mal'āk* as an envoy of God, the singular form clearly predominates (only 15 pl. forms occur). God sends his heavenly and earthly envoys one by one; a plurality of messengers is not necessary, since God himself protects both his messengers and his message (cf. Jer. 1:7f.).[27]

2. *Prophets.* The designation *mal'āk* is parallel to *nābî',* "prophet" (once in the sg., 4 times in the pl.). Haggai is called a "prophet" (Hag. 1:3) and *mal'āk YHWH* (v. 13). The passage reveals two basic concepts concerning prophets: prophets are fundamentally messengers sent by Yahweh; and they are commissioned to proclaim the message of their superior (Yahweh), not their own message. Thus, in the passage which recounts Jeremiah's call (Jer. 1:4-10), Yahweh declares: "For you shall go to all to whom I send you, and you shall speak whatever I command you" (v. 7). God's words are put into the mouth of the prophet (v. 9). Thus both prophets and messengers have the same function: they are sent by their superior to speak *his* words.

The pl. *mal'ākîm* refers to prophets in 2 Ch. 36:15f.; Isa. 44:26; Ezk. 30:9. In 2 Ch. 36:15f., the Chronicler summarizes the reasons for Judah's destruction: Yahweh con-

---

27. In contrast with messengers sent by human beings, see IV.1 above.

tinually sent his word to the people by "his messengers" (*mal'āḵāw,* v. 15), but the people mocked the "messengers of God" (*mal'ᵃḵê hā'ᵉlōhîm,* v. 16), despised his words, and scoffed at "his prophets" (*nᵉḇî'āw,* v. 16). Thus the *mal'āḵ* as a *nāḇî'* speaks God's word, not his own, and the term *nāḇî'* is the title for the one who functions as a *mal'āḵ* by proclaiming God's word.

In Isa. 44:24-28, the prophet pronounces God's decree to restore Jerusalem through Cyrus. In v. 26a, in a section proclaiming the glory of Yahweh,[28] Yahweh reveals himself as *mēqîm dᵉḇar ʿᵃḇāḏāw* (MT *ʿaḇdô*) *waʿᵃṣaṯ mal'āḵāw yašlîm,* "who confirms the word of his servants (following LXX), and performs the counsel of his messengers." In contrast to *'ôṯôṯ baddîm,* "omens of soothsayers," *qôsᵉmîm,* "diviners," and *ḥᵃḵāmîm,* "the wise" (v. 25), *ʿᵃḇāḏāw* and *mal'āḵāw* clearly refer to prophets. Yahweh confirms the message of the prophets because the prophet speaks what Yahweh orders him to speak. When the *mal'āḵîm* say that Yahweh will rebuild Jerusalem and the temple, it will happen because the message comes from Yahweh. The terms *ʿᵃḇāḏāw* and *mal'āḵāw* are interchangeable, the former referring to status, the latter to function.

Prophets appear as political *mal'āḵîm* in Ezk. 30:9 (the situation being similar to that discussed above regarding Isa. 18). They are sent out to pronounce doom upon the Egyptians and those who support them.

The term *mal'āḵî* in Mal. 1:1 may be a personal name, the singular form of *mal'āḵ* with the 1st person singular suffix, "my messenger," i.e., "my prophet" (cf. Mal. 3:1); or an apocopated form of *mal'āḵ YHWH,* "messenger of Yahweh" (cf. Hag. 1:13); or, following the LXX versions of Aquila, Symmachus, and Theodotion (Μαλαχιας, *Malachias*), a clausal name *mal'ᵃḵîyâ,* "my messenger is Yahweh,"[29] or perhaps better "my [guardian] angel is Yahweh"[30] or "sent by Yahweh."[31] This debate has never been settled.

If the word is a common noun, referring to a prophet, we would expect the 3rd person masculine singular suffix to be used: "the oracle of the word of Yahweh to Israel through his messenger." This is a superscript, an editorial notation, and grammatical agreement would be appropriate. As an apocopation, *mal'āḵî* is suspect because of the lack of parallel occurrences. Therefore it can only be interpreted as the clausal name or personal name "my messenger," deriving from the appellative.

3. *Priests.* There are 2 instances of *mal'āḵ* as priest. Mal. 2:6f. reads: "True torah was in his mouth, and no wrong was found on his lips. He walked with me in peace and justice, and he turned many from evil. For from the lips of a priest *(kōhēn)* they guard knowledge, and they seek torah from his mouth, for he is the messenger *(mal'āḵ)* of Yahweh of hosts."

This passage not only indicates the use of *mal'āḵ* for *kōhēn,* but shows in detail the

---

28. → כבוד *kāḇôḏ* (VII, 22-38).
29. Cf. G. J. Botterweck, "Jakob habe ich lieb — Esau hasse ich," *BiLe,* 1 (1960), 28.
30. H. Junker, *Die zwölf kleinen Propheten. HS,* VIII/3 (1938), *in loc.*
31. W. Rudolph, *Haggai — Sacharja 1–8 — Sacharja 9–14 — Maleachi. KAT,* XIII/4 (1976).

role of the priest as a messenger of Yahweh. He teaches the torah (note the chiasm: *b^epîhû . . . biśpāṯāw . . . śiptê . . . mippîhû,* which emphasizes oral communication of the torah), his teaching is less prophetic word than traditional wisdom and truth, the *da'aṯ*[32] by which people live. As a priest he is very close to God (Mal. 2:6b), and his instruction resulted in turning many from evil ways. Next to this priestly aspect, his activity is designated as that of a *mal'āk̲,* i.e., that of delivering the message of his superior, not his own message. As *mal'āk̲* he delivers it; as *kōhēn* he guards and transmits it.

The author of Ecclesiastes counsels his audience against the thoughtless participation in religious observances, particularly the making of precipitous vows upon entering the house of God (Eccl. 4:17–5:6[5:1-7]). In this context he admonishes: "Do not let your mouth lead you into sin, and do not [then] say to the messenger that it was a mistake." The author is emphasizing one's obligation to fulfill one's vows; it is a sin not to make good on a commitment, and then even to offer cheap excuses. The *mal'āk̲* is the priest or temple official charged with collecting on the vow.

4. *mal'ak̲ YHWH / mal'ak̲ '^elōhîm.* These two phrases are construct chains occurring 56 and 10 times respectively. In addition, *mal'^ak̲ê '^elōhîm* appears 3 times, and *mal'ak̲ habb^erîṯ* (Mal. 3:1) and *mal'ak̲ pānāw* (Isa. 63:9) once each. Although the word *mal'āk̲* is not always in construct with the divine name when it refers to angels, the context in these situations suggests this meaning. Furthermore, this combination is at least implied in 11 additional passages; *mal'āk̲* is associated another 13 times with God by means of a suffix, and, finally, can be shown another 24 times to refer to the "*the* angel [of God]."[33] Several areas of concentration emerge: Gen. 16, 22; Nu. 22; Jgs. 6, 13; 2 S. 24 par. 1 Ch. 21; 1 K. 19; 2 K. 1; 19 par. Isa. 37 par. 2 Ch. 32; Zec. 1–6, 12; Mal. 2, 3. It also frequently occurs in the traditions surrounding the exodus and conquest (e.g., Ex. 23, 32, 33; Jgs. 2).[34]

The use of *mal'āk̲* in Zec. 1:9–6:5 illustrates that one of the primary functions of the angel of God is to communicate God's message, especially to his prophets, who themselves are messengers to humankind (cf. 1 K. 13:18). The angel repeatedly "speaks" to Zechariah (Zec. 1:11,12; 3:4,6; cf. Gen. 16:7f.,9,10f.).

Nonetheless, the function of the angel of Yahweh goes beyond the communication of God's message. He is not only a messenger delivering God's words, but is also a minister or agent authorized to perform them. Thus he is sent by God to go before Abraham's servant (Gen. 24:7,40), to go before Israel (Ex. 23:20,23; 32:2,34), to deliver them (Nu. 20:16), and to lead them into the land of Canaan (Ex. 23:20; cf. Mal. 3:1, where God's angel will clear the way before him by punishing sinners, a moralizing reappearance of the exodus motif). The angel protects the Israelites at the Reed Sea (Ex. 14:19), resists Balaam (Nu. 22:22), helps Elijah (1 K. 19:7), and smites the foes

32. → ידע *yāḏa'* (V, 448-481).
33. Documentation in Röttger, 8f.
34. For further details, see *ibid.,* 6f.

of Israel (2 K. 19:35 par. Isa. 37:36). These examples illustrate that in the religious thought of Israel the angel of Yahweh was understood as the agent of Yahweh's assistance to Israel. Although the notion of angels was otherwise very much associated with fear, the angel of Yahweh was understood not as Israel's enemy, but as the benefactor sent to help Israel. The appearance of angels is welcomed (1 S. 29:9), their wisdom extolled (2 S. 14:17,20; 19:27). From the passage in 2 S. 14 it is apparent that one of the highest compliments one can pay the king is to compare him favorably to the angel of Yahweh. According to Zec. 12:8, at the restoration of Israel the house of David will be compared with the angel of Yahweh. Nor was this basically positive estimation of the angel of Yahweh mitigated by the fact that this angel could also assume the role of the *mašḥîṯ,* the "destroyer."[35]

Another concept of the angel of Yahweh is expressed in Israel's blessing of Joseph (Gen. 48:15f.): "The God before whom my fathers Abraham and Isaac walked, the God who has led me throughout my life to this day, the angel, the one who has redeemed me from all evil." The *mal'āk̲* is the *gō'ēl;*[36] he redeems the elect from all evil (Isa. 63:9) and avenges the blood of those who are persecuted (Ps. 35:4-6). This notion also informs the understanding of the *mal'āk̲* in the Exodus Narrative.

In the narrative of Sennacherib's siege of Jerusalem (2 K. 19:35 par. Isa. 37:36; 2 Ch. 32:21), Yahweh's agent who destroys the Assyrian army is called the *mal'ak̲ YHWH:* he "goes out" *(yṣ')* and "smites" *(nkh,* hiphil); Yahweh "sends" *(šlḥ)* him and he "destroys" *(kḥd).* The angel of Yahweh is the instrument of Yahweh's favor to Israel, and he acts by redeeming, protecting, and defending them. The Chronicler, by emphasizing particularly the sending *(šlḥ),* may be discouraging any identification of the angel with Yahweh himself.

The only example of the angel of Yahweh turning against Israel occurs in 2 S. 24 par. 1 Ch. 21, where the angel of God is the agent of God's punishment upon David because of his census. Yahweh sent a plague *(deb̲er)* upon Israel, but when the angel stretched forth his hand to destroy Jerusalem, Yahweh commanded the "destroying angel" *(mal'ak̲ hammašḥîṯ; mal'ak̲ hammakkeh)* to stop (2 S. 24:15f. par. 1 Ch. 21:14f.).

The parallel in 1 Ch. 21 is important for another reason: it substantiates an earlier perception of the angel of Yahweh as a being of superhuman size and strength. David was able to see the destroying angel (v. 16) "standing between earth and heaven, and in his hand a drawn sword stretched out over Jerusalem."

In earlier passages, angels speak to human beings from the heavens (Gen. 21:17; 22:11,15), from fire (Ex. 3:2), or in dreams (Gen. 28:12; 31:11). They appear to animals as well as to human beings (Nu. 22), often disappear from view (Jgs. 6:21; 13:21), and are often unrecognized as angels by those to whom they are sent (Jgs. 13). They ascend to heaven in fire (Jgs. 13:20), and ascend and descend on a ladder (Gen. 28:12). These passages illustrate that the angel of Yahweh often performs his tasks with abilities beyond those of human beings.

---

35. See discussion below.
36. → גאל *gā'al* (II, 350-55).

In some passages it is no longer possible to distinguish God from his *mal'āḵ* in interactions with human beings. Gerhard von Rad has disclosed a system in this apparently inconsistent usage: "When the reference is to God apart from man, Yahweh is used; when God enters the apperception of man, the *[mal'āḵ YHWH]* is introduced."[37] Several examples can illustrate this. In Gen. 16:7-14 (J), Yahweh hears the cry of Hagar and sends the *mal'aḵ YHWH* to communicate with her directly. After the angel has communicated with her, she calls the name of Yahweh: "You are the God who sees me!" She then cries: "I have indeed seen God" (read *'ᵉlōhîm* contra MT *hᵃlōm*). Yet the actual intercessor with Hagar is the angel of Yahweh, not Yahweh himself. Hagar's comment that she has seen an *'ᵉlōhîm* may indicate that she is herself clear about having seen "a divine being" rather than God himself. The same relationship appears in the Elohistic narrative. According to Gen. 21:15-21, God hears the cry of Ishmael; the angel of God calls to Hagar from heaven; and God himself opens her eyes.

God tested Abraham by asking him to sacrifice Isaac (Gen. 22:1-19), but it is the angel of Yahweh who spoke to Abraham from heaven (vv. 11,15); according to v. 1, however, the initial command was given by *'ᵉlōhîm.* Since in Gen. 22:1-19 one cannot determine the E source with any certainty,[38] *'ᵉlōhîm* may very well be a generic term here for "a divine being." Be that as it may, the author did not distinguish between God who tested and the angel who spoke the command, though this does not mean that the two are to be identified. In any case, it does not appear that distinctions between various strata and sources can resolve this problem in Gen. 22.[39]

According to Gen. 31:1-16, Yahweh commanded Jacob to leave Laban and return to his homeland (v. 3). It is Jacob's belief, however, that the command is given by the *mal'aḵ 'ᵉlōhîm* (v. 11,13).

It is the *mal'aḵ YHWH* who speaks to the people concerning their disregard of the covenant stipulations (Jgs. 2:1,4), and who appeared to the wife of Manoah (Jgs. 13:2-25), though after the appearance of the angel she reports that she has seen a "man of God" *('îš 'ᵉlōhîm),* like the appearance of the angel of God (v. 6). Manoah entreated Yahweh to send the *'îš 'ᵉlōhîm* again (v. 8); God listened, and the *mal'aḵ hā'ᵉlōhîm* appeared again (v. 9). After repeated appearances and conversations with Manoah and his wife, the *mal'aḵ YHWH* ascended in the flame of the altar (v. 20) and appeared no more (v. 21). Manoah's response to his wife was: "We shall surely die, for we have seen *'ᵉlōhîm.*" Either Manoah was mistaken (they did not see God because they did not die), or he had seen "only" a divine being *('ᵉlōhîm).* Jgs. 13 shows with marvelous clarity the overlapping terminology, and further examples can be found in Gen. 32:22-32(21-31); 2 S. 24:17; Hos. 12:5(4); Zec. 1:9–6:5.

The question of the relationship between Yahweh and his angel would not be complete without a discussion of Ex. 3. The *mal'aḵ YHWH* appeared to Moses in a flame of fire from the midst of a bush (Ex. 3:2; cf. Jgs. 13:20). But throughout the

---

37. *TDNT,* I, 77.
38. C. Westermann, *Genesis 12–36* (Eng. trans., Minneapolis, 1985), 354, 360f.
39. Cf. *ibid.,* 354f., contra R. Kilian, *Isaaks Opferung. SBS,* 44 (1970), and Röttger.

subsequent dialogue the voice from the bush is referred to as Yahweh (Ex. 3:4,7) or *'elōhîm* (vv. 11,13,15). Moses hides his face from *'elōhîm* (v. 6). Thus this is the only place where the *mal'āḵ* is only at the very beginning of the narrative.

This terminological confusion might be explained in three ways.

(1) Yahweh might have transmitted his message to Moses by his *mal'āḵ,* but the author used the terms Yahweh and *'elōhîm* since in his opinion the message came directly from God. The occurrence of *mal'āḵ* at the beginning of the narrative qualifies the subsequent use of Yahweh and *'elōhîm.*

(2) The importance of the call of Moses, the initiation of God's personal relationship with Israel, and the revealing of God's personal name did not allow the narrative to be dominated by a *mal'āḵ.* The significance of the narrative itself required the direct intervention of God.

(3) Yahweh himself spoke to Moses, but since Moses was not allowed to see him, the intercession of the *mal'āḵ* was necessary.

Freedman-Willoughby

Recent interpretation does not consider Ex. 3 to be a literary unity,[40] so an identification of sources should to a large extent resolve the confusion in Ex. 3. Werner H. Schmidt asserts that without argumentation concerning the divine name an identification of sources succinctly shows that the mention of Yahweh does indeed come from J, and the mention of *'elōhîm* from E. The issue then focuses on v. 2a, which Schmidt attributes to J. H. Röttger, however, considers the *mal'aḵ YHWH* to be a secondary insertion resulting quite consistently from the intention of the Elohist. "Here the Elohistic redactor establishes an element of continuity between the time of the patriarchs and that of the people of Israel, simultaneously anticipating the role of the *mal'āḵ* in the events of the exodus."[41] Such longitudinal argumentation, however, is not compelling from the perspective of literary criticism, so that the juxtaposition of *mal'aḵ YHWH* and *'elōhîm* remains unresolved. Peter Weimar[42] has refined Schmidt's literary critical position, suggesting that the Yahwist is at work in v. 2a anticipating in an interpretive manner the second part of the bush scene as a theophany of Yahweh. Werner Fuss[43] presents the same literary critical distinctions, but views the mention of the messenger as a more forceful emphasis on Yahweh's transcendence by the redactor. Although this probably takes the argument in the right direction, it does not contradict Claus Westermann's clear statement[44] that the shift between Yahweh and *mal'aḵ YHWH* did not result from any theological reflection, but rather "is much more a case of narrative transmission of actual and varied experience of an encounter in which the messenger pronounced the oracle that changed the course of events."

Fabry

---

40. Cf. the resolute position of W. H. Schmidt, *Exodus 1–6. BK,* II/1 (1988), 106-10.
41. P. 89.
42. *Die Berufung des Mose. OBO,* 32 (1980), 233.
43. *Die deuteronomistische Pentateuchredaktion in Exodus 3–17. BZAW,* 126 (1972), 26.
44. *Genesis 12–36,* excursus on "The Messenger of God (מלאך יהוה) in the OT," 243.

Ex. 23, 33 shed additional light on the divine manifestation in Ex. 3. Ex. 23:20-22a read: "I am sending an angel in front of you to guard you . . . listen to his voice . . . for my name is in him. But if you completely obey him and do all that I say. . . ." The importance of this passage for the interpretation of Ex. 3 is twofold. The *mal'aḵ YHWH* is so closely associated with Yahweh that Yahweh's name is in him. When Moses speaks with God, he obeys the voice of the *mal'āḵ*. Thus the *mal'aḵ YHWH* is the intermediary between God and human beings. When God speaks, he speaks through the angel bearing his name. When a person hears God's commands through this mediator, he is to comply fully, for the message of the *mal'āḵ* is Yahweh's message. The *mal'āḵ* is "not a figure or representative or mode of God's manifestation . . . he is only the one who actually engages in the encounter."[45] He approaches the person with the authority, commission, and name of Yahweh.

Finally, Ex. 33 should be examined briefly. Although the narrative states that Yahweh spoke to Moses "face to face" (v. 11), the context clearly indicates that the manifestation of the divine presence here was the function of the "pillar of cloud" (vv. 9,10). The entire narrative emphasizes as forcefully as possible that any direct experience of God is fatal for a human being, even for Moses, and that this experience must be mediated by a mitigation of such immediacy. In Ex. 33, such means include fire, cloud, and the *mal'āḵ*.

From these passages it is evident that the *mal'aḵ YHWH* is closely associated with Yahweh in name, authority, and message, and that he represents Yahweh in the human realm, whereas Yahweh's own immediacy is actualized in realms outside human perception.

Freedman-Willoughby

The shift between Yahweh and *mal'aḵ YHWH* does not involve the substitution of an anthropomorphic portrayal of the deity by theological speculation as suggested by the interpolation theory,[46] but rather the living portrayal of an encounter with God, which because of the dangers of an immediate theophany was also understood as having been mediated in some way. As is the case in the secular sphere regarding the *mal'āḵ*, the identification of the party issuing the commission and the messenger is customary.[47] This is essentially the revelation hypothesis as already proposed by Hubert Junker,[48] according to which "the 'angel of Yahweh,' as the companion and bearer of Yahweh's glory, reveals to human beings through his appearance Yahweh's own presence, though Yahweh himself remains mysteriously invisible."[49] This interpretation also closely approximates the representation theory as developed by Jerome and Augustine,[50] according to which the angel as Yahweh's creature, by virtue of his special commission

45. Schmidt, 290, with W. Zimmerli.
46. M. J. Lagrange, "L'Ange de Jahvé," *RB*, 12 (1903), 212-225.
47. Cf. Ficker, 907.
48. *Genesis. EB*, I (^{2}1955), 76f.
49. Cf. also Gross, 35.
50. Cf. J. Rybinski, *Der Mal'akh Jahwe* (Paderborn, 1929).

and endowed with divine authority, appears as Yahweh's representative. This theory was modified by Fridolin Stier[51] into the vizier theory. Interpretations using function as their point of departure doubtlessly do better justice to the biblical evidence than theories that speculate on essence, among which one should mention the identity theory (the *mal'āḵ* and Yahweh are identical)[52] and the hypostasis theory (which views the *mal'āḵ* as an hypostasis of Yahweh),[53] modified as the logos theory (as early as the church fathers). All these theories must be measured by how well they address the messenger's function, for "God is present not in the messenger, but in the message."[54]

Fabry

The term *mal'aḵ YHWH* / *'ᵉlōhîm* denotes in mythic contexts the retainers of God. They are the heavenly beings who accompany him, praise him, and are present in his court. They are his hosts[55] (Ps. 103:20; 148:2), his servants (*'eḇeḏ*)[56] (Job 4:18, the term denoting status more than function), who guard the righteous (Ps. 34:8[7]; 91:11) and punish the wicked (Ps. 78:49; Prov. 16:14). In addition to the *mal'āḵîm,* this court also includes the cherubim[57] and seraphim;[58] a more difficult question is that of the *bᵉnê 'ᵉlōhîm ('ēlîm).*[59] The functions of this heavenly court emerge from several psalms. Ps. 103:20f.: "Bless Yahweh, O you his angels, you mighty warriors who perform his word. Bless Yahweh, all his hosts, his ministers that do his will!" Ps. 104:4 offers a further perspective: "Who makes the winds his messengers *(mal'āḵāw),* and the flaming fire his servants *(mᵉšārᵉṯāw).*" The traditional interpretation[60] understands the messengers and servants as metaphors for wind and fire, and characterizes them as being obedient to God. This translation, however, is unintelligible embedded as it is in the evocation of a myth of traversing the sky (cf. Ps. 104:3). Rather, the translation should be: "Who with his retainers makes the winds kindle with fire." The messengers and servants together with God set the wind's activity into motion; as companions of the sun-god in pulling the sun across the skies with his chariot, they set the winds on fire. Also in Ps. 104:2 one can readily imagine God's messengers stretching out the heavens, similar to Isa. 42:5, "who created the heavens and stretched them out."[61] This interpretation of Ps. 104:4 is supported by the striking accumulation of participles in vv.

---

51. *Gott und sein Engel im AT. ATA,* 12/2 (1934).
52. Cf. B. Stein, "Der Engel des Auszugs," *Bibl,* 19 (1938), 286-307.
53. Cf. G. van der Leeuw, *Religion in Essence and Manifestation* (Eng. trans., London, 1938), 141-46; A. Lods, "L'Ange de Yahvé et l''âme extérieure,'" *Studien zur semitischen Philologie und Religionsgeschichte. Festschrift J. Wellhausen. BZAW,* 27 (1914), 263-278.
54. Westermann, *Genesis 12–36,* 244.
55. → צבאת *ṣᵉḇā'ōṯ.*
56. → עבד *'āḇaḏ.*
57. → כרוב *kᵉrûḇ* (307-319).
58. → שׂרף *śārāp.*
59. Cf. F. Dexinger, *Sturz der Göttersöhne; oder, Engel vor der Sintflut? WBTh,* 13 (1966).
60. Cf. H.-J. Kraus, *Psalms 60-150* (Eng. trans., Minneapolis, 1989), 295.
61. Cf., however, the different view held by K. Elliger, *Deuterojesaja. BK,* XI/1 (1978), 222, 231f.

2-4 (*'ōṭeh-'ôr, nôṭeh šāmayîm, 'ōśeh . . rûḥôṯ*). The expression *'ēš lōhēṭ* (v. 4b) corresponds structurally and grammatically. Yahweh is the subject of *lōhēṭ,* i.e., *lōhēṭ* does not function as the predicate of *'ēš* (it would have to be a fem. ptcp.). The winds are thus set ablaze with the fire of Yahweh's chariot as he, accompanied by his angels, traverses the sky.

Freedman-Willoughby

This new interpretation presupposes a comprehensive spectrum of mythological motifs behind the text of Ps. 104, though this need not contradict the clear focus of the psalm on the theology of creation. This interpretation does not, however, explain syntactically the inversion involving *'ēš lōhēṭ,* and it overlooks the fact that for the meaning "ignite, set ablaze" actually the piel participle would be expected (cf. Job 41:13[21]). Textual corruption may be a factor here, as suggested already by the LXX and Qumran (1QH 1:11).

Fabry

Two other passages are important for an understanding of the role and function of the *mal'aḵ YHWH* because they focus on a particular angel among the hosts of the heavenly court. Elihu's first speech in Job 33:22-25 reads: "His soul draws near to the pit, and his life to those who bring death, unless there is for him an angel, a defender ("intercessor, spokesman"[62]), one of a thousand to declare to a person his rights, and he is kind to him and says, 'Deliver him from going down into the Pit; I have found a ransom for him; let his flesh become plump with youth; let him return to the days of his youthful vigor." The *mal'āḵ* here represents the heavenly defender in Yahweh's court. He steps in for the accused and argues for a verdict of acquittal by enumerating what the man has a right to in the way of justice and fair treatment and delivers him by offering a ransom. Yahweh listens, is convinced by the argument, and restores the man's health. The term *mēlîṣ* as a characterization of the *mal'āḵ* is not quite clear. In Gen. 42:23, it means "interpreter," so that Job 33:22-25 might be thinking of the "interpreting angel" (*angelus interpres*) familiar from apocalyptic and rabbinic writings (cf. Zec.1–6).[63] Here the *mēlîṣ* is the heavenly defense attorney who argues a person's case before Yahweh (and against Satan).

The *mal'āḵ* appears with the opposite function in Mal. 3:1-5. Yahweh intends to send his messenger, the "messenger of the covenant" (*mal'aḵ habbᵉrîṯ*), to refine and purify the sons of Levi and bring testimony against sorcerers, adulterers, those who swear falsely, and those who oppress the poor. Here the *mal'āḵ* (like Satan) functions as the heavenly prosecutor who pleads for a guilty verdict against those who disobey the covenant.

Prov. 16:14 presents the *mal'āḵ* in the role of an outsider: "The king's anger is like

---

62. → ליץ *lyṣ* III (VII, 550-52).

63. Cf. C. Westermann, *God's Angels Need No Wings* (Eng. trans., Philadelphia, 1979), 117-124; P. Schäfer, *Rivalität zwischen Engeln und Menschen. SJ,* 8 (1975), 10-18.

a messenger of death, but a wise man will appease it." The concept of the *mal'aḵ māweṯ* derives from the familiar mythic notion of the summons to meet one's fate, just as Mot, the god of the underworld, sends messengers to bring victims to him. The association with the king's wrath is apparent, for the anger of the king is equated with a sentence of death (cf. Prov. 19:12; 20:2). Like the angel of death, the "angels of evil" *(mal'ᵃḵê rā'îm)* are agents of Yahweh's wrath and indignation (cf. Ps. 78:49).

VI. Metaphorical Usage. The "servant" in Deutero-Isaiah is almost always Israel rather than a prophet or some other individual. In Isa. 42:19, *'aḇdî, mal'āḵî,* and *mᵉšullām* are parallel terms referring to the blind servant Israel. Here the terms "servant" and "messenger" are interchangeable, the former referring to status, the latter to function. The role of Israel as a *mal'āḵ* is broader than merely its function as messenger. Israel is Yahweh's instrument, a people performing his word and representing his divine love and commitment to human beings.

Freedman-Willoughby

VII. Qumran. The *mal'āḵ* appears *ca.* 50 times in the Qumran writings, with an abundance of synonymous terms as well, which can function as genuine replacements *('ēlîm, bᵉnê šāmayim, mᵉlāḵîm, qᵉḏôšîm, rûḥôṯ, gibbôrîm, kᵉrûḇîm, ṣîrîm, nᵉśî'îm, rā'šîm, kōhᵃnîm,* and *mᵉšārᵉṯîm),* as well as the names of specific angels.[64] This terminological multiplicity indicates the presence of a well-defined Qumran-Essene angelology,[65] something underscored by the existence of what is known as the "angelic liturgy" (4QŠirᵇ). The doctrine of angels is an essential component of Qumran-Essene ecclesiology insofar as the community understood itself in various respects as a fellowship with these angels.[66] This informed first of all the community's self-understanding as an eschatological alliance of warriors: not only is the encampment itself sanctified by the presence of angels (1QM 7:1-17; in contrast to Dt. 23:15[14], God's presence in the camp is replaced by the that of the angels), the Qumranites also viewed the angels as fellow warriors (1QM 12:4,8; cf. 4Q491-495 and *passim*). Furthermore, the community considered itself to be in liturgical fellowship with the angels (1QSa 2:8; 1QSb 4:22-26, with an interesting equivalency between the priest of the community and the "Angel of the Presence"; 1QH 6:13; 4Q511 35:4) in their common worship of God in the community as the new temple.

Consistent with the dualism of the Qumran-Essene worldview, the world of angels was viewed as being divided into two realms. The first is that of Belial as the "Angel of Malevolence" (*mal'aḵ maśṭēmâ,* 1QM 13:11), with his retinue, the "angels of destruction" (*mal'ᵃḵê ḥeḇel,* 1QM 1:15; 13:12; CD 2:6; 4Q510 1:5 par. Lilith) and the

---

64. Cf. J. Strugnell, "The Angelic Liturgy at Qumrân: 4Q Serek šîrôt 'ôlat haššabbāt," *Congress Volume, Oxford 1959. SVT,* 7 (1960), 318-345, esp. 331ff.

65. Cf. F. Nötscher, "Geist und Geister in den Texten von Qumran," *Vom Alten zum NT. BBB,* 17 (1962), 175-187; J. A. Fitzmyer, "A Feature of Qumrân Angelology and the Angels of 1 Cor. xi.10," *NTS,* 4 (1957/58), 48-58; M. Delcor, "Qumran angélologie," *DBS,* IX, 970ff.

66. Cf. Schäfer, 33-40.

"angel of darkness" (*mal'aḵ ḥôšeḵ,* 1QS 3:20) against which a person could effectively protect himself only through obedience to the Torah (CD 16:5). The other realm is that of God with the "Angels of Holiness" (*mal'^aḵê qôḏeš,* 1QSa 2:8; 1QSb 3:6; 1QM 7:6), the "Angel of his Truth" (*mal'aḵ '^amittô,* 1QS 3:24), and the "angels of the luminaries of his glory" (*ml'k m'wrwt kbwdw,* 4Q511 2 I 8; 20 I 2). They function to assist and to rescue (1QM 13:14; 17:6). That they are viewed as preexistent beings is attested by their presence at creation (11QtgJob 30:5). They participate in God's plans (1QM 10:11) and glorify his name (1QM 12:1; 4QDibHam 7:6).

Fabry

מְלָאכָה *m^elā'kâ*

Contents: I. The Root and Cognates. II. Definition: 1. Skilled Work; 2. Project; 3. Manufacture; 4. Commission or Business. III. Summary. IV. Qumran.

I. The Root and Cognates. The root of *m^elā'kâ* is *l'k,* which, although unattested in Hebrew in its verbal form, is attested in other Semitic languages, e.g., Ugar. *làak,* "to send,"[1] Arab. *la'aka* and *'alaka,* "to send," and Ethiop. *la'aka,* "to send (a message)." Nominal derivatives in these languages show the extension of the meaning "to send": Ugar. *ml'k,* "messenger,"[2] *ml'kt,* "mission, embassy,"[3] Arab. *mal'ak,* "angel, messenger, envoy," and Ethiop. *mal'ak,* "angel, messenger." Hebrew derivatives besides *m^elā'kâ* include → מלאך *mal'āḵ,* "messenger, angel," and *mal'āḵûṯ,* "mission, commission, message" (Hag. 1:13). In addition to the foregoing derivatives, Phoenician and Punic exhibit *ml'kt* and *mlkt,* "work."[4]

The word *m^elā'kâ* occurs 166 times in the OT in its various forms. Even its distribution in the OT shows that the word is closely associated with work in the sanctuary or involving sacred objects (62 occurrences in the Pentateuch, 33 of those in Ex. 31ff.; 13 in Lev. 23; 7 in Nu. 8). The Deuteronomistic history uses it 19 times (primarily in the account of the temple construction in 1 K. 6f.), the Chronicler 63 times (primarily

---

m^elā'kâ. W. F. Albright, "Specimens of Late Ugaritic Prose," *BASOR,* 150 (1958), 36-38; Z. Ben-Ḥayyim, "Word Studies II," *H. Yalon Memorial Volume* (Jerusalem, 1974), 46; E. L. Greenstein, "Trans-Semitic Idiomatic Equivalency and the Derivation of Hebrew *ml'kh,*" *UF,* 11 (1979), 329-336; J. Milgrom, *Studies in Levitical Terminology, I: The Encroacher and the Levite: The Term 'Abodah, UCPNES,* 14 (1970); A. Silitonga, *The Comprehension of Work (Mela'kah) in the OT* (diss., South East Asia Graduate School of Theology, Singapore, 1974).

1. *KTU,* 1.4 V, 41, 42; VII, 45; 1.5 IV, 23, 24; 1.13, 27; 1.14 III, 19, 20; 1.24, 16; 2.10, 10; 2.14, 7; 2.26, 4; 2.31, 43; 2.42, 12; 2.63, 7, 10, 13.
2. E.g., *ibid.,* 1.14 III, 20, 33; VI, 35.
3. *Ibid.,* 2.17, 7; 2.23, 3; 2.31, 49; 2.33, 35.
4. *DISO,* 151.

in the context of the temple construction and renovation in 1 Ch. 22ff.; 2 Ch. 24, 34). The term occurs only sporadically in the prophetic and wisdom literature.

Its meanings can be subdivided into four areas: (1) skilled work, craftsmanship; (2) general work (including physical labor); (3) the result of work, manufacture, movable property; (4) mission, commission, errand, or business.

The association between the verb "to send" and the noun "work" derives from a postulated **ml'kt yd,* analogous to *mišlaḥ yāḏ* (e.g., Dt. 12:7,18), "work of the hands," lit. "the outstretching of one's hand,"[5] semantically equivalent to Akk. *šipir idim/qāti(m),* "work of the hands."[6]

Sirach uses *mᵉlā'ḵâ* 6 times, generally with the meaning "labor, work" (Sir. 3:17; 4:29f.), "business" (37:11), or with the explicit connotation "toilsome labor," par. agricultural work in the field (7:15).

The LXX translates fairly consistently with *érgon* (127 times) or something similar, although it occasionally interprets it by *latreutós* or *leitourgía, ephēmería,* or *kataskeuē* (once each).

II. Definition.

1. *Skilled Work.* The idea expressed by *mᵉlā'ḵâ* in the majority of cases in the OT is that of "work entailing skill" as opposed to work entailing physical labor *(ʿᵃḇôḏâ).*[7]

a. The types of skills encompassed by *mᵉlā'ḵâ* include: working in precious metals (Ex. 38:24), with precious stones (Ezk. 28:13), agricultural skill (1 Ch. 27:26; Prov. 24:27), working in ceramics (Jer. 18:3), navigation (Ps. 107:23), working with ropes (Jgs. 16:11), working in a royal function (Gen. 39:11; Est. 3:9; 9:3; Dnl. 8:27), cultic service (Jer. 48:10), bearing holy objects (Nu. 4:3), functioning as judges and officers (1 Ch. 26:29), executing a work suitable for God (1 Ch. 29:1), an occupation (Jon. 1:8),[8] planning and execution (1 Ch. 28:19; Ezr. 10:13), and executive prowess (1 K. 11:28).

God's works are skilled works: creation (the planning and skill of execution, Gen. 2:2f.; Ps. 73:28) and punishment of nations (Jer. 50:25).

b. One of the most instructive series of instances which demonstrate the semantic connotations of *mᵉlā'ḵâ* is that of the tabernacle and temple construction and the repairs made on the temple. Bezalel was full of "wisdom, understanding, knowledge and all craftsmanship" or "skill" (Ex. 31:3; 35:21,31). Hiram had the ability to perform skillful work with bronze (1 K. 7:14). Men "of wisdom" were those involved in the tent's construction (Ex. 36:4,8). Other skills represented in this series include: skill in working with stone, wood, and metals (Ex. 31:4,5; 35:33; 38:24; 1 K. 7:14,22; 1 Ch. 22:15,16; 29:5), textile work (Ex. 35:35), and making temple vessels (1 K. 7:40). Repairs of buildings also involve skill (2 K. 12:12,15,16[Eng. vv. 11,14,15];

5. So Ben-Ḥayyim.

6. E.g., CH, §188; D. D. Luckenbill, ed., *The Annals of Sennacherib. OrIP,* 2 (1924), 133; 79f. (Greenstein).

7. Cf. Milgrom, 60-87.

8. See II.4 below.

22:5,9; 2 Ch. 24:13; 34:10,12,13,17; Ezr. 3:8,9; Hag. 1:14). The general activity of building is viewed under the idea of skilled work (Ex. 39:43; 1 K. 7:51; 2 Ch. 4:11; 5:1; 8:16; Neh. 2:16).

c. One aspect of *mᵉlā'ḵâ* as skilled work is that of cultic tasks, especially well attested in the Chronicler's history (1 Ch. 9:13,19,33; 23:4,24; 26:30; 2 Ch. 13:10; Neh. 10:34[33]; 11:12,16,22; 13:10,30). A prime example of *mᵉlā'ḵâ* as cultic tasks is found in 2 Ch. 29:34, where the priests were too few to flay all the offerings, so the Levites helped them until *hammᵉlā'ḵâ,* "the cultic task," was finished. Some other types of cultic duties were the playing of musical instruments and singing (1 Ch. 9:33; 25:1; Neh. 13:10), guarding the thresholds (1 Ch. 9:19), and performing the most holy tasks (1 Ch. 6:34[49]).

The phrase *mᵉle'ḵeṯ ʿᵃḇôḏâ* (1 Ch. 9:13,19) means "cultic service." This is due to the Chronicler's transfer of the meaning of *ʿᵃḇôḏâ,* "physical labor," to "cult service, worship." Hence *mᵉle'ḵeṯ ʿᵃḇôḏâ* literally says "the skilled work of the cult service."[9] The understanding of the idiom occurs in this sense only in Chronicles, whereas the original meaning was "construction project"[10] or "occupational work."[11]

2. *Project.* The term *mᵉlā'ḵâ* is used in a more general sense to cover the whole spectrum of the idea of "work," from mental activities such as planning together to execution by skill and by physical labor. This general usage seems to be best rendered by the word "project."

a. The episodes of sanctuary construction and repair offer examples of the use of *mᵉlā'ḵâ* in this sense. Here, too, this signification is elucidated by the use of *mᵉlā'ḵâ* with *ʿᵃḇôḏâ,* "physical labor" or "execution." The phrase *ʿᵃḇōḏaṯ mᵉlā'ḵâ* means the "execution of the work" (Ex. 35:21,24; 36:1,3; 1 Ch. 28:13,20; 2 Ch. 24:12). The construction of the sanctuary is conceived of as the execution of a plan or project (Ex. 36:2,5,7; 40:33); so also the construction of Solomon's temple (1 K. 5:30[16]; 9:23; 1 Ch. 28:19,21; 29:1; 2 Ch. 8:16), the temple renovation of Ezra's time (Ezr. 2:69; cf. Neh. 7:70f.; Ezr. 3:8f.; 6:22), Nehemiah's wall building (Neh. 2:16; 4:5,9,10,11, 13,15,16[11,15,16,17,19,21,22]; 5:16; 6:3,9,16), and the repair work on the temple (2 Ch. 24:12f.; 34:10,12,13,17).

The meaning of "project" is also found in 2 Ch. 16:5, where Baasha stopped the project of building Ramah. Prov. 24:27 also conveys the idea of planning and executing, thus indicating a general work project. 1 S. 8:16 uses *mᵉlā'ḵâ* to mean the "king's projects" or "official works" (cf. 1 K. 9:23, although here [otherwise only 1 K. 5:30(16)] the "king's [Solomon's] project" might refer to *mas,* "compulsory service"; cf. the Akk. equivalent *šipar šarri*[12]). The work of creation can also be understood as a "project" (Gen. 2:2,3).

Thus in the earliest sources *mᵉlā'ḵâ* is used as a general term for work or project including both skilled work and planning and the physical labor attending its execution, while *ʿᵃḇôḏâ* refers exclusively to physical labor. In postexilic texts *ʿᵃḇôḏâ* takes on

9. Cf. Milgrom, §72.
10. Cf. II.2.a below.
11. Cf. II.2.b below.
12. Middle Assyrian laws, A, §§18, 19, 40, cited in Greenstein.

the meaning of "cult service" and "worship" (e.g., 1 Ch. 6:17[32]; 23:28-32; 2 Ch. 8:14). Consequently, there results a semantic gap without a word for physical labor. Early rabbinic literature shows how this gap was filled: here *mᵉlāʾḵâ* takes on, in addition to its other meanings, the idea of physical labor (e.g., Mishnah *Šabb.* vii.1,2; Tosefta *Šabb.* vii.8; ix.5; *Parah* ii.6). In the later writings of the OT, however, *mᵉlāʾḵâ* has not yet taken on this specific meaning. The cases which one might at first glance explain by the meaning of "physical labor" turn out to be best understood as meaning "project." 2 Ch. 8:9 relates that Solomon did not make the Israelites into slaves *limlaʾḵtô,* "for his project(s)." This use is the Chronicler's own, since the parallel passage 1 K. 9:22 does not use *mᵉlāʾḵâ* at all. Likewise, 2 Ch. 16:5 uses *mᵉlaʾḵtô* for Baasha's projects (*mᵉlāʾḵâ* is missing in the parallel 1 K. 15:21). (An earlier, related passage from the antimonarchical criticisms of the nomistic Deuteronomistic source [1 S. 8:16] talks of the king who might confiscate slaves from his people *limlaʾḵtô,* "for his projects.") The pronominal suffixes in these examples of *mᵉlāʾḵâ* are in a subjective genitive relationship to the noun, "project of the king," and not an objective genitive relationship, "labor for the king" (cf. Gen. 2:2f.; Ex. 20:9; 1 Ch. 29:6; 2 Ch. 8:16). The *ʿōśê mᵉlāʾḵâ* (2 Ch. 34:13)[13] are project workers who have responsibility for every kind of labor *(laʿᵃḇôḏâ waʿᵃḇôḏâ).* Thus in Chronicles *mᵉlāʾḵâ* is not used specifically for "physical labor," but is still used in the general sense of "project."

b. A use of *mᵉlāʾḵâ* in the comprehensive meaning of physical and mental work is found in the prescriptions against *mᵉlāʾḵâ* on the Sabbath and festivals (Ex. 12:16; 20:9f.; 31:14f.; 35:2; Lev. 16:29; 23:3,7f.,21,25,28,30f.,35f.; Nu. 28:18,25f.; 29:1,7, 12,35; Dt. 5:13f.; 16:8; Jer. 17:22,24). Of these instances, 12 which pertain to festivals use the construction *kol-mᵉleʾḵet ʿᵃḇōḏâ* (Lev. 23:7,8,21,25,35,36; Nu. 28:18,25,26; 29:1,12,35), while the passages concerning the Sabbath and the Day of Atonement use *kol-mᵉlāʾḵâ* (Lev. 23:3,28; Nu. 29:7; cf. Ex. 31:14f.). The same distinction between these holy days is highlighted by the use of the word *šabbaṯ šabbāṯôn,* "sabbath of solemn rest" (par. *kol-mᵉlāʾḵâ*), used only in reference to the Sabbath and the Day of Atonement (Ex. 16:23; 31:15; 35:2; Lev. 23:3,32; for festivals, see Lev. 23:24,39). Thus *kol-mᵉlāʾḵâ* proves to be more comprehensive than *kol-mᵉleʾḵet ʿᵃḇōḏâ.* From this study, *mᵉlāʾḵâ* is thus the inclusive word for work, and the prohibition against *kol-mᵉlāʾḵâ* conveys the idea that on the Sabbath and the Day of Atonement there is to be "absolute rest" where "every conceivable kind of exertion, skilled and unskilled, heavy or light (physical or mental), is proscribed."[14] The use of *ʿᵃḇōḏâ* in the phrase *mᵉleʾḵet ʿᵃḇōḏâ* modifies the general sense of *mᵉlāʾḵâ* in the same way that *zayiṯ* modifies the general sense of *ʿēṣ,* "tree," to "olive tree." Thus not every kind of *mᵉlāʾḵâ* is proscribed, but only that which consists of physical labor (i.e., occupational work). It then follows that a lesser prohibition of labor prevails on the festivals (with the exception of the Sabbath and the Day of Atonement) and that light physical activities, such as household cleaning or concentrated study, would be allowed.

---

13. Cf. *BHS.*
14. Cf. Milgrom, §69 and n. 297.

In the case of the Passover Festival, P gives a definition of what *m^ele'k̲et̲ ^ab̲ōd̲â* (Lev. 23:7; Nu. 28:25) means: "No activity *(kol-m^elā'k̲â lō')* should be carried out on them: only *('ak̲)* what everyone must eat, that alone may be prepared for you" (Ex. 12:16). This would mean that the only difference between the two prescriptions *m^ele'k̲et̲ ^ab̲ōd̲â* and *kol-m^elā'k̲â* is the preparation of food. But this raises questions such as whether the literary sources (Ex. 12 as opposed to Lev. 23; Nu. 28) represent the same ideology, i.e., that all physical labor is forbidden, or whether the Passover Festival is actually more severe than other festivals in that all work except food preparation is forbidden in order to prevent contamination by leaven of food prepared before the festival.

3. *Manufacture.* Not only does *m^elā'k̲â* represent skilled work (activity), but it also represents the "finished product, that which the skill has wrought."[15]

a. The idea of "manufacture" is borne out in Lev. 13:48, which speaks of the plague of leprosy being "in any manufacture of leather." In Ex. 36:6, the people were not to produce any more "manufactured goods" for the sanctuary offering. Ex. 39:43 says that Moses saw all the *m^elā'k̲â* of the holy tent, referring to the finished product. The parable of the vine (Ezk. 15:3-5) poses the question whether or not vine wood can be made into a manufactured "product" (cf. Lev. 7:24; 11:32; 13:51).

Another semantic extension of *m^elā'k̲â* is found in 2 Ch. 17:13, where Jehoshaphat had great "provisions" or "supplies" in the cities of Judah. The use of *m^elā'k̲â* in Ex. 36:7 similarly indicates amassed manufactured goods to be used in the construction of the holy tabernacle.

b. A more specific application of *m^elā'k̲â* as manufactured goods is in reference to "movable property." Ex. 22:7,10(8,11) utilizes *m^elā'k̲â* in this sense regarding the oath one takes that he "has not laid hands on the property (or goods) of the other." In two passages *m^elā'k̲â* even has the meaning "flocks, herds, cattle." Saul kept alive the good animals for sacrifices to God and destroyed *kol-hamm^elā'k̲â n^emib̲zâ w^enāmēs,* "all despised and rejected animals" (1 S. 15:9,15). Esau slowly follows the *m^elā'k̲â,* "cattle" (Gen. 33:14). The meaning "cattle, herd" for *m^elā'k̲â* conforms to the idea that the herd is the result of skilled labor in breeding and feeding.

4. *Commission or Business.* Many passages yet exhibit a semantic connection to the original meaning of the verb *l'k,* "to send." A simple extension of the nominal idea "mission" would be "commission, errand, charge," a further extension being "business, business affair(s)."

a. The idea of errand or commission is seen in Gen. 39:11, where Joseph comes to perform Potiphar's "commission/business." Jonah was asked by the sailors what his "errand" or "business" was (Jon. 1:8). Prov. 18:9 mentions that the one who is slack in his "business" or "duty" is a brother to one who destroys. Prov. 22:29 talks of one skillful *(māhîr)* in his "business," and Ps. 107:23 speaks of those doing "business" on the seas (i.e., perhaps "trading mission, mission abroad"[16]).

---

15. *Ibid.,* §67.
16. Cf. Albright, 38.

A similar understanding is found in Est. 3:9; 9:3. Here the *ʿōśê hammᵉlāʾḵâ* are those who perform the king's commission, i.e., stewards or lesser officials (cf. Gen. 39:11). Dnl. 8:27 can be interpreted similarly.

We have examined above the use of *mᵉlāʾḵâ* in the sense of "project, plan" in connection with the king,[17] especially in reference to construction projects. However, *mᵉlāʾḵâ* in connection with the king might at times also be understood as "service" or "commission." Thus 1 Ch. 4:23 says that the potters and inhabitants of Netaim and Gederah dwelt there with the king *bimᵉlaʾḵtô,* "in his service/commission"; cf. also 1 Ch. 29:6; Est. 3:9; 9:3; Dnl. 8:27 and the similar list of officers in 1 Ch. 27:1,25. Here *mᵉlāʾḵâ* seems to refer to the responsibilities of governmental service.

III. Summary. Thus *mᵉlāʾḵâ* is a term covering a wide range of meaning from general "work" to specific aspects and extensions of the work concept such as "craftsmanship, manufactured objects, business, commission," etc. The striking aspect of *mᵉlāʾḵâ* is that nowhere in the Bible is it used specifically for the idea of physical labor, and, conversely, that it always implies a work involving skill. Although *mᵉlāʾḵâ* as a general term for "work" does include the idea of physical labor, it is not until rabbinic times that it comes to stand for physical labor exclusively. This semantic development follows naturally from the etymology of *mᵉlāʾḵâ,* since the root *lʾk,* "to send," and its nominal derivatives would tend to signify a non-physical activity. Thence derive the simple extensions in meaning like "commission" or "business," which lead to more abstract usages such as the work which one is commissioned to perform, e.g., skilled work and entire projects. This development from simple to more abstract is not, however, indicative of the ages of the respective passages. The various semantic aspects of *mᵉlāʾḵâ* may have existed early. The text of the OT does not portray any noticeable diachronic development in the meaning of *mᵉlāʾḵâ.*

Milgrom-Wright

IV. Qumran. In the Qumran writings *mᵉlāʾḵâ* first refers quite generally to "work" (11QT 47:9), and in connection with the stipulations concerning communal property it means "work force" (par. *māmôn,* 1QS 6:3; par. *hôn,* 1QS 6:19). In this sense its meaning seems also to move in the direction of "income for work rendered" (cf. 1QS 6:20). The Temple scroll then uses the term consistently in proscriptions against work, whereby here, too, a terminological differentiation seems to apply[18]: *mᵉleʾḵeṯ ʿᵃḇōḏâ* is prohibited on the first day of the month (11QT 14:10), completely during the Feast of Unleavened Bread (17:11), specifically on the seventh day of the Feast of Unleavened Bread (17:16), during the Feast of Weeks (19:8), on the first day of the seventh month (25:9), and during the Feast of Tabernacles (29:10). In contrast, on the Sabbath (CD 10:15) and on the Day of Atonement (11QT 27:6,7,10) *kol-mᵉlāʾḵâ* is prohibited. Indeed, according to CD 10:19 a person is not even permitted to speak about "things having

17. See II.2.a above.
18. See II.2.b above.

to do with work" *(diḇrê hammᵉlā'ḵâ).* 11QT 27:7 threatens transgressors with being "cut off from the midst of his people."

Fabry

מֶלַח *melaḥ*

Contents: I. Occurrences. II. Seasoning. III. Symbol of Disaster. IV. 1. Healing Agent; 2. Salt in the Cult; 3. Covenant of Salt.

I. Occurrences. The use of salt is attested in the earliest human civilizations. Its designation by *mlḥ* is shared by all Semitic languages with Israel.[1] The noun *melaḥ* occurs 22 times in the OT, 7 of those in geographical names. The Aram. *mᵉlaḥ* occurs 3 times, and the verb *mālaḥ* 4 times. Mention should also be made of the 7 passages in the LXX where salt occurs, and the 4 occurrences of *mᵉlēḥâ,* "salty, barren land."

II. Seasoning. Salt is highly valued as a seasoning. Sir. 39:26 counts it among the "basic necessities of human life." Without salt, foods have no taste (Job 6:6), a view richly attested both in Israel's immediate environs and elsewhere in antiquity.[2] Because of its white color and grainy texture, salt serves in Sir. 43:19 as a metaphor for hoarfrost. According to Sir. 22:15, it is difficult to bear, and was thus probably transported in bags or blocks. Precisely because it was indispensable and so valuable, the state used the salt trade as a source of taxes (1 Mc. 10:29; 11:35).[3]

III. Symbol of Disaster. Considering the high estimation of salt it is striking to find it associated with misfortune and destruction as well, an association Anton Jirku actually considers to be the original.[4] The "symbol of the dead and past" gradually became "an object evoking the feeling of sacred awe."[5] However, considering the overwhelmingly positive estimation of salt it was more likely the desolate, infertile region around

---

melaḥ. H. Blümner, "Salz," *PW,* II/2 (1920), 2075-99; G. Dalman, *AuS,* IV (1935), 49-58; E. P. Deatrick, "Salt, Soil, Savior," *BA,* 25 (1962), 41-48; F. C. Fensham, "Salt as Curse in the OT and the Ancient Near East," *BA,* 25 (1962), 48-50; R. J. Forbes, "Salz," *BHHW,* III (1966), 1653f.; F. Hauck, "ἅλας," *TDNT,* I, 228f.; V. Hehn, *Das Salz* (Berlin, ²1901); E. Hertzsch, "Salz," *RGG*³, V (1961), 1347f.; A. M. Honeyman, "The Salting of Shechem," *VT,* 3 (1953), 192-95; A. Jirku, *Materialien zur Volksreligion Israels* (Leipzig, 1914); *HAL,* II (1995), 588; H. Lesêtre, "Sel," *DB,* V (1912), 1568-1572; B. Meissner, *BuA,* I, 415, 425; II, 87, 240, 228f., 309; St.-B., I (1922), 232-36.

1. *HAL,* II, 588.
2. Cf. Hehn, 6f.; *BuA,* 415.
3. Cf. also Blümner, 2096ff.
4. Pp. 13, 15.
5. *Ibid.,* 19f.

the Dead Sea and the legend of its origin (Gen. 19) that shaped this negative connotation. Both Dt. 29:22(Eng. v. 23) and Zeph. 2:9 explicitly mention the destruction of Sodom and Gomorrah as God's punishment. According to Wis. 10:7, the salt region around the Dead Sea and the pillar of salt there (Gen. 19:26) are evidence of human wickedness and its chastisement. Only wild asses live there (Job 39:5f.), and the only food to be found is saltwort (*mallûaḥ,* 30:4). Jer. 17:6-8 significantly juxtaposes the blessed person, who is like a green tree planted by water, and the cursed person in the parched desert "in an uninhabited salt land." God is known to turn "rivers into a desert, . . . a fruitful land into a salty waste" (Ps. 107:33f.; cf. also Sir. 39:23). Thus the same could happen when Abimelech symbolically strews salt over Shechem after its destruction so that, like a salt desert, it would be unfruitful and uninhabitable (Jgs. 9:45); that the city's subsequent history does not support this kind of ban has prompted A. M. Honeyman[6] to interpret salt here as a kind of apotropaic agent for securing oneself against the avenging spirits of the slain Shechemites.

The negative symbolic connotations of salt are in any case consistent with the name "Salt Sea" in reference to the Dead Sea (Gen. 14:3; Josh. 3:16; 12:3; 18:19), as well as with the fact that one city there is called the "City of Salt" (Josh. 15:62) and one valley the "Valley of Salt" (2 S. 8:13; 1 Ch. 18:12; 2 K. 14:7; 2 Ch. 25:11; Ps. 60:2[superscription]). The extent to which the bleak wilderness of Judah was perceived as desolation can be seen in Ezk. 47 with its vision of the healing *(rp')* effects of the temple spring, which transforms the desert into paradisaic fruitfulness.

IV. 1. *Healing Agent.* And yet the swamps and marshes will not be so affected (Ezk. 47:11)! For whence would one then acquire life-sustaining salt, which in the hand of Elisha can even make the spring at Jericho "wholesome (*rp'*)" (2 K. 2:20-22)? The custom of rubbing a newborn child with salt probably also constitutes a measure thought to enhance health (Ezk. 16:4), something also consistent with the estimation of salt in antiquity as a medicine[7] and its use in religious rites of healing.[8] A petitioner can even entreat salt in prayer to deliver him from a spell, after the success of which the petitioner vows to venerate it as his creator-god.[9] Compare also Homer *Iliad* ix.214, where salt is called "divine." Ex. 30:35 designates as "pure and holy" the incense seasoned with salt.

2. *Salt in the Cult.* Thus salt also plays a part in the cultic sphere, so much so that in Ashur even the gods were included in its enjoyment with the invocation: "You are salt, begotten in a pure place, created by Ellil as the food of the great gods. Without you no feast is held in the temple. Without you the king, lord, and prince smell no sacrificial fragrance."[10] The OT mentions salt 9 times in connection with sacrifices.

6. P. 194.
7. Blümner, 2090.
8. *BuA,* II, 228f., 240, 309.
9. *Ibid.,* 228f.
10. *Idem.*

Lev. 2:13 prescribes its use with cereal offerings, whereby v. 13b, with its prescription for using salt "with all your offerings," probably does not go beyond this, since the stipulations concerning other kinds of sacrifices (Lev. 3–7) do not mention salt. Although Ezk. 43:24 does say that the animal used for the burnt offering is to be sprinkled with salt, this is probably a case of subsequent expansion of the custom (attested by Josephus *Ant.* iii.9.1; Jub. 21:11). T.Lev. 9:14 also states that "[you shall] salt with salt every sacrificial offering." While according to Lev. 24:7 incense was probably sprinkled between the breads of the Presence, but no salt, the LXX mentions salt as well. (Compare also the use of salt with incense in Sir. 49:1.) This, too, probably constitutes a later expansion. In any case, salt must have been used extensively in the temple, since Ezr. 6:9; 7:22 mention stipulations involving its delivery, 7:22 even with the remark "salt without prescribing how much." The use of salt as a part of sacrifices is attested outside Israel neither in the Egyptian nor in the Assyrian sphere, although it was used later in Greece and Rome (the sacrificial animal is sprinkled with *mola salsa*[11]).

3. *Covenant of Salt.* The regulations involving the use of salt with cereal offerings in Lev. 2:13 emphatically call this the "salt of the covenant with your God." Since evidence shows that outside Israel salt was even considered to be a food of the gods, one cannot with Jirku[12] understand this salt of the covenant as a kind of self-imprecation in the case of covenant violation. Since salt is a part of every meal among human beings, and since it is used primarily with cereal offerings, then the sacrifice and sacrificial meal would more likely be the constitutive factors influencing such linguistic usage. What is fundamental is that "the communal partaking of salt is a sign of friendship and a symbol of communality."[13] The same was true for the Greeks and Romans;[14] cf. also *synalízomai* in Acts 1:4.

Binding mutual commitments result from the hospitality of table fellowship. Thus the scribes writing to Artaxerxes emphasize that they are bound to watch out for his interests because they "eat the salt of the palace" (Ezr. 4:14). Just as the covenant was enacted through eating and drinking before God and with God (Ex. 24:11), so did God allot to the priests their portion of the sacrifice through a "covenant of salt forever" (Nu. 18:19). In 2 Ch. 13:5, Abijah asserts against Jeroboam that Yahweh had given the kingship over Israel to David and his sons for all time by a "covenant of salt."

The "covenant of salt" transfers to the divine covenant the notion of hospitality associated with table fellowship, with its subsequent commitment to loyalty and solicitude; Israel is to keep its covenantal obligations, although God, too, is to provide for the election and rights of the covenantal partner.

Eising(†)

---

11. Lesêtre, 1569; Blümner, 2093f.
12. Pp. 18f.
13. W. Rudolph, *Esra und Nehemiah. HAT,* XX (1949), 43.
14. Blümner, 2089, 2091-93.

מִלְחָמָה *milḥāmâ;* לָחַם *lāḥam*

Contents: I. The Noun: 1. Root, Meaning, Distribution, Semantic Field; 2. Ancient Near East; 3. Historical and Theological Focal Points; 4. Yahweh and War; 5. Overcoming War; War and Peace. II. The Verb.

---

milḥāmâ. R. Bach, *Die Aufforderungen zur Flucht und zum Kampf im alttestamentlichen Prophetenspruch. WMANT,* 9 (1962); *idem,* " '. . . der Bogen zerbricht, Spiesse zerschlägt und Wagen mit Feuer verbrennt,' " *Probleme biblischer Theologie. Festschrift G. von Rad* (Munich, 1971), 13-26; R. Bartelmus, *Heroentum in Israel und seiner Umwelt. AThANT,* 65 (1979); O. Bauernfeind, "πόλεμος," *TDNT,* VI, 507-513; *idem,* "στρατεύομαι," *TDNT,* VII, 705-7; M. J. Benedict, *The God of the OT in Relation to War* (New York, 1927, repr. 1972); A. Bertholet, *Religion und Krieg* (Tübingen, 1915); C. M. Carmichael, "A Time for War and a Time for Peace: The Influence of the Distinction upon some Legal and Literary Material," *JJS,* 25 (1974), 50-63; W. Caspari, "Was stand im Buch der Kriege Jahwes?" *ZWTh,* 54 (1912), 110-158; D. L. Christensen, *Transformations of the War Oracle in OT Prophecy* (Missoula, 1975); J. J. Collins, "The Mythology of Holy War in Daniel and the Qumran War Scroll," *VT,* 25 (1975), 596-612; P. C. Craigie, "Yahweh Is a Man of War," *SJT,* 22 (1969), 183-88; *idem, The Problem of War in the OT* (Grand Rapids, 1978); F. M. Cross, "The Divine Warrior in Israel's Early Cult," in A. Altmann, ed., *Biblical Motifs* (Cambridge, Mass., 1966), 11-30; P. R. Davies, "Dualism and Eschatology in the Qumran War Scroll," *VT,* 28 (1978), 28-36; *idem,* "Dualism and Eschatology in 1QM: A Rejoinder," *VT,* 30 (1980), 93-97; S. J. DeVries, "Temporal Terms as Structural Elements in the Holy-War Tradition," *VT,* 25 (1975), 80-105; J. Ebach, *Das Erbe der Gewalt* (Gütersloh, 1980); O. Eissfeldt, *Krieg und Bibel* (Tübingen, 1915); D. Ellul, "Variations sur la thème de la guerre sainte dans le Deutéro-Zacharie," *La guerre sainte. ETR,* 56/1 (1981), 55-71; G. Fohrer, *Glaube und Welt im AT* (Frankfurt, 1948), 230-258; H. Fredriksson, *Jahwe als Krieger* (Lund, 1945); R. Gale, *Great Battles of Biblical History* (New York 1970); N. K. Gottwald, " 'Holy War' in Deuteronomy: Analysis and Critique," *RevExp,* 61 (1964), 296-310; H. Gunkel, *Israelitisches Heldentum und Kriegsfrömmigkeit im AT* (Göttingen, 1916); J.-G. Heintz, "Prophetisme et guerre sainte salon les archives royales de Mari et AT," *La guerre sainte. ETR,* 56/1 (1981), 47-49 (for further bibliog. on the topic "La guerre sainte," see *idem,* 39-45); K.-J. Illman, *OT Formulas about Death* (Åbo, 1979), 88f.; W. Janzen, "War in the OT," *Mennonite Quarterly Review,* 46 (1972), 155-166 = *Still in the Image. Institute of Mennonite Studies,* 6 (Newton, Kans., 1982), 173-186; *idem,* "God as Warrior and Lord," *BASOR,* 220 (1975), 73-75; G. H. Jones, " 'Holy War' or 'Yahweh War'?" *VT,* 25 (1975), 642-658; O. Keel, *The Symbolism of the Biblical World* (Eng. trans., New York, 1978), 219-225; J. Kegler, *Politisches Geschehen und theologisches Verstehen. CThM,* A, 8 (1977), 113ff., 253ff.; R. Kittel, *Das AT und unser Krieg* (Leipzig, 1916); H.-J. Kraus, "Vom Kampf des Glaubens: Eine biblisch-theologische Studie," *Beiträge zur alttestamentlichen Theologie. Festschrift W. Zimmerli* (Göttingen, 1977), 239-256; W. Lienemann, *Gewalt und Gewaltverzicht* (Munich, 1982), 36-48; M. C. Lind, *Yahweh Is a Warrior* (Scottdale, Pa., 1980); N. Lohfink, "Die Schichten des Pentateuch und der Krieg," *Gewalt und Gewaltlosigkeit im AT. QuaestDisp,* 96 (1983), 51-110; A. Malamat, *Early Israelite Warfare and the Conquest of Canaan* (Oxford, 1978); *idem,* "Israelite Conduct of War in the Conquest of Canaan According to the Biblical Tradition," in F. H. Cross, ed., *Symposia,* ZRFOP, 1f. (Cambridge, Mass., 1979), 35-55; P. D. Miller, Jr., " 'God the Warrior,' " *Int,* 19 (1965), 39-46; *idem,* "El the Warrior," *HThR,* 60 (1967), 411-431; *idem,* "The Divine Council and the Prophetic Call to War," *VT,* 18 (1968), 100-107; *idem, The Divine Warrior in Early Israel. HSM,* 5 (1973); L. Perlitt, "Israel und die Völker," *Studien zur Friedensforschung,* 9 (1972), 17-64;

I. The Noun.

1. *Root, Meaning, Distribution, Semantic Field.* The noun *milḥāmâ* (occurring as the segolate *milḥemeṯ* only in 1 S. 13:22) is a *miqṭal(at)* form constructed from the root *lḥm I.* Such forms often refer to the place, means, or result of the action described by the verbal root in question.[1] Both the root and the noun itself are attested in other Semitic languages,[2] namely, in Arabic, Christian Palestinian, Syriac, Mandaic, Ethiopic (Tigré), Ugaritic,[3] and for Middle Hebrew also the numerous occurrences in the Qumran writings.

The semantic scope of the root and its derivative extends from crowding and shoving to conflict and antagonism (Ps. 120:7; 144:3; Mic. 3:5), to skirmish (2 S. 10:9), battle, and war. In addition, in Ps. 76:4(Eng. v. 3); Hos. 2:20(18) (less so in Hos. 1:7; Isa. 30:32b), *milḥāmâ* seems possibly to refer to a specific weapon (a lance or mace?[4]).

Textually uncertain passages include 2 Ch. 35:21; Ps. 27:3;[5] Isa. 27:4; 30:32 (a verb?); and probably also 1 S. 13:22; 2 S. 1:27.

H. D. Preuss, "Alttestamentliche Aspekte zu Macht und Gewalt," in H. Greifenstein, ed., *Macht und Gewalt* (Hamburg, 1978), 113-134; A. de Pury, "La guerre sainte israélite: Rélité historique oufiction littéraire?," *La guerre sainte. ETR,* 56/1 (1981), 5-38; P. de Robert, "Arche et guerre sainte," *La guerre sainte. ETR,* 56/1 (1981), 51-53; G. von Rad, *Holy War in Ancient Israel* (Eng. trans., Grand Rapids, 1991) (and other works); W. Richter, *Traditionsgeschichtliche Untersuchungen zum Richterbuch. BBB,* 18 (^{2}1966), 177-186, 338; M. Rose, " 'Entmilitarisierung des Kriegs'? (Erwägungen zu den Patriarchen-Erzählungen der Genesis)," *BZ,* N.S. 20 (1976), 197-211; *idem, Deuteronomist und Jahwist. AThANT,* 67 (1981); L. Ruppert, *Der leidende Gerechte und seine Feinde* (Würzburg, 1973), 22f., 104f., 156f., 159ff., 177, 221; F. Schwally, *Semitische Kriegsaltertümer, I: Der heilige Krieg im alten Israel* (Leipzig, 1901); M. S. Seale, *The Desert Bible* (New York, 1974), 24-52; R. Smend, *Yahweh War and Tribal Confederation* (Eng. trans., Nashville, 1970); J. A. Soggin, "The Prophets on Holy War as Judgement against Israel," *OT and Oriental Studies. BietOr,* 29 (1975), 67-71; F. Stolz, *Jahwes und Israels Kriege. Kriegstheorien und Kriegserfahrungen. AThANT,* 60 (1972); M. E. Tate, "War and Peacemaking in the OT," *RevExp,* 79 (1982), 587-596; R. de Vaux, *AncIsr,* 213-267; *Warfare in the Ancient Near East. Iraq,* 25/2 (1963); P. Weimar, "Die Yahwekriegserzählungen in Exodus 14, Josua 10, Richter 4 und 1 Samuel 7," *Bibl,* 57 (1976), 38-73; *idem* and E. Zenger, *Exodus: Geschichten und Geschichte der Befreiung Israels. SBS,* 75 (1975); M. Weippert, " 'Heiliger Krieg' in Israel und Assyrien," *ZAW,* 84 (1972), 460-493 (additional bibliog. 463f.); P. Welten, *Geschichte und Geschichtsdarstellung in den Chronikbüchern. WMANT,* 42 (1973), 79ff., 115ff., 201ff.; A. S. van der Woude, "צָבָא *ṣābā'* Heer," *THAT,* II, 498-507, esp. 502f.; Y. Yadin, *The Art of Warfare in Biblical Lands* (Eng. trans., New York, 1963); W. Zimmerli, *The OT and the World* (Eng. trans., Atlanta, 1976), 53-66 (cf. also *idem, OT Theology in Outline* [Eng. trans., Atlanta, 1978], 59-64).

1. See II below; cf. E. Jenni, *Lehrbuch der hebräischen Sprache des ATs* (Basel, 1978), 182.
2. Cf. *HAL,* II (1995), 526, 589; *DISO,* 137, 152; *KAI,* 181 (Mesha inscription); 24, 6 (Zinjirli); then also J. J. Glück, *OuTWP,* 19 (1976), 41-43.
3. Cf. Ugar. *mlḥmt, UT,* no. 1367.
4. Cf. *HAL,* II, 589. Concerning the (relatively varied) rendering of *milḥāmâ* in the LXX and its use in the Apocrypha, cf. E. Hatch and H. A. Redpath, *A Concordance to the Septuagint* (1897; repr. Grand Rapids, 1983), II, 1172f.; also Bauernfeind, *TDNT,* VI, 511f.; VII, 705-7. See further W. Foerster, "ἐχθρός," *TDNT,* II, 811f.; O. Bauernfeind, "μάχομαι," *TDNT,* IV, 527.
5. Cf. M. Dahood, "Hebrew-Ugaritic Lexicography IV," *Bibl,* 47 (1966), 419, who reads "troops."

The approximately 320 occurrences of the noun are found both in the older and more recent OT texts, although its distribution[6] does exhibit clear focal points (1 + 2 Samuel; 1 + 2 Chronicles; 1 + 2 Kings; Jeremiah; Judges; Deuteronomy; Joshua; Isaiah; Numbers), i.e., those texts that recount wars or make extensive thematic use of war as a means of divine intervention in history.[7] Its absence in Genesis (occurring only in Gen. 14:2,8) can probably better be explained on the basis of sociological and social-historical factors than as a result of redactional considerations.[8] Furthermore, there are no occurrences (typically) in Leviticus, Ruth, Ezra, Nehemiah, Esther, Trito-Isaiah, Lamentations, Jonah, Nahum, Habakkuk, Zephaniah, Haggai, and Malachi, even though the only genuinely "non-bellicose" books in the OT are Ruth and Canticles.

Not only this particular distribution of occurrences, but also the extensive semantic field into which *lḥm* and *milḥāmâ* belong make it quite clear that the idea of war (with whatever content and however understood) plays an important role in the OT. In addition to the verbs → בוא *bô'* and → יצא *yṣ'* (often used in connection with *lḥm* or *milḥāmâ*, e.g., Jgs. 9:38f.; 1 S. 8:20; 28:1; 2 S. 11:17; 2 K. 19:9; 2 Ch. 26:6; Neh. 4:2; Isa. 37:9; Jer. 32:29; Dnl. 11:11; Zec. 14:3), this field includes the following roots or terms: *'sp, 'ôyēḇ, 'ᵃrôn, gibbôr, grh, dbq* (1 S. 14:22), *hlk* (Jgs. 8:1), *hmm, ḥayil, ḥlṣ, ḥrb, ḥrm, yr', yrd, yš', kōaḥ, maḥᵃneh, mûṯ* (to die in war, e.g., Dt. 20:5-7), *ngš, nkh, nûs, ntn (bᵉyaḏ* or *lipnê), 'br, 'zr, 'am, 'lh, 'rk, 'śh, pḥd, pûṣ, ṣāḇā', qbṣ, qûm* (Ps. 27:3; Jer. 49:14; Ob. 1), *qrb, šālôm,* and *tᵉrû'â*. The evidence presented by this wide semantic field also makes it clear, for example, that one cannot, on the basis of an investigation into *lḥm* and *milḥāmâ* alone, determine "the" definitive OT witness concerning war, and the present study accordingly makes no attempt to do so. Furthermore, the literature on this topic is not seldom colored by (apologetic or even "national") ancillary interests, and is thus occasionally quite problematical.[9]

2. *Ancient Near East.* The OT understanding of battle and war, an understanding in which the use of *lḥm* and *milḥāmâ* play an essential if not exclusive role, follows and is indebted to the practice and ideology of war shared not only by the ancient Near East specifically, but by antiquity in general.[10] Both earlier and later scholars have confirmed that this is the case, and their studies make it clear both that and how in its own understanding of war and especially in its synoptic view of war and divine action ancient Israel understood itself to be both connected with and separated from other nations of the ancient Near East.[11]

---

6. Cf. A. S. van der Woude, "צָבָא *ṣābā'* Heer," *THAT,* II, 502.
7. See I.3 below.
8. Cf. Lind, 35ff. contra Rose, 197ff.
9. E.g., Gunkel, R. Kittel; apologetic interests color the work of Benedict, and to a certain extent also Craigie; Gale is problematical because of methodological considerations. Concerning (semantic) antitheses, see I.5 below.
10. Weippert, 485; cf. 491.
11. Among earlier scholars, cf. Bertholet and (with less differentiation in detail) Schwally (esp. in view of the various customs and rituals associated with the practice of war); cf. also (*s.v.*

3. *Historical and Theological Focal Points.* a. After the brief remark in Ex. 13:17,[12] according to which Yahweh did not lead his people through the land of the Philistines lest they see war (E?), the first, more extensive focal point in the OT concerning battle and war is found in the narratives of (the wilderness wanderings and especially the immediately following) conquest (Nu. 31:14,21,27,28,49; 32:6,20; cf. 32:27,29; note already the attendant word field[13]). What is begun in Nu. 31f. is continued in Joshua (Josh. 4:13; 6:3; 8:1,3,11,14; 10:7,24; 11:19f.), in the form both of specific details and of summary notices (e.g., Josh. 11:18,23; 14:15; cf. 14:11; 17:1).[14] According to Sir. 46:3, Joshua was conducting the "wars of Yahweh" (cf. v. 6). The experience of Yahweh's skill in war was thus important for this early period of Israel with the (doubtlessly not always peaceful) conquest of the land,[15] and not only or even first of all for the Deuteronomic/Deuteronomistic theology (cf. Dt. 2:9; 3:1; 29:6[7]; also 2:24).[16] Battles and the problem of securing the land are then the subjects of Jgs. 3:10 and 8:13; Jgs. 20[17] (cf. 21:22), with its 12 occurrences, then constitutes a special focal point, although in this case concerning a war or battle between "Israel" and Benjamin. The verbs associated with *milḥāmâ* include → בוא *bô'*, → נגשׁ *ngš*, → הלך *hlk*, → ערך *'rk*, → עשׂה *'śh*, → עלה *'lh*, → יצא *yṣ'*. Only Jer. 6:4; 51:27f.; Joel 4:9(3:9); and Mic. 3:5 speak of "consecrating" a war.[18]

b. Discussion of the wars and battles of the various kings and their adversaries becomes more frequent after the inception of the Israelite-Judean monarchy. Israel and Judah fight against one another or against their neighbors or other attackers (separately or occasionally as allies). The people's wish is for the king to conduct "our" wars (1 S. 8:20), wars fought first of all against the Philistines (often qualified as "heavy" or "hard"[19]): 1 S. 4:2; 13:22 (unclear text); 14:20,22,23,52; 17:1,2,20,28,33; 2 S. 21:15,18,20; 23:9 (cf. 1 Ch. 10:3; 11:13; 20:4-6), then also against the Amalekites (2 S.

"Krieg") A. van den Born, "Krieg," *BL*², 994; H.-J. Kraus, *RGG*³, IV (1960), 64f. ("Krieg II: Im AT"); B. Reicke, *BHHW,* II (1964), 1005-10. Among more recent scholars, cf. Craigie, *The Problem of War in the OT,* 115ff. (with further bibliog.); Keel; Stolz; Weippert; then also S. Curto, "Krieg," *LexÄg,* III (1980), 765-786, concerning Egypt; and H. Klengel, "Krieg, Kriegsgefangene," *RLA,* VI, 241-43 (1983), concerning Mesopotamia. The various contributions by Ellul, Heintz, de Pury, and de Robert to *ETR,* 56/1, should also be consulted. Finally, concerning the Assyrian practice and understanding of war, see H. Spieckermann, *Juda unter Assur in der Sargonidenzeit. FRLANT,* 129 (1982), 344ff. Finally, cf. additionally L. Schmidt, *Menschlicher Erfolg und Jahwes Initiative. WMANT,* 38 (1970); Kegler.

12. On Gen. 14, see I.1 above.

13. See I.1 above; on this matter specifically, see esp. Lind, 65ff.; Lohfink; Malamat; Seale; Stolz, 69ff.; Yadin.

14. Cf. here J. S. Ascaso, *Las guerras de Josué* (Valencia, 1982).

15. Cf. I.4 below.

16. → ירשׁ *yrš* (VI, 368-396); on this matter specifically, see von Rad, 187f.; Lind, 145ff.; Perlitt, 50ff.; Rose, *Deuteronomist und Jahwist;* Stolz, 17ff.; for a more detailed study of the Pentateuch and the narratives of the land conquest, cf. Lohfink.

17. Cf. DeVries, 89ff.

18. → קדשׁ *qdš;* see also Bach, *Die Aufforderungen zur Flucht.*

19. → כבד *kāḇēḏ* (II.1.d) (VII, 18); → חזק *ḥāzaq (chāzaq)* (IV, 301-8).

1:4). The followers of Saul conduct war against those of David (2 S. 3:6,30; compare 20:9f. and 1 K. 2:5!). Other wars conducted by David are described in 2 S. 8:10 (1 Ch. 18:10); 10:8; 11:15,18f. (cf. 1 Ch. 19:7,9,10,14) as battles against the Arameans (cf. 1 Ch. 19:17; cf. also Sir. 47:5f.; 1QM 11:2-4 for an evaluation of David the warrior).[20] In and of itself, the theologically interesting remark in 1 K. 5:17(3), according to which David could not build the temple because of the warfare surrounding him,[21] contradicts the otherwise positive view of the wars of Yahweh in 1-2 Samuel. Since it is even amplified in 1 Ch. 22:8 (cf. 28:3) (Yahweh-discourse and the addition of → דם *dām*), it more likely represents (if understood causally) a later evaluation.

In the (subsequent) period of the monarchy Israel and Judah then fight against one another, or wars occur within Israel itself (2 S. 2:17; 3:1; 18:6,8; 1 K. 14:30; 15:6,7,16,32; 2 Ch. 12:15; 13:2). Jehoshaphat and Ahab conduct wars against the Syrians (1 K. 20; cf. 2 Ch. 18), Ben-hadad against Israel (1 K. 20:26; cf. v. 39), Israel against the Syrians (1 K. 20:29; 22:1,35; 2 Ch. 18:34), or against the Moabites or their King Mesha (2 K. 3:7,26).

c. As in the world at large, so also in Israel there is a time for → שלום *šālôm* and a time for *milḥāmâ* (Eccl. 3:8), and war should be conducted with wisdom and reflection (Prov. 20:18; cf. 24:6). It is, of course, inappropriate to discuss war with a prisoner (Sir. 37:11). That a person cannot, as a human being, conquer the → לויתן *liwyāṯān* in battle (Job 40:32[41:8]) is a singular but logical statement. The reality of war is that it involves not only plundering (Mic. 2:8), but above all also manifold death (Dt. 20:5-7; 2 S. 1:25; 3:30; 11:25; cf. also 1 Ch. 22:8; 28:3; 2 S. 11:15; 19:11[10]; 21:17; Isa. 22:2).[22] Wars are also the topic in 2 K. 8:28; 13:25; 14:7; 16:5; cf. Isa. 7:1.

d. Both the concentration of occurrences and their content disclose an ideology of war peculiar to 1-2 Chronicles. Those skilled in war are specially mentioned and enumerated, and since war is "from God," numerous adversaries are slain. One cries to God in battle,[23] God himself goes out to battle, and the Levites are put in charge of the spoils of war (1 Ch. 5:18-20,22; 7:4,11,40; 12:1,9,20,34,36-39[1,8,19,33,35-38]; 14:15; 26:27; cf. 2 Ch. 13:14f.). Consequently, it is to be expected that Chronicles picks up corresponding remarks in the books of Kings (2 Ch. 6:34f.; 8:9; 11:1; 18:3,5,14,29; 22:5). Of greater significance, however, are the additional statements and judgments concerning the wars of specific kings not found in Kings (2 Ch. 13:3; 14:9[10]; 17:13; 20:1; cf. 2 Ch. 20 as a whole with its war narrative; cf. also 25:8,13; 26:11,13; 27:7; 32:2,6,8; 35:21 and also 14:5[6]; 15:19; 16:9). Peter Welten has undertaken thorough studies of these texts and has attempted to evaluate both historically and theologically the concerns and background of the accounts of the organization of the armies and of the wars themselves (especially in the case of important and positively judged kings)

---

20. For a discussion of the textual types in 1-2 Samuel, cf. Kegler, 113ff.; also Stolz, 139ff. On the catalog of virtues involving David in 1 S. 16:18 (*"kalokagathía,"* "nobility of character," so von Rad, *Holy War in Ancient Israel,* 83) and on 1 S. 17, cf. also Bartelmus and Ebach, 15ff.

21. → סבב *sbb;* causal or temporal usage?

22. Cf. Illman, 88ff.; → מות *mûṯ* (VIII, 185-209).

23. → זעק *zāʿq* (IV, 112-122).

as well as the war discourses[24] (cf. Ex. 14:13f.; Dt. 20:1-20; 1QM 10–13, esp. 10:8bff., an extensive prayer). Considerations include the influence of Greek mercenary forces during the period of Chronicles, problems of delimitation, and hopes of expansion during this period.

e. The understanding of war (the day of Yahweh as war and as eschatological war?) in Daniel (Dnl. 9:26; 11:20,25) is illuminated by comparison with the Maccabean (religious) wars, especially with the battles of Judas according to 1 Maccabees.[25]

f. More than 100 occurrences (with 14 verbal forms) attest the popularity and importance of the idea of war to the Qumran community.[26] As a body of men organized for war, the Qumran community is organized according to principles reflecting such an identity and even precisely lists its inventory of weapons. There are battles within the group, battles directed toward the outside world (with clearly dualistic features) against the group's adversaries, and against the nations in the larger sense and taken together; these wars are both historical and eschatological, undertaken with the aid of heavenly powers which both struggle among one another and teach the art of combat. In both theory and execution, the war of the Sons of Light against the Sons of Darkness is a "battle of God" or "his war."[27]

g. Finally, the construct chains involving *milḥāmâ* are extremely numerous, and considerably expand its word field.[28] These include the battle horse (Jer. 8:6; Job 39:25) and the noise or alarm of war and the battle cry (Ex. 32:17; Jer. 4:19; 49:2; 50:22). The battle bow is mentioned (Zec. 9:10), as well as weapons of war in the more general sense[29] (Dt. 1:41; Jgs. 18:11,16f.; 1 S. 8:12; 2 S. 1:27 [textual problems?]; 1 Ch. 12:34,38[33,37]; Jer. 21:4; 51:20; Ezk. 32:27). The man or men of war are frequently mentioned, referring not only to special warriors, but also to soldiers in general (e.g., Nu. 31:28,49; Dt. 2:14,16; Josh. 5:4,6; 6:3; 17:1; Jgs. 20:17; 1 S. 16:18; 17:33; 2 S. 17:8; Isa. 41:12; Jer. 6:23; 38:4; 39:4; 41:3; 48:14; 49:26; 50:30,42; 51:32; 52:7,25; Ezk. 27:10,27; Joel 2:7; cf. also 1 Ch. 5:18; 2 Ch. 13:3: apparently especially popular in writings influenced by Deuteronomistic thought). Frequent mention is made, together with → עם *ʿam,* of "people of war" (or "fighting men"; Nu. 21:33; Dt. 2:32; Josh. 8:1,3,11; 10:7,24; 1 S. 23:8; here the term *ʿam* can designate the warring people without the addition of *milḥāmâ:* e.g., Dt. 3:1; Josh. 6:5; 8:14; Jgs. 4:13; 2 S. 1:4; 10:13; 19:4[3]; also 1 K. 8:44?). These people of war are more often additionally characterized by "strength, power"[30] or as "hero"[31] (e.g., 1 S. 16:18; 2 Ch. 17:13; Isa. 3:2; Jer. 41:16; 48:14; Joel 2:7; 4:9[3:9];[32] on the plural

---

24. Cf. also Weimar-Zenger, 57ff.

25. Cf. Kraus, 246ff.; Collins; and further E. Janssen, *Das Gottesvolk und seine Geschichte* (Neukirchen, 1971), 36ff.

26. Cf. (for Daniel as well) Collins; Davies; Kraus, 247f.

27. Cf. I.4 below.

28. See I.1 above.

29. → כלי *kᵉlî,* II.4 (172).

30. → חיל *ḥayil (chayil)* (IV, 349-355).

31. → גבר *gibbôr,* II, 373-77.

32. On the sequence of these attributes, cf. K. Elliger, *Deuterojesaja. BK,* XI/1 (1978), 249f.

form, cf. 2 S. 8:10; 1 Ch. 18:10; 28:3[33]). Mention is made of the "blood of war" (1 K. 2:5, *dām*), and of those who render services in war (1 Ch. 12:1, *'zr*) as vassals;[34] even in a festive procession (at a wedding?) "experts in war" make an appearance (Cant. 3:8).[35] All these things are involved in battle (2 S. 11:18f.),[36] although mere words do not constitute the strength and power necessary for battle (2 K. 18:20; Isa. 36:5).

4. *Yahweh and War.* The discussion to this point has already made it clear that both battle and war in general as well as *milḥāmâ* (and *lḥm*) in particular are associated with Yahweh, his character, and his actions. We can now consider those passages explicitly, emphasizing the connection between Yahweh and *milḥāmâ*.

a. First of all, mention should be made of "Yahweh's wars" (1 S. 18:17; 25:28: David is to conduct them, as in the older story of David's rise to power; cf. Sir. 46:3; 1 Ch. 5:22; 2 Ch. 20:15), and of the alleged "Book of the Wars of Yahweh" (Nu. 21:14). 1 S. 17:47 and (in the "banner song"?) Ex. 17:16 both assert that "the battle is Yahweh's." Yahweh is a "man of war" (Ex. 15:3; cf. Isa. 42:13), a mighty hero in battle (Ps. 24:8; cf. Jgs. 5:23; Isa. 42:13). Several key passages assert that he alone fights, and not the people itself,[37] for as Israel's God he fights for Israel (Josh. 10:42). The usual opinion is that the people participate actively in Yahweh's war, a divine oracle before the battle (Jgs. 1:1; 20:18,23,28; 1 K. 22:6,15; cf. 1 K. 20:14)[38] answering the question whether and precisely who is to mobilize for battle. One girds oneself for war[39] before Yahweh (Nu. 32:20,27,29), and Yahweh himself prepares his people for battle (Zec. 10:3-5: a conscious shift of emphasis? cf. Chronicles). He bestows victory (Prov. 21:31) to the steeds being prepared for the day of battle (cf. Ps. 20:8[7]). Yahweh instructs in the art of war and provides the strength for it (2 S. 22:35,40 par. Ps. 18:35,40[34,39]; cf. Ps. 144:1; Isa. 28:6), and according to Jgs. 3:1f. he left Canaanites in the land so that the Israelites, who knew nothing of the wars in Canaan, might later experience war. Yahweh provides succor in war (1 S. 14:23; cf., however, Eccl. 9:11) and is able to preserve against its negative consequences (Ps. 27:3). Yahweh as the leader of hosts and Yahweh as an individual warrior belong together,[40] since (according to Deuteronomistic theology as explicated in Ex. 14/15) Yahweh took his people through war (Dt. 4:34; *lqḥ*), and both in and through battle will insure their cause[41] (1 K. 8:44f. as a Deuteronomistic prayer; cf. 2 Ch. 6:34). Yahweh conducts "our battles" (2 Ch. 32:8) and in that way is "with us";[42] many are

33. On the combination of attributes, cf. also Welten, 119, n. 20.
34. Cf. M. Dahood, "Ugaritic-Hebrew Parallel Pairs," *RSP,* II, 74f., 105.
35. → למד *lāmad* (VIII, 4-10).
36. → דבר *dāḇār (dābhar)* (III, 84-125).
37. See II below.
38. → שׁאל *šā'al.*
39. → חלץ *ḥālaṣ (chālats)* (IV, 436-441).
40. Cf. Fredriksson.
41. → משׁפט *mišpaṭ.*
42. → את *'ēṯ* (I, 449-463).

slain, because the war is from God (1 Ch. 5:22), and God also goes along into battle (1 Ch. 14:15).

These statements of faith concerning the wars of Yahweh are thus quite old, going back at least as far as the Davidic period. Yahweh lends legitimacy to these wars, aids in them, and ultimately himself participates in battle (cf. the verbal form in Sir. 4:28). It is then the Deuteronomistic writing that develops a more or less extensive "theory" of Yahweh's war,[43] a theory finding its fullest development in the Chronicler's history. However, the age of many of the texts as well as the (older) parallels from the ancient Near East[44] militate against viewing this theory in its totality as a recent one. Yahweh was conceived as active, living, and a force in history; such a view also included, or even necessitated, the association of Yahweh with war (according to Rudolf Smend this was for the tribe of Rachel a principle of faith generated by the exodus experience). That this association could also emerge in ways other than through a direct combination of Yahweh and *lḥm/milḥāmâ* is shown by the war narratives involving Yahweh in which these terms do not play any decisive role.

b. The same Yahweh that fights for his people, however, can also turn *against* his people in war. He prevents the king from maintaining himself in battle (Ps. 89:44[43]),[45] and the command to retreat is now given not to Israel's adversaries, but to Israel itself, just as in a reverse fashion the enemies, and not Israel, are now exhorted to battle,[46] although these exhortations to battle do not always (have to) include the catchword *milḥāmâ*. It is Yahweh's judgment against his people which (according to the message of the prophets) is now fulfilled through war (Isa. 3:25; 13:4; 21:15; 22:2; 30:32; 42:25; Jer. 4:19; 6:4,23; 18:21; 21:4f.; 28:8[!]; 46:3; 49:2,14; Ezk. 27:27; 39:20; Hos. 10:9,14;[47] Ob. 1; Joel 2:5; Am. 1:14; Zec. 14:2; cf. Job 38:22f; Ps. 144:3; often used together with → אֵשׁ *'ēš;* → לַהַב *lahab̲;* → לַהַט *lahaṭ*).[48] Although Yahweh's judgment through war is fulfilled against Israel just as it is against hybrid foreign peoples, it is also fulfilled precisely through such peoples and their wars.[49] The day of Yahweh[50] will be a war against Israel or was already such a war (e.g., Ezk. 7:14; 13:5; 17:17; cf. Dt. 28:25f.). Yahweh will even take away the men of war[51] (Isa. 3:2), so that in the face of such an event there will be no alternative but to flee (Jer. 42:14) before this war; yet even flight offers no assurance (despite Mic. 3:5). Israel found itself forced and indeed in a position to understand Yahweh's judgment upon his own people in

43. On this topic, see Jones; Miller, 155ff.; Perlitt; von Rad; Smend; Stolz; Weippert; also Zimmerli.

44. Cf. I.2 above and the bibliog. cited there.

45. On the historical and theological considerations here, cf. T. Veijola, *Verheissung in der Krise* (Helsinki, 1982).

46. Cf. Bach.

47. Cf. here H. W. Wolff, *Hosea. Herm* (Eng. trans., 1974), 187f.

48. On Jer. 21:4f., cf. W. Thiel, *Die deuteronomistische Redaktion von Jeremia 1–25. WMANT,* 41 (1973), 233f. with bibliog.

49. On this topic, cf. Christensen; Soggin.

50. → יוֹם *yôm,* VI, 28-31.

51. Cf. I.3.g above.

connection with its faith in Yahweh the warrior. War also constitutes judgment, and not merely a positive experience for the people of God.

It was perhaps the experience of Yahweh's power in war that brought together and bonded Israel's tribes. War was by no means particularly "holy," but for the OT it is quite naturally also a matter of religion. War itself is not praised; rather, Yahweh is experienced, probably even primarily, as a warring God of deliverance (cf. the famous remark by Julius Wellhausen[52]: "Yahweh was the battle cry of this league of war. . . . The military encampment in time of war was both the nation's cradle and its oldest sanctuary. Israel was there, and Yahweh was there"). This does not imply that war constituted a cultic act or that there was ever any cultic representation of Yahweh's battles. There is no textual evidence for this, and the portrait painted by Chronicles is theoretical wishful thinking. Although some assertions (e.g., portraying Yahweh as *gibbôr:* cf. Isa. 9:6[7]; 10:21 or *meleḵ*) are also attested in reference to El,[53] this says nothing about Yahweh's wars (e.g., in Ex. 15; Ps. 18; Isa. 13; Joel 4)[54] also originally having been cosmic struggles. Israel was Yahweh's people and Yahweh's community — this was the presupposition for the OT political theology of war. This is far removed, however, from any high ethical estimation of war; rather, war was exposed (David; kingship) as an instrument of human power politics. While it is not glorified, however, neither is it underestimated. Yahweh's help was experienced through it, so that the assertion was often made that in the final analysis it was Yahweh's war, not that of human beings (cf. only Dt. 1:41f.). To label this as mere theological ideology is unacceptable in view of the overall OT witness, especially when one recalls that war also constituted judgment upon Israel itself.

One important factor illuminating the OT view and understanding of the practice of war is that specific statutes of war are traced back to Yahweh (Dt. 20:1-7,20 with the catchwords *lḥm/milḥāmâ;* 21:10; Nu. 10:9; cf. Dt. 7:20-26; 2 Ch. 20:1; 1 Mc. 3:56; also 1QM 7:1-7; 10:2-4[55]).

5. *Overcoming War; War and Peace.* It was certainly not a matter of indifference to the ancient Israelites whether there was war or peace. The OT says nothing about war as a locus for the development of manly virtues. War is also full of violence (cf. merely Dt. 20), violence which P was not the first to view negatively (Gen. 6:12f.).[56] Thus the best antithesis to war is peace, and *šālôm* accordingly constitutes the fullest semantic opposite to *milḥāmâ* (1 K. 20:18; Ps. 120:7; Eccl. 3:8; Mic. 3:5; Zec. 9:10; cf. also Dt. 20:12; Josh. 11:19; 2 S. 8:10; 11:7; 1 K. 2:5;[57] 1 Ch. 18:10; Isa. 27:4f.).[58]

---

52. *Israelitische und jüdische Geschichte* (Berlin, ^{9}1958), 23f.
53. → אל *'ēl* (I, 242-261).
54. So Miller.
55. On these texts, cf. esp. Stolz, 25ff.; Carmichael's views here are somewhat problematical.
56. → חמס *ḥāmās (chāmās)* (IV, 478-487).
57. On this passage, cf. M. Noth, *Könige 1–16. BK,* IX/1 (^{2}1983).
58. Cf. also M. Dahood and T. Penar, "Ugaritic-Hebrew Parallel Pairs," *RSP,* I, 262, for Ugaritic evidence.

2 S. 11:7 and also Jgs. 8:9; 1 K. 2:5, however, show that → שלום *šālôm* does not always mean simply the "absence of war."

It is then especially postexilic texts (or additions from this period) that speak of peace and hope (often as eschatological promises) that Yahweh will destroy all weapons (Jer. 49:35; Hos. 1:5; 2:20[18]; Mic. 5:9f.[10f.]; Zec. 9:10).[59] Originally this probably meant (only) that he would do this because of and through his intervention in war on Israel's behalf. However, such statements concerning the war of Yahweh (!) were modified and expanded into positive, general anticipation, developing probably from the basis of Ps. 46:10(9) (cf. 76:4[3]). Isa. 41:12 foretells an end to the (Babylonian) men of war, and the promise in 28:5f. (secondary) probably also referred initially only to one quite specific enemy before receiving a more expanded interpretation. According to Hos. 1:7 (addition), Yahweh will no longer deliver through war; yet next to Zec. 4:6 we later have the evidence of 10:3-5 or ch. 14;[60] and even the beautiful testimony of hope in Isa. 2:4 (= Mic. 4:3) finds not only its antithesis in Ps. 18:35,40(34,39) par., but also its negative counterpart in Joel 4:10(3:10), even if according to the context there those who so speak will come to ruin. The notion of peace among nations was not primarily, and certainly not exclusively, Israelite, nor was such hope able to establish itself as the predominant one within the OT, as shown by the book of Daniel and other texts of early Jewish apocalypticism.[61] At this point one should not be too quick to harmonize, nor to read the OT too one-sidedly in its testimony concerning war and peace. Although as a statement of trust Job 5:20 does indeed occupy a weighty position within its own context, it also finds its direct corrective and counterargument in Eccl. 8:8.

II. The Verb. The preceding discussion of the noun already prompted several references to the verb. The discussion commenced with the noun because of the wider and more comprehensive scope of its usage, to which that of the verb can then be referred (only 4 occurrences in the qal, 164 in the niphal; one should probably also add Dt. 32:24, though not Jgs. 5:8). As far as distribution is concerned,[62] it occurs primarily in Exodus, Numbers–2 Kings, Nehemiah, Chronicles, and Jeremiah, though not, e.g., in Genesis, Leviticus, Deutero-Isaiah, or Ezekiel; among the Minor Prophets only in Deutero-Zechariah; no occurrences in the Wisdom Literature. The verb means "to fight, do battle with," rarely also "to besiege" (a city: Jer. 32:24,29; 34:1,22), and is often used with the preps. *'ēṯ/'im, 'el,* or *'al* when the sense is "against" and with *l^e* in the sense of "for." The verb and noun often appear together within the same context, a fact underscoring anew their close association (1 S. 8:20; 2 S. 11:17,20; 1 K. 12:21; 2 K. 16:5; 2 Ch. 11:1; 32:8; Zec. 10:5). Subjects of the verb include individuals as warriors (e.g., Dāvid against Goliath), kings, who then naturally also represent their people (Saul, then analogously also Gideon or Jephthah), further the people of Israel, a foreign nation, and other nations (usually as Israel's enemies). One particular textual

59. Cf. Bach, *Festschrift von Rad.*
60. On Deutero-Zechariah, cf. Ellul.
61. Cf. Preuss, 132ff., on the question of Yahweh's eschatological power.
62. Cf. *THAT,* II, 502.

group includes the statements concerning the belligerent adversaries of the psalmist (Ps. 35:1; 56:2f.[1f.]; 109:3);[63] here, too, Yahweh is ultimately invoked as warrior (Ps. 35:3).

Fighting is discussed without any particular emphasis as a human activity (especially of kings) (1 S. 4:10; 13:5; 2 S. 8:10; 2 K. 3:21; 6:8; 8:29; 9:15; 16:5 [cf. Isa. 7:1]; 2 Ch. 26:6; 27:5; Isa. 20:1; Jer. 33:5; 34:7; 41:12; cf. also the summaries of the kings of Israel/Judah in 1 K. 14:19; 22:46; 2 K. 13:12; 14:15,28; also those with specific names, e.g., 2 Ch. 27:7).

A smaller group includes texts concerning the wilderness wanderings. Here adversaries war with Israel as it journeys to the promised land. These narratives are by no means concerned only with the theme of creaturely survival, but rather also with that of deliverance (in war) (Ex. 17:8; Nu. 21:1,23; 22:11).

Analogous to the usage of the noun, the verb is also used in the narratives of Israel's conquest of the land or of its efforts to secure the land against surrounding hostile neighbors (Josh. 9:2; 10:5,29,31,34,36; 11:5; 24:8,9,11; Jgs. 1:1,3,5,8,9; 5:19f.; Josh. 19:47 in reference to Dan and its territory). Here it is especially the Ammonites who fight against Israel (and vice versa): Jgs. 10:9,18; 11:4f.,6,8,9; 11:20,25,27,32; cf. 11:12; 12:1,3,4: i.e., altogether 15 occurrences as a recurring thematic word in the account of Jephthah's wars against the Ammonites, or in retrospect.[64]

Furthermore, the verb is used (like the noun) in the accounts of the wars of Saul and David against the Philistines (1 S. 4:9f.; 13:5; 31:1; 1 Ch. 10:1) and Syrians (2 S. 10:17; 1 Ch. 19:17). Israel wants to have a king go into battle both along with it and on its behalf (1 S. 8:20). Saul is also to fight against the Amalekites and to execute the ban[65] against them (1 S. 15:18, cited as divine discourse). The verb then quite naturally also occurs in the narrative of the battle between David and Goliath (1 S. 17:9f.,32f. [4 occurrences]; cf. the subst. in v. 47).

Jeremiah twice receives the following salvific promise accompanied by the formula of succor: "They will fight against you; but they shall not prevail against you" (Jer. 1:19; 15:20).[66] Jer. 21:5 even employs the Deuteronomic/Deuteronomistic expression "with outstretched hand and mighty arm."[67]

The previously discussed[68] ideology of war unique to Chronicles also manifests itself there in the use of the verb. Here 9 occurrences come from the hand of the Chronicler independent of the source documents and parallels in Samuel and Kings.

---

63. See Ruppert.

64. Cf. J. A. Soggin, *Judges. OTL* (Eng. trans. 1981), 202-222; W. Richter, "Die Überlieferungen um Jephtah Ri 10,17–12,6," *Bibl,* 47 (1966), 485-556; Stolz, 123ff.; R. M. Polzin, *Moses and the Deuteronomist* (New York, 1980), 176-181.

65. → חרם *ḥāram* (V, 180-199).

66. For a discussion of the relationship between these two texts, cf. N. Ittmann, *Die Konfessionen Jeremias. WMANT,* 54 (1981), 182ff. On Jer. 21:4 (cf. 34:7; 37:8 and elsewhere), cf. I.4.b above; in addition to Thiel (see n. 48 above), cf. also H. Weippert, *Die Prosareden des Jeremiabuches. BZAW,* 132 (1973), 67-86, on the identification of textual strata and linguistic features.

67. See H. D. Preuss, *Deuteronomium. EdF,* 164 (1982), 187.

68. See I.3.d.

2 Ch. 26:6; 27:5 are narratives; 2 Ch. 35:20,22 give slightly more emphatic statements; and 2 Ch. 13:12; 20:17; 32:8 are then war orations. Yahweh ultimately always fights with and for Judah, and the mere knowledge of this brings the "fear of Yahweh"[69] upon the enemies (2 Ch. 17:10; 20:29). Concerning the pointed mention by Chronicles of fighting among brethren (Israel and Judah), cf. also the use of the verb in 1 K. 12:24; 2 Ch. 11:4; Zec. 14:14.[70]

At times, however, Yahweh himself fights (14 occurrences; usually salvific promises: Ex. 14:14,25 [J]; Dt. 1:30; 3:22; 20:4; Josh. 10:14,42; 23:3; cf. v. 10; Neh. 4:8,14[14,20]; Jer. 21:5: in Nebuchadnezzar against Israel!; Zec. 14:3; however, cf. also 2 Ch. 13:12). And according to Jgs. 5:20, the stars fight for Israel from the heavens (all occurrences usually niphal, with no significant difference from the qal; compare Ex. 14:14 and 25). One should also consider the plea in Ps. 35:1; references to Isa. 7:1-9; 30:15f.; 31:1,3 also seem in order (cf. also Isa. 60:10; 30:32). As in Dt. 20:4, statements concerning Yahweh's own fighting are often combined with the assurance of his accompaniment or active presence[71] (Jer. 1:19; 15:20; Zec. 10:5); Yahweh must be "in the midst of Israel" if Israel is to fight and be victorious (Dt. 1:41f.; cf. 20:4: "goes with you"). Yahweh's fighting, however, is often closely associated and interwoven with Israel's own fighting; according to Chronicles (2 Ch. 13:12; 20:17; 32:8), Yahweh directs Judah's wars (as already in 1 S. 18:17; 25:28; cf. Zec. 10:5; compare also Josh. 10:25,29 in connection with v. 42; Dt. 20:4,10,19; 1 S. 17:47 alongside vv. 9f.,32f.). Although such thinking in and of itself is especially characteristic of Deuteronomy and the Deuteronomistic history,[72] it is precisely there that the verb *lḥm* is seldom used, prompting anew the question whether such references to Yahweh's fighting really are always a result of Deuteronomic/Deuteronomistic thought.[73] The assertion in 1 S. 12:9 (Deuteronomistic) that Yahweh gives Israel into the hands of its enemies, so that they fight against Israel, is a different (clearly Deuteronomistic) interpretive category, since certain prophetic texts represent a similar view (Jer. 21:2,5; 32:24,29; cf. 34:22; 37:8,10: here, too, often with Deuteronomistic redaction; cf. Isa. 63:10), and Yahweh's own fighting is often the content of prophetic oracles of judgment against Israel/Judah (Isa. 30:32 [textual emendation necessary?]; Jer. 21:1-7; 34:22; 37:8,10; 51:30 [usually with the perf. or perf. consecutive]). Consequently, although the use of both the verb and the noun testify to the understanding and continued hopeful anticipation of Yahweh as a warring God, both events and words showed that Yahweh's fighting could also direct itself against his own people.

Preuss

69. → פחד *paḥaḏ*.

70. On the ideology of war in Chronicles, see Welten; on the "fear of Yahweh," see Welten, 97.

71. → את *'ēṯ* (I, 449-463).

72. Cf. Preuss, *Deuteronomium,* 188f.

73. Cf. Rose, *Deuteronomist und Jahwist.*

מלט mlṭ → פלט plṭ

מֶלֶךְ melek; מָלַךְ mālak; מְלוּכָה m^elûkâ; מַלְכוּת malkût; מַמְלָכָה mamlākâ; מַמְלָכוּת mamlākût

Contents: I. Royal Titles and the Understanding of Kingship in the Ancient Near East: 1. Egypt; 2. Mesopotamia; 3. West Semites. II. The Word Group *mlk:* 1. Origin and Distribution; 2. Derivations; 3. LXX Renderings. III. General Usage of the Word Group *mlk:* 1. Occurrences and Distribution in the OT; 2. Semantic Field Associations; 3. The Verb; 4. Fixed Expressions; 5. Abstract Expressions; 6. OT Notions of Kingship; 7. *mlk* in the Prophetic Criticism of Kings; 8. The Problem of an OT Ideology of Kingship. IV. Theological Usage: Yahweh as King — Yahweh *mlk:* 1. Occurrences; 2. Origin of the Predication "Yahweh as King"; 3. Use in Theophoric Personal Names; 4. The Preexilic Zion Tradition; 5. Other Divine Kings in the OT; 6. Notions of *mlk* in Prophecy; 7. "Yahweh *mālak*"; 8. The So-called Enthronement Festival of Yahweh; 9. The Yahweh-Kingship Hymns; 10. Other Psalms; 11. Late Prophecy and Apocalypticism. V. Qumran.

---

melek. G. W. Ahlström, *Psalm 89: Eine Liturgie aus dem Ritual des leidenden Königs* (Lund, 1959); A. Alt, "The Monarchy in the Kingdoms of Israel and Judah," *Essays on OT History and Religion* (Eng. trans., Garden City, 1966), 311-335; *idem* and H. Donner, "Königtum in Israel," *RGG*[3], III (1959), 1709-12; S. Amsler, *David, Roi et Messie. CahTh,* 49 (1963); A. Bentzen, *King and Messiah* (Eng. trans., London, 1955); *idem, Det sakrale Kongedømme* (Copenhagen, 1945); K. H. Bernhardt, *Das Problem der altorientalischen Königsideologie im AT. SVT,* 8 (1961); H. J. Boecker, *Die Beurteilung der Anfänge des Königtums in den deuteronomistischen Abschnitten des 1. Samuelbuches. WMANT,* 31 (1969); P. A. H. de Boer, " 'Vive le roi!,' " *VT,* 5 (1955), 225-231; G. Buccellati, *Cities and Nations of Ancient Syria. StSem,* 26 (1967); H. Cazelles, "De l'idéologie royale," *Festschrift T. H. Gaster. JANES,* 5 (1973), 59-73; *idem,* "La titulature du roi David. Mélanges Bibliques. Festschrift A. Robert. Travaux de l'Institut Catholique de Paris, 4 (1957), 131-36; G. Cooke, "The Israelite King as Son of God," *ZAW,* 73 (1961), 202-225; J. Coppens, *Le messianisme royal. LD,* 54 (1968); F. M. Cross, "Kings and Prophets," *Canaanite Myth and Hebrew Epic* (Cambridge, Mass., 1973), 217-289; F. Crüsemann, *Der Widerstand gegen das Königtum. WMANT,* 49 (1978); I. Engnell, *Studies in Divine Kingship in the Ancient Near East* (1943, repr. Oxford, 1967); J. de Fraine, *L'aspect religieux de la royauté israélite. AnBibl,* 3 (1954); H. Frankfort, *Kingship and the Gods* (Chicago, 1948, repr. 1978); E. Galbiati, "Il carattere sacro della regalità nell'antico Israele," *BeO,* 19 (1977), 89-100; A. Gelston, "Kingship in the Book of Hosea," *Language and Meaning. OTS,* 19 (1974), 71-85; E. R. Goodenough, "Kingship in Early Israel," *JBL,* 48 (1929), 169-205; M. Görg, *Gott-König-Reden in Israel und Ägypten. BWANT,* 105[6/5] (1975); H. Gressmann, *Der Messias. FRLANT,* 26[43] (1929); J. H. Grønbek, "Kongens kultiske funktion i det forexilske Israel," *DTT,* 20 (1957), 1-16; S. Herrmann, "Die Königsnovelle in Ägypten und in Israel," *Festschrift A. Alt. WZ Leipzig,* 3 (1953/54), 32-44, 87-91; H.-R. Hölzel, *Die Rolle des Stammes* "mlk" *und seiner Ableitungen für die Herrschaftsvorstellungen der vorexilischen Zeit* (diss., Hamburg, 1971); S. H. Hooke, ed., *The Labyrinth* (London, 1935);

W. Huss, "Der 'König der Könige' und der 'Herr der Könige,' " *ZDPV,* 93 (1977), 131-140; T. Ishida, "נָגִיד: A Term for Legitimation of the Kingship," *AJBI,* 3 (1977), 35-51; *idem, The Royal Dynasties in Ancient Israel. BZAW,* 142 (1977); A. R. Johnson, *Sacral Kingship in Ancient Israel* (Cardiff, [2]1967); E. Kutsch, *Salbung als Rechtsakt im AT und im alten Orient. BZAW,* 87 (1963); M. Liverani, "La royauté syrienne de l'âge du bronze récent," in P. Garelli, ed., *Le palais et la royauté, archéologie et civilization. XIXe Rencontre assyriologique internationale 1971* (Paris, 1974), 329-356; N. Lohfink, "*melek, šallîṭ* und *môšel* bei Kohelet und die Abfassungszeit des Buchs," *Bibl,* 62 (1981), 535-543; D. Lys, "De l'onction à l'intronisation royale," *ETR,* 29/3 (1954), 1-54; C. Macholz, "Nagid — der Statthalter, 'praefectus,' " *Sefer Rendtorff. Festschrift R. Rendtorff. BDBAT,* 1 (1975), 59-72; *idem,* "Die Stellung des Königs in der israelitischen Gerichtsverfassung," *ZAW,* 84 (1972), 157-182; R. Martin-Achard, "L'institution de la royauté en Israel," *BCPE,* 29 (1977), 45-50; A. D. H. Mayes, "The Rise of the Israelite Monarchy," *ZAW,* 90 (1978), 1-19; T. N. D. Mettinger, *King and Messiah. CB,* 8 (1976); D. Michel, "Studien zu den sogenannten Thronbesteigungspsalmen," *VT,* 6 (1956), 40-68; S. Morenz, "Ägyptische und davidische Königstitulatur," *ZÄS,* 79 (1954), 77f.; S. Mowinckel, *He That Cometh* (Eng. trans., Nashville, 1956); L. M. Muntingh, "Some Aspects of West-Semitic Kingship in the Period of the Hebrew Patriarchs," *Biblical Essays* (Potchefstroom, 1966), 106-115; C. R. North, "The Religious Aspects of Hebrew Kingship," *ZAW,* 50 (1932), 8-38; M. Noth, "God, King, and Nation in the OT," *The Laws in the Pentateuch"* (Eng. trans. 1966, repr., London, 1984), 145-178; N. Poulssen, *König und Tempel im Glaubenszeugnis des AT. SBM,* 3 (1967); G. von Rad, "βασιλεύς," *TDNT,* I, 565-571; further bibliog. in *TWNT,* X/2 (1979), 1008-1014; *idem,* "The Royal Ritual in Judah," *The Problem of the Hexateuch* (Eng. trans., New York, 1966), 222-231; H. Ringgren, "König und Messias," *ZAW,* 64 (1952), 120-147; *idem, The Messiah in the OT. SBT,* 18 (1956); E. I. J. Rosenthal, "Some Aspects of the Hebrew Monarchy," *JJS,* 9 (1958), 1-18; L. Schmidt, *Menschlicher Erfolg und Jahwes Initiative. WMANT,* 38 (1970); W. H. Schmidt, "Kritik am Königtum," *Probleme biblischer Theologie. Festschrift G. von Rad* (Munich, 1971), 440-461; K. Seybold, *Das davidische Königtum im Zeugnis der Propheten. FRLANT,* 107[125] (1972); J. A. Soggin, *Das Königtum in Israel. BZAW,* 104 (1967); *idem,* "מֶלֶךְ melek," *THAT,* I, 908-920; *idem,* "Zur Entwicklung des alttestamentlichen Königtums," *ThZ,* 15 (1959), 401-418; T. C. G. Thornton, "Charismatic Kingship in Israel and Judah," *JTS,* N.S. 14 (1963), 1-11; R. de Vaux, "The King of Israel, Vassal of Yahweh," *The Bible and the Ancient Near East* (Eng. trans., Garden City, 1971), 152-180; T. Veijola, *Die ewige Dynastie. AnAcScFen,* B, 193 (1975); *idem, Das Königtum in der Beurteilung der deuteronomistischen Historiographie. AnAcScFen,* B, 198 (1977); A. Weiser, "Die Legitimation des Königs David," *VT,* 16 (1966), 325-354; G. Widengren, "King and Covenant," *JSS,* 2 (1957), 1-32; *idem, Sakrales Königtum im AT und im Judentum* (Stuttgart, 1955); H. Wildberger, "Die Thronnamen des Messias, Jes. 9,5b," *ThZ,* 16 (1960), 314-332 = *Jahwe und Sein Volk. ThB,* 66 (1979), 56-74.

I: W. Barta, *Untersuchungen zur Göttlichkeit des regierenden Königs. MÄSt,* 32 (1975); R. Labat, *Le caractère religieux de la royauté assyro-babylonienne. Études d'Assyriologie,* 2 (Paris, 1939); A. Lemaire, "Note sur le titre *bn hmlk* dans l'ancien Israel," *Sem,* 29 (1979), 59-65; A. Moret, *Du caractère religieux de la royauté pharaonique. BdÉ,* 15 (1902); G. Posener, *De la divinité du Pharaon. Cahiers de la Societé Asiatique,* 15 (Paris, 1960); E. Ringgren, *Religions of the Ancient Near East* (Eng. trans., Philadelphia, 1973), 36-42, 99-107, 169-173; *idem, Die Religionen des Alten Orients. ATDSond* (1979), 46-50; W. O. P. Römer, *Sumerische 'Königshymnen' der Isin-Zeit. DMOA,* 13 (1965); B. Schmitz, *Untersuchungen zum Titel* sȝ — njswt *"Königssohn". Habelts Diss. Ägyptologie,* 2 (Bonn, 1976); Seux.

IV: A. Alt, "Gedanken über das Königtum Jahwes," *KlSchr,* I ([3]1964), 345-357; J. Bonsirven, "Le règne de Dieu suivant l'AT," *Mélanges Bibliques A. Robert,* 295-302; M. Buber, *Kingship of God* (Eng. trans., New York, 1967); F. M. Cross, *Canaanite Myth and Hebrew Epic* (Cambridge, Mass., 1973); W. Dietrich, "Gott als König," *ZThK,* 77 (1980), 251-268; O. Eissfeldt,

"Jahwe als König," *ZAW,* 46 (1928), 81-105 = *KLSchr,* I (1962), 172-193; *idem,* "Jahwes Königsprädizierung als Verklärung national-politischer Ansprüche Israels," *Wort, Lied, und Gottesspruch. Festschrift J. Ziegler, II. FzB,* 2 (1972), 51-55 = *KlSchr,* V (1973), 216-221; I. Engnell, *The Call of Isaiah. UUÅ,* 1949/4; J. de Fraine, "La royauté du Yahvé dans les textes concernant l'arche," *Volume de Congrès, Genève 1965. SVT,* 15 (1966), 134-149; J. Gray, *The Biblical Doctrine of the Reign of God* (Edinburgh, 1979); *idem,* "The Hebrew Conception of the Kingship of God," *VT,* 6 (1956), 268-285; *idem,* "The Kingship of God in the Prophets and Psalms," *VT,* 11 (1961), 1-29; H. Gross, *Weltherrschaft als religiöse Idee im AT. BBB,* 6 (1953), 113-129; J. Hempel, "Königtum Gottes im AT," *RGG*[3], III (1959), 1706-9; A. A. Koolhaas, *Theocratie en monarchie in Israel* (Wageningen, 1957) [Eng. summary]; H.-J. Kraus, *Die Königsherrschaft Gottes im AT. BHTh,* 13 (1951); W. Küppers, "Gottesherrschaft und Königtum in Israel," *IKZ,* 25 (1935), 148-160; J. Lindblom, "The Idea of the Kingdom of God," *ExpT,* 51 (1939/1940), 91-96; V. Maag, "Malkût Jahweh," *Congress Volume, Oxford 1959. SVT,* 7 (1960), 129-153 = *Kultur, Kulturkontakt und Religion* (Göttingen, 1980), 145-169; H.-P. Müller, "Die himmlische Ratsversammlung: Motivgeschichtliches zu Apc 5_{1-5}," *ZNW,* 54 (1963), 254-267; L. Rost, "Königsherrschaft Jahwes in vorköniglicher Zeit?" *ThLZ,* 85 (1960), 721-24; H. H. Schmid, "Jahwe und die Kulttraditionen von Jerusalem," *ZAW,* 67 (1955), 168-197; W. H. Schmidt, *Königtum Gottes in Ugarit und Israel. BZAW,* 80 ([2]1966); J. Schreiner, *Sion-Jerusalem Jahwes Königssitz. StANT,* 7 (1963); F. Stolz, *Strukturen und Figuren im Kult von Jerusalem. BZAW,* 118 (1970); P. Welten, "Die Vernichtung des Todes und die Königsherrschaft Gottes," *ThZ,* 38 (1982), 129-146; H. W. Wolff, "Herrschaft Jahwes und Messiasgestalt im AT," *ZAW,* 54 (1936), 168-202.

IV.7-10: A. Bentzen, "King Ideology — "Urmensch" — "Thronbestijgingsfeest," *StTh,* 3 (1949), 143-157; F. M. T. de Liagre Böhl, *Nieuwjaarsfeest en Koningsdag in Babylon en Israël* (diss., Groningen, 1927) = *Opera Minora* (Groningen, 1953), 263-281; A. Caquot, "Le psaume 47 et la royauté de Yahwé," *RHPR,* 39 (1959), 311-337; H. Cazelles, "Le Nouvel An en Israél," *DBS,* VI (1960), 620-645; J. Coppens, "La date des Psaumes de l'Intronisation de Yahvé," *ETL,* 43 (1967), 192-97; *idem, "Les Psaumes de l'Intronisation de Yahvé et de la Royauté de Yahvé," ETL,* 42 (1966), 225-231; A. Feuillet, "Les Psaumes eschatologiques du règne de Jahweh," *NRTh,* 83 (1951), 244-260, 352-363; A. Gelston, "A Note on יהוה מלך," *VT,* 16 (1966), 507-512; H. Gross, "Läst sich in den Psalmen ein 'Thronbesteigungsfest Gottes' nachweisen?" *TrThZ,* 65 (1956), 24-40; A. S. Kapelrud, "Jahves tronstigningsfest og funnene i Ras Sjamra," *NTT,* 41 (1940), 38-58; *idem,* "Nochmals *Jahwä mālāk,*" *VT,* 13 (1963), 229-231; L. Köhler, "Jahwäh mālāk," *VT,* 3 (1953), 188f.; E. Lipiński, "Les Psaumes de la royauté de Yahwé dans l'exégèse moderne," in R. de Langhe, ed., *Le Psautier. OrBibLov,* 4 (1962), 133-272; *idem,* "Les Psaumes du Règne," *Assemblées du Seigneur,* 9 (1964), 7-22; *idem, La royauté de Yahwé dans la poésie et le culte de l'ancien Israël. VVAW.L,* 27/55 ([2]1968); *idem,* "Yāhweh mâlāk," *Bibl,* 44 (1963), 405-460; W. S. McCullough, "The 'Enthronement of Yahweh' Psalms," *A Stubborn Faith. Festschrift W. A. Irwin* (Dallas, 1956), 53-61; J. Morgenstern, "The Cultic Setting of the 'Enthronement Psalms,'" *HUCA,* 35 (1964), 1-42; S. Mowinckel, *Psalmenstudien,* II: *Das Thronbesteigungsfest Jahwäs und der Ursprung der Eschatologie. SNVAO,* 1922 (repr. Amsterdam, 1961); *idem,* "Tronstigningssalmerne og Jahves tronstigningsfest," *Norsk teologi til reformationsjubileet. NTT,* 1917, 13-79; J. Muilenburg, "Psalm 47," *JBL,* 63 (1944), 235-256; L. I. Pap, *Das israelitische Neujahrsfest* (Kampen, 1933); E. Peterson, Εἷς Θεός. *FRLANT,* 24[41] (1926), 141ff.; J. Ridderbos, "Jahwäh malak," *VT,* 4 (1954), 87-89; R. A. Rosenberg, "Yahweh Becomes King," *JBL,* 85 (1966), 297-307; H. Schmidt, *Die Thronfahrt Jahves am Fest der Jahreswende im alten Israel* (Tübingen, 1927); N. H. Snaith, *The Jewish New Year Festival* (London, 1947); J. H. Ulrichsen, "*JHWH mālāḵ:* einige sprachliche Beobachtungen," *VT,* 27 (1977), 361-374; P. Volz, *Das Neujahrsfest Jahwes* (Tübingen, 1912); J. D. W. Watts, "Yahweh Mālak Psalms," *ThZ,* 21 (1965), 341-48; P. Welten, "Königsherrschaft Jahwes und Thronbesteigung," *VT,* 32 (1982), 297-302.

I. Royal Titles and the Understanding of Kingship in the Ancient Near East.

1. *Egypt.* The usual Egyptian word for "king" is *nśw,* more completely rendered as *nśw byty,* "King of Upper and Lower Egypt"; other words include *ỉty,* "ruler," *nb,* "lord," and *nb tꜣ.wy,* "lord of the two lands." One frequent designation is *ḥm.f,* "his majesty." The OT term *parʿōh,* "pharaoh," corresponding to *pr ʿꜣ,* "great house," refers in the Old Kingdom to the palace, and from the twelfth dynasty on in specific formulas to the king; beginning with the nineteenth dynasty it is used as a title for the king.

At his enthronement the king received what is known as the royal protocol *(nḫb.t)* with the five royal names designating him as Horus, the protégé of the two crown goddesses *(nb.ty),* as "Horus of Gold," as King of Upper and Lower Egypt *(nśw byty),* and as the Son of Re. As Horus he is the legitimate heir to the throne, following his deceased father, who has become Osiris. As King of Upper and Lower Egypt he embodies in his own person the unity of the two halves of the empire. As Son of Re he represents the sun-god and creator who made and maintains the cosmic order. He represents the latter also in the verbal expression *ḫʿy,* "appear": just as the primeval god appeared at the beginning and created the world, and just as Re appears each morning, so also does the king now appear on his throne and create order in the land. The cosmic and social order is called *mꜣʿ.t* (often translated as "truth"); on the one hand, Maat is the daughter of the sun-god, and on the other the sacrifice the king brings to the god. The king's cultic actions thus maintain *mꜣʿ.t.*

The divine procreation and birth of the king is represented by pictorial illustrations with accompanying texts (in Deir el-Bahri for Hatshepsut, and in Luxor for Amenhotep III). Amon assumes the form of the reigning king and begets with the queen the royal child. The child's name is spoken, and the future of the new ruler is proclaimed (cf. Isa. 7:14-16). Thus the king is predestined to rule; indeed, he is even said to "rule already within the egg."

The king is thus god and the son of a god, but is so only by virtue of his office. Otherwise he is a human being with human characteristics.

The king's task is to "make the land flourish again as it did in primeval times by the plans of Maat." In this respect he embodies the creator-god. Just as the creator-god, through Hu (proclamation, command) and Sia (knowledge, wisdom), made the world and Maat ruling in it, so also is it said of the king: "Hu is in your mouth, Sia in your heart, your speech is the shrine of Maat." Just as the creator was alone at the beginning, so also does the king vanquish his enemies alone (e.g., Rameses II at the battle of Kadesh).

The king is the shepherd of his people, and is to care for them just as a shepherd does for his flock. An effective reign of a king also enhances the fruitfulness of nature: the inundation of the Nile, the growth of grain, and so on. Thus new kings are greeted as the bringers of a time of salvation with rich harvests, good fortune, and joy throughout the land.[1]

---

1. "Joy at the Accession of Mer-ne-Ptah," *ANET,* 378; similarly "Joy at the Accession of Ramses IV," 378f.; also in A. Erman, *The Literature of the Ancient Egyptians* (Eng. trans. 1927, repr. New York, 1971), 278f., 279f. Cf. the royal texts in W. Beyerlin, ed., *Near Eastern Religious Texts. OTL* (Eng. trans. 1978), 27-30.

Akhenaten claims a special position as revealer of the one god: "There is no other who knows you, but your son [Akhenaten]."[2]

The king as ruler is responsible for the establishment and maintenance of temples. The procedure of temple establishment as a result of divine command is occasionally narrated in what is known as a royal novella.[3]

2. *Mesopotamia.* a. The Sumerian king is called *lù.gal,* "great man." Kingship itself "comes down from heaven," and is thus a divine institution; each individual king also derives his majesty from the gods and is considered to be the son of a god and/or a goddess. Šulgi was "carried in the sacred womb of the goddess Ninsuna." Gudea names the goddess Gatumdug as mother and father and says: "You took my father's seed into your womb. You bore me in the sanctuary." Whereas some expressions seem to suggest physical procreation, others suggest that enthronement was viewed as symbolic rebirth.[4] Occasionally the king is called the "god of the land" or something similar, and in certain periods his name is written with the divine determinative. Some evidence suggests that the king's divinity is connected with his role in the celebration of the sacred wedding.[5]

The king is thought to be extraordinarily wise; he "loves justice and despises wickedness," maintains law and order, protects widows and orphans, and is the shepherd of his people, "like father and mother for his people." He is responsible for the maintenance of the cult and often appears as the founder of temples; Gudea, e.g., constructs a temple according to a heavenly model.[6]

b. The Akkadian word for king is *šarru,* which is etymologically related to Heb. → שַׂר *śar.* In addition, the term *malku* is used.

Royal ideology changes with Hammurabi inasmuch as the name of the king is no longer written with the divine determinative, although the king's sacral duties and functions do remain intact. As before, kingship "comes down from heaven." The gods have chosen the king for his office even before his birth and have predetermined his destiny; he is "sent" by them. He is called the son of a particular god or goddess, referring in this case probably more to divine protection — every person, after all, is (symbolically) the son (daughter) of his own particular god. The king can be called the shadow or representation *(tamšīlu)* of the god. Especially Assyrian kings are often described as being surrounded by divine radiance *(mēlammu)* which prompts terror among enemies. The divine nature of kingship is also attested by the fact that several epithets apply both to kings and to gods,[7] although this does not change the fact that the king stands before the gods as a mere human being.

---

2. Beyerlin, ¶46.
3. Cf. III.6 below.
4. Å. Sjöberg, review of Römer, *Or,* 35 (1966), 288f.; *idem, RoB,* 20 (1961), 20, 25.
5. Römer, 57; cf. also M.-J. Seux, "Königtum," *RLA,* VI (1983), 140-173.
6. *ANET,* 268; also *SAHG,* 137ff.
7. Engnell, 178ff.

Through the appropriate titles the king claims world dominion: *šar kiššati,* "king of the totality," *šar kibrāt(im) arba'i(m)/erbetti,* "king of the four corners of the universe."[8] He rules "from the upper to the lower sea" (or the Mediterranean and Persian Gulf). He is also *šarru dannu,* "mighty king," *šarru rabû,* "great king," etc.[9]

The king represents the divine world to his subjects. He is the *iššakku,* something like the "prefect/governor" of the god. With the god's power he fights against enemies. He is the shepherd of the people, and is to maintain justice and righteousness *(mêšaru, kettu)* throughout the land and preserve the life of the land, i.e., he is to insure growth, fruitfulness, and the welfare of the land, a function occasionally expressed in "messianic" statements.

On the other hand, he is answerable to the gods. In the Babylonian New Year Festival the king must atone in order to renew his kingship. And if through the king's own guilt misfortune threatens, the king can install a substitute king *(šar pūḫi)* to accept the gods' punishment.

c. The appellation "king," however, was also a divine epithet designating the god as lord or possessor of something.[10] Enlil is "king of the lands," Ea "king of the waters' depths" *(šar apsī);* Anu, Enlil, Ashur, Marduk, and others are "king of the gods" *(šar ilāni).* Šamaš in particular is the "king of heaven and earth" *(šar šamê u erṣeti).*

In the Babylonian creation epic Marduk, before his battle with Tiamat, is proclaimed king by the gods with the words *Marduk šar;* a similar formula is applied to Ashur in what is known as the Assyrian royal ritual (representing perhaps a renewal of kingship).

3. *West Semites.* Within the Ugaritic pantheon El is the only real king *(mlk);* "he is king in the larger sense, indeed, he can be called the 'king of eternity' (*mlk ʿlm*)."[11] In addition, however, Baʿal also acquires the title of king through his victory over Yam: "Our king is Baʿal, our sovereign second to none."[12] As king he then also receives a house, i.e., a palace or temple.

The Keret and Aqhat epics, although mythologically colored, probably reflect notions associated with earthly kingship. Keret is viewed as the son of El, and his son is nursed by the goddess Aṯirat. He is the mediator of divine power and divine blessing for the community, and when he falls ill, the entire country suffers: no rain falls, and the land bears no fruit.

The figure of Danel in the Aqhat epic, although not specifically designated as king, nonetheless is a just judge and otherwise exercises the usual regnal functions. Among other things, he, like Keret, protects the rights of the poor, of widows, and of orphans. When his son Aqhat dies, the land bears no fruit.

---

8. Seux, 305f., 308ff.
9. *Ibid.,* 292ff.
10. K. Tallqvist, *Akkadische Götterepitheta. StOr,* 7 (1938, repr. 1974), 232ff.
11. H. Gese, *Die Religionen Altsyriens, Altarabiens und der Mandäer. RdM,* 10/2 (1970), 97.
12. *KTU,* 1.3 V, 32; also *ANET,* 133.

West Semitic inscriptions attest the general notion of sacral kingship. The king is installed in his office by the gods,[13] is responsible for the construction of temples,[14] and is to be just.[15] Kilamuwa was like a father and mother to his people, and took care of them all.[16]

Ringgren

II. The Word Group mlk.

1. *Origin and Distribution.* The Hebrew terms *meleḵ* — *mālaḵ* belong to a Northwest Semitic word group deriving from the root *mlk* with the general meaning "king," "to be king." This root is attested as early as the third millennium B.C. in northern Syrian Ebla, where various theophoric personal names occur, e.g., *A-bù-ma-lik, Eb-du-ma-lik, Gibil-ma-lik,* and in similar constructions,[17] and in the abstract *ma-li-ku-um,* "kingship,"[18] and in the feminine form *ma-lik-tum,* "queen," frequently juxtaposed with a Sumerian personal name;[19] thus far, however, the masculine form *ma-lik* does not seem to be attested in independent usage. The etymology is unknown. Derivations from (1) *mā lāḵa* (exclamation: "What [belongs] to you?")[20] or (2) *hlk* (ptcp. *mōlîḵ*) cannot be substantiated. Both the noun and verb are considered loanwords in Akkadian, where they refer primarily to foreign rulers and compete with the homonymous word group *malāku,* "to advise, counsel," *māliku,* "adviser, counselor," *malku,* "advice, counsel,"[21] both probably influenced by *šarru* and its derivatives. The appearance of precisely this special meaning in Northwest Semitic should probably be viewed as a retro-development[22]: Hebrew in Neh. 5:7, *mlk niphal,* "to take counsel with oneself" (conj. in Job 12:17; Hos. 8:4); Aram. *meᵉlaḵ*,* "advice, counsel" (Dnl. 4:24[Eng. v. 27], immediately next to *malkā'*!); *mlk,* "to ask for advice," *mlkh,* "advice."[23] Both the noun and the verb are also attested in South Semitic, again — as well as can be determined — with semantic differences: OSA, Arab. "king"; Arab., Ethiop. "possession," "to possess," and similar examples.[24] It is likely that a Paleo–West Semitic, perhaps even Proto-Semitic root *mlk*[25] underwent a different semantic development in

---

13. *KAI,* 10, 2; 202 A, 3; 214, 2f.
14. *Ibid.,* 14, 15ff.
15. *Ibid.,* 4, 6f.; 10, 8f.
16. *Ibid.,* 24, 10-13; also *ANET,* 654f.
17. G. Pettinato, *Catalogo dei testi cuneiformi di Tell Mardikh-Ebla. MEE,* I (1979), see index; H.-P. Müller, "Religionsgeschichtliche Beobachtungen zu den Texten von Ebla," *ZDPV,* 96 (1980), 11ff.
18. Cf. G. Garbini, "La Lingua di Ebla," *La parola del passato,* 33 (1978), 254.
19. G. Pettinato, *Culto ufficiale ad Ebla durante il regno di Ibbi-sipiš* (Rome, 1979), *passim,* see index.
20. W. Eilers, *WO,* 3 (1949), 142f.
21. *AHw,* II (1972), 593ff.; *CAD,* X/1 (1977), 154ff.
22. Cf. *HAL,* II (1995), 591: *mlk* II.
23. J. Hoftijzer and G. van der Kooij, *Aramaic Texts from Deir ʿAlla. DMOA,* 19 (1976), II, 9.
24. Cf. L. Kopf, "Arabische Etymologien und Parallelen zum Bibelwörterbuch," *VT,* 9 (1959), 261f. = *Studies in Arabic and Hebrew Lexicography* (Jerusalem, 1976); Wehr, *s.v.*
25. P. Fronzaroli, "Studi sul lessico comune semitico," *AANLR,* N.S. 20 (1965), 246-269.

each of the three Semitic linguistic branches, governed in Akkadian by semantic competition (displacement and semantic restriction by *šarru*), in Arabic by politico-cultural peculiarities (semantic modification), and variously influenced in a secondary fashion by the development of the word group in West Semitic (the effects of loan-words).

The noun is attested by the following phonetic forms: Eb. **ma-lik;* Amor. *milk;* Ugar. *malk* (literary language);[26] Ugar. (vernacular), South Can. (EA) *milk;* Akk. *malk(u), mālik(u);* Gk. *malch-, melch* (μελ[ε]χ, μελεϰ) (LXX transcriptions of names); Mand. *malēk;*[27] Heb. (MT) *meleḵ,* const. *malk-;* Gk. *malachei/chēm.*[28]

2. *Derivations.* The intransitive verb *mālaḵ* seems to derive from the primary noun *mlk,* and remains within the same semantic sphere. The Hebrew term *meleḵ* is paralleled by the feminine form *malkâ,* "queen," with the special derivative *meleḵeṯ (haššāmayim),* "queen (of heaven)," and the West Semitic divine names or epithets → *Mōleḵ* (MT), *Milkôm.* Abstract constructions, in part influenced by Aramaic, include the feminine forms *meluḵâ,* "kingship," *malḵûṯ,* "kingdom" (Biblical Aram. *malḵû*), and the verbal nouns *mamlāḵâ* and *mamlāḵûṯ,* "dominion, kingdom." The personal names constructed with *mlk,* frequently attested since the Mari period and then also attested in Hebrew, are also of West Semitic provenance: *Meleḵ, Mōleḵeṯ, Milkâ, Malkām, Yamlēḵ, Malkî'ēl, Malkiyyâ (Malkiyyāhû), Malkî-ṣeḏeq, Malkîrām, Malkîšûa', 'Aḇîmeleḵ, 'Aḥîmeleḵ, 'Elîmeleḵ, Mallûḵ, 'Anammeleḵ, 'Aḏrammeleḵ, 'Eḇeḏ-meleḵ, Neṯan-meleḵ* (all OT), and similar constructions (cf. *'Allameleḵ,* "king's terebinth").

3. *LXX Renderings.* As a rule, the LXX translates *mlk* forms with *basil* equivalents; since the exceptions usually are prompted by context or are in any case explainable, they thus confirm the rule. In 13 instances *meleḵ* is rendered by *árchōn.* Regarding passages from the Pentateuch (Gen. 49:20; Nu. 23:21; Dt. 17:14,15[twice]; 28:36), this is usually explained by the obvious assumption (cf. Dt. 17; 28) that during the "Mosaic period" Israel did not yet have a king[29] (cf., however, Gen. 14; 36 LXX). A similar explanation can be given for the rendering *árchōn* for MT *mōleḵ* in Lev. 18:21; 20:2,3,4,5 (differently in the other, non-Pentateuchal passages 1 K. 11:7; 2 K. 23:10; Jer. 32:35). The LXX translators correctly view the existence both of the king and of the *Moloch* in Israel as a post-Mosaic phenomenon. The passages from Isaiah are influenced by the context (more frequent use of *árchōn,* 1:10ff.), as are Ezk. 28:12 (the *árchōn* of Tyre, after *nāgîḏ* in 28:2) and 37:22,24 (assimilated to *nāśî'* in 34:24; 37:25, usually translated by *árchōn*). Dnl. 10:13 is a special case (cf. LXX *stratēgós;* Theodo-

---

26. Cf. J. Nougayrol, "Textes Suméro-accadiens des archives et bibliothèques privées d'Ugarit," *Ugaritica,* 5. *MRS,* 16 (1968), 234f., 244f.

27. *MdD,* 244f., 273.

28. For suffixal and plural forms, in texts of Epiphanius, cf. A. Jepsen, "Zur Kanongeschichte des ATs," *ZAW,* 71 (1959), 115ff.

29. See the following remarks on *archḗ.*

tion *árchōn basileías Persṓn*). The singular translation *hēgoúmenoi* occurs 3 times within the context of Ezk. 43:7,9 (the graves of the kings), probably in the sense of an actualization during a period without kings. Twice the term *stratēgós,* and once *boulḗ* are used for *melek̲*. The former occurs in Job 15:24 quite consistent with the adaptation of the parable: it is not the king, but rather the field general who prepares for battle. Regarding Dnl. 10:13, see the preceding discussion. In Dnl. 4:24(27) (Theodotion), the term *boulḗ* is the equivalent of Aram. *mᵉlak̲,* "advice, counsel," which the LXX might also have read in Eccl. 2:12 (MT *melek̲*).

The derivatives offer a similar picture. Although the verb naturally is variously rendered in its various forms, there is nonetheless little deviation from *basileu* forms, such as *krateín* in Est. 1:1 and naturally Neh. 5:7 *(mlk* niphal = *bouleúein).* Similarly, hardly any significant exceptions occur among the abstract constructions (cf. Est. 1:2; Dnl. 4:23,34[26,37]: circumscriptions with *thrónos*). Of some note are the renderings of *mamlāk̲â* by *archḗ* in Dt. 17:18,20; Isa. 10:10; Ezk. 29:14 (referring to Egypt, see the above discussion concerning *árchōn*) or by *nómos,* "district, province," in Isa. 19:2 (adaptation to the internal structure of the Egyptian state: "cities" and "districts," but no [longer] "kingdoms").

III. General Usage of the Word Group mlk.

1. *Occurrences and Distribution in the OT.* The word group of the root *mlk* occurs more than 3,000 times in the OT.[30] After *YHWH, ʾᵉlōhîm,* and *bēn,* the term *melek̲* is the fourth most frequently occurring noun in the OT, more frequent even than *yiśrāʾēl* (with *ca.* 2,500 occurrences), attesting its historical and religious significance for biblical themes. Its distribution among literary works, collections, and books corresponds to the various themes. In the Pentateuch (with only *ca.* 120 occurrences), this word group refers with few exceptions (Yahweh: Gen. 48:16[Sam.]; Ex. 15:18; Nu. 23:21; Dt. 33:5; also Gen. 17:6,16; 35:11; Nu. 24:7; Dt. 17:14f.; 28:36) to non-Israelite kings. The Deuteronomistic history offers the most occurrences (more than 1,400), a bit less than half of the total number, statistically attesting this work's special interests. The high number of occurrences in Esther is striking (more than 250 in ten chapters). Concentrations in lists and enumerations are found, e.g., in Gen. 14,36; Josh. 10,12.

2. *Semantic Field Associations.* The diverse use of *melek̲* to refer to a wide variety of monarchical forms of rule, from Late Bronze Age municipal kingship to national kingship to vast empires, references occurring both within and outside of the immediate Israelite sphere, suggests that this term encompassed a very broad and comprehensive semantic horizon, and that it was actually a skeleton term that acquired concrete meaning only through its context. Its semantic essence can be described with Jgs. 9:2 approximately as follows: *melek̲* refers to the "one man" *(ʾîš ʾeḥād̲)* who alone rules *(mšl bᵉ)* over a specific (larger) group, e.g., over the citizens of a

30. For exact statistics, see Soggin, *THAT,* I, 910.

"city" *(baʿᵃlê ʿîr)*, whereby a subordination *(ʿal)* of the many to the one is established, a system vividly illustrated by Jotham's fable (Jgs. 9:7-15; cf. also Gen. 37:7f.; in Joseph's dream the sheaves bowing down to the one upright sheaf constitute a *mlk* model). This general meaning becomes associated with specific historico-political circumstances by the addition of more specific qualifications, usually genitive constructions circumscribing the sphere of rule (cf. the list in Josh. 12 or Gen. 14:1f.), although such additions alone do not yet offer anything concrete about the nature of that rule. The scope and openness of the term leaves room for notions emerging from the world of the text and of its spokespersons. The extraordinarily frequent use of the term at all levels of language shows that both as a concretely qualified designation for a ruling figure and as a general term for a certain form of rule, *melek̲* became a fundamental term playing an enormous role in the life of the people of the OT.

In contradistinction with *melek̲*, *rōʾš* is semantically a functional term referring to the head or leadership position as such which an individual acquires or occupies by virtue of being suited for such a position or by having proved himself, especially at the tribal or clan level, as the leader of military units, and as the head of legal bodies. The term and title have preserved the semantic components "head and chief" (figurative), "office and aptitude" (functional), and "director and chairperson" in a homogeneous social group (terminological).[31] The instances of direct contact between *rōʾš* and *melek̲* are revealing, since emphasis on the functional aspect of *rōʾš* results in a conscious weakening of the *melek̲* statement. Jgs. 10:18; 11:8-11 recount that Jephthah was made the *rōʾš* (and *qāṣîn*) "over all the inhabitants of Gilead." This is juxtaposed with Jotham's fable in Jgs. 9:7-15, which illuminates Abimelech's city kingship (cf. 9:2: the functional definition is associated with the expression *mšl b*). The Canaanite institution of kingship in the description of 1 S. 8:11-18 is about to displace the old tradition of the tribal leader, relegating it to a lower level. Even 1 S. 15:17 (Deuteronomistic?) still resonates with this conflict in its criticism of Saul as the simultaneous "head of the tribes of Israel" and as the "anointed king over Israel." The prophets were especially keen in picking up on this conflict. Hos. 2:2(1:11) anticipates the reunification of the two kingdoms of Judah and Israel under *one* head *(rōʾš ʾeḥād̲)* without using the title of king, and with obvious criticism of the current political circumstances. Isa. 7:8,9 similarly reduces the current political systems (implicitly also the Judean, in addition to the Syrian and Ephraimite) to their skeletal structures of a pyramidal cosmic system, and criticizes the alleged absolute nature of the monarchies.[32] Ps. 18:44(43), citing the king's praise at having been made the "head of the nations," also contains an admonition regarding the concomitant obligations of such a position (v. 45[44]). In this sense the two "leadership functions" can appear together in a comparison as in Job 29:25: the chief of a public municipal council and the king on

---

31. Cf. J. R. Bartlett, "The Use of the Word רֹאשׁ as a Title in the OT," *VT,* 19 (1969), 1-10; H.-P. Müller, "רֹאשׁ *rōš* Kopf," *THAT,* II, 701-15.
32. Cf. Seybold, 66ff., and III.7 below.

his throne amid his warriors, again throwing into relief the differing orders of magnitude.[33]

The term → שׂר *śar* also has its own semantic history and its own semantic scope, limited on the whole to lesser circumstances and to organizational forms of a subordinate nature.[34] At an early stage *śar* (usually pl.) refers absolutely to a leading class in the clan and tribal organization (often translated not quite adequately by "prince"), e.g., in the Song of the Well (Nu. 21:18: "the well that the nobles dug" par. *nᵉḏîḇê hāʿām;* cf. the *mᵉḥōqēq*-scepter) in reference to the "Israelites," although it applies equally to the Moabites (Nu. 22:8-14) and Midianites (Jgs. 7:25; other passages: Jgs. 5:15,29; 8:6,14 next to the "elders"; Ps. 68:28[27]).

The term *śar* is then applied especially in the context of municipal government and military organization to refer to a man authorized to command and direct, authority bestowed upon him by superiors. The *nomen rectum* variously indicates the scope of power: the chief of a band, leader of chariot corps, captain of fifty/a hundred, head of an army, troup leader, taskmaster, supervisor, foreman, etc. "Who made you *ʾîš śar* and judge over us?" Moses is asked (Ex. 2:14). The competency attributable to a *śar* of this kind (rendered approximately "chief") is exemplified by the ostracon found in Yabneh-yam (Mīnet Rūbīn)[35] with a petition to the *śar* (perhaps "governor") as well as by the title *śar-ṣᵉḇāʾ* (Josh. 5:14) referring the commanding officer of the army. Finally, *śar* can be used as the designation for a royal official and functionary (e.g., Gen. 12:15; 1 K. 4:2; 5:30). Hence the appearance of the two terms *meleḵ* and *śar* together evokes the semantic notion of a courtly system and a royal power apparatus, whereby the subordination of *śar* is presupposed (Jgs. 4:2; Jer. 1:18; 4:9; Hos. 3:4).[36] This juxtaposition confirms the constitutive meaning of *meleḵ* as an autocrat, a ruler by one's own authority, a completely independent potentate who employs subordinated officials in the exercise of power. Thus it is all the more striking when a "king" is refused the *meleḵ* title and instead is given a predication constructed with *śar: śar-šālôm* (Isa. 9:5[6]), referring to the future Davidic ruler (cf. also Isa. 10:8; 23:8).

The title → נגיד *nāgîḏ* contributes little to the semantic determination of *meleḵ*. Recent investigation[37] has shown that it refers to the designated successor of the king, i.e., to the crown prince (after 1 K. 1:35; cf. v. 20), and probably does not derive from any tribal-historical circumstances.[38] The two terms hardly come into substantive contact. Only within the context of royal-theological concepts does the metaphorical use of *nāgîḏ* — as the designation of the king as ruler over Yahweh's people, both in northern Israelite and Judean contexts — bestow sacral dignity upon the bearer, although this does not affect the use of *meleḵ* in any discernible fashion.[39]

---

33. Regarding the Chronicler's usage, cf. Müller.
34. J. A. Soggin, "משׁל *mšl* herrschen," *THAT,* I, 932.
35. *KAI,* 200; *ANET,* 568.
36. See also O. Tufnell, *et al., Lachish,* IV (Oxford, 1958), 4.
37. E. Lipiński, "*NĀGĪD,* der Kronprinz," *VT,* 24 (1974), 497-99; Mettinger, 151ff.
38. So W. Richter, "Die nāgīd-Formel," *BZ,* N.S. 9 (1965), 71-84; L. Schmidt, 141ff.
39. Cf. J. W. Flanagan, "Chiefs in Israel," *JSOT,* 20 (1981), 47-73.

The same is true of the title → משח *māšîaḥ,* "anointed," which, in contrast to *melek,* and except for two late exceptions (Dnl. 9:25,26), is never used absolutely, but rather only in syntagmatic connection with Yahweh, demonstrating thereby its theological function.

The term → שפט *šōpēṭ*[40] probably refers to a specific office during the premonarchical period (e.g., Jgs. 4:4). As the official title "judge" it first appears during the middle period of the monarchy along with other functionaries, e.g., *śārîm, yōʿaṣîm,* etc. It occasionally appears in connection with *melākîm* (only in the pl.), where it draws attention perhaps to the jurisdictional aspect of the office of the king (possibly also intended only as a parallel term: "regents" next to "kings"; Ps. 2:10; Hos. 7:7). The application of the *šōpēṭ*-title probably to the reigning Judean king in Mic. 4:14(5:1) is unique: *šōpēṭ* Israel — a prophetic theologoumenon.[41]

The same is true of the relationship between *melek* and *nāśî'*. This official title, probably of early Israelite origin from the time of the tribal confederation,[42] is used with increasing frequency during the waning years of the monarchy to refer both to Davidic and to foreign kings (especially in Ezekiel), and parallel with that usage also in the Priestly Document as a designation for the "tribal prince." Both instances are attended by an element of theologically based *melek* criticism resulting in the repression of the *melek* term.[43]

3. *The Verb.* The meaning of the verb *mlk* is usually given as "become/be king, reign as king, reign, function as king"; it occurs primarily in the qal and hiphil, with 1 occurrence in the hophal (Dnl. 9:1) and 1 in the niphal (Neh. 5:7). Derivation of the verb from the noun is confirmed by primarily nominal use. Nominal forms and forms with a 3rd person singular subject predominate. Combinations with *melek/malkûṯ* are common (e.g., *mlk melek,* "to reign as king"), underscoring the secondary, dependent nature of the verbal meaning. With very few exceptions the subject of the qal passages is the 3rd "person," best exemplified by *melek.* Of the approximately 300 occurrences, only 7 have a 2nd person subject (Gen. 37:8; 1 S. 23:17; 24:21; 2 S. 3:21; 16:8; 1 K. 11:37; Jer. 22:15), 2 have a 1st person subject (1 K. 1:5: Adonijah; Ezk. 20:33: *YHWH*), and 4 a 3rd person plural subject (Gen. 36:31; 1 K. 11:24; 1 Ch. 1:43; Prov. 8:15). These passages are in any event particularly significant. Among the hiphil passages (with a primary and secondary subject), the agents actually installing the king are of

---

40. Cf. G. Liedke, "שׁפט *špṭ* richten," *THAT,* II, 1003f.

41. Cf. K.-D. Schunck, "Die Richter Israels und ihr Amt," *Volume de Congrès, Genève 1965. SVT,* 15 (1966), 252-262; M. Weinfeld, "Judge and Officer in Ancient Israel and in the Ancient Near East," *Proceedings of the Sixth World Congress of Jewish Studies 1973* (1977), 73-81 [Eng. summary]; J. A. Soggin, "Das Amt der 'kleinen Richter' in Israel," *VT,* 30 (1980), 245-48.

42. So M. Noth.

43. Cf. O. Calderini, "Evoluzione della funzione del *NĀŚÎ:* il libro dei numeri," *BeO,* 20 (1978), 123-133; *idem,* "Considerazioni sul *NĀŚÎ'* ebraico, il *NAŠI biltim* babilonese e il *NĀŠû* assiro," *BeO,* 21 (1979), 273-281. On the distinction between *melek, šallîṭ,* and *mōšēl* during the Hellenistic period, cf. Lohfink.

particular interest: Yahweh (6 times; with Saul in 1 S. 15:11,35; with Solomon in 1 K. 3:7; 2 Ch. 1:8ff.), Samuel, David, the "people of the land," the king of Babylon, etc., and especially plural agents again (e.g., Jgs. 9:6; 1 S. 11:15; 1 K. 12:20; 16:16; Hos. 8:4). The formulaic use of the verb both with the prepositions *ʿal, bᵉ, lᵉ, taḥaṯ* and in stereotypical formulations with the 3rd person and infinitive (*bᵉmolḵô,* etc.) suggests the presence of official language. This accords with the fact that the overwhelming majority of occurrences in the books of Samuel and Kings are found in annals.[44]

4. *Fixed Expressions.* As the human subject par excellence in the OT, *meleḵ* naturally occurs in every conceivable syntactical construction, among which several especially significant examples may be singled out.

a. Constructions with the verb *mlk* in the qal emphasize the nominal meaning (1 S. 8:9,11: "the king who shall reign over them [allegedly, just as you want]"; Jer. 23:5: "to reign as [a proper] king"). In the hiphil, the form expressing the installation of the king (e.g., Jgs. 9:6; 1 S. 15:11; Isa. 7:6), the constructions correspond to formulations with *śîm, qûm, kûn,* and *mšḥ.*

b. More specific qualifications of kingship are added with the genitive (king of the Philistines, of Babylon, of Edom) or prepositionally (over Israel, in Jerusalem). Conversely, *meleḵ* in the position of the *rectum* qualifies persons and things as royal or as having something to do with the king: *ben meleḵ,* "king's son"; *mištēh meleḵ,* "king's meal"; *miqdaš meleḵ,* "royal sanctuary" (Am. 7:13); *ʾeḇen hammeleḵ,* "royal (official) weight" (2 S. 14:26); *dereḵ hammeleḵ,* "king's highway" (Nu. 20:17; 21:22). Such examples include the royal impression on vessels, seals, etc.: *lmlk,* whereby the two notions associated with *meleḵ* come to bear the subjective, personal association and the institutional, official association.

c. Apart from specific expressions and official designations, *meleḵ* also occurs in fixed forms of address, titles, and predications, including the "courtly" form of address *ʾaḏōnî hammeleḵ,* "my lord the king" (2 S. 3:21; 15:21; cf. Gen. 40:1; on *ʾāḏôn* as a royal title, cf. Ps. 110:1; Jer. 22:18; 34:5). The entire arsenal of courtly forms of address are collected together, e.g., in 2 S. 14:1ff.; 1 K. 1:11ff.). This context includes the acclamatory formulas *yᵉḥî hammeleḵ,* "Long live the king!" (1 S. 10:24; 2 S. 16:16; 1 K. 1:34),[45] and "May the king live forever" (1 K. 1:31; Neh. 2:3; Dnl. 2:30; 4:14,31[17,34]; 6:21,27[20,26] [Aram.]). Appropriations include the Assyrian royal title "great king" (Isa. 36:4,13 par. 2 K. 18:19,28: *šarru rabû;* cf. Ps. 47:3[2]; Mal. 1:14) and the corresponding Babylonian title "king of kings" (e.g., Ezr. 7:12; Ezk. 26:7; Dnl. 2:37: *šar šarrāni*).

The metaphorical usage of *meleḵ* is semantically revealing: king over the trees (Jgs. 9:8ff.), over all great creatures (= Leviathan, Job 41:26[34]), over locusts (Prov. 30:27; cf. the animal comparisons in vv. 29ff. emended text), and over terrors (= death, Job 18:14).

---

44. On the theological use of the verb, see IV.7 below.
45. → חיה *ḥāyâ (chāyāh),* III.6 (IV, 335f.).

e. The feminine form *malkâ* occurs in the OT in the singular only with reference to foreign queens: the queen of Sheba (1 K. 10 par. 2 Ch. 9) and Queen Esther (25 occurrences in Esther), and in the plural only in poetic reference to the sixty wives of the king (Cant. 6:8f.). This form was apparently not commonly used (cf. in contrast *g^e^bîrâ*). Not even Athaliah receives this designation, although the only feminine form of the verb *mlk* in the qal refers to her reign (ptcp. in 2 K. 11:3; 2 Ch. 22:12).

5. *Abstract Expressions.* An evaluation of the four abstract constructions with *mlk* can draw on elements of word construction and on characteristic usage, whereby several delimitations emerge militating against the assumption of indiscriminate usage.

a. Throughout its usage, the term *m^e^lûḵâ,* a deverbal adjectival *qāṭûl* form (fem.), remains subordinated to the verbal form insofar as it refers to the function of *mlk,* and that means to the office of the king, the majesty of the king, the "status as king,"[46] the status of being king, and royal actions associated with reigning in general (usually with the article; the exceptions are influenced by context: 1 K. 21:7; Isa. 34:12; 62:3; Ezk. 16:13). Saul takes *(lkd)* the kingship (1 S. 14:47; cf. 10:16; 11:14; 18:8). According to 1 S. 10:25, certain rights *(mišpāṭ)* attend this office. The office passes to Absalom (2 S. 16:8; 1 K. 2:15,22), as well as to Jeroboam (1 K. 11:35; 12:21). A new reign is proclaimed (Isa. 34:12). Jezebel accuses Ahab of not properly exercising the office of king (*'śh,* 1 K. 21:7, lit., "Do what is royal!"). According to Ezk. 16:13, Jerusalem acquired royal status, which included the throne (1 K. 1:46), a royal residence (2 S. 12:26), and the emblems and insignia of kingship (cf. Isa. 62:3). In theological metaphors such royal status can also be attributed to Yahweh (Ps. 22:29[28]; Ob. 21). The adjectival semantic element emerges in the occasionally attested expression "of royal lineage" (*mizzera' hamm^e^lûḵâ,* e.g., 2 K. 25:25; Ezk. 17:13; Dnl. 1:3). The restricted use of this term, which is probably rooted in the court language of the early monarchy, suggests that it apparently never really acquired definite contours; rather, as the obligatory article shows, it was characterized by a certain element of ambiguity and even vagueness (pertaining to things royal, that which is royal), but to that extent was indeed suited for expressions of a more general nature ("the matter of the kingdom of Saul," e.g., 1 S. 10:16; cf. Jezebel's reproach in 1 K. 21:7).

b. The term *mamlāḵâ,* an *m*-preformative of *mlk,* which can express an action and its results, place, type, and manner of an event, and finally the instrument of action, is thus predisposed to bring to expression the functional system "kingship" in all these aspects: as dominion, residence and reign, power apparatus — in a word, as an institution. And indeed, this term (together with *malḵût*) is the most common expression for the monarchical governmental form ("kingdom"). There is almost no need to list examples for the use of this term, which itself was especially widespread during the preexilic period.[47] The more official forms of usage are especially informative: *bêṯ*

46. *HAL,* II, 587.
47. Cf. the entry in *HAL,* II.

mamlāḵâ, "imperial temple" (Am. 7:13); *bêṯ^e^ḵā ûmamlaḵt^e^ḵā,* "your house and your kingdom" (2 S. 7:16; cf. 12:13; Isa. 9:6); "two kingdoms" (Ezk. 37:22; cf. the concentration of occurrences in 1 K. 11); and the juxtaposition with *gôy,* "national people" (1 K. 18:10; Ps. 46:7[6]; Isa. 60:12). The theological expression *mamleḵeṯ kōh^a^nîm,* "a kingdom of priests" (Ex. 19:6), is unique; parallel with *gôy qāḏôš,* "a holy nation,"[48] its intention is to characterize Israel's special position in the family of kingdoms and nations with respect to its priestly status as a sacral theocracy. Although this term does appear in later writings such as Chronicles and Psalms, it appears nonetheless to have been displaced by *malkûṯ* during the (late) postexilic period.

c. The Middle Hebrew term *malkûṯ,* a denominative construction from *meleḵ* resulting from Aramaic influence (analogous to Akkadian), almost completely displaces *mamlāḵâ* in the later OT writings. Apparently the Aramaic term, with its more sharply accentuated phonetic character, was better suited as a designation for an institution that was largely dominated by foreign influence. Especially, though, it seems to correspond to Official Aramaic usage (cf., e.g., Ezr. 4:5f.,24; 6:15). Although older material does attest a few occurrences (Nu. 24:7; 1 S. 20:31; 1 K. 2:12; Ps. 45:7[6]; Jer. 10:7; 49:34; 52:31), these can be explained either as early Aramaic influences (Nu. 24:7, Balaam), as regional dialects (Ps. 45:7[6]?), or as Masoretic corrections. Its meaning is indistinguishable from that of *mamlāḵâ:* "kingdom" (as a comprehensive term).

d. The term **mamlāḵûṯ* (attested 9 times, 5 of those in Josh. 13, and only in the sg. const.) seems to be a hybrid construction involving the two previously discussed nominal forms; it can probably be traced back to the Masoretes, where it may have resulted either from the misreading of a *kethibh* plene form or from scribal error. No semantic distinction is discernible (compare Jer. 26:1 with 49:34; 1 S. 15:28 with 1 K. 11:11).

6. *OT Notions of Kingship.* The repertoire of notions associated with the word group surrounding *meleḵ,* notions fairly sated by usage and experience, was in certain contexts able to crystallize into fixed notions of kingship, dominion, monarchical self-expression, and political value systems, i.e., into forms representing a certain royal ideology or understanding of the state; in its own turn, such ideology exercised influence at the level of consciousness, style, and tradition. The diachronic use of the *meleḵ* group through the course of Israel's history shows that the simple, fundamental idea of the exercise of power by a single individual over others was also able to establish itself and become accepted in Israel despite all the complications this kind of social system must have presented to traditional faith. This *meleḵ* system of rule, a system whose manifestations one could experience in the model of Late Bronze Age municipal organization, whose roots extended back into the Early Bronze Age, was both simple and effective in its organization of manifold energies, centrally controlled, under a single will, establishing thereby well-ordered power relationships.

48. → גוי *gôy,* II.2 (II, 429f.).

Several OT statements characteristic of Israel's encounter with this *melek̲* system derive from the sphere of Wisdom:

Prov. 30:27: "The locusts have no *melek̲,* yet all of them march in rank (LXX: *eutáktōs*)." The king guarantees ordered leadership for the many, for the larger group that can no longer be organized and ruled by other social systems (e.g., that of the family, clan, or army), and replaces the "wisdom" of societal instincts natural to the "lesser creatures." According to the formula in Jgs. 17:6; 18:1; 19:1; 21:25, "in those days there was not yet a *melek̲* in Israel"; the period of the monarchy put an end to a time of anarchy.

Gen. 37:8: The reaction of Joseph's brothers to his dream of the one, erect sheaf and the sheaves bowing before it is significant: "Are you indeed to become king over us *(mlk ʿal)* or even have dominion over us *(mšl bᵉ)*?" This twofold question expresses an intensification. While the application of the *melek̲* principle to the sphere of the family and clan is already perverse enough, the repression implied by *mšl* seems completely unacceptable. Both the implications and the limits of the *melek̲* principle resonate here.

Jgs. 9:8-15: Jotham's fable offers evidence of intense concern with this problem. Such a reign *(mlk ʿal),* although apparently unavoidable for the trees as a whole (and installed through anointing[49]), nonetheless constitutes in the opinion of the more valuable and useful trees an (unapproachable) "swaying and waving" (*nûaʿ* "over the trees"), a renunciation of all meaningful activity. The trees are forced to seek out the bramble, the dry scrub which in fires is dangerous even to cedars (addendum in v. 15b); it offers itself as king and makes an elaborate proclamation in a grotesque overestimation of its own capacity (v. 15; cf. Lam. 4:20; Ezk. 17:23). The fable originally addressed itself not against the institution of kingship as such, but rather against its negative estimation and the resulting refusal of those capable of occupying it.

In context, 1 S. 8:11-17 constitutes the royal privileges (*mišpaṭ hammelek̲,* "the privilege/right of the king") announced by Samuel at the establishment of Saul's kingship; apparently it, too, did not in principle originally evaluate the office negatively (v. 17 [D]). It is self-evident that agreements such as this were concerned with a balance of interests and obligations. The advantages attending this new institution were countered by the rights to be surrendered to the central governmental power, the services to be rendered, and the taxes to be paid (the tenth). Hence more is said about social changes: the establishment of a power apparatus (v. 11), of a court (v. 13), of a standing army (v. 12a), of a feudal agricultural system and the means to manufacture implements of war (v. 12b), a system of fiefs and tribute (vv.14f.), and of compulsory state service (v. 16); conversely, less is said about the negative consequences (such as vv. 17ff. [D]), whereby those affected do have opportunities as officers, court officials, and feudal tenants. It is still disputed whether the real-life basis of the royal privileges recorded here derive from the feudal municipal kingship of Late Bronze age Canaan,[50] from

---

49. → משח *māšaḥ.*

50. I. Mendelsohn, "Samuel's Denunciation of Kingship in the Light of the Akkadian Documents from Ugarit," *BASOR,* 143 (1956), 17-22.

experiences with Solomon's reign,[51] or in actual agreements in connection with the establishment of Saul's kingship.

The notion of kingship most widespread and theologically most influential in the OT is the Judean-Jerusalemite royal ideology as exemplified especially in what are known as the Royal Psalms (e.g., Pss. 2,18,20,21,45?,72,89,101,132,144?) and related texts (e.g., 2 S. 7,23; the so-called messianic prophecies). This theologically based and cultically rooted conception, one upon which apparently all the essential authorities were able to agree over the course of time, was developed and promulgated at the Zion sanctuary in Jerusalem and probably represented the official state doctrine during the time of the Judean monarchy. It served to legitimize and codify the monarchical-dynastic system which the Davidic house was able to maintain — probably also thanks to this conception — for more than four centuries in Jerusalem.

One component of this royal conception is the probably pre-Davidic tradition associated with the earlier city of the Jebusites concerning a sacred city kingship "according to the order of Melchizedek" (Ps. 110:4; Gen. 14), which the Davidic house apparently appropriated as an inheritance for itself (2 S. 5:6-12). With it, however, they also appropriated at least parts of a Canaanite notion of rule (priestly kingship, city sanctuary, and similar aspects) with the attendant sacral implications, much of which had to come into conflict with the traditions of the Yahweh faith (2 S. 7). Egyptian influence was added as early as David's own reign, and even more so during the Solomonic period. This young kingdom seems to have oriented itself according to Egyptian models, and only during the middle and later monarchy do Assyrian-Babylonian influences also become discernible in Jerusalem.

A *second* component which was decisive for this Judean notion of kingship is the enduring influence exerted by the two founders of the kingdom, David and Solomon. David was the model for the official image of the king, one that became increasingly fixed as an ideal, while Solomon created the prerequisites for the maintenance and propaganda of the royal ideal (construction of temple and palace, establishment of the various court institutions). It was also probably during the Solomonic period that the document known as the "royal novella,"[52] which found expression in 2 S. 7, was developed, the official document legitimizing under prophetic sanction (Nathan) the dynastic notion of rule as the ideal basis of the kingdom. Elements of what is known as Nathan's oracle were also included (vv. 11, 16). This royal novella seems to establish the idea of kingdom that accompanied and supported the Davidic kingship.

This notion of kingdom also already contains the *third* component, one deriving from the premonarchical traditions of Israel.[53] Theological notions of the traditional Yahweh faith influenced the idea of the state and created a counterbalance against the "imperial magic"[54] and against the temptation of a sacral-ideological stylization of

---

51. R. E. Clements, "The Deuteronomistic interpretation of the founding of the monarchy in I Sam. VIII," *VT,* 24 (1974), 398-410.
52. S. Herrmann.
53. M. Noth.
54. V. Maag.

this kingship. The prophetic resistance against kings of Judah and Israel is directing itself against the same tendencies of an autonomous development of the monarchical system.

A *fourth* component, and one which was of constitutive significance for the continued existence and expansion of the Judean-Jerusalemite royal ideology, is what is called the "royal ritual in Judah."[55] Although the enthronement ceremony cannot be reconstructed in all its parts, the extant material does make it clear that this ceremony was of fundamental significance for the Davidic kingship.

Its most important elements include: anointing *(mšḥ)* with the concomitant, probably Egyptian understanding of the office (high official, vassal of the highest royal authority); adoption as the son of God in the sense of Ps. 2; bestowal of honorific names and titles (corresponding to the pharaonic royal titles; cf. 2 S. 23; Isa. 9:6[7]); delivery of the royal protocol with the fixing of the royal privileges in written form (Ps. 2:7; 2 K. 11:12); enthronement as ruler "by divine grace" and installation in the residence of the "lord of the world" (Ps. 110:1; 18:44[43]; 2:8; 132); and the bestowal of the royal insignia.[56]

Presumably, the northern kingdom of Israel also developed an ideology of the state (cf. 1 K. 12); unfortunately, it is no longer discernible as a whole.[57]

7. *mlk in the Prophetic Criticism of Kings.* The prophetic criticism of kingship and of the royal ideal in Israel continues in its own way earlier opposition against the monarchical system, opposition which was never fully silenced. It is of concern here only to the extent that it is related to the word group *mlk* or employs its terminology.[58] It is not particularly noteworthy that the prophets took over common terminology and its fixed semantic content (e.g., in the indication of dates: "in the year that King Uzziah died" [Isa. 6:1], or in statements such as Isa. 23:15: "seventy years, the lifetime of one king," or in expressions such as "on the day of our king" [Hos. 7:5]); what is of significance is that they extract or inject their own semantic substance from or into the *mlk* words within the framework of their critical pronouncements and predictions for the future. Several passages can serve as examples *pars pro toto*:

a. The prophetic narrative tradition shows that the prophets, especially the circle around Elijah/Elisha, influenced the installation of kings particularly in the northern kingdom by undertaking the specific designation of kings by ritual anointing (cf. 1 K. 19:15f.). Hosea, probably the most incisive critic of kingship in the northern kingdom (next to Amos; cf. 7:10ff.; 9:11f.?), refers to this tradition in his judgment: "They have made kings (*mlk* hiphil), but not through my [Yahweh's] will" (Hos. 8:4). Such rulers thus lack legitimacy, and Yahweh keeps them on the throne only for the sake of the negative consequences: "I gave you a king in my anger, and I took him away in my

---

55. G. von Rad.
56. On this entire complex, cf. von Rad, *The Problem of the Hexateuch.*
57. On this problem, see Alt, Mettinger.
58. On this problem as a whole, cf. W. H. Schmidt, *Festschrift G. von Rad.*

wrath" (Hos. 13:11). The Samaritan kingship is handled with what amounts to despotic arbitrariness — doubtlessly the talionic reaction against the despotic nature of these regents — until the "king of Israel" is swept away once and for all "at dawn" (Hos. 10:15?) and perishes "like a chip on the face of the waters" (v. 7, uncertain text). In any event, Hosea viewed kingship as one of the institutions that had become too destructive for Israel and should thus be eliminated, together with the governmental apparatus *(śar),* sacrificial cult, and sacral institutions. The only remedy is to forsake such institutions entirely (Hos. 3:3f.; cf. 10:1-8).

b. Isaiah's criticism of kingship is documented in what are known as the messianic oracles (to the extent they are Isaianic), Isa. 7, 9, and 11. Emphatic use of *mlk* words, however, occurs only in two passages, 7:6; 9:11(12): in 7:6, coalition members in the Syro-Ephraimite war intend "to set up a king (as king)" in Judah (namely, Ben Tabe-el), disregarding the political cosmic order which according to Isaiah Yahweh has sanctioned, an order which foresees a member of the house of David as "head" of Jerusalem rather than some arbitrary *meleḵ*. Isa. 9:6(7) speaks of the future establishment of a kingdom which will again be Davidic in the original sense.

c. Jeremiah's critical attitude expresses itself in the question he puts to the contemporary King Jehoiakim, whether being *meleḵ,* i.e., the first, can exhaust itself merely in one's effort to promote prosperity and fortune (Jer. 22:15; cf. 21:11-14). The anticipated future king, in contrast to Zedekiah, will be a "legitimate branch." He will also do what one hopes such a *meleḵ* will do: *mālaḵ meleḵ,* reign wisely and establish justice and order in the land (23:5f.).

d. Ezekiel's basic criticism of the Davidic kingship, developed in the extended parables in chs. 17 and 19 (cf. also Ezk. 34; 37; 43:7-9) is characterized by his juxtaposition of the venerable title → **נשׂיא** *nāśî'* with the term *meleḵ,* lending expression to his notions of a theocratic state form.

e. Deutero-Isaiah completely unravels the older Judean-Davidic conception of state. His worldview no longer reserves a place for the Jerusalem monarchy.

f. Postexilic prophecy once again develops a royal-messianic image of the future, although quite often the word *meleḵ* is not applied to the coming ruler (but cf. Isa. 32:1; Zec. 9:9), a sign that the Yahweh faith still encounters difficulties with the concept and its inherent notion of rule.

8. *The Problem of an OT Ideology of Kingship.* The question of the uniqueness of the religious component of the ideology of kingship has generated a lively discussion during the past decades, a discussion variously portrayed and documented.[59] The debate was precipitated primarily by the thesis of English-speaking scholars under the aegis of S. H. Hooke, the assertion being that throughout the entire ancient Near East the ideology of kingship in principle followed a single basic pattern whose structure can

---

59. C. M. Edsmann, "Zum sakralen Königtum in der Forschung der letzten hundert Jahre," *The Sacral Kingship. SNumen,* 4 (1959), 3-17; Bernhardt; H.-J. Kraus, *Geschichte der historisch-kritischen Erforschung des ATs* (Neukirchen, ^{3}1982), 460ff.

be traced back to its provenance in myth and cult. This notion of kingship was structured according to a fixed, enduring schema (myth and ritual pattern), and viewed the king in the center of a mythic-cultic drama that was to guarantee the stability of the cosmic order. Thus sacral majesty and even divinity were attributed to the king (sacral, divine kingship).

Although this discussion was conducted on extremely diverse levels, the results relating to the present semantic-theological evaluation of the *mlk* word group pertain primarily to methodology, consisting in my opinion in the need for contextual differentiation. Such differentiation should be made according to (a) the cultural spheres and historical epochs in which the ideology of kingship under discussion developed (e.g., Syro-Canaanite city culture of the Amarna period; the Persian period); (b) politico-historical developments prompting localized versions of these systems of rule (e.g., kingship in Jerusalem, in the northern kingdom, and in the southern kingdom); (c) the different bearers and representatives of the various notions of kingship (e.g., as imperial self-representation, mythic-religious legitimation, or a specific understanding of the state); (d) the linguistic level of the life setting for the various conceptions of royal ideology (catchwords: courtly style,[60] imperial magic,[61] mythopoetics); (e) the various aspects of both "civil" and "sacral" legitimation;[62] (f) the experiential horizon and spiritual environment (e.g., kingship hymns, prophetic criticism). Questions concerning the religious connotations inherent in the *mlk* group can be answered, if at all, only on the basis of the situational, literary, and socio-cultural context.

IV. Theological Usage: Yahweh as King — Yahweh mlk.

1. *Occurrences.* Yahweh occurs 13 times as the subject of *mlk* (Ex. 15:18; 1 S. 8:7; Ps. 47:9[8]; 93:1; 96:10 par. 1 Ch. 16:31; 97:1; 99:1; 146:10; Isa. 24:23; 52:7; Ezk. 20:33; Mic. 4:7). Several points are noteworthy. Only 1 of these passages is prose (1 S. 8:7). The hymnic genres predominate (8 times with Isa. 52:7; 1 Ch. 16:31, 7 times in what are known as the Yahweh-kingship hymns). The combination *YHWH mlk* often occupies a prominent position (3 times at the beginning of a psalm, twice at the conclusion). And, finally, there is an affinity with the Yahweh-Zion theme (explicitly in Ex. 15:18; Isa. 24:23; 52:7; Mic. 4:7; Ps. 146:10; implicitly in almost all the passages). Yahweh is qualified with the epithet *melek̲* 41 times (Nu. 23:21; Dt. 33:5; 1 S. 12:12; Ps. 5:3[2]; 10:16; 24:7,8,9,10; 29:10; 44:5[4]; 47:3,7,8[2,6,7]; 48:3[2]; 68:25[24]; 74:12; 84:4[3]; 95:3; 98:6; 99:4; 145:1; 149:2; Isa. 6:5; 33:22; 41:21; 43:15; 44:6; Jer. 8:19; 10:7,10; 46:18; 48:15; 51:57; Dnl. 4:34[37]; Mic. 2:13; Zeph. 3:15 (cf. LXX); Zec. 14:9,16,17; Mal. 1:14). Again, only 1 passage is genuine prose (1 S. 12:12). The strong representation among the Psalms is also noteworthy (20 times), as is what amounts to merely secondary mention in the prophetic tradition (besides Isa. 6:5; Jer. 8:19 and perhaps Mal. 1:4; Zec. 14:9) in fixed formulations resembling titles. The

60. H. Gressmann.
61. V. Maag.
62. Cf. Mettinger.

reference to Zion emerges quite strongly, and again the Yahweh-kingship hymns constitute an inner circle (Pss. 29,47,95,98,99). The abstract constructions derived from *mlk* refer to Yahweh in 9 instances, largely in later passages (1 Ch. 29:11; Ps. 22:29[28]; 103:19; 145:11,12,13; Dnl. 3:33[4:3]; 4:31[34]; Ob. 21). If one also orders chronologically the passages in which references to the throne, etc. occur (e.g., Ps. 9:5,8[4,7]; 47:9[8]; 89:15[14]; 93:2; 103:19; Isa. 6:1; 66:1; Jer. 3:17; 17:12; Ezk. 1:26[63]), discounting certain questionable premonarchical passages (Nu. 23:21; Dt. 33:5; Ps. 24), there emerges a significant number from the period of the monarchy (Isa. 6:5; Jer. 8:19; Micah? Zephaniah? and several psalms which can be dated: Pss. 29,48,68,89; Ex. 15) and from the exilic period (Deutero-Isaiah); the majority, however, comes from the postexilic period, suggesting a relatively late beginning with constant growth up till the late OT period (Isaiah Apocalypse; Second Zechariah; Daniel). The history of this theologoumenon is reflected in the statistical evidence.

2. *Origin of the Predication "Yahweh as King."* There is reason to believe that the notion of Yahweh as king was not first appropriated during the period of the monarchy itself,[64] but rather at an earlier date.[65] First of all, certain individual passages suggest this, such as Dt. 33:5; Nu. 23:21, which, while not completely undisputed, probably do not refer to political kingship, but rather presuppose in Jacob-Israel the notion of Yahweh's kingship "in Jeshurun, when the heads of the people assembled, all the tribes of Israel together" (Dt. 33:5): "Yahweh, his God, with him, and the shout of a king is in him" (Nu. 23:21). Accordingly, Yahweh would be "king" at least over "the people, the tribes of Israel, Jacob," who hail him; and this is the Yahweh of Sinai, of Seir (Dt. 33:2), "the El of Jeshurun" (Dt. 33:26 MT). Apparently, contact with the notions of the kingship of god cultivated by the sedentary Canaanite religion,[66] and specifically with the notion of the kingship of the highest god El,[67] led to a similar amplification of the Yahweh faith, which until then had not been so defined. Traces of this appropriation can be found especially in psalm texts from the (early) period of the monarchy (Ps. 24:7-10; 29:10; 68:25[24]; 82), although also in the frequent resonance of certain notions of courtly institutions in the narrative material of older Pentateuchal strata (Gen. 3:22; 6:1ff.; 11:7; 18:1ff.). It is difficult to determine the extent to which the ark as a throne symbol[68] influenced the evolution of the notion of kingship in the Yahweh faith. The hypothesis that the notion emerged in the temple sanctuary at Shiloh (according to Ps. 24:7-10) must remain an assumption. Judging from the meager evidence, it apparently did not play any significant role in the period before Israel became a state[69] (1 S. 8:7; 12:12 derive from the later theological discussion surrounding the monarchi-

---

63. → כסא *kissē'* (VII, 232-259).
64. So Eissfeldt, von Rad, and others.
65. Alt, Maag, W. H. Schmidt, and others.
66. Maag.
67. W. H. Schmidt.
68. → ארון *'arôn* (I, 363-374).
69. A different view is taken by M. Buber, who probably overinterprets Jgs. 6:22f.

cal constitution). This did not change until Israel was involved in establishing its own state and acquired a politically different consciousness in its encounter with the religious forms of the Canaanite world, and until in confrontation and conflict it was forced to expand and interpret anew its traditional ideas of faith.

3. *Use in Theophoric Personal Names.* These findings are confirmed by the OT personal names constructed with *mlk.* Although with *'bymlk, 'ḥymlk, 'lymlk* (*milkâ* does not seem to be theophoric) the OT does indeed exhibit various name constructions attesting the notion of God as king — regardless of how the element *mlk* is interpreted here: as subject (divine name[70]) or as predicate ("father-[God-]is-king," etc.[71] — these constructions nonetheless appear to have been originally pre- and non-Israelite (cf. the examples in EA): *'bymlk,* king of Gerar (Gen. 20:2–26:26); *'ḥymlk,* priest of Nob (1 S. 21:2[21:1]–23:6); *'limlk* from Bethlehem in Judah (Ruth 1:2ff.). This suggests that the notion (par. *'āḇ, 'āḥ, 'ēl*) derives from the Canaanite religion of El. The name of the priest-king of Salem, *malkîṣeḏeq* (Gen. 14:18; Ps. 110:4; 1QapGen 22:14) points in this direction: "king(-god)-is-*ṣdq*'. Not until the name of Saul's son, *Malkîšûaʿ* ("my-king-is-help" or vice versa, 1 S. 14:49; 31:2), can one date a theophoric *mlk* name in Israel, although the occurrence of individual names naturally leaves many unresolved questions, cf. *Malkî'ēl* (Gen. 46:17 [P]; Nu. 26:45; 1 Ch. 7:31). Analogous to the earlier occurrences, such personal names become more widespread only toward the end of the monarchy. The *mlk* names containing the element *YHWH* come from the 7th-6th centuries B.C.: *Malkiyyâ (Malkiyyāhû)* (Jer. 21:1);[72] *Yhwmlk* (seal *ca.* 7th century[73]); *Malkîrām* (son of King Jeconiah, 1 Ch. 3:18). The shorter forms are more difficult to date: *Meleḵ* (descendant of Saul, 1 Ch. 8:35; 9:41); *Malkām* (1 Ch. 8:9); *Yamlēḵ* (1 Ch. 4:34); *Mallûḵ* (Ezra; Nehemiah; 1 Chronicles).

4. *The Preexilic Zion Tradition.* One group of apparently older preexilic passages presents the Yahweh-*mlk* statement in connection with the Zion tradition (Ex. 15; Pss. 24,29; Isa. 6), whence it evidently derived. The reference and point of departure seem according to Ps. 24; Isa. 6 to have been in a cultic-symbolic sense the ark and throne of the cherubim in the Jerusalem temple. From there evidence leads back possibly to the sanctuary at Shiloh (Ps. 24) and to the Jebusite sanctuary in pre-Davidic Jerusalem (Ps. 29). Use of the theologoumenon in this traditio-historical context is characterized by the following:

(a) The still discernible adaptation of the *meleḵ* predication as expressed, e.g., in the interrogative form of Ps. 24: "Who is this [overly] mighty king?" (*mî zeh meleḵ hakkāḇôḏ,* vv. 8, 10). The title *meleḵ hakkāḇôḏ* alone obviously does not yet contain

---

70. E.g., Eissfeldt.

71. E.g., Noth.

72. Y. Aharoni, "Three Hebrew Ostraca from Arad," *Festschrift W. F. Albright. ErIsr,* 9 (1969), 11 [Heb.]; *ANET,* 568f.

73. G. R. Driver, "Brief Notes. (I) A New Israelite Seal," *PEQ,* 77 (1945), 5; F. Vattioni, "I sigilli ebraici," *Bibl,* 50 (1969), 376, no. 162.

any definitive answer. Clarity emerges only with the identification as Yahweh *ṣ*^e^*ḇā'ôṯ*. Other identifications were apparently also possible. The adaptation can be recognized in the presumed Canaanite source document for Ps. 29 and its Baʿal-hadad model, e.g., v. 10a: "Yahweh sits enthroned over the flood," interpreted by v. 10b: "Yahweh sits enthroned as king forever." Ugaritic texts confirm the earlier provenance of the structure of this notion.

(b) The semantic relation of superiority is established by the element *mlk:* the foremost, the mightiest, the highest. This comes to expression in the confession of Yahweh's singularity. What Ps. 24:8,10; Ex. 15:11 formulate interrogatively (who . . .?) and Ps. 29:10 as struggle and conflict (Yahweh among the "sons of gods," *bᵉnê 'ēlîm,* v. 1), is in the hymnic predications of Isa. 6:3 and especially Ex. 15:11,18 a thetic confession: Yahweh is *the* holy one; his power extends over the *entire* earth; he is *the* lord and *the* king (*hammeleḵ YHWH,* Isa. 6:5; cf. vv. 1,8; the "great king," Ps. 48:3[2]; cf. 47:3[2]). The *mlk* concept reflects polemical-apologetic concerns.

(c) Motivated by its cultic-symbolic substratum and supported by its unique matrix of associations, this notion acquires elective affinity for related and neighboring theologoumena, generating an expandable network of associations expressed in stereotypical terminology (cf. Pss. 24,29; Isa. 6 as well as the Yahweh-kingship hymns[74]). E.g., in Ps. 29 the *mlk* theme is characterized by the Baʿal-hadad topos "storm theophany and struggle with the dragon," in Isa. 6 by the typically Isaianic Judeo-Egyptian figures (seraphim), in Ps. 89:15f.,19(14f.,18) by the idea of the pharaonic royal throne and its foundation (Maat), whereby in each case various theological implications and extensions emerge establishing the specific meaning of each text. At the same time, however, this openness was accompanied by the possibility that notions of divine kingship both similar and alien to Yahweh could be assimilated.[75]

These three aspects apply in equal fashion to the Yahweh-kingship hymns, at least to their older parts.[76]

5. *Other Divine Kings in the OT.* Other divine names constructed with *mlk* occur in the OT analogous to, e.g., Phoen. *Melkart* (< *milk-qart,* "king of the city") or to the Tyrian Baʿal,[77] including:

a. Milcom (< *mlk-m,* mimation form with determinative, also attested outside the OT, and within the OT itself also pointed as *Malkām:* 2 S. 12:30; Jer. 49:1,3; Zeph. 1:5, "the king[-god]"), the primary national god of the Ammonites. After Solomon introduced his cult (1 K. 11:5,7,33), Milcom apparently did not constitute a syncretistic religious threat until toward the end of the monarchy (parallel expressions being "to worship Yahweh" and "to swear by Milcom," Zeph. 1:5 conj.; 2 K. 23:13).

b. Moloch[78] (< *mlk,* MT *mōleḵ,* cacophonously pointed; LXX *Moloch;* originally

74. See IV.7-9 below.
75. See IV.5 below.
76. See IV.7-9 below.
77. Cf. Gese, 194f.; 193 A.109; G. Wallis, "Melkart," *BHHW,* II (1964), 1186f.
78. → מֹלֶךְ *mōleḵ* (VIII, 375-388).

probably *Melek̲;* like Milcom usually with the article, e.g., Lev. 20:5; 1 K. 11:7, and possibly still used appellatively as a title: "the king[-god]"). This name, which appears at approximately the same (late preexilic) time, cannot be identified unequivocally.[79] According to Lev. 18:21; 20:2-5, it seems probably to have been a deity, and not a sacrifice,[80] associated with Topheth in the Valley of Hinnom near Jerusalem, to whom the Israelites probably consecrated children (not burned, as some have concluded from the formula "make go through the fire"; 2 K. 23:10; Jer. 32:35).[81]

c. Adrammelech and Anammelech (probably < "Adad-king," "ʿAnat-king"[82]). According to 2 K. 17:31, these were deities worshipped (along with Yahweh) by the Syrians from Sepharvaim who were forcefully deported to Samaria.

d. The "queen of heaven" *(mᵉleḵeṯ* [< *malkaṯ*], *haššāmayim).*[83] According to Jer. 7:18; 44:17-19,25, she was already worshipped in Israel during the preexilic period, probably as a result of Assyrian-Babylonian influence.[84]

6. *Notions of mlk in Prophecy.* Although the prophets do not employ the kingship theologoumenon very frequently, this does not, as Isa. 6 shows, necessarily constitute rejection. They refer rather to the circumstances of the Zion tradition, and although they develop their call schemata with the aid of the court model (1 K. 22; Isa. 6; Ezk. 1–3; Isa. 40:1-8), use of this terminology occurs in only a few, albeit significant passages. The vision of the Pharaoh-like king *YHWH ṣᵉḇā'ôṯ* in Isa. 6:1ff. is paralleled by Ezekiel's throne chariot vision (Ezk. 1:15ff.). Both are sated with tradition. The people's "cry for help" (Jer. 8:19 [8:18-22]) is noteworthy, if not completely clear, since it calls into question the Zion confession: Is Yahweh not in Zion? Is Zion's king [?] no longer there?" The theologoumenon plays a significant role in Isa. 40–55. The notion of court institutions in Isa. 40:1ff. presupposes the idea of kingship just as does the royal predication in Isa. 42:1ff. The *melek̲* theologoumenon is used in a completely traditional fashion in the religious polemic of Deutero-Isaiah, as shown by the occurrences in the trial scenes: "King of Jacob" (Isa. 41:21); "Creator of Israel, your King" (43:15); "King of Israel" (44:6). The antithetical usage in connection with the Zion tradition thus can come as no surprise: *mālak̲ 'ᵉlōhāyik̲,* "your God reigns as king" (Isa. 52:7). And yet this traditional royal predication acquires new actuality with Deutero-Isaiah. The "king" of the heavenly court controls the affairs of the world's kingdoms (the royal highway in the desert, Isa. 40:3; "all flesh" — all people are your

79. Cf. K.-H. Bernhardt, "Moloch," *BHHW,* II, 1232; W. Kornfeld, "Moloch," *BL,* 1163f. with bibliog.

80. So Eissfeldt.

81. On this cultic rite, cf. D. Plataroti, "Zum Gebrauch des Wortes *mlk* im AT," *VT,* 28 (1978), 286-300.

82. Cf. Gese, 110.

83. Cf. *ibid.,* 191 A.90.

84. Cf. M. Weinfeld, "The Worship of Molech and of the Queen of Heaven and its Background," *UF,* 4 (1972), 139; M. Delcor, "Le culte de la 'Reine du Ciel' selon Jer 7,18; 44,17-19,25 et ses survivances," *Von Kanaan bis Kerala. Festschrift J. P. M. van der Ploeg. AOAT,* 211 (1982), 101-122.

subjects, vv. 5,6-8; world theophany, v. 5). He stands over against the nations and their gods explicitly as *meleḵ* of Israel, proving himself in the divine trial as the superior, singular, and unique God. These predications apparently also function to subsume under the Yahweh-Zion-king concept various political ideas from the inheritance of Israel's monarchy and royal history. Deutero-Isaiah's intentions here coincide both with those of the Deuteronomistic historian (1 S. 8,12) and with the theocratic ideology of the Chronicler (cf. the notion of the "throne of God" of the house of David, 1 Ch. 28:5; 29:23[85]). The theophany of the world king serves to reestablish the former residence Zion; thus the news is to be proclaimed that once again Zion's God and no other will reign there as king (Isa. 52:7, perfect aspect in visionary perspective). By metaphorically expanding along previously established lines, Deutero-Isaiah accentuates (1) the universal and simultaneously particular, (2) the superlative, and (3) the eschatological aspects of the kingship theologoumenon. In this sense he "rehabilitated the title of King as applied to Yahweh."[86]

Various anonymous and probably postexilic prophetic sayings attempt to renew the notion of Yahweh as king by picking up the Zion tradition once again. These are totally oriented toward the future: Jer. 3:17; 10:7,10; 17:12; 51:57 (46:18; 48:15); Ob. 21; Mic. 2:13; 4:7; Zeph. 3:15; Mal. 1:14.

7. *"Yahweh mālaḵ."* Scholars seem to have reached a certain degree of clarity concerning the much discussed formulaic expression *YHWH mālaḵ.* The following factors are important in its understanding:

a. The *x-qāṭal* formulation (inverted verbal clause or compound nominal clause) accentuates *x,* i.e., Yahweh, which — especially at the beginning of a psalm — generates strong emphasis. It is Yahweh who . . . ; Yahweh — he. . . .

b. The *x-qāṭal* formulation should be distinguished from all *qāṭal-x* analogies. An exact syntactical-formal analogy occurs in prose only in 1 K. 1:18: "And now, behold, Adonijah-*mālaḵ,"* which confirms the preceding consideration (a). To this extent the statement implies a negation: *x* and not *y,* an aspect explicated in various contexts (1 K. 1:18; Pss. 93,96,97,99).

c. The meaning of the verb[87] in the perfect with Yahweh as subject is the same as the normal meaning, generally circumscribed by "to be king, become king, rule as king, reign," without any partial aspect (e.g., "to become") exhibiting any discernible priority or becoming fixed in any specific contexts. There is no temporal reference apart from the perfect aspect of the verb *mlk* with a durative semantic component, and would have to be determined from context (in contrast to the imperfect forms with and without *waw*-consecutive, e.g., 1 K. 1:18, and statements with temporal indicators, e.g., Ex. 15:18).

d. The expression should be characterized form-critically not as an "enthronement cry"[88] or the like, but rather, like the frequently cited parallels from the Marduk or

---

85. See also Dietrich, 265f.; → כסא *kissē',* III.2 (VII, 245-47).
86. W. Eichrodt, *Theology of the OT,* I. *OTL* (Eng. trans. 1961), 198.
87. See III.3 above.
88. Mowinckel.

Horus rituals, as a "cry of acclamation or proclamation."[89] This formula does not automatically allow one to conclude by analogy the existence of an enthronement ritual and enthronement festival.

e. Both the formulaic character and the accentuated position within the psalm texts suggest that the various contexts constitute "explications of the statement *YHWH mālak̲,*"[90] explications developing hymnically and theologically the substance of the short formula, which itself had apparently acquired the status of dogma.

8. *The So-called Enthronement Festival of Yahweh.* In his investigation into the cultic life setting of the *YHWH mālak̲* formula, Sigmund Mowinckel[91] took various routes in arriving at a synthesis in reconstructing an ancient Israelite festival focusing on Yahweh's enthronement. As a cultic drama with liturgical symbolism, this festival creatively actualized Yahweh's enthronement by portraying it according to the earthly model; it was repeated annually, and during the preexilic period was combined with the autumnal and New Year's festival. It is within this cultic framework that the *YHWH mālak̲* expression originally functions. In the context of Yahweh's cultic presence, the expression does not mean "Yahweh is king, but rather Yahweh has (now) become king." The expression thus functions in paying homage to the king Yahweh during the enthronement.[92] Here, too, the enthronement psalms in both the narrower sense (according to Mowinckel, Pss. 47,93,95–100) and wider sense (altogether more than forty psalms) have their original setting and exhibit their original meaning as a reflex to the cultic events within the overall course of these "festival plays," plays during which all the individual elements and themes of the Jerusalem cultic hymn are presented: creation and struggle with the primeval dragon, conflict with the gods, exodus, battle of the nations, judgment and renewal, deliverance epiphany, etc. This cult-functional interpretation of these psalms constitutes the true alternative to both the historical and the eschatological interpretations.

This hypothesis, which had already been sketched out earlier independently of Mowinckel,[93] was well received both directly[94] and with creative expansion into the "cultic pattern,"[95] although also with critical modification by other festival theories.[96] The discussion of this topic has not yet reached a conclusion. Although it is generally

---

89. Michel.

90. *Ibid.*

91. NTTSup, 1917, 13-79; then in his classic work *Psalmenstudien, II* (1922). In English, see especially *The Psalms in Israel's Worship,* I (Eng. trans., Nashville, 1962), ch. 5, "Psalms at the Enthronement Festival of Yahweh."

92. E.g., p. 6.

93. Volz.

94. Cf. H. Schmidt.

95. Engnell and others.

96. Variously a "royal festival of Zion," H.-J. Kraus, *Psalms 1–59* (Eng. trans., Minneapolis, 1987), 56f.; or a "Covenant Festival of Yahweh," A. Weiser, *Psalms. OTL* (Eng. trans. 1962), 35-52.

recognized that the narrower group of enthronement psalms were indeed associated with the cult, the existence of a central festival of this sort is not beyond dispute.

9. *The Yahweh-Kingship Hymns.* The enthronement psalms, or better, the Yahweh-kingship hymns (viewing the *mlk* predication as the central element), Pss. 47,93,95–99, are complex literary constructions. Generally viewed as postexilic, one of their primary characteristics is that the *YHWH mlk* statement occupies a dominant position within a strongly anthological textual structure. The notion of Yahweh as king holds together the collage-like series of individual elements which are in part preformed and appropriated as citations (cf. esp. Ps. 96). This framing function is given to the *YHWH-mlk* expression apparently in its role as a central theological statement which the Jerusalem Zion tradition is attempting to codify. The concomitant psalm statements then develop and establish this confession, whose recognition and acceptance apparently have to be reaffirmed.

Ps. 93 positions this confession thetically at the beginning ("Yahweh reigns as king") and supports it (1) with a tripartite hymnic textual section dealing with Yahweh's victory over the waters of chaos (vv. 1aβ-δ,3,4, probably preexilic), (2) with a reference to creation cast in the style of a prayer (the earth is Yahweh's everlasting throne; vv. 1b,2[v. 1b is a displaced verse; cf. Ps. 96:10]), and (3) with praise of his manner of ruling through his decrees (*'ēḏôṯ*) and through his presence (the holy temple) (93:5). In this way the various aspects of Yahweh's rule (creation, cosmic order, and revelation) are encompassed and appended to the confession itself as concrete examples, whereby the polemical fundamental character of the formula comes to expression.

Ps. 97 can be understood in basically the same way. The Yahweh-king formula, positioned at the beginning, is explicated by different elements within the psalm, including various psalm citations (v. 2b par. 89:15[14]; v. 4a par. 77:19b[18b]; v. 6a par. 50:6a; v. 8 par. 48:12[11]; v. 9a par. 83:19[18]; v. 12b par. 30:5b[4b]), introducing the following aspects of Yahweh's reign as king: the theophany as the lord of the entire world, the reaction of the cosmic elements, and the subjection of all the gods; for Yahweh proves to be the "most high over all the earth," "exalted far above all gods" (97:1,2a,3-6,7b,9); justice and righteousness are the signs of his pharaonic throne (v. 2b); next to him, other alleged gods are merely "little gods" (*'ᵉlîlîm,* v. 7a); Zion and the daughters of Judah can rejoice in his judgments (*mišpāṭeyḵā.* v. 8), because under his rule "light shines[97] for the righteous" (vv. 10-12).

Ps. 99 proclaims Yahweh's kingship from the perspective of his holy presence on Zion. Mention of the "cherubim throne" (v. 1) is amplified by the predications "great," "exalted over all the gods [MT people]" (v. 2), and "holy" (vv. 3,5,9), whom one can approach only in subjection, yet who — as shown by the classic examples of Moses, Aaron, and Samuel (vv. 6-8) — always remained cultically accessible. The *'ōz meleḵ* in v. 4 is a *crux interpretum;* in any case, the verse is emphasizing the love of justice and of order exhibited by this king in Israel.

97. All or most versions read thus, instead of "is sown."

Although Pss. 96,95,98, and 47 do not position the proclamatory *YHWH mālak̲* at the beginning, they, too, are guided by this royal theologoumenon, which holds together the various individual parts in a kind of mosaic. Ps. 96 asks for a "new song" for the nations (vv. 1f.) whose content is to be Yahweh's glory and salvific deeds. It even offers an example of such singing in vv. 4-6 (composed of citations in part from Pss. 29,93,98). Ps. 96:10-13 summarizes what is to be said to the nations: Yahweh is the king of the world and the judge of the nations.

Ps. 95 uses the statement in its traditional function: "For Yahweh is the [a] great God *('ēl)* and the [a] great King above all gods *('ᵉlōhîm)"* (v. 3). The psalm exhorts those who may call themselves the "people of his pasture" (v. 7) to extol him as the "rock of our salvation" (v. 1).

Ps. 98 also calls out for people to join in the worldwide festive rejoicing "before the face of King Yahweh" (v. 6). Here "king" has become the title representing a plethora of notions concerning faith.

Finally, Ps. 47 casts its statement in the style of the hymnic imperative from elements of traditional notions of Yahweh as king; the term *melek̲* occurs twice in the hymnic section (vv. 3,9[2,8]) and twice in the confessional sections (vv. 7-10[6-9]). The immediate context shows which aspects the psalm is seeking to evoke with the expression: (1) The predication *melek̲ gād̲ôl* evokes by its association with royal titles a universal horizon and categories of world power ("all peoples," "over all the earth"). (2) The variously cited "vertical" prep. *ʿal* (3 times; *ʿālâ,* 2 times; *ʿelyôn* next to *taḥat̲,* 2 times) adds the superlative aspect: Yahweh is *the* most high God (cf. Ps. 95:3; 96:4, etc.). (3) The combination of throne and regnal shout *(tᵉrûʿâ)* evokes the familiar associations with Zion. This might even be evoking a cultic procession (47:6[5]). (4) The form "our king" (v. 7[6]), together with the urgent tone of the fourfold exhortation to sing, is able to generate especially strong emotional elements when those who are exhorted do indeed surrender to the enthusiastic mood of the psalm and freely appropriate in their own confession (v. 8a[7a]) the royal proclamation of vv. 3,6,9(2,5,8).

10. *Other Psalms.* Use of the *melek̲* theologoumenon in the other psalms exhibits relationships with the ideas associated with the Yahweh-kingship hymns. The theologoumenon is reflected: (1) in several individual confessions of trust (1st person sg. suf.): "my King and my God" (Ps. 5:3[2]; probably as an addendum in Ps. 84:4[3]); "my God, the King" (Ps. 145:1; cf. vv. 11-13); strikingly, also in collective psalms we read "you are my King, God (Yahweh)" (Ps. 44:5[4]), and par.: "yet God is my King from of old" (Ps. 74:12 MT). A personal *ʿeb̲ed̲* relationship probably resonates here as well (cf. also Ps. 149:2: "let the sons of Zion rejoice in their King"; Isa. 33:22: "Yahweh is our king");[98] (2) in the confessional statements that temporally (with *ʿôlām:* Ps. 29:10b; Ex. 15:18; Ps. 9:5[4]; 146:10; 145:13 pl.; Jer. 10:10; with *qed̲em* in Ps. 74:12) or spatially (e.g., Ps. 9:8[7]; 10:16; Jer. 10:7) expand Yahweh's royal dominion — "king of the gods" according to the archaic predication (Ps. 95:3 and the expansion to Ps.

98. On the construction of personal names, see IV.3 above.

135:6 according to 11QPs[a]: *mlk 'lwhym*); (3) in hymnic predications with the abstract constructions *malkûṯ/m^elûkâ,* terms which also flirt with this kind of expansion into the universal: Ps. 22:29(28) (cf. vv. 28,30-32[27,29-31); 103:19 *(bakkōl);* 145:11-13. The doxologies in 1 Ch. 29:11 ("thine is the kingdom") and at the conclusion to the book of Obadiah (Ob. 21: "the kingdom shall be Yahweh's") also belong within the horizon of these hymnic statements.

11. *Late Prophecy and Apocalypticism.* Evidence also occurs in the later parts of several prophetic books and in apocalyptic literature. Zec. 14:16f. announces that at the Feast of Booths "every one that survives of all the nations" will go up to Zion "to worship the King, Yahweh *ṣ^eḇā'ôṯ*" and (according to v. 17) to petition for rain. According to Isa. 24:21-23, in the future ("on that day") *YHWH ṣ^eḇā'ôṯ* will gather together the heavenly hosts and earthly kings in a pit, will punish them, and will himself take over dominion in Zion *(mālaḵ YHWH),* so that even the moon and sun will be diminished.[99] These features recall Dnl. 2,7. Finally, in Dnl. 3:33[4:3]; 4:31,34[34,37] Nebuchadnezzar speaks the doxology to "the King of heaven," a doxology which considering 1 Ch. 29:11; Ps. 145:13; Ob. 21 has apparently been taken from the liturgical repertoire: "His kingdom is an everlasting kingdom, and his sovereignty endures from generation to generation" (Dnl. 3:33[4:3]; cf. 4:31[34]).[100]

Seybold

V. Qumran. The root *mlk* is attested more than 50 times in the writings of Qumran. What is surprising, however, is its weak representation in the larger scrolls: no occurrences at all in 1QS (in contrast, 8 in CD), 2 in 1QH; 9 in 1QM (plus 4 occurrences in parallel 4QM fragments); the texts of 3Q, 5Q, and 6Q contain 1 occurrence each, although the fragmentary nature of the texts hardly allows any real conclusions. 4QpNah attests 5, 11QT 7 occurrences.

An evaluation of these occurrences first finds that the institution of the monarchy, while certainly playing a role for the community historically (cf. 1QM 11:3), by no means played any relevant contemporary role. Earthly kings had no place in their eschatologically charged anticipation (CD 20:16; cf. 1:6; also Hos. 3:4; 1QM 12:7). Not surprisingly, however, the Temple scroll deviates from this line.[101] God is the "king of glory" (4Q510 1:1; 4Q511:52-59 III 4; 4QFlor 1:3), who is "with" his community (1QM 12:3,8; 19:1); he is the ruler of all creatures (1QH 10:8) and bears the title "great king" (5Q10 1:3) and "king of kings" (4QM[a] I 13 par. 1QM 14:16). The "kings of the nations" (1QM 12:14; 19:6) will serve him. CD 8:10; 19:23f. even refer to the "kings of the nations" as serpents spewing poison. Their head is the king of Yawan (Ionia, Greece) (CD 8:11; cf. 4QpNah 1:2f.). The earthly adversaries of the Qumran

99. Cf. Welten.

100. On post-OT literature, cf. H. Kleinknecht, G. von Rad, K. G. Kuhn, K. L. Schmidt, "βασιλεύς," *TDNT,* I, 564-593 (further bibliog. in *TWNT,* X/2, 1008-1014); J. Gray, *The Biblical Doctrine of the Reign of God;* J. Coppens and J. Carmignac, "Règne de Dieu," *DBS,* 54, 1-252.

101. See following discussion.

community in the decisive eschatological battle include the king of the Kittim (1QM 15:2) and the kings of the north (1QM 1:4 par. 4Q496 3:3). Some passages contain vague historical allusions (4QpNah 2:9; 4:2), and CD 3:9 even an obvious anachronism in its assertion that because of the murmuring during the wilderness wanderings the "kings" of the Israelites were destroyed. The unclear textual context in the "Song of Michael" seems to suggest that Michael is to be counted among the circle of the gods, to which even the mighty "kings of the east" have no access (4QM[a] 11 I:12,18). One ecclesiological surprise is found in CD 7:16f.: the tabernacle of David which in Am. 9:11 is supposed to be rebuilt is now interpreted within the framework of realized eschatology as the books of the Torah, and the congregation understands itself as this king (*hammelek̲ hû' haqqāhāl,* "the king is the congregation"). Since 4QFlor 12f. interprets Am. 9:11 messianically, one cannot exclude the possibility that the equation *melek̲* = *qāhāl* is a messianic notation.

The regulations concerning kings in the Temple scroll (11QT 56–59) are based on the laws of kingship in Dt. 17:14-20, which have, however, been considerably expanded, perhaps in an anti-Hasmonean spirit. The function of the king seems in many ways to parallel that of the high priest. In the case of a war of aggression the king is subject to high priestly oracular guidance.

Fabry

מֹלֶךְ *mōlek̲*

Contents: I. *mlk* in Phoenician-Punic: 1. *mlk/molch-/mlkt* "Offering"; 2. The Semantic Field of *mlk;* a. *molchomōr* etc. and *mlk 'mr;* b. *mlk 'dm;* c. *mlk b'l;* d. *nṣb mlk(t) (b'l);* e. *mlk bšr* etc.; f. *'zrm (h)'š/'št.* 3. Function of the *mlk* Sacrifice; a. Thanksgiving Ceremony; b. Ceremony of Lament or Petition. II. Related Constructions in the Ancient Near East Outside the Phoenician-Punic Sphere? III. *mōlek̲* in Hebrew: 1. Linguistic Considerations; a. Form and Meaning; b. The Semantic Field of *mōlek̲;* 2. Occurrences and Dating; 3. The Function and the Recipient of the *mōlek̲* Sacrifice.

---

mōlek̲. A. Alt, "Zur Talionsformel," *ZAW,* 52 (1934), 303-5; A. Bea, "Kinderopfer für Moloch oder für Jahwe?" *Bibl,* 18 (1937), 95-107; H. Cazelles, "Molok," *DBS,* V (1957), 1337-1346; K. Dronkert, *De Molochdienst in het OT* (Leiden, 1953) [Eng. summary]; J. Ebach and U. Rüterswörden, "ADRMLK, 'Moloch' und BA'AL ADR," *Festschrift C. F. A. Schaeffer. UF,* 11 (1979), 219-226; O. Eissfeldt, *Molk als Opferbegriff im Punischen und Hebräischen, und das Ende des Gottes Moloch. BRA,* 3 (1935); J.-G. Février, "Les rites sacrificiels chez les Hébreux et à Carthage," *REJ,* 123 (1964), 7-18; W. Kornfeld, "Der Moloch: Eine Untersuchung zur Theorie O. Eissfeldts," *WZKM,* 51 (1948-1952), 287-313; M. J. Mulder, *Kanaänitische Goden in het OT* (Hague, 1965), 57-64; W. Röllig, "Moloch," *WbMyth,* I (1965), 299f.; M. Weinfeld, "The Worship of Molech and of the Queen of Heaven and its Background," *UF,* 4 (1972), 133-154.

I. mlk in Phoenician-Punic.

1. *mlk/molch-/mlkt* "Offering." The only Phoenician attestation for *mlk* is in *RÉS* 367, a 3rd/2nd-century-B.C. votive inscription from Nebi Yūnis; although Mark Lidzbarski[1] still considered this to be inauthentic, its reconsideration by Bernard Delavault and André Lemaire has probably established its authenticity. This then constitutes the only example of an offering plate of the kind frequently attested in the Punic sphere, being explicitly associated through its inscription with the *mlk* sacrifice.[2]

The term *mlk* is profusely attested in Punic on votive stelae from the beginning of the 6th century B.C. till the period following the Roman conquest of Carthage;[3] in addition, four stelae from Algerian Ngaus (Nicivibus) attest the 2nd/3rd-century-A.D. Latin transcriptions *morch-, moch-, molch-,* and *morc-,* among which *molch-* probably best approximates the contemporary pronunciation.[4] In *CIS* I, 198, 4; 5684, 1, the fem. (pl.?) *mlkt* is used instead of *mlk.*

The Phoenician-Punic term *mlk(t)/molch-* is probably to be explained as a causative nominal *maqṭil(at)* form from *ylk (< wlk),* suggesting the pronunciation *môlēk* (< *mawlik*).

I: J. Alquier and P. Alquier, "Stèles votives à Saturne découvertes près de N'gaous [Algérie]," *CRAI,* 1931, 21-26, with an addendum by J.-B. Chabot, 26f.; J. Carcopino, "Survivances par substitution des sacrifices d'enfants dans l'Afrique romaine," *RHR,* 106 (1932), 592-99; J.-B. Chabot, "Punica XI: Les inscriptions néopuniques de Guelma," *JA,* 11/8 (1916), 483-520; *idem,* "Punica XVIII: Stèles puniques de Constantine," *JA,* 11/10 (1917), 38-79; G. Charles-Picard, *Les religions de l'Afrique antique* (Paris, 1954), 42-52; R. Charlier, "La nouvelle série de stèles puniques de Constantine et la question des sacrifices dits 'molchomor,' en relation avec l'expression 'bsrm btm,' " *Karthago,* 4 (1953), 3-49; P. Cintas, "Le sanctuaire punique de Sousse," *Revue africaine,* 91 (1947), 1-80; B. Delavault and A. Lemaire, "Une stèle 'molk' de Palestine dédiée à Eshmoun? RES 367 reconsidéré," *RB,* 83 (1976), 569-583; R. Dussaud, "Précisions épigraphiques touchants les sacrifices puniques d'enfants," *CRAI,* 1946, 371-387; J.-G. Février, "Essai de reconstruction du sacrifice molek," *JA,* 248 (1960), 167-187; *idem,* "Molchomor," *RHR,* 143 (1953), 8-18; *idem,* "Le rite de substitution dans les textes de N'Gaous," *JA,* 250 (1962), 1-10; "Le vocabulaire sacrificiel punique," *JA,* 243 (1955), 49-63; G. Garbini, "L'iscrizione cartaginese CIS I 5510 e il sacrificio 'molk,' " *RSO,* 42 (1967), 8-13; *idem,* "מלך בעל e מלך אמר: A proposito di CIS I 123 B," *RSO,* 43 (1968), 5-11; *idem,* "Il sacrificio dei bambini nel mondo punico," *Atti della Settimana di Studio "Sangue e Anthropologia Biblica" Roma, 10-15 marzo 1980,* I (Rome, 1981), 127-134; S. Gsell, *Histoire ancienne de l'Afrique du nord,* IV (repr. Paris, 1972), 404-410; J. Guey, " 'Moloch' et 'Molchomor': A propos des stèles votives," *MAH,* 54 (1934), 83-102; J. Hoftijzer, "Eine Notiz zum punischen Kinderopfer," *VT,* 8 (1958), 288-292; C. Picard, "Le monument de Nebi-Yunis," *RB,* 83 (1976), 584-89.

III: E. Dhorme, *La religion des Hébreux nomades* (Paris, 1937), 201-219; *idem,* "Le dieu Baal et le dieu Moloch dans la tradition biblique," *AnSt,* 6 (1956), 57-61; A. Jirku, "Gab es im AT einen Gott Molok (Melek)?" *ARW,* 35 (1938), 178f.; O. Kaiser, "Den Erstgeborenen deiner Söhne sollst du mir geben. Erwägungen zum Kinderopfer im AT. Denkender Glaube. FS C. H. Ratschow (Berlin/New York, 1976), 24-48; D. Plataroti, "Zum Gebrauch des Wortes *mlk* im AT," *VT,* 28 (1978), 286-300; R. de Vaux, *Studies in OT Sacrifice* (Cardiff, 1964), 73-90.

1. *LidzEph,* I (1902), 285-87.
2. Picard.
3. *DISO, s.v. mlk* V; R. S. Tomback, *A Comparative Lexicon of the Phoenician and Punic Languages. SBL Diss,* 32 (1978), *s.v. mlk* IV.
4. Texts in Alquier-Alquier.

The defective orthography of the preformative syllable occurs frequently in derivatives of nouns with *mem*-preformative from I-*waw/yodh* roots; cf., e.g., *mṣ',* "place or act of going forth," or *mtnt,* "gift."[5] The defective orthography of the stem vowel, however, corresponding to the *o*-phoneme between *l* or *r* and *c* or *ch* in the Latin transcriptions, apparently derives from the short *i* in the stem syllable of the Phoenician-Punic causative. The vowel is additionally attested by the rendering *ml'k,*[6] in which ' replaces *ē.* The vowel sequence *ô* — *ē* in the root *hlk* is illuminated by comparison with *thuulek,* "guest."[7] The absence of the vowel in the Latin transcriptions may have resulted from subsequent linguistic degeneration, something also attested by the orthographical variation.

Since the causative (yiphil) of *ylk* means "to offer, present" (cf. Phoen. *wylk zbḥ,* "and they will present a burnt offering"[8]), the *maqṭil* noun refers to the result of the particular action expressed ("that which is presented/offered") or to the action itself ("presenting, the act of offering or sacrificing"); the feminine construction *mlkt* refers to the latter, more abstract usage.

Contextual considerations also suggest that *mlk(t)* functions as a sacrificial term.[9] Since *mlk* frequently occurs as the object of *ndr,* "to vow, pledge,"[10] Otto Eissfeldt's suggestion that *mlk* itself refers to a "vow, pledge" is unacceptable. Primarily, however, *mlk,* "offering," and the prepositional object *bmlk 'zrm (h)'š/'št,* "as offering . . . ," are used with verbs such as *ytn,* "to give,"[11] *zbḥ,* etc., "to sacrifice,"[12] and *nš',* "to present, offer."[13] Finally, *mlk b'l* occurs as a predicative of *mtnt,* "his gift (consecrated to the deity)."[14]

Correspondingly, the inscriptions of Ngaus identify the terms constructed with *molch-* etc. as *sacrum magnum nocturnum*[15] or as *sacrum.*[16]

Sacrificial terms are also constructed as causatives from verbs of movement in other Semitic languages: Heb. *'lh* hiphil (e.g., Gen. 8:20; 22:2; cf. Pun. *h'l'*[17]); Heb. *'br* hiphil; and Aram. *nsq/slq* aphel (variously "to present, offer"), from the latter of which the nouns (Late Babylonian) *massaqtu,* "burnt offering," and (Mand.) *masiqtā,* referring to the sacramental meal, are derived.[18]

---

5. J. Friedrich and W. Röllig, *Phönizisch-punische Grammatik. AnOr,* 46 (^{2}1970), §202b.
6. A. Berthier and R. Charlier, *Le sanctuaire punique d'El-Hofra à Constantine* (Paris, 1955), 54, 2.
7. Plautus *Poenulus* 934.
8. *KAI,* 26, II, 19.
9. Eissfeldt, Dussaud, Février, Hoftijzer, and others.
10. *RÉS,* 367, I, 2; *CIS,* I, 307, 3f.; Berthier-Charlier, 42, 1-3; 54, 2f.; 55, 1f.; *KAI,* 105, 2f.
11. *RÉS,* 367, I, 2; *CIS,* I, 5685, 2.
12. *Neupunische Inschriften* (numbering follows P. Schröder; cf. the list in *KAI,* III, 74-77), 15, 1; 18, 1; 19, 1; 20, 1/2; 74, 1; 75, 1/2; 77, 2; 85,1; cf. further Chabot, *JA,* 11/8 (1916), 509.
13. *Neupunische Inschriften,* 21 (= *KAI,* 167), 1,3; on *zbḥ b,* "to sacrifice as," cf. Friedrich-Röllig, §283, 10.
14. *KAI,* 99, 2.
15. 1, 4/5; 3, 1/2.
16. 2, 5/6; 4, 4/5.
17. *KAI,* 159, 8.
18. Cf. W. von Soden, "*n* als Wurzelaugment im Semitischen," *Studia orientalia. Festschrift C. Brockelmann. WZ Halle-Wittenberg,* 17, 2/3 (1968), G, H. 2/3, 175-184.

The most recently suggested identification[19] of Pun. *mlk* V[20] with *mlk* II, "king," in the fashion of an epithet of the divine recipient of the sacrifice named in the inscription, is unacceptable not least because no divine name occurs before *mlk* to which the epithet might refer;[21] even in the expression *mtnt' mlk b'l,*[22] the combination *mlk b'l,* used predicatively, would exhibit no satisfactory syntactical connection even if it were the reference to a deity. In most instances, however, an epithet *mlk* would compete with other epithets appended to the name of the god honored by the sacrifice. Furthermore, the feminine construction *mlkt*[23] would not agree in gender with *b'l ḥmn;*[24] conversely, the masc. *mlk* would be referring to the feminine divine name *tnt.*[25] Finally, assuming that *mlk* is functioning as an epithet, then the *molch-* of the Latin transcriptions would have to be separated from Phoen.-Pun. *mlk,*[26] especially since an interpretation of *molch-* as "king" is still impeded by the fact that Phoen.-Pun. *mlk,* "king," attests the stem vowel *i* or *a.*[27]

The frequency of Semitic causative constructions from verbs of movement for sacrificial terminology also militates against associating *mlk* in the sense of "royal sacrifice"[28] or of "(compelling) power"[29] with the root *mlk,* "king."

2. *The Semantic Field of mlk.* Since *mlk* occurs without more specific attributive qualifications only in a few texts,[30] a more exact determination of its meaning can only be attained by analyzing its attendant semantic field.

a. *molchomōr etc. and mlk 'mr.* The construction *molchomōr* in the Ngaus inscriptions corresponds according to J.-B. Chabot[31] and many others to the expression *mlk 'mr* already attested in the earliest votive stelae from Carthage and Constantine.[32] The interpretation of Pun. *'mr* corresponding to Heb. *'immēr,* "lamb,"[33] is supported, despite

19. Charlier, 15-19.
20. *DISO.*
21. *CIS,* I, 307, 4; Berthier-Charlier, 36, 2; 42, 3; *Neupunische Inschriften,* 30, 2.
22. *KAI,* 99, 2.
23. *CIS,* I, 5684, 1.
24. *Ibid.,* lines 3/4.
25. Berthier-Charlier, 37, 2.
26. This is the consistent position of Weinfeld.
27. Friedrich-Röllig, §193b.
28. W. F. Albright, *Yahweh and the Gods of Canaan* (London, 1968), 210; *idem* (with a different semantic determination), *Archaeology and the Religion of Israel* (Garden City, ⁵1968), 156-58.
29. R. Dussaud, review of Février, *JA,* 243 (1955), 49-63; and *idem,* "Les découvertes épigraphiques puniques et néopuniques depuis la guerre," *Studi Orientalistici. Festschrift G. Levi della Vida,* I (Rome, 1956), 274-286, *Syr,* 34 (1957), 394; cf. already Dussaud, *CRAI,* 1946, 372.
30. *RÉS,* 367, I, 1; Berthier-Charlier, 42, 4; 43, 4; *Neupunische Inschriften,* 30, 2; *KAI,* 159 (= *Neupunische Inschriften,* 124), 9.
31. *CRAI,* 1931, 26f.
32. *KAI,* 61 B, 1/2; *CIS,* I, 307, 4/5; Chabot, *JA,* 11/10 (1917), 49f.; Berthier-Charlier, 54, 2/3; 55 (= *KAI,* 109), 1/2.
33. *DISO,* 18; further parallels in Tomback, 24.

the *o* of the Latin transcriptions,[34] both by the expression *agnum pro vikario*[35] and by the portrayals on the Ngaus stelae of a bearded Saturn with a sacrificial knife before whom a sheep lies. Archaeological evidence points in the same direction: in addition to the remains of children, the tophets of Punic sanctuaries also increasingly yield those of calves, sheep, lambs, young goats, and even birds.[36]

Apparently, *mlk 'mr* always occurs without any more specific attributive qualifications.[37]

b. *mlk 'dm.* The expression *mlk 'dm* is attested in Constantine and Altiburos;[38] with the frequent addendum *bšrm . . . ,*[39] it can probably best be explained philologically as "human sacrifice."[40] The interpretation of *'dm* as a subjective genitive in the sense of "layman"[41] is excluded as a possibility because the donor of a *mlk 'dm bšʿrm btm*[42] refers to himself as a "priest";[43] derivation from *dm,* "blood," with *aleph*-prostheticum,[44] however, is inconsistent with phonetic laws.[45] Even when *mlk 'dm* occurs without more specific attributive qualifications,[46] the expression can admittedly refer metonymically to a substitute sacrifice; in that case, the cultic terminology no longer reflects the actual custom. To be sure, the expression *mlk 'dm* never occurs in combination with *'mr,* "lamb," or *bʿl,* "instead of an infant," expressions almost certainly referring to substitutions.

c. *mlk bʿl.* That *mlk bʿl* does indeed mean "offering in place of an infant"[47] is shown by the parallel formulation to *KAI,* 61 A, 1/2, *mlk 'mr,* "offering of a lamb."[48] The parallel nature of *mlk bʿl* and *mlk 'mr* in *KAI,* 61, A and B, also militates against the interpretation of *bʿl* as a subjective genitive (in the sense of "citizen"[49] or "donor, giver"[50]) or as the divine name *bʿl;*[51] this latter suggestion is also problematical because

---

34. Which is why E. Lipiński (in W. Beyerlin, ed., *Near Eastern Religious Texts. OTL* [Eng. trans. 1978], 234) reads the ptcp. qal active of *'mr,* the votive offering "of one who promises."
35. Ngaus cited in Alquier-Alquier, 3, 6; 4, 4.
36. Bibliog. in Kaiser, 29f., no. 15.
37. The expression *mlk 'ṭr* (Berthier-Charlier, 56 [= *KAI,* 110]) is an isolated occurrence and apparently represents a scribal error, as does *mlk 'šr* (*CIS,* I, 123 B, 1/2).
38. Examples in *DISO, s.v. mlk* V, 1; see also *ANET,* 658.
39. Cf. I.2.e below.
40. E.g., Eissfeldt, 16; Hoftijzer, 289; Röllig, *KAI,* II, 114.
41. Investigated as a possibility by Eissfeldt; similarly Lipiński, 234.
42. Berthier-Charlier, 29, 3.
43. Février, *RHR,* 143 (1953), 10f.
44. So Février, *JA,* 243 (1955), 54.
45. On *ēdōm* in Augustine, cf. Hoftijzer, 289, no. 2, and again Février, *JA,* 248 (1960), 186, no. 17.
46. Berthier-Charlier, 39, 1; 40, 3; 41, 3; *KAI,* 103, 1/2; Altiburos 2 (*LidzEph,* I, 42, no. 1).
47. Février, *RHR,* 143 (1953), 16; *idem, JA,* 243 (1955), 53; *idem, JA,* 248 (1960), 177; Röllig, *KAI,* II, 76f.
48. *KAI,* 61, B, 1/2; further examples of *mlk bʿl* in *DISO s.v. mlk,* V, 4; see also *mlkt bʿl, CIS,* I, 5684, 1, as well as *bʿl* alone, Berthier-Charlier, 114, 4. See also *ANET,* 658.
49. Cazelles, *DBS,* V, 1342.
50. Lipiński, 234.
51. Weinfeld, 139.

of (1) the absence of a prep. *l* for *bʿl,* (2) the competing reference to the recipient of the sacrifice by *lbʿl ḥmn,*[52] and (3) the lack of gender agreement in *mlkt bʿl.*[53] The substitution of a lamb for a child is suggested both by the expression *agnum pro vikario*[54] and by the apparently formulaic sequence *anima pro anima, sanguis pro sanguine, vita pro vita.*[55]

d. *nṣb mlk(t) (bʿl).* The combinations *nṣb mlk,*[56] *nṣb mlk bʿl* [*ʾzrm*],[57] *nṣb mlkt bʿl,*[58] *nṣb mlk ʾs̊/m̊r,*[59] and *nṣb mlkt bmṣrm*[60] show that the locus of the *mlk* sacrifice was designated by a stela *(nṣb).* The remains of sacrifices are often found beneath such stelae, and occasionally — though not always[61] — the erection of such a stela itself seems to have been viewed as the substitute *bšry,* "instead of flesh."[62]

e. *mlk bšr etc.* The expression *mlk bšr* should be interpreted from the perspective of Carthaginian *ʾš ndr knmy . . . bšry,* "that which KNMY pledged . . . instead of his flesh."[63] The terms *bšry, bšryʾ,* and *bšrm* are composed of *b,* "instead of," and *šr,* "flesh"[64] and the 3rd person masculine/feminine singular suffix.[65] The renderings collected by René Charlier[66] and Jacob Hoftijzer[67] also suggest the lexeme *šr;* the frequent occurrence of a vowel letter between *š* and *r* suggests an equivalent to Heb. *šeʾēr,* "flesh."[68] The possible combination *bšr* with suffix[69] or plural ending[70] is less persuasive, since *b-šʾr̊rm,* "instead of his flesh,"[71] occurs parallel after *b̊-ṣmḥ,* "instead of his descendant."[72] The parallel *bṣmḥ* par. *bšʾr̊rm*[73] additionally confirms the euphemistic use of *šr* for "child"; correspondingly, the expression *b̊ṣmḥ šʾrm*[74]

---

52. *KAI,* 61, A, 4/5 and *passim.*
53. *CIS,* I, 5684, 1.
54. Ngaus, 3, 6; 4, 4.
55. *Ibid.,* 2, 3/4; 3, 3/4; and in a different order: 4, 2/3.
56. *RÉS,* 367, I, 1.
57. Examples in *DISO s.v. mlk,* V, 4; see also *KAI,* 98, 2; *CIS,* I, 2613; 5685, 1.
58. *CIS,* I, 5684, 1.
59. *Ibid.,* 123B, 1/2.
60. *Ibid.,* I, 198, 4/5.
61. Contra Weinfeld, 135.
62. Cf. I.2.e below; *KAI,* 79, 5/6; cf. 163, 2 and the sparse inscriptions on the stelae from Nora; cf. here S. Moscati, *Le stele puniche di Nora nel Museo Nazionale di Cagliari. StSem,* 35 (1970).
63. *KAI,* 79, 3-6 (cf. *CIS,* I, 296, 2; 3822, 2-5; 5688, 2-5; N. Slouszch, *ʾÔṣar hakkᵉt̲ûb̲ôt̲ happᵉnîqiyyôt̲* (Tel Aviv, 1942), 471, 3-6. On *mlk bšr* as an object of *ndr,* "to vow, pledge," cf. *CIS,* I, 306, 5.
64. *DISO,* 288; Tomback, 311.
65. Février, *RHR,* 143 (1953), 12ff., and elsewhere.
66. P. 32.
67. P. 290, no. 1.
68. A different opinion is expressed by Cazelles, 1342.
69. Hoftijzer, 292; *DISO,* 45.
70. Dussaud, 380.
71. *KAI,* 162, 2.
72. Cf. l. 4 and *bkny,* "instead of his descendant[?]," *CIS,* I, 5688, 4/5.
73. *KAI,* 162, 2.
74. *Ibid.,* 163, 3.

seems to mean "instead of an offspring of their [?] flesh" (cf. the use of Heb. *šᵉʾēr,* "flesh," in Lev. 18:3; 20:19; and Pun. *šʾr*[75] for "relatives").

The term *bšrm* also occurs in the following combinations: *bšrm btm;*[76] *bšrm bntm;*[77] *mlk ʾdm bš(ʿ)rm btm;*[78] *mlk ʾdm bšrm bnʿ tm;*[79] and *mlk ʾdm ʾzrm ʾš . . . bšrn̊ btn̊.*[80]

The problematical element here is the relationship between *bntm* and *btm* (> *btn*). Eissfeldt[81] resolves *btm* into the prep. *b* with the subst. *tm* ("in perfection/completeness"), whereby *tm,* like the Hebrew adj. *tāmîm* (Ex. 12:5; Lev. 1:3; 10:3), evokes the idea of unblemished ritual purity as a prerequisite for sacrifices.[82] It must be pointed out that in inscriptions[83] *btm* corresponds to Lat. *de pecunia sua,*[84] "at one's own cost," which can be transferred to *mlk* as a substitute offering and which James-Germaine Février[85] also applies to *bntm* as *b* + *tmm* niphal; here one can point out also that *RÉS* 367 consists of an enumeration of persons who have made a financial contribution *(ʿrkt)* to a *mlk* sacrifice. It seems more likely, however, that *bšrm bntm* and *bšrm btm* both should be understood from the perspective of *bšrm bnʿ tm,* "instead of his flesh, instead of his unblemished son";[86] it is of no consequence that the 3rd person masculine singular suffix is actualized in two sequential words by the allomorphs *-m* and -ʿ.[87] *btm* then arises from *bntm* through assimilation of *n* to *t; bntm* and *btm* never occur together.

f. *ʾzrm (h)ʾš/ʾšt.* Special problems are presented by *ʾzrm (h)ʾš,* etc., and *ʾzrm ʾšt,* etc. Although the expressions do occur alone,[88] they are usually found in combinations: as genitive to *mlk,*[89] to *mlk ʾdm,*[90] and to [*nṣ*]*b mlk bʿl;*[91] the expression *bmlk ʾzrm (h)ʾš/ʾšt* seems specifically to be characteristic for Guelma (Calama).[92] The verbs with which *ʾzrm* is used as an object show that it is a sacrificial designation: *nšʾ,* "to

75. Tomback, 310.
76. *JA,* 11/10 (1917), 76, 3; *KAI,* 104, 2-6; Slouszch, 228, 2.
77. *CIS,* I, 3746, 6/7 (similarly 4929, 3; 5741, 8); Berthier-Charlier, 38, 3/4; 45, 3/4.
78. *KAI,* 105, 3; 106 (= Berthier and Charlier, 28), 1; Berthier-Charlier, 29, 1/2; 30, 1/2; 32, 2; 34, 3/4; 36, 3.
79. *KAI,* 107 (= Berthier-Charlier, 35), 4.
80. Berthier-Charlier, 37, 2/3.
81. P. 20.
82. Hoftijzer, 291, no. 1.
83. *KAI,* 72, B, 4, and elsewhere.
84. *KAI,* 124; 125; 126.
85. *JA,* 248 (1960), 172.
86. *KAI,* 107, 4.
87. Cf. the corresponding juxtaposition of -ʿ and -ʾ in Berthier-Charlier, 4, 4; 104, 2/3; cf. Röllig, *KAI,* II, 115.
88. *CIS,* I, 3781, 2; 3783, 2; 5550, 2; 5702, 2/3; 5741, 6/7; Berthier-Charlier, 162, 1/2; *Neupunische Inschriften,* 11, 2.
89. Examples in *DISO, s.v. mlk,* V, 3.
90. *Idem.*
91. *KAI,* 98, 2.
92. *Neupunische Inschriften,* 15, 2; 18, 2/3; 21 (= *KAI,* 167), 2/3.

present, offer,"[93] *pg'*, "to honor (a vow, etc.),"[94] and probably also *ndr,* "to pledge, vow."[95]

Since the *'zrm 'š/'št* in certain instances[96] is apparently preceded by a *bšrnl/m* with the same function, the afformative *-m* might be the 3rd person masculine singular suffix; admittedly, to my knowledge a masculine form without a suffix is nowhere attested for *'zrm.* The singular character of its presumed apposition *'š* militates against taking *-m* as a plural ending, and the absence of such a morpheme in the extant Phoenician-Punic evidence militates against taking it as an adverbial ending. Given its morphological uncertainty, explanations of this semanteme on the basis of Ugar. *ỉzr* (a type of sacrifice)[97] or Pun. *'zrt,* "family, descendants,"[98] are still questionable. If, on the other hand, *-m* is not an afformative, this makes unlikely any connection with Phoenician *'zrm* in *KAI,* 14, 3, 13, not least because this is a verbal form (1st person singular prefixing conjugation *zrm* niphal, "I was snatched/carried away," corresponding to *ngzlt,* 1st person singular affixing conjugation *gzl* niphal with the same meaning[99]) which does not fit the Punic passage.

The (appositional?) *'š,* etc., and *'št,* etc., as in *'îš wᵉ'ištô* (Gen. 7:2), signals the opposition "masculine — feminine," apparently with respect to the sacrificial elements themselves.[100] The sequence *'zrm 'š w'zrm 'št*[101] refers to the juxtaposition of a male and a female sacrifice, whereas a pronominal interpretation of *'š/'št*[102] in this passage yields no sense; the subjects of the pledging and offering are precisely here probably not coincidentally father and daughter (ll. 3-5).

3. *Function of the mlk Sacrifice.* If in the Phoenician-Punic sphere the *mlk* was thus probably originally a child sacrifice or its later substitution by a lamb or something similar,[103] we must now inquire regarding the function of this sacrifice.

a. *Thanksgiving Ceremony.* As far as information concerning its *reasons* is concerned, the *mlk* stelae admittedly do not deviate from the other extant votive stones: They mention an answered prayer (e.g., *kšm' ql',* "because he heard his voice"[104]) and refer to the blessing received (*brk',* "he blessed him"). To that extent the *mlk* sacrifice,

---

93. *CIS,* I, 3781; 3783; 5550.

94. *Neupunische Inschriften,* 11.

95. *CIS,* 5702; 5741. Cf. now [*lnš*]*'.'zr,* J. Hoftijzer, G. van der Kooij, and H. J. Franken, *Aramaic Texts from Deir 'Alla. DMOA,* 19 (1976), I, 14(12).

96. Berthier-Charlier, 37, 2, and *CIS,* I, 5741, 6-8.

97. R. de Vaux, review of C. Virolleaud, *La Légende phénicienne de Danel* (Paris, 1936), and *idem,* review of C. Virolleaud, *La Légende du roi Keret des Sidonens* (Gembloux, 1936), *RB,* 46 (1937), 442.

98. J.-G. Février, *JA,* 239 (1951), 9f.; cf. *BAr,* (1946/49, 1953), 168.

99. Ll. 2, 12, contra Février, JA, 243 (1955), 57-63.

100. On the appositional designation of such elements, cf. Friedrich-Röllig, §309.

101. *CIS,* I, 5702, 2/3.

102. Most recently Tomback, 9.

103. Cf. also K. Jaroš, *Die Stellung des Elohisten zur kanaanäischen Religion. OBO,* 4 (1974), 296ff.

104. This and the following citation, *KAI,* 110, 4; *ANET,* 658.

like most votive offerings, represents a thanksgiving ceremony. The *purpose* of the *mlk* sacrifice resides accordingly in the hope of future blessing (*tbrk'*, "may she [the goddess] bless him"[105]). Most of the inscriptions also reveal that the offering and the erection of the stela were carried out as the fulfillment of a vow made in a situation of distress, whereby one can compare the expression *ex voto* from Ngaus (1, 5, etc.) with the previously mentioned occurrences of *ndr,* "to vow, pledge."

The admittedly extremely fragmentary text of *KAI* 162 suggests that the answer to the prayer consisted in the gift of pregnancy, and since the ones making the offering seldom amplify their names with a title,[106] we can assume that the *mlk* sacrifice derives from the familial sphere, a fact consistent perhaps with its atavistic character. In the substitution sacrifice the previously requested child is then returned to the deity as a symbolic gift. Substitute sacrifices probably were not offered when the god — as in Jgs. 11:30-40 — provided deliverance from a different kind of distress and danger.

Such future blessing was probably almost always intended to benefit the actual donor. In other instances, the concern may have been for the child delivered by the substitute, as evidenced perhaps by the expressions *pro salute Concess*[*e*],[107] *pro Con*[*ces*]*se salute*,[108] and *pro salut*[*e*] *Donati,*[109] if Concessa and Donatus are the names of the children involved.[110]

b. *Ceremony of Lament or Petition.* In contrast, the *mlkt bmṣrm* in *CIS,* I, 198, 4/5, apparently represent(s) a ceremony of lament and petition, if, that is, *bmṣrm* can be understood with Eissfeldt[111] as the prep. *b* + the noun *mṣrm,* "in situations of distress," after the analogy of Heb. *m*^{e}*ṣārîm* (Lam. 1:3) and *min-hammēṣar* (Ps. 118:5). In the case of *CIS,* I, 198, the reference is to the distress of a person different from the person offering the sacrifice, a person for whom the *mlkt* sacrifice(s) *bmṣrm* is/are made. Only the *mlkt* sacrifice(s) *bmṣrm,* "in situations of distress," can be compared with the Phoenician and Punic child sacrifices made in catastrophic situations as attested by Philo Byblius (in Eusebius *Praep. ev.* i.10.44; cf. Porphyry, in Eusebius *Praep. ev.* iv.16.6) and other ancient authors, though both this procedure and that in 2 K. 3:27 derive from the public-political sphere rather than the private sphere.

Regardless of whether the Punic *mlk* sacrifice actually constitutes a ceremony of thanksgiving or of petition, it was in any case prompted by a specific, given occasion and was never a regularly performed institution.

II. Related Constructions in the Ancient Near East Outside the Phoenician-Punic Sphere? There do not appear to be any institutions outside the Phoenician-Punic sphere corresponding to Heb. *mōlek̲*.

---

105. *KAI,* 79, 6.
106. So Berthier-Charlier, 29, 3; 41, 2; 42, 2.
107. Ngaus, 2, 4/5.
108. *Ibid.,* 3, 4.
109. *Ibid.,* 4, 3.
110. Carcopino.
111. Pp. 28-30; cf. the bibliog. in *DISO, s.v. mlk* V, 5.

Because of its nonreligious usage, the Late Egyptian term *mrk,* "(royal) gift" (for a king),[112] although apparently a Canaanite loanword,[113] is not to be associated in any way with the Phoen.-Pun. or Heb. *mlk* attested at a so much later date; perhaps *mrk,* if it is not a derivation of *mlk,* "king,"[114] can be explained as a derivation of a root meaning "dowry" attested in Akkadian *(mulūgu/mulīgu),*[115] Ugaritic *(mlg),*[116] and Rabbinic Hebrew *(m^e lûg).*[117]

The nouns *mlk* and *mlkt,* which in *UM* (no. 1119) Cyrus H. Gordon still assigns to Ugar. *mlk* II ("a kind of sacrifice"), he in *UT* (no. 1483) assigns to *mlk* I, "king." The expression [*šlm.mlk.šlm*]*mlkt,* too, involves the opposition "king — queen," since the following genitive attributes to *šlm* are also actually designations of class standing.[118]

The *dbḥ.mlk* par. *dbḥ.ṣpn*[119] refers to a sacrifice for Il which is here associated with Zaphon;[120] here *mlk* has become a fixed, independent epithet like Akk. *māliku(m),* "counselor," or *mal(i)ku(m),* "king," which is applied as an epithet to a whole series of Mesopotamian gods.[121] Similarly, one can compare ᵈMA.LIK.MEŠ = *mlkm*[122] with the *malikū* or *mālikū* of Mari.[123]

The term *Malik,* attested in Mesopotamia as early as the pre-Sargonic period,[124] or *Malku(m),*[125] is also attested in personal names from Ugarit[126] and recently also from Ebla.[127] Neither this term nor the *malikū/mālikū* from Mari, given their association with the netherworld, has anything to do with the Phoen.-Pun. or Heb. *mlk.*[128] The divine

---

112. *Wen-amon,* II, 12 (*ANET,* 27); Chester-Beatty, I, vo. B, 31 (*WbÄS,* II, 113.3).

113. M. Burchardt, *Die altkanaanäischen Fremdworte und Eigennamen im Ägyptischen* (Leipzig, 1909f.), no. 481.

114. W. F. Albright, review of J. B. Pritchard, *ANET* (Princeton, 1950), *JAOS,* 72 (1951), 261.

115. *AHw,* II (1972), 671b; *CAD,* X/2 (1977), 193f.

116. *UT,* no. 1480.

117. Cf. Cazelles, 1343.

118. Contra Cazelles, 1345.

119. *KTU,* 1.91, 2/3.

120. As also in *KTU,* 1.47, 1; cf. also 1.148:1.

121. Contra Eissfeldt, *Neue keilalphabetische Texte aus Ras Schamra-Ugarit. SDAW,* 1965/6, 14, and many others; cf. K. L. Tallqvist, *Akkadische Götterepitheta. StOr,* 7 (1938, repr. 1974), 128f.

122. *Ugaritica,* 5 (1968), 45, 35.

123. Examples in *CAD,* X/1 (1977), 168; cf. J. F. Healy, "*MLKM/RP'UM* and the *KISPUM,*" *UF,* 10 (1979), 89-91; M. Dietrich and O. Loretz, "Neue Studien zu den Ritualtexten aus Ugarit (I) Ein Forschungsbericht," *UF,* 13 (1981), 69-74.

124. J. J. M. Roberts, *The Earliest Semitic Pantheon* (Baltimore, 1972), 42f. and *passim.*

125. Examples in *CAD,* X/1 (1977), 168f. (with bibliog.!).

126. *Ugaritica,* 5, 60; *PNU,* 79.157f.

127. G. Pettinato, "Testi cuneiformi des 3. millennio in paleo-cananeo rinvenuti nella campagna 1974 a Tell Mardīkh = Ebla," *Or,* 44 (1975), 370f.; *idem,* "The Royal Archives of Tell Mardikh-Ebla," *BA,* 39 (1976), 50; *idem,* "Aspetti amministrativi e topografici di Ebla nel III millenni av. Cr.," *RSO,* 50 (1976), 1-14 and elsewhere.

128. Cf. W. F. Albright, *Archaeology and the Religion of Israel* (Baltimore, 1954), 162-64, 218; Cazelles, 1344f.; de Vaux, 88f., and many others.

name *Muluk,* occurring in the place name *Ilum-Muluk,*[129] in the North Semitic personal name *I-tar-mu-luk,*[130] and in Ugaritic personal names,[131] is probably merely a phonetic variation of *Malik* belonging to the larger context of the "Canaanite" phonetic shift *ā* > *ō;* the place name *Ilum-Muluk* also occurs in the form *I-lu-ma-li-ka-wi^ki^.*[132] On the other hand, *Malik/Malku(m)/Muluk* and the *malikū/mālikū* of Mari are ultimately probably identical with the *meleḵ* of Isa. 57:9.

III. mōleḵ in Hebrew.

1. *Linguistic Considerations.* In my opinion, the connection between Heb. *l^e^mōleḵ*[133] and Phoen.-Pun. *mlk/molch-*[134] seems even more likely now that the "missing link" between Hebrew and Punic has emerged in the inscriptional casts of *RÉS* 367 from *Nēbi Yūnis,* even though this Phoenician inscription is also more recent than the OT occurrences.

a. *Form and Meaning.* In the Hebrew expression *l^e^mōleḵ,* "as an offering," the prep. *l^e^* is not a dative particle (e.g., "for *mōleḵ*"), but rather has the same function as the Punic *b*-essentiae in *bmlk 'zrm (h)'š/'št;*[135] Eissfeldt[136] early compared *l^e^mōleḵ* with *l^e^ʿôlâ,* "as a burnt offering" (Gen. 22:2), and *l^e^'āšām,* "as a guilt offering" (Lev. 5:18). In Ezk. 23:37, the *l^e^*-essentiae in *l^e^'oḵlâ,* "as food," is accompanied by the dative-*l^e^* referring to the divine recipients of the sacrifice *(lāhem),* whereby the two functions of *l^e^* can be clearly distinguished. The first misunderstanding of the sacrificial term as the designation of a deity might be the expression *zānâ 'aḥ^a^rê hammōleḵ,* "play the harlot after Molech" (Lev. 20:5), as shown by the parallel use of *zānâ* in v. 6. This misunderstanding of *l^e^mōleḵ* as the designation of a deity then manifests itself in the Masoretic vocalization according to *habbōšeṯ,* in the translation *ho Móloch* (*basileús,* 1 K. 11:7; or *árchōn,* Lev. 18:21; 20:2-5) in the later LXX passages (2 K. 23:10; Jer. 32:35; Am. 5:26), in Aquila, Symmachus, and Theodotion, and in the construction *Moloch* in the Vulg.

The suggestion that *mōleḵ* represents an earlier, independent divine designation[137] seems unlikely not least because *mōleḵ* does not occur apart from the context of sacrifice in the OT.

The correct pronunciation of Heb. *mlk* might be similar to that disclosed for Phoen.-Pun. *môlēk,* especially since a transition to the Masoretic *mōleḵ* is easy to imagine from that basis.

b. *The Semantic Field of mōleḵ.* The Hebrew term *ʿbr* hiphil, "to offer," corresponds

---

129. Examples in M. Birot, J. R. Kupper, and O. Rouault, *Répertoire analytique. ARM.T,* XVI/1 (1979), 17.

130. *CT,* 33, 29, 15.

131. *PRU,* IV, 215, 27; RS 17.242.

132. G. Dossin, "Signaux lumineux au pays de Mari," *RA,* 35 (1938), 178, no. 1.

133. On *l^e^,* cf. Eissfeldt, 36.

134. After Eissfeldt this connection is postulated esp. by Dussaud, Guey, Carcopino, Charles-Picard, and Cazelles.

135. Cf. I.1, 2.f. above.

136. Pp. 38f.

137. So Bea, Kornfeld, Dronkert, Weinfeld, Plataroti, and many others.

as a morphological-semantic parallel to Phoen.-Pun *ylk* yiphil, "to offer,"[138] whereby *l^eha'^ab̲îr* (Lev. 18:21; Jer. 32:35) is tautologically related to *l^emōlek̲*. The combination *'br* hiphil with *l^eYHWH* (Ex. 13:12) makes it plausible that *l^emōlek̲* could also be misunderstood as the dative of a divine name. The expression *nāt̲an l^emōlek̲* (Lev. 20:2-4; cf. *nāt̲an* + object *b^ek̲ôr* in Ex. 22:28f.[Eng. vv. 29f.]; Mic. 6:7) is apparently an early component of Canaanite sacrificial language;[139] cf. also *ytn* with the object "sacrificial gifts,"[140] *ytn* with the object *mlk (b'l),*[141] and the use of the noun *mtnt',* "gift," with the predicative *mlk b'l.*[142] Then, however, *bā'ēš (l^emōlek̲),* "with [RSB 'through'] fire (as a *mlk* sacrifice)" in connection with *'br* hiphil (Dt. 18:10; 2 K. 16:3; 17:17; 21:6; 23:10; 2 Ch. 33:6; Ezk. 20:31) is doubtlessly to be taken just as literally as in combination with *śrp,* "to burn" (Dt. 12:31; 2 K. 17:31; Jer. 7:31; 19:5).[143] The expression *wayyab̲'ēr bā'ēš* (2 Ch. 28:3) also refers to actual burning of the *mlk* sacrifice. Furthermore, in contrast to the Phoenician-Punic evidence, the idea of substitution for the sacrifice is excluded for Heb. *mōlek̲* by the mention of "seed" (Lev. 18:21; 20:2-4) and especially of sons and daughters (2 K. 23:10; Jer. 32:35; cf. Dt. 12:31; Jer. 7:31; 19:5; 2 K. 17:31).

2. *Occurrences and Dating.* The expression *l^emōlek̲* definitely occurs in Lev. 18:21; 20:2,3,4; 2 K. 23:10; Jer. 32:35; to these we may add *hammōlek̲* in Lev. 20:5. The expression *lammelek̲* in the gloss to Isa. 30:33 probably also refers to the *mlk* sacrifice, whereas in 1 K. 11:7 one should proabably read *l^emilkōm* instead of *l^emōlek̲*. Hence all occurrences are found either within the context of the Holiness Code or within that of the Deuteronomistic literature.

Although the formulations in Lev. 20:2-4 contain older linguistic elements, in their present form they also exhibit stylistic features of later literary rhetoric; in fact, the whole of v. 5bβ, with *zānâ 'ah̲^arê hammōlek̲,* may be the work of a glossarist.[144] However, the doubling of the verbs *nāt̲an* and *l^e* + *'br* hiphil + *l^emōlek̲* in Lev. 18:21, where furthermore the placing of the object in the initial position can be explained as literary imitation of vv. 7-19, does not at all give a stronger impression of originality than does Lev. 20:2-4, especially since Lev. 18:21 stands isolated within its own context.[145] Thus Lev. 18:4; 20:2-5 contribute to the dating of the *mlk* sacrifice in Israel only to the extent that the present secondary stratum of the Holiness Code underwent its literary reworking at earliest during the exilic period, and more likely during the postexilic period.

---

138. *KAI,* 26, II, 19.
139. Contra Kaiser, 42.
140. *KAI,* 43, 9; 68, 18; 137, 6; 163, 1.
141. *RÉS,* 367, I, 1/2; *CIS,* I, 5685, 2.
142. *KAI,* 99, 2; see I.1 above.
143. With Kaiser, 33f.; contra Weinfeld, 141, and Plataroti, 292f.
144. Cf. M. Noth, *Leviticus. OTL* (Eng. trans. 1965), 147-49; cf., however, also W. Thiel, "Erwägungen zum Alter des Heiligkeitsgesetzes," *ZAW,* 81 (1969), 53ff.
145. Cf. Kaiser, 43.

Otto Kaiser[146] has interpreted the plerophoric expression *heʿeḇîr (bāʾēš) lᵉmōleḵ* (2 K. 23:10; Jer. 32:35) as a secondary literary enhancement of *śārap bāʾēš* (Jer. 7:31). Particularly the (post-Deuteronomistic?) reference to Josiah's defilement of the Topheth (2 K. 23:10) might owe more to the Deuteronomistic ideal of this king than to actual historical events.[147] This terminology derives from the Deuteronomic-Deuteronomistic criticism of the cult, whereby child sacrifice, on the basis of a (secondary?) combination in Dt. 18:10, also appears together with sorcery and necromancy in Lev. 20:5f.; 2 K. 17:17; 21:6; 2 Ch. 33:6. The offer of sacrifice of the first-born as an atonement rite in Mic. 6:7 must then belong to the exilic period just as do its devaluation (Ezk. 20:25f.) or the denial (Jer. 7:31 > 19:5; 32:35 [Deuteronomistic]) of any corresponding commandment from Yahweh.[148] In contrast, the references to child sacrifice in the secondary passages in Ezekiel (Ezk. 16:20f.; 20:31; 23:37,39; as well as Isa. 57:5; Ps. 106:37) suggest a provenance during the postexilic period.

The cause of the relatively late, episodic emergence of the *mlk* sacrifice in Israel was not only crisis-related religious excesses, but simultaneously the Phoenician influence in Judah during both the exilic and postexilic periods, an influential infiltration manifesting itself in other areas as well.[149] Contemporary influence exerted on Phoenicia itself might also have occasioned the numerous Punic *mlk* sacrifices, which on the basis of *RÉS* 367 and the Hebrew evidence cannot be viewed as indigenous there. Occurrences of comparable sacrifices during earlier periods (Gen. 22; Jgs. 11:30-40; 2 K. 3:27) are rare, and lack any terminologically demonstrated specificity.

3. *The Function and the Recipient of the mōleḵ Sacrifice.* Only Mic. 6:7 makes what might be a reference to the function of the Israelite *mlk* sacrifice. According to this passage, both it and the action in 2 K. 3:27 — in a manner different from most of the Punic *mlk* sacrifices — functioned as a ceremony of lament and petition pushed to its most extreme limits, as an act of atonement; this also explains why substitutes were unacceptable. Its connection with the Topheth is not sufficient evidence to show that this was a regular institution[150]: on the one hand, according to Isa. 57:5, child sacrifice was not bound to the Topheth; on the other hand, according to Isa. 30:33, the Topheth apparently also involved the sacrifice of prisoners, which a gloss here probably incorrectly designates as *mlk.* To that extent the *mlk* sacrifice should thus be differentiated from the regular consecration of the first-born (Ex. 34:19a and *passim*); at the same time, when in cases such as Mic. 6:7 it refers to the killing of the first-born, it might

---

146. *Ibid.,* 34, 39, 43.

147. *Ibid.,* 33f.; E. Würthwein, "Die Josianische Reform und das Deuteronomium," *ZThK,* 73 (1976), 395-423, esp. 415; H. Hollenstein, "Literarkritische Erwägungen zum Bericht über die Reformmassnahmen Josias 2 Kön. XXIII 4ff.," *VT,* 27 (1977), 334.

148. On the dating of Mic. 6:7, cf. G. Fohrer, *Intro. OT* (Eng. trans., Nashville, 1968), 446; O. Kaiser, *Intro. OT* (Eng. trans., Minneapolis, 1975), 228f.

149. Cf. H.-P. Müller, "Phönizien und Juda in exilisch-nachexilischer Zeit," *WO,* 6 (1971), 189-204.

150. Contra Weinfeld, 133f.

have been understood as an exceptional intensification of the consecration of the first-born.

Postexilic considerations concerning a corresponding Yahweh-commandment (Jer. 7:31 [Deuteronomistic]; Ezk. 20:25; Mic. 6:7) suggest that the *mlk* sacrifice was probably intended for Yahweh. There was no cogent reason to dispute in the later redactional texts Jer. 19:5; 32:35 that Yahweh had never commanded that corresponding sacrifices be offered to Baʿal. If, however, the *mlk* sacrifice derives from Phoenician influence during the exilic and postexilic periods, then the gloss to Ps. 106:38 justifiably associates it with the "idols of Canaan"; Dt. 12:31 (Deuteronomistic); 2 K. 17:31; Ezk. 16:21; 20:31; 23:37 (secondary) also understand this ritual as a sacrifice to idols.

The question remains open whether temporal priority should be attributed to the prohibition of the *mlk* sacrifice in Lev. 18:21; 20:2-5 or to its condemnation in 2 K. 23:10; Jer. 32:35. In either case, both prohibition and condemnation show that the *mlk* sacrifice was perceived as incompatible with Yahweh's character, which accords with its episodic emergence prompted by Phoenician influence. The question must similarly remain open whether Yahweh's judgment, since it could not be deterred by the *mlk* sacrifice, was specifically understood as having been prompted by it (e.g., in view of the Deuteronomistic school).[151]

Kaiser[152] justifiably disputes the historical value of the mention of sacrifices offered by the Sepharvites to *ʾaḏrammeleḵ* and *ʿanammeleḵ* (2 K. 17:31). Whereas *ʾaḏrammeleḵ* recalls the Assyrian God Adad-milki,[153] the divine designation *ʿanammeleḵ* is composed of fem. *ʿanaṯ* + masc. *meleḵ* corresponding to the Phoen.-Pun. *mlkʿštrt*,[154] which makes it probable that the model was a Phoenician deity.[155] On the other hand, the different vocalization of the element *-mlk* by the (post-?) Deuteronomistic author of 2 K. 17:31 more likely suggests that he was not thinking of any connection with *hammôlēḵ*.

H.-P. Müller

151. Kaiser, 40.

152. *Ibid.*, 35f.

153. E.g., O. Eissfeldt, "Adrammelek und Demarus," *KlSchr,* III (1966), 335-39.

154. *KAI,* 19, 2/3; 71, 2; 119, 1; additional examples in Röllig, *KAI,* II, 28.

155. On *ʿnt* in Phoenician, cf. *KAI,* 42, 1, and the examples in Röllig, *KAI,* II, 59.

מָן mān

Contents: I. Occurrences. II. Etymology. III. The Tamarisk Manna. IV. Literary-Critical and Theological Considerations.

I. Occurrences. The term *mān,* "manna," occurs 13 times in the OT: 5 times without the article (Ex. 16:31,33; Dt. 8:16; Josh. 5:12aβ; Ps. 78:24; according to some scholars also in Ex. 16:15), 7 times with the article (Ex. 16:35a,b; Nu. 11:6,7,9; Dt. 8:3; Josh. 5:12aα), and once with a suffix as *manᵉḵā* (Neh. 9:20). The LXX transcribes it only in Ex. 16 according to the Hebrew with *man,* otherwise it follows the Aramaic (cf. the st. emph. מנא of the Targumim) with *manna* (in Bar. 1:10 a scribal error for *manaa* = *minḥâ,* "sacrificial offering"). The NT also employs the form *mánna* (Jn. 6:31,49; He. 9:4; Rev. 2:17). In Ex. 16, the Vulg. renders it as does the LXX as *man* (also in Nu. 11), otherwise as *manna.* Both in Greek (where except for Ex. 16:31; Josh. 5:12b; Ps. 77:24[Eng. 78:24] it is always used with the article) and in Latin the word is an undeclinable neuter noun (cf. Ex. 16:35: *tó man;* Neh. 9:20: *manna tuum* = LXX 2 Esd.19:20: *tó manna soú;* Rev. 2:17). The Greek word was never declined, and the Latin word was declined only by a few of the Church Fathers.

II. Etymology. The etymology of *mān* is disputed because the third radical necessary

---

mān. W. Baumgartner and M. Eglin, "Ein Gegenstück zum biblischen Manna," *ThZ,* 4 (1948), 235-37; F. S. Bodenheimer, "The Manna of Sinai," *BA,* 10 (1947), 2-6 = G. E. Wright and D. N. Freedman, eds., *BA Reader,* I (Garden City, 1961), 76-80; *idem* and O. Theodor, eds., *Ergebnisse der Sinai-Expedition 1927 der Hebräischen Universität, Jerusalem* (Leipzig, 1929); J. Buxtorf the Younger, "Historia Mannae," *Exercitationes ad Historiam* (Basel, 1659), 336-390; repr. B. Ugolinus, *Thesaurus Antiquitatum Sacrarum VIII* (Venice, 1747), 587-640; J. Coppens, "Les traditions relatives à la Manne dans Exode, XVI," *EstEcl,* 34 (1960), 473-489 = *Miscelánea bíblica. Festschrift A. Fernández* (Madrid, 1961), 169-185; A. de Guglielmo, "What was the Manna?" *CBQ,* 2 (1940), 112-129; P. Haupt, "Biblical Studies: The Etymology of Manna," *AJP,* 43 (1922), 247-49; *idem,* "Manna, Nectar, and Ambrosia," *PAPS,* 61 (1922), 227-236; A. Kaiser, *Der heutige Stand der Mannafrage* (Arbon, 1924); *idem,* "Neue wissenschaftliche Forschungen auf der Sinai-Halbinsel (besonders zur Mannafrage)," *ZDPV,* 53 (1930), 63-75; R. B. Kenney, *Ante-Nicene Greek and Latin Patristic Uses of the Biblical Manna Motif* (diss., Yale, 1968); L. Köhler, "Plinius weiss, was Manna bedeutet," *Neue Zürcher Zeitung und schweizerisches Handelsblatt,* 1943, no. 822; P. Maiberger, *Das Manna: Eine literarische, etymologische und naturkundliche Untersuchung. Ägypten und AT,* 6 (Wiesbaden, 1983); B. J. Malina, *The Palestinian Manna Tradition: The Manna Tradition in the Palestinian Targums and its Relationship to the NT Writings. AGSU,* 7 (1968); R. Meyer, "Μάννα," *TDNT,* IV, 462-66; N. Peters, "Zu Man hu, Ex 16,15," *ZKTh,* 23 (1899), 371; E. Rupprecht, "Stellung und Bedeutung der Erzählung vom Mannawunder (Ex 16) im Aufbau der Priesterschrift," *ZAW,* 86 (1974), 269-307; H. Schult, "Mān hū' und mah-hū' in Exodus 16,15," *Diehlheimer Blätter,* 1 (1972), 1-9; A. Tschirch, *Handbuch der Pharmakognosie,* II/1 (Leipzig, 1912), 103-114, 131-36, 147, 151f. (various types of manna); M. Walther, *Tractatus plenus & planus de Mannâ* (Leiden, 1633 [Rostock, [1]1631]); J. K. Zenner, "מן הוא Man hu. Ex 16,15," *ZKTh,* 23 (1899), 164-66.

for determining the fundamental meaning is itself uncertain due to the limited word field. Theoretically the roots *mnh, mnn, mwn,* and *myn* might be considered. At least since the 5th century, the Jews (Amoraim) derive the word from *mnh,* "to count, allot." In this sense they see in *mān* an abbreviated form from *māneh* with the meaning "gift," "allotment," "prepared food." Thus in the Babylonian Talmud in the Gemara to the tractate *Sukkah* 39b[1] we read: "How do we know that *vm* means food? From the passage (Dnl. 1:5): 'The king assigned them a daily portion."

This derivation might go back as far as the 1st century B.C., as the circumscription of manna as *"hétoimon" árton* in Wis. 16:20 suggests, and it might also have inspired Philo (*Leg. all.* iii.166) in the 1st century A.D. to use the *figura etymologica: kaí epí toú mánna oún kaí epí pásēs "dōreás," hḗn ho theós "dōreítai."* This etymological explanation was also supported in the Middle Ages by Rashi, Ibn Ezra, Kimḥi, Baḥya, and Arema,[2] and came by way of Nicholas of Lyra[3] to Martin Luther. In his own translation of the OT (1523), Luther renders *mān hû'* in Ex. 16:15 as a nominal clause: "that is Man," and in a marginal gloss says: "*Man* in Hebrew means 'a gift, portion.'" Thenceforward this derivation was accepted by almost all Christian theologians and predominated into the past century. Against this view F. R. Fay[4] derived *mān* from the uncommon Hebrew root *mnn* (cf. the rendering *mannᵉḵā*), whose meaning he gives as "to divide, to part, to measure," comparing it with what in his opinion was the semantically equivalent derivative *mēn,* "part," which is attested only once with a suffix: *minnēhû* (Ps. 68:24[23]). J. G. Murphy[5] associated the word with the root *myn,* "to split, divide," taking *mān* to refer to a "secretion," namely, the manna which in his opinion was secreted from the tamarisk. Paul Haupt[6] arrived at the same conclusion by way of the prep. *min,* originally a substantive with the meaning "separation," with which he associated *mîn,* "kind, type," i.e., that through which something "separates or distinguishes" itself, and *mîn,* "heretic, sectarian." Militating against this etymology, however, is the fact that modern science was the first to recognize manna as the secretion from a plant or animal.

There have also been attempts to explain the word as deriving from other Semitic or non-Semitic languages. Thus as early as 1661 Johann Heinrich Hottinger[7] referred to the Arabic noun *mann,* "gracious bestowal; favor; benefit," interpreting *mān* then as "quasi beneficium, donum, munus Dei" ("like a benefaction, a gift, a favor of God"). A relationship between the two words was still considered a possibility both by Wilhelm Gesenius since the second edition of his Hebrew dictionary[8] and by Eduard

1. L. Goldschmidt, *Der Babylonische Talmud,* III (Berlin, 1933), 108.
2. Cf. Buxtorf (1659), 338f. = (1747), 590.
3. *Postilla* to Ex. 16:15.
4. *The Book of Joshua* (Edinburgh, 1871), 66.
5. *A Critical and Exegetical Commentary on the Book of Exodus* (Edinburgh, 1866), 156.
6. *AJP,* 43 (1922), 248; *PAPS,* 61 (1922), 235.
7. *Etymologicum Orientale* (Frankfurt, 1661), 248.
8. F. H. W. Gesenius, *Hebräisch-Deutsches Handwörterbuch über die Schriften des AT* (Leipzig, ²1823), 427; cf. also *idem, GesTh,* II (1840), 799.

König in his own dictionary.[9] In the Koran,[10] Muhammad seems through popular etymology to have associated the Aramaic loanword[11] *al-mannu,* "manna," from the expression "eat of the good things with which we have supplied you," with the Arabic verb *manna,* "to show grace, favor, benefaction; to grant, give as a gift, bestow with grace," which he uses primarily in connection with Allah.[12] Thus in the *Muḫtār aṣ-ṣiḥāḥ* by Muḥammad al-Razi[13] one finds the (already older) definition: "*al-mannu* is every benefaction granted by Allah, exalted is he, for which a person has neither toiled nor striven."

Georg Ebers[14] suggested a derivation from daily life. Among the sacrificial offerings intended for the Horus temple in Edfu (3rd millennium B.C.) mention is made of a substance similar to myrrh with the consonants *mnn,* which he vocalizes as *mannu* and identifies as manna. In contrast, Victor Loret[15] reads *"mennen,"* and interprets it as bitumen or asphalt. In addition, *GesB,* to the extent that this word *mn(n?)w,* which occurs only in Late Egyptian, is the equivalent of manna at all, views it as a Semitic loanword.

Even less persuasive is the meaning "drop, resin," determined by Julius Fürst[16] on the basis of Sanskrit *maṇi,* "pearl, precious stone, jewel," which alludes (given the comparison with bdellium in Nu. 11:7) to the resinlike drops of the (tamarisk) manna.

Ludwig Köhler[17] and Walter Baumgartner[18] think that the original meaning of *mān* has been transmitted to us through Pliny, who says the following in *Hist. nat.* xii.32 concerning incense: "Micas concussu elisas mannam vocamus." Köhler translates: "The crumbs which are shaken away we call manna," from which he concludes that *mān* originally meant "something fine, grainlike, tiny crumbs"; this, he asserts, suits Ex. 16:14 well, which in his opinion would then read: "There was on the face of the wilderness a fine, grainlike thing." Because of the small grains, this Semitic name was given both to incense and to the tamarisk manna. This explanation is, however, already quite old, and was offered as early as 1644 by Claudius Salmasius. However, the idea of something "grainlike" suggested by many dictionaries[19] is not contained in the Lat. *manna.* This word, which derives from the Greek and is first used by Hippocrates, occurs in classical literature primarily in medicinal works, where it always refers to finely ground incense or "incense powder," which in the medicine of antiquity served as an astringent.

---

9. *Hebräisches und aramäisches Wörterbuch zum AT* (Leipzig, $^{6/7}$1937), 228.
10. 2:57 (54); 7:160 (160); 20:80f. (82).
11. Cf. J. Horovitz, "Jewish Proper Names and Derivatives in the Koran," *HUCA,* 2 (1925), 222 and 210f.
12. Cf. Sura 3:164 (158); 4:94 (96); 6:53; 12:90, and elsewhere.
13. (Cairo, ^{3}1329 = 1911), 662.
14. *Durch Gosen zum Sinai* (Leipzig, ^{2}1881), 226f.
15. "Études de droguerie égyptienne," *RT,* 16 (1894), 159f.
16. *Concordantiae Hebraicae* (Leipzig, 1840), 648.
17. No. 822; cf. *HAL,* II (1995), 596.
18. P. 235.
19. Including Meyer, *TDNT,* IV, 462.

The tamarisk manna of the Sinai peninsula, however, is called *mann* by the indigenous population, a name doubtlessly connected with Heb. *mān.* Since, however, given its usage it must be an originally Arabic word rather than a loanword from Hebrew, it might be the best candidate to illuminate the biblical name, if, that is, this natural product is indeed the reference in Ex. 16. The Arabs, however, did not give this name merely to the tamarisk manna; the polyhistorian Šihāb al-Nuwairī (1279-1332) already enumerates thirteen different kinds of manna.[20] According to him, the Arabs use the word *mann* among others to refer to honey, stick-lac, labdanum, the powdery leaf covering *wars* and *qinbîl,* dodder, the waxen layer on palm leaves, the Persian *tarangubîn* or alhagi manna, to which he also assigns the manna which falls upon the tamarisk, and then finally the honeydew on oaks, peach, and apricot trees. Although these are extremely varied substances, all involve thin, fine plant coverings, which, since their plant or animal origin was unknown, were assumed to have fallen from heaven. Hence the fundamental meaning emerging for Arab. *mann* is "thin layer, fine covering; something thin, fine," whereby the notion of "falling from heaven" is an essential component. Accordingly, the classical μάννα/*manna,* the incense powder, might have been a Semitic loanword which as *terminus technicus* came to the Greeks and Romans along with incense. Although it has nothing to do with the Greek-Latin biblical homonym (as also shown by its declinable feminine gender), it is etymologically related to it.

In Hebrew the root *mnn,* "to be thin, fine," is attested only in *minnîm* (Ps. 150:4) and *minnî* (Ps. 45:9[8]), "stringed instruments" (loanword?); cf. Syr. *mennā, menntā',* "hair; pelt; string (of a musical instrument)."

The Bible then also speaks of manna in fashion consistent with the basic meaning of Arab. *mann:* it falls with the dew from heaven, as one must doubtlessly conclude along with Nu. 11:9 from the covering of dew mentioned in Ex. 16:13, and covers the ground in a thin layer "fine as hoarfrost" (Ex. 16:14). This "fine covering" is called *daq* in Hebrew, a word which surprisingly is used in precisely the same sense as Arab. *mann.* It also exhibits the fundamental meaning "to be thin, fine," and refers to finely ground incense (Lev. 16:12), dust (Isa. 29:5; 40:15), thin hair (Lev. 13:30), a lean or gaunt man (Lev. 21:20; in reference to cows: Gen. 41:3,4; to ears of grain: vv. 6,7,23f.), and to a faint sound (1 K. 19:12).

III. The Tamarisk Manna. Thus *daq* provides a precise etymological explanation for *mān,* and this usage shows that the author of Ex. 16:14 knew perfectly well what notions lay behind this name. When furthermore he mentions that the manna "fell from heaven" with the dew, this clearly shows that he is referring to the natural product. He is doubtlessly thinking here of the Sinaitic tamarisk manna, since this is the only one occurring in the southern Sinai among those regions traversed during Israel's wilderness wanderings, however one may reconstruct that route; here the original author of the manna narrative might indirectly be pointing out that he considers Mt. Sinai to be located in the mountain range there. That the tamarisk manna is meant is also suggested

20. *Nihāyat al-Arab fī Funūn al-Adab,* 18 vols. (Cairo, 1923-55).

by the precise description in Ex. 16:31, according to which the manna consisted of white, honey-sweet grains about the size of coriander seeds. Since these tiny fruitbuds are yellowish-brown, the comparison here is with the form rather than with the color, something also attested by Nu. 11:7.

Arab scholars considered manna to be "a kind of dew." So also according to Nu. 11:7, the honeylike manna fell from heaven with the dew. The tamarisk manna of the Sinai peninsula is indeed nothing other than a kind of honeydew also produced in other regions, primarily during the summer by aphids and shield lice on certain leaf trees (e.g., oaks, linden, willows, maples, cherry, and peach trees) and conifers (silver firs, spruce, Scotch pine, and larch), as well as on other plants. Since these saps are low in nutrients, the insects need extremely large quantities to cover their nutritional needs, quantities they transform into valuable construction materials and excrete as so-called honeydew, which like raindrops or dewdrops adheres to the branches in large quantities or falls to the ground. Although this substance retains its firmness in the coolness of the night and in the early morning, it quickly dissolves in the warmth of the sun because of its soluble composition (cf. Ex. 16:21), covering leaves and branches with a thin layer of glaze. It is this layer that is evoked by the fundamental meaning of the name *mān/mann.* Because this sticky manna is difficult to harvest from trees, it is collected during the early morning in the form of the still firm manna globules. In lower temperatures these globules crystallize over the course of a few days and acquire in their pure form a milky-white color. Hence it is not a contradiction when on the one hand Ex. 16:14 speaks of a "flakelike layer," and on the other v. 31 speaks of "tiny grains." Verse 14 offers an etymological explanation in its description of the essential feature of the name *mān,* while in contrast v. 31 offers a botanical explanation in its description of the characteristics of a certain kind of manna, namely, the tamarisk manna.

In the Sinai peninsula the tamarisk manna was found only in a few valleys of the southern mountain range and on the southwestern coast (at *aṭ-Ṭūr*), a peculiar situation resulting from climatological conditions. That is, only in the central mountains does enough rain fall (up to 200 mm. [*ca.* 8 in.] annually) to provide the necessary water to the tamarisks in the form of perennial groundwater streams, including in the more arid regions (along the coast of the Gulf of Suez). If this quantity is not attained during winters with little rain, then the entire manna production can cease even for years at a time, which is why such production is not possible in areas that consistently fall short of this limit (e.g., Kadesh).[21]

The identification of biblical manna with the naturally occurring (tamarisk) manna can be traced back as far as Flavius Josephus (*Ant.* iii.1.6).

IV. Literary-Critical and Theological Considerations. The manna narrative in Ex. 16 is one of the most disputed and difficult chapters in the OT as far as literary-critical considerations are concerned. There is agreement only concerning its lack of unity.

---

21. Contra H. Gressmann, *Mose und seine Zeit. FRLANT,* N.S. 1 (1913), 137; Guglielmo, 122; E. Auerbach, *Moses* (Eng. trans., Detroit, 1975), 83-86.

The confusing variety of opinions, however, can for the most part be reduced to three basic positions, with more or less strong deviations: (1) The predominating theory attributes the main components of Ex. 16 to P and finds (esp. in vv. 4+5,13-15,27-31,35) fragments of a tradition coming from J.[22] (2) The opposing view is less well represented; it asserts that the basic narrative comes from J and was expanded by redactional, specifically Priestly (P) additions (esp. in vv. 1+2,6-13a,32-36).[23] (3) According to some literary critics, J is to be discounted completely; what we have is the more or less extensive (in part Deuteronomistic) reworking of a P narrative.[24] Joseph Coppens and Bruce J. Malina ascertain yet a different stratification.[25]

More recent literary critical investigation[26] has concluded that the basic components of Ex. 16 are the result of a Priestly (P) author, and that all other writers dealing with manna are dependent on his variously expanded account. The basic narrative of P (Ex. 16:1-3,6+7,9-14abα,15,21,31,35a) belongs to the genre of "murmuring stories" (cf. Nu. 14:1-38; 16:1-35; 17:6-28[16:41–17:13]; 20:1-13), and its intention is to show that against all merit and expectation, God did indeed provide nourishment for his rebellious, faithless people in the barren and hostile wilderness. Both the great temporal distance of P from these events and the absence of older traditions militate against a historical and naturalistic interpretation of the giving of the manna, which is based on theological reflection. Although the author does draw on a phenomenon characteristic of the Sinai peninsula with this reference to the manna (as is also the case with the quail in Ex. 16:13), he elevates it into the miraculous by having the people be provided with manna every day for forty years.

Since the Israelites later (v. 31) give this unknown nourishment the name *mān,* it would create tension if they had earlier already used this very name in the cry *mān hû'* (v. 15) at their first encounter with it and had meant "that is man(na)." Thus although this translation, suggested again most recently by Hermann Schult, is grammatically possible, its substance is problematical; it was, to be sure, suggested quite frequently even centuries ago. The current, generally accepted translation, "what is that?" (following the LXX and Vulg.), more readily does justice to the context than to the grammar, since an impersonal interrogative pronoun *mān* exists neither in Hebrew nor in any other Semitic language. We must assume, then, that the

---

22. So following J. Wellhausen, "Die Composition des Hexateuchs II. Die Erzählung der übrigen Bücher des Hexateuchs," *Jahrbücher für deutsche Theologie,* 21 (1876), 531-602, esp. 547-49 = *Die Composition des Hexateuchs und der historischen Bücher des AT* (Berlin, ^{3}1899), 78f.; G. von Rad, *Die Priesterschrift im Hexateuch. BWANT,* 65[4/13] (1934); G. W. Coats, *Rebellion in the Wilderness* (Nashville, 1968), 83-87; M. Noth, *Exodus. OTL* (Eng. trans. 1962), 129-137; N. Negretti, *Il Settimo giorno. AnBibl,* 55 (1973), 173-224; B. S. Childs, *The Book of Exodus. OTL* (1974), 271-304.

23. R. Smend, *Die Erzählung des Hexateuch auf ihre Quellen untersucht* (Berlin, 1912), 148-151, 158; O. Eissfeldt, *Hexateuch-Synopse* (Darmstadt, ^{2}1962; repr. 1973), 37-39; W. Rudolph, *Der "Elohist" von Exodus bis Josua. BZAW,* 68 (1938), 34-37, 275.

24. Rupprecht.

25. See bibliog.

26. Maiberger.

author transformed the interrogative particle *mâ,* "what?" into an interrogative word *mān,* explained by the following *mah-hû'* (whereby the homonymous Aramaic personal interrogative pronoun might have functioned as a kind of godparent), in order to allude to the later name.

Picking up on the "morning by morning" in v. 21 with "and it happened on the sixth day," the expanded unit B (16:22aαb,23-24aα,25-26) was added to the basic narrative (unit A), the expanded unit then associating the giving of the manna with the introduction of the Sabbath. To this end the manna is made even more miraculous by having it fall doubly on the sixth day and not at all on the Sabbath; and even though it melted in the sun, it could nonetheless be cooked and baked at will, enabling it to replace all other foods.

The expanded unit C (16:16-20,32-34) picks up on the honeylike taste of the manna (v. 31) and discovers in the manna a symbol of the "honey-sweet" word of God that nourishes the soul (cf. Ps. 19:11[10]; 119:103; Prov. 24:13f.; Ezk. 2:8; 3:1-3; Sir. 24:20), a word available in the same "measure" to each person (Ex. 16:18). As a reminder of that divine word, an *'ōmer* of manna is kept before the covenant testimony (v. 34)! The cubic measure *'ōmer,* which is attested only in this unit and nowhere else either in or outside the OT, is presumably the tenth part of an *'êpâ* (v. 36), a name laden with symbolism which the author invented *ad hoc* after the model of the similarly sounding *ḥōmer,* the tenfold measure of an *'êpâ* as an allusion to *'ōmer,* "word of God" (Ps. 68:12[11]; 77:9[8]; cf. also Ps. 19:3f.[2f.]).

The expanded unit D (Ex. 16:4+5,27-30) subsumes the giving of the manna, which B had associated with the Sabbath commandment, under the theme "temptation" by concretizing within the context of the Sabbath regulation the abstract concepts "temptation" and "the giving of the law" mentioned in the account of Ex. 15:25b-26. The manna, which the basic narrative called "bread" (v. 15), already derives from the otherworldly realm as "bread from heaven" (v. 4).

Nu. 11:6-9 is a gloss insertion dependent on the basic narrative and the expanded unit B (boiling and baking), whereas Dt. 8:2-4,16, in which manna is to remind the people tested by hunger of the vital importance of the word of God, is based on the expanded units C and D. Josh. 5:12 looks back at Ex. 16:35. The expression "bread from heaven" in Neh. 9:15; Ps. 105:40 is based on D, whereas in Neh. 9:20 the context recalls Dt. 8:3+4. And Ps. 78:23-25 picks up the transcendentally charged notion of unit D and idealizes manna as "grain of heaven" and "bread of the mighty/of angels."

Manna is also called the "food of angels" in the Wisdom of Solomon (Wis. 16:20). Idealized into the epitome of pleasing taste, it symbolizes the sweetness (*glykýtēta,* v. 21) of God to his children. Here, too, as in the expanded unit C and in Dt. 8:3, manna is spiritualized into food for the soul; as the "all-nourishing" food "suiting every taste" (Wis. 16:25) it is to function as a reminder of the life-giving word of God (v. 26). The statement recalling this notion, namely, that the "righteous are nourished" by it (v. 23), as well as the adjective "ambrosial" (19:21), which again emphasizes the exquisite heavenly taste, both probably contributed to the late Jewish idea of manna as the nourishment of the future world (*'ôlām habbā';* cf. Rev. 2:17).

Maiberger

מָנָה *mānâ;* מְנָת *m^{e}nāt̲;* מְנִי *m^{e}nî*

Contents: I. 1. Etymology, Occurrences; 2. LXX Rendering. II. The Verb *mnh:* 1. Qal and Niphal (Pe'il); 2. Piel (Pael) and Pual. III. *mānâ, m^{e}nāt̲, m^{e}nî.*

I. 1. *Etymology, Occurrences.* The root *mnw/y* with the basic meaning "to count" is common to the Semitic languages[1] (although it is absent in Ethiopian). Numerous occurrences are attested in Akkadian (*manû,* "to count, figure," also "to recite [an incantation],"[2] along with several derivatives, including *mīnu,* "number"). In Northwest Semitic the word group is attested especially in Aramaic (*mny,* "to count";[3] the most important derivatives are *mnh/mnt,* "part, portion," and *mnyn,* "number"). It is also relatively well attested in Biblical Aramaic (the verb *mnh* 6 times, including once each in the qal and pe'il [Dnl 5:25][4], 4 times in the pael; once *minyān*). In contrast, the root recedes in the other representatives of Northwest Semitic. Ugaritic attests the noun *mnt,* "numbering, part,"[5] only in isolated instances. OT Hebrew also attests only a limited number of occurrences.[6] The verb occurs 28 times (12 times in the qal, 6 in the niphal, 8 in the piel [discounting Ps. 61:8(Eng. v. 7): *mn* is a textual error or cannot be derived from *mnh*],[7] and once in the pual). Derivatives include *mānâ* (12 occurrences) and *m^{e}nāt̲* (9 occurrences; cf. also the conj. in Neh. 13:5 [instead of *mṣwt*],[8] as well as the divine name *m^{e}nî* (a hapex legomenon; in addition, **mōneh* occurs twice in the sense of "time, multiple"). The fact that these occurrences derive for the most part from the postexilic period suggests Aramaic influence (*m^{e}nāt̲* may even constitute an Aramaic loanword[9]; and the piel of *mnh,*

---

mānâ. W. Borée, *Die alten Ortsnamen Palästinas* (1930, Hildesheim, ^{2}1968); O. Eissfeldt, "Eine Einschmelzstelle am Tempel zu Jerusalem," *FuF,* 13 (1937), 163f. = *KlSchr,* II (1963), 107-9; *idem,* "Die Menetekel-Inschrift und ihre Deutung," *ZAW,* 63 (1951), 105-114 = *KlSchr,* III (1966), 210-17; J. A. Fitzmyer and D. J. Harrington, *A Manual of Palestinian Aramaic Texts. BietOr,* 34 (1978); H. Gese, M. Höfner, and K. Rudolph, *Die Religionen Altsyriens, Altarabiens und der Mandäer. RdM,* 10/2 (1970); E. Jenni, *Das hebräische Pi'el* (Zurich, 1968); K. Rupprecht, *Der Tempel von Jerusalem. BZAW,* 144 (1977); T. Veijola, *Die ewige Dynastie. AnAcScFen,* B, 193 (1975); M. Wagner, *Die lexikalischen und grammatikalischen Aramaismen im alttestamentlichen Hebräisch. BZAW,* 96 (1966); H. W. Wolff, *Studien zum Jonabuch. BSt,* 47 (^{2}1975).

1. See *HAL,* II (1995), 599; P. Fronzaroli, "Studi sul lessico comune semitico," *AANLR,* N.S. 20 (1965), 260, 266, 269.
2. *CAD,* X/1 (1977), 221-27; *AHw,* II (1972), 603f.
3. Cf. *DISO,* 159; *LexSyr,* 394; *WTM,* III, 156f.; *MdD,* 274a; on the Aramaic texts from Qumran and from the Wilderness of Judah, see Fitzmyer-Harrington, 328.
4. See II.1 below.
5. *WUS,* no. 1600; *UT,* no. 1502.
6. Cf. in contrast *spr;* see II.1 below.
7. Cf. *BHS; HAL,* II, 597, 599.
8. Cf. *BHS;* W. Rudolph, *Esra und Nehemia. HAT,* XX, 204.
9. Wagner, 78f.

which occurs only in late texts, could also be modeled after the Aramaic pael[10]). The word group is attested only sparingly in the extant Hebrew portions of Sirach and in the Hebrew Qumran writings (*mnh* qal, Sir. 40:29; niphal?, 1QSb 4:2[11]; *mnh* [*mānâ*], Sir. 26:3;[12] 41:21; *mnt* [*m^enāṯ*], 1QS 10:8; 11QT 22:10).[13]

The place name *timnâ* (e.g., Gen. 38:12; Josh. 15:10; cf. *timnî,* Jgs. 15:6), which also occurs in compounds (Josh. 19:50; 24:30; Jgs. 2:9), probably also derives from *mnh.*[14] It is uncertain whether this also applies to the PN *yimnâ,* which occurs in Gen. 46:17; Nu. 26:44 (the second occurrence in this passage should probably read *yimnî*[15]); 1 Ch. 7:30; 2 Ch. 31:14. According to *KBL*^{3}, 397, this is a theophoric name: may he (God) bestow (bestowed) dominion to (*mnh* piel); and according to Martin Noth,[16] a derivation of *ymn:* "[child of] happiness."[17]

2. *LXX Rendering.* The term *mnh* in the qal (Aramaic as well) and the niphal is rendered in the LXX overwhelmingly by *arithméō,* although other verbs are used in 1 K. 20:25; Isa. 53:12 (*logízō;* cf. *logismós,* Sir. 40:29); 65:12; Dnl. 5:26 Theodotion; the peʿil in Dnl. 5:25 has no LXX equivalent[18]). The piel (pael) and pual are covered by *kathístēmi* or a compound of *tássō (diatássō, ektássō, prostássō)* (other verbs are used in Job 7:3; Dnl. 1:5 LXX; 1:11 LXX). The nouns *mānâ* and *m^enāṯ* are always rendered by *merís.* The DN *m^enî* is rendered by *týchē.*

II. The Verb mnh. 1. *Qal and Niphal (Peʿil).* All forms in the qal and niphal (including the qal and peʿil of Biblical Aramaic) presuppose the basic meaning "to count," although this implies consciously directed counting in the sense of "to calculate, order," rather than neutral enumeration. In this sense collected silver is counted to be paid out again as wages for workers (2 K. 12:11f.[10f.]).[19] The shepherd counts his animals to check the size of the flocks (Jer. 33:13). The king of Syria is encouraged to "count out" a new army so as to have access again to an effective instrument of power in battle against Israel (1 K. 20:25). David conducts a census in order to learn the precise number of men capable of being mustered for military purposes (2 S. 24:1; 1 Ch. 21:1; cf. 2 S. 24:9, and the discussion below). The Suffering Servant was "numbered" with the *pōš^eʿîm* and thus given over to death (Isa. 53:12).[20]

Conversely, the impossibility of so numbering or counting means that every calculation or controlled accessibility is excluded. Where nothing is present, nothing can be

---

10. *Idem.*
11. Cf. D. Barthélemy and J. T. Milik, *Qumran Cave I. DJD,* I (1955), 125f.
12. See III below.
13. On the later Hebrew literature, cf. *WTM,* III, 149f., 154-56, 157f., 161f.
14. Borée, 41, 74.
15. See *BHK, BHS.*
16. *IPN,* 224.
17. → ימין *yāmîn,* VI, 102f.
18. See II.1 below.
19. On the process of counting, see Eissfeldt, *KlSchr,* II (1963), 107-9.
20. → פשע *pšʿ.*

numbered, and nothing can be controlled (Eccl. 1:15). The same holds true for incomprehensibly high numbers. Thus Israel is characterized as an immeasurably large people to emphasize that it is invulnerable to external enemies (Nu. 23:10), and cannot be governed by an inexperienced king (1 K. 3:8). Occasionally the promise of descendants to the patriarchs emphasizes the innumerability of those descendants, whereby in Gen. 13:16 the verb *mnh* occurs twice (qal and niphal). This passage, too, wants to express that the future descendants, i.e., the Israelites, will acquire an unanticipated significance and that no power in the world will be able to call that significance into question. Finally, the mention of the sacrifice of innumerable animals in connection with the dedication of the temple (1 K. 8:5; 2 Ch. 5:6; cf. 1 K. 8:62-64) intends to portray this as an event whose dimensions transcend the capacity of normal human perception and comprehension.

Such limitations do not apply to Yahweh. His emergence as the subject of the various forms of *mnh* brings to expression his unlimited sovereignty. He decides concerning the number of stars and determines their names (Ps. 147:4), i.e., he exercises the power of control and accessibility over them.[21] He "counts out" the apostates for the sword, giving them over thus to destruction (Isa. 65:12).[22] He "numbers" the days of the rule of Belshazzar (Dnl. 5:26), i.e., he has calculated it like a sum of money and now draws the bottom line. Dnl. 5:25b is probably also to be understood as such a reckoning. The first *mᵉnēʾ* (secondarily eliminated in the LXX [Theodotion]; cf. also the summary before 5:1 LXX) might be a participle peʿil preceding the three following weight or money values "as a kind of check or verification notice in the sense of 'counted' "[23] (the logical subject of the participle is again Yahweh; it is in fact questionable whether v. 25b is referring to Belshazzar alone; it was probably originally a statement addressing the declining value of Neo-Babylonian kings, which in the present context, especially through vv. 26-28, acquired a new interpretation[24]). Even the previously mentioned assertions concerning the immeasurable greatness of Israel (Gen. 13:16; Nu. 23:10; 1 K. 3:8) ultimately serve to demonstrate Yahweh's limitless sovereignty. For they all presuppose that this people is his work and that he never loses control of it; i.e., his powers of control and accessibility transcend the possibilities of human reckoning and decision.

A human being can, of course, become culpable in appropriating for himself such divine power of control. David's autocratically undertaken census (2 S. 24; 1 Ch. 21; see discussion above) is considered a grievous offense prompting an appropriate punishment (2 S. 24:1; 1 Ch. 21:1,17; 27:24; cf. 2 S. 24:10; 1 Ch. 21:3[25]). The offense may consist precisely in the fact that such a counting of the people illegitimately subjects to human control the divine authority over Israel.[26]

---

21. → קרא *qārāʾ;* → שׁם *šēm.*
22. → חרב *ḥereḇ* (V, 155-165).
23. Eissfeldt, *KlSchr,* III (1966), 213f.
24. *Ibid.,* 210-17, and the comms.
25. → דבר *deḇer (debher)* (III, 125-27).
26. On this notion, one also attested outside Israel, → פקד *pqd;* cf. also W. Schottroff, "פקד *pqd* heimsuchen," *THAT,* II, 472f.; G. André, *Determining the Destiny: PQD in the OT. CB,* 16 (1980).

2 S. 24, upon which 1 Ch. 21 depends, is admittedly not a unified whole. Verse 1 might derive from later redaction through which the original text of the census (vv. 2,4b-9) is subjected to theological interpretation.[27] The fact, however, that precisely here the verb *mnh* appears (whereas the original text used *pqd*) makes it especially clear that this verb is firmly associated with the notion of calculation and control. Verse 10, in which *spr* is used, possibly derives from yet further redactional activity.[28]

On the other hand, Yahweh can prompt a person to undertake a self-examination transcending normal human capacity. According to Ps. 90 (postexilic), he can teach those who trust him to "number" their days (v. 12a), i.e., to settle frankly and straightforwardly with life's futility and transience (vv. 9-11) in order to become truly wise (v. 12b). Here wisdom concepts are appropriated and revised.[29] This kind of frank, direct settling is the prerequisite for wisdom commensurate with that of God, wisdom which in its own turn issues into trust in Yahweh's compassion and succor (vv. 1,13-17).

In Hebrew the qal and niphal of *mnh* are to a large extent semantic equivalents of the corresponding stem forms of → ספר *spr,* and the two verbs can thus also appear in immediate juxtaposition as synonyms (1 K. 3:8; 8:5; cf. also 2 S. 24:1,10 [see also preceding discussion]); of the two, however, the latter is attested in the qal much more frequently, and the customary noun for "number" *(mispār;* cf. in contrast Aram. *minyān),* attested exclusively in Hebrew, derives from it. This is probably a case of Canaanite influence (cf. Ugar. *spr,*[30] Phoen.-Pun. *mspr*[31]). In Sir. 40:29, *mnh* in the qal exhibits a meaning comparable to that of the verb *ḥšb* ("to figure as").[32]

2. *Piel (Pael) and Pual.* The piel or pael of *mnh* means "to distribute, allot, commission, install in office" (resultative[33]). Accordingly, the pual participle (1 Ch. 9:29) has the meaning "commissioned, appointed." The characteristic feature of all the occurrences in the piel or pael is that they variously bring to expression the powers of command of a highest authority. Both in the Biblical Aramaic texts and in Dnl. 1, the reference is to the powers of disposal of the Babylonian or Persian kings as the highest human authority (Dnl. 1:5,10; 2:24,49; 3:12) or to derivative authorization or power of authority (Ezr. 7:25; Dnl. 1:11 [different in the LXX]). The remaining occurrences refer to Yahweh's own powers of disposal, powers transcending all human possibilities and comprehension. According to the book of Jonah, he is able to commission natural forces like servants (Jon. 2:1[1:17]; 4:6-8), his sovereignty impressively underscored by the fourfold occurrence of the form *wayᵉman.*[34] He is

---

27. Veijola, 108-117; Rupprecht, 6.
28. Veijola, 108-117; on *spr,* see following discussion.
29. → חכם *ḥāḵam (chākham),* V (IV, 379-384).
30. *WUS,* no. 1947; *UT,* no. 1793.
31. *DISO,* 161.
32. → חשב *ḥāšaḇ* (IV, 228-245).
33. Cf. Jenni, 213.
34. Cf. Wolff, 38.

also the logical subject in Job 7:3, as the continuation of the chapter shows (cf. vv. 12ff.); i.e., for Job it is he who assigns a person his destiny and who in so doing incomprehensibly leads him into distress and misery. The PN *yimnâ* can possibly be interpreted in the same sense.[35]

III. mānâ, m^enāṯ, m^enî. The nouns *mānâ* and *m^enāṯ* variously refer to a specific portion allotted or accessible to a person or group of persons (in Ps. 63:11[10] also animals). In the literal sense the reference is always to natural products, whereby both nouns refer primarily to the cultic sphere. In the texts of P, *mānâ* refers to the priests' portion of the (animal) sacrifices (Ex. 29:26; Lev. 7:33;[36] 8:29; 11QT 22:10); in texts of the Chronicler, *m^enāṯ* refers to the portion of the temple contributions allotted to the priests and Levites (Neh. 12:44,47; 13:10; 2 Ch. 31:4; Neh. 13:5 conj.;[37] also *mānâ,* 2 Ch. 31:19). In two older texts, *mānâ* refers to the portion of the participants in a sacrificial meal (1 S. 1:4f.; 9:23). The sending of portions of food at the time of a great feast, which occurred primarily as an act of charity, probably also grew out of the notion of participation in a sacrificial meal (*mānâ:* Neh. 8:10,12; Est. 9:19,22 [Feast of Purim]; perhaps Sir. 41:21b also belongs in this context). Purely secular usage is attested only in Est. 2:9 *(mānâ)* and Ps. 63:11(10) *(m^enāṯ).* In the figurative sense *m^enāṯ* refers to one's portion in life, i.e., the fate allotted by Yahweh to an individual or a collective. According to Ps. 16:5f., Yahweh himself constitutes that portion, i.e., the vital ground of the individual.[38] Here it is especially notions concerning land possession which are appropriated and applied to the fate of the individual.[39] Conversely, destruction is the fate apportioned to the wicked (the portion of their cup, *kôs,* Ps. 11:6), while Jerusalem in its harlotry will suffer shameful violation (Jer. 13:25; *m^enāṯ middayiḵ* should probably be translated "the portion of your measure," i.e., "the portion measured out for you" [the LXX variant is probably secondary[40]]; the parallel here is *gôrāl*). The same figurative meaning is also found in the divine name *m^enî* occurring in Isa. 65:11, a god of destiny or fortune (accordingly rendered as *týchē* in the LXX), apparently a counterpart to the god Gad also mentioned here.[41] He is probably to be associated with the god of destiny *manāt,* a deity widespread in the Arabic sphere during the pre-Islamic period and also attested among the Nabateans *(mnwtw).*[42]

In Sir. 26:3, *mnh (mānâ)* is also used with figurative meaning (the Talmudic variant

---

35. See I.1 above. On Ps. 61:8[7], see I.1 above.

36. On the delimitation of this term over against *ḥōq* and *t^erûmâ* in Lev. 7:33, cf. R. Hentschke, *Satzung und Setzender. BWANT,* 83[5/3] (1963), 34f.

37. See I.1 above.

38. → חלק II, *ḥālaq (chālaq)* (IV, 447-451).

39. → גורל *gôrāl* (II, 450-56); → חבל I *ḥbl* (IV, 172-79); → נחלה *naḥ^alâ;* cf. also the notion of the drinking cup, → כוס *kôs* (101-4).

40. Cf. here *BHK, BHS.*

41. On this god and on gods of fate in general, → גד *gāḏ (gadh),* III.1 (II, 383f.).

42. See *HAL,* II, 602; cf. also Gese-Höfner-Rudolph, 205, 361f., 370, 377.

mtnh[43] is probably secondary;[44] cf. also *merís* in the LXX[45]). In 2 Ch. 31:3, *m*^{e}*nāṯ* refers not to the portion received, but rather to the portion given (the king's contribution to public sacrifices). Although this usage is singular within the OT, it also occurs both in 1QS 10:8 ("contribution of my lips," understood as a sacrificial offering; cf. *trwmt śptym* in 10:6) and in later Jewish writings.[46] Textual emendation is therefore unnecessary.

Conrad

---

43. Cf. R. Smend, *Die Weisheit des Jesus Sirach* (Berlin, 1906), 44.
44. See J. Schirmann, "Some Additional Leaves from Ecclesiasticus in Hebrew," *Tarbiz,* 29 (1959/1960), 133 [Heb.].
45. See I.2 above.
46. Cf. *WTM,* III, 161 (Aramaic 162).

מְנוֹרָה *m*^{e}*nôrâ*

Contents: I. Meaning, Occurrences. II. Cultic Usage: 1. Tabernacle: a. Construction; b. Symbolism; 2. First (Solomonic) Temple; 3. The Second Temple; 4. LXX, Qumran.

---

m^e*nôrâ.* P. R. Ackroyd, "The Temple Vessels — a continuity theme," *Studies in the Religion of Ancient Israel. SVT,* 23 (1972), 166-181; R. J. Clifford, *The Cosmic Mountain in Canaan and the OT. HSM,* 4 (1972); F. M. Cross, "The Tabernacle," *BA,* 10 (1947), 45-68; M. Görg, "Zur Dekoration des Leuchters," *BN,* 15 (1981), 21-29; E. R. Goodenough, *Jewish Symbols in the Greco-Roman Period,* 13 vols. (New York, 1953-1968); M. Haran, "The Complex of Ritual Acts Performed Inside the Tabernacle," *Studies in the Religion of the Bible. ScrHier,* 8 (1961), 272-302; *idem,* "The Divine Presence in the Israelite Cult and the Cultic Institutions," *Bibl,* 50 (1969), 251-267; *idem,* "The Nature of the 'ʾohel moʿedh' in Pentateuchal Sources," *JSS,* 5 (1960), 50-65; Z. Ilan, "Jewish Menorot from the Golan," *Qadmoniot,* 13 (1980), 117-19 [Heb.]; C. L. Meyers, *The Tabernacle Menorah. ASOR Diss.,* 2 (Missoula, 1975); *idem,* "Was there a Seven-Branched Lampstand in Solomon's Temple?" *BAR,* 5/5 (1979), 46-57; *idem,* "Jachin and Boaz in Religious and Political Perspective," *CBQ,* 45 (1983), 167-178; *idem,* "Lampstand," *ABD,* 4, 141-43; *idem,* "Temple, Jerusalem," *ABD,* 6, 350-369; *idem* and E. M. Meyers, "Fourth Vision: The Lampstand and the Two Olive Trees," *Haggai, Zechariah 1–8. AB* 25 (1987), 227-277; A. de Nicola, "La lucerna cultuale in Israele," *BeO,* 14 (1972), 79-91; R. North, "Zechariah's Seven-Spout Lampstand," *Bibl,* 51 (1970), 183-206; J. Nougayrol, *Cylindres-sceaux et empreintes de cylindres trouvés en Palestine* (Paris, 1939); N. Perrot, "Les représentations de l'arbre sacré sur les monuments de Mésopotamie et d'Élam," *Babyloniaca,* 17 (Paris, 1937); L. Y. Rahmani, "Depictions of Menorot on Ossuaries," *Qadmoniot,* 13 (1980), 114-17 [Heb.]; R. H. Smith, "The Household Lamps of Palestine in OT Times," *BA,* 27 (1964), 1-31; V. Sussmann, "Astragal Menorah on Clay Lamps," *Qadmoniot,* 13 (1980), 119-121 [Heb.]; L. E. Toombs, "Lampstand," *IDB,* III, 64-66; L. H. Vincent, "La peinture céramique Palestinienne," *Syr,* 5 (1924), 81-107; L. Yarden, *The Tree of Light* (Uppsala, 1972).

I. Meaning, Occurrences. The word *m^e^nôrâ* is rendered "lampstand" in most English translations. It is a nominal form from the common root *nyr (nwr),* from which the noun *nēr,* "lamp," is also derived. The Hebrew root, which probably originally meant "to flame," can be compared with Ugar. *nyr,* "to flame,"[1] and Akk. *nūru,* "light,"[2] both of which have celestial or light-giving associations. Arabic and Aramaic cognates have similar meanings. Since the *mem*-preformative added to the verbal stem transforms the root into a noun indicating the place or instrument of the verbal action, *m^e^nôrâ* is thus a generic term for the repository or support of a lamp, a thing that "flames."

The only biblical synonym is *neb̲raštā'* (Dnl. 5:5), corresponding to Mishnaic *nib̲rešet̲,* which is of obscure origin; it derives perhaps from a Persian root meaning "to shine, flame."[3]

The term *m^e^nôrâ* occurs 41 times in the Hebrew Bible; the preponderance of these occurrences (26) are in the Priestly writings of the Pentateuch, where it refers to the single golden lampstand of the tabernacle sanctuary,[4] constructed under the guidance of Moses in the wilderness period. Detailed information about the fabrication of the *m^e^nôrâ* can be found in the prescriptive (Ex. 25:31-40) and descriptive (Ex. 37:17-24) portions of the tabernacle texts. In addition, references to this lampstand are scattered in other Priestly sections (Ex. 30:27; 31:8; 35:14; 39:37; 40:4,24; Lev. 24:4; Nu. 3:31; 4:9; 8:2,3,4). There are 12 references to the lampstands of the First Temple: in the brief description of 1 K. 7:49; then in 1 Ch. 28:15; 2 Ch. 4:7,20; 13:11, and in the Jeremianic description of the Babylonian spoiling of the Jerusalem temple (Jer. 52:19). One of Zechariah's visions includes a lampstand, which may preserve some memory of the First Temple artifacts, since this vision (Zec. 4) predates the postexilic rebuilding of the temple. Only once does a lampstand appear in a noncultic context; the guestroom prepared for Elisha in Shunem contained a lampstand (2 K. 4:10). Archaeological evidence of lampstands in domestic contexts is rare;[5] but the fact that Elisha's hostess is a "wealthy woman" may provide the reason for the special kind of furnishing. This lampstand is the only one that is not specifically said to be made of metal (silver or gold). It may thus be a ceramic stand, for which there is some archaeological evidence; or alternatively it may be a wooden stand.

II. Cultic Usage.

1. *Tabernacle.* The extremely precise and elaborate description of the fabrication of the *m^e^nôrâ* in the texts of Exodus was long considered a projection, to a greater or lesser degree, back into the earliest Israelite cult of cultic circumstances existing during the period of the Second Temple. However, postwar biblical scholarship[6] has now

1. *WUS,* no. 1850.
2. *AHw,* II (1972), 805.
3. F. Rosenthal, *A Grammar of Biblical Aramaic. PLO,* N.S. 5 (^{2}1963), §190.
4. → משכן *miškān.*
5. Cf. Smith, 23.
6. E.g., Cross.

established the great antiquity of many of the priestly traditions connected with the tabernacle, while still recognizing that the final written document was probably not established before the exile. A thorough philological, archaeological, and art-historical analysis of the detailed presentation of the tabernacle lampstand allows it to be dated at the end of the Late Bronze Age or shortly thereafter, i.e., within range of the Mosaic era.[7] Both the technological and the artistic aspects of its construction are also attested in the Egyptian-Aegean-Canaanite sphere of Late Bronze Age II, which is important for an assessment of the symbolism of the tabernacle lampstand.

a. *Construction.* The word *m^enôrâ* in the Priestly texts refers in some texts (as Ex. 26:35; 40:4,24; Nu. 8:2f.) to the entire branched object — three branches issuing forth from either side of a central shaft — and in other texts (Ex. 25:31-35; 37:17-21) only to the central portion thereof. It is the latter which constitutes the functional stand or support for the lamp(s). The seven lamps themselves are not an integral part of the lampstand; nor is their placement on the stand explicit. They are *not* said to be placed at the end of each branch; such an inference comes from early extrabiblical Jewish sources and not from the OT. Rather, it is quite likely that they were all situated on the central stand itself. If Lev. 24:4 is referring to the placement of the lamps "on" (*ʿal*) the *m^enôrâ,* meaning the central stand, such an understanding would be verified. A similar intent can be seen in the formulation *ʾel-mûl p^enê hamm^enôrâ* (Nu. 8:2,3), a phrase designating where the light from the lamps should fall. In its utilization of *mûl,* "in front of" or "before," along with *p^enê* the latter becomes an architectonic specification of a part of the total lampstand, i.e., its "face" or the central, light-bearing portion of its shaft, rather than a general indication of "front."

In two instances (Ex. 27:20; Lev. 24:2f.; perhaps also Ex. 25:37) the text refers to the illumination provided by a single lamp. Both these passages also make reference to the *ʾōhel môʿēḏ* and thus may represent a conflation of the "tent of meeting" tradition with the "tabernacle" tradition of the Priestly Code.[8]

The central shaft, or lampstand proper, consists of *yārēḵ w^eqāneh.* This pair is a hendiadys referring to a base-forming shaft, thickened or flaring outward toward the bottom, forming a stable, free-standing object. Such cultic stands are attested by archaeological evidence in the ancient Near East.[9] They are cylindrical shafts, with a wider diameter at the bottom than at the top, and can be found in metal or stone as well as in pottery examples.

The language used for the branches as well as for the decorative aspects is derived from ancient architectonic vocabulary, doubtlessly archaic already by the time of the LXX and other ancient versions, which do not understand the technical nuances and which are influenced by the somewhat different lampstand of the Second Temple. Perhaps the most noteworthy feature of this terminology (*qāneh, peraḥ, kaptôr, m^ešuqqāḏîm*) is the fact that it shows the translation of botanical motifs into architectural features (cf. Egyptian art).

---

7. Cf. Meyers, *Tabernacle Menorah,* 182ff. and *passim.*
8. Cf. Haran.
9. Cf. Meyers, *Tabernacle Menorah,* ch. III and figs. 1-19.

The terms *kaptôr ûperaḥ* also constitute a hendiadys and refer to a "floral capital," a thrice-repeated feature on each of the branches as well as a fourfold repetition on the central stand. Repetition as an artistic motif conveys the idea of continuity and permanence, and finds its specific and prolific expression in the art of the eighteenth dynasty in Egypt. This feature is related to a development, which can be seen in the graphically preserved stands known from wall paintings or seals and in the archaeologically known cylindrical stands of Palestine, that occurs at the end of the Late Bronze Age. The botanical *qāneh* also suggests Egyptian influence. It is a generic term for "reed" and generally specifies the "Persian reed" *(arundo donax),* a gigantic grass common along the Nile and in the Nile Delta. Accordingly, *qāneh* nearly always appears in the OT in Egyptian contexts, or in contexts where it symbolizes Egypt itself (cf. Isa. 36:6 par. 2 K. 18:21).

The "bowls" *(g^eḇiʿîm)* of the lampstand are more difficult to identify. In connection with the *m^enôrâ* this term refers perhaps to a somewhat rare kind of double-bowl lamp consisting of a ceramic bowl containing a smaller bowl or cup.[10] This Palestinian vessel of the Late Bronze and Iron Ages, with antecedents in Egypt and the Aegean, comes perhaps from tent traditions that presuppose only one lamp, later merged with a conception of seven discrete lamps. Alternatively, it may refer to a wide bowl on which the discrete lamps were placed, the equivalent of the *gullâ* of Zechariah. The Hebrew word *gullâ* is related to Akk. *gullatu,* whereas *g^eḇīʿâ* seems to be an Egyptian loanword.

Both the material and the fabrication of the tabernacle lampstand (cf. the expressions "pure gold" [Ex. 25:31,36; 37:17,22] and "one piece of hammered work" [Ex. 25:36; 37:22]) are rooted in ancient metallurgical traditions. The former expression, *zāhāḇ ṭāhôr,* as distinct from other words for "gold" in the Bible, reflects a gold-working tradition associated with Egyptian practices. As for the second term, *kullāh . . . 'aḥaṯ,* "of one piece," seems to refer to the use of sheet gold or gold foil, and implies that a wooden model was utilized for construction of the lampstand. The term *miqšâ* is not clearly understood. The root may signify a rubbing or back-and-forth motion, compatible with the process of rubbing sheet gold over a wooden mold.

b. *Symbolism.* The functional purpose of the *m^enôrâ* was performed by its central stand. Thus the additional six branches and the elaborate, botanically inspired floral capitals must be understood aside from a functional context. The form of the lampstand as a whole, consisting of three pairs of two branches and a central shaft, is to be morphologically identified with a convention found in Near Eastern iconography. This convention, derived from a stylized tree design, expressed the theme of the fertility of nature and/or the sustenance of life. The Near Eastern version of this convention that most closely parallels the form of the branched lampstand of Exodus is found in the Late Bronze Age culture of the eastern Mediterranean. In Palestine in particular, there appeared precisely at this time artistic renderings of the stylized tree design that had no local antecedents and which did not continue much beyond the very beginning of the succeeding Iron Age. These renderings are found in glyptic art and on painted

10. Cf. Smith, 14-17; H. Weippert, "Lampe (3.)," *BRL*², 200.

pottery. The largest portion of all Palestinian seals is of the Mitanni type and occurs in Late Bronze Age II; the most popular motif is that of the "seven-ball branch" (six branches plus axis), often resting on a stylized mountain[11] or on a stand. Likewise, during the Late Bronze Age II somewhat crude paintings of the stylized tree design appear on pottery.[12]

This seven-branched form (six branches plus axis) was a powerful symbol of the fructifying and life-giving power of various deities.[13] With its botanical details, it utilizes a powerful symbolic vehicle to convey the notion of God's presence within the aniconic precincts of the Yahweh temple. While the graphic expression of the *m^enôrâ* can be clearly related to this tree symbol denoting fertility and life, the symbolic meaning for ancient Israel would not necessarily be expected to follow such a pattern, since the migration of symbol from one culture to another is rarely accompanied by the explanations or mythology that previously accompanied it.[14] An examination of tree motifs in ancient Israel[15] indicates that the themes of fertility and immortality have largely been replaced by other concepts. The demythologized tree signifies a *hieros topos* as part of the widespread paradigm of the sacred center as the meeting place between God and human beings. Particularly in a portable shrine where a permanent mountaintop shrine is precluded,[16] it would represent the cosmic center and thus the meeting place between God and human beings. Thus while the fertility aspects of the tree form were removed, the lampstand itself retained the value of a symbol of the constant accessibility to divine presence and power within the context of a mobile sanctuary.[17] Within the context of the Priestly documents, the *m^enôrâ* was a constituent part of the daily order of priestly attendance, a ritual complex encompassing the Near Eastern concept of the temple service as caring for a deity.[18]

2. *First (Solomonic) Temple.* The ten lampstands of Solomon's temple, to be placed five on the north side and five on the south side before the inner sanctuary, are briefly described in 1 K. 7:49 par. 2 Ch. 4:7. There is no mention of branches; only a "flower" is spoken of, along with the "lamps." This would suggest, on the basis of archaeological evidence of early Iron Age II, that cylindrical stands (of the same sort as that comprising the central part of the tabernacle lampstand) featuring one (or several) floral capital(s) were utilized. The lamps that surmounted these ten stands were likely to have been seven-spouted, of the sort found in cultic contexts in Iron Age Palestine.[19] If Zechariah's vision has any validity as a witness for the First

---

11. Cf. Nougayrol.
12. Cf. Vincent.
13. Cf. Parrot, *passim;* Meyers, *Tabernacle Menorah,* ch. IV.
14. For a discussion of symbols in general, cf. Goodenough, IV, 25-62; XII, 64-77.
15. Cf. Meyers, *Tabernacle Menorah,* 133-156.
16. Cf. Clifford.
17. Cf. Haran, *Bibl,* 50 (1969), 251-267.
18. Cf. Haran, *ScrHier,* 8 (1961), 272-302.
19. Cf. North, 183-206; Meyers, *BAR,* 5/5 (1979), 46-57.

Temple, the existence therein of this kind of stand with multispouted lamps would be supported. However, it is unlikely that the lampstands constructed in Solomon's reign, probably by Tyrian workmen using *zāhāḇ sāg̱ûr,* would have survived the Babylonian conquest in 587 B.C. In any case, the symbolic value of the single arboreal-branched *m^enôrâ* of the tabernacle would be obviated by the largely functional (i.e., providing illumination) unbranched Solomonic stands. Perhaps there was also a competitive relationship between the *m^enôrâ* symbolism and that of the temple pillars Jachin and Boaz, assuming these did indeed function for illumination.[20] The Jerusalem sanctuary had its own cosmic symbolism within the land of Israel as well as its own tree symbolism in the botanical carvings of its cedar panels (1 K. 6:15,18,29) and the cypress doors (1 K. 6:34,35), perhaps also in a grove (cf. Ps. 52:10[8]), apart from a branched lampstand.

3. *The Second Temple.* The OT gives no indication concerning the existence of a lampstand in the postexilic temple. The single possible exception is Zechariah's vision, which does, however, predate the temple restoration. Yet this vision of a single lampstand may represent the postexilic attention to priestly matters, including their attempt to restore the temple consistent with the Priestly "blueprint" and to replace its sacred furniture. The concern for the continuity of God's presence meant a return to the ancient traditions[21] and thus the fabricature, as best as could be executed according to late 5th/early 6th-century technology, of a *m^enôrâ* according to the Pentateuchal pattern established in the premonarchic era. At this point, however, the arboreal symbolism of the lampstand seems to have receded after centuries in which the light-giving aspects of the Solomonic lampstands were prominent. In the postexilic temple the light motif represented God's presence. Ultimately, while the actual *m^enôrâ* of the temple was carried off, the idea of the *m^enôrâ* survived the destruction of the Jerusalem temple in A.D. 70. Eventually it became the most prominent symbol of postbiblical Judaism in synagogues and tombs, on oil lamps and glass vessels, on seals and coins.[22] These later representations of the *m^enôrâ* provide a direct link with the oldest tabernacle traditions while being given new shapes and meanings.

Meyers

4. *LXX, Qumran.* The LXX translates *m^enôrâ* with *lychnía* (31 times). In rendering the Priestly account of the lampstand's fabrication in the wilderness sanctuary it varies between *lychnía* (Ex. 37:17 [LXX 38:13]) and *lampádion* (Ex. 37:19 [LXX 38:16]). According to LXX 38:16(MT 37:19), *lampádia* can also function as a part of the lampstand when the individual lamps are so referred.

---

20. W. F. Albright; cf., however, 1 K. 7:41ff. and M. Noth, *Könige 1–16. BK,* IX/1 (^{2}1983), 154. See also C. Meyers, *CBQ,* 45 (1983), 167-178.

21. Cf. Ackroyd, 66-81.

22. Cf. Goodenough, IV, 77-92; XII, 79-83.

The term *mᵉnôrâ* occurs only rarely in Qumran. The occurrence in 11QT 3:13 is poorly preserved and stands in the context of instructions concerning the materials for temple construction and furnishing. The term itself is no longer preserved in the candlestick description in 11QT 9.

Fabry

מִנְחָה *minḥâ*

Contents: I. 1. Etymology; 2. Extrabiblical Occurrences. II. 1. Semantic Field; 2. Syntactic Combinations; 3. LXX. III. Distribution and Linguistic Patterns: 1. Pentateuch; 2. Deuteronomistic History and Chronicler's History; 3. Prophets. IV. Secular Usage: 1. Gift; 2. Tribute. V. Theology: 1. Sacrifice or Offering; 2. Designation of Time. VI. Qumran.

I. 1. *Etymology.* Scholarship offers contradictory answers to the question concerning the etymology of *minḥâ.* Is it a primary noun itself or a deverbal nominal construction? Although *KBL*³ treats *minḥâ* as a primary noun, in its discussion of the lexeme *mnḥ* it draws attention to a possible relationship with *minḥâ.*[1] Hebrew, however, does not attest any verb *mnḥ.* Since the previously known occurrences of this root are to be dated significantly later (Arab. *manaḥa,* "to give, loan"; cf. also Tigr. and Geez "give someone [e.g., a poor person] a cow on loan" [the cow belongs to the owner, and the

---

minḥâ. P. A. H. de Boer, "An Aspect of Sacrifice," *Studies in the Religion of Ancient Israel. SVT,* 23 (1972), 27-47; J. R. Brown, *Temple and Sacrifice in Rabbinic Judaism* (Evanston, 1963); A. Charbel, "Offerta di prodotti vegetali nei sacrifice *šᵉlāmîm,*" *Euntes docete,* 26 (1974), 398-403; G. B. Gray, *Sacrifice in the OT: Its Theory and Practice* (1925, repr. New York, 1981); R. D. Hecht, *Sacrifice: Comparative Study and Interpretation* (diss., UCLA, 1976); W. Herrmann, "Götterspeise und Göttertrank in Ugarit und Israel," *ZAW,* 72 (1960), 205-216; J. Hoftijzer, "Das sogenannte Feueropfer," *Hebräische Wortforschung. Festschrift W. Baumgartner. SVT,* 16 (1967), 114-134; B. A. Levine, *In the Presence of the Lord: A Study of Cult and Some Cultic Terms in Ancient Israel. StJLA,* 5 (1974); *idem* and W. W. Hallo, "Offerings to the Temple Gates at Ur," *HUCA,* 38 (1967), 17-58; A. F. Rainey, "The Order of Sacrifices in OT Ritual Texts," *Bibl,* 51 (1970), 485-498; M. Rehm, "Das Opfer der Völker nach Mal 1,11," *Lex tua veritas. Festschrift H. Junker* (Trier, 1961), 193-208; R. Rendtorff, *Studien zur Geschichte des Opfers im alten Israel. WMANT,* 24 (1967); H. Ringgren, *Israelite Religion* (Eng. trans., Philadelphia, 1966), 166-178; L. Rost, *Studien zum Opfer im alten Israel. BWANT,* 113 (1981); H. H. Rowley, "The Meaning of Sacrifice in the OT," *BJRL,* 33 (1950-51), 74-110 = *From Moses to Qumran* (New York, 1963), 67-107; R. J. Thompson, *Penitence and Sacrifice in Early Israel Outside the Levitical Law* (Leiden, 1963); R. de Vaux, *Studies in OT Sacrifice* (Eng. trans., Cardiff, 1964; cf. *CahRB,* 1 [1964]). → זבח *zāḇaḥ (zābhach)* (IV, 8-29); → לבנה *lᵉḇōnâ* (VII, 441-47); → עולה *ʿôlâ;* → קטר *qiṭṭēr.*

1. P. 568.

milk is used by the poor person][2]), *mnḥ* has probably legitimately been viewed as a denominative until now.

The Ugaritic text RS 1957.701, however,[3] contains an important occurrence which may attest the existence of a verb *mnḥ* as early as Ugaritic literature. Line 5, *'lp.ṯmn mt kḇd d.mnḥt,* which Mitchell Dahood translates as "one thousand eight hundred heavy (jars) of cereals," presupposes either a feminine singular or a feminine plural substantive. Michael Heltzer[4] thinks that *mnḥt* is a sacrificial term meaning "gift" or "offering," even though the text itself represents a commercial document. Oswald Loretz and others, following Mario Liverani,[5] correctly point out that the form *mnḥt* can be interpreted as the passive participle of *mnḥ,* "to hand out, distribute." If this interpretation should prove correct, then a deverbal origin for *minḥâ* cannot be excluded. If, however, *minḥâ* derives from *mnḥ,*[6] then the noun is a *qaṭl* or *qiṭl* form.[7] In this context it should be pointed out that the Middle Hebrew plural form *m^enāḥôṯ* (Mishnah *Zebaḥ.* ix.5) points to a root *mnḥ,* since a prefigured *mem* would presuppose **minḥôṯ*.[8] Such a plural is indeed attested 3 times in Biblical Hebrew.

This leads to the assumption of a different verbal root as the basis for the nominal construction. One suggestion is *nḥy/w* → נחה I *(nāḥâ),* "to lead, guide,"[9] which is well attested in the OT, while its extrabiblical occurrences clearly direct us to the South Semitic sphere.[10] A deverbalization of *nḥy/w* is to that extent not problematical, since now *minḥâ* has developed in a fully regular fashion as a *maqṭal/miqṭal* form with a feminine ending. The verb's semantic point of departure, however, then generates a virtually insoluble problem.

These findings suggest that *minḥâ* represents a primary noun from which a verb *mnḥ* then developed. This denomination likely occurred already in the second half of the second millennium B.C.

2. *Extrabiblical Occurrences.* The term *minḥâ* is only infrequently attested outside

2. Cf. Leslau, "Observations on Semitic Cognates in Ugaritic," *Or,* 37 (1968), 358; *Contributions,* 31.

3. Published by M. Dahood in L. R. Fisher, *et al., The Claremont Ras-Shamra Tablets. AnOr,* 48 (1971), 32.

4. Review of Fisher, *et al., IEJ,* 22 (1972), 254.

5. "Il talento di Ashdod," *OrAnt,* 11 (1972), 193-99.

6. Cf. *GesB,* 437; *WTM,* III, 153; J. C. de Moor, *The Seasonal Pattern in the Ugaritic Myth of Ba'lu. AOAT,* 16 (1971), 132.

7. The former is supported by the early readings given in *KBL*³, 568: *mānā* (Sam.), *manaa* (LXX, Jerome).

8. Cf. J. Blau and S. E. Loewenstamm, "Zur Frage der scriptio plena im Ugaritischen und Verwandtes," *UF,* 2 (1970), 28, n. 57.

9. Cf. already F. Perles, *Analekten zur Textkritik des ATs* (Munich, 1895), 78; F. Hommel; M. Lidzbarski ; then T. F. McDaniel, "Philological Studies in Lamentations, I," *Bibl,* 49 (1968), 35; H. L. Ginsberg, *ANET,* 130.

10. Cf. E. Jenni, "נחה *nḥh* leiten," *THAT,* II, 53-55.

the Bible. The earliest extant occurrences point to Ugarit, where *mnḥ* occurs with the general meaning "gift, tribute,"[11] whereas the meaning "sacrifice, offering" posited by Cyrus Gordon[12] cannot be derived from these few occurrences.

In *KTU,* 1.2 I, 38, the suffixed *mnḥyk* (masc. pl.) means "your gifts," and parallels *'rgmnk,* "your tribute," whereby one must consider whether the suffixes should not be understood as markers of dative usage.[13] Within the context of the divine struggle between Baʿal and the sea god Yamm, Baʿal is to acknowledge his own subordination by presenting tribute to Yamm. The parallel *'rgmn,* "tribute," makes it unlikely that *mnḥ* carries any sacrificial connotations. The accompanying verb *ybl* also occurs biblically in connection with *minḥâ* (Hos. 10:6; Zeph. 3:10).[14] The parallels noted in *RSP,* I, §II.210, for *ybl* and *nḥh* (Ps. 60:11[Eng. v. 9]; 108:11[10]) are probably deceptive, and the reference to Job 29:25 is incorrect.

In *KTU,* 4.91, 1, *mnḥ.bd.ybnn* means "tribute from the hand of PN," and contains no religious connotation whatever.[15] The same then also holds true for line 4 if the present text *šmn nḥ* ("oil in skins"[16]) were to be emended with Yigael Sukenik to *šmn mnḥ,* "sacrificial/offering oil."[17] Finally, the root probably also occurs in the Akkadian text *PRU* 293,2 and 5 from Ugarit, where the word *manaḫati* has been interpreted by Jean Nougayrol as the plural of Akk. *mānaḫtu,* "work."[18] William F. Albright claimed that this word was actually Heb. *minḥâ.* Akkadian, however, does not attest this root.[19]

Late Egyptian attests *mnḥt* with the meaning "gift of homage," although this might be a loanword from Hebrew.[20]

Although *mnḥh* I-III does occur within Hebrew, Aramaic, and Phoenician-Punic epigraphy, *mnḥh* I can be eliminated as an Egyptian loanword.[21] Neither does *mnḥh* III, "grave, tomb,"[22] belong to this etymon.[23] *mnḥh* II,[24] "sacrifice, offering" in the form of a stela, a temple, or a vegetable gift, is profusely attested both in the Elephantine Aramaic papyri of the fifth century B.C.[25] and in Phoenician-Punic and Neo-Punic inscriptions. A Phoenician votive inscription to Melqart (Lapethos) mentions *mnḥh* in

11. *WUS,* no. 1579.
12. *UT,* no. 1500.
13. Cf. Blau-Loewenstamm, 28, n. 58; see also *ANET*³, 130.
14. Cf. L. Sabottka, *Zephanja. BietOr,* 25 (1972), 121f.
15. Cf. J.-M. de Tarragon, *Le Culte à Ugarit. CahRB,* 19 (1980), 71.
16. Cf. M. Dietrich, O. Loretz, and J. Sanmartín, "Zur ugaritischen Lexikographie (VIII)," *UF,* 5 (1973), 113.
17. "An Ugaritic List of Spices and Ointments," *Tarbiz,* 18 (1946/47), 126 [Heb.]. On the possible attestation of a verbal root *mnḥ* in Ugarit in the text RS 1957.701, cf. above.
18. Cf. *AHw,* II (1972), 602.
19. Cf. further J. L. Boyd III, "Two Misunderstood Words in the Ras Shamra Akkadian Texts," *Or,* 46 (1977), 229.
20. Cf. *WbÄS,* II, 84.
21. *DISO,* 158.
22. N. Avigad, "Excavations at Beth Sheʿarim, 1955," *IEJ,* 7 (1957), 239.
23. → נוח *nwḥ.*
24. *DISO,* 159.
25. Cf. *AP,* 30, 21, 25; 31, 21; 32, 9; 33, 11; cf. also E. Vogt, title, 107.

a general sense.[26] The Punic Marseilles Tariff[27] clearly picks up OT sacrificial terminology when *minḥâ* — together with *bll,* as is frequently the case in P — occurs next to *zeḇaḥ* (l. 14). The meaning "cereal offering," however, seems too vague, since a *zbḥ ṣd* (l. 12) already covers this type. Neither is the content of the *minḥâ* specified: Baked goods, milk, fat, and *kl zbḥ* can be included.

Thus outside the OT, too, the meaning of *minḥâ* is fairly broad; cf. also the Neo-Punic inscription of Mactar,[28] where *minḥâ* functions as the summary term for the oblations of a cultic gathering.[29] In an addendum to the Neo-Punic inscription of Altiburos,[30] *minḥâ* and the parallel *ʿōlâ* refer to the sacrificial offerings to Baʿal Hammon.[31]

Finally, the root is also attested in Arab. *manaḥa,* "to give, loan," and *minḥat,* "gift," as well as in additional South Semitic dialects (see preceding discussion).

Rabbinic literature attests only the noun *minḥâ,* in the Targumim *minḥāṯāʾ,* with the meanings "gift, sacrificial offering, especially cereal offering," figuratively "the time of the afternoon sacrifice" (cf. 1 K. 18:29,36; 2 K. 3:20; 16:13,15; Ezr. 9:4f.; Isa. 43:23; Mal. 1:10,11) and the "prayer at the afternoon sacrifice."[32]

II. 1. *Semantic Field.* The semantic field of *minḥâ* emerges from the many parallels and series of sacrificial terms accompanying it (Ex. 30:9; Lev. 7:37; 9:4; 23:13,18,37; Nu. 4:16; 6:15; 7:87; 15:24; 29:39).

The classification of the individual sacrificial terms is difficult to evaluate and probably assumed various forms during various periods. In early texts *minḥâ* is of equal value with *ʿōlâ, ḥaṭṭāʾṯ, ʾāšām,* and *zeḇaḥ,* while in P^S and R^P it, like *neseḵ,* is demoted by means of suffixes into a complementary offering accompanying these greater sacrifices. The term *minḥâ* never occurs as a generic term like *qorbān, kālîl,* and *ʾiššeh,* and since its content is frequently explained, the concrete realization of that content must have been variable within certain parameters.

2. *Syntactic Combinations.* Syntactically, *minḥâ* exhibits a certain awkwardness. In half of its occurrences it appears undeclined in the singular absolute state with (40 times) or without (73 times) the article. Here it governs the following construct chains: *qorban minḥâ* (Lev. 2:1); *tôraṯ hamminḥâ* (Lev. 6:7[14]); *sōleṯ hamminḥâ* (Lev. 6:8[15]), and *nôśᵉʾê minḥâ* (Jgs. 3:18). It occurs 23 times in the singular construct state, including the following occurrences in the Pentateuch: *minḥaṯ habbōqer* (Ex. 29:41); *minḥaṯ marḥešeṯ* (Lev. 2:7); *minḥaṯ bikkûrîm* (Lev. 2:14); *minḥaṯ pittîm* (Lev. 6:14); *minḥaṯ kōhēn* (Lev. 6:16[23]); *minḥaṯ hattāmîḏ* (Nu. 4:16); *minḥaṯ qᵉnāʾōṯ* (Nu. 5:15);

26. *KAI,* 43, 13.
27. *KAI,* 69; cf. the Carthaginian "duplicate," *KAI,* 74; see also *ANET*³, 656f.
28. *KAI,* 145, 13.
29. → מרזח *marzēaḥ.*
30. *KAI,* 159, 8.
31. For further discussion of Punic sacrificial terminology cf. J.-G. Février, "Le vocabulaire sacrificiel punique," *JAs,* 243 (1955), 49-63.
32. Cf. *WTM,* III, 153.

and *minḥaṯ zikkārôn* (Nu. 5:15); and outside the Pentateuch additionally: *minḥaṯ hā'āreḇ* (2 K. 16:15; Ps. 141:2); *minḥaṯ šāw'* (Isa. 1:13); *minḥaṯ y^ehûḏâ* (Mal. 3:4); *minḥaṯ yiśrā'ēl* (1 S. 2:29); and only once *minḥaṯ YHWH* (1 S. 2:17). This latter expression probably corresponds to the customary formulation *minḥâ l^eYHWH* (Nu. 28:26; Isa. 66:20; Joel 2:14; Mal. 2:12; 3:3), which indicates the target object by means of a dative particle (cf. also the king in Hos. 10:6; Jehoshaphat in 2 Ch. 17:5; Uzziah in 2 Ch. 26:8).

minḥâ is seldom used with adjectives. Occurrences include: *minḥâ ḥ^aḏāšâ* (Lev. 23:16); *minḥâ ḥ^arēḇâ* (Lev. 7:10); and *minḥâ ṭ^ehôrâ* (Mal. 1:11).

3. *LXX.* The LXX renders *minḥâ* 142 times with *thysía,* twice with *thysíasma,* and once each with *holokaútōma* and *prosphorá.* In language related to sacrifice and offering it does not differentiate between *minḥâ* and *zeḇaḥ,* rendering both terms with *thysía;* neither is *'iššeh* clearly set off, since it is rendered 8 times by *thysía* in addition to *kárpōma.* Apparently the semantic shifts between *minḥâ* and *qorbān* within the Priestly traditions are also noted by the LXX, since *qorbān* — rendered by the general term *dṓron* — is set apart from the specification *minḥâ = thysía.* The extreme proximity of these two terms, however, also manifests itself in the fact that *minḥâ* is also rendered 30 times by *dṓron,* although primarily outside of sacrificial texts. The LXX makes clear distinctions between *'ōlâ (holokaútōma, holokaútōsis,* and only 6 times *thysía), ḥaṭṭā'ṯ (hamartía), 'āšām (plēmméleia), q^eṭōreṯ (thymíama),* and *neseḵ (spondḗ).*

What is striking is the frequent rendering by *maná* (once: Dnl. 2:46), *manaá* (16 times), *manach* (once: 2 K. 17:3), *mánna* (12 times; *mánna* otherwise refers 10 times to → מן *mān*), and *mannaeím* (once: Neh. 13:9). Rather than marking distinctions in content, these different forms more likely represent linguistic variants in the LXX versions and recensions. The question is unavoidable, however, just how *mánna* can be used for *minḥâ.* We find that this rendering occurs only outside the Pentateuch, especially in Jeremiah, Nehemiah, Daniel, and consistently above all in Ezk. 45ff. (in the Codex Alexandrinus). On the one hand, it may have resulted from a consistent scribal error involving *manaá,* as suggested by Paul Maiberger in the case of Bar. 1:10,[33] an explanation supported by the variants between codices A and B, although the frequency is nonetheless striking. Thus this is probably not a case of scribal error, and this particular translation can be traced back rather to the textual history of the LXX itself: (1) the meaning of *mān = mánna* remained undefined for a long period, since *mān* was understood in an indefinite sense as "gift, present";[34] (2) Gk. *mánna,* "frankincense, incense powder, granular sacrificial substance,"[35] offers itself as a likely, albeit one-sided, translation, since the *minḥâ* is often associated with incense; (3) it must be assumed that the morpheme *minḥâ* does not represent the genuine

---

33. → מן *mān,* I (VIII, 389-395); cf. also R. Meyer, "Μάννα," *TDNT,* IV, 462f.
34. Cf. Maiberger.
35. Cf. H. G. Liddell, R. Scott, and H. S. Jones, *Greek English Lexicon,* II (Oxford, ⁹1940, repr. 1948), 1079.

phonetic value of the word, since the first syllable probably originally contained an a-vowel (see preceding discussion); (4) rabbinic occurrences suggest that an identification between *minḥâ* and manna was conceivable; how else was one to explain that the taste of manna was considered like that of "finely ground flour and oil" (and honey)?[36]

III. Distribution and Linguistic Patterns. The noun *minḥâ* occurs 211 times in the Hebrew OT, twice in the Aramaic sections (Ezr. 7:17; Dnl. 2:46), and twice in Sirach (45:14; 50:9).

Of these, 113 occurrences are in the Pentateuch, 44 in the Prophets, 33 in the Deuteronomistic history, 16 in the Chronicler's history, and only 6 in the Psalms. This distribution derives not least from the two main semantic specifications "sacrifice, offering" and "gift." Given the broad temporal distribution, the occurrences in the Pentateuch are especially ill-served by a summary definition.

1. *Pentateuch.* The term *minḥâ* occurs in all the temporal strata of the Pentateuch's development; at the same time, specific linguistic patterns in connection with the use of *minḥâ* characterize the individual segments.

a. Very few occurrences derive from the pre-Yahwistic/Yahwistic literary stage. Gen. 4:3,4,5 all derive from a Kenite source: the *minḥâ* both of Cain and Abel are referred to the respective sacrificer by means of a suffix. Similarly, suffixed *minḥâ* also occurs in the (pre-)Yahwistic Dathan-Abiram episode (Nu. 16:15). This stage is characterized by weak semantic specification of the term: *minḥâ* refers to a "sacrificial offering" in a broad, general sense; indeed, one cannot yet strictly ascertain that it even constitutes a sacrificial term. It probably refers rather to a "gift/offering to a superior," as the contemporaneous occurrences in the story of Joseph seem to suggest (Gen. 43:11, 15,25,26). At this early stage, *minḥâ* consistently occurs only as an object within the given sentence structure, i.e., mention of this term always simultaneously evokes the controlling subject.

b. The linguistic usage of the Elohist differs sharply from this, since in the Jacob-Esau controversy he views *minḥâ* as the subject of participial constructions (Gen. 32:21f.[20f.]). At the same time, such linguistic specification signals a substantive aspect to the extent that *minḥâ* here encompasses livestock, flocks, and other movable possessions (cf. Gen. 32:14[13]). In the phrase *minḥâ hû'* (Gen. 32:19[18]) E already coins a formulaic expression that will later be used in the addenda to the Priestly Document as a sacrificial declaration (cf. Lev. 2:6,15). E does not seem to have used a suffixed form of *minḥâ*.

Neither J nor E uses specific verbs with *minḥâ,* and although *bô'* hiphil and *lāqaḥ* do reflect common later usage as well, *kûn* hiphil (cf. Ps. 141:2) and *yāraḏ* hiphil are unique. Linguistic usage has not yet become fixed.

36. Examples in St.-B., II (1924), 481; cf. further B. J. Malina, *The Palestinian Manna Tradition. AGSU,* 7 (1968), 66; R. Le Déaut, "Une aggadah targumique et les 'murmures' de Jean 6," *Bibl,* 51 (1970), 80-83.

c. Over 100 occurrences of *minḥâ* are found in the Priestly Document alone and in the redactional activity undertaken by it in the Pentateuch. In this context, P^G seems still to have dealt in a restrained fashion with this word, for only 10 occurrences can be attributed to this basic stratum (Ex. 29:41; 30:9; Lev. 2:1,4,8,9; 5:13?; 7:37; 9:4,17). Now *minḥâ* occurs consistently without suffixes, for it is removed completely from secular language and reserved for sacrificial terminology, in which as a sacrifice or offering it is similarly transferred from the individual sphere to the ecclesiological sphere of the congregation Israel. At the same time, P^G carries through a specification, since now → קרבן *qorbān* becomes the designation for the unspecified "sacrificial offering," while *minḥâ* is co- or subordinated to it as a more exact specification or is classified as a partial sacrifice or offering. The sacrificial regulations in Lev. 2 especially reflect source-specific linguistic usage. Here P^G speaks of a *qorban minḥâ lᵉYHWH* (vv. 1,4), whereas later addenda speak only of *minḥâ* (vv. 3,7,10,11) or of *nôṯereṯ min-hamminḥâ* (vv. 3,10). P^G almost always uses *qāraḇ* hiphil as the sacrificial verb, and also gives information concerning the scope of the *minḥâ*-materials. It consists basically of finely ground flour *(sōleṯ)* which is mixed *(bll)* with oil *(šemen)* (Lev. 2:1; 9:4); it can additionally contain frankincense (2:1) and unleavened bread (2:4f.). The ingredients are so fixed that P^G usually can speak simply of *minḥâ* without any more specific information (e.g., 9:4), whereas later addenda again consider more specific information to be necessary (compare Lev. 7:9,10 with 9:4).

d. P^S addenda which focus on the "sacrificial portions of the priests" (Lev. 2:3,10; 6:7,8[14,15]; 7:9,10; 10:12) no longer perceive any connection between *qorbān* and *minḥâ;* they now subordinate *minḥâ* to the fire offering *('iššeh)* (2:3,10; 10:12). The presentation term is *qāraḇ* hiphil. According to this tradition, the *minḥâ* can also be prepared without oil, i.e., "dry" *(ḥᵃrēḇâ)* (7:10; cf. 6:13[20]).

Other P^S addenda seem to equate *minḥâ* and *qorbān* again (2:5,7). A singular tradition in Lev. 2:13-16 ("first fruits") speaks of the *qorban minḥāṯᵉḵā* (2:13), which is to be prepared with salt. In the same verse this tradition can even replace *minḥâ* with *qorbān.* The singular tradition "Tamid offering" (Lev. 6:12-16[19-23]) subordinates *minḥâ* to the generic terms *qorbān* (v. 13[20]) and *kālîl* (v. 16[23]), something also observable in the later P^S addenda (cf., e.g., Nu. 5:15). Here *qorbān* functions in a general fashion as a designation for any kind of presentation or offering, e.g., also for materials to be added to the temple treasury, whereas *minḥâ* remains limited to sacrifices or offerings within the context of a cultic activity. These later traditions also show that the ingredients (by the addition of roasting corn and groats, Lev. 2:14,15) and manner of preparation (by the addition of the griddle in v. 5 and the pan in v. 7) have been expanded. The term of presentation is again *qāraḇ* hiphil.

Further individual traditions associated with P^S are found in the sacrificial laws concerning leprosy (Lev. 14), the offering of jealousy (Nu. 5), and the Naziriteship (Nu. 6); extremely old individual traditions are also found in the regulations concerning the consecration offerings of the tribal princes (Nu. 7) and the levitical consecration (Nu. 15). The language is unremarkable: *minḥâ* is the *terminus technicus* for the cereal offering, whose ingredients are specially mentioned only when they are to be varied at certain occasions (cf. Lev. 14:10,21; Nu. 15:4,6,9). The offering of jealousy plays a special role and apparently reflects a singular tradition. Here *minḥâ* occurs only in construct: *minḥaṯ qᵉnā'ōṯ* (Nu. 5:15,25), *minḥaṯ zikkārôn mazkereṯ ʿāwōn* (vv. 15,18) (*minḥâ* elsewhere in the construct state only in Ex. 29:41; Lev. 2:14; 6:7,16[14,23]; Nu. 4:16, all P^S). The singularity of this tradition also manifests itself in the fact that in Nu. 5:15 a jealousy *minḥâ* is to be prepared which, in contrast to all others, is to be prepared not from *sōleṯ,* but rather from *qemaḥ śᵉʿōrîm* without oil and without frankincense. Only occasionally do these later traditions associate the *minḥâ* with a drink offering *(nesek̲)* (Nu. 6:15,17; 15:24). It is also noteworthy that *minḥâ* now once again occurs with suffixes, suffixes which usually connect the offering itself with the person making the offering (e.g., Nu. 6:17); at the same time, however, an incipient linguistic relaxation can be observed insofar as the suffixes now also serve to subordinate *minḥâ* (and *nesek̲*) to a more comprehensive offering and to degrade it into a secondary offering (cf. Nu. 8:8). Increasingly, *lāqaḥ* joins *qārab̲* hiphil as the term of presentation.

e. The 4 occurrences in the Holiness Code can be subsumed under these linguistic auspices (Lev. 23:13,16,18,37). H views the *minḥâ* consistently in connection with other types of sacrifice and offering: *ʿōlâ, zeb̲aḥ,* and especially *nesek̲.* These are all component offerings of the *'iššeh lᵉYHWH.* H pays attention to the specification of the *minḥâ* materials (v. 13) and introduces a *minḥâ ḥᵃd̲āšâ* (v. 16; cf. Nu. 28:26) in connection with the harvest festival. The term *ʿāśâ* now joins *qārab̲* hiphil.

f. The final stage is probably represented by the sacrificial calendar in Nu. 28:1–30:1 (32 occurrences), "one of the latest sections of the Pentateuch."[37] What the previous sacrificial laws prescribed (Lev. 1–7; 23; Nu. 15) is now presupposed as the obtaining order. The subordination of *minḥâ* to the *ʿōlâ* is completely variable (cf. Nu. 28:12,31; 29:6), and the specification of the actual content of the *minḥâ* is no longer presented according to a unified model (cf. P^S in Nu. 15:6,9: *minḥâ sōleṯ* [quantity] *bālûl baššemen* [quantity], and the variety of formulations used by R^P in Nu. 28:5,9,12ab,13,26; 28:20, 28; 29:3,9,14 and elsewhere). Consistently *minḥâ* is associated with a primary sacrifice or offering by means of suffixes, and is constantly associated with *nesek̲.* The presentation term is increasingly *ʿāśâ.* The concluding formulation in Nu. 29:39 contains in *minḥōṯêk̲em* the only plural construction in the Pentateuch.

2. *Deuteronomistic History and Chronicler's History.* The term *minḥâ* occurs 32 times in the Deuteronomistic history and 16 times in the Chronicler's history. The portion of the occurrences exhibiting the meaning "gift, present, tribute" (14 and 6 occurrences) is significantly higher than in the Pentateuch. The number of parallel series of sacrificial terms naturally quickly diminishes (cf. Josh. 22:23,29; 1 K. 8:64; 2 K. 16:15; 2 Ch. 7:7). With few exceptions *minḥâ* occurs in the absolute state, and suffixed forms are rare (1 S. 2:29; 1 K. 10:25; 2 K. 16:13,15; 2 Ch. 9:24). Thus also outside the Pentateuch no real tendency toward fixed usage can be clearly ascertained. Statements concerning content are rarely made, since as one of the classical sacrifices or offerings the *minḥâ* is ritually fixed and familiar (exceptions include: Jgs. 6:18f.

37. M. Noth, *Numbers. OTL* (Eng. trans. 1968), 219.

[kids and unleavened cakes]; 1 Ch. 21:23 [wheat]; 1 Ch. 23:29 [fine flour]); similarly, the meaning "tribute" is only rarely accompanied by more specific references to content (exceptions: 1 K. 10:25 par. 2 Ch. 9:24 [silver and gold vessels, garments, weapons, balsam, horses, and mules]; 2 K. 8:9 [precious things]), so that here, too, one can already ascertain an advanced technical understanding of the term.

In the Deuteronomistic history, *minḥâ* occurs almost exclusively as the object of the verbs *ʿālâ* hiphil, *qāraḇ* hiphil, *šālaḥ;* in isolated instances the verbs *bô'* hiphil, *nāśā',* *br'* II hiphil, *bʿṭ, qṭr* hiphil, and others occur. The Chronicler's history attests clearly altered linguistic usage, since here *nāṯan* and *bô'* hiphil are used, and only 3 times *nāśā'* and once *šûḇ* hiphil.

3. *Prophets.* The term *minḥâ* occurs 8 times in Isaiah (3 times in Proto-Isaiah, once in Deutero-Isaiah, 4 times in Trito-Isaiah); 4 times in Jeremiah (at the earliest in his second proclamation period); 15 times in Ezekiel (exclusively in the draft constitution); twice in Amos (5:22 as an original part of the text; 5:25 as a secondary insertion); once in Hosea; 3 times in Joel; once in Zephaniah; and 7 times in Malachi. The Psalms mention *minḥâ* 6 times, Daniel mentions it twice. Despite the enormous temporal-historical scope encompassed by these writings, it is striking that *minḥâ* here is almost never understood as "tribute" or "gift" (exceptions: Hos. 10:6 [gift (RSV tribute) to the great king]; Isa. 39:1 [to Hezekiah]). In all other cases Yahweh is either explicitly or implicitly the goal of the *minḥâ.* Not only do the prophets rarely use this word (the occurrences in Ezekiel do not belong to the basic stratum of the draft constitution, but rather to the late exilic *nāśî'* and Zadokite strata[38]), but with few exceptions they also always use it in parallel constructions with other sacrificial terms. That is, they view the *minḥâ* basically only in connection with the other sacrifices and offerings. This also means, however, that neither the *minḥâ* nor any other offering is singled out for attention, but rather that the entire sacrificial cult is the focus of their prophetic proclamation. Once again *minḥâ* is used in the absolute state (exceptions: *minḥaṯ ʿāreḇ* in Ps. 141:2; Dnl. 9:21; *minḥaṯ yᵉhûḏâ* in Mal. 3:4), suffixes are not common (exceptions: Ps. 20:4[3]; Am. 5:22; Zeph. 3:10), and related verbs do not really reveal any fixed linguistic structures: Trito-Isaiah uses *ʿālâ* hiphil and *bô'* hiphil; *ʿāśâ* predominates in Ezekiel's draft constitution, and Malachi adds *nāgaš* hiphil, which is attested only twice previously as the presentation term with *minḥâ* (Am. 5:25 [secondary]; Lev. 2:8 P^{G}; with *minḥâ* as "tribute" in 1 K. 5:1; with other sacrificial terms cf. Ex. 32:6; Lev. 8:14). Finally, the fundamental association of *minḥâ* and *neseḵ* is noteworthy in Joel.

IV. Secular Usage. In secular usage *minḥâ* appears with the meaning "gift, present," or "tribute," although some passages already exhibit a semantic progression toward the meaning "sacrifice, offering."

1. *Gift.* With the meaning "gift," *minḥâ* occurs with a variety of contexts, and the content of such a *minḥâ* is accordingly quite variable. A *minḥâ* as a gift is never

38. W. Zimmerli, *Ezekiel 2. Herm* (Eng. trans. 1983), *in loc.*

presented completely unintentionally; that is, in every instance it is more or less obvious that the presentation of this gift is directed toward attaining a specific goal. Thus in the first instance the *minḥâ* is intended to make the person receiving it well-disposed toward the giver (2 K. 8:8f.). The sons of Jacob seek to win Joseph's favor and to ward off Joseph's claims to the youngest son Benjamin by bringing to him — quite independent of the *kesep* for the grain — a rich *minḥâ* consisting of balsam, honey, tragacanth gum, myrrh, pistachio nuts, and almonds (Gen. 43:11,15,25,26 J). Presenting this kind of *minḥâ* to the head of a country for the sake of securing his favor was customary (cf. 2 K. 20:12 par. Isa. 39:1; Ps. 45:13[12]), although it is not in every case clear whether such a *minḥâ* does not already exhibit the character of a payment of tribute (cf. Ps. 72:10: *minḥâ* par. *'eškār,* "tribute"). A *minḥâ* is also presented to the newly chosen king as a gift of homage (cf. 2 Ch. 17:5; 32:23 *migdānôṯ*). Refusing to present it is the same as refusing loyalty (1 S. 10:27). Before his own meeting with Esau Jacob sends him an enormous *minḥâ* consisting of livestock in order to acknowledge Esau as the land's sovereign and to prevent possible hostilities (Gen. 32:14, 19,21,22[13,18,20,21] E). According to J, this *minḥâ* and Esau's acceptance of it function representatively by signaling "favor" *(ḥēn)* and "favorable acceptance" *(rāṣâ)* between the two hostile brothers. J pointedly draws out the meaning of this *minḥâ* for the sphere of human relationships by using it like a sacrificial term: "If I find favor with you, then accept my present from my hand; for truly to see your face is like seeing the face of God" (Gen. 33:10). Thus even in the case of the profane *minḥâ* the term's cultic-sacral connotation can adroitly be brought into play; this presupposes that the *minḥâ* offering was accorded an extremely wide sphere of efficacy in mollifying the deity (see discussion below) and similarly presupposed such efficacy being operative in the secular sphere.

At least in the language of the Chronicler it seems possible to view a *minḥâ* to Yahweh primarily under the aspect of a gift and less as a sacrifice or offering; cf. the parallels *minḥâ l^eYHWH* and *migdānôṯ lîḥizqîyāhû* (2 Ch. 32:23; cf. also 1 Ch. 16:29; Ps. 96:8). Of particular interest is Zeph. 3:10 with its Jewish interpretation: "From beyond the rivers of Cush my suppliants shall bring me the *minḥâ*."[39] Into this universalistic statement a "Jewish particularist" inserted a *baṯ pûṣay,* "daughter of my dispersions." Despite the textual difficulties here, this insertion seems to be giving information concerning the content of the *minḥâ*. The *minḥâ* is the "congregation of my dispersed ones," the Diaspora itself.

2. *Tribute*. Regarding both its scope and its addressee, a *minḥâ* as a "gift" is presented *sua sponte*. Though scholarship peculiarly never presses the question,[40] it does indeed come as a surprise that this term can now also refer to a "tribute," a levy that hardly has anything in common with a gift. A tribute is a levy coerced by military superiority from a subject to the more powerful party. Since any irregularity in paying

39. W. Rudolph, *Zephanja. KAT,* XIII/3 (1975), 291.
40. Cf. R. de Vaux, *AncIsr,* 415-432.

the tribute (cf. Hoshea's suspension of the *minḥâ* to Shalmaneser in 2 K. 17:3f. and its consequences) threatened the *status quo,* prompting a declaration of war which ended with the destruction of the inferior party, one must view this as a significant semantic component of the term *minḥâ*. OT Hebrew does not otherwise attest a term for "tribute." The previously mentioned *'eškār* occurs only in Ezk. 27:15; Ps. 72:10, and in neither of these passages can this meaning be determined exactly. Similarly, *middâ II* suggested by *GesB* more likely refers to a domestically induced tax levy (Neh. 5:4). Either as a designation for "tribute" *minḥâ* is a euphemism, or the semantic perspectives "gift," "tribute," and "cereal offering" reveal a common fundamental perception. This does not seem a superfluous point, since especially in the theological sphere (see discussion below) — although not only there — the appeasing effects of the *minḥâ* are everywhere evident. Does this signal perhaps an etymological relationship with the root → נוח *nwḥ,* "to settle, rest"? Since foreign payments of tribute reflect the greatness of one's own kingship, one must suspect a tendentious portrayal on the part of the court reporter behind the fantasy payments of tribute by King Mesha to Ahab (2 K. 3:4) and by the Philistines to Jehoshaphat (2 Ch. 17:11). David obliged the Syrians (2 S. 8:6 par. 1 Ch. 18:6) and the Moabites (2 S. 8:2; 1 Ch. 18:2) to pay tribute, while Solomon brought everything from the Euphrates to the Philistines and the Egyptian border under his control (1 K. 5:1[4:21]). The payments to him constitute tribute, since they are made *šānâ bᵉšānâ,* "year by year" (1 K. 10:25; 2 Ch. 9:24). Finally, Uzziah also obliged the Ammonites to pay tribute (2 Ch. 26:8).

In contrast, information is scarce concerning one's own tribute payments using the term *minḥâ*. Jgs. 3:15,17,18 speak of tribute to the Moabites, 2 K. 17:3f. of tribute paid by the northern kingdom to the Assyrians, and Hos. 10:6 shows the failure of the politics of 2 K. 17:3f.: "The calf itself shall be carried to Assyria as *minḥâ* to the great king."

Fabry

V. Theology. 1. *Sacrifice or Offering*. The term *minḥâ,* "gift, present," early acquired the specialized meaning of a sacrifice or offering which was to be a "pleasing odor" *(rê[a]ḥ nîḥô[a]ḥ)* to the deity and was to soothe its senses. Thus David says to Saul: "If it is Yahweh who has stirred you up against me, then give him a *minḥâ* to smell (*rwḥ* hiphil)" (1 S. 26:19). This pleasing smell of the sacrifice's fragrance is also implied even if the term *minḥâ* is not explicitly mentioned. Thus it also happens that when Noah makes an offering to Yahweh after the deluge, and Yahweh smells its pleasing fragrance *(wayyāraḥ YHWH 'eṯ-rêaḥ hannîḥōaḥ),* he pledges not to curse the earth a second time (Gen. 8:21); cf. negatively Lev. 26:31: "I will no longer smell the fragrance of your sacrifices"; Amos 5:21: "I take no pleasure in smelling your solemn assemblies."

And indeed, the *minḥâ* constitutes that part of the ritual which creates the fragrance: corn, flour, baked bread, or cakes mixed with oil and frankincense and presented before Yahweh (Lev. 2:14f.). The *minḥâ* constitutes the high point of the sacrificial ritual, since it insures that God is able to smell the pleasing fragrance of the offering.

Although the term *minḥâ* frequently occurs in connection with or parallel to *zeḇaḥ,* *'ôlâ* (see earlier discussion), it usually constitutes a fixed ritual together with the *qᵉṭōreṯ* and the incense offering *(lᵉḇônâ);* cf. Isa. 1:13: "It is futile to bring me *minḥâ;* incense *(qᵉṭōreṯ)* is an abomination to me." Isa. 43:23: "I have not burdened you with *minḥâ,* or wearied you with frankincense *(lᵉḇônâ)*" (cf. also Neh. 13:5-9; Isa. 66:3; Jer. 17:26; 41:5). The tandem *minḥâ* and *lᵉḇônâ* also appears in the Elephantine papyri, indeed exclusively in this combination.[41]

Ps. 141:2 is of significance regarding the association of *minḥâ* (especially the evening *minḥâ*) with the incense offering: "Let my prayer be counted as incense before thee, and the lifting up of my hands as an evening *minḥâ*" (cf. discussion below).

The *minḥâ,* mixed with oil and frankincense, was blended from flour or meal and could be offered by anyone, independent of animal sacrifice (cf. Lev. 2). Indeed, the *minḥâ* and the incense offering *(qᵉṭōreṯ, lᵉḇônâ)* developed into a kind of universal ritual; cf., e.g., Mal. 1:11: "For from the rising of the sun to its setting my name is great among the nations, and in every place incense *(muqṭār)* is offered to my name, and a pure *minḥâ.*"

Reference should be made also to the eighty men who go up to Jerusalem bringing *minḥâ* and *lᵉḇônâ* (Jer. 41:5).

Offerings of the *minḥâ* type are attested throughout the ancient Near East. Thus in a Kassite votive inscription we read: "For Adad . . . he libated from seeds and . . . roots, he caused incense to go up in smoke" *(i-na ŠE.NUMUN ù ḫir-ṣa-ti qut-ri-nam ú-ša-aq-ti-ir)*.[42] In Mesopotamia we also find fragrant offerings whose odor is meant for the deity: "Without you [Šamaš] the great gods of heaven and earth cannot smell the incense offerings" *(ul iṣ-ṣi-nu qut-rin-nu)*.[43]

In the official cult, however, the *minḥâ* was normally connected with animal sacrifice, something already attested by ancient Israelite sources. Gideon takes for his offering a kid and unleavened bread, baked from an ephah of flour (Jgs. 6:19); Manoah, the father of Samson, takes a kid and a *minḥâ* (Jgs. 13:19; cf. v. 23); Hannah, the mother of Samuel, prepares a thank offering consisting of three bulls (LXX and 4QSam: "a three-year-old bull"), an ephah of flour, and a skin of wine (1 S. 1:24). The Priestly Document provides precise instructions concerning the quantities of grain or flour for such offerings. The *minḥâ* consists of a tenth of an ephah of fine meal *(sōleṯ)* for a lamb offering, two tenths for a ram offering, and three tenths for a bull offering (cf. Nu. 15:1-15; 28; 29).

It should be pointed out that, in contrast to the usual interpretation, this *sōleṯ* does not strictly speaking mean "fine flour," but rather "meal," i.e., ground, pulverized grain (cf. Akk. *siltu* and Bab. *Šabb.* 74b: *slt slty,* "cut into pieces, cut evenly"; cf. Akk. *salātu*), which — one assumed — was more finely sifted than flour and contained no husks.[44]

---

41. Cf. *AP,* 30.21, 25; 31.21; 32.9; 33.10f.; cf. also Vogt, 107.
42. *BM* 92699; E. Sollberger, "Two Kassite Votive Inscriptions," *JAOS,* 88 (1968), 191-95.
43. J. Nougayrol, "Textes Religieux (I)," *RA,* 65 (1971), 162, 3.
44. See recently J. Milgrom, *Leviticus 1–16. AB* 3 (1991), 179.

In his temple vision, Ezekiel mentions other quantities for the *minḥâ:* "one ephah for a ram, one ephah for a bull, and for a lamb as much as he has at hand" (Ezk. 46:4; cf. 45:24). The determination of such recipes for the preparation of ritual sacrifices is also regulated in Mesopotamia: "three sheep . . . three *ṣimid*-measures *(= s^eʾîm)* of grain."[45] The proportions of grain/flour per animal sacrifice derive from current customs at the court or among the populace for the preparation of meals and feasts. Accordingly, Abraham prepares as a hospitality meal for his guests one calf and three measures *(s^eʾîm)* of meal *(sōleṯ)* (Gen. 18:6f.). Similarly, a list for deliveries to soldiers found at Ugarit reads: "one lamb and a *lth̩* of flour."[46] One *lth̩* (cf. Heb. *lēṯeḵ,* Hos. 3:2) corresponds roughly to one tenth of an ephah (2.2 l. [2.3 qt.]),[47] which in Israel accompanied a lamb offering.

2. *Designation of Time.* Since the *minḥâ* together with frankincense constituted the high point of the sacrificial ritual, namely, the presentation of the "pleasing fragrance" *(rêaḥ nîḥôaḥ),* the time of this offering was viewed as the most favorable time of the day. Thus Elijah offers his prayer to God at the time of the *minḥâ* offering *(baʿ^alôṯ hamminḥâ,* 1 K. 18:36), and his prayer is answered (vv. 38f.). Ps. 141:2 also attests that the hour of the *minḥâ* and of the incense offering was viewed as the most favorable time of the day: "Let my prayer be counted as incense before thee, and the lifting up of my hands as an evening *minḥâ.*" In fact, the expression "favorable time" is itself attested in the Psalms: "But as for me, my prayer is to thee, Yahweh, at a favorable time *(ʿēṯ rāṣôn).* O God, in the abundance of thy steadfast love, with thy faithful help answer me" (Ps. 69:14[13]). This verse is recited in the synagogue at the *minḥâ* prayer on the Sabbath,[48] a tradition that seems to go back very far. Here, too, the petitioner uses the formula *ʿ^anēnî,* "answer me," which goes back to Elijah's evening prayer. It is of further significance that the prayer of fasting days "*ʿ^anēnî*" is recited only in connection with the *minḥâ* prayer.[49] The burning of incense offerings within the context of liturgy is also reflected in Isaiah's inaugural vision (Isa. 6). The angels' trisagion is accompanied by the filling of the temple with smoke, directly recalling the smoke ascending from the incense altar (v. 6). Solomon's prayer of consecration in 1 K. 8:12ff. should probably also be understood against this background (cf. the description of the cloud in the temple in vv. 10f.), namely, as a prayer accompanied by an incense offering (cf. Lev. 16:2,13).

The literature from the period of the Second Temple as well as rabbinic writings richly attest this understanding of the time of the *minḥâ* as the appropriate time for prayer. It is said that Ezra offered his penitential prayer (in connection with the problem of mixed marriages) at the time of the evening *minḥâ* (Ezr. 9:5); similarly, the angel Gabriel reveals

---

45. T. G. Pinches, *The Babylonian Tablets of the Berens Collection* (London, 1915), 110, 8.
46. *KTU,* 4.751.
47. Cf. Heltzer.
48. Cf. I. Elbogen, *Der jüdische Gottesdienst in seiner geschichtlichen Entwicklung* (Leipzig, 1913), 118.
49. *Ibid.,* 55.

himself at just this time to Daniel (Dnl. 9:21) or to the priest Zechariah (Lk. 1:9f.). As was the custom, the people prayed "outside the house of God" while the priests presented the incense offering. This is picked up in a regulation in the Mishnah (*Tamid* vi.3; *Kelim* i.9), according to which the people were not permitted to enter the area between the porch and the altar *(byn h'wlm wlmzbḥ)* while the priest presented the incense offering. The people assembled in the outer court *(ʿ^{a}zārâ)* for prayer. Finally, Judith prays in the house of God at the time of the evening *minḥâ* (Jth. 9:1).

It is said that the Hasmonean high priest John Hyrcanus received his revelation at the time of the incense offering (Josephus *Ant.* xiii.282f.).

The Targum understood the various references to incense and offering fragrance in Cant. 4:11-16 as if they were referring to the incense offering in the temple, whereby the priests and people prayed: "May God, my beloved, enter the temple and readily accept the offerings of his people" (Targ. to vv. 11,16). The blessing of Isaac in Gen. 27:27f. ("Ah, the smell of my son is like the smell of a field that Yahweh has blessed") was similarly interpreted with an eye on the incense offering in the temple (cf. further the apocryphal Life of Adam and Eve 29; *T. Levi* 3:5f.).[50]

All these examples illuminate the rabbinic designation "*minḥâ* prayer" *(t^{e}pillaṯ minḥâ)* as the afternoon prayer. Although the *minḥâ* was also presented in the morning as a cereal offering, the actual time of prayer was associated with the evening offering at which the people were assembled. This *minḥâ* worship took place at the ninth hour (3 p.m.), when the evening offering, the cereal offering, and the incense offering were presented (cf. Mishnah *Pesaḥ.* v.1; Acts 3:1; 10:3,30).

Ezra's penitential prayer (Ezr. 9:5) showed that the time of the *minḥâ* was also the most appropriate time for confession, a custom continued later. On the eve of the Day of Atonement the confession of sin was spoken shortly before darkness (*ʿm ḥškh;* Tosefta *Kippurim* iv.14). A similar confession over the tithe was spoken at the *minḥâ* offering at the Passover Festival (Mishnah *Maʿaś. Š.* v.10; cf. Lev. 2). The Talmud also sees in *minḥâ* the appropriate time for prayer *(bʿy rḥmy)* (cf. Bab. *Taʿan.* 12b and *passim*). Midrash Psalms even views the confession of sin and the *minḥâ* prayer as the continuation of the presentation of the burnt offering in the period without temple and priest.[51]

Weinfeld

VI. Qumran. In the writings of Qumran the term *minḥâ* occurs quite frequently. Although the term appears only 4 times in writings concerned with the community rule (twice each in 1QS and CD) and is picked up in a few fragments from 4Q with clear invocation of OT sacrificial terminology (cf. 4QDibHam 4:10; 4QOrd 12:2; 4Q508 (4QPrFêtes^{b}) 9:1; cf. also 11QPs^{a} 18:8), the Temple scroll uses it over 40 times. The Aramaic 1QapGen contains 2 occurrences (21:2,20) referring to Abraham's sacrifices. The occurrences within the context of the community rule are characteristic for the

---

50. → לבונה *l^{e}ḇônâ* (VII, 441-47).

51. Cf. A. Jellinek, בית המדרש: *Sammlung kleiner Midraschim und vermischter Abhandlungen aus der älteren jüdischen Literatur* (Jerusalem, 1967), IV, 104ff. [Heb.; Ger. intro.).

Qumran-Essenic understanding of sacrifice. 1QS 9:5 speaks of heave offerings of the lips (= prayer), interpreted as *niḏbaṯ minḥaṯ rāṣôn,* a "delectable freewill offering." The spiritualization of the cult evidenced here[52] is also attested in CD 11:21: The animal sacrifice of the wicked is an abomination, but the prayer of the just is an agreeable *minḥâ.* In 11QT we encounter the linguistic usage of P virtually unchanged: through suffixes the *minḥâ* is self-evidently and consistently referred to more comprehensive sacrifices. Qumran attests both "morning" (11QT 13:15) and "evening" *minḥâ* (17:7). Noteworthy is the consistent combination of the *minḥâ* with the drink offering (cf. 11QT 15:9; 16:18; 17:14; 20:8f. 22:3,7; 23:5,17; 24:5,8; 25:6,14; 28:11). Specifications of content also correspond to P (1QT 11:11; 34:12 wheat flour; 20:10 mixed with frankincense).

Fabry

52. Cf. G. Klinzing, *Die Umdeutung des Kultus in der Qumrangemeinde und im NT. StUNT,* 7 (1971), 64ff.

מָנַע *mānaʿ*

Contents: I. Etymology and Range. II. 1. Distribution in the OT; 2. Meaning, Synonyms, Antonyms; 3. Sirach; 4. LXX; 5. Qumran. III. OT Usage: 1. Secular Sphere; 2. Religious Sphere; 3. Theological Contexts.

I. Etymology and Range. Attestations for this root clearly point to the West[1] and South Semitic spheres. It occurs once in a Ya'udic curse formula[2]: May the God Hadad "keep sleep away" from the enemy (*lmnʿ;* the precative particle *l* as a Canaanism). The only attestation in Official Aramaic is found in Ahikar 136: "Do not despise that which is your lot, nor covet some great thing which is withheld from you" *(zy ymnʿ mnk)* (cf. Ps. 131:1), using *mnʿ* in the peal imperfect, to be translated as an internal passive,[3] a forerunner of the "divine passive" of late Hebrew.

The root is probably already attested in Canaanite. In one letter from the Amarna period[4] we read in the upper margin *a-na minim [t]a-me-na ú-nu-tu,* "why do you withhold our utensils?" The meaning of the root *mnʿ* is secured by the antithesis of *tu-ud-da-nu-n[a],* "may they be given over" (l. 21).

The same meaning is exhibited by Mand. *mna II,* "to keep away, withhold,"[5] and

1. *DISO,* 159.
2. *KAI,* 214, 24.
3. J. M. Lindenberger, *The Aramaic Proverbs of Ahiqar* (Baltimore, 1983), 133 with n. 412.
4. G. Wilhelm, "Ein Brief der Amarna-Zeit aus Kāmid el-Lōz (KL 72:600)," *ZA,* 29[63] (1973), 75.
5. *MdD,* 274b.

Talmudic *mn'*, "prevent, hold back, hinder,"[6] whereas Syr. *män'*, "to come through, arrive at; to come to, become,"[7] has already distanced itself semantically.

In contrast, the South Semitic languages have preserved the fundamental meaning, as in OSA Sabaean *mn'*, "to defend (militarily), hold back, restrain"[8] (par. *ḏ'*, "bring low, defeat," *ṯbr,* "break into pieces," and *'ḫrn,* "remove";[9] however, cf. the semantically progressive adj. *manī'*, "mighty, noble, excellent"). In Sabaean, Safaitic, and Liḥyanite personal names the root occurs apparently with the meaning "to protect."[10] In Arabic *mana'a,* "to stop, detain, keep from entering or passing,"[11] also occurs in many nominal forms: *man'a,* "resistance," *manā'a,* "inaccessibility," *mumāna'a,* "opposition," etc.

In Ethiopic the root occurs only in Tigre *man^{e}'a,* "to withhold, refuse," and *man^{e}'āy^{e}t,* "that which is refused."[12] In rabbinic writing *māna'* tends to be used in connection with the terminology of abstinence, especially in connection with the Nazirite vows of abstinence.[13]

II. 1. *Distribution in the OT.* The root *mn'* occurs 29 times in the OT (25 times in the qal, 4 the niphal). The oldest occurrences derive from the early monarchy (Nu. 22:16; 24:11 [J];[14] Prov. 11:26; Gen. 30:2 [E]); undetermined preexilic occurrences (once in Amos, 6 times in Jeremiah, 4 times in Proverbs, twice in the Psalms) and exilic-postexilic occurrences (4 times in the Deuteronomistic history, Job; once in Ezekiel, Joel, Ecclesiastes, Nehemiah). God is the subject 13 times (including *passivum divinum,* Jer. 3:3; Joel 1:13; Job 38:15), twice the king, 13 times a person, and once a person's sins (Jer. 5:25).

Syntactic combinations are unremarkable: the object is added asyndetically or with *'eṯ,* the *dativus incommodi* is designated either by suffixes or, in most cases, by *min* or *l^{e}* (Ps. 84:12[Eng. v. 11]).[15]

2. *Meaning, Synonyms, Antonyms.* The semantic scope of this verb extends from "hold back" to "withhold something from someone, deny a person something," to "restrain someone, keep someone away from."[16] The original meaning may be "to withhold" in the sense of a denial of possession.

The most comprehensive synonym is *kālā',* then also *'āṣar,* → חשׂך *ḥāśaḵ,* and *'āṣal;*

6. *WTM,* III, 159.

7. *LexSyr,* 395.

8. ContiRossini, 179a.

9. *CIH,* 573, 5 = Ja 853 A/5, B/5, C/5, D/4, E/5, F/5; cf. A. Jamme, *Sabaean Inscriptions from Maḥram Bilqîs (Mârib)* (Baltimore, 1962), 269ff.

10. *RyNP,* 1, 128f.

11. Wehr (^{4}1979), 1087; Lane, 3024f.

12. *TigrWb,* 129.

13. Citations in *WTM,* III, 159.

14. W. Gross, *Bileam. StANT,* 38 (1974), 427 and *passim,* considers this a part of nonsource unit I.

15. Cf. *HAL,* II (1995), 508.

16. *HAL,* II, 602.

individual aspects are covered by *ṣāpan,* "to hide," with the undertone "to lie in wait," *'āḇar* hiphil, *sûr min* hiphil, and *rāḥaq* hiphil, "keep far away, remove" (primarily in the spatial sense), *nw'* hiphil, "to hinder, prevent," *šûḇ* hiphil, and others, "to hold back,"[17] and *nzr* niphal, although only with the semantic implication "to abstain from" (cf. the rabbinic usage of *māna'*). The antonyms of *māna'* derive first from the semantic field "to bring near" (*qāraḇ* hiphil, *bô'* hiphil), then "to give" (*nāṯan, šā'al* hiphil, *pwq* hiphil), "to bestow" *(śîm* hiphil, *šāpaṯ),* "to pour out" (*nāsaḵ* hiphil, *rûm* hiphil), "to lead astray" (*ṯ'h* hiphil, *swt* hiphil, *ndh* hiphil, *nś', pth* piel, *šûḇ* polel), and *dibber,* "to speak readily," *'ānâ,* "to answer," as an antonym to "withholding a response" (Jer. 42:4).

3. *Sirach.* Sirach attests *mn'* 9 times, exclusively in the qal. In all instances the subject is a person. The Greek rendering varies enormously.

4. *LXX.* In its own rendering, the LXX uses 23 different verbs: the dominant ones include *apokōlýein* (5 times), *ap/an/epéchein* (5 times), *aph/exaírein* (3 times), *aphysterein* (twice), as well as *krýptein, ókneiṇ,* and others.

5. *Qumran.* The root *mn'* has thus far been attested only twice in Qumran. 11QtgJob 18:9 (text?) cites Job 31:16; and in 11QPs^a 24 (a Hebrew version of an apocryphal psalm long familiar in Syriac[18]) — an individual lament — the psalmist petitions: "Incline your ear and grant to me what I ask, and that which I am petitioning may you not withhold from me" (v. 5 *wbqšty 'l tmn' mmny*).[19] The Syriac text replaces *mn'* with the synonym *kl'* (cf. Ps. 84:12[11]; Job 31:16).

III. OT Usage. 1. *Secular Sphere.* In the secular sphere *māna'* in the first instance means "to keep someone away from something" or "to withhold something from someone," whereby the semantic aspect of the etymon fully resonates. This notion of withholding is understood primarily as the non-granting of things to which the addressee in any event has no recognizable legal claims. The king can grant or withhold his daughter from a suitor (2 S. 13:13). The vassal can preempt even greater misfortune for himself and his country by not refusing to pay tribute to the stronger party (1 K. 20:7). Older proverbial wisdom already formulates the phenomenon of ingratitude toward the politically and economically perspicacious person: "The people curse him who holds back *(mn')* grain, but a blessing is on the head of him who sells it" (Prov. 11:26; a different view is taken by Helmer Ringgren,[20] who sees the virtues of generosity and compassion to be the focal point here; the purely mercantile *šāḇar* in v. 26b, however, militates against this view). For the sphere of instruction the axiom is offered that one should not withhold discipline

17. → שׁוּב *šûḇ.*
18. Cf. M. Noth, "Die fünf syrisch überlieferten apokryphen Psalmen," *ZAW,* 48 (1930), 1-23.
19. Cf. J. A. Sanders, *The Psalms Scroll of Qumrân Cave 11 (11QPs^a). DJD,* IV, 70f.
20. *Sprüche. ATD,* XVI/1 (^{3}1980), *in loc.*

(mûsār)[21] from a child (Prov. 23:13), a clear reference to corporeal punishment, as v. 13b unmistakably shows.[22]

A similar counsel might be found in Sir. 4:23 (MS A) if Tadeusz Penar[23] is correct in pointing *'l tmn' dbr b'wlm* in the text to *be'ûlîm:* "Do not withhold your maxim from *children,* and do not hide your wisdom." According to MS C, however, the intention of the text seems to point in another direction: its *b'ytw,* "at the proper time,"[24] suggests the presence of *be'ôlām* for MS A, so that the text offers a general exhortation to be helpful: "Never remain silent (when a word might put things right)."[25]

Otherwise the expression "to hold back/withhold words" means a limitation of the full message and a violation of the obligation to truth; the reverse, however, "not to withhold words," does not simply mean the correct status of the message and of the obligation to truth, but rather can — especially in the mouth of a prophet — constitute a radical intensification, namely: merciless frankness. Thus Jeremiah will withhold nothing in the situation immediately preceding the fall of Jerusalem (Jer. 42:4). In so doing, he not only meets his own obligation over against the word of God — it needs no special explication — but he will also not attempt to make the message more bearable by couching it in some deft formulation. The listeners' answer (vv. 5f.) shows that they are prepared for anything.

The term *māna'* elsewhere means "to hold back oneself (or someone) from a certain action": from undertaking a journey (Nu. 22:16), going barefoot (Jer. 2:25), and weeping (Jer. 31:16). Precisely as an expression of self-limitation (and its absence) the term *māna'* occurs appropriately in hedonistically colored proverbs: "And whatever my eyes desired I did not keep from them *('āṣal);* I kept my heart from no pleasure *(lō' māna'tî)*" (Eccl. 2:10). At a critical distance from traditional solutions of wisdom, Qoheleth views joy as the best portion human beings have in life.[26] Thus he sees no sense in ascetic self-limitation over against such joy, although he also knows that ultimately it, too, is merely breath, or vanity[27] (Eccl. 2:1f.,11). In Sir. 14:14, the classical formulation of the hedonistic imperative of Aristippus resonates: "Do not deprive yourself of a day's enjoyment; do not let your share of desired good pass by you."

Penar[28] incorrectly views the morality of correct payment as the focal point here ("do not withhold a part of daily pay"), since the meaning of *ṭôḇâ* may not be stretched to include "daily pay." All work and all renunciation ultimately benefit someone else (Sir. 14:4,15; cf. Sir. 11:18f.; Prov. 11:24; cf. also Homer *Odyssey* i.248, 375, and

---

21. → יסר *yāsar* (VI, 127-134).

22. On the problem of corporeal and verbal punishment, cf. L. Dürr, *Das Erziehungswesen im AT und im Alten Orient. MVÄG,* 36/2 (1932), esp. 114ff.; M. Sæbø, "יסר *jsr* züchtigen," *THAT,* I, 738-742; R. D. Branson, → מסר *mûsār,* VI, 131f.

23. *Northwest Semitic Philology and the Hebrew Fragments of Ben Sira. BietOr,* 28 (1975), 16f.

24. Cf. H. P. Rüger, *Text und Textform im hebräischen Sirach. BZAW,* 112 (1970), 34.

25. J. G. Snaith, *Ecclesiasticus, or the Wisdom of Jesus Son of Sirach. CBC* (1974), 28.

26. Cf. O. Loretz, *Qohelet und der alte Orient* (Freiburg, 1964), 244f.

27. → הבל *heḇel (hebhel)* (III, 313-320).

28. P. 44.

passim). It is unclear whether Sir. 35:3 (MS B), "Speak, you who are older, for it is your right, but with accurate knowledge, and do not interrupt the music *('l tmn' šyr),*" also belongs in this hedonistic context.

2. *Religious Sphere.* Within religious contexts *māna'* frequently appears in connection with social themes. Eliphaz sees one cause of Job's misfortune in his allegedly asocial behavior, namely, that he gave no water to the thirsty and "withheld" (*māna',* Job 22:7) bread from the hungry. In an extensive oath of purgation[29] Job rejects this accusation: he never withheld anything that the poor[30] desired (Job 31:16), whereby that which is desired[31] goes beyond what is actually necessary[32] (cf. Sir. 4:3; 41:19), meaning that Job more than fulfilled his social obligation. This social obligation is generalized as early as in proverbial wisdom: a person should willingly support not only the poor, but anyone in need of something (Prov. 3:27). Sirach also reflects on this axiom, expressing it in various formulations, e.g., "Give graciously to all the living, and withhold not *ḥesed* even from the dead" (Sir. 7:33; but cf. 12:1-6); or: "Give to the good person, but refuse the sinner" (Sir. 12:4,7).

Sir. 7:21 invokes a complex legal background: "Do not withhold from him [the slave] his freedom *(ḥwpš).*" On the one hand, this exhortation refers to the legally prescribed emancipation of slaves in the Sabbath and Jubilee Year[33] (Ex. 21:2;[34] Dt. 15:12), although there is evidence of an extension to include non-Hebrew slaves as well;[35] on the other hand, the first half-verse, "love like yourself an intelligent slave," is able to generalize the emancipation of slaves into a fundamental humanitarian directive independent of any legal prescription.

Only twice does *māna'* occur in ethical contexts. Prov. 1:15 admonishes to hold back one's foot from the path of sinners and not to walk in the way with them (v. 15a), nor to give in to their enticements (v. 10). Zophar (Job 20:12-14) vividly characterizes the wicked *(rāšā')* and perverse person *(ḥānēp)* who holds wickedness like candy under his tongue, i.e., who gleefully lets it dissolve on his tongue. Yet during such enjoyment it turns to poison.

3. *Theological Contexts.* The OT text also recounts that Yahweh variously withholds things from human beings. The oldest occurrence is found in Gen. 30:2. This verse, which occurs in the context of what is primarily a Yahwistic narrative concerning the birth and naming of the sons of Jacob, has often been attributed to E on account of the

---

29. On the analogous "negative confession" in the Egyptian Book of the Dead (ch. 125), cf. R. Kilian, "Apodiktisches und kasuistisches Recht im Licht ägyptischer Analogien," *BZ,* N.S. 7 (1963), 185-202.

30. → דל *dal* (III, 208-230).

31. → חפץ *ḥāpēṣ* (V, 92-107).

32. → שאל *šā'al.*

33. Cf. R. North, → דרור *d^erôr,* II.2 (III, 267f.).

34. → חפשי *ḥopšî* (V, 114-18).

35. Cf. Snaith, 45.

divine name ("Am I in the place of Elohim, who has withheld from you the fruit of the womb?");[36] Claus Westermann,[37] however, with good reason sees J at work here as well. Now, since Yahweh has "withheld" the fruit of the womb, Rachel views adoption ("to bear upon the knees") the only possibility of having her "own" children.

Yahweh's withholding especially of the gifts of nature is a component of prophetic proclamation of judgment. Yahweh withholds rain (Am. 4:7; Jer. 3:3) in order to chastise his people. He restrains rivers so that the cosmos mourns (Ezk. 31:15). He also withholds (divine passive) cereal and drink offerings from his temple in order to lead his people to genuine repentance (Joel 1:13). According to Job 38:15, he withholds the morning light from the wicked, which Georg Fohrer[38] takes as a reference to a positive outcome to legal proceedings. Finally, Yahweh can indirectly withhold blessing when a person's own sins erect a divisive barrier between himself and God (Jer. 5:25).

Everywhere, however, the believer trusts in Yahweh's succor. The early preexilic[39] liturgy of the temple gates[40] recognizes that God withholds no good thing from those who walk uprightly (Ps. 84:12[11]; cf. 11QPs[a] 24). The king, too, could rely on a special measure of certainty that God would indeed answer him, so that Yahweh "has not withheld the request of his lips" (Ps. 21:3[2]). Finally, the people itself confesses in a postexilic atonement service that Yahweh, despite the people's own disobedience during the exodus, did not withhold the manna, but rather granted them food in abundance (Neh. 9:20). The faithful Agur amplifies his petition for honesty and contentedness in life with the following entreaty to Yahweh: *'al-timna' mimmennî b^{e}ṭerem 'āmûṯ* (Prov. 30:7), "Do not deny them to me before I die."

God sovereignly guides human plans and action. This occurs not only in the form of positive guidance, but also — as the David-Nabal narrative shows — when God deftly restrains him from evil (*māna',* 1 S. 25:26,34) and keeps him back from blood guilt (v. 39).[41] To show this paradigmatically, the Deuteronomistic historian expands his source in 1 S. 25: Whereas the basic stratum emphasizes the origin and character of Queen Abigail,[42] the Deuteronomistic historian recasts the story into a paradigm showing how God used Abigail as an instrument to preserve the anointed from blood guilt.[43] Even if one follows Hans Joachim Stoebe[44] and takes issue on the basis of source and transmission-historical considerations with Hans-Ulrich Nübel's (and also

36. E.g., H. Gunkel, *Genesis. HAT,* I (1917); O. Eissfeldt, "Jakob-Lea und Jakob-Rahel (Gen 29, 16-30,24; 35,16-20)," *Gottes Wort und Gottes Land. Festschrift H. W. Hertzberg* (Göttingen, 1965), 50-55.

37. *Genesis 12–36* (Eng. trans., Minneapolis, 1985), 472.

38. G. Fohrer, *Das Buch Hiob. KAT,* XVI (1963), 504.

39. H.-J. Kraus, *Psalms 60–150* (Eng. trans., Minneapolis, 1989), 167.

40. H. Schmidt, *Die Psalmen. HAT,* I/15 (1934), 160.

41. → חשׂך *ḥāśaḵ,* V, 224-28, esp. 227f.

42. Cf. J. H. Grønbæk, *Die Geschichte von Aufsteig Davids. Acta Theol. Danica,* 10 (Ger. trans. 1971), 170-75.

43. → דם *dām* (III, 234-250); cf. H.-U. Nübel, *Davids Aufstieg in der frühe israelitischen Geschichtsschreibung* (diss., Bonn, 1959), 51ff.

44. *Das erste Buch Samuelis. KAT,* VIII/1 (1973), 454.

Timo Veijola's[45]) literary-critical differentiation, this does not address the real intention of the story: a confession of faith in Yahweh's solicitude for his anointed and the idealization of David.[46]

Fabry

45. *Das Königtum in der Beurteilung der deuteronomistischen Historiographie. AnAcScFen,* B, 198 (1977).
46. Cf. further K.-H. Bernhardt, *Das Problem der altorientalischen Königsideologie im AT. SVT,* 8 (1961), 120.

מַס *mas;* סֵבֶל *sēḇel*

Contents: I. Etymology; Related Expressions in the Ancient Near East. II. 1. Slavery in Egypt; 2. *mas ʿōḇēḏ.* III. Occurrences and Understanding of *mas* in the OT. IV. Postexilic and Extrabiblical Occurrences. V. Summary.

I. Etymology; Related Expressions in the Ancient Near East. The word *mas* is of unknown origin. According to Martin Noth,[1] it derives "perhaps" from Egyp. *ms,* "to bring." J. A. Montgomery[2] associates it with OSA *mnšʾ,* "gift, present."[3] Although compulsory labor was common in Egypt, it cannot be associated with a particular word.[4]

Akk. *massu,* "person liable for service,"[5] occurs primarily as a loanword in Alalakh around 1700 B.C.[6] A later occurrence from Alalakh (*ca.* 1500) mentions two *LÚ mas*

mas. P. Artzi, "סֵבֶל," *EMiqr,* V (1968), 995f.; *idem,* "*Sablum* = סבל," *BIES,* 18 (1954), 66-70; A. M. Bakir, *Slavery in Pharaonic Egypt. ASAE Sup.,* 18 (1952), 14-40; A. Biram, "מס עובד (Corvée)," *Tarbiz,* 23 (1952), 137-142 [Heb.]; D. G. Evans, "The Incidence of Labour-Service in the Old-Babylonian Period," *JAOS,* 83 (1963), 20-26; Z. Falk, *Hebrew Law in Biblical Times* (Jerusalem, 1964), 117-122; M. Haran, "The Gibeonites, the Nethinim and the Sons of Solomon's Servants," *VT,* 11 (1961), 159-161; M. Held, "The Root *ZBL/SBL* in Akkadian, Ugaritic and Biblical Hebrew," *JAOS,* 88 (1968), 90-96; D. Künstlinger, "I. עֲדֵי אֹבֵד. II. לְמַס עֹבֵד," *OLZ,* 34 (1931), 609-612; B. Levine, "The Netînîm," *JBL,* 82 (1963), 207-212; I. Mendelsohn, "State Slavery in Ancient Palestine," *BASOR,* 85 (1942), 14-17; *idem,* "On Corvée Labor in Ancient Canaan and Israel," *BASOR,* 167 (1962), 31-35; T. N. D. Mettinger, *Solomonic State Officials, CB,* 5 (1971), 128-139; A. Rainey, "מַס עֹבֵד," *EMiqr,* V (1968), 55f.; *idem,* "Compulsory Labour Gangs in Ancient Israel," *IEJ,* 20 (1970), 191-202; G. Sauer, "Fronarbeit," *BHHW,* I (1962), 502; M. Weber, *Ancient Judaism* (Eng. trans., New York, 1952), 55, 59, 256.

1. *Könige 1-16. BK,* IX/1 (^{2}1983), 212.
2. "Some Hebrew Etymologies," *JQR,* 25 (1934-35), 267.
3. ContiRossini, 191; cf. Ethiop. *měnšāʾ,* "dues, levy."
4. Bakir.
5. *AHw,* II (1972), 619.
6. Mettinger, 130.

āli among the *ḫabiru.* In addition, the word is found once in Amarna[7] in reference to workers who receive their "wages" (or more likely "rations," although only four months out of the year) like other employees.[8] In Old Babylonian *massu* can be compared with *muškēnum.*[9] "Forced labor" in conjunction with watering was the only way agriculture was possible.

Ugaritic does not attest *ms;* as a synonym for New Babylonian *pilku,* "feudal obligation,"[10] and Old Babylonian *ilku,* "obligatory service for land allotment,"[11] the term *ỉnṯ* is used.[12] In contrast, Reuven Yaron[13] associates *ỉnṯ* with *'ᵃḥuzzâ* in Josh. 22:4.

II. 1. *Slavery in Egypt.* The term *mas* refers to "compulsory service," a kind of labor to which a person is "forced" without it constituting "slavery" in the formal sense. The only Hebrew word for slavery, however, is also used to refer to normal, voluntary work;[14] only the combination *bêṯ ʿᵃḇāḏîm* unmistakably refers to slavery (Ex. 20:2 par. Dt. 5:6 and 11 further occurrences), the designation for the Israelites' compulsory service in Egypt, which is usually called *siḇlōṯ* (Ex. 1:11; 2:11; 5:4f.; 6:6f.). Only once, and then indirectly, is there mention of *missîm* overseers (Ex. 1:11).

2. *mas ʿōḇēḏ.* The expression *mas ʿōḇēḏ* occurs 3 times; despite attempts to interpret this as an expression for particularly hard compulsory labor for non-Israelites,[15] it is only a synonym for *mas,*[16] for Josh. 16:10 (likewise the substance of Jgs. 1:30) with *ʿōḇēḏ* is identical with Josh. 17:13 par. Jgs. 1:28,(33,35) without *ʿōḇēḏ,* and refers to the somewhat theoretical fate of the tribes whose areas were conquered but who were not annihilated.[17] The reference is thus to groups among the Canaanite population who were subjected to compulsory service after the conquest of their areas; according to T. N. D. Mettinger,[18] the prerequisites for this were not given until the time of David. According to the Deuteronomic laws of war (Dt. 20:11; cf. 11QT 62:8), this is the procedure to be followed regarding places which capitulate without resistance, whereas

7. EA, 365; F. Thureau-Dangin, "Nouvelles lettres d'el-amarna," *RA,* 19 (1922), 97f.; A. Rainey, *El Amarna Tablets* 359-379. *AOAT,* 8 (^{2}1978), 81.

8. On this letter, cf. also A. Alt, "Neues über Palästina aus dem Archiv Amenophis' IV," *KlSchr,* III (1959), 169-174.

9. Evans, 23, who distinguishes the classification by age (of young men and women) regarding *guruš.*

10. *AHw,* II, 863.

11. *AHw,* I (1965), 371f.

12. *WUS,* no. 325; Hurrian loanword? = Akk. *unuššu, AHw,* III (1981), 1422; cf. J. Nougayrol, *PRU,* I, 226; a different view is taken by I. M. Diakonoff, "A Babylonian Political Pamphlet from about 700 B.C.," Festschrift B. Landsberger. AS, 16 (1965), 345.

13. "A Document of Redemption from Ugarit," *VT,* 10 (1960), 88.

14. Sauer.

15. Haran, 163; Mettinger, 129.

16. According to Rainey, the expression consists of a Canaanite term with a Hebrew gloss; cf. Biram, 138.

17. → חרם *ḥērem* (V, 180-199).

18. P. 133.

a different procedure is prescribed for "cities far away," whereby the expression "far" in Dt. 20:15 probably does not refer to expansionist conquests outside Canaan, but is alluding rather to the cunning of the Gibeonites in Josh. 9:6.[19]

Since in 1 K. 9:21 *mas-ʿōḇēḏ* is followed by the prepositional phrase "to this day," a longer period of compulsory service might be implied, although it hardly represents, as David Künstlinger believes with reference to Nu. 24:20,24, a variant of *'bd* = Arab. *'abadan,* "for ever." The parallel 2 Ch. 8:8 has the simple *mas,* as does the comparable passage 1 K. 9:15. The term *ʿeḇeḏ* is again the key word in the postexilic continuation of this institution.[20]

III. Occurrences and Understanding of mas in the OT.

1. The Israelites despised their own *mas* in Egypt and considered their deliverance from it to be Yahweh's greatest act in history. The fact that Israel itself was once a slave *(ʿeḇeḏ)* serves in Deuteronomy as the reason for the humane treatment of the → גור *gēr* (Dt. 15:15; 16:12; 24:18,22). This view stands over against the endorsement of compulsory service in Joshua-Judges. No such endorsement is evident for genuine compulsory labor under David (2 S. 20:24; 1 Ch. 22:2) or Solomon (1 K. 9:20f. par. 2 Ch. 8:8, where peculiarly "Canaanites" are not mentioned among the peoples obligated to service). This *mas* is, however, portrayed as requisite for the completion of the temple.

The *mas* organization carried out by Solomon is reproved beforehand in 1 S. 8:11 (despite Isaac Mendelsohn's attempt[21] to interpret this as feudalism operative during the period of Samuel — the reference to Ugar. *msm* is based on a misreading [*msm* for *mdm*]). The negative estimation of Solomon is doubtlessly based to a large extent on the fact that he did not pay the workers for constructing his palace (Jer. 22:13 alludes to this). However, no biblical author rejects *mas* for good and necessary purposes, and for this reason J. A. Wainwright[22] believes one should not associate the character of "forced labor" with *mas,* and should refer instead to the work of unskilled laborers to which one can assign a neutral ethical character.

Probably, however, Solomon's *mas* stands opposed to the divine will insofar as it also — or even primarily — affected the Israelites themselves (1 K. 5:27[13] = LXX 5:27 with *phóros*[23]). This is not obviated by the remark that Solomon never used Israelites as slaves (*ʿeḇeḏ,* 1 K. 9:22), if one does not insert *mas* here with *BHK*³ — not *BHS;* nor by 2 Ch. 8:9, if one does not eliminate *'ᵃšer* with *BHK*³ and *BHS.* It was probably only in Deuteronomistic wishful thinking that the Israelites were exempted from *mas.*[24]

---

19. Cf. A. Rofé, "The Laws of War in Deuteronomy," *Zion,* 39 (1974), 143-156 [Heb.], XXII [Eng. summary].
20. See IV.1 below.
21. *BASOR,* 85, 15.
22. "Zoser's Pyramid and Solomon's Temple," *ExpT,* 91 (1979/1980), 137-140.
23. See IV.2 below.
24. R. de Vaux, *AncIsr,* 141f.

Disapproval of the Solomonic system of compulsory service is also evidenced by the stoning of the *mas* overseer Ado(ni)ram (2 S. 20:24; 1 K. 12:18).[25] One must remember, however, that the strict condemnation of the "sins of Jeroboam" (1 K. 15:30, etc.; 20 times) ignores the fact that he was an opponent of every abuse of the *mas* (1 K. 11:28, which does, however, use the term *sēḇel,* which according to Mettinger is a northern Israelite synonym for *mas;* cf. Mari *sablum*[26]). The final example of compulsory service is recounted under Asa (1 K. 15:22).

2. Several other occurrences of *mas* should be mentioned here. According to Gen. 49:15, the Israelite tribe of Issachar was subjected to forced labor in Canaan, a condition interpreted as the demeaning consequence of its passivity.[27] The condition of *mas* is presented in a generalized fashion as the consequence of defeat in war (Isa. 31:8; Lam. 1:1). According to Prov. 12:24, the slothful person must resort to compulsory labor in order to earn his livelihood.

IV. Postexilic and Extrabiblical Occurrences.

1. The "sons of Solomon's slaves *(ʿbd)*" in Neh. 11:3 (cf. 7:57,60 par. Ezr. 2:55,58) are mentioned together with the *nᵉṯînîm.* The expression "*mas ʿōḇēḏ* to this day" in 1 K. 9:21 serves as an etiological explanation for their presence.[28] The *nᵉṯînîm* represent in the Talmud the temple *mas,* while the "Gibeonites" stand for the state *mas*.

2. The LXX consistently renders *mas* with *phóros,* which here does not mean "tax" as it does in the NT.[29] However, in the Talmud and in Modern Hebrew *mas* also takes on this meaning, allegedly on the basis of Est. 10:1,[30] although there it is probably a case of misunderstanding a decree concerning compulsory labor.[31]

V. Summary. What emerges is thus a general biblical view that work is good in and of itself and a necessary component of human life, even when it is "mobilized by force" for worthy, although not private purposes: here the danger of misuse arises, which must be countered.

North

---

25. On this name, see Mettinger, 133.
26. See Artzi.
27. G. von Rad, *Genesis. OTL* (Eng. trans., 1961) *in loc.*
28. J. Liver, "The Literary History of Joshua X," *JSS,* 8 (1963), 233.
29. K. Weiss, "φόρος," *TDNT,* IX, 80.
30. D. Daube, "The Last Chapter of Esther," *JQR,* 37 (1947), 140; Rainey, *EMiqr,* V, 55f.
31. H. Bardtke, *Das Buch Esther. KAT,* XVII/5 (1963), 402; a different view is taken by G. Gerleman, *Esther. BK,* XXI (^{2}1981), 143f.

מַסֵּכָה *massēḵâ*

Contents: I. Vocabulary Associated with Idols: Delimitation, Etymology, and Meaning. 1. *massēḵâ;* 2. *neseḵ;* 3. *ʿaṣabbîm;* 4. *pesel;* 5. *ṣelem;* 6. *semel.* II. Modes of Production. III. OT. 1. Occurrences and Distribution; 2. Expressions; 3. Theological Meaning; 4. LXX.

I. Vocabulary Associated with Idols: Delimitation, Etymology, and Meaning.

1. *massēḵâ.* The noun *massēḵâ* is usually taken as the *maqṭil* form of the verb *nsk,* "to pour out"[1] (or, in Isa. 25:7; 28:20, *massēḵâ* II, "covering" from *nsk* II, "to weave"[2]), with the meaning "molten image (of a deity)"[3] or "cast [poured] image."[4] This derivation implies that the underlying verb *nsk* means "to pour metal," a meaning not attested with certainty in the OT; in the passages in question (Isa. 40:19; 44:10) the general expression *nsk pesel* might be circumscribing a different method of working metal. Furthermore, these translations of the term *massēḵâ,* which occurs primarily in fixed expressions,[5] frequently present considerable problems not completely ameliorated by the additional rendering suggested by *KBL*[3], namely, "metal-casting." That *massēḵâ* derives from the vocabulary of metallurgy is demonstrated by the passages which describe the production materials and methods (cf., e.g., Ex. 32:2; Isa. 30:22; 40:19; 44:9-17; Hos. 13:2) and by parallel formulations such as *ʾelōhê massēḵâ* (Ex. 34:17) — *ʾelōhê zāhāḇ* (Ex. 32:31), so that José Faur's hypotheses[6] that the *massēḵâ* is related to *neseḵ,* "libation," or to *swk* II, "to anoint," suggesting a consecrated image, are unpersuasive. The root *nsk,* attested in numerous Semitic languages, does not exhibit a unified semantic field. Two separate semantic aspects do, however, emerge more

---

massēḵâ. K.-H. Bernhardt, *Gott und Bild. ThArb,* 2 (1956); J. Boese and U. Rüss, "Goldschmiedetechniken," *RLA,* III (1957-1971), 519-531; O. Eissfeldt, "Gott und Götzen im AT," *ThStKr,* 103 (1931), 151-160 = *KlSchr,* I (1962), 266-273; E. Feucht, "Goldschmiedearbeiten," *LexÄg,* II (1977), 751-54; K. Galling, "Götterbild, weibliches," *BRL*[2], 111-19; W. Helck, "Kultstatue," *LexÄg,* III (1980), 859-863; H.-D. Hoffmann, *Reform und Reformen. AThANT,* 66 (1980); C. R. North, "The Essence of Idolatry," *Von Ugarit nach Qumran. Festschrift O. Eissfeldt. BZAW,* 77 (²1961), 151-160; H. D. Preuss, *Die Verspottung fremder Religionen im AT. BWANT,* 92[5/12] (1971); J. Renger and U. Seidl, "Kultbild," *RLA,* VI (1981), 307-319; M. Weippert, "Gott und Stier," *ZDPV,* 77 (1961), 93-117; P. Welten, "Götterbild, männliches," *BRL*[2], 99-111; *idem,* "Göttergruppe," *BRL*[2], 119-122; W. Zimmerli, "Das Bilderverbot in der Geschichte des alten Israel," *Schalom. Festschrift A. Jepsen. ArbT,* 1/46 (1971), 86-96 = *Studien zur alttestamentlichen Theologie und Prophetie. Gesammelte Aufsätze,* 2. *ThB,* 51 (1974), 247-260; → נסך *nsk;* פסל *psl;* → צלם *ṣelem.*

1. *BLe,* §492t.
2. *HAL,* II (1995), 605.
3. *GesB,* 440.
4. *HAL,* II, 605.
5. See III.2 below.
6. "The Biblical Idea of Idolatry," *JQR,* 69 (1978), 1-15.

strongly: sacrifice or offering (libation) on the one hand, and the working of metals on the other. West Semitic *nsk* can be traced back to Akk. *nasāku,* "to cast or hurl out flat."[7] The West Semitic occurrences of *nsk* show that the aspect of "rendering into a flat surface" probably stands in the foreground regarding the metal-working technology in question.[8] Since *massēḵâ* is associated only with the materials gold and silver, the actual method of working these materials was probably hammering or plating,[9] particularly considering that Hebrew uses a different verb to refer to the pouring of metal, namely, → יצק *yṣq.*[10] Thus *massēḵâ* might refer to a beaten (hammered) piece (in silver or gold) or to precious metal plating, although the latter might sooner be suggested by *ṣph* II, and *rq*ʿ piel might then originally refer perhaps to the manufacture of the precious metal sheeting required for these methods.[11] In the case of *massēḵâ,* then, such wooden or metal statues or objects overlaid with precious metal are probably the primary reference (as mentioned in Isa. 40:19; Jer. 10:3f., and elsewhere). The total absence of the term in secular contexts can be explained by its use in texts characterized by iconoclastic polemics, to which are also limited the other terms such as *pesel* and *ʿaṣabbîm,* all of which also derive from the activities of handiwork artisans. This also explains why in languages independent of Hebrew the term *massēḵâ* is not attested with this meaning.[12]

2. *neseḵ.* The term *neseḵ,* deriving from the same root as *massēḵâ,* is usually used in the OT with the meaning "libation," and occurs in 4 exilic-postexilic passages as a synonym for *massēḵâ* (Isa. 41:29; 48:5; Jer. 10:14 par. 51:17[13]); in contrast, *massēḵâ* does not occur in these texts (Deutero-Isaiah–Jeremiah[14]). These texts using *neseḵ* in place of *massēḵâ* more strongly emphasize the characterization and evaluation as foreign idolatry present in the wordplay of Isa. 30:1.[15] This parallel is also supported by those expressions using *neseḵ* which correspond exactly to the familiar expressions using *massēḵâ,* such as *pislî wᵉniskî* (Isa. 48:5; cf. *pesel ûmassēḵâ*) or the sundered and juxtaposed word combinations in Jer. 10:14 par. 51:17. Dnl. 11:8 uses *nāsîḵ,* which derives from the root *nsk,* in the sense of *massēḵâ* perhaps in order to create in this passage an additional association in the expression *ʾᵉlōhêhem ʿim-nᵉsiḵêhem* with *nāsîḵ,* "prince."

---

7. *AHw,* II (1972), 752f.; *CAD,* XI/2 (1980), 15-20.
8. For details, cf. → נסך *nsk.*
9. Cf. Boese-Rüss.
10. Cf. also the Ugaritic examples in *KTU,* 1.4 I, 23-43; M. Dietrich and O. Loretz, "Die sieben Kunstwerke des Schmiedegottes in KTU 1.4 I 23-43," *UF,* 10 (1978), 57-63, and R. Heyer, "Ein archäologischer Beitrag zum Text KTU 1.4 I 23-43," *UF,* 10 (1978), 93-109.
11. See II below.
12. Both the reading and the interpretation of the only two occurrences (*KAI,* 26 A III, 1; C IV, 3) are uncertain; cf. *DISO,* 160 *s.v.*
13. Cf. A. Weiser, *Das Buch Jeremia 1–25,14. ATD,* X ([7]1976), 87.
14. On Isa. 42:17, cf. K. Elliger, *Deuterojesaja.* BK, XI/1 (1978), *in loc.*
15. See III.1 below.

3. *ʿaṣabbîm.* In contrast to the other terms associated with idols, which do not refer to a specific group of images, the *pluralia tantum* *ʿaṣabbîm*[16] functions as a collective term for the idols of non-Israelite religions, something explicitly stated in 9 of 17 passages (1 S. 31:9; 2 S. 5:21; 1 Ch. 10:9; Isa. 46:1; Jer. 50:2; Ps. 106:36,38; 115:4; 135:15). The particular character of the noun *ʿaṣabbîm* derives from the homonymous root *ʿṣb* I, "to shape, create, form," and *ʿṣb* II, "to pain, grieve." Its earliest occurrences are found in Hosea.

On the basis of tensions with v. 10 involving content, 1 S. 31:9 is considered a secondary addition to 31:8-13. It can be recognized here as a redactional organizational insertion within the story of David's accession, influenced by the model of 1 S. 17:51,54. Similarly, 2 S. 5:21 can be taken as secondary following the suggestion of Timo Veijola,[17] v. 21 being related to the loss of the ark in 1 S. 4:1-11.

Among the various transgressions reproved by Hosea, one consistent motif — although applied only to Ephraim — is the association with foreign peoples and thereby also with their idols and cults (Hos. 4:17; 5:8,11,13; 7:8,11; 8:11; 12:2[Eng. v. 1]). Since the 4 occurrences of *ʿaṣabbîm* (4:17; 8:4; 13:2; 14:9[8]) also refer to Ephraim, the reference here is probably exclusively to foreign idols,[18] something also suggested by the only occurrence of *massēḵâ* in Hosea (13:2); here *massēḵâ* is explicated as regards form by the term Hosea otherwise usually employs to refer to idols, namely, *ʿaṣabbîm: massēḵâ* manufactured according to the model of foreign gods *(keṯaḇniṯ ʿaṣabbîm,* conj. *BHS).* This linguistic usage and the explanatory comparison between *massēḵâ* and *ʿaṣabbîm* might have something to do with the prophet's Judean sphere of activity.[19]

Regarding the term *massēḵâ,* Hans Walter Wolff[20] suggests a poured metal image, just as *massēḵâ* is also used in Ex. 32:4,8 for the image of a calf, although in 13:2 after the model of "small bronze statuettes overlaid with silver (cf. 8:4b[2:10bβ(8bβ)] and the commentary)."

In later texts the term's semantic nuances are partially weakened (2 Ch. 24:18; Zec. 13:2), or even completely lost in texts whose polemical character has been intensified by a concentration of terms from the same semantic field (Isa. 10:10f.; 48:5; Mic. 1:7). Two passages with text-critical problems (Isa. 48:5; Ps. 139:24)[21] attest the special, semantically undifferentiated form *ʿōṣeḇ.*

4. *pesel.* The nominal constructions of *psl,* which the Masoretes divided among two lexemes (*pesel* + **pāsîl*),[22] together constitute the most frequent term in the OT

---

16. → עצב *ʿṣb.*

17. *Die ewige Dynastie. AnAcScFen,* B, 193 (1975), 97ff.

18. Cf. also J. P. Floss, *Jahwe dienen, Göttern dienen. BBB,* 45 (1975), 161f.

19. Cf. H. W. Wolff, *Hosea. Herm* (Eng. trans., 1974), 219, 225; a different view is taken by H. Motzki, "Ein Beitrag zum Problem des Stierkultes in der Religionsgeschichte Israels," *VT,* 25 (1975), 470-485, who suspects the presence of a Deuteronomistic gloss.

20. P. 225 and n. 28.

21. Cf. E. Würthwein, "Erwägungen zu Psalm cxxxix," *VT,* 7 (1957), 173f.

22. Regarding this discussion, cf. C. Dohmen, "על־(ה)מזבח — Zur Bedeutung und Verwendung von hebr. על," *BN,* 16 (1981), 11f.

used to refer to idols (with 54 occurrences). Unaccompanied by qualifications this term refers to any kind of cultic image, both the idols of foreign religions (e.g., 2 K. 21:7; Jer. 51:47) and those forbidden for Israel by the prohibition of images (Ex. 20:4; Dt. 5:8). Neither is *pesel* limited to the meaning inherent in the root, "to hew, cut," encompassing rather also idols manufactured in other ways (Isa. 44:10).[23] It occurs in numerous combinations with more specific qualifications, such as *pesel ûmassēḵâ* (e.g., Dt. 27:15; Jgs. 17:3,4); *pᵉsîlê ʾᵉlōhîm* (Dt. 12:3); *pesel hāʾᵃšērâ* (2 K. 21:7).[24]

5. *ṣelem.* The actual meaning of *ṣelem* in the OT is "concrete representation," then also "image," etc. The meaning "idol" for *ṣelem* first arises through expressions such as *ṣalmê massēḵōṯām* (Nu. 33:52), *ṣalmê tōʿᵃḇōṯām* (Ezk. 7:20), or through substantive references such as that in 2 K. 11:18 par. 2 Ch. 23:17.[25]

6. *semel.* Among terms referring to images, the term *semel,* attested only in Phoenician-Punic and 5 times in the OT (Dt. 4:16; 2 Ch. 33:7,15; Ezk. 8:3,5), is a functional term which defines an object belonging to another in terms of that other.[26]

II. Modes of Production. Throughout the ancient Near East the most varied sorts of representations of deities are attested (statuary, reliefs, paintings, and glyptics).[27] In the case of precious metals, full casting was limited to smaller figurines both because of technical considerations[28] and because of the value of the materials.

Greater significance was early acquired by the various methods of goldsmithing,[29] which applied thin layers of precious metal onto parts made of wood, bronze, or even silver.[30] A concretely formed core could be "overlaid" with hammered sheets of precious metal attached by nails and rivets (plating);[31] especially in the case of hollow objects and those similar to reliefs, the sheeting of precious metal was hammered over an elastic core (bitumen, clay, soft wood) into the corresponding form (beating).[32] Since for reasons of stability such pieces were often filled or attached to a core, it is not always easy to determine exactly what methods were used in their production. In addition to idols produced in these ways, one also finds

23. → עשה *ʿāśâ;* → יצר *yāṣar* (VI, 257-265); → נסך *nāsaḵ.*

24. On this whole complex, → פסל *psl.*

25. On the term's etymology and range, → צלם *ṣelem;* H. Wildberger, "צֶלֶם *ṣælæm* Abbild," *THAT,* II, 556-563.

26. On its etymology and meaning, cf. C. Dohmen, "Heisst סֶמֶל 'Bild, Statue'?" *ZAW,* 96 (1984), 263-66.

27. Cf. E. Unger, "Götterbild," *RLV,* IV (Berlin, 1926), 412-16.

28. M. Weippert, "Metall und Metallbearbeitung," *BRL*², 222f.

29. Cf. Boese-Röss; E. Feucht, *LexÄg,* II, 751-54.

30. Cf. EA, 14, I, 68; 14, II, 11ff. On the relative value of gold and silver in the ancient Near East, → זהב *zāhāḇ (zāhābh),* IV, 36; W. F. Leemans, "Gold," *RLA,* III, 512f.

31. Cf. Boese-Rüss, 522.

32. *Ibid.,* 523.

in Syria and Palestine medallion-like plates of precious metal which hung as pendants.[33]

III. OT. 1. *Occurrences and Distribution.* The noun *massēḵâ* occurs 28 times in the MT of the OT, although only 25 of these occurrences are to be classified as terms for idols, since in Isa. 25:7; 28:20 a derivation of *nsk* II, "to weave," is evident, and in 2 Ch. 28:2 the Peshitta reads *mdbḥ'* = *mizbᵉḥôṯ* instead of *massēḵôṯ;* this reading is supported by the following *labbᵉʿālîm* along with the *lᵉ* + suffix of the acting person, attested exclusively with idols, as well as by the substantive context of vv. 1-4. Isa. 30:1, where *massēḵâ* is frequently rendered by "alliance" or similar terms, contains in the variously explained *figura etymologica nsk massēḵâ*[34] an allusion to two acts attested during the preexilic period designating a connection with foreign gods. The linguistic form *nsk massēḵâ* recalls *nsk neseḵ,* "present a drink offering," as a sign of veneration toward foreign gods (cf. Jer. 7:18; 19:13; 32:29; 44:17, and elsewhere); by replacing *neseḵ* with *massēḵâ,* which derives from the same root, the author additionally establishes an association with the production of an idol. A synoptic evaluation of different interpretations of *ʿśh ʿṣh* shows that the preceding portion of the verse also contains such a wordplay.[35]

No particular pattern in the distribution of *massēḵâ* occurrences can be discerned, since small concentrations such as Jgs. 17; 18 are based on narrative pieces. If one considers, however, that in several instances *massēḵâ* in its present positions stands in secondary textual material (e.g., Nu. 33:52; Isa. 30:22), one focal point in its usage does emerge in Deuteronomic/Deuteronomistic passages. Of even greater significance is the observation that the noun occurs primarily in the unaltered form *massēḵâ* — the plural occurs only 4 times (*massēḵôṯ:* Nu. 33:52; 1 K. 14:9; 2 Ch. 34:3,4) and the construct form only once (*massēḵaṯ:* Isa. 30:22) — and in fixed expressions.

2. *Expressions.* In addition to the variously attested pair *pesel ûmassēḵâ, massēḵâ* occurs as a *nomen rectum* in construct chains: *ʿēgel massēḵâ* (Ex. 32:4,8; Dt. 9:12[?[36]],16; Neh. 9:18); *'ᵉlōhê massēḵâ* (Ex. 34:17; Lev. 19:4); *ṣalmê massēḵôṯām* (Nu. 33:52). The expression *'ᵉlōhîm 'ᵃḥērîm ûmassēḵôṯ* (1 K. 14:9, its only occurrence) seems to correspond formally to *pesel ûmassēḵâ.* Both types of expressions, the construct chain and that with *w,* can be divided in the same way, their component parts then being juxtaposed in parallelism (Isa. 30:22; 42:17; Hab. 2:18[?]; Ps. 106:19). Only in 2 K. 17:16; Hos. 13:2 does *massēḵâ* stand alone. In both passages, however, *massēḵâ* is explicated further, in 2 K. 17:16 by *šᵉnê(m) ʿᵃḡālîm.*[37] In addition to the expressions

---

33. Cf. K. Galling, "Götterbild, weibliches," *BRL*², 116; on the corresponding archaeological evidence cf. in addition to the lexica already cited also Elliger, esp. 76f.

34. Cf. H. Wildberger, *Jesaja. BK,* X/3 (1982), 1147f.

35. M. Dahood, "Accusative *ʿēṣāh,* 'Wood,' in Isaiah 30,1b," *Bibl,* 50 (1969), 57f.; Wildberger, *BK,* X/3, 1151f.

36. Cf. *BHS.*

37. On Hos. 13:2, see I.3 above.

mentioned above, several parallel formulations also occur which make it clear that *massēḵâ* has to do with goldsmithing. In Ex. 32:31, the formulation *'elōhê zāhāḇ* occurs in place of *'ēgel massēḵâ,* and in 1 K. 12:28; 2 K. 10:29; 2 Ch. 13:8 Jeroboam's calf images are referred as *'eglê (haz)zāhāḇ.*

3. *Theological Meaning.* Like most of the terms used in the OT in reference to idols, the term *massēḵâ* originally referred to a product created and shaped by human hands. A synoptic consideration of both etymology and OT usage reveals that *massēḵâ* refers to the goldsmithing on an idol, and primarily not to the image itself. Considering the magical and mythical notions associated with gold, which in the ancient Near East were especially widespread in connection with idols,[38] it is easy to see why this particular aspect of the image was specifically singled out or subjected to polemic. This is also shown by Hos. 10:5, where the golden brilliance of the image of the calf, called its *kāḇôḏ,* is the object of the priests' cultic exultation.[39]

Even though archaeological evidence for these valuable precious metal components of idols is understandably meager,[40] neither their quantity nor their significance throughout the ancient Near East should be underestimated. One particularly good example of confrontation with these notions is Isa. 30:22.[41] The parallelism of v. 22a emphasizes that the idol's *ṣippûy* and *'ēpôḏ* are to be discarded because of their cultic uselessness *(ṭm'),* leaving open the question whether this parallelism is synonymous ("silver-covered graven images — gold-plated molten images") or synthetic ("the covering of the silver graven images — the *'ēpôḏ* of the gold plating").

In the first case the term *pesel ûmassēḵâ* (comparable to Ps. 109:19) would be divided, and then the other members of the parallelism also would correspond to one another;[42] in the other case one would have a silver core covered with gold bearing a precious garment *('ēpôḏ).*[43]

Despite these difficulties, the intention of this verse emerges quite clearly. By drawing attention to the accumulation of such precious metals, it specifically criticizes the notions associated with them. It is also of significance that in the case of such idols the *massēḵâ* reference evokes not only official cultic images such as Jeroboam's bull symbols, but also the smaller, amulet-like representations used privately, something also alluded to, e.g., by the context of the *'ārûr* series in Dt. 27; the narrative Jgs. 17; 18; and Nah. 1:14.

---

38. → זהב *zāhāḇ (zāhābh)* (IV, 32-40); L. Störck, "Gold," *LexÄg,* II (1977), 725-731; Leemans, *et al., RLA,* III, 504-531; E. Hornung, *Conceptions of God in Ancient Egypt* (Eng. trans., Ithaca, 1982).

39. Wolff, 175.

40. Welten, *BRL*², 110; however, cf. also the Hittite examples in M. Weippert, *ZDPV,* 77 (1961), 100.

41. Cf. L. Laberge, "Is 30,19-26: A Deuteronomic Text?" *Église et Théologie,* 2 (1971), 35-54.

42. Wildberger, *BK,* X/3, *in loc.*

43. Cf. Unger, 414f.

Although the two occurrences in Ex. 34:17; Lev. 19:4[44] with the prohibition of *'ᵉlōhê massēḵâ* (only here) do not polemicize as strongly as does the Deuteronomistic theology against the notions associated with costly idols, they do tend in the same direction.

4. *LXX.* As a translation for *massēḵâ* the LXX offers *chōneutós* (17 times), *chōneuma* (twice), and *glyptós* (twice). The most frequent renderings of the other terms used in reference to idols clearly show their semantic differences. Thus the LXX renders *pesel, *pāsîl* primarily with *glyptós; *ʿaṣaḇ* with *eídōlon;* and *ṣelem, semel* with *eikōn.*

Dohmen

---

44. Cf. J. Halbe, *Das Privilegrecht Jahwes: Ex 34, 10-26. FRLANT,* 114 (1975), 216ff.

מסס *mss;* מסה *msh*

Contents: I. Etymology. II. Occurrences, LXX. III. OT Usage. IV. Derivatives, Secondary Forms. V. Qumran.

I. Etymology. The root *mss* is attested only in Hebrew and in Jewish Aramaic (ethp. "fail, break down," palpel "make dissolve"); Arab. *mašša,* "dissolve in water," does not fully correspond phonetically. The secondary form *msh,* attested 4 times, has Arabic, Jewish Aramaic, Syriac, and Mandaic parallels;[1] in addition, a few forms in the MT with *m's* seem to be related semantically to *mss* (see below).

II. Occurrences, LXX. In the MT *mss* occurs once in the qal (3 times if one counts the two forms *mᵉśôś;* see below), 18 times in the niphal, and once in the hiphil. The derivative *massâ* occurs once, as does *temes.*[2]

In the majority of instances the LXX translates with *tḗkō;* other translations include *bréchō* (Ps. 6:7; Jer. 34:3), *ptoéō* (Josh. 7:5), *dialýō* (Jgs. 15:11), *exístēmi* (Josh. 2:11; Ps. 39:12), *thraúō, thrausmós* (Ezk. 21:12; Nah. 2:11), *deiliaínō* (Dt. 20:8), and various circumlocutions.

---

mss. G. Gerleman, "Der Sinnbereich 'fest — los(e)' im Hebräischen," *ZAW,* 92 (1980), 405f.; D. J. McCarthy, "Some Holy War Vocabulary in Joshua 2," *CBQ,* 33 (1971), 228-230; R. Lauha, *Psychophysischer Sprachgebrauch im AT. AnAcScFen, DHL,* 35 (1983).

1. Cf. A. Guillaume, "Hebrew and Arabic Lexicography: A Comparative Study, II," *Abr-Nahrain,* 2 (1960/61), 22.

2. The semantic field is discussed by Gerleman.

III. OT Usage. 1. In the first instance, *mss* means "to flow," "to dissolve," "to melt": wax melts in the fire (Ps. 68:3[Eng. v. 2]; 97:5; Mic. 1:4; cf. Ps. 22:15[14]); manna melts in the sun (Ex. 16:21); cf. also "turned to water" (Josh. 7:5) and the associations with water in Ezk. 21:12[7];[3] Ps. 22:15(14). Mountains flow with blood (Isa. 34:3). Jgs. 15:14 uses the term figuratively: the cords around Samson's arms become weak and dissolve.

Melting wax serves as an image of the annihilation of God's enemies in theophany (Ps. 68:3[2]) or of the melting of mountains at his appearance (Ps. 97:5; Mic. 1:4).

2. One group of 8 occurrences associates *mss* niphal with the despairing human heart. The simple expression is used 3 times in Joshua, twice in reference to Israel's enemies (the Canaanites), with the additional remark that they had no more courage (*rûaḥ;* Josh. 2:11; 5:1), and once in reference to the Israelites themselves after the defeat at Ai, with the additional commentary that their heart became "as water" (7:5). The image of water recurs in Ezk. 21:12(7), where the anticipated reaction of the people to the coming catastrophe is described: All hearts will despair *(mss),* every hand will fall limply down *(rāp̄â),* all "spirits" will become faint, and all knees will "run with water." This concentration of expressions provides a vivid picture of the people's "utter despair."[4] The limp hands recur in Isa. 13:7: all hands will be feeble, and all hearts will melt when the day of Yahweh comes; v. 8 contains additional synonyms: "become dismayed" (*bhl* niphal), pangs and agony *(ṣîrîm, ḥ^{a}b̲ālîm),* "to writhe *(ḥîl)* like a woman in travail." Nah. 2:11(10) contains further synonyms: faint hearts, tottering knees, trembling loins; cf. also Isa. 19:1: the idols of Egypt will tremble *(nûaʿ),* and the hearts of the Egyptians will despair (melt). Finally, in Ps. 22:15(14) the heart melting like wax represents the psalmist's own sufferings.[5]

Even without *lēb̲* the term *mss* niphal can refer to a person's sinking spirits. After Absalom's defeat even the most valiant man will lose all courage (despair, *mss* niphal; 2 S. 17:10). A warrior can be disheartened by his less courageous brothers (Dt. 20:8; perhaps hiphil is to be read); cf. also Dt. 1:28: "Our brethren [the scouts] have made our hearts melt" (hiphil). In contrast, Ps. 112:10 speaks of languishing away in a general sense: "The wicked man sees it [the good fortune of the righteous person] and is angry; he gnashes his teeth and 'melts away.'" Similarly Isa. 10:18: "as when a sick man wastes away."

IV. Derivatives, Secondary Forms. 1. The noun *massâ* occurs only once, namely, in Job 9:23, which focuses on the mockery of the wicked at the despair of the innocent.[6] Similarly, the derivative *temes* is used only once; one of the curses in Ps. 58 refers to the slime of the snail, illustrating the destruction of the cursed persons.

---

3. However, cf. W. Zimmerli, *Ezekiel 1. Herm* (Eng. trans. 1979), 425.
4. *Idem.*
5. On this whole complex, cf. Lauha, 149f.
6. Cf. É. P. Dhorme, *A Commentary on the Book of Job* (Eng. trans., Nashville, 1967), *in loc.*

2. When Bildad in his first discourse speaks of the fate of the godless person, he says among other things: God destroys him (Job 8:18), and then he continues (v. 19): "Behold, this is *mᵉśôś darkô,*" which with the orthography employing *ś* could mean: "That is the joy [ironically] of his life's way." Usually, however, one derives the infinitive from *mss:* "That is the passing away of his life's way," which yields good sense. Then, however, the question arises whether yet another *mᵉśôś* can be so interpreted, namely, in Isa. 8:6. The inhabitants of Jerusalem refuse the waters of Shiloah *ûmᵉśôś 'eṯ-rᵉṣîn ûḇen-rᵉmalyāhû.* Either one interprets *mᵉśôś* here as "joy," meaning that the Jerusalemites were prepared to greet the hostile princes with royal exultation (it is not otherwise known that such a party existed advocating this), or one derives *mᵉśôś* from *mss* and translates: "It will certainly [inf. abs.] languish away (NRSV 'melt in fear') with Rezin and the son of Remaliah."[7]

3. A couple of passages suggest that one secondary form of *mss* was *m's.* Job 7:5 reads: "My skin hardens *(rāḡa')* and *yimmā'ēs*"; one would expect "dissolves" or a similar term. Either this is a form of *mss* itself, or *m's* constitutes a secondary form. Édouard P. Dhorme[8] suspects the same verb in v. 16: *ma'astî lō'-lᵉ'ôlām 'eḥyeh,* "I am languishing away, I will/do not want to live for ever."

4. The concrete meaning predominates in the case of *māsâ.* God's word melts the ice (Ps. 147:18); the petitioner in a psalm of lament floods his bed (makes it flow) with his own tears (Ps. 6:7[6]); God makes human splendor *(ḥāmûḏ)* dissolve like the moth (Ps. 39:12[11]). Only in Josh. 14:8 is it combined with *lēḇ:* the brethren (scouts) made the people's courage melt (cf. Dt. 1:28 and *BHS*).

V. Qumran. In Qumran *mss* has thus far been attested 18 times, with a clear accumulation in 1QM. The stereotypical OT usage is taken over. The references are almost exclusively to the *lēḇ nāmēs,* the melting heart of the enemies of the Qumran Essenes (1QM 1:14; 8:10; 9:11; 4Q161 8–10:4), or of the inconstant believer (1QM 10:6 [cf. 11QT 62:4]; 11:9).[9] The call to the final battle will give courage to the fearful of heart (1QM 14:6; 4Q491 11 II.15). The occurrences in 1QH could have been taken from the OT book of Psalms (compare 1QH 2:28; 4:33; 8:32; fr. 4:14 with Ps. 22:15[14]).

Ringgren

---

7. Cf. the comms.
8. P. 107f.
9. Cf. here esp. H. Bardtke, "Acedia in Qumrān," *Qumran-Probleme. DAWB,* 42 (1963), 29-51.

מָעַד *māʿaḏ*

Contents: I. Etymology, Occurrences. II. Usage. III. LXX.

I. Etymology, Occurrences. The Hebrew term *māʿaḏ,* "to wobble, shake," corresponds to Syr. *m*^{e}*ʿaḏ* with the same meaning, and perhaps also to Arab. *maʿada,* "to hasten through the land, draw one's sword," passive "to be weak, sick at one's stomach." It occurs 7 times in the MT of the OT (5 times qal, once each pual and hiphil). It is not attested in Qumran.

II. Usage. This verb refers to a wobbly gait or stance, evoking the idea of unsteadiness.

Ps. 18:35-37(Eng. vv. 34-36) (par. 2 S. 22) portrays a military situation in which the psalmist achieves victory through divine succor. In v. 37(36) we read: "You gave me a wide place for my steps under me, so that my feet did not wobble," i.e., God gives him room to move (cf. v. 20[19]) so that he is not surrounded and brought down; his feet and his steps are secure.

Ps. 26 is the prayer of an innocent person introduced by the assurance that the petitioner has walked in integrity and trusted in Yahweh without wavering (v. 1). The reference is thus to the stability and constancy of one's conduct.

Ps. 37, a song influenced by the wisdom tradition, asserts in v. 31 that the righteous person has the law of God in his heart, the result being that his steps do not slip or wobble. Slipping here can refer either to misfortune (cf. 38:17[16] with *mwṭ*) or to moral lapse; the context seems to support the first meaning better.

In Job 12:5, Job replies to Zophar's first discourse: *lappîḏ bûz l*^{e}*ʿaštuṯ šaʾ*^{a}*nān nāḵôn l*^{e}*môʿ*^{a}*ḏê rāgel.* This is a difficult verse and was not understood by early translations; most commentaries emend the text. Édouard Dhorme[1] attempts a rather verbatim translation of the MT: "For misfortune, derision (so think the fortunate ones!), A blow for those whose feet slip!" The carefree speak derisively of those who cannot stand firm and thus fall into misfortune.

Prov. 25:19 should read *môʿāḏeṯ* instead of *mûʿāḏeṯ* (pual) and be translated "Trust in a faithless man in time of trouble is like a bad tooth or a foot that slips." One cannot bite with a bad tooth, nor walk securely with a wobbly foot; both are unreliable. Just as little can one rely on a deceptive man in times of distress.[2]

---

māʿaḏ. H. A. Brongers, "Darum, wer fest zu stehen meint, der sehe zu, dass er nicht falle: 1 Kor X 12," *Symbolae biblicae et mesopotamicae. Festschrift F. M. T. de Liagre Böhl. StFS,* 4 (1973), 56-70, esp. 61.

1. *A Commentary on the Book of Job* (Eng. trans., Nashville, 1967), 169f.
2. H. Ringgren, *Sprüche. ATD,* XVI/1 (^{3}1980), 101.

One should probably also read a participial form of *m'd* in Sir. 16:18: The heavens, the cosmic sea, and the earth all tremble at God's visitation.

In a prayer of execration directed at adversaries in Ps. 69:24(23), the hiphil form occurs with the plea that God "darken" their eyes and make their loins tremble, once again a reference to a secure step in the sense of a happy, secure life. Ezk. 29:7 also uses *m'd* (to be read instead of *'md*) together with *moṯnayim:* those who lean upon Egypt will be made to wobble.

*KBL*³ also suggests reading *m'd* hiphil for *wayᵉmōḏeḏ* in Hab. 3:6: Yahweh's appearance in a theophany causes the earth to tremble (cf. Sir. 16:18 above).

III. LXX. The LXX translates twice with *astheneō*, once with *hyposkelízomai,* and once with *saleúomai.* Job 12:5; Prov. 25:19 are understood differently.

Ringgren

מָעוֹז *mā'ôz*

Contents: I. Etymology. II. 1. Occurrences; 2. Meaning; 3. Equivalents in the LXX. III. Secular Usage. IV. Religious Usage: 1. Yahweh as Fortress and Mighty Helper; 2. Yahweh as Refuge and Protective Retreat; 3. Merging of the Two Statements; 4. Yahweh's Sanctuary; 5. "The God of Fortresses"; 6. Summary. V. Qumran.

I. Etymology. The noun *mā'ôz* is attested in Hebrew and as *ma'āḏ* also in Arabic. Perhaps Ugar. *'d* IV, "protection,"[1] is also related. *KTU,* 1.65, a liturgy,[2] contains in ll. 9-10 the entreaty to El that he hasten and come quickly "to the protection of Zaphon, to the protection of Ugarit" *(b'd ṣpn b'd ỉgrt).* The second occurrence[3] reads *b'd b'lkm,* "to the protection of Ba'al[?]," but permits no clear explication due to the absence of its context.

It is indisputable that the first element in this noun is a *mem* prefix. Derivation of the second element, however, is more problematical. Just as Ugar. *'d* derives from the root *'wd,* and Arab. *ma'āḏ* from the root *'wḏ,* so also would it seem likely that *mā'ôz* derives from *'wz* inasmuch as similar nouns are the derivatives of biliteral roots. The Masoretic pointing, however, does contradict this, according to which the *ā* is preserved unaltered as the initial vowel[4] and the second radical undergoes gemination. In this

---

mā'ôz. D. Eichhorn, *Gott als Fels, Burg und Zuflucht. EH,* 23/4 (1972), 114-120.

1. *WUS,* no. 2000; differently in *UT,* no. 1814; cf. also this difference in the interpretation of personal names in *WUS* and *PNU,* 106f.
2. O. Eissfeldt, "Bestand und Benennung der Ras-Schamra-Texte," *KlSchr,* II (1963), 346.
3. *KTU,* 4.17, 16.
4. *BLe,* §26t′; O. Grether, *Hebräische Grammatik für den akademischen Unterricht* (Munich, ²1955), §57i; E. Jenni, *Lehrbuch der hebräischen Sprache des ATs* (Basel, 1981), §11, 3, 4; cf. also *VG,* I, 375f.

case *mā'ôz* would derive from the root *'zz,*[5] as the comparable noun *māgēn* derives from *gnn*.

More recent lexica and grammars agree in their assertion that *mā'ôz* can be traced back to the root *'zz* as well as to the root *'wz,* which are "formed by elision and difficult to separate semantically."[6]

It is difficult to determine whether *mā'ôzen* in Isa. 23:11 is a secondary form of our noun lengthened by an afformative *n,*[7] or has resulted from scribal error.[8]

II. 1. *Occurrences.* The term *mā'ôz* occurs 36 times in the OT, to which can be added 1 occurrence in Sirach. It appears either 6 or 7 times in the Qumran writings. Three additional occurrences result from the probable conjecture of → מעון *mā'ôn* to *mā'ôz* in Ps. 71:3; 90:1; 91:9.[9]

An overview of the distribution reveals the following: 10 occurrences in Proto-Isaiah (3 in chs. 24–27); 9 in the Psalms; 7 in Daniel; twice each in Ezekiel and Nahum; once each in Judges, Samuel, Jeremiah, Joel, Proverbs, and Nehemiah. Six Qumran occurrences are found in the Hodayoth. If we also count the three conjectures, the number within the Psalter rises to 12. This reveals a clear concentration on the one hand in the spiritual songs of Israel, and on the other in the apocalyptic writings.

2. *Meaning.* This distribution is explained by the meaning and content of *mā'ôz.* Derivation from the root *'zz,* "to be strong," gives the meaning "strength," "bulwark";[10] given its rottage in *'wz,* "to seek refuge," however, it might yield "place of refuge," "succor."

This allows us to distinguish the proximity of the two semantic spheres and also explains their confluence, for *GesB* offers the following: "1. mountain stronghold or mountain peak . . . ; bulwark, fortress . . . 2. protection, shelter," and *KBL*[3] reads: "1. mountain stronghold, place of refuge . . . 2. God as *mā'ôz.*"

3. *Equivalents in the LXX.* The Greek expressions in the LXX also correspond to this broader semantic duality. They can be grouped as follows: "strength," "bulwark" on the one hand, and "protection," "succor," "help" on the other. The first group includes: *ischýs* (8 times) along with *enischýō* (once) or *katischýō* (once), *ochýrōma* (3 times), *krataiōsis* (once) and *krataióō* (once) as well as *hypostḗrigma* (once). The following words can be assigned to the second group: *hyperaspistḗs* (6 times), *boēthós* (4 times) along with *boēthéō* (3 times) and *boḗtheia* (once), *kataphygē* (3 times), *sképḗ*

---

5. *BLe,* §61dη.

6. *HAL,* II (1995), 610; also *GesB; GK,* §85k.

7. So *HAL,* II.

8. *GesB;* cf. 1QIs[a].

9. A different view is taken by O. Eissfeldt, "Jahwes Verhältnis zu 'Eljon und Schaddaj nach Psalm 91," *KlSchr,* III (1966), 445; "Eine Qumran-Textform des 91. Psalms," *KlSchr,* V (1973), 46, who rejects the conjecture in Ps. 91:9.

10. *GK,* §85k.

(twice) along with *skepastḗs* (once), *antílēmpsis* (once) and perhaps also *hypoménō* (once), *stásis* (once) and *hai enkataleleimménai* (once). The LXX should be followed in emending 2 S. 22:33 according to Ps. 18:33(Eng. v. 32) to *m^e'azz^erēnî.*

III. Secular Usage. In OT secular usage *mā'ôz* refers to a "citadel," a "fortress," a military "bulwark." The enemy penetrates into "the fortress of the king of the north" (Dnl. 11:7), advances to the fortress of the adversary (Dnl. 11:10), turns back toward "the fortresses of his own land" (Dnl. 11:19) or toward the "fortified citadels" (*mibṣ^erê mā'uzzîm,* Dnl. 11:39). The oracle concerning Tyre contains Yahweh's order to level the fortresses of Canaan (Isa. 23:11), referring to the destruction by the Persians of the Phoenician maritime fortresses including Sidon and Tyre,[11] just as the gloss Isa. 23:4 directly refers to Sidon as the "fortress of the sea" *(mā'ôz hayyām).* Isa. 23:14 also refers to the destruction of Sidon, the bulwark of the ships of Tarshish, expressed in v. 1 by *bayiṯ,* "house." Similarly, in Ezk. 30:15 the city of *sîn* (the Vulg. mentions instead the port city Pelusium) is called "the stronghold of Egypt," and in vv. 13-19 the fall of Egypt can be portrayed paradigmatically in the destruction of its most famous fortresses.

That the word "fortress" is always synonymous with "fortified city" is corroborated by the expression *'ārê mā'uzzô,* "his fortified cities" (Isa. 17:9). At the same time, the notion of protection resonates in this expression, protection which such cities are able to offer to the person seeking refuge. Thus Nineveh is warned that it will have to seek a *mā'ôz* from its enemy (Nah. 3:11), just as Sidon, as the bulwark of the ships of Tarshish, also constituted their protection and as it were their port of refuge (Isa. 23:14).

It is not quite clear just what Jgs. 6:26 is presupposing. Gideon is instructed to build an altar to Yahweh "on the top of this stronghold" *('al rō'š hammā'ôz hazzeh).* Some MSS facilitate the text by reading *mā'ôn;*[12] the LXX^A understands the word as a personal name *Maōz* (LXX^B: *Maouek*). Ernst Bertheau[13] translates "on the top of this fortress"; Otto Eissfeldt[14] says "on the top of this high place"; Hans Wilhelm Hertzberg[15] "up high upon the mountain stronghold"; and Friedrich Nötscher[16] "on the fortified elevation." Scholars as early as C. F. Keil[17] explicated this expression as meaning "possibly upon the top of the mountain, upon which the fortress belonging to Ophrah was situated." More recently, J. Alberto Soggin,[18] following this line of thinking a bit further, associated *mā'ôz* with the sanctuary and interpreted the entire bulwark as "a version of the fortified Canaanite temple." As attractive as this suggestion might well be, it encounters difficulties when we try to imagine an altar on the top of

11. → כנען *k^ena'an*, VII, 219.
12. Cf. *BHS.*
13. *Das Buch der Richter und Ruth. KEHAT,* VI (²1883), 139.
14. *Die Quellen des Richterbuches* (Leipzig, 1925), 41.
15. *Die Bücher Josua, Richter und Ruth. ATD,* IX (⁴1974), 183.
16. *Richter. EB,* I (1955), 650.
17. *Judges. KD,* II, 336.
18. *Judges. OTL* (Eng. trans. 1981), 123f.

such a *mā'ôz*. Given the use of *rō'š* in geographical descriptions, the passage seems more likely to be suggesting a largely inaccessible mountaintop or a predominantly rocky region which, like a fortress, is virtually impregnable. This might be supported by the *parallelismus membrorum* of *mā'ôz* and *ṣûr/sela'*, "rock," in many of Israel's religious songs.

IV. Religious Usage. The term *mā'ôz* is used with far greater frequency in religious contexts, the most important of which are the statements referring to Yahweh.

1. *Yahweh as Fortress and Mighty Helper.* A clearly circumscribed vocabulary appears in a series of pertinent passages either parallel to *mā'ôz* or in its immediate context. In the individual lament Ps. 31:3[2], the plea to Yahweh, "be a rock of the bulwark (NRSV 'refuge,' *leṣûr-mā'ôz*) for me," is paralleled by the expression "a mountain fortress" *(lebêṯ meṣûḏôṯ);* and in the individual lament Ps. 71:3 the same plea, "be to me a rock of the 'bulwark,' " issues into the confident confession "for you are my rock *(sal'î)* and my mountain fortress (*meṣûḏāṯî*)." In Ps. 31:5[4], the petitioner's confession is brief: "For you are my citadel." The positioning of → מצודה *meṣûḏâ* thus clearly defines our noun as a "citadel," "bulwark." It expresses insuperable strength and, underscored additionally by its association with *ṣûr* or *sela',* unchanging stability and solidity. This explains how our noun could be associated with Yahweh in metaphorical speech. It characterizes the believer's rock-like trust in God's omnipotence.

At the same time, however, this knowledge of God's superior power and strength stands behind the believer's plea for succor and deliverance by Yahweh. Thus the root *yš'* hiphil, "to rescue, save," occurs in the context of the two citations from the Psalms (Ps. 31:3[2]; 71:3); in addition, the verb *nṣl* hiphil, "to help," also occurs in Ps. 31:3(2). This leads to other passages in which the theme of "divine help" similarly occurs with the metaphor of the "citadel." Isa. 17:10 accuses the northern kingdom Israel of having forgotten God, of not having remained loyal to him, and of having turned to a different god that cannot help.[19] In this context the expressions "the God of your help (NRSV 'salvation,' *'elōhê yiš'ēḵ*)" and "the rock of your bulwark (NRSV 'refuge,' *ṣûr mā'uzzēḵ*)" parallel one another in referring to the reliability of Yahweh's succor. The individual lament Ps. 28:8 proclaims in a confessional formulation: Yahweh is the strength *('ôz)* of his people, and a "saving bulwark (NRSV 'refuge,' *mā'ôz yešû'ôṯ*)" for his anointed. This context would also include the reference to Yahweh as the "stronghold of my life" *(mā'ôz-ḥayyay)* from Ps. 27:1 (and Sir. 51:2), since it, too, is found in a confessional statement and has as its parallel the sentence Yahweh is "my light *('ôrî)* and my salvation *(yiš'î).*"

By way of comparison *KBL*[3] refers to the Greek-Phoenician bilingual text from Larnax Lapethos, in which the goddess 'Anat is called *m'z ḥym,* or her Greek equivalent Athena is called *Sōteírą Níkę*.[20] W. W. Graf Baudissin[21] renders this expression as

19. Cf. W. Schottroff, *"Gedenken" im alten Orient und im AT. WMANT,* 15 (1964), 171.
20. *KAI,* 42, 1.
21. *Adonis und Esmun* (Leipzig, 1911), 18, 457.

"power of life," or better "power of the living," meaning that 'Anat's power intervenes for the living, that she stands by them and helps them in the fullness of her power.[22]

Finally, two further passages can be presented in this context, since they similarly associate *mā'ôz* with assistance, succor, and security for the believer. In Dnl. 11:1, Gabriel tells Daniel that Michael stands by him "as a helper" *(l^e^maḥ^a^zîq)* and "as refuge" *(l^e^mā'ôz).* And Prov. 10:29 focuses on the experience that he who walks uprightly in Yahweh's way possesses *mā'ôz,* which v. 9 circumscribes by saying that he can live "securely" *(beṭaḥ).*

In Ps. 60:9(7) par. 108:9(8), *mā'ôz* is similarly to be understood in the sense of the power with which Yahweh intervenes on behalf of his believers. In the style of an oracle of good news the passage reads: "Gilead is mine; Manasseh is mine; Ephraim is the *mā'ôz* of my head, Judah my scepter." Yahweh is conceived as a warrior-ruler with the ruler's scepter in his hand and the helmet on his head. Thus the helmet could figuratively quite well be called "the fortress of the head," expressing thereby the inviolable association of Ephraim with Yahweh, out of which hope and consolation regarding Yahweh's succor emerges for the northern kingdom.

This is also the sense of the masculine personal name *ma'azyāhû* (1 Ch. 24:18), *ma'azyâ* (Neh. 10:9[8]), or *m'wzyh, m'wzy,* and *m'zyh.*[23] This name is composed of the noun *mā'ôz* and the theophoric element Yahweh, with the resultant meaning "Yahweh is my fortress, my succor, my refuge."[24]

2. *Yahweh as Refuge and Protective Retreat.* In yet a different group of passages the term *maḥ^a^seh,* "place of refuge," "refuge,"[25] occurs as a parallel for our noun. This suggests that *mā'ôz* in these texts conceives of God as the refuge of the hard-pressed believer, as his protection and shelter. Thus the two expressions "a refuge for his people" and "a stronghold for the people of Israel" stand as a parallel apposition to Yahweh (Joel 4:16[3:16]). In the "prophetic song of thanksgiving"[26] the two statements that in times of distress Yahweh is a "refuge to the poor" and a "refuge to the needy" are illustrated by the images of "shelter from the rainstorm" *(maḥseh mizzerem)* and "shade from the heat" *(ṣēl mēḥōreḇ)* (Isa. 25:4), drawing attention thus to the existential shelter of Yahweh as the true refuge for the believer in times of distress.

The MT of Ps. 91:9, "For you have with your 'Yahweh is my refuge' made Elyon your habitation (citadel, *m^e'^ôneḵā*)," [27] is almost always emended to "For you — Yahweh is 'your' refuge, you took Elyon for your 'bulwark' *(mā'ûzzeḵā).*"[28] Quite aside from the fact that 11QPs^b^ reads *mḥmdk,* "your bliss," for *m'wnk,* "your habitation," the understanding of this psalm as a whole is not at all a matter of unanimous

22. A different view is taken by Donner, *KAI,* II, 59: "refuge of the living."
23. *AP,* 22, 70; 109.
24. Cf. M. Noth, *IPN,* 157.
25. → חסה *ḥāsâ* (V, 64-75).
26. O. Kaiser, *Isaiah 13–39. OTL* (1974), 197.
27. According to Eissfeldt, *KlSchr,* V, 47.
28. Cf., e.g., H.-J. Kraus, *Psalms 60–150* (Eng. trans., Minneapolis, 1989), 220.

agreement. While one usually takes it as a didactic poem, as instruction and guidance, or even as a song of trust, Eissfeldt[29] suggests understanding Ps. 91 as a conversion psalm. A believer who so far has experienced protection from Elyon/Shadday now confesses that Yahweh will be his refuge and fortress (vv. 1-2). A third party encourages the believer in this decision, emphasizing by explicitly picking up in v. 9 the expression "my refuge" from v. 2 "that only the confession to Yahweh makes it possible to participate fully in Elyon's complete fullness of power, and that thus only Yahweh represents the complete revelation of Elyon."[30]

Drawing on familiar expressions from the language of the Psalter, Isaiah criticizes his people's unnatural behavior. Because they set out to go down to Egypt "to take refuge in the protection of Pharaoh *(lā'ôz bᵉmā'ôz par'ōh),* and to seek shelter in the shadow of Egypt *(laḥsôṯ bᵉṣēl miṣrāyim),*" that refuge will turn to their shame, and the shelter to their humiliation (Isa. 30:2).

As Bernard Duhm[31] correctly points out, the infinitive construct associated with *mā'ôz* in Isa. 30:2 does not derive from the root *'zz,* but rather from *'wz.* This root also occurs in Ps. 52:9(7), where *mā'ôz* is understood as the refuge God represents for the believer, although here actually the opposite is stated insofar as it is characteristic of the godless person that he in fact does not seek refuge in God, but rather in his own wealth.

Jer. 16:19 also uses *mānôs* (→ נוס), "refuge," as an explication for *mā'ôz.* Again, the statement is formulated as a confession: "Yahweh is my strength *('uzzî)* and my stronghold *(mā'uzzî)* and my refuge in the day of trouble." The acrostic hymn Nah. 1:7 reads similarly: "Yahweh is good, a stronghold in the day of trouble." And Ps. 90:1 confesses with thanksgiving: "Yahweh, thou hast been a 'refuge' to us in all generations."

3. *Merging of the Two Statements.* As clearly distinguishable as these two aspects of the usage of *mā'ôz* are in many passages, there are also indications that a merging occurred in the form of a concentration of all the substantive associations evoked by the expression *mā'ôz.* This is most clearly the case in Ps. 37:39: the righteous person experiences deliverance *(tᵉšû'â)* from Yahweh; he is his refuge *(mā'ôz)* in the time of trouble. While the expectation and assurance of deliverance by Yahweh correspond to the meaning of *mā'ôz* as bulwark and strength discussed earlier, the second statement, along with its reference to the time of trouble, precisely reflects the context of *mā'ôz* just discussed, namely, as refuge. This combination of the two semantic aspects becomes even more evident subsequently in v. 40, since one after another the verbs *'zr* hiphil, *plṭ* piel (twice), *yš'* hiphil, and as a concluding justification *ḥsh* are used. God is the helper, savior, and deliverer, and for that reason the petitioner trusts in the shelter of his refuge. Ps. 43:2 is to be interpreted similarly, since the confession "you are the

29. *KlSchr,* III, 441-47.
30. *Ibid.,* 445.
31. *Das Buch Jesaja. HKAT* (⁵1968), 215.

God in whom I take refuge" is the reason for the confident plea in v. 1: "Vindicate me *(špṭ),* defend my cause *(rîḇ),* deliver me (*plṭ* piel)."

A clear distinction is not possible in Neh. 8:10. The exhortation to the people to be carefree and joyful is justified by the statement: "for joy in Yahweh is your *mā'ôz.*" This could mean "is your strength,"[32] although it could also be understood such that joy is the best aid against the fear of God's wrath.[33]

4. *Yahweh's Sanctuary.* In a few instances *mā'ôz* refers to Yahweh's sanctuary, the Jerusalem temple. Ezk. 24:25 foretells the destruction of Jerusalem and of the temple itself, whereby "the meaning of God's temple for the house of Israel is described with a threefold predication"[34]: it is their bulwark, whereby v. 25 varies the statement of v. 21, "my sanctuary, your proud treasure" *(miqdāšî gᵉ'ôn 'uzzᵉḵem),* and understands *mā'ôz* as an impregnable citadel; it is their eminent joy, "the delight of their eyes and their heart's desire." Dnl. 11:31, which foretells the profanation of the Jewish temple by Antiochus Epiphanes, also inserts *hammā'ôz* as an apposition to *hammiqdāš,* although not in reference to the sanctuary and the citadel,[35] but rather to the sanctuary as the bulwark and place of refuge for the persecuted Jews.

Isa. 27:5 also refers to the temple as a place of refuge. Here the assertion is made that one can "lay hold" *(ḥzq* piel) of Yahweh's refuge and make peace with him. As recent commentaries consistently point out, this presupposes the function of the Jerusalem sanctuary as a place of asylum.[36] Adonijah "grasps" (*ḥzq* piel) the horns of the altar (1 K. 1:50), just as does Joab (1 K. 2:28).

5. *"The God of Fortresses."* Antiochus' idolatrous behavior also involved his veneration of the "god of fortresses" *('ᵉlōah mā'uzzîm)* instead of the gods of his fathers (Dnl. 11:38). Both the LXX and the Vulg. view this as a proper name; it is probable that Zeus Olympius, Jupiter Capitolinus, is meant.[37]

6. *Summary.* The majority of *mā'ôz* statements referring to Yahweh are found in laments from the Psalter. They are largely confessional in nature or formulated as supplications, and represent expressions of trust by the petitioners. They express Israel's faith in Yahweh's invincible strength and in his unique power, both of which his people and every individual have experienced and hope to continue experiencing anew as succor, deliverance, and divine assistance. Although no indications or allusions are made, one can nonetheless take as the background to these statements of faith the salvific deeds of Israel's God, deeds which undergird the Yahweh-faith itself, such as the exodus events, the bestowal of the land, or the postexilic revivification; at the same

32. So RSV; also K. Galling, *Die Bücher der Chronik, Esra, Nehemia. ATD,* XII (1954), 232.
33. W. Rudolph, *Esra und Nehemia. HAT,* XX (1949), 149.
34. W. Zimmerli, *Ezekiel 1. Herm* (Eng. trans. 1979), 507.
35. N. W. Porteous, *Das Buch Daniel. ATD,* XXIII (^{3}1978), 122.
36. Cf. L. Delekat, *Asylie und Schutzorakel am Zionheiligtum* (Leiden, 1967).
37. A. Bentzen, *Daniel. HAT,* XIX (^{2}1952), 83.

time, one must consider that a transformation or reforming of these expressions, which largely concern the people as a whole, has taken place into the realm of individual-personal piety.

That Yahweh represents refuge for the believer in distress, and is able to provide both shelter and protection for him, is doubtlessly an expression of God's abundant goodness; at the same time, it anticipates the concretizing that takes place in the form of an identification between God and his sanctuary, so that the temple, in its function as a place of asylum, probably provides the background for a whole series of statements in the Psalter that confess Yahweh as refuge. Ultimately, however, this notion was itself spiritualized again to the extent that the holy place of refuge became a metaphor for the sheltering protection of the heavenly Lord.

Dieter Eichhorn[38] offers the following as a summary: "The horizon for the designation of Yahweh as *mā'ôz* is Yahweh's mighty theophany in its double aspect as salvation for those 'who hope in him' and destruction for those 'who rise up against him.' The petitioners who refer to Yahweh as *mā'uzzî* or entreat Yahweh to step forward as their *mā'ôz* are persons whose existence stands and falls with the mediation of Yahweh's function as *mā'ôz* for the community in his appropriate revelation on Zion." This includes first of all the prophet (Ps. 28), then also the levitical temple singer and preacher (Ps. 31) as well as the wisdom teacher loyal to Yahweh (Ps. 37). Further "democratization" is not discernible.

V. Qumran. The few Qumran occurrences approximately correspond to the biblical statements already discussed. Here, too, *mā'ôz* means "power." The petitioner laments that the strength has left his body, and the strength of his loins has left him (1QH 8:32,33). And in 1QH 8:23f. the reference is probably to a tree or something similar which maintains its strength even during the season of heat.

With equal frequency *m'wz* means "refuge." The petitioner laments that he is forsaken and no longer has any refuge (1QH 8:27). Or in a thanksgiving confession he acknowledges that God has given him "no fleshly refuge" (1QH 10:23) and that his support is "in the refuge on high" *(bm'wz mrwm),* paralleled by the expression "everlasting fountain" (1QH 10:32).

The fragment 1Q35 1:1 contains only the textually problematical reading *lm'wz,* which does not allow any interpretation.

Zobel

38. P. 120.

מָעוֹן *mā'ôn;* מְעֹנָה *me'ōnâ*

Contents: I. Occurrences, Meaning, Semantic Field. II. Usage: 1. Lair of Animals; 2. God's Dwelling Place; 3. God as Refuge; 4. Place Name.

I. Occurrences, Meaning, Semantic Field. The noun *mā'ôn* is a so-called *maqṭal* construction (*mem*-preformative) from the (inferred, although not attested!) root *'ûn/'în.*[1] Wolfram von Soden[2] also assigns *'ônâ,* "dwelling" (not "cohabitation!"), to this root (Ex. 20:10). In addition to the Arabic verb *ǵyn*[3], evidence within its linguistic field includes Akk. *mā'unnu,* "dwelling,"[4] and possibly also a Punic equivalent.[5] Five OT passages use *mā'ôn* with the meaning "lair or habitation/dwelling place for (wild) animals" (Jer. 9:10[Eng. v. 11]; 10:22; 49:33; 51:37; Nah. 2:12[11]; regarding this final passage cf. 1QH 5:13). In the remaining passages *mā'ôn* refers to the temple as the earthly, or to heaven as the celestial dwelling of God[6] (Dt. 26:15; 2 Ch. 30:27; 36:15; Ps. 26:8; 68:6[5]; Jer. 25:30; Zec. 2:17[13]). Disputed passages include first of all 1 S. 2:29,32;[7] Jgs. 6:26; Zeph. 3:7 (cf. LXX). Paul Hugger[8] includes *mā'ôn* as a conjecture in Ps. 84:7[6]; 87:7 as well. Other disputed passages from the Psalms include Ps. 71:3; 90:1; 91:9, so that the total number of occurrences can vary widely[9] (from 15 [or only 12/13] to 18/19).

---

mā'ôn. R. E. Clements, *God and Temple* (Philadelphia, 1965); L. Delekat, *Asylie und Schutzorakel am Zionheiligtum* (Leiden, 1967); D. M. Eichhorn, *Gott als Fels, Burg und Zuflucht. EH,* 23/4 (1972); S. D. Goitein, " 'Mā'ōn' — A Reminder of Sin," *JSS,* 10 (1965), 52f.; P. Hugger, *Jahwe, meine Zuflucht. Münsterschwarzacher Studien,* 13 (1971), 152-55; O. Keel, *The Symbolism of the Biblical World* (Eng. trans., New York, 1978), 179-198; *idem* and M. Küchler, *Orte und Landschaften der Bibel: Ein Handbuch und Studienreiseführer zum Heiligen Land,* II: *Der Süden* (Zurich, 1982); M. Metzger, "Himmlische und irdische Wohnstat Jahwes," *UF,* 2 (1970), 139-158; F. Stolz, *Strukturen und Figuren im Kult von Jerusalem. BZAW,* 118 (1970), 213; G. Westphal, *Jahwes Wohnstätten nach den Anschauungen der alten Hebräer. BZAW,* 15 (1908).

1. Cf. also W. Borée, *Die alten Ortsnamen Palästinas* (1930, Hildesheim, ^{2}1968), 72; see also Y. Aharoni, *The Land of the Bible* (Eng. trans., Philadelphia, 1967, ^{2}1979), 354; cf. L. Kopf, "Arabische Etymologien und Parallelen zum Bibelwörterbuch," *VT,* 9 (1959), 261f. = *Studies in Arabic and Hebrew Lexicography* (Jerusalem, 1976), 187f.: Arab. *'wn,* "to help."

2. "Zum hebräischen Wörterbuch," *UF,* 13 (1981), 159f.

3. Cf. *HAL,* II (1995), 610.

4. EA, 116, 11; but cf. *AHw,* II (1972), 637.

5. *DISO,* 161: uncertain text; for a less cautious view see R. S. Tomback, *A Comparative Semitic Lexicon of the Phoenician and Punic Language. SBL Diss.,* 32 (1978), 190.

6. On the distinction and accompanying context, see II.2 below.

7. Cf. A. Guillaume, "Hebrew and Arabic Lexicography: A Comparative Study, II," *Abr-Nahrain,* 2 (1960/61), 9.

8. P. 154.

9. Cf. R. Knierim, "עָוֹן *'āwōn* Verkehrtheit," *THAT,* II, 243; F. Stolz, "צִיּוֹן *Ṣijjōn* Zion," *THAT,* II, 547; S. Amsler, "קוּם *qūm* aufstehen," *THAT,* II, 639; A. R. Hulst, "שׁכן *škn* wohnen," *THAT,* II, 909.

The noun *mᵉ'ōnâ* exhibits a similar semantic scope: lair of wild animals (Job 37:8; 38:40; Ps. 104:22; Cant. 4:8; Am. 3:4; Nah. 2:13[12]); God's dwelling place (Ps. 76:3[2]); place of refuge (Dt. 33:27). The fact that the temple and ultimately also God himself can be a "refuge" at least preserves the possibility of discounting conjectures affecting *mā'ôn* for Ps. 71:3; 90:1;[10] 91:9.[11]

Since *mā'ôn/mᵉ'ōnâ* can refer to the temple as well as to heaven as Yahweh's habitation or dwelling place,[12] its semantic field is correspondingly expansive.[13]

Consequently, the LXX interprets and differentiates more strongly. Thus *hagíasma* (2 Ch. 36:15) occurs along with *kataphygḗ* (Ps. 90:1; 91:9), then *diatribḗ* (Jer. 49:33[LXX 30:28]) along with *koítē* (Jer. 10:22); further also *euprépeia* (Ps. 26:8[LXX 25:8]), *tópos* (Ps. 68:6[5][LXX 67:6]; 71:3[LXX 70:3]), *oíkos* (Dt. 26:15), *katoikētḗrion* (2 Ch. 30:27; Nah. 2:12[11]; Jer. 9:10[11]), and *mouṓn* (1 S. 2:32[?]).

In the Qumran texts *mā'ôn* occurs 11 times in reference to a den of lions (1QH 5:13; cf. Nah. 2:12[11]), to heaven (as God's dwelling place: 1QS 10:3; 1QM 12:2; 1QSb 4:25; also 1QH 12:2, or is this referring to the temple?), to heaven as the place of light (and of darkness: so with *mᵉ'ōnâ:* 1QH 12:5+7), 1QS 10:1; 1QH 12:5; the text of 1QH 12:2 is uncertain; cf. also 1Q36 12:2. With its reference to the congregation (!) as God's temple/dwelling place (1QS 8:8) the Qumran community goes beyond OT usage.[14]

II. Usage. 1. *Lair of Animals.* Whenever *mā'ôn* refers to the dwelling place or abode of wild animals, it never does so simply for the sake of neutral portrayal; rather, the context always involves judgment, i.e., a place (Jerusalem, the cities of Judah, Hazor, Nineveh, or Babylon) is warned that wild animals will seek and find their dwelling place there. This is first the case in Nahum's ironic lament[15] (Nah. 2:12[11]); cf. the repetition in 1QH 5:13) over the predicted destruction of Nineveh, which did indeed come to pass, Nineveh becoming a den for lions.[16] The context involving an oracle of judgment and (this time genuine) lament is also found in Jer. 9:10(11), according to which Jerusalem will become the lair of jackals *(tan),* something even expressed in the form of a divine lament (after the model of prophetic discourse? however, cf. the LXX regarding v. 9[10]).[17] Similar proclamations in Jer. 10:22; 49:33; 51:37 (regarding the cities of Judah, Hazor, and Babylon) are secondary, more recent texts constructed analogously to Jer. 9:10(11).

---

10. See esp. Goitein, Kopf.

11. Cf. II.3.

12. Cf. II.2.

13. → ישב *yāšaḇ* (VI, 420-438); → מקום *māqôm* (VIII, 531-544); *miqdāš; miškān; mākôn;* → קדש *qōdeš;* → שכן *škn;* cf. also → כסא *kissēʾ* (VII, 232-259) and → היכל *hêyḵāl,* III, 386f., as well as → ציון *ṣiyyôn* and ירושלם *yᵉrûšālēm* (VI, 347-355).

14. Cf. B. Gärtner, *The Temple and the Community in Qumran and the NT. SNTS Mon,* 1 (1965).

15. So K. Elliger, *Das Buch der zwölf kleinen Propheten, II: Nahum. ATD,* XXV (^{8}1982), *in loc.*

16. → ארי *ʾᵃrî,* I, 386.

17. On the connection between judgment oracle and lament, cf. F. Ahuis, *Der klagende Gerichtsprophet* (Stuttgart, 1982).

2. *God's Dwelling Place.* According to Ps. 26:8, the temple is Yahweh's habitation, which the psalmist loves. 2 Ch. 36:15 asserts that God himself had compassion on his temple as his dwelling place.[18] Both Sir. 50:1(2); Jgs. 6:26 probably also belong in this context. In none of these passages, however, does *mā'ôn* say anything substantive concerning the question whether Yahweh's temple was understood primarily as the locus of dwelling or of encounter. The answer to this question requires an evaluation of the entire semantic field.[19]

Despite the considerable theological emphasis on the (Jerusalem?) temple in Deuteronomy, here, too, it is clear that Yahweh's dwelling place is (in) heaven (Dt. 26:15; cf. Dt. 4:36; 1 K. 8:30-39 Deuteronomistic).[20] According to Jer. 25:30, Yahweh sounds his voice from his heavenly habitation, something that in Am. 1:2 occurs from Zion. According to 2 Ch. 30:27, Yahweh's heavenly habitation is the goal of prayer. The reference in the liturgical addendum Zec. 2:17(13) (cf. v. 14[10]) as well as in Ps. 68:6(5) might be both to Yahweh's heavenly and to his earthly habitation (cf. the context and the relationship with Jgs. 5:4f.). When reference is made in this way to Yahweh's habitation in heaven or in the temple, a qualifying *qdš* is usually added (although not in Ps. 26:8; 2 Ch. 36:15).

The real reason one can argue over this question of whether in a given instance the reference is to Yahweh's heavenly or to his earthly habitation (the temple) is that a clean theological distinction neither can nor should be made between the two.[21] That is, with regard to the sanctuary the boundaries between heavenly and earthly are suspended,[22] and in the temple itself the heavenly sphere reaches into the earthly (or vice versa).[23] Thus Israel's immediate environs attest the divine address "house, dwelling place,"[24] and the ancient Near East, like the OT itself, could speak similarly about the dwelling place of the gods whether the focus was a temple or heaven.[25]

3. *God as Refuge.* As a result of this understanding, not only was Yahweh's presence experienced in the temple, but ultimately Yahweh himself was viewed as the dwelling place, i.e., refuge, for the petitioner. Thus in the disputed passages from the Psalter (Ps. 71:3; 90:1; 91:9) one must consider more carefully than has often been the case the necessity of textual emendation (usually to → מעוז *mā'ôz*). Not only can the name of the dwelling place have become an epithet here,[26] but *mā'ôn* as a metaphor for Yahweh's

18. Cf. H. D. Preuss, "Barmherzigkeit I," *TRE,* V, 222f.
19. See I above.
20. On this question, see H. D. Preuss, *Deuteronomium. EdF,* 164 (1982), 49.
21. On the attendant relationships, see Clements; Keel; Metzger, whereby the latter peculiarly does not pursue the question of *mā'ôn*.
22. So Metzger.
23. So Keel.
24. As regards Nergal, cf. Hugger, 154, n. 107.
25. On this subject, cf. Keel; Metzger; then also *WbMyth,* I, index (1965) *s.v.* "Wohnsitz der Götter."
26. Stolz, 213, n. 178.

protection is comprehensible as a substitute divine appellative[27] (cf. Ps. 76:3[2]; Dt. 33:27). In view of the clearly evident democratization of this assertion of trust, it is of no significance whether one must consider the possibility of a cultic mediator as the original speaker.[28] Both the temple and Yahweh himself are the "place" to which the petitioner flees and where he experiences refuge and protection.

4. *Place Name.* The locale *mā'ôn,* situated 13 km. (8 mi.) southwest of Hebron in the vicinity of Carmel, is mentioned in Josh. 15:55; 1 S. 25:2 (cf. 1 S. 23:24f. and the conj. in 1 S. 25:1 and possibly in Jgs. 10:12).[29] Today it is called Khirbet Ma'în. Ma'ôn, situated southwest of Hebron, has now also been attested on an ostracon from Arad.[30] There was also a locale called *(bêṯ) ba'al mā'ôn* in Transjordan, mentioned in Jer. 48:23 (and Nu. 32:3?) as well as in the Mesha inscription[31]

Preuss

---

27. Hugger, 155.
28. Eichhorn, 121ff.
29. In addition to the information given in *HAL,* II, 610 *s.v. mā'ôn* IV, one can now refer to the thorough discussion of this locale's name, location, history, significance, and exploration in Keel-Küchler, 756f. and index; cf. also *GTTOT,* 15, 22, 149, 320f.; Aharoni; Hugger, 153.
30. 25:4; cf. Y. Aharoni, *Arad Inscriptions* (Jerusalem, 1981), 50f.
31. *KAI,* 181, 9, 30.

מָעַט *mā'aṭ;* מְעַט *me'aṭ*

Contents: I. 1. Occurrences; 2. Meaning. II. Secular Usage: 1. Idiomatic Expressions; 2. Wisdom Language. III. Expressions of Small Quantity in Religious Contexts: 1. Temporal Aspect; 2. Quantitative Aspect; 3. Much or Little as a Term for "Enough"; 4. Prayer; 5. Accusations; 6. Ps. 8:6(Eng. v. 5); 6. Ezk. 11:16.

I. 1. *Occurrences.* The noun *me'aṭ* occurs 101 times in the OT, and the verb derived from it (qal, piel, hiphil) another 22 times (or 23 counting Sir. 3:18). Constructions from this root are attested in Arabic (*ma'iṭa,* "become fewer," *ma'aṭa,* "take away, out"), Akkadian (*maṭû,* "become lesser, be small/few"), as well as in Ethiopic and Tigre. The distribution of the noun in the OT is as follows: It occurs 11 times in Genesis; 10 each in the Psalms and Proverbs; 7 each in Numbers and Proto-Isaiah; 6 in Deuteronomy; 5 each in Ezekiel and Job; 4 each in Ecclesiastes and 1 Samuel; 3 each in Exodus, 2 Samuel, and Haggai; twice each in Joshua, 1 Kings, Jeremiah, Hosea, Ezra, Nehemiah, Daniel, and 2 Chronicles; and once each in Leviticus, Judges, 2 Kings, Zechariah, Canticles, Ruth, and 1 Chronicles.

2. *Meaning.* The fundamental meaning of *me'aṭ* emerges clearly from the contextual parallel in 1 K. 17:12: *kap̱-qemaḥ* and *me'aṭ šemen,* "a handful of meal/a little oil,"

and from the antithesis, the latter indicated in several instances by constructions of the root *rbh: rbh* (Ex. 16:17f.; 30:15; Lev. 25:16; Nu. 26:54; 33:54; 35:8; Ps. 107:38; Prov. 13:11; Jer. 29:6; 30:19); *raḇ* (Nu. 13:18; 26:54,56; 33:54; 35:8; Dt. 26:5; 28:38; 1 S. 14:6; Prov. 15:16); *rōḇ* (Lev. 25:16; Dt. 7:7; 28:62; Prov. 16:8); *harbēh* (2 K. 10:18; Eccl. 5:11[12]; Jer. 42:2; Hag. 1:6,9). In Ps. 37:16, the parallel noun is *hāmôn,* "abundance." In addition, the fundamental meaning of *m'ṭ,* "little, few" as opposed to "much, many," emerges clearly in what is apparently a fixed expression put into the mouth of Jonathan: "For nothing can hinder Yahweh from saving by many or by few" (1 S. 14:6; cf. also Eccl. 5:11[12]).

The noun can be used absolutely as in Dt. 28:38: "You will gather little in," or in tandem with another noun, as in 1 S. 14:29,43: "a little of this honey." An intensification is expressed by the typically Isaianic expression *mᵉ'aṭ miz'ār,* "a very little," i.e., a very little while (Isa. 10:25; 16:14; 29:17).

Although the noun is combined with *bᵉ,* "by," in 1 S. 14:6, and with *lᵉ,* "to," in 2 Ch. 29:34; Hag. 1:9, in the majority of instances it is used with *kᵉ,* "how." Here, too, the various semantic nuances of *mᵉ'aṭ* emerge, since this combination can be taken temporally with the meaning "quickly, almost, just about, soon" (2 Ch. 12:7; Job 32:22; Ps. 2:12; 73:2 [here par. *kᵉ'ayin*]; 81:15[14]; 94:17; 119:87; Prov. 5:14; Cant. 3:4; Ezk. 16:47), plerophorically *(kim'aṭ-regaʿ)* with the meaning "a brief moment" (Ezr. 9:8; Isa. 26:20), quantitatively with the meaning "few, little" (Isa. 1:9; perhaps also Gen. 26:10; 2 S. 19:37[36]; Ps. 105:12 par. 1 Ch. 16:19), or qualitatively with the meaning "little worth" (Prov. 10:20).

The verb exhibits the basic meaning "to be few, small."

II. Secular Usage.

1. *Idiomatic Expressions.* There were apparently several idiomatic expressions in Hebrew using *mᵉ'aṭ.* They are consistently embedded in direct discourse. In 4 instances a guest expresses upon arrival the request: "Give me a little water to drink" (Gen. 24:17,43; Jgs. 4:19; 1 K. 17:10). The formulas of greeting probably also include Abraham's order that a little water be brought for washing his guests' feet (Gen. 18:4).

Yet another, similarly fixed expression seems to be that which refers to the brevity of life. Thus Jacob pronounces before Pharaoh: "Few and evil have been the days of the years of my life" (Gen. 47:9), and Job inquires: "Are not the days of my life few?" (Job 10:20); a similar wish is directed to the wicked, namely, that "his days be few" (Ps. 109:8).

Finally, mention should be made of the apparently popular idiomatic expression *hamᵉ'aṭ min* + suffix/noun, "is it too small a thing for you (sg. or pl., your harlotries)" (Nu. 16:9; Job 15:11; Isa. 7:13; Ezk. 16:20; 34:18; without *min* in Gen. 30:15; Nu. 16:13; with *lᵉ* + suf. Josh. 22:17).

2. *Wisdom Language.* From this perspective the use of *mᵉ'aṭ* in the language of wisdom is also not surprising. The stylistic device of comparison (*ṭôḇ min,* "better . . . than") is used in Prov. 15:16; 16:8 in connection with *mᵉ'aṭ* and corresponding antithetical expressions: "Better is a little with the fear of Yahweh than great treasure

and trouble with it" (15:16), "better is a little with righteousness than great revenues with injustice" (16:8). In Ps. 37:16, such comparison is tied to the antithesis "the righteous — the wicked." The end of the wicked is also the focus in Ps. 37:10: "Yet a little (while), and the wicked will be no more"; Job 24:24: "They are exalted a little, and then are gone." In contrast to the value of the tongue of the righteous, the heart of the wicked is of little worth (Prov. 10:20).

Prov. 6:10; 24:33 characterize the slothful person, who says: "A little sleep, a little slumber, a little folding of the hands to rest."[1] Prov. 13:11 finds that quickly accumulated wealth "dwindles," while enduring work "increases" one's possessions. In contrast to the rich, whose surfeit does not let him sleep, the laborer finds sweet respite whether he has little or much (Eccl. 5:11[12]). Eccl. 5:1(2), evoking Prov. 10:19, admonishes to let one's words be few in prayer to God; Eccl. 10:1 offers the proverb which the LXX finds "offensive": "A little folly outweighs wisdom and honor."[2] According to Eccl. 12:3, the burdens of old age include the "grinders (teeth) becoming few." And in Eccl. 9:14 a wisdom parable begins with the words "There was a little city, with only a few people dwelling in it."

III. Expressions of Small Quantity in Religious Contexts. Israel's religious language also displays the various semantic nuances of *me'aṭ* in a variety of contexts.

1. *Temporal Aspect.* The temporal aspect of *me'aṭ* refers to a brief period of time. The reference can be to Yahweh's salvific activity or judgment, whereby the further distinction can be made whether this activity is acknowledged as having occurred in the past or is being foretold for the future.

The fact that a remnant is saved that can live again in the holy place in Jerusalem is viewed by Ezr. 9:8 as a sign that "for a brief moment favor has been shown us." Similarly, the Babylonian exile or the Assyrian oppression can be described as a short period of Yahweh's wrath (Isa. 10:25; Zec. 1:15).

The following passages focus on foretelling Yahweh's future intervention. Here the predominating expression *'ôḏ me'aṭ* in initial position is noteworthy in Jer. 51:33; Hos. 1:4; Hag. 2:6. It "sets a time limit for the fulfillment of judgment"[3]: In a short while the time of Babylon's harvest will come, I will punish the house of Jehu for the blood of Jezreel, I will shake the entire world. The advent of salvation, however, can also be foretold in this way: "Is it not yet a very little while until Lebanon shall be turned into a fruitful field?" (Isa. 29:17). Simple *me'aṭ* or *kim'aṭ* express the same thing. In an allusion to the merely "temporary occupation of Jerusalem,"[4] the city's imminent deliverance is announced (2 Ch. 12:7). If Israel would but obey its God, he would soon subdue their enemies (Ps. 81:15[14]). To preserve itself from Yahweh's wrath, Yahweh advises the people to hide itself for a little while (Isa. 26:20). And in view of the

---

1. So H. Ringgren, *Sprüche. ATD,* XVI/1 (^{3}1980), *in loc.*
2. So W. Zimmerli, *Prediger. ATD,* XVI/1 (^{3}1980), 225.
3. H. W. Wolff, *Hosea. Herm* (Eng. trans., 1974), 17.
4. W. Rudolph, *Chronikbücher. HAT,* XXI (1955), 233.

imminent conquest Yahweh promises that "little by little" *(me'aṭ me'aṭ)* he will drive out the inhabitants of Canaan (Ex. 23:30; Dt. 7:22).

Hos. 8:10 should be understood temporally, and refers to imminent judgment.[5] In Ps. 105:12 par. 1 Chr. 16:19, one cannot determine unequivocally whether *kim'aṭ* is to be interpreted temporally[6] or quantitatively;[7] for it is asserted that Yahweh did not allow the Israelites to be oppressed during the patriarchal period, since they were "still few in number (*kim'aṭ,* 'had been in the land for only a short while' or 'were only a small group, a minority'), and were sojourners in it." In comparison with similar statements that also justify Yahweh's compassion and protection with reference to a lesser party,[8] the latter alternative seems more probable.

Finally, brief reference should be made to Ps. 2:12; Job 32:22, where righteous behavior is prompted by the belief that God's wrath is quickly or easily inflamed, or that the creator God could soon put an end to Elihu.

2. *Quantitative Aspect.* The quantitative aspect of *me'aṭ* emerges in the conclusion to Deuteronomy. One of the consequences of disobedience to the commandments is that Israel will sow much seed but gather little in (Dt. 28:38). Hag. 1:6 asserts the same thing, stimulating thereby the temple reconstruction. And Hag. 1:9 reveals the discrepancy between the people's high expectations and paltry results. Just as a smaller quantity is understood here in a general fashion as the consequence of curse, so are increase and multiplicity understood as the consequences of blessing (Ps. 107:38f.).

The theme of the increase or decrease of a people as the result of divine blessing or curse occurs relatively frequently. Yahweh's compassion toward the exiles is expressed in the fact that he does not diminish their number (Jer. 30:19; cf. 29:6). Although not uttered by Yahweh *expressis verbis,* the statement in the small historical credo nonetheless clearly refers to him, namely, that the patriarch sojourned in Egypt as a stranger with few men, and became a great nation (Dt. 26:5). In a reverse fashion, God's punishment consists in only a few men remaining from Israel, although it was once as numerous as the stars of heaven (Dt. 28:62; similarly Lev. 26:22). Applied to a foreign people such as Egypt, such divine judgment again means a reduction in number (Ezk. 29:15). In all these statements, however, a direct relationship obtains between quantity and quality. A great nation is "strong" (*'āṣûm,* Dt. 26:5), while a lesser nation is so weak that it is no longer able to rule over others (Ezk. 29:15; also Nu. 13:18). Dnl. 11:23 asserts the unthinkable, namely, that someone with only a small people shall become strong.

Regarding Yahweh's attitude toward Israel within the context of Israel's size, two considerations are of importance. Even when not expressed by the root *m'ṭ,* the substance of, e.g., Jgs. 7:1-8 remains in effect: Gideon is to diminish drastically the number of warriors with him so that Israel will be unable to boast before Yahweh that it delivered

5. So Wolff, 144.
6. As does the Zürcher Bible.
7. So H.-J. Kraus, *Psalms 60–150* (Eng. trans., Minneapolis, 1989), 306; Rudolph, 122.
8. Cf. II.2 above.

itself. This notion is then given a precise theological formulation in Dt. 7:7f.: not because Israel was the greatest nation did Yahweh choose it — since, in fact, it is the fewest *(hamm^{e}'aṭ)* of all peoples — but because he loved Israel. Thus Yahweh's compassionate election can find no justification in Israel itself. Here the idea is carried to the extreme that was sketched, e.g., in the plea made by Amos that Israel be spared: "Jacob is so small" (Am. 7:2,5). The smallness of a people, like the helplessness of an infant, evokes the gentleness, concern, and caring love of its God. Such a notion is also expressed in the plea to the prophet Jeremiah made by the confused forces after the murder of Gedaliah, namely, that he pray to Yahweh on behalf of this remnant: "for there are only a few of us left out of many" (Jer. 42:2). This dependent clause again appeals to one's sense of compassion, either that of the prophet[9] or of Yahweh himself.

Finally, statements concerning small quantity are also associated with notions of a remnant; here the idea of divine judgment can be reflected. When Isa. 16:14 asserts that the remnant of Moab will be "very few," this simultaneously implies complete weakness and subjection to contempt. Similarly, the announcement that the glory of Kedar will come to an end is explicated by the assertion that "the remainder of the archers will be few" (Isa. 21:16f.). The idea of the small remnant of Israel, however, despite the attendant reality of judgment, can nonetheless express an element of forbearance and preservation, and of Yahweh's steadfast love for his people, whose further history he will renew. Because Yahweh has left his people a few survivors, it is far better off than Sodom and Gomorrah (Isa. 1:9). The symbolic act Ezekiel is instructed to perform consists in taking only a small number of hairs from the final third of his shorn hair and beard, and binding them into the skirts of his robe (Ezk. 5:3), a reference to the preservation of a small remnant of people who will stay alive. And Jeremiah entreats Yahweh to correct him, although not to do so in anger, but rather in his divine moderation so that Yahweh not "bring him to nothing" (Jer. 10:24), i.e., he entreats Yahweh to preserve him and to keep him alive. Ezr. 9:8 renders this as *miḥyâ m^{e}'aṭ,* "a little reviving," the basis of which is similarly Yahweh's compassion.

3. *Much or Little as a Term for "Enough."* When one person gathers much nourishment but has nothing over, and the other gathers less but has no lack (Ex. 16:17f.), this is an expression of Yahweh's grace and compassion for the people wandering in the wilderness. "Little or much" thus points out that each receives enough from Yahweh. One receives what he or she needs. The same idea lies behind 1 S. 14:6: Jonathan is convinced that it is easy for Yahweh to help "by many or by few." 2 S. 12:8 recalls that Yahweh also generously compensates David: if that which you have already received were too little, Yahweh would add much more as well.

4. *Prayer.* Such references to small quantity are also embedded in prayers, laments, and indictments. Thus Moses cries to Yahweh: "They are almost *(m^{e}'aṭ)* ready to stone

---

9. A. Weiser, *Das Buch Jeremia 25,15–52,54. ATD,* XXI (^{8}1983), 368.

me" (Ex. 17:4). Similar formulations are found in Ps. 73:2; 119:87; Prov. 5:14: My feet almost stumbled, they (godless men) have almost made an end of me, I was almost in utter ruin. This reference to "almost" or "nearly" always expresses the conviction that God came to the petitioner's aid at just the right time (Ps. 94:17). And in the great prayer of confession the congregation asks that all its hardships not seem little to God (Neh. 9:32). Finally, knowing that the days of his life are few, Job asks at least that they be a bit brighter (Job 10:20).

5. *Accusations.* The interrogative *ham'aṭ* represents a typical formulation expressing indictment and indignation. It expresses Israel's murmuring in the wilderness (Nu. 16:13), or is directed as an indictment against the company of Korah (Nu. 16:9), against those building an altar by the Jordan (Josh. 22:17), or against Job (Job 15:11). This figure of speech is also appropriated by Isaiah (Isa. 7:13) and Ezekiel (Ezk. 16:20; 34:18) in order to accuse the house of David of rebellion against God, the "unfaithful wife" of harlotry and child sacrifice, and the animals of the flocks of lack of consideration toward one another. The skeptical question "is it not enough" drastically evokes the enormous intensification of sinful behavior: not only rebellion against human beings, but even against God; not only harlotry, but even human sacrifice; not only eating the grass of the pasture, but treading down what is left over as well. This makes the indictment so grievous that no doubt can remain concerning the verdict. The interrogative formulation challenges the addressee to respond, who can but confirm and secure the indictment.

6. *Ps. 8:6(5).* Ps. 8:6(5) makes a special assertion. The dignity of human beings as the most excellent of God's creatures is rendered in the prayer assertion: "Yet you have made him little less than God" *(ḥsr* [piel] *me'aṭ min).* Whether the sense is that "human beings have their station, given to them by God in creation, immediately below the heavenly beings,"[10] or that, more likely, one must interpret the statement thus: "Thou hast made him lack but little of the divine,"[11] is in this context less significant, since here, too, *me'aṭ* refers to something slight, little, infinitesimally small.[12] The LXX understands the expression temporally: *brachý ti* (cf. He. 2:7,9).

7. *Ezk. 11:16.* For the sake of completeness, let us refer in conclusion to Ezk. 11:16. Yahweh speaks: "Though I removed them far away among the nations, and though I scattered them among the countries, yet I have been a sanctuary to them in small measure *(lemiqdaš me'aṭ).*" Here *me'aṭ* again evokes the element of hope. Although Israel had to go into distant exile, it is "not a place abandoned by God,"[13] since there, too, Yahweh became a sanctuary to them, granting them thus his continued presence.

---

10. H.-J. Kraus, *Psalms 1–59* (Eng. trans., Minneapolis, 1987), 183.
11. H. W. Wolff, *Anthropology of the OT* (Eng. trans., Philadelphia, 1974).
12. → חסר *ḥāsēr,* V, 89f.
13. W. Zimmerli, *Ezekiel 1. Herm* (Eng. trans. 1979), 262.

The lesser element associated with such a sanctuary probably resides in the fact that such worship in a distant land was only a shadow of the services conducted in the Jerusalem sanctuary. Thus Yahweh's salvific will manifests itself in this expression even in the midst of judgment over his people, guaranteeing his loyalty in determining Israel's future.

Zobel

מְעִים *mēʿîm*

Contents: I. Etymology, Occurrences. II. Usage. III. LXX.

I. Etymology, Occurrences. The Hebrew term **mēʿîm,* "inner parts, entrails" (the absolute form is not attested in the OT; Modern Hebrew also attests the dual *mēʿayim*) corresponds etymologically to Aram. *m^{e}ʿā', m^{e}ʿayyā'* (Syr. *maʿyā'*), Arab. *maʿy, miʿā,* and Ethiop. *'amāʿūt* with the same meaning; an element of uncertainty attaches to the Akkadian form *amūtu,* "sheep liver, liver omen."[1]

The word occurs 30 times in the MT of the OT, as well as once in Sirach. The distribution pattern of occurrences is unremarkable.

II. Usage. In some cases the word refers concretely to "entrails": Joab struck his sword into Amasa's body, causing the entrails to flow out onto the ground (2 S. 20:10); Joram is struck by a disease that causes his bowels to fall out (2 Ch. 21:15,18f.). The reference can even be to the external part of the body, as in the descriptive song Cant. 5:14.

In an extended sense *mēʿîm* refers to what is filled with food, i.e., the "stomach": Ezekiel fills his stomach with the scroll, i.e., he eats it (Ezk. 3:3); on the day of the wrath of Yahweh the people are able neither to satisfy their hunger nor to fill their stomachs (Ezk. 7:19); Zophar says that the wicked person's food turns to poison in his *mēʿîm* (Job 20:14, par. *qereḇ*); Jon. 2:1f.(Eng. 1:17–2:1) is comparable: Jonah is in the *mēʿîm* of the fish. According to Nu. 5:22, the water of execration brings a curse into the *mēʿîm* of the woman.[2] In Ps. 22:15(14), *mēʿîm* refers to the inner parts of the body in general: "my heart is melted within my insides."

The term *mēʿîm* refers further to the body or to the inner parts of the body as the

---

mēʿîm. H. Holma, *Die Namen der Körperteile im Assyrisch-Babylonischen. AnAcScFen,* B, 7/1 (1911); H. W. Wolff, "The Inner Parts of the Body," *Anthropology of the OT* (Eng. trans., Philadelphia, 1974), 63-66.

1. *AHw,* I (1965), 46; cf. Holma, 88. Concerning the topic in general, cf. F. Rundgren, "Semitische Wortstudien. 8: Geʿez *'amāʿūt* 'Eingeweide,' " *OrSuec,* 10 (1961), 121-27.

2. → בטן *beṭen,* II, 98; cf. G. Giesen, *Die Wurzel* שבע *"schwören." Eine semasiologische Studie zum Eid im AT. BBB,* 56 (1981), 124-132.

seat of origin of a person, "the internal sexual organs."[3] In this sense it often parallels *beṭen,* e.g., in Gen. 25:23: "Two nations are in your [Rebekah's] body *(beṭen),* and two peoples from your womb *(mēʿîm)* shall be divided"; Isa. 49:1: "Yahweh called me from the *beṭen,* from my mother's womb *(mēʿîm)* he named my name" (Yahweh's servant is appointed to his task even before birth; cf. Jer. 1:5[4]); Ps. 71:6: "Upon you I have leaned from the *beṭen* on; from the womb on *(mᵉʿê ʾimmî)* you have been my protection" (cf. Ps. 22:10f.[9f.] with different vocabulary). Reference is often made to a son or heir who goes forth from the *mēʿîm* of his father (Gen. 15:4; 2 S. 7:12; 16:11; perhaps also 2 K. 20:18; Isa. 39:7 [conj.[5]]; Isa. 39:7, where 1QIs[a] reads *mimmᵉʿê* instead of *mimmê*). 2 Ch. 32:21 emphasizes how Hezekiah is slain by "his own sons" *(yᵉṣîʾê mēʿāw).* In Isa. 48:19, the terms *zeraʿ,* "offspring," and *ṣeʾᵉṣāʾê mēʿeykā* are parallel. Finally, Ruth 1:11 also belongs in this context: "Have I yet children in my *mēʿîm?*"

In the figurative sense *mēʿîm* refers to a person's inner parts as the seat of the emotions. Here it stands in 5 of 8 occurrences together with *hāmâ,* "to surge, rush, get excited" (or *hāmôn*). The context can be that of love, as in Cant. 5:4: the bride is inwardly thrilled by her love for the groom; and in Sir. 51:21, where the relationship with wisdom is described in the terminology of love[6] (the Hebrew text has "*yehᵉmû mēʿay* like an oven," which leads to the reading represented by the Peshitta; the LXX presupposes the Hebrew text, although without "oven"). In other occurrences the reference is to divine compassion. Thus in Isa. 63:15 God is implored to look down from heaven, and the question is raised: "Where are the yearning of your heart and your compassion *(raḥᵃmîm)?*" In Jer. 31:20, God characterizes Ephraim as his favorite son and says: "My heart is stirred; I will surely have mercy *(rḥm)* on him." In Isa. 16:11, we read: "Therefore my soul moans [or 'is agitated,' *hāmâ*] for Moab, my *qereḇ* for Kir-heres." In one instance *hāmâ* occurs not with *mēʿîm,* but rather with par. *lēḇ,* namely, in the temperamental outcry in Jer. 4:19: "*mēʿay mēʿay* [NRSV 'My anguish! My anguish!']! I writhe in pain! Oh, the walls of my heart! My heart [or 'soul'][7] is beating wildly *(hāmâ);* I cannot keep silent." This verse evokes Jeremiah's profound anguish in the face of the coming catastrophe.

In contrast, twice in Lamentations the verb is *ḥᵒmarmar,*[8] and the verses employ several synonyms: "I am in distress *(ṣar-lî),* my soul is in tumult, my heart *(lēḇ)* is wrung within me *(bᵉqirbî)*" (Lam. 1:20); and: "My eyes are spent with weeping *(kālû),* my soul is in tumult, my liver *(kāḇēḏ)* is poured to the ground because of the destruction of the daughter of my people" (Lam. 2:11). Both cases evoke the grief caused by the great catastrophe of the year 586. Yet another image is used in Job 30:27: the heart is in turmoil *(rtḥ)* and is never still.

---

3. Wolff, 63.
4. L. Schmidt, "Die Berufung Jeremias (Jer 1,4-10)," *ThViat,* 13 (1975/77), 189-209, esp. 205f., suspects that the Judean ideology of kingship provides the background for this formulation; cf. already O. Kaiser, *Der königliche Knecht. FRLANT,* N.S. 52[70] (1959), 57.
5. *HAL,* II (1995).
6. See H. Ringgren, *Word and Wisdom* (Lund, 1947), 113.
7. See *BHS.*
8. → חמר *ḥmr* (V, 1-4).

Thus *mēʿîm* can be associated with the most varied emotions: love, compassion, anguish, grief.

Finally, this context also includes Ps. 40:9(8), where the psalmist says: "Your law is within my *mēʿîm*" (cf. Ps. 37:31 with *lēḇ*).

III. LXX. The LXX usually translates *mēʿîm* with *koilía,* although in isolated cases it uses *éleos* (Isa. 63:15) and *gastḗr* (Job 20:14). In Gen. 15:4, the LXX simply reads *ek soú,* and in Jer. 31:20(LXX 38:20) it uses a circumscription.

Ringgren

מָעַל *māʿal;* מַעַל *maʿal*

Contents: I. Etymology. II. Occurrences. III. LXX. IV. OT Usage: 1. Unfaithfulness Toward Human Beings; 2. Unfaithfulness Toward God; 3. Special Cases. V. Qumran.

I. Etymology. *KBL*[3] follows Jakob Barth[1] in associating Heb. *māʿal* with Arab. *maǵila,* "to be vicious, wicked," and *maǵālat,* "betrayal, deception." The Arabic verb, however, can perhaps be translated better as "to be rotten, depraved," and is used only in reference to a person's eye. There is, however, a verb *maǵala,* "to slander, calumniate," whence derives the term *maǵālat,* "slander, calumniation." In addition, *maǵālat* can also be derived from *ǵāla(i)* VIII, "to deceive." The meaning here thus does correspond very well to the Hebrew "to act counter to one's duty, to be unfaithful." Considering that the Hebrew verb often has the connotation "to deprive/take away something due a person," another possibility might be Arab. *maʿala,* "to snatch away, damage, slander." Otherwise the verb is attested both in Middle Hebrew and in Jewish Aramaic with the meaning "to misappropriate, to misuse something sacred," apparently reflecting biblical influence.

J. L. Palache[2] points out that the relationship between *māʿal* and *meʿîl,* "cloak," resembles that between *bāḡaḏ,* "to deceive, mislead," and *beḡeḏ,* "clothing, garment": a piece of clothing "covers" the body; "to cover or clothe something" means "to deceive." This suggestion, however, presupposes a completely different original meaning for the root than that suggested by the etymology.

II. Occurrences. The term *māʿal* occurs noticeably often in the paronomastic expression *māʿal maʿal* (20 times); the verb occurs alone 15 times, and the noun 9 times

---

1. *Etymologische Studien zum semitischen, insbesondere zum hebräischen Lexicon* (Leipzig, 1893), 62f.

2. *Semantic Notes on the Hebrew Lexicon* (Eng. trans., Leiden, 1959), 45.

alone. All occurrences are late: Ezekiel, Deuteronomistic history, Holiness Code, Priestly Code, Chronicler's history, Daniel (Prov. 16:10; Job 21:34 are difficult to date).

Words that accompany *mā'al* include *ḥṭ', 'āwōn, 'āšam, māraḏ, mārâ,* and *rš'*.

III. LXX. The LXX does not have a consistent translation for *mā'al,* translating instead according to context. Thus the following paronomastic expressions are used for *mā'al ma'al: lanthánō — lḗthē* (Lev. 5:15; Nu. 5:27), *plēmmeléō — plēmméleia* (Josh. 7:1; 22:16,20,31; Dnl. 9:7), *parapíptō — paráptōma* (Ezk. 14:13; 15:8; 18:24; 20:27), *adikéō — adikía* (Ezk. 39:26), *anoméō — anomía* (1 Ch. 10:13), *aphístēmi — apóstasis* (2 Ch. 28:19), *athetéō — athétēma* (2 Ch. 36:14), *paroráō* with participle (Lev. 5:21[Eng. 6:2]; Nu. 5:6; Nu. 5:12 even has *eán parídę̄ autón hyperidoúsa*). When *mā'al* stands alone, it is also variously rendered by *adikéō, anoméō, aphístēmi,* and *athetéō,* as well as *apeithéō, asynthetéō,* and *hamartánō* (2 Ch. 12:2; Ezr. 10:2). The noun is rendered in several instances by *anomía,* and in isolated cases by *apostasía* and *apóstasis,* and by circumscriptions such as those in Nu. 31:16; Josh. 22:22.

IV. OT Usage. The act of *mā'al* can direct itself either toward human beings or toward God.

1. *Unfaithfulness Toward Human Beings.* The law concerning the so-called jealousy offering (Nu. 5:11-31) describes the presupposed case as follows: if a woman leaves her husband *(śāṭâ)* and acts unfaithfully against him (commits a *ma'al)* and has sexual relations with another man . . . (v. 12). Verse 27 describes the same case as *niṭmā',* "to defile oneself," and as *mā'al ma'al.* The reference is thus to marital infidelity; from a different perspective the verb could be circumscribed by the expression "to deprive someone of something to which he is entitled."

The sacrificial laws of Lev. 5 require an *'āšām* offering when a person sins *(ḥāṭā')* and commits a *ma'al* by deceiving another person in a matter of deposit or security (v. 21[6:2]). On the one hand, the person deprives someone of something rightfully his, and on the other hand he shows unfaithfulness. Nu. 5:6 seems to presuppose a similar case: when a person commits a sin *(ḥaṭṭa'ṯ),* a *ma'al* against Yahweh, becoming guilty thereby *('āšam),* he is to make restitution regarding the object which led to that guilt. Although strictly speaking this disloyalty is directed against a person, the act itself is simultaneously judged as disloyalty toward God. In contrast, in Lev. 5:15, which requires an *'āšām* offering, the *ma'al* is expressly associated with God when someone unwittingly *(bišgāgâ)* sins *(ḥāṭā')* regarding any of the gifts consecrated to Yahweh *(qoḏšê YHWH);* even if this has occurred unwittingly, Yahweh nonetheless has been deprived of something rightfully his.

2. *Unfaithfulness Toward God.* This marks the transition to unfaithfulness toward God. A concrete example is found in Josh. 7:1: by misappropriating some of the devoted things *(ḥērem),* Achan deprives God of what belongs to him. This event is then recalled in Josh. 22:16,20,22 (here + *māraḏ*) and in 1 Ch. 2:7 (verb only).

Ezekiel uses the term *mā'al* in the general sense of religious disloyalty toward God.

Ezk. 14:13-20 is composed in the style of casuistic cultic law. Verse 13 presupposes the case that a land sins *(ḥāṭā')* and commits *ma'al,* so that Yahweh must punish it; although the righteous men Noah, Daniel, and Job will be able to deliver their own lives, they will not be able to save the land itself. No further information is given regarding the exact nature of the sin or unfaithfulness.

In a similarly casuistic context, Ezk. 18:24 asserts that a righteous person who turns away from righteousness and commits iniquity *('āwel)* after the model of the wicked *(rāšā')* is to die for his *ma'al* and his sin. Hence *ma'al* is equated with iniquity, godlessness, and sin; or rather, *ma'al* encompasses the entire essence of the wicked, which does not acknowledge God as God.

Ezk. 20:27 associates *ma'al* with defamation or blasphemy (*gdp* piel) against God; the following verse reveals that the reference is to worship on the high places. Accordingly, *ma'al* involves denying Yahweh the veneration due him. Since vv. 27-29 are clearly to be taken as an exegetical elaboration of the preceding material,[3] the terms *mā'al* and *giddēp* must refer to v. 24, which defines sin as rejection *(mā'as)* of the statutes and profanation (*ḥll* piel) of the Sabbath. The term *mā'al* thus refers to transgression against the sacred.

The remaining passages from Ezekiel are of a more general nature. Ezk. 15:8 asserts that Yahweh will make the land desolate because the people committed *ma'al,* and 17:20 that Zedekiah will be condemned for the same reason; 39:23 states that the Israelites were led into exile because of their *'āwōn* and *ma'al,* and v. 24 additionally mentions their uncleanness *(ṭum'â)* and *peša'*. According to 39:26, however, they will forget their shame and their *ma'al* after the restoration.

Lev. 26:40 (Holiness Code) is similarly generalized: when the Israelites experience God's punishment, they will have to confess their guilt (*'āwōn,* NRSV 'iniquity'), which consisted in their having committed *ma'al* and having resisted Yahweh *(hālaḵ baqqerî).* Then, according to v. 42, Yahweh will remember his covenant.

In contrast, Dt. 32:51 (P) establishes a clear connection with the violation of what is sacred: "You committed *ma'al* at Meribath-kadesh and did not revere me as holy (*qdš* piel)." Instead of *ma'al,* the parallel passage Nu. 27:12-14 uses *mārâ* and "did not sanctify me" (so RSV).

The occurrences in the Chronicler's history offer several examples indicating the actual content of *mā'al.* According to 1 Ch. 5:25, the tribes of Reuben, Gad, and Manasseh committed *ma'al* against the God of their fathers by playing the harlot after the gods of the land *(zānâ 'aḥarê);* according to 1 Ch. 10:13, Saul committed *ma'al* by seeking guidance from a spirit (instead of from Yahweh!). Uzziah commits *ma'al* by entering the temple to make an incense offering, a presumption *(gāḇah lēḇ)* which simultaneously constitutes a violation of the sanctity of the temple (2 Ch. 26:16,18). The remark in 2 Ch. 28:19, namely, that Ahaz acted wantonly (*hipria'*) and committed *ma'al* against Yahweh, is left quite general, although v. 23 explicates it by revealing that he sacrificed to the gods of Damascus.

---

3. W. Zimmerli, *Ezekiel 1. Herm* (Eng. trans. 1979), 412.

In 2 Ch. 29:6, Hezekiah says: "for our fathers have committed *ma'al,*" adding by way of explication: they have done what was evil *(ra')* in the sight of Yahweh, they have forsaken him *('āzaḇ),* have turned away from Yahweh's habitation *(miškān)* and turned their backs on him *(nāṯan 'ōrep).* This verse serves to justify the order to the Levites (v. 5) to carry out the filth *(niddâ)* from Yahweh's house and to sanctify the temple again (*qdš* piel). That is, the temple's sanctity has been violated and must be reestablished. 2 Ch. 30:7 is similar, where Hezekiah says in a general sense that the fathers committed *ma'al* against Yahweh, whereupon he gave them up to desolation. The context in v. 8 shows what the positive requirement is: to come to the sanctuary, which he has sanctified (hiphil), and to serve him *('bd);* hence *ma'al* constitutes the neglect of precisely these demands.

2 Ch. 29:19 mentions the restoration and sanctification of the temple utensils which King Ahaz had discarded in his *ma'al.* 2 Ch. 33:19 specifies the sin and *ma'al* of Manasseh as the building of sacrificial high places and the erection of Asherim and *pᵉsîlîm.* 2 Ch. 36:14 again refers to the sanctity of the temple: the priests committed *ma'al* following all the abominations of the nations and polluted *(ṭm'* piel) the house of Yahweh, which he had hallowed (hiphil).

Several times the book of Ezra refers to marriages with foreign women as *ma'al.* Such marriages constitute unfaithfulness toward Yahweh (Ezr. 9:2,4; 10:2,6,10; cf. Neh. 13:27).

Nu. 31:16 briefly mentions worship of Ba'al as *ma'al,* again underscoring idolatry as a breach of faith. In contrast, Neh. 1:8; Dnl. 9:7 make only general references.

3. *Special Cases.* Job 21:34 represents a special case. Job says to his friends: "How then will you comfort me with empty nothings *(heḇel)?* There is nothing left of your answers but *ma'al.*" This apparently does not refer to unfaithfulness toward God, but rather to a deceptive interpretation of facts that does not correspond to reality. In Prov. 16:10, *mā'al* refers to mistaken legal judgment: the king speaks the correct judgment and does not deceive, since he exercises his office by divine authority (cf. LXX: *planáō,* "to err, go astray").

V. Qumran. In Qumran the term *ma'al* has simply become one of many expressions for sin. The objects of *mā'al* can include the Torah (CD 9:16f.) or one's fellow human being (lit., "flesh," as in Isa. 58:7: CD 7:1). To forsake God *('āzaḇ)* is *ma'al* (CD 1:3; cf. Ezk. 39:23; Lev. 26:40). One often encounters combinations such as "guilty rebellion and sins of unfaithfulness" (*'ašmaṯ peša' ûma'al ḥaṭṭā'ṯ,* 1QS 9:4), "abominable uncleanness *(niddâ)* and guilty faithlessness" (*'ašmaṯ ma'al,* 1QH 11:11). 1QH 10:23 juxtaposes the terms *ma'al* and *peša',* 1QH 4:30,34 the terms *ma'al* and *'ašmâ.* Apparently no substantive distinction was perceived between the various terms used to refer to sin.

Ringgren

מַעֲלָל *maʿ^a lāl* → עלל *ʿll*

מַעֲשֶׂה *maʿ^a śeh* → עָשָׂה *ʿāśâ*

מֹץ *mōṣ*

Contents: I. Etymology, Occurrences. II. Usage.

I. Etymology, Occurrences. The term *mōṣ*, "chaff," is a primary noun corresponding etymologically to Arab. *mauṣ*, "straw." It occurs 8 times in the OT, always metaphorically in poetical texts. The LXX usually translates it with *chnoús*, although occasionally with *ánthos* and *koniortós* (dust).

II. Usage. The metaphor derives from the practice of threshing. After threshing with the threshing sledge[1] the grain was winnowed onto the threshing floor, the wind blowing away the chaff and the seeds falling to the floor.[2]

The most extensive use of this metaphor is found in Deutero-Isaiah (Isa. 41:15f.): "Now, I will make of you a threshing sledge . . . you shall thresh the mountains and crush them, and you shall make the hills like chaff. You shall winnow them and the wind shall carry them away, and the tempest shall scatter them." The objects "mountains" and "hills" do not really fit with the metaphor, which otherwise is used to refer to the destruction of the enemies. These mountains and hills are probably the same as in 40:4, i.e., obstacles standing in the way of the returning exiles. These obstacles are thus to disappear like chaff in the wind.

Isa. 17:13; 29:5, on the other hand, speak about the annihilation of enemies. The first passage describes the storm of nations against Zion; as soon as God intervenes, however, this storm collapses: "He will rebuke them, and they will flee far away, chased like chaff on the mountains before the wind and whirling dust before the storm." The second passage also speaks of the hostile attack on Zion and its repulsion: "But the multitude of your strangers (NRSV 'foes') shall be like small dust, and the multitude of the ruthless like flying chaff." Every attack against Zion will founder, the enemies will be blown away like chaff over the threshing floor when Yahweh intervenes in defense of his holy city.

Hos. 13:3 blends the metaphor of chaff with other imagery in its portrayal of

---

1. → דוש *dûš (dûsh)* (III, 182-86).
2. *AuS*, III (1933), 126-139.

judgment over Israel: "Therefore they shall be like the morning mist or like the dew that goes early away, like chaff that swirls from the threshing floor or like smoke from a window." All these images evoke the notion of swift dispersion (if "morning mist" and "dew" are not glosses from 6:4[3]).

Although the text of Zeph. 2:2 may be corrupt, the point of comparison is in any case the swiftness with which chaff blows away. Gillis Gerleman[4] translates the MT: "Like chaff a day has passed away"; otherwise the text is usually emended as follows[5]: "before you are driven away like the drifting chaff," which of course better corresponds to the usual intent of the metaphor.

Ps. 1:4 is unequivocal: "The wicked . . . are like chaff which the wind drives away,"[6] they do not endure, but quickly pass away. Ps. 35:5 similarly wishes upon the petitioner's adversaries: "Let them be like chaff before the wind, with the angel of Yahweh driving them on!" (cf. v. 6: "Let their way be dark and slippery, with the angel of Yahweh pursuing them!"); they should receive the proper punishment.

The same principle underlies Job 21:18, which calls into question whether this really does happen: "How often are they [the wicked] like straw before the wind, and like chaff that the storm carries away?" The anticipated answer: only rarely.

Ringgren

---

3. Cf. A. Weiser, *Das Buch der zwölf Kleinen Propheten, I: Hosea. ATD,* XXIV (^{7}1979), *in loc.*
4. *Zephanja* (Lund, 1942), 26.
5. Cf., e.g., K. Elliger, *Das Buch der zwölf Kleinen Propheten, II: Zephanja. ATD,* XXV (^{8}1982), *in loc.*
6. Cf. *AuS,* III, 126-139.

מָצָא *māṣā'*

Contents: I. Derivation, Meaning, Occurrences. II. Finding as the Result of Seeking. III. "Finding Favor in Someone's Eyes." IV. "Encountering Someone," "Meeting Someone." V. Niphal "To Be Found, Detected, Caught." VI. Qal and Niphal "To Be Present," "To Be." VII. "To Find, Deem, Evaluate, Judge." VIII. "Meeting" in the Impersonal Sense. IX. Seeking and Finding God. X. Israel's Election as an Activity of God's "Finding." XI. Yahweh as Subject. XII. Hiphil. XIII. Idiomatic Expressions. XIV. Other Considerations. XV. 1. Biblical Aramaic *mṭ'* in Daniel; 2. Qumran.

---

māṣā'. A. R. Ceresko, "The Function of *Antanaclasis* (*mṣ'* 'to find' // *mṣ'* 'to reach, overtake, grasp') in Hebrew Poetry, Especially in the Book of Qoheleth," *CBQ,* 44 (1982), 551-569; J. Eaton, "Some Misunderstood Hebrew Words for God's Self-Revelation," *BT,* 25 (1974), 331-38; G. Gerleman, "מצא *mṣ'* finden," *THAT,* I, 922-25; M. Z. Kaddari, "Syntactic Presentation of a Biblical Hebrew Verb (*mṣ'*)," in G. B. Sarfatti, ed., *Studies in Hebrew and Semitic*

I. Derivation, Meaning, Occurrences. The OT concept articulated in the various forms of *mṣ'* makes use of a common Semitic root which occurs as such or in a similar form in virtually all the older and more recent Semitic languages. An element of motion similar to that inherent in Heb. *mṣ'* also manifests itself in Ugar. *mǵy, mṣ', mz',*[1] "to come, come to someone, arrive at, reach to something," OSA *mṭ', mz',* "to arrive," Arab. *mṣy,* "to go away, depart," and Aram., Biblical Aram. *mṭ', mṭy,* "to come, meet, arrive at, reach to." The same is true of Middle Hebrew, Jewish Aramaic, Egyptian Aramaic,[2] Palmyrene, Mandaic, Ethiopic, Tigre, and Amharic. As a verb indicating condition, Akk. *maṣû,* "to suffice, be enough,"[3] probably does not belong together with the transitive Hebrew verb *māṣā'.* One meaning attested everywhere except in Akkadian is "to find."[4]

The English equivalent "to find" constitutes the primary meaning of Biblical Heb. *mṣ',* whence the multiplicity of semantic extensions attested in the OT can easily be derived. The element of movement already mentioned precedes the act of finding and to that extent is always implied. The occasional stronger emphasis on this element is a secondary manifestation from which one can frequently enough get back to the original meaning. The act of finding is the result of conscious effort or intentional endeavor, in a great many cases the result of seeking, as well as the result of unintentional encounter, of a chance discovery or meeting. The act of "seeking," which in connection with *mṣ'* is rendered in the majority of instances by → בקשׁ *bqš* piel, less often by → דרשׁ *drš* (or occasionally a verb of hoping or anticipation, → קוה *qwh* piel), should not be characterized as an oppositional or antithetical term, but rather as a corresponding or complementary term. The opposite is actually "to lose," "to have gotten lost," "to hide," and "to be hidden." The second semantic field of "to find" mentioned above (in the sense of unintentional finding) also presupposes an element of action or movement.

The root *mṣ'* occurs 449 times in the OT.[5] The OT attests only verbal forms in the stem modifications qal (302), niphal (140), and hiphil (7). The distribution in the OT is widespread, with occurrences in almost every OT book (except Joel, Obadiah, Nahum, and Haggai). Even the Hebrew portion of Daniel attests 4 occurrences of *mṣ',* while Biblical Aram. *mṭ'* occurs 8 times in Daniel. A certain concentration of occurrences emerges in the narrative texts (e.g., 56 times in Genesis; 38 in 1/2 Samuel; 41

Languages (Ramat-Gan, 1980), 18-25 [Heb.], LVI [Eng. summary]; R. Kümpel, *Die Berufung Israels: Ein Beitrag zur Theologie des Hosea* (diss., Bonn, 1973), esp. 18-32; H. Preisker, "εὑρίσκω," *TDNT,* II, 769f.

1. *WUS*³, no. 1627, 1634, 1649; *UT,* no. 1520, 1524; cf. M. Dahood, "Northwest Semitic Philology and Job," *The Bible in Current Catholic Thought. M. J. Gruenthaner Memorial Volume. St. Mary's Theology Studies,* 1 (New York, 1962), 57, esp. on Job 11:7ab.

2. *DISO,* 164; cf. J. Blau, "Marginalia Semitica II," *Israel Oriental Studies,* 2 (1972), 67-72.

3. *AHw,* II (1972), 621b.

4. Cf. *HAL,* II (1995), 714.

5. According to G. Lisowsky; 462 occurrences according to *KBL*³; 454 according to *THAT;* 455 according to A. Even-Shoshan, *A New Concordance of the OT* (Jerusalem, 1983), 694-98.

in 1/2 Kings; 38 in 1/2 Chronicles) and in the Wisdom Literature (25 times in Proverbs; 17 in Ecclesiastes; 19 in Job; 9 in Canticles). Astonishingly few occurrences are found in the prophetic writings (most frequently in Jeremiah, with 26 occurrences; Jeremiah does, of course, contain extensive narrative passages). Heb. *mṣ'* is a commonly used term employed both in theological and in secular contexts. No special factors affecting its use are discernible. Depending on the context, a broad range of meanings emerges which can usually be traced back without much difficulty to the equivalent "to find." This is confirmed by the observation that the LXX translates the overwhelming majority of *mṣ'* passages with *heurískein,* although one does encounter numerous additional equivalents as well.[6] The Qumran texts also attest the use of *mṣ',* with approximately 35 occurrences thus far (qal and niphal).

II. Finding as the Result of Seeking. The story of Saul's accession as king in 1 S. 9:1–10:16 vividly illustrates the matrix of getting lost (or having become lost), seeking, and finding (or not finding). The asses of Kish, Saul's father, were lost (1 S. 9:3, *wattō'ḇaḏnâ*). He tells his son to go and look for them with the aid of one of the servants (*wᵉqûm lēḵ baqqēš,* v. 3), whereupon the two pass through long stretches of land without finding what they are seeking (*wᵉlō' māṣā'û,* v. 4). The element of movement preceding the actual finding is indicated verbally. This story portrays how Saul "meets up with" the "kingmaker" Samuel (circumscribed again with *mṣ'*[7]). The fact that the asses have nonetheless been found is repeated several times in the course of the story (1 S. 9:20, *kî nimṣā'û;* cf. 10:2,16), a motif woven like a red thread through the narrative fabric. According to another version of Saul's accession, at Mizpah he is taken by lot, sought, but not found (1 S. 10:21, *mṣ'* niphal). The OT often tells how someone is sought by others and is either found or not found: the spies by their pursuers in Josh. 2:22; the priests of David by Absalom's servants (2 S. 17:20); a young maiden for David, Abishag the Shunammite (1 K. 1:3, here as previously always with *bqš* piel and *mṣ'* qal); Elijah (on Ahab's orders) by Obadiah (1 K. 18:10,12); Elijah by members of the prophetic order after he is taken up to heaven (2 K. 2:17); the lover by the beloved (Cant. 3:1,2,4; 5:6, where seeking can be circumscribed by calling [*qr'*], and finding by answering [*'nh*]). Of course, besides persons, objects can also be the object of seeking and finding, e.g., the cup hidden in the brothers' "baggage" in the story of Joseph (Gen. 44:12, with *ḥpś* piel for "searching"; cf. the context), and the *tᵉrāp̄îm* Rachel steals and hides from Laban in the cycle of legends surrounding Jacob (Gen. 31:32-35, in v. 35 again *ḥpś* piel for "searching"). The harlot seeks and finds her lover as well as the path to him, unless Yahweh obstructs both, as in the case of adulterous Israel (Hos. 2:8f.[Eng. vv. 6f.]). In all these examples (which can represent many others), *mṣ'* is a common word that can be applied to a multitude of objects.

The metaphorical figure of seeking and not finding can proverbially refer to the fact

---

6. Cf. Preisker.
7. See IV below.

that a given danger is no longer a threat, or that God has eliminated it. This is the vision of salvation of Deutero-Isaiah (Isa. 41:12), according to which the adversaries and opponents of the chosen people of God will be put to shame *(bôš)* and become as nothing *(kᵉ'ayin), tᵉḇaqqᵉšēm wᵉlō' timṣā'ēm* (cf. the context), "you shall seek them but you shall not [be able to] find them [any longer]." Wisdom Literature ultimately views the *rāšāʿ,* despite his apparent well-being, as precarious and doomed to perish: "he will not be found" (Job 20:8; cf. Ps. 1:5).

That which is sought and then found can be a plethora of different abstractions, e.g., the *mᵉnûḥâ* which Naomi's two widowed daughters-in-law are to seek and find in the house of the men they will marry (Ruth 1:9; in view of 3:1 the mother-in-law helps with the search). Cant. 8:10 might be referring to the same thing when it describes the ultimate union of the lovers as the bride "finding *šālôm.*" According to Jer. 6:16, those persons will "find rest" in the theologically fulfilled sense who inquire about the proven paths to the good *(lintiḇôṯ ʿôlām 'ê-zeh ḏereḵ haṭṭôḇ)* and then walk in those paths. In inquiry, in asking about the good path, and in walking in that path those whom Jeremiah is addressing will find *margôaʿ lᵉnapšᵉḵem* (*miṣ'û* as the final in a string of imperatives, lit., "and find rest for your souls!" Jer. 6:16). The word of consolation to Baruch addresses his lament that he, Baruch, is unable to find rest *(mᵉnûḥâ)* in the oppressive present (Jer. 45:3). What Jeremiah laments for Baruch as an individual, Lamentations laments for exiled Judah as a collective (Lam. 1:3). "Rest" is sometimes understood concretely as a "resting place" which is either found or not found. The dove flying around outside the ark finds no *mānôaḥ* (Gen. 8:9 [J]). In contrast, in the judgment upon Edom the nocturnal demon Lilith will indeed (be permitted to) find a *mānôaḥ* among the ruins of the fortresses and palaces (Isa. 34:14).[8]

In various figures of speech Wisdom Literature extols the wisdom and understanding *(ḥoḵmâ, tᵉḇûnâ)* one seeks and finds (Prov. 3:13, *'ašrê 'āḏām māṣā' ḥoḵmâ*). Inclining one's ear to the sayings of wisdom, and heeding her words, means life for all who find them (4:22; cf. v. 21). Righteousness and truth are promised to those who find wisdom (8:9; cf. the context; wisdom herself is speaking in 8:35: *kî mōṣᵉ'î māṣā' ḥayyîm;*[9] see also vv. 12 + 17). Wisdom will open the future *('aḥᵃrîṯ)* and grant well-being to a person, but that person must first seek her diligently (8:17, *šḥr* piel) and "find" her (24:14). According to Elihu, Job's friends have obviously not found it in regard to Job himself (Job 32:13).

The abstractions attested as objects of *mṣ'* in the OT also include the solution to a riddle (Jgs. 14:12,18, *ḥîḏâ*) and the answer to a question, however posed (Job 32:3, *maʿaneh;* see also v. 13, where "answer" is equated with *ḥoḵmâ;* cf. also Neh. 5:8, *māṣā' dāḇār,* "to answer"). An even more general object is *ṭôḇ,* which can be found or missed; only the wise person, the person who keeps understanding (*šōmēr tᵉḇûnâ,* Prov. 19:8), finds it; the *ʿiqqēš-lēḇ* does not find it, but rather falls to evil (Prov. 17:20). The objects found by the person who pursues *(rdp)* righteousness and kindness are

---

8. Cf. O. Kaiser, *Isaiah 13–39. OTL* (Eng. trans. 1974), *in loc.*
9. *Qere;* see *BHS.*

more concrete; he finds life *(ḥayyîm)*, righteousness and honor (*ṣ^eḏāqâ w^eḵāḇôḏ*, Prov. 21:21). The weighty term *'ēzer k^enegdô* (Gen. 2:18,20 [J]) as a circumlocution for the man's partner, the woman, is the sought or chosen object prompted by male appraisal of the given circumstances. Among animals the man has found "no helper appropriate for him." Only Yahweh's own creative act creates the possibility of finding such an *'ēzer* (Gen. 2:20 [+ 21ff.] [J]). The investigation into a conspiracy (*bqš* pual) brings the matter *(dāḇār)* to light (Est. 2:23, *mṣ'* niphal). The attainment of results in an investigation, research, and appraisal is frequently expressed by *mṣ'*.[10] The procedure of indictment apparently employs the expression "to find a matter *(dāḇār)* against (*b^e*; NRSV 'in') someone" (Job 19:28). As a result of the intense proclivity toward imagery and metaphor in OT thought and speech, abstract content is expressed through descriptions of concrete activities. Thus a reference to not finding one's way or dwelling place expresses the condition of wandering about (Ps. 107:4). A hart that finds no pasture and is nonetheless driven even further is a symbol for debility and misery (Lam. 1:6). The agony of the Babylonian catastrophe consists for Jerusalem in the deportation of the king and his officials to a place where the law cannot be kept and prophets find no *ḥāzôn* (Lam. 2:9).

III. "Finding Favor in Someone's Eyes." The expression "to find favor or approval *(māṣā' ḥēn)* in someone's eyes (*b^e'ênê* NN)" occurs 43 times in the OT. Although it is especially well attested in narrative contexts, it does not occur in the traditions of the prophetic books except in Jer. 31:2, nor in the Psalms, Job, and hardly in Wisdom Literature. The various contexts in which the expression occurs show that it apparently derives from courtly style: in the book of Esther, 5:8; 7:3; 8:5 (cf. the parallel formulation with *nś' ḥēn b^e'ênê* in 5:2); in the Joseph story in Gen. 39:4; 50:4; in the story of David's accession and succession (see David's relationship with Saul and Jonathan, 1 S. 16:22; 20:3,29; with the Philistine king Achish of Gath, 27:5; Joab's relationship with David, 2 S. 14:22; cf. 16:4). This expression is also applied to the relationship between man and woman, whereby consonant with the sociological conditions obtaining in the ancient Near East the woman is to "find favor or approval in the eyes of the man" (Ruth 2:2,10,13, Levirate marriage; Dt. 24:1, in divorce proceedings, where a bill of divorce may be composed and handed over if among other things the wife *lō' timṣā'-ḥēn b^e'ênāw*). It is clear that this figure of speech applies to an encounter between two unequals. The socially-sociologically inferior party must "find" favor in the eyes of the superior party, the person of higher standing. This kind of unequal relationship can also occasionally emerge as a result of self-diminution or voluntary subjection. One such example is the relationship between Jacob and Esau, at whose encounter Jacob (for the familiar reasons presented in the narrative) subjects himself to Esau (Gen. 32:6[5]; 33:8,10,15). Beyond this, the expression is "reduced" to a courtesy formula, particularly when a petitioner encounters the person before whom he is making the petition (Laban before Jacob, Gen.

10. See discussion below.

30:27; Shechem before Jacob and his sons, the brothers of Dinah, whom he desires, Gen. 34:11; Jacob before Joseph, Gen. 47:29; David's followers before Nabal, 1 S. 25:8). This seems generally to be an element that is part and parcel of the context implied by the expression, namely, that "finding favor" in the eyes of a person either actually or temporarily of higher standing accompanies a request to the superior party, superior in the sense of the potential capacity for actually fulfilling that request. There are, however, isolated instances in which such bestowing of favor by a "superior" is justified quite simply by the remark that the person favored has indeed "found favor" in the eyes of the person bestowing it, or that the former has directed a request to the latter (1 S. 16:22, David is brought to Saul's court; cf. 1 K. 11:19). This entire complex is also applied to a person's relationship with God, although here the relationship cannot be reversed. A person attains, strives for, or receives favor in the eyes of God. The latter was the case for Noah when Yahweh made the decision concerning the deluge (Gen. 6:8 [J]). Finding favor in Yahweh's eyes is also indicated by the granting of the request not to pass by Abraham (Gen. 18:3 [J]). For Lot, too, this idiom stands in connection with a request (Gen. 19:19 [J]). The formula occurs especially frequently when Moses intercedes on behalf of his (sinful) people at Sinai (Ex. 33:12,13,16,17 [J]); in one instance, the people itself (as a corporate person), and not merely an individual, is conceived as standing before God to receive this show of favor (v. 16). This passage also includes a reflection concerning just how one is to recognize *(bammeh yiwwāḏa')* that both Moses and the people have found favor. The answer supplied in the rhetorical question is: "[by] thy [God's] going with us, so that we are distinct, I and thy people, from all other people that are upon the face of the earth." The burden weighing upon Moses, namely, the people murmuring in the wilderness, is proof for him that he has not "found favor" in Yahweh's eyes (Nu. 11:11,15 [J]). Finding favor *(māṣā' ḥēn)* with God is not an abstract experience of favor, but acquires rather concrete, substantive fulfillment in God's salvific actions on behalf of the person or group concerned (e.g., David's hope that after Absalom's conspiracy Yahweh will bring him back to Jerusalem and allow him to see the ark of God again, 2 S. 15:25). According to the vision of salvation of Jer. 31:2, the people who survived the sword by fleeing into the wilderness find the *ḥēn* of rest. The theological use of this formula can also easily be traced back to the courtly background of the expression. One notices that *māṣā' ḥēn* is well attested in the Yahwistic stratum of the Pentateuch. The word group is used in a weakened and generalized sense in the few examples from Wisdom Literature. Specific behavior advocated by wisdom enhances one's chances of finding favor in the sight of both God and human beings (Prov. 3:4; 28:23).[11]

IV. "Encountering Someone," "Meeting Someone." This particular semantic nuance, of course, is easily understood as an extension of the actual equivalent "to find." Both the circumstances and the context as they emerge from the various

11. → חנן *ḥānan* (V, 22-36).

passages, however, do suggest occasionally seeking a more appropriate translation for *mṣ'*. The intentional finding of one person by another can also be rendered as "to seek out," as might perhaps be the case in the angel's encounter with Hagar at the well in the desert (Gen. 16:7 [E]). The same might apply to the consciously arranged encounter between Elijah and Elisha (1 K. 19:19), in which context we might use the expression "to come across or meet a person." Elijah is sent by God to Ahab, and "seeks" the latter out in Naboth's vineyard (1 K. 21:20). Such conscious encounter between two persons can certainly also occur in the hostile sense. Cain, who has been driven from his field, laments that his existence is now threatened by every person who comes upon him (who encounters him) (Gen. 4:14,15 [J], *kol-mōṣ*^{e}*'î yahargēnî*). This refers first of all to the anticipated blood avengers from the slain person's family, but is then consciously expanded to refer to Cain's complete defenselessness in the face of every potential enemy after his banishment. The same expression is used once more in retrospect concerning the defeated people of God during the time of Nebuchadnezzar: "All who encountered them (in hostility) have devoured them" (Jer. 50:7, *kol-môṣ*^{e}*'êhem '*^{a}*ḵālûm*). During the conquest involving the tribe of Judah the "Judeans" come upon Adoni-bezek *(wayyimṣ*^{e}*'û)* and fight against him (Jgs. 1:5). The Chronicler's account of a battle between King Jehoshaphat and the Ammonites and Moabites uses *mṣ'* in the hostile sense (2 Ch. 20:16); the same applies to Jehu's battle against the Judean collaborators of Ahab (2 Ch. 22:8; the Deuteronomistic version in 2 K. 10:13 speaks only of a chance encounter between Jehu and the Judeans). Saul is astonished that David finds his enemy, namely, Saul himself, and nonetheless spares him (1 S. 24:20[19], *w*^{e}*ḵî-yimṣā' 'îš 'eṯ-'ōy*^{e}*ḇô w*^{e}*šill*^{e}*ḥô b*^{e}*ḏereḵ ṭôḇâ*). Of course, an unintentional meeting with a personal counterpart can also ultimately be translated as "finding," though the expressions "to meet, encounter" also suggest themselves, e.g., for Jacob's servant, whom Jacob instructs how to behave if the servant should encounter Esau (Gen. 32:20[19]); or for the man gathering sticks on the sabbath day in the wilderness, whom the Israelites come upon and take into custody (Nu. 15:32,33); or, finally, for the Egyptian servant of an Amalekite whom David's mercenaries come upon and seize in the Negeb after the Amalekite raid upon Ziklag (1 S. 30:11). It is difficult to say whether Jehu's meeting with Jehonadad the son of Rechab occurred by chance, though the formulation in 2 K. 10:15 at least allows for this possibility. The same uncertainty attaches to the account of the designation of Jeroboam by Ahijah the Shilonite, who (by chance?) meets Jeroboam on the road outside Jerusalem and performs the symbolic act on him (1 K. 11:29). One might also imagine that Ahijah lay in wait and watched for Jeroboam (*wayyimṣā' 'ōṯô . . . badderek̲*).

This example leads us to a group of passages in which *mṣ'* is used the sense of an intentional, positive or neutral encounter with another person. As Saul and his servant are looking for the seer Samuel, who is to tell them where the lost asses are, they chance upon young maidens coming out of the city to draw water; the maidens advise them to go up to the city in order to meet the *rō'eh* (1 S. 9:11,13). The signs confirming Saul's designation by Samuel include meetings. In one instance Saul will himself encounter two men at Rachel's tomb, and in another instance three men going up to Bethel with sacrifices will meet him at the oak of Tabor (1 S. 10:2,3). Joram of Israel and Ahaziah of Judah set out to meet Jehu in order to ascertain why he is coming (2 K. 9:21).

V. Niphal "To Be Found, Detected, Caught." In casuistic law *mṣ'* niphal is used in the sense of being detected or caught. The Book of the Covenant uses the niphal to describe the detection, finding, and seizing of a thief (Ex. 22:1,6,7[2,7,8]); according to the Deuteronomic version of the crime of kidnapping, *mṣ'* niphal is used to refer to the seizing of the thief, and in the recension of the Book of the Covenant for the discovery in the thief's possession of what has been stolen, Dt. 24:7; Ex. 21:16). In one of his judgment oracles, Jeremiah refers to the shame of the thief who has been caught and exposed (Jer. 2:26; cf. 48:27). According to Prov. 6:31, adultery is worse than theft. The thief who is caught can at least make recompense (sevenfold compensation); the adulterer cannot. Deuteronomy prescribes quite detailed regulations for marital law. Here, too, the point of departure is the adulterer who is "caught" (handed over, detected, circumscribed with *mṣ'* niphal) (Dt. 22:22). If a man lies with a virgin who is not betrothed and this becomes "known" (found out; v. 28, even the meeting with the young woman is described with *mṣ'* qal), he is to pay the usual brideprice and marry the girl. Nor can he ever divorce her. The expression "to be discovered," "to be happened upon," also occurs outside legal regulations, e.g., in the story of the five Canaanite kings who have hidden from Joshua and his victorious Israelite army in the cave at Makkedah and are discovered (Josh. 10:17, *nimṣᵉ'û*). Similarly, according to one Jeremianic judgment oracle Yahweh discovers *rᵉšā'îm* among his people (Jer. 5:26), and according to another oracle he finds, as an expression of criminal activity on the part of the people, the blood of innocent poor people (on their hands, 2:34, perhaps following the LXX and Peshitta reading *bᵉḵappayiḵ* instead of *biḵnāp̄ayiḵ; see BHS*). Furthermore, he uncovers *qešer* among the men of Judah and the inhabitants of Jerusalem (Jer. 11:9). This passage is part of the Deuteronomistic discourse; following upon Jeremianic proclamation and picking up on prophetic forms of speech, it justifies with vv. 9 + 10 the following announcement of disaster (v. 11). The extensive, detailed oracle against Babylon contains a sentence foretelling that the former world power will itself also be "found," and that it, too, will one day be "caught" and destroyed (Jer. 50:24, *nimṣē'ṯ;* the parallel term is *tpś* niphal; cf. v. 23).

VI. Qal and Niphal "To Be Present," "To Be." The verb *mṣ'* niphal is frequently used to refer to the presence or existence or a person, thing, or abstraction at a specific place or in a given situation (cf. Fr. *se trouver* and Ger. *sich befinden*) . The qal occurs in this sense in only a very few instances. There is some doubt whether Josh. 2:23 belongs here. The spies sent out by Joshua return and report all that was there (*'ēṯ kol-hammōṣᵉ'ôṯ 'ōṯām,* where *mṣ'* still exhibits strong verbal characteristics, and *kōl* is the subject, lit., "what had happened to [encountered] them"). Yahweh's instruction to Ezekiel in Ezk. 3:1 is more unequivocal: "eat what you find" *('ēṯ 'ᵃšer-timṣā' 'ᵉḵôl).* The passages using the qal increase in number when one considers the figure of speech in which *yāḏᵉḵā* (your hand) is the subject of a form of *mṣ'*. This figure of speech expresses the authorization of action (which itself is to be freely chosen). Abimelech is to ambush the rebellious city of Shechem and do "what your hand finds to do (RSV 'as occasion offers')" to the men who come out against him (Jgs. 9:33). Samuel says the same thing to Saul, who has been designated as king: when all the confirming signs have occurred, then Saul should do *'ašer timṣā' yāḏeḵā* (1 S. 10:7). According to the wisdom of Ecclesiastes (9:10; cf. v. 9), a person should energetically use the free space that constitutes life for all sorts of activity, since this is no longer possible in death. Generosity in a sense similar to this expression is what David demands from Nabal, whereby the actual, original sense of the idiom yet resonates (1 S. 25:8, to the effect, give generously, as much as you have at hand, or "what your hand finds").

The use of *mṣ'* niphal in the sense of "to be present, to be," is far more common, though correspondingly more generalized. Persons "are present" ("find themselves") in a city or with a leader (or king), i.e., they are present at this particular place or with this particular person; such is the case, e.g., with Lot's wife and daughters, who are with Lot (Gen. 19:15 [J], *hannimṣā'ōṯ*), and Saul musters the people (warriors) who were with him *('immô),* and he and Jonathan *wᵉhā'ām hannimṣā' 'immām* stay in Geba of Benjamin (1 S. 13:15,16). During Ishmael's revolt against Gedaliah ten of the eighty pilgrims from the north present in Mizpah are spared because they are able to provide food (Jer. 41:8). In the palace in Susa all sorts of people are present at the banquet of the Persian king (Est. 1:5). And Mordecai is to gather all the Jews present in Susa (NRSV "to be found in Susa") for prayer and fasting for Esther so that she might fulfill her mission with the Persian king on behalf of the Jews (Est. 4:16). Thus a considerable number of passages can be adduced in which the presence or co-presence of persons at a specific, concrete event is noted with *mṣ'* niphal (2 Ch. 29:29; 30:21, passover during the time of Hezekiah with all the participants present in Jerusalem, the Israelites; 2 Ch. 34:32f., the Josianic covenant, into which Josiah made those present in Jerusalem and in Benjamin enter, *kol-hannimṣā';* 2 Ch. 35:7,17,18, being present at the Josianic passover; Ezr. 8:25). Especially in the case of war and misfortune (Ex. 9:19), those present in this region and situation and who are thus affected are so described (Dt. 20:11; Isa. 13:15; 22:3; 37:4; 2 K. 25:19; 1 Ch. 4:41). Frequently those affected include not only the human beings themselves, but also any animals or livestock present in the besieged city as well as goods and supplies, so that the summary includes *'aḏ kol-nimṣā',* "and all that they found" (Jgs. 20:48; even all the cities found in a specific region, v. 48b). Before the plague of hail the Egyptians are to be warned so they can rescue and shelter any people and beasts in the fields (Ex. 9:19). Legal language also employs the formulation with *yimmāṣē' bᵉ* + suffix, e.g., in deliberations concerning what to do when a criminal is found (is present) in the community (Dt. 17:2), or in instructions insuring that certain kinds of wicked persons not be found among the Israelites (Dt. 18:10). Prophets point out that Yahweh is aware of the presence of *rᵉšā'îm* among his people, whose pernicious activities can be described (Jer. 5:26). The legal prescriptions of the Book of the Covenant include things found in the presence of a person that can be used as evidence against him (Ex. 22:3[4], the ox, ass, or sheep found in the thief's possession; Ex. 21:16, in the case of kidnapping, the person found in the thief's possession and obviously intended for sale). In inheritance law, the total inheritance, from which the first-born (even if not the son of the favorite wife) is to receive a double portion, is called *kōl 'ašer-yimmāṣē' lô* (Dt. 21:17).

References to the presence of "things" is equally frequent, generalized, and varied. The money necessary as payment to the seer "is found" in the hand of Saul's servant (1 S. 9:8). Joseph gathers up all the money present in Egypt and Canaan in order to buy the stored grain in the time of need (Gen. 47:14). According to P voluntary contributions (*t^e^rûmaṯ YHWH,* Ex. 35:5) were raised for equipping the tent of meeting and its worship service, the people bringing what they had with them (Ex. 35:22,23; cf. 1 Ch. 29:8; *mṣ'* with suffixed *'ēṯ*). David, fleeing from Saul, demands from the priest Ahimelech at Nob the holy bread to eat along the way, or "whatever else is at hand" (1 S. 21:4[3], *'ô hannimṣā'*). Hezekiah showed the Babylonians "all that was present" in his treasure house, armory, and storehouses (2 K. 20:13; cf. Isa. 39:2). Because of the Philistine monopoly on iron during the time of Saul, there were in Israel no swords or spears nor even a smith (1 S. 13:19,22).

Finally, abstractions can also be the references of *mṣ'* niphal. Yahweh finds that revolt is present among the men of Judah and the inhabitants of Jerusalem (Jer. 11:9, *nimṣā'-qešer b^e^ . . .*), and is thus prompted to intervene. One characteristic of the time of salvation is that Zion will be comforted by Yahweh, its wilderness will be like the garden of Eden, and joy, gladness, praise, and thanksgiving will then be found there (Isa. 51:3). Neither will wild, ravenous beasts molest anyone, since they will not be present there *(šām)* (Isa. 35:9).

VII. "To Find, Deem, Evaluate, Judge." The OT contains a series of passages in which *mṣ'* (qal = active; niphal = passive) is used to designate the results of an investigation or evaluation. Here the term acquires declarative features. In most instances the reference is to the evaluation of circumstances, characteristics, and ethical qualities regarding certain people; in a few instances, however, objects or things are also the focus of the verb. Thus during the time of King Jehoash the need for repairs *(beḏeq)* was "found" regarding the temple, necessitating renovations (2 K. 12:6, *mṣ'* niphal). After Joab's campaign against the Ammonites, the Ammonite crown is placed on David's head, who evaluates it with regard to its gold content and precious stones; the result is: "he found that it weighed a talent of gold . . ." (1 Ch. 20:2, *mṣ'* qal; according to the LXX possibly niphal with regards to its weight: "its weight was found . . ."). An entire matter is investigated and found to be just as thought, e.g., the conspiracy discovered by Mordecai which Esther then makes known to the Persian king (Est. 2:23, *way^e^ḇuqqaš haddāḇār wayyimmāṣē'*).

As already mentioned, one's personal mode of behavior toward other persons, toward a collective, and finally also toward God, can be the object of investigation and evaluation. The falsely accused person knows that God will find nothing if he subjects the person to a thorough examination (Ps. 17:3, *bḥn, pqd,* and *ṣrp* are followed by *bal-timṣā'*). It is the ideal and desire of the righteous person that no evil *(rā'â)* be found in him (1 S. 25:28, *mṣ'* niphal with *b^e^*), but that God find his heart to be faithful, as was that of Abram in the version of Neh. 9:8 in the historical summary from v. 6 on. Contexts are more concrete that take the loyalty of one person to another or to an entire group as the object of such investigation and evaluation. David's loyalty to the Philistine king Achish of Gath is confirmed by the latter in the face of suspicions involving David's participation in a campaign against Saul (1 S. 29:3,6, *mṣ'* with suffixed b^e = "to find in him"; the object is in v. 3 *lô' m^e'ûmâ,* and in v. 6 *rā'â,* while in v. 8 the object is represented only by the interrogative pronoun *mah*[*-māṣā'ṯā b^e'aḇd^{e}ḵā*], with which David's own question is introduced regarding just why he is to be excluded from the campaign). Solomon similarly demands the agreed upon loyalty from Adoniah: *w^e'im-rā'â ṯimmāṣē'-ḇô wāmēṯ;* if he is found to be disloyal, he must die (1 K. 1:52). The same kind of loyalty is maintained on the part of God toward the human (covenantal) partner, e.g., in the (Deuteronomistically influenced) question God puts to his people (the house of Jacob and all the families of the house of Israel), namely, what wrong *('āwel)* the fathers may have found in him *(bô)* that prompted them to go astray from him (Yahweh) and to go after *heḇel* (Jer. 2:5; cf. vv. 4-9, Deuteronomistic discourse). This entire passage serves to attest Yahweh's loyalty toward his people. The lamentation over the fall of the king of Tyre portrays the king as the primordial man in his splendor and beauty in paradise, who is then driven out of paradise when *'awlā(ṯā)h* (iniquity) is found in him (Ezk. 28:15). One part of the body, e.g., the mouth, can stand as *pars pro toto:* no wrong is found on (or in) his lips (Mal. 2:6, where the ideal priest is juxtaposed with the disloyal, despicable one, vv. 4-7), or with reference to the people of the time of salvation: "nor shall a deceitful tongue be found in their mouths" (Zeph. 3:13, together with other positive behavioral characteristics). The time of salvation also includes the confirmation of Israel's sinlessness (Jer. 50:20), since Yahweh will have forgiven its sins; one cannot, however, attest such for oneself (Hos. 12:9[8]: "Ephraim says [erroneously]: In all my toils they can find no *'āwōn* in me," qal impf., 3rd masc. pl., although the text is uncertain; see *BHS*); such confirmation can only come from an external source (from God, e.g., through a prophet, 1 K. 14:13; here Ahijah of Shiloh determines this for an individual, namely, Jeroboam's dying son: *dāḇār ṭôḇ 'el-YHWH '^{e}lōhê yiśrā'ēl;* cf. 2 Ch. 19:3: *d^{e}ḇārîm ṭôḇîm* are found in Jehoshaphat [*'imm^{e}ḵā*] because he sought God and destroyed the Asherahs). Elihu accuses Job of considering himself without sin (Job 33:9), and of believing that God is (unjustly) accusing him (v. 10, *hēn t^{e}nû'ôṯ 'ālay yimṣā'*). The direct opposite of confirmed or attested sinlessness is the actual finding of sin, as exposed in the prophetic justification of disaster (Mic. 1:13; referring to Lachish, since the *piš'ê yiśrā'ēl* were found in [or on] this city, *mṣ'* niphal with b^e).

The individual marital regulations in Dt. 22:13-21 address the complications arising in marriage when the married girl was actually not a virgin. In this case, procedures are ordered with corresponding consequences for both the husband and the wife depending on the findings of the examination of the girl (*mṣ'* with suffixed l^e and with *b^{e}ṯûlîm* as the object, Dt. 22:14,17,20).[12] Here *mṣ'* is used to refer to the concrete (medical) findings of an examination.

VIII. "Meeting" in the Impersonal Sense. The term *mṣ'* is used not only in the personal sense of encounter and meeting, but also in the material or objective sense. An axe head slips from its handle while being used to cut wood and (accidentally)

12. On *mṣ'* in Dt. 22:13-29, cf. M. Fishbane, "Biblical Colophons, Textual Criticism and Legal Analogies," *CBQ,* 42 (1980), 438-449.

strikes (finds) a person, so that the person dies as a result (Dt. 19:5, *mṣ'* qal). The unfortunate individual who unintentionally caused this accident is permitted to flee into one of the three cities of refuge in order to stay alive. The Philistine archers find (i.e., strike) Saul in battle with the help of their weapons *(qešeṯ),* so that he is seriously wounded (1 S. 31:3). A person's hand is occasionally mentioned as the "weapon" that "finds" (= strikes) the opponent, e.g., Saul's hand, which would find (strike) David (1 S. 23:17). The king (at his enthronement) is assured (in an oracle of good news) that his hand (his right hand) will "find," i.e., strike, all his enemies and those who hate him (Ps. 21:9[8]). This figure of speech can also be applied to Yahweh. Just as Yahweh has struck the nations (with his hand), so also will he strike Jerusalem because of its idolatry (Isa. 10:10; vv. 10-12 are a Deuteronomistic insertion disrupting the context of vv. 5-9 + 13-15 and reversing the logical sequence[13]). The metaphor changes in Isa. 10:14, where in the establishment of Assyria's guilt its international politics is compared with the activity of a person who robs nests. Although the hand finds both the baby birds and the eggs and as it were destroys them in this way, the substance of the metaphor is different: the nest robber takes out the nest itself.

A person's "hand" can function not only as the subject of *mṣ'* activity initiated by God or human beings, it can also be the object. The expression "to use one's hands," although admittedly accompanied by the idea of then striking out with them, comes across as an idiom for describing "mustering up the energy or courage" (Ps. 76:6[5]). A whole series of negative abstractions (sg. + pl.) functions as the subjects for forms of *mṣ',* appearing both in secular and sacral (theological) contexts. Such abstractions include sin, transgression, misdeeds, calamity, misfortune, distress, affliction, shame, fear, and so on. The four lepers who increase their own wealth by seizing the possessions of the Syrians after the latter's miraculous flight from the Israelites, believe that this *ʿāwōn* will find them (RSV 'overtake' them) if they do not report the affair to the Israelite king (2 K. 7:9). The term *ʿāwōn* is not only transgression, but also the consequence of transgression that overtakes the perpetrator. A similar situation obtains regarding the *ḥaṭṭā'ṯ* of the transjordanian tribes, which will surely find them if after acquiring their own land portions they do not also (out of loyalty to the collective of tribes) participate in the "conquest" of the regions allotted to the other tribes (Nu. 32:23). The Deuteronomistic divine discourse in Dt. 31 anticipates the apostasy of the people of God after it enters the promised land. The result will be *rāʿôṯ rabbôṯ* and *ṣārôṯ,* which will "find" them (come upon, afflict, vv. 17,21; cf. Dt. 4:30, God's judgmental acts, *kol hadd^eḇārîm hā'ēlleh*). These can also be the historical oppression and affliction of the sort Gideon points out to the divine messenger who calls on him (Jgs. 6:13, *w^elāmmâ m^eṣā'aṯnû kol-zō'ṯ*). Of course, misfortune can also come upon an individual, e.g., Jacob, whose favorite son Benjamin fails to return with his brothers from Egypt because Joseph has held him back as a hostage (Gen. 44:34, *rāʿ*). In asserting his own integrity, Job points out that he would not have rejoiced if evil *(rāʿ)* had overtaken those who hate him (Job 31:29). Esther intercedes with the Persian king on

13. See H. Wildberger, *Isaiah 1–12* (Eng. trans., Minneapolis, 1991), *in loc.*

behalf of her people, which is threatened by *rā'â* resulting from Haman's pogrom (Est. 8:6). A summary term for the afflictions and hardships of the exodus and wilderness wanderings, and in general for the arduous ups and downs of history, is *t^elā'â,* which has come upon the people (Ex. 18:8; Nu. 20:14; Neh. 9:32, variously with *mṣ'* as predicate and an object in the form of a verbal suffix). The psalmist who has been delivered from fear and distress offers his song of thanksgiving in which he recounts his own catastrophe. "Snares of death" and the pangs of *š^e'ôl* "found" him (Ps. 116:3). In contrast, in Ps. 119:143 the misery of having been struck by *ṣar-ûmāṣôq* is countered by the delight in God's commandments. Finally, Prov. 6:33 warns against adultery, which merely delivers the adulterer over to *nega'-w^eqālôn* (plague and dishonor will find him). Despite being summarized in an abstract negative term, the misfortune itself is then always concrete, e.g., in 1 K. 13:24; 20:36 in the figure of a lion which "finds" and kills the unfortunate person.

IX. Seeking and Finding God. The simple matrix of seeking and finding is also applicable to the relationship between human beings and God. Several passages portray this process from the perspective of the person who is seeking God. This expression is a characteristic element of Deuteronomistic discourse in Dt. 4, which assures us that that person will find Yahweh who searches after him with all his heart (*bqš* piel and *drš,* v. 29). The context speaks of idolatry, pointing out that Yahweh nonetheless does receive back the person who returns to him (v. 30). The announcement of good news in Jer. 29 is also indebted to Deuteronomistic preaching; appended to Jeremiah's letter to the exiles, it similarly assures that a person will find Yahweh if he, Yahweh, is sought with all one's heart (Jer. 29:13f., initially *mṣ'* in the qal, then understood as a tolerative in the niphal: *w^enimṣē'tî lāḵem,* "and I will let myself be found by you"[14]). The preaching of the Chronicler also exhorts a person to seek Yahweh diligently, and promises (or confirms) that Yahweh will indeed let himself be found (1 Ch. 28:9; 2 Ch. 15:2,4,15). On the other hand, it threatens with rejection (*lā'aḏ,* "forever") the person who forsakes Yahweh (1 Ch. 28:9, *'āzaḇ*). In the older literature, namely, in prophetic proclamation, the disaster attending all predictions of concrete historical and natural catastrophes consists (also as an intensification) in the fact that the Israelites will seek (out) Yahweh (with offerings at the sanctuaries), but be unable to find him (Hos. 5:6; Am. 8:12). In Amos, the *d^eḇar YHWH* represents Yahweh himself as the object of this seeking and finding (or not finding; in both instances "seeking" is rendered by *bqš* piel; according to Jer. 15:16, Yahweh's words are there [found, *mṣ'* niphal] as a joy and consolation, indeed even as a source of strength and as food). Material deriving from the tradition of Deutero-Isaiah still focuses on this potentially futile search for Yahweh when it exhorts to seek Yahweh while he may still be found (Isa. 55:6). The parallel stich specifies this more closely by inviting its readers to call upon Yahweh while he is still near *(qārôḇ; diršû YHWH b^ehimmāṣ^e'ô).* Trito-Isaiah foresees for the

---

14. W. Thiel, *Die deuteronomistische Redaktion von Jeremia 26–45. WMANT,* 52 (1981), 15-17.

end time that Yahweh will be "found" by those who did not seek him, i.e., not only by his own people, but by the nations (Isa. 65:1, *nimṣē'ṯî lᵉlō' ḇiqᵉšunî*). In a general sense Yahweh is considered the well-"proved" help, refuge, and strength in trouble (Ps. 46:2[1], in a creed preceding the song of Zion: *'ᵉlōhîm lānû . . . bᵉṣārôṯ nimṣā' mᵉ'ōḏ*).

Later Wisdom Literature reflects on the possibility and impossibility of finding God. Zophar points out to Job that he, Job, is unable to find God's *ḥēqer,* or to penetrate to the *taḵlîṯ šadday,* despite all his efforts (Job 11:7). Here *mṣ'* acquires the meaning of intellectual mastery and control of a problem. Job confirms this in one of his own discourses (23:3). This actually constitutes his existential distress, namely, that God is inaccessible. Finally, Elihu also underscores the same assertion (in the typical style of rhetorical questions, as already employed by Zophar, 37:23). In this evocation of the impossibility of grasping God through human means, wisdom reflection acquires an element of hymnic predication for the incomparable majesty of God as opposed to human beings.

In the proverbs of Solomon wisdom itself as a divine gift and human task syntactically occupies the position of God. Wisdom should be sought, i.e., a person should diligently strive toward it, and should try to find it. If a person despises it, he will not find it even if he searches for it (*šḥr,* Prov. 1:28). Wisdom has many names and functions: *ḥoḵmâ, tᵉḇûnâ, da'aṯ, yir'aṯ YHWH, tôḵaḥaṯ,* and many others. At the same time wisdom mediates essential worldly and spiritual goods, e.g., the finding of *da'aṯ 'ᵉlōhîm* (Prov. 2:5) or *da'aṯ mᵉzimmôṯ* (8:12), even those of life and favor with Yahweh (8:35, *kî mōṣᵉ'î māṣā' ḥayyîm*). Even "eschatological" goods are associated with that wisdom which can and should be found, such as the future itself and unshakable hope (Prov. 24:14[15]). In Ecclesiastes, God's unfathomable nature is played out in "God's work" *(ma'ᵃśēh hā'ᵉlōhîm),* which cannot be found (out). The expression "work" must be taken in the broad sense of God's activity in nature, the cosmos, and history, activity that comes about unquestioned and uninterrupted according to its own plan and meaning, although without any human being — and be he ever so wise — being able to fathom and understand it *(mṣ')* (Eccl. 3:11; 8:17, with threefold use of *lō' māṣā'* or *lō' yûḵal limṣō'*).

X. Israel's Election as an Activity of God's "Finding." A small number of passages in the OT, passages whose assertions are nonetheless quite striking and cannot be overlooked, speaks of Yahweh's election of Israel in the wilderness by employing the verb *mṣ'* (known as the "discovery tradition"[16] or the "*mṣ'* tradition"[17]). The earliest clearly recognizable *mṣ'* occurrence is in Hosea (9:10[18]). There

15. The first part of this verse is uncertain; see *BHS* and *BHK*³ as well as H. Ringgren, *Sprüche. ATD,* XVI/1 (³1980), *in loc.*

16. R. Bach, *Die Erwählung Israels in der Wüste* (diss., Bonn, 1951), reviewed in *ThLZ,* 78 (1953), 687.

17. Kümpel, 18ff.

18. Kümpel takes a different view; see following discussion.

Yahweh's earlier discovery and free selection (Yahweh, as it were, picked the grapes he [unexpectedly] found in the wilderness and the early fruit on the fig tree, because they apparently were "according to his taste"[19]) is juxtaposed with Israel's subsequent behavior, and its exposed apostasy serves to justify the anticipated disaster initiated by Yahweh. This idea is picked up in the Song of Moses, which particularly underscores Yahweh's caring concern after his "find in the wilderness" (Dt. 32:10; cf. vv. 11ff.; not until v. 15b is the discussion continued with reference to Israel's apostasy from Yahweh[20]). Jer. 31:2 also employs the topos of Yahweh's compassionate concern for his people as experienced in the wilderness to refer to the (coming) salvation. Here the "tradition of the finding" (Gerhard von Rad) is admittedly to be gleaned from the reflection of the people's own experience. The verse uses the stereotypical formulation *māṣā' ḥēn bammidbār.*[21] To that extent this example is only an indirect witness to the use of *mṣ'* in this strand of tradition. Allusions to this tradition (although without *mṣ'*) can also be found in Jer. 2:2; Hos. 13:5. In contrast, Yahweh's election of David is circumscribed by *mṣ'* in Ps. 89:21(20) *(māṣā'ṯî dāwiḏ ʿaḇdî)* and paralleled by the stich with *mšḥ* (anointing with "my" holy oil). The substance of Hos. 12:5(4) might belong in the discussion of this passage; it speaks of God "finding" Jacob in Bethel, although in this case for the purpose of speaking with and encouraging Jacob, who weeps and beseeches the angel there (this passage is not easy to understand, since it draws in individual features from the Jacob stories as comparative material, then alters and updates them to fit the present circumstances; see, e.g., the peculiar *ʿimmānû* [instead of *ʿimmô*][22]). "Yahweh's find" at Bethel can be understood as a topos of Yahweh's salvific devotion to his people, as a confirmation of its election, when Israel, Ephraim, and Jacob are called there to penitence and to turn away from sin (cf. Hos. 12:7[6]).

Wagner

In his Bonn dissertation, Robert Kümpel[23] finds in Hos. 9:10 a *mṣ'* tradition deriving from an Israelite tribal and cultic tradition from Beer-lahai-roi (oldest stratum of Gen. 16:7-14). "According to this tradition, the tribal ancestress Hagar, fleeing and in mortal danger, experiences an encounter with God" (i.e., God finds her), "receives a divine directive and the promise of a son, accompanied by a confirmation of freedom. Through the theophany she is at the same time delivered from the life-threatening situation. . . . This . . . Ishmaelite tradition . . . became familiar in northern Israel (Hos. 9; 12; Jer. 31; 1 K. 19), although it also found its way into the imagery of the Jerusalem royal festival (Ps. 89; 1 K. 11)."[24]

---

19. H. W. Wolff, *Hosea. Herm* (Eng. trans. 1974), 163f.
20. Cf. G. von Rad, *Deuteronomy. OTL* (Eng. trans. 1966), *in loc.*
21. W. Rudolph, *Jeremia. HAT,* XII (^{3}1968), *in loc,* reads *kammiḏbār.*
22. Cf. Wolff, *in loc.*
23. See bibliog.
24. Kümpel, 30. On the possibility of an election tradition behind the phrase *mṣ' bammiḏbār,* cf. S. Talmon, → מדבר *miḏbār* (VIII, 87-118).

Hosea appropriates the substantive aspects of this tradition, i.e., for *mṣ'* the "salvific significance and necessity of an encounter with God for his (a person's) life."[25] Thus Yahweh's encounter with Israel is evaluated by the מצא formula on the one hand as deliverance from great distress, and on the other as promise and challenge.

Fabry

XI. Yahweh as Subject. Yahweh's response to Abraham's petition that Yahweh spare the righteous *(ṣaddîqîm)* of Sodom and Gomorrah from the imminent disaster about to overtake these places is that Yahweh will spare the city and its people if he does indeed find the number of righteous persons mentioned by Abraham (Gen. 18:26,28,30, *'im-'emṣā' šām* or *bisᵉḏōm*). Abraham's repeated plea is accompanied by the phrase *'ûlay yimmāṣᵉ'û šām,* and by an ever smaller number of righteous persons (Gen. 18:29,30,31,32, "suppose one finds there"). Yahweh's forbearance would be based on his forgiveness *(nś')* for the sake of the righteous *(baʿᵃḇûrām).* Von Rad is probably correct in pointing out that this piece (Gen. 18:20-33) derives not from an older saga, but rather from the theological reflection of the Yahwist.[26]

It is impossible to say whether a prophetic intercession preceded the divine directive in Jer. 5:1, according to which Jerusalem was to be traversed to see whether an *'îš ʿōśeh mišpāṭ mᵉḇaqqēš 'ᵉmûnâ* might be found *('im-timṣᵉ'û),* so that Yahweh might pardon Jerusalem *(wᵉ'eslaḥ lāh).* In any event, the passage strongly recalls Gen. 18. Ezk. 22:30 can probably be included in this series even though the formulation and point of departure are different. Yahweh is seeking a "mediator" who might stand in the breach before him for the land, which is itself characterized by injustice and violence, so that he, Yahweh, will not have to devastate it. Yahweh, however, finds none. Only once is direct reference made to what is said indirectly in the previous passages, namely, that Yahweh finds nothing but transgression *(ʿāwōn)* where he hoped to find faithfulness. This passage, however, sounds like a proverb (Gen. 44:16). It describes God's omniscience, before which even hidden and concealed transgressions are revealed (found). Furthermore, an element of divine judgment attaches to the context of this passage. Joseph's brothers genuinely believe that Joseph's missing cup is not in their baggage. Joseph, however, had it secretly hidden in Benjamin's possessions and then ordered these to be checked. The ones thus "convicted" exclaim: God has found out the *ʿᵃwōn ʿᵃḇāḏeyḵā.*

XII. Hiphil. The causative meaning "to cause to find" provides the point of departure for understanding the few hiphil occurrences within the OT (only 7 total). The individual contexts determine the more specific meaning of the verb, e.g., in the account of the various acts involved in the ceremonial sacrifices which according to Lev. 9 Aaron and his sons perform. Twice it is said that after Aaron slaughters the sacrificial animal, his sons bring ("deliver") the blood to him, which they have apparently

---

25. P. 31.
26. *Genesis. OTL* (Eng. trans. 1961), *in loc.*

collected, so that he can then sprinkle it upon the altar round about *(sāḇîḇ)* (Lev. 9:12, regarding the *'ôlâ,* and in v. 18 the *zeḇaḥ haššᵉlāmîm*). A second act seems to be the presentation of the *'ôlâ* in divided (prepared) pieces for Aaron to burn upon the altar (v. 13). The parallel term in this context is *qrb* hiphil.

Yet another use of *mṣ'* hiphil, construed with *bᵉyaḏ* + person, is attested in the account of the dispute between Abner and Ishbosheth. The former points out the various proofs of his loyalty toward the latter, and notes that he "has not delivered" Ishbosheth "over into the hand of David" (2 S. 3:8). The same expression appears in an insertion in Deutero-Zechariah's vision of the shepherds (Zec. 11:6) to refer to Yahweh's acts of judgment coming upon the entire earth; Yahweh will cause every person to fall into the hand of his neighbor (and his king), and there will be no escape.[27] In the discourses of Elihu *mṣ'* hiphil is in one instance a term of requital next to *šlm* piel in the sense of the close relationship between act and consequence (Job 34:11, *ûḵᵉ'ōraḥ 'îš yamṣî'ennû*); in another instance it is a term of execution or fulfillment ("he, God, causes it to happen," "brings it about," Job 37:13) as a circumlocution for God's power over storm phenomena, which he causes to happen as judgment or grace on his world.

XIII. Idiomatic Expressions. Ecclesiastes uses *mṣ'* as a term for evaluation and consolidation of what he has gleaned from experience ("I have found," etc., Eccl. 7:14,26,29). "Finding a word to say" effectively means the same thing as "to answer" (Neh. 5:8). Praying to God at the right time is what the righteous person is wont to do, who after his confession of sin has experienced God's forgiveness (Ps. 32:6, *lᵉ'ēṯ mᵉṣō',* although this phrase is somewhat difficult, since the word *raq* follows immediately upon the infinitive[28]). The realization that something is so, or the fact that one notices it, can also be expressed by *mṣ'* (2 K. 17:4, the Assyrian king "finds," i.e., notices the defection of the last Israelite king, Hoshea, *mṣ' bᵉ;* Jer. 10:18: Yahweh intends to make his acts of judgment genuinely palpable, tangible). "Finding one's heart" means "to find courage," "to gain confidence" (2 S. 7:27). The parallel passage in 1 Ch. 17:25 only uses *mṣ'* without *lēḇ.* A similar expression associates the verb with "hand" in the sense of "to be courageous," and in the negative sense of "to become discouraged" (Ps. 76:6[5]). As an indication of sufficient possessions, livestock, or land, *mṣ'* is used with suffixed *lᵉ* in an apparently abbreviated manner of expression ("there is for the person concerned," "there is sufficient," "it is enough"). In all likelihood that which is deemed sufficient was originally mentioned concretely as well, as is still the case in Hos. 12:9(8): "Ephraim has said, 'Ah, but I am rich, I have found *'ôn* for myself,' " i.e., "I have enough." Only the aforementioned abbreviated form is found in Nu. 11:22 as well as in Josh. 17:16 (niphal).

That which "the hand (of a person) finds" refers to that which the person does or does not *(lō')* possess. This figure of speech occurs in Lev. 12:8; 25:28 (cf. vv. 26-28); 1 S. 25:8; Job 31:25. Finding booty corresponds to distributing the same sort of spoils

---

27. Cf. W. Rudolph, *Sacharja 9–14. KAT,* XIII/4 (1976), *in loc.*
28. H.-J. Kraus, *Psalms 1-59* (Eng. trans., Minneapolis, 1987), *in loc.*

(Nu. 31:50; 1 S. 14:30; 2 Ch. 20:25), i.e., the joyous concluding act of a military campaign; thus Ps. 119:162 can compare the joy one finds in God's word with that of the person who finds a wealth of booty. In the Deuteronomic regulations regarding sexual coercion applied to a betrothed young woman, *mṣ'* describes the process during which the man actually meets the woman (Dt. 22:23,25,27). The same applies to the regulations concerning the unbetrothed young woman (Dt. 22:28).

Occasionally *mṣ',* "to find," can take on the meaning of "to seek," although in this case various attendant sequential activities are tacitly implied. The signal Jonathan is to give his ally David, whom Saul is pursuing, involves the shooting of arrows, and the direction the lad takes in searching for the arrows constitutes part of the agreed upon signal. That is, Jonathan's servant is to go, search for the arrows, find them, and bring them back. All that is said, however, is: *lēḵ mᵉṣā'* (or *ruṣ mᵉṣā' nā',* 1 S. 20:21,36; cf. 1 Ch. 10:3,8).

XIV. Other Considerations. Not only seeking, but also hoping and anticipating address the goal of finding (Ps. 69:21[20], *qwh* piel). The sower anticipates the harvest. Isaac sows, *wayyimṣā' baššānâ hahî' mē'â šᵉʿārîm* (Gen. 26:12 [J]). Jacob hunts and catches *(mṣ')* the game (Gen. 27:20 [JE]; cf. vv. 3,7), just as Isaac expects and anticipates receiving from Esau. Fire breaks out and burns what it finds (Ex. 22:5[6], *mṣ'* next to *'kl*). At the revolt of Sheba David worries that the rebel might reach *(mṣ')* one of the fortified cities and elude his pursuer (2 S. 20:6). Jerusalem's enemies deride the fallen city and cry: "Now we have attained it" (Lam. 2:16, with *mṣ'* also *qwh* piel, *blʿ* piel, and *r'h*). Whereas the ambitious person reaches his goal, the person who counts reaches his result, the end sum (2 Ch. 2:16[17], *mṣ'* niphal, "153,600 aliens were counted").

XV. 1. *Biblical Aramaic mṭ' in Daniel.* Daniel attests 8 occurrences for Biblical Aram. *mṭ',* although with varying meanings. Nebuchadnezzar's dream of the great tree reports that the top of the tree reached to heaven (Dnl. 4:8,17[11,20], *mṭ'* with *lᵉ*). The interpretation takes this as referring to the king's power and dominion (4:19[22]). As the story progresses, the decree of God contained in the dream is related, and it turns out that the decree of the Most High is coming to the king (4:21[24], *mṭ'* with *ʿal*). By way of summary the assertion follows that all this came upon King Nebuchadnezzar (v. 25[28] in the same formulation as in v. 21[24]). In the remaining passages *mṭ'* expresses an external element of movement: "to reach, arrive at" (6:25[24]; 7:13,22). The place of arrival is indicated by means of *lᵉ,* the corresponding person with *ʿaḏ.* Abstractions such as time and hour can also function as subjects of *mṭ'.* The time and hour come, or are there for a specific event (7:22).[29] The semantic fields of the Biblical Aramaic root *mṭ'* can be reduced to two elements: it functions first as an indication of extension (an object, a symbolically represented dominion extends or reaches to a specified place, "finds" that place), and second as the description of movement ("to come"), something also attested within the semantic field of the Hebrew root *mṣ'.*

29. Cf. O. Plöger, *Das Buch Daniel. KAT,* XVIII (1965), for further discussion of these passages.

2. *Qumran.* The approximately 35 occurrences of *mṣ'* in the texts of Qumran offer nothing new regarding the understanding and use of the root. Here, too, *mṣ'* appears only in its verbal manifestation with the usual OT meanings. It refers to persons and objects finding or being found (CD 9:14-16; 1QM 15:11; 11QT 55:15; 60:17; 62:7), whereby "objects" actually usually refer to abstractions, the matter a person investigates and finds (1 QS 8:11, *dāḇār*), the *śēḵel,* understanding (1QS 9:13), everything a person finds to do in the law of Moses (CD 15:10), or in general everything there is to do (1QS 9:20), fraud, transgression, deception and abominations on the tongue, where praise of God's righteousness should be on one's lips (1QS 10:22,23). However, the general indication that persons "are present" at a certain place is also attested as a meaning for *mṣ'* (1QS 6:2). The same applies to legal language, which stipulates that a person caught (found) to have made false statements concerning his property is to be subjected to certain rules of punishment (1QS 6:24; cf. the legal stipulations taken over from Dt. 22 concerning the case of "rape" in 11QT 65:9,12; 66:4,7,10; compare also 11QT 60:17 with Dt. 18:9-13). As a result of God's judgment, all "men of lies" and "seers of error" will no longer be present (i.e., will no longer be found; 1QH 4:20). The same will happen to the wicked (4QpPs37:2,7; cf. Ps. 37:10).

Wagner

מַצֵּבָה *maṣṣēḇâ*

Contents: I. Term and Object. II. Ancient Near East: 1. General Considerations; 2. *nṣb/yṣb;* 3. Basic Meaning. III. OT: 1. Archaeological Evidence; 2. Literary Evidence; 3. Related and Substitute Terms; 4. Verbs; 5. Topography and Setting. IV. Theological Background: 1. Acceptance; 2. Theological Doubts: a. Gen. 28:18,22 and Related Texts; b. Land Conquest and Israel's Nationhood; 3. Rejection: a. Destruction of Pre-Israelite Cultic Massebahs; b. Prohibition; 4. Reflections in Deuteronomistic and Later Literature. V. Priestly Concerns Regarding the First Commandment.

---

maṣṣēḇâ. A. Aharoni, "Chronique archéologique: Lakish," *RB,* 76 (1969), 576-78; *idem,* "Arad: Its Inscriptions and Temple," *BA,* 31 (1968), 2-32; W. F. Albright, "The High Place in Ancient Palestine," *Volume du Congrès, Strasbourg 1956. SVT,* 4 (1957), 242-258; W. B. Barrick, "The Funerary Character of 'High-Places' in Ancient Palestine: A Reassessment," *VT,* 25 (1975), 565-595; *idem,* "What Do we Really Know about 'High-Places'?" *SEÅ,* 45 (1980), 50-57; G. Beer, *Steinverehrung bei den Israeliten. Schriften der Strassburger Wissenschaftlichen Gesellschaft,* N.S. 4 (1921); K. Budde, "Zur Bedeutung der Mazzeben," *OLZ,* 15 (1912), 248-252; J. V. Canby, "The Stelenreihen at Assur, Tell Halaf, and *Maṣṣēbôt,*" *Iraq,* 38 (1976), 113-132; É. Cothenet, "Onction," *DBS,* VI (1960), 701-732; W. G. Dever, "Chronique archéologique: Gezer," *RB,* 76 (1969), 563-67; *idem, et al.,* "Further Excavations at Gezer, 1967-1971," *BA,* 34 (1971), 94-132; H. Donner, "Zu Gen 28,22," *ZAW,* 74 (1962), 68-70; K. Elliger, "Chammanim = Masseben?" *ZAW,* 57 (1939), 256-265; J. P. Fokkelmann, *Narrative Art in Genesis.*

I. Term and Object. In the OT, the term *maṣṣēḇâ* refers to a stone erected by human hands, though not conceived as serving architectonic purposes. Since neither the form nor the function is ever specifically described, and at best can only be surmised, the word is for normal purposes not translated ("massebah").

Although the LXX uses the term *stēlē* in 32 of 36 instances to render *maṣṣēḇâ* (only in 4 instances does the word render Heb. *bāmâ*), modern scholarship prefers to reserve the word "stela" for "artistically" worked columns or raised stone plates with inscriptions and/or pictures.[1]

SSN, 17 (1975); V. Fritz, *Tempel und Zelt. WMANT,* 47 (1977); K. Galling, "Erwägungen zum Stelenheiligtum von Hazor," *ZDPV,* 75 (1959), 1-13; C. F. Graesser, "Standing Stones in Ancient Palestine," *BA,* 35 (1972), 34-63; *idem, Studies in Maṣṣēbôt* (diss., Harvard, 1969); R. J. Griffeth, *Maṣṣēbāh* (diss., Yale, 1938 [unavailable to author]); J. Halbe, *Das Privilegrecht Jahwes, Ex 34,10-26. FRLANT,* 114 (1975); Z. Herzog, "On the Meaning of Bama in the Light of Archaeological Data," BethM, 73 (1978), 177-183 [Heb.], 254 [Eng. summary]; K. Jaroš, *Die Stellung des Elohisten zur kanaanäischen Religion. OBO,* 4 (1974); C. A. Keller, "Über einige alttestamentliche Heiligtumslegenden," *ZAW,* 67 (1955), 141-168; 68 (1956), 85-97; K. M. Kenyon, *Jerusalem: Excavating 3000 Years of History* (New York, 1967); A. Lemaire, "Les Inscriptions de Khirbet El-Qôm et l'Ashérah de YHWH," *RB,* 84 (1977), 595-608; J. L'Hour, "L'alliance de Sichem," *RB,* 69 (1962), 5-36, 161-184, 350-368; *idem,* "Les interdits toʿeba dans le Deutéronome," *RB,* 71 (1964), 481-503; G. Lilliu, "Betilo," *Enciclopedia dell'arte antica, classica e orientale,* II, 72-76; V. Maag, "Zum Hieros Logos von Beth-El," *Asiatische Studien,* 5 (1951), 122-133 = *idem, Kultur, Kulturkontakt und Religion* (Göttingen, 1980), 29-37; Z. Meshel, "Did Yahweh Have a Consort?" *BAR,* 5/2 (1979), 24-35; T. Mettinger, "The Veto on Images and the Aniconic God in Ancient Israel," *Religious Symbols and their Functions. SIDA,* 10 (1979), 15-29; D. Neiman, "PGR: A Canaanite Cult-Object in the OT," *JBL,* 67 (1948), 55-60; M. Ottosson, *Temples and Cult Places in Palestine. Acta Universitatis Upsaliensis; Boreas: Uppsala Studies in Ancient Mediterranean and Near Eastern Civilizations,* 12 (1980); J. Pirenne, "Sud-Arabe: QYFQF/MQF: De la lexicographie à la spiritualité des 'idolâtres,' " *Sem,* 30 (1950), 93-124; A. de Pury, *Promesse divine et légende cultuelle dans le cycle de Jacob. ÉtB* (1975); A. Reichert, "Massebe," *BRL*^{2}, 206-9; M. Rose, *Der Ausschliesslichkeitsanspruch Jahwes. BWANT,* 106[6/6] (1975); G. Schmitt, *Du sollst keinen Frieden schliessen mit den Bewohnern des Landes. BWANT,* 91[5/11] (1970); Y. Shiloh, "Iron Age Sanctuaries and Cult Elements in Palestine," in F. M. Cross, ed., *Symposia. ZRFOP,* 1f. (Cambridge, Mass., 1979), 147-157; E. Stockton, "Sacred Pillars in the Bible," *ABR,* 20 (1972), 16-32; *idem,* "Stones at Worship," *AJBA,* 1 (1970), 58-81; *idem,* "Phoenician Cult Stones," *AJBA,* 2/3 (1974/75), 1-27; S. Swiderski, *Megalithische und kultische Objekte Palästinas und die monotheistischen Ideen Israels im AT* (diss., Vienna, 1960); S. du Toit, "Aspects of the Second Commandment," *OuTWP,* 12 (1969, ed. 1971), 101-10; P. H. Vaughan, *The Meaning of "bāmâ" in the OT. SOTSMon,* 3 (1974); R. de Vaux, "Chronique archéologique: Jérusalem," *RB,* 71 (1964), 253-58; P. Welten, "Stele," *BRL*^{2}, 321-25; *idem,* "Kulthöhe und Jahwetempel," *ZDPV,* 88 (1972), 19-37; G. E. Wright, "Samaria," *BA,* 22 (1959), 67-78; W. Zimmerli, "Das Bilderverbot in der Geschichte des alten Israel," *Schalom. Festschrift A. Jepsen. ArbT,* 1/46 (1971), 86-96 = *Studien zur alttestamentlichen Theologie und Prophetie. Gesammelte Aufsätze,* 2. *ThB,* 51 (1974), 247-260; *idem,* "Das zweite Gebot," *Festschrift A. Bertholet* (Tübingen, 1950), 550-563 = *Gottes Offenbarung. Gesammeltes Aufsätze,* 1. *ThB,* 19 (^{2}1969), 234-248; G. Zuntz, "Βαίτυλος and Bethel," "Classica et Mediaevalia," *Revue Danoise de philologie et d'histoire,* 8 (1947), 169-219.

1. Cf. Welten, 322; Reichert.

II. Ancient Near East.

1. *General Considerations.* In the ancient Near East intentionally raised stones are much more widely attested in various forms and roles within religious and cultic contexts[2] than is the etymon *maṣṣēḇâ.*[3] Despite all variety, the common element is their erect position, the intentional result of human activity. They can be crude and unhewn, or more or less intentionally worked, with varying height and form, with or without inscriptions and pictures.

2. *nṣb/yṣb.* The verbal base *nṣb* (including in Hebrew the root variation *yṣb*[4]) is widely attested in the West Semitic sphere (including EA, as a loanword), though otherwise Akkadian does not even attest any derivations in any meaning related to the present discussion.[5] The nominal forms (with or without preformative: *nṣb:* Old South Arabic, Punic, and Aramaic; *nṣyb:* Nabatean; *mṣb:* Nabatean, Palmyrene, also Ugaritic, though in the sense of "frame, stand"[6]; *mṣbt* and *mnṣbt:* Phoenician and Punic; *nṣbt:* Ugaritic, Arabic[7]) evoke the meaning of (physical) erection or erect position. Figurative usage does not seem to occur.

3. *Basic Meaning.* Pictures and inscriptions, i.e., stelae, offer especially promising clues to functional modes and concrete meaning. However, apart from the frequent uncertainty regarding interpretation, one cannot presuppose that all possibilities have been articulated, so that questions remain regarding these silent stones.

Regarding the stone massebahs without images or inscriptions attested in the OT, the ancient Near East offers three salient points: a) Although the concrete meaning of a given massebah depends on its actual founder (an office holder, a private individual, a collective), this original intention is not necessarily understood and transmitted without alteration later; that is, one must reckon with both conscious and unconscious reinterpretations and rededications. b) The fundamental intention or common denominator of all the various concrete functions might have been the visible perpetuation (or creation?) of an aspect that endures beyond temporary acts and events, applicable in many different dimensions, not least the religious and cultic. To this extent the massebah can portray or represent the worshiper, and not always (merely) the venerated deity.[8] c) Similar to the evidence for writing and language, the many semantic possi-

---

2. Cf. M. Eliade, "Sacred Stones: Epiphanies, Signs and Forms," *Patterns in Comparative Religion* (Eng. trans., New York, 1958), 216-238; H. Möbius, "Stele," *PW,* III A/2, 2307-2325; K. Latte, "Steinkult," *PW,* III A/2, 2295-2305.

3. Cf. H. Ringgren, *Die Religionen des Alten Orients. ATDSond* (1979), 190; *idem, Religions of the Ancient Near East* (Eng. trans., Philadelphia, 1973), 159.

4. Cf. *HAL,* II (1995), 427.

5. Cf. *AHw,* II (1972), 755, 756f.; R. S. Tomback, *A Comparative Lexicon of the Phoenician and Punic Languages. SBL Diss.,* 32 (Missoula, 1978), 219f.

6. Cf. *WUS,* no. 1831; *KTU,* 1.65; *HAL,* II, 620.

7. Cf. Tomback, 193f., 219f.; *DISO,* 164, 184; M. Broshi, "מַצֵּבָה," *EMiqr,* V (1968), 221-23.

8. De Pury, 2, 415.

bilities are concretized in varying contexts, contexts which can, however, be all the more puzzling the more complicated and archaeologically well-preserved they are. Approximately from the Middle Bronze Age onward one encounters stones lacking pictures or inscriptions grouped with one bearing a picture, with a statue, or with both (e.g., at Hazor[9]), with a horizontal stone plate (Hazor[10]), or with a stone cube (e.g., Gezer[11]); several massebahs are often concentrated at a single locale (e.g., Byblos, Ashur[12]). Scholarship has hardly addressed the question of the external form of the individual massebahs.

III. OT. 1. *Archaeological Evidence.* As far as the environment of the OT itself is concerned, archaeological evidence is limited almost exclusively to inscriptionless massebahs.[13] These were customary among the preceding Canaanite population of Palestine.[14] From certain massebahs there emanated in fact a kind of sacral aura that endured beyond the various changes in understanding and perception. Thus massebahs were respectfully "buried" in Lachish, apparently toward the end of the 8th century, and perhaps during a reform as a result of which they were to be withdrawn from cultic usage as illegitimate objects.[15] In Arad, in the Holy of Holies of the temple dating from Israelite times, a massebah with traces of paint was found *in situ* with others outside its original position.[16] The cultic interpretation of two juxtaposed monoliths from the period of the monarchy found by K. M. Kenyon in northeast Jerusalem (on the slope of the Ophel)[17] is disputed.[18]

2. *Literary Evidence.* The word *maṣṣēḇâ* occurs 34 times in the OT unequivocally in this form, and additionally once in the variation *maṣṣeḇeṯ* in the absolute state (2 S. 18:18).

In Isa. 6:13 the terms *maṣṣeḇeṯ* and *maṣṣaḇtāh* apparently have as little to do with massebahs[19] as do several other rare nominal constructions from the same base *(maṣṣāḇ, muṣṣāḇ, maṣṣāḇâ, miṣṣāḇâ).*

---

9. Reichert, 208, pl. 49, 4.

10. *Idem.*

11. *Ibid.,* 207, pl. 49, 2.

12. Cf. Stockton, *AJBA,* 1 (1970), 58-81; Graesser, *Studies in Maṣṣēbôt; idem, BA,* 35 (1972), 34-63; Canby. Regarding the difficulties involved in the "Canaanite dogmatics," cf. Ottosson, 40.

13. Regarding the single small fragment of an inscription stela from Samaria, cf. Welten, 322; Wright, 77.

14. Cf. Reichert, 206-9.

15. Cf. Fritz, 84.

16. M. Wüst, "Arad," *BRL*², 11f.

17. Kenyon, 65, and pls. 33-35.

18. Cf. Ottosson, 105; B. Mazar, "Jerusalem," *EAEHL,* II (1976), 589; Graesser, *BA,* 35 (1972), 54f.; de Vaux, 253f.

19. Cf. the comms.; see also G. W. Ahlström, "Isaiah vi.13," *JSS,* 19 (1974), 169-172; contra F. F. Hvidberg, "The Masseba and the Holy Seed," *Interpretationes ad VT pertinentes. Festschrift S. Mowinckel NTT.* 56 (1955), 97-99; S. Iwry, "*maṣṣēbāh* and *bāmāh* in 1Q Isaiah 6_{13}," *JBL,* 76 (1957), 225-232.

3. *Related and Substitute Terms.* Related terms seem to be *ṣiyyûn,* "gravestone" (2 K. 23:17), a kind of signpost (Jer. 31:21) or funerary sign (Ezk. 39:15) that cannot be determined more specifically; *yāḏ,* "monument" (1 S. 15:12; 2 S. 18:18; cf. 1 Ch. 18:3; Isa. 56:5). Apparently early, perhaps as early as the Yahwist[20] (see also Dt. 27:2,4), reservation and ultimately complete rejection resulted in an avoidance of the word "massebah," which in given instances was replaced by other terms, above all by → אבן *'eḇen* (Dt. 27:2,4; Josh. 4:9,20; 24:26-27; cf. Gen. 31:45), → מזבח *mizbēaḥ* (Gen. 33:20; 35:1), *gal* (Gen. 31:46,48,51f.), *miṣpâ* (Gen. 31:49), perhaps by reading the ptcp. *muṣṣāḇ* (Jgs. 9:6b; cf. Gen. 28:12). Other constructions are used for architectonic columns (with the possible exception of Ezk. 26:11) and for naturally occurring forms (e.g., Gen. 19:26: *nṣyb*). Attempts to interpret *miḵtāḇ, peger,* and *ḥammānîm* as massebahs can only be viewed as unsuccessful.

4. *Verbs.* Verbs with the meaning "to erect, set up" are used to indicate the standard vertical position effected by human beings as applied to every physical, naturally occurring, or artificial artistic form: especially the *figura etymologica* with *y(n)ṣb* hiphil (Gen. 35:14,20; 2 K. 17:10; cf. 2 S. 18:18), then also *rwm* hiphil (Gen. 31:45), *qwm* hiphil (Dt. 16:22; Lev. 26:1; cf. Josh. 4:9). Less characteristic verbs include *śym* (Gen. 28:18,22), *'śh* (2 K. 3:2), *bnh* (Ex. 24:4, probably only because of the [secondary?] zeugma with *mizbēaḥ;* cf. 1 K. 14:23 with the tripartite formulation *bāmôṯ ûmaṣṣēḇôṯ wa'ᵃšērîm*). The verb *ṭwb* hiphil suggests artistic formation (Hos. 10:1; cf. Mic. 5:12[Eng. v. 13]). Negative verbs refer to the crushing or comminution of hard and brittle material: *šbr* piel (Ex. 23:24; 34:13; Dt. 7:5; 12:3; 2 K. 18:4; 23:14; 2 Ch. 14:2[3]; 31:1; Jer. 43:13), *ntṣ* (2 K. 10:27), *krt* hiphil (Mic. 5:12[13]), *yrd* (Ezk. 26:11: to fall over); defacement: *šdd* poel (Hos. 10:2); or probably removal in general: *yṣ'* hiphil (2 K. 10:26), *swr* hiphil (2 K. 3:2).[21] Any stone *('eḇen)* can serve as the material (Gen. 28:18,22; 31:45; cf. 35:14; Jer. 2:27; 3:9).

5. *Topography and Setting.* Except in those exceptional cases of what are better described as secular signs (such as Absalom's personal monument in the "King's Valley" [2 S. 18:18; cf. 1 S. 15:12] or Rachel's tomb [Gen. 35:20]), massebahs in stories and other accounts are located at already existing sanctuaries, where they function less as the basis or expression of that sanctuary's fundamental holiness, than as documentation of a concrete (additional) dedication; such is the case at Bethel in the Jacob narratives (Gen. 28:18,22 and ancillary references, cf. v. 11), the temple in Samaria (2 K. 10:26; cf. 3:2), and in the vicinity of Jerusalem (2 K. 23:14). In given instances massebahs are mentioned after altars (Ex. 24:4; Hos. 10:1f.; Isa. 19:19; cf. Dt. 16:22) or (from the hand of the Deuteronomist) at the end of a tripartite series along with the Asherim (Ex. 34:13; Dt. 7:5; 12:3). Probably as a result of the uncomfortable fact that altars maintained their legitimacy in Israel, and were not simply to be dismissed

---

20. Cf. de Pury, 2, 557 and *passim.*
21. On *śrp* in 2 K. 10:26, cf. J. Gray, *I & II Kings. OTL* (^{2}1970), 558 (^{3}1977).

or condemned completely (cf. 1 K. 19:10,14), they were replaced by the term *bāmôṯ* and incorporated into the not quite logical series *bāmôṯ ûmaṣṣēḇôṯ wa'ᵃšērîm* (1 K. 14:23; 2 K. 18:4; cf. 23:13f.).[22] Hence in this sort of fixed expression the *bāmôṯ* does not necessarily indicate the actual location of the massebahs (cf. 2 Ch. 14:2[3]; 31:1, and the other expression "on [every] mountain/[high] hill and under [every] green tree": 1 K. 14:23; 2 K. 17:10; cf. Dt. 12:2). The double expression *maṣṣēḇôṯ wa'ᵃšērîm* occurs only once (2 K. 17:10). The attitude of condemnation is especially emphasized in later texts by the proximity to consistently despised or forbidden cultic symbols: *pesel/*pāsîl* (Dt. 7:5; 12:3; Mic. 5:12[13]), *'ᵉlîlîm,* and *'eḇen maśkîṯ* (Lev. 26:1).

IV. Theological Background. The change attested here in use and theology regarding the massebahs remains unclear and uncertain. It does not seem likely that we are dealing with a clearly differentiated sequence of developments; differing, even contradictory notions can coexist.

1. *Acceptance.* In the older traditions, the legitimacy of massebahs is not called into question. Jacob marks and honors Rachel's grave with a massebah (Gen. 35:20 E; cf. 2 S. 18:18). The massebah erected by Jacob marks the place of encounter with YHWH (Gen. 28:11-22), an encounter both rich in consequences and richly commemorated (cf. Gen. 31:13; 35:24) and that forever lends significance to the location; the massebah functions as a perpetual proclamation of the place's association with God.[23] Even the ardent Yahwist Hosea counts massebahs among the cultic symbols whose temporary removal is to prompt repentance among the people (Hos. 3:4; on 10:1f. see discussion below). In the late period the positive perception occasionally resurfaces in view of the coming age: "In that day there will be an altar to Yahweh in the midst of the land of Egypt, and a *maṣṣēḇâ* for Yahweh at its border. It [probably generic, the subject is not clear — probably massebah and altar] will be a sign *('ôṯ)* and witness *('ēḏ)* to Yahweh . . . he will send them a savior *(môšîa')* . . ." (Isa. 19:19f.). One recalls the altars built by the patriarchs at the occasion of epiphanies, not for the purpose of sacrifice, but rather probably as enduring signs.[24] In contrast: At the defeat of the Egyptians the destruction of their cultic places includes the "massebahs," obelisks of Beth-shemesh (Heliopolis) (Jer. 43:13).[25] When no questions of faith arose, perhaps *yṣb* hiphil was left unchanged and without commentary (Gen. 35:20 E; 2 S. 18:18; cf. 1 S. 15:12; 2 S. 18:17; 2 K. 17:10 is condemnatory from the outset).

2. *Theological Doubts.* Texts reflecting traditions which in and of themselves are neutral toward massebahs nonetheless betray a certain reservation and independence on the part of their final redactors.

---

22. → במה *bāmâ (bāmāh),* II, 142.
23. Cf. C. Westermann, *Genesis 12–36* (Eng. trans., Minneapolis, 1985), 459.
24. Cf. H. Wildberger, *Jesaja. BK,* X/2 (1978), 727-746.
25. Cf. W. Rudolph, *Jeremia. HAT,* XII (^{3}1968), 258f.

a. *Gen. 28:18,22 and Related Texts.* In the most extensive passage in the Jacob tradition, Gen. 28:18,22 (E?), the nonspecific verb *śym* qal is used in reference to the massebah, just as in v. 11 (E) and 18 it is used in the non-cultic context for *m^e ra'^a šōṯāw.* Furthermore, v. 11 underscores the fortuitous, unintentional nature of this choice: *mē'aḇnê hammāqôm* (usually *lqḥ 'eḇen:* Gen. 31:45; Josh. 24:26; cf. Josh. 4:3,5; 1 K. 18:31; 2 S. 18:18). Any possible sacral associations (incubation) are thus more likely weakened or averted. The contradiction of this tendency immediately thereafter is only apparent: *wayyiṣōq šemen 'al-rō'šāh* (28:18b). Although this is the only such act performed on an object outside the tent precinct, in contradistinction with P (*mšḥ:* Ex. 30:26-33; Lev. 8:10f.; Nu. 7:1; cf. Dnl. 9:24b), it is not understood as an act of anointing,[26] something which, in contrast, is unequivocally the case in Gen. 31:13 (secondary).[27] Interpretations which likely accrued gradually remained in various initial stages. The *bêṯ 'elōhîm* is according to the stelae of Sefire[28] probably not a temple structure, but more likely the massebah itself as a kind of indirect symbol of the deity, or more precisely: the deity's earthly dwelling place. If the "house of Elohim" — which is certainly possible — is yet a part of the protasis, the "conditions" of the vow, and the final clause commences only with 22b, then it follows that the real significance of the massebah emerges only in the salvation that has been petitioned and granted, similar to the way Jacob anticipates in 21b that Yahweh will prove to be Elohim (cf. Gen. 17:7).[29]

In Gen. 35:14 the syntactically repetitious *maṣṣeḇeṯ 'eḇen* sounds like a warning against Asherim and images made of wood (Jgs. 6:26; Isa. 45:20) and evokes the notion of an altar made of stones (Ex. 20:25; Dt. 27:5f.; 1 K. 18:31). This is also suggested by the additional mention of the drink offering: *wayyassēḵ 'āleyhā neseḵ.* Though this does not constitute a rite of consecration, the altar and making of the "covenant" are its most frequent locus.[30] (Concerning the altar in place of the massebah cf. Gen. 33:20; 35:1,7; Josh. 22:10-34.) In a manner somehow contrary to the context, the massebah itself does not receive a name; only "the place" does (Gen. 28:19; 35:15; cf. v. 7). With this gesture the final redaction places the sanctuary as such at the center of attention, perhaps as a corrective to any unwelcome overestimation of the massebah.

b. *Land Conquest and Israel's Nationhood.* Along with writing and the altar, massebahs play a role in cultic events in which Israel's special relationship with God is portrayed or commemorated. This is expressly the case only at Sinai: "And Moses wrote all the words of Yahweh . . . and built *(wayyiḇen)* an altar . . . and twelve massebahs, according to *(l^e)* the twelve tribes of Israel." The massebahs are incongruous with the verb and are not mentioned again in the course of the narrative, and thus probably constitute a learned requisite, commemorative stones corresponding to the

26. → יצק *yāṣaq,* VI, 255f.
27. Cf. Westermann, *Genesis 12–36,* 492.
28. *KAI,* 223 C, 2/3,7,9/10; cf. Donner.
29. Fokkelmann, 67-70; Keller, 166.
30. Cf. O. Michel, "σπένδω," *TDNT,* VII, 531-33.

number considered sacred for Israel's constitution (Ex. 24:4 [E?]; cf. 1 K. 18:31). In the considerably reworked construction Josh. 3:7–5:1 two sets of twelve stones each are "set up" (4:9,20: *qwm* hiphil) in the midst of the Jordan (4:3,9) or in Gilgal (4:20) and interpreted focusing on the twelve tribes as a "sign" (*'ôṯ,* 4:6) and "as a memorial" (*lᵉzikkārôn,* 4:7) of the crossing and entry granted by God (cf. the — ritual — "children's question": Josh. 4:6-7,21-22, as well as Dt. 6:20-25; Ex. 12:26f.; 13:14-16). Possibly an older group of idols or images *(pᵉsîlîm)* "at Gilgal" (Jgs. 3:19,26) was reinterpreted to preserve the notion of later cultic centralization.

In connection with the land conquest, Dt. 27:1-8 mentions that an undetermined number of "stones" are to be erected (vv. 2,4: *qwm* hiphil; doublets) surrounding the altar (vv. 5-7; pre-Deuteronomic; cf., e.g., Ex. 20:25). The reference here is to stelae, since one is to write (on plaster, vv. 2,4) "all the words of this law" (vv. 3,8), revealing their redactional, literary character, independent of any material or archaeological considerations.

Josh. 8:30-32, influenced by Dt. 27:2,4,8 among others, completely ignores technical considerations. Joshua seems to write "a copy of the law of Moses" (cf. Dt. 17:18) on the (unhewn) stones used to construct the altar.[31] Thus tensions between older traditions and later (Deuteronomic and Deuteronomistic) customs are theologically disarmed and exploited.[32] Within the framework of the *bᵉrîṯ*-ceremony concluding the land conquest Joshua "took a great stone, and set it up (*qwm* hiphil) there under the terebinth in the sanctuary of Yahweh" (Josh. 24:26b; cf. Gen. 35:4).[33] The stone is declared to be a "witness,"[34] not as a bearer of writing as in the aforementioned case, but rather "because it has heard all the words of Yahweh (*'imrê YHWH* occurs only here in the entire OT!) . . . lest you deal falsely with your God" (v. 27).[35] Although the positive reference to the sanctuary is pre-Deuteronomic, the interpretation of the stone itself may be Deuteronomic. In Sefire "not a single word of this inscription *(spr')* is to be silent."[36] The stone as a "witness" fulfills a function analogous to that of the regular reading of the Torah (Dt. 31:9-13).[37] This silent witness doubtlessly does not proclaim any details of the "words," but rather contributes to the constant presence and openly acknowledged character of the special relationship between the people and God.

Gen. 31:44-55 actualizes the same understanding of the *maṣṣēḇâ* (v. 51: *yrh* qal) through its declared function as a document of the contract between Jacob and Laban and as a border marker. The additional *gal* (vv. 51,52, cf. vv. 46,47,48) reflects the redactional interest in thwarting inappropriate cultic and theological associations.

31. Cf. J. A. Soggin, *Joshua. OTL* (Eng. trans., 1972), 242-44.
32. Cf. L'Hour, *RB,* 69 (1962), 29-36.
33. Reichert, 207, pl. 49, 1.
34. Cf. C. van Leeuwen, "עֵד *'ēd* Zeuge," *THAT,* II, 212, 214-16.
35. Cf. M. A. Klopfenstein, "כחשׁ *kḥš* pi. leugnen," *THAT,* I, 825-28.
36. *KAI,* 222B, 8.
37. Cf. D. J. McCarthy, *Treaty and Covenant. AnBibl,* 21A (^{2}1978), 98-105, here 103.

3. *Rejection.* Massebahs are not only reinterpreted, neutralized, or appropriated linguistically and theologically in this fashion, they also encounter rejection (as early as pre-Deuteronomic writings).

a. *Destruction of Pre-Israelite Cultic Massebahs.* In connection with the land conquest, several older texts in the Pentateuch demand the destruction of the massebahs of the country's previous inhabitants (Ex. 23:24; 34:13; Dt. 7:5; 12:3). Most recently, scholars consider Ex. 34:13 (perhaps Deuteronomistic?) to be the earliest witness of this sort: *kî 'eṯ-mizb^{e}ḥōṯām tittōṣûn w^{e}'eṯ-maṣṣēḇōṯām t^{e}šabbērûn w^{e}'eṯ-'^{a}šērāw* (!) *tiḵrōṯûn.*[38] This stark tripartite formula is a result of pragmatic considerations along with the general prohibition against social contact *(b^{e}rîṯ),* since such contacts would be a temptation and thus a threat to the exclusive worship of Yahweh (Ex. 34:12,14-16).[39] The massebahs are to be destroyed as a Canaanite cultic requisite just like altars and Asherim. The prohibition against "molten gods" (Ex. 34:17; cf. Lev. 19:4) is independent and does not constitute an argument for interpreting the massebahs as icons. Ex. 34:13 thus does not contain any elements describing the massebahs more specifically.

In contrast, in Ex. 23:24a the words with which Ex. 20:5a prohibits the worship of such forbidden images (20:4) are addressed directly to "their [the previous inhabitants'] gods" (*hištaḥ^{a}wâ* and *'bd* hophal in the same order), thus subsuming "other," foreign gods and images under the same rubric as far as actual cultic practice is concerned.[40] The comparison *lō' ṯa'^{a}śeh k^{e}ma'^{a}śêhem* (Ex. 23:24aβ) might be intentionally construed for multiple interpretation regarding cultic practices and be focusing especially on images,[41] whether appropriated from others or from one's own manufacture.[42] This perspective also applies to what follows. The unique *kî hārēs t^{e}hār^{e}sēm* (Deuteronomistic?) refers via *ma'^{a}śêhem* to *'^{e}lōhêhem.*[43] Thus "their massebahs" at the conclusion of the verse (*w^{e}šabbēr t^{e}šabbēr maṣṣēḇōṯêhem* [Deuteronomistic?], cf. Ex. 34:13) also includes the massebahs of foreigners, since there really are no others, not even if they have been used or manufactured by the Israelites themselves. They are mentioned as the only detail presumably because they were not only easily "set up," but one perceived in them a particular affinity to one's own graphic representation of the deity. This iconic aspect, clearly discernible over against the previously mentioned texts, fundamentally excludes massebahs by alluding to Ex. 20:3-5, not just from the perspective of socio-religious inappropriateness (cf. Dt. 12:2,30).

In Dt. 7:5, a reworking[44] of Ex. 34:13, the substantively unaltered trio addressed by the commandment of destruction (altars, massebahs, Asherim) has been expanded by a fourth member: "And you shall burn their graven images with fire." This is hardly

38. Cf. Halbe, 116-18; a different view is taken, e.g., by Jaroš, 28.
39. Cf. Schmitt, 24-30.
40. Cf. P. Welten, "Bilder II: AT," *TRE,* VI (1980), 520f.
41. Cf. G. Beer, *Exodus. HAT,* III (1939), 120: "Nor shall you imitate their idols."
42. Cf. Halbe, 490, 491, n. 20.
43. Cf. Zimmerli, *ThB,* 19 (1969), 238-246.
44. Pre-Deuteronomistic according to Halbe, 112; cf. in contrast Jaroš, 31.

to be taken as instructions for action, since although the preceding passages point out that the Canaanites have been decimated by God and the Israelites (cf. vv. 1-2: ban, extermination[45]), every *b^erîṯ* with them (v. 2b) and all connubiality are prohibited because of the danger of being led astray (vv. 3f.). Fixed motifs and expressions remind Israel of its special position (v. 6). This is not done without admonishments regarding the cult. Massebahs have disappeared from the fixed series; the virulent problem is that of actual images (cf. Dt. 4:9-28). The substantively identical, four-part commandment of destruction is in Dt. 12:3 directed at the inner-Israelite centralization of worship. This applies not simply to specific Canaanite symbols, but rather to all cultic places without distinction (*min hammāqôm hahû',* 12:3b),[46] apart from the one, specifically chosen location (v. 5; compare 12:4 with 7:5a). Massebahs share both the estimation and the fate of the entire inventory of such cultic places. The commandments of destruction, which even in the oldest passages are directed as literary fiction at the impending land conquest, are in reality directed toward cultic separation from the Canaanites. To the extent the massebahs do attract a certain amount of attention, this seems to derive from their particular proximity to imagery, at least in the Deuteronomic/Deuteronomistic passages. Their temptation was omnipresent precisely because they were so easily set up (cf. the possible allusion to spontaneity and chance in *lāqaḥ 'eḇen:* Gen. 28:11,18; 31:45,46; Josh. 24:26; similarly Josh. 4:20; 1 S. 7:12; 1 K. 18:31). The centralization of the cult offered new arguments against all massebahs. Recent archaeology, however, shows that theory and practice did not always coincide.

b. *Prohibition.* Dt. 16:22: "And you shall not set up a massebah, which [because] Yahweh your God hates [it]." This prohibition stands after one against Asherim and before one against blemished sacrificial animals. This group has no apparent connection with the present context, and constitutes, along with part of the textual expansions, the remainder of a larger, pre-Deuteronomic unit (16:21 knows as little about the unity of centralized worship as does Ex. 20:24f.[47]). Because of the close connection with 26:21, the massebah is also to be visualized "beside the altar." Yahweh's "hatred" as a motivating factor behind the prohibition is substantively the same as the *tô'^aḇaṯ YHWH* (17:1), which in Deuteronomy summarizes Canaanite cultic practices (cf. Dt. 12:31, *kol-tô'^aḇaṯ YHWH '^ašer śānē',* and the parenetic amplification 12:29-31; Jer. 44:4).[48] Here the massebah is viewed as something endemically Canaanite and as incompatible with the Yahweh cult.

In Lev. 26:1 the prohibition is rhetorically embellished by means of a literary device (chiasmus) and interpreted thus: A prohibition against making *'^elîlîm,* against setting up *pesel ûmaṣṣēḇâ,* against erecting an *'eḇen maśkîṯ* "in your land," explicitly *l^ehištaḥ^awōṯ 'āleyhā.* The spiritual environment of the first and second commandments clearly emerges from what immediately precedes (25:55) and from the concluding

45. → חרם *ḥāram* (V, 180-199).
46. Cf. Halbe, 112.
47. Cf. Halbe, 116f.; Graesser, *Studies,* 248-254; Rose, 51-59.
48. On this entire complex, see L'Hour, *RB,* 71 (1964), 486-89.

motif: *ʾanî YHWH ʾelōhêḵem.* The prohibition is thus directing itself against impermissible cultic liberties. Only in this rhetorical context is the massebah this closely associated with the graven image[49] under the auspices of a single verb, and also associated even more clearly with the sphere of graphic representation through the final member (*ʾeḇen maśkîṯ*[50]). Whatever specific historical events might have caused the massebah to acquire its bad reputation, here it is subjected to the same verdict as is the worship of graven images and foreign gods (cf. Mic. 5:12[13]; Hos. 10:1f.).

4. *Reflections in Deuteronomistic and Later Literature.* Although the appropriation of this prohibition into Deuteronomy (16:22; Lev. 26:1) may well be a symptom of justified apprehension, the older formula does exhibit a certain theoretical character. In any event, despite such rejection the massebahs do not occupy the central position in Deuteronomic/Deuteronomistic or later criticism. Rather, they are actually not mentioned that often. As far as specifics are concerned, although Ahab is accused of erecting a massebah to Baʿal, this accusation is actually only made retrospectively at the reform of his son Jehoram (2 K. 3:3; cf. 1 K. 16:32f.; 2 K. 21:3). Only Jehu is reported, in an independent, non-formulaic remark, of having destroyed the "massebahs of the temple of Baʿal" (2 K. 10:26f.). For the rest, massebahs appear in the summaries, apparently incorporated into the older, threefold, expanded and accommodated formula (1 K. 14:23; 2 K. 17:9f.; 18:4 and 2 Ch. 31:1; 2 K. 23:13f.).[51] The massebah is not mentioned in 1 K. 15:12, in contrast to the parallel passage 2 Ch. 14:2(3). Even one such as Josiah is tolerant when the cult is not threatened (*ṣiyyûn,* 2 K. 23:17f.; cf. Gen. 35:20; 2 S. 18:18). Archaeological evidence (in Arad and Lachish) suggests that in reality it may not even have been the massebahs themselves that were targeted; rather, the entire cultic site *(bāmâ)* was to be defiled and made unsuitable for any cult, be it Canaanite (syncretistic) or that of Yahweh.[52]

V. Priestly Concerns Regarding the First Commandment. The question arises concerning just why the massebahs were ultimately done away with, in principle from the time of the Deuteronomistic writing, and in reality no later than the postexilic period; this was not the case, e.g., regarding altars, which were, after all, closely related to them (though cf. Jgs. 6:25f.). Although their association with Yahweh is positively established, e.g., by Jacob (Gen. 28:11-22), so also is that with Baʿal (2 K. 3:2; 10:26f.). The earlier openness disappeared probably as a result of the Yahwistic reaction to the experience of a very real amalgamation with the Canaanite cult. The occasion was thus probably quite pragmatic. A particular inner proximity to Baʿal, e.g., as a specifically or emphatically masculine symbol, is attested neither by the (formulaic) proximity to the Asherim (1 K. 14:23; 2 K. 17:10; 18:4; 23:14)[53] nor by the unprecedented expres-

---

49. → פסל *pesel.*
50. Cf. *HAL,* II, 641.
51. Cf. III.5 above.
52. Cf. Rose, 187-192; Vaughan, 12; Boyd Barrick, *SEÅ,* 45 (1980), 56.
53. → אשׁרה *ʾašērâ (ʾashērāh),* I, 443f.

sion, recently attested in the far south: "Yahweh and his Asherah."[54] The centralization of worship, itself a result of this reaction, was especially incompatible with the wide distribution of the massebahs (cf. the pertinent formula in Dt. 12:2; 1 K. 14:23; 2 K. 16:4; 17:10; 2 Ch. 28:4; Hos. 4:13; Jer. 2:20; 3:6; 17:2), particularly since the ultimately exclusive Jerusalem temple never seems to have included any massebahs; at least none is ever mentioned, in contrast to the Asherim (2 K. 21:3-7; 23:6 with vv. 14-15; cf. 18:22).

Furthermore, the proximity of the massebah to graven images may have provided the fluid transition to complete rejection, at least as a (subsequent) additional justification (cf. Hos. 10:1; Lev. 26:1), since here one did perceive a threat to the exclusive worship of Yahweh (compare 2 K. 17:7-18 with Ex. 20:2-5, as well as Dt. 4:16-18,25,28; Jer. 2:27; Ezk. 20:32; Mic. 5:9-13[10-14]; Hab. 2:19). The ultimately decisive Deuteronomic opposition directed itself more indirectly against the massebahs. The salient dogmatic considerations resulted from priestly concern for Yahweh's exclusive claims.

Gamberoni

---

54. Cf. Lemaire; Meshel; J. A. Emerton, "New Light on Israelite Religion: The Implications of the Inscriptions from Kuntillet ʿAjrud," *ZAW,* 94 (1982), 2-20.

מַצָּה *maṣṣâ;* מַצּוֹת *maṣṣôṯ*

Contents: I. 1. Etymology; 2. Occurrences. II. 1. Noncultic Texts; 2. Sacrificial Regulations; 3. The Feast of Unleavened Bread.

---

maṣṣâ. C. W. Atkinson, "The Ordinances of Passover-Unleavened Bread," *ATR,* 44 (1962), 70-85; E. Auerbach, "Die Feste im alten Israel," *VT,* 8 (1958), 1-18, esp. 1-10; G. Beer and O. Holtzmann, eds., *Pesachim. Die Mischna,* II/3 (Giessen, 1912); F. Cabrol, "Azymes," *DACL,* I/2 (1924), 3254-3260; B. D. Eerdmans, "Das Mazzoth-Fest," *Orientalische Studien. Festschrift T. Nöldeke* (Giessen, 1906), II, 671-79; I. Engnell, "Pæsaḥ-Maṣṣōt a Hebrew Annual Festival of the Ancient Near East Pattern," in C. J. Bleeker, ed., *Proceedings of the 7th Congress for the History of Religions 1950* (Amsterdam, 1951), 111-13; *idem,* "Pæsaḥ-Maṣṣōt and the Problem of 'Patternism,'" *OrSuec,* 1 (1952), 39-50; G. B. Gray, "Passover and Unleavened Bread: The Laws of J, E, and D," *JTS,* 37 (1936), 241-253; H. Haag, "Das Mazzenfest des Hiskia," *Wort und Geschichte. Festschrift K. Elliger. AOAT,* 18 (1973), 87-94 = *Das Buch des Bundes* (Düsseldorf, 1980), 216-225; *idem, Vom alten zum neuen Pascha. SBS,* 49 (1971); J. Halbe, "Erwägungen zu Ursprung und Wesen des Massotfestes," *ZAW,* 87 (1975), 324-346; *idem,* "Passa-Massot im deuteronomischen Festkalender," *ZAW,* 87 (1975), 147-168; *idem, Das Privilegrecht Jahwes: Ex 34,10-26. FRLANT,* 114 (1975); H.-J. Kraus, "Zur Geschichte des Passah-Massot-Festes im AT," *EvTh,* 18 (1958), 47-67; E. Kutsch, "Erwägungen zur Geschichte der Passafeier und des Massotfestes," *ZThK,* 55 (1958), 1-35; P. Laaf, *Die Pascha-Feier Israels. BBB,* 36

I. 1. *Etymology.* The derivation of the word *maṣṣâ* from the root *mṣṣ,* "to suck,"[1] in the sense that *maṣṣâ* refers to something "which is, as it were, sucked, i.e., eagerly or gladly eaten,"[2] can hardly be maintained, not least because of the rather distant semantic detour involved. Associations with Heb. *mṣh,* "to press or drain out," or with Arab. *muzz,* "sourish, acidulous," *mazza,* "to suck," or Ethiop. *maḏaḏa* (cf. Arab. *maḏaḏ,* "sour milk"), "to drink sour milk," are all "merely expedients designed to aid the word in somehow finding a Semitic father."[3] In contrast, one can hardly deny that some connection exists between Gk. *máza* (Hellenistic *máza,* Megarian *mádda*), "barley dough, barley bread/cakes," and Heb. *maṣṣâ.*[4] However, rather than Gk. *máza* representing a Semitic loanword,[5] it is more likely that Heb. *maṣṣâ* was borrowed from the Greek,[6] unless a word from Asia Minor or of Hurrian origin provided the point of departure for both the Greek and the Hebrew.[7]

2. *Occurrences.* The terms *maṣṣâ* and *maṣṣôṯ* occur altogether 54 times in the OT. In the singular *maṣṣâ* occurs only in Lev. 2:5 in the general sense referring to the regulation that the cereal offering may not contain leaven, and Lev. 8:26 (twice) in the expression *ḥallaṯ maṣṣâ,* "an unleavened cake," and Nu. 6:19 next to *rᵉqîq maṣṣâ,* "a thin unleavened wafer." The majority of occurrences (24 total) can be attributed to P. The expression *ḥag hammaṣṣôṯ* in reference to the feast occurs 9 times. The verb *'āḵal* occurs 18 times in connection with *maṣṣôṯ*.

Thus far, the Qumran writings attest *maṣṣâ/maṣṣôṯ* only in the Temple scroll in 3 passages (11QT 15:9; 17:11; 20:12).

(1970); H. G. May, "The Relation of the Passover to the Festival of Unleavened Cakes," *JBL,* 55 (1936), 65-82; O. Michel, "Azyma," *RAC,* 1, 1056-1062; J. Morgenstern, "The Origin of *Maṣṣoth* and the *Maṣṣoth*-Festival," *AJT,* 21 (1917), 275-293; E. Otto, *Das Mazzotfest in Gilgal. BWANT,* 107[6/7] (1975); S. Ros Garmendia, *La Pascua en al AT. Biblia Victoriensia,* 3 (1978); L. Rost, "Massoth," *BHHW,* II (1964), 1169f.; *idem, Studien zum Opfer im alten Israel. BWANT,* 113 (1981); G. Sauer, "Israels Feste und ihr Verhältnis zum Jahweglauben," *Studien zum Pentateuch. Festschrift W. Kornfeld* (Vienna, 1977), 135-141; J. Schreiner, "Exodus 12,21-23 und das israelitische Pascha," *Festschrift W. Kornfeld,* 69-90; J. B. Segal, *The Hebrew Passover, from the Earliest Times to A.D. 70.* London Oriental Series, 12 (1963); C. Steuernagel, "Zum Passa-Maṣṣotfest," *ZAW,* 31 (1911), 310; B. N. Wambacq, "Les Maṣṣôt," *Bibl,* 61 (1980), 31-54; J. Wellhausen, *Prolegomena zur Geschichte Israels* (Berlin, [6]1927), 82ff.; H. Windisch, "ζύμη, ζυμόω, ἄζυμος," *TDNT,* II, 902-6; F. Zeilinger, *Das Passionsbrot Israels* (diss., Graz, 1963); P. Zerafa, "Passover and Unleavened Bread," *Ang,* 41 (1964), 235-250.

1. Still advocated by E. König, *Hebräisches und aramäisches Wörterbuch zum AT* (Leipzig, 1910; [6,7]1937), *s.v.,* and *BDB*.

2. So König.

3. Beer-Holtzmann, 21.

4. Cf. H. Frisk, *Griechisches Etymologisches Wörterbuch. Indogermanische Bibliothek,* ser. 2, 2 (Heidelberg, 1970), II, 158f.

5. So E. Assmann, "Zur Vorgeschichte vom Kreta," *Philologus,* 67 (1908), 199.

6. So C. H. Gordon, "Homer and Bible," *HUCA,* 26 (1955), 61; "The Rôle of the Philistines," *Antiquity,* 30 (1956), 24.

7. Cf. Rost, *Studien zum Opfer im Alten Israel,* 19, n. 8.

As a rule, the LXX translates with *ázyma*.[8]

II. 1. *Noncultic Texts.* Although the Israelites probably originally became acquainted with the word *maṣṣâ* "as a foreign word applied to the cult,"[9] it is advisable to begin with those few passages in which *maṣṣôṯ* are attested in noncultic contexts. After Lot urges the two men to come into his house in Sodom, he prepares a feast *(mišteh)* for them and has *maṣṣôṯ* baked (Gen. 19:3). The reference here is to unleavened wafers baked when there is no time for fermentation. The *ʿugôṯ* which Sarah is to bake (Gen. 18:6) and with which Abraham treats the two visitors were probably unleavened wafers, for they, too, are hastily prepared so they can be eaten immediately. And when according to 1 S. 28:24 the "medium of Endor" not only slaughters a fatted calf for Saul but also bakes *maṣṣôṯ,* here, too, the focus is probably on serving the guest something quickly. To all this one can add the story of Gideon serving the *mal'āḵ* (Jgs. 6:11ff.),[10] which apparently reflects a widespread custom for offering food to the deity, although here the intervention of the *mal'aḵ YHWH* transforms it into an *ʿôlâ;* one cannot avoid the suspicion that also in Gen. 19:3 (18:6) the background of the story is the notion that the *maṣṣôṯ* are baked goods for serving the gods. Thus one cannot completely discount the possibility that the narrator in 1 S. 28:24[11] was identifying this meal as a sacrificial meal for conjuring the spirit of the dead.

2. *Sacrificial Regulations.* In the sacrificial regulations of P unleavened bread plays a certain role independent of the Feast of Unleavened Bread and the Passover celebration. According to Lev. 2:4, the prepared form of the cereal offering consists of unleavened cakes, *ḥallôṯ maṣṣôṯ,* whose dough is already mixed with oil, and of thin unleavened wafers, *reqîqê maṣṣôṯ,* which are spread with oil. The semolina cakes baked on the griddle must also be unleavened, as Lev. 2:5 explicitly emphasizes. Lev. 6:9(Eng. v. 16) underscores once again that the unburned remainder of the cereal offering must be eaten by the priests in a holy place, and must be in the form of unleavened cakes.

According to Lev. 7:12, the bread involved in the peace offering, as was the case with the cereal offering in Lev. 2, consists of unleavened cakes mixed with oil and unleavened wafers spread with oil. It is noteworthy that an apparent concession to earlier praxis is made by 7:13 in its allowance for leavened cakes as an offering (cf. Am. 4:5). In connection with the priestly regulations, Lev. 10:12 once more points out that it a priestly obligation to consume the cereal offering unleavened in a holy place.

The consecration of priests in Ex. 29 par. Lev. 8 includes unleavened bread among the offerings. The installation offering consists of a young bull and two rams without blemish, and according to Ex. 29:2 also unleavened bread *(leḥem maṣṣôṯ),* unleavened cakes, and unleavened wafers made of fine wheat flour. The basket of unleavened bread

---

8. Cf. esp. Windisch and Michel.
9. Rost, *Studien zum Opfer im Alten Israel,* 19, n. 8.
10. Cf. recently Rost, *Studien zum Opfer im Alten Israel,* 17ff.
11. Contra H. J. Stoebe, *Das erste Buch Samuelis. KAT,* VIII/1 (1973), *in loc.*

(*sal hammaṣṣôṯ,* Ex. 29:23; Lev. 8:2,26; Nu. 6:15,17 next to simple *sal* Ex. 29:3[twice], 32; Nu. 6:19) standing before Yahweh can be viewed as a permanent fixture in the later cult even if more specific information is lacking.[12] From this basket the priest takes the bread and places it into the hands of the priestly candidates in order to complete the wave offering before Yahweh.

Finally, the Nazirite regulations in Nu. 6 also emphasize that the cereal offering required among the offerings for consecration is to be a basket of unleavened cakes and unleavened wafers (Nu. 6:15). As was the case with the priestly consecration in Lev. 8 par. Ex. 29, explicit reference is again made to the basket in which the bread is to be brought. The cakes and wafers are precisely defined with the same formulations as in Lev. 2:4 (also 7:12).[13]

The occurrence of *maṣṣôṯ* in 2 K. 23:9 is difficult to interpret and thus disputed. According to 2 K. 23:9a, the former priests of the high places are not admitted to sacrificial service in the Jerusalem temple. The following clause (v. 9b), *kî 'im-'āḵᵉlû maṣṣôṯ bᵉṯôḵ 'ᵃḥêhem,* "but they ate unleavened bread among their kindred," presents a variety of interpretative difficulties. It is hardly the case[14] that the priests of the high places, just as they were not permitted to participate in the sacrificial services, also had to stay "to themselves," *bᵉṯôḵ 'ᵃḥêhem,* for meals. Similarly off the mark is the interpretation of *bᵉṯôḵ 'ᵃḥêhem* in the sense of "among their previous fellow citizens," i.e., "at their former residences,"[15] since "to eat *maṣṣôṯ*" is not the equivalent of "to eat bread" in the sense of "to live" (cf. Am. 7:12). Since *maṣṣôṯ* did not constitute the priests' normal food, nor even an essential part of it, one suspects that 2 K. 23:9 constitutes an observation originally belonging to the portrayal of the Passover celebration in 2 K. 23:21ff. indicating that although the priests of the high places indeed were not admitted to altar service, their participation in the Passover Festival was viewed as a confession of faith to Yahweh;[16] or that v. 9b is pointing out that the priests of the high places had to celebrate "the Passover Festival among and in the same way as the lay people with whom they had come."[17] If one prefers not to take v. 9b as a displaced text referring to the Passover celebration, then it seems likely that this statement is to be viewed as a reference to the regulation of the livelihood of the unemployed rural priests. The suggestion that one must thus repoint *maṣṣôṯ* to *miṣwôṯ* with reference to Neh. 13:5, where the tithe for the Levites is called *miṣwaṯ halᵉwîyim,* raises doubts because *miṣwôṯ* or *miṣwâ* cannot be used in connection with the verb *'āḵal,*[18] and because in Neh. 13:5, too, the text probably should be emended with the Vulg. *(partes Levitarum)* to *mᵉnāyôṯ.* Reading *mᵉnāyôṯ* instead of *maṣṣôṯ* in 2 K.

---

12. Cf. K. Elliger, *Leviticus. HAT,* IV (1966), 109.
13. Cf. D. Kellermann, *Die Priesterschrift von Numeri 1_1 bis 10_{10}. BZAW,* 120 (1970), 91.
14. Cf. O. Thenius, *Die Bücher der Könige. KEHAT,* IX (²1873), 441f.
15. Cf. W. W. Graf Baudissin, *Die Geschichte des alttestamentlichen Priesterthums* (1889, repr. Osnabrück, 1967), 236f.
16. Cf. R. Kittel, *Die Bücher der Könige. HKAT,* V (1900), 301f.; A. Šanda, *Die Bücher der Könige. EHAT,* IX/2 (1912), 345.
17. So H. Schmidt, *Die grossen Propheten. SAT,* II/2 (²1923), 177.
18. Cf. B. Stade and F. Schwally, *The Books of Kings. SBOT,* IX (1904), 294.

23:9 as well is attractive, and thus instead of the unleavened bread one has a general word for portion or allotment.[19] If one recalls, however, that according to Lev. 6:9 it is the special obligation of the priests to eat in a holy place the remaining portions of the cereal offering in the form of unleavened bread to preserve the holy character of this food, it is not surprising that 2 K. 23:9 mentions *maṣṣôṯ* representatively as an especially important part of the priestly portion of the offering. Rashi[20] also views it thus when he says that although the priests of the high places were indeed not permitted to offer sacrifices, they were permitted to eat part of the offerings, and were thus viewed as priests with a blemish *(kbʿly mwmyn).* 2 K. 23:9 thus reveals that the demand made in Dt. 18:6,7, namely, to regard the priests of the high places who came to Jerusalem as equal to those already in Jerusalem, encountered opposition and was not able to be implemented in its entirety. One could hardly, however, deny these rural priests the right of priestly provision, the result being that at least their livelihood was secured by their participation in the offering perquisites, referred to here representatively by the *maṣṣôṯ*.

3. *The Feast of Unleavened Bread.* The sparse information concerning the *maṣṣôṯ* festival (Feast of Unleavened Bread) offers few concrete details about the actual festival customs, so that the character and history of the festival are not easily traced. The *maṣṣôṯ* festival is treated as an independent festival in Ex. 34:18; 23:15 as well as Dt. 16:16; Ex. 12:15-20; 13:3-10; Lev. 23:6-8; Nu. 28:17-25 as well as 2 Ch. 8:13. The festival sequence of the pre-Deuteronomic period as passed down in Ex. 34:18-24; 23:14-17 associates the *maṣṣôṯ* festival with the Feast of Weeks and of Ingathering *(ḥag šāḇuʿōṯ* and *ḥag hāʾāsîp̄).* This provided the basis for the thesis advocated since Julius Wellhausen with only minor modifications and still currently representing the widespread *communis opinio,* namely, that the *maṣṣôṯ* festival was an agricultural festival of Canaanite origin. The removal of the old leaven and the eating of the unleavened bread during the seven-day festival week is interpreted such that this celebration introduced the new agricultural year. As is apparent from Ex. 34:18; 23:15, the *maṣṣôṯ* festival was not originally associated with a fixed date. The actual date was determined by the condition of the grain and the beginning of the harvest, which was itself dependent on that condition; this can be seen in Dt. 16:9, which refers to "the time the sickle is first put to the standing grain" *(mēhāḥēl ḥermēš baqqāmâ),* i.e., from the sickle's first cut into the standing grain of the barley harvest. However, the harvest of barley, as the earliest type of grain, does not occur, e.g., until June in the fertile Valley of Jezreel,[21] so that this general designation is difficult to reconcile with the later, specific dating on the fifteenth day of the first month (= Nisan = Abib = March/April).

The seven-day duration of the *maṣṣôṯ* festival is closely associated with the notion

---

19. Cf. A. Kuenen, *Historisch-kritische Einleitung in die Bücher des ATs,* I/1 (Leipzig, 1887), 281, and still *HAL,* II (1995), *s.v. maṣṣâ.*

20. *Miqraʾôt gedōlôt, in loc.*

21. Cf. G. Dalman, *AuS,* I/2 (1928), 333.

of the week attested by Yahweh as the Lord of work and rest. The establishment of the "day after the Sabbath" (Lev. 23:11), i.e., the first day of the week, as the beginning of the festival week is probably not part of the original stipulations. However, after this fixing of the seven-day *maṣṣôṯ* festival the feast itself coincided exactly with one week. Later praxis in fact relinquished this connection between the festival and the single week and oriented itself according to the date of the Passover.

After these two festivals had become pilgrimage festivals (at least since Deuteronomy and the reform of Josiah), it seemed plausible to combine the Passover with the *maṣṣôṯ* festival. The *maṣṣôṯ* festival is explicitly called *ḥag* in Ex. 34:18; 23:15; Lev. 23:6; Dt. 16:16; 2 Ch. 8:13; 30:13,21; 35:17; Ezr. 6:22. However, it is noteworthy that according to Dt. 16:7 one's presence at the sanctuary is required only for the Passover, but not for the *maṣṣôṯ* festival. The older prescription requiring the eating of unleavened bread at the Passover (Ex. 12:8) accommodated the combination of the two festivals.

After in this way the secondary calendric dating of the beginning of the *maṣṣôṯ* festival on the fifteenth day of the first month was established,[22] it was inevitable that difficulties would arise if as before one insisted on maintaining the connection of the *maṣṣôṯ* festival with the single week (cf. Ex. 23:15; 34:18; and Ex. 12:16; Dt. 16:8; Lev. 23:6,8). In interpreting the expression *mimmoḥᵒraṯ haššabbāṯ* (Lev. 23:16) the rabbis availed themselves of the understanding of *šabbāṯ* here as "festival day," namely, as the first day after the Passover night, while the Boethusians *(bytwsyn)* took the expression literally and reckoned from the first regular Sabbath after the Passover celebration day (Bab. *Menaḥ.* 65a). Thus in actual practice one gave up the connection between the *maṣṣôṯ* festival and the week and oriented the celebration entirely according to the date determined by the full moon of the fourteenth day of the first month (= Nisan) for the Passover. This abolished the connection between the *maṣṣôṯ* festival and the beginning of the harvest. Lev. 23:9-19 shows that the original significance of the festival, namely, as a celebration of the beginning of the harvest, had been forgotten;[23] for in this text the waving of the first sheaf (*ʿōmer rēʾšîṯ,* Lev. 23:10; *ʿōmer hattᵉnûp̱â,* v. 15) appears as an independent celebration of the beginning of the harvest completely void of any reference to the *maṣṣôṯ* festival.

An independent *maṣṣôṯ* festival seems to have been celebrated under Hezekiah, as 2 Ch. 30 reveals. The reference to the Passover in this text can be traced back to a redactor associated with the Chronicler's portrayal; this redactor oriented himself according to 2 Ch. 35:1-7 because at his time "a Festival of Unleavened Bread without the preceding passover was unthinkable."[24]

The Passover papyrus from Elephantine,[25] as well as the commentary and emendations suggested for the textual lacunae by Pierre Grelot[26] shows that in 419 B.C. both

---

22. Cf. Kutsch, 14ff.; Elliger, *HAT,* IV, 315.
23. Cf. Elliger, *HAT,* IV, 314f.
24. Cf. Haag, *AOAT,* 18, 91.
25. *AP,* no. 21, pp. 60-65.
26. "Etudes sur le 'Papyrus Pascal' d'Éléphantine," *VT,* 4 (1954), 349-384.

a Passover and *maṣṣôṯ* festival were familiar to the settlement at Elephantine. If Hananiah's instructions from Jerusalem for the Jews in Elephantine are not intended to reintroduce the celebration of the *maṣṣôṯ* festival, then the preserved portions of the text do indicate clearly that they represent the demand not to celebrate the Passover without also celebrating the *maṣṣôṯ* week immediately thereupon, and to do so on the fixed date (15-21 Nisan), i.e., in the sense of the Jerusalem priesthood.[27] As a festival offering for the Passover-*maṣṣôṯ* festival at the Jerusalem temple, P stipulates the following in Nu. 28:16-23: on each of the seven festival days two young bulls and a ram as well as seven lambs a year old are to be offered as a burnt offering with the requisite cereal offerings.

The textual evidence available to us associates the *maṣṣôṯ* festival (Ex. 34:18; 23:15; Dt. 16:3) as well as the Passover (Dt. 16:1,6) or the Passover-*maṣṣôṯ* festival (Ex. 12:23-27,39; Ex. 12:12,17) with the deliverance from Egypt. Reference to the *maṣṣôṯ* in Dt. 16:3 as *leḥem ʿonî,* "bread of affliction," recalls the plight of the people of Israel in Egypt (cf. Ex. 3:17, *ʿonî miṣrayim;* Gen. 41:52, *ʾereṣ ʿonî*) and during the exodus. This association with the exodus from Egypt is most extensively treated in Ex. 12, which discusses the two festivals in more detail in its account of the exodus. Both festivals are "historicized," and both are to serve later to recall the decisive event in Israel's salvation history, deliverance from Egypt through Yahweh's intervention. As Herbert Haag observes, "In this way the festival becomes a 'memorial' to the historically tangible salvific acts of God. The singular, one-time historical event becomes a personal, salvific presence for all generations through this commemorative cultic celebration."[28]

More recent interpretations have yet to prove their merit. Ivan Engnell understands the Passover as a southern Canaanite form of the New Year Festival celebrated in the spring, and the *maṣṣôṯ* festival as a northern Canaanite form of the same festival, so that the two festivals represent merely different versions of the same celebration. Similarly, Otto Procksch thinks it conceivable that the *maṣṣôṯ* festival was unique to the tribes of Leah, while the Feasts of Weeks and Tabernacles "belonged to the tribes of Rachel, since references to wheat and fruit suggest a provenance in fertile regions."[29]

According to Jörn Halbe,[30] the *maṣṣôṯ* festival does not represent an originally Canaanite agricultural festival which was then secondarily reconstituted according to the Yahweh faith; rather, this festival for farmers "originated as the response of the Yahweh faith to settled life."[31] Its origin can be explained as a result of the *maṣṣôṯ* element within the older Passover ritual having become independent. In contrast, Eberhard Otto assumes that the Israelites became familiar with the *maṣṣôṯ* festival in Gilgal, and attempts to trace the eating of the *maṣṣôṯ* back to the conditions of the wilderness period. In view of both these theories, however, one must not forget that

27. Haag, *SBS,* 49, 95f.
28. *Ibid.,* 59.
29. *Theologie des ATs* (Gütersloh, 1950), 549.
30. *ZAW,* 87 (1975), 324-356.
31. *Ibid.,* 345.

the word *maṣṣâ* exhibits no etymological roots in the Semitic linguistic sphere, so that the suspicion cannot be so easily dismissed that the Israelites appropriated from external sources not only the word itself, but also the custom of eating unleavened bread during the seven-day *maṣṣôṯ* festival.[32]

Kellermann

32. On the literary-critical evaluation of the *maṣṣôṯ*-festival in Josh. 5, cf. H.-J. Fabry, *BETL* (1984).

מְצוּדָה *m^eṣûḏâ;* *מָצוֹד *māṣôḏ;* מְצוֹדָה *m^eṣôḏâ;* מְצָד *m^eṣāḏ*

Contents: I. 1. Root Differentiation; 2. Etymology, Occurrences in the Ancient Near East; 3. Occurrences, Meanings. II. Secular Usage: 1. Derivatives of the Root *ṣwd;* 2. Derivatives of the Basic Form **mṣd.* III. Religious Contexts and Figurative Theological-Religious Meaning: 1. Derivatives of the Root *ṣwd;* 2. Derivatives of the Basic Form **mṣd.*

I. 1. *Root Differentiation.* The various nouns belonging to the word group *m^eṣûḏâ* probably derive from two different Hebrew roots or basic forms: either from *ṣwd* = "to hunt," "to lie in wait for," "to apprehend," or from the root **mṣd* (cf. Arab. *maṣd, maṣād,* "summit," "place of refuge"[1]). In this connection, the root *ṣwd* is associated not only with **māṣôḏ* (I), but also with *m^eṣûḏâ* (I) and *m^eṣôḏâ,* while derivatives from the basic form **mṣd* include *m^eṣāḏ* (*m^eṣaḏ,* which occurs as such only in 1 Ch. 12:9[Eng. v. 8], can be viewed in light of the LXX as a later addendum and can probably be attributed to scribal error[2]) as well as **māṣôḏ* (II) and *m^eṣûḏâ (m^eṣuḏâ)* (II..

2. *Etymology, Occurrences in the Ancient Near East.* Derivatives of both basic forms are attested also beyond Hebrew in other Semitic languages. The root *ṣwd* derives from Akk. *ṣādu* as well as Ugar. *ṣd,* and also appears in Middle Hebrew, Jewish-Aramaic, Syriac, and Arabic; the term **māṣôḏ* (I) also attests parallel terms in Christian-Palestinian *mṣd'* = "net," while *m^eṣûḏâ* (I) has related terms in Middle Heb. *m^eṣāḏâ,* Jewish-Aram.

m^eṣûḏâ. G. Dalman, *AuS,* VI (1939), 328, 335-340, 359-362; D. Eichhorn, *Gott als Fels, Burg und Zuflucht. EH,* 23/4 (1972), 96-99; K. Galling, "Fisch und Fischfang," *BRL*², 83f.; G. Gerleman, *Contributions to the OT Terminology of the Chase* (Lund, 1946); O. Keel, *The Symbolism of the Biblical World* (Eng. trans., New York, 1978); M. Metzger, "Festung," *BHHW,* I (1962), 475-79; K.-D. Schunck, "Davids 'Schlupfwinkel' in Juda," *VT,* 33 (1983), 110-13; J. Simons, *Jerusalem in the OT. StFS,* 1 (1952), 60-64; H. Weippert, "Festung," *BRL*², 80-82; Y. Yadin, *Masada* (Eng. trans., New York, 1967).

1. See *HAL,* II (1995), 622.
2. Cf. W. Rudolph, *Chronikbücher. HAT,* XXI (1955), 104.

m^eṣûḏtā', Syr. mṣīḏtā, and Arab. miṣyadat = "net," "snare, trap." Similarly, not only is the basic form *mṣd taken up again in Arab. maṣd and maṣād = "summit," "place of refuge," but m^eṣāḏ finds its continuation in Jewish-Aram. m^eṣāḏtā' = "stronghold," and m^eṣûḏâ (II) in Middle Heb. m^eṣāḏâ and Jewish-Aram. m^eṣûḏtā'.

3. a. *Occurrences.* This word group occurs 42 times in the OT and in the extracanonical writings and manuscripts from the Dead Sea and from the Judean Desert. Of these, only 9 occurrences, including several conjectures, are to be attributed to derivatives of the root *ṣwd,* appearing above all in Ezekiel (3 times), Ecclesiastes (twice), and Sirach (twice including Sir. 26:22, attested only in Greek, where *pýrgos* constitutes the erroneous translation of *m^eṣûḏâ* II instead of I[3]). In contrast, nouns deriving from the form **mṣd,* including several conjectures, occur 32 times, primarily in Samuel (11 times) and the Psalms (7 times), whereby *m^eṣāḏ* originally only occurred in the plural (in 1 Ch. 12:9,17[8,16] *m^eṣāḏ* or *m^eṣaḏ* is a later insertion; 1 Ch. 11:7 contains an early scribal error resulting from *m^eṣûḏâ,* as shown by 1 Ch. 11:5 and the parallel 2 S. 5:9), while *m^eṣûḏâ (m^eṣuḏâ)* II (with the exception of Ps. 31:3[2]; 71:3a conj.) was used only in the singular.

b. *Meanings.* Consistent with the original meaning of the root *ṣwd* = "to hunt," "to capture," the derivative **māṣôḏ* (I) from this root has the meaning "snare, net" (Job 19:6; Eccl. 7:26; in Ps. 116:3 read *m^eṣōḏê*). Similarly, the additional derivative *m^eṣûḏâ* (I), representing the feminine form of **māṣôḏ* (I), also exhibits meanings derived from notions of the hunt: "hunting net" (Ezk. 12:13; 17:20; Sir. 9:3; 26:22 conj.) and "huntsman's bag, prey" (Ezk. 13:21), while the third derivative of this root, *m^eṣôḏâ,* again only exhibits the meaning "hunting net" (Eccl. 9:12), a meaning thus common to all the derivatives of the root *ṣwd.*

In contrast, the fundamental meaning common to the nouns derived from the basic form **mṣd* is "place with difficult access." From this meaning the term *m^eṣāḏ* has acquired the specialized meaning "hiding place," "hideout" (Jgs. 6:2; 1 S. 23:14,19; 24:1[23:29]; 1 Ch. 12:9,17[8,16]; Ezk. 33:27) and "place of refuge" (Isa. 33:16; Jer. 48:41; 51:30); the additional specialized meaning "stronghold" first appears in the manuscripts from the Dead Sea and from the Judean Desert.[4] Similarly, the derivative **māṣôḏ* (II) also developed the specialized meaning "hiding place," "hideout" (Prov. 12:12). The third, most frequently occurring derivative, *m^eṣûḏâ,* in addition to the basic meaning "place with difficult access" (Job 39:28), largely attests the specialized meaning "hiding place," "hideout" (1 S. 22:4,5; 24:23[22]; 2 S. 5:17; 23:14; 1 Ch. 11:16; 12:9,17[8,16]), and "place of refuge" (Pss. 18:3[2]; 31:3,4[2,3]; in 71:3a read *m^eṣûḏôṯ,* 3b; 91:2; 144:2). In contrast, the additional specialized meaning "stronghold," which is often erroneously understood as the primary meaning,[5] is limited to 4 passages (2 S.

3. Cf. P. W. Skehan, "Tower of Death or Deadly Snare? (Sir 26,22)," *CBQ,* 16 (1954), 154; *HAL,* II, 622.

4. Cf. P. Benoit, J. T. Milik, and R. de Vaux, *Les grottes de Murabb'ât. DJD,* II (1961), 164, no. 45; M. Baillet, J. Tadeusz, and R. de Vaux, *Les 'petites grottes' de Qumrân. DJD,* III (1962), 269, 37; on *m^eṣāḏ* in 1 Ch. 11:7, see I.3.a above.

5. So *GesB,* 452; *HAL,* II, 622.

5:7,9; in 1 Ch. 11:5,7 read *m*^{e}*ṣuḏâ*), all of which refer to pre-Israelite Jerusalem, conquered by David = Zion = the city of David, and all of which are clearly set apart from the other occurrences of this derivative by the defective orthography *m*^{e}*ṣuḏâ*. It is possible that in this way the meaning "stronghold" was first attached to the noun *m*^{e}*ṣuḏâ* in connection with David's conquest of the acropolis or city enclosure of Jerusalem, considered virtually impregnable; later it was then likely also transferred to the noun *m*^{e}*ṣāḏ* as well as other strongholds (cf. also the *n.l.* Μασαδα).

II. Secular Usage. Nouns deriving from the root *ṣwd* as well as constructions based on the basic form **mṣd* are used in secular contexts both in the OT and in extrabiblical writings, usage accounting for approximately half of all occurrences of this word group.

1. *Derivatives of the Root ṣwd.* In ancient Israel, the *ṣwd*-derivatives **māṣôḏ, m*^{e}*ṣûḏâ,* and *m*^{e}*ṣôḏâ,* like the Hebrew word *rešeṯ,* were designations for the net used both in hunting and in fishing (Eccl. 9:12), to be differentiated from the casting net or snare net *(mikmār)* and the dragnet *(ḥērem),* also used in connection with fishing.[6] From this completely concrete point of departure, the terms **māṣôḏ* and *m*^{e}*ṣûḏâ* serve in wisdom literature as symbols for women and their behavior to the extent that it results in the suspension of the physical and psychological independence of another person. Thus Eccl. 7:26 describes the woman as a being consisting of snares and nets, while Sir. 9:3 warns against the snares of a loose woman, and Sir. 26:22 (conj.) refers to the married woman as a deadly snare for her lovers.

2. *Derivatives of the Basic Form *mṣd.* Secular usage of derivatives of the basic form **mṣd* in the OT is limited almost exclusively to the historical books. In this connection, the meaning "hiding place," "hideout" predominates, in several instances associated with *m*^{e}*ʿārâ,* "cave" (Jgs. 6:2; 2 S. 23:13f.; 1 Ch. 11:15f.; Ezk. 33:27; compare also 1 S. 22:1 with 22:4f., and 1 S. 24:1,23[23:29; 24:22] with 24:4[3]). Thus in Jgs. 6:2 *m*^{e}*ṣāḏ* refers to the hiding places the Israelite clans made for themselves to be used together with caves as protection from the Midianites; similarly, *m*^{e}*ṣāḏ* or *m*^{e}*ṣûḏâ* refers to the cave of Adullam which served as David's hiding place from Saul (1 S. 22:4f.; 2 S. 23:14; 1 Ch. 11:16), as well as to David's hiding places in the hill country of Ziph (1 S. 23:14,19) or to his hideout in the caves of En-gedi (1 S. 24:1,23[23:29; 24:22]). David probably finally expanded one of these hiding places into a fixed headquarters in which he also took refuge later (2 S. 5:17). No evidence, however, suggests associating this or David's other hideouts with the idea of a mountain stronghold.[7]

The derivative *m*^{e}*ṣûḏâ* is also used in secular contexts in the basic meaning "place with difficult access"; in Job 39:28 it and the rocky crag refer to the inaccessible resting place of the eagle. Above all, however, *m*^{e}*ṣuḏâ* (written defectively) in the meaning "stronghold" exhibits secular character. Such is the case when Zion is so referred to

6. Dalman, 335f., 361f.
7. Cf. *HAL,* II, 622, and the comms.

in its identity as the pre-Davidic acropolis or city enclosure of Jerusalem, which David renamed the city of David (2 S. 5:7,9; 1 Ch. 11:5,7 [conj.]). Analogously, the writings from the Dead Sea and from the Judean Desert also use *m*^e*ṣāḏ* as a designation for a stronghold,[8] including the expression *mṣd ḥsdn,* probably a reference to the settlement of Qumran in its character as a stronghold.[9]

III. Religious Contexts and Figurative Theological-Religious Meaning. The OT uses both the derivatives of the root *ṣwd* and the nouns derived from the basic form **mṣd* in religious contexts and with figurative theological-religious meaning.

1. *Derivatives of the Root ṣwd.* The general meaning "snare, net" occurs first of all in Ezekiel and Job with Yahweh as the subject as a metaphorical expression for Yahweh's omnipotence and control of human beings. It was Yahweh's net in which King Zedekiah was captured when he came into Babylonian captivity (Ezk. 12:13; 17:20), and it is Yahweh's net that closes around Job when Yahweh persecutes and torments him (Job 19:6). Analogously, the netherworld, *š*^e*'ôl,* can also be the subject in connection with such a "net" as a metaphor for the mortal threat to human life (Ps. 116:3 conj.). Ezekiel uses the additional meaning "prey," actually a semantic extension of "net"; in an oracle against the false prophetesses, Yahweh announces that no more will persons become their "prey" whom they have hexed through practices hostile to God, i.e., such persons will no longer fall into their power (Ezk. 13:21).

2. *Derivatives of the Basic Form *mṣd.* Use in religious contexts of nouns deriving from the basic form **mṣd* is governed largely by the meaning "place of refuge." This is particularly clear in the Psalms; in passages from laments and thanksgiving psalms (Pss. 18:3[2]; 31:3,4[2,3]; 71:3a[conj.],3b; 91:2; 144:2), among which 2 S. 22:2 should also be included, *m*^e*ṣûḏâ* consistently refers to Yahweh as a place or house of refuge for human beings. In this connection, the association with analogous terms such as *miśgāḇ, mānôs, mā'ôn, maḥseh,* and *sela'* is noteworthy.[10]

Similarly, prophetic literature also largely associates the meaning "place of refuge" with its preferred noun *m*^e*ṣāḏ*. In Isa. 33:16, within the framework of a little apocalypse, the righteous are assured that at Yahweh's eschatological judgment over the nations they will dwell on the heights and find refuge in places among the rocks. Likewise, a redactor establishes in Jeremiah's oracles a connection between Yahweh's own actions and the seeking of places of refuge. According to Jer. 51:30, after Yahweh has called the nations to war against Babylon, her warriors give up the fight and are now crouching in their places of refuge; and according to Jer. 48:41f., Yahweh himself proclaims that in Moab the cities have been taken and the places of refuge seized, so that Moab has been destroyed as a people because it magnified itself against Yahweh. On the other hand, although Ezekiel ties *m*^e*ṣāḏ* in with a Yahweh-oracle in Ezk. 33:27, he uses it

---

8. *DJD,* II, 164, no. 45; III, 269, 37.
9. Cf. R. Meyer, *Das Gebet des Nabonid. BSAW,* 107/3 (1962), 9, n. 3.
10. Cf. Eichhorn.

with the general meaning "hiding place," "hideout" (cf. also the parallel mention of "caves"), which is probably to be explained by the concrete reference in Ezk. 33:24-29 to conditions among the Judeans who were not deported.

In wisdom literature, the form **māṣôḏ* with the meaning "hiding place," "hideout" similarly serves as a metaphorical circumlocution, e.g., for the heart of the wicked as the hiding place of evil (Prov. 12:12).

Schunck

מִצְוָה *miṣwâ*

Contents: I. *miṣwâ* as an Expression of Authority. II. 1. Etymology, Meaning; 2. Semantic Field, Synonyms. III. *miṣwâ* in Human Contexts. IV. God's *miṣwâ.* V. Expressions for Obedience and Disobedience. VI. Qumran.

I. miṣwâ as an Expression of Authority. The word *miṣwâ* is one of the expressions for God's will and authority, and as such refers to his "order" or his "commandment." It is thus a term of great significance for understanding the OT's notion of the relationship between God and human beings. Although we will not deal here with the postbiblical traditions (with the exception of Qumran), it should be pointed out that the term *miṣwâ* became centrally important in the practice of Jewish religion and retains this eminent position in Judaism even today.

The concept of a divine command represents the transfer of certain formal relations from the human to the theological sphere. The God of Israel is at once father, judge, and king in the traditional sense of these terms, and it is thus possible to say that he issues orders, though not all biblical traditions understand divine authority in this way.

II. 1. *Etymology, Meaning.* The etymology of *miṣwâ* is unequivocal: It derives from the verb → צוה *ṣiwwâ,* "to appoint, order, direct," and evokes the same connotations. It is a nominal construction of the *miqṭāl*-type and means literally "command, order," though like other nouns of this pattern it designates both the action itself and its consequences or results. It thus means "that which is ordered,

---

miṣwâ. G. Braulik, "Gesetz als Evangelium: Rechtfertigung und Begnadigung nach der deuteronomischen Tora," *ZThK,* 79 (1982), 127-160; A. Deissler, *Psalm 119(118) und seine Theologie. MThS,* 1/11 (1955); H. Gese, "The Law," *Essays on Biblical Theology* (Eng. trans., Minneapolis, 1981), 60-92; A. Marmorstein, *Studies in Jewish Theology* (Oxford, 1950); L. Monsengwo Pasinya, *La notion de nomos dans le Pentateuque grec. AnBibl,* 52 (1973); M. Steckelmacher, "Etwas über die leichten und schweren Gebote in der Halacha und Agada," *Festschrift A. Schwarz* (Berlin, 1917); G. Wallis, "Torah und Nomos," *ThLZ,* 105 (1980), 321-332. → חקק *ḥāqaq* (V, 139-147).

the commandment," and from the perspective of the person so addressed it implies "duty, obligation."[1]

2. *Semantic Field, Synonyms.* The word *miṣwâ* belongs to a group of terms which are often used together and which express the various aspects of authority, including *mišpāṭ,* "judgment, justice, right," *ḥōq* (fem. *ḥuqqâ*), "statute," and *tôrâ,* "instruction," "law." None of these terms in and of itself has anything to do with God's authority.

The Hebrew term → משפט *mišpāṭ* reflects the notion of legal proceedings, and since the maintenance of justice was the responsibility of the kings, the word is often also used in connection with royal functions. Thus 1 S. 8:11 speaks of the *mišpaṭ hammelek̠,* "the ordinances/legal claims of the king." First of all, *mišpāṭ* refers to that which is contained in legal proceedings, i.e., the legal norm or judgment. It refers as well, however, to the anticipated result of those proceedings, "justice." The *mišpāṭ* should be followed because it represents the accepted standard of justice.

The Hebrew term *ḥōq*[2] actually refers to what is inscribed or written and thus made public and approved. It directs attention to the mediation of authority. The *ḥōq* should be followed because someone with authority has written or "promulgated" it.

The word → תורה *tôrâ* also reflects the mediation of authority ("direction, instruction"). A *tôrâ* should be followed because it has been presented or shown to someone. The term *tôrâ* often designates cultic directions or instructions given by the priest, doubtlessly reflecting the origin of the term. It represents the correct procedure to be followed.

Other, less fixed terms contributing to the definition of *miṣwâ* include *'ēmer* (fem. *'imrâ*), "utterance, word," *dāb̠ār,* "word, oracle," and *'ēd̠ûṯ,* a word of problematical origin meaning either "witness" or "covenant" (that which binds a community together). At least two if not all three of these terms direct attention to the spoken word as authoritative. The words should be followed because the person who has spoken them possesses authority.

The dynamics obtaining between these various terms shows how *miṣwâ* fits into the system of authority. The word *miṣwâ* is authoritative in and of itself. A *miṣwâ* should be followed because it has been given by someone with authority. Just how the command has been mediated is not specified, but only *that* it was.

III. miṣwâ in Human Contexts. It is advisable first to discuss several examples for *miṣwâ* from specifically human contexts. In this connection the verb *ṣiwwâ,* whence the noun derives, is also of significance. We find that the verb also exhibits a certain orientation toward the notion of authority.

1. The term *miṣwâ* can refer to the transfer directive in a legal document. Jer. 32:6-14 speaks of the purchase of a field by a relative. In this case Jeremiah is the → גאל *gō'ēl*

---

1. Cf. J. Barth, *Die Nominalbildung in den semitischen Sprachen* ([2]1894; repr. Hildesheim, 1967), 243, no. 161.

2. → חקק *ḥāqaq* (V, 139-147).

who intends to prevent the sale of family property. The purchase is symbolic, but the terminology is legal-technical. Verse 11 reads: "Then I took the sealed deed of purchase — i.e., the transfer directive *(miṣwâ)* and the conditions *(ḥuqqîm)* — and the open copy, and I gave them to Baruch the son of Neriah. . . ." The documents were deposited in an earthenware vessel so that Jeremiah's purchase should later confirm his prophecy, according to which "fields and vineyards shall again be bought in this land." The sealed portion of the document contained the essential conditions, while the open portion served as an index for identifying the property, the main participants, and so on.

*W. Rudolph finds this interpretation grammatically problematical; he moves the words *hammiṣwâ wᵉhaḥuqqîm* with the preceding *ʿal* ("according to precept and order") to the conclusion of v. 10.

Ringgren

This passage thus suggests a juridical origin for the term *miṣwâ:* A document for the transfer of right of possession was called *miṣwâ;* the word is used together with *ḥōq*.

2. The term *miṣwâ* designates the last will and testament of a father. Jer. 35 repeatedly states that the sons of Jonadab the son of Rechab kept the final instructions of their father *(miṣwaṯ ʾᵃḇîhem)* to refrain from drinking wine (v. 14). Gen. 50:16 uses the verb *ṣiwwâ* in connection with Joseph's final instructions.

3. The *miṣwâ* can be a royal decree. Numerous examples show that the *miṣwâ* represents the expression of royal authority, and even more examples attest the verb *ṣiwwâ* in this connection. In 2 K. 18:36 (par. Isa. 36:21) the expression *miṣwaṯ hammeleḵ* is best rendered "the standing command of the king." Jerusalem's inhabitants, who had to listen to the words of the Assyrian commander, were instructed by Hezekiah not to respond to the propaganda. In 1 K. 2:41-43 Solomon summons Shimei and addresses him abruptly: "Why have you not kept your oath to Yahweh and the standing order *(miṣwâ)* with which I charged you?" Solomon had enjoined Shimei not to leave Jerusalem, and since the order was corroborated by an oath, the king could not alter it. Est. 3:3f. contains a similar reference to standing royal orders. Ahasuerus had given the order that all persons were to bow down before Haman, and when Mordecai repeatedly refused, the courtiers say to him: "Why do you transgress against the king's (current) command *(miṣwaṯ hammeleḵ)?*"

In two later passages the term *miṣwâ* refers to the royal order to carry out a given action. Zechariah, the son of the priest Jehoiada, was murdered by command of King Joash (2 Ch. 24:21), and as a result of Josiah's decree people from the northern part of the country came to Jerusalem to celebrate Passover (2 Ch. 30:12). Similarly, the

---

*[Ed. note: Wilhelm Rudolph (*Jeremia. HAT,* XII [³1968], 176) finds this interpretation grammatically problematical; he moves the words *hammiṣwâ wᵉhaḥuqqîm* with the preceding *ʿal* ("according to precept and order") to the conclusion of v. 10. — Ringgren]

Chronicler ascribes the regular duties of the Levites to the commandment of David which was carried out by Solomon (Neh. 12:24f.; 2 Ch. 29:35; 35:10, etc.).

4. The term *miṣwâ* can also mean "portion, claim." Neh. 13:5 reads: "He [the priest Eliashib] prepared a large chamber where they had previously put the cereal offering, the frankincense, the vessels, and the tithes of grain, wine, and oil, the portion of the Levites [*miṣwaṯ hallᵉwiyyîm:* "by commandment to the Levites," so RSV], the singers and gatekeepers, and the contributions of the priests *(tᵉrûmaṯ hakkōhᵃnîm)."* Here *miṣwâ* has replaced an earlier term with the same meaning, probably *ḥōq,* which in Gen. 47:22 and Ezk. 45:14 refers to the fees and income due the priests.

5. The term *miṣwâ* can mean "obligation, dues." In Neh. 10:33(Eng. v. 32) the pl. *miṣwôṯ* designates that which the people under Nehemiah's leadership imposed upon themselves as a tax for the maintenance of the temple and cult: "We also lay upon ourselves the obligation to charge ourselves yearly with the third part of a shekel for the service of the house of our God." This single passage anticipates the meaning "obligation" which developed later in the postbiblical period.

6. In Isa. 29:13 *miṣwâ* has a negative connotation in reference to something carried out without the proper motivation: "This people draw near with their mouth and honor me with their lips . . . so that their fear of me is a commandment of men learned by rote *(miṣwaṯ 'ᵃnāšîm mᵉlummāḏâ)*" — the people's worship has become purely a formality.

7. In the book of Proverbs the teacher appears as the wise and experienced father who instructs his son concerning the hazards of life. The father's advice must be understood in the context of a patrician society in which sons were prepared for court life. Although the passages in which *miṣwâ* occurs presuppose the father-son relationship, they do imply connections with royal authority.

Since wisdom literature often repeats the same ideas in a variety of forms, we often encounter different terms relating to authority, as is the case in the following three statements:

Prov. 1:8: "Hear, my son, your father's instruction *(mûsār),* and reject not your mother's teaching *(tôrâ).*"

Prov. 6:20: "My son, keep your father's commandment *(miṣwâ),* and forsake not your mother's teaching *(tôrâ).*"

Prov. 6:23: "For the commandment *(miṣwâ)* is a lamp and the teaching *(tôrâ)* a light, and the reproofs of discipline *(tôḵᵃḥôṯ mûsār)* are the way of life."

In 6:20 *mûsār* is replaced by *miṣwâ,* and 6:23 includes all three terms. In other proverbs *miṣwâ* parallels *'ēmer,* "speech, utterance" (Prov. 2:1; 7:1), and in one case *dāḇār,* "word" (13:13). We find that in wisdom literature *miṣwâ* often refers to what a person should *not* do, and thus to that which should be avoided. The purpose of the *miṣwâ* imparted by the father is the avoidance of life's hazards.

In the later *midrāš*-tradition the father's commandments and prescriptions were regularly reinterpreted to apply to the relationship between a person and God, a situation resulting from the identification of wisdom with the revealed law. God revealed wisdom, and the instructions of wisdom became divine commandments.[3]

IV. God's miṣwâ. Relationships based on authority, in both human and divine contexts, permeate OT literature. Here we must pay attention to *how* such authority is expressed. In this connection it should be pointed out that *miṣwâ* and *ṣiwwâ* do not occur with the same frequency in all biblical writings; in some strata of tradition they occur hardly or not at all. This fact should enable us to track down the origin of the *miṣwâ*-term in the sense of the divine commandment. Although the terms *miṣwâ* and *ṣiwwâ* involve law and administration (especially royal administration, which includes both military and cultic institutions), *miṣwâ* itself occurs only relatively late as a term for formal human relations. In early poetic texts and in the earliest laws *miṣwâ* does not occur at all. Neither is it the case that the *miqṭāl*-construction only emerges late, since the verb *ṣiwwâ* attests almost the same distribution. We must conclude that the term "order, command" as an expression of authority emerged later than other terms such as "word," "(written) statute," *tôrâ,* or "legal norm."

Here we must also note that the Israelite understanding of law as directly given by God is virtually unique in the ancient Near East. According to the Mesopotamian laws Shamash as the god of righteousness bestows upon the king a sense for righteousness (Akk. *kettu*), which guides him to a just promulgation of laws.[4]

According to OT understanding, God reveals laws and legal norms; he directly formulates those laws. It was thus only to be expected that sooner or later *miṣwâ* and *ṣiwwâ* would attain the dominant position among expressions for divine authority and, as it were, obfuscate the clear background of prescriptive law visible in terms such as *mišpāṭ, tôrâ, ḥōq,* and so on.

This development can be illustrated by an investigation into the prophetic books.

The term *miṣwâ* does not occur at all in the preexilic prophets, and *ṣiwwâ* only rarely. Jeremiah is the first to use *ṣiwwâ.* When it does occur in earlier prophetic literature, it evokes specific connotations and does not refer to divine authority in law or administration. Amos reproves the people in one instance for having "commanded" the prophets not to proclaim God's word (2:12). In two other oracles Amos uses the verb with God as subject in what is perhaps its original sense, "to command, order": God will give the command that the house of Israel be smitten into bits (6:11), and he will send out the serpent and the sword to destroy the people (9:3f.), or will order the people's banishment (9:9).

Similar meanings are found in Isa. 5:6 and 10:6: God commands the forces of nature or sends Assyria to chastise the people. A late echo of this idea occurs in Nah. 1:14.

Jeremiah is the first prophet to use *ṣiwwâ* in its full measure, and the term *miṣwâ* occurs in his writings at least in human contexts (on 32:11 and 35:14 see discussion

3. Cf. G. F. Moore, *Judaism in the First Centuries of the Christian Era: The Age of the Tannaim,* I (Cambridge, 1927, ²1966), 38, 263f.
4. J. J. Finkelstein, "מִשְׁפָּט," *EMiqr,* V (1968), 609f.

above). Jeremiah mentions royal decrees as *miṣwâ* (Jer. 27:4; 36:8; 38:27; 39:11; 51:59). In connection with divine chastisement he uses the verb in the same way as Amos and Isaiah (Jer. 34:22; 47:7), though he also says that God "commanded" him to prophesy, and "appointed" him as a prophet even before his birth (Jer. 1:7,17; 26:2,8; 50:21). Of particular interest is the reference to what God did or did not command the people to do during the exodus: He did not command them to bring sacrifices, but rather to obey his will in regard to human relationships (Jer. 7:22f.; 14:14; 23:32; 29:23). Ezekiel follows Jeremiah's example when he speaks of God's "commandments, orders" (Ezk. 9:11; 12:7; 24:18; 37:7,10).

The pre-Jeremianic prophets prefer *dāḇār* and *dibber* in such situations, expressions which Jeremiah frequently uses in connection with *ṣiwwâ.* This corresponds to the use of *miṣwâ* in the law collections. In the Covenant Code (Ex. 21–23) the predominating term is *mišpāṭ,* while *miṣwâ* does not occur at all. The verb occurs once (23:15) in connection with the commandment to celebrate the Feast of Unleavened Bread; considerable evidence, however, suggests that the words "as I commanded you" constitute a gloss.

The Exodus version of the Decalog uses *miṣwâ* once (Ex. 20:6): "I show steadfast love to thousands of those who love me and keep my commandments." This sentence might be a Deuteronomistic addendum, since the language, as shown by Dt. 7:9, is Deuteronomistic. The term *miṣwâ* is probably not part of the original vocabulary of the Decalog.

In the Deuteronomic laws (12–27) *miṣwâ* occurs only in superscriptions and postscripts which probably constitute redactional addenda, or in Deuteronomistic interpolations. Even the poetic chapter 33 contains a reference to the commandment of Moses (not of God): "Moses commanded us a law" (v. 4). In section 12–27 *miṣwâ* never functions as a primary term.

A similar situation obtains in the Deuteronomistic history. Occurrences of *ṣiwwâ* with God as subject usually derive from Deuteronomistic redaction, with the exceptions exhibiting the older meaning "to appoint, commission."

The word *miṣwâ* first functions as a primary term in the Deuteronomic prologue (1–11) and in the final section of the book. Here *miṣwâ* is introduced along with the older terms for authority *dāḇār, ḥōq, mišpāṭ, ʿēḏûṯ,* and so on.

The verb *ṣiwwâ* occurs first in Dt. 1:3, recurring frequently, while *miṣwâ* occurs for the first time in 4:2 (*miṣwôṯ YHWH,* "the commandments of Yahweh"), then again in 6:25 in the expression *kol-hammiṣwâ hazzōʾṯ,* "all this commandment." Chs. 4–6 consistently use others terms as well, though in chs. 8–11 *miṣwâ* is a fixed part of the language. Dt. 1–11 thus constitutes the reworking of an earlier text whose original vocabulary did not include *miṣwâ.* While in several important sections *miṣwâ* does not occur at all, this is not a result of the fact that the content of those sections has nothing to do with the divine will or with law.

In summary we thus can say that the Deuteronomistic school, with which Jeremiah had clear connections, was the first to understand as an order or commandment the divine will expressed in the law. Although this notion may well have older roots, the Deuteronomistic school was the first to make more extensive use of it. This orientation of authority was well suited to the environment of the royal court and influenced

Jeremiah's manner of expression, who maintained continued contact with that court. It should be noted that the verb *ṣiwwâ* occurs in the approximately contemporaneous Arad letters: *ṣiwwᵉkā ḥᵃnanyāhû ʿal bᵉʾēršebaʿ,* "Hananyahu hereby orders you to Beersheba"; *wᵉladdābār ʾᵃšer ṣiwwîtanî,* "as regards the matter concerning which you gave me orders."[5] In the subsequent period various priestly authors, chroniclers, and several psalmists and wisdom authors employed the "order"-concept further.

V. Expressions for Obedience and Disobedience. Just as *miṣwâ* functions as one of the many terms for authority, so also several verbs expressing obedience or disobedience occur together with the other expressions involving authority. In some instances it is clear that, e.g., *ḥōq* or *mišpāṭ* rather than *miṣwâ* was the original term for authority associated with the given verb.

1. The most frequent verb expressing obedience to God's *miṣwâ* is → שׁמר *šāmar,* "to observe, keep," a term which designates obedience in connection with other words for authority as well. It is frequently combined with → עשׂה *ʿāśâ,* "to do, perform," which also occurs alone. In the relatively early passage Hos. 12:7 the objects of *šāmar* are *ḥeseḏ,* "steadfast love," and *mišpāṭ,* "justice, right," though this does not mean that *šāmar* originated in connection with one of these words. (Later sources replace *šāmar* with *nāṣar:* Pss. 78:7; 119:115; Prov. 3:1; 6:20.)

2. In the case of *šāmaʿ,* "to hear," which is used in several different constructions in connection with *miṣwâ,* one might surmise that it originally referred to a reaction to the spoken word (e.g., *dāḇār*), an observation confirmed by the distribution of occurrences. Furthermore, the expression *šāma bᵉqôl,* "to heed someone's voice," occurs as a designation for obedience.

3. Several other verbs designating the performance of a *miṣwâ* seem to have been appropriated by other terms of authority. Thus the expression *yiqqaḥ miṣwôṯ,* "he will accept [heed, so RSV] commandments" (Prov. 10:8) clearly derives from the idiom *lāqaḥ mûsār,* "to accept correction" (Jer. 2:30; 5:3, etc.). The expression *yārēʾ miṣwôṯ,* "who respects the commandments" (Prov. 13:13), similarly derives from *yārēʾ dᵉḇar YHWH* (Ex. 9:20).

One can also "remember" God's commandments (Nu. 15:39f.), which guide a person to their fulfillment *(ʿāśâ!),* since *zāḵar* normally also implies the action itself.[6] Several late expressions clearly reveal a development from other terms for authority, e.g., the assertion made in Ezr. 10:4 that one trembles *(ḥrd)* before God's commandments; cf. Isa. 66:5, "to tremble at God's word."

All this shows that the OT authors often used different terms together to refer to authority and to the act of heeding such authority, so that the original distinctions were obfuscated. The predominating element in all this is a comprehensive system of obedience, and in this system *miṣwâ* occupies its own position.

---

5. See D. Pardee, *Handbook of Ancient Hebrew Letters. SBLSBS,* 15 (Chico, 1982), 3.4 = Arad 3 (catalogue #4), pp. 34f.; 3.18 = Arad 18 (catalogue #18), pp. 54f.

6. → זכר *zāḵar (zākhar)* (IV, 64-82).

The same juxtaposition characterizes the expressions for disobedience. The most simple method is to negate the verbs of obedience: one does not keep or does not heed, and so on. There are, however, other possibilities. A person can "turn aside" (*sûr,* Dt. 17:20) from the commandments, an expression deriving from the notion of turning aside from the correct way (Ex. 32:8; Dt. 31:29; cf. Dt. 28:14 with *dāḇār*). A person can "break"[7] the commandments (Nu. 15:31; Ezr. 9:14), an expression originally referring to the covenant. A person can also "forsake" the commandments of God (*ʿāzaḇ,* 1 K. 18:18; 2 K. 17:16; 2 Ch. 7:19; Ezr. 9:10), "transgress" (*ʿāḇar,* 2 Ch. 24:20; cf. Est. 3:3 referring to the king's command), "forget" (*šāḵaḥ,* Ps. 119:176), or "despise" (not used with *miṣwâ; bāzâ* with *dāḇār,* Nu. 15:31; *nāʾaṣ* with *ʾimrâ,* Isa. 5:24; *māʾas* with *tôrâ,* Isa. 5:24; Jer. 6:19; with *ḥōq,* Lev. 26:15; 2 K. 17:15; Ezk. 20:24; with *dāḇār,* 1 S. 15:23,26; Jer. 8:9; with *mišpāṭ,* Lev. 26:43; Ezk. 5:6; 20:13,16). In every case *miṣwâ* shares the particular linguistic expression with other terms for authority, and it is doubtful whether any verb referred specifically to the reaction to *miṣwâ.*

This interrelation emerges clearly in two psalms that speak of God's law and commandments, Pss. 19 and 119. Whereas Ps. 19 speaks more about the characteristic features of the commandments, Ps. 119 describes primarily the attitude of the believer toward the commandments. In Ps. 19 *miṣwâ* is one of six expressions for authority, including *yirʾâ,* "fear" (if the text is correct; cf. *BHS*). In Ps. 19 as well as in Ps. 119 yet another term is used which is actually younger than *miṣwâ,* namely, *piqqûḏîm,* "directions, orders," like *miṣwâ* a military-administrative term which in later writings can replace *miṣwâ.*

Ps. 19:8-10(7-9) says the following about the value of the commandments:

> The teaching *(tôrâ)* of Yahweh is perfect, reviving the soul;
> the testimony *(ʿēḏûṯ)* of Yahweh is sure, making wise the simple;
> the precepts *(piqqûḏîm)* of Yahweh are right, rejoicing the heart;
> the commandment *(miṣwâ)* of Yahweh is pure, enlightening the eyes;
> the fear *(?yirʾâ)* of Yahweh is clean, enduring for ever;
> the ordinances *(mišpāṭîm)* of Yahweh are true and righteous altogether.

Ps 119 uses ten different terms for the expression of authority, including also *piqqûḏîm* and *yirʾâ,* combined with various expressions denoting the attendant reactions, some of which transcend simple obedience and designate emotional attitudes such as love, rejoicing, the desire to learn, and so on. Both psalms share the concern that the commandments might be transgressed as a result of oversight. In this respect these psalms reflect the priestly regulations concerning carelessness (cf. especially Lev. 4–5). Here the most important term is *miṣwâ,* and the laws reflect the spirit of the Deuteronomic prologue. In general, the verb *ṣiwwâ* occupies the central position in the Priestly laws of the Pentateuch, something shown not least from the frequent use of the formula *kaʾ*ᵃ*šer ṣiwwâ YHWH ʾeṯ-mōšeh,* "as Yahweh commanded Moses." Whereas the older law collections only rarely attest *miṣwâ* or *ṣiwwâ,* the Priestly laws increasingly use *miṣwâ* in addition to the older terms for expressions of divine authority.

---

7. → פרר *pārar.*

This imitation of Deuteronomistic linguistic usage was consistent with the Priestly view, since the Priestly school was of the opinion that every detail of the cult originated directly with God and was just as authoritative as the older laws. It is apparent that the notion of commandments structured as orders was directed not only to the individual Israelite, but even more to the entire people. It became a constituent part of the Deuteronomistic and Priestly understanding of the general relationship between God and Israel, and derives from the notion of the law as having been revealed by God.[8]

Both in Dt. 28 and in Lev. 26, where blessing and curse are portrayed as consequences of obedience or disobedience, *miṣwâ* is the decisive term (3 occurrences in Lev. 26, 4 in Dt. 28). The same applies to Dt. 11:13-28, where the alternative blessing-curse is similarly clearly delineated. The first section (vv. 13-21) uses only two terms of authority, *miṣwâ* (twice, at the beginning and end) and *dāḇār* (once); the reference is to rain and fruitfulness as a reward for worship in love and obedience toward the commandments, and to aridity and poverty as punishment for disobedience consisting in the worship of other gods. The words of God should be taught anew to every generation, should be written upon the doorposts and born as a sign upon one's body.[9] The second section promises victory over enemies and possession of the land as a consequence of obedience toward the *miṣwâ,* and the final section (vv. 26-28) summarizes obedience and disobedience as conditions of the promise; "Behold, I set before you this day a blessing and a curse: the blessing, if you obey the commandments of Yahweh your God, which I command you this day, and the curse, if you do not obey the commandments of Yahweh your God, but turn aside from the way which I command you this day, to go after other gods which you have not known."

What is the content of the "commandments of God"? From the Deuteronomist onward and in the Priestly Document the *miṣwôṯ* are the totality of laws. Only the pre-Deuteronomistic laws do not mention the notion of commandments structured as orders. This applies both to the Covenant Code and to the older parts of the passover laws in Ex. 12–13. The short collection in Ex. 34, which already exhibits Deuteronomistic influence, uses the verb *ṣiwwâ,* but not *miṣwâ.* In other words, the emergence of the term *miṣwâ,* which says that God "orders" or "commands" laws, marks a new understanding of divine authority as it refers to law and covenant: The laws have become commandments (orders).

VI. Qumran. It is to be expected that the Qumran texts maintain a certain continuity with the OT commandment terms, but also that they exhibit a further development of the same; and indeed, this is the case. For the most part we encounter here reflexes of the Deuteronomistic and Priestly emphasis on the "commandments" as the most important expression of divine authority. Thus we find, e.g., variations of the assertion in Dt. 7:9 that God shows steadfast love toward those who "love me and keep my commandments" (1QH 16:13,17; CD 19:28). In the Damascus Document the usual term for the Torah and

---

8. Cf. Braulik.

9. → מזוזה *m^ezûzâ* (VIII, 225-27).

its laws is *miṣwôṯ 'ēl,* which a person either "keeps," "fulfills," or "holds fast to," or from which a person "turns away" by despising them, or against which one preaches rebellion or conspires (CD 2:18,21; 3:2,6,8,12; 5:21; 8:19, etc.). The Temple Scroll contains only a few occurrences of *miṣwâ* and *ṣiwwâ* (55:13; 59:14-16, etc.).

Two passages deserve special attention:

1. CD 7:2 says that a person should correct his brother "according to the commandment," a clear reference to Lev. 19:17, which remarks that one should correct one's brother if he transgresses the law. What is important here is the use of the specific form *hammiṣwâ* to refer to the Torah as a whole. In later rabbinic usage one would read *kakkāṯûḇ,* "as it is written," i.e., in the Torah.

2. CD 10:2f. says that no man shall be declared a trustworthy witness who "has wilfully transgressed something ('a word') of the commandment *('ôḇēr dāḇār min hammiṣwâ).*" A similar expression is found in 1QS 8:17: "who deliberately, on any point whatever, turns aside from all that is commanded *('^{a}šer yāsûr mikkōl hammiṣwâ dāḇār).*" Here *hammiṣwâ* means the same as *hattôrâ;* rabbinic language even attests the expression *dāḇār min hattôrâ.*

The Qumran writings thus represent a transition from the OT understanding to later Jewish understanding of *miṣwâ* as law, a transition prefigured by Deuteronomistic and Priestly usage.

Levine

מְצוּלָה *m^eṣûlâ;* מְצוֹלָה *m^eṣôlâ;* צוּלָה *ṣûlâ* II; צָלַל *ṣālal* II

Contents: I. 1. Distribution, Etymology, Occurrences; 2. LXX. II. Semantic Field. III. Theological Contexts: 1. Cosmology; 2. The Exodus; 3. Anthropology.

I. 1. *Distribution, Etymology, Occurrences.* The term *m^eṣûlâ* occurs 12 times in the OT, almost exclusively in postexilic texts (the single exception being Ps. 68:23[Eng. v. 22]). Its distribution (5 times in the Psalms, twice in Zechariah, once each in Exodus, Nehemiah, Job, Jonah, Micah) shows that it does not really belong in narrative, but occurs rather almost exclusively in poetically structured literature. It is probably an artificial word constructed deverbally — but from which root?

a. Franz Zorell[1] suggests the root **ṣwl.* It occurs only in Arab. *ṣāla,* "to spring, leap, attack," II "to soften (with water)," "to wash" (grain, gold), "to clean a threshing-floor."[2] This group probably also includes Middle Heb. *m^eṣûlôṯ,*[3] "grain dust" (like Arab. *ṣuwālat*) and Arab. *miṣwal,* a basin sunk into the ground for cleansing grain.[4]

1. *LexHebAram,* 465.
2. Wehr (^{4}1979), 621.
3. *WTM,* III, 209.
4. *AuS,* III (1933), 257f., 278; on Aram. *ṣwlh,* "depths of the sea," see III.1 below.

b. *ṣwl, a secondary form of *ṣll*,[5] allows for three possibilities: *ṣll* I (attested only late) means "to ring"; derivation from this root[6] does not seem likely. Similarly, *ṣll* III (denominative from *ṣēl*, "shadow"), "become shady, dark, peaceful," can for semantic reasons hardly be considered, although a connection with this root has repeatedly been proposed (cf. already the LXX: *skía thanátou* for *m^eṣôlâ*, Ps. 88:7(6)(LXX 87:7); and *tṓn kataskiṓn* for *'^ašer bamm^eṣulâ*, Zec. 1:8).[7] Only *ṣll* II seems to lead in the right direction. The OT attests it in the meaning "to sink down" only in Ex. 15:10; *KBL*³, however, correctly refers to the even older Akk. *ṣalālu*, "to lie down, lie, sleep."[8] This verb is also attested in Arab. *ḍalla*, "to go astray," "to disappear,"[9] OSA *ḍll*, "demise, fall,"[10] and perhaps Ethiop. "to swim."[11] Modern Heb. and Jewish Aram. *ṣll*, "to sink down, become clarified," might belong here as well,[12] then probably also the root *ṣll* attested in Syr. *ṣal* and Arab. *ṣalla*, "to filter, cleanse"[13] (cf. Arab. *maṣala*, "to curdle [milk], strain, filter"[14]).

c. The association of *m^eṣûlâ* with *nāṣal* piel, "to plunder,"[15] in the rabbinic explanation of Ex. 12:36 (cf. *Ber.* 9b) is more a case of catchword association than etymology.

If a deverbalization of צלל II must thus be assumed, it can only have taken place via a secondary form of *ṣwl*, since otherwise one would expect *m^eṣullâ*.[16] We are thus dealing with a feminine *maqṭul* of a verb ע״ו,[17] a construction that generates intransitive abstractions[18] or designates the "bearer of a completely finished condition, though also the object of the term or concept."[19] The variation in orthography *m^eṣûlâ/m^eṣôlâ* is a familiar linguistic-historical phenomenon[20] and is semantically irrelevant.

The term *m^eṣûlâ* thus refers to something which is "sunken down, deep." On the one hand it can refer to a "spring" (Ugar. *mṣlt*[21]), and on the other it can refer in

5. *KBL*³, 589, 949; *HAL*, II (1995), 623.
6. E. König, *Hebräisches und aramäisches Wörterbuch zum AT* (Leipzig, 1910; [6,7]1937), 240.
7. Cf. further H. Ewald, *Beiträge zur Geschichte der seltesten Auslegung und Spracherklärung des ATs* (Stuttgart, 1844); F. Hitzig; Zorell, 466.
8. *KBL*³, 962; *AHw*, III (1981), 1075f.; *CAD*, XVI (1962), 67-70.
9. Cf. F. M. Cross and D. N. Freedman, "The Song of Miriam," *JNES*, 14 (1955), 247; K. Vollers, "Arabisch und Semitisch: Gedanken über eine Revision der semitischen Lautgesetze," *ZA*, 9 (1894), 179.
10. ContiRossini, 227.
11. *LexLingAeth*, 1256.
12. *KBL*¹, *GesB*.
13. *KBL*³, 962.
14. Wehr ([4]1979), 1070.
15. → נצל *nṣl*.
16. Cf. *BLe*, 493dη.
17. *Ibid.*, 493bη; cf. *GK*, §85k.
18. Cf. J. Barth, *Die Nominalbildung in den semitischen Sprachen* ([2]1894; repr. Hildesheim, 1967), §166.
19. Cf. V. Christian, *Untersuchungen zur Laut- und Formenlehre des Hebräischen. SAW*, 228/2 (Vienna, 1953), 142.
20. *BLe*, § 61iζ.
21. Cf. *CML*², 151b; contra *WUS*, no. 1641.

Hebrew to "depths" in general. In this respect the term can easily take on cosmological features, especially in the later period,[22] something attested by the fluctuation characterizing its rendering in the LXX.

2. *LXX.* The LXX translates 6 times with *bythós,* "depth, depth of the sea," and 3 times with *báthos,* "depth," a term referring to the "overarching dimension, both of the world and of life," the "totality of the dimension named," though also to that which is inexhaustible and unfathomable.[23] The translator renders *mᵉṣûlâ* (Job 41:23[31]) and *ṣûlâ* (Isa. 44:27) with *ábyssos,* evoking on the one hand a cosmological-mythological aspect of the kind normally attaching to → תהום *tᵉhôm* and *rahab;* on the other hand, he transposes the word into the contextual horizon of Hades or the Netherworld, the "prison for the powers opposed to God."[24] Twice the LXX interprets the Hebrew word as a formative of *ṣēl,* "shadow" (Ps. 88:7[6]; Zec. 1:8), and translates *ṣālal* II (Ex. 15:10) with *dýein,* "to sink down, go under."

The Vulg. does not make these distinctions, translating consistently with *profundum* and reserving the cosmological-mythological term *abyssus* for *tᵉhôm.* In Ps. 88:7(6), it follows the mistaken reading of the LXX: *umbra mortis.*

II. Semantic Field. The semantic field of *mᵉṣûlâ* is influenced by the fact that the word belongs to poetic language and exhibits obvious affinity with mythological notions. Parallel constructions show *mᵉṣûlâ* next to *tᵉhôm,* "primeval ocean," *yām,* "sea," *mayim,* "waters," *mayim rabbîm,* "great waters," *mayim ʾaddîrîm,* "powerful waters," *mayim ʿazzîm,* "mighty waters," *gallîm,* "waves," and *nahᵃrôṯ,* "floods."

In anthropological contexts the semantic field shifts, and now includes *bôr taḥtiyyôṯ,* "lowest pit," *maḥᵃšakkîm,* "darkness," *mišbār,* "breakers of the seashore," *ṭîṭ,* "mud," *maʿᵃmaqqê-mayim,* "deep waters," *šibbōleṯ mayim,* "torrent of water," *bᵉʾēr,* "well," *ḥᵃmôṯ yammîm, zaʿap̱ yammîm,* "raging of the seas," and *šᵉʾôl, ʾᵃḇaddôn,* "netherworld."

These semantic fields clearly show that an exact definition of the term *mᵉṣûlâ* is not possible, and there is certainly no indication that the translation "depth" should necessarily evoke some sort of vertical dimension.

III. Theological Contexts. The word *mᵉṣûlâ* is not one deriving from the secular language of everyday life, for it occurs in the OT and in 1QH exclusively in theologically relevant contexts. Here the themes "Yahweh's cosmic power," "exodus," and "theological anthropology" can be taken as focal points.

1. *Cosmology.* The earliest and only preexilic occurrence is found in Ps. 68:23(22). This psalm is a witness to the harsh confrontation between Canaanite and Israelite

---

22. Cf. H. F. Weiss, *Untersuchungen zur Kosmologie des hellenistischen und palästinensischen Judentums. TU,* 97 (1966).
23. Cf. A. Strobel, "βάθος," *EDNT,* I, 190.
24. Cf. O. Böcher, "ἄβυσσος," *EDNT,* I, 4.

religion and portrays Yahweh as the universal cosmic lord with immeasurable reach. He seizes his enemies from the highest mountain (Bashan) and from the *m^eṣulôṯ yām*. The power of this Israelite god is thus not territorially defined. Despite the interpretative difficulties attaching to Bashan, this statement should be understood as a merism for cosmic omnipotence. (The only extrabiblical occurrence of *ṣûlâ* [Sefire I] should be understood similarly. There the person concluding the contract calls all the gods as witnesses, including heaven, earth, *ṣûlâ* and the springs, day and night.[25]) A reference to the events at the Red Sea cannot be substantiated.[26]

This all-encompassing power is then the faith motif of the OT psalmist. As an example of especially effective help he adduces God's deliverance of the shipwrecked, recalling the terminology of the mythological chaos struggles (Ps. 107:24; cf. 2 Cor. 11:25). Isa. 44:24-28 and Job also pick up on this tradition. With such cosmological vocabulary Deutero-Isaiah may well be referring to the Babylonian power "in which the exiles are in danger of sinking and drowning."[27] By merely uttering the word Yahweh can put an end to its existence (v. 27). According to Job 41:23(31), Leviathan[28] lives in the *m^eṣûlâ,* which he causes to boil like a pot. Yet even the *m^eṣûlâ* is within reach of Yahweh's power; here, too, the "king over all creatures of pride" can testify to Yahweh's power as creator.

2. *The Exodus.* Although *m^eṣûlâ* does not occur in the Red Sea narrative of the older Pentateuchal sources, later sources did insert the word here in the course of tradition history. In the course of this interpretation the cosmological struggle of chaos has been evoked, Yahweh being reinterpreted from the "one who acts" into a "warrior."[29] As seen above,[30] the term *m^eṣûlâ* also introduced such a connotation into the narrative. The Song of Moses (Ex. 15:1-18),[31] whose final form is ultimately postexilic, doubtlessly contains elements deriving from different sources, as a comparison between vv. 4 and 5 shows[32]: v. 4, "Pharaoh's chariots and his army he cast into the sea; his picked officers were sunk in the Red Sea," contains a completely realistic description that could come from a source quite close to the actual event, while v. 5 (cf. Neh. 9:11), "the (primeval) floods *(t^ehōmōṯ)* covered them; they went down into the *m^eṣôlōṯ* like a stone," constitutes a subsequent interpretation. Erich Zenger suggests that the neutral *yām* or *yam sûp̱* here is interpreting the cosmological *t^ehôm* and *m^eṣôlâ* in order better

25. *KAI,* 222A, 11f.
26. A. Weiser, *Psalms. OTL* (Eng. trans. 1962), *in loc.*
27. K. Elliger, *Deuterojesaja. BK,* XI/1 (1978), 474, citing G. Fohrer, *Das Buch Jesaja III. ZBK* (1964), 82.
28. → לויתן *liwyāṯān* (VII, 504-9); cf. also R. Kratz, *Rettungswunder. EH,* 23/123 (1979), 30ff.
29. Cf. W. H. Schmidt, *Exodus, Sinai und Moses. EdF,* 191 (1983), 65.
30. See III.1.
31. Cf. E. Zenger, "Tradition und Interpretation in Exodus xv 1-21," *Congress Volume, Vienna 1980. SVT,* 32 (1981), 452-483.
32. On the literary criticism of this passage, cf. Zenger, 462f.

to accommodate the Song of Moses to historical tradition. Ex. 15:10 says that the Egyptians sink *(ṣll)* like lead *(ʿôpereṯ)* in the mighty waters.

Zec. 10:11 (text?) portrays the homecoming of the exiles with the colors of the exodus motif, colors which unequivocally try to render the actual events transparent in the sense of a typological interpretation. That is, postexilic Israel should view this homecoming as "its" exodus, and should recognize in it the cosmic power of its God Yahweh. Zechariah does not delineate the transition from typology to a cyclical understanding of history as strongly as does the Priestly source[33] or R^P.[34] What is also of significance here is the pointed emphasis on Yahweh's omnipotence, which brings about Israel's liberation simply by means of a whistle signal (v. 8). Zechariah's portrayal of the *m^eṣûlôṯ y^{e}ʾōr,* or "depths of the Nile," drying up at Yahweh's signal might simultaneously constitute an ironic religio-polemical response to a boastful citation from the Assyrian king Sennacherib passed down in 2 K. 19:24.

3. *Anthropology.* In anthropologically textured laments the chaotic, threatening powers of the *m^eṣûlâ* predominate along with the motif of answered prayer, according to which God exercises his power over these forces as well. Jon. 2:4(3) might serve as a *locus classicus:* "You cast me into the *m^eṣûlâ bilḇaḇ yammîm,* and the flood *(nāhār)* surrounded me; all your waves *(mišbārîm)* and your billows *(gallîm)* passed over me." Considering this concentrated terminology reflecting distress at sea, this entire psalm (Jon. 2:3-11[2-10]) was probably composed as an independent literary unit based on an earlier Jonah narrative and then subsequently inserted here.[35] In the process, the author combined through association several motifs familiar to individual psalms of lament (cf. Ps. 69:3,16[2,15]; 88:7[6], where *m^eṣûlâ* is also mentioned). As a text-critical consideration one cannot overlook that *m^eṣûlâ* without a preposition is syntactically problematical. Yet even as a subsequent interpretation of the possibly ambiguous *l^eḇaḇ yammîm*[36] it is completely consonant with the spirit of the passage and corresponds well with *t^ehôm* (Jon. 2:6[5]). The subjective disposition of the person in distress — evoked by the image of the shipwrecked person — is objectified into the disposition of any person over against the primeval cosmic powers. To the extent, however, that God does indeed exercise power over these forces, the petitioner's own present distress turns into a crisis of faith (v. 5[4]). This is also how 1QH 3:6,14; 8:19 are to be understood. Here the *m^eṣôlôṯ* are taken as metaphors for uncertainty and danger in the larger sense, and are reckoned to the sphere of *$š^{e}$ʾôl* and *ʾ^{a}baddôn.* For the petitioner in 1QH there is no need for any special act of deliverance on the part of God, since he knows that his own membership in the congregation fundamentally removes him from such dangers.

---

33. Cf. esp. N. Lohfink, "Die Priesterschrift und die Geschichte," *Congress Volume, Göttingen 1977. SVT,* 29 (1978), 189-255, esp. 213ff.
34. H.-J. Fabry, *BETL* (1984).
35. Cf. H. W. Wolff, *Obadiah and Jonah* (Eng. trans., Minneapolis, 1986), 131f.
36. → לב *lēḇ* (VII, 399-437).

Mic. 7:19 is to be understood as a syndrome of cosmological and anthropological notions taken into association with the exodus motif: "He will again have compassion upon us; he will tread our iniquities under foot. You will cast all our [?] sins into the *m^{e}ṣulôṯ yām.*" Hans Walter Wolff is probably correct in his assertion that this unique passage is comparing the act of forgiveness with Israel's liberation at the exodus.[37]

Fabry

---

37. *Micah* (Eng. trans., Minneapolis, 1990), 231.

מִצְרַיִם *miṣrayim*

Contents: I. Etymology. II. OT: 1. Table of Nations (Gen. 10); 2. Ideological Considerations; 3. Egyptian Religion. III. Historical Relationships Between Israel and Egypt. IV. 1. The Joseph Story; 2. The Exodus: a. The Exodus Narrative; b. Evaluation of the Exodus in the Psalms, Prophetic Texts, etc.; c. The Exodus in the Wisdom of Solomon; d. The Exodus in the Prophetic Books. V. Egypt in the Prophetic Oracles Concerning Foreign Nations: 1. Isaiah; 2. Jeremiah; 3. Ezekiel. VI. Qumran.

---

miṣrayim. A. Alt, *Israel und Ägypten. BZAW,* 6 (1909); P. Barguet, *La stèle de la famine à Séhel. BdÉ,* 24 (1953); A. Barucq, *L'expression de la louange divine et de la prière dans la Bible et en Egypte. BdÉ,* 33 (1962); J. Bergman, "Atonhymn och skaparpsalm," *RoB,* 39 (1980), 3-23; L. Boadt, *Ezekiel's Oracles Against Egypt. BietOr,* 37 (1980); H. Brunner, "Gerechtigkeit als Fundament des Thrones," *VT,* 8 (1958), 426-28; G. E. Bryce, *A Legacy of Wisdom: The Egyptian Contribution to the Wisdom of Israel* (Lewisburg, 1979); B. Couroyer, "Amenemopé, XXIV, 13-18," *RB,* 75 (1968), 549-561; *idem,* "L'origine égyptienne de la Sagesse d'Amenemopé," *RB,* 70 (1963), 208-224; *idem,* "Quelques égyptianismes dans l'Exode," *RB,* 63 (1956), 209-219; H. Donner, *Die literarische Gestalt der alttestamentlichen Josephsgeschichte. SHAW,* 1976/2; E. Drioton, "Le Livre des Proverbes et la Sagesse d'Aménémopé," *Sacra Pagina,* I, *BETL,* 12f. (1959), 229-241; E. Erman, *"Eine ägyptische Quelle der 'Sprüche Salomos,'" SPAW,* 15 (1924), 86-93; G. Gerleman, "Die Bildsprache des Hohenliedes und die altägyptische Kunst," *ASTI,* 1 (1962), 24-30; I. Grumach, *Untersuchungen zur Lebenslehre des Amenemope. MÄSt,* 23 (1972); H. W. Helck, *Die Beziehungen Ägyptens zu Vorderasien im 3. und 2. Jahrtausend v. Chr. ÄgAbh,* 5 (^{2}1971); S. Herrmann, *Israels Aufenthalt in Ägypten. SBS,* 40 (1970); *idem, "Die Königsnovelle in Ägypten und in Israel," WZLeipzig,* 3 (1953/54), 51-62; P. Humbert, *Recherches sur les sources égyptiennes de la littérature sapientiale d'Israël* (Neuchâtel, 1929); O. Kaiser, "Der geknickte Rohrstab," *Wort und Geschichte. Festschrift K. Elliger. AOAT,* 18 (1973), 99-106; *idem,* "Zwischen den Fronten," *Wort, Lied, und Gottesspruch. Festschrift J. Ziegler, FzB,* 2 (1972), II, 197-206; C. Kayatz, *Studien zu Proverbien 1–9. WMANT,* 22 (1966); O. Keel, *The Symbolism of the Biblical World* (Eng. trans., New York, 1978); *idem, Yahwes Entgegnung an Ijob. FRLANT,* 121 (1978); *idem* and U. Winter, *Vögel als Boten: Studien zu Ps 68,12-14, Gen 8,6-12, Koh 10,20 und dem Aussenden von Botenvögeln in Ägypten. OBO,* 14 (1977); F. K. Kienitz, *Die politische Geschichte Ägyptens vom 7. bis zum 4. Jahrhundert vor der Zeitwende* (Berlin, 1953); K. A. Kitchen, *The Third Intermediate Period in Egypt (1100-650 B.C.)* (Warminster, 1972); B. Mazar, "The Campaign of Pharaoh Shishak to Palestine," *Volume du Congrès, Strasbourg 1956. SVT,* 4 (1957),

I. Etymology. The Hebrew name for Egypt, *miṣrayim,* corresponds to Ugar. *mṣrm,*[1] Phoen. *mṣrym,*[2] Egyptian Aram. *mṣryn,* Syr. *meṣrēm,* Akk. *Muṣur/Muṣru/Miṣri,* Old Persian *Mudrāya,* Arab. *Miṣr;* the word is not, however, attested in Old Egyptian. The Egyptians themselves called their land *km.t, the* "black (land)" (Copt. *kēme, khēmi*), *tȝ.wy,* the "two lands" (referring to Upper and Lower Egypt), occasionally also *ỉdb.wy,* the "two shores" (of the Nile). The Greek term *Aígyptos* derives from Egyp. *ḥ.t-kȝ-ptḥ,* "chapel of Ptah" (central sanctuary in Memphis during the Amarna period, cuneiform *ḫikuptaḫ* as the city's name), thence also the designation "Coptic." The Talmud attests the term *gip̱ṭîṯ* for "Egyptian."[3] If *miṣrayim* constitutes a genuine dual form, and if it is connected with Akk. *miṣru,* "border, region,"[4] and Arab. *miṣr,* "border, land, capital city," it might be a translation of *tȝ.wy,* although this explanation is extremely uncertain. Meir Fraenkel's derivation of *miṣrayim,* associating it with *māṭār,* "rain," "water," is untenable.[5]

The singular form *māṣôr* also occurs in the OT (Mic. 7:12; 2. K. 19:24 par. Isa. 37:25; Isa. 19:6), and the gentilic form *miṣrî* is richly attested.

II. OT.

1. *Table of Nations (Gen. 10).* In the Table of Nations in Gen. 10 (J and P), *miṣrayim* appears as the son of Ham together with Cush (Nubia), Put (Libya), and Canaan (v. 6 [P]). Since the Table of Nations likely reflects politico-historical groupings rather than racial-linguistic relationships, it provides a picture of the political situation in pre-

---

57-66; T. N. D. Mettinger, *Solomonic State Officials. CB,* 5 (1971); P. Montet, *Egypt and the Bible* (Eng. trans., Philadelphia, 1968); S. Morenz, "Ägyptologische Beiträge zur Erforschung der Weisheitsliteratur Israels," *Les sagesses du Proche-Orient ancien* (Paris, 1963), 63-71; *idem,* "Die ägyptische Literatur und die Umwelt," *Ägyptologie. HO,* I/2 (1952), 194-206; G. Nagel, "A propos des rapports du Psaume 104 avec les textes égyptiens," *Festschrift A. Bertholet* (Tübingen, 1950), 395-403; S. I. L. Norin, *Er spaltete das Meer. CB,* 9 (Ger. trans. 1977); T. E. Peet, *A Comparative Study of the Literatures of Egypt, Palestine and Mesopotamia* (London, 1931); G. von Rad, "The Royal Ritual in Judah," *The Problem of the Hexateuch* (Eng. trans., New York, 1966), 222-231; D. B. Redford, *A Study of the Biblical Story of Joseph (Genesis 37–50). SVT,* 20 (1970); E. Ruprecht, "Das Nilpferd im Hiobbuch," *VT,* 21 (1971), 209-231; S. Ö. Steingrimsson, *Vom Zeichen zur Geschichte. CB,* 14 (1979); J. Vandier, *La famine dans l'Égypte ancienne* (Paris, 1936); J. A. L. M. Vergote, *Joseph en Égypte. OrBibLov,* 3 (1959); W. A. Ward, "The Egyptian Office of Joseph," *JSS,* 5 (1960), 144-150; H. Wildberger, "Das Abbild Gottes, Gen 1,26-30," *ThZ,* 21 (1965), 245-259, 481-501; *idem,* "Die Thronnamen des Messias, Jes 9,5b," *ThZ,* 16 (1960), 314-332 = *Jahwe und Sein Volk. ThB,* 66 (1979), 56-74; R. J. Williams, "Ägypten und Israel," *TRE,* I (1977), 492-505; *idem,* " 'A people come out of Egypt': An Egyptologist looks at the OT," *Congress Volume, Edinburgh 1974. SVT,* 28 (1975), 231-252; E. Würthwein, "Egyptian Wisdom and the OT" (Eng. trans.), in J. L. Crenshaw, ed., *Studies in Ancient Israelite Wisdom* (New York, 1976), 113-133; A. S. Yahuda, *The Language of the Pentateuch in its Relation to Egyptian* (London, 1933); J. Zandee, "Egyptological Commentary on the OT," *Travels in the World of the OT. Festschrift M. A. Beek* (Leiden, 1974), 269-281.

1. *WUS,* no. 1645.
2. *KAI,* 5, 2; 49, 34.
3. A. Erman, *ZÄS,* 35 (1897), 109.
4. *AHw,* II (1972), 659.
5. "Zur Deutung von biblischen Flur- und Ortsnamen: *Miṣrajim,*" *BZ,* N.S. 5 (1961), 86.

Israelite times, and the "brothers" of *miṣrayim* represent regions dependent on Egypt. The names of the "sons" of *miṣrayim* (Gen. 10:13f. [J]) are all plural gentilic forms and thus refer to ethnic units: *lûdîm* (Jer. 46:9; Ezk. 30:5), *ʿanāmîm, lehāḇîm, napṯuḥîm, paṯrusîm,* and *kasluḥîm,* "whence came the Philistines and the *kaptōrîm.*" Besides the Philistines and Caphtorim, only *napṯuḥîm* (Lower Egypt) and *paṯrusîm* (Upper Egypt) can be identified with certainty.

2. *Ideological Considerations.* Ideologically, the OT associates Egypt primarily with the land of slavery ("house of bondage," *bêṯ ʿaḇāḏîm:* Ex. 13:3; 20:2; Dt. 5:6; 6:12; 7:8; 8:14; 13:6,11[Eng. vv. 5,10]; Jgs. 6:8; Jer. 34:13; Mic. 6:4 — almost exclusively Deuteronomistic material) from which Israel was delivered (see discussion below). Otherwise, Egypt was also viewed as a rich, fruitful land where one could find refuge in times of drought and famine (Gen. 12:10; 42:1ff.; 43:1f.). In the stories of the murmuring in the wilderness, Egypt is remembered as the land where the people had plenty to eat (Ex. 16:3: "when we sat by the fleshpots and ate our fill of bread"; Nu. 11:5: "we remember the fish we used to eat in Egypt for nothing, the cucumbers, the melons, the leeks, the onions, and the garlic"). Only in exceptional instances are references made to the harsh work of artificial irrigation in Egypt in contrast to Canaan, which receives its water from rain (Dt. 11:10).

The Egyptians are a foreign people with an incomprehensible language (*ʿam lōʿēz,* Ps. 114:1; cf. also Dt. 28:49; Isa. 28:11; 33:19; Jer. 5:15), a people whose customs are strange and must be explained (Gen. 43:33; 46:34; cf. Ex. 8:22[26]).

According to 1 K. 5:10(4:30), Solomon's wisdom "surpassed the wisdom of all the people of the east, and all the wisdom of Egypt." The reference in v. 13(33) to his familiarity with the "trees . . animals, birds, reptiles, and fish" is often taken as a counterpart to what has been called the Egyptian "wisdom of lists."[6] Indeed, the preeminent position occupied by wisdom within Egyptian literature is well known,[7] and the various relationships between Egyptian and Israelite wisdom literature are quite multifarious. Prov. 22:17–23:14 seem to exhibit literary dependence on the Egyptian teaching of Amenemope,[8] and Prov. 1–9 share extensive structural and ideological agreement with Egyptian wisdom.[9]

3. *Egyptian Religion.* Surprisingly, the OT says very little about Egyptian religion, and only indirectly might one conclude the presence of Egyptian influence on Solomon. 1 K. 3:1; 7:8; 9:16,24 report that Solomon married a daughter of the Pharaoh and built her a house — for political reasons, of course. This is also mentioned in 1 K. 11:1 in a gloss dealing with the king's foreign wives. Since 11:4 asserts that "his wives turned

---

6. G. von Rad, "*Job* XXXVIII and Ancient Egyptian Wisdom," *The Problem of the Hexateuch* (Eng. trans., New York, 1966), 281-291.

7. Cf. H. Brunner, "Die Weisheitsliteratur," *Ägyptologie. HO,* I/2 (1952), 90-110; H. Ringgren, *Sprüche. ATD,* XVI/1 (^{3}1980), introduction.

8. Cf. Ringgren, *in loc.*

9. See Kayatz.

away his heart after other gods," at least the redactor's opinion seems to be that Solomon also worshipped the gods of Egypt, although nothing concrete is reported about such worship.[10]

Ezk. 8:10 is also often adduced as a reference to the cult of Egyptian gods. The abominations the prophet finds in the Jerusalem temple include "portrayals of all kinds of creeping things and loathsome beasts" etched on the walls. Considering the animal forms of most of the Egyptians gods, several scholars take this as a reference to Egyptian idols[11] (cf. also Ezk. 20:7f.; 23:19-21,27).

The first thorough critique of idolatry in general and of the Egyptian cult of animals in particular is found in Wis. 13–15.[12] The Egyptian *ḥarṭummîm* are mentioned in the Joseph story and in the plague narratives as soothsayers and magicians.[13] The word also occurs in Akkadian as a loanword, and then in Daniel as well.

Historical considerations prevent the acceptance of older theories of the monotheism of Akhenaten having influenced Israelite religion. The question remains, however, concerning the striking agreement between certain sections of Ps. 104 and the great sun hymn ("Hymn to the Aton") from Amarna. Since the solar religion of Akhenaten was forgotten shortly after his death, it is difficult to determine the path such influence might have taken. One possibility would be a continued transmission of the older Amon hymn which underlies this sun hymn;[14] another would be the fact that both the sun hymn and Ps. 104 exhibit a certain similarity with the wisdom of lists.[15] The fact remains, however, that the agreements are in part almost verbatim (esp. Ps. 104:20-30).

An additional example of Egyptian influence is alleged for the titles of the coming king in Isa. 9:5(6). At his enthronement, the Egyptian king received a document known as the royal protocol *(nḫb.t)* with his five royal names. If the *ʿēḏûṯ* of 2 K. 11:12 and the *ḥōq* of Ps. 2:7 reflect similar usage, the four (!) royal names in Isa. 9:5(6) might have been influenced by such a protocol.[16] The content of the names, however, more likely suggests polemic against the titles of the Assyrian kings.[17]

III. Historical Relationships Between Israel and Egypt. Over the course of time, diverse relationships quite naturally developed between the neighboring lands of Egypt

---

10. On the Yahwist's criticism of the infiltration of Egyptian religion during the Solomonic age, cf. W. von Soden, "Verschlüsselte Kritik an Salomo in der Urgeschichte des Jahwisten?" *WO,* 7/2 (1973/74), 228-240; M. Görg, "Die 'Sünde' Salomos," *BN,* 16 (1981), 42-59.

11. So A. Bertholet, *Hesekiel. HAT,* XIII (1936), *in loc.;* W. F. Albright, *Archaeology and the Religion of Israel* (Baltimore, ^{2}1946), 166f.; cf. W. Zimmerli, *Ezekiel 1.* Herm (Eng. trans. 1979), 240f.

12. Cf. V below.

13. → חרטם *ḥarṭōm* (V, 176-79).

14. A. Erman, *Literature of the Ancient Egyptians* (Eng. trans., New York, 1927; repr. 1971), 138f..

15. See Bergman, with additional bibliog.

16. G. von Rad, *The Problem of the Hexateuch,* 229.

17. R. A. Carlson, "The anti-Assyrian character of the oracle in Is. IX 1-6," *VT,* 24 (1974), 130-35.

and Canaan. As already seen,[18] the Table of Nations in Gen. 10 mentions Canaan among the brothers of *miṣrayim,* reflecting political relationships during the pre-Israelite period. The Amarna Letters and other sources testify to these relationships in the 14th century B.C.

The Joseph story as well as the stories of the emigration of Jacob's family to Egypt reflect events which, although not historically verifiable, nonetheless can be viewed as fairly typical and thus cannot be dismissed as completely unhistorical[19] (we will speak later about the deliverance from Egypt). It is reported that during the Solomonic age a certain (unnamed) Pharaoh undertook a military campaign against Gezer (1 K. 9:16); the city was captured and given to Pharaoh's daughter (who became Solomon's wife) as a dowry *(šilluḥîm).* We also hear of the importation of chariots and horses from Egypt and Kue (Cilicia) (1 K. 10:28f.; cf. 2 Ch. 1:16f.; 9:28). The wording seems to imply that Solomon had acquired a kind of monopoly in this trade, although this seems improbable. Different explanations have been advanced: either one identifies *miṣrayim* with the region *Muṣru* in the Taurus Mountains, where horses were indeed bred, or one assumes with Kurt Galling[20] that "horses were bought up in Cilicia, and at the same time experienced horse teams along with chariots were already being acquired from Egypt."[21] In any case, passages such as Dt. 17:16 (an apparent allusion to Solomon); Isa. 30:16; 31:1 testify to the fact that one was accustomed in Judea to associating Egypt with horses. Finally, T. N. D. Mettinger has shown that Solomon's administration was probably largely organized according to an Egyptian model.

Egypt also plays a role as a place refuge for Jeroboam (1 K. 11:40); after Solomon's death Jeroboam returns from Egypt and becomes king in northern Israel (1 K. 12:2f.). Just five years later, according to 1 K. 14:25, Pharaoh Shishak (or Shushak, Egyp. *ššnq)* I of the twenty-second dynasty attacked Rehoboam, acquiring rich booty from Jerusalem as a result. As a matter of fact, he also penetrated into the northern kingdom and into Transjordan.

2 Ch. 14:9-14(10-15) reports a renewed attack under Asa: a certain "Zerah of Cush (NRSV 'the Ethiopian')" (an Egyptian field general?) attacked Judah, but was defeated by Asa. Nothing more is known of this event.

Egypt does not reenter biblical purview until the time of Isaiah. In approximately 715 B.C. the Ethiopian prince Shabaka was able to bring all Egypt under his rule, founding the twenty-fifth dynasty. Egypt, thus newly strengthened, emerged as a counter to the great Assyrian power, renewing the hope of the Palestinian princes for deliverance from the Assyrian yoke. 2 K. 17:4 reports that in the northern kingdom King Hoshea made contact with Pharaoh So (*sw',* either = Egyp. *ṯ3y,* "vizier," or an

18. See II.1 above.

19. Herrmann.

20. *Die Bücher der Chronik, Esra, Nehemiah. ATD,* XII (1954), 81.

21. See the discussion in E. Würthwein, *Die Bücher der Könige. ATD,* XI/1 (1977), *in loc.;* cf. also H. Cazelles, "מצר (1 Reg 10,28," *Hommages à A. Dupont-Sommer* (Paris, 1971), 17-26; P. Garelli, *ibid.,* 37-48.

abbreviation of the name Osorkon IV [730-715][22]) and ceased paying tribute to Assyria. The mention of ambassadors from Ethiopia (Cush) in Isa. 18:1ff. is generally taken to refer to this situation (see below). Statements such as those in Isa. 20 and 30, warning against trust in Egypt, clearly derive from this situation.

Yet another "king of Ethiopia" appears in 2 K. 19:9. During his own military campaign to Palestine (701), Sennacherib learns that Tirhakah (Taharkah) had "set out to fight against him." It is not clear whether this report had anything to do with Sennacherib's unexpected withdrawal (1 K. 19:36). Because of the historical and chronological problems attaching to this event, the reader should refer to the more comprehensive works on the history of Israel.

The power struggle between Egypt and Assyria continued, and was made even more complicated by the emergence of the Babylonians as adversaries of Assyria. In 2 K. 23:29, we find Pharaoh Neco II (twenty-sixth dynasty) marching "toward Assyria" (likely to the assistance of Assyria against the Babylonians); Josiah confronts him and is defeated and killed at Megiddo (609 B.C.; 2 K. 23:29). Neco's expedition was unsuccessful, although while returning he did claim dominion over Syria-Palestine, installing Josiah's son Jehoiakim as an Egyptian vassal prince in Jerusalem (2 K. 23:34). A few years later (605), Neco was defeated by Nebuchadnezzar at Carchemish (Jer. 46:2), and 2 K. 24:7 reports briefly that "the king of Egypt did not come again out of his land, for the king of Babylon had taken over all that belonged to the king of Egypt from the Brook of Egypt to the river Euphrates."

During Zedekiah's reign plans seemed to have developed for an anti-Babylonian coalition with the aid of Egypt. Jeremiah opposed it, although without success. According to Jer. 37:5,7, Egyptian troops did indeed appear in Judah, forcing the Babylonians to give up their siege of Jerusalem temporarily (cf. Jer. 34:21). After the fall of Jerusalem in 587 and the murder of the governor Gedaliah, many Judeans fled to Egypt (Jer. 42f.), taking Jeremiah along with them against his will (43:6).

IV. Two great OT narrative complexes use Egypt as their setting: the Joseph story (Gen. 37–50) and the Exodus story (Ex. 1–15). However, both Egypt's role and the traditio-historical problems involved are in each case completely different.

1. *The Joseph Story.* From a composition-technical perspective, the Joseph story functions as a connecting link between the patriarchal stories and the Exodus Narrative, explaining why and how the Israelites came to Egypt. Its literary genre is generally characterized as a novella. Although post-Wellhausen scholars usually identify the two sources J and E at work here (with short insertions by P), the criteria for source differentiation are extraordinarily weak,[23] which is why many scholars are now inclined to understand the Joseph story as a unified composition. According to Herbert Donner,

---

22. See *TRE,* I, 495; D. B. Redford, "A Note on II Kings, 17,4," *Journal of the Society for the Study of Egyptian Antiquities,* 11 (1981), 75f., suggests that So is actually = *s3w,* "Saʿidic."
23. Cf. recently Donner.

only 41:50-52; 46:1-5; 48; 50:23-25 might contain material possibly deriving from the traditional Pentateuchal sources.

As a whole the narrative is permeated by elements testifying to a fairly close acquaintance with Egyptian conditions (some scholars suggest it reflects the conditions around 1200 B.C.[24]): names such as Potiphar and Potiphera (Gen. 39:1ff.; 41:45,50; both *pꜣ-dy-pꜣ-rʿ*), *ṣāpᵉnaṯ-paʿnēaḥ* (41:45)[25] (the last portion of which in any case contains the word *ʿnḫ,* "life"), Asenath ("belonging to the goddess Neith"), as well as several details concerning courtly life and Egyptian customs. The only problematical element attaches to the cup divination (44:5), which thus far has not been attested with certainty in Egypt.[26] In contrast, the interpretation of dreams (ch. 40) is well-attested in Egyptian sources.[27] Neither is the east wind (41:6) quite Egyptian, since in Egypt it is actually the south wind which is known as the searing wind. Thus Egypt and Egyptian conditions are described here from the perspective of a foreigner, although a perspective for the most part well acquainted with those conditions.

Of particular interest are the Egyptian parallels to the story of Joseph and Potiphar's wife (Gen. 39:6-20) and of the seven years of famine (41:53-57). In the first instance we can refer to the *Tale of Two Brothers,* and in the second to an inscription from Siheil which tells how the Nile inundation failed to occur for seven years during the time of Djoser (third dynasty); although the inscription derives from the Ptolemaic period, it might well preserve an older tradition.[28] Although the connection with the *Tale of Two Brothers* is clear, most commentaries merely mention it rather than fully exploit it. Claus Westermann,[29] e.g., points out that the continuation of the tale deviates from the Joseph story. Precisely this continuation, however, might provide the key to solving the problem, since it exhibits a striking similarity with the circle of myths surrounding Osiris. At issue is the indestructibility of (Osiric) life and the miraculous procreation of a new ruler, motifs also found in the Joseph story. The purpose of the whole is given in Gen. 50:20 as "to preserve a numerous people." Osiris is the god of grain, and Joseph becomes the provider for his people through his grain trade. Joseph's path to eminence leads through dangers designated by the word *bôr* (37:22,24, "pit, well"; 40:15; 41:14, "dungeon"); the same word is also used to refer to the netherworld. This does not mean, however, that Joseph is a disguised fertility god (Tammuz, Adonis, etc.),[30] but rather only that fertility motifs permeate the story and apparently have contributed to its formation. One should also note that against this Egyptian backdrop Canaanite-Israelite features also emerge: *bôr,* "I shall go down to Sheol" (37:35), *qāḏîm* (see above). (The Potiphar episode also has a Canaanite parallel in the myth of the storm-god and the goddess Ashertu,[31] although this myth has a different focus.)

---

24. So Vergote.
25. For several possible interpretations, see Vergote, 141ff.
26. Despite Vergote, 172ff.
27. → חלם *ḥālam (chālam),* IV, 432.
28. See *ANET*³, 31f.; for the *Tale of Two Brothers,* see *ANET*³, 23-25.
29. C. Westermann, *Genesis 37–50* (Eng. trans., Minneapolis, 1986), 60f.
30. Cf. Albright; B. Reicke, *Die kultischen Hintergründe der Josepherzählung* (1948).
31. *ANET*³, 519; Westermann does not render this quite correctly.

Bo Reicke[32] attempts to support his view of Joseph as a fertility-god by assuming that the Joseph story served as a cultic legend for the autumnal festival. And indeed, Ps. 81:6(5) asserts of the *ḥag* of the autumnal festival that "he [Yahweh] made it a decree in Joseph (spelled *yᵉhôsēp*) *bᵉṣē'ṯô ʿal-'ereṣ miṣrayim.*" The last clause is usually translated "when he [Yahweh] went out against the land of Egypt," and is associated with the exodus events (or one reads *mē'ereṣ miṣrayim,* "from the land of Egypt"). This may, however, be an allusion to Gen. 41:45: *wayyēṣē' yôsēp ʿal-'ereṣ miṣrayim,* i.e., to inspect the land after his rise to eminence. In this case Joseph's advance is associated with the autumnal *ḥag,* and one might find an allusion to Joseph in the name of the festival, *ḥag hā'āsîp.* Since Joseph is not otherwise associated with the autumnal festival, however, this thesis must remain somewhat uncertain.

Gerhard von Rad's understanding of the Joseph story as a wisdom story of exemplary behavior is much disputed. Scholars tend rather to find other familiar narrative motifs, such as, e.g., the rise to eminence of a younger brother. Without a doubt, however, the focus is on the rise of a righteous person after many tribulations and much suffering. Cf. Ps. 34:20(19): "Many are the afflictions of the righteous, but Yahweh delivers him out of them all"; this psalm does admittedly also exhibit wisdom features.

2. *The Exodus.* Israel's deliverance from Egypt occupies considerable space in the OT tradition. Apart from the Exodus Narrative as such, it is also recalled as the fundamental act of election in the context of Deuteronomic parenesis, in the creed Dt. 26:5, in the Deuteronomistic history, in historiographic psalms (see below), and in the prophetic books (Isa. 10:24,26; 11:15f.; Jer. 2:6; 7:22,25; 11:4,7; 16:14; 23:7; 31:32; 32:20f.; 34:13; Ezk. 20:6,9f.; Hos. 2:17[15]; 12:10,14[9,13]; Am. 2:10; 3:1; 4:10; 9:7; Mic. 6:4; 7:15; Hag. 2:5).

a. *The Exodus Narrative.* The actual Exodus Narrative is preceded by the account of the "Egyptian plagues" (Ex. 7:8-10,29). In its present form it is generally taken to be a compilation of a J narrative and a P narrative.[33] The entire course of the narrative is portrayed as a struggle between Moses and Aaron as leaders of the Israelites on the one hand, and Pharaoh and his magicians *(ḥarṭummîm)* on the other; or, viewed theologically, as a struggle between Yahweh and the gods of Egypt. Yahweh emerges victorious from this struggle only through the tenth plague, the slaughter of the first-born. The procession through the Red Sea is yet another triumph for Yahweh; in the song of the sea in Ex. 15 it is portrayed with military terminology (Yahweh as a man of war, *'îš milḥāmâ,* v. 3) and in semimythological colors as a struggle against the sea (cf. Baʿal and Yam in Ugarit).[34] Despite its mythological coloring, the song does refer to concrete events (chariots, sinking into the sea), although this can in part be attributed to subsequent redactional activity.[35]

---

32. Pp. 25f.
33. See the comms.; Steingrimsson distinguishes the sources differently.
34. Norin, 77ff.
35. Norin; E. Zenger, "Tradition und Interpretation in Exodus xv 1-21," *Congress Volume, Vienna 1980. SVT,* 32 (1981), 462f. → מצולה *mᵉṣûlâ* (VIII, 514-19).

b. *Evaluation of the Exodus in the Psalms, Prophetic Texts, etc.* Similar mythologizing features are found in several psalms. Ps. 77:14-21(13-20) contains expressions such as "when the waters saw you, they were afraid; the very deep *(tᵉhōmôṯ)* trembled" (v. 17[16]) and "the skies thundered; your arrows flashed on every side" (v. 18[17], here as a storm theophany). Ps. 106:9 uses the verb → גער *gāʿar,* otherwise associated with the struggle with chaos, to portray how Yahweh rebukes *(gāʿar)* the Red Sea. (Two other psalms often adduced in this context, Ps. 74 and 89, refer to creation, as the context shows.[36]) Isa. 51:9f. associates an allusion to the exodus with motifs otherwise deriving from the struggle with chaos: the context implies that the killing of Rahab-*tannîn* causes the sea to dry up for the redeemed people to pass over; furthermore, the sea is referred to as *tᵉhôm rabbâ.* In other words, Israel's deliverance from Egypt was a victory over the powers of chaos comparable to Yahweh's primeval victory at creation: creation and redemption are one.[37] Isa. 51:10f. uses the verbs *gāʾal* and *pāḏâ* for the deliverance from Egypt — and Babylon. The term *gāʾal* also occurs in Ex. 6:6; 15:13; Ps. 77:16[15]; 106:10; cf. also Ps. 74:2; and *pāḏâ* occurs in Dt. 9:26; 13:6; Ps. 78:42. This characterizes the liberation as a ransom from slavery (expressly *pāḏâ mibbêṯ ʿᵃḇāḏîm,* Dt. 13:6[5]; Mic. 6:4). Other comparable expressions include *hiṣṣîl* (Ex. 3:8; 6:6) and *hôšîaʿ* (Ps. 106:8,10). Simple descriptive expressions include *hôṣîʾ*[38] and *heʿᵉlâ.*[39]

Other expressions interpret the deliverance as a sign of Yahweh's might: *ʾōṯôṯ ûmôpᵉṯîm*[40] (Ex. 7:3; Dt. 4:34; 7:19; Ps. 78:43; 105:27; 135:9; only *ʾôṯ* in Dt. 11:3; only *môpēṯ* in Ex. 4:21; 7:9; 11:9f.). Yahweh's show of power is expressed by the tandem "by a mighty hand and an outstretched arm"[41] (Dt. 4:34; 5:15; 7:19; 11:2; 26:8; Ps. 136:12; cf. *yāḏ ḥᵃzāqâ* in Dt. 9:26, *zᵉrôaʿ nᵉṭûyâ* + *šᵉp̄āṭîm gᵉḏōlîm* in Ex. 6:6 [P]; *zᵉrôaʿ* alone in Ps. 77:16[15]). Ex. 3:20; Ps. 106:7 use *nip̄lāʾôṯ,* Ps. 78:12 *peleʾ.*[42] The purpose of this demonstration of power is given in Ex. 6:7 (P) by the recognition formula "so that you know that I am Yahweh your God" (cf. Ex. 7:5; 9:29; 12:12).

c. *The Exodus in the Wisdom of Solomon.* In Deutero-Isaiah the exodus becomes the model for the imminent liberation from the exile, succinctly summarized in the passage cited above, Isa. 51:9-11, although also evoked several times by exodus typology within the book.

A completely different picture emerges in Ps. 80:9f.(8f.), where Israel is portrayed

---

36. So Norin, 110ff.; see H. Ringgren, "Yahvé et Rahab-Léviatan," *Mélanges bibliques et orientaux. Festschrift H. Cazelles. AOAT,* 212 (1981), 387-393.

37. G. von Rad, "Das theologische Problem des alttestamentlichen Schöpfungsglaubens," in P. Volz, *et al.,* eds., *Werden und Wesen des ATs. BZAW,* 66 (1936), 138-147.

38. → יצא *yāṣāʾ* (VI, 225-250).

39. → עלה *ʿālâ;* → יצא *yāṣāʾ,* VI, 238f.

40. → אות *ʾôṯ (ʾôth)* (I, 167-188); → מופת *môpēṯ* (VIII, 174-181).

41. → יד *yāḏ* (V, 393-426); → זרוע *zᵉrôaʿ* (IV, 131-140).

42. → פלא *plʾ.*

as a vine which Yahweh brings out of Egypt to transplant in Canaan.[43] Yet another picture is found in Hos. 11:1f.; here Israel is the son Yahweh calls out of Egypt.

The Exodus story is given a unique interpretation in the final section of the Wisdom of Solomon. Chapter 10 elaborates the view that the history of the world is guided by wisdom rather than directly by God. In Wisd. 10:15ff., we read that wisdom delivered "a holy people . . . from a nation of oppressors," and that she entered the soul of Moses, withstanding dread kings (i.e., Pharaoh) amid wonders and signs. It was she who guided the people through the Red Sea, while the Egyptians drowned. The following chapters (11–19) develop the entire exodus occurrence in a series of antitheses: the Egyptians are tormented by plagues, while the Israelites escape. Of particular interest is 11:15-27, which first mocks the Egyptian cult of animals ("they worshipped irrational serpents and worthless animals," 11:15; developed further and substantiated in 13:1-9; 15:14-19) — for precisely this reason the Egyptians are punished by animal plagues (11:23-25).

d. *The Exodus in the Prophetic Books.* The prophets only occasionally refer to the exodus, and then usually as a basic historical fact (see above; cf. also comparisons such as that in Am. 4:10: "a pestilence after the manner of Egypt"; Isa. 10:24,26: "lift up their staff against you as the Egyptians did"). God's universal might is illustrated in Am. 9:7 by the fact that he brought up Israel from Egypt, the Philistines from Caphtor, and the Syrians from Kir to their present dwelling places, and in Isa. 43:3 by the fact that he gave Egypt and Cush as ransom for his people Israel. Hosea foresees a return to Egypt for Israel, a return that will bring about a kind of new beginning (Hos. 8:13; 9:3,6 compared with 2:16[14]). According to the allegory of Ezk. 23, the two sisters Oholah and Oholibah played the harlot in Egypt (v. 3), which seems to suggest (cf. 20:7f.) that while in Egypt Israel worshipped the idols of the land; this completely isolated assertion might at most be supported by Josh. 24:14.

In Mic. 6:3f., Yahweh accuses Israel of ingratitude: though he led the people out of Egypt, they have forgotten his salvific deeds. Jeremiah also recalls the deliverance from Egypt, "the iron-smelter," and the resulting covenant (Jer. 11:4).

V. Egypt in the Prophetic Oracles Concerning Foreign Nations. The prophets Isaiah, Jeremiah, and Ezekiel mention Egypt several times in their oracles concerning foreign nations, where they take a stand regarding the various problems attending the current historical situation.

1. *Isaiah.* Isaiah experienced Egypt's renewal under Shabaka as well as the resultant unrest in Palestine. In connection with the Philistine uprising in 713-711 he goes naked and barefoot "as a sign and a portent against Egypt and Cush," to show how the Assyrians will lead away the Egyptian captives (Isa. 20:1-6). Hence one should place no hope in Egypt. The utterances in 31:1-3 were probably made a short while later; here Isaiah castigates reliance on Egyptian horses and chariots ("for the Egyptians are human, and not God; their horses are flesh, and not spirit," v. 3). The same is true of 30:1-5, where only shame and humiliation are foretold for those who seek refuge with

---

43. → גפן *gep̱en (gephen)* (III, 53-61).

Pharaoh. The following, rather dark verses (30:6f.) portray Egypt as Rahab, although as useless and inactive (the MT *rahaḇ hēm šāḇeṯ* has probably been corrupted). Rather than rise up to take part in the battle as he once did, Rahab will remain seated and inactive.[44]

The oracle against Cush (NRSV 'Ethiopia,' Isa. 18:1-7) may derive from the same situation (since Shabaka came from Cush); Egypt is not actually mentioned here, however, and the scarcity of concrete features does make dating the oracle somewhat difficult.[45]

The series of statements in Isa. 19:1-15 is more problematical, and its authenticity is generally disputed based on stylistic considerations. A prediction is made for the dissolution of national order, the collapse of economic life, and the confusion of Egypt's rulers. "A fierce king will rule over them" (v. 4: historical allusion or a prediction for the future?). Isaiah's usual warning against reliance on Egyptian aid is absent. These assertions are followed by a series of statements introduced by *bayyôm hahû'* which are doubtlessly secondary and which among other things foretell Egypt's conversion to the worship of Yahweh and a covenant between Egypt and Assyria blessed by Yahweh (a similar universalist prediction is found in Mic. 7:12).

2. *Jeremiah.* Jeremiah mentions Egypt in a variety of contexts. In Jer. 2:6, he recalls Israel's deliverance: the people has forgotten that Yahweh led it out of Egypt, and instead has gone after idols (v. 5). Because of this apostasy Israel has had to live under foreign rule, first Assyria, and now (under Jehoiakim) Egypt. The search for help in Egypt and Assyria is reprimanded in a reproachful double question (v. 18).

Egypt then appears among the nations to whom Jeremiah is to extend Yahweh's cup of wrath (Jer. 25:15-29).[46] The oracles against foreign nations in Jer. 45–51 appropriately also include a chapter on Egypt (ch. 46). The first part of the chapter (46:2-12) announces Neco's defeat at the Euphrates. Although Pharaoh intends to inundate the entire world just as the Nile overflows its banks each year, and to become ruler of the world, he "has not reckoned with the cosmic lord, the Lord Yahweh of hosts."[47] Not even Egypt's famous medicinal arts can heal the wounds of this grievous defeat (v. 11). The second section (vv. 13-26) foretells Nebuchadnezzar's imminent entry into Egypt. Here Egypt is portrayed as a beautiful heifer being attacked by a gadfly from the north, as a moaning woman in travail, and as a forest cut down by axes (vv. 20-23). The same theme is struck in 48:8-13 in connection with a symbolic act.

3. *Ezekiel.* Ezekiel's oracles against foreign nations include a whole series of statements concerning Egypt, most of which can be dated (the exception being ch. 30).

The first oracle (Ezk. 29:1-10) describes the king of Egypt as a dragon, full of

---

44. O. Kaiser, *Isaiah 13–39. OTL* (Eng. trans. 1974), 290.
45. Cf. *ibid.*, 90-93.
46. → כוס *kōs* (VII, 101-4).
47. W. Rudolph, *Jeremia. HAT,* XII (^{3}1968), 233.

presumptuous arrogance, lying in the Nile (such comparison with a crocodile is attested in praise of the Egyptian king[48]); Yahweh captures him, however, and casts him out into the wilderness. Here (as already in Isa. 36:6) Egypt is compared to a staff of reed which wounds the person leaning upon it (Ezk. 29:6f.).

Chapter 30, in its first, undated section (vv. 1-19), employs the familiar motif of the day of Yahweh (v. 3) in several oracles concerning Nebuchadnezzar's destruction of Egypt and its allies (v. 10). Ezk. 30:20-26 can be dated in April 587, approximately three months before the fall of Jerusalem: although Pharaoh raises his hand in battle, Yahweh will break it by means of the king of Babylon. Chapter 31 portrays Pharaoh as a proud tree competing with the trees of Eden, yet a tree which foreigners will cut down. Ezk. 32:1-16, which v. 16 designates as a *qînâ,* returns to the image of the dragon from ch. 29, asserting that Yahweh will capture it in his net and strew its flesh over the earth. Ezk. 32:17-32, also a lament, describes how Egypt will descend into the realm of the dead, where all the other nations hostile to God have already gone.

Finally, Ezk. 29:17-21 can be dated in April 571, making it the latest of the prophet's oracles which can be dated. Here Yahweh promises through the prophet to give Egypt to Nebuchadnezzar as compensation for his not altogether successful military campaign against Tyre. The course of history itself confirmed this prediction a few years later.[49]

Ringgren

IV. Qumran. Thus far, the Qumran texts have attested 15 occurrences of the term *miṣrayim.* To the extent that the context of these texts is still discernible (4QDibHam 1:9; 4Q158 14 I 4,5,6; both 4Q163 28:1 and 4Q167 17:1 can be eliminated), here, too, the deliverance from Egypt constitutes the most important context in which *miṣrayim* appears. In this connection it is astonishing that the Qumran-Essene literature does not exhibit any independent *miṣrayim* theology. The term occurs in a positive sense only in citations (from Lev. 25:42 [4Q 159:2-4,3); Dt. 13:6[5] [4Q158 14 I 5; 11QT 54:16]; Dt. 17:16 [11QT 56:16]; Dt. 20:1 [11QT 61:14]; Dt. 32:48f. [1Q22 1:1]), remaining thus within OT parameters. This can also be seen in the remarkably pale exhortation to remember the miracles in Egypt (4Q185 1f. I.15). The traditions unique to Qumran itself seem to associate only negative connotations with the term, the most significant negative factor being the simple fact that *miṣrayim* does not occur in the classical Qumran scrolls. 1QM 1:4 counts the Kittim of Egypt among the eschatological enemies, and 1QM 14:1 (text?) recalls the annihilation of the *'ᵉlîlê miṣrayim.* Finally, CD 3:5 expands the murmuring motif to include the time in Egypt as well: "And their sons in Egypt walked in the stubbornness of their hearts."

Fabry

---

48. W. Eichrodt, *Ezekiel. OTL* (Eng. trans. 1970), 403.
49. *Ibid.,* 279f.

מַקֶּבֶת *maqqeḇeṯ;* פַּטִּישׁ *paṭṭîš;* מַפֵּץ *mappēṣ*

Contents: I. Etymology. II. Usage. III. Synonyms: *paṭṭîš, mappēṣ.* IV. Later Derivations.

I. Etymology. The noun *maqqeḇeṯ* derives from the verb *nqb,* which means "to bore a hole" (2 K. 12:10[Eng. v. 9]; Hag. 1:6). The term *n*^{e}*qēḇâ,* deriving from the same verb, refers to a female, or to something feminine (Dt. 4:16; Jer. 31:22).

The Siloam Inscription refers to the breakthrough in the tunnel with the noun *hnqbh.* In Akkadian the term *naqābu* means "to hollow out," though it is usually used in the meaning "to deflower (a virgin)."[1] The Akkadian term *maqqabu,* "hammer,"[2] occurs as a loanword from Northwest Semitic.

Accordingly, the Hebrew word *maqqeḇeṯ* refers on the one hand to a cavity or hollow, and on the other to an object into which a hole has been bored (or with which one makes such a cavity?). This object was the hammer, which in the early period was made of stone into which a hole was bored for the handle.

II. Usage. In Isa. 51:1 *maqqeḇeṯ* is used clearly with the meaning "cavity, hollow." Here Abraham is designated as the "rock" and Sarah as the "cavity of the cistern" (wordplay with *n*^{e}*qēḇâ?*) from which the people once came. It is uncertain whether this is actually an allusion to mythological notions of the birth of human beings from a rock.[3] In any event, the rock does not refer to God.[4]

Otherwise the word always refers to the hammer as a tool, and occasionally as a weapon. The early account in Jgs. 4:21 already tells how Jael used a hammer to kill Sisera by driving a tent peg through his temple.

1 K. 6:7 shows that during the monarchy hammers were made of iron, since no iron hammer was permitted to be used in Solomon's temple. Since it had been appropriated from the Philistines, it was viewed during Solomon's time as something alien and thus dangerous. (This might reflect a notion similar to that in Ex. 20:25: Iron profanes the stone.)

The hammer was the tool used by smiths who made idols (Isa. 44:12), a notion also reflected in Jer. 10:4 (men fasten the idol with hammer and nails so that it will not tip

---

maqqeḇeṯ. A. A. Bevan, "The Origin of the Name Maccabee," *JTS,* 30 (1929), 191-93; R. Marcus, "The Name Makkabaios," *Joshua Starr Memorial Volume. Jewish Social Studies,* 5 (1953), 205ff.; E. Schürer, *The History of the Jewish People in the Age of Jesus Christ (175* B.C.–A.D. 135), I (Edinburgh, ^{2}1973), 158, n. 49.

1. *AHw,* II (1972), 743.
2. *AHw,* II, 607; J. C. Greenfield, "Ugaritic Lexicographical Notes," *Festschrift A. Goetze. JCS,* 21 (1967), 92, takes this as referring to a different tool, namely, a "trimmer, hedge cutter."
3. P. Volz, *Jesaja II. KAT,* IX/2 (1932), *in loc.;* C. Westermann, *Isaiah 40–66. OTL* (1969), *in loc.*
4. As suggested by P. A. H. de Boer, *Second-Isaiah's Message. OTS,* 11 (1956), 58ff.

over). This seems to confirm that the (iron) hammer was still perceived as a foreign tool as late as the exilic period.

III. Synonyms: paṭṭîš, mappēṣ. The word *paṭṭîš* is used in a similar context in Isa. 41:7 to refer to the hammer used by those who make idols: The image is secured so that it will not totter.[5] In Jer. 23:29 the same word refers to the power of the divine word: It is like fire and like a hammer that breaks a rock into pieces. Jer. 50:23 offers a picture of Babylon, which once smashed the entire world like a hammer, but now itself lies completely cut down and broken.

The word *mappēṣ* is also used to refer to the hammer of war in Jer. 51:20, where it parallels *k^elê milḥāmâ* in reference (as in 50:23, see above) to Babylon as the instrument with which Yahweh smashes nations and kingdoms.

IV. Later Derivations. It is disputed whether the name *Makkabaíos* (1 Mc. 2:4,66; 3:1, etc.) derives from *maqqeḇeṯ*. The objection has been raised that the *maqqeḇeṯ* was actually a small hand tool unsuitable as a symbol of war. Furthermore, we have already seen that at least in the earlier period the hammer was not viewed as an Israelite tool, though this may have changed in the later period. The name may also have some connection with Isa. 62:2, which reads: "a new name which the mouth of Yahweh will give *(yiqq^obennû)*." The books of the Maccabees themselves offer no explanation for the name.

Kapelrud

---

5. → מוט *mwṭ* (VIII, 152-58).

מָקוֹם *māqôm*

Contents: I. Occurrences: 1. Outside the OT; 2. In the OT; 3. LXX. II. Conceptual and Semantic Field: 1. Local-Adverbial; 2. Related Words and Terms. III. Outside the Cult: 1. Physical-Spatial Notions; 2. Notions of Order: a. The Cosmic Order; b. Mystery; c. Social Standing; d. The Question of Meaning; 3. The Grave; 4. Personification of the World of Life and of One's Surroundings; 5. The Land: a. Neutral Usage; b. The Promised Land. IV. Priestly Rubrics. V. Holy Places of the Preceding Ages. VI. Cultic Sites in the Present: 1. *māqôm* in the Altar Regulations; 2. The *māqôm* of the Ark; 3. The Chosen *māqôm* (Deuteronomic); 4. "My *māqôm* in *šîlô*" (Jer. 7:12); 5. Ambiguity (Deuteronomistic and Later). VII. Metaphorical Usage: 1. Elements of the Earthly Sanctuary; 2. Independent Usage; 3. God Himself. VIII. Qumran.

---

māqôm. F.-M. Abel, "L'apparition du Chef de l'Armée de Yahweh à Josué (Jos. 5,13-15)," *Miscellanea Biblica et Orientalia. Festschrift A. Miller. StAns,* 27f. (1951-52), 109-113; P. R. Ackroyd, "Two Hebrew Notes," *ASTI,* 5 (1966-67), 82-86; S. Amsler, "קום *qûm* aufstehen,"

THAT, II, 635-641; J. Barr, *Comparative Philology and the Text of the OT* (1968, repr. Winona Lake, 1987); W. W. Graf Baudissin, "El Bet-el (Genesis 31,13; 35,7)," *Vom AT. Festschrift K. Marti. BZAW,* 41 (1925), 1-11; J. Begrich, "Die priesterliche Tora," in P. Volz, *et al.,* eds., *Werden und Wesen des ATs. BZAW,* 66 (1936), 63-88 = *GSAT. ThB,* 21 (1964), 232-260; A. Biran, " 'To the God who is in Dan,' " *Temples and High Places in Biblical Times* (Jerusalem, 1981), 142-151; D. Conrad, *Studien zum Altargesetz: Ex 20:24-26* (Marburg, 1968); M. J. Dahood, "Hebrew-Ugaritic Lexicography V," *Bibl,* 48 (1967), 421-438; *idem,* "Northwest Semitic Philology and Job," *The Bible in Current Catholic Thought. M. J. Gruenthaner Memorial Volume. St. Mary's Theology Studies,* I (New York, 1962), 55-74; *idem,* "Qohelet and Northwest Semitic Philology," *Bibl,* 43 (1962), 349-365; *idem,* review of P. Benoit, J. Milik, and R. de Vaux, *Les grottes de Murabbʿat. DJD,* II (1961), *Bibl,* 44 (1963), 230f.; J. Day, "The Destruction of the Shiloh Sanctuary and Jeremiah VII 12,14," in J. A. Emerton, ed., *Studies in the Historical Books of the OT. SVT,* 30 (1979), 87-94; H. Donner, " 'Hier sind deine Götter, Israel!,' " *Wort und Geschichte. Festschrift K. Elliger. AOAT,* 18 (1973), 45-50; F. Dumermuth, "Zur deuteronomischen Kulttheologie und ihren Voraussetzungen," *ZAW,* 70 (1958), 59-98; D. T. Fenton, "בכל־אות נפשו Phraseological Criteria for the Study of Deuteronomic Cult Restriction," *Studies in the Bible and the Hebrew Language. Sefer M. Wallenstein* (Jerusalem, 1979), 21*-35*; J. G. Février, "Paralipomena Punica. VIII: Le mot MĀQÔM en phénicien-punique," *CahB,* 9 (1960/61), 33-36; G. Fohrer, "Zion-Jerusalem in the OT," *TDNT,* VII, 293-319; D. N. Freedman, "The Massoretic Text and the Qumran Scrolls: A Study in Orthography," *Textus,* 2 (1962), 87-102 = F. M. Cross and S. Talmon, eds., *Qumran and the History of the Biblical Text* (Cambridge, Mass., 1975), 196-211; V. Fritz, *Tempel und Zelt. WMANT,* 47 (1977); K. Galling, "Die Ausrufung des Namens als Rechtsakt in Israel," *ThLZ,* 81 (1956), 65-70; G. Garbini, " 'Paleo-siriano' meqūm = 'lega, federazione,' " *AION,* 36 (1976), 222-25; H. Gese, "Der Davidsbund und die Zionserwählung," *Vom Sinai zum Zion. BEvTh,* 64 (1974), 113-129; J. Halbe, *Das Privilegrecht Jahwes: Ex 34,10-26. FRLANT,* 114 (1975); B. Halpern, "The centralization formula in Deuteronomy," *VT,* 31 (1981), 20-38; M. Haran, *Temples and Temple-Service in Ancient Israel* (Oxford, 1978); B. Holwerda, "De altaarwet, Ex 20,24-26," = *Oudtest. Voordrachten II = Bijzondere Canoniek* (Kampen, 1972), 233-268; M. P. Horgan, *Pesharim: Qumran Interpretations of Biblical Books. CBQMon,* 8 (1979); J. Jeremias, *Theophanie. WMANT,* 10 (^{2}1977); A. F. Key, "The Giving of Proper Names in the OT," *JBL,* 83 (1964), 55-59; K. Koch, "Zur Geschichte der Erwählungsvorstellung in Israel," *ZAW,* 67 (1955), 205-226; E. König, "Stimmen Ex 20,24 und Dtn 12,13f. zusammen?" *ZAW,* 42 (1924), 337-346; H. Koester, "τόπος," *TDNT,* VIII, 187-208; E. Lipiński, *La royauté de Yahwé dans la poésie et le culte de l'ancien Israël. VVAW.L,* 27 (^{2}1968), no. 55; J. Lust, "Elia and the Theophany on Mount Horeb," *BETL,* 41 (1976), 91-100; G. C. Macholz, *Israel und sein Land* (Habilitationsschrift, Heidelberg, 1969); T. N. D. Mettinger, *The Dethronement of Sabaoth. CB,* 18 (1982); M. Metzger, "Himmlische und irdische Wohnstatt Jahwes," *UF,* 2 (1970), 139-158; E. Otto, "Jakob in Bethel," *ZAW,* 88 (1976), 165-190; L. Perlitt, "Sinai und Horeb," *Beiträge zur alttestamentlichen Theologie. Festschrift W. Zimmerli* (Göttingen, 1977), 302-322; R. Rendtorff, "Jakob in Bethel," *ZAW,* 94 (1982), 511-523; H. Graf Reventlow, "Gebotskern und Entfaltungsstufen in Deuteronomium 12," *Gottes Wort und Gottes Land. Festschrift H. W. Hertzberg* (Göttingen, 1965), 174-185; E. Robertson, "The Altar of Earth (Ex 20:24-26)," *JJS,* 1 (1948), 12-21; B. E. Shafer, "The Root *bḥr* and Pre-Exilic Concepts of Chosenness in the Hebrew Bible," *ZAW,* 89 (1977), 20-42; J.-L. Ska, "La place d'Ex 6_{2-8} dans la narration de l'exode," *ZAW,* 94 (1982), 530-548; J. J. Stamm, "Zum Altargesetz im Bundesbuch," *ThZ,* 1 (1945), 304-6; Y. Tesfai, *This is my Resting Place: An Inquiry into the Role of Time and Space in the OT* (diss., Lutheran School of Theology, Chicago, 1975) (unavailable to author; cf. review by M. J. Buss, *ZAW,* 90 (1978), 122; N. J. Tromp, *Primitive Conceptions of Death and the Nether World in the OT. BietOr,* 21 (1969); R. de Vaux, " 'Le lieu que Yahvé a choisi pour y établir son nom,' " *Das ferne und nahe Wort. Festschrift L. Rost. BZAW,* 105 (1967), 219-228; P. Weimar, *Die Berufung des Mose. OBO,* 32 (1980); H. Weippert, " 'Der Ort,

I. Occurrences.

1. *Outside the OT.* The Hebrew term *māqôm* is a *ma*-noun deriving from → קום *qûm.* Outside the OT, similar deverbal constructions[1] are attested in Ugarit (in a problematical formula concerning gold[2]), in Aramaic in Zincirli[3] and later,[4] frequently in Phoenician-Punic,[5] in Hebrew inscriptions,[6] in both biblical[7] and nonbiblical texts[8] (1QapGen XIX 26) from Qumran, and in Old South Arabic[9] but not in Akkadian.[10] Variations of the basic type cover a wide semantic spectrum: place (location), holy place, cult functionary,[11] grave, surface,[12] reserves, supplies,[13] goods, etc.[14]

2. *In the OT.* Among the approximately 400 occurrences in the OT,[15] only about one tenth function as subject and one tenth as object; four fifths constitute amplifications or qualifications of circumstance, a situation testifying to the weakly delineated meaning inhering in the term itself and to its strong semantic dependence on context. With decreasing frequency it occurs above all in narrative and cultic sections of the Pentateuch; in historical works; Jeremiah, Isaiah, Ezekiel, Job, Ecclesiastes, Psalms.

3. *LXX.* The LXX translates almost exclusively with *tópos* (363 times), though occasionally also with *chṓra, pólis, themélion, thrónos,* and *hópou.*

II. Conceptual and Semantic Field.

1. *Local-Adverbial.* The generic, local-adverbial meaning occurs quite frequently in formulaic expressions: *māqôm* with a possessive suffix (largely third person singular),

---

den Jahwe erwählen wird, um dort seinen Namen wohnen zu lassen,' " *BZ,* N.S. 24 (1980), 76-94; P. Welten, "Kulthöhe und Jahwetempel," *ZDPV,* 88 (1972), 19-37; C. Westermann, "Die Herrlichkeit Gottes in der Priesterschrift," *Wort–Gebot–Glaube. Festschrift W. Eichrodt. AThANT,* 59 (1970), 227-249 = *Forschung am AT. ThB,* 55 (1974), 115-137; G. Westphal, *Jahwes Wohnstätten nach den Anschauungen der alten Hebräer. BZAW,* 15 (1908); W. C. van Wyk, "The Translation of מקום in the Temple Speech of Jeremiah," *OuTWP,* 24 (1982), 103-9.

1. Cf. *KBL*³, 592f., 1018; Freedman, 97f.
2. *KTU,* 1.14 II, 1; III, 35; VI, 19; see also W. Johnstone, "OT Technical Expressions in Property Holding," *Ugaritica,* 6 (1969), 314f.
3. *KAI,* 214, 14.
4. *KAI,* 253, 1.
5. R. S. Tomback, *A Comparative Lexicon of the Phoenician and Punic Languages. SBL Diss.,* 32 (Missoula, 1978), 195-97.
6. *CIJ,* 974, 1; 1002, 1.
7. Cf. Horgan, 299.
8. See VIII below.
9. ContiRossini, 230.
10. Cf. *AHw,* II (1972), 896b; I (1965), 82b.
11. Tomback, 195-97.
12. *DISO,* 165.
13. *WUS,* no. 2417; cf., however, *CML*², 83, 86, 89.
14. *WTM,* III, 223f.
15. Cf. *THAT,* II, 636.

attached to a usually singular noun, often with a preceding particle *(b^e, l^e, min);* in relative clauses employing the Masoretic construct form *m^{e}qôm,*[16] often with retrospective *šām* or *bô.* This local meaning can be generalized to the point of complete dissolution of the reference to any specific point, in the sense of generic "where," "there," "everywhere": *kōl māqôm* (insofar as this expression is not referring to one or several specific places): e.g., Nu. 18:31; Josh. 1:3; Dt. 11:24; Prov. 15:3; Am. 8:3; probably Mal. 1:11; differently in Isa. 7:23: every piece of property (real estate); Dt. 12:13: every pagan cultic place. The expression *m^{e}qôm p^{e}lōnî 'almōnî* intentionally leaves the exact location unspecified for narrative reasons (1 S. 21:3[Eng. v. 2]; 2 K. 6:8).

2. *Related Words and Terms.* Poetic and prayer-texts frequently use similar constructions from other roots either instead of or in addition to *māqôm:* on the one hand *māqôm* with *qdš* (Ezr. 9:8; Ps. 24:3; Isa. 60:13; Jer. 17:12), and on the other *mā'ôn* with *qdš* (Dt. 26:15; 2 Ch. 30:27; Ps. 68:6[5]; Jer. 25:30; Zec. 2:17[13]), *mākôn* with *qdš* (Dnl. 8:11); next to *māqôm* with *yšb* (1 K. 8:30; 2 Ch. 6:21) we find *mākôn* with *yšb* (1 K. 8:13,39,43,49 par. 2 Ch. 6:2,30,33,39; Ps. 33:14); on the one hand *m^{e}qôm kis'î* (Ezk. 43:7), on the other *m^{e}kôn kis'ekā* (Ps. 89:15[14]), *kis'ô* (Ps. 97:2); as an utterance of God: *'el-m^{e}qômî* (Hos. 5:15), though also *bimkônî* (Isa. 18:4); the location of the temple is called *māqôm* (Jer. 17:12) and *mākôn* (Ezr. 2:68); cf. Ps. 26:8: *YHWH 'āhabtî m^e'ôn bêtekā ûm^{e}qôm miškan k^{e}bôdekā.* One and the same psalm, in speaking of the creation *(ysd)* of the cosmos, uses *māqôm* and *mākôn* (Ps. 104:8,5). Such alternation is a stylistic device occurring with particular animation in connection with the sanctuary in Jerusalem (see below). In Isa. 45:19 the construct state *bim^{e}qôm* is hardly saying anything different or more than the *nomen rectum 'ereṣ ḥōšek* alone (Job 10:21), and at most is emphasizing the element of unworthiness: "in a dark corner of the world."[17]

III. Outside the Cult. The semantic spectrum outside the cult is extraordinarily broad.

1. *Physical-Spatial Notions.* In the physical sense *māqôm* can refer to the following: spatial distance (1 S. 26:13); a dwelling place (to be expanded) (2 K. 6:1,2); living space (Isa. 5:8; Ezk. 45:4); lack of space for graves (Jer. 7:32; 19:11); the absence of any clean surface on a table (Isa. 28:8), or of space for a mount to pass through (Neh. 2:14); a locality or city (e.g., Gen. 19:12-14: *hammāqôm hazzeh* par. *hā'îr;* "the men of the place," Gen. 26:7; 29:22; 38:21,22; Jgs. 19:16; Ezr. 1:4; cf. 1 S. 7:16); the (appointed) place to stay (1 S. 27:5); one's place at a table (1 S. 9:22); ground given up tactically in battle (Jgs. 20:36); an *'ereṣ* suitable for pasturing and human settlement (Nu. 32:1; Jgs. 18:9-10); one's home (Isa. 14:2; Jer. 27:22). In connection with these notions and their attendant legal, social, and emotional content, *māqôm* is often used with a possessive suffix and a verb of movement, e.g., Jgs. 7:7; Nu. 24:11; Job 27:21;

16. *GK,* 130cd; *Synt,* §§144, 162.

17. P.-E. Bonnard, *Le second Isaïe. ÉtB* (1972), 166; → חשך *ḥāšak,* V, 252.

Prov. 27:8; 2 S. 15:19;[18] Sir. 41:19, and elsewhere. In a similar sense, suffixes are usually used with the terms *'ereṣ* (Gen. 30:25; Ezk. 21:35[30]), *'am* (Nu. 24:14), *naḥ^alâ* (Josh. 24:28), *'ōhel* (1 K. 8:66 par. 2 Ch. 7:10; 1 K. 12:16 par. 2 Ch. 10:16; 2 K. 14:12 par. 2 Ch. 25:22; 2 K. 13:5; cf. Isa. 13:14; Jer. 12:15). In the later period the plural form *kol-m^eqômôṯ* appears in formulaic expressions in reference to the exile and Diaspora (Jer. 24:9; 29:14; 40:12; 45:5; Ezk. 34:12; cf. Neh. 4:6[12]).

2. *Notions of Order.* The term *māqôm* can evoke various notions of order or organization.

a. *The Cosmic Order.* Although the term is attested once in connection with the technology associated with wells (Gen. 29:3), it occurs more frequently in the context of the cosmos. Wisdom understands that each and every thing has its "place" there (Eccl. 1:4-7; Bar. 3:24; cf. Gen. 1:9), so that *māqôm* and *g^eḇûl* can stand parallel (Ps. 104:8-9; cf. Dt. 11:24). In an historical-geographical context the *'allûpîm* of the Edomites are enumerated (Gen. 36:15-43) among other qualifications also "according to their *m^eqômôṯ*" (Gen. 36:40; cf. 10:5,20,31,32).[19] Images of catastrophes (of judgment) include the interruption of stability and violent removal of things from their appropriate *māqôm* (Isa. 13:13; Job 9:6; 14:18; 18:4).

b. *Mystery.* Since order in the larger sense is in many ways unfathomable to human beings, the term *māqôm* can also function as an expression of mystery, of that which is inaccessible to human beings in both the cosmic (Job 38:12,19; cf. Isa. 45:19) and the spiritual realm: "But where shall *ḥoḵmâ* be found [v. 20: whence does it come]? And where is [a/the] *māqôm* of *bînâ*?" (Job 28:12,20; cf. v. 14). Positively: "God understands the way to it, and he knows its *māqôm*" (Job 28:23).

c. *Social Standing.* Qoheleth is probably referring to a person's social station or professional, official position when he warns in 10:4: *m^eqôm^eḵā 'al-tannaḥ* (cf. 8:1-4,5-9). The sense of "office," or better, "official place," is clearer in 3:16,[20] and of "official position" in 1 K. 20:24 (cf. Gen. 40:13; 41:13: *kēn* with possessive suffix[21]).

d. *The Question of Meaning.* In Qoheleth's lament, the *māqôm 'eḥāḏ* is the end fated for every person (3:20) according to the senseless order of death, probably also referring simply to the netherworld, Sheol (6:6b; Tob. 3:6).[22]

3. *The Grave.* In Eccl. 8:10 the expression *m^eqôm (māqôm?) qāḏôš* refers perhaps to a burial place.[23] Given the context, a reference to an extensive burial place in Ezk. 39:11 (11-16) (*m^eqôm šēm* instead of *m^eqôm šām?*[24]) is no less probable than other

---

18. Cf. *BHS.*
19. *KBL*³, 52f.
20. Cf. N. Lohfink, *Kohelet. NEB* (1980), *in loc.*
21. See also *WTM,* III, 223f.
22. Cf. Ackroyd, 84f.
23. Cf. Dahood, *Bibl,* 43 (1962), 349-365; *idem, Bibl,* 44 (1963), 230f., and the reference to Phoenician inscriptions in *KAI,* 14, 4; 214, 14; *DISO,* 165, 30f.; Sir. 49:10 LXX; cautious: Barr, 292; Lohfink, 62.
24. Cf. *BHS.*

attempts at explanation. According to Jer. 7:32; 19:11, people will be buried in the abhorrent (Jer. 19:6,12,13; also 2 K. 23:10) Topheth because the appropriate burial place is not large enough (cf. Ex. 14:11).

4. *Personification of the World of Life and of One's Surroundings.* In a negative sense the *māqôm* of the wicked appears in poetic personification almost as an accomplice who turns against him (Job 8:18; 20:9; Ps. 103:16), though Job laments that the same thing happens to the righteous (7:10). "His *māqôm*" refers to a person's immediate surroundings along with the various people associated with it (Job 6:17; 27:23; Nah. 1:8 according to MT; cf. Dt. 33:9). The following positive prediction is made concerning Eliakim: "I will fasten him like a (tent) peg *bemāqôm ne'emān*" (Isa. 22:23).

5. *The Land.*

a. *Neutral Usage.* The term *māqôm* can refer without theological overtones to the land of one's birth (Ezk. 21:35[30]) or of certain peoples (Ex. 3:8; cf. 3:17[25]).

b. *The Promised Land.* In Gen. 13:14-17 the *māqôm 'ašer 'attâ šām* (v. 14) is not just an arbitrary location, but rather the promised land itself (overview, measuring off as a legal act;[26] see also Gen. 13:3,4 coll. with 12:8). The goal is *hammāqôm 'ašer hakinōṯî* (Ex. 23:20b).

IV. Priestly Rubrics. The Priestly Document binds specific ceremonies to specific "places" inside or outside the temple, the tent, the camp, or the city: *bimqôm* (always thus!) *qāḏôš* (8 times[27]), *meqôm haqqōḏeš* (twice[28]), *māqôm* outside the camp (Lev. 4:12; 6:4[11]; Nu. 19:9), or without any more specific qualification (Lev. 10:14), *māqôm ṭāmē'* outside the city (Lev. 14:40,41,45), the place where the sacrificial animal is slaughtered (relative clause; Lev. 4:24,33; 14:13), the place where ashes are poured out (Lev. 4:12; 1:16). These are rubrics from the perspective of the priests, oriented from the interior of the temple outward. The "place" is "sacred" because it belongs to the temple. More specific theological qualification is needed as little here as in the case of the designation of a diseased bodily part as *meqôm haššeḥîn* (Lev. 13:19).[29]

V. Holy Places of the Preceding Ages.

1. A particular *māqôm* may be of interest to tradition because a certain encounter with God occurred there (theophany).

a. In Josh. 5:15 *(hammāqôm 'ašer 'attâ 'ōmēḏ 'ālāw qōḏeš hû')* and Ex. 3:5 (J; with an expanded predicate: *'aḏmaṯ qōḏeš hû';* similarly only in Zec. 2:16[12]) the model of the familiar priestly declaratory formula[30] is applied to a ritual of introduction.

25. Cf. also W. H. Schmidt, *Exodus 1–6. BK,* II/1 (1988), 140f.
26. Cf. C. Westermann, *Genesis 12–36* (Eng. trans., Minneapolis, 1985), 178-181.
27. So K. Elliger, *Leviticus. HAT,* IV (1966), 96 A.22.
28. *Idem.*
29. On this entire complex, cf. Haran, 184-87.
30. Cf. Begrich, *ThB,* 21, 254, n. 157; Schmidt, 158f.

Although theophanies are usually mediated through optical and/or acoustic means, whereupon the person involved reacts appropriately (Jgs. 6:22; 13:22; Ex. 20:19; Dt. 5:23-27; Isa. 6:5), here the manifestation enlists the setting both as scenic development and as intensification. Both Ex. 3:5 and Josh. 5:15 stand in the foreground of the deliverance from Egypt or the entry itself, i.e., within the horizon of the land (Ex. 3:8; *śar ṣᵉḇā' YHWH,* Josh. 5:14,15; with Jericho as the background, Josh. 5:13; 6:1ff.). This piece of earth mediates perhaps typologically and parenetically the holiness both of God and of the land. Whatever the prehistory may have been, those involved with transmitting this tradition were not focused on the subsequent identification of this place as one of Israel's cultic sites. It is no accident that the P-commentary to Ex. 3 (Ex. 6:2-8) does not speak of what for P might be an ambiguous *māqôm.*[31]

b. Gen. 28:11-22 mentions "the *māqôm*" with no prior identification or introduction (v. 11, 3 times),[32] as if it were an already familiar (cultic) place.[33] Both strands of tradition assert that what Jacob recognizes both during the nocturnal experience and in his subsequent conscious reflection is attached to and concentrated in "this *māqôm*" (v. 16 J; v. 17 E).[34] Jacob expresses in words the same feelings and the same confession as do Moses and Joshua through their behavior (Ex. 3:5,6b; Josh. 5:15): contrite admission of one's own ignorance and terror, and a confession of Yahweh's presence. The following acts enduringly imbue the appropriate status, recognition, and confession into the *māqôm* and dedicate it (also) to Yahweh. Other deities who might be worshiped there are not an issue. Even the naming of the *māqôm,* rather than the massebah, as *bêṯ-'ēl* (v. 19 J; cf. 35:15b P?) shows where the focal point lies.

Later tradition is interested primarily in the place itself. In Gen. 35:1,3,7,[35] in connection with other scenes from the patriarchal history, an altar is built there. In Gen. 35:13 (P?[36]) Yahweh departs the *māqôm* after he has spoken (cf. Gen. 17:22), which means that he is present at the *māqôm* for the purpose of or during temporary audiences at a specific time. The place identified by a certain (etiological) name (cf. also Gen. 32:3,31[2,30]), the patriarch, and God become inextricable in their mutual association. Thus does God introduce himself: *'ānōḵî hā'ēl bêṯ-'ēl* (Gen. 31:13 E; cf. the "God of Jerusalem," 2 Ch. 32:19).[37] The naming of the *māqôm* itself with "El of Beth-El" might be the result of conscious replication in connection with place names containing the name *ba'al* (Gen. 35:7),[38] especially since "the Israelites did not name newly

---

31. Cf. Ska, *ZAW,* 94 (1982), 530-548.

32. Cf. Westermann, *Genesis 12–36,* 453-55.

33. Cf. Rendtorff.

34. → ירא *yārē',* VI, 301f.

35. According to K. Jaroš, *Die Stellung des Elohisten zur kanaanäischen Religion. OBO,* 4 (1974), 25, this is to be attributed to E, though it has also been partially reworked by the Deuteronomist.

36. Cf. *BHS.*

37. J. Naveh, "Old Hebrew Inscriptions in a Burial Cave," *IEJ,* 13 (1963), 84f., 90f.; *yhwh šmrn:* Z. Meshel, "Did Yahweh Have a Consort?" *BAR,* 5 (1979), 30f.; "the God who is in Dan": Biran, 142-151.

38. Cf. *BHS.*

founded settlements after their God,"[39] nor indeed did they even found new *m^eqômôṯ*, but rather took over those already existing[40] (cf. *m^eqôm š^eḵem,* Gen. 12:6; a similar construction is found in Jer. 19:13a).

The problematical expression *hinnēh māqôm 'ittî* uttered by God (Ex. 33:21)[41] can perhaps be resolved by reference to the notion that on the top of the mountain Moses situates himself next to Yahweh (Ex. 34:2: *nṣb* hiphil + *lî* + *šām;* 34:5: *nṣb* hithpael + *'immô* + *šām* and the proclamation of Yahweh's name), and Yahweh passes by (*'br,* Ex. 33:19,22-23; 34:6-8; 1 K. 19:11). At the *māqôm,* a piece of land which the authors hardly viewed as an already existing sanctuary, God presents himself to the appointed person. This may also constitute a more moderate interpretation of the harsh principle in Ex. 33:20: *lô-yir'anî hā'āḏām wāḥāy* (cf. the — protective? — cleft in the rock, or cave, in Ex. 33:22; 1 K. 19:9,13).

2. The (etiological) names given to the sites of theophanies or of other significant events in the form of fixed formulas,[42] regardless of whether such sites were already cultic sites according to previous traditions, infuse Israel's identity and tradition, as it were, into the land, and Israel thereby appropriates the land both in an actual and in a theological sense.[43] Such "places" constitute memorials, as shown especially by the (later) literary imitations of this procedure (e.g., Gen. 22:14; Jgs. 18:12; 1 S. 23:28; 2 S. 6:8 par. 1 Ch. 13:11; 1 Ch. 14:11; 2 Ch. 20:26). The term *māqôm* often serves as a substitute and reference; it is not used when other landmarks are already known: wells (Gen. 16:14), erected stones (Gen. 31:47,48), Beer-sheba (Gen. 26:33[44]). Or no name may be given at all, e.g., in the case of the oaks of Mamre. In his own polemic, Amos calls the locales by their actual names (5:4-5; 7:9; 8:14), and has no occasion to use secondary reminiscences or *māqôm* (differently in 2 Ch. 3:1[45]).

VI. Cultic Sites in the Present.

1. *māqôm in the Altar Regulations.* In the "altar regulations" of Ex. 20:24-26 the distributive or collective expression *b^eḵol-hammāqôm*[46] approaches the meaning "everywhere," though with qualitative limitations. The word *māqôm* — with article — might have been prompted associatively by the altars (vv. 24a,25). At issue is the legitimate form of altars, not of buildings, a presumably archaic feature (cf. Josh.

39. W. Borée, *Die alten Ortsnamen Palästinas* (1930, Hildesheim, ^{2}1968), 94.
40. Schmidt, 113.
41. Cf. A. B. Ehrlich, *Randglossen zur hebräischen Bibel* (1908, repr. Hildesheim, 1968), I: *Genesis und Exodus,* 407; J. Jeremias, *WMANT,* 10 (^{2}1977), 202; *KBL*^{3}, 97f.
42. Cf. Key, 55-59.
43. Cf. H. Köster, "τόπος," *TDNT,* VIII, 195f.
44. On Gen. 21:31, cf. Westermann, *Genesis 12–36,* 349.
45. Cf. R. Mosis, *Untersuchungen zur Theologie des chronistischen Geschichtswerkes. FThS,* 92 (1973), 107.
46. Cf. Conrad, 5-7, 9-11, 212; Halbe, 369-383, 421f., 442; → זכר *zāḵār (zākhar),* IV, 74f.

8:30-31; 22; Jgs. 6:24-32; 13:20; 21:4; 1 S. 14:35; 2 S. 24:18,21,25; 1 K. 18:30); neither is the issue exclusively the initial or one-time "revelation,"[47] but rather the remembrance or acknowledgment of Yahweh's "name" (cf. Isa. 26:13; Ex. 23:13; Ps. 16:4).[48] Thus wherever Yahweh is worshiped and proclaimed at an appropriate altar, Yahweh "comes,"[49] or is present.[50] The reference here is not to a selection; rather, a criterion is given for the evaluation of actual *m*^e^*qômôṯ* and of the actual worship service, though this also, of course, constitutes requirement and instruction. That is, it is not the *māqôm* that makes the cult legitimate, but rather the cult that makes the *māqôm* legitimate. "The question of the true cultic place is here programmatically removed from any administratively decreed solution."[51]

Mal. 1:11 goes even further, especially since one must read this passage against the background of the later centralization of the cult. While the expression *bēḵol-māqôm* is adverbial, it is not additive in the cumulative sense, but rather "sweeping" or "all-encompassing." The quality of cultic capability is delimited. Both *muqṭār* and *minḥâ ṭ*^e^*hôrâ* will be real without either external spatial delimitation or specific internal determination. The expressions are unusual, and there is no mention of any cultic accoutrements or organization. Every traditional rubrical sense is eclipsed. There is no longer any topographically circumscribed holy precinct. Although the ultimate consequence would be that the entire world would be *māqôm,*[52] this transcends the word's possibilities.

2. *The māqôm of the Ark.* The Philistines realize that the ark must leave their land and return "to its own *māqôm*" if the disasters befalling them are to end (1 S. 5:11; 6:2; cf. 5:3). The term *māqôm* is not used in reference to the various stages of return (1 S. 6:19–7:1; 2 S. 6:10-11); only when David finally places it back in the tent (2 S. 6:17; cf. in contrast the par. 1 Ch. 16:1; though cf. also 1 Ch. 15:1,3, material exclusive to Chronicles) or Solomon returns it to the temple (1 K. 8:6,7 par. 2 Ch. 5:7,8) is it said to return to "its *māqôm.*" Although reference is occasionally made to this *māqôm* as if to the ark itself (1 K. 8:7 par. 2 Ch. 5:8), this seems to be a figure of speech prompted perhaps by the concern for preserving certain traditions by means of localization even after the ark itself no longer existed.

3. *The Chosen māqôm (Deuteronomic).* The basic framework of the Deuteronomic selection-formula, the standing relative clause *hammāqôm ʾ*^a^*šer yiḇḥar YHWH* (Dt. 12:5; 15:20; 16:15,16; 17:10; 31:11) announces God's (fictional) future act and does not constitute a prescription, not even with its amplifications: *b*^e^*ʾaḥaḏ š*^e^*ḇāṭeyḵā*

---

47. Cf. Halbe, 371-76, contra W. Schottroff, *"Gedenken" im alten Orient und im AT. WMANT,* 15 (²1967), 248.

48. *KAI,* 214, 16, 21.

49. On God's "coming," → בוא *bôʾ,* II, 44-49; → בחר *bāḥar (bāchar),* II, 80f.

50. Concerning the unusual 1st person singular of Yahweh, cf. Halbe, 375f., 481f.

51. Halbe, 379.

52. Cf. R. Pautrel, "Malachie," *DBS,* V (1957), 743-45.

(12:14) or *mikkol-šiḇṭêḵem* (12:5), *lāśûm šᵉmô šām* (12:5,21; 14:24) or *lᵉšakkēn šᵉmô šām* (12:11; 14:23; 16:2,6,11; 26:2; 12:5, *lectio conflata*[53]). The chosen *māqôm* is the sanctioned and obligatory site for sacrifices, offerings, and joyful repast (12:6-7,11b, 14,18,27; 26:2), for the fulfillment of vows (12:26), the delivery or eating of tithes (14:22-23), of the firstlings, the first-born (15:19-20), for the administration of the portions of the priests and Levites (18:6-8), for the main festivals (16:1-17), for judgment in difficult legal cases (17:8,10), and finally for the regular reading of "this Torah" (31:11). Only sections generally judged as later speak about movement from different places and pilgrimages, especially in the summarizing initial verse: *tiḏrᵉšû ûḇā'ṯā šāmmâ* (12:5; cf. 12:26; 14:25; 16:16; also coll. Ex. 23:14,17; 34:23,26). The inner logic of certain new regulations presupposes that the chosen *māqôm* is not (or no longer) situated at one's own dwelling place; such indications include the permission for sacrificial slaughter at one's own home (12:15-16,21; 15:22); financial provisions for certain cases (14:24-26); and concern for Levites from other places (18:6-8).[54] Such measures are justified by the fact that the chosen place is too "far" (12:21; 14:24), a situation itself arising from the fact that, following his promise, God "enlarged" the land through his blessing (12:20; 19:8). The singularity of one cultic site for all Israel, i.e., the strict demand for cultic centralization, does not inhere from the very beginning in this formula,[55] but rather was imbued into it as a result of circumstances.[56] An inadvertent remark in Dt. 12:3 still shows traces of this process: Although the verse speaks of the *mᵉqômôṯ* of the pagans which are to be demolished (only here does the word refer unequivocally to pagan cultic sites[57] and include a description), it ends with a syntactically problematical reference to a certain *māqôm (min-hammāqôm hahû')*. Apparently the notion of the single *māqôm* asserted itself here by sheer force.[58] The ultimately unexplained fact that the *māqôm* in Deuteronomy was never given a name may be a result of, among other things, the fundamental nature precisely of the incomplete formula itself: Yahweh's selection is the primary issue. According to one series of admonitions the pagan cultic sites are to be avoided (12:8,13,30,31; 2 K. 17:33), and on the other hand they are to be physically demolished (12:2f.). 12:3b interprets this as the destruction of "their [the gods portrayed on the graven images] names" (*'bd* piel as at the beginning, v. 2a). The idea that the "names" of the others are to be removed is not new to this context (Dt. 7:24; Hos. 2:19[17]; Zeph. 1:4; cf. Ps. 9:6[5]; Zec. 13:2). 1 K. 8:27 literally calls into question the older, unaffected notion that Yahweh dwells in the temple and "on the earth" (cf. 1 K. 8:12,13). According to Deuteronomy God chooses the place to "make his name dwell there" (*škn* piel; Dt. 12:11) or to "lie down there" *(śwm)*, whereby it remains unresolved whether one must refer here to an actual Deuteronomic "name

53. Cf. Weippert, 93; Halpern, 23f.
54. Cf. H. D. Preuss, *Deuteronomium. EdF,* 164 (1982), 118.
55. So Fenton.
56. Halpern, 36f.
57. Reventlow, 177f.
58. Cf. Halbe, 112f.

theology"[59] or not.[60] Outside the Deuteronomic parenesis itself many (Deuteronomistic) variations occur without the term *māqôm* (1 K. 8:43,44,48; 11:13,32; 14:21; 2 K. 21:7; 23:27; 2 Ch. 6:33,38; 33:7; Jer. 7:10,11,14,30; 32:34; 34:15). The historicizing expression *'el hammāqôm 'ᵃšer 'āmartā yihyeh šᵉmî šām* (occurring only in 1 K. 8:29; cf. Neh. 1:9) remains close to the Deuteronomic form, while the parallel 2 Ch. 6:20 is more reserved: *'el hammāqôm 'ᵃšer 'āmartā lāśûm šimkā šām* (analogous expressions without *māqôm* occur in 2 K. 21:4 par. 2 Ch. 33:4; 2 K. 23:27; 2 Ch. 6:6; 20:9). Only in the material exclusive to Chronicles in 2 Ch. 7:12 has the Deuteronomic formula been cultically fixed in the extreme: *ûḇāḥartî bammāqôm hazzeh lî lᵉḇêṯ zāḇaḥ,* while the corresponding passage in 1 K. 9:3 only speaks of the prayer *lᵉpānay.*

4. *"My māqôm in šîlô" (Jer. 7:12).* In the expression *mᵉqômî 'ᵃšer bᵉšîlô . . . bāri'šônâ* (Jer. 7:12) *māqôm* refers with rare explicitness to a circumscribed holy precinct, the temple, located in but not identical with Shiloh.[61] When Shiloh is not mentioned by name, it is referred to only as *māqôm,* perhaps because the appropriate organization and accoutrements are absent. The consistent use of *bayiṯ* for Jerusalem (7:10,11,14; 26:6), the contextually unusual relative clause following *māqôm,* and the emphatic *bāri'šônâ* all emphasize the difference between the (former) Shiloh and the (present) Jerusalem, but do so such that every legitimate sanctuary — including Jerusalem — can be destroyed if the people disregard Yahweh's claim (notwithstanding, e.g., Jer. 7:7b). Thus amid its destruction the *māqôm* of Shiloh yet remains an unnerving illustration of God's judgment (cf. Jer. 26:6).

5. *Ambiguity (Deuteronomistic and Later).* In the book of Jeremiah, particularly, it seems, in the sections affected by Deuteronomistic redaction, the term *māqôm* hovers with a certain ambiguity between the Jerusalem temple, Topheth (7:32; 19:6-14), the city, and the land.[62] This can hardly be viewed as merely the unintentional result of literary development; rather, later readers, in the shadow of the great catastrophe, expanded to all of Israel the threats which in what was probably original, authentic Jeremianic material had only been directed at the temple.[63] This semantic ambiguity coincides with the existing circumstances, which though hardly articulated can nonetheless be illustrated by various examples. In Jeremiah alone the expression *hammāqôm hazzeh* occurs at least 30 times in all the aforementioned contexts. Within the framework of Deuteronomy (1:31; 9:7; 11:5; 29:6[7]) it refers to the decisive setting at the end of the wilderness wanderings, immediately before entry into the land. Following this situation Dt. 26:9 speaks of the sanctuary in a formulation evoking the notion of being

---

59. Cf. M. Weinfeld, *Deuteronomy and the Deuteronomic School* (1972, repr. Winona Lake, 1992), 193f.; Halpern, *passim.*

60. Cf. R. de Vaux, *BZAW,* 105 (1967), 219-228.

61. W. Thiel, *Die deuteronomistische Redaktion von Jeremia 1–25. WMANT,* 41 (1973), 112f.

62. Cf. van Wyk.

63. Cf. Thiel, 224; M. Rose, *Der Ausschliesslichkeitsanspruch Jahwes. BWANT,* 106[6/6] (1975), 217-220.

led there. The reference within the historical overview is to the land itself (1 S. 12:8). In other Deuteronomistic passages it refers to the temple (1 K. 8:30,35), and in Huldah's utterance and its expansions to the temple along with the city, not excluding the land (2 K. 22:16,17,19,20). In Zeph. 1:4 the expression (as a secondary limitation?) is probably concentrating judgment on the temple.[64] In Hag. 2:9 God proclaims the temple (and Jerusalem?) as the earthly center of worldwide *šālôm.*[65] In other contexts, too, *māqôm* sometimes hovers between the meanings temple and land (2 S. 7:10 par. 1 Ch. 17:9; Ex. 23:20b). The expression *hammāqôm hazzeh* occurs without any theological connection only in 1 K. 13:8,16 (Bethel) and 2 K. 6:9 (military tactics).

VII. Metaphorical Usage. The term *māqôm* is used metaphorically in various poetic and prophetic contexts to refer to the sanctuary.

1. *Elements of the Earthly Sanctuary.* The expression *t^e^pillaṯ hammāqôm hazzeh* (2 Ch. 7:15; 6:40; material exclusive to Chronicles) is not really a metaphor, but employs rather the notion of the "house of prayer" (Isa. 56:7; cf. Jer. 7:11). Isa. 18:7c, *m^e^qôm šēm YHWH ṣ^e^ḇā'ôṯ har ṣiyyôn,* possibly the source of the Deuteronomic name formula, is a theological confession to Zion (cf. Ps. 68:30[29]; Isa. 8:18[66]). Poetically David seeks a *māqôm* for Yahweh as or for his *miškānôṯ* (Ps. 132:5; cf. 78:60). Yahweh answers by choosing Zion (Pss. 132:13a; 78:68), spontaneously and as a result of unfathomable "love" (Pss. 132:13b,14b; 78:68b), to be his habitation (*yšb,* Ps. 132:13b,14b) and resting place (*m^e^nûḥāṯî:* Ps. 132:8a,14a; cf. 78:69). This constitutes a development of the notion of Zion as the final *māqôm* of the ark (2 S. 6:1-19; 7:2,7; 1 K. 8:1-13; cf. Ps. 132:7-8; Nu. 10:35-36). Despite the close connection between temple, dynasty, and residence, the term *māqôm* is never used to refer to the latter, even though virtually everything constituting the external, public prestige of that center uses the word for the sake of localization, either because of its dramatic effect or as a syntactical device serving the simultaneous celebration of the greatness both of the temple and of the near God. For Ezekiel, Yahweh's *kāḇôḏ* rises *mimm^e^qômô* (Ezk. 3:12; cf. *BHS*). Notions of Yahweh's dignity are combined: *m^e^qôm kis'î . . . m^e^qôm kappôṯ raglay* (Ezk. 43:7; cf. Isa. 6:1); *kissē' kāḇôḏ . . . m^e^qôm miqdāšēnû* (Jer. 17:12; cf. 3:17); a more clearly eschatological reference: the return of former glory *l^e^pā'ēr m^e^qôm miqdāšî ûm^e^qôm raglay '^a^kabbēḏ* (Isa. 60:13; cf. 14). The term *māqôm* thus becomes a kind of logogram for the Zion theology with its transcendent dimension.[67]

2. *Independent Usage.* Some doxologies and theophanies with no reference to the temple of Zion transcend these parameters. Yahweh's works are exhorted to praise him *b^e^kol-m^e^qōmôṯ memšaltô* (Ps. 103:22). This rather weak localization probably results from the hymnic élan that recognizes no conceivable boundaries (cf. Pss. 96:9-13;

---

64. Cf. W. Rudolph, *Micha, Nahum, Habakuk, Zephanja. KAT,* XIII/3 (1975), 262.
65. Cf. W. Rudolph, *Haggai, Sacharja 1–8, 9–14, Maleachi. KAT,* XIII/4 (1976), 43.
66. H. Wildberger, *Isaiah 1–12* (Eng. trans., Minneapolis, 1991), 370.
67. Cf. Mettinger, 24-32.

98:4-9). Only once in Solomon's prayer of dedication is heaven referred as *m^eqôm šib̲t^ek̲ā* (1 K. 8:30 par. 2 Ch. 6:21; cf. 1 K. 8:39,43,49 par. 2 Ch. 6:30,33,39), influenced perhaps by the two immediately preceding occurrences (?). Do Deuteronomistic ears perceive the term *māqôm* as being too earthbound or limited?[68] In Isa. 26:21 and Mic. 1:3 God comes forth to judgment: *yōṣēʾ mimm^eqômô*. In Mic. 1:3 the reference can hardly be taken to mean anything other than that he comes forth from heaven, since God enters the world from outside.[69] Since this is not as unequivocal in Isaiah, some suggest that God comes forth from the temple, Zion,[70] though without being able to disprove the opposite view.[71] The question is justified whether such attempts at a more precise identification of locale perhaps fail to recognize the intentional ambiguity and poetically suggestive character of the passage.

In Hos. 5:15 God announces that as punishment he will withdraw *ʾel-m^eqômî* until the people repent. An identification of this place as Zion or the temple is an utter impossibility.

3. *God Himself?* On the whole, the term *māqôm* in its theological usage rarely occurs apart from some connection with the temple theology. As a mediating auxiliary term it relativizes limitations that may seem excessively earthbound or vivid, so that under the influence of altered perceptions new readings are facilitated. To a certain extent it functions as do other various abstract or indefinite, though indispensable terms from our theological language, and lends itself to overcoming the limitations of mere sense perception. From this perspective the interpretation of the famous *māqôm ʾaḥēr* in Est. 4:14 as God seems in order.[72]

Gamberoni

VIII. Qumran. The writings of Qumran offer virtually nothing new concerning the use of *māqôm*. We read about the place where ten men are present (1QS 6:3,6; CD 13:12) and about the place where the army is assembled (1QM 19:9; 1Q33 2:4; cf. 1QM 14:3). In a couple of instances *māqôm* parallels *maʿ^amād̲* in reference to the place or rank occupied by the individual within the community (1QS 2:23; cf. CD 13:12). In 1QS 8:8 the congregation is described as a plantation and a temple that will not sway *(mûš)* from its place. In 1QM 7:7 and 11QTemple 46:13, as in Dt. 23:13, the *m^eqôm yād̲* is the latrine. The 23 occurrences in the Temple Scroll include several references to the chosen place (42:9,16; 53:9; 56:5; 60:13), as well as references to places set apart for a particular purpose *(mub̲dāl)* (15:12; 35:13). In addition, *māqôm* is used in a general sense to refer to places in the temple, outside the city, for burial, and so on.

Ringgren

---

68. Cf. Metzger.
69. Cf. Rudolph, *KAT,* XIII/3, 40.
70. H. Wildberger, *Jesaja 13–27. BK,* X/2 (1978), 999.
71. Jeremias, 19.
72. Cf. Ackroyd, 82-84; on this understanding in the Targums, cf. C. A. Moore, *Esther. AB,* VII B (1971), 50; G. Gerleman, *Esther. BK,* XXI/2 ([2]1982), 19.

מָקוֹר *māqôr*

Contents: I. Etymology. II. Occurrences, LXX. III. OT Usage. IV. Qumran.

I. Etymology. The etymology of *māqôr* is not entirely clear. It looks like a *ma*-construction from *qwr.* A verb *qûr* is attested in Hebrew only in 2 K. 19:24 par. Isa. 37:25: *qartî wᵉšāṯîṯî mayim,* "I dug wells and drank water." If *qûr* means "to dig for water," then *māqôr* in the sense of "spring" or "well" might derive from it. The equivalents of Heb. *qûr* in other languages are uncertain: Arab. *qāra* means not only "to make a round hole,"[1] but probably even more specifically "to cut a hole in fabric" and also "to cut (a melon) into round slices," "to walk on tiptoes," etc., cases which hardly seem to exhibit any connection with "spring, fountain"; although OSA *wqr* does mean "to split,"[2] it also means "to sculpt";[3] a connection with Heb. *nāqar,* Jewish-Aram., Syr. *nᵉqar,* "to poke out, pick out," Arab. *naqara,* "to hollow out," can be established by the assumption of a root *qr* which has been expanded by various means. An unequivocal correspondence is found only in Ugaritic, where *qr* and *mqr* both mean "spring, fountain," or something similar[4]: *qr ʿnk,* "the spring of your eye" in reference to the source of tears;[5] *b.mqr mmlʾt,* "[women,] who fill [their buckets] from the fountain [the well]"[6] par. *bnpk šîbt,* "those who draw from the fountain," whereby *npk* is to be associated with *nbk* and *mbk* (Heb. *nēḇeḵ* and *mabbāḵ*).[7] Syr. *maqûra,* "cistern," is probably a Canaanite loanword.[8] Although *KBL*³ also adduces Egyp. *ḳrr.t,* "cave," a more likely candidate would be *ḳr.t,* "spring, source" (in reference to, among other things, the "two sources" of the Nile).

II. Occurrences, LXX. The term *māqôr* occurs 18 times in the OT (Ps. 68:27[Eng. v. 26] is uncertain), as well as twice in Sirach. With the exception of 3 occurrences in Leviticus with the specialized meaning "blood flow," the word occurs only in poetic texts: 7 times in Proverbs, twice in the Psalms, 4 times in Jeremiah, and once each in Hosea and Zechariah.

The LXX translates almost exclusively with *pēgḗ: phléps,* "vein," is used in Hos. 13:15, once also *rýsis,* and both Sirach passages show a variant text form.

---

1. So *KBL*³.
2. *KBL*³.
3. ContiRossini, 140.
4. *WUS,* no. 2443.
5. *KTU,* 1.16 I, 27.
6. *KTU,* 1.14 V, 2; the parallel III, 9 has *bbqr*!
7. *WUS,* no. 1738.
8. H. Bauer, "Überreste der kanaanäischen Unterschicht in den aramäischen Sprachen," *OLZ,* 29 (1926), 801.

III. OT Usage. Twice *māqôr* parallels *maʿyān,* "spring, source": on the one hand in Hos. 13:15, where we read that the east wind, representing Yahweh's coming judgment, will dry up (the MT has a form of *bôš,* read *ybš*) the *māqôr* in Ephraim–northern Israel and parch *(ḥrb)* its spring *(maʿyān);* and on the other in Prov. 25:26, where a righteous person who falters before the wicked is compared with a muddled spring *(maʿyān)* and a polluted fountain: When a righteous person cannot assert himself over against the wicked, he is like a fountain or spring rendered unusable, i.e., the expected function is absent. The term *māqôr* is also used with a purely concrete reference in Jer. 51:36: Yahweh causes the river (*yām* in reference to the Euphrates as in Isa. 18:2; 19:5 for the Nile) of Babylon to run dry *(ḥrb)* and its fountain or spring to dry up *(ybš).* As in Hos. 13:15, the disruption of the water supply is expressed by the two verbs *ybš* and *ḥrb,* presented in both instances as a result of Yahweh's chastising judgment.

Deutero-Zechariah's vision for the future foretells for the house of David and the inhabitants of Jerusalem an open fountain "for *(l*^{e}*),*" i.e., for the purpose of cleansing them from sin and uncleanness (Zec. 13:1). The reference is to a purificatory ritual washing in the water from the spring which Yahweh — perhaps under the temple, as in Ezk. 47:1ff.; Joel 4:18(3:18) — will cause to come forth.

The Hebrew text of Sir. 43:20 is problematical. In connection with praise of God's revelations in nature we read: "The cold north wind blows, and the fountains (Heb. *m*^{e}*qôrô;* the LXX has "water"; read *m*^{e}*qôrôṯ*) freeze to ice (read with LXX *qeraḥ* instead of *rqb*)."

Jeremiah's lament uses *māqôr* in the metaphorical sense (Jer. 8:23[9:1]): "O that my head were waters, and my eyes a fountain of tears, that I might weep day and night for the slain of the daughter of my people!" The prophet's profound sympathy with his people breaks forth here in the wish that he might be able to weep sufficiently over the people's suffering. A different image emerges in Sir. 10:13: "For an accumulation (*miqweh* as in Gen. 1:10 in reference to the sea) of pride *(zāḏôn)* is sin (LXX and Peshitta: "For the beginning of sin is pride"), and its fountain causes abomination *(zimmâ)* to pour forth." According to v. 12, sin is apostasy from God, whence emerges a sea of pride which like a fountain causes abominable acts to gush forth. The essence of sin is hybris, and from that hybris all sinful deeds flow.

In Prov. 5:18 *māqôr* is used as a symbolic expression for "the wife of your youth," to which the wisdom apprentice should hold fast so that strangers not enjoy it. In vv. 15ff. the same reference is made with *bôr, b*^{e}*'ēr,* and *maʿyān.* The question is whether this admonition is merely an admonition to exercise marital fidelity or is to be taken allegorically as a warning against foolishness ("the strange [loose] woman").[9]

According to Ps. 36:10(9) "the fountain of life" *(m*^{e}*qôr ḥayyim)* is with *(ʿim)* Yahweh, as explained in the second half of the verse: "In thy light do we see light,"[10]

---

9. → זור *zûr,* זר *zār,* IV, 56; cf. H. Ringgren, *Sprüche. ATD,* XVI/1 (^{3}1980), 30.
10. → אור *'ôr,* III.1.c (I, 161).

i.e., it is Yahweh who bestows blessing. The preceding v. 9(8) indicates that this experience of blessing comes about in the temple worship service.

Several proverbs apply the attribute "fountain of life" to wisdom. "The teaching *(tôrâ)* of the wise is a fountain of life, that one may avoid the snares of death" (Prov. 13:14), i.e., whoever heeds the admonitions of the wise will enjoy success and a happy life. 14:27 says the same thing about the fear of Yahweh. Although it is possible that this statement represents a later, "religious" stage of wisdom thought, the collectors of the proverbs apparently viewed wisdom and the fear of God as being fundamentally the same. Prov. 16:22 uses the term *śēkel,* "insight," for wisdom, though the content is the same: It is beneficial to life. The background for this image, of course, is the general observation that a fountain yields water and thus life, though it should be pointed out that wisdom is associated with life in other ways as well: as the way or path of life (Prov. 2:19; 5:6; 6:23; 15:24), or as the tree of life (Prov. 3:18; cf. 15:4).[11]

The mouth, i.e., the words of the righteous, can also be called a fountain of life (Prov. 10:11); the antithesis in v. 11b shows what is meant: The mouth of the wicked conceals violence. In other words, wise speech is beneficial to life, wicked speech detrimental.[12] Prov. 18:4 also speaks about such words, though here they are called the "fountain of wisdom" (the LXX, however, reads "fountain of life" here as well[13]).

Jeremiah juxtaposes Yahweh himself as a fountain of living (i.e., fresh) water over against the idols which are like broken cisterns (Jer. 2:13). Forsaking Yahweh is as foolish as trying to quench one's thirst with stale water, and from a leaking cistern at that.[14] This expression recurs in Jer. 17:13, a small pericope (vv. 12f.) that probably does not come from Jeremiah himself even though its mode of expression is at least in part Jeremianic. Here Yahweh, present in the temple, is called the fountain of living water (i.e., of life), while all who forsake him are put to shame.

Ps. 68:27(26) is doubtful. Here the cultic congregation receives the predicate *mimmᵉqôr yiśrā'ēl,* which can hardly be the correct reading. One should probably read *miqrā'ê* with *bᵉ:* "in the congregations of Israel."

Finally, in Leviticus the blood of the menstruating woman (Lev. 20:18) or of the woman in childbed (12:7) is called *mᵉqôr dāmîm;* in both cases blood is viewed as unclean.

IV. Qumran. The term *māqôr* occurs fairly frequently in the Qumran writings. The dualistic community rule speaks of "the fountain *(ma'yān)* of light and the source of darkness," from which truth or wickedness comes (1QS 3:19). The combination *māqôr — ma'yān* occurs elsewhere as well: God is the "fountain of knowledge *(dē'â)* and the source *(ma'yān)* of holiness" (1QS 10:12); he is "a fountain of righteousness, a reservoir

---

11. → חיה *ḥāyâ (chāyāh),* IV, 335.
12. On this passage, cf. W. Bühlmann, *Vom rechten Reden und Schweigen. OBO,* 12 (1976), 270ff.
13. *Ibid.,* 275f.
14. W. Rudolph, *Jeremia. HAT,* XII (³1968), 17.

(miqweh, cf. the previous discussion of Sir. 10:13) and a spring *(ma'yān)* of glory *(kāḇôḏ)*" (1QS 11:6f.). "My light has sprung from the source of his knowledge" (1QS 11:3; cf. Ps. 36:10[9]), "from the source of his righteousness is my justification *(mišpāṭ),* and from his marvelous mysteries is the light in my heart" (1QS 11:5). Thus does God emerge as the source of all that is good.

In the thanksgiving hymn 1QH 8:4ff. the singer describes himself as "a fountain of streams in an arid land (Isa. 44:3) and a spring of waters *(mabbûa' mayim)* in a dry land (Isa. 35:7; cf. 41:18)," i.e., his teaching bestows life upon the believers. This metaphor is continued in what follows. All animals find nourishment at the everlasting spring *(mᵉqôr 'ôlām)* (8:8), all trees take root, and a new Eden emerges (several allusions, e.g., 8:20: the "everlasting spring as an Eden ['*ēḏen*] of glory"). In conclusion the singer asserts: "By my hand thou hast opened for them a well-spring" (8:21; on the open well-spring cf. Zech. 13:1). Several references are made to this opening of the spring, e.g., 1QH 2:18: "thou hast put teaching and understanding, that I might open a fountain of knowledge to all men of insight"; 18:10: "thou didst open a fountain in the mouth of thy servant"; cf. 11:19: "a fountain of bitter mourning opens for me" (negative); 10:31: "my heart shall be open to the everlasting fountain"; cf. also 18:12f.

There is also, however, a fountain of uncleanness, as shown, e.g., by 1QH 1:22, which describes human beings as, among other things, *sôḏ 'erwâ* and *mᵉqôr niddâ.* Since *niddâ* refers in the OT to menstruation, it seems logical to interpret *māqôr* against the backdrop of Lev. 20:18 and to understand the real meaning of the expression as "menstrual blood." One is then tempted to read *sôḏ 'erwâ* as *sôr* . . . and to translate "filth (froth) of shame." We would then have two expressions for sexual impurity as images for human sinfulness. 1QH 12:25 speaks similarly about the "source of uncleanness and of shameful disgrace" (*qālôn*)" in a description of human beings. The War Scroll (1QM 7:6) is clearly referring to sexual uncleanness when it stipulates that no man "who is impure because of his *māqôr*" may take part in battle, since holy angels will be taking part as well.

Ringgren

מַקֵּל *maqqēl*

Contents: I. Etymology. II. OT Usage: 1. Riding Crop; 2. Shepherd's Staff; 3. As a Weapon of War; 4. As a Symbol of Dominion; 5. The Almond Branch in Jer. 1:11; 6. In Soothsaying; 7. Gen. 30:37-43. III. LXX.

---

maqqēl. H. Bonnet, *Die Waffen der Völker des alten Orients* (Leipzig, 1926); E. Power, "The Shepherd's Two Rods in Modern Palestine and in Some Passages of the OT," *Bibl,* 9 (1928), 434-442; G. Sauer, "Mandelzweig und Kessel in Jer $1_{11ff.}$," *ZAW,* 78 (1966), 56-61; G. von Welsenburg, *Das Versehen der Frauen in Vergangenheit und Gegenwart* (Leipzig, 1899); P. S. Wood, "Jeremiah's Figure of the Almond Rod," *JBL,* 61 (1942), 99-103.

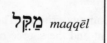

I. Etymology. The etymology of *maqqēl* is uncertain. Earlier scholars derive it from *qll,* "to shake (the staff used during the oracle of the lot)"[1] (cf. Ezk. 21:26) or from a stem *qlw* attested in Arab. *qalā,* "to drive" (thus: "driving stick").[2] Others associate it with the root *bql* attested in many of the Semitic languages[3]: Arab. and Ethiop. *baqala,* "to sprout"; cf. Arab. *baql,* "growth, herb, plant," Akk. *baqlu,* "sprout,"[4] Syr. *buqlā',* "sprout," Ethiop. *baq^{w}el,* "herb, plant"; Akk. *buqlu,* on the other hand, means "malt"[5] (cf. Ugar. *bql,* "groats[?]"[6]).

Considering, however, that *maqqēl* occurs as a loanword in Egyptian in the form *maqira,*[7] it should probably be understood as a West Semitic primary noun.

Its semantic field includes → מטה *maṭṭeh,* → שׁבט *šēḇeṭ,* and *maš'ēn.*[8]

II. OT Usage. The term *maqqēl* refers to a somewhat slender branch, though rarely such a branch in its natural condition; that is, it is usually an implement of some sort or is used symbolically.

1. *Riding Crop.* Balaam used a *maqqēl* to drive the ass he was riding (*nāṭâ,* Nu. 22). He struck it (*nkh* hiphil, vv. 23,25,28,32) when it refused to obey him, and the context seems to indicate that he used his rod in an unusually harsh manner.

2. *Shepherd's Staff.* When little David set out to meet the heavily armed Goliath (1 S. 17), he was equipped with his *maqqēl,* a shepherd's bag (*yalqûṭ,* explicated by *k^{e}lî hārō'îm*[9]) with five carefully chosen stones and a sling *(qela').* Goliath's remark, "Am I a dog, that you come to me with sticks (*maqlôṯ,* v. 43)," expresses his disdain for his seemingly weak opponent, and suggests that he took the rod in David's hand to be David's only weapon, in contrast to his own conventional weapons (vv. 5-7,45,47,51; cf. 2 S. 23:21, *ḥ^{a}nîṯ — šēḇeṭ*); the remark also presupposes that a *maqqēl* was normally used to drive away attacking animals. This is precisely the situation David presents to Saul with some exaggeration in order to impress him (vv. 32-37; cf. Am. 3:12; Isa. 31:4). David goes into battle with the equipment of a shepherd (on the rod, cf. Zec. 11:7,10,14; on the bag with stones, cf. the pouch [*ṣ^{e}rôr*] in 1 S. 25:29;[10] on the sling cf. 1 S. 25:29). In view of the many examples in which a battle is won by means of the cunning of an individual or of a small band, it is likely that the narrator wanted to portray David as cunning (cf. 2 S.

---

1. F. Schwally, "Miscellen: 2. קָלַל, מַקֵּל," *ZAW,* 11 (1891), 170f.
2. L. Kopf, "Arabische Etymologien und Parallelen," *VT,* 8 (1958), 186 = *Studies in Arabic and Hebrew Lexicography* (Jerusalem, 1976).
3. On the interchange of *b* and *m,* cf. S. Moscati, *An Introduction to the Comparative Grammar of the Semitic Languages. PLO,* N.S. 6 (^{2}1969), 8, 8.
4. *AHw,* I (1965), 105.
5. *AHw,* I, 139.
6. *WUS,* no. 556.
7. W. F. Albright, *The Vocalization of the Egyptian Syllabic Orthography. AOS,* 5 (1934), 45.
8. Cf. Sauer, 58.
9. Cf. H. J. Stoebe, "Die Goliathperikope 1 Sam. XVII 1–XVIII 5 und die Textform der Septuaginta," *VT,* 6 (1956), 409.
10. Cf. also O. Eissfeldt, *Der Beutel der Lebendigen. BSAW,* 105/6 (1960).

21:19; 1 Ch. 20:5): His appearance as a shepherd distracts Goliath's attention from his real weapon, which he conceals in an unexpected place.

Neither Gen. 32:11(Eng. v. 10) nor Ex. 12:11 indicates more specifically the purpose of the rods or staffs (as a defense weapon?), though in both cases a journey is involved (Jacob leaves Canaan, the Israelites in Egypt prepare to depart). Jacob mentions his *maqqēl* as a sign of his earlier low status *(bᵉmaqlî ʿāḇartî)* in contrast to his present greatness *(hāyîṯî lišnê maḥᵃnôṯ)*.

The term *maqqēl* occurs with figurative meaning as a shepherd's staff in Zec. 11:7,10,14. The shepherd = the prophet/Yahweh takes two staffs, which he calls *nōʿam* and *ḥōḇᵉlîm,* and tends the sheep = the people *(rāʿâ ʾeṯ-haṣṣōʾn).* The names allude to the shepherd's dual function: first, to protect the animals against external danger (*nōʿam,* "grace"), and second, to keep the herd together (*ḥōḇᵉlîm,* "connection, unity"). The decision the prophet/Yahweh makes to annul the covenant guaranteeing the people protection against foreign nations is expressed by the breaking *(gāḏaʿ)* of the *nōʿam*-staff (v. 10). The annulment of the brotherhood between Judah and Israel is symbolized by the breaking of the *ḥōḇᵉlîm*-staff (v. 14). This results in a situation quite the opposite of that in Ezk. 34:11-16, where the promised *nōʿam*-relationship with the people is depicted in shepherding terminology, and of that in Ezk. 37:16-28, where the *ḥōḇᵉlîm*-relationship is expressed by the joining together of two wooden sticks *(ʿēṣ . . . lîhûḏâ wᵉliḇnê yiśrāʾēl ḥᵃḇērāw* and *ʿēṣ . . . lᵉyôsēp ʿēṣ ʾeprayim wᵉkol-bêṯ yiśrāʾēl ḥᵃḇērāw)* into a single staff (*lᵉʿēṣ ʾeḥāḏ wᵉhāyû laʾᵃḥāḏîm bᵉyāḏeḵā,* vv. 16f.).

3. *As a Weapon of War.* The term *maqqēl* occurs once in an enumeration of war booty which Israel is to burn after its victory (shields, bows, arrows, *maqqēl yāḏ* and spears, Ezk. 39:9). A striking stick for individual combat is not attested in the ancient Near East, though it does occur in Egypt; significantly, Ezk. 39:9 is referring to the weapons of a foreign (Scythian?) people (Magog).[11] Other scholars take *maqqēl yāḏ* to refer to a sharpened staff, possibly with an iron tip and comparable perhaps to the *maṭṭeh* of 1 S. 14:43.[12]

4. *As a Symbol of Dominion.* The expression *maqqēl tip̄ʾārâ* as a symbol of dominion parallels *maṭṭēh ʿōz* in Jer. 48:17, a passage referring to the fall of Moab. The lament *ʾêḵâ nišbar maṭṭēh ʿōz maqqēl tip̄ʾārâ* recalls the beginning of the song about the fall of the Babylonian king in Isa. 14:4b,5: *ʾêḵ . . . šāḇar YHWH maṭṭēh rᵉšāʿîm šēḇeṭ mōšᵉlîm.* Ezk. 19:10-14 shows that *maṭṭeh* and *šēḇeṭ* could also be understood as fresh tree branches.[13]

5. *The Almond Branch in Jer. 1:11.* In one of his visions Jeremiah sees an almond branch (*maqqēl šāqēḏ,* Jer. 1:11; "rod of almond," so RSV). The interpretation of the vision (*šōqēḏ ʾᵃnî ʿal dᵉḇārî laʿᵃśōṯô,* v. 12) shows that the association "almond branch

11. Bonnet, 1f.

12. W. Zimmerli, *Ezekiel 2. Herm* (Eng. trans. 1983), *in loc.*

13. Cf. G. Widengren, *The King and the Tree of Life in Ancient Near Eastern Religion. UUÅ,* 1951/4, 37.

(šāqēḏ) — to watch (over the performance of the word)" is the primary one. If, however, that were the only association evoked by the prophet, one would have to ask why the vision is limited to one branch of the tree. It is likely that the notions of shepherding and ruling evoked by *maqqēl* also played a part in the prophet's psychological process, so that Yahweh's protection and power also resonate as a presupposition and guarantee of the fulfillment of his word. G. Sauer[14] argues similarly by referring to the origin of the *maqqēl* in divination. It is not the word conjured by the oracle sticks which endures; Yahweh himself will watch over his own word.

6. *In Soothsaying.* Hos. 4:12 reproves the use of a *maqqēl* for divination, though the exact procedure cannot be specified more closely. The parallel *b*ᵉ*ʿēṣô yišʾāl* is just as indefinite as *maqlô yaggîḏ lô*. The first expression might refer to the kind of procedure mentioned in Nu. 17 and Isa. 17:10f., where conclusions are drawn based on whether a rod does or does not blossom. The reference might also be to the techniques of rhabdomancy (cf. Ezk. 21:26f.[21f.]).[15] Perhaps these are two expressions for the same thing.[16] In any case, the mention of *maqqēl* excludes any interpretation as the oracular practice involving holy trees and Asherim.[17]

7. *Gen. 30:37-43.* A praiseworthy example of the cunning of a patriarch is recounted in Gen. 30:37-43, which tells how Jacob established a great flock of speckled and spotted animals. During breeding he lay fresh[18] rods *(maqlôṯ),* which he made striped by peeling white streaks in them, into the watering troughs from which the flocks drank. This is obviously an example of the popular notion of being frightened at the sight of a person or thing during pregnancy, i.e., the notion that the development of a fetus is influenced by what the mother (human being or animal) sees or otherwise experiences at conception and during pregnancy.[19]

III. LXX. The LXX usually translates *maqqēl* with *rhábdos,* though occasionally also with *baktēría*. In 1 S. 17:43 the LXX includes the addendum: *(en rhábdǭ) kaí líthois; kaí eípen Dauid ouchí all' ḗ cheírō kynós.*

André

14. P. 59.

15. → קסם *qsm.*

16. Cf. S. Küchler, "Das priesterliche Orakel in Israel und Juda," *Abhandlungen zur semitischen Religionskunde und Sprachwissenschaft. Festschrift G. von Baudissin. BZAW,* 33 (1918), 292f.

17. T. H. Robinson, *Die Zwölf Kleinen Propheten: Hosea bis Micha. HAT,* XIV (²1954), *in loc.*

18. → לח *laḥ* (VII, 512-17).

19. Cf. B. Kummer, "Schwangerschaft," in H. Bächtold-Stäubli, ed., *Handwörterbuch des deutschen Aberglaubens,* VII (Berlin, 1927), 1406-1427, esp. 1422.

מִקְלָט *miqlāṭ*

Contents: I. Etymology, Meaning. II. Legal Regulations Regarding Asylum in Israel: 1. Before the Priestly Source; 2. In the Priestly Source. III. Summary. IV. LXX.

I. Etymology, Meaning. The word *miqlāṭ* derives from the root *qlṭ,* attested with a double meaning in Middle Hebrew. Based possibly on an original meaning of "to separate, divide, cut off," in its passive form the verb exhibits the meaning "cut off, not fully developed." The term *qālûṭ* is used with this meaning once in the Bible (Lev. 22:23). In contradistinction with *śārû(a)ʿ* (the stem has the fundamental meaning "to stretch out, extend"), *qālûṭ* probably refers to the malformation consisting in the shortening of a particular bodily part (cf. LXX: *kolobókerkos,* "with a docked tail"). This meaning is also suggested by Arab. *qalaṣa* (change from *ṭ* to *ṣ*), "to contract, shrink, draw in."

On the other hand, the substantive *miqlāṭ* attests a root *qlṭ* suggested by Jewish-Aramaic with the meaning "to take up, harbor." The verb is used in this sense in connection with rainwater, grafting, and male semen.

The substantive derived from this root, *miqlāṭ,* occurs 20 times in the Bible, the occurrences being limited to later strata and to only a few chapters: Nu. 35; Josh. 20f.; 1 Ch. 6. The word always refers to the cities into which a person who has unintentionally killed another person can flee and be taken in. Thus in the majority of cases the word occurs in the combination *ʿārê (ham)miqlāṭ,* "cities of refuge." The term *miqlāṭ* thus means "(place of) refuge" or — expressed in legal terminology — "(place of) asylum." It should be pointed out that in the Bible the term *miqlāṭ* is not used to refer to every kind of asylum, but rather in a limited fashion only to that involving manslaughter.

II. Legal Regulations Regarding Asylum in Israel. The notion of asylum is rooted in the experience of Israel's early legal circumstances. The family unit, grounded in the clan-based community, guaranteed both the personal development and legal protection of each individual. When this intact sphere was disrupted, the avenger of blood

---

miqlāṭ. M. David, "Die Bestimmungen über die Asylstädte in Josua XX," *OTS,* 9 (1951), 30-48; L. Delekat, *Asylie und Schutzorakel am Zionheiligtum* (Leiden, 1967); B. Dinur, "The Religious Character of the Cities of Refuge and the Ceremony of Admission into Them," *ErIsr,* 3 (1954), 135-146 [Heb.], VIII-IX [Eng. summary]; M. Greenberg, "The Biblical Conception of Asylum," *JBL,* 78 (1959), 125-132; S. Klein, "Cities of the Priests and Levites and Cities of Refuge," *Qobeṣ JPES* (1934/35), 81-107 [Heb.]; M. Löhr, *Das Asylwesen im AT. SKG.G,* 7/3 (1930), 177-217; J. Milgrom, "Sancta contagion and altar/city asylum," *Congress Volume, Vienna 1980. SVT,* 32 (1981), 278-310; N. M. Nicolsky, "Das Asylrecht in Israel," *ZAW,* 48 (1930), 146-175; G. Pidoux, "Quelques allusions au droit d'asile dans les psaumes," *Maqqél shāqedh. Festschrift W. Vischer* (Montpellier, 1960), 191-97; J. de Vaulx, "Refuge," *DBS,* IX (1979), 1480-1510; R. de Vaux, *AncIsr,* 160-63; L. Wenger, "Asylrecht," *RAC,* I (1950), 836-844.

(gō'ēl haddām)[1] was obligated to carry out his responsibility. Accordingly, leaving this community simultaneously meant the loss of legal protection (cf. Gen. 4:14; 12:1). This loss could be ameliorated if in the foreign land a family took up the new arrival as a protected citizen *(gēr),*[2] thereby accepting responsibility for his legal protection. The same concept is transferred to the divine sphere, where a person could find refuge in the sanctuary of a given deity. In this way the right of asylum, which in Israel and the entire ancient Near East was recognized as a legal institution, imposed limits on blood revenge where the avenger of blood might have exercised his right unjustly. In the course of Israel's history this right of asylum was circumscribed in different ways.

1. *Before the Priestly Source.* Legal prescriptions concerning this legal institution without using the term *miqlāṭ* are found in Ex. 21:13f. and Dt. 4:41-43; 19:1-13.

a. In connection with a number of crimes deserving the death penalty (Ex. 21:12-17), the Covenant Code prescribes as a fundamental rule in Ex. 21:12-14 the death of the murderer (v. 12). The exception involves the person who did not lie in wait for the victim *(ṣāḏâ),* but rather caused the death as a result of God's (unfortunate) providence. The place of asylum God appoints is circumscribed in a general fashion as a "place to which he may flee" (v. 13). In the following verse, which denies the right of asylum to the deceitful person, the place becomes more clearly recognizable as an altar, which is why in this instance this "place" is actually a sanctuary. Just who is to decide whether the circumstances involve "deceit" or "treachery" remains open. Avengers of blood, priests associated with the sanctuary, or community elders are all equally possible.

This corresponds approximately to 1 K. 1:50-53, where Adonijah flees to the altar and is subsequently released home by Solomon, though the incident admittedly does not involve the manslaughter case addressed in Ex. 21:13. In contrast, the case of Joab involves unpunished murder (Abner, Amasa; cf. 1 K. 2:5), which is why his flight to the altar does not save him. Because he refuses to leave the sanctuary, he is killed at the altar (cf. 1 K. 2:28-34). This is the only example corresponding to the sense of Ex. 21:13f.

The place of asylum is left completely undetermined, which might reflect the early conditions in Israel inasmuch as several sanctuaries (as was the case among other peoples of the ancient Near East) could offer the fugitive protection.

b. Dt. 19:1-13 and 4:41-43 describe the places of refuge as "cities to which the manslayer (*rōṣē(a)ḥ* = murderer and manslayer) can flee." The following elucidations emerge in comparison with Ex. 21:13f.:

1. These places are now cities rather than sanctuaries.
2. Their number is limited. Dt. 19 reckons initially with three cities, which in the event of territorial expansion into West Jordan[3] (vv. 8f.) are complemented by three more (no names are mentioned).

---

1. → גאל *gā'al* (II, 350-55, esp. 352).
2. → גור *gûr* (II, 439-449, esp. 446f.).
3. Milgrom interprets this as an expansion *of* West Jordan.

3. The perpetrator's preceding attitude and behavior are taken into consideration (Ex. 21 mentions only what happens during the deed itself).
4. If the perpetrator is to be removed from the place of asylum, the "elders of his city" are to function as adjudicators. In accordance with the task of the elders in the legal investigation (cf. Dt. 21:1-9; 22:13-21; 25:5-10), this refers to those from the city from which the perpetrator fled.
5. The example offered is that of accidental death caused during the felling of trees, though God's providence is no longer mentioned.
6. The distribution of places of refuge (Dt. 19:3) must guarantee that the perpetrator can escape the avenger of blood within a reasonable period of time to avoid the shedding of innocent blood.
7. Dt. 4:41-43 (conclusion to the introductory address) mentions the three cities Bezer, Ramoth, and Golan by name for the area east of the Jordan. This geographical distribution meets the requirements and offers refuge for the Reubenites, Gadites, and Manassites.

The prescriptions of Deuteronomy show a more specific delineation of legal practice. It doubtlessly corresponds better to the theological presupposition of the one sanctuary in Jerusalem by speaking now of the city rather than of the "place" (sanctuary). However, this neither presupposes that the freedom of movement of the person seeking asylum was earlier restricted to the sanctuary, nor excludes the possibility that after the judgment of his deed and after having been declared innocent the person had to remain at the place of asylum (cf. the testimonies to innocence in the Psalms). The doubtlessly secondary expansion to six cities leaves open the question just which of the three derive from the earlier time. Since in my opinion in Josh. 20 the west Jordanian cities have been added, it would be possible that the east Jordanian cities already enjoyed a longer prehistory. This might be confirmed by the fact that as late as the period of the monarchy there were still several sanctuaries in the west Jordanian region of the kingdom, while none are attested for East Jordan. Since the places of refuge in East Jordan are distributed among the tribal areas, one suspects that Deuteronomy transferred an institution associated with the eastern tribes onto the promised land itself when in the course of centralization a corresponding organization became pressing in West Jordan as well. Unfortunately, the biblical traditions contain no corresponding examples from concrete daily life. As far as language is concerned, Dt. 4:41-43 is doubtlessly dependent on Dt. 19 and is to be viewed as more recent.

2. *In the Priestly Source.* The biblical texts employing the term *miqlāṭ* belong to the tradition of the Priestly Source or are dependent upon it.

a. The language of Josh. 20f. resembles that of Dt. 19 inasmuch as the unintentional element is circumscribed by the expressions "unwittingly" and "having had no enmity against him in times past [yesterday and three days ago]." Furthermore, the city elders function in the role of adjudicators. This additional element fits with Israel's legal customs beginning with the land allotment and thus might reflect actual law. The fugitive is to explain his legal case to the elders at the city gate, who take him into protective custody, give him a place to stay, and protect him against the avenger of blood (vv. 4f.).

b. Nu. 35 offers the full text, even though the cities themselves are not mentioned by name. Lack of intentionality is designated by the term *šᵉgāgâ,* "inadvertence," which P uses in the case of unwitting transgressions (e.g., Lev. 4; Nu. 15). Most noticeable here is the significance of the congregation,[4] before whose judgment the asylum seeker must stand. At the same time, the sojourn of the manslayer in the city is fixed as the time "until the death of the high priest" (vv. 25,28), a period which can also not be shortened by a ransom payment *(kōp̱er).* Nu. 35:16-18 excludes the possibility of manslaughter when a normally lethal instrument is used. The three cities of asylum beyond the Jordan and in the land of Canaan (v. 14) are not mentioned by name. According to Nu. 35:15 these prescriptions apply equally to Israelites, strangers *(gēr),* and sojourners *(tôšāḇ),* whereas Josh. 20:9 mentions only strangers.

c. The statements in 1 Ch. 6:42,52(57,67) add nothing substantively new concerning the term *miqlāṭ,* since the list of Levitical cities merely designates Hebron and Shechem as cities of asylum.

As far as the significance of the "congregation" in the evaluation of the appropriateness of granting asylum is concerned, one should consider the larger context involving its task in adjudication in Israel. Dt. 17:8-13 foresees the possibility that a local court might turn to the place chosen by God when the legal case before it seems too difficult (Dt. 17:8). There "the Levitical priests" and "the judge" are to deliver the binding verdict. Since here, too, more precise information concerning actual legal practice is lacking, one suspects that the royal judge of the earlier period was secondarily superseded by the Levitical priests,[5] or that the two possibilities existed simultaneously. The second possibility is supported by references in the Psalms which both presuppose royal adjudication (cf. Pss. 72:1; 122:5, and others) and reckon with priestly decisions (cf. the asseverations of innocence and the accompanying rituals). That one's enduring place in the cultic community *(ʿēḏâ)* depends on such judgment is doubtlessly the case concerning the sacral sphere (cf. Pss. 15; 24), and may also have applied to other legal situations (cf. Ps. 1:5). In any event, Nu. 35 tries to preserve for the congregation such powers of decision at the central sanctuary. It provides for the return of the innocent person to the place of asylum he has sought out (v. 25).

It is commensurate with the orientation of P to associate an act of atonement with inadvertent transgressions as well. This is apparently how P interprets the obligation of the manslayer to remain at the place of asylum until the death of the high priest. A corresponding penitential sum is thus designated as a ransom, but is rejected as an actual substitute (Nu. 35:32). The final cessation of obligation is not justified. The widespread assumption that the death of the high priest was associated in the postexilic period with an amnesty (comparable to the change in kings) might have played a part. Since the ancient Near East also attests the notion that an asylum seeker was obligated

---

4. → עדה *ʿēḏâ.*

5. Cf., e.g., G. von Rad, *Deuteronomy. OTL* (Eng. trans. 1966), 117f.

to serve in the sanctuary, it is conceivable that after the judgment of the central congregation P considered the fugitive obligated to the high priest until the high priest's death.[6]

The number and actual significance of the cities of refuge must remain a largely open question. Given the present understanding of biblical sources, one must assume that the number grew from three to six in the course of transmission, since Nu. 35:14 is the first to present the six cities in a linguistically unified form. The enumeration in Dt. 4:43 is probably not dependent on Josh. 20:8, since the formulation of Josh. 20:8 presupposes the notion of appointing *(nāṯan)* Levitical cities from tribal areas, while Dt. 4:43 speaks of setting apart *(hiḇdîl)* places of refuge for members of specific tribes. On the other hand, concerning the west Jordanian cities Josh. 20:7 attests a similar notion of setting apart *(hiqdîš)* three cities, chosen not according to tribal area, but rather according to geographical location. This is also the only occurrence of the designation *ʿārê hammûʿāḏâ,* "designated cities," for the places of refuge. We are thus dealing here with an independent tradition which was later considerably reworked in light of Nu. 35. All these findings are probably best explained by assuming that two originally independent traditions concerning places of refuge and hence also differing legal customs were later combined and to a certain extent harmonized. The fact that the recognizable elements of legal practice fit relatively easily into the legal institutions of Israel already known to us militates against the opinion that these are merely theoretical legal postulates.

III. Summary. Although the term *miqlāṭ* emerges rather late in the biblical tradition, i.e., in the postexilic period, it nonetheless picks up an older legal institution with which Israel sought to protect from blood revenge the manslayer who acted without malicious intent. Because this situation could involve misuse, the elders as the local bearers of justice and the priestly court of the central sanctuary were called upon to carry out their own responsibility, namely, that of excluding from asylum the intentional murderer and of preventing the avenger of blood from exercising revenge in the case of genuinely unintentional slaying. The biblical traditions offer neither consistent nor contradictory accounts, so that one recognizes less the concrete implementation of these laws than the theological concern with having justice predominate even when it is threatened by human passions.

IV. LXX. The LXX renders *miqlāṭ* with *phygadeutḗrion* (14 times), and in isolated instances with *kataphygḗ* and *phygádion.* In Josh. 21:27,32 it translates verbally with *aphorízein.*

Schmid

---

6. Cf. H. Cazelles, review of *OTS,* 9 (1951), *VT,* 2 (1952), 380.

מֹר *mōr*

Contents: I. 1. Meaning; 2. Etymology and Ancient Near East; 3. LXX; 4. Occurrences. II. OT Usage.

I. 1. *Meaning.* The Hebrew subst. *mōr (môr)* refers in the OT to myrrh, i.e., to the resin of the terebinth *Commiphora abessinica* from southern Arabia, which occurs both as a solid and as a liquid.[1] Although in the ancient Near East myrrh also played a significant role as a healing substance[2] or was used in mummification (cf. Jn. 19:39f.), the OT mentions it only as a substance used in connection with incense and fragrance.

2. *Etymology and Ancient Near East.* The bitter taste of myrrh suggests deriving the noun from the verb *mrr* I.[3] An analogous term occurs in Ugaritic.[4] In all three Ugaritic occurrences[5] *mr* occurs in connection with *šmn.* According to Mitchell Dahood,[6] this suggests proximity to Est. 2:12. Akkadian attests *murru* I with the meaning "bitterness" next to "myrrh."[7] Syriac Mandaic attests *mûrā',* Arabic *murr,* and Old South Arabic *mrt.*[8] Uncertain occurrences include a reading in Imperial Aramaic *mwr'*[9] as well as one in Neo-Punic.[10] A paleo-Canaanite occurrence for *mu-ur-ra* is also attested.[11] In *KAI,* 161, 8, we find *mrdr,* presumably with the meaning "myrrh drops" as an equivalent to Heb. *mor-d^e^rôr.* Egyptian attestations for myrrh include *ʿntyw.*[12] There it is used in

---

mōr. G. W. van Beek, "Frankincense and Myrrh," *BA,* 23 (1960), 69-95 = E. F. Campbell and D. N. Freedman, eds., *BA Reader,* 2 (1961, repr. Winona Lake, 1975), 99-126; H. Frehen, "Myrrhe," *BL*², 1189; R. K. Harrison, *Healing Herbs of the Bible* (Leiden, 1966), 45f.; G. Krinetzki, *Kommentar zum Hohenlied. BETL,* 16 (1981); E. Löw, *Die Flora der Juden,* I/1 (Vienna, 1926), 299-311; H. N. and A. L. Moldenke, *Plants of the Bible. Chronica Botanica,* 28 (New York, 1952), 82-84; G. E. Post and J. E. Dinsmore, *Flora of Syria, Palestine and Sinai* (Beirut, ²1932/33), I, 284; G. Ryckmans, "De l'or(?), de l'encens et de la myrrhe," *RB,* 58 (1951), 372-76; A. Steier, "Myrrha," *PW,* XVI/1 (1933), 1134-1146; A. van der Wal, *Planten uit de Bibel* (Amsterdam, ²1982), 51-53 (extensive bibliog.); M. Zohary, *Plants of the Bible* (New York, 1982).

1. For a more detailed description, cf. van Beek; Steier.
2. Cf., among others, EA, 269, 16f.; probably also Mk. 15:23.
3. *BLe,* 455f.
4. Cf. *RSP,* I, III, 78.
5. *KTU,* 4.14, 2, 8, 15; *KTU,* 4.91, 16; *UT,* 173:22.
6. M. Dahood, *Ugaritic-Hebrew Philology. BietOr,* 17 (1965), 65.
7. *AHw,* II (1972), 676.
8. Cf. *HAL,* II (1995), 630.
9. *CIS,* II, 147 AB⁴ = *AP,* 73, 4.
10. Cherchel, II, 8; *DISO,* 145.
11. Cf. EA, 269, 16f.; 25:IV, 51.
12. Cf. the plentiful Egyptian equivalents in *WbÄS,* VI, 107.

mummification as an embalming substance, in connection with incense[13] as a censing substance in the cult, and as a medicinal healing substance.[14] Myrrh also occurs in Egyptian in connection with love poetry.[15] This further confirms the proximity of Egyptian love poetry to Canticles noted in other contexts (see discussion below).

The word has not been attested thus far in the Qumran writings.

3. *LXX.* The LXX renders *mōr* as *krónikos* or *krókos* in Prov. 7:17, as *staktē* in Cant. 1:13, and as *smýrnikos* in Est. 2:12. Other occurrences use *smýrna,* as is the case in Sir. 24:15, which lacks a Hebrew equivalent. The term *mýron* is not used for *mōr,* but rather for *šmn.*

4. *Occurrences.* The term *mōr* occurs 11 times in the OT in the singular: Ex. 30:23; Ps. 45:9(Eng. v. 8); Prov. 7:17; Cant. 1:13; 3:6; 4:6,14; 5:1,5,13; Est. 2:12. The targum on Ex. 30:23 uses *mwr'* and *myr'*.[16]

II. OT Usage. The concentration of occurrences in Canticles is striking, specifically within the so-called "descriptive songs" (Cant. 4:6; 5:13; probably also 1:13; 4:14) and the so-called "experience account" (5:5). References to myrrh are clearly part of the language of love both on the side of the woman (1:13; 5:13) and on that of the man (4:6,14; 5:1). In these texts *mōr* acquires the status of a symbol. Cant. 4:12–5:1 extols the beloved as a locked garden, mentioning *mōr* as one precious growth among many others (e.g., frankincense and aloe). These are not to be taken as images for individual bodily parts, but rather underscore metaphorically the emphasis on splendor, since gardens of the kind described here were unknown in Palestine, and thus considered something quite extraordinary. According to 5:1, the garden does not remain locked, and the lover gains access to it. His partaking of the garden is expressed by his gathering myrrh and spices and drinking honey, wine, and milk, images representing the pleasures of love. Cant. 1:13; 4:6 are possibly corresponding verses. In a fashion analogous to 1:3, the woman describes her beloved in 1:13 as a fragrant bag of myrrh *(ṣ^e^rôr hammōr)* between her breasts, alluding to the custom of applying fragrances, including myrrh, between one's breasts.[17] The song describing the beloved woman in Cant. 4:1-7 speaks in v. 6 of the mountain of myrrh and hill of frankincense to which the lover yearns to go.

---

13. → לבנה *l^e^ḇōnâ* (VII, 441-47).

14. R. Germer, "Myrrhe," *LexÄg,* IV (1982), 275f.; on the peculiar association of the dead king and myrrh, cf. H. Grapow, *Vergleiche und andere bildliche Ausdrücke im Ägyptischen. AO,* 21/1f. (1920, repr. 1983), 147.

15. S. Schott, ed., *Altägyptische Liebeslieder* (Zurich, ²1950), 50, 88, 90, and *passim.*

16. Cf. G. H. Dalman, *Aramäisch-neuhebräisches Handwörterbuch zu Targum, Talmud und Midrasch* (³1938, repr. Hildesheim, 1967), 228; cf. there also *mwry.*

17. On the notion of the lover as fragrant breast adornment, cf. H. Schmökel, *Heilige Hochzeit und Hoheslied. AKM,* 32/1 (1956), 101f., who adduces similar references in the Tammuz liturgy; on the possible "rhyme" *ṣ^e^rôr hammōr,* see L. Krinetzki, *Das Hohe Lied. KBANT* (1964), 55.

Contra Gillis Gerleman,[18] who considers this a literary topos, these two expressions should on the basis of the preceding verses as well as 1:12 be understood as references to the breasts of the beloved.[19] Cant. 4:6 need not be an insertion, since the desire to be close to the woman can very easily have emerged from the preceding description. In 5:13, the woman compares the lips (moustache?) of her beloved with "lilies distilling liquid myrrh."[20] The same expression is also found in 5:5, where the woman describes her own hands as dripping with myrrh. Contra Wilhelm Rudolph's[21] suggestion that the lover smeared dripping myrrh on the door latch, the verb *ntp* indicates that her hands were already rubbed with myrrh[22] (cf. also the prep. *ʿal*). One must admittedly still ask whether here, too, *môr (ʿōḇēr)* does not refer to the woman's passionate yearning.

Cant. 3:6-10, in the form of a choral song, describes a wedding procession. In addition to frankincense and fragrant powders, myrrh is also mentioned as a censing substance.[23] According to Est. 2:12, myrrh along with other substances served the beautification of the royal concubines before they went in to Ahasuerus. This text accordingly stands in a certain proximity to the occurrences in Canticles. Ps. 45:9(8) describes the clothes of the royal bridegroom with references to myrrh, aloe, and cassia, probably alluding to their fragrance. Here, too, *mōr* is used in connection with the language of weddings and love. The completely positive language of love attested in the previous texts is reversed in Prov. 7:17, although the erotic evocation is maintained: a married woman entices a young man to sleep with her by referring to her bed, which she has perfumed with myrrh, aloes, and cinnamon. "Her words here strongly recall the description of the bed at the sacred wedding as well as the invitation of the ancient Near Eastern love-goddess to the wedding celebration."[24]

Whereas in these texts *mōr* is consistently used in secular contexts (at most Ps. 45 might yet exhibit a theological orientation[25]), Ex. 30:23 belongs to the cultic sphere. Probably reflecting postexilic custom,[26] Ex. 30:22-33 gives instructions for producing the sacred anointing oil, which includes in addition to cinnamon, calamus, cassia, and olive oil also myrrh *(mōr-d^eròr)*.

Finally, in wisdom's self-commendation the fragrance of myrrh again is taken as the superior point of comparison for other fragrances (Sir. 24:20).

It becomes clear that in all these texts the term *mōr* is associated with something

---

18. *Das Hohelied. BK,* XVIII (²1981), 150.

19. W. Rudolph, *Das Hohelied. KAT,* XVII/2 (1962), 145f.; H. Ringgren, *Das Hohe Lied. ATD,* XVI/2 (³1981), 271.

20. On *môr ʿōḇēr,* cf. H.-P. Stähli, "עבר *ʿbr* vorüber, hinübergehen," *THAT,* II, 202.

21. *KAT,* XVII/2, 156.

22. Gerleman, *BK,* XVIII, 166f.

23. Concerning the procession, cf. Gerleman's reference to parallels in the funerary festival of Thebes and in the offering festival at Luxor, *BK,* XVIII, 136.

24. H. Ringgren, *Sprüche. ATD,* XVI/1 (³1980), 36.

25. Contra Ringren, *ATD,* XVI/1, concerning Prov. 7:17; Cant. 5:1; possibly also Cant. 4:6, Ringgren, *ATD,* XVI/2, *in loc.*

26. M. Noth, *Exodus. OTL* (Eng. trans. 1962), 238.

extraordinary and beautiful. Myrrh is counted among the precious things reserved for extraordinary things or ideas (anointing oil, wisdom), events (weddings), and people (the beloved), something whose fragrance makes these things even more attractive and more precious. The term *mōr* does not, however, exhibit any special theological significance.

Hausmann